Fodor's

JAPAN
17TH EDITION

Where to Stay and Eat
for All Budgets

Must-See Sights
and Local Secrets

Ratings You Can Trust

Fodor's Travel Publications   New York, Toronto, London, Sydney, Auckland
www.fodors.com

FODOR'S JAPAN
EDITORS: Emmanuelle Alspaugh, Deborah Kaufman

Editorial Contributors: Dominic Al-Badri, Collin Campbell, Paul Davidson, Justin Ellis, Amanda Harlow, Constance Jones, Jared Lubarsky, Deidre May, Sarah Richards, Steve Trautlein, John Malloy Quinn, James Vardaman, and Matt Wilce
Editorial Production: Linda K. Schmidt, Bethany Cassin Beckerlegge, Kazumi Pestka
Maps: David Lindroth, *cartographer*; Rebecca Baer and Robert Blake, *map editors*
Design: Fabrizio La Rocca, *creative director*; Guido Caroti, *art director*; Moon Sun Kim, *cover designer*; Melanie Marin, *senior picture editor*
Production/Manufacturing: Robert B. Shields
Cover Photograph: Chad Ehlers/Photo Network/PictureQuest

SPECIAL SALES
This book is available for special discounts for bulk purchases for sales promotions or premiums. Special editions, including personalized covers, excerpts of existing books, and corporate imprints, can be created in large quantities for special needs. For more information, write to Special Markets/Premium Sales, 1745 Broadway, MD 6-2, New York, New York 10019, or e-mail specialmarkets@ randomhouse.com.

IMPORTANT TIP & AN INVITATION
Although all prices, opening times, and other details in this book are based on information supplied to us at press time, changes occur all the time in the travel world, and Fodor's cannot accept responsibility for facts that become outdated or for inadvertent errors or omissions. So **always confirm information when it matters,** especially if you're making a detour to visit a specific place. Your experiences—positive and negative—matter to us. If we have missed or misstated something, **please write to us.** We follow up on all suggestions. Contact the Japan editor at editors@fodors.com or c/o Fodor's at 1745 Broadway, New York, New York 10019.

PRINTED IN THE UNITED STATES OF AMERICA

10 9 8 7 6 5 4 3 2 1

DESTINATION JAPAN

elicate cherry blossoms stir in the wind, centuries-old villages hide in mountain valleys, sacred structures whisper of history and lore: You've entered Japan, a land of exquisite and ancient beauty. Temples from the 6th century, castles that cascade in tiers down to earth, and venerated shrines transport you across vast, turbulent, and colorful time periods. Bullet trains, meanwhile, shuttle you between these sights and beyond, to gorgeous undeveloped natural areas, to fantastic restaurants serving exotic foods you've never tried before, and to traditional craft houses producing pottery and paper. Crackling with energy, Japan's cities remind you that this country is a postindustrial giant, a critical player in the global economy. If you've come to discover a world completely different from your own, there's no doubt you'll succeed.

Tim Jarrell, Publisher

CONTENTS

Maps

CloseUps

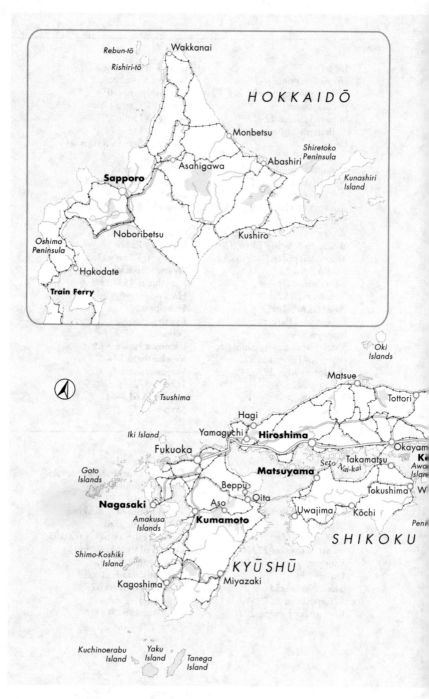

Rebun-tō

Rishiri-tō

Wakkanai

HOKKAIDŌ

Monbetsu

Shiretoko Peninsula

Asahigawa

Abashiri

Kunashiri Island

Sapporo

Noboribetsu

Kushiro

Oshima Peninsula

Hakodate

Train Ferry

Oki Islands

Matsue

Tsushima

Tottori

Hagi

Yamaguchi

Hiroshima

Iki Island

Fukuoka

Okayam

Seto Nai-kai

Takamatsu

Kō

Matsuyama

Awa Islan

Goto Islands

Beppu

Tokushima

W

Nagasaki

Aso

Oita

Uwajima

Kōchi

Amakusa Islands

Kumamoto

Peni

Shimo-Koshiki Island

SHIKOKU

KYŪSHŪ

Kagoshima

Miyazaki

Kuchinoerabu Island

Yaku Island

Tanega Island

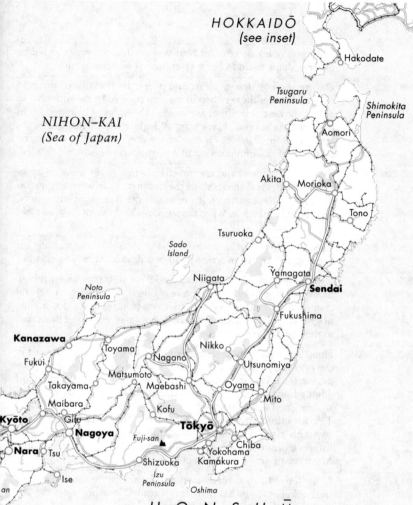

> 🅕9

ABOUT THIS BOOK

Once you've learned to find your way around our pages, you'll be in great shape to find your way around your destination.

RATINGS

Orange stars ★ denote sights and properties that our editors and writers consider the very best in the area covered by the entire book. These, the best of the best, are listed in the Fodor's Choice section in the front of the book. Black stars ★ highlight the sights and properties we deem Highly Recommended, the don't-miss sights within any region. It goes without saying that no property pays to be included.

SPECIAL SPOTS

Pleasures & Pastimes and text on chapter title pages focus on experiences that reveal the spirit of the destination. Also watch for Off the Beaten Path sights. Some are out of the way, some are quirky, and all are worthwhile. When the munchies hit, look for Need a Break? suggestions.

TIME IT RIGHT

Check On the Calendar up front and chapters' Timing sections for weather and crowd overviews and best days and times to visit.

SEE IT ALL

Use Fodor's Great Itineraries as a model for your trip. Either follow those that begin the book, or mix regional itineraries from several chapters. In cities, Good Walks guide you to important sights in each neighborhood; ► indicates the starting point of walks and itineraries in the text and on the map.

BUDGET WELL

Hotel and restaurant price categories from ¢ to $$$$ are defined in the opening pages of each chapter—expect to find a balanced selection for every budget. For attractions, we always give standard adult admission fees; reductions are usually available for children, students, and senior citizens. Look in Discounts & Deals in Smart Travel Tips for information on destination-wide ticket schemes. Want to pay with plastic? AE, D, DC, MC, V following restaurant and hotel listings indicate whether American Express, Discover, Diner's Club, MasterCard, or Visa are accepted.

BASIC INFO

Smart Travel Tips lists travel essentials for the entire area covered by the book. For the best ways to travel around local areas, see the Getting Around sections within chapters.

ON THE MAPS

Maps throughout the book show you what's where and help you find your way around. Black and orange numbered bullets ❶ ❶ in the text correlate to bullets on maps.

BACKGROUND

We give background information within the chapters in the course of explaining sights as well as in CloseUp boxes and in the chapters at the end of the book. The Glossary of Key Japanese Words & Suffixes at the end of the book can be invaluable.

FIND IT FAST

Within the book, chapters are arranged in geographical order beginning with Tōkyō and fanning out to the surrounding cities and regions. Chapters covering regions are divided into smaller areas, within which towns are covered in logical geographical order; attractive routes and interesting places between towns are flagged as En Route. Heads at the top of each page help you find what you need within a chapter.

DON'T FORGET

Restaurants are open for lunch and dinner daily unless we state otherwise; we mention dress only when there's a specific requirement and reservations only when they're essential or not accepted—it's always best to book ahead. Also unless stated otherwise, hotels have private baths, phone, TVs, and air-conditioning and operate on the European Plan (aka EP, meaning without meals). We always list facilities but not whether you'll be charged extra to use them, so when pricing accommodations, find out what's included.

SYMBOLS

Many Listings

★ Fodor's Choice
★ Highly recommended
⊠ Physical address
✢ Directions
⬠ Mailing address
☎ Telephone
⎗ Fax
⊕ On the Web
✉ E-mail
⊞ Admission fee
☉ Open/closed times
► Start of walk/itinerary
Ⓜ Metro stations
⊟ Credit cards

Outdoors

🏌 Golf
⛺ Camping

Hotels & Restaurants

⊡ Hotel
⇆ Number of rooms
⟳ Facilities
⦿ Meal plans
✕ Restaurant
⬧ Reservations
⌂ Dress code
⤬ Smoking
⌦ BYOB
✕⊡ Hotel with restaurant that warrants a visit

Other

⟲ Family-friendly
🛈 Contact information
⇨ See also
⊠ Branch address
☞ Take note

ON THE ROAD WITH FODOR'S

The more you know before you go, the better your trip will be. Japan's best sushi bar could be just around the corner from your hotel, but if you don't know it's there, it might as well be on the other side of the globe. That's where this book comes in. It's a great step toward making sure your next trip lives up to your expectations. As you plan, check out the Web as well. Whatever reference you consult, be savvy about what you read, and always consider the source. Here at Fodor's, and at our online arm, Fodors.com, our focus is on providing you with information that's accurate and on target. Every day Fodor's editors put enormous effort into getting things right, beginning with the search for the right contributors—people who have objective judgment, broad travel experience, and the writing ability to put their insights into words. There's no substitute for advice from a like-minded friend who has just come back from where you're going, but our writers, having seen all corners of Japan, are the next best thing. They're the kind of people you'd poll for tips yourself if you knew them.

Dominic Al-Badri studied biochemistry at the University of London's Imperial College but wound up teaching, writing, and editing English for 12 years in Japan. Between 1997 and 2004 he was the editor of the venerable English-language monthly *Kansai Time Out*. After revising the Ōsaka, Kōbe, and Smart Travel Tips chapters for *Fodor's Japan,* Dominic left Japan to pursue graduate studies at the London School of Economics. However, he misses quality *shōchū* (a spirit distilled from sweet potatoes or grains) so much that he intends to return to Japan as soon as he can.

Paul Davidson first came to Japan in 1995 to work as an extra in a karate film by the B-movie director Pepe Baba. The picture went straight to video, and Paul went to Changsha, China. He lived in China and São Tomé, a small island nation off the coast of West Africa, until his return to Japan in 2000. Currently based in Yokohama, outside of Tōkyō, Paul works as a writer and translator when he isn't playing the *biwa* (Japanese lute) with the Tengu-kai sextet. He has contributed to several editions of *Fodor's China* and *Fodor's Japan*. For this edition, he updated the Shikoku and Nagoya, Ise-Shima & the Kii Peninsula chapters, as well as the essays at the end of the book.

Justin Ellis, a native of Australia and graduate of the University of Sydney has been living and writing in Japan since 1999. He has contributed countless restaurant reviews, features, and other articles to *Kansai Time Out* and the *Kyoto Journal*. Being more familiar with 19th-century Japanese history, Justin was thrilled to cover Nara, whose important temples date to the 7th century. He remains entranced by the classical simplicity of Nara architecture, especially Nandai-mon. Most of his free time is spent seeking out new food heavens, exotic hotels, and ryokan gems in the hope of one day making a television program about them.

Hokkaidō updater **Amanda Harlow** dropped out of provincial journalism in the south of England to travel the world for a year—and never went back. She settled in Japan in 1993, first in Saitama and finally in Hokkaidō, where she now works proofreading, teaching, and narrating government videos about clearing snow from roads. Her perfect Hokkaidō day is skiing followed by a hot spring, sushi, and a beer.

Jared Lubarsky, who revised the Exploring, Where to Eat, Where to Stay, and Sports sections of the Tōkyō chapter, has lived in Japan since 1973. He has worked for cultural exchange organizations, taught at public and private universities, and written extensively for travel publications. He still ponders the oddities of Japanese culture, wondering why, for instance, the signs that advise you not to ride in elevators during an earthquake are posted *inside* the elevators.

In 2001 Kyōto updater Deidre May left her native South Africa, where she directed an animated television series, to take a year off. Drawn to Eastern ways and philosophies, she came to Japan, where she now lives in an old Japanese house with two cats among the foothills of Mount Hiei in northeastern Kyōto, at the site of one of the original Buddhist enclaves. She is a regular contributor and editor for the *Kyoto Journal*. Her other interests include Tibetan Buddhism, *reiki* (energy healing), and calligraphy.

John Malloy Quinn suspects that the origins of his orbits can be traced back to his high-school-era, part-time job at a Japanese restaurant. After earning a master's in English from the University of Colorado at Boulder, where he published articles in the *Colorado Daily* and *Boulder Magazine*, John moved to Japan to teach English. He spent two years in Shizuoka, seven years in Ishikawa, and for the last three years he has made his home in the leafy, hip labyrinth of Tōkyō's Setagaya Ward. He teaches at Tōkai and Kyōrin Universities. John has contributed to several editions of *Fodor's Japan*, and for this edition he wrote the Okinawa chapter and revised the Western Honshū chapter.

Sarah Richards completed her Bachelor of Arts in Japanese Studies and Linguistics at McGill University in Montréal, Canada, before stumbling on a teaching job that led her to a small fishing village in a quiet corner of Shikoku Island. After two years of frolicking in the rice paddies, she took a position at a big publishing company in Tōkyō. Aside from all the warm smiles and steamy *onsen* she encountered while updating the Kyūshū and Japan Alps chapters, Sarah's memorable moments include sampling bright-green horseradish ice cream at the Daiō Wasabi Farm in Matsumoto and taking a helicopter ride into the ferocious Nakadake, one of Kyūshū's active volcanoes.

Steve Trautlein is a writer and editor at *Metropolis* magazine, a weekly publication focusing on entertainment and lifestyles in Japan. He has reviewed dozens of bars, restaurants, and shops in Tōkyō and the surrounding area. With Matt Wilce, Steve revised the Nightlife and Shopping sections of the Tōkyō chapter, as well as the Side Trips from Tōkyō chapter.

Matt Wilce first came to Japan in 1993 and has lived in Tōkyō since 1998. He has done everything from teaching government employees to being knifed by a yakuza on a TV police show, but prefers to stick to more sedate activities such as writing. Matt has written and edited articles on the Japanese entertainment industry for *Eye-Ai* and *Metropolis* magazines, and he has also written features for *The Rochester Review, The Lantern, Ikebana International, POL Oxygen,* and *JapanInc.* He contributed to the Nightlife and Shopping sections of the Tōkyō chapter, and the Side Trips from Tōkyō chapter.

Tennessee-born James Vardaman wrote the guidebook *In and Around Sendai* and coauthored *Japanese Etiquette Today* and *Japan from A to Z: Mysteries of Everyday Life Explained.* He has been a professor of English at Surugadai University in Saitama Prefecture and has worked as a translator. James updated the Tōhoku chapter.

WHAT'S WHERE

(1) Tōkyō

Immense and sprawling, Tōkyō commands a prominent position on the southern coast of Honshū, Japan's largest island. Some 12 million people live in or within commuting distance of the capital. Like most big cities, Tōkyō stitches together several colorful neighborhoods—Asakusa, Ginza, Tsukiji, Shinjuku, and dozens more—each with its own texture.

(2) Side Trips from Tōkyō

If Tōkyō were rows of Quonset huts, it would still be worth staying in for the side trips nearby. Start with lunch in Yokohama's Chinatown, where more than 150 restaurants serve every major regional Chinese cuisine. Here silks, spices, herbal medicines, and all things Chinese beckon from a warren of shops in narrow lanes. Far removed from such urban bustle lie Nikkō and the Tōshō-gū shrine complex, stirring in its sheer scale alone. Some call it sublime, some excessive, but no one finds it dull. At a nearby national park, Chūzenji-ko (Lake Chūzenji) and waterfalls like Kegon-no-taki nourish the spirit. The national park and resort area of Hakone puts you close to majestic Fuji-san, which you can climb in summer without special gear. In Hase, the 37-ft Daibutsu—the Great Buddha—has sat for seven centuries, serenely gazing inward. The temples and shrines of nearby Kamakura, 13th-century capital of Japan, remind you that this was an important religious as well as political center. Break away from the tourists and enjoy a moment of peace: the clamor of Tōkyō falls silent here in the ancient heart of Japan.

(3) Nagoya, Ise-Shima & the Kii Peninsula

Sacred sites, traditional crafts, and untamed natural beauty head the list of reasons to visit this region west of Tōkyō. At Ise-Shima National Park the highly venerated Ise Jingū (Grand Shrines of Ise) sit amid groves of ancient trees and, in accordance with Shintō tradition, are rebuilt with new wood every 20 years. A loop around the Kii Peninsula takes you past magnificent coastal scenery, fishing villages, and Yoshino-san, with perhaps the finest springtime display of cherry blossoms in Japan. Inland, the mountain monastery of Kōya-san, founded in 816, looms almost as large as myth with its 120 temples. Old Japan resonates in Gifu, famous for its oiled-paper umbrellas, paper lanterns, and for U-kai, the ancient practice of fishing with cormorants. And though not especially handsome, Japan's fourth-largest city, Nagoya, with its easygoing residents, can grow on you. It has some sightseeing moments, notably at Nagoya-jō and the Tokugawa Art Museum, whose many priceless objects include a National Treasure: 12th-century illustrated hand scrolls of *The Tale of Genji,* widely considered the world's first novel.

(4) The Japan Alps & the North Chūbu Coast

Soaring mountains, slices of old Japan, and superb hiking, skiing, and *onsen* soaking make this region enticing. So does the gorgeous natural color, from the flowering trees of spring to the rich hues of autumn. Nagano is a good base if taking the waters is high on your list. Yudanaka Onsen's thermal springs are popular with people bent on relaxing, and with snow monkeys, who gather for warmth. Nearby at the renowned hot springs at

Kusatsu, a bracing pinch of arsenic (far from toxic levels) spikes the mineral waters. Hiking in the mountains around the towns of Karuizawa and Kamikōchi tones both body and soul. In the friendly city of Kanazawa, you can find fine museums, shrines, traditional crafts, and the enchanting Naga-machi (Samurai District). The city's Kenroku Garden ranks as one of the three finest gardens in the country. Traditional Japan also remains alive in Takayama, where in April and October drummers set the pulse for raucous ancient festivals. A trip around the north Chūbu coast and the Noto-hantō (Noto Peninsula) rewards you with dreamlike seascapes and charming villages such as Wajima, renowned for its lacquerware. On Sado Island (Sado-ga-shima) the pace of life recalls centuries past. Japan changes slowly in these mountains and along these shores. Savor it.

(5) Kyōto

Whatever you do, don't miss a trip to gracious Kyōto, where 12 centuries of history and tradition echo in beautiful gardens, castles, and museums, and nearly 2,000 temples and shrines. The city is near the middle of Honshū, Japan's biggest island, and only 20 minutes by train from Ōsaka. Kyōto is the city that gave birth to classical Japanese customs, aesthetics, and arts—to be sure, glorious sights abound here, with gold-leaf Kinkaku-ji topping nearly any list of favorites. At Kiyomizu-dera, built on a steep hillside, views of the temple match views from it, while Kōryū-ji serves as both a place of worship and a trove of National Treasures. Secular, but no less devoted to ceremony, are the geisha of the Gion district. Secular, too, but with a religious following, are the gastronomic shrines serving *kaiseki ryōri*, an elegant meal that engages all senses. Like the food, the crafts here approach perfection: dolls, fans, ceramics, and creations by masters of the Kyō-yūzen silk-dyeing technique. Pick up your mementos here; you won't find better.

(6) Nara

Ancient Nara, south of Kyōto, may not match that great city for sheer volume of sacred sites, but its shrines and parks count among Japan's finest, and its crafts and cuisine are superb. Head straight for Nara Kōen, a splendid park with about 1,000 tame deer, and to the Kasuga Taisha temple complex. Its main shrines are National Treasures. Other must-sees near the park are the resplendent Tōdai-ji and the Daibutsu-den, which houses a 53-ft bronze Buddha. From here, it's a train or bus ride to the temples of western Nara. The finest is Hōryū-ji, with its Great Treasure Hall and 7th-century wooden buildings. It's possible to visit Nara in one day, but you may find yourself wanting to linger.

(7) Ōsaka

Ōsaka is on the south shore of western Honshū. Unlike Kyōto or Nara, Ōsaka dazzles you with bright lights rather than tradition, but it does possess Ōsaka-jō, a match for any castle in the country, and sumō wrestling at the Ōsaka Furitsu Taiikukaikan. Japan is passionate about sumō, whose origins are tied to ancient Shintō rites, and Osakans are among its biggest fans. Despite the bulk of the wrestlers, their quickness is amazing; some years ago in an exhibition, novice sumō wrestlers tossed beefy

NFL linemen around like schoolboys. The Americans never asked for a rematch. Bunraku puppet masters ply a gentler art at the National Bunraku Theater. Ōsaka is famous for the perfection of this dramatic form. For neon and nightlife, hop on a subway to Dōtombori-dōri. Unwind and dine among the locals, who have a reputation as food-lovers. Be sure to sample delicacies like okonomiyaki, grilled pancakes with vegetables and meat. You won't spend a week in Ōsaka, but a day or two has its rewards.

8 Kōbe

For a break from traditional Japan, try Kōbe—typified more by its harbor skyline, with the Hotel Ōkura Kōbe rising above the water, than by sights like Ikuta Jinja, a Shintō shrine. European and Japanese influences have long mingled in this city on Ōsaka Bay. One result is Kitano-chō, worth a visit for its old Western-style homes, including delightful Choueke Yashiki. Shopping is one of Kōbe's strong points, and at the Tasaki Shinju company you can learn how pearls get from mollusk to necklace. International accents lace the culinary scene, where pride of place goes to pricey, world-famous Kōbe beef. Yes, it's marbled, but don't worry: you'll be eating fish again soon.

9 Western Honshū

Mountains divide this region into an urban south and a rural north. Today Hiroshima stands tall and modern in the south, while the charred A-Bomb Dome, a sobering icon of the atomic age, testifies to darker times. Offshore at Miyajima, the famous Ō-torii appears to float on the water. Also in the south is Himeji-jō, one of Japan's most beloved castles. In nearby Bizen, masters craft the famous local pottery, while Kurashiki, with its buildings and willow-shaded canals, envelops you in an older time. On the northern coast, don't miss history-rich Hagi and the gems called Tsuwano and Matsue, two towns special even in this lovely corner of Japan.

10 Shikoku

Thanks to its isolation—now ended by bridges to Honshū—the southern island of Shikoku has held on to its traditions, and staved off the industry that blights parts of Japan. Your rewards for leaving the beaten path to come here include great hiking with dramatic scenery, some of the freshest seafood in the country, and a chance to make a fool of yourself (that's the idea) at the rollicking Awa Odori festival in Tokushima. Tokushima is also a good place to try your hand at traditional crafts, such as papermaking, or to watch masters at work. Visit the mellow city of Kōchi, rugged Shōdo-shima island, and the superb Takamatsu gardens. Take the waters at Dōgo Onsen Hon-kan and at the beach. This is a Japan you've never dreamed of.

11 Kyūshū

Lush Kyūshū, southernmost of Japan's main islands, has everything from an active and accessible volcano, at Aso-san National Park, to the quiet hills of charming Nagasaki, a harbor town often called the San Francisco of Japan. Not far from the artsy spa of Yufuin, volcanic grandeur accents pastoral views, and at the Beppu hot springs, kitsch, neon, and tour groups prevail.

12 Okinawa

Okinawa, an archipelago 400 km (250 mi) south of Kyūshū, is known as the Hawaii of Japan. Calm, shallow bodies of water with soft, white sand underfoot satisfy the casual swimmer and sun-tan seeker, while teeming reefs, canyons, and shelves of coral under less than 10 meters (30 feet) of water attract the snorkeler and scuba diver. The islands are surrounded by some of the clearest, cleanest, warmest waters in the world. They are also the temporary home of some 20,000 U.S. troops on bases established there at the end of World War II.

13 Tōhoku

If you overlook Tōhoku—Honshū's six northern prefectures—you'll be among millions of travelers, Japanese and foreign, who do. That's their loss and, potentially, yours. The main island's urban metabolism slows down here; friendliness rises and natural beauty abounds. Zaō-san draws skiing enthusiasts, and even nonskiers come for the *juhyō*, snow-covered fir trees that resemble fairy-tale monsters. With its caldera lake and great hiking, the mountain also merits a visit in summer. A short hop east lies modern Sendai, Tōhoku's largest city and a good base for trips to Zaō-san and Matsu-shima, a bay studded with 250 pine-clad islands that is one of Japan's three official scenic wonders. In southern Tōhoku, the five lakes of different hues, known as Go-shiki-numa, and Inawashiro-ko, Japan's third-largest lake, are neighbors. In nearby Kitakata, mud-wall storehouses will eat up your film, and in Aizu-Wakamatsu you can see how a wealthy Samurai lived (in 38 rooms, for starters). Let your hair down at celebrations up north, such as the lively Nebuta Festival in Aomori and the Kantō Festival in Akita. Make time for traditional Kakunodate, a kind of Kyōto in miniature, and nearby alpine Tazawa-ko, Japan's deepest lake. Top it off with a day trip to wind-blown Tappi-Zaki. Honshū ends here; across the chilly water lies Hokkaidō. You've come far from Tōkyō, in every imaginable way.

14 Hokkaidō

Barely tamed and beautiful, Japan's northernmost island is also its last frontier—a world away from Honshū's urban hives. You won't find shrines or castles here; the Japanese started settling Hokkaidō in earnest in the 19th century. What you will find are glorious landscapes, abundant hiking and skiing opportunities, and a good, modern base in the island's capital, Sapporo. In February the Sapporo Snow Festival dazzles with huge ice sculptures, and the city's nightlife zone, Susukinō, glitters with neon year-round. To the south lie famous hot springs at Noboribetsu Onsen and, next door, Jigokudani (Valley of Hell), a volcanic crater that belches boiling water and sulfurous vapors. To the east is the town of Nibutani, a last toehold of the indigenous Ainu people, muscled aside as Japanese from the south moved to Hokkaidō. Northeast lie three great national parks: wild Shiretoko by the sea, lake-filled Akan, and mountainous Daisetsu-zan. You can walk the northern tip of Japan at Sōya-misaki. Feel the peace. And if you're returning to any big Japanese city, brace yourself for the shock.

Many people don't see much more of Japan than Tōkyō, Kyōto, and the blur of the suburbs through the windows of a bullet train. If you want to explore the country at a slower pace, reduce the journey from a 170-mph whiz to a slow meander among temples, shrines, hot springs, mountains, and major cities.

Highlights of Japan
14 to 16 days

TŌKYŌ 3 days. Begin with three days in Tōkyō. So few days in a megalopolis of millions may seem brief, but once you get caught up in the buzz of the city you'll soon be dashing from Shinjuku's skyscrapers to Ginza's boutiques. Be sure to take advantage of your jet lag and start your first day off with the early morning tuna auction at the Chūō Oroshiuri Ichiba, the Tsukiji fish market. If you have an extra day to spare, consider using it for a day trip to nearby Kamakura, the 13th-century capital of Japan, or to Fuji-san. ⇨ *Chapters 1 & 2*

NIKKŌ 1 to 2 days. If you're still in big-city mode you may wish to approach Nikkō as a day trip, but a longer stay will allow you to soak up the atmosphere of the ancient temples and shrines in a gorgeous mountain setting. Tōshō-gū ranks as one of Japan's best shrines, and nearby Chūzenji-ko (Lake Chūzenji) and the Kegon-no-taki (Kegon Falls) are impressive. ⇨ *Nikkō in Chapter 2*

ISE 1 day. Ise Jingū (Grand Shrines of Ise), with their harmonious architecture and cypress-forest setting, provide one of Japan's most spiritual experiences. The nearby city of Toba is an introduction to Japan's pearl-diving traditions. ⇨ *Ise-Shima National Park & the Kii Peninsula in Chapter 3*

NARA 1 day. During the 8th century Nara served as the capital of Japan, and many cultural relics of that period, including some of the world's oldest wooden structures, still stand among forested hills and parkland. You can cover most major sights on foot in a day. Be sure to visit Nara's 53-ft-high Daibutsu (Great Buddha) and to make friends with the affable deer of Nara Kōen. ⇨ *Chapter 6*

KYŌTO 3 days. For many visitors Kyōto is Japan, and few leave disappointed. Wander in and out of temple precincts like Ginkaku-ji, spot geisha strolling about Gion, and dine on kaiseki ryōri, an elegant culinary event that engages all the senses. Outside the city center, day-trip to hillside Arashiyama, the gardens of the Katsura Rikyū, and the temple of Enryaku-ji atop Hiei-zan. ⇨ *Chapter 5*

KURASHIKI 1 day. This rustic town, an important trading port in centuries past, retains its picturesque 17th-century buildings. The 1930s classical-style Ōhara Art Museum houses a fine collection of European art. The Kurashiki Craft Museum displays crafts from around the world, including pottery from nearby Bizen. ⇨ *The San-yō Region in Chapter 9*

HIROSHIMA 2 days. A quick glance at the busy, attractive city of Hiroshima gives no clue to the events of August 6, 1945. Only the city's Peace Memorial Park (Heiwa Kinen Kōen)—with its memorial museum and its A-Bomb Dome (Gembaku Dōmu), a twisted, half-shattered structural ruin—serves as a reminder of the horror of the day the world first saw the destructive potential of atomic weapons. From Hiroshima, make a quick trip to the island of Miyajima to see the famous floating torii of the Itsukushima Jinja, a shrine built on stilts above a tidal flat. ⇨ *The San-yō Region in Chapter 9*

BEPPU OR YUFUIN **2 days.** You don't need to be shaken by an earthquake to realize that Japan is very seismically active. One of the locals' favorite pastimes is relaxing in an *onsen* (hot spring), and Beppu, on the southernmost island of Kyūshū, has been a hot-springs resort for centuries. You can soak in mineral water or bubbling mud or bury yourself in therapeutic sand. With entertainment complexes, neon signs, and souvenir shops, Beppu can be a bit much. A quiet alternative is nearby Yufuin, with crafts galleries and thermal baths. ⇨ *Beppu & Yufuin in Chapter 11*

By Public Transportation The train ride from Tōkyō's Asakusa Station to Nikkō takes less than two hours. Return to Tōkyō to catch either the Hikari or Kodama Shinkansen (bullet train) from Tōkyō Station to Nagoya. The private Kintetsu Railway can take you from Nagoya south to Ise in 80 minutes. This railway can also take you from Ise to Kyōto, with connections to Nara. Less than two hours away from Kyōto by the San-yō Shinkansen is Kurashiki; you may need to change trains at Okayama. This same line will connect you to Hiroshima and Fukuoka, where you can catch the JR Nichirin Line to Beppu. Regular bus service connects Beppu and Yufuin.

Traditional & Contemporary
9 days

Yes, Japan is a modern country with its skyscrapers, lightning-fast train service, and splendid neon lights. But it's also rich in history, culture, and tradition. Japan is perhaps most fascinating when you see these two faces at once: a 17th-century shrine sitting defiantly by a tower of steel and glass and a geisha chatting on a cell phone. A trip to Japan's major cities and holiest mountains combines the best of both worlds.

ŌSAKA **1 day.** Ōsaka's amazing airport serves as an impressive gateway to Japan. But the high-tech, undulating terminal is usually all that visitors see of this city before catching the express to nearby Kyōto. Although by no means picturesque, Ōsaka does provide a taste of urban Japan outside the capital, along with a few traditional sights. The handsome castle Ōsaka-jo nestles among skyscrapers, and the neon of Dōtombori flashes around the local Kabuki theater. Osakans are passionate about food, and you're bound to find some of the finest in the country here. ⇨ *Chapter 7*

KŌYA-SAN **1 day.** More than 100 temples belonging to the Shingon sect of Buddhism stand on one of Japan's holiest mountains, 30 mi south of Ōsaka. An exploration of the atmospheric cemetery of Okuno-in takes you past interesting examples of headstone art and 300-year-old cedar trees. ⇨ *Kōya-san & Yoshino-san in Chapter 3*

KYŌTO **3 days.** With nearly 2,000 temples and shrines, exquisite crafts, and serene gardens, Kyōto embodies traditional Japan. But the city is a bustling metropolis in its own right, with high-tech industries and contemporary architecture. A splendid modern-art gallery, National Museum of Modern Art, cozies up to the buildings of the Heian Jingū (Heian Shrine). I. M. Pei designed the main structure of the Miho Museum, built into a hillside to the north of Kyōto and displaying traditional Japanese art and Asian and Western antiquities. And Kyōto Eki, Hiroshi Hara's modern, once-controversial, marble-and-glass train station, is as significant as any of Kyōto's ancient treasures. ⇨ *Chapter 5*

HIMEJI **1 day.** The city's most famous sight, Himeji-jō, also known as the White Egret Castle (Shirasag-jō), dominates the city and its skyline. The castle takes only an afternoon to see, but museums near the train station are also worth a visit if you have an interest in Japan's modern architecture. Kenzō Tange designed the informative Hyōgo Prefectural Museum of History, and boxer-turned-architect Tadao Andō is responsible for the Himeji Museum of Literature, which is celebrated more for its unique minimalist exterior than for the exhibits inside. ⇨ *The San-yō Region in Chapter 9*

TŌKYŌ **3 days.** Japan's capital, it seems, has much in common with everyone's vision of the future. The neon of Kabuki-chō, the city's wildest nightlife venue, is said to have inspired the cityscapes in *Blade Runner,* and Andrei Tarkovsky used images of the Tōkyō Metropolitan Expressway in his futuristic film masterpiece *Solaris.* Shibuya's bottle-blonde schoolgirls and the chic twentysomethings of Aoyama beat the nation's fashion drum, and buildings such as Philippe Starck's imaginative Asahi Beer headquarters tower over traditional structures like Asakusa's Sensō-ji. Sumō wrestlers observe centuries-old rituals before grappling in an ultramodern stadium. The venue sits next door to a space-age museum, the Edo-Tōkyō Museum, that houses the treasures of Old Edo, a stimulating contrast typical of Tōkyō. ⇨ *Chapter 1*

By Public Transportation From Ōsaka's Nankai Namba Station you can reach Kōya-san in 90 minutes by the private Nankai Line and a cable car. You have to pass through Ōsaka again to get to Kyōto; frequent daily Hikari and Kodama Shinkansen make the 15-minute trip from Ōsaka to Kyōto. From Kyōto the Shinkansen will whisk you to Himeji in 45 minutes. Head back to Kyōto to catch the Shinkansen to Tōkyō.

Lakes & Mountains
8 days

With 80% of Japan's surface covered by mountains, you're bound to meet up with one sooner or later. Fuji-san, Japan's tallest peak, is one of the country's most enduring images, but several other mountains also provide a focus for a wonderful visit. Most of the country's lakes are small and shallow, but usually clear and scenic.

SAPPORO **2 days.** This pleasant and accessible city serves as a good base for exploring the dramatic landscape of Hokkaidō. Mountains encircle

Sapporo, the venue for the 1972 Olympic Games, and draw Japanese skiers in winter. Take day trips out to Tōya-ko or Shikotsu-ko, picturesque caldera lakes where you can boat or fish, and Noboribetsu Onsen, where you can soak in hot springs set against striking mountain scenery. ⇨ Sapporo & Otaru & the Shakotan-hantō in Chapter 14

DAISETSU-ZAN NATIONAL PARK 2 days. One of Japan's most popular spots for hiking and skiing reflects the essence of Hokkaidō: soaring mountain peaks, hidden gorges, cascading waterfalls, forests, and hot springs. Sheer cliff walls and stone spires make for a stunning drive through the Sōun-kyō ravine. Take a cable car up to the top of Hokkaidō's tallest mountain, Asahi-dake; hike or ski for a couple of hours; and then unwind at a hot spring below. ⇨ *Central & Northern Hokkaidō in Chapter 14*

HAGURO-SAN 2 days. This mountain, the most accessible of the Dewa-san range, a trio of sacred mountains in Tōhoku, is worth the trip not only for the lovely climb past cedars, waterfalls, and shrines but also for the thatched shrine at the top. You may even happen upon one of the many festivals and celebrations that take place at the shrine throughout the year. The rigorous climb itself, up 2,446 stone steps to the summit, is the main draw; however, it's possible to take a bus up or down the mountain. ⇨ Tōhoku West Coast in Chapter 13

FUJI-SAN & FUJI GO-KO 2 days. Climbing Mount Fuji requires an early start, ideally you should reach the summit before dawn in order to greet the sunrise. The climb takes five hours but is not arduous. The trip up is safe only in July and August, but the views of the mountain are rewarding any time of year. The nearby resort area at Fuji Go-ko (Fuji Five Lakes) is one place to take in some of those views, and it's the best place to set up base camp for your climb. You can skate and fish here in the winter, boat and hike in the summer. ⇨ *Fuji-Hakone-Izu National Park in Chapter 2*

Transportation Many countryside areas are difficult to reach by public transportation, so you may want to rent a car for parts of this trip, and combine it with trains, buses, and even flights. Note that flights, in addition to being quicker, are often equal in price to if not cheaper than trains. Although Sapporo has some direct flights from Europe and the United States, if you're bound for Hokkaidō you usually have to transfer in Tōkyō. If you do choose to use the train to Daisetsu-zan National Park, it'll take two hours from Sapporo to Kamikawa, the nearest station. Heading to Haguro-san by rail is possible, but it's easier to take the hour-long flight out of Sapporo to tiny Shōnai Airport in Sakata, only 30 minutes away by bus or car from Haguro-san. You can hop on a plane from Shōnai Airport for the hour-long trip toTōkyō, or use the Shinkansen, which takes more than four hours to reach Tōkyō and may require you to change trains. From Tōkyō a bus or train will take you to Fuji-san.

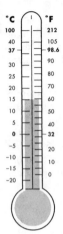

The best seasons to travel to Japan are spring and fall, when the weather is at its best. In spring the country is warm, with only occasional showers, and flowers grace landscapes in both rural and urban areas. The first harbingers of spring are plum blossoms in early March; *sakura* (cherry blossoms) follow, beginning in Kyūshū and usually arriving in Tōkyō by mid-April. Summer brings on the rainy season, with particularly heavy rains and stifling humidity in July. Avoid July and August if at all possible, unless you're visiting Hokkaidō, where temperatures are a little more bearable. Fall is a welcome relief, with clear blue skies and glorious foliage. Occasionally a few surprise typhoons occur in early fall, but the storms are usually as quick to leave as they are to arrive. Winter is gray and chilly, with little snow in most areas along the Pacific Ocean side of the country, where temperatures rarely fall below freezing. Hokkaidō and the Japan Sea side of the country (facing Korea and Russia) are a different story, however, and heavy snow falls can be expected in the winter months.

For the most part, the climate of Japan is temperate and resembles that of the east coast of the United States. The exceptions are the subtropical southern islands of Okinawa, south of Kyūshū, and the northern island of Hokkaidō.

To avoid crowds, **do not plan a trip for times when most Japanese are vacationing.** For the most part, Japanese cannot select when they want to take their vacations; they tend to do so on the same holiday dates. As a result, airports, planes, trains, and hotels are booked far in advance. Many businesses, shops, and restaurants are closed during these holidays. Holiday periods include the few days before and after New Year's; Golden Week, which follows Greenery Day (April 29); and mid-August at the time of the Obon festivals, when many Japanese return to their hometowns. March to September 2005 is an exciting time to visit the Nagoya area for the much-anticipated 2005 World Expo. See chapter 3 for details.

Climate

The following is a list of average daily maximum and minimum temperatures for major cities in Japan.

🎬 Forecasts **Weather Channel** ⊕ www.weather.com.

TŌKYŌ

Jan.	46F	8C	May	72F	22C	Sept.	78F	26C
	29	2		53	12		66	19
Feb.	48F	9C	June	75F	24C	Oct.	70F	21C
	30	1		62	17		56	13
Mar.	53F	12C	July	82F	28C	Nov.	60F	16C
	35	2		70	21		42	6
Apr.	62F	17C	Aug.	86F	30C	Dec.	51F	11C
	46	8		72	22		33	1

KYŌTO

Jan.	48F	9C	May	75F	24C	Sept.	82F	28C
	35	2		56	13		68	20
Feb.	53F	12C	June	82F	28C	Oct.	74F	23C
	32	0		66	19		53	12
Mar.	59F	15C	July	93F	34C	Nov.	62F	17C
	40	4		72	22		46	8
Apr.	65F	18C	Aug.	89F	32C	Dec.	53F	12C
	44	7		74	23		33	1

FUKUOKA

Jan.	53F	12C	May	74F	23C	Sept.	80F	27C
	35	2		57	14		68	20
Feb.	58F	14C	June	80F	27C	Oct.	74F	23C
	37	3		68	20		53	12
Mar.	60F	16C	July	89F	32C	Nov.	65F	18C
	42	6		75	24		48	9
Apr.	62F	17C	Aug.	89F	32C	Dec.	53F	12C
	48	9		75	24		37	3

SAPPORO

Jan.	29F	2C	May	60F	16C	Sept.	72F	22C
	10	12		40	4		51	11
Feb.	30F	1C	June	70F	21C	Oct.	60F	16C
	13	11		50	10		40	4
Mar.	35F	2C	July	75F	24C	Nov.	46F	8C
	20	7		57	14		29	2
Apr.	51F	11C	Aug.	78F	26C	Dec.	33F	1C
	32	0		60	16		18	8

NAHA

Jan.	65F	19C	May	80F	26C	Sept.	86F	30C
	56	14		57	14		60	16
Feb.	66F	19C	June	84F	29C	Oct.	81F	27C
	65	19		71	22		76	24
Mar.	69F	21C	July	88F	31C	Nov.	75F	24C
	79	26		78	26		77	25
Apr.	75F	24C	Aug.	87F	31C	Dec.	69F	21C
	72	22		66	19		60	16

Matsuri (festivals) are very important to the Japanese, and a large number are held throughout the year. Many of them originated in folk and religious rituals and date back hundreds of years. Gala matsuri take place annually at Buddhist temples and Shintō shrines, and many are associated with the changing of the seasons. Most are free and attract thousands of visitors as well as locals. If you're going to be in a city or town when a festival is taking place, make sure to book your hotel room well in advance. You can find more about the important matsuri, such as the big three festivals of Kyōto (the Gion, Jidai, and Aoi festivals), in individual chapters.

To find out specific matsuri dates, contact the Japan National Tourism Organization (☎ 212/757–5640 in U.S., 03/3201–3331 in Tōkyō). Note that when national holidays fall on Sunday, they are celebrated on the following Monday. Museums and sights are often closed the days after these holidays.

WINTER

January 1	New Year's Day, along with the days preceding and following, is the festival of festivals for the Japanese. Some women dress in traditional kimonos, and many people visit shrines and hold family reunions. Although the day is solemn, streets are often decorated with pine twigs, plum branches, and bamboo stalks.
February	During the first week more than 300 pieces of ice sculpture, some huge, populate the Sapporo Snow Festival, bringing some 2 million people to the city to see them.
February	Asahikawa's Ice Festival is a smaller counterpart to Sapporo's, with more of a country-fair atmosphere.
February 11	National Foundation Day celebrates accession to the throne by the first emperor.
February 13–15	Akita (in Tōhoku) City's Namahage Sedo Festival enacts in public a ritual from nearby Oga of threatening "good-for-nothings": men in demon masks carrying buckets and huge knives issue dire warnings to loafers.

SPRING

On or near March 21	Vernal Equinox Day celebrates the start of spring. On or around this date, Buddhists visit family graves and tombs to remember and pay their respects to their ancestors.
March 25– Sept.25, 2005	The 2005 World Exposition held near Nagoya is expected to host more than 125 nations and 15 million visitors.
April 14 and 15	Takayama's Sannō Festival transforms this sleepy time machine of a town into a rowdy party.

April 29	Greenery Day marks the first day of Golden Week—when many Japanese take vacations, and hotels, trains, and attractions are booked solid. This is *not* a good time to visit Japan.
May 3–5	Nanao's 400-year-old Seihakusai Festival enlivens the rustic Noto Peninsula fishing town with three days and nights of pulling huge 10-ton floats called *deka-yama* through the streets amid much all-night revelry. Okinawa's Naha Hāri, or Naha Dragon-Boat Races, are held May 3–5, and again in early June.
May 3	Constitution Memorial Day commemorates the adoption of the Japanese constitution.
May 5	On Children's Day, once more-appropriately called Boys' Day, families with little boys display paper or cloth carp on bamboo poles outside the house or a set of warrior dolls inside the home.
Weekend before May 15	The Kanda Festival, a loud Tōkyō blowout that takes place in odd-numbered years, is all about taking the Kanda shrine's gods out for some fresh air in their *mikoshi* (portable shrines)—not to mention drinking plenty of beer and having a great time.
May 15	Dating to the 6th century, the Aoi Festival, also known as the Hollyhock Festival, is the first of Kyōto's three most popular celebrations. An "imperial" procession of 300 courtiers starts from the Imperial Palace and makes its way to Shimogamo Jinja to pray for the prosperity of the city. Today's participants are local Kyōtoites.
3rd weekend in May	The Sanja Festival, held at Tōkyō's Asakusa Jinja, is the city's biggest party. Men, often naked to the waist, carry palanquins through the streets amid revelers. Many of these bare bearers bear the tattoos of the Yakuza, Japan's Mafia.
June	On Miyajima near Hiroshima, the lunar calendar determines the timing of three stately barges that cross the bay to the island's shrine for the Kangen-sai Festival.
1st weekend in June	The Yosakoi Soran Festival explodes with 41,000 noisy and colorful dancers on the streets of Sapporo. Yosakoi Soran is based on a blending of Koichi's Yosako dance festival and Hokkaidō's fishing folk-song Soran-bushi.
June 13–15	Hyaku-man-goku means the rice needed to feed one for a year, and Kanazawa's festival of the same name commemorates the city's rich rice-growing history with celebrations with floating lanterns, an amazing variety of parades, and a great deal of merrymaking.
SUMMER	
July 16 and 17	The Gion Festival, which dates to the 9th century, is perhaps Kyōto's most popular festival. Events are held throughout July, but the climax is this event in the middle of the month. Twenty-nine huge floats sail along downtown streets and make their way to Yasaka Jinja to

	thank the gods for protection from a pestilence that once ravaged the city.
July 20	A recent addition to the calendar, Umi no hi (Marine Day) marks the start of school summer holidays.
July 24 and 25	Ōsaka's Tenjin Festival is a major event, with parades of floats, night-time fireworks, and processions of 100-plus lighted vessels on the city's canals.
August	The first week's dreamlike Neputa Festival, held in the Tōhoku city of Hirosaki, involves nightly processions of floats, populated with illuminated paintings of faces from mythology, through the streets.
1st Saturday in August	At Noto Peninsula's Ishizaki Hōtō Festival celebration, paper lanterns more than 6 feet tall are carried on the shoulders of townsfolk, who open their houses to all guests for one night of lavish feasting and drinking.
August 3–7	The Nebuta Festival in northern Tōhoku's Aomori noisily celebrates an ancient battle victory with a nighttime parade of illuminated floats.
August 5–7	At Yamagata's Hanagasa Festival, in southern Tōhoku, celebrants dance through the streets in local costume among floats. Food and drink are on hand for spectators.
August 6–8	Sendai's Tanabata celebrates two legendary astrological lovers with a theatrical rendition of their tale, and city residents decorate their streets and houses with colorful paper and bamboo streamers.
August 13–16	During the Obon Festival, a time of Buddhist ceremonies in honor of ancestors, many Japanese take off the entire week to travel to their hometowns—try to avoid travel on these days.
August 15	Okinawa's Eisā Festival coincides with Obon. During this time, everyone is on holiday, and dancers and musicians keep to the streets.
August 16	For the Daimonji Gozan Okuribi, huge bonfires in the shape of kanji characters illuminate five of the mountains that surround Kyōto. The most famous is the *Dai*, meaning "big," on the side of Mt. Daimonji in Higashiyama (Kyōto's eastern district). Dress in a cool yukata (cotton robe) and walk down to the banks of the Kamo-gawa to view this spectacular summer sight, or catch all five fires from the rooftop of your hotel downtown or a spot in Funaoka-yama or Yoshida-yama parks. There are Bon dances as well as the floating of lanterns in Arashiyama.
FALL	
September 15	Keiro-no-hi is Respect for the Aged Day.
On or near September 23	Shubun-no-hi is the Autumnal Equinox Day.

2nd Monday in October	Health-Sports Day commemorates the Tōkyō Olympics of 1964.
Mid-October	The Dai-Ryūkyū Matsuri (The Big Ryūkyū Festival) is held in Naha, Okinawa, for a week in October, and is in fact a series of about a dozen smaller festivals highlighting aspects of local culture. One of these is known as the Naha Festival, held annually on October 10, which culminates in the "Great Naha Tug of War."
October 22	Kyōto's Jidai Festival, the Festival of Eras, features a colorful costume procession of fashions from the 8th through 19th century. The procession begins at the Imperial Palace and winds up at Heian Jinja. More than 2,000 Kyōtoites voluntarily participate in this festival, which dates to 1895.
October 22	The Kurama Fire Festival, at Kurama Shrine, involves a roaring bonfire and a rowdy portable shrine procession that makes its way through the narrow streets of the small village in the northern suburbs of Kyōto. If you catch a spark, it's believed to bring good luck.
November 3	Culture Day, established after World War II, encourages the Japanese to cherish peace, freedom, and culture, both old and new.
November 23	Kinro Kansha-no-hi (Labor Thanksgiving Day) is recognized by harvest celebrations in some parts of the country.
December 23	On Tennō Tanjōbi (the Emperor's Birthday), Emperor Akihito makes an appearance on the balcony of the Imperial Palace in Tōkyō.
December 27	Travel is *not* recommended on the first day of the weeklong New Year celebrations.

PLEASURES & PASTIMES

Bathing Partly because of the importance of purification rites in Shintō, Japan's ancient indigenous religion, the art of bathing has been a crucial element of Japanese culture for centuries. Baths in Japan are as much about pleasure and relaxation as they are about washing and cleansing. Traditionally, communal bathhouses served as centers for social gatherings, and even though most modern houses and apartments have bathtubs, many Japanese still prefer the pleasures of communal bathing—either at *onsen* (⇨ *below*) while on vacation or in public bathhouses closer to home. For tips on bathhouse etiquette, *see* "Bathing: An Immersion Course" in Chapter 16.

Beaches For a country that consists entirely of islands, Japan has surprisingly few good beaches. Those accessible from Tōkyō, around Kamakura and the Izu Peninsula, are absolutely mobbed all summer long. The beaches of Kyūshū and Shikoku are less crowded, more pleasant, and have clear blue water. The country's best beaches are on the subtropical Ryūkyū Islands, which include Okinawa (⇨ Chapter 12). But bear in mind that many Japanese find it less expensive to fly to Hawaii than to go to the Ryūkyū.

Bicycling With its narrow roads and largely mountainous terrain, Japan does not offer ideal conditions for long cycling trips. In certain towns, however, it's feasible, inexpensive, and delightful to see the sights by bicycle. Where this is the case, there are bicycle-rental shops near the main railway station, as in Kanazawa, Takayama, and Hagi. One region that is flatter and less trafficked than most of Japan is the San-in coast of Western Honshū (⇨ Chapter 9). You can do some serious cycling on some of the remote islands, such as Sado, on the Sea of Japan, and Iki, off the coast of Kyūshū. Wherever you ride, don't forget that cars drive on the left side of the road in Japan.

Dining Japanese food is not only delicious and healthy but also arranged to please the eye. In fact the aesthetic experience of food is of utmost importance to the Japanese. Even the most humble box lunch (*bentō*) from a railway station or on a train will have been created with careful attention to color combinations and overall presentation. This guide's regional chapters discuss local specialties in detail, and the Japanese are very proud of their local specialties—from Kyōto's *kaiseki ryōri* (elaborate, multicourse set meals) to the Japan Alps region's use of mountain vegetables and tasty local miso. For an introduction to the delights of Japanese cooking, turn to Chapter 15, The Discreet Charm of Japanese Cuisine, and Chapter 18, where you'll find our Japanese Vocabulary & Menu Guide.

Language As difficult as it can be, learning Japanese is also a delight. You'll see many Japanese terms throughout this book. If you're wondering if "-san" really does mean "mountain," and "kōen" means "park," *check* the Glossary of Key Japanese Words and Suffixes at the end of this book. It will help you understand basic travel terms. For tips on how to communicate and more information on the Japanese language in general, *see* Language *in* Smart Travel Tips A to Z *and* the English–Japanese Traveler's Vocabulary at the end of this book.

Onsen

No doubt the Japanese love of bathing has something to do with the hundreds of *onsen* (natural hot springs) that bubble out of their volcanic islands. Many onsen are surrounded by resorts, ranging from overlarge Western-style hotels to small, humble inns; all are extremely popular among Japanese tourists. Traditionally the curative value of hot-spring water was strongly emphasized. Add to that today's need to get away from the frantic pace of life and relax. At resorts, onsen water is usually piped in to hotel rooms or large, communal indoor baths. And some onsen have *rotemburo* (open-air baths) where you can soak outdoors in the midst of a snowy winter landscape. Some of the best-known spas near Tōkyō are at Atami, Hakone, Itō, and Nikkō; in Kōbe, at Arima; in Kyūshū, at Beppu and Yufuin; and in Hokkaidō, at Noboribetsu.

Shopping

Japan's *depāto* (pronounced "deh-*pah*-to, meaning department stores) have to be seen to be believed—from their automatonlike white-gloved elevator operators to their elaborate wrapping of even the most humble purchase. Items made by every international designer you can name sit alongside the best of traditional Japanese arts and crafts items, and most stores have at least two basement levels devoted entirely to the selling of food, from international grocery fare to ready-to-eat Japanese delicacies and everyday menu items.

For a view of how the middle class manages its daily shopping, head to one of the shopping arcades that are often an extension of urban and suburban train or subway stations. Everything—clothes, stationery, books, CDs, electronic goods, food, housewares—is sold in these arcades, which can be madhouses during the evening rush hour. Markets are another way to get closer to everyday Japanese life. The warrens of shops outside Tōkyō's fish market in Tsukiji are full of interesting wares. Kyōto's Nishi-kōji market and its monthly Tō-ji and Kitano Tenman-gū markets are essential experiences. Takayama's Asa-ichi (morning market) is another must for local items.

Skiing

Japan's mountains are beautiful and snowy in winter, with very good skiing conditions. Many ski areas are near natural hot springs, so you can end a chilly day on the slopes with a hot soak. The most popular ski areas are around central Honshū's Nagano, site of the 1998 Winter Olympics; in northern Honshū at Mt. Zao; and in Hokkaidō at Niseko (west of Sapporo) and Daisetsu-zan National Park (in the central part of the island).

But be forewarned: The major drawback of skiing in Japan is crowds, especially on weekends and holidays. The slopes can become more heavily packed with people than snow, and trains and highways leading to the ski areas are also congested. If you're set on skiing in Japan, try to go on a weekday or head for Hokkaidō during a nonholiday period.

Sumō

If baseball can be called Japan's modern national pastime, surely sumō is its traditional national pastime, and it remains tremendously popular, even at 2,000 years old. A Shintō-style roof is hung from the ceiling over a circular clay ring in which two enormous wrestlers face off. After various preliminary rites, some of which involve tossing handfuls of salt into the ring to symbolize purification, the actual wrestling begins. A match ends when any part of a wrestler's body (other than the soles of his feet) touches the ground or when he is pushed out of the ring. Wrestlers wear only a loincloth-type garment and have slick topknot hairstyles.

Six 15-day sumō tournaments are held each year, selling out stadiums that seat around 10,000 people; millions more watch on television. The matches are shown on huge screens in major train stations and elsewhere—if a tournament is under way while you're in Japan, you'll know it. Tickets can be difficult to obtain, but it's definitely worth a try. If you go, buy the more expensive seats, both because they give you a better view of the action and because they include a bagful of a generous amount of food and sumō-theme souvenirs, such as a tea or sake set whose cups feature drawings of the major wrestlers.

Knowing some big-time sumō names might prove useful for conversations with Japanese about this sport so dear to their hearts. Chionofuji, one of the first trim sumō wrestlers, retired into a status much revered. Asashōryū is one of the recent popular yokozuna, hailing from Mongolia.

FODOR'S CHOICE

> The sights, restaurants, hotels, and other travel experiences on these pages are our writers' and editors' top picks—our Fodor's Choices.

LODGING

$$$$	**Grand Hyatt Tōkyō.** Lavish materials, from sheets to showerheads, are the main claim to fame of this hotel.
$$$$	**Hotel Ōkura,** Tōkyō. The Ōkura is an old favorite among diplomats and business travelers for its good service, spacious rooms, and understated sophistication. There's a small museum on-site.
$$$$	**Imperial Hotel,** Kamikōchi, the Japan Alps. Beautiful woodwork, velvet rugs, fireplaces, and exemplary service are the trademarks of this high-end alpine lodge.
$$$$	**Miyakojima Tōkyū Resort,** Miyako-jima, Okinawa. On Japan's finest beach in subtropical Okinawa, this resort delivers everything you could want from a beach vacation.
$$$$	**Nagoya Kankō Hotel,** Nagoya. The city's oldest hotel, the choice of royalty and celebrities, has a satisfying contemporary interior.
$$$$	**Nara Hotel,** Nara. Be sure to ask for a room in the old wing of this early-20th-century hotel overlooking several famous temples.
$$$$	**Ritz-Carlton Ōsaka.** The ultimate in luxury, the Ritz's exemplary service is matched by its lavish guest rooms.
$$$$	**Tawaraya,** Kyōto. Presidents and celebrities stay at this famous inn, founded at the turn of the 18th century.
$$$$	**The Windsor Hotel,** Tōya-ko, Hokkaidō. Perched on the edge of a volcanic lake, this resort hotel offers incredible views over the rugged territory of Hokkaidō's Shikotsu-Tōya National Park.
$$$–$$$$	**Four Seasons Hotel Chinzan-sō,** Tōkyō. Every polished inch is evidence of the million dollars or so that it cost to complete each guest room.
$$$–$$$$	**Ryokan Kurashiki,** Kurashiki. This rare, ultra-traditional ryokan offers guests a picturesque setting and constant, attentive service but few of the amenities you're used to.
$$$–$$$$	**Westin Miyako Hotel,** Kyōto. Atop Mt. Kacho near the Eastern temples, this hotel has a walking trail and several Japanese gardens, as well as tastefully furnished rooms.
$$$–$$$$	**Yoshimizu Ginza,** Tōkyō. Artistic minimalism is the style of this simple, traditional inn, which aims to provide a total escape from the crowded streets of the city.
$$$	**Shin-Kōbe Oriental Hotel,** Kōbe. For the best views of downtown and the harbor, book a room in this Morgan Stanley–owned hotel, Kōbe's tallest building.

$$ **Furusato Kankō Hotel,** Kagoshima, Kyūshū. Enjoy a dip in the onsen, sea-water pool, or indoor lap pool before views of the bay and the Mt. Sakurajima volcano.

$$ **Pension Angelica,** Mt. Aso National Park. The coziest chalet in all of Japan, the Angelica has pretty, sunny rooms, and a restaurant serving delicious Western-style meals.

BUDGET LODGING

$ **Holiday Inn Nagasaki.** Oil paintings, leather chairs, and old-fashioned telephones give this affordable hotel a bit of sophistication.

$ **Sawanoya Ryokan,** Tōkyō. Rooms are basic and the bathroom is shared, but you can't beat the warm welcome at this family-run inn. Rooms book up quickly.

RESTAURANTS

$$$$ **Aragawa,** Kōbe. The finest Kōbe beef—thoroughly marbled and exquisitely tender—is served in delicate, costly portions at this renowned restaurant.

$$$$ **Kagetsu,** Nagasaki. Elaborate, multicourse Japanese and Asian-European meals are served at this restaurant in a 17th-century former brothel.

$$$$ **Mankamerō,** Kyōto. Experience traditional Japanese cuisine as it was enjoyed by members of the imperial court, at king's-ransom prices.

$$$$ **Yagembori,** Kyōto. In a teahouse near a little brook in the heart of the geisha district, this restaurant serves the finest kaiseki (Japanese haute cuisine) on handmade ceramics. Try the shabu-shabu.

$$$–$$$$ **Sagenta,** near Kyōto. After a train ride to the mountain town of Kibune, you'll be seated on an outdoor dining platform over a gurgling stream and served a meal of delicious Japanese cuisine.

$$–$$$$ **Hyakuman-goku,** Hagi. This restaurant on western Honshū's San-in coast serves some of the finest raw seafood in the world, including tuna, sea urchin, and crab.

$$–$$$$ **Inakaya,** Tōkyō. Cooks in traditional dress grill skewers of meat, seafood, and vegetables as you look on.

$$–$$$$ **Tableaux,** Tōkyō. Red leather meets antique gold at Tableaux. Although the design is over-the-top, it doesn't outshine the contemporary Asian-Italian dishes.

$$–$$$ **Kawakyō,** Matsue. Famous delicacies from Shinji-ko lake served here include freshwater eel, whitefish, smelt, small black-shelled clams, and shrimp.

$$–$$$ **Robata,** Tōkyō. Home-style Japanese food, including steamed fish and beef stew, is served on beautiful pottery in this small eatery.

$$–$$$	Sasashū, Tōkyō. This traditional-style pub pairs the finest sakes in Japan with the best izakaya food in town.
$$–$$$	Mimiu, Ōsaka. Warm up around a pot of thick noodle-and-seafood soup stewed over a burner at your table.
$$	Ganchan, Tōkyō. Squeeze into this tiny, cluttered restaurant for some of the best charcoal-grilled yakitori in town.
$$	Sagano, Kyōto. Tofu simmered in savory broth is subtle and delicate at this gorgeous Arashiyama-district retreat.

BUDGET RESTAURANTS

$–$$	Aoi-Marushin, Tōkyō. Loads of tempura are served fresh from the fryer at this Asakusa staple, a short walk from Sensō-ji temple. English menus make ordering a snap.
¢–$$	Ume no Hana, Tōkyō. A traditional stone walkway lined with lanterns leads up to this restaurant, which takes the simple ingredient tofu and transforms it into delicious, creative dishes.

CASTLES

Himeji-jō, Himeji, western Honshū. Japan's most spectacular castle has four stone strongholds to support its gorgeous, tiered towers and protect its other buildings.

Kōchi-jō, Kōchi, Shikoku. The elegant white walls of Japan's best-preserved castle rise above a dramatic cliff face.

Nijō-jō, Kyōto. Big, elaborate Nijō-jō was built to impress, and it still succeeds. Inside is a fine art collection.

Ōsaka-jō, Ōsaka. Enormous, majestic, and especially beautiful when illuminated at night, Ōsaka Castle presides over the city on a foundation of immense granite rocks.

ISLANDS & BEACHES

Miyako-shōtō, Okinawa. This group of islands has white-sand beaches, coral reefs teeming with rainbow-color fish, and just enough development to assure comfort.

Mae-hama, Miyako-jima, Okinawa. Widely regarded as Japan's best beach, Mae-hama offers miles of smooth, white sand extending into warm, clear, turquoise water.

Yaeyama-shōtō, Okinawa. If you can travel the distance to this remote island chain, you'll be rewarded by unblemished underwater scenery and a jungle-like national park.

MUSEUMS & MEMORIALS

A-Bomb Dome, Hiroshima. Only this building was left unreconstructed after an atomic bomb leveled this Western Honshū city.

Great Hanshin-Awaji Earthquake Memorial, Kōbe. This museum commemorates the thousands who lost their lives in Kōbe's 1995 earthquake, and teaches you everything you ever wanted to know about the cause and effect of this type of natural disaster.

Hyōgo Prefectural Museum of Art, Kōbe. Inside a striking, postmodern, concrete building on the waterfront, this leading museum houses works by Koiso Ryohei and August Rodin.

Nezu Institute of Fine Arts, Tōkyō. A fantastic collection of Japanese and Chinese art, a lovely 5-acre garden, and several tea pavilions make the Nezu Institute the perfect destination for a leisurely afternoon.

Nibutani Ainu Culture Museum, Nibutani, Hokkaidō. Artifacts and videos illustrate life in an Ainu community.

Ōsaka Aquarium. At Japan's best aquarium, and one of the world's largest, you can admire whale sharks, king penguins, and giant spider crabs.

Tōkyō National Museum. This is where to get your fill of East Asian art and archaeology, including pottery, scrolls, swords, armor, and masks.

NATURAL WONDERS

Fuji-san, Fuji-Hakone-Izu National Park. Whether you climb to the summit or view it from afar, beautiful, symmetrical, snow-capped Mt. Fuji is bound to make an impression.

Kegon Falls, Chūzenji. You can view Japan's most famous waterfall from either the top or the bottom of the 318-ft drop.

Nakadake, Mt. Aso National Park. Ever wanted to look into the caldera of a still-active volcano? Go ahead and satisfy your curiosity. You won't be disappointed.

Shimanami Kaidō, Shikoku. A series of bridges lets you island-hop between Shikoku and Western Honshū by bus, bicycle, or on foot.

PARKS & GARDENS

Daisetsu-zan National Park, Hokkaidō. Japan's largest national park, Daisetsu-zan has vast plains, soaring mountain peaks, endless hiking trails, and, of course, onsen.

Ginkaku-ji, Kyōto. One of the two gardens at this tranquil temple provides changing perspectives as you stroll through it; the other is a dry garden with dazzling sand shapes for quiet contemplation.

Glover Garden, Nagasaki. This minivillage of 19th-century Western-style houses includes the former mansion of Scottish merchant Thomas Glover. The community and surrounding gardens were supposedly the setting for Puccini's *Madame Butterfly*.

Gyokusen Garden, Kanazawa. Step into this intimate sculpted garden for a total escape into a land of natural yet cultivated beauty.

Imperial Palace East Garden, Tōkyō. This wonderfully sculpted garden has tree-shaded walkways, rows of rhododendrons, a pond, a waterfall, several fine old structures, and unbeatable views of the Imperial Palace.

Katsura Rikyū, Kyōto. The loveliness of this vast estate's numerous gardens and rustic teahouses makes it worth your while to plan a visit in advance—as you must.

Kōinzan Saihō-ji, Kyōto. An extraordinary multilevel garden covered with 120 varieties of moss give this temple its nickname: the Moss Temple (Koke-dera).

ONSEN

Sakino-yu Onsen, Kii Peninsula. One of the best cheap thrills in southern Japan, these rocky hot springs let you soak in warm water while facing the chilly Pacific Ocean.

Kamuiwakka Onsen, Shiretoko National Park. A hot-water stream tumbles down a mountainside in a series of waterfalls and pools at this heavenly onsen.

SIGHTS & SCENES

Backstreet shops of Tsukiji, Tōkyō. Besides its lively fish market, Tsukiji has countless small stores selling snacks, kitchenware, baskets, and knickknacks, plus dozens of tiny sushi bars.

Gion, Kyōto. Geisha in richly brocaded kimono hurry down alleys to appointments in this Kyōto neighborhood.

Hida Folk Village, Takayama. Here you can walk through a reconstructed village of *gasshō-zukuri*—traditional farmhouses with steep, A-frame, thatched roofs.

Kabuki-za, Tōkyō. A night of Kabuki is a quintessential Japanese experience and there's no better place to catch a performance than at this theater.

Matsue, western Honshū. A lovely, remote town on the northern shore, Matsue offers delectable seafood, beautiful scenery, and elegant architecture.

Ryōgoku, Tōkyō. A sumō tournament or the elaborate Edo-Tōkyō Museum may draw you out to this working-class neighborhood west of the Sumida-gawa River.

Takayama, the Japan Alps. This wonderfully quaint, quiet, mountain town has a downtown area arranged like a museum, with rows of traditional wood-lattice buildings housing charming shops and restaurants.

Tsuwano, western Honshū. Stucco-and-tile walls, old castle ruins, and clear streams running beside the streets all contribute to the beauty of this unique mountain hamlet.

U-kai, Gifu. You won't see this at Disney World, but u-kai, or fishing with cormorants, is some of the liveliest, if un-PC, entertainment you're ever likely to witness.

TEMPLES & SHRINES

Daibutsu-den, Tōdai-ji, Nara. The world's largest wooden structure houses a colossal 8th-century bronze Buddha.

Great Buddha statue, Kamakura. This 37-ft, 700-year old bronze statue about 40 mi southwest of Tōkyō is one of Japan's most enduring symbols.

Hase-dera Temple, Kamakura. The haunting sight of hundreds of statues of Jizō—the bodhisattva associated with the souls of lost children—will stay with you after seeing this temple.

Hōryū-ji, Nara. Japan's oldest temple compound houses a fine collection of Buddhist art.

Ise Jingū, Ise-Shima. The austere beauty of the Grand Shrines of Ise is especially intriguing when you consider that the structures are completely rebuilt every 20 years.

Kinkaku-ji, Kyōto. Gold leaf covers this shining three-story temple, which is brilliantly reflected in the calm water of the pond it overlooks.

Kiyomizu-dera, Kyōto. You get a splendid panorama of the city from the cliff-side main hall of this spacious temple complex.

Myōryū-ji, Kanazawa. This deceptively modest-looking temple hides dozens of secret passageways, staircases, and trap doors—even a hidden tunnel to the castle.

Sensō-ji, Tōkyō. A walk through the serene gardens and Shintō shrine of this Edo-period temple complex is a must for any visitor to Tōkyō.

Tōshō-gū, Nikkō. Anyone with more than four or five days to spend in Tōkyō should make a trip out to Nikkō to see the resplendent world-renowned shrine to Ieyasu Tokugawa.

SMART TRAVEL TIPS

ADDRESSES

The simplest way to decipher a Japanese address is to break it into parts. For example: 6-chōme 8–19, Chūō-ku, Fukuoka-shi, Fukuoka-ken. In this address the "chōme" indicates a precise area (a block, for example), and the numbers following "chōme" indicate the building within the area. Note that buildings aren't always numbered sequentially; numbers are often assigned as buildings are erected. Only local police officers and mail carriers in Japan seem to be familiar with the area defined by the chōme. Sometimes, instead of "chōme," "machi" (town) is used. Written addresses in Japan also have the opposite order of those in the West, with the city coming before the street.

"Ku" refers to a ward (a district) of a city, "shi" refers to a city name, and "ken" indicates a prefecture, which is roughly equivalent to a state in the United States. It's not unusual for the prefecture and the city to have the same name, as in the above address. There are a few geographic areas in Japan that are not called ken. One is greater Tōkyō, which is called Tōkyō-to. Other exceptions Kyōto and Ōsaka, which are followed by the suffix "-fu"—Kyōto-fu, Ōsaka-fu. Hokkaidō, Japan's northernmost island, is also not considered a ken. Not all addresses conform exactly to the above format. Rural addresses, for example, might use "gun" (county) where city addresses have "ku" (ward).

Even Japanese people cannot find a building based on the address alone. If you get in a taxi with a written address, do not assume the driver will be able to find your destination. Usually, people provide very detailed instructions or maps to explain their exact locations. It's always good to know the location of your destination in relation to a major building or department store.

AIR TRAVEL

You can fly nonstop to Tokyo from Chicago, Detroit, New York, Los Angeles, San Francisco, Portland (OR), Seattle, Minneapolis, and Washington, D.C., in the United States; from London; from Brisbane, Sydney, and Melbourne in Australia; and from Auckland in New Zealand.

You can also fly nonstop to Ōsaka from Chicago, Detroit, Pittsburgh, and San Francisco in the United States; and from Brisbane and Sydney in Australia. Because of the distance, fares to Japan from the United States tend to be expensive, usually between $900 and $1,200 for a seat in coach. But it's possible to get a ticket for as low as $700 from a discount travel Web site, depending on the time of year.

BOOKING

When you book, look for nonstop flights and remember that "direct" flights stop at least once. Try to avoid connecting flights, which require a change of plane. Two airlines may operate a connecting flight jointly, so ask whether your airline operates every segment of the trip; you may find that the carrier you prefer flies you only part of the way. To find more booking tips and to check prices and make online flight reservations, log on to www.fodors.com.

CARRIERS

Japan Airlines (JAL) and United Airlines are the major carriers between North America and Narita Airport in Tōkyō; Northwest, American Airlines, Delta Airlines, and All Nippon Airways (ANA) also link North American cities with Tōkyō. JAL, Cathay Pacific, Virgin Atlantic Airways, and British Airways fly between Narita and Great Britain; JAL, United, and Qantas fly between Narita and Australia; and JAL and Air New Zealand fly between Narita and New Zealand. Most of these airlines also fly into and out of Japan's number two international airport, Kansai International Airport, located south of Ōsaka.

🛪 Airlines & Contacts **Air Canada** ☎ 888/247-2262, 0120/04-8048 in Japan ⊕ www.aircanada.ca. **All Nippon Airways** ☎ 800/235-9262 in U.S. and Canada, 0120/02-9222 in Japan for domestic flights, 0120/02-9333 in Japan for international flights ⊕ www.anaskyweb.com or www.ana.co.jp. **American** ☎ 800/433-7300, 0120/00-0860 in Japan ⊕ www.aa.com. **British Airways** ☎ 0345/222-111 in U.K., 03/3593-8811 in Japan ⊕ www.british-

airways.com. **Continental** ☎ 800/525-0280 ⊕ www.continental.com. **Delta** ☎ 800/221-1212 ⊕ www.delta.com. **Japan Airlines** ☎ 800/525-3663, 0845/7747-700 in U.K., 0120/25-5931 international in Japan, 0120/25-5971 domestic in Japan ⊕ www.jal.co.jp. **Korean Air** ☎ 800/438-5000, 0800/413-000 in U.K., 03/5443-3311 in Japan ⊕ www.koreanair.com. **Lufthansa** ☎ 0870/837-7737 in U.K. ⊕ www.lufthansa.com. **Northwest** ☎ 800/447-4747, 03/3533-6000 or 0120/12-0747 in Japan ⊕ www.nwa.com. **Swiss** ☎ 800/221-4750, 020/7434-7300 in U.K., 03/5156-9090 in Japan ⊕ www.swissair.com. **Thai Airways International** ☎ 800/426-5204, 020/7499-9113 in U.K., 03/3503-3311 in Japan ⊕ www.thaiair.com. **United** ☎ 800/241-6522, 0120/11-4466 in Japan ⊕ www.united.com.

CHECK-IN & BOARDING

Always **find out your carrier's check-in policy.** Plan to arrive at the airport about 1½ hours before your scheduled departure time for domestic flights and 2½ hours before international flights. You may need to arrive earlier if you're flying from one of the busier airports or during peak air-traffic times. To avoid delays at airport-security checkpoints, try not to wear any metal. Shoes without laces that you can slip off and on are convenient when you have to pass them through the baggage scanners. Belt and other buckles, shoes with nails or steel toes, and keys are among the items that can set off detectors.

Assuming that not everyone with a ticket will show up, airlines routinely overbook planes. When everyone does, airlines ask for volunteers to give up their seats. In return, these volunteers usually get a several-hundred-dollar flight voucher, which can be used toward the purchase of another ticket, and are rebooked on the next flight out. If there are not enough volunteers, the airline must choose who will be denied boarding. The first to get bumped are passengers who checked in late and those flying on discounted tickets, so get to the gate and check in as early as possible, especially during peak periods.

Always **bring a government-issued photo ID** to the airport; even when it's not required, a passport is best.

CUTTING COSTS

The least expensive airfares to Japan are priced for round-trip travel and must usually be purchased in advance. Airlines generally allow you to change your return date for a fee; most low-fare tickets, however, are nonrefundable. It's smart to call a number of airlines and check the Internet; when you are quoted a good price, book it on the spot—the same fare may not be available the next day, or even the next hour. Always check different routings and look into using alternate airports. Also, price off-peak flights, which may be significantly less expensive than others. Travel agents, especially low-fare specialists (⇨ Discounts & Deals), are helpful.

Consolidators are another good source. They buy tickets for scheduled flights at reduced rates from the airlines, then sell them at prices that beat the best fare available directly from the airlines. (Many also offer reduced car-rental and hotel rates.) Sometimes you can even get your money back if you need to return the ticket. Carefully read the fine print detailing penalties for changes and cancellations, purchase the ticket with a credit card, and confirm your consolidator reservation with the airline.

When you fly as a courier, you trade your checked-luggage space for a ticket deeply subsidized by a courier service. There are restrictions on when you can book and how long you can stay. Some courier companies list with membership organizations, such as the Air Courier Association and the International Association of Air Travel Couriers; these require you to become a member before you can book a flight.

Many airlines, singly or in collaboration, offer discount air passes that allow foreigners to travel economically in a particular country or region. These visitor passes usually must be reserved and purchased before you leave home. Information about passes often can be found on most airlines' international Web pages, which tend to be aimed at travelers from outside the carrier's home country. Also, try typing the name of the pass into a search engine, or search for "pass" within the carrier's Web site.

Both of Japan's major carriers offer reduced prices for flights within the country, though tickets must be booked outside Japan. JAL offers the Yōkoso Japan Airpass; ANA has the Visit Japan Fare.

Consolidators AirlineConsolidator.com ☎ 888/468-5385 ⊕ www.airlineconsolidator.com, for international tickets. **Best Fares** ☎ 800/880-1234 or 800/576-8255 ⊕ www.bestfares.com; $59.90 annual membership. **Cheap Tickets** ☎ 800/377-1000 or 800/652-4327 ⊕ www.cheaptickets.com. **Expedia** ☎ 800/397-3342 or 404/728-8787 ⊕ www.expedia.com. **Hotwire** ☎ 866/468-9473 or 920/330-9418 ⊕ www.hotwire.com. **Now Voyager Travel** ✉ 45 W. 21st St., Suite 5A, New York, NY 10010 ☎ 212/459-1616 🖷 212/243-2711 ⊕ www.nowvoyagertravel.com. **Onetravel.com** ⊕ www.onetravel.com. **Orbitz** ☎ 888/656-4546 ⊕ www.orbitz.com. **Priceline.com** ⊕ www.priceline.com. **Travelocity** ☎ 888/709-5983, 877/282-2925 in Canada, 0870/876-3876 in U.K. ⊕ www.travelocity.com.

Courier Resources Air Courier Association/Cheaptrips.com ☎ 800/280-5973 or 800/282-1202 ⊕ www.aircourier.org or www.cheaptrips.com; $34 annual membership. **International Association of Air Travel Couriers** ☎ 308/632-3273 in U.S., 0800/0746-481 in U.K. ⊕ www.courier.org ⊕ www.aircourier.co.uk; $45 annual membership. **Now Voyager Travel** ✉ 45 W. 21st St., Suite 5A, New York, NY 10010 ☎ 212/459-1616 🖷 212/243-2711 ⊕ www.nowvoyagertravel.com.

Discount Passes Visit Japan Fare All Nippon Airways ☎ 800/235-9262 in U.S. and Canada, 870/837-8866 in U.K. ⊕ www.anaskyweb.com or www.ana.co.jp. **All Asia Pass** Cathay Pacific ☎ 800/233-2742, 800/268-6868 in Canada ⊕ www.cathay-usa.com or www.cathay.ca. **Yōkoso Japan Airpass** Japan Airlines ☎ 800/525-3663, 0845/7747-700 in U.K. ⊕ www.jal.co.jp.

ENJOYING THE FLIGHT

State your seat preference when purchasing your ticket, and then repeat it when you confirm and when you check in. For more legroom, you can request one of the few emergency-aisle seats at check-in, if you're capable of moving obstacles comparable in weight to an airplane exit door (usually between 35 pounds and 60 pounds)—a Federal Aviation Administration requirement of passengers in these seats. Seats behind a bulkhead also offer more legroom, but they don't have under-seat storage. Don't sit in the row in front of the emergency aisle or in front of a bulkhead, where seats may not recline.

Ask the airline whether a snack or meal is served on the flight. If you have dietary concerns, request special meals when booking. These can be vegetarian, low-cholesterol, or kosher, for example. It's a good idea to pack some healthful snacks and a small (plastic) bottle of water in your carry-on bag. On long flights, try to maintain a normal routine, to help fight jet lag. At night, get some sleep. By day, eat light meals, drink water (not alcohol), and **move around the cabin** to stretch your legs. For additional jet-lag tips consult *Fodor's FYI: Travel Fit & Healthy* (available at bookstores everywhere).

All domestic flights in Japan are no-smoking.

FLYING TIMES

Flying time to Japan is 13¾ hours from New York, 12¾ hours from Chicago, 9½ hours from Los Angeles, 9½ hours from Sydney, 11–12 hours from the United Kingdom. Japan Airlines' GPS systems allow a more direct routing, which reduces its flight times by about 30 minutes. Your trip east, because of tailwinds, can be about 45 minutes shorter.

HOW TO COMPLAIN

If your baggage goes astray or your flight goes awry, complain right away. Most carriers require that you **file a claim immediately.** The Aviation Consumer Protection Division of the Department of Transportation publishes *Fly-Rights*, which discusses airlines and consumer issues and is available online. You can also find articles and information on mytravelrights.com, the Web site of the nonprofit Consumer Travel Rights Center.

Airline Complaints Air Transport Users Council ⊠ For inquiries: FAA, Room K201, CAA House, 45–59 Kingsway, London, WC2B 6TE ☎ 020/7240–6061 ⊕ www.caa.co.uk/auc/. **Aviation Consumer Protection Division** ⊠ U.S. Department of Transportation, Office of Aviation Enforcement and Proceedings, C-75, Room 4107, 400 7th St. SW, Washington, DC 20590 ☎ 202/366–2220 ⊕ airconsumer.ost.dot.gov. **Federal Aviation Administration**

Consumer Hotline ⊠ For inquiries: FAA, 800 Independence Ave. SW, Washington, DC 20591 ☎ 800/322–7873 ⊕ www.faa.gov.

RECONFIRMING

Check the status of your flight before you leave for the airport. You can do this on your carrier's Web site, by linking to a flight-status checker (many Web booking services offer these), or by calling your carrier or travel agent. Always confirm international flights at least 72 hours ahead of the scheduled departure time.

AIRPORTS

The major gateway to Japan is Tōkyō's Narita Airport (NRT), 80 km (50 mi) northeast of the city. To alleviate the congestion at Narita, Kansai International Airport (KIX) opened in 1994 outside Ōsaka to serve the Kansai region, which includes Kōbe, Kyōto, Nara, and Ōsaka. It's also possible to fly from the United States, the United Kingdom, New Zealand, and Australia into Nagoya Airport. Fares are generally cheapest into Narita, however. A few international flights use Fukuoka Airport, on the island of Kyūshū; these include Continental flights from Guam, JAL from Honolulu, and flights from other Asian destinations. Shin-Chitose Airport, outside Sapporo on the northern island of Hokkaidō, handles some international flights, mostly to Asian destinations such as Seoul and Shanghai. Most domestic flights to and from Tōkyō are out of Haneda Airport.

Two new airports were in the works at this writing—one in Nagoya (the Central Japan International Airport, slated to open before the 2005 World Expo) and one in Kōbe, which will handle only domestic flights.

Tōkyō Narita's Terminal 2 has two adjoining wings, north and south. When you arrive, your first task should be to convert your money into yen; you need it for transportation into Tōkyō. In both wings ATMs and money exchange counters are in the wall between the customs inspection area and the arrival lobby. Both terminals have a Japan National Tourist Organization's Tourist Information Center, where you can get free maps, brochures, and other visitor information. Directly across from the customs-area exits at both terminals are the ticket counters for airport limousine buses to Tōkyō.

If you plan to skip Tōkyō and center your trip on Kyōto or central or western Honshū, Kansai International Airport (KIX) is the airport to use. Built on reclaimed land in Ōsaka Bay, it's laid out vertically. The first floor is for international arrivals; the second floor is for domestic departures and arrivals; the third floor has shops and restaurants; and the fourth floor is for international departures. A small tourist information center on the first floor of the passenger terminal building is open daily 9–5. Major carriers are Air Canada, Japan Airlines, and Northwest Airlines. The trip from KIX to Kyōto takes 75 minutes by JR train; to Ōsaka it takes 45–70 minutes.

🛩 Fukuoka Airport (FUK) ☎ 092/483-7007 ⊕ www.fuk-ab.co.jp. Haneda Airport (HND) ☎ 03/5757-8111 ⊕ www.tokyo-airport-bldg.co.jp. Kansai International Airport (KIX) ☎ 0724/55-2500 ⊕ www.kansai-airport.or.jp. Narita Airport (NRT) ☎ 0476/34-5000 ⊕ www.narita-airport.or.jp. New Chitose Airport (CTS) ☎ 0123/23-0111.

DUTY-FREE SHOPPING

While Narita's selection of shops is pretty good, duty-free shopping at Kansai International Airport is surprisingly poor, though there's a good shopping plaza opposite the airport entrance.

BIKE TRAVEL

Cycling is a very popular means of transport in Japan—at the neighborhood level. Because of the country's mountainous terrain, however, long-distance cycling is not really an option, except for the most determined traveler. Daily bike rental is available at tourist information offices in many cities and towns, and can often be had for free. Due to the popularity of this kind of service, however, it's best to turn up as early as possible in the morning before all the bikes are taken out for the day. Cycling on the sidewalks is common, and not frowned upon.

BIKES IN FLIGHT

Most airlines accommodate bikes as luggage, provided they are dismantled and boxed; check with individual airlines about packing requirements. Some airlines sell bike boxes, which are often free at bike shops, for about $20 (bike bags can be considerably more expensive). International travelers often can substitute a bike for a piece of checked luggage at no charge; otherwise, the cost is about $100. Most U.S. and Canadian airlines charge $40–$80 each way.

BOAT & FERRY TRAVEL

Ferries connect most of the islands of Japan. Some of the more popular routes are from Tōkyō to Tomakomai or Kushiro in Hokkaidō; from Tōkyō to Shikoku; and from Tōkyō or Ōsaka to Kyūshū. You can **purchase ferry tickets in advance** from travel agencies or before boarding. The ferries are inexpensive and are a pleasant, if slow, way of traveling. Private cabins are available, but it's more fun to travel in the economy class, where everyone sleeps in one large room. Passengers eat, drink, and enjoy themselves in a convivial atmosphere. For information on local ferries *see* the A to Z sections at the end of the individual chapters.

BUS TRAVEL

Japan Railways (JR) offers a number of long-distance buses that are comfortable and inexpensive. You can use Japan Rail Passes (⇨ Train Travel, *below*) on some, but not all, of these buses. In the 1990s, as the economy stagnated and people spent less, numerous private companies established long-distance bus routes as an economical alternative to the nation's trains and planes. Routes and schedules are constantly changing, but tourist information offices will have up-to-date details. It's now possible to travel from Ōsaka to Tōkyō for as little as ¥5,000 one-way. Buses are generally modern and very comfortable, though overnight journeys are best avoided. Nearly all are now no-smoking. Foreign travelers are not often seen on these buses, and they remain one of the country's best-kept travel secrets. Japan Rail Passes are not accepted by private bus companies. City buses outside of Tōkyō are quite convenient, but **be sure of your route and destination,** because the bus driver probably won't speak English.

FARES & SCHEDULES

Some buses have a set cost, anywhere from ¥100 to ¥200, depending on the route and municipality, in which case you board at the front of the bus and pay as you get on. On other buses cost is determined by the distance you travel. You take a ticket when you board at the rear door of the bus; it bears the number of the stop at which you boarded. Your fare depends on your destination and is indicated by a board at the front of the bus. Japan Railways also runs buses in some areas that have limited rail service. Remember, these buses are covered by the JR Pass, even if some JR reservation clerks tell you otherwise. Bus schedules can be hard to fathom if you don't read Japanese, however, so it's best to ask for help at a tourist information office.

RESERVATIONS

Reservations are not always essential, except at peak holiday times and on the most popular routes, like Tōkyō–Ōsaka.
🚌 Bus Information **JR Kantō Bus** ☎ 03/3516-1950. **Nishinihon JR Bus** ☎ 06/6466-9990.

BUSINESS HOURS

General business hours in Japan are weekdays 9–5. Many offices also open at least half of the day on Saturday but are generally closed on Sunday.

BANKS & OFFICES

Banks are open weekdays from 9 to at least 3, with some now staying open until 4 or 5. As with shops, there's a trend toward longer and later opening hours.

GAS STATIONS

Gas stations follow usual shop hours, though 24-hour stations can be found near major highways.

MUSEUMS & SIGHTS

Museums generally close on Monday and the day following national holidays. They are also closed the day following special exhibits and during the weeklong New Year celebrations.

SHOPS

Department stores are usually open 10–7 but close one day a week, which varies from store to store. Other stores are open from 10 or 11 to 7 or 8. There's a trend toward longer and later opening hours in major cities, and 24-hour convenience stores, many of which now have ATM facilities, can be found across the whole country.

CAMERAS & PHOTOGRAPHY

If your camera or laptop was made in Japan, you should consider registering it with U.S. Customs (⇨ Customs & Duties, *below*) to avoid having to pay duties on it when returning home.

Fluorescent lighting, which is common in Japan, gives photographs a greenish tint. You can counteract this discoloration with an FL filter.

The Japanese love photography, and taking photographs at temples or shrines is perfectly acceptable. Digital photography is all the rage now, and Japan is the world-leader in camera-equipped mobile phones. The *Kodak Guide to Shooting Great Travel Pictures* (available at bookstores everywhere) is loaded with tips.
📷 Photo Help **Kodak Information Center** ☎ 800/242-2424 🌐 www.kodak.com.

EQUIPMENT PRECAUTIONS

Don't pack film or equipment in checked luggage, where it is much more susceptible to damage. X-ray machines used to view checked luggage are extremely powerful and therefore are likely to ruin your film. Try to ask for hand inspection of film, which becomes clouded after repeated exposure to airport X-ray machines, and keep videotapes and computer disks away from metal detectors. Always keep film, tape, and computer disks out of the sun. Carry an extra supply of batteries, and be prepared to turn on your camera, camcorder, or laptop to prove to airport security personnel that the device is real.

FILM & DEVELOPING

Film is very easy to find, and is reasonably priced (a 36-exposure color print film costs ¥400, but cheap multipacks are very easy to find). Developing, however, can be a hit-and-miss affair, and is expensive compared to developing costs in the United States.

VIDEO
Japan uses the same standard for videotape as the U.S., so non-U.S. visitors should ensure an adequate supply of videotape. A 60-minute camcorder tape costs ¥1,300.

CAR RENTAL
Rates in Tōkyō begin at ¥6,300 a day and ¥37,800 a week, including tax, for an economy car with unlimited mileage.
🗺 Major Agencies **Alamo** ☎ 800/522-9696 ⊕ www.alamo.com. **Avis** ☎ 800/331-1084, 800/ 879-2847 in Canada, 0870/606-0100 in U.K., 02/ 9353-9000 in Australia, 09/526-2847 in New Zealand ⊕ www.avis.com. **Budget** ☎ 800/527- 0700, 0870/156-5656 in U.K. ⊕ www.budget.com. **Dollar** ☎ 800/800-6000, 0800/085-4578 in U.K. ⊕ www.dollar.com. **Hertz** ☎ 800/654-3001, 800/ 263-0600 in Canada, 0870/844-8844 in U.K., 02/ 9669-2444 in Australia, 09/256-8690 in New Zealand ⊕ www.hertz.com. **National Car Rental** ☎ 800/227-7368, 0870/600-6666 in U.K. ⊕ www. nationalcar.com.

INSURANCE
When driving a rented car you are generally responsible for any damage to or loss of the vehicle. You also may be liable for any property damage or personal injury that you may cause while driving. Before you rent, see what coverage you already have under the terms of your personal auto-insurance policy and credit cards.

REQUIREMENTS & RESTRICTIONS
In Japan your own driver's license is not acceptable. You need an international driver's permit; it's available from the American or Canadian Automobile Association, or, in the United Kingdom, from the Automobile Association or Royal Automobile Club (⇨ Auto Clubs *under* Car Travel, *below*). By law, car seats must be installed if the driver is traveling with a child under six.

SURCHARGES
Before you pick up a car in one city and leave it in another, ask about drop-off charges or one-way service fees, which can

be substantial. Also inquire about early-return policies; some rental agencies charge extra if you return the car before the time specified in your contract while others give you a refund for the days not used. To avoid a hefty refueling fee, fill the tank just before you turn in the car, but be aware that gas stations near the rental outlet may overcharge. It's almost never a deal to buy the tank of gas that's in the car when you rent it; the understanding is that you'll return it empty, but some fuel usually remains. Child seats generally cost about ¥500 a day, and must be ordered at the time of reservation.

CAR TRAVEL
You need an international driving permit (IDP) to drive in Japan. IDPs are available from the American and Canadian automobile associations and, in the United Kingdom, from the Automobile Association and Royal Automobile Club. These international permits, valid only in conjunction with your regular driver's license, are universally recognized; having one may save you a problem with local authorities.

Major roads in Japan are sufficiently marked in the Roman alphabet, and on country roads there's usually someone to ask for help. However, it's a good idea to have a detailed map with town names written in *kanji* (Japanese characters) and *romaji* (romanized Japanese).

Car travel along the Tōkyō–Kyōto–Hiroshima corridor and in other built-up areas of Japan is not as convenient as the trains. Within the major cities, the trains and subways will get you to your destinations faster and more comfortably. Roads are congested, gas is expensive (about ¥110 per liter, or $4.80 per gallon), and highway tolls are exorbitant (tolls between Tōkyō and Kyōto amount to ¥10,550). In major cities, with the exception of main arteries, English signs are few and far between, one-way streets often lead you off the track, and parking is often hard to find and usually expensive.

That said, a car can be the best means for exploring cities outside the metropolitan areas and the rural parts of Japan, especially Kyūshū and Hokkaidō. Consider taking a train to those areas where exploring the countryside will be most interesting and renting a car locally for a day or even half a day.

AUTO CLUBS

🚗 In Australia **Australian Automobile Association (AAA)** ☎ 02/6247-7311 ⊕ www.aaa.asn.au.
🚗 In Canada **Canadian Automobile Association (CAA)** ☎ 613/247-0117 ⊕ www.caa.ca.
🚗 In New Zealand **New Zealand Automobile Association** ☎ 09/377-4660 ⊕ www.aa.co.nz.
🚗 In the U.K. **Automobile Association (AA)** ☎ 0870/550-0600 ⊕ www.theaa.com. **Royal Automobile Club (RAC)** ☎ 0870/572-2722 ⊕ www.rac.co.uk.
🚗 In the U.S. **American Automobile Association (AAA)** ☎ 800/564-6222 ⊕ www.aaa.com.

EMERGENCY SERVICES

Emergency telephones along the highways can be used to contact the authorities. A nonprofit service, JHelp.com, offers a free, 24-hour emergency assistance hotline. Car-rental agencies generally offer roadside assistance services.
🚗 **Police** ☎ 110. **Fire** ☎ 119. **JHelp.com** ☎ 0570/00-0911.

GASOLINE

Gas stations are plentiful along Japan's toll roads, and prices are fairly uniform across the country. Credit cards are accepted everywhere and are even encouraged—there are discounts for them at some places. Self-service stations have recently become legal, so if you pump your own gas you may get a small discount. Often you pay after putting in the gas, but there are also machines where you put money in first and then use the receipt to get change back. Tipping is not customary.

ROAD CONDITIONS

Roads in Japan are often narrower than those found in the United States, but they're well maintained in general. Driving in Tōkyō and other cities can be troublesome, as there are many narrow, one-way streets and little in the way of English road signs except on major arteries. Wild boars are not uncommon in rural districts, and have been known to block roads and ram into cars in moun-

tainous parts of the city of Kōbe, and in Kyūshū, especially at night.

ROAD MAPS

Mapple is the most famous map company in Japan. Their maps can be found at any convenience store or bookshop, but they are only available in Japanese.

RULES OF THE ROAD

In Japan, people **drive on the left.** Speed limits vary, but generally the limit is 80 kph (50 mph) on highways, 40 kph (25 mph) in cities. Penalties for speeding are severe. By law, car seats must be installed if the driver is traveling with a child under six, while the driver and all passengers in cars must wear seat belts at all times. Legislation banning the use of hand-held mobile phones is expected to be passed in 2005.

Many smaller streets lack sidewalks, so cars, bicycles, and pedestrians share the same space. Motorbikes with engines under 50 cc are allowed to travel against automobile traffic on one-way roads. Fortunately, considering the narrowness of the streets and the volume of traffic, most Japanese drivers are technically skilled. They may not allow quite as much distance between cars as you're used to. Be prepared for sudden lane changes by other drivers. When waiting at intersections after dark, many drivers, as a courtesy to other drivers, turn off their main headlights to prevent glare.

Japan has very strict laws concerning the consumption of alcohol prior to getting behind the wheel. Given the almost zero-tolerance for driving under the influence and the occasional evening police checkpoint set up along the roads, it's wisest to avoid alcohol entirely if you plan to drive.

CHILDREN IN JAPAN

Western children are adored in Japan and visitors with young children, especially blond ones, should expect lots of attention, especially in rural areas. If you are renting a car, don't forget to arrange for a car seat when you reserve. For general advice about traveling with children, consult *Fodor's FYI: Travel with Your Baby* (available in bookstores everywhere).

BABYSITTING

Some very expensive Western-style hotels and resorts have supervised playrooms where you can drop off your children. The babysitters, however, are unlikely to speak English. Child-care arrangements can also be made through your hotel's concierge, but some properties require up to a week's notice.

FLYING

If your children are two or older, ask about children's airfares. As a general rule, infants under two not occupying a seat fly at greatly reduced fares or even for free. But if you want to guarantee a seat for an infant, you have to pay full fare. Consider flying during off-peak days and times; most airlines will grant an infant a seat without a ticket if there are available seats. When booking, confirm carry-on allowances if you're traveling with infants. In general, for babies charged 10% to 50% of the adult fare you are allowed one carry-on bag and a collapsible stroller; if the flight is full, the stroller may have to be checked or you may be limited to less.

Experts agree that it's a good idea to use safety seats aloft for children weighing less than 40 pounds. Airlines set their own policies: if you use a safety seat, U.S. carriers usually require that the child be ticketed, even if he or she is young enough to ride free, because the seats must be strapped into regular seats. And even if you pay the full adult fare for the seat, it may be worth it, especially on longer trips. Do **check your airline's policy about using safety seats during takeoff and landing.** Safety seats are not allowed everywhere in the plane, so get your seat assignments as early as possible.

When reserving, request children's meals or a freestanding bassinet (not available at all airlines) if you need them. But note that bulkhead seats, where you must sit to use the bassinet, may lack an overhead bin or storage space on the floor.

FOOD

Western-style fast-food restaurants, coffee shops, and ice-cream chains are common in Japan. Many of the most popular U.S. chains are represented. Two very good local chains to watch out for are MOS Burger and Freshness Burger. First Kitchen is similar, but has more than just burgers, offering hot dogs and healthy sandwiches too. Pizzas are readily available across the country. *Okonomiyaki,* a kind of pancake stuffed with beef, pork, or shrimp and common in West Japan, is very popular with Japanese children.

LODGING

Most hotels in Japan allow children under a certain age (usually 12) to stay in their parents' room at no extra charge, but others charge for them as extra adults; be sure to find out the cutoff age for children's discounts.

SIGHTS & ATTRACTIONS

Places that are especially appealing to children are indicated by a rubber-duckie icon (ⓒ) in the margin.

SUPPLIES & EQUIPMENT

Disposable diapers are widely available in large supermarkets, pharmacies, and Toys R Us stores. Formula is available in powdered form, in tins or packs of sachets, which are more convenient for travelers.

COMPUTERS ON THE ROAD

Phone jacks are the same in Japan as in the United States. Many hotels have ADSL or Ethernet connections for high-speed Internet access. Ethernet cables are usually available to buy at hotels if you don't bring your own. Wireless Internet access (Wi-Fi) is increasingly popular and available for free at certain coffee shops and in many hotel lobbies across the country.

CONSUMER PROTECTION

Honesty and integrity are important values in Japan, and tourist scams uncommon. Note, however, that luxury-brand goods bought from street vendors are not likely to be the real thing.

Whether you're shopping for gifts or purchasing travel services, **pay with a major credit card** whenever possible, so you can cancel payment or get reimbursed if there's a problem (and you can provide documentation). If you're doing business with a particular company for the first time, contact your local Better Business Bureau and the attorney general's offices in your state and (for U.S. businesses) the company's home state as well. Have any complaints been filed? Finally, if you're buying a package or tour, always consider travel insurance that includes default coverage (⇨ Insurance).

▌ BBB Council of Better Business Bureaus ✉ 4200 Wilson Blvd., Suite 800, Arlington, VA 22203 ☎ 703/276-0100 🖷 703/525-8277 ⊕ www. bbb.org.

CUSTOMS & DUTIES

When shopping abroad, keep receipts for all purchases. Upon reentering the country, **be ready to show customs officials what you've bought.** Pack purchases together in an easily accessible place. If you think a duty is incorrect, appeal the assessment. If you object to the way your clearance was handled, note the inspector's badge number. In either case, first ask to see a supervisor. If the problem isn't resolved, write to the appropriate authorities, beginning with the port director at your point of entry.

IN AUSTRALIA

Australian residents who are 18 or older may bring home A$400 worth of souvenirs and gifts (including jewelry), 250 cigarettes or 250 grams of cigars or other tobacco products, and 1,125 ml of alcohol (including wine, beer, and spirits). Residents under 18 may bring back A$200 worth of goods. Members of the same family traveling together may pool their allowances. Prohibited items include meat products. Seeds, plants, and fruits need to be declared upon arrival.

▌ Australian Customs Service 🕮 Regional Director, Box 8, Sydney, NSW 2001 ☎ 02/9213-2000 or 1300/363263, 02/9364-7222 or 1800/020-504 quarantine-inquiry line 🖷 02/9213-4043 ⊕ www. customs.gov.au.

IN CANADA

Canadian residents who have been out of Canada for at least seven days may bring in C$750 worth of goods duty-free. If you've been away fewer than seven days but more than 48 hours, the duty-free allowance drops to C$200. If your trip lasts 24 to 48 hours, the allowance is C$50.

You may not pool allowances with family members. Goods claimed under the C$750 exemption may follow you by mail; those claimed under the lesser exemptions must accompany you. Alcohol and tobacco products may be included in the seven-day and 48-hour exemptions but not in the 24-hour exemption. If you meet the age requirements of the province or territory through which you reenter Canada, you may bring in, duty-free, 1.5 liters of wine or 1.14 liters (40 imperial ounces) of liquor or 24 12-ounce cans or bottles of beer or ale. Also, if you meet the local age requirement for tobacco products, you may bring in, duty-free, 200 cigarettes and 50 cigars. Check ahead of time with the Canada Customs and Revenue Agency or the Department of Agriculture for policies regarding meat products, seeds, plants, and fruits.

You may send an unlimited number of gifts (only one gift per recipient, however) worth up to C$60 each duty-free to Canada. Label the package UNSOLICITED GIFT—VALUE UNDER $60. Alcohol and tobacco are excluded.

▌ Canada Customs and Revenue Agency ✉ 2265 St. Laurent Blvd., Ottawa, Ontario K1G 4K3 ☎ 800/461-9999 in Canada, 204/983-3500, 506/636-5064 ⊕ www.ccra.gc.ca.

IN JAPAN

Japan has strict regulations about bringing firearms, pornography, and narcotics into the country. Anyone caught with drugs is liable to be detained, deported, and refused reentry into Japan. Certain fresh fruits, vegetables, plants, and animals are also illegal. Nonresidents are allowed to bring in duty-free: (1) 400 cigarettes or 100 cigars or 500 grams of tobacco; (2) three 760-ml bottles of alcohol; (3) 2 ounces of perfume; (4) other goods up to ¥200,000 value.

▌ Ministry of Finance, Customs and Tariff Bureau ✉ 3-1-1 Kasumigaseki, Chiyoda-ku, Tōkyō, 100-8940 ☎ 03/3581-4111 ⊕ www.customs.go.jp/index_e.htm.

IN NEW ZEALAND

All homeward-bound residents may bring back NZ$700 worth of souvenirs and gifts; passengers may not pool their allowances, and children can claim only the concession on goods intended for their own use. For those 17 or older, the duty-free allowance also includes 4.5 liters of wine or beer; one 1,125-ml bottle of spirits; and either 200 cigarettes, 250 grams of tobacco, 50 cigars, *or* a combination of the three up to 250 grams. Meat products, seeds, plants, and fruits must be declared upon arrival to the Agricultural Services Department.

🔲 **New Zealand Customs** ✉ Head office: The Customhouse, 17–21 Whitmore St., Box 2218, Wellington ☎ 09/300–5399 or 0800/428–786 ⊕ www.customs. govt.nz.

IN THE U.K.

From countries outside the European Union, including Japan, you may bring home, duty-free, 200 cigarettes, 50 cigars, 100 cigarillos, or 250 grams of tobacco; 1 liter of spirits or 2 liters of fortified or sparkling wine or liqueurs; 2 liters of still table wine; 60 ml of perfume; 250 ml of toilet water; plus £145 worth of other goods, including gifts and souvenirs. Prohibited items include meat and dairy products, seeds, plants, and fruits.

🔲 **HM Customs and Excise** ✉ Portcullis House, 21 Cowbridge Rd. E, Cardiff CF11 9SS ☎ 0845/010–9000 or 0208/929–0152 advice service, 0208/929–6731 or 0208/910–3602 complaints ⊕ www.hmce. gov.uk.

IN THE U.S.

U.S. residents who have been out of the country for at least 48 hours may bring home, for personal use, $800 worth of foreign goods duty-free, as long as they haven't used the $800 allowance or any part of it in the past 30 days. This exemption may include 1 liter of alcohol (for travelers 21 and older), 200 cigarettes, and 100 non-Cuban cigars. Family members from the same household who are traveling together may pool their $800 personal exemptions. For fewer than 48 hours, the duty-free allowance drops to $200, which may include 50 cigarettes, 10 non-Cuban cigars, and 150 ml of alcohol (or 150 ml of perfume containing alcohol). The $200 allowance cannot be com-

bined with other individuals' exemptions, and if you exceed it, the full value of all the goods will be taxed. Antiques, which U.S. Customs and Border Protection defines as objects more than 100 years old, enter duty-free, as do original works of art done entirely by hand, including paintings, drawings, and sculptures. This doesn't apply to folk art or handicrafts, which are in general dutiable.

You may also send packages home duty-free, with a limit of one parcel per addressee per day (except alcohol or tobacco products or perfume worth more than $5). You can mail up to $200 worth of goods for personal use; label the package PERSONAL USE and attach a list of its contents and their retail value. If the package contains your used personal belongings, mark it AMERICAN GOODS RETURNED to avoid paying duties. You may send up to $100 worth of goods as a gift; mark the package UNSOLICITED GIFT. Mailed items do not affect your duty-free allowance on your return.

To avoid paying duty on foreign-made high-ticket items you already own and will take on your trip, register them with Customs before you leave the country. Consider filing a Certificate of Registration for laptops, cameras, watches, and other digital devices identified with serial numbers or other permanent markings; you can keep the certificate for other trips. Otherwise, bring a sales receipt or insurance form to show that you owned the item before you left the United States.

For more about duties, restricted items, and other information about international travel, check out U.S. Customs and Border Protection's online brochure, *Know Before You Go*.

🔲 **U.S. Customs and Border Protection** ✉ For inquiries and equipment registration, 1300 Pennsylvania Ave. NW, Washington, DC 20229 ⊕ www.cbp. gov ☎ 877/287–8667 or 202/354–1000 ✉ For complaints, Customer Satisfaction Unit, 1300 Pennsylvania Ave. NW, Room 5.2C, Washington, DC 20229.

DISABILITIES & ACCESSIBILITY

Though wheelchair navigation is possible and elevators are common, the sheer numbers of people in Tōkyō and other large cities may cause some frustration. However, strangers and service people are exceptionally kind and willing to help. Many shrines and temples are set on high ground, but most have ramps. Visit http://accessible.jp.org for lists of accessible sights, hotels, shops, and more.

LODGING

Staying in a traditional Japanese inn, where guests sleep on futons laid out on *tatami*-mat floors and usually use a communal bath, is difficult, if not impossible, for those with mobility problems. In other hotels, ask for the lowest floor on which accessible services are offered. If you have a hearing impairment, check whether the hotel has devices to alert you visually to the ring of the telephone, a knock at the door, and a fire/emergency alarm. Some hotels provide these devices without charge. Discuss your needs with hotel personnel if this equipment isn't available, so that a staff member can personally alert you in the event of an emergency.

In Tōkyō, the Imperial Hotel is the top choice for travelers with wheelchairs. In Ōsaka, the Hilton Ōsaka is a good high-end in a central location, while those looking for something more reasonable should head for the Hotel New Hankyū, close to Shin-Ōsaka Station. In Kyōto, the Westin Miyako Hotel is a good choice.

🏨 Best Choices **Imperial Hotel** ⊠ 1-1-1 Uchisai-wai-chō, Chiyoda-ku, Tōkyō 100-8558 ☎ 03/3504-1251 ⊕ www.imperialhotel.co.jp. **Hilton Ōsaka** ⊠ 8-8 Umeda 1-chōme, Kita-ku, Ōsaka 530-0001 ☎ 06/6347-7111 ⊕ www.hilton.co.jp/osaka. **Hotel New Hankyū** ⊠ 1-1-35 Shibata, Kita-ku, Ōsaka 530-8310 ☎ 06/6372-5101 ⊕ www.hotel.newhankyu.co.jp. **Westin Miyako Hotel** ⊠ Sanjō-Keage, Higashiyama-ku, Kyōto-shi 605-0052 ☎ 075/771-7111 ⊕ www.westinmiyako-kyoto.com.

RESERVATIONS

When discussing accessibility with an operator or reservations agent, ask hard questions. Are there any stairs, inside *or* out? Are there grab bars next to the toilet *and* in the shower/tub? How wide is the doorway to the room? To the bathroom? For the most extensive facilities meeting the latest legal specifications, opt for newer accommodations. If you reserve through a toll-free number, consider also calling the hotel's local number to confirm the information from the central reservations office. Get confirmation in writing when you can.

TRANSPORTATION

Main train stations often have elevators, and station staff will be happy to assist travelers using wheelchairs. Many private train and bus companies, including the Shinkansen (bullet train), are equipped to serve passengers with disabilities. Reservations are essential. Taxi trunks are large enough to hold folded wheelchairs.

🏨 Complaints **Aviation Consumer Protection Division** (⇨ Air Travel) for airline-related problems. **Departmental Office of Civil Rights** ⊠ For general inquiries, U.S. Department of Transportation, S-30, 400 7th St. SW, Room 10215, Washington, DC 20590 ☎ 202/366-4648 🖷 202/366-9371 ⊕ www.dot.gov/ost/docr/index.htm. **Disability Rights Section** ⊠ NYAV, U.S. Department of Justice, Civil Rights Division, 950 Pennsylvania Ave. NW, Washington, DC 20530 🖷 ADA information line 202/514-0301, 800/514-0301, 202/514-0383 TTY, 800/514-0383 TTY ⊕ www.ada.gov. **U.S. Department of Transportation Hotline** 🖷 For disability-related air-travel problems, 800/778-4838, 800/455-9880 TTY.

TRAVEL AGENCIES

In the United States, the Americans with Disabilities Act requires that travel firms serve the needs of all travelers. Some agencies specialize in working with people with disabilities.

🏨 Travelers with Mobility Problems **Access Adventures/B. Roberts Travel** ⊠ 206 Chestnut Ridge Rd., Scottsville, NY 14624 ☎ 585/889-9096 ⊕ www.brobertstravel.com ✎ dltravel@prodigy.net, run by a former physical-rehabilitation counselor. **Flying Wheels Travel** ⊠ 143 W. Bridge St., Box 382, Owatonna, MN 55060 ☎ 507/451-5005 🖷 507/451-1685 ⊕ www.flyingwheelstravel.com.

DISCOUNTS & DEALS

Be a smart shopper and compare all your options before making decisions. A plane ticket bought with a promotional coupon from travel clubs, coupon books, and direct-mail offers or purchased on the Internet may not be cheaper than the least expensive fare from a discount ticket agency. And always keep in mind that what you get is just as important as what you save.

DISCOUNT RESERVATIONS

To save money, look into discount reservations services with Web sites and toll-free numbers, which use their buying power to get a better price on hotels, airline tickets ($\Rightarrow$ Air Travel), even car rentals. When booking a room, always **call the hotel's local toll-free number** (if one is available) rather than the central reservations number—you can often get a better price. Always ask about special packages or corporate rates.

When shopping for the best deal on hotels and car rentals, look for guaranteed exchange rates, which protect you against a falling dollar. With your rate locked in, you won't pay more, even if the price goes up in the local currency.

Airline Tickets Air 4 Less ☎ 800/AIR4LESS; low-fare specialist.

Hotel Rooms Accommodations Express ☎ 800/444-7666 or 800/277-1064 ⊕ www.acex.net. **Hotels.com** ☎ 800/246-8357 ⊕ www.hotels.com. **Steigenberger Reservation Service** ☎ 800/223-5652 ⊕ www.srs-worldhotels.com. **Turbotrip.com** ☎ 800/473-7829 ⊕ www.turbotrip.com. **VacationLand** ☎ 800/245-0050 ⊕ www.vacation-land.com.

PACKAGE DEALS

Don't confuse packages and guided tours. When you buy a package, you travel on your own, just as though you had planned the trip yourself. Fly/drive packages, which combine airfare and car rental, are often a good deal. In cities, ask the local visitor's bureau about hotel and local transportation packages that include tickets to major museum exhibits or other special events.

EATING & DRINKING

The restaurants we list are the cream of the crop in each price category. Food, like many other things in Japan, is expensive. Eating at hotels and famous restaurants is costly; however, you can eat well and reasonably at standard restaurants that may not have signs in English. Many less expensive restaurants have plastic replicas of the dishes they serve displayed in their front windows, so you can always point to what you want to eat if the language barrier is insurmountable. A good place to look for moderately priced dining spots is in the restaurant concourse of department stores, usually on the bottom floor. Properties indicated by an ✕🏠 are lodging establishments whose restaurant warrants a special trip.

In general, Japanese restaurants are very clean (standards of hygiene are very high). Tap water is safe, and most hotels have Western-style restrooms, although restaurants may have Japanese-style toilets, with bowls recessed into the floor, over which you must squat.

If you're in a hurry and looking for something different yet familiar, a visit to one branch of the MOS Burger, Freshness Burger, or First Kitchen will fit the bill. These nationwide chains offer familiar hamburgers, but they also have local variations. Yoshinoya is another popular chain, serving grilled salmon, rice and miso soup for breakfast (until 10), and then hearty portions of rice and beef for the rest of the day.

Local and regional specialties are discussed at the beginning of each chapter in this book; for more general information on dining in Japan, *see* The Discreet Charm of Japanese Cuisine at the end of this book.

MEALTIMES

Note that many restaurants in rural towns are shut by 9. Unless otherwise noted, the restaurants listed in this guide are open daily for lunch and dinner.

PAYING

Credit cards are increasingly widely accepted at cheaper establishments, but definitely check before sitting down for dinner if you don't have much cash with you.

RESERVATIONS & DRESS

Reservations are always a good idea; we mention them only when they're essential or not accepted. Book as far ahead as you can, and reconfirm as soon as you arrive. (Large parties should always call ahead to check the reservations policy.) We mention dress only when men are required to wear a jacket or a jacket and tie.

ECOTOURISM

Vending machines dispensing cans and bottles of juice, tea, and beer can be found all over the country. They nearly always have a plastic recycling bin next to them for you to pop your empty container into afterward. These recycling bins can also be found in front of convenience stores.

ELECTRICITY

To use electric-powered equipment purchased in the U.S. or Canada, **bring a converter and adapter.** The electrical current in Japan is 100 volts, 50 cycles alternating current (AC) in eastern Japan, and 100 volts, 60 cycles in western Japan; the United States runs on 110-volt, 60-cycle AC current. Wall outlets in Japan accept plugs with two flat prongs, like in the United States, but do not accept U.S. three-prong plugs.

If your appliances are dual-voltage, you'll need only an adapter. Don't use 110-volt outlets marked FOR SHAVERS ONLY for high-wattage appliances such as blow-dryers. Most laptops operate equally well on 110 and 220 volts and so require only an adapter.

EMBASSIES

The following embassies and consulates are open weekdays, with one- to two-hour closings for lunch. Call for exact hours.

🏛 Australia **Australian Embassy and Consulate** ✉ 2-1-14 Mita, Minato-ku ☎ 03/5232-4111 ⊕ www.australia.or.jp/english Ⓜ Toei Mita Line, Shiba-Kōen station [Exit A2]; Toei Ōedo and Namboku lines, Azabu-jūban station [Exits 2 and 4].

🏛 Canada **Canadian Embassy and Consulate** ✉ 7-3-38 Akasaka, Minato-ku ⊕ www.fac-aec.gc.ca ☎ 03/5412-6200 Ⓜ Hanzō-mon and Ginza lines, Aoyama-itchōme station [Exit 4].

🏛 New Zealand **New Zealand Embassy** ✉ 20-40 Kamiyama-chō, Shibuya-ku ☎ 03/3467-2271 ⊕ www.nzembassy.com Ⓜ Chiyoda Line, Yoyogi-kōen station [Minami-guchi/South Exit].

🏛 United Kingdom **British Embassy and Consulate** ✉ 1 Ichiban-chō, Chiyoda-ku, Imperial Palace District ☎ 03/5211-1100 ⊕ www.uknow.or.jp Ⓜ Hanzō-mon Line, Hanzō-mon station [Exit 4].

🏛 United States **U.S. Embassy and Consulate** ✉ 1-10-5 Akasaka, Minato-ku, Toranomon ☎ 03/322-4500 ⊕ http://tokyo.usembassy.gov/ Ⓜ Namboku Line, Tameike-Sannō station [Exit 13].

EMERGENCIES

Assistance in English is available 24 hours a day on the toll-free Japan Helpline.

🏛 **Ambulance and Fire** ☎ 119. **Japan Helpline** ☎ 0120/46-1997 or 0570/00-0911. **Police** ☎ 110.

ENGLISH-LANGUAGE MEDIA

BOOKS

English-language books are easy to find at bookshops in Japan's major cities, but if you're planning an extended stay in the countryside, stock up before you go. Because almost all English-language books are imported, they are generally 20%–50% more expensive than at home.

NEWSPAPERS & MAGAZINES

The *Daily Yomiuri*, an English-language sibling of the *Yomiuri Shimbun*; the *Japan Times*, a daily English-language newspaper; and the *International Herald Tribune/Asahi Shimbun* are reliable for national and international news coverage, as well as for entertainment reviews and listings. They're available at newsstands and in bookstores that carry English-language books, and they have Web sites (⇨ *below*)—handy if you want to brush up on current events before your trip.

RADIO & TELEVISION

The national broadcaster, NHK, has a number of bilingual programs on TV, including the news. Popular international cable and satellite TV channels, like BBC World and CNN, are widely available in hotels. There's very little in English on the radio in Japan, though you can hear plenty of Western pop and classical music.

GAY & LESBIAN TRAVEL

A few words about the Japanese attitude toward homosexuality will help you in Japan. Because Japan does not have the religious opposition to homosexuality that the West does, the major barrier that continues to suppress gay lifestyle in Japan is the Confucian duty to continue the family line, to bring no shame to the family, and to fit into Japanese society. So gay and lesbian travelers aren't likely to stumble upon many establishments that cater to a gay clientele.

There *are* gay bars, karaoke lounges, discos, "snacks" (a type of bar), hostess bars, host bars, and drag king/queen bars—the trick is finding them. Even the gay district of Tōkyō, Shinjuku 2-chōme (a 15-minute walk west of Shinjuku Station) leaves you wondering if you've found the place. When you get there, look for people who live in the area, particularly Westerners, and approach them. The Japanese would never broach the subject except, perhaps, at the end of a night of drinking. In fact, it's a bad idea to broach the subject with a Japanese: it will cause much awkwardness, and the response will be nowhere near as sophisticated as it has become in the West. All of this said, homosexuality (as an interest but not a life choice) is more accepted in the realm of human expression than it is in the West. This may sound quite discouraging, but in actuality, Japan can prove to be an outlet of immense freedom for gays if you are successful in making friends in Tōkyō, the Kansai area (Kyōto–Ōsaka–Kōbe), and Hiroshima.

International Gay Friends is a gay meeting group in Tōkyō. Occur Help Line sets aside different days of the month for women and men. *Out in Japan* magazine is available at Tower Records in Tōkyō.

F Contacts & Information **International Gay Friends** ☎ 03/5693-4569. **Occur Help Line** ☎ 03/3380-2269.

F Gay- & Lesbian-Friendly Travel Agencies **Different Roads Travel** ✉ 8383 Wilshire Blvd., Suite 520, Beverly Hills, CA 90211 ☎ 323/651-5557 or 800/429-8747 (Ext. 14 for both) 🖷 323/651-5454 ✉ lgernert@tzell.com. **Kennedy Travel** ✉ 130 W. 42nd St., Suite 401, New York, NY 10036 ☎ 212/840-8659 or 800/237-7433 🖷 212/730-2269 ⊕ www.kennedytravel.com. **Now, Voyager** ✉ 4406 18th St., San Francisco, CA 94114 ☎ 415/626-1169 or 800/255-6951 🖷 415/626-8626 ⊕ www.nowvoyager.com. **Skylink Travel and Tour/Flying Dutchmen Travel** ✉ 1455 N. Dutton Ave., Suite A, Santa Rosa, CA 95401 ☎ 707/546-9888 or 800/225-5759 🖷 707/636-0951; serving lesbian travelers.

HEALTH

Tap water everywhere is safe in Japan. Medical treatment varies from highly skilled and professional treatment at major hospitals to somewhat less advanced procedures in small neighborhood clinics. At larger hospitals you have a good chance of encountering English-speaking doctors who have been partly educated in the West.

OVER-THE-COUNTER REMEDIES

It may be difficult to buy the standard over-the-counter remedies you're used to, so it's best to bring with you any medications (in their proper packaging) you may need. Medication can only be bought at pharmacies in Japan, but every neighborhood seems to have at least one. *Kusuri-ya* is the word for "pharmacy" in Japanese. Pharmacists in Japan are usually able to manage at least a few words of English, and certainly are able to read some, so have a pen and some paper ready, just in case. In Japanese, aspirin is *asupirin* and Tylenol is *Tairenōru*.

PESTS & OTHER HAZARDS

Mosquitoes can be a minor irritation during the rainy season, though you are never at risk of contracting anything serious, like malaria. If you're staying in a *ryokan* or somewhere without air-conditioning, anti-mosquito coils, or an electric-powered spray will be provided. Dehydration and heatstroke could be concerns if you spend a long time outside during the summer months, so isotonic sports drinks are readily available from the nation's ubiquitous vending machines.

HOLIDAYS

As elsewhere, peak times for travel in Japan tend to fall around holiday periods. You want to avoid traveling during the few days before and after New Year's; during Golden Week, which follows Greenery Day (April 29); and in mid-July and mid-August, at the time of Obon festivals, when many Japanese return to their hometowns (Obon festivals are celebrated July or August 13–16, depending on the location). Note that when a holiday falls on a Sunday, the following Monday is a holiday.

January 1 (*Ganjitsu*, New Year's Day); the second Monday in January (*Senjin-no-hi*, Coming of Age Day); February 11 (*Kenkoku Kinen-bi*, National Foundation Day); March 20 or 21 (*Shumbun-no-hi*,

Vernal Equinox); April 29 (*Midori-no-hi,* Greenery Day); May 3 (*Kempō Kinen-bi,* Constitution Day); May 5 (*Kodomo-no-hi,* Children's Day); the third Monday in July (*Umi-no-hi,* Marine Day); the third Monday in September (*Keirō-no-hi,* Respect for the Aged Day); September 23 or 24 (*Shūbun-no-hi,* Autumnal Equinox); the second Monday in October (*Taiiku-no-hi,* Sports Day); November 3 (*Bunka-no-hi,* Culture Day); November 23 (*Kinrō Kansha-no-hi,* Labor Thanksgiving Day); December 23 (*Tennō Tanjōbi,* Emperor's Birthday).

INSURANCE

The most useful travel-insurance plan is a comprehensive policy that includes coverage for trip cancellation and interruption, default, trip delay, and medical expenses (with a waiver for preexisting conditions).

Without insurance you'll lose all or most of your money if you cancel your trip, regardless of the reason. Default insurance covers you if your tour operator, airline, or cruise line goes out of business—the chances of which have been increasing. Trip-delay covers expenses that arise because of bad weather or mechanical delays. Study the fine print when comparing policies.

If you're traveling internationally, a key component of travel insurance is coverage for medical bills incurred if you get sick on the road. Such expenses aren't generally covered by Medicare or private policies. U.K. residents can buy a travel-insurance policy valid for most vacations taken during the year in which it's purchased (but check preexisting-condition coverage). British and Australian citizens need extra medical coverage when traveling overseas.

Always **buy travel policies directly from the insurance company;** if you buy them from a cruise line, airline, or tour operator that goes out of business you probably won't be covered for the agency or operator's default, a major risk. Before making any purchase, review your existing health and home-owner's policies to find what they cover away from home.

🛈 Travel Insurers In the U.S.: **Access America** ✉ 2805 N. Parham Rd., Richmond, VA 23294 ☎ 800/284-8300 🖷 804/673-1491 or 800/346-9265 ⊕ www.accessamerica.com. **Travel Guard International** ✉ 1145 Clark St., Stevens Point, WI 54481 ☎ 715/345-0505 or 800/826-1300 🖷 800/955-8785 ⊕ www.travelguard.com.

🛈 Insurance Information In the U.K.: **Association of British Insurers** ✉ 51 Gresham St., London EC2V 7HQ ☎ 020/7600-3333 🖷 020/7696-8999 ⊕ www.abi.org.uk. In Canada: **RBC Insurance** ✉ 6880 Financial Dr., Mississauga, Ontario L5N 7Y5 ☎ 800/668-4342 or 905/816-2400 🖷 905/813-4704 ⊕ www.rbcinsurance.com. In Australia: **Insurance Council of Australia** ✉ Insurance Enquiries and Complaints, Level 12, Box 561, Collins St. W, Melbourne, VIC 8007 ☎ 1300/780808 or 03/9629-4109 🖷 03/9621-2060 ⊕ www.iecltd.com.au. In New Zealand: **Insurance Council of New Zealand** ✉ Level 7, 111-115 Customhouse Quay, Box 474, Wellington ☎ 04/472-5230 🖷 04/473-3011 ⊕ www.icnz.org.nz.

LANGUAGE

Throughout this book, names of sights and properties are listed first in the language they are best known to English speakers in Japan. When the English is listed first, as in the case of the Tōkyō National Museum, a transliteration is provided afterward in parentheses. When the Japanese transliteration is listed first, as in the case of Dembō-in, the English translation comes afterward in parentheses.

Communicating in Japan can be a challenge. This is not because the Japanese don't speak English but because most English speakers know little, if any, Japanese. Take some time before you leave home to **learn a few basic words,** such as where (*doko*), what time (*nan-ji*), bathroom (*o-te-arai*), thank you (*arigatō gozaimasu*), excuse me (*sumimasen*), and please (*one-gai shimasu*).

English is a required subject in Japanese schools, so most Japanese study English for at least six years. This does not mean everyone *speaks* English. Schools emphasize reading, writing, and grammar. As a result, many Japanese can read English but can speak only a few basic phrases. Furthermore, when asked, "Do you speak English?" many Japanese, out of modesty, say no, even if they do understand and speak a fair amount of it. It's usually best to simply ask what you really want to know slowly, clearly, and as simply as possible. If the person you ask understands, he or she will answer or perhaps take you where you need to go.

Although a local may understand your simple question, he or she cannot always give you an answer that requires complicated instructions. For example, you may ask someone on the subway how to get to a particular stop, and he may direct you to the train across the platform and then say something in Japanese that you do not understand. You may discover too late that the train runs express to the suburbs after the third stop; the person who gave you directions was trying to tell you to switch trains at the third stop. To avoid this kind of trouble, **ask more than one person for directions every step of the way.** You can avoid that trip to the suburbs if you ask someone *on* the train how to get to where you want to go. Also, remember that politeness is a matter of course in Japan and that the Japanese won't want to lose face by saying that they don't know how to get to somewhere. If the situation gets confusing, **bow, say *arigatō gozaimashita* ("thank you" in the past tense), and ask someone else.** Even though you are communicating on a very basic level, misunderstandings can happen easily. When asking for directions, it's best to ask a "where is" type question—at least the person you've asked can point in the general direction, even if they can't explain themselves to you clearly.

Traveling in Japan can be problematic if you don't read Japanese. Before you leave home, **buy a phrase book** that shows English, English transliterations of Japanese (*romaji*), and Japanese characters (*kanji* and *kana*). You can read the romaji to pick up a few Japanese words and match the kanji and kana in the phrase book with characters on signs and menus. When all else fails, ask for help by pointing to the Japanese words in your book.

The Japan National Tourist Organization (JNTO) manages a free English-language tourist information line (0088/22–4800) in daily operation 9–5, and if there's an emergency you can always call the free, 24-hour Japan Helpline (0120/46–1997 or 0570/00–0911).

For information on pronouncing Japanese words, notes on how Japanese words are rendered in this guide, and a list of useful words and phrases, *see* An English-Japanese Traveler's Vocabulary *in* Chapter 14.

Note: There's some disagreement over the use of gaijin (literally, "outside person") as opposed to *gai-koku-jin* (literally, "outside country person") because the former has negative echoes of the days of Japanese isolationism. In the 17th and 18th centuries, when the Japanese had contact only with Dutch traders, Westerners were called *batā-kusai* (literally, "stinking of butter")—obviously a derogatory term. Gai-koku-jin, on the other hand, has a softer, more polite meaning, and many Westerners in Japan prefer it because it has no xenophobic taint.

Gaijin is used to translate the word *foreigner* throughout this guide for two reasons. First, it's commonly used in books written by Westerners who have lived in Japan, and as such it has wider recognition value. Second, as Japan becomes more global—especially its younger generation—gaijin is losing its negative sense. Many Japanese use gaijin as the one word they know to describe non-Japanese and most often mean no offense by it.

So if children giggle and point at the *gaijin-san,* know that it's meant with only the kindest fascination. And if you feel that extra politeness is appropriate, use gai-koku-jin with colleagues whom you respect—or with whomever might be using gaijin a bit too derogatorily.

LODGING

Overnight accommodations in Japan run from luxury hotels to *ryokan* (traditional inns) to youth hostels and even capsules. Western-style rooms with Western-style bathrooms are widely available in large cities, but in smaller, out-of-the-way towns it may be necessary to stay in a Japanese-style room—an experience that can only enhance your stay.

The lodgings we list are the cream of the crop in each price category. We always list the facilities that are available—but we don't specify whether they cost extra: when pricing accommodations, always ask what's included and what costs extra. Properties indicated by an ✕🏠 are lodging establishments whose restaurant warrants a special trip.

Assume that hotels operate on the European Plan (EP, with no meals) unless we specify that they use the Continental Plan (CP, with a Continental breakfast), Breakfast Plan (BP, with a full breakfast), Modified American Plan (MAP, with breakfast and dinner), or the Full American Plan (FAP, with all meals).

Outside cities and major towns, most lodgings quote prices on a per-person basis with two meals, exclusive of service and tax. If you do not want dinner at your hotel, it is usually possible to renegotiate the price. Stipulate, too, whether you wish to have Japanese or Western breakfasts, if any. When you make reservations at a noncity hotel, you are usually expected to take breakfast and dinner at the hotel—this is the rate quoted to you unless you specify otherwise. In this guide, properties are assigned price categories based on the range between their least and most expensive standard double rooms at high season (excluding holidays).

APARTMENT & VILLA (OR HOUSE) RENTALS

If you want a home base that's roomy enough for a family and comes with cooking facilities, consider a furnished rental. These can save you money, especially if you're traveling with a group. Home-exchange directories sometimes list rentals as well as exchanges.

In addition to the agents listed below, English language-newspapers and magazines, such as the *Hiragana Times, Kansai Time Out* or *Metropolis*, or the *City-Source English Telephone Directory* may be helpful in locating a rental property. Note that renting apartments or houses in Japan is not that common a way to spend a vacation.

🏠 International Agent **Hideaways International** ✉ 767 Islington St., Portsmouth, NH 03801 ☎ 603/430-4433 or 800/843-4433 🖷 603/430-4444 🌐 www.hideaways.com, annual membership $145.

Moveandstay ✉ Sabaai Concept Co., Ltd., 163 Ocean Insurance Bldg., Unit 17H, Surawongse Rd., Suriyawongse, Bangkat, Bangkok, Thailand 10500 ☎ 02/235-6624 🖷 02/235-6626 🌐 www.moveandstay.com.

🏠 Local Agents **Tsukasa Weekly/Monthly Mansion** ✉ 6-4-14 Koyama, Shinagawa-ku, Tōkyō 142-0062 ☎ 03/3784-0631 or 03/3440-0111 🖷 03/3784-1167 ✉ 1-3-2 Tokui-machi, Chūō-ku, Ōsaka 540-0025 ☎ 06/6949-4471 🖷 06/6942-9373; Japanese guarantor required. **The Mansions** ✉ 3-8-5 Roppongi, Minato-ku, Tōkyō 106-0032 ☎ 03/5414-7070 🖷 03/5414-7088 ✉ 2-1-3 Azabudai, Minato-ku, Tōkyō 106-0041 ☎ 03/5575-3232 🖷 03/5575-3233 🌐 www.themansions.jp.

🏠 Rental Listings **Metropolis** ✉ 3F Maison Tomoe Bldg., 3-16-1 Minami-Aoyama, Minato-ku, Tōkyō 107-0062 ☎ 03/3423-6932 🖷 03/3423-6931 🌐 www.metropolis.japantoday.com. **Kansai Time Out** ✉ 1-1-13 Ikuta-chō, Chūō-ku, Kōbe 651-0092 ☎ 078/232-4517 🖷 078/232-4518 🌐 www.kto.co.jp.

CAMPING

Camping is popular with the young and with families and there are designated campgrounds around the country. Beach and mountain areas are particularly popular and facilities are good. Camping outside of designated areas is permitted except in national parks.

HOME EXCHANGES

If you would like to exchange your home for someone else's, join a home-exchange organization, which will send you its updated listings of available exchanges for a year and will include your own listing in at least one of them. It's up to you to make specific arrangements.

🏠 Exchange Clubs **Intervac U.S.** ✉ 30 Corte San Fernando, Tiburon, CA 94920 ☎ 800/756-4663 🖷 415/435-7440 🌐 www.intervacus.com; $125 yearly for a listing, online access, and a catalog; $65 without catalog.

HOME VISITS

Through the home visit system, travelers can get a sense of domestic life in Japan by visiting a local family in their home. The program is voluntary on the homeowner's part, and there's no charge for a visit. The system is active in many cities throughout the country, including Tōkyō, Yokohama, Nagoya, Kyōto, Ōsaka, Hiroshima, Nagasaki, and Sapporo. To make a reservation, **apply in writing for a home visit at least a day in advance** to the local tourist information office of the place you are visiting. Contact the Japan National Tourist Organization (⇨ Visitor Information, *below*) before leaving for Japan for more information on the program.

HOSTELS

No matter what your age, you can save on lodging costs by staying at hostels. In some 4,500 locations in more than 70 countries around the world, Hostelling International (HI), the umbrella group for a number of national youth-hostel associations, offers single-sex, dorm-style beds and, at many hostels, rooms for couples and family accommodations. Membership in any HI national hostel association, open to travelers of all ages, allows you to stay in HI-affiliated hostels at member rates; one-year membership is about $28 for adults (C$35 for a two-year minimum membership in Canada, £14 in the U.K., A$52 in Australia, and NZ$40 in New Zealand); hostels charge about $10–$30 per night. Members have priority if the hostel is full; they're also eligible for discounts around the world, even on rail and bus travel in some countries.

Hostels in Japan run about ¥2,000–¥3,000 per night for members, usually ¥1,000 more for nonmembers. The quality of hostels varies a lot in Japan, though the bad ones are never truly terrible, and the good ones offer memorable experiences. Most offer private rooms for couples or families, though you should call ahead to be sure. Tourist information offices can direct you to a local hostel. Note that hostels tend to be crowded during school holidays, when university students are traveling around the country.

 Organizations **Japan Youth Hostels, Inc.** ✉ Suidō-bashi Nishiguchi Kaikan, 2-20-7 Misaki-chō, Chiyoda-ku, Tōkyō 101-0061 ☎ 03/3288-1417. **Hostelling International–USA** ✉ 8401 Colesville Rd., Suite 600, Silver Spring, MD 20910 ☎ 301/495-1240 🖷 301/495-6697 ⊕ www.hiusa.org. **Hostelling International–Canada** ✉ 205 Catherine St., Suite 400, Ottawa, Ontario K2P 1C3 ☎ 613/237-7884 or 800/663-5777 🖷 613/237-7868 ⊕ www.hihostels.ca.

YHA England and Wales ✉ Trevelyan House, Dimple Rd., Matlock, Derbyshire DE4 3YH, U.K. ☎ 0870/870-8808, 0870/ 770-8868, or 0162/959-2600 🖷 0870/770-6127 ⊕ www.yha.org.uk. **YHA Australia** ✉ 422 Kent St., Sydney, NSW 2001 ☎ 02/9261-1111 🖷 02/9261-1969 ⊕ www.yha.com.au. **YHA New Zealand** ✉ Level 1, Moorhouse City, 166 Moorhouse Ave., Box 436, Christchurch ☎ 03/379-9970 or 0800/278-299 🖷 03/365-4476 ⊕ www.yha.org.nz.

HOTELS

Full-service, first-class hotels in Japan resemble their counterparts all over the world, and because many of the staff members speak English, these are the easiest places for foreigners to stay. They are also among the most expensive, tending to fall into the $$$ and $$$$ categories.

Business hotels are a reasonable alternative. These are clean, impersonal, and functional. All have Western-style rooms that vary from small to minuscule; service is minimal. However, every room has a private bathroom, albeit cramped, with tub and handheld shower, television (no English-language channels), telephone, and a hot-water thermos. Business hotels are often conveniently located near the railway station. The staff may not speak English, and there's usually no room service, but the rates fall into the $ and $$ categories.

Designed to accommodate the modern Japanese urbanite, the capsule hotel is a novel idea. The rooms are a mere 3½ foot wide, 3½ foot high, and 7¼ foot long. They have an alarm clock, television, and phone, and little else. Capsules are often used by commuters who have had an evening of excess and cannot make the long journey home. Although you may want to try sleeping in a capsule, you probably won't want to spend a week in one.

Some useful words when checking into a hotel: air-conditioning *eakon*, private baths *o-furo*, showers *shawā*, double beds *daburubeddo*, twin beds *tsuinbeddo*, separate *betsu*, pushed together *kuttsukerareta*, queen bed *kuīn saizun-no-beddo*, king bed *kingu saizu-no-beddo*.

All hotels listed have private bath unless otherwise noted.

RESERVING A ROOM

🔢 **Toll-Free Numbers Best Western** 🕾 800/528–1234 ⊕ www.bestwestern.com. **Choice** 🕾 800/424–6423 ⊕ www.choicehotels.com. **Clarion** 🕾 800/424–6423 ⊕ www.choicehotels.com. **Comfort Inn** 🕾 800/424–6423 ⊕ www.choicehotels.com. **Four Seasons** 🕾 800/332–3442 ⊕ www.fourseasons.com. **Hilton** 🕾 800/445–8667 ⊕ www.hilton.com. **Holiday Inn** 🕾 800/465–4329 ⊕ www.ichotelsgroup.com. **Hyatt Hotels & Resorts** 🕾 800/233–1234 ⊕ www.hyatt.com. **Inter-Continental** 🕾 800/327–0200 ⊕ www.ichotelsgroup.com. **Marriott** 🕾 800/228–9290 ⊕ www.marriott.com. **Le Meridien** 🕾 800/543–4300 ⊕ www.lemeridien.com. **Nikko Hotels International** 🕾 800/645–5687 ⊕ www.nikkohotels.com. **Radisson** 🕾 800/333–3333 ⊕ www.radisson.com. **Renaissance Hotels & Resorts** 🕾 800/468–3571 ⊕ www.renaissancehotels.com/. **Ritz-Carlton** 🕾 800/241–3333 ⊕ www.ritzcarlton.com. **Sheraton** 🕾 800/325–3535 ⊕ www.starwood.com/sheraton. **Sleep Inn** 🕾 800/424–6423 ⊕ www.choicehotels.com. **Tōkyū Hotels** 🕾 03/3462–0109 ⊕ www.tokyuhotels.co.jp/en. **Washington Hotels** 🕾 03/3433–4253 ⊕ www.wh-rsv.com/english/index.html. **Westin Hotels & Resorts** 🕾 800/228–3000 ⊕ www.starwood.com/westin.

INEXPENSIVE ACCOMMODATIONS

JNTO publishes a listing of some 700 accommodations that are reasonably priced. To be listed, properties must meet Japanese fire codes and charge less than ¥8,000 (about $70) per person without meals. For the most part, the properties charge ¥5,000–¥6,000 ($44–$54). These properties welcome foreigners (many Japanese hotels and ryokan do not like to have foreign guests because they might not be familiar with traditional-inn etiquette). Properties include business hotels, *ryokan* of a very rudimentary nature, *minshuku* (Japanese bed-and-breakfasts), and pensions. It's the luck of the draw whether you choose a good or less-than-good property. In most cases rooms are clean but very small. Except in business hotels, shared baths are the norm, and you are expected to have your room lights out by 10 PM.

Many establishments on the list of reasonably priced accommodations—and many that are not on the list—can be reserved through the nonprofit organization **Welcome Inn Reservation Center.** Reservation forms are available from your nearest JNTO office (⇨ Visitor Information, *below*). The Japanese Inn Group, which provides reasonable accommodations for foreign visitors, can be reserved through this same service. The center must receive reservation requests at least one week before your departure to allow processing time. If you are already in Japan, JNTO's Tourist Information Centers (TICs) at Narita Airport, Kansai International Airport, downtown Tōkyō, and Kyōto can make immediate reservations for you at these Welcome Inns.

🔢 Reservations **Japanese Inn Group** Ryokan Asakusa Shigetsu ✉ 1-31-11 Nishi-Asakusa, Taitō-ku, Tōkyō 111-0032 🕾 03/3252-1717 ⊕ www.jpinn.com. **Welcome Inn Reservation Center** ✉ Tōkyō International Forum B1, 3-5-1 Marunouchi, Chiyoda-ku, Tōkyō 100-0005 🕾 03/3211-4201 🖷 03/3211-9009 ⊕ www.itcj.or.jp.

MINSHUKU

Minshuku are private homes that accept guests. Usually they cost about ¥6,000 (about $54) per person, including two meals. Although in a ryokan you need not lift a finger, don't be surprised if you are expected to lay out and put away your own bedding in a minshuku. Meals are often served in communal dining rooms. Minshuku vary in size and atmosphere; some are private homes that take in only a few guests, while others are more like no-frill inns. Some of your most memorable stays could be at a minshuku, as they offer a chance to become acquainted with a Japanese family and their hospitality.

🔢 **Japan Minshuku Center** ✉ Tōkyō Kōtsū, Kaikan Bldg., B1, 2-10-1 Yūrakuchō, Chiyoda-ku, Tōkyō 🕾 03/3216-6556 🖷 03/3216-6557 ⊕ www.minshuku.co.jp.

RYOKAN

If you want to sample the Japanese way, **spend at least one night in a ryokan (inn).** Usually small, one- or two-story wooden structures with a garden or scenic view, they provide traditional Japanese accommodations: simple rooms in which the bedding is rolled out onto the floor at night.

Ryokan vary in price and quality. Some older, long-established inns cost as much as ¥80,000 ($700) per person, whereas humbler places that are more like bed-and-breakfasts are as low as ¥6,000 ($54). Prices are per person and include the cost of breakfast, dinner, and tax. Some inns allow you to stay without having dinner and lower the cost accordingly. However, this is not recommended, because the service and meals are part of the ryokan experience. It is important to **follow Japanese customs in all ryokan.** For more information, *see* the Ryokan Etiquette box *in* Chapter 5.

Japan Ryokan Association ✉ 1-8-3 Maru-no-uchi, Chiyoda-ku, Tōkyō ☎ 03/3231-5310. JNTO (⇨ Visitor Information, *below*).

TEMPLES

You can also arrange accommodations in Buddhist temples. JNTO has lists of temples that accept guests. A stay at a temple generally costs ¥3,000–¥9,000 ($27–$80) per night, including two meals. Some temples offer instruction in meditation or allow you to observe their religious practices, while others simply offer a room. The Japanese-style rooms are very simple and range from beautiful, quiet havens to not-so-comfortable, basic cubicles. Either way, temples provide a taste of traditional Japan.

MAIL & SHIPPING

The Japanese postal service is very efficient. Air mail between Japan and the United States takes between five and eight days. Surface mail can take anywhere from four to eight weeks. Express service is also available through post offices.

Although there are numerous post offices in every city, it's probably best to **use the central post office near the main train station,** because the workers speak English and can handle foreign mail. Some of the smaller post offices are not equipped to send packages. Post offices are open weekdays 9–5 and Saturday 9–noon. Some of the central post offices have longer hours, such as the one in Tōkyō, located near Tōkyō Eki (train station), which is open 24 hours year-round. Most hotels supply stamps and mail your letters and post-cards, usually with no service fee.

The Japanese postal service has implemented use of three-numeral-plus-four postal codes, but its policy is similar to that in the United States regarding ZIP-plus-fours; that is, addresses with the three-numeral code will still arrive at their destination, albeit perhaps one or two days later. Mail to rural towns may take longer.

OVERNIGHT SERVICES

FedEx has drop-off locations at branches of Kinko's in all major cities. A 1 kg/2.20 lb package from central Tōkyō to Washington, D.C., would cost about ¥7,200 ($64) and take two days to be delivered.

Major Services FedEx ☎ 0120/00-320 toll-free, 043/298-1919 ⊕ www.fedex.com/jp_english.

POSTAL RATES

It costs ¥110 (98¢) to send a letter by air to North America and Europe. An airmail postcard costs ¥70 (63¢). Aerograms cost ¥90 (81¢).

RECEIVING MAIL

To get mail, have parcels and letters sent "poste restante" to the central post office in major cities; unclaimed mail is returned after 30 days.

SHIPPING PARCELS

The Japanese Post Office is very efficient and domestic mail rarely goes astray. To ship a 5 kg/11.02 lb parcel to the U.S., Canada, the U.K., Australia, or New Zealand costs ¥10,150 ($91) if sent by airmail, ¥7,300 ($65) by SAL (economy airmail) and ¥4,000 ($36) by sea. Allow a week for airmail, 2 to 3 weeks for SAL, and up to 6 weeks for packages sent by sea. Large shops usually ship domestically, but not overseas.

MONEY MATTERS

Japan is expensive, but there are ways to cut costs. This requires, to some extent, an adventurous spirit and the courage to stray from the standard tourist paths. One good way to hold down expenses is to **avoid taxis** (they tend to get stuck in traffic anyway) and **try the inexpensive, efficient subway and bus systems;** instead of going to a restaurant with menus in English and Western-style food, go to places where you can rely on your good old index finger to point to the dish you want, and try food that the Japanese eat (⇨ The Discreet Charm of Japanese Cuisine *in* Chapter 15).

A regular cup of coffee costs ¥250–¥600 ($2–$5.50); a bottle of beer, ¥350–¥800 ($3–$7); a 2-km (1-mi) taxi ride, ¥660 ($6); a McDonald's hamburger, ¥84 (75¢); a bowl of noodles, ¥600 ($5.50); an average dinner, ¥2,500 ($22); a double room in Tōkyō, ¥11,000–¥45,000 ($98–$403).

Prices throughout this guide are given for adults. Substantially reduced fees are almost always available for children, students, and senior citizens. For information on taxes, *see* Taxes.

ATMS

ATMs at many Japanese banks do not accept foreign-issue cash or credit cards. Citibank has centrally located branches in most major Japanese cities and ATMs that are open 24 hours. Japan's most progressive bank, UFJ, is a member of the Plus network. Some convenience stores have also have cash machines in the Plus network. Post offices have ATMs that accept Visa, MasterCard, American Express, Diners Club, and Cirrus cards. Elsewhere, especially in more rural areas, it's difficult to find suitable ATMs. PIN numbers in Japan are comprised of four digits. In Japanese, an ATM is commonly referred to by its English acronym, while PIN is *anshō bangō*.

CREDIT CARDS

MasterCard and Visa are the most widely accepted credit cards in Japan. Many vendors don't accept American Express. Throughout this guide, the following abbreviations are used: **AE**, American Express; **DC**, Diners Club; **D**, Discover; **MC**, MasterCard; and **V**, Visa.

🔢 Reporting Lost Cards **American Express** ☎ 0120/02-0120. **Diners Club** ☎ 0120/07-4024. **Discover** ☎ 001801/902-3100 **MasterCard** ☎ 00531/11-3886. **Visa** ☎ 0120/13-3173.

CURRENCY

The unit of currency in Japan is the yen (¥). There are bills of ¥10,000, ¥5,000, ¥2,000, and ¥1,000. Coins are ¥500, ¥100, ¥50, ¥10, ¥5, and ¥1. Japanese currency floats on the international monetary exchange, so changes can be dramatic. Some vending machines will not accept the newly introduced ¥2,000 bill or the new version of the ¥500 coin, but these older machines are gradually being replaced.

CURRENCY EXCHANGE

At this writing, the exchange rate was ¥104 for U.S. $1, ¥86 for Canadian $1, ¥200 for British £1, ¥82 for Australian $1, and ¥76 for New Zealand $1.

For the most favorable rates, **change money through banks.** Although ATM transaction fees may be higher abroad than at home, ATM rates are excellent because they're based on wholesale rates offered only by major banks. You won't do as well at exchange booths in airports or rail and bus stations, in hotels, in restaurants, or in stores. To avoid lines at airport exchange booths, get a bit of local currency before you leave home.

🔢 Exchange Services **International Currency Express** ✉ 427 N. Camden Dr., Suite F, Beverly Hills, CA 90210 ☎ 888/278-6628 orders 🖷 310/278-6410 ⊕ www.foreignmoney.com. **Travel Ex Currency Services** ☎ 800/287-7362 orders and retail locations ⊕ www.travelex.com.

TRAVELER'S CHECKS

Traveler's checks are widely accepted at major businesses in cities, though not in small businesses or rural areas. Lost or stolen checks can usually be replaced within 24 hours. To ensure a speedy refund, buy your own traveler's checks— don't let someone else pay for them: irregularities like this can cause delays. The person who bought the checks should make the call to request a refund.

PACKING

Because porters can be hard to find and baggage restrictions on international flights are tight, pack light. What you pack depends more on the time of year than on any dress code. For travel in the cities, pack as you would for any American or European city. At more expensive restaurants and nightclubs, men usually need to wear a jacket and tie. Wear conservative-color clothing at business meetings. Casual clothes are fine for sightseeing. Jeans are as popular in Japan as they are in the United States and are perfectly acceptable for informal dining and sightseeing.

Although there are no strict dress codes for visiting temples and shrines, you will be out of place in shorts or immodest outfits. For sightseeing leave sandals and open-toe shoes behind; you'll need sturdy walking shoes for the gravel pathways that surround temples and fill parks. Make sure to bring comfortable clothing that isn't too tight to wear in traditional Japanese restaurants, where you may need to sit on tatami-matted floors. For beach and mountain resorts pack informal clothes for both day and evening wear.

Japanese do not wear shoes in private homes or in any temples or traditional inns. Having shoes you can quickly slip in and out of is a decided advantage. Take some wool socks along to help you through those shoeless occasions during the winter.

If you're a morning coffee addict, **take along packets of instant coffee.** All lodgings provide a thermos of hot water and bags of green tea in every room, but for coffee you can call room service, buy very sweet coffee in a can from a vending machine, or purchase packets of instant coffee at local convenience stores. If you're staying in a Japanese inn, they probably won't have coffee.

Sunglasses, sunscreen lotions, and hats are readily available, and these days they're not much more expensive in Japan. It's a good idea to carry a couple of plastic bags to protect your camera and clothes during sudden cloudbursts.

Take along small gift items, such as scarves or perfume sachets, to thank hosts (on both business and pleasure trips), whether you've been invited to their home or out to a restaurant.

In your carry-on luggage, pack an extra pair of eyeglasses or contact lenses and enough of any medication you take to last a few days longer than the entire trip. You may also ask your doctor to write a spare prescription using the drug's generic name, as brand names may vary from country to country. In luggage to be checked, **never pack prescription drugs, valuables, or undeveloped film.** And don't forget to carry with you the addresses of offices that handle refunds of lost traveler's checks. Check *Fodor's How to Pack* (available at online retailers and bookstores everywhere) for more tips.

To avoid customs and security delays, carry medications in their original packaging. Don't pack any sharp objects in your carry-on luggage, including knives of any size or material, scissors, nail clippers, and corkscrews, or anything else that might arouse suspicion.

To avoid having your checked luggage chosen for hand inspection, don't cram bags full. The U.S. Transportation Security Administration suggests packing shoes on top and placing personal items you don't want touched in clear plastic bags.

CHECKING LUGGAGE

You're allowed to carry aboard one bag and one personal article, such as a purse or a laptop computer. Make sure what you carry on fits under your seat or in the overhead bin. Get to the gate early, so you can board as soon as possible, before the overhead bins fill up.

Baggage allowances vary by carrier, destination, and ticket class. On international flights, you're usually allowed to check two bags weighing up to 70 pounds (32 kilograms) each, although a few airlines allow checked bags of up to 88 pounds (40 kilograms) in first class. Some international carriers don't allow more than 66 pounds (30 kilograms) per bag in business class and 44 pounds (20 kilograms) in economy. On domestic flights, the limit is usually 50 to 70 pounds (23 to 32 kilograms) per bag. In general, carry-on bags shouldn't exceed 40 pounds (18 kilograms). Most airlines won't accept bags that weigh more than 100 pounds (45 kilograms) on domestic or international flights. Expect to pay a fee for baggage that exceeds weight limits. Check baggage restrictions with your carrier before you pack.

Airline liability for baggage is limited to $2,500 per person on flights within the United States. On international flights it amounts to $9.07 per pound or $20 per kilogram for checked baggage (roughly $640 per 70-pound bag), with a maximum of $634.90 per piece, and $400 per passenger for unchecked baggage. You can buy additional coverage at check-in for about $10 per $1,000 of coverage, but it often excludes a rather extensive list of items, shown on your airline ticket.

Before departure, itemize your bags' contents and their worth, and label the bags with your name, address, and phone number. (If you use your home address, cover it so potential thieves can't see it readily.) Include a label inside each bag and **pack a copy of your itinerary.** At check-in, make sure each bag is correctly tagged with the destination airport's three-letter code. Because some checked bags will be opened for hand inspection, the U.S. Transportation Security Administration recommends that you leave luggage unlocked or use the plastic locks offered at check-in. TSA screeners place an inspection notice inside searched bags, which are re-sealed with a special lock.

If your bag has been searched and contents are missing or damaged, file a claim with the TSA Consumer Response Center as soon as possible. If your bags arrive damaged or fail to arrive at all, file a written report with the airline before leaving the airport.

🅰 Complaints **U.S. Transportation Security Administration Contact Center** ☎ 866/289–9673 ⊕ www.tsa.gov.

PASSPORTS & VISAS

When traveling internationally, carry your passport even if you don't need one (it's always the best form of ID) and **make two photocopies of the data page** (one for someone at home and another for you, carried separately from your passport). If you lose your passport, promptly call the nearest embassy or consulate and the local police.

U.S. passport applications for children under age 14 require consent from both parents or legal guardians; both parents must appear together to sign the application. If only one parent appears, he or she must submit a written statement from the other parent authorizing passport issuance for the child. A parent with sole authority must present evidence of it when applying; acceptable documentation includes the child's certified birth certificate listing only the applying parent, a court order specifically permitting this parent's travel with the child, or a death certificate for the nonapplying parent. Application forms and instructions are available on the Web site of the U.S. State Department's Bureau of Consular Affairs (⊕ travel.state.gov).

ENTERING JAPAN

Visitors from the United Kingdom can enter Japan and stay for up to six months with a valid passport; Canadian citizens are allowed three months; and visitors from the United States, Australia, and New Zealand can stay for 90 days; no visa is required.

PASSPORT OFFICES

The best time to apply for a passport or to renew is in fall and winter. Before any trip, check your passport's expiration date, and, if necessary, renew it as soon as possible.

🅰 Australian Citizens **Passports Australia** Australian Department of Foreign Affairs and Trade ☎ 131-232 ⊕ www.passports.gov.au.

🅰 Canadian Citizens **Passport Office** ✉ To mail in applications: 200 Promenade du Portage, Hull, Québec J8X 4B7 ☎ 819/994-3500 or 800/567-6868 ⊕ www.ppt.gc.ca.

🅰 New Zealand Citizens **New Zealand Passports Office** ☎ 0800/22-5050 or 04/474-8100 ⊕ www.passports.govt.nz.

🅰 U.K. Citizens **U.K. Passport Service** ☎ 0870/521-0410 ⊕ www.passport.gov.uk.

🅰 U.S. Citizens **National Passport Information Center** ☎ 877/487-2778, 888/874-7793 TDD/TTY ⊕ travel.state.gov.

RESTROOMS

The most hygienic restrooms are found in hotels and department stores, and are usually clearly marked with international symbols. You may encounter Japanese-style toilets, with bowls recessed into the floor, over which you squat facing the hood. This may take some getting used to, but it's completely sanitary as you don't come into direct contact with the facility.

In many homes and Japanese-style public places, there will be a pair of slippers at the entrance to the restrooms. Change into these before entering the room, and change back when you exit.

Some public toilets don't have toilet paper, though there are dispensers where packets can be purchased for ¥50 (45¢) or so. Similarly, paper towel dispensers or hand dryers are not always installed, so a small handkerchief is useful to dry your hands.

SAFETY

Even in its major cities, Japan is a very safe country with one of the lowest crime rates in the world. You should, however, **avoid Ura-Kabuki-chō in Tōkyō's Shinjuku district and some of the large public parks at nighttime.**

Be aware that a money belt or a waist pack pegs you as a tourist, so be careful of placing money and valuables in these. A better idea is to distribute your cash and valuables (including your credit cards and passport) between a deep front pocket, an inside jacket or vest pocket, and a hidden money pouch.

SENIOR-CITIZEN TRAVEL

Senior citizens often qualify for discounts at museums. To qualify for age-related discounts, mention your senior-citizen status up front when booking hotel reservations (not when checking out) and before you're seated in restaurants (not when paying the bill). Be sure to have identification on hand. When renting a car, ask about promotional car-rental discounts, which can be cheaper than senior-citizen rates.

🎓 Educational Programs **Elderhostel** ✉ 11 Ave. de Lafayette, Boston, MA 02111-1746 ☎ 877/426-8056, 978/323-4141 international callers, 877/426-2167 TTY 🖷 877/426-2166 ⊕ www.elderhostel.org. **Interhos-**

tel ✉ University of New Hampshire, 6 Garrison Ave., Durham, NH 03824 ☎ 603/862-1147 or 800/733-9753 🖷 603/862-1113 ⊕ www.learn.unh.edu.

SHOPPING

Despite the high price of many goods, shopping is one of the great pleasures of a trip to Japan. You may not find terrific bargains here, but if you know where to go and what to look for, you can purchase unusual gifts and souvenirs at reasonable prices. In particular, **don't shop for items that are cheaper at home;** Japan is not the place to buy a Gucci bag. Electronics, too, are generally cheaper in the United States. Look for things that are Japanese made for Japanese people and sold in stores that do not cater primarily to tourists.

Don't pass up the chance to purchase Japanese crafts. Color, balance of form, and absolutely superb craftsmanship make these items exquisite and well worth the price you'll pay. Some items can be quite expensive; for example, Japanese lacquerware carries a hefty price. But if you like the shiny boxes, bowls, cups, and trays and consider that quality lacquerware is made to last a lifetime, the cost is justified. Be careful, though: some lacquer items are made from a pressed-wood product rather than solid wood, and only experts can tell the difference. If the price seems low, it probably means the quality is low, too. Note that, except at street markets, bargaining is not usually possible.

KEY DESTINATIONS

Akihabara in Tōkyō or Den-Den Town in Ōsaka are must-visit destinations for fans of computers and electrical gadgets; major department stores, like Daimaru or Hankyū are a safe bet in any major city for high-quality clothes, crafts, and pottery. Ōsaka's Amerika-Mura and Tōkyō's Shibuya districts are essential stopping-off points for the latest in teen fashion. For full shopping details, *see* the shopping section *in* each chapter.

WATCH OUT

The export of antiques is controlled, and items such as firearms and Japanese swords cannot be exported without special documentation. A reputable dealer can ad-

vise about particular items and paperwork. Some street vendors purport to sell
brand-name products at very cheap prices,
but often the goods are fakes from China
or Thailand.

SIGHTSEEING GUIDES

The Japan Guide Association will introduce you to English-speaking guides. You
need to negotiate your own itinerary and
price with the guide. Assume that the fee
will be ¥25,000–¥30,000 for a full eight-
hour day. The Japan National Tourist Organization can also put you in touch with
various local volunteer groups that conduct tours in English; you need only to
pay for the guide's travel expenses, admission fees to cultural sites, and meals if you
eat together.

The Japan National Tourist Organization
(JNTO) sponsors a Good-Will Guide program in which local citizens volunteer to
show visitors around; this is a great way
to meet Japanese people. These are not
professional guides; they usually volunteer
both because they enjoy welcoming foreigners to their town and because they
want to practice their English. The services of Good-Will Guides are free, but
you should pay for their travel costs, their
admission fees, and any meals you eat
with them while you are together. To participate in this program, make arrangements for a Good-Will Guide in advance
through JNTO in the United States or
through the tourist office in the area
where you want the guide to meet you.
The program operates in 75 towns and
cities, including Tōkyō, Kyōto, Nara,
Nagoya, Ōsaka, and Hiroshima.

🔼 Tour Contacts **Japan Guide Association** ☎ 03/
3213-2706. **Japan National Tourist Organization**
✉ Tōkyō International Forum B1, 3-5-1
Marunouchi, Chiyoda-ku ☎ 03/3201-3331
Ⓜ Yūraku-chō Line, Yūraku-chō station [Exit A-4B].

STUDENTS IN JAPAN

Discounts for students are sometimes
available at museums and other tourist attractions. You must show an International
Student Identity Card.

🔼 IDs & Services **STA Travel** ✉ 10 Downing St.,
New York, NY 10014 ☎ 212/627-3111, 800/777-0112

24-hr service center ☎ 212/627-3387 ⊕ www.sta.
com. **Travel Cuts** ✉ 187 College St., Toronto, Ontario M5T 1P7, Canada ☎ 800/592-2887 in U.S.,
416/979-2406 or 866/246-9762 in Canada ☎ 416/
979-8167 ⊕ www.travelcuts.com.

TAXES

HOTEL

A 5% national consumption tax is added
to all hotel bills. Another 3% local tax is
added to the bill if it exceeds ¥15,000
(about $134). You may **save money by
paying for your hotel meals separately**
rather than charging them to your bill.

At first-class, full-service, and luxury hotels, a 10% service charge is added to the
bill in place of individual tipping. At the
more expensive ryokan, where individual-
ized maid service is offered, the service
charge is usually 15%. At business hotels,
minshuku, youth hostels, and economy
inns, no service charge is added to the bill.

SALES & VALUE-ADDED TAX

There's an across-the-board, nonrefundable 5% consumption tax levied on all
sales, which is included in the ticket price.
Authorized tax-free shops will knock the
tax off purchases over ¥10,000 if you
show your passport and a valid tourist
visa. A large sign is displayed at such
shops. A 5% tax is also added to all
restaurant bills. Another 3% local tax is
added to the bill if it exceeds ¥7,500
(about $67). At the more expensive restau-
rants, a 10%–15% service charge is added
to the bill. Tipping is not customary.

TAXIS

Taxis are an expensive way of getting
around cities in Japan, though nascent
deregulation moves are easing the market a
little. The first 2 km (1 mi) cost ¥540–¥660
($4.82–$5.88), and it's ¥80 (71¢) for every
additional 280 meters (400 yards). If possible, avoid using taxis during rush hours
(7:30 AM–9:30 AM and 5 PM–7 PM).

In general, it's easy to hail a cab: do not
shout or wave wildly—simply raise your
hand if you need a taxi. Japanese taxis
have automatic door-opening systems, so
do not try to open the taxi door. Stand
back when the cab comes to a stop—if you

are too close, the door may slam into you. When you leave the cab, do not try to close the door; the driver will do it automatically. Only the curbside rear door opens. A red light on the dashboard indicates an available taxi, and a green light indicates an occupied taxi.

Drivers are for the most part courteous, although sometimes they balk at the idea of a foreign passenger because they do not speak English. Unless you're going to a well-known destination such as a major hotel, it's advisable to **have a Japanese person write out your destination in Japanese.** Remember, there is no need to tip.

TELEPHONES

AREA & COUNTRY CODES
The country code for Japan is 81. When dialing a Japanese number from outside of Japan, drop the initial "0" from the local area code. The country code is 1 for the United States and Canada, 61 for Australia, 64 for New Zealand, and 44 for the United Kingdom.

DIRECTORY & OPERATOR ASSISTANCE
Operator assistance at 104 is in Japanese only. Weekdays 9–5 (except national holidays), English-speaking operators can help you at the toll-free NTT Information Customer Service Centre.

 Directory Assistance ☎ 104. **NTT Information Customer Service Centre** ☎ 0120/36-4463.

INTERNATIONAL CALLS
Many gray, multicolor, and green phones have gold plates indicating, in English, that they can be used for international calls. Three Japanese companies provide international service: KDDI (001), Japan Telecom (0041), and IDC (0061). Dial the company code + country code + city/area code and number of your party. Telephone credit cards are especially convenient for international calls. For operator assistance in English on long-distance calls, dial 0051.

LONG-DISTANCE SERVICES
AT&T, MCI, and Sprint access codes make calling long-distance relatively convenient, but you may find the local access

number blocked in many hotel rooms. First ask the hotel operator to connect you. If the hotel operator balks, ask for an international operator, or dial the international operator yourself. One way to improve your odds of getting connected to your long-distance carrier is to travel with more than one company's calling card (a hotel may block Sprint, for example, but not MCI). If all else fails, call from a pay phone.

 Access Codes For local access numbers abroad, contact one of the following: **AT&T Direct** ☎ 800/222-0300. **MCI WorldPhone** ☎ 800/444-4444. **Sprint International Access** ☎ 800/877-4646.

MOBILE PHONES
Japan is the world leader in mobile phone technology, but overseas visitors cannot easily use their handsets in Japan. Phones can be rented on arrival at Vodafone outlets at both Narita and Kansai airports. Rental rates start at ¥525 ($5) a day, excluding insurance.

PHONE CARDS
Telephone cards for ¥1,000 ($9) can be bought at station kiosks or convenience stores and can be used in virtually all public telephones.

PUBLIC PHONES
Telephones come in various colors, including pink and green. Most pink-and-red phones, for local calls, accept only ¥10 coins. Green-and-gray phones accept ¥10 and ¥100 coins as well as prepaid telephone cards. Domestic long-distance rates are reduced as much as 50% after 9 PM (40% after 7 PM). Green-and-gray phones take coins and accept telephone cards—disposable cards of fixed value that you use up in increments of ¥10. Telephone cards, sold in vending machines, hotels, and a variety of stores, are tremendously convenient because you will not have to search for the correct change.

TIME
All of Japan is in the same time zone, 1 hour behind Sydney, 9 hours ahead of London, 14 hours ahead of New York, and 17 hours ahead of San Francisco. Daylight saving time is not observed.

TIPPING

Tipping is not common in Japan. It's not necessary to tip taxi drivers, or at hair salons, barbershops, bars, or nightclubs. A chauffeur for a hired car usually receives a tip of ¥500 ($4.50) for a half-day excursion and ¥1,000 ($9) for a full-day trip. Porters charge fees of ¥250–¥300 (about $2.50) per bag at railroad stations and ¥200 ($1.80) per piece at airports. It's not customary to tip employees of hotels, even porters, unless a special service has been rendered. In such cases, a gratuity of ¥2,000–¥3,000 ($18–$26) should be placed in an envelope and handed to the staff member discreetly.

TOURS & PACKAGES

Because everything is prearranged on a prepackaged tour or independent vacation, you spend less time planning—and often get it all at a good price.

BOOKING WITH AN AGENT

Travel agents are excellent resources. But it's a good idea to collect brochures from several agencies, as some agents' suggestions may be influenced by relationships with tour and package firms that reward them for volume sales. If you have a special interest, find an agent with expertise in that area. The American Society of Travel Agents (ASTA) has a database of specialists worldwide; you can log on to the group's Web site to find one near you.

Make sure your travel agent knows the accommodations and other services of the place being recommended. Ask about the hotel's location, room size, beds, and whether it has a pool, room service, or programs for children, if you care about these. Has your agent been there in person or sent others whom you can contact?

Do some homework on your own, too: local tourism boards can provide information about lesser-known and small-niche operators, some of which may sell only direct.

BUYER BEWARE

Each year consumers are stranded or lose their money when tour operators—even large ones with excellent reputations—go out of business. So check out the operator.

Ask several travel agents about its reputation, and try to **book with a company that has a consumer-protection program.** (Look for information in the company's brochure.) In the United States, members of the United States Tour Operators Association are required to set aside funds ($1 million) to help eligible customers cover payments and travel arrangements in the event that the company defaults. It's also a good idea to choose a company that participates in the American Society of Travel Agents' Tour Operator Program; ASTA will act as mediator in any disputes between you and your tour operator.

Remember that the more your package or tour includes, the better you can predict the ultimate cost of your vacation. Make sure you know exactly what is covered, and beware of hidden costs. Are taxes, tips, and transfers included? Entertainment and excursions? These can add up.

◪ Tour-Operator Recommendations **American Society of Travel Agents** (⇨ Travel Agencies). **National Tour Association** (NTA) ⊠ 546 E. Main St., Lexington, KY 40508 ☎ 859/226-4444 or 800/682-8886 ⊟ 859/226-4404 ⊕ www.ntaonline.com. **United States Tour Operators Association** (USTOA) ⊠ 275 Madison Ave., Suite 2014, New York, NY 10016 ☎ 212/599-6599 ⊟ 212/599-6744 ⊕ www.ustoa.com.

TRAIN TRAVEL

Riding Japanese trains is one of the pleasures of travel in the country. Efficient and convenient, trains run frequently and on schedule. The Shinkansen (bullet train), one of the fastest trains in the world, connects major cities north and south of Tōkyō. It is only slightly less expensive than flying but is in many ways more convenient because train stations are more centrally located than airports (and, if you have a Japan Rail Pass [⇨ Cutting Costs, *below*], it's extremely affordable). On the main line that runs west from Tōkyō, there are three types of Shinkansen. The *Nozomi* makes the fewest stops, which can cut as much as an hour from long, cross-country trips; it's the only Shinkansen on which you cannot use a JR Pass. The *Hikari* makes just a few more stops than the Nozomi. The *Kodama* is the equivalent of a Shinkansen local, making all stops along the Shinkansen lines. The same principal of faster and slower Shinkansen also applies on the line that runs north from Tōkyō to Morioka, in the Tōkyō region.

Other trains, though not as fast as the Shinkansen, are just as convenient and substantially cheaper. There are three types of train services: *futsū* (local service), *tokkyū* (limited express service), and *kyūkō* (express service). Both the tokkyū and the kyūkō offer a first-class compartment known as the Green Car. Smoking is allowed only in designated carriages on long-distance and Shinkansen trains. Local and commuter trains are entirely no-smoking.

Because there are no porters or carts at train stations, and the flights of stairs connecting train platforms can turn even the lightest bag into a heavy burden, it's a good idea to **travel light when getting around by train.** Savvy travelers often have their main luggage sent ahead to a hotel that they plan to reach later in their wanderings. It's also good to know that every train station, however small, has luggage lockers, which cost about ¥300 for 24 hours.

CUTTING COSTS

If you plan to travel by rail, **get a Japan Rail Pass,** which offers unlimited travel on Japan Railways (JR) trains. You can purchase one-, two-, or three-week passes. A one-week pass is less expensive than a regular round-trip ticket from Tōkyō to Kyōto on the Shinkansen. You must **obtain a rail pass voucher prior to departure for Japan** (you cannot buy them in Japan), and the pass must be used within three months of purchase. The pass is available only to people with tourist visas, as opposed to business, student, and diplomatic visas.

When you arrive in Japan, you must exchange your voucher for the Japan Rail Pass. You can do this at the Japan Railways desk in the arrivals hall at Narita Airport or at the JR stations of major cities. When you make this exchange, you determine the day that you want the rail pass to begin, and, accordingly, when it ends. You do not have to begin travel on the day you make the exchange; instead, **pick the starting date to maximize use.** The Japan Rail Pass allows you to travel on all JR-operated trains (which cover most destinations in Japan) but not lines owned by other companies.

The JR Pass is also valid on buses operated by Japan Railways (⇨ Bus Travel, *above*). You can make seat reservations without paying a fee on all trains that have reserved-seat coaches, usually the long-distance trains. The Japan Rail Pass does not cover the cost of sleeping compartments on overnight trains (called blue trains), nor does it cover the newest and fastest of the Shinkansen trains, the *Nozomi,* which make only one or two stops on longer runs. The pass covers only the *Hikari* Shinkansen, which make a few more stops than the *Nozomi,* and the *Kodama* Shinkansen, which stop at every station along the Shinkansen routes.

Japan Rail Passes are available in coach class and first class (Green Car), and as the difference in price between the two is relatively small, it's worth the splurge for first class, for real luxury, especially on the Shinkansen. A one-week pass costs ¥28,300 coach class, ¥37,800 first class; a two-week pass costs ¥45,100 coach class, ¥61,200 first class; and a three-week pass costs ¥57,700 coach class, ¥79,600 first class. Travelers under 18 pay lower rates. The pass pays for itself after one Tōkyō–Kyōto round-trip Shinkansen ride. Contact a travel agent or Japan Airlines to purchase the pass.

Japan Railways Group ✉ 1 Rockefeller Plaza, Suite 1622, New York, NY 10020 ☎ 212/332-8686 🖷 212/332-8690.

Buying a Pass Japan Airlines (JAL) ✉ 655 5th Ave., New York, NY 10022 USA ☎ 212/838-4400. **Japan Travel Bureau (JTB)** ✉ 810 7th Ave., 34th fl., New York, NY 10019 ☎ 212/698-4900 or 800/223-6104. **Nippon Travel Agency (NTA)** ✉ 111 Pavonia Ave., Suite 317, Jersey City, NJ 07310 ☎ 201/420-6000 or 800/682-7872.

FARES & SCHEDULES

Train Information JR Hotline ☎ 03/3423-0111 is an English-language information service, open weekdays 10-6.

RESERVATIONS

Many travelers assume that rail passes guarantee them seats on the trains they wish to ride. Not so. If you're using a rail pass, there's no need to buy individual tickets, but you should **book seats ahead.** This guarantees you a seat and is also a useful reference for the times of train departures and arrivals. You can reserve up to two weeks in advance or just minutes before the train departs. If you fail to make a train, there's no penalty, and you can reserve again.

Seat reservations for any JR route may be made at any JR station except those in the tiniest villages. The reservation windows or offices, *midori-no-madoguchi,* have green signs in English and green-stripe windows. If you're traveling without a Japan Rail Pass, there's a surcharge of approximately ¥500 (depending upon distance traveled) for seat reservations, and if you miss the train, you'll have to pay for another reservation. When making your seat reservation, you may request a no-smoking or smoking car. Your reservation ticket shows the date and departure time of your train as well as your car and seat number. On the platform you can figure out where to wait for a particular train car. Notice the markings painted on the platform or on little signs above the platform; ask someone which markings correspond to car numbers. If you don't have a reservation, ask which cars are unreserved. Sleeping berths, even with a rail pass, are additional. Unreserved tickets can be purchased at regular ticket windows. There are no reservations made on local service trains. For traveling short distances, tickets are usually sold at vending machines. A platform ticket is required if you go through the wicket gate onto the platform to meet someone coming off a train. The charge is ¥140 (in Tōkyō and Ōsaka, the tickets are ¥130).

Most clerks at train stations know a few basic words of English and can read roman script. Moreover, they are invariably helpful in plotting your route. The complete railway timetable is a mammoth book written only in Japanese; however, you can **get an English-language train schedule from the Japan National Tourist Organization** (JNTO; ⇨ Visitor Information, *below*) that covers the Shinkansen and a few of the major JR Limited Express trains. JNTO's booklet *The Tourist's Handbook* provides helpful information about purchasing tickets in Japan.

TRANSPORTATION AROUND JAPAN

Japan's public transport networks are second to none. Unless you're traveling to Hokkaido, a Japan Rail Pass is all you need. Trains are fast, frequent, clean, and punctual. Long-distance buses are a good low-budget alternative to train travel. You don't need to rent a car in Japan unless you're planning to explore central Kyūshū or rural Hokkaido.

TRAVEL AGENCIES

A good travel agent puts your needs first. Look for an agency that has been in business at least five years, emphasizes customer service, and has someone on staff who specializes in your destination. In addition, **make sure the agency belongs to a professional trade organization.** The American Society of Travel Agents (ASTA) has more than 10,000 members in some 140 countries, enforces a strict code of ethics, and will step in to mediate agent-client disputes involving ASTA members. ASTA also maintains a directory of agents on its Web site. (If a travel agency is also acting as your tour operator, *see* Buyer Beware *in* Tours & Packages.)

🔢 Local Agent Referrals **American Society of Travel Agents (ASTA)** ✉ 1101 King St., Suite 200, Alexandria, VA 22314 ☎ 703/739-2782 or 800/965-2782 24-hr hotline 🖷 703/684-8319 ⊕ www. astanet.com. **Association of British Travel Agents** ✉ 68-71 Newman St., London W1T 3AH ☎ 020/7637-2444 🖷 020/7637-0713 ⊕ www.abta.com. **Association of Canadian Travel Agencies** ✉ 130 Albert St., Suite 1705, Ottawa, Ontario K1P 5G4 ☎ 613/237-3657 🖷 613/237-7052 ⊕ www.acta.ca. **Australian Federation of Travel Agents** ✉ Level 3, 309 Pitt St., Sydney, NSW 2000 ☎ 02/9264-3299 or 1300/363-416 🖷 02/9264-1085 ⊕ www.afta.com. au. **Travel Agents' Association of New Zealand** ✉ Level 5, Tourism and Travel House, 79 Boulcott St., Box 1888, Wellington 6001 ☎ 04/499-0104 🖷 04/499-0786 ⊕ www.taanz.org.nz.

VISITOR INFORMATION

Learn more about foreign destinations by checking government-issued travel advisories and country information. For a broader picture, consider information from more than one country.

For information before you go, contact the Japan National Tourist Organization (JNTO). You may also want to check out their Web site at www.jnto.go.jp. When you get there, call or stop by one of the Tourist Information Centers (TIC) for information on western or eastern Japan and use the Japan Travel Phone (daily 9–5); for recorded information 24 hours a day, call the Teletourist service.

🄵 Japan National Tourist Organization (JNTO) **Canada:** ✉ 165 University Ave., Toronto, Ontario M5H 3B8 ☎ 416/366–7140. **Japan:** ✉ 2-10-1 Yūrakuchō 1-chōme, Chiyoda-ku, Tōkyō ☎ 03/3502–1461 ✉ 9F, JR Kyōto Station Bldg., Hachijō-guchi, Minami-ku, Kyōto ☎ 075/344–3300. **United Kingdom:** ✉ Heathcoat House, 20 Savile Row, London W1X 1AE ☎ 020/7734–9638. **United States:** ✉ 1 Rockefeller Plaza, Suite 1250, New York, NY 10020 ☎ 212/757–5640 ✉ 401 N. Michigan Ave., Suite 770, Chicago, IL 60611 ☎ 312/222–0874 ✉ 1 Daniel Burnham Court, San Francisco, CA 94109 ☎ 415/292–5686 ✉ 515 S. Figueroa St., Suite 1470, Los Angeles, CA 90071 ☎ 213/623–1952.

🄵 Japan Travel Phone **Throughout Japan** ☎ 0088/22–4800 throughout Japan outside Tōkyō and Kyōto, 03/3201–3331 in Tōkyō, 075/344–3300 in Kyōto.

🄵 Teletourist Service **Tōkyō** ☎ 03/3201–2911.

🄵 Tourist Information Centers (TIC) **Tōkyō International Forum B1** ✉ 3-5-1 Marunouchi, Chiyoda-ku, Tōkyō ☎ 03/3201–3331 ✉ Main Terminal Bldg., Narita Airport, Chiba Prefecture ☎ 0476/34–6251 ✉ 2F, JR Kyōto Station Bldg., Hachijō-guchi, Minami-ku, Kyōto ☎ 075/343–6655 ✉ Kansai International Airport, Ōsaka ☎ 0724/56–6025.

🄵 Government Advisories **U.S. Department of State** ✉ Overseas Citizens Services Office, 2100 Pennsylvania Ave. NW, 4th fl., Washington, DC 20520 ☎ 202/647–5225 interactive hotline, 888/407–4747 ⊕ www.travel.state.gov. **Consular Affairs Bureau of Canada** ☎ 800/267–6788 or 613/944–6788 ⊕ www.voyage.gc.ca. **U.K. Foreign and Commonwealth Office** ✉ Travel Advice Unit, Consular Division, Old Admiralty Bldg., London SW1A 2PA ☎ 0870/606–0290 or 020/7008–1500 ⊕ www.fco.gov.uk/travel. **Australian Department of Foreign Affairs and Trade** ☎ 300/139–281 travel advice, 02/6261–1299 Consular Travel Advice Faxback Service ⊕ www.dfat.gov.au. **New Zealand Ministry of Foreign Affairs and Trade** ☎ 04/439–8000 ⊕ www.mft.govt.nz.

WEB SITES

You can research prices and book plane tickets, hotel rooms, rental cars, vacation packages, and more at ⊕ www.fodors.com. In addition, you can post your pressing questions in the Travel Talk section. Other planning tools include a currency converter and weather reports, and there are loads of links to travel resources.

Cultural resources and travel-planning tools abound for the cybertraveler to Japan. Good first stops include the Web sites of Japan's three major English-language daily newspapers, the *Asahi Shimbun* (⊕ www.asahi.com), *Daily Yomiuri* (⊕ www.yomiuri.co.jp/index-e.htm), and the *Japan Times* (⊕ www.japantimes.co.jp).

For travel updates, visit the Web site of the Japan National Tourist Office (JNTO ⊕ www.jnto.go.jp). You can also find a links page, which connects you to an amusing if random assortment of sites that somehow relate to Japan.

Metropolis (⊕ http://metropolis.japantoday.com) and *Tokyo Journal* (⊕ www.tokyo.to/index.html), slick online magazines for the English expat community in Tōkyō, will catch you up on the latest goings-on in the capital city. Both have up-to-date arts, events, and dining listings. In the Kansai region, *Kansai Time Out* (⊕ www.kto.co.jp) is definitely worth a look.

Online resources abound for information on traveling by public transportation. Visit Jorudan's invaluable "Japanese Transport Guide" (⊕ www.jorudan.co.jp/english/norikae/e-norikeyin.html), which has a simple, uncluttered interface. You enter the station from which you're departing and your destination, and the planner presents you with the travel time, fare, and distance for all possible routes. Japan Rail's sites are handy planning tools as well, and provide fare and ticket information. The JR East (⊕ www.jreast.co.jp/e), the JR West

(⊕ www.westjr.co.jp/english/english/ index.html), and the main JR (⊕ www. japanrailpass.net) sites will direct you to detailed information about the Japan Rail Pass (⇨ Train Travel, *above*). For local info, RATP (⊕ www.subwaynavigator. com), the French rail-transit authority, maintains a useful subway navigator, which includes the subway systems in Ōsaka, Tōkyō, and Sapporo. The Metropolitan Government Web site (⊕ www. metro.tokyo.jp), incidentally, is an excellent source of information on sightseeing and current events in Tōkyō.

On the Web site of the Japan City Hotel Association (⊕ www.jcha.or.jp/english) you can search member hotels by location and price and make reservations online. Japan Economy Hotels Reservation Service Inc. (⊕ www.inn-info.co.jp/english/home.html) is another online lodging resource.

Japanese-Online (⊕ www.japanese-online. com) is a series of online language lessons that will help you pick up a bit of Japanese before your trip. (The site also, inexplicably, includes a sampling of typical Japanese junior high school math problems.) Kabuki for Everyone (⊕ www.fix.co.jp/ kabuki/kabuki.html) provides a comprehensive and accessible introduction to the dramatic form; on the site you can find video clips of Kabuki performances, summaries of major plays, an audio archive of Kabuki sounds, and a bibliography for further reading. Finally, for fun, stop by the Web site of Tōkyō's Tsukiji Central Wholesale Market (⊕ www.tsukiji-market. or.jp/tukiji_e.htm)—where else can you see tuna as big as cars online?

TŌKYŌ 東京

(1)

MOST IMPORTANT TEMPLE COMPLEX
Sensō-ji in Asakusa ⇨*p.38*

SHARPEST WEAPON COLLECTION
Japanese Sword Museum in Shibuya ⇨*p.60*

BEST SUSHI BAR
Edo-Gin in Tsukiji ⇨*p.89*

FRESH FROM THE FRYER
Tempura at Aoi-Marushin in Asakusa ⇨*p.81*

BEST MINIMALIST ESCAPE
The elegant Yoshimizu Ginza ⇨*p.94*

***LOST IN TRANSLATION* BEHEMOTH**
Park Hyatt Tōkyō in Shinjuku ⇨*p.98*

WHEN IN JAPAN, SING KARAOKE
Smash Hits in Shibuya ⇨*p.115*

By Jared
Lubarsky, Steve
Trautlein, and
Matt Wilce

Of all major cities in the world, it is perhaps the hardest to understand or to see in any single perspective. To begin with, consider the sheer, outrageous size of it. Tōkyō incorporates 23 wards, 26 smaller cities, 7 towns, and 8 villages—altogether sprawling 88 km (55 mi) from east to west and 24 km (15 mi) from north to south. The wards alone enclose an area of 590 square km (228 square mi), which in turn house some 12 million people. More than 3 million of these residents pass through Shinjuku Station, one of the major hubs in the transportation network, every day.

Space, that most precious of commodities, is so scarce that pedestrians have to weave in and around utility poles as they walk along the narrow sidewalks—yet mile after mile, houses rise only one or two stories, their low uniformity broken here and there by the sore thumb of an apartment building. Begin with that observation, and you discover that the very fabric of life in this city is woven of countless, unfathomable contradictions.

Tōkyō is a state-of-the-art financial marketplace, where billions of dollars are whisked electronically around the globe every day in the blink of an eye—and where all but a handful of ATMs shut down at 9 PM. A city of astonishing beauty in its small details, Tōkyō also has some of the ugliest buildings on the planet and generates more than 20,000 tons of garbage a day. It installed its first electric light in 1877, yet still has hundreds of thousands of households without a bathtub.

Outsiders rarely venture very far into the labyrinths of residential Tōkyō. Especially for travelers, the city defines itself by its commercial, cultural, and entertainment centers: Ueno, Asakusa, Ginza, Roppongi, Shibuya, Harajuku, Shinjuku, and an ever-growing list of new developments. The attention of Tōkyō shifts constantly, seeking new patches of astronomically expensive land on which to realize its enormous commercial energy. Nowadays, you can't buy a square yard anywhere in the city's central wards for less than $1,000.

Tōkyō has no remarkable skyline, no prevailing style of architecture, no real context into which a new building can fit. Every new project is an environment unto itself. Architects revel in this anarchy, and so do the designers of neon signs, show windows, and interior spaces. The kind of creative energy you find in Tōkyō could flower only in an atmosphere where there are virtually no rules to break.

Not all of this is for the best. Many of the buildings in Tōkyō are merely grotesque, and most of them are supremely ugly. In the large scale, Tōkyō is not an attractive city—nor is it gracious, and it is certainly not serene. The pace of life is wedded to the one stupefying fact of population: within a 36-km (22-mi) radius of the Imperial Palace live almost 30 million souls, all of them in a hurry and all of them ferocious consumers—not merely of things but of culture and leisure. Still uncertain about who they are and where they are going, they consume to identify themselves—by what they wear, where they eat, and how they use their spare time.

Sooner or later everything shows up here: Van Gogh's *Sunflowers*, the Berlin Philharmonic, Chinese pandas, Mexican food. Even the Coney

You need three days just to take in the highlights of Tōkyō and still have time for some shopping and nightlife. With four or five days you can explore the city in greater depth, wander off the beaten path, and appreciate Tōkyō's museums at leisure. More time would allow for day trips to the scenic and historical sights in communities outside the city.

If you have 3 days

Start *very* early (why waste your jet lag?) with a visit to the **Tōkyō Central Wholesale Market in Tsukiji** while it's still in high gear; then use the rest of the day for a tour of the **Imperial Palace** and environs.

Spend the morning of Day 2 at Buddhist **Sensō-ji** in Asakusa, and from there head to **Ueno** for an afternoon with its many museums, vistas, and historic sites.

Start Day 3 with a morning stroll through **Ginza** to explore its fabled shops and depāto. In the afternoon, see the Shintō **Meiji Jingū** and take a leisurely walk through the nearby Harajuku and Omotesandō fashion districts to the **Nezu Institute of Fine Arts**—a perfect oasis for your last impressions of the city.

If you have 5 days

Follow the itinerary above and add to it (or punctuate it with) a morning of browsing in **Akihabara**, Tōkyō's electronics discount quarter, visiting the nearby Shintō **Kanda Myōjin** as well. Spend the afternoon on the west side of **Shinjuku**, Tōkyō's 21st-century model city; savor the view from the observation deck of architect Kenzō Tange's monumental **Tōkyō Metropolitan Government Office**; and cap off the day with a walk through the greenery of **Shinjuku Gyoen National Garden**.

The luxury of a fifth day would allow you to fill in the missing pieces that belong to no particular major tour: the Buddhist **Sengaku-ji** in Shinagawa, the remarkable **Edo-Tōkyō Museum** in **Ryōgoku**, a tea ceremony, or any of the shops that haven't yet managed to stake a claim on your dwindling resources. See a sumō tournament, if there's one in town; failing that, you could still visit the **Kokugikan,** the National Sumō Arena, in the Ryōgoku district, and some of the sumō stables in the neighborhood.

If you have more time

With a week or more, you can make Tōkyō your home base for a series of side trips (⇨ Chapter 2).

Island carousel is here—lovingly restored down to the last gilded curlicue on the last prancing unicorn, back in action at an amusement park called Toshima-en (としまえん). Tōkyō is a magnet, and now the magnet is drawing you. What follows here is an attempt to chart a few paths for you through this exciting and exasperating city.

See the glossary at the end of this book for definitions of the common Japanese words and suffixes used in this chapter.

EXPLORING TŌKYŌ

The distinctions between Shitamachi (literally "downtown," to the north and east) and Yamanote (literally "uptown," to the south and west) have shaped the character of Tōkyō since the 17th century and will guide you as you explore the city. At the risk of an easy generalization, it might be said that downtown has more to *see*, uptown more to *do*. Another way of putting it is that Tōkyō north and east of the Imperial Palace embodies more of the city's history and traditional way of life; the glitzy, ritzy side of contemporary, international Tōkyō generally lies south and west.

The city has been divided into eight exploring sections in this chapter, six in Shitamachi—starting in central Tōkyō with the Imperial Palace District—and two uptown in Yamanote. It can be exhausting to walk from one part of Tōkyō to another—you can look in vain for places outdoors just to sit and rest en route—and bus travel can be particularly tricky. Fortunately, no point on any of these itineraries is very far from a subway station, and you can use the city's efficient subway system to hop from one area to another, to cut a tour short, or to return to a tour the next day. The area divisions in this book are not always contiguous—Tōkyō is too spread out for that—but they generally border each other to a useful degree. As you plan your approach to the city, by all means skip parts of an area that don't appeal or combine parts of one tour with those of another to get the best of all worlds.

The listings in this chapter include subway and Japan Rail (JR) train lines and stops, as well as station exit names and numbers in cases where they're most helpful—which is quite often, as several stations have multiple (sometimes more than 15) exits.

Imperial Palace District 皇居近辺

Kōkyo, the Imperial Palace, occupies what were once the grounds of Edo Castle. When Ieyasu Tokugawa chose the site for his castle in 1590, he had two goals in mind. First, it would have to be impregnable. Second, it would have to reflect the power and glory of his position. He was lord of the Kantō, the richest fief in Japan, and would soon be shōgun, the military head of state. The fortifications he devised called for a triple system of moats and canals, incorporating the bay and the Sumida-gawa into a huge network of waterways that enclosed both the castle keep (the stronghold, or tower) and the palaces and villas of his court—in all, an area of about 450 acres. The castle had 99 gates (36 in the outer wall), 21 watchtowers (of which 3 are still standing), and 28 armories. The outer defenses stretched from present-day Shimbashi Station to Kanda. Completed in 1640 (and later expanded), it was at the time the largest castle in the world.

The walls of Edo Castle and its moats were made of stone from the Izu Peninsula, about 96 km (60 mi) to the southwest. The great slabs were brought by barge—each of the largest was a cargo in itself—to the port of Edo (then much closer to the castle than the present port of Tōkyō

Performing Arts

Japan is justly proud of its music, dance, and theater traditions, which are quite unique: unless you happen to catch one of the infrequent (and expensive) performances of a company on tour abroad, you'll never really see the like of Kabuki, Nō, or Bunraku outside of Japan.

Combining music, dance, drama, and spectacular costumes, acrobatics, and special effects, Kabuki is the sort of performance you can enjoy without understanding a word the actors say. Nō, on the other hand, is an acquired taste. A ritual masked drama that has remained virtually unchanged since the 14th century, Nō moves at a stately—nay, glacial—pace to music and recitation utterly different from anything Western. Bunraku is Japan's puppet theater, like Kabuki a popular form of entertainment, but with roots in the western part of the country. The puppets themselves are so expressive and intricate in their movements that each requires three people to move it around on stage.

Three theaters in Tōkyō present Kabuki, including the landmark Kabuki-za, first built exclusively for that purpose in 1925. Four traditional schools, each with its own performance space, specialize in Nō; there's also the National Nō Theater, and—on rare occasions—night performances by torchlight in the courtyards of temples. Bunraku is not found as often in Tōkyō as it is in Ōsaka, but if there's a performance anywhere in town during your stay, it's worth seeing.

The Restaurant Scene

The sushi style most familiar to Westerners—slices of raw fish on vinegared rice, with a bit of wasabi—developed in Tōkyō, and today you'll find countless sushi bars here. Tempura, served in stalls and restaurants throughout the city and particularly in the Shitamachi area, is another specialty. Tōkyō also brims with countless international restaurants. The range of dining options is astonishing: it's hard to think of a national cuisine of any prominence that goes unrepresented. Some of those choices can be hideously expensive. For every budget-buster, however, there are any number of bargains—good cooking of all sorts, at prices ordinary travelers can afford. The options, in fact, go all the way down to street food and *yakitori* (Japanese-style chicken kebabs) joints under railroad trestles.

Shopping

In the late 1990s upscale consumer goods in Tōkyō—designer clothing, cultured pearls, home electronics—spiraled down from the insanely expensive to the merely costly. Fashions by internationally known designers like Issey Miyake, Rei Kawakubo, Hanae Mori, Yohji Yamamoto, Hiroko Koshino, and Kansai Yamamoto are priced more reasonably in Tōkyō's boutiques and department stores than they are abroad. Among things more traditionally Japanese, good buys include pottery, fabrics, folk-craft objects in wood and bamboo, cutlery, lacquerware, and handmade paper. You can find regional specialties from all over Japan, amounting to an enormous range of goods from which to choose. The selections in conveniently located arcades and the crafts sections of major department stores make one-stop shopping easy.

Tōkyō Overview

TO ROPPONGI HILLS →

Asakusa

Kappa-bashi-dōri

Asakusa-dōri

Kokugikan (National Sumo Area)

Ryōgoku

Tōkyō Expwy No.7

SHINJUKU LINE

TŌEI ASAKUSA LINE

E. EXPWY No.6

Kiyosu-bashi-dōri

Kura-mae-dōri

Akihabara

GINZA LINE

Asakusa-bashi

Nihombashi

Shōwa-dōri

HIBIYA LINE

Okachi-machi

Kanda

Tōkyō Expwy No. 1

Tōkyō

Nippori

Uguisudani

Ueno Kōen

Ueno

Ueno

Asakura Sculpture Gallery

Nishi-Nippori

CHIYODA LINE

Akihabara & Jimbō-chō

Ochanomizu

Kanda

Nihombashi, Ginza, & Yūraku-chō

Meiji-dōri

Hongo-dōri

Kasuga-dōri

Jimbo-chō

Hakusan-dōri Ave.

Kōrakuen

Tōkyō Dome

Sudō-bashi

Yasukuni-dōri

Imperial Palace

TŌEI MITA LINE

Rikugien Gardens

Koishikawa Botanical Gardens

Shinobazu-dōri

Iida-bashi

Nakasendo

Tōkyō Expwy No.5

Ichigaya

Yotsuya

← TO ŌJI

Otsuka

MARUNOUCHI LINE

Waseda-dōri

Shinjuku-dōri

Higashi-Ikebukuro

Zōshigaya

ARAKAWA LINE

Aoyama & Harajuku

Sendagaya

TO TOSHIMA-EN ↑

Sunshine International Aquarium

Meiji-dōri

Meijiro-dōri

MARUNOUCHI LINE

Shinjuku Gyo-en

YŪRAKUCHŌ LINE

Ikebukuro

Mejiro

Takada-no-baba

Shin-Ōkubo

Seibu-Shinjuku

Shinjuku

Shinjuku-dōri

TŌZAI LINE

Ōkubo

Ome-kaidō

Shinjuku

Yoyogi

Tama Dōbutsu Kōen Shinjuku

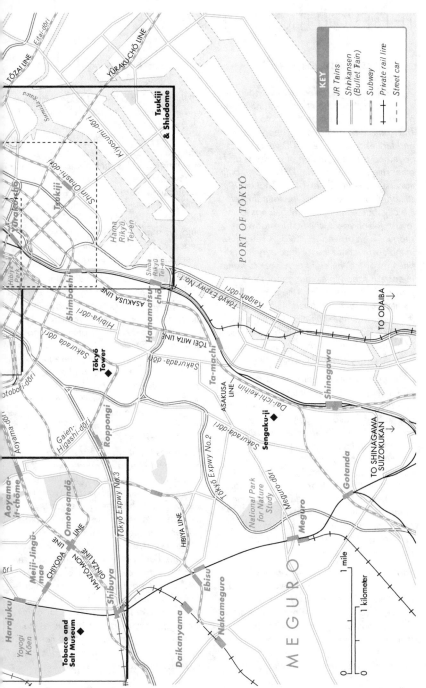

THE EVOLUTION OF TŌKYŌ

L IFE WAS SIMPLER HERE in the 12th century, when Tōkyō was a little fishing village called Edo (pronounced eh-doh), near the mouth of the Sumida-gawa (Sumida River) on the Kantō Plain. The Kantō was a strategic granary, large and fertile; over the next 400 years it was governed by a succession of warlords and other rulers. One of them, Dōkan Ōta, built the first castle in Edo in 1457. That act is still officially regarded as the founding of the city, but the honor really belongs to Ieyasu (ee-eh-ya-su), the first Tokugawa shōgun, who arrived in 1590. A key figure in the civil wars of the 16th century, he had been awarded the eight provinces of Kantō in eastern Japan in exchange for three provinces closer to Kyōto, the imperial capital. Ieyasu was a farsighted soldier; the swap was fine with him. On the site of Ōta's stronghold he built a mighty fortress of his own—from which, 10 years later, he was effectively ruling the whole country.

By 1680 there were more than a million people here, and a great city had grown up out of the reeds in the marshy lowlands of Edo Bay. Tōkyō can only really be understood as a jō-ka-machi—a castle town. Ieyasu had fought his way to the shogunate, and he had a warrior's concern for the geography of his capital. Edo Castle had the high ground, but that wasn't enough; all around it, at strategic points, he gave large estates to allies and trusted retainers. These lesser lords' villas also served as garrisons, outposts on a perimeter of defense.

Farther out, Ieyasu kept the barons he trusted least of all—whom he controlled by bleeding their treasuries. He required them to keep large, expensive establishments in Edo; to contribute generously to the temples he endowed; to come and go in alternate years in great pomp and ceremony; and, when they returned to their estates, to leave their families—in effect, hostages—behind.

All this, the Edo of feudal estates, of villas and gardens and temples, lay south and west of Edo Castle. It was called Yamanote—the Bluff, the uptown. Here, all was order, discipline, and ceremony; every man had his rank and duties (very few women were within the garrisons). Those duties were less military than bureaucratic. Ieyasu's precautions worked like a charm, and the Tokugawa dynasty enjoyed some 250 years of unbroken peace, during which nothing very interesting ever happened uptown.

But Yamanote was only the demand side of the economy: somebody had to bring in the fish, weed the gardens, weave the mats, and entertain the bureaucrats. To serve the noble houses, common people flowed into Edo from all over Japan. Their allotted quarters of the city were jumbles of narrow streets, alleys, and cul-de-sacs in the low-lying estuarine lands to the north and east. Often enough, the land assigned to them wasn't even there; they had to make it by draining and filling the marshes (the first reclamation project in Edo dates to 1457). The result was Shitamachi—literally "downtown"—the part below the castle, which sat on a hill. Bustling, brawling Shitamachi was the supply side: it had the lumberyards, markets, and workshops; the wood-block printers, kimono makers, and moneylenders. The people here gossiped over the back fence in the earthy, colorful Edo dialect. They went to Yoshiwara—a walled and moated area on the outskirts of Edo where prostitution was under official control (Yoshiwara was for a time the biggest licensed brothel area in the world). They supported the bathhouses and Kabuki theaters and reveled in their spectacular summer fireworks festivals. The city and spirit of the Edokko—the people of Shitamachi—have survived, while the great estates uptown are now mostly parks and hotels.

The shogunate was overthrown in 1867 by supporters of Emperor Meiji. The following year, the emperor moved his court from Kyōto to Edo and renamed it Tōkyō: the Eastern Capital. By now the city was home to nearly 2 million people, and the geography was vastly more complex. As it grew, it became not one but many smaller cities, with different centers of commerce, government, entertainment, and transportation. In Yamanote rose the commercial emporia, office buildings, and public halls that made up the architecture of an emerging modern state. The workshops of Shitamachi multiplied, some of them becoming small jobbers and family-run factories. Still, there was no planning, no grid. The neighborhoods and subcenters were worlds unto themselves, and a traveler from one was soon hopelessly lost in another.

The firebombings of 1945 left Tōkyō, for the most part, in rubble and ashes. That utter destruction could have been an opportunity to rebuild on the rational order of cities like Kyōto, Barcelona, or Washington. No such plan was ever made. Tōkyō reverted to type: it became once again an aggregation of small towns and villages. One village was much like any other; the nucleus was always the shōten-gai, the shopping arcade. Each arcade had at least one fishmonger, grocer, rice dealer, mat maker, barber, florist, and bookseller. You could live your whole life in the neighborhood of the shōten-gai. It was sufficient to your needs.

People seldom moved out of these villages. The vast waves of new residents who arrived after World War II—about three-quarters of the people in the Tōkyō metropolitan area today were born elsewhere—just created more villages. People who lived in the villages knew their way around, so there was no particular need to name the streets. Houses were numbered not in sequence but in the order in which they were built. No. 3 might well share a mailbox with No. 12. People still take their local geography for granted—the closer you get to the place you're looking for, the harder it is to get coherent directions. Away from main streets and landmarks, even a taxi driver can get hopelessly lost.

Fortunately, there are the kōban: small police boxes, or substations, usually with two or three officers assigned to each of them full time, to look after the affairs of the neighborhood. You can't go far in any direction without finding a kōban. The officer on duty knows where everything is and is glad to point the way. (The substation system, incidentally, is one important reason for the legendary safety of Tōkyō: on foot or on white bicycles, the police are a visible presence, covering the beat. Burglaries are not unknown, of course, but street crime is very rare.)

Tōkyō is still really two areas, Shitamachi and Yamanote. The heart of Shitamachi, proud and stubborn in its Edo ways, is Asakusa; the dividing line is Ginza, west of which lie the boutiques and department stores, the banks and engines of government, the pleasure domes and cafés. Today there are 13 subway lines in full operation that weave the two areas together.

is now) and hauled through the streets on sledges by teams of 100 or more men. Thousands of stonemasons were brought from all over the country to finish the work. Under the gates and castle buildings, the blocks of stone are said to have been shaped and fitted so precisely that a knife blade could not be slipped between them.

The inner walls divided the castle into four main areas, called *maru.* The *hon-maru,* the principle area, contained the shōgun's audience halls, his private residence, and, for want of a better word, his seraglio—the *ō-oku,* where he kept his wife and concubines, with their ladies-in-waiting, attendants, cooks, and servants. At any given time, as many as 1,000 women might be living in the ō-oku. Intrigue, more than sex, was its principal concern, and tales of the seraglio provided a rich source of material for the Japanese literary imagination. Below the hon-maru was the *ni-no-maru,* where the shōgun lived when he transferred his power to an heir and retired. Behind it was the *kita-no-maru,* the northern area, now a public park; south and west was the *nishi-no-maru,* a subsidiary fortress.

Not much of the Tokugawa glory remains. The shogunate was abolished in 1868, and when Emperor Meiji moved from Kyōto to Edo, which he renamed Tōkyō, Edo Castle was chosen as the site of the Imperial Palace. Many of its buildings had been destroyed in the turmoil of the restoration of the emperor, others fell in the fires of 1872, and still others were simply torn down. Of the 28 original *tamon* (armories), only 2 have survived. The present-day Imperial Palace, which dates to 1968, is open to the general public only twice a year: on January 2 and December 23 (the Emperor's Birthday), when thousands of people assemble under the balcony to offer their good wishes to the imperial family. On other days during the year, the Imperial Household Agency conducts guided group tours of the palace grounds by reservation. In 1968, to mark the completion of the current palace, the area that once encompassed the hon-maru and ni-no-maru was opened to the public as the Imperial Palace East Garden. There are three entrance gates—Ōte-mon, Hirakawa-mon, and Kita-hane-bashi-mon. You can easily get to any of the three from the Ōte-machi or Takebashi subway station.

Numbers in the text correspond to numbers in the margin and on the Imperial Palace map.

a good walk

A good place to start is **Tōkyō Station** ❶ ▐⎺. The Ōte-machi subway stop (on the Chiyoda, Marunouchi, Tōzai, Hanzō-mon, and Toei Mita lines) is a closer and handier connection, but the old redbrick Tōkyō Station building is a more compelling choice. Leave the station by the Marunouchi Central Exit, cross the street in front at the taxi stand, and walk up the broad divided avenue that leads to the Imperial Palace grounds. To your left is Marunouchi, to your right Ōte-machi: you're in the heart of Japan, Incorporated—the home of its major banks and investment houses, its insurance and trading companies. Take the second right, at the corner of the New Marunouchi Building; walk two blocks, past the gleaming brown-marble fortress of the Industrial Bank of Japan, and turn left. Ahead of you, across Uchibori-dōri (Inner Moat Avenue) from the Palace Hotel, is **Ōte-mon** ❷, one of three entrances to the **Imperial Palace East Garden** ❸.

Turn right as you leave the East Garden through Ōte-mon. Where the wall makes a right angle, you will see the Tatsumi, or Ni-jū Yagura (Double-Tiered Watchtower), one of three surviving watchtowers on the original fortifications. Here the sidewalk opens out to a parking lot for tour buses and the beginning of a broad promenade. In the far corner to your right, where the angle of the wall turns again, is the Kikyō-mon, a gate used primarily for deliveries to the palace. At the far end of the parking lot is Sakashita-mon, the gate used by the officials of the Imperial Household Agency.

From here to Hibiya Kōen (Hibiya Park), along both sides of Uchibori-dōri, stretches the concourse of the **Imperial Palace Outer Garden** ④. This whole area once lay along the edge of Tōkyō Bay. Later, the shōgun had his most trusted retainers build their estates here. These in turn gave way to the office buildings of the Meiji government. In 1899 the buildings were relocated, and the promenade was planted with the wonderful stands of pine trees you see today.

Walk along the broad gravel path to the **Two-Tiered Bridge** ⑤ and the Sei-mon (Main Gate). The bridge makes its graceful arch over the moat here from the area inside the gate. The building in the background, completing the picture, is the Fushimi Yagura, built in the 17th century. It is the last of the three surviving original watchtowers.

Continue on the gravel walk past the Sei-mon, turn right, and pass through the gate known as **Sakurada-mon** ⑥. Before you do, turn and look back down the concourse: you will not see another expanse of open space like this anywhere else in Tōkyō.

Look south across the street as you pass through the gate; the broad avenue that begins on the opposite side is Sakurada-dōri. World-renowned architect Kenzō Tange's Metropolitan Police Department building is on the west corner. The stately brick building on the east corner is the old Ministry of Justice. Sakurada-dōri runs through the heart of official Japan; between here and Kasumigaseki are the ministries—from Foreign Affairs and Education to International Trade and Industry—that compose the central government. Turn right at Sakurada-mon and follow the Sakurada Moat uphill along Uchibori-dōri.

A five-minute walk will bring you to where Roppongi-dōri branches in from the left; look in that direction and you will see the approach to the squat pyramid of the **National Diet Building** ⑦, which houses the Japanese parliament. Bear right as you continue to follow the moat along Uchibori-dōri to the next intersection, at Miya-zaka. Across the street are the gray-stone slabs of the **Supreme Court** ⑧. This and the **National Theater** ⑨, next door, are worth a short detour.

Cross back to the palace side of the street and continue north on Uchibori-dōri. At the top of the hill, on your right, a police contingent guards the road to the **Hanzō-mon** ⑩—the western gate to the new Imperial Palace. Here, where the road turns north again, begins the Hanzō Moat.

North along the Hanzō Moat is a narrow strip of park; facing it, across the street, is the British Embassy. Along this western edge of his fortress,

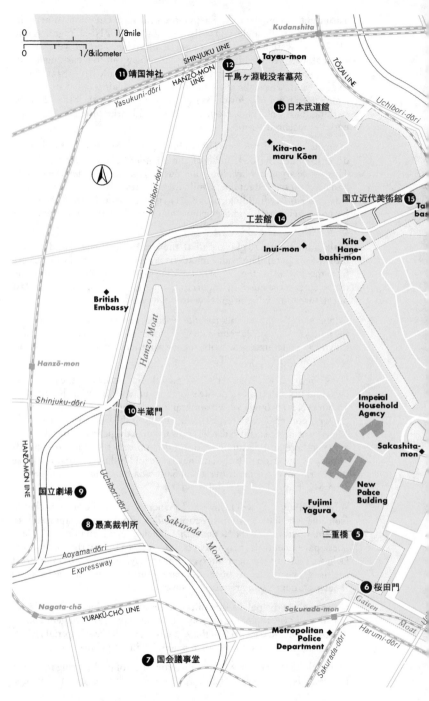

0 ————— 1/8mile
0 ————— 1/8kilometer

Kudanshita

SHINJUKU LINE

HANZŌ-MON LINE

TŌZAI LINE

Uchibori-dōri

11 靖国神社

Yasukuni-dōri

12 千鳥ヶ淵戦没者墓苑

◆ Tayau-mon

13 日本武道館

◆ Kita-no-maru Kōen

Uchibori-dōri

国立近代美術館 15

Ta ba

工芸館 14

Inui-mon ◆

Kita Hane-bashi-mon ◆

◆ British Embassy

Hanzo Moat

Hanzō-mon

Shinjuku-dōri

10 半蔵門

HANZŌ-MON LINE

Imperial Household Agency

Sakashita-mon ◆

9 国立劇場

Uchibori-dōri

New Palace Bulding

8 最高裁判所

Fujimi Yagura ◆

二重橋 5

Aoyama-dōri

Expressway

Sakurada Moat

6 桜田門

Gatsen Mo

Nagata-chō

YURAKŪ-CHŌ LINE

Sakurada-mon

Harumi-dōri

Metropolitan Police Department ◆

7 国会議事堂

the shōgun kept his personal retainers, called *hatamoto,* divided by *ban-chō* (district) into six regiments. Today these six ban-chō are among the most sought-after residential areas in Tōkyō, where high-rise apartments commonly fetch ¥100 million or more.

At the next intersection, review your priorities again. You can turn right and complete your circuit of the palace grounds by way of the Inui-mon, or you can continue straight north to the end of Uchibori-dōri to **Yasukuni Jinja** ⑪, the Shrine of Peace for the Nation.

Leave Yasukuni Jinja the way you came in, cross the street, turn left, and walk down the hill. The entrance to **Chidori-ga-fuchi National Memorial Garden** ⑫ is about 50 yards from the intersection, on the right. The green strip of promenade is high on the edge of the moat, lined with cherry trees. Halfway along, it widens, and opposite the Fairmount Hotel a path leads down to the Chidori-ga-fuchi Boathouse. Beyond the boathouse, the promenade leads back in the direction of the Imperial Palace.

If you have the time and stamina for a longer tour, retrace your steps from the boathouse, leave Chidori-ga-fuchi the way you came in, turn right, and continue down the hill to the entrance to Kita-no-maru Kōen (Kita-no-maru Park), on the west side of the Imperial Palace. To get to this park you'll have to pass through Tayasu-mon, one of the largest and finest of the surviving *masu* (box) gates to the castle. The first building you come to in the park is the octagonal **Japan Martial Arts Hall** ⑬, site of major rock concerts and martial arts contests.

Opposite the main entrance to the Japan Martial Arts Hall, past the parking lot, a pathway leads off through the park back in the direction of the palace. Cross the bridge at the other end of the path, turn right, and then right again before you leave the park on the driveway that leads to the **Kōgeikan** ⑭. This museum is devoted to works of traditional craftsmanship by the great modern masters.

Return to the park exit and cross the street to the palace side. Ahead of you is the Inui-mon, a gate used primarily by members of the imperial family and invited guests. A driveway here leads to the Imperial Household Agency and the palace. A bit farther down the hill is the Kita-Hane-bashi-mon, one of the entrances to the Imperial Palace East Garden.

At the foot of the hill is Takebashi—although the name means Bamboo Bridge, the original construction has long since given way to reinforced concrete. Cross the street here to see the collection of modern Japanese and Western artwork in the **National Museum of Modern Art, Tōkyō** ⑮. On the palace side of Takebashi sits the finely reconstructed **Hirakawa-mon** ⑯, the East Garden's third entrance, which will complete the loop on this walk. From here follow the moat as it turns south again around the garden. In a few minutes you'll find yourself back at Ōte-mon, tired, perhaps, but triumphant.

TIMING   The Imperial Palace area covers a lot of ground—uphill and down—and even in its shorter versions the walk includes plenty to see. Allow at least an hour for the East Garden and Outer Garden of the palace itself. Plan to visit Yasukuni Jinja after lunch and spend at least an hour there. The Yūshūkan (at Yasukuni Jinja) and Kōgeikan museums are both small and should engage you for no more than a half hour each, but the modern art museum requires a more leisurely visit—particularly if there's a special exhibit. Set your own pace, but assume that this walk will take you the better part of a full day.

Avoid Monday, when the East Garden and museums are closed; the East Garden is also closed Friday. In July and August, heat will make the palace walk grueling—bring hats and bottled water.

What to See

⑫ Chidori-ga-fuchi National Memorial Garden (千鳥ヶ淵戦没者墓苑). High on the edge (*fuchi* means "edge") of the Imperial Palace moat, this park is pleasantly arrayed with cherry trees. Long before Edo Castle was built, there was a lovely little lake here, which Ieyasu Tokugawa incorporated into his system of defenses. Now you can rent a rowboat at **Chidori-ga-fuchi Boathouse**, roughly in the middle of the park, and explore it at your leisure. The park entrance is near Yasukuni Jinja, west and downhill from the corner of Yasukuni-dōri and Uchibori-dōri. ⊠ *Chiyoda-ku* ☎ *03/3234–1948* ⌨ *Park free, boat rental ¥500 for 30 min* ☉ *Park daily sunrise–sunset, boathouse daily 10–5; opens at 9 in cherry-blossom season, usually late Mar.–early Apr.* Ⓜ *Hanzō-mon and Shinjuku subway lines, Kudanshita Station (Exit 2).*

⑩ Hanzō-mon (Hanzō Gate, 半蔵門). The house of the legendary Hattori Hanzō once sat at the foot of this small wooden gate. Hanzō was the leader of the shōgun's private corps of spies and infiltrators—and assassins, if need be. They were the menacing, black-clad ninja, perennial material for historical adventure films and television dramas. The gate is a minute's walk east from the subway. ⊠ *Chiyoda-ku* Ⓜ *Hanzō-mon subway line, Hanzō-mon Station (Exit 3).*

⑯ Hirakawa-mon (Hirakawa Gate, 平川門). The approach to this gate crosses the only wooden bridge that spans the Imperial Palace moat. The gate and bridge are reconstructions, but Hirakawa-mon is especially beautiful, looking much as it must have when the shōgun's wives and concubines used it on their rare excursions from the seraglio. Hirakawa-mon is the north gate to the East Garden, southeast of Bamboo Bridge. ⊠ *Chiyoda-ku* Ⓜ *Tōzai subway line, Takebashi Station (Exit 1A).*

❸ Imperial Palace East Garden (Kōkyo Higashi Gyo-en, 皇居東御苑). The entrance to the East Garden is the ⇨ **Ōte-mon**, once the main gate of Ieyasu Tokugawa's castle. In lieu of an admission ticket, collect a plastic token at the office on the other side of the gate. As you walk up the driveway, you pass on the left the National Police Agency dōjō (martial arts hall). The hall was built in the Taishō period (1912–25) and is still used for kendō (Japanese fencing) practice. On the right is the Ōte Rest House, where for ¥100 you can buy a simple map of the garden.

Fodor'sChoice
★

There was once another gate at the top of the driveway, where feudal lords summoned to the palace would descend from their palanquins and proceed on foot. The gate itself is gone, but two 19th-century guardhouses survive, one outside the massive stone supports on the right and a longer one inside on the left. The latter, known as the **Hundred-Man Guard-house,** was defended by four shifts of 100 soldiers each. Past it, to the right, is the entrance to what was once the ni-no-maru, the "second circle" of the fortress. It's now a grove and garden, its pathways defined by rows of perfect rhododendrons; a pond and a waterfall are in the northwest corner. At the far end is the **Suwa Tea Pavilion,** an early-19th-century building relocated here from another part of the castle grounds.

The steep stone walls of the **hon-maru** (the "inner circle"), with the Moat of Swans below (the swans actually swim in the outer waterways), dominate the west side of the garden. Halfway along, a steep path leads to an entrance in the wall to the upper fortress. This is **Shio-mi-zaka,** which translates roughly as "Briny View Hill," so named because in the Edo period the ocean could be seen from here.

The foundations of the keep make a platform with a fine view of Kita-no-maru Kōen and the city to the north. The view must have been even finer from the keep itself. Built and rebuilt three times, it soared more than 250 feet over Edo. The other castle buildings were all plastered white; the keep was black, unadorned but for a golden roof. In 1657 a fire destroyed most of the city. Strong winds carried the flames across the moat, where it consumed the keep in a heat so fierce that it melted the gold in the vaults underneath. The keep was never rebuilt.

To the left of the keep foundations there's an exit from the hon-maru that leads northwest to the Kita-Hane-bashi-mon. To the right, another road leads past the **Tōka Music Hall**—an octagonal tower faced in mosaic tile, built in honor of the empress in 1966—down to the ni-no-maru and out of the gardens by way of the northern ⇨ Hirakawa-mon. If you decide to leave the hon-maru the way you came in, through the Ōte-mon, stop for a moment at the rest house on the west side of the park before you surrender your token, and look at the photo collection. The pairs of before-and-after photographs of the castle, taken about 100 years apart, are fascinating. ⊠ *Chiyoda-ku* ⬚ *Free* ☉ *Mar.–Oct., weekends and Tues.–Thurs. 9–4; Nov.–late Dec. and early Jan. and Feb., weekends and Tues.–Thurs. 9–3:30* Ⓜ *Tōzai, Marunouchi, and Chiyoda subway lines, Ōte-machi Station (Exit C13b).*

❹ **Imperial Palace Outer Garden** (Kōkyo-Gaien, 皇居外苑). When the office buildings of the Meiji government were moved from this area in 1899, the whole expanse along the east side of the palace was turned into a public promenade and planted with stands of pine. The Outer Garden affords the best view of the castle walls and their Tokugawa-period fortifications: Ni-jū-bashi and the Sei-mon, the 17th-century Fujimi Yagura watchtower (the only surviving watchtower of the hon-maru), and the Sakurada-mon. ⊠ *Chiyoda-ku* ⬚ *Free* Ⓜ *Chiyoda subway line, Ni-jū-bashi-mae Station (Exit 2).*

⓭ **Japan Martial Arts Hall** (Nippon Budōkan, 日本武道館). With its eight-sided plan based on the Hall of Dreams of Hōryū-ji in Nara, the Budōkan was built as a martial arts arena for the Tōkyō Olympics of 1964. It still hosts tournaments and exhibitions of jūdō, karate, and kendō, as well as concerts. Tōkyō promoters are fortunate in their audiences, who don't seem to mind the exorbitant ticket prices and poor acoustics. To get here from the Kudanshita subway stop, walk west uphill toward Yasukuni Jinja; the entrance to Kita-no-Maru Kōen and the Budōkan is a few minutes' walk from the station, on the left. ☒ *2–3 Kitano Maru Kōen, Chiyoda-ku* ☎ *03/3216–5100* Ⓜ *Tōzai, Hanzō-mon, and Shinjuku subway lines, Kudanshita Station (Exit 2).*

❶❹ **Kōgeikan** (Crafts Gallery of the National Museum of Modern Art, 工芸館). Built in 1910, the Kōgeikan, once the headquarters of the Imperial Guard, is a rambling redbrick building, Gothic Revival in style, with exhibition halls on the second floor. The exhibits are all too few, but many of the craftspeople represented here—masters in the traditions of lacquerware, textiles, pottery, and metalwork—have been designated by the government as Living National Treasures. The most direct access to the gallery is from the Takebashi subway station on the Tōzai Line. Walk west and uphill about 10 minutes, on the avenue between Kita-no-maru Kōen and the Imperial Palace grounds; the entrance is on the right. ☒ *1–1 Kita-no-maru Kōen, Chiyoda-ku* ☎ *03/3211–7781* ☒ *¥420, includes admission to National Museum of Modern Art; additional fee for special exhibits; free 1st Sun. of month* ☉ *Tues.–Sun. 10–5* Ⓜ *Hanzō-mon and Shinjuku subway lines, Kudanshita Station (Exit 2); Tōzai subway line, Takebashi Station (Exit 1b).*

❼ **National Diet Building** (Kokkai-Gijidō, 国会議事堂). This chunky pyramid, completed in 1936 after 17 years of work, houses the Japanese parliament. It's a building best contemplated from a distance. On a gloomy day it seems as if it might well have sprung from the screen of a German Expressionist movie. ☒ *1–7–1 Nagata-chō, Chiyoda-ku* Ⓜ *Marunouchi subway line, Kokkai-Gijidō-mae Station (Exit 2).*

❶❺ **National Museum of Modern Art, Tōkyō** (Tōkyō Kokuritsu Kindai Bijutsukan, 国立近代美術館). Founded in 1952 and moved to its present site in 1969, this was Japan's first national art museum. It mounts major exhibitions of 20th- and 21st-century Japanese and Western art throughout the year, but tends to be rather stodgy about how it organizes and presents these exhibitions and is seldom on the cutting edge. The second through fourth floors house the permanent collection, which includes the painting, prints, and sculpture of Rousseau, Picasso, Tsuguji Fujita, Ryūzaburo Umehara, and Taikan Yokoyama. ☒ *3–1 Kita-no-maru Kōen, Chiyoda-ku* ☎ *03/3214–2561* ⊕ *www.momat.go.jp* ☒ *¥420, includes admission to the Kōgeikan); free 1st Sun. of month* ☉ *Tues.–Thurs. and weekends 10–5, Fri. 10–8* ☉ *Closed July 20 and Sept. 13* Ⓜ *Tōzai subway line, Takebashi Station (Exit 1b); Hanzō-mon and Shinjuku subway lines, Kudanshita Station (Exit 2).*

❾ **National Theater** (Kokuritsu Gekijō, 国立劇場). Architect Hiroyuki Iwamoto's winning entry in the design competition for the National Theater building (1966) is a rendition in concrete of the ancient *azekura* (storehouse) style, invoking the 8th-century Shōsōin Imperial Repository in Nara. The large hall seats 1,746 and presents primarily Kabuki theater, ancient court music, and dance. The small hall seats 630 and is used mainly for Bunraku puppet theater and traditional music. ✉ *4–1 Hayabusa-chō, Chiyoda-ku* ☎ *03/3265–7411* ⊘ *Varies depending on performance* Ⓜ *Hanzō-mon subway line, Hanzō-mon Station (Exit 1).*

❷ Ōte-mon (Ōte Gate, 大手門). The main entrance to the Imperial Palace East Garden, Ōte-mon was in former days the principal gate of Ieyasu Tokugawa's castle. The masu style was typical of virtually all the approaches to the shōgun's impregnable fortress: the first portal leads to a narrow enclosure, with a second and larger gate beyond, offering the defenders inside a devastating field of fire upon any would-be intruders. Most of the gate was destroyed in 1945 but was rebuilt in 1967 on the original plans. The outer part of the gate, however, survived. ✉ *Chiyoda-ku* Ⓜ *Tōzai, Marunouchi, and Chiyoda subway lines, Ōte-machi Station (Exit C10).*

❻ Sakurada-mon (Gate of the Field of Cherry Trees, 桜田門). By hallowed use and custom, the small courtyard between the portals of this masu gate is where joggers warm up for their 5-km (3-mi) run around the palace. ✉*Chiyoda-ku* Ⓜ *Yūraku-chō subway line, Sakurada-mon Station (Exit 3).*

❽ Supreme Court (Saikō Saibansho, 最高裁判所). The Supreme Court's fortresslike planes and angles, in granite and concrete, speak volumes about the role of the law in Japanese society—here is the very bastion of the established order. Designed by Shinichi Okada, the building was the last in a series of open architectural competitions sponsored by the various government agencies charged with the reconstruction of Tōkyō after World War II. Okada's winning design was one of 217 submitted. Before the building was finished, in 1974, the open competition had generated so much controversy that the government did not hold another one for almost 20 years. Guided tours are available, but under restrictive conditions: you must be at least 16 years old to take part, tours musts be reserved two weeks in advance, and there is no interpretation in English. Tours are conducted weekdays (except July 20–August 31 and national holidays); they begin at 3 and take about an hour. ✉ *4–2 Hayabusa-chō, Chiyoda-ku* ☎ *03/3264–8111 for public relations office (Kōhōka) for tours* Ⓜ *Hanzō-mon subway line, Hanzō-mon Station (Exit 1).*

▶ **❶ Tōkyō Station** (東京駅). The work of Kingo Tatsuno, one of Japan's first modern architects, Tōkyō Station was completed in 1914. Tatsuno modeled his creation on the railway station of Amsterdam. The building lost its original top story in the air raids of 1945, but it was promptly repaired. In the late 1990s, plans to tear it down entirely were scotched by a protest movement. Inside, it has been deepened and tunneled and redesigned any number of times to accommodate new commuter lines, but the lovely old redbrick facade remains untouched. Inside is the Tōkyō Station Hotel, on the west side on the second and third floors. ✉ *1–9–1 Marunouchi, Chiyoda-ku* ☎ *03/3231–2511.*

❺ Two-Tiered Bridge (Ni-jū-bashi, 二重橋). Making a graceful arch across the moat, this bridge is surely the most photogenic spot on the grounds of the former Edo Castle. Normally you can approach no closer than the head of Sei-mon Sekkyō, a short stone bridge that arcs over the moat to the Sei-mon—the Main Gate. Ordinary mortals may pass through this gate only on December 23 and January 2 to pay their respects to the imperial family. The guards in front of their small, octagonal, copper-roof sentry boxes change every hour on the hour—alas, with nothing like the pomp and ceremony of Buckingham Palace. ✉ *Chiyoda-ku* Ⓜ *Chiyoda subway line, Ni-jū-bashi-mae Station (Exit 2).*

★ ⑪ **Yasukuni Jinja** (Shrine of Peace for the Nation, 靖国神社). Founded in 1869, this shrine is dedicated to the approximately 2.5 million Japanese who have died since then in war or military service. Since 1945 Yasukuni has been the periodic focus of passionate political debate, given that the Japanese constitution expressly renounces both militarism and state sponsorship of religion. Even so, hundreds of thousands of Japanese come here every year, simply to pray for the repose of friends and relatives they have lost.

The shrine is not one structure but a complex of buildings that include the **Main Hall** and the **Hall of Worship**—both built in the simple, unadorned style of the ancient Shintō shrines at Ise—and the **Yūshūkan,** a museum of documents and war memorabilia. The Yūshūkan, which has limited English notes and labels, presents Japan at its most ambivalent—if not unrepentant—about its more recent militaristic past. Critics charge that the newer exhibits glorify the nation's role in the Pacific War as a noble struggle for independence.

Also here are a Nō theater and, in the far western corner, a sumō-wrestling ring. Both Nō and sumō have their origins in religious ritual, as performances offered to please and divert the gods. Sumō matches are held at Yasukuni in April, during the first of its three annual festivals.

You can pick up a pamphlet and simplified map of the shrine in English just inside the grounds. Just ahead of you, in a circle on the main avenue, is a statue of Masujirō Ōmura, commander of the imperial forces that subdued the Tokugawa loyalist resistance to the new Meiji government. From here, as you look down the avenue to your right, you can see the enormous steel outer torii of the main entrance to the shrine at Kudanshita; to the left is a bronze inner torii, erected in 1887. (These Shintō shrine arches are normally made of wood and painted red.) Beyond the inner torii is the gate to the shrine itself, with its 12 pillars and chrysanthemums—the imperial crest—embossed on the doors.

If time permits, turn right as you leave the Yūshūkan and walk to the pond at the rear of the shrine. There's no general admittance to the teahouses on the far side, but the pond is among the most serene and beautiful in Tōkyō, especially in spring, when the irises are in bloom. ✉ *3–1–1 Kudankita, Chiyoda-ku* ☎ *03/3261–8326* 💴 *¥800* 🕐 *Grounds daily, usually 9–9. Museum Mar.–Oct., daily 9–5; Nov.–Feb., daily 9–4:30* Ⓜ *Hanzō-mon and Shinjuku subway lines, Kudanshita Station (Exit 1).*

need a break? The specialty at the moderately priced **Tony Roma's** (トニーローマ), as it is in this chain's umpteen locations, is charcoal-broiled spareribs. It's on the west side of Uchibori-dōri north of the British Embassy, at the intersection straight west of Inui-mon. ✉ *1 Samban-chō, Chiyoda-ku* ☎ *03/3222–3440.*

Akihabara & Jimbō-chō 秋葉原・神保町

This is it: the greatest sound-and-light show on earth. Akihabara is a merchandise mart for anything—and everything—that runs on electricity, from microprocessors and washing machines to television sets and gadgets that beep when your bathwater is hot. Wherever you go in the world, if people know nothing else about Japan, they recognize the country as a cornucopia of electronics equipment and household appliances. About 10% of what Japan's electronics industry makes for the domestic market passes through Akihabara.

Some 400 years ago this was a residential district for the lower-ranked samurai retainers of the Tokugawa military government. Later, it evolved into a commercial center—known especially for leather goods—and in 1929 the nation's largest wholesale produce market was located here. Surrounding the market were small shops making and selling vacuum tubes and radio parts for customers who wanted to build their own sets and catch the programs aired by the newly created Japan Broadcasting Corporation. Just after World War II a black market sprang up around the railroad station, where the Yamanote Line and the crosstown Sōbu Line intersect. In time, most of the stalls were doing a legitimate business in radio parts, and in 1951 they were all relocated in one dense clump under the tracks. Retail and wholesale suppliers then spread out into the adjacent blocks and made the area famous for cut-rate prices. In 1989 the produce market was torn down and relocated; still under construction on that site is the Akihabara Information Technology Center, slated for completion in 2006.

Few visitors to Tōkyō neglect this district; the mistake is to come here merely for shopping. Akihabara may be consumer heaven, but it's also the first stop on a walking tour through the general area known as Kanda—where the true Edokko, the born-and-bred Tōkyōites of the old town, claim their roots—to the bookstalls of Jimbō-chō. In a sense this tour is a journey through time: it's a morning's walk from satellite broadcast antennas to the hallowed precincts of the printed word.

Numbers in the text correspond to numbers in the margin and on the Akihabara & Jimbō-chō map.

a good walk

Start at the west exit of JR Akihabara Station. (There's also a stop, Nakaokachi-machi, nearby on the Hibiya subway line, but the JR provides much easier access.) Come out to the left after you pass through the wicket, head into the station square, turn right, and walk to the main thoroughfare. Ahead of you on the other side of the street you can see the **LAOX** (ラオックス) ❶ ► building, one of the district's major discount stores.

Before you get to the corner, on the right is a little warren of stalls and tiny shops that cannot have changed an iota since the days of the black market—except for their merchandise. A stroll through the narrow passageways will reveal an astonishing array of switches, transformers, resistors, semiconductors, printed circuit cards, plugs, wires, connectors, and tools. The labyrinth is especially popular with domestic and foreign

techno mavens, the people who know—or want to know—what the latest in Japanese electronic technology looks like from the inside.

If you turn left at the corner and cross the small bridge over the Kanda-gawa (Kanda River), you'll soon come to the **Transportation Museum** ❷— a detour you might want to make if you have children in tow. If not, turn right at the corner and walk north on Chūō-dōri. Music blares at you from hundreds of storefronts as you walk along; this is the heart of the district. Most larger stores on the main drag have one floor—or even an entire annex—of products for the foreign market, staffed by clerks who speak everything from English to Mandarin to Portuguese. Prices are duty-free (don't forget to bring your passport). One of the biggest selections can be found at **Yamagiwa** ❸, just past the second intersection, on the right.

At Yamagiwa, cross the street, continue north to the Soto Kanda 5-chōme intersection (there's an entrance to the Suehiro-chō subway station on the corner), and turn left onto Kuramae-bashi-dōri. Walk about five minutes—you'll cross one more intersection with a traffic light—and in the middle of the next block you can see a flight of steps on the left, between two brick buildings. Red, green, and blue pennants flutter from the handrails. This is the back entrance to **Kanda Myōjin** ❹.

Leave the shrine by the main gate. The seated figures in the alcoves on either side are its guardian gods; carved in camphor wood, they are depicted in Heian costume, holding long bows. From the gate down to the copper-clad torii on Hongō-dōri is a walk of a few yards. On either side are shops that sell the specialties famous in this neighborhood: pickles, miso, and sweet sake laced with ground ginger. On the other side of the avenue are the wall and wooded grounds of the **Yushima Seidō** ⑤ Confucian shrine.

Cross Hongō-dōri and turn left, following the wall downhill. Turn right at the first narrow side street, and right again at the bottom; the entrance to Yūshima Seidō is a few steps from the corner. As you walk up the path, you can see a statue of Confucius on your right; where the path ends, a flight of stone steps leads up to the main hall of the shrine.

Retrace your steps, turn right as you leave the shrine, and walk along the continuation of the wall on the side street leading up to Hijiri-bashi (Bridge of Sages), which spans the Kanda-gawa at Ochanomizu Station on the JR Sōbu Line. Cross the bridge—you're now back on Hongō-dōri—and ahead of you, just beyond the station on the right, you can see the dome of the Russian Orthodox Nikolai Cathedral.

Continue south to the intersection of Hongō-dōri and Yasukuni-dōri. Surugadai, the area to your right as you walk down the hill, is a kind of fountainhead of Japanese higher education: two of the city's major private universities—Meiji and Nihon—occupy a good part of the hill. Not far from these are a score of elite high schools, public and private. In the 1880s several other universities were founded in this area. They have since moved away, but the student population here is still enormous.

Turn right on Yasukuni-dōri. Between you and your objective—the **bookstores of Jimbō-chō** ⑥—are three blocks of stores devoted almost exclusively to electric guitars, records, travel bags, skis, and skiwear. The bookstores begin at the intersection called Surugadai-shita and continue along Yasukuni-dōri for about ½ km (¼ mi), most of them on the south (left) side of the street. This area is to print what Akihabara is to electronics.

What about that computer or CD player you didn't buy at the beginning of your walk because you didn't want to carry it all this way? No problem. There's a subway station (Mita Line) at the Jimbō-chō main intersection; go one stop north to Suidō-bashi, transfer to the JR Sōbu Line, and five minutes later you're back in Akihabara.

TIMING Unless you do a lot of shopping, this walk should take you no more than a morning. Cultural landmarks are few, and you can explore them thoroughly in a half hour each. Getting from place to place will take up much of your time. Keep in mind that most stores in Akihabara do not open until 10 AM. Weekends draw hordes of shoppers, especially on Sunday, when the four central blocks of Chūō-dōri are closed to traffic and become a pedestrian mall.

What to See

 Bookstores of Jimbō-chō (神保町書店街). For the ultimate browse through art books, catalogs, scholarly monographs, secondhand paperbacks, and dictionaries in most known languages, the bookstores of Jimbō-chō are the place to go. A number of the antiquarian booksellers here carry not only rare typeset editions but also wood-block-printed books of the Edo period and individual prints. At shops like **Isseidō** (一誠堂) and **Ohya Shōbō** (大屋書房), both open Monday–Saturday 10–6, it's still possible to find genuine 19th- and 20th-century prints—if not in the best condition—at affordable prices. Many of Japan's most prestigious publishing houses make their home here in this area as well. The bookstores run for ½ km (¼ mi) on Yasukuni-dōri beginning at the Surugadai-shita intersection. ⊠ *Isseido: 1–7–4 Kanda Jimbō-chō, Chiyoda-ku* ☎ *03/3292–0071* ⊠ *Ohya Shōbō: 1–1 Kanda Jimbō-chō, Chiyoda-ku, Jimbō-chō* ☎ *03/3291–0062* Ⓜ *Shinjuku and Mita subway lines, Jimbō-chō Station (Exit A7).*

❹ **Kanda Myōjin** (Kanda Shrine, 神田明神). This shrine is said to have been founded in 730 in a village called Shibasaki, where the Ōte-machi financial district stands today. In 1616 it was relocated, a victim of Ieyasu Tokugawa's ever-expanding system of fortifications. The present site was chosen, in accordance with Chinese geomancy, to afford the best view from Edo Castle and to protect the shrine from evil influences. The shrine itself was destroyed in the Great Kantō Earthquake of 1923, and the present buildings reproduce in concrete the style of 1616. Ieyasu preferred the jazzier decorative effects of Chinese Buddhism to the simple lines of traditional Shintō architecture. This is especially evident in the curved, copper-tile roof of the main shrine and in the two-story front gate.

Three principle deities are enshrined here: Ōkuninushi-no-Mikoto and Sukunohikona-no-Mikoto, both of whom appear in the early Japanese creation myths, and Taira-no-Masakado. The last was a 10th-century warrior whose contentious spirit earned him a place in the Shintō pantheon: he led a revolt against the Imperial Court in Kyōto, seized control of the eastern provinces, declared himself emperor—and in 940 was beheaded for his rebellious ways. The townspeople of Kanda, contentious souls in their own right, made Taira-no-Masakado a kind of patron saint, and even today—overlooking somehow the fact that he lost—they appeal to him for victory when they face a tough encounter.

Some of the smaller buildings you see as you come up the steps and walk around the main hall contain the *mikoshi*—the portable shrines that are featured in one of Tōkyō's three great blowouts, the **Kanda Festival.** (The other two are the Sannō Festival of Hie Jinja in Nagata-chō and the Sanja Festival of Asakusa Shrine.) The essential shrine festival is a procession in which the gods, housed for the occasion in their mikoshi, pass through the streets and get a breath of fresh air. The Kanda Festival began in the early Edo period. Heading the procession then were 36 magnificent floats, most of which were destroyed in the fires that raged through the city after the earthquake of 1923. The floats that lead the procession today move in stately measure on wheeled carts, attended by the priests and officials of the shrine dressed in Heian-period (794–1185) costume. The mikoshi, some 70 of them, follow behind, bobbing and weaving, carried on the shoulders of the townspeople. Shrine festivals like Kanda's are a peculiarly competitive form of worship: piety is a matter of who can shout the loudest, drink the most beer, and have the best time. The festival takes place in August in odd-numbered years. Kanda Myōjin is on Kuramae-bashi-dōri, about a five-minute walk west of the Suehiro-chō subway stop. ⊠ *2–16–2 Soto Kanda, Chiyoda-ku* ☎ *03/3254–0753* Ⓜ *Ginza subway line, Suehiro-chō Station (Exit 3).*

▶ ❶ **LAOX** (ラオックス). Of all the discount stores in Akihabara, LAOX has the largest and most comprehensive selection, with four buildings in this area—one exclusively for musical instruments, another for duty-free appliances—and outlets in Yokohama and Narita. This is a good place to find the latest in digital cameras, watches, and games. ⊠ *1–2–9 Soto Kanda, Chiyoda-ku* ☎ *03/3253–7111* ⊗ *Mon.–Sat. 10–8, Sun. 10–7:30* Ⓜ *JR Akihabara Station (Nishi-guchi/West Exit).*

☺ ❷ **Transportation Museum** (Kōtsū Hakubutsukan, 交通博物館). Displays at this fun museum explain the early development of the railway system and include a miniature layout of the rail services, as well as Japan's first airplane, which took off in 1903. To get here from JR Akihabara Station, cross the bridge on Chūō-dōri over the Kanda River, and turn right at the next corner. ⊠ *1–25 Kanda Sudachō, Chiyoda-ku* ☎ *03/3251–8481* ▭ *¥310* ⊗ *Tues.–Sun. 9:30–5* Ⓜ *JR Akihabara Station (Denki-gai Exit).*

❸ **Yamagiwa** (ヤマギワ). Entire floors of this discount electronics giant are devoted to computer hardware and software, fax machines, and copiers. Yamagiwa has a particularly good selection of lighting fixtures, most of them 220 volts, but the annex has export models of the most popular appliances and devices, plus an English-speaking staff to assist you with selections. You should be able to bargain prices down a bit—especially if you're buying more than one big-ticket item. ⊠ *1–5–10 Soto Kanda, Chiyoda-ku* ☎ *03/3253–5111* ⊗ *Weekdays 11–7:30, weekends 10:30–7:30* Ⓜ *JR Akihabara Station (Nishi-guchi/West Exit).*

❺ **Yushima Seidō** (Yushima Shrine, 湯島聖堂). The origins of this shrine date to a hall, founded in 1632, for the study of the Chinese Confucian classics. The original building was in Ueno, and its headmaster was Hayashi Razan, the official Confucian scholar to the Tokugawa government. The shogunal dynasty found these Chinese teachings—with their emphasis on obedience and hierarchy—attractive enough to make Confucianism a kind of state ideology. Moved to its present site in 1691 (and destroyed by fire and rebuilt six times), the hall became an academy for the ruling elite. In a sense, nothing has changed: in 1872 the new Meiji government established the country's first teacher-training institute here, and that, in turn, evolved into Tōkyō University—the graduates of which still make up much of the ruling elite. The hall could almost be in China: painted black, weathered and somber, it looks like nothing else you're likely to see in Japan. ⊠ *1–4–25 Yūshima, Bunkyō-ku* ☎ *03/3251–4606* ▭ *Free* ⊗ *Apr.–Sept., Fri.–Wed. 10–5; Oct.–Mar., Fri.–Wed. 10–4* ⊗ *Closed Aug. 13–17 and Dec. 19–31* Ⓜ *Marunouchi subway line, Ochanomizu Station (Exit B2).*

Ueno 上野

JR Ueno Station is Tōkyō's version of the Gare du Nord: the gateway to and from Japan's northeast provinces. Since its completion in 1883, the station has served as a terminus in the great migration to the city by villagers in pursuit of a better life.

Ueno was a place of prominence long before the coming of the railroad. When Ieyasu Tokugawa established his capital here in 1603, it was merely a wooded promontory, called Shinobu-ga-oka (Hill of Endurance), overlooking the bay. Ieyasu gave a large tract of land on the hill to one of his most important vassals, Takatora Toda, who designed and built Edo Castle. Ieyasu's heir, Hidetada, later commanded the founding of a temple on the hill. Shinobu-ga-oka was in the northeast corner of the capital. In Chinese geomancy, the northeast approach required a particularly strong defense against evil influences.

That defense was entrusted to Tenkai (1536–1643), a priest of the Tendai sect of Buddhism and an adviser of great influence to the first three Tokugawa shōguns. The temple he built on Shinobu-ga-oka was called Kan'ei-ji, and he became the first abbot. The patronage of the Tokugawas and their vassal barons made Kan'ei-ji a seat of power and glory. By the end of the 17th century it occupied most of the hill. To the magnificent Main Hall were added scores of other buildings—including a pagoda and a shrine to Ieyasu—and 36 subsidiary temples. The city of Edo itself expanded to the foot of the hill, where Kan'ei-ji's main gate once stood. And most of what is now Ueno was called *Mon-zen-machi*: "the town in front of the gate."

The power and glory of Kan'ei-ji came to an end in just one day: April 11, 1868. An army of clan forces from the western part of Japan, bearing a mandate from Emperor Meiji, arrived in Edo and demanded the surrender of the castle. The shogunate was by then a tottering regime; it capitulated, and with it went everything that had depended on the favor of the Tokugawas. The Meiji Restoration began with a bloodless coup.

A band of some 2,000 Tokugawa loyalists assembled on Ueno Hill, however, and defied the new government. On May 15 the imperial army attacked. The Shōgitai (loyalists), outnumbered and surrounded, soon discovered that right was on the side of modern artillery. A few survivors fled; the rest committed ritual suicide, and took Kan'ei-ji with them—torching the temple and most of its outbuildings.

The new Meiji government turned Ueno Hill into one of the nation's first public parks. The intention was not merely to provide a bit of greenery but to make the park an instrument of civic improvement and to show off the achievements of an emerging modern state. It would serve as the site of trade and industrial expositions; it would have a national museum, a library, a university of fine arts, and a zoo. The modernization of Ueno still continues, but the park is more than the sum of its museums. The Shōgitai failed to take everything with them: some of the most important buildings in the temple complex survived or were restored and should not be missed.

Numbers in the text correspond to numbers in the margin and on the Ueno map.

a good
walk

The best way to begin is to head to JR Ueno Station on the JR Yaman-ote Line and leave the station by the Kōen-guchi (Park Exit), upstairs. Directly across from the exit is the Tōkyō Metropolitan Festival Hall, one of the city's major venues for classical music. Follow the path to the right of the hall to the information booth, where you can pick up a useful detailed map of the park in English; northwest of the booth (turn left, away from Ueno Station) is the **National Museum of Western Art ❶** ▶. The Rodins in the courtyard—*The Gate of Hell, The Thinker,* and the magnificent *Burghers of Calais*—are authentic castings from Rodin's orig-inal molds.

Turn right at the far corner of the museum and walk along a stretch of wooded park; you come next to the **National Science Museum ❷**. At the next corner is the main street that cuts through the park. Turn left on this street, and cross at the traffic signal some 50 yards west to the main entrance of the **Tōkyō National Museum ❸**, which has one of the world's greatest collections of East Asian art and archaeology.

Turn right as you leave the museum complex, walk west, and turn right at the first corner; this road dead-ends in about five minutes in the far northwest corner of the park, opposite the gate to **Kan'ei-ji ❹**. (The gate is usually locked; use the side entrance to the left.) Stretching away to the right is the cemetery of Kan'ei-ji, where several Tokugawa shōguns had their mausoleums. These were destroyed in the air raids of 1945, but the gate that led to the tomb of the fourth shōgun, Ietsuna, remains.

Retrace your steps to the main gate of the Tōkyō National Museum, and cross the street to the long esplanade, with its fountain and reflecting pool. Keep to the right as you walk to the south end of the esplanade, where you'll come to the central plaza of the park. (Look to your left for the police substation, a small steel-gray building of futuristic design.) To the right is the entrance to Ueno Zoo (上野動物園).

A few steps farther south, on the continuation of the esplanade, is the path that leads to **Tōshō-gū ❺**—the shrine to the first Tokugawa shōgun, Ieyasu. The entrance to the shrine is marked by a stone torii built in 1633.

From Tōshō-gū, return to the avenue, turn right, and continue walking south. Shortly you can see a kind of tunnel of red-lacquered torii, with a long flight of stone steps leading down to the shrine to Inari, a Shintō deity of harvests and family prosperity. Just below the Inari shrine is a shrine to Sugawara Michizane (854–903), a Heian-period nobleman and poet worshipped as the Shintō deity Tenjin. Because he is associated with scholarship and literary achievement, Japanese students visit his vari-ous shrines by the hundreds of thousands in February and March to pray for success on their college entrance exams.

Return to the avenue and continue south. On the left side is a flight of stone steps to **Kannon Hall ❻**, one of the important temple structures that survived the Meiji-Tokugawa battle of 1868.

Leave the temple by the front gate, on the south side. Continue south, and you soon come to where the park narrows to a point. Two flights of steps lead down to the main entrance on Chūō-dōri. Before you

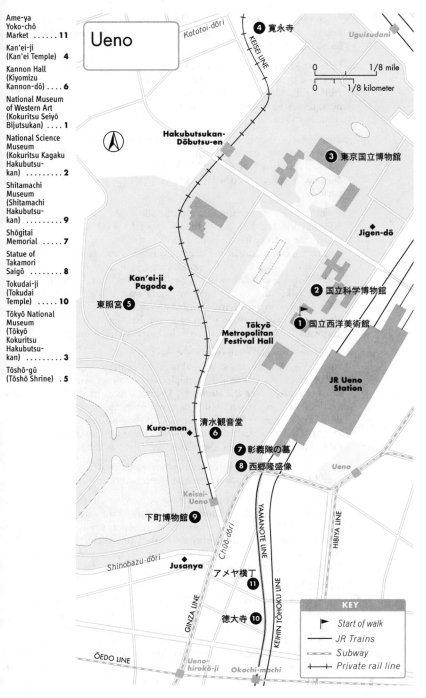

Ueno

Kototoi-dōri

4 寛永寺

KEISEI LINE

Uguisudani

0   1/8 mile

0   1/8 kilometer

Hakubutsukan-
Dōbutsu-en

3 東京国立博物館

Jigen-dō

Kan'ei-ji
Pagoda ◆

2 国立科学博物館

東照宮 5

1 国立西洋美術館

Tōkyō
Metropolitan
Festival Hall

JR Ueno
Station

Kuro-mon ◆

清水観音堂 6

7 彰義隊の墓

8 西郷隆盛像

Ueno

Keisei-
Ueno

下町博物館 9

YAMANOTE LINE

HIBIYA LINE

Shinobazu-dōri

Jusanya ◆

Chūō-dōri

アメヤ横丁 11

徳大寺 10

GINZA LINE

KEIHIN TŌHOKU LINE

KEY

▶   *Start of walk*

—   *JR Trains*

= =   *Subway*

+ +   *Private rail line*

ŌEDO LINE

Ueno-
hirokō-ji

Okachi-machi

reach the steps, you can see the **Shōgitai Memorial** ❼, on the left, and a few steps away, with its back to the gravestone, the **statue of Takamori Saigō** ❽.

Leave the park and walk south, keeping to the west side of Chūō-dōri, until you get to the corner where Shinobazu-dōri comes in on the right. About a block beyond this corner, you see a building hung with banners; this is Suzumoto, a theater specializing in a traditional narrative comedy called *rakugo*.

Turn right at the Shinobazu-dōri intersection and walk west until you come to an entrance to the grounds of Shinobazu Pond (不忍池); just inside, on the right, is the small black-and-white building that houses the **Shitamachi Museum** ❾, which celebrates the working-class folk of the Edo period.

From in front of the museum, a path follows the eastern shore of Shinobazu Pond. On the island in the middle of the pond is Benzaiten (弁財天), a shrine to the patron goddess of the arts. You can walk up the east side of the embankment to the causeway and cross to the shrine. Then cross to the other side of the pond, turn left in front of the boathouse, and follow the embankment back to Shinobazu-dōri. Off to your right as you walk, a few blocks away and out of sight, begin the precincts of Tōkyō University, the nation's most prestigious seat of higher learning, alma mater to generations of bureaucrats. Turn left as you leave the park and walk back in the direction of the Shitamachi Museum.

When you reach the intersection, cross Chūō-dōri and turn right; walk past the ABAB clothing store and turn left at the second corner. At the end of this street is **Tokudai-ji** ❿, a temple over a supermarket, and the bustling heart of **Ame-ya Yoko-chō Market** ⓫. There are more than 500 little shops and stalls in this market, which stretches from the beginning of Shōwa-dōri at the north end to Ōkachi-machi at the south end. Ōkachi-machi means "Ōkachi Town"; the *ōkachi*—the "honorable infantry," the samurai of lowest rank in the shōgun's service—lived in the area.

From here follow the JR tracks as you wander north. In a few minutes you'll find yourself back in front of Ueno Station.

TIMING Exploring Ueno can be one excursion or two: an afternoon of cultural browsing or a full day of discoveries in one of the great centers of the city. Avoid Monday, when most of the museums are closed. Ueno out of doors is no fun at all in February or the rainy season (late June–mid-July); mid-August can be brutally hot and muggy. In April, the cherry blossoms of Ueno Kōen are glorious.

What to See

⓫ **Ame-ya Yoko-chō Market** (アメヤ横丁). The history of Ame-ya Yoko-chō (often shortened to Ameyoko) begins in the desperate days immediately after World War II. Ueno Station had survived the bombings—virtually everything around it was rubble—and anyone who could make it here from the countryside with rice and other small supplies of food could sell them at exorbitant black-market prices. Sugar was a commodity that couldn't be found at any price in postwar Tōkyō. Before long, there were

Over 700 monthly
furnished apartments
and guest houses
in Tokyo

Why SAKURA HOUSE ?

Economical - Monthly rents start from 80,000 yen for private apartments and 48,000 yen for guest houses, including utility expense and internet. Rents payable with VISA or MasterCard.

Easy - No key money, agent fee or guarantor required. All rooms furnished, just pop in with a suitcase.

Enjoyable - For guest houses, you will share a house with other sojourners from all over the world. Make friends, and share your Tokyo experience with them.

E-friendly - Check **http://www.sakura-house.com** for the latest availabilities. You can book a room online before coming to Japan.

❁ SAKURA HOUSE

Nishi-Shinjuku K-1 building 2F, 7-2-6 Nishi-Shinjuku, Shinjuku-ku, Tokyo
TEL: +81-3-5330-5250 (from abroad) **/ 03-5330-5250** (inside Japan)
For daily stays, check our sister hotel : **http://www.sakura-hotel.co.jp**

hundreds of stalls in the black market selling various kinds of *ame* (confections), most of them made from sweet potatoes. These stalls gave the market its name: Ame-ya Yoko-chō means "Confectioners' Alley."

Shortly before the Korean War, the market was legalized, and soon the stalls were carrying watches, chocolate, ballpoint pens, blue jeans, and T-shirts that had somehow been "liberated" from American PXs. In years to come the merchants of Ameyoko diversified still further—to fine Swiss timepieces and French designer luggage of dubious authenticity, cosmetics, jewelry, fresh fruit, and fish. The market became especially famous for the traditional prepared foods of the New Year, and during the last few days of December as many as half a million people crowd into the narrow alleys under the railroad tracks to stock up for the holiday. ⊠ *Ueno 4-chōme, Taitō-ku* ☾ *Most shops and stalls daily 10–7* Ⓜ *JR Ueno Station (Hirokō-ji Exit).*

❹ **Kan'ei-ji** (Kan'ei Temple, 寛永寺). In 1638 the second Tokugawa shōgun, Hidetada, commissioned the priest Tenkai to build a temple on the hill known as Shinobu-ga-oka in Ueno to defend his city from evil spirits. Tenkai turned for his model to the great temple complex of Enryaku-ji in Kyōto, established centuries earlier on Mt. Hiei to protect the imperial capital. The main hall of Tenkai's temple, called Kan'ei-ji, was moved to Ueno from the town of Kawagoe, about 40 km (25 mi) away, where he had once been a priest; it was moved again, to its present site, in 1879, and looks a bit weary of its travels. The only remarkable remaining structure here is the ornately carved vermilion gate to what was the mausoleum of Tsunayoshi, the fifth shōgun. Tsunayoshi is famous in the annals of Tokugawa history for his disastrous fiscal mismanagement and his *Shōrui Awaremi no Rei* (Edicts on Compassion for Living Things), which, among other things, made it a capital offense for a human being to kill a dog. ⊠ *1–14–11 Ueno Sakuragi, Taitō-ku* ☎ *03/3821–1259* 🖙 *Free, contributions welcome* ☾ *Daily 9–5* Ⓜ *JR Ueno Station (Kōen-guchi/Park Exit), JR Uguisudani Station.*

❻ **Kannon Hall** (Kiyomizu Kannon-dō, 清水観音堂). This National Treasure was a part of Abbot Tenkai's grand attempt to echo in Ueno the grandeur of Kyōto, but the echo is a little weak. The model for it was Kyōto's magnificent Kiyomizu-dera, but where the original rests on enormous wood pillars over a gorge, the Ueno version merely perches on the lip of a little hill. And the hall would have a grand view of Shinobazu Pond—which itself was landscaped to recall Biwa-ko (Lake Biwa), near Kyōto—if the trees in front of the terrace were not too high and too full most of the year to afford any view at all. The principal Buddhist image of worship here is the Senjū Kannon (Thousand-Armed Goddess of Mercy). Another figure, however, receives greater homage. This is the Kosodate Kannon, who is believed to answer the prayers of women having difficulty conceiving children. If their prayers are answered, they return to Kiyomizu and leave a doll, as both an offering of thanks and a prayer for the child's health. In a ceremony held every September 25, the dolls that have accumulated during the year are burned in a bonfire. ⊠ *1–29 Ueno Kōen, Taitō-ku* ☎ *03/3821–4749* 🖙 *Free* ☾ *Daily 7–5* Ⓜ *JR Ueno Station (Kōen-guchi/Park Exit).*

★ ▶ **①** **National Museum of Western Art** (Kokuritsu Seiyō Bijutsukan, 国立西洋美術館). Along with castings from the original molds of Rodin's *Gate of Hell, The Burghers of Calais,* and *The Thinker,* the wealthy businessman Matsukata Kojiro (1865–1950) acquired some 850 paintings, sketches, and prints by such masters as Renoir, Monet, Gauguin, Van Gogh, Delacroix, and Cézanne. Matsukata kept the collection in Europe, but he left it to Japan in his will. The French government sent the artwork to Japan after World War II, and the collection opened to the public in 1959 in a building designed by Swiss-born architect Le Corbusier. Since then, the museum has diversified a bit; more recent acquisitions include works by Rubens, Tintoretto, El Greco, Max Ernst, and Jackson Pollock. The Seiyō is one of the best-organized, most pleasant museums to visit in Tōkyō. ⊠ *7-7 Ueno Kōen, Taitō-ku* ☎ *03/3828–5131* ⊕ *www.nmwa.go.jp* ✉ *¥420; additional fee for special exhibits* ☉ *Tues.–Thurs. and weekends 9:30–4:30, Fri. 9:30–7:30* Ⓜ *JR Ueno Station (Kōen-guchi/Park Exit).*

☾ **②** **National Science Museum** (Kokuritsu Kagaku Hakubutsukan, 国立科学博物館). The six buildings of this museum complex house everything from fossils to moon rocks. And what self-respecting institution of its kind would be without a dinosaur collection? Look for them in the B2F Exhibition Hall, in the newest annex. Although the museum occasionally outdoes itself with special exhibits, it's pretty conventional, and provides relatively little in the way of hands-on learning experiences. Kids seem to like it anyway—but this is not a place to linger if your time is short. ⊠ *7-20 Ueno Kōen, Taitō-ku* ☎ *03/3822–0111* ⊕ *www. kahaku.go.jp/english* ✉ *¥420; additional fees for special exhibits* ☉ *Tues.–Thurs. 9–5, Fri. 9–8, weekends 9–6* Ⓜ *JR Ueno Station (Kōen-guchi/Park Exit).*

★ **❾** **Shitamachi Museum** (Shitamachi Hakubutsukan, 下町博物館). Japanese society in the days of the Tokugawa shōguns was rigidly stratified. Some 80% of the city was allotted to the warrior class and to temples and shrines. The remaining 20% of the space—between Ieyasu's fortifications on the west, and the Sumida-gawa on the east—was known as Shitamachi, literally, "downtown" or the "lower town" (as it expanded, Shitamachi came to include what today constitutes the Chūō, Taitō, Sumida, and Kōtō wards). It was here that the common folk, who made up more than half the population, lived. Most of them inhabited long, single-story tenements called *nagaya,* one jammed up against the next along the narrow alleys and unplanned streets of Ueno and the areas nearby. They developed a unique culture and way of life. The people here were hardworking, short-tempered, free-spending, quick to help a neighbor in trouble, and remarkably stubborn about their way of life. The Shitamachi Museum preserves and exhibits what remained of that way of life as late as 1940.

The two main displays on the first floor are a merchant house and a tenement, intact with all their furnishings. This is a hands-on museum: you can take your shoes off and step up into the rooms. On the second floor are displays of toys, tools, and utensils donated, in most cases, by people who had grown up with them and used them all their lives. There are also photographs of Shitamachi and video documentaries of crafts-people at work. Occasionally various traditional skills are demonstrated, and you're welcome to take part. This don't-miss museum makes great use of its space, and there are even volunteer guides (available starting at 10) who speak passable English. ⊠ *2–1 Ueno Kōen, Taitō-ku* ☎ *03/3823–7451* ⊡ *¥300* ⊘ *Tues.–Sun. 9:30–4:30* Ⓜ *JR Ueno Station (Kōen-guchi/Park Exit); Keisei private rail line, Keisei-Ueno Station (Higashi-guchi/East Exit).*

❼ Shōgitai Memorial (彰義隊の墓). Time seems to heal wounds very quickly in Japan. Only six years after the Shōgitai had destroyed most of Ueno Hill in 1868, the Meiji government permitted these Tokugawa loyalists to be honored with a gravestone, erected on the spot where their bodies had been cremated. ⊠ *Taitō-ku* Ⓜ *JR Ueno Station (Kōen-guchi/Park Exit); Keisei private rail line, Keisei-Ueno Station (Higashi-guchi/East Exit).*

❽ Statue of Takamori Saigō (西郷隆盛像). As chief of staff of the Meiji imperial army, Takamori Saigō (1827–77) played a key role in forcing the surrender of Edo and the overthrow of the shogunate. Ironically, Saigō himself fell out with the other leaders of the new Meiji government and was killed in an unsuccessful rebellion of his own. The sculptor Takamura Kōun's bronze, made in 1893, sensibly avoids presenting Saigō in uniform. ⊠ *Taitō-ku* Ⓜ *JR Ueno Station (Kōen-guchi/Park Exit); Keisei private rail line, Keisei-Ueno Station (Higashi-guchi/East Exit).*

❿ Tokudai-ji (Tokudai Temple, 徳大寺). This is a curiosity in a neighborhood of curiosities: a temple on the second floor of a supermarket. Two deities are worshipped here. One is the bodhisattva Jizō, and the act of washing this statue is believed to help safeguard your health. The other, principal image is of the Indian goddess Marishi, a daughter of Brahma, usually depicted with three faces and four arms. She is believed to help worshippers overcome various sorts of difficulties and to help them prosper in business. ⊠ *4–6–2 Ueno, Taitō-ku* Ⓜ *JR Yamanote and Keihin-tōhoku lines, Ōkachi-machi Station (Higashi-guchi/East Exit) or Ueno Station (Hirokō-ji Exit).*

❸ Tōkyō National Museum (Tōkyō Kokuritsu Hakubutsukan, 東京国立博物館). This complex of four buildings grouped around a courtyard is one of the world's great repositories of East Asian art and archaeology. Altogether, the museum has some 87,000 objects in its permanent collection, with several thousand more on loan from shrines, temples, and private owners.

Fodor'sChoice
★

The Western-style building on the left (if you're standing at the main gate), with its bronze cupolas, is the **Hyōkeikan.** Built in 1909, it was devoted to archaeological exhibits; aside from the occasional special exhibition, the building is closed today. The larger **Heiseikan,** behind the Hyōkeikan, now houses the archaeological exhibits. Look for the flamelike sculpted rims and elaborate markings of Middle Jōmon–period pottery (circa 3500 BC–2000 BC)—so different from anything produced in Japan before or since. Also look for the terra-cotta figures called *haniwa,* unearthed at burial sites dating from the 4th to the 7th centuries. The figures are deceptively simple in shape, and mysterious and comical at the same time in effect.

In the far left corner of the museum complex is the **Hōryū-ji Hōmot-sukan** (Gallery of Hōryū-ji Treasures). In 1878 the 7th-century Hōryū-ji in Nara presented 319 works of art in its possession—sculpture, scrolls, masks, and other objects—to the Imperial Household. These were transferred to the National Museum in 2000 and now reside in this gallery designed by Yoshio Taniguchi. There's a useful guide to the collection in English, and the exhibits are well explained. Don't miss the hall of carved wooden *gigaku* (Buddhist processional) masks.

The central building in the complex, the 1937 **Honkan**, houses Japanese art exclusively: paintings, calligraphy, sculpture, textiles, ceramics, swords, and armor. Also here are 84 objects designated by the government as National Treasures. The Honkan rotates the works on display several times during the year. It also hosts two special exhibitions a year (April and May or June, and October and November), which feature important collections from both Japanese and foreign museums. These, unfortunately, can be an ordeal: the lighting in the Honkan is not particularly good, the explanations in English are sketchy at best, and the hordes of visitors make it impossible to linger over a work you especially want to study. The more attractive **Tōyōkan**, to the right of the Honkan, completed in 1968, is devoted to the art of other Asian cultures. ✉ *13–9 Ueno Kōen, Taitō-ku* ☎ *03/3822–1111* ⊕ *www.tnm.go.jp/en* 🎫 *¥420* 🕙 *Tues.–Sat. 9:30–5, Sun. 9:30–6* Ⓜ *JR Ueno Station (Kōen-guchi/Park Exit).*

★ ❺ **Tōshō-gū** (Tōshō Shrine, 東照宮). Ieyasu, the first Tokugawa shōgun, died in 1616 and the following year was given the posthumous name Tōshō-Daigongen (The Great Incarnation Who Illuminates the East). The Imperial Court declared him a divinity of the first rank, thenceforth to be worshipped at Nikkō, in the mountains north of his city, at a shrine he had commissioned before his death. That shrine is the first and foremost Tōshō-gū. The one here, built in the ornate style called *gongen-zukuri,* dates to 1627. Miraculously, it survived the disasters that destroyed most of the other original buildings on the hill—the fires, the 1868 revolt, the 1923 earthquake, the 1945 bombings—making it one of the few early-Edo-period buildings in Tōkyō. The shrine and most of its art are designated National Treasures.

Two hundred *ishidōrō* (stone lanterns) line the path from the stone entry arch to the shrine itself. One of them, just outside the arch to the left, is more than 18 feet high—one of the three largest in Japan. This particular lantern is called *obaketōrō* (ghost lantern) because of a story connected to it: it seems that one night a samurai on guard duty slashed at the ghost (*obake*) that was believed to haunt the lantern. His sword was so good it left a nick in the stone, which can still be seen. Beyond these lanterns is a double row of 50 copper lanterns, presented by the feudal lords of the 17th century as expressions of their piety and loyalty to the regime.

The first room inside the shrine is the **Hall of Worship;** the four paintings in gold on wooden panels are by Tan'yū, one of the famous Kano family of artists who enjoyed the patronage of emperors and shōguns from the late 15th century to the end of the Edo period. Tan'yū was appointed *goyō eshi* (official court painter) in 1617. His commissions included the Tokugawa castles at Edo and Nagoya as well as the Nikkō Tōshō-gū. The framed tablet between the walls, with the name of the shrine in gold, is in the calligraphy of Emperor Go-Mizuno-o (1596–1680). Other works of calligraphy are by the abbots of Kan'ei-ji. Behind the Hall of Worship, connected by a passage called the *haiden,* is the sanctuary, where the spirit of Ieyasu is said to be enshrined.

The real glories of Tōshō-gū are its so-called **Chinese Gate,** which you reach at the end of your tour of the building, and the fence on either side. Like its counterpart at Nikkō, the fence is a kind of natural history lesson, with carvings of birds, animals, fish, and shells of every description; unlike the one at Nikkō, this fence was left unpainted. The two long panels of the gate, with their dragons carved in relief, are attributed to Hidari Jingorō—a brilliant sculptor of the early Edo period whose real name is unknown (*hidari* means "left"; Jingorō was reportedly left-handed). The lifelike appearance of his dragons has inspired a legend. Every morning they were found mysteriously dripping with water. Finally it was discovered that they were sneaking out at night to drink from the nearby Shinobazu Pond, and wire cages were put up around them to curtail this disquieting habit. ✉ *9–88 Ueno Kōen, Taitō-ku* ☎ *03/3822–3455* 🎫 *¥200* 🕐 *Daily 9–5* Ⓜ *JR Ueno Station (Kōen-guchi/Park Exit).*

Asakusa   浅草

In the year 628, so the legend goes, two brothers named Hamanari and Takenari Hikonuma were fishing on the lower reaches of the Sumidagawa when they dragged up a small, gilded statue of Kannon—an aspect of the Buddha worshipped as the goddess of mercy. They took the statue to their master, Naji-no-Nakamoto, who enshrined it in his house. Later, a temple was built for it in nearby Asakusa. Called Sensō-ji, the temple was rebuilt and enlarged several times over the next 10 centuries—but Asakusa itself remained just a village on a river crossing a few hours' walk from Edo.

Then Ieyasu Tokugawa made Edo his capital and Asakusa blossomed. Suddenly, it was the party that never ended, the place where the free-spending townspeople of the new capital came to empty their pockets. For the next 300 years it was the wellspring of almost everything we associate with Japanese popular culture.

The first step in that transformation came in 1657, when Yoshiwara—the licensed brothel quarter not far from Nihombashi—was moved to the countryside farther north: Asakusa found itself square in the road, more or less halfway between the city and its only nightlife. The village became a suburb and a pleasure quarter in its own right. In the narrow streets and alleys around Sensō-ji, there were stalls selling toys, souvenirs, and sweets; acrobats, jugglers, and strolling musicians; and sake shops and teahouses—where the waitresses often provided more than tea. (The Japanese have never worried much about the impropriety of such things; the approach to a temple is still a venue for very secular enterprises of all sorts.) Then in 1841 the Kabuki theaters—which the government looked upon as a source of dissipation second only to Yoshiwara—moved to Asakusa.

Highborn and lowborn, the people of Edo flocked to Kabuki. They loved its extravagant spectacle, its bravado, and its brilliant language. They cheered its heroes and hissed its villains. They bought wood-block prints, called *ukiyo-e*, of their favorite actors. Asakusa was home to the Kabuki theaters for only a short time, but that was enough to establish it as *the* entertainment quarter of the city—a reputation it held unchallenged until World War II.

When Japan ended its long, self-imposed isolation in 1868, where else would the novelties and amusements of the outside world first take root but in Asakusa? The country's first photography studios appeared here in 1875. Japan's first skyscraper, a 12-story mart called the Jū-ni-kai, was built in Asakusa in 1890 and filled with shops selling imported goods. The area around Sensō-ji had by this time been designated a public park and was divided into seven sections; the sixth section, called Rok-ku, was Tōkyō's equivalent of 42nd Street and Times Square. The nation's first movie theater opened here in 1903—to be joined by dozens more, and these in turn were followed by music halls, cabarets, and revues. The first drinking establishment in Japan to call itself a "bar" was started in Asakusa in 1880; it still exists.

Most of this area was destroyed in 1945. As an entertainment district, it never really recovered, but Sensō-ji was rebuilt almost immediately. The people here would never dream of living without it—just as they would never dream of living anywhere else. This is the heart and soul of Shitamachi, where you can still hear the rich, breezy downtown Tōkyō accent of the 17th and 18th centuries. Even today the temple precinct embraces an area of narrow streets, arcades, restaurants, shops, stalls, playgrounds, and gardens. It's home to a population of artisans and small entrepreneurs, neighborhood children and their grandmothers, and hipsters and hucksters and mendicant priests. In short, if you have any time at all to spend in Tōkyō, you really should devote at least a day of it to Asakusa.

Numbers in the text correspond to numbers in the margin and on the Asakusa map.

a good walk

For more information on individual shops mentioned in this walk, *see* Shopping, *below.*

Start at Asakusa Station, at the end of the Ginza Line. Opened in 1927, this was Tōkyō's first subway, running from Asakusa to Ueno; it later became known as the Ginza Line when it was extended through Ginza to Shimbashi and Shibuya. Follow the signs, clearly marked in English, to Exit 1. When you come up to the street level, turn right and walk west along Kaminari-mon-dōri. In a few steps you come to a gate on your right with two huge red lanterns hanging from it: this is **Kaminari-mon** ❶ ▶, the main entrance to the grounds of Sensō-ji.

Another way to get to Kaminari-mon is via the "river bus" ferry from Hinode Pier, which stops in Asakusa at the southwest corner of the park called Sumida Kōen. Walk out to the three-way intersection, cross two sides of the triangle, and turn right. Kaminari-mon is in the middle of the second block.

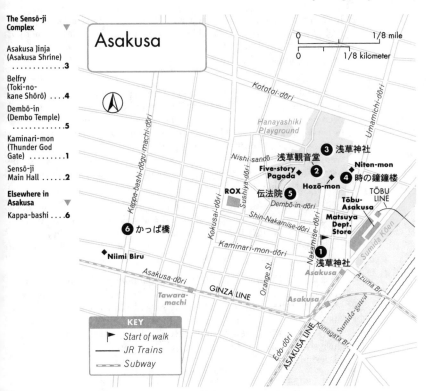

Take note of the Asakusa Tourist Information Center (Asakusa Bunka Kankō Center), across the street from Kaminari-mon. A volunteer staff with some English is on duty here daily 10–5 and will happily load you down with maps and brochures.

From Kaminari-mon, Nakamise-dōri—a long, narrow avenue lined on both sides with small shops—leads to the courtyard of Sensō-ji. One shop worth stopping at is Ichiban-ya, about 100 yards down on the right, for its handmade, toasted *sembei* (rice crackers) and its seven-pepper spices in gourd-shape bottles of zelkova wood. At the end of Nakamise-dōri, on the right, is Sukeroku, which specializes in traditional handmade dolls and models clothed in the costumes of the Edo period. Just beyond Sukeroku is a two-story gate called Hōzō-mon.

At this point, take an important detour. Look to your left as you pass through the gate. Tucked away in the far corner is a vermilion-color building in the traditional temple style (just to the left of the pagoda, behind an iron railing) that houses the Sensō-ji administrative offices: walk in, go down the corridor on the right to the third door on the left, and ask for permission to see the Garden of Dembō-in. There's no charge. You simply enter your name and address in a register and receive a ticket. Hold on to the ticket: you'll need it later.

Return to Hōzō-mon and walk across the courtyard to the **Sensō-ji Main Hall** ❷. To the left of the Main Hall is the Five-Story Pagoda. To the right is **Asakusa Jinja** ❸; near the entrance to this shrine is the east gate to the temple grounds, Niten-mon.

From Niten-mon, walk back in the direction of Kaminari-mon to the southeast corner of the grounds. On a small plot of ground here stands the shrine to Kume-no-Heinai, a 17th-century outlaw who repented and became a priest of one of the subsidiary temples of Sensō-ji. Late in life he carved a stone statue of himself and buried it where many people would walk over it. In his will, he expressed the hope that his image would be trampled upon forever. Somehow, Heinai came to be worshipped as the patron god of lovers—as mystifying an apotheosis as you will ever find in Japanese religion.

Walk south from Heinai's shrine along the narrow street that runs back to Kaminari-mon-dōri, parallel to Nakamise-dōri. On the left you pass a tiny hillock called Benten-yama and the 17th-century **Belfry** ❹. Opposite Benten-yama is a shop called Naka-ya, which sells all manner of regalia for Sensō-ji's annual Sanja Festival.

Next door is Kuremutsu, a tiny century-old *nomiya* (Japanese pub); it's open only in the evening, but is worth admiring any time of day as a remnant of the Meiji era. Just up the street from Kuremutsu is Hyaku-suke, an unusual shop selling traditional Japanese cosmetics. Three doors up, on the same side of the street, is Fuji-ya, a shop that deals exclusively in *tenugui*: cotton hand towels, hand-printed from original stencil designs.

Turn right at the corner past Fuji-ya and walk west on Dembō-in-dōri until you cross Nakamise-dōri. On the other side of the intersection, on the left, is Yono-ya, purveyor of pricey handmade boxwood combs for traditional Japanese coiffures and wigs.

Now it's time to cash in the ticket you've been carrying around. Walk west another 70 yards or so, and on the right you can see an old dark wooden gate; this is the side entrance to **Dembō-in** ❺, the living quarters of the abbot of Sensō-ji. The only part of the grounds you can visit is the garden: go through the small door in the gate, across the courtyard and through the door on the opposite side, and present your ticket to the caretaker in the house at the end of the alley. The entrance to the garden is down a short flight of stone steps to the left.

Turn right as you leave Dembō-in and continue walking west on Dembō-in-dōri. You pass a small Shintō shrine with numerous little statues of the bodhisattva Jizō; this is a shrine for prayers for the repose of the souls of *mizuko*—literally "water children"—those who were aborted or miscarried.

Farther on, at the corner of Orange-dōri, is the redbrick Asakusa Public Hall; performances of Kabuki and traditional dance are sometimes held here, as well as exhibitions on life in Asakusa before World War II. Across the street is Nakase, one of the best of Asakusa's many fine tempura restaurants.

If you have the time and energy, you might want to explore the warren of streets and covered arcades on the south and west sides of Dembō-in, where you can find kimonos and *yukata* (cotton kimono) fabrics, traditional accessories and festival costumes, and purveyors of crackers, seaweed, and tea. Otherwise, walk south, away from Dembō-in, on any of these arcades to return to Kaminari-mon-dōri; turn right, and walk to the end of the avenue. Cross Kokusai-dōri, turn left, and then right at the next major intersection onto Asakusa-dōri; on the corner is the entrance to Tawara-machi Station on the Ginza subway line. Head west on Asakusa-dōri; at the second traffic light, you can see the Niimi Building across the street, crowned with the guardian god of the Kappa-bashi neighborhood: an enormous plastic chef's head, 30 feet high, beaming, mustached, and crowned, as every chef in Japan is crowned, with a tall white hat. Turn right onto Kappa-bashi-dōgu-machi-dōri to explore the shops of **Kappa-bashi** ⑥, Tōkyō's wholesale-restaurant-supply district.

At the second intersection, on the right, is the main showroom of Maizuru, virtuosos in the art of counterfeit cuisine—the plastic food models displayed at many Japanese restaurants. A few doors down is Biken Kōgei(美研工芸), a good place to look for the folding red-paper lanterns that grace the front of inexpensive bars and restaurants. Across the street from Maizuru is Nishimura, a shop specializing in the traditional restaurant entrance curtains called *noren*.

On the next block, on the right (east) side of the street, is Kondo Shōten (近藤商店), which sells all sorts of bamboo trays, baskets, scoops, and containers. A block farther, look for Iida Shōten(飯田商店), with a good selection of embossed cast-iron kettles and casseroles, called *nambu* ware. On the far corner is Union Company, which sells everything you need to run a coffee shop (or the make-believe one in your own kitchen): roasters, grinders, beans, flasks, and filters of every kind.

There's more of Kappa-bashi to the north, but you can safely ignore it. Continue east, straight past Union Company down the narrow side street. On the next block, on the left, look for Tsubaya Hōchōten, which sells cutlery for professionals. Continue on this street east to Kokusai-dōri and then turn right (south). As you walk, you can see several shops selling *butsudan,* Buddhist household altars. The most elaborate of these, hand-carved in ebony and covered with gold leaf, are made in Toyama Prefecture and can cost as much as ¥1 million. No proper Japanese household is without at least a modest butsudan; it's the spiritual center of the family, where reverence for ancestors and continuity of the family traditions are expressed. In a few moments you'll be back at Tawara-machi Station—the end of the Asakusa walk.

TIMING Unlike most of the other areas to explore on foot in Tōkyō, Sensō-ji is admirably compact. You can easily see the temple and environs in a morning. The garden at Dembō-in is worth a half hour. If you decide to include Kappa-bashi, allow yourself an hour more for the tour. Some of the shopping arcades in this area are covered, but Asakusa is essentially an outdoor experience. Be prepared for rain in June, heat and humidity in July and August.

The Sensō-ji Complex 浅草寺

Dedicated to the goddess Kannon, the Sensō-ji Complex is the heart and soul of Asakusa. Come for its local and historical importance, its garden, its 17th-century Shintō shrine, and the wild Sanja Festival in May. ✉ *2-3-1 Asakusa, Taitō-ku* ☎ *03/3842-0181* 🎫 *Free* 🕐 *Temple grounds daily 6–sunset* Ⓜ *Ginza subway line, Asakusa Station (Exit 1/ Kaminari-mon Exit).*

❸ Asakusa Jinja (Asakusa Shrine, 浅草神社). Several structures in the temple complex survived the bombings of 1945. The largest, to the right of the Main Hall, is this Shintō shrine to the Hikonuma brothers and their master, Naji-no-Nakamoto—the putative founders of Sensō-ji. In Japan, Buddhism and Shintoism have enjoyed a comfortable coexistence since the former arrived from China in the 6th century. It's the rule, rather than the exception, to find a Shintō shrine on the same grounds as a Buddhist temple. The shrine, built in 1649, is also known as Sanja Sanma (Shrine of the Three Guardians). The **Sanja Festival,** held every year on the third weekend in May, is the biggest, loudest, wildest party in Tōkyō. Each of the neighborhoods under Sanja Sanma's protection has its own mikoshi, and on the second day of the festival, these palanquins are paraded through the streets of Asakusa to the shrine, bouncing and swaying on the shoulders of the participants all the way. Many of the "parishioners" take part naked to the waist, or with the sleeves of their tunics rolled up, to expose fantastic red-and-black tattoo patterns that sometimes cover their entire backs and shoulders. These are the tribal markings of the Japanese underworld.

Near the entrance to Asakusa Shrine is another survivor of World War II: the east gate to the temple grounds, **Niten-mon,** built in 1618 for a shrine to Ieyasu Tokugawa (the shrine itself no longer exists) and designated by the government as an Important Cultural Property. ✉ *Taitō-ku.*

❹ Belfry (Toki-no-kane Shōrō, 時の鐘鐘楼). The tiny hillock Benten-yama, with its shrine to the goddess of good fortune, is the site of this 17th-century belfry. The bell here used to toll the hours for the people of the district, and it was said that you could hear it anywhere within a radius of some 6 km (4 mi). The bell still sounds at 6 AM every day, when the temple grounds open. It also rings on New Year's Eve—108 strokes in all, beginning just before midnight, to "ring out" the 108 sins and frailties of humankind and make a clean start for the coming year. Benten-yama and the belfry are at the beginning of the narrow street that parallels Nakamise-dōri. ✉ *Taitō-ku.*

need a break? Originally a teahouse, **Kuremutsu** (暮六つ), a tiny pub, has been sitting—precariously—on its site, a stone's throw from the Asakusa Kannon Temple, for more than 100 years. Narrow your field of vision, to shut out the buildings on either side, and you could be back in the waning days of Meiji-period Japan. Open only in the evenings, 4–10 (closed Mon.), Kuremutsu specializes in premium sake, with set courses of food and drink that range from ¥5,000 to ¥10,000. ✉ *2-2-13 Asakusa, Taitō-ku* ☎ *03/3842-0906.*

★ ❺ **Dembō-in** (Dembo Temple, 伝法院). Believed to have been made in the 17th century by Kōbori Enshū, the genius of Zen landscape design, the garden of Dembō-in, part of the living quarters of the abbot of Sensō-ji, is the best-kept secret in Asakusa. Anyone can see the front entrance to Dembō-in from Nakamise-dōri—behind an iron fence in the last block of shops—but the thousands of Japanese visitors passing by seem to have no idea what it is. (And if they do, it somehow never occurs to them to visit it themselves.) The garden of Dembō-in is usually empty and always utterly serene, an island of privacy in a sea of pilgrims. Spring, when the wisteria blooms, is the ideal time to be here. As you walk along the path that circles the pond, a different vista presents itself at every turn. The only sounds are the cries of birds and the splashing of carp.

A sign in English on Dembō-in-dōri, about 150 yards west of the intersection with Naka-mise-dōri, indicates the entrance, through the side door of a large wooden gate. For permission to see the abbot's garden, you must first apply at the temple administration building, between Hōzō-mon and the Five-Story Pagoda, in the far corner. ⊠ *Taitō-ku* ☎ *03/ 3842–0181 for reservations* ⊠ *Free* ⊗ *Daily 9–4; may be closed if abbot has guests.*

need a break?

The tatami-mat rooms in **Nakase** (中瀬), a fine tempura restaurant, look out on a perfect little interior garden that's hung in May with great fragrant bunches of white wisteria. Carp and goldfish swim in the pond, and you can almost lean out from your room and trail your fingers in the water as you listen to the fountain. Nakase is expensive: lunch (11:30–3) at the tables inside starts at ¥3,000; more elaborate meals by the garden start at ¥7,000. It's across Orange-dōri from the redbrick Asakusa Public Hall. ⊠ *1–39–13 Asakusa, Taitō-ku* ☎ *03/ 3841–4015* ⊟ *No credit cards* ⊗ *Closed Tues. and 2nd and 4th Mon. of month.*

▶ ❶ **Kaminari-mon** (Thunder God Gate, 雷門). This is the proper Sensō-ji entrance, with its huge red-paper lantern hanging in the center. The original gate was destroyed by fire in 1865; the replica you see today was built after World War II. Traditionally, two fearsome guardian gods are installed in the alcoves of Buddhist temple gates to ward off evil spirits. The Thunder God (Kaminari-no-Kami) of the Sensō-ji main gate is on the left. He shares his duties with the Wind God (Kaze-no-Kami) on the right. Few Japanese visitors neglect to stop at **Tokiwa-dō** (常盤堂), the shop on the west side of the gate, to buy some of Tōkyō's most famous souvenirs: *kaminari okoshi* (thunder crackers), made of rice, millet, sugar, and beans.

Kaminari-mon also marks the southern extent of **Nakamise-dōri** (仲見世通り), the Street of Inside Shops. The area from Kaminari-mon to the inner gate of the temple was once composed of stalls leased to the townspeople who cleaned and swept the temple grounds. The rows of redbrick buildings now technically belong to the municipal government, but the leases are, in effect, hereditary: some of the shops have been in the same families since the Edo period. ⊠ *Taitō-ku.*

❷ Sensō-ji Main Hall (浅草観音堂). The Main Hall and Five-Story Pagoda of Sensō-ji are both faithful copies in concrete of originals that burned down in 1945. During a time when most of the people of Asakusa were still rebuilding their own bombed-out lives, it took 13 years to raise money for the restoration of their beloved Sensō-ji. To them—and especially to those involved in the world of entertainment—it's far more than a tourist attraction: Kabuki actors still come here before a new season of performances, and sumō wrestlers visit before a tournament to pay their respects. The large lanterns in the Main Hall were donated by the geisha associations of Asakusa and nearby Yanagi-bashi. Most Japanese stop at the huge bronze incense burner, in front of the Main Hall, to bathe their hands and faces in the smoke—it's a charm to ward off illnesses—before climbing the stairs to offer their prayers.

The Main Hall, about 115 feet long and 108 feet wide, is not an especially impressive piece of architecture. Unlike in many other temples, however, part of the inside has a concrete floor, so you can come and go without removing your shoes. In this area hang Sensō-ji's chief claims to artistic importance: a collection of 18th- and 19th-century votive paintings on wood. Plaques of this kind, called *ema*, are still offered to the gods at shrines and temples, but they are commonly simpler and smaller. The worshipper buys a little tablet of wood with the picture already painted on one side and inscribes a prayer on the other. The temple owns more than 50 of these works, which were removed to safety in 1945 and so escaped the air raids. Only eight of them, depicting scenes from Japanese history and mythology, are on display. A catalog of the collection is on sale in the hall, but the text is in Japanese only.

Lighting is poor in the Main Hall, and the actual works are difficult to see. This is also true of the ceiling, done by two contemporary masters of Nihon-ga (traditional Japanese-style painting); the dragon is by Ryūshi Kawabata, and the motif of angels and lotus blossoms is by Inshō Dōmoto. One thing that visitors cannot see at all is the holy image of Kannon itself, which supposedly lies buried somewhere deep under the temple. Not even the priests of Sensō-ji have ever seen it, and there is in fact no conclusive evidence that it actually exists.

Hōzō-mon (宝蔵門), the gate to the temple courtyard, is also a repository for sutras (Buddhist texts) and other treasures of Sensō-ji. This gate, too, has its guardian gods; should either god decide to leave his post for a stroll, he can use the enormous pair of sandals hanging on the back wall—the gift of a Yamagata Prefecture village famous for its straw weaving. ⊠ *Taitō-ku.*

Elsewhere in Asakusa

★ **❻ Kappa-bashi** (かっぱ橋). In the 19th century, so the story goes, a river (crossed by a bridge) ran through the present-day Kappa-bashi district. The surrounding area was poorly drained and was often flooded. A local shopkeeper began a project to improve the drainage, investing all his own money, but met with little success until a troupe of *kappa*—mischievous green water sprites—emerged from the river to help him. A more prosaic explanation for the name of the district points out that the lower-ranking retainers of the local lord used to earn extra money by making straw raincoats, also called kappa, that they spread to dry on the bridge.

Today, Kappa-bashi's more than 200 wholesale dealers sell everything the city's restaurant and bar trade could possibly need to do business, from paper supplies and steam tables to signs and soup tureens. In their wildest dreams the Japanese themselves would never have cast Kappa-bashi as a tourist attraction, but indeed it is.

For one thing, it is *the* place to buy plastic food. The custom of putting in restaurant windows models of the food served inside is said to date to the early days of the Meiji Restoration, when anatomical models made of wax first came to Japan as teaching aids in the new schools of Western medicine. A businessman from Nara decided that wax models would also make good point-of-purchase advertising for restaurants. He was right: the industry grew in a modest way at first, making models mostly of Japanese food. In the boom years after 1960, restaurants began to serve all sorts of dishes most people had never seen before, and the models provided much-needed reassurance: "So *that's* a cheeseburger. It doesn't look as bad as it sounds. Let's go in and try one." By the mid-1970s, the makers of plastic food were turning out creations of astonishing virtuosity and realism, and foreigners had discovered in them a form of pop art. ⊠ *Nishi-Asakusa 1-chōme and 2-chōme, Taitō-ku* ⊘ *Most shops daily 9–6* Ⓜ *Ginza subway line, Tawara-machi Station (Exit 1).*

Tsukiji & Shiodome   築地・汐留

Although it's best known today as the site of the largest fish market in Asia, Tsukiji is also a reminder of the awesome disaster of the great fire of 1657. In the space of two days, it killed more than 100,000 people and leveled almost 70% of Ieyasu Tokugawa's new capital. Ieyasu was not a man to be discouraged by mere catastrophe, however; he took it as an opportunity to plan an even bigger and better city, one that would incorporate the marshes east of his castle. Tsukiji, in fact, means "reclaimed land," and a substantial block of land it was, laboriously drained and filled, from present-day Ginza to the bay.

The common people of the tenements and alleys, who had suffered most in the great fire, benefited not at all from this project; land was first allotted to feudal lords and to temples. After 1853, when Japan opened its doors to the outside world, Tsukiji became Tōkyō's first foreign settlement—the site of the American legation and an elegant two-story brick hotel, and home to missionaries, teachers, and doctors.

To the west of Tsukiji lie Shiodome and Shimbashi. In the period after the Meiji Restoration, Shimbashi was one of the most famous geisha districts of the new capital. Its reputation as a pleasure quarter is even older. In the Edo period, when there was a network of canals and waterways here, it was the height of luxury to charter a covered boat (called a *yakata-bune*) from one of the Shimbashi boathouses for a cruise on the river; a local restaurant would cater the excursion, and a local geisha house would provide the companionship. Almost nothing remains in Shimbashi to recall that golden age, but as its luster has faded, adjacent Shiodome has risen—literally—in its place as one of the most ambitious redevelopment projects of 21st-century Tōkyō.

Shiodome (literally "where the tide stops") was an area of saltwater flats on which in 1872 the Meiji government built the Tōkyō terminal—the original Shimbashi Station—on Japan's first railway line, which ran for 29 km (18 mi) to nearby Yokohama. Later a freight yard, the area eventually became Japan Rail's (JR) most notorious white elephant: a staggeringly valuable hunk of real estate, smack in the middle of the world's most expensive city, that JR no longer needed and couldn't seem to sell. By 1997 a bewildering succession of receivers, public development corporations, and zoning commissions had evolved an urban renewal plan for the area, and the land was auctioned off. Among the buyers were Nippon Television and Dentsū, the largest advertising agency in Asia and the fourth largest in the world.

In 2002 Dentsū consolidated its scattered offices into the centerpiece of the Shiodome project: a 47-story tower and annex designed by Jean Nouvel. With the annex, known as the Caretta Shiodome, Dentsū aspired not just to a new corporate address, but an "investment in community," a complex of cultural facilities, shops, and restaurants that has turned Shiodome into one of the most fashionable places in the city to see and be seen. The 1,200-seat Dentsū Shiki Theater SEA here has become one of Tōkyō's major venues for live performances; its resident repertory company regularly brings long-running Broadway hits like *Mamma Mia* to eager Japanese audiences.

Numbers in the text correspond to numbers in the margin and on the Tsukiji & Shiodome map.

a good walk

TSUKIJI

Take the Ōedo Line to Tsukiji-shijō Station. Leave the station by Exit A1 onto Shin-Ōhashi-dōri and turn right. After walking about 30 paces, you come to the back gate of the fish market, which extends from here southeast toward the bay. Alternatively, take the Hibiya Line to Tsukiji Station (FISH MARKET signs in English are posted in the station), come up on Shin-Ōhashi-dōri (Exit 1), and turn southeast. Cross Harumi-dōri, walk along the covered sidewalk for about 110 yards to the traffic light, and turn left. Walk to the end of the street (you can see the stone torii of a small shrine) and turn right. If you reach this point at precisely 5 AM, you can hear the signal for the start of Tōkyō's greatest ongoing open-air spectacle: the fish auction at the **Tōkyō Central Wholesale Market** ❶ ⏰.

By 9 AM the business of the fish market is largely finished for the day, but there's still plenty to see and do in the area. After the auctions you can explore the **backstreet shops of Tsukiji** ❷, in the maze of alleys between the market and Harumi-dōri. Here you can find a fascinating collection of small restaurants, stalls, fish markets, and other stores. For a close-up view of Japanese daily life, this is one of the best places in Tōkyō to visit.

Return to Shin-Ōhashi-dōri and walk northeast, past Harumi-dōri. On the right, as you approach the Hibiya subway line's Tsukiji Station, are

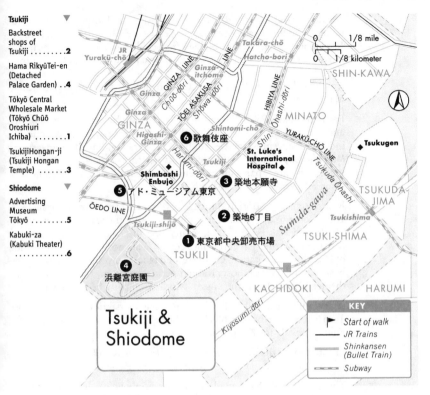

the grounds of **Tsukiji Hongan-ji** ❸. Looking much like a transplant from India, this temple is the main branch in Tōkyō of Kyōto's Nishi Hongan-ji. A short walk north of Tsukiji Hongan-ji are the grounds of St. Luke's International Hospital (founded in 1900 by Dr. Rudolf Teusler, an American medical missionary), which are not in themselves worth a detour but are of historical note. Here, in the 18th century, scholars Ryōtaku Maeno and Gempaku Sugita translated a Dutch book on anatomy, thereby ushering in Japan's interest in Western science. Covering the several square blocks north of the hospital was the foreign settlement created after the signing of the U.S.-Japan Treaty of Commerce in 1858. Among the residents here in the late 19th century was a Scottish surgeon and missionary named Henry Faulds. Intrigued by the Japanese custom of putting their thumbprints on documents for authentication, he began the research that established for the first time that no two people's fingerprints are alike. In 1880 he wrote a paper for *Nature* magazine suggesting that this fact might be of some use in criminal investigation.

After visiting Tsukiji Hongan-ji, walk southwest on Shin-Ōhashi-dōri, past the Asahi Newspapers Building and the National Institute for Cancer Research on your right. The street will curve to the right; dead ahead, across the intersection of Kaigan-dōri at Shiosaki-bashi, are Shiodome and the skyscraper headquarters of the advertising giant Dentsū. Just before the intersection, on the left, the old Nanmon-bashi stone bridge crosses a canal to the entrance of the **Hama Rikyū Tei-en** ❹. (The path to the left as you enter the garden leads to the "river bus" ferry landing, from which you can leave this excursion and begin another: up the Sumida to Asakusa.)

SHIODOME   From the Hama Rikyū Tei-en, cross Shōwa-dōri by the pedestrian bridge and spend some time exploring the shops and arcades of Caretta Shiodome, adjacent to the Dentsū headquarters building. The **Advertising Museum Tokyo** ❺, on the B1 level of Caretta, is especially worth visiting. It presents Japan's unique sense of graphic design in the context of some 300 years of advertising history.

Return to Shōwa-dōri and turn left. (If you were to turn right instead, you'd come to a "0" marker commemorating the starting point of the 1872 railway service to Yokohama.) At the next major intersection turn right and then left at the third corner. Walk northeast in the direction of Higashi-Ginza Station. On the second block, on your right, is the Shimbashi Enbujo, which hosts Kabuki performances and other traditional theater. On the left is the Nissan Motor Company headquarters.

A brisk minute's walk will bring you to the intersection of Harumi-dōri. Turn left, and on the next block, on the right, you can see the **Kabuki-za** ❻, built especially for Kabuki performances.

Just in front of the Kabuki-za is the Hibiya subway's Higashi-Ginza stop, where you can make your way back to where you started.

TIMING   The Tsukiji walk has few places to spend time *in*; getting from point to point, however, can consume most of a morning. The backstreet shops will probably require no more than an hour. Allow yourself about an hour to explore the fish market; if fish in all its diversity holds a special fascination for you, take two hours. Remember that in order to see the fish auction in action, you need to get to the market before 6:30 AM; by 9 AM the business of the market is largely finished for the day.

This part of the city can be brutally hot and muggy in August; during the O-bon holiday, in the middle of the month, Tsukiji is comparatively lifeless. Mid-April and early October are best for strolls in the Hama Rikyū Tei-en.

What to See

❺ **Advertising Museum Tokyo** (アド・ミュージアム東京). ADMT puts the unique Japanese gift for graphic and commercial design into historical perspective, from the sponsored "placements" in 18th-century woodblock prints to the postmodern visions of fashion photographers and video directors. The museum is maintained by a foundation established in honor of Hideyo Yoshida, fourth president of the mammoth Dentsū Advertising Company, and includes a digital library of some 130,000 entries on everything you ever wanted to know about hype. There are no explanatory panels in English—but this in itself is a test of how well the visual vocabulary of consumer media can communicate across cultures. ⊠ *1–8–2 Higashi-Shimbashi, Caretta Shiodome B1F–B2F, Chūō-ku* ☎ *03/6218–2500* ⊕ *www.admt.jp* 🎟 *Free* 🕐 *Tues.–Fri. 11–6:30, Sat. 11–4:30* Ⓜ *Ōedo subway line, Shiodome Station (Exit 7); JR (Shiodome Exit) and Asakusa and Ginza lines (Exit 4), Shimbashi Station.*

② **Backstreet shops of Tsukiji** (築地6丁目). Tōkyō's markets provide a vital coun-
terpoint to the museums and monuments of conventional sightseeing:
they let you see how people really live in the city. If you have time for
only one market, this is the one to see. The three square blocks between
the Tōkyō Central Wholesale Market and Harumi-dōri have, naturally
enough, scores of fishmongers, but also shops and restaurants. Stores
sell pickles, tea, crackers and snacks, cutlery (what better place to pick
up a professional sushi knife?), baskets, and kitchenware. Hole-in-the-
wall sushi bars here have set menus ranging from ¥1,000 to ¥2,100; look
for the plastic models of food in glass cases out front. The area includes
the row of little counter restaurants, barely more than street stalls,
under the arcade along the east side of Shin-Ōhashi-dōri, each with its
one specialty. If you haven't had breakfast by this point in your walk,
stop at **Segawa** (瀬川) for *maguro donburi*—a bowl of fresh raw tuna
slices served over rice and garnished with bits of dried seaweed (Segawa
is in the middle of the arcade, but without any distinguishing features
or English signage; your best bet is to ask someone). Some 100 of the
small retailers and restaurants in this area are members of the Tsukiji
Meiten-kai (Association of Notable Shops), and promote themselves by
selling illustrated maps of the area for ¥50; the maps are all in Japanese, but with proper frames they make great souvenirs. ⊠ *Tsukiji 4-
chōme, Chūō-ku* Ⓜ *Ōedo subway line, Tsukiji-shijō Station (Exit A1);
Hibiya subway line, Tsukiji Station (Exit 1).*

④ **Hama Rikyū Tei-en** (Detached Palace Garden, 浜離宮庭園). The land here
was originally owned by the Owari branch of the Tokugawa family from
Nagoya, and it extended to part of what is now the fish market. When
one of the family became shōgun in 1709, his residence was turned into
a shogunal palace—with pavilions, ornamental gardens, pine and cherry
groves, and duck ponds. The garden became a public park in 1945, although a good portion of it is fenced off as a nature preserve. None of
the original buildings has survived, but on the island in the large pond
is a reproduction of the pavilion where former U.S. president Ulysses S.
Grant and Mrs. Grant had an audience with the emperor Meiji in 1879.
The building can now be rented for parties. The path to the left as you
enter the garden leads to the "river bus" ferry landing, from which you
can leave this excursion and begin another: up the Sumida-gawa to
Asakusa. Note that you must pay the admission to the garden even if
you're just using the ferry. ⊠ *1–1 Hamarikyū–Teien, Chūō-ku* ☎ *03/
3541–0200* 🎟 *¥300* 🕐 *Daily 9–4:30* Ⓜ *Ōedo subway line, Shiodome
Station (Exit 8).*

⑥ **Kabuki-za** (Kabuki Theater, 歌舞伎座). Soon after the Meiji Restoration
and its enforced exile in Asakusa, Kabuki began to reestablish itself in
this part of the city. The first Kabuki-za was built in 1889, with a European facade. Here two of the hereditary theater families, Ichikawa and
Onoe, developed a brilliant new repertoire that brought Kabuki into the

modern era. In 1912 the Kabuki-za was taken over by the Shochiku theatrical management company, which replaced the old theater building
in 1925. Designed by architect Shin'ichirō Okada, it was damaged during World War II but was restored soon after. ⊠ *4–12–15 Ginza, Chūō-
ku* ☎ *03/3541–3131* ⊕ *www.shochiku.co.jp/play/kabukiza/theater*
Ⓜ *Hibiya subway line, Higashi-Ginza Station (Exit 3).*

★ ▶ ❶ **Tōkyō Central Wholesale Market** (Tōkyō Chūō Oroshiuri Ichiba,
東京都中央卸売市場). The city's fish market used to be farther uptown,
in Nihombashi. It was moved to Tsukiji after the Great Kantō Earthquake of 1923, and it occupies the site of what was once Japan's first
naval training academy. Today the market sprawls over some 54 acres
of reclaimed land and employs approximately 15,000 people, making
it the largest fish market in the world. Its warren of buildings houses
about 1,200 wholesale shops, supplying 90% of the seafood consumed
in Tōkyō every day—some 2,400 tons of it. Most of the seafood sold
in Tsukiji comes in by truck, arriving through the night from fishing ports
all over the country.

What makes Tsukiji a great show is the auction system. The catch—more
than 100 varieties of fish in all, including whole frozen tuna, Styrofoam
cases of shrimp and squid, and crates of crabs—is laid out in the long
covered area between the river and the main building. Then the bidding
begins. Only members of the wholesalers' association can take part. Wearing license numbers fastened to the front of their caps, they register their
bids in a kind of sign language, shouting to draw the attention of the
auctioneer and making furious combinations in the air with their fingers. The auctioneer keeps the action moving in a hoarse croak that sounds
like no known language, and spot quotations change too fast for ordinary mortals to follow.

Different fish are auctioned off at different times and locations, and by
6:30 AM or so this part of the day's business is over, and the wholesalers
fetch their purchases back into the market in barrows. Restaurant owners and retailers arrive about 7, making the rounds of favorite suppliers for their requirements. Chaos seems to reign, but everybody here knows
everybody else, and they all have it down to a system.

The 52,000 or so buyers, wholesalers, and shippers who work at the
market may be a lot more receptive to casual visitors than they were in
the past, but they are not running a tourist attraction. They're in the
fish business, moving more than 600,000 tons of it a year to retailers
and restaurants all over the city, and this is their busiest time of day.
The cheerful banter they use with each other can turn snappish if you
get in their way. Also bear in mind that you are not allowed to take photographs while the auctions are under way (flashes are a distraction).
The market is kept spotlessly clean, which means the water hoses are
running all the time. Boots are helpful, but if you don't want to carry
them, bring a pair of heavy-duty trash bags to slip over your shoes and
secure them above your ankles with rubber bands. ⊠ *5–2–1 Tsukiji, Chūō-
ku* ☎ *03/3542–1111* ⊕ *www.shijou.metro.tokyo.jp* 🎫 *Free* ◷ *Business
hrs Mon.–Sat. (except 2nd and 4th Wed. of month) 5 AM–3 PM* Ⓜ *Ōedo*

subway line, Tsukiji-shijō Station (Exit A1); Hibiya subway line, Tsuk-iji Station (Exit 1).

 Tsukiji Hongan-ji (Tsukiji Hongan Temple, 築地本願寺). Disaster seemed to follow this temple, the main branch in Tōkyō of Kyōto's Nishi Hon-gan-ji, since it was first located here in 1657: it was destroyed at least five times thereafter, and reconstruction in wood was finally abandoned after the Great Kantō Earthquake of 1923. The present stone building dates from 1935. It was designed by Chūta Ito, a pupil of Tatsuno Kingo, who built Tōkyō Station. Ito's other credits include the Meiji Shrine in Harajuku; he also lobbied for Japan's first law for the preservation of historic buildings. Ito traveled extensively in Asia; the evocations of clas-sical Hindu architecture in the temple's domes and ornaments were his homage to India as the cradle of Buddhism. But with stained-glass win-dows and a pipe organ as well, the building is nothing if not eclectic. ⊠ *3–15–1 Tsukiji, Chūō-ku* ☎ *03/3541–1131* ⊟ *Free* ⊙ *Daily 6–4* Ⓜ *Hi-biya subway line, Tsukiji Station (Exit 1).*

need a break? **Edo-Gin** (江戸銀), one of the area's older sushi bars, founded in 1924, is legendary for its portions—slices of raw fish that almost hide the balls of rice on which they sit. Dinner is pricey, but the set menu at lunch is a certifiable *bāgen* (bargain) at ¥1,000. Walk southwest on Shin-Ōhashi-dōri from its intersection with Harumi-dōri. Take the first right and look for Edo-Gin just past the next corner, on the left. ⊠ *4–5–1 Tsukiji, Chūō-ku* ☎ *03/3543–4401* ⊟ *AE, MC, V* ⊙ *Closed early Jan.* Ⓜ *Hibiya subway line, Tsukiji Station (Exit 1); Ōedo subway line, Tsukiji-shijō Station (Exit A1).*

Nihombashi, Ginza & Yūraku-chō   日本橋・銀座・有楽町

Tōkyō is a city of many centers. The municipal administrative center is in Shinjuku. The national government center is in Kasumigaseki. For almost 350 years Japan was ruled from Edo Castle, and the great stone ramparts still define—for travelers, at least—the heart of the city. His-tory, entertainment, fashion, traditional culture: every tail you could want to pin on the donkey goes in a different spot. Geographically speaking, however, there's one and only one center of Tōkyō: a tall, black, iron pole on the north side of Nihombashi—and if the tail you were hold-ing represented high finance, you would have to pin that one right here as well.

When Ieyasu Tokugawa had the first bridge constructed at Nihom-bashi, he designated it the starting point for the five great roads lead-ing out of his city, the point from which all distances were to be measured. His decree is still in force: the black pole on the present bridge, erected in 1911, is the Zero Kilometer marker for all the national highways.

In the early days of the Tokugawa Shogunate, Edo had no port; almost everything the city needed was shipped here. The bay shore was marshy and full of tidal flats, so heavily laden ships would come only as far as Shinagawa, a few miles down the coast, and unload to smaller vessels. These in turn would take the cargo into the city through a network of canals to wharves and warehouses at Nihombashi. The bridge and the area south and east became a wholesale distribution center, not only for manufactured goods but also for foodstuffs. The city's first fish market, in fact, was established at Nihombashi in 1628 and remained here until the Great Earthquake of 1923.

All through the Edo period, this area was part of Shitamachi. Except for a few blocks between Nihombashi and Kyō-bashi, where the city's deputy magistrates had their villas, it belonged to the common people— not all of whom lived elbow to elbow in poverty. There were fortunes to be made in the markets, and the early millionaires of Edo built their homes in the Nihombashi area. Some, like the legendary timber magnate Bunzaemon Kinokuniya, spent everything they made in the pleasure quarters of Yoshiwara and died penniless. Others founded the great trading houses of today—Mitsui, Mitsubishi, Sumitomo—which still have warehouses nearby.

It was appropriate, then, that when Japan's first corporations were created and the Meiji government developed a modern system of capital formation, the Tōkyō Stock Exchange (Shōken Torihikijo) would go up on the west bank of the Nihombashi-gawa (Nihombashi River). A stone's throw from the exchange now are the home offices of most of the country's major securities companies, which in the hyperinflated bubble economy of the 1980s and early '90s were moving billions of yen around the world electronically—a far cry from the early years of high finance, when the length of a trading day was determined by a section of rope burning on the floor of the exchange. Trading finished when the rope had smoldered down to the end.

A little farther west, money—the problems of making it and of moving it around—shaped the area in a somewhat different way. In the Edo period there were three types of currency in circulation: gold, silver, and copper, each with its various denominations. Determined to unify the system, Ieyasu Tokugawa started minting his own silver coins in 1598 in his home province of Suruga, even before he became shōgun. In 1601 he established a gold mint; the building was only a few hundred yards from Nihombashi, on the site of what is now the Bank of Japan. In 1612 he relocated the Suruga plant to a patch of reclaimed land west of his castle. The area soon came to be known informally as Ginza (Silver Mint).

The value of these various currencies fluctuated. There were profits to be made in the changing of money, and this business eventually came under the control of a few large merchant houses. One of the most successful of these merchants was a man named Takatoshi Mitsui, who had a dry-goods shop in Kyōto and opened a branch in Edo in 1673. The shop, called Echigo-ya, was just north of Nihombashi. By the end of the 17th century it was the base of a commercial empire—in retailing, banking, and trading—known today as the Mitsui Group. Not far from the site of Echigo-ya stands its direct descendant: Mitsukoshi department store.

"*Rui wa tomo wo yobu*" goes the Japanese expression: "like calls to like." From Nihombashi through Ginza to Shimbashi is the domain of all the noble houses that trace their ancestry back to the dry-goods and kimono shops of the Edo period: Mitsukoshi, Takashimaya, Matsuzakaya, Matsuya. All are intensely proud of being at the top of the retail business, as purveyors of an astonishing range of goods and services.

The district called Yūraku-chō lies west of Ginza's Sukiya-bashi, stretching from Sotobori-dōri to Hibiya Kōen and the Outer Garden of the Imperial Palace. The name derives from one Urakusai Oda, younger brother of the warlord who had once been Ieyasu Tokugawa's commander. Urakusai, a Tea Master of some note (he was a student of Sen no Rikyū, who developed the tea ceremony) had a town house here, beneath the castle ramparts, on land reclaimed from the tidal flats of the bay. He soon left Edo for the more refined comforts of Kyōto, but his name stayed behind, becoming Yūraku-chō—the Pleasure (*yūraku*) Quarter (*chō*)—in the process. Sukiya-bashi was the name of the long-gone bridge near Urakusai's villa that led over the moat to the Silver Mint.

The "pleasures" associated with this district in the early postwar period stemmed from the fact that a number of the buildings here survived the air raids of 1945 and were requisitioned by the Allied forces. Yūraku-chō quickly became the haunt of the so-called *pan-pan* women, who provided the GIs with female company. Because it was so close to the military post exchange in Ginza, the area under the railroad tracks became one of the city's largest black markets. Later, the black market gave way to clusters of cheap restaurants, most of them little more than counters and a few stools, serving yakitori and beer. Office workers on meager budgets and journalists from the nearby *Mainichi, Asahi,* and *Yomiuri* newspaper headquarters would gather here at night. Yūraku-chō-under-the-tracks was smoky, loud, and friendly—a kind of open-air substitute for the local taproom. The area has long since become upscale, and no more than a handful of the yakitori stalls remains.

Numbers in the text correspond to numbers in the margin and on the Nihombashi, Ginza, and Yūraku-chō map.

a good walk

For more information on department stores and individual shops mentioned in this walk, *see* Shopping, *below.*

Begin at Tōkyō Station. Take the Yaesu Central Exit on the east side of the building, cross the broad avenue in front of you (Sotobori-dōri), and turn left. Walk north until you cross a bridge under the Shuto Express

NIHOMBASHI way and turn right at the second corner, at the **Bank of Japan** ❶ ▐ . From here walk east two blocks to the main intersection at Chūō-dōri. On your left is the Mitsui Bank, and on your right is **Mitsukoshi** ❷ department store. The small area around the store, formerly called Suruga-chō, is the birthplace of the Mitsui conglomerate.

Turn right on Chūō-dōri. As you walk south, you can see on the left a shop founded in 1849, called Yamamoto Noriten, which specializes in *nori*, the ubiquitous dried seaweed used to wrap *maki* (sushi rolls) and *onigiri* (rice balls); nori was once the most famous product of Tōkyō Bay.

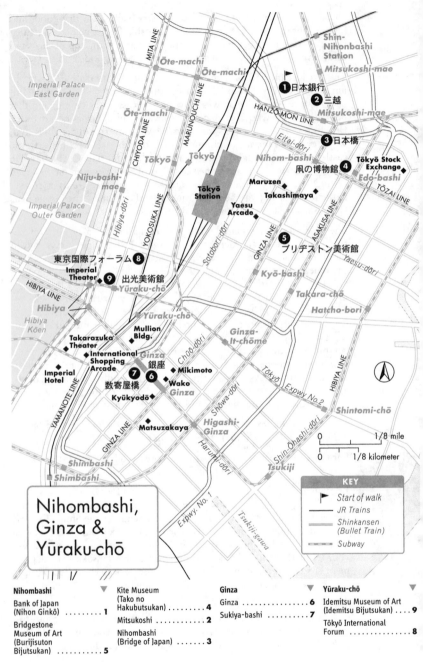

Imperial Palace East Garden

MITA LINE

Ōte-machi

Ōte-machi

Shin-Nihonbashi Station

Mitsukoshi-mae

MARUNOUCHI LINE

CHIYODA LINE

Ōte-machi

❶日本銀行

❷三越

HANZO-MON LINE

Mitsukoshi-mae

Eitai-dōri

❸日本橋

Niju-bashi-mae

Tōkyō

Tōkyō

Nihom-bashi

❹ 凧の博物館

Tōkyō Stock Exchange

Edo-bashi

TŌZAI LINE

Imperial Palace Outer Garden

Hibiya-dōri

YOKOSUKA LINE

Tōkyō Station

Maruzen

Takashimaya

Yaesu Arcade

Sotobori-dōri

ASAKUSA LINE

GINZA LINE

Yaesu-dōri

❺ ブリヂストン美術館

東京国際フォーラム ❽

HIBIYA LINE

Imperial Theater

❾ 出光美術館

Yūraku-chō

Kyō-bashi

Yūraku-chō

Hibiya

Hibiya Kōen

Yūraku-chō

Takara-chō

Hatcho-bori

Mullion Bldg.

Ginza-It-chōme

Takarazuka Theater

International Shopping Arcade

Chūō-dōri

Ginza

銀座

TŌKYŌ Expwy No. 2

HIBIYA LINE

YAMANOTE LINE

Imperial Hotel

❼

❻

数寄屋橋

Mikimoto

Wako

Ginza

Shintomi-chō

GINZA LINE

Kyūkyodō

Shōwa-dōri

Higashi-Ginza

Shin-Ōhashi-dōri

Matsuzakaya

Haru̅mi-dōri

Tsukiji

0 _____ 1/8 mile

0 _____ 1/8 kilometer

Shimbashi

Shimbashi

KEY

▶ Start of walk

— JR Trains

Shinkansen (Bullet Train)

▭ Subway

Tsukiji-gawa

Expwy. No. 1

Nihombashi, Ginza & Yūraku-chō

At the end of the next block is **Nihombashi** ❸ (this is the name of the bridge itself, as well as the neighborhood), shaken but not stirred by the incessant rumbling of the expressway overhead. Before you cross the bridge, notice on your left the small statue of a sea princess seated by a pine tree: a monument to the fish market that stood here before the 1923 quake. To the right is the Zero Kilometer marker, from which all highway distances are measured. On the other side, also to the right, is a plaque depicting the old wooden bridge. In the Edo period the south end of the bridge was set aside for posting public announcements—and for displaying the heads of criminals.

Turn left as soon as you cross the bridge and walk past the Nomura Securities Building to where the expressway loops overhead and turns south. This area is called Kabuto-chō, after the small Kabuto Jinja (Kabuto Shrine, 兜神社) here on the left, under the loop. Across the street from the shrine is the Tōkyō Stock Exchange.

At the main entrance to the Stock Exchange, turn right. Walk south two blocks to the intersection at Eitai-dōri and turn right again. Walk west on Eitai-dōri, turn right onto Shōwa-dōri, and then make a left onto the first small street behind the Bank of Hiroshima. Just off the next corner is a restaurant called Taimeiken. On the fifth floor of this building is the delightful little **Kite Museum** ❹—well worth the detour for visitors of all ages.

Retrace your steps to Eitai-dōri, continue west, and turn left onto Chūō-dōri. One block south, on the left, is Takashimaya department store; on the right is Maruzen, one of Japan's largest booksellers.

Look right at the next intersection; you can see that you've come back almost to Tōkyō Station. Below the avenue from here to the station runs the Yaesu Underground Arcade, with hundreds of shops and restaurants. The whole area here, west of Chūō-dōri, was named after Jan Joosten, a Dutch sailor who was shipwrecked on the coast of Kyūshū with William Adams—hero of James Clavell's novel *Shōgun*—in 1600. Like Adams, Joosten became an adviser to Ieyasu Tokugawa, took a Japanese wife, and was given a villa near the castle. "Yaesu" (originally Yayosu) was as close as the Japanese could come to the pronunciation of his name. Adams, an Englishman, lived out his life in Japan; Joosten drowned off the coast of Indonesia while attempting to return home.

On the southeast corner of the intersection is the **Bridgestone Museum of Art** ❺, one of Japan's best private collections of early modern painting and sculpture, both Western and Japanese.

GINZA   Consider your feet. By now they may be telling you that you'd really rather not walk to the next point on this excursion. If so, get on the Ginza Line—there's a subway entrance right in front of the Bridgestone Museum of Art—and ride one stop to **Ginza** ❻. Take any exit directing you to the 4-chōme intersection (yon-*chō*-me kō-sa-ten). When you come up to the street level, orient yourself by the Ginza branch of the Mitsukoshi department store, on the northeast corner, and the round Sanai Building on the southwest.

From Ginza 4-chōme, walk northwest on Harumi-dōri in the direction of the Imperial Palace. From Chūō-dōri to the intersection called **Sukiya-bashi ❼**, named for a bridge that once stood here, your exploration should be free-form: the side streets and north–south parallel streets are ideal for wandering, particularly if you're interested in art galleries—of which there are 300 or more in this part of Ginza.

YŪRAKU-CHŌ
有楽町 From the Sukiya-bashi intersection, walk northwest on the right side of Harumi-dōri. Pass the curved facade of the Mullion Building department store complex and cross the intersection. After passing through the tunnel under the JR Yamanote Line tracks, turn right. Walk two long blocks east, parallel to the tracks, until you come to the gleaming white expanse of the **Tōkyō International Forum ❽**. You can relax in the open space of the Forum's plaza and perhaps grab a pastry and coffee at Café Wien, next to the Plaza Information Center.

From the southwest corner of the Forum, turn left and walk halfway down the block to the main entrance of the International Building, which houses the **Idemitsu Museum of Art ❾** on the ninth floor. After a stop inside, continue west along the side of the International Building toward the Imperial Palace to Hibiya-dōri. Turn left; less than a minute's walk along Hibiya-dōri will bring you to the Dai-ichi Mutual Life Insurance Company Building (第一生命館), which survived World War II intact; General Douglas MacArthur directed the affairs of Japan from 1945 to 1951 in an office here. Across the avenue is the pleasant Hibiya Kōen, Japan's first Western-style public park, which dates to 1903. Press on, past the Hibiya police station, across the Harumi-dōri intersection; at the second corner, just before you come to the Imperial Hotel, turn left.

At the end of the block, on the corner, is the Takarazuka Theater, where all-female casts take the art of musical review to the highest levels of camp. Continue southeast, and on the next block, on both sides of the street (just under the railroad bridge), are entrances to the International Shopping Arcade. Stores here sell kimonos and happi coats, pearls and cloisonné, prints, cameras, and consumer electronics: one-stop shopping for presents and souvenirs.

Turn left down the narrow side street that runs along the side of the arcade to the Hankyū department store and you can find yourself back on Harumi-dōri, just a few steps from the Sukiya-bashi crossing. From here you can return to your hotel by subway, or a minute's walk will bring you to JR Yūraku-chō Station.

TIMING There's something about this part of Tōkyō—the traffic, the number of people, the way it exhorts you to keep moving—that can make you feel you've covered a lot more ground than you really have. Take this walk in the morning; when you're done, you can better assess the energy you have left for the rest of the day. None of the stops along the way, with the possible exception of the Bridgestone and Idemitsu museums, should take you more than 45 minutes. The time you spend shopping, of course, is up to you. In summer make a point of starting early, even though many stores and attractions don't open until 10 or 11: by midday the heat and humidity can be brutal. On weekend afternoons (October–March, Saturday 3–5 and Sunday noon–5; April–September, Saturday 2–6 and Sunday noon–6), Chūō-dōri is closed to traffic from Shimbashi all the way to Kyō-bashi and becomes a pedestrian mall with tables and chairs set out along the street. Keep in mind that some of the museums and other sights in the area close on Sunday.

What to See

❶ Bank of Japan (Nihon Ginkō, 日本銀行). The older part of the Bank of Japan is the work of Tatsuno Kingo, who also designed Tōkyō Station. Completed in 1896, on the site of what had been the Edo-period gold mint, the bank is one of the few surviving Meiji-era Western buildings in the city. The annex building houses the **Currency Museum,** a historical collection of rare gold and silver coins from Japan and other East Asian countries. There's little English information here, but the setting of muted lighting and plush red carpets evokes the days when the only kind of money around was the kind you could heft in your hand. ✉ 2–1–1 Nihombashi Hongoku-chō, Chūō-ku ☎ 03/3279–1111 bank, 03/3277–3037 museum ⊕ www.boj.or.jp/en ☜ Free ✆ Museum Tues.–Sun. 9:30–4:30 Ⓜ Ginza (Exit A5) and Hanzō-mon (Exit B1) subway lines, Mitsukoshi-mae Station.

❺ Bridgestone Museum of Art (Burijisuton Bijutsukan, ブリヂストン美術館). This is one of Japan's best private collections of French impressionist art and sculpture and of post-Meiji Japanese painting in Western styles by such artists as Shigeru Aoki and Tsuguji Fujita. The collection, assembled by Bridgestone Tire Company founder Shōjiro Ishibashi, also includes work by Rembrandt, Picasso, Utrillo, and Modigliani. The small gallery devoted to ancient art has a breathtaking Egyptian cat sculpture dating to between 950 and 660 BC. The Bridgestone also puts on major exhibits from private collections and museums abroad. ✉ 1–10–1 Kyō-bashi, Chūō-ku ☎ 03/3563–0241 ⊕ www.bridgestone-museum.gr.jp/e/ ☜ ¥700 ✆ Tues.–Sat. 10–8, Sun. 10–6 Ⓜ Ginza subway line, Kyō-bashi Station (Meijiya Exit) or Nihombashi Station (Takashimaya Exit).

❻ Ginza (銀座). Ieyasu's Silver Mint moved out of this area in 1800. The name Ginza remained, but only much later did it begin to acquire any cachet for wealth and style. The turning point was 1872, when a fire destroyed most of the old houses here. The main street of Ginza, together with a grid of parallel and cross streets, was rebuilt as a Western quarter. It had two-story brick houses with balconies, the nation's first sidewalks and horse-drawn streetcars, gaslights, and, later, telephone poles. Before the turn of the 20th century, Ginza was already home to the great mercantile establishments that still define its character. The **Wako** (和光) department store, for example, on the northwest corner of the 4-chōme intersection, established itself here as Hattori, purveyors of clocks and watches. The clock on the present building was first installed in the Hattori clock tower, a Ginza landmark, in 1894.

Many of the nearby shops have lineages almost as old, or older, than Wako's. A few steps north of the intersection, on Chūō-dōri, **Mikimoto** sells the famous cultured pearls first developed by Kokichi Mikimoto in 1883. His first shop in Tōkyō dates to 1899. South of the intersection, next door to the Sanai Building, **Kyūkyodō** (鳩居堂) carries a variety of handmade Japanese papers and related goods. Kyūkyodō has been in business since 1663 and on Ginza since 1880. Across the street and one block south is the **Matsuzakaya** (松坂屋) department store, which began as a kimono shop in Nagoya in 1611.

There's even a name for browsing this area: Gin-bura, or "Ginza wandering." The best times to wander here are Saturday afternoons and Sunday from noon to 5 or 6 (depending on the season), when Chūō-dōri is closed to traffic between Shimbashi and Kyō-bashi. ⊠ *Chūō-ku* Ⓜ *Ginza and Hibiya subway lines, Ginza Station.*

★ ❾ **Idemitsu Museum of Art** (Idemitsu Bijutsukan, 出光美術館). The strength of the collection in these four spacious, well-designed rooms lies in the Tang- and Song-dynasty Chinese porcelain and in the Japanese ceramics—including works by Nonomura Ninsei and Ōgata Kenzan. On display are masterpieces of Old Seto, Oribe, Old Kutani, Karatsu, and Kakiemon ware. The museum also houses outstanding examples of Zen painting and calligraphy, wood-block prints, and genre paintings of the Edo period. Of special interest to scholars is the resource collection of shards from virtually every pottery-making culture of the ancient world. The museum is on the ninth floor of the Teikoku Gekijō building. ⊠ *3–1–1 Marunouchi, Chiyoda-ku* ☎ *03/3213–9402* ⚏ *¥800* ⊙ *Tues.–Sun. 10–4:30* Ⓜ *Yūraku-chō subway line, Yūraku-chō Station (Exit A1).*

☾ ❹ **Kite Museum** (Tako no Hakubutsukan, 凧の博物館). Kite flying is an old tradition in Japan. The collection here includes examples of every shape and variety of kite from all over the country, hand-painted in brilliant colors with figures of birds, geometric patterns, and motifs from Chinese and Japanese mythology. You can call ahead to arrange a kite-making workshop (in Japanese) for groups of children. ⊠ *1–12–10 Nihombashi, Chūō-ku* ☎ *03/3271–2465* ⊕ *www.tako.gr.jp* ⚏ *¥210* ⊙ *Mon.–Sat. 11–5* Ⓜ *Tōzai subway line, Nihombashi Station (Exit C5).*

❷ **Mitsukoshi** (三越). Takatoshi Mitsui made his fortune by revolutionizing the retail system for kimono fabrics. The drapers of his day usually did business on account, taking payments semiannually. In his store (then called Echigo-ya), Mitsui started the practice of unit pricing, and his customers paid cash on the spot. As time went on, the store was always ready to adapt to changing needs and merchandising styles: garments made to order, home delivery, imported goods, and even—as the 20th century opened and Echigo-ya changed its name to Mitsukoshi—the hiring of women to the sales force. The emergence of Mitsukoshi as Tōkyō's first *depāto* (department store), also called *hyakkaten* (hundred-kinds-of-goods emporium), actually dates to 1908, with the construction of a three-story Western building modeled on Harrods of London. This was replaced in 1914 by a five-story structure with Japan's first escalator. The present flagship store is vintage 1935. Even if you don't plan to shop, this branch merits a visit. Two bronze lions, modeled on those at London's Trafalgar Square, flank the main entrance and serve as one of Tōkyō's best-known meeting places. Inside, a sublime statue of Magokoro, a Japanese goddess of sincerity, rises four stories through the store's central atrium. ⊠ *1–4–1 Nihombashi Muromachi, Chūō-ku* ☎ *03/ 3241–3311* ◷ *Daily 10–7:30* Ⓜ *Ginza and Hanzō-mon subway lines, Mitsukoshi-mae Station (Exits A3 and A5).*

❸ Nihombashi (Bridge of Japan, 日本橋). Why the expressway *had* to be routed directly over this lovely old landmark back in 1962 is one of the mysteries of Tōkyō and its city planning—or lack thereof. There were protests and petitions, but they had no effect. At that time Tōkyō had only two years left to prepare for the Olympics, and the traffic congestion was already out of control. So the bridge, with its graceful double arch, ornate lamps, and bronze Chinese lions and unicorns, was doomed to bear the perpetual rumble of trucks overhead—its claims overruled by concrete ramps and pillars. ⊠ *Chūō-ku* Ⓜ *Tōzai and Ginza subway lines, Nihombashi Station (Exits B5 and B6); Ginza and Hanzō-mon subway lines, Mitsukoshi-mae Station (Exits B5 and B6).*

❼ Sukiya-bashi (数寄屋橋). The side streets of the Sukiya-bashi area are full of art galleries, which operate a bit differently here than they do in most of the world's art markets. A few, like the venerable **Nichidō** (日動画廊; 5–3–16 Ginza), **Gekkōsō** (月光荘; 7–2–8 Ginza), **Yoseidō** (養清堂画廊; 5–5–15 Ginza, and **Kabuto-ya** (兜屋画廊; 8–8–7 Ginza), actually function as dealers, representing particular artists, as well as acquiring and selling art. The majority, however, are rental spaces. Artists or groups pay for the gallery by the week, publicize their shows themselves, and in some cases even hang their own work. It's not unreasonable to suspect that a lot of these shows, even in so prestigious a venue as Ginza, are vanity exhibitions by amateurs with money to spare—but that's not always the case. The rental spaces are also the only way for serious professionals, independent of the various art organizations that might otherwise sponsor their work, to get any critical attention; if they're lucky, they can at least recoup their expenses with an occasional sale. ⊠ *Chiyoda-ku* Ⓜ *Ginza, Hibiya, and Marunouchi subway lines, Ginza Station (Exit C4).*

❽ Tōkyō International Forum (東京国際フォーラム). This postmodern masterpiece, the work of Uruguay-born American architect Raphael Viñoly, is the first major convention and art center of its kind in Tōkyō. Viñoly's design was selected in a 1989 competition that drew nearly 400 entries from 50 countries. The plaza of the Forum is that rarest of Tōkyō rarities, civilized open space: a long, tree-shaded central courtyard with comfortable benches. Freestanding sculpture, triumphant architecture, and people strolling—actually *strolling*—past in both directions are all here. The Forum itself is really two buildings. On the east side of the plaza is Glass Hall, the main exhibition space—an atrium with an 180-ft ceiling, a magnificent curved wooden wall, and 34 upper-floor conference rooms. The west building has six halls for international conferences, exhibitions, receptions, and concert performances—the largest with seating for 5,012. ⊠ *3–5–1 Marunouchi, Chiyoda-ku* ☎ *03/5221–9000* ⊕ *www.t-i-forum.co.jp/english* Ⓜ *Yūraku-chō subway line, Yūraku-chō Station (Exit A-4B).*

need a break?

Amid all of Tōkyō's bustle and crush, you actually can catch your breath in the open space of the plaza of the Tōkyō International Forum. If you also feel like having coffee and a bite of pastry, stop in at **Café Wien** (カフェ・ウィーン), next to the Plaza Information Center. ✉ *3–5–1 Marunouchi, Chiyoda-ku* ☎ *03/3211–3111* ⏱ *Daily 10 AM–10 PM* Ⓜ *Yūraku-chō subway line, Yūraku-chō Station (Exit A-4B).*

Aoyama & Harajuku 青山・原宿

Who would have known? As late as 1960 this was as unlikely a candidate as any area in Tōkyō to develop into anything remotely chic. True, there was the Meiji Shrine, which gave the neighborhood a certain solemnity and drew the occasional festival crowd. Between the shrine and the Aoyama Cemetery to the east, however, the area was so unpromising that the municipal government designated a substantial chunk of it for low-cost public housing. Another chunk, called Washington Heights, was being used by U.S. occupation forces—who spent their money elsewhere. The few young Japanese people in Harajuku and Aoyama were either hanging around Washington Heights to practice their English or attending the Methodist-founded Aoyama Gakuin (Aoyama University)—and seeking their leisure farther south in Shibuya.

Then Tōkyō won its bid to host the 1964 Olympics, and Washington Heights was turned over to the city for the construction of Olympic Village. Aoyama-dōri, the avenue through the center of the area, was improved. Under it ran the extension of the Ginza Line subway and later the Hanzō-mon Line. Public transportation is the chief ingredient in Tōkyō's commercial alchemy: suddenly, people could get to Aoyama and Harajuku easily, and they did—in larger and larger numbers, drawn by the Western-style fashion houses, boutiques, and design studios that decided this was the place to be. By the 1980s the area was positively *smart*. Today most of the older buildings along Omotesandō, many of them put up originally as low-cost public housing, are long gone, and in their place are the glass-and-marble emporia of *the* preeminent fashion houses of Europe: Louis Vuitton, Chanel, Armani, and the like. Their showrooms here are the Japanese cash cows of their worldwide empires.

Numbers in the text correspond to numbers in the margin and on the Aoyama & Harajuku map.

a good walk

For more information on department stores and individual shops mentioned in this walk, *see* Shopping, *below.*

Begin outside of the Gaien-mae subway station on Aoyama-dōri. This is also the stop for the Jingū Baseball Stadium, home field of the Yakult Swallows. You can see it across the street from the Chichibu-no-miya Rugby and Football Ground. The stadium is actually within the **Meiji Shrine Outer Gardens** ❶ ▶. The National Stadium—Japan's largest sta-

AOYAMA 青山

THE TEENYBOPPER SHOPPERS OF HARAJUKU

On weekends, the heart of Harajuku, particularly the street called Takeshita-dōri, belongs to high school and junior high school shoppers, who flock here with hoarded sums of pocket money and for whom last week was ancient history. Harajuku is where market researchers come, pick 20 teenagers off the street at random, give them ¥2,000, and ask them to buy a tote bag. Whole industries convulse themselves to keep pace with those adolescent decisions. Stroll through

Harajuku—with its outdoor cafés, its designer-ice-cream and Belgian-waffle stands, its profusion of stores with names like Rap City and Octopus Army, its ever-changing profusion of mascots and logos—and you may find it impossible to believe that Japan is in fact the most rapidly aging society in the industrial world.

dium, with room for 75,000 people, and the seat from which the city hosted the 1964 Summer Olympics—sits on the other side of this park.

From Gaien-mae, walk west some five blocks toward Shibuya (渋谷), and turn left at the intersection where you see the Omotesandō subway station on the right-hand side of the avenue. Hold tight to your credit cards here: this is the east end of Omotesandō, Tōkyō's premier fashion boulevard, lined on both sides with the boutiques of couturiers like Issey Miyake, Missoni, Calvin Klein, and Comme des Garçons. Midway along the avenue is the quirky, high-tech (to some critics, even fetishistic) Tōkyō showroom of the Prada fashion house, built by Swiss-based architects Jacques Herzog and Pierre de Meuron. At the far end of the street (a 15-minute walk at a brisk pace), across the intersection to the right, you can see the walls of the **Nezu Institute of Fine Arts ❷**.

From the Nezu Institute of Fine Arts, retrace your steps to Aoyama-dōri. If you turned left here, you would come in due course (it's a longish walk) to Shibuya, by way of the Aoyama Gakuin University campus on the left. To make your way to Harajuku, continue straight across Aoyama-dōri northwest on Omotesandō.

HARAJUKU North of Aoyama-dōri, Omotesandō becomes a broad divided boulevard lined with ginko trees, sloping gently downhill to the intersection with Meiji-dōri and to the neighborhood of Harajuku. Upscale brands have laid claim to the higher ground of the boulevard, but the commercial pulse of this area beats faster in the maze of side streets and alleys off to the left (south side) of Omotesandō; here, the hole-in-the-wall boutiques of hundreds of domestic designers cater to a young market. Japan's adolescents may have less to spend than a couturier's clientele, but they still take their apprenticeship as consumers very seriously.

On the left side of the boulevard as you approach the Meiji-dōri intersection is the Oriental Bazaar, a store especially popular with foreign

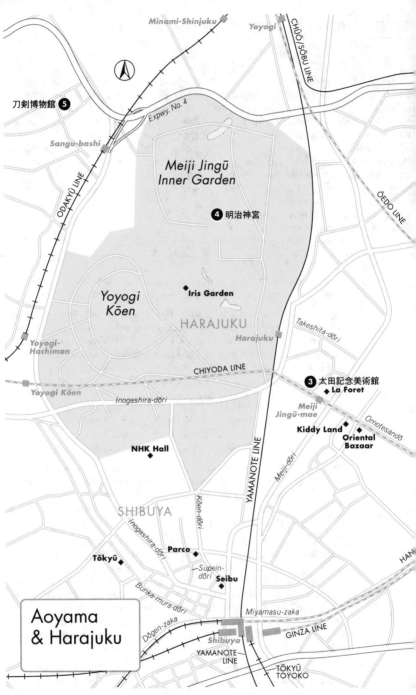

Minami-Shinjuku

Yoyogi

CHŪŌ/SŌBU LINE

刀剣博物館 **5**

Expwy. No. 4

Sangu-bashi

ŌDEO LINE

Meiji Jingū Inner Garden

4 明治神宮

ODAKYŪ LINE

◆ Iris Garden

Yoyogi Kōen

HARAJUKU

Yoyogi-Hachiman

Harajuku ◼

Takeshita-dōri

CHIYODA LINE

Yoyogi Kōen

3 太田記念美術館
◆ La Foret

Inogashira-dōri

Meiji Jingū-mae

Omotesandō

Kiddy Land ◆

◆ Oriental Bazaar

YAMANOTE LINE

Meiji-dōri

NHK Hall ◆

SHIBUYA

Kōen-dōri

Inogashira-dōri

Parco ◆

Tōkyū ◆

Supein-dōri

Seibu ◆

Bunka-mura-dōri

HAN

Miyamasu-zaka

Aoyama & Harajuku

Dōgen-zaka

Shibuya ◼

GINZA LINE

YAMANOTE LINE

TŌKYŪ TOYOKO

visitors for its extensive stock of Japanese, Korean, and Chinese souvenirs at reasonable prices; browse here for scroll paintings and screens, kimono fabrics, antiques, ceramics, and lacquerware. A few doors down is Kiddy Land, one of the city's largest toy stores. On the northwest corner of the intersection itself is La Foret. With some 110 boutiques on five floors, this was one of the earliest of Tōkyō's characteristic vertical malls.

Here you might want to make a brief detour to the right on Meiji-dōri and left at the corner of the third narrow side street, called Takeshita-dōri, which rises to JR Harajuku Station at the other end. This is where the youngest of Harajuku's consumers gather from all over Tōkyō and the nearby prefectures, packing the street from side to side and end to end, filling the coffers of countless faddish shops. If Japanese parents ever pause to wonder where their offspring might be on a Saturday afternoon, Takeshita-dōri is the likely answer.

Retrace your steps to La Foret, turn right, and walk uphill on the right side of Omotesandō to the first corner. Turn right again, and a few steps from the corner on this small street you can find the **Ōta Memorial Museum of Art** ❸—an unlikely setting for an important collection of traditional wood-block prints. Return to Omotesandō and walk up (northwest) to the intersection at the top. Across the street to your right look for JR Harajuku Station; straight ahead are the entrance to the Meiji Shrine Inner Garden and the **Meiji Shrine** ❹ itself.

When you finish exploring the grounds of the shrine, you have two options. You can leave the Inner Garden on the northwest side and walk west about five minutes from Sangū-bashi Station along the private Odakyū railway line to the **Japanese Sword Museum** ❺ to see its collection of swords. From there you can return to Sangū-bashi Station and take the train two stops north to Shinjuku, the next major exploring section.

TIMING Aoyama and Harajuku together make a long walk, with considerable distances between the sights. Ideally, you should devote an entire day to these two areas, giving yourself plenty of time to browse in shops. You can see Meiji Shrine in less than an hour; the Nezu Institute warrants a leisurely two-hour visit. Don't be afraid to visit on weekends; there are more people on the streets, of course, but people-watching is a large part of the experience of Harajuku. Spring is the best time of year for the Meiji Shrine's Inner Garden. As with any other walk in Tōkyō, the June rainy season is horrendous, and the humid heat of midsummer can quickly drain your energy and add hours to the time you need for a comfortable walk.

What to See

★ ❺ **Japanese Sword Museum** (Tōken Hakubutsukan, 刀剣博物館). It's said that in the late 16th century, before Japan closed its doors to the West, the Spanish tried to establish a trade here in weapons of their famous Toledo steel. The Japanese were politely uninterested; they had been making blades of incomparably better quality for more than 600 years. Early Japanese swordsmiths learned the art of refining steel from a pure iron sand called *tamahagane,* carefully controlling the carbon content by adding straw to the fire in the forge. The block of steel was repeatedly folded, hammered, and cross-welded to an extraordinary strength, then "wrapped" around a core of softer steel for flexibility. At one time there were some 200 schools of sword making in Japan; swords were prized not only for their effectiveness in battle but for the beauty of the blades and fittings and as symbols of the higher spirituality of the warrior caste. There are few inheritors of this art today. The Japanese Sword Museum offers a unique opportunity to see the works of noted swordsmiths, ancient and modern—but don't expect any detailed explanations of them in English. ⊠ *4–25–10 Yoyogi, Shibuya-ku* ☎ *03/3379–1386* 💴 *¥525* ⏱ *Tues.–Sun. 10–4:30* Ⓜ *Odakyū private rail line, Sangū-bashi Station.*

★ ❹ **Meiji Shrine** (Meiji Jingū, 明治神宮). The Meiji Shrine honors the spirits of Emperor Meiji, who died in 1912, and Empress Shōken. It was established by a resolution of the Imperial Diet the year after the emperor's death to commemorate his role in ending the long isolation of Japan under the Tokugawa Shogunate and setting the country on the road to modernization. Completed in 1920 and virtually destroyed in an air raid in 1945, it was rebuilt in 1958 with funds raised in a nationwide public subscription.

Made from 1,700-year-old cypress trees from Mt. Ari in Taiwan, the two torii at the entrance to the grounds of the shrine rise 40 feet high; the crosspieces are 56 feet long. Torii are meant to symbolize the separation of the everyday secular world from the spiritual world of the Shintō shrine. The buildings in the shrine complex, with their curving green copper roofs, are also made of cypress wood. The surrounding gardens have some 100,000 flowering shrubs and trees, many of which were donated by private citizens.

An annual festival at the shrine takes place on November 3, Emperor Meiji's birthday, which is a national holiday. On the festival day and at New Year's, as many as a million people come to offer prayers and pay their respects. Several other festivals and ceremonial events are held here throughout the year; check by phone or on the shrine Web site to see what's scheduled during your visit. Even on a normal weekend the shrine draws thousands of visitors, but this seldom disturbs its mood of quiet gravitas: the faster and more unpredictable the pace of modern life, the more respectable the Japanese seem to find the certainties of the Meiji era.

The peaceful **Inner Garden** (Jingū Nai-en, 神宮内苑), where the irises are in full bloom in the latter half of June, is on the left as you walk in from the main gates, before you reach the shrine. Beyond the shrine is the **Treasure House** (宝物殿), a repository for the personal effects and clothes of Emperor and Empress Meiji—perhaps of less interest to foreign visitors than to the Japanese. ⊠ *1–1 Kamizono-chō, Yoyogi, Shibuya-ku* ☎ *03/3379–9222* ⊕ *www.meijijingu.or.jp* 💴 *Shrine free, Inner Garden ¥500, Treasure House ¥500* ⏱ *Shrine daily sunrise–sunset; Inner Garden Mar.–Nov., daily 9–4; Treasure House daily 10–4* ⏱ *Closed 3rd Fri. of month* Ⓜ *Chiyoda subway line, Meiji-jingū-mae Station; JR Yamanote Line, Harajuku Station (Exit 2).*

▶ **❶ Meiji Shrine Outer Gardens** (Meiji Jingū Gai-en, 明治神宮外苑). This rare expanse of open space is devoted to outdoor sports of all sorts. The Yakult Swallows play at **Jingū Baseball Stadium** (神宮球場; ⊠ 13 Kasumigaoka, Shinjuku-ku ☎ 03/3404–8999); the Japanese baseball season runs from April to October. The main venue of the 1964 Summer Olympics, **National Stadium** (国立競技場; ⊠ 10 Kasumigaoka, Shinjuku-ku ☎ 03/3403–1151) now hosts soccer matches. Some of the major World Cup matches were played here when Japan co-hosted the event with Korea in autumn 2002. ⊠ *Shinjuku-ku* Ⓜ *Ginza and Hanzō-mon subway lines, Gai-en-mae Station (Exit 2); JR Chūō Line, Shina-no-machi Station.*

❷ Nezu Institute of Fine Arts (Nezu Bijutsukan, 根津美術館). This museum houses the private art collection of Meiji-period railroad magnate and politician Kaichirō Nezu. The permanent display in the main building and the annex includes superb examples of Japanese painting, calligraphy, and ceramics—some of which are registered as National Treasures—plus Chinese bronzes, sculpture, and lacquerware. The institute also has one of Tōkyō's finest gardens, with more than 5 acres of shade trees and flowering shrubs, ponds, and waterfalls, as well as seven tea pavilions. To get here walk southeast on Omotesandō-dōri from the intersection of Aoyama-dōri for about 10 minutes to where the street curves away to the left. The Nezu Institute is opposite the intersection, on the right, behind a low sandstone-gray wall. ⊠ *6–5–1 Minami-Aoyama, Minato-ku* ☎ *03/3400–2536* ⊕ *www.nezu-muse.or.jp/index_e.html* ⊠ *¥1,000* ☉ *Tues.–Sun. 9–4* Ⓜ *Ginza and Hanzō-mon subway lines, Omotesandō Station (Exit A5).*

FodorsChoice
★

need a break?

How can you resist a café with a name like **Yokku Mokku** (ヨックモック)? Tables in the tree-shaded courtyard continue to make this place, which established itself as Japan's primo confectionery just after World War II, an Aoyama favorite. Its blue-tile front is on Omotesandō-dōri near the Nezu Institute. As you approach, you'll probably notice a steady stream of very smartly dressed young people on their way in and out. The café is open daily 10–7. ⊠ *5–3–3 Minami-Aoyama, Shibuya-ku* ☎ *03/5485–3340* Ⓜ *Ginza, Chiyoda, and Hanzō-mon subway lines, Omotesandō Station (Exit A4).*

★ **❸ Ōta Memorial Museum of Art** (Ōta Kinen Bijutsukan, 太田記念美術館). The gift of former Tōhō Mutual Life Insurance chairman Seizō Ōta, this is probably the city's finest private collection of ukiyo-e, traditional Edo-period wood-block prints. *Ukiyo* means "the floating world" of everyday life; *e* (pronounced eh) means "picture." The genre flourished in the 18th and 19th centuries. The works on display are selected and changed periodically from the 12,000 prints in the collection, which includes some extremely rare work by artists such as Hiroshige, Sharaku, and Utamaro. From JR Harajuku Station, walk southwest downhill on Omotesandō-dōri and turn left on the narrow street before the intersection of Meiji-dōri. The museum is less than a minute's walk from the corner, on the left. ⊠ *1–10–10 Jingū-mae, Shibuya-ku* ☎ *03/3403–0880* ⊠ *¥500–¥800, depending on exhibi-*

tion ⊗ Tues.–Sun. 10:30–5; may be closed 1st–4th of the month for new installations, so call ahead.

Shinjuku 新宿

If you have a certain sort of love for big cities, you're bound to love Shinjuku. Come here, and for the first time Tōkyō begins to seem *real*. Shinjuku is where all the celebrated virtues of Japanese society—its safety and order, its grace and beauty, its cleanliness and civility—fray at the edges.

To be fair, the area has been on the fringes of respectability for centuries. When Ieyasu, the first Tokugawa shōgun, made Edo his capital, Shinjuku was at the junction of two important arteries leading into the city from the west. It became a thriving post station, where travelers would rest and refresh themselves for the last leg of their journey; the appeal of this suburban pit stop was its "teahouses," where the waitresses dispensed a good bit more than sympathy with the tea.

When the Tokugawa dynasty collapsed in 1868, 16-year-old Emperor Meiji moved his capital to Edo, renaming it Tōkyō, and modern Shinjuku became the railhead connecting it to Japan's western provinces. As the haunt of artists, writers, and students, it remained on the fringes of respectability; in the 1930s Shinjuku was Tōkyō's bohemian quarter. The area was virtually leveled during the firebombings of 1945—a blank slate on which developers could write, as Tōkyō surged west after the war. By the 1970s property values in Shinjuku were the nation's highest, outstripping even those of Ginza.

Today three subways and seven railway lines converge here. Every day more than 3 million commuters pass through Shinjuku Station, making this the city's busiest and most heavily populated commercial center. The hub at Shinjuku—a vast, interconnected complex of tracks and terminals, department stores and shops—divides the area into two distinctly different subcities, Nishi-Shinjuku (West Shinjuku) and Higashi-Shinjuku (East Shinjuku).

After the Great Kantō Earthquake of 1923, Nishi-Shinjuku was virtually the only part of Tōkyō left standing; the whims of nature had given this one small area a gift of better bedrock. That priceless geological stability remained largely unexploited until the late 1960s, when technological advances in engineering gave architects the freedom to soar. Some 20 skyscrapers have been built here since then, including the Tōkyō Metropolitan Government Office complex, and Nishi-Shinjuku has become Tōkyō's 21st-century administrative center.

By day the quarter east of Shinjuku Station is an astonishing concentration of retail stores, vertical malls, and discounters of every stripe and description. By night it's an equally astonishing collection of bars and clubs, strip joints, hole-in-the-wall restaurants, pinball parlors, and peep shows—just about anything that amuses, arouses, alters, or intoxicates is for sale in Higashi-Shinjuku, if you know where to look. Drunken fistfights are hardly unusual here, and petty theft is not unknown. Not surprisingly, Higashi-Shinjuku has the city's largest—and busiest—police substation.

Numbers in the text correspond to numbers in the margin and on the Shinjuku map.

For more information on department stores and individual shops mentioned in this walk, *see* Shopping, *below.*

a good
walk

NISHI-SHINJUKU

JR trains and subways will drop you off below ground at Shinjuku Station; head for the west exit. You need to get up to the street level in front of the Odakyū department store, with the Keiō department store on your left, to avoid the passageway under the plaza. Walk across the plaza, through the bus terminal, or take the pedestrian bridge on the north side. Traffic in front of the station is rather confusing—what you're looking for is the wide, divided, east–west avenue on the other side, called Chūō-dōri (YON-GŌ GAIRO on some street markers), between the Fuji Bank on the left and the Dai-ichi Kangyō Bank on the right. Walk west on Chūō-dōri one block to the Shinjuku Center Building, cross at the traffic light, and turn right. On the next block is the tapering shape of the Yasuda Fire and Marine Insurance Building; the **Seiji Tōgō Memorial Sompo Japan Museum of Art** ❶ ☞ is on the 42nd floor.

Retrace your steps to Chūō-dōri, turn right, and walk west to where the avenue dead-ends at Kyū-gō Gairo, also called Higashi-dōri. You can see the 52-story Shinjuku Sumitomo Building ahead of you to the right, and to the left the unmistakable shape of the Tōkyō Metropolitan Government Office complex—but you need to make a slight detour to reach it. Cross Kyū-gō Gairo, turn left, and walk south past the front of the Keiō Plaza Inter-Continental, the first of the high-rise hotels to be built in the area, to the next corner.

Across the street you can see the blue phallic shape of the sculpture in front of the Shinjuku Monolith Building. Turn right and walk downhill on Fureai-dōri. In the middle of this next block, on the left, is the Shinjuku NS Building. Opposite the NS Building, to the right, are the steps to the Citizens' Plaza of the adored and reviled **Tōkyō Metropolitan Government Office** ❷.

From here turn east and walk along any of the streets parallel to Chūō-dōri that lead back to Shinjuku Station. You may want to stop (especially if you haven't included Akihabara on your Tōkyō itinerary) at one of the giant discount electronics stores in the area—Yodobashi and Doi are a block from the station—to get an eye- or bagful of the latest gadgets that Japan is churning out.

HIGASHI-
SHINJUKU

From the east exit of Shinjuku Station you can't miss the huge video screen on the facade of Studio Alta. Under this building begins Subnade—the most extensive underground arcade in Tōkyō, full of shops and restaurants. Studio Alta is at the northwest end of Shinjuku-dōri, which on Sunday, when the area is closed to traffic, becomes a sea of shoppers. Turn right, and as you walk southeast, Kinokuniya Bookstore looms up on your left; the sixth floor is devoted to foreign-language books, including some 40,000 titles in English. On the next block, on the same

Shinjuku

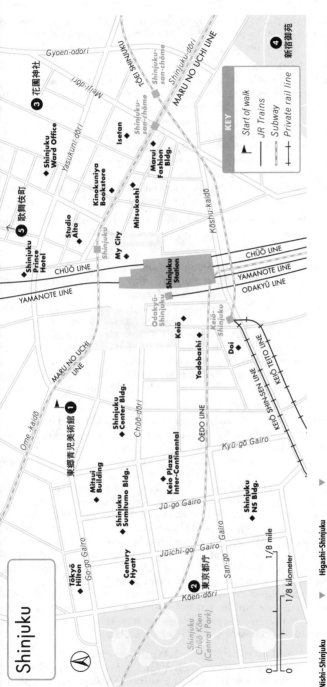

KEY

▲ Start of walk
— JR Trains
— Subway
++ Private rail line

Gyoen-odori

Shinjuku-dōri

TOEI SHINJUKU

MARU NO UCHI LINE

新宿御苑 ❹

❸ 花園神社

Meiji-dōri

Shinjuku-san-chōme

Shinjuku-san-chōme

Shinjuku Ward Office

Yasukuni-dōri

Isetan

Kōshū-kaidō

Marui Fashion Bldg.

歌舞伎町 ❺

Kinokuniya Bookstore

Mitsukoshi

Studio Alta

Shinjuku

My City

Shinjuku Prince Hotel

CHŪŌ LINE

Shinjuku Station

CHŪŌ LINE

YAMANOTE LINE

YAMANOTE LINE

ODAKYŪ LINE

Odakyū-Shinjuku

Keiō-Shinjuku

Keiō

Doi

MARU NO UCHI LINE

Keiō

Yodobashi

KEIŌ SHIN-SEN LINE

KEIŌ TEITO LINE

Ome-kaidō

東郷青児美術館 ❶

Shinjuku Center Bldg.

Chūō-dōri

ŌEDO LINE

Kyū-gō Gairo

Mitsui Building

Shinjuku Sumitomo Bldg.

Keio Plaza Inter-Continental

Jū-go Gairo

Shinjuku NS Bldg.

Tōkyō Hilton

Go-gō Gairo

Century Hyatt

東京都庁 ❷

Jūichi-go Gairo

San-gō Gairo

Kōen-dōri

Shinjuku Chūō Kōen (Central Park)

0   1/8 mile
0   1/8 kilometer

▶ **Nishi-Shinjuku**
Seiji Tōgō Memorial
Sompo Japan Museum of Art
(Sompo Japan Tōgō
Seiji Bijutsukan) **1**

Tōkyō Metropolitan
Government Office
(Tōkyō Tochō) **2**

▶ **Higashi-Shinjuku**
Hanazono Jinja
(Hanazono Shrine) **3**
Kabuki-chō **5**

Shinjuku Gyo-en
National Garden **4**

side of the street, is Isetan department store, with a foreign customer-service counter on the fifth floor. Mitsukoshi department store and the Marui Fashion Building are on the opposite side of Shinjuk-dōri.

At the Isetan corner, turn left onto Meiji-dōri and walk north. Cross Yasukuni-dōri and walk for another minute until you reach **Hanazono Jinja ③**. From here you can head in two different directions—indeed, to two different worlds. You can retrace your steps to Isetan department store and the Shinjuku-san-chōme subway station, and take the Marunouchi Line one stop east to Shinjuku-Gyo-en-mae, a few steps from the north end of **Shinjuku Gyo-en National Garden ④**. Visit the gardens and take the subway back to Shinjuku Station. Another option is to walk back from Hanazono Jinja as far as Yasukuni-dōri and take a right. Two blocks farther is the south end of rough-and-tumble **Kabuki-chō ⑤**. From here you can easily return to Shinjuku Station on foot.

If you'd like to finish the day with a kaiseki or *bentō* (box) meal, head for Yaozen (八百膳), on the 14th floor of Takashimaya Times Square (5–24–2 Sendagaya).

TIMING Plan at least a full day for Shinjuku if you want to see both the east and west sides. Subway rides can save you time and energy on the longer versions of these walks, but walking distances are still considerable. The Shinjuku Gyo-en National Garden is worth at least an hour, especially if you come in early April, during *sakura* (cherry blossom) season. The Tōkyō Metropolitan Government Office complex can take longer than you might expect; lines for the elevators to the observation decks are often excruciatingly long. Sunday, when shopping streets are closed to traffic, is the best time to tramp around Higashi-Shinjuku. The rainy season in late June and the sweltering heat of August are best avoided.

What to See

③ Hanazono Jinja (Hanazono Shrine, 花園神社). Constructed in the early Edo period, Hanazono is not among Tōkyō's most imposing shrines, but it does have one of the longest histories. Chief among the deities enshrined here is Yamato-takeru-no-Mikoto, a legendary 4th-century imperial prince whose heroic exploits are recounted in the earliest Japanese mythologies. His fame rests on the conquest of aboriginal tribes, which he did at the bidding of the Yamato Court. When he died, legends say his soul took the form of a swan and flew away. Prayers offered here are believed to bring prosperity in business. The shrine is a five-minute walk north on Meiji-dōri from the Shinjuku-san-chōme subway station. The block just to the west (5-chōme 1) has the last embattled remaining bars of the "Golden-Gai": a district of tiny, unpretentious, even seedy, nomiya that in the '60s and '70s commanded the fierce loyalty of fiction writers, artists, freelance journalists, and expat Japanophiles—the city's hard-core outsiders. ⊠ *5–17–3 Shinjuku, Shinjuku-ku* ☎ *03/3209–5265* ⓩ *Free* ⊘ *Daily sunrise–sunset* Ⓜ *Marunouchi subway line, Shinjuku-san-chōme Station (Exits B2 and B3).*

⑤ Kabuki-chō (歌舞伎町). In 1872 the Tokugawa-period formalities governing geisha entertainment were dissolved, and Kabuki-chō became Japan's largest center of prostitution. Later, when vice laws got stricter, prostitution just went a bit deeper underground, where it remains—deeply deplored and widely tolerated.

In an attempt to change the area's image after World War II, plans were made to replace Ginza's fire-gutted Kabuki-za with a new one in Shin-juku. The plans were never realized, however, as the old theater was re-built. But the project gave the area its present name. Kabuki-chō's own multipurpose theater is the 2,000-seat **Koma Gekijō** (コマ劇場); ✉ 1–19–1 Kabuki-chō, Shinjuku-ku ☎ 03/3200–2213). The building, which also houses several discos and bars, is a central landmark for the quarter.

Kabuki-chō means unrefined nightlife at its best and raunchy seediness at its worst. Neon signs flash; shills proclaim the pleasures of the places you particularly want to shun. Even when a place looks respectable, ask about prices first: *bottakuri*—overcharging for food and drink—is the regional sport here, and watered-down drinks can set you back ¥5,000 or more in a hostess club. Avoid the cheap nomiya under the railway tracks; chances are there's a client in at least one of them looking for a fight. All that said, you needn't be intimidated by the area: use your street-smarts, and it *can* be fun. ✉ *Shinjuku-ku* Ⓜ *JR (Higashi-guchi/East Exit) and Marunouchi subway line (Exits B10, B11, B12, and B13), Shin-juku Station.*

▶ ❶ **Seiji Tōgō Memorial Sompo Japan Museum of Art** (Sompo Japan Tōgō Seiji Bijutsuka, 東郷青児美術館). The painter Seiji Tōgō (1897–1978) was a master of putting on canvas the grace and charm of young maidens. More than 100 of his works from the museum collection are on display here at any given time, along with other Japanese and Western artists. The museum also houses Van Gogh's *Sunflowers*. Yasuda Fire & Marine In-surance Company CEO Yasuo Gotō acquired the painting in 1987 for ¥5.3 billion—at the time the highest price ever paid at auction for a work of art. He later created considerable stir in the media with the ill-con-sidered remark that he'd like the painting cremated with him when he died. The gallery has an especially good view of the old part of Shin-juku. ✉ *Yasuda Fire and Marine Insurance Bldg., 42nd fl., 1–26–1 Nishi-Shinjuku, Shinjuku-ku* ☎ *03/5777–8600* ⊕ *www.sompo-japan. co.jp/museum/english/index.html* ✑ *¥500; additional fees for special ex-hibits* ◉ *Tues.–Sun. 10–6* ◉ *Closed Dec. 27–Jan. 4* Ⓜ *Marunouchi and Shinjuku subway lines, JR, and Keiō Shin-sen and Teitō private rail lines; Shinjuku Station (Exit A18 for subway lines, Nishi-guchi/West Exit or Exit N4 from the underground passageway for all others).*

★ ❹ **Shinjuku Gyo-en National Garden** (新宿御苑). This lovely 150-acre park was once the estate of the powerful Naitō family of feudal lords, who were among the most trusted retainers of the Tokugawa shōguns. In 1871, after the Meiji Restoration, the family gave the grounds to the govern-ment, which—not quite ready yet to put such gems at the disposal of ordinary people—made it an imperial property. After World War II the grounds were finally opened to the public. It's a perfect place for leisurely walks: paths wind past ponds and bridges, artificial hills, thoughtfully placed stone lanterns, and more than 3,000 kinds of plants, shrubs, and trees. There are different gardens in Japanese, French, and English styles, as well as a greenhouse (the nation's first, built in 1885) filled with tropical plants. The best times to visit are April, when 75 different species of cherry trees—some 1,500 trees in all—are in bloom, and the first two weeks of November, during the chrysanthemum exhibition. ⊠ *11 Naitō-chō, Shinjuku-ku* ☎ *03/3350–0151* 💴 *¥200* ☉ *Tues.–Sun. 9–4; also open Mon. 9–4 in cherry-blossom season (Mar. 25–Apr. 24) and for chrysanthemum show (Nov. 1–15)* Ⓜ *Marunouchi subway line, Shinjuku Gyo-en-mae Station (Exit 1).*

★ ❷ **Tōkyō Metropolitan Government Office** (Tōkyō Tochō, 東京都庁). Dominating the western Shinjuku skyline and built at a cost of ¥157 billion, Kenzō Tange's grandiose city hall complex is clearly meant to remind observers that Tōkyō's annual budget is bigger than that of the average developing country. The late-20th-century complex consists of a main office building, an annex, the Metropolitan Assembly building, and a huge central courtyard, often the venue of open-air concerts and exhibitions. The design has inspired a passionate controversy: Tōkyōites either love it or hate it. The main building soars 48 stories, splitting on the 33rd floor into two towers. On a clear day, from the observation decks on the 45th floors of both towers, you can see all the way to Mt. Fuji and to the Bōsō Peninsula in Chiba Prefecture. Several other skyscrapers in the area have free observation floors—among them the Shinjuku Center Building, the Shinjuku Nomura Building, and the Shinjuku Sumitomo Building—but city hall is the best of the lot. The Metropolitan Government Web site, incidentally, is an excellent source of information on sightseeing and current events in Tōkyō. ⊠ *2–8–1 Nishi-Shinjuku, Shinjuku-ku* ☎ *03/5321–1111* ⊕ *www.metro.tokyo.jp* 💴 *Free* ☉ *North observation deck daily 9:30–10:30; south observation deck daily 9:30–5:30* Ⓜ *Marunouchi and Shinjuku subway lines, JR, Keiō Shin-sen and Teitō private rail lines; Shinjuku Station (Nishi-guchi/West Exit).*

Elsewhere in Tōkyō   その他の楽しいスポット

The sheer size of the city and the diversity of its institutions make it impossible to fit all of Tōkyō's interesting sights into neighborhoods and walking tours. Plenty of worthy places—from Tōkyō Disneyland to sumō stables to the old Ōji district—fall outside the city's neighborhood repertoire. Yet no guide to Tōkyō would be complete without them.

Amusement Centers & Aquariums

Ⓒ **Kasai Seaside Park** (葛西臨海公園). With two artificial beaches, a bird sanctuary, and the **Tōkyō Sea Life Park** aquarium spread over a stretch of landfill between the Arakawa and the Kyū-Edogawa rivers, Kasai Seaside Park is one of the major landmarks in the vast effort to transform Tōkyō Bay into Fun City. The **Great Ferris Wheel of Diamonds and Flowers** (Daia to Hana no Dai-kanransha), the tallest Ferris wheel in Japan, takes passengers on a 17-minute ride to the apex, 384 feet above the ground, for a spectacular view of the city. On a clear day you can see all the way to Mt. Fuji; at night, if you're lucky, you reach the top just in time for a bird's-eye view of the fireworks over the Magic Kingdom, across the river. To get here, take the JR Keiyō Line local train from Tōkyō

Station to Kasai Rinkai Kōen Station; the park is a five-minute walk from the south exit. ⊠ *Rinkai-chō, Edogawa-ku* ☎ *03/3686–6911* 💰 *Free, Ferris wheel ¥700* ⊙ *Ferris wheel Sept.–July, Tues.–Fri. 10–8, weekends 10–9; Aug., weekdays 10–8, weekends 10–9.*

🌀 **Kōrakuen** (後楽園). The Kōrakuen stop on the Marunouchi subway line, about 10 minutes from Tōkyō Station, lets you out in front of the **Tōkyō Dome,** Japan's first air-supported indoor stadium, built in 1988 and home to the Tōkyō Giants baseball team. Across the Tōkyō Expressway from the stadium is **LaQua,** formerly the Kōrakuen Amusement Park. It's chiefly noted for its stomach-churning Thunder Dolphin giant roller coaster, which runs at one point straight through what the management touts as the world's first centerless Ferris wheel. ⊠ *1–3–61 Kōraku, Bunkyō-ku* ☎ *03/5800–9999* 💰 *LaQua: ¥4,000 for full day, ¥3,000 after 5 PM* ⊙ *LaQua daily 10–10.*

🌀 **Shinagawa Aquarium** (Shinagawa Suizokukan, しながわ水族館). The fun part of this aquarium in southwestern Tōkyō is walking through an underwater glass tunnel while some 450 species of fish swim around and above you. There are no pamphlets or explanation panels in English, however. Avoid Sunday, when the dolphin and sea lion shows draw crowds in impossible numbers. Take the local Keihin-Kyūkō private rail line from Shinagawa to Ōmori-kaigan Station. Turn left as you exit the station and follow the ceramic fish on the sidewalk to the first traffic light; then turn right. You can also take the JR Tōkaidō Line to Oimachi Station; board a free shuttle to the aquarium from the No. 6 platform at the bus terminal just outside Oimachi Station. ⊠ *3–2–1 Katsushima, Shinagawa-ku* ☎ *03/3762–3433* 💰 *¥1,100* ⊙ *Wed.–Mon. 10–4:30; dolphin and sea lion shows 3 times daily, on varying schedule.*

🌀 **Tōkyō Disneyland** (東京デイズニーランド). At Tōkyō Disneyland, Mickey-san and his coterie of Disney characters entertain just the way they do in the California and Florida Disney parks. When the park was built in 1983 it was much smaller than its counterparts in the United States, but the construction in 2001 of the adjacent DisneySea, with its seven "Ports of Call" with different nautical themes and rides, added more than 100 acres to this multifaceted Magic Kingdom.

The simplest way to get to Disneyland is by JR Keiyo Line from Tōkyō Station to Maihama; the park is just a few steps from the station exit. From Nihombashi you can also take the Tōzai subway line to Urayasu and walk over to the Tōkyō Disneyland Bus Terminal for the 25-minute ride, which costs ¥230. You can buy tickets in advance in Tōkyō Station, near the Yaesu North Exit—look for red-jacketed attendants standing outside the booth—or from any travel agent, such as the Japan Travel Bureau. ⊠ *1–1 Maihama, Urayasu-shi* ☎ *045/683–3333* ⊕ *www. tokyodisneyresort.co.jp* 💰 *1-day pass for Disneyland or DisneySea ¥5,500; 2-day pass for both parks ¥9,800* ⊙ *Daily 9–10; seasonal closings in Dec. and Jan. may vary, so check before you go.*

🌀 **Tōkyō Tower** (東京タワー). In 1958 Tōkyō's fledgling TV networks needed a tall antenna array to transmit signals. Trying to emerge from the devastation of World War II, the nation's capital was also hungry for a landmark—a symbol for the aspirations of a city still without a skyline. The result was the 1,093-foot-high Tōkyō Tower: an unabashed (though taller) knockoff of Paris's Eiffel Tower. The Grand Observation Platform, at an elevation of 492 feet, and the Special Observation Platform, at an elevation of 820 feet, quickly became major tourist attractions; they still draw some 3 million visitors a year, the vast majority of them Japanese youngsters on their first trip to the big city. A modest aquarium and a wax museum round out the tower's appeal as an amusement complex. The tower does provide a spectacular view of the city, and it gives Godzilla something to demolish periodically. This is a good diversion for kids, but get here soon: the antennas were originally built for analog broadcasting, and with Japan set to convert entirely to digital communications by 2010, a real demolition is already on the planning board. ⊠ *4–2–8 Shiba-Kōen, Minato-ku* ☎ *03/3433–5111* ☞ *¥820 for Grand Observation Platform, ¥600 extra for Special Observation Platform; aquarium ¥1,000; wax museum ¥870* ⊙ *Tower, daily 9–10. Wax museum, daily 10–9. Aquarium, Sept.–July, daily 10–7; Aug., daily 10–8* Ⓜ *Hibiya subway line, Kamiyachō Station (Exit 2).*

off the
beaten
path

ODAIBA (お台場). Tōkyō's "offshore" leisure and commercial-development complex rises on more than 1,000 acres of landfill, connected to the city by the Yurikamome monorail from Shimbashi. People come here for the arcades, shopping malls, and museums, as well as the city's longest (albeit artificial) stretch of sand beach, along the boat harbor. There's also a Ferris wheel—a neon phantasmagoric beacon for anyone driving into the city across the Rainbow Bridge. With hotels and apartment buildings as well, this is arguably the most successful of the megaprojects on Tōkyō Bay.

From Shimbashi Station (JR, Karasumori Exit; Asakusa subway line, Exit A2; Ginza subway line, Exit 4) follow the blue seagull signs to the monorail. You can pick up a map of Odaiba in English at the entrance. The Yurikamome Line makes 10 stops between Shimbashi and the terminus at Ariake; fares range from ¥310 to ¥370, but the best strategy is to buy a ¥1,000 prepaid card that allows you to make multiple stops at different points in Odaiba. The monorail runs every three to five minutes from 5:46 AM to 11:56 AM.

Architecture buffs should make time for Daiba, the second stop on the monorail, if only to contemplate the futuristic **Fuji Television Nippon Broadcasting Building** (フジテレビ; ⊠ 2–4–8 Daiba, Minato-ku ☎ 03/5500–8888 ☞ ¥500 ⊙ Tues.–Sun. 10–8). From its fifth-floor Studio Promenade, you can watch programs being produced. The observation deck on the 25th floor affords a spectacular view of the bay and the graceful curve of the Rainbow Bridge.

The third stop on the monorail from Shimbashi is the **Museum of Maritime Science** (Fune-no-Kagakukan, 船の科学館; ⊠ 3–1 Higashi-Yashio, Shinagawa-ku ☎ 03/5500–1111 ☞ ¥1,000 ⊙ Weekdays 10–5, weekends 10–6), which houses an impressive collection of models and displays on the history of Japanese shipbuilding and navigation. Built in the shape of an ocean liner, the museum is huge; if you're interested in ships, plan at least an hour here to do it justice. There are no English-language explanations at the museum. Anchored alongside the museum are the ferry *Yōtei-maru*, which for some 30 years plied the narrow straits between Aomori and Hokkaidō, and the icebreaker *Sōya-maru*, the first Japanese ship to cross the Arctic Circle.

The fun part of the **National Museum of Emerging Science and Innovation** (Nihon Kagaku Miraikan, 日本科学未来館; ✉ 2–41 Aomi, Kōtō-ku ☎ 03/3570–9151 🔁 ¥500 ⊙ Mon. and Wed.–Sat. 10–7, Sun. 10–5), the third stop on the monorail from Shimbashi, is on the third floor, where you can watch robots in action, write with light pens, and play with various things that move. The rest of the museum is what the Japanese call *ō-majime* (deeply sincere)—five floors of thematic displays on environment-friendly technologies, life sciences, and the like with high seriousness and not much fun. Some of the exhibits have English-language explanations. It's a short walk here from the Museum of Maritime Science.

A two-minute walk south from the fourth stop on the monorail, at Telecom Center, brings you to **Odaiba's Hot Spring Theme Park** (Ōedo Onsen Monogatari, 大江戸温泉物語); ✉ 2–57 Ōmi, Kōtō-ku ☎ 03/5500–1126 🔁 ¥2,700; ¥1,500 surcharge for entrance after midnight). This *onsen* (thermal spring) draws water from a mineral-rich underground supply. No more than a handful of such places survive in Tōkyō, but the Ōedo Onsen managed to tap a source some 4,600 feet below the bay, and parlayed this into a tourist attraction that should not be missed.

At the entrance, designed to evoke an Edo-era gate, remove your shoes and store them in a locker. Attendants in period wigs and *hakama* (culottes) guide you to a dressing room, where you exchange your street clothes for a yukata, which you can wear for the rest of your stay in the park. Choose from several indoor and outdoor pools, with different temperatures and motifs—but remember that you must soap up and rinse off before you enter any of them. Follow up with a massage and a stroll through the food court—modeled on a street in Yoshiwara, the licensed red-light district of the Edo period—for sushi or noodles. On any given day, Ōedo Onsen draws 2,000 to 4,000 visitors; getting naked with strangers may be daunting at first, but the baths are gender-segregated, and hygiene is absolutely no problem. The park is open daily from 11 AM to 9 AM; the front desk closes at 2 AM. Charges include the rental of a yukata and a towel.

Roppongi Hills (六本木ヒルズ). During the last quarter of the 20th century, Roppongi was a better-heeled, better-behaved version of Shinjuku or Shibuya, without the shopping: not much happening by day, but by night an irresistible draw for young clubbers with foreign sports cars and wads of disposable income. In 2003, Mori Building Company—Japan's biggest commercial landlord—transformed this area and created Roppongi Hills, a complex of shops, restaurants, residential and commercial towers, a nine-screen cineplex, a luxury hotel, and a major art museum, wrapped around the TV Asahi studios and sprawled out in five zones from the Roppongi intersection to Azabu-jūban. To navigate this minicity, you need a 12-page floor guide with color-coded maps; luckily, the guide is available in English, and most of the staff members at the omnipresent information counters speak a modicum of English as well. At the center of Roppongi Hills is the 54-story **Mori Tower** (森タワー; ☎ 03/5777–8600 🖼 Museum and observation promenade ¥1,800 weekdays, ¥2,000 weekends ⊘ Mon., Wed., and Thurs. 10–10; Fri.–Sun. 10–5). On a clear day, from the Tokyo City View observation promenade on the 52nd floor, you can see Mt. Fuji in the distance, and by night the panoramic view of the city is spectacular. The promenade encircles three of the nine galleries of the Mori Art Museum, which showcases contemporary art in several different media. You enter the six main galleries, where the major exhibitions are mounted, from the floor above. The Mori is well-designed, intelligently curated, and hospitable to big crowds. ✉ 6–10–1 Roppongi, Minato-ku ⊕ www.roppongihills.com Ⓜ Hibiya subway line, Roppongi Station (Exit C-1).

FodorśChoice
★

Ryōgoku (両国). Two things make this working-class Shitamachi neighborhood worth a special trip: this is the center of the world of sumō wrestling as well as the site of the extraordinary Edo-Tōkyō Museum. Five minutes from Akihabara on the JR Sōbu Line, Ryōgoku is easy to get to, and if you've budgeted a leisurely stay in the city, it's well worth a morning's expedition.

The **Edo-Tōkyō Museum** (江戸東京博物館; ✉ 1–4–1 Yokoami, Sumida-ku ☎ 03/3626–9974 ⊕ www.edo-tokyo-museum.or.jp 🖼 ¥600; additional fees for special exhibits ⊘ Tues., Wed., and weekends 9:30–5; Thurs. and Fri. 9:30–8 ⊘ Closed Dec. 28–Jan. 4 and on Tues. when Mon. is a national holiday) opened in 1993, more or less coinciding with the collapse of the economic bubble that had made the project possible. Money was no object in those days; much of the large museum site is open plaza—an unthinkably lavish use of space. From the plaza the museum rises on massive pillars to the permanent exhibit areas on the fifth and sixth floors. The escalator takes you directly to the sixth floor—and back in time 300 years. You cross a replica of the Edo-period Nihombashi Bridge into a truly remarkable collection of dioramas, scale models, cutaway rooms, and even whole buildings: an intimate and convincing experience of everyday life in the capital of the Tokugawa shōguns. Equally elaborate are the fifth-floor re-creations of early modern Tōkyō, the "enlightenment" of Japan's headlong embrace of the West, and the twin devastations of the Great Kantō Earthquake and World War II. If you only visit one nonart museum in Tōkyō, make this it.

To get to the museum, leave Ryōgoku Station by the west exit, immediately turn right, and follow the signs. The moving sidewalk and the stairs bring you to the plaza on the third level; to request an English-speaking volunteer guide, use the entrance to the left of the stairs instead, and ask at the General Information counter in front of the first-floor Special Exhibition Gallery.

Walk straight out to the main street in front of the west exit of Ryōgoku Station, turn right, and you come almost at once to the Kokugikan (National Sumō Arena), with its distinctive copper-green roof. If you can't attend one of the Tōkyō sumō tournaments, you may want to at least pay a short visit to the **Sumō Museum** (相撲博物館; ✉ 1–3–28 Yokoami, Sumida-ku ☎ 03/3622–0366 💴 Free ⏰ Weekdays 10–4:30), in the south wing of the arena. There are no explanations in English, but the museum's collection of sumō-related wood-block prints, paintings, and illustrated scrolls includes some outstanding examples of traditional Japanese fine art.

Sumō wrestlers are not free agents; they must belong to one or another of the **sumō stables** officially recognized by the Sumō Association. Although the tournaments and exhibition matches take place in different parts of the country at different times, all the stables—now some 30 in number—are in Tōkyō, most of them concentrated on both sides of the Sumida-gawa near the Kokugikan. Wander this area when the wrestlers are in town (January, May, and September are your best bets) and you're more than likely to see some of them on the streets, in their wood clogs and kimonos. Come 7 AM–11 AM, and you can peer through the doors and windows of the stables to watch them in practice sessions. One of the easiest to find is the Tatsunami Stable (立浪部屋; 3–26–2 Ryōgoku), only a few steps from the west end of Ryōgoku Station (turn left when you go through the turnstile and left again as you come out on the street; then walk along the station building to the second street on the right). Another, a few blocks farther south, where the Shuto Expressway passes overhead, is the Izutsu Stable (井筒部屋; 2–2–7 Ryōgoku).

★ **Sengaku-ji** (Sengaku Temple, 泉岳寺). One day in the year 1701, a young provincial baron named Asano Takumi-no-Kami, serving an official term of duty at the shōgun's court, attacked and seriously wounded a courtier named Yoshinaka Kira. Kira had demanded the usual tokens of esteem that someone in his high position would expect for his goodwill; Asano refused, and Kira humiliated him in public to the point that he could no longer contain his rage.

Kira survived the attack. Asano, for daring to draw his sword in the confines of Edo Castle, was ordered to commit suicide. His family line was abolished and his fief confiscated. Headed by Kuranosuke Ōishi, the clan steward, 47 of Asano's loyal retainers vowed revenge. Kira was rich and well protected; Asano's retainers were *rōnin*—masterless samurai. It took them almost two years of planning, subterfuge, and hardship, but on the night of December 14, 1702, they stormed Kira's villa in Edo, cut off his head, and brought it in triumph to Asano's tomb at Sengaku-ji, the family temple. Ōishi and his followers were sentenced to commit suicide—which they accepted as the reward, not the price, of their honorable vendetta—and were buried in the temple graveyard with their lord.

The event captured the imagination of the Japanese like nothing else in their history. Through the centuries it has become the national epic, the last word on the subject of loyalty and sacrifice, celebrated in every medium from Kabuki to film. The temple still stands, and the graveyard is wreathed in smoke from the bundles of incense that visitors still lay reverently on the tombstones.

The story gets even better. There's a small museum on the temple grounds with a collection of weapons and other memorabilia of the event. One of these items dispels forever the myth of Japanese vagueness and indirection in the matter of contracts and formal documents. Kira's family, naturally, wanted to give him a proper burial, but the law insisted this could not be done without his head. They asked for it back, and Ōishi—mirror of chivalry that he was—agreed. He entrusted it to the temple, and the priests wrote him a receipt, which survives even now in the corner of a dusty glass case. "Item," it begins, "One head."

Take the Asakusa subway line to Sengaku-ji Station (Exit A2), turn right when you come to street level, and walk up the hill. The temple is past the first traffic light, on the left. ⊠ *2–11–1 Takanawa, Minato-ku* ☎ *03/3441–5560* 🔄 *Temple and grounds free, museum ¥200* ☉ *Temple Apr.–Sept., daily 7–6; Oct.–Mar., daily 7–5. Museum daily 9–4.*

Sōgetsu School (Sōgetsu Kaikan, 草月会館). The schools of ikebana, like those of other traditional arts, from music and dance to calligraphy and tea ceremony, are highly stratified organizations. Students rise through levels of proficiency, paying handsomely for lessons and certifications as they go, until they can become teachers themselves. At the top of the hierarchy is the *iemoto,* the head of the school, a title usually held within a family for generations. The Sōgetsu School of flower arrangement is a relative newcomer to all this. It was founded by Sōfū Teshigahara in 1927, and, compared to the older schools, it espouses a style flamboyant, free-form, and even radical. Detractors call it overblown, but it draws students and admirers from the world over, and it has made itself wealthy in the process. Lessons in flower arrangement are given in English on Monday from 10 to noon. Reservations must be made a day in advance. The main hall of the Sōgetsu Kaikan, created by the late Isamu Noguchi, one of the masters of modern sculpture, is well worth a visit. Noguchi's moving composition of carved stone slabs, cantilevered walkways, and flowing water is typical of his later career and reflects the influence of Zen aesthetics. Sōgetsu Kaikan is a 10-minute walk west on Aoyama-dōri from the Akasaka-mitsuke intersection or east from the Aoyama-itchōme subway stop. ⊠ *7–2–21 Akasaka, Minato-ku* ☎ *03/3408–1209* 🔄 *¥4,850 for 1st lesson, ¥3,800 per lesson thereafter* Ⓜ *Ginza and Marunouchi subway lines, Akasaka-mitsuke Station; Ginza and Hanzō-mon subway lines, Aoyama-itchōme Station (Exit 4).*

Tobacco and Salt Museum (Tobako to Shio Hakubutsukan, たばこと塩の博物館). A museum that displays examples of every conceivable artifact associated with tobacco and salt since the days of the Maya might not seem, at first, to serve a compelling social need, but the existence of the T&S reflects one of the more interesting facts of Japanese political life. Tobacco and salt were both made government monopolies at the beginning of the 20th century. Sales and distribution were eventually liberalized, but production remained under exclusive state control until 1985 through the Japan Tobacco and Salt Public Corporation. The corporation was then privatized. Renamed Nihon Tabako Sangyō (Japan Tobacco, Inc.), it continues to provide comfortable, well-paying second careers—called *amakudari* (literally "descent from Heaven")—for retired public officials. It remains Japan's exclusive producer of cigarettes, still holds a monopoly on the sale of salt, and dabbles in real estate, gardening supplies, and pharmaceuticals—ringing up sales of some $17 billion a year. Japan Tobacco, Inc., in short, has more money than it knows what to do with: so why not put up a museum? What makes this museum noteworthy is the special exhibit on the fourth floor of ukiyo-e on the themes of smoking and traditional salt production. T&S is a 10-minute walk on Kōen-dōri from Shibuya Station. ⊠ *1–16–8 Jinnan, Shibuya-ku* ☎ *03/3476–2041* ⊕ *www.jtnet.ad.jp/Culture/museum/ Welcome.html* ⊠ *¥100* ⊗ *Tues.–Sun. 10–5:30* ⊗ *Closed Sept. 1 and Dec. 29–Jan. 3* ⓜ *Subway, JR, and private rail lines, Shibuya Station (Kita-guchi/North Exit).*

Toden Arakawa Line (都電荒川線). Want to take a trip back in time? Take the JR Yamanote Line to Ōtsuka, cross the street in front of the station, and change to the Toden Arakawa Line—Tōkyō's last surviving trolley. Heading east, the trolley takes you through the back gardens of old neighborhoods on its way to Ōji—once the site of Japan's first Western-style paper mill, built in 1875 by Ōji Paper Company, the nation's oldest joint-stock company. The mill is long gone, but the memory lingers on at the **Asuka-yama Ōji Paper Museum**(紙の博物館). Some exhibits here show the process of milling paper from pulp. Others illustrate the astonishing variety of products that can be made from paper. The museum is a minute's walk from the trolley stop at Asuka-yama Kōen: you can also get here from the JR Ōji Station (Minami-guchi/South Exit) on the Keihin–Tōhoku Line, or the Nishigahara Station (Asuka-yama Exit) on the Namboku subway line. ⊠ *1–1–3 Ōji, Kita-ku* ☎ *03/ 3916–2320* ⊠ *¥300* ⊗ *Tues.–Sun. 10–4:30.*

WHERE TO EAT

At last count there were more than 200,000 bars and restaurants in Tōkyō. Since the collapse of the bubble economy in the 1990s, you might expect people to be a bit more cautious with their disposable income, but Tōkyōites seem—on the surface, at least—undismayed. Megalithic development projects, like those in Shiodome, Roppongi, Odaiba, and Ebisu, continue to rise and vie among themselves for tenant lists of first-rate places to wine and dine. The high end of the market (especially in the "anchor" luxury hotels of these major developments) can be grotesquely expensive, but Tōkyō's myriad choices also include a fair number of bargains—good cooking of all sorts that you can enjoy even on a modest budget. Food and drink, even at street stalls, are safe wherever you go.

For an international city, Tōkyō is still stubbornly provincial in many ways. Whatever the rest of the world has pronounced good, however, eventually makes its way here: French, Italian, Chinese, Indian, Middle Eastern, Latin American. It's hard to think of a cuisine of any prominence that goes unrepresented, as Japanese chefs by the thousand go abroad, hone their craft, and bring it home to this city.

Restaurants in Japan naturally expect most of their clients to be Japanese, and the Japanese are the world's champion modifiers. Only the most serious restaurateurs refrain from editing some of the authenticity out of foreign cuisines; in areas like Shibuya, Harajuku, and Shinjuku, all too many of the foreign restaurants cater to students and young office workers who come mainly for the *fun'iki* (atmosphere). Choose a French bistro or Italian trattoria in these areas carefully, and expect to pay dearly for the real thing. That said, you can count on the fact that the city's best foreign cuisine is world-class.

Several of France's two- and three-star restaurants, for example, have established branches and joint ventures in Tōkyō, and they regularly send their chefs over to supervise. The style almost everywhere is still nouvelle cuisine: small portions, with picture-perfect garnishes and light sauces. More and more, you find interesting fusions of French and Japanese culinary traditions. Meals are served in poetically beautiful presentations, in bowls and dishes of different shapes and patterns. Recipes make imaginative use of fresh Japanese ingredients, like *shimeji* mushrooms and local wild vegetables.

Tōkyōites have also had more and more opportunities to experience the range and virtuosity of Italian cuisine; chances are good that the finer trattorias here will measure up to even Tuscan standards. Indian food is also consistently good—and relatively inexpensive. Chinese food is the most consistently modified; it can be very good, but for repertoire and richness of taste, it pales in comparison to Hong Kong or Beijing fare. Significantly, Tōkyō has no Chinatown. Many of the city's newest restaurants can only be classified as "fusion" or "eclectic," quoting liberally—like California cuisine—from several Eastern and Western culinary traditions.

The quintessential Japanese restaurant is the *ryōtei,* something like a villa, most often walled off from the bustle of the outside world and divided into several small, private dining rooms. These rooms are traditional in style, with tatami-mat floors, low tables, and a hanging scroll or a flower arrangement in the alcove. One or more of the staff is assigned to each room to serve the many dishes that compose the meal, pour your sake, and provide light conversation. Think of a ryōtei as an adventure, an encounter with foods you've likely never seen before and with a centuries-old graceful, almost ritualized style of service unique to Japan. Many parts of the city are proverbial for their ryōtei; the top houses tend to be in Akasaka, Tsukiji, Asakusa and nearby Yanagi-bashi, and Shimbashi.

A few pointers are in order on the geography of food and drink. The farther "downtown" you go—into Shitamachi—the less likely you are to find the real thing in foreign cuisine. There's superb Japanese food all over the city, but aficionados of sushi swear (with excellent reason) by Tsukiji, where the fish market supplies the neighborhood's restaurants with the freshest ingredients; the restaurants in turn serve the biggest portions and charge the most reasonable prices. Asakusa takes pride in its tempura restaurants, but tempura is reliable almost everywhere, especially at branches of the well-established, citywide chains. Every department store and skyscraper office building in Tōkyō devotes at least one floor to restaurants; none of them stand out, but all are inexpensive and quite passable places to lunch. When in doubt for dinner, note that Tōkyō's top-rated international hotels also have some of the city's best places to eat and drink.

Dining out in Tōkyō does not ordinarily demand a great deal in the way of formal attire. If it's a business meal, of course, and your hosts or guests are Japanese, dress conservatively: for men, a suit and tie; for women, a dress or suit in a basic color, stockings, and a minimum of jewelry. On your own, you'll find that only a very few upscale Western venues (mainly the French and Continental restaurants in hotels) will even insist on ties for men; follow the unspoken dress codes you'd observe at home and you're unlikely to go wrong.

Prices

Price-category estimates are based on the cost of a main course at dinner, excluding drinks, taxes, and service charges; once you add in these costs, a restaurant listed as $$ can easily slide up a category to $$$ when it comes time to pay the bill.

WHAT IT COSTS In yen					
	$$$$	$$$	$$	$	¢
AT DINNER	over 3,000	2,000–3,000	1,000–2,000	800–1,000	under 800

Prices are per person for a main course.

Akasaka

Indian

★ $$ ✕ **Moti** (モテイ). Vegetarian dishes at Moti, especially the lentil and eggplant curries, are very good; so is the chicken masala, cooked in butter and spices. The chefs here are recruited from India by a family member who runs a restaurant in Delhi. As its reputation for reasonably priced North Indian cuisine grew, Moti established branches in nearby Akasakamitsuke, Roppongi, and farther afield in Yokohama. They all have the inevitable Indian friezes, copper bowls, and white elephants, but this one—popular at lunch with the office crowd from the nearby Tōkyō Broadcasting System headquarters—puts the least into decor. ✉ *Kimpa Bldg., 3rd fl., 2-14-31 Akasaka, Minato-ku* ☎ *03/3584–6640* ▤ *AE, DC, MC, V* Ⓜ *Chiyoda subway line, Akasaka Station (Exit 2).*

Italian

$$$–$$$$ ✕ **La Granata** (ラ・グラナータ). In the Tōkyō Broadcasting System Garden building, La Granata is very popular with the media crowd in this neighborhood, and deservedly so: the chefs prepare some of the most accomplished, professional Italian food in town. La Granata is decked out trattoria style, with brickwork arches, red-checkered tablecloths, and a display of antipasti to whet the appetite. Whether you order the *tagliolini* (thin ribbon noodles) with porcini mushrooms, the spaghetti with garlic and red pepper, or another dish as your main meal, start with an appetizer of the wonderful batter-fried zucchini flowers filled with mozzarella and asparagus. ✉ *5-1-3 Akasaka, Minato-ku* ☎ *03/3582–5891* ▤ *AE, MC, V* Ⓜ *Chiyoda subway line, Akasaka Station (Exit 1A).*

Where to Eat in Tōkyō

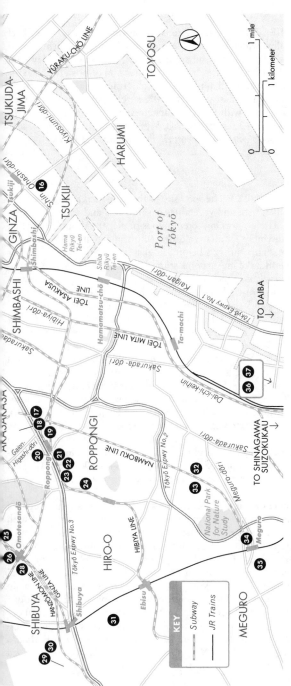

Adjanta **5**
Aoi-Marushin **3**
Barbacoa Grill **26**
Chez Matsuo **29**
Den-En Kyo **32**
Edo-Gin **16**
Erawan **22**
Ganchan **18**
Heichinrou **10**
Higo-no-ya **25**

Homeworks **17**
Inakaya **21**
Jidaiya **20**
Keawjai **34**
Kisoji **9**
La Granata **8**
Le Papillon de Paris . . **28**
Maisen **27**
Manhattan Grill **36**
Moti **7**

Naokyū **14**
Ōshima **15**
Rangetsu **13**
Restorante Carmine . . **4**
Robata **11**
Roti **23**
Sabado Sabadete **33**
Sankō-en **24**
Sasa-no-yuki **2**
Sasashin **12**

Sasashū **1**
Spago **19**
Tableaux **31**
Tenmatsu **30**
Tonki **35**
T. Y. Harbor Brewery . . **37**
Ume no Hana **6**

Japanese

$$$-$$$$ ✕ **Kisoji** (木曽路). The specialty here is shabu-shabu: thin slices of beef cooked in boiling water at your table and dipped in sauce. Normally this is an informal, if pricey, sort of meal; after all, you do get to play with your food a bit. Kisoji, however, adds a dimension of posh to the experience, with all the tasteful appointments of a traditional ryōtei: private dining rooms with tatami seating (at a 10% surcharge), elegant little rock gardens, and alcoves with flower arrangements. ⊠ *3–10 Akasaka, Minato-ku* ☎ *03/3588–0071* ▤ *AE, MC, V* Ⓜ *Ginza and Marunouchi subway lines, Akasaka-mitsuke Station (Belle Vie Akasaka Exit).*

Aoyama

Japanese

$$$ ✕ **Higo-no-ya** (肥後の屋). The specialty of the house is *kushi-yaki*: small servings of meat, fish, and vegetables cut into bits and grilled on bamboo skewers. There's nothing ceremonious or elegant about kushi-yaki; it resembles the more familiar yakitori, with somewhat more variety to the ingredients. Higo-no-ya's helpful English menu guides you to other delicacies like shiitake mushrooms stuffed with minced chicken; bacon-wrapped scallops; and bonito, shrimp, and eggplant with ginger. The restaurant is a postmodern-traditional cross, with wood beams painted black, paper lanterns, and sliding paper screens. There's tatami, table, and counter seating. ⊠ *AG Bldg. B1, 3–18–17 Minami-Aoyama, Minato-ku* ☎ *03/3423–4461* ▤ *AE, DC, MC, V* ⊘ *No lunch* Ⓜ *Ginza, Chiyoda, and Hanzō-mon subway lines, Omotesandō Station (Exit A4).*

$-$$ ✕ **Maisen** (まい泉). Converted from a *sentō* (public bathhouse), Maisen still has the old high ceiling (built for ventilation) and the original signs instructing bathers where to change out of their street clothes. Bouquets of seasonal flowers help transform the large, airy space into a pleasant dining room. Maisen's specialty is *tonkatsu*: tender, juicy, deep-fried pork cutlets served with a spicy sauce, shredded cabbage, miso soup, and rice. A popular alternative is the *Suruga-zen* set, a main course of fried fish served with sashimi, soup, and rice. There are no-smoking rooms upstairs. ⊠ *4–8–5 Jingū-mae, Shibuya-ku* ☎ *03/3470–0071* ▤ *AE, DC, MC, V* Ⓜ *Ginza, Chiyoda, and Hanzō-mon subway lines, Omotesandō Station (Exit A2).*

¢-$$ ✕ **Ume no Hana** (梅の花). The exclusive speciality here is tofu, prepared in more ways than you can imagine—boiled, steamed, stir-fried with minced crabmeat, served in a custard, wrapped in thin layers around a delicate whitefish paste. Tofu is touted as the perfect high-protein, low-calorie health food; at Ume no Hana it is raised to the elegance of haute cuisine. Enter this restaurant from a flagstone walk lined with traditional stone lanterns, and remove your shoes when you step up to the main room; the tables are divided into intimate spaces with latticed wooden screens. Private dining rooms have tatami seating with recesses under the tables so you can stretch your legs. Prix-fixe meals include a complimentary aperitif. ⊠ *2–14–6 Kita-Aoyama, Bell Commons 6F, Minato Ward* ☎ *03/3475–8077* ⚲ *No smoking* ▤ *AE, DC, MC, V* Ⓜ *Ginza Line, Gaien-mae Station (Exit 3).*

Fodor'sChoice ★

ON THE MENU IN TŌKYŌ

FIRST, THINK SUSHI. *The style popular now everywhere—slices of raw fish or shellfish on a hand-formed portion of vinegared rice, with a dab of wasabi for zest—developed in Edo (present-day Tōkyō) in the early 19th century. The local name for this style, in fact, is Edo-mae. (Go west, to Ōsaka or Kyōto, and you find a very different kettle of fish, called oshi-zushi: the fish and rice are pressed together in a box mold, then sliced into individual servings.) Originally, Edo-mae was pure street food, sold at stalls as a quick snack; today the best sushi restaurants send buyers early every morning to the Central Wholesale Market in Tsukiji for the freshest ingredients: maguro (tuna) and hamachi (yellowtail), tako (octopus) and ika (squid), ikura (salmon roe) and uni (sea urchin), ebi (shrimp) and anago (conger eel).*

Next, think tempura: fresh fish, shellfish, and vegetables delicately batter-fried in oil. This kind of cooking dates to the mid-16th century, with the earliest influences of Spanish and Portuguese culture on Japan, and you find it today all over the country. But nowhere is it better than in Tōkyō, and nowhere in Tōkyō is it better than in the tempura stalls and restaurants of Shitamachi—the older commercial and working-class districts of the eastern wards—or in the restaurants that began there in the 19th century and moved upscale. Typical ingredients are shrimp, kisu (smelt), shirauo (whitebait), shiitake mushrooms, lotus root, and green peppers. To really enjoy tempura, you want to be at the counter, in front of the chef: these individual portions should be served and eaten the moment they emerge from the oil.

Asakusa

Japanese

$–$$ ✕ **Aoi-Marushin** (葵丸進). The largest tempura restaurant in Tōkyō, with

FodorsChoice six floors of table and tatami seating, welcomes foreign customers and

★ makes a visit easy with English menus. This is a family restaurant. Don't expect much in the way of decor—just lots of food at very reasonable prices. Asakusa is a must on any itinerary, and tempura *teishoku* (an assortment of delicate batter-fried fish, seafood, and fresh vegetables) is the specialty of the district. Aoi-Marushin's location, just a few minutes' walk from the entrance to Sensō-ji temple, makes it an obvious choice after a visit to the temple. ✉ *1–4–4 Asakusa, Taitō-ku* ☎ *03/3841–0110* ▤ *AE, MC, V* Ⓜ *Ginza and Asakusa subway lines, Asakusa Station (Exit 1).*

Azabu-jūban

American/Casual

$–$$ ✕ **Homeworks** (ホームワークス). Every so often, even on alien shores, you've got to have a burger. When the urge strikes, the Swiss-and-bacon special at Homeworks is an incomparably better choice than anything you can get at one of the global chains. Hamburgers come in three sizes on white or wheat buns, with a variety of toppings. There are also hot teriyaki chicken and pastrami sandwiches and vegetarian options like hummus and eggplant. Desserts, alas, are so-so. With its hardwood banquettes and French doors open to the street in good weather, Homeworks is a pleasant place to linger over lunch. ⊠ *Vesta Bldg. 1F, 1–5–8 Azabu-jūban, Minato-ku* ☎ *03/3405–9884* ▤ *No credit cards* Ⓜ *Namboku and Ōedo subway lines, Azabu-jūban Station (Exit 4).*

Korean

$$–$$$$ ✕ **Sankō-en** (三幸園). With the embassy of South Korea a few blocks away, Sankō-en stands out in a neighborhood thick with Korean-barbecue joints. Customers—not just from the neighborhood but from nearby trendy Roppongi as well—line up at all hours (from 11:30 AM to midnight) to get in. Korean barbecue is a smoky affair; you cook your own food, usually thin slices of beef and vegetables, on a gas grill at your table. The *karubi* (brisket), which is accompanied by a great salad, is the best thing to order. ⊠ *1–8–7 Azabu-jūban, Minato-ku* ☎ *03/3585–6306* 🍴 *Reservations not accepted* ▤ *MC, V* ⊗ *Closed Wed.* Ⓜ *Namboku and Ōedo subway lines, Azabu-jūban Station (Exit 4).*

Daikanyama

Contemporary

$$–$$$$
FodorśChoice
★

✕ **Tableaux** (タブローズ). The mural in the bar depicts the fall of Pompeii, the banquettes are upholstered in red leather, and the walls are papered in antique gold. So with ponytailed waiters gliding about, you suspect that somebody here really *believes* in Los Angeles. Tableaux may lay on more glitz than is necessary, but the service is cordial and professional, and the food is superb. Try batter-fried zucchini flowers with mozzarella and anchovy; spaghettini with baby clams, lobster meat, and green olives; or the miso-glazed black cod with sour-plum sauce, garnished with mushrooms and shrimp wontons. The bar is open until 1:30 AM. ⊠ *Sunroser Daikanyama Bldg. B1, 11–6 Sarugaku-chō, Shibuya-ku* ☎ *03/5489–2201* ▤ *AE, DC, MC, V* ⊗ *No lunch* Ⓜ *Tōkyū Toyoko private rail line, Daikanyama Station (Kita-guchi/North Exit).*

Ginza

Japanese

$$$$ ✕ **Ōshima** (大志満). The draw at Ōshima is the *Kaga ryōri* cooking of Kanazawa, a small city on the Sea of Japan known as "Little Kyōto" for its rich craft traditions. Waitresses dress in kimonos of Kanazawa's famous Yūzen dyed silk; Kutani porcelain and Wajima lacquerware grace the exquisite table settings. Seafood at Ōshima is superb, but don't ignore the specialty of the house: a stew of duck and potatoes called *jibuni*. Kaiseki full-course meals are pricey, but there's a reasonable lunchtime set menu for ¥1,800. ⊠ *Ginza Core Bldg. 9F, 5–8–20 Ginza, Chūō-ku* ☎ *03/3574–8080* ▤ *AE, MC, V* Ⓜ *Ginza, Hibiya, and Marunouchi subway lines, Ginza Station (Exit A5).*

$$$–$$$$ ✕ **Rangetsu** (らん月). Japan enjoys a special reputation for its lovingly raised, tender, marbled domestic beef. Try it, if your budget will bear the weight,

WHERE TO REFUEL

When you don't have time for a leisurely meal, you might want to try a local chain restaurant. **Yoshinoya,** popular with Tōkyōites, serves grilled salmon, rice, and miso soup for breakfast (until 10), and then hearty portions of rice and beef for the rest of the day. **Sen Zushi, Chiyoda Sushi,** and **Kyoutaru** dish out sushi and sashimi, and at **Ichiran** you can customize a bowl of ramen. Nearly all of these counter-service restaurants also sell onigiri (rice balls), the easiest snack to pick up when you're on the go. Often shaped like a thick triangle small enough to fit in your palm, the sticky rice balls come stuffed with a bit of salmon, kelp, or meat and wrapped in nori, so you can handle them. Rice balls cost about ¥100. If you want to eat something familiar, check out **MOS Burger, Freshness Burger,** or **First Kitchen,** which serve classic hamburgers as well as some Japanese snacks.

at Rangetsu, in the form of this elegant Ginza restaurant's signature shabu-shabu or sukiyaki course. Call ahead to reserve a private alcove, where you can cook for yourself, or have a kaiseki meal brought to your table by kimono-clad attendants. Rangetsu is a block from the Ginza 4-chōme crossing, opposite the Matsuya Department Store. ⊠ *3–5–8 Ginza, Chūō-ku* ☎ *03/3567–1021* ▤ *AE, DC, MC, V* Ⓜ *Marunouchi and Ginza subway lines, Ginza Station (Exits A9 and A10).*

¢ ✕ **Naokyū** (直久). Ramen is the quintessential Japanese fast food in a bowl: thick Chinese noodles in a savory broth, with soybean paste, diced leeks, slices of pork loin, and spinach. No neighborhood in Tōkyō is without at least one ramen joint—often serving only at a counter, where you eat standing up. In Ginza, the hands-down favorite—for prices that have hardly changed since the 1970s, as well as for taste—is Naokyū, in the basement of Hankyū Department Store. There's limited seating here at the Formica-top tables; at lunch the line of waiting customers extends halfway down the corridor. ⊠ *Hankyū Department Store H2, 5–2–1 Ginza, Chūō-ku* ☎ *03/3571–0957* ▤ *MC, V* Ⓜ *Marunouchi and Ginza subway lines, Ginza Station (Sukiyabashi Exit C3 for Ginza Palmy).*

Ichiyaga

Italian

$$ ✕ **Restorante Carmine** (カルミネ). Everybody pitched in, so the story goes, when chef Carmine Cozzolino left his job at an upscale restaurant in Aoyama and opened this unpretentious neighborhood bistro in 1987: friends designed the logo and the interior, painted the walls (black and white), and hung the graphics, swapping their labor for meals. The five-course dinner (¥3,800–¥5,000) here could be the best deal in town. The menu changes daily; specialties of the house include pasta twists with tomato-and-caper sauce, and veal scallopini à la Marsala. The wine list is well chosen, and the tiramisu is a serious dessert. ⊠ *1–19 Saiku-chō,*

Shinjuku-ku ☎ *03/3260–5066* 🗔 *AE, MC, V* Ⓜ *Ōedo subway line, Ushigome-Kagurazaka Station (Exit 1).*

Ikebukuro

Japanese

$$–$$$ ✕ **Sasashū** (笹周). This traditional-style pub is noteworthy for stocking
Fodor'sChoice only the finest and rarest, the Latours and Mouton-Rothschilds, of sake:
★ these are the rice wines that take gold medals in the annual sake competition year after year. It also serves some of the best izakaya food in town—and the Japanese wouldn't dream of drinking well without eating well. Sasashū purports to be the only restaurant in Tōkyō that serves wild duck, brushed with sake and soy sauce and broiled over a hibachi. This is a rambling, two-story, traditional-style building, with thick beams and step-up tatami floors. ⊠ *2–2–6 Ikebukuro, Toshima-ku* ☎ *03/3971–6796* 🗔 *AE, DC, V* ☽ *Closed Sun. No lunch* Ⓜ *JR Yamanote Line; Yūrakuchō, Marunouchi, and Ōedo subway lines: Ikebukuro Station (Exit 19).*

Meguro

Japanese

★ **¢–$$** ✕ **Tonki** (とんき). Meguro, a neighborhood distinguished for almost nothing else culinary, has arguably the best tonkatsu restaurant in Tōkyō. It's a family joint, with Formica-top tables and a server who comes around to take your order while you wait the requisite 10 minutes in line. And people do wait in line, every night until the place closes at 10:45. Tonki is a success that never went conglomerate or added frills to what it does best: deep-fried pork cutlets, soup, raw cabbage salad, rice, pickles, and tea. That's the standard course, and almost everybody orders it, with good reason. ⊠ *1–1–2 Shimo-Meguro, Meguro-ku* ☎ *03/3491–9928* 🗔 *DC, V* ☽ *Closed Tues. and 3rd Mon. of month* Ⓜ *JR Yamanote and Namboku subway lines, Meguro Station (Nishi-guchi/West Exit).*

Thai

★ **$$** ✕ **Keawjai** (ゲウチャイ). Blink and you miss the faded sign of this little basement restaurant a minute's walk from Meguro Station. Keawjai is one of the few places in Tōkyō to specialize in the subtle complexities of Royal Thai cuisine, and despite its size—only eight tables and four banquettes—it serves a remarkable range of dishes in different regional styles. The spicy beef salad is excellent (and *really* spicy), as are the baked rice and crabmeat served in a whole pineapple and the red-curry chicken in coconut milk with cashews. The staff is Thai, and the service is friendly and unhurried. ⊠ *Meguro Kōwa Bldg. B1, 2–14–9 Kami Ōsaki Meguro-ku* ☎ *03/5420–7727* 🗔 *AE, DC, MC, V* ☽ *Closed 2nd and 3rd Mon. of month* Ⓜ *JR Yamanote and Namboku subway lines, Meguro Station (Higashi-guchi/East Exit).*

Niban-chō

Indian

$$ ✕ **Adjanta** (アジャンタ). In the mid-20th century, the owner of Adjanta came to Tōkyō to study electrical engineering. He ended up changing careers and establishing what is today one of the oldest and best Indian restaurants in town. There's no decor to speak of at this 24-hour restaurant. The emphasis instead is on the variety and intricacy of Indian cooking—and none of its dressier rivals can match Adjanta's menu for sheer depth. The curries are hot to begin with, but you can order them even hotter. There's a small boutique in one corner, where saris and imported Indian foodstuffs are sold. ⊠ *3–11 Niban-chō, Chiyoda-ku* ☎ *03/3264–6955* ▤ *AE, DC, MC, V* Ⓜ *Yūraku-chō subway line, Kōji-machi Station (Exit 5).*

Nihombashi

Japanese

$$ ✕ **Sasashin** (笹新). Like most izakaya, Sasashin spurns the notion of decor: there's a counter laden with platters of the evening's fare, a clutter of rough wooden tables, and not much else. It's noisy, smoky, crowded—and great fun. Like izakaya fare in general, the food is best described as professional home cooking, and is meant mainly as ballast for the earnest consumption of beer and sake. Try the sashimi, the grilled fish, or the fried tofu; you really can't go wrong by just pointing your finger to anything on the counter that takes your fancy. ⊠ *2–20–3 Nihombashi-Ningyōchō, Chūō-ku* ☎ *03/3668–2456* ⌕ *Reservations not accepted* ▤ *No credit cards* ☽ *Closed Sun. and 3rd Sat. of month. No lunch* Ⓜ *Hanzō-mon subway line, Suitengū-mae Station (Exit 7); Hibiya and Asakusa subway lines, Ningyōchō Station (Exits A1 and A3).*

Omotesandō

Brazilian

$$–$$$ ✕ **Barbacoa Grill** (バルバッコアグリル). Carnivores flock here for the great-value all-you-can-eat Brazilian grilled chicken and barbecued beef, which the efficient waiters will keep bringing to your table on skewers until you tell them to stop. Those with lighter appetites can choose the less-expensive salad buffet and feijoada pork stew with black beans; both are bargains. Barbacoa has hardwood floors, lithographs of bull motifs, warm lighting, salmon-color tablecloths, and roomy seating. This popular spot is just off Omotesandō-dōri on the Harajuku 2-chōme shopping street (on the north side of Omotesandō-dōri), about 50 yards down on the left. ⊠ *4–3–24 Jingū-mae, Shibuya-ku* ☎ *03/3796–0571* ▤ *AE, DC, MC, V* Ⓜ *Ginza, Chiyoda, and Hanzō-mon subway lines, Omotesandō Station (Exit A2).*

French

$$$$ ✕ **Le Papillon de Paris** (ル・パピヨン・ド・パリ). This very fashion-minded restaurant is a joint venture of L'Orangerie in Paris and couturier Hanae Mori. Muted elegance marks the dining room, with cream walls and deep-brown carpets; mirrors add depth to a room that actually seats only 40. The ambitious prix-fixe menus change every two weeks; the recurring salad of sautéed sweetbreads is excellent. This is a particularly good place to be on Sunday between 11 and 2:30, for the buffet brunch (¥3,500), during which you can graze through to what is arguably the best dessert tray in town. ⊠ *Hanae Mori Bldg., 5th fl., 3–6–1*

Kita–Aoyama, Minato-ku ☎ *03/3407–7461* ✍ *Reservations essential* ▭ *AE, DC, MC, V* ✆ *No dinner Sun.* Ⓜ *Ginza, Chiyoda and Hanzō-mon subway lines, Omotesandō Station (Exit A1).*

Roppongi

American

$$$$ ✕ **Spago** (スパゴ). Celebrity-chef Wolfgang Puck, who created the original Spago in Los Angeles, still checks in periodically to oversee the authenticity of his California cuisine at this Tōkyō branch. Most diners here content themselves with a starter like mango-and-Brie quesadilla with tomato salsa, and an equally eclectic pasta or pizza—but such entrées as grilled snapper with lemongrass and chardonnay or roast duck breast with Cointreau sauce and beet risotto are not to be ignored. This is a clean, well-lighted place, painted pink and white and adorned with potted palms. The best seats in the house are on the glassed-in veranda. ✉ *5–7–8 Roppongi, Minato-ku* ☎ *03/3423–4025* ▭ *AE, DC, MC, V* Ⓜ *Hibiya subway line, Roppongi Station (Exit 3).*

Contemporary

$$–$$$ ✕ **Roti** (ロティ). Billing itself a "modern American brasserie," Roti takes pride in the creative use of simple, fresh ingredients, and a fusing of Eastern and Western elements. For an appetizer, try the Vietnamese sea-bass carpaccio with crisp noodles and roasted garlic, or the calamari batter-fried in ale with red-chili tartar sauce. Don't neglect dessert: the espresso-chocolate tart is to die for. Roti stocks some 60 Californian wines, microbrewed ales from the famed Rogue brewery in Oregon, and Cuban cigars. The best seats in the house are in fact outside: at one of the dozen tables around the big glass pyramid on the terrace. ✉ *Piramide Bldg. 1F, 6–6–9 Roppongi, Minato-ku* ☎ *03/5785–3671* ▭ *AE, MC, V* Ⓜ *Hibiya subway line, Roppongi Station (Exit 1).*

Japanese

$$–$$$$ ✕ **Inakaya** (田舎屋). The style here is *robatayaki,* a dining experience that
Fodor'sChoice   segues into pure theater. Inside a large U-shape counter, two cooks in
★   traditional garb sit on cushions behind a grill, with a cornucopia of food spread out in front of them: fresh vegetables, seafood, skewers of beef and chicken. You point to what you want, and your server shouts out the order. The cook bellows back your order, plucks your selection up out of the pit, prepares it, and hands it across on an 8-foot wooden paddle. Inakaya is open from 5 PM to 5 AM, and fills up fast after 7. ✉ *Reine Bldg., 1st fl., 5–3–4 Roppongi, Minato-ku* ☎ *03/3408–5040* ✍ *Reservations not accepted* ▭ *AE, DC, MC, V* ✆ *No lunch* Ⓜ *Hibiya subway line, Roppongi Station (Exit 3).*

$$–$$$ ✕ **Jidaiya** (時代屋). The Roppongi branch of this restaurant evokes the feeling of an Edo-period tavern with a good collection of antiques: *akadansu* (red-lacquered chests), Nambu ironware kettles, and low *horigotatsu* tables, with recesses beneath which you can stretch out your legs. All the tables are for six people or more; you're bound to be sharing yours. The later you dine (the place stays open until 4 AM), the more boisterous and friendly your tablemates will be. Jidaiya serves a bit of everything in its prix-fixe courses: shabu-shabu, tempura, sushi, steamed rice with seafood. The food is nothing fancy, but it's delicious and filling. ⊠ *Uni Roppongi Bldg., B1, 7–15–17 Roppongi, Minato-ku* ☎ *03/3403–3563* 🖃 *AE, DC, MC, V* Ⓜ *Hibiya subway line, Roppongi Station (Exit 2).*

$$ ✕ **Ganchan** (がんちゃん). The Japanese expect their yakitori joints—restaurants that specialize in bits of charcoal-broiled chicken and vegetables—to be just like Ganchan: smoky, noisy, and cluttered. The counter seats barely 15, and you have to squeeze to get to the chairs in back. Festival masks, paper kites and lanterns, and greeting cards from celebrity patrons adorn the walls. The cooks yell at each other, fan the grill, and serve up enormous schooners of beer. Try the *tsukune* (balls of minced chicken) and the fresh asparagus wrapped in bacon. The place stays open until 1 AM (11 PM on Sunday). ⊠ *6–8–23 Roppongi, Minato-ku* ☎ *03/3478–0092* 🖃 *MC, V* Ⓜ *Hibiya subway line, Roppongi Station (Exit 1A).*

Fodor'sChoice ★

Thai

$$–$$$ ✕ **Erawan** (エラワン). Window tables at this sprawling Thai "brasserie" on the top floor of a popular Roppongi vertical mall afford a wonderful view of the Tōkyō skyline at night. Black-painted wood floors, ceiling fans, Thai antiques, and rattan chairs establish the mood, and the space is nicely broken up into large and small dining areas and private rooms. The service is cheerful and professional. Specialties of the house include deep-fried prawn and crabmeat cakes, spicy roast-beef salad, sirloin tips with mango sauce, and a terrific dish of stir-fried lobster meat with cashews. For window seating, it's best to reserve ahead. ⊠ *Roi Bldg. 13F, 5–5–1 Roppongi, Minato-ku* ☎ *03/3404–5741* 🖃 *AE, DC, M, V* Ⓜ *Hibiya subway line, Roppongi Station (Exit 3).*

Shibuya

Japanese

★ **$$–$$$** ✕ **Tenmatsu** (天松). The best seats in the house at Tenmatsu, as in any tempura-*ya*, are at the immaculate wooden counter, where your tidbits of choice are taken straight from the oil and served up immediately. You also get to watch the chef in action. Tenmatsu's brand of good-natured professional hospitality adds to the enjoyment of the meal. Here you can rely on a set menu or order à la carte tempura delicacies like lotus root, shrimp, *unagi* (eel), and *kisu* (a small white freshwater fish). Call ahead to reserve counter seating or a full-course kaiseki dinner in a private tatami room. ⊠ *1–6–1 Dōgen-zaka, Shibuya-ku* ☎ *03/3462–2815* 🖃 *DC, MC, V* Ⓜ *JR Yamanote Line, Shibuya Station (Minami-guchi/South Exit); Ginza and Hanzō-mon subway lines, Shibuya Station (Exit 3A).*

Shinagawa

Contemporary

$$–$$$$ ✕ **Manhattan Grill** (マンハッタングリル). Only in hypereclectic Japan can you have a French-Indonesian meal at a restaurant called the Manhattan Grill in a food court dubbed the "Foodium." Chef Wayan Surbrata, who trained at the Four Seasons Resort in Bali, has a delicate, deft touch with such dishes as spicy roast-chicken salad, and steak marinated in cinnamon and soy sauce, served with shiitake mushrooms and *gado-gado* (shrimp-flavor rice crackers). One side of the minimalist restaurant is open to the food court; the floor-to-ceiling windows on the other side don't afford much of a view. The square black-and-white ceramics set off the food especially well. ⊠ *Atré 4F, 2–18–1 Konan, Minato-ku* ☎ *03/6717–0922* ▤ *AE, MC, V* Ⓜ *JR Shinagawa Station (Higashi-guchi/East Exit).*

★ **$$–$$$** ✕ **T. Y. Harbor Brewery** (T.Y.ハーバーブルワリーレストラン). A converted warehouse on the waterfront houses this restaurant, a Tōkyō hot spot for private parties. Chef David Chiddo refined his signature California-Thai cuisine at some of the best restaurants in Los Angeles. Don't miss his grilled mahimahi with green rice and mango salsa, or the grilled jumbo-shrimp brochettes with tabbouleh. True to its name, T. Y. Harbor brews its own beer, in a tank that reaches all the way to the 46-ft-high ceiling. The best seats in the house are on the bayside deck, open from May to October. Reservations are a good idea on weekends. ⊠ *2–1–3 Higashi-Shinagawa, Shinagawa-ku* ☎ *03/5479–4555* ▤ *AE, DC, MC, V* Ⓜ *Tōkyō Monorail or Rinkai Line, Tennoz Isle Station (Exit B).*

Shirokanedai

Chinese

$$–$$$ ✕ **Den-En Kyo** (田燕居). Pale-green walls with black trim, antique chests, and chic geometric screens announce that this is not your typical Chinese-food joint. Chef Son You-Ting puts forth the high cuisine of his native Beijing, varied with the spicy style of Szechuan Province. There's no English menu, but you can always order the seven-course set meal (for two people or more), which includes Den-En Kyo's wonderful fried spring rolls with minced shrimp, and braised pork with lotus root. The 11-course menu features quail-egg soup, Peking duck, and jumbo scallops braised in brandy. ⊠ *Creer Bldg. 2F, above the Garden supermarket, 3–16–8 Shirokanedai, Minato-ku* ☎ *03/3440–6635* ▤ *DC, MC, V* Ⓜ *Mita and Namboku subway lines, Shirokanedai Station (Exit 2).*

Spanish

$$ ✕ **Sabado Sabadete** (サバドサバデテ). Catalan jewelry designer Mañuel Benito used to rent a bar in Aoyama on Saturday nights and cook for his friends, just for the fun of it. Word got around: eventually there wasn't room in the bar to lift a fork. Inspired by this success, Benito opened this Spanish restaurant. The highlight of every evening is still the moment when the chef, in his bright red cap, shouts out "Gohan desu yo!"—the Japanese equivalent of "Soup's on!"—and dishes out his bubbling-hot paella. Don't miss the empanadas or the *escalivada* (Spanish ratatouille with red peppers, onions, and eggplant). ⊠ *Genteel Shirokanedai Bldg., 2nd fl., 5–3–2 Shirokanedai, Minato-ku* ☎ *03/3445–9353* ▤ No credit cards ⊘ Closed Sun. Ⓜ *Mita and Namboku subway lines, Shirokanedai Station (Exit 1).*

Shōtō

French

$$$$ ✕ **Chez Matsuo** (シェ・松尾). With its stately homes, Shōtō, a sedate sort of Beverly Hills, is the kind of area you don't expect Tōkyō to have—at least not so close to Shibuya Station. In the middle of it all is Chez

Matsuo, in a lovely two-story Western-style house. The dining rooms overlook the garden, where you can dine by candlelight on spring and autumn evenings. Owner-chef Matsuo studied as a sommelier in London and perfected his culinary finesse in Paris. His pricey food is nouvelle; the specialty of the house is *suprême* (breast and wing) of duck. ⊠ *1–23–15 Shōtō, Shibuya-ku* ☎ *03/3465–0610* 🍴 *Reservations essential* ⊟ *AE, DC, MC, V* Ⓜ *JR Yamanote Line, Ginza and Hanzō-mon subway lines, and private rail lines: Shibuya Station (Exits 5 and 8 for Hanzō-mon, Kita-guchi/North Exit for all others).*

Tsukiji

Japanese

★ **$–$$$** ✕ **Edo-Gin** (江戸銀). In an area that teems with sushi bars, this one maintains its reputation as one of the best. Edo-Gin serves generous slabs of fish that drape over the vinegared rice rather than perch demurely on top. The centerpiece of the main room is a huge tank in which the day's ingredients swim about until they are required; it doesn't get any fresher than this. Set menus here are reasonable, especially for lunch, but a big appetite for specialties like sea urchin and *ōtoro* tuna can put a dent in your budget. ⊠ *4–5–1 Tsukiji, Chūō-ku* ☎ *03/3543–4401* 🍴 *Reservations not accepted* ⊟ *AE, DC, MC, V* ☺ *Closed early Jan.* Ⓜ *Hibiya subway line, Tsukiji Station (Exit 1); Ōedo subway line, Tsukiji-shijō Station (Exit A1).*

Uchisaiwai-chō

Chinese

★ **$$–$$$$** ✕ **Heichinrou** (聘珍楼). A short walk from the Imperial Hotel, this branch of one of Yokohama's oldest and best Chinese restaurants commands a spectacular view of the Imperial Palace grounds. Call ahead to reserve a table by the window. The cuisine is Cantonese; pride of place goes to the *kaisen ryōri*, a banquet of steamed sea bass, lobster, shrimp, scallops, abalone, and other seafood dishes. Much of the clientele comes from the law offices, securities firms, and foreign banks in the building. The VIP room at Heichinrou, with its soft lighting and impeccable linens, is a popular venue for power lunches. ⊠ *Fukoku Seimei Bldg., 28th fl., 2–2–2 Uchisaiwai-chō, Chiyoda-ku* ☎ *03/3508–0555* ⊟ *AE, DC, MC, V* ☺ *Closed Sun.* Ⓜ *Mita Line, Uchisaiwai-chō Station (Exit A6).*

Ueno

Japanese

$$–$$$ ✕ **Sasa-no-yuki** (笹の雪). In the heart of Shitamachi, Tōkyō's old downtown working-class neighborhood, Sasa-no-yuki has been serving meals based on homemade tofu for the past 300 years. The food is inspired in part by *shōjin ryōri* (Buddhist vegetarian cuisine). The basic three-course set menu includes *ankake* (bean curd in sweet soy sauce), *uzumi* tofu (scrambled with rice and green tea), and *unsui* (a creamy tofu crepe filled with sea scallops, shrimp, and minced red pepper). For bigger appetites, there's also an eight-course banquet. The seating is on tatami, and the garden has a waterfall. ⊠ *2–15–10 Negishi, Taitō-ku* ☎ *03/*

3873–1145 🗔 *AE, DC, V* ⊘ *Closed Mon.* Ⓜ *JR Uguisudani Station (Kita-guchi/North Exit).*

Yūraku-chō

Japanese

$$–$$$ ✕ **Robata** (炉端). Old, funky, and more than a little cramped, Robata is
Fodor'sChoice   a bit daunting at first. But fourth-generation chef-owner Takao Inoue
★   holds forth here with an inspired version of Japanese home cooking. He's
also a connoisseur of pottery; he serves his food on pieces acquired at
famous kilns all over the country. There's no menu; just tell Inoue-san
(who speaks some English) how much you want to spend, and leave the
rest to him. A meal at Robata—like the pottery—is simple to the eye
but subtle and fulfilling. Typical dishes include steamed fish with vegetables, stews of beef or pork, and seafood salads. ⊠ *1–3–8 Yūraku-
chō, Chiyoda-ku* ☎ *03/3591–1905* 🗔 *No credit cards* ⊘ *Closed 3rd
Mon. of month. No lunch* Ⓜ *JR Yūraku-chō Station (Hibiya Exit); Hibiya, Chiyoda, and Mita subway lines, Hibiya Station (Exit A4).*

WHERE TO STAY

There are three things you can take for granted almost anywhere you set
down your bags in Tōkyō: cleanliness, safety, and good service. The fac-
tors that will probably determine your choice, then, are cost and location.

It's not at all easy to find a *moderately* priced lodging in this city. The
cost of commercial real estate in Tōkyō has come down from the in-
sane levels of the 1980s and early 1990s, but lodging prices never really
took a nosedive. It doesn't pay to build small or to convert an existing structure to a boutique hotel; when developers build, they build
on a grand scale, and when the project includes a hotel—more often
than not, nowadays, on the upper floors of an office tower—it's invariably at the high end of the market. Most of the hotels that have
opened in Tōkyō since 2002, or are slated to open by 2006, are managed by international luxury chains like the Hyatt, Four Seasons, and
Mandarin Oriental groups.

These ventures add pricy lodgings to the overall supply at an astonishing rate: analysts predict that by 2007 travelers will have some 84,000
rooms at their disposal. Does that presage a glut? Bargains to be had?
Probably not. Hoteliers are predicting that visitors to Tōkyō are willing to pay well to be pampered, and the spare-no-expense approach to
hotel design remains the norm: soaring atriums, concierges, oceans of
marble, interior decorators fetched in from London, New York, and Milan.
The results—some of which are listed here—rival the quality of luxury
accommodations anywhere in the world.

Hotels in the middle market provide less in the way of services and decor,
but this affects the cost of accommodations less than you might imagine. Deluxe hotels make a substantial part of their profits from their banquet and dining facilities; they charge you more, but they can also give
you more space. Farther down the scale, you pay less—but not re-

markably less—and the rooms are disproportionately smaller. By and large, these are the hotels that remain under local management and ownership; some of them, aware at last of the threat posed by their international rivals, are undertaking major expansion and renovation projects to stay competitive.

With Tōkyō's down-market business hotels, inns, and guesthouses, what you sacrifice is essentially location. You pay significantly less for the minimal benefits of a roof overhead, but you might have to travel farther to and from sights you want to see. That said, the sacrifice is not really very great. Many of these accommodations are still within the central wards; some of them have an old-fashioned charm and personal touch the upscale hotels can't offer. Nor should transportation be a concern: wherever you're staying, Tōkyō's subway and train system—comfortable (except in rush hours), efficient, inexpensive, and safe—will get you back and forth.

Unless otherwise specified, all rooms at the hotels listed here have private baths and are Western style.

Prices

	WHAT IT COSTS In yen				
	$$$$	$$$	$$	$	¢
FOR 2 PEOPLE	over 22,000	18,000–22,000	12,000–18,000	8,000–12,000	under 8,000

Price categories are assigned based on the range between the least and most expensive standard double rooms in nonholiday high season. Taxes (5%, plus 3% for bills over ¥15,000) are extra.

Akasaka-mitsuke

$$$$ 🏨 **Hotel New Ōtani Tōkyō and Towers** (ホテルニューオータニ). The New Ōtani is virtually a city unto itself. When the house is full and all the banquet facilities are in use (this is a popular venue for weddings and tour groups), the traffic in the restaurants and shopping arcades seems like rush hour at a busy railway station. The hotel's redeeming feature is its spectacular 10-acre Japanese garden, complete with a pond and a red-lacquer bridge; the rooms overlooking the garden are the best in the house. Among the many restaurants and bars are La Tour d'Argent, Japan's first Trader Vic's, and the revolving Sky Lounge. ✉ 4–1 Kioi-chō, Chiyoda-ku, Tōkyō-to 102-0094 ☎ 03/3265–1111, 0120/11–2211 toll-free 🖷 03/3221–2619 ⊕ www.newotani.co.jp 🛏 1,549 rooms, 30 on 21st floor for women only, 51 suites ⚒ 33 restaurants, cafeteria, coffee shop, grocery, patisserie, room service, in-room data ports, in-room safes, minibars, refrigerators, cable TV with movies, driving range, 2 tennis courts, indoor pool, health club, hair salon, 4 bars, beer garden, shops, babysitting, dry cleaning, laundry service, business services, convention center, travel services, no-smoking rooms ⊟ AE, DC, MC, V Ⓜ Ginza and Marunouchi subway lines, Akasaka-mitsuke Station (Exit 7).

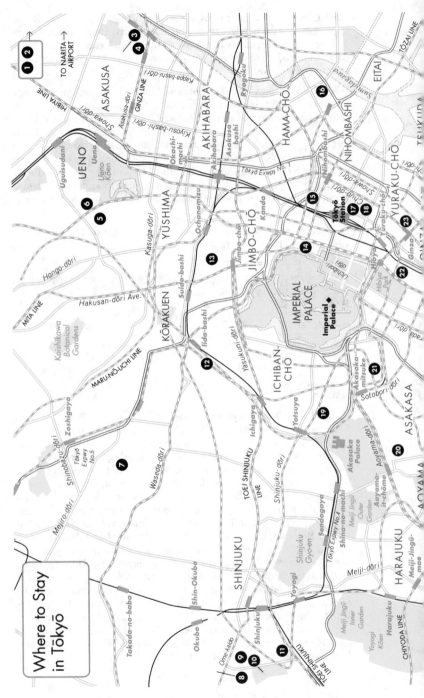

Where to Stay in Tōkyō

TO NARITA → AIRPORT

HIBIYA LINE

ASAKUSA

Asakusa-dōri

Showa-dōri

Kappa-bashi-dōri

GINZA LINE

Kiyosu-bashi-dōri

AKIHABARA

Okachi-machi

Asakusa-bashi

Akihabara

Ryōgoku

HAMA-CHŌ

Sumida-gawa

EITAI

TŌZAI LINE

Kanda

Tōkyō Exwy No.1

UENO

Uguisudani

Ueno

Ueno Kōen

Tōkyō Exwy No.1

YUSHIMA

Ochanomizu

Suida-bashi

Kanda

Nihombashi

Chūo-dōri

Showa-dōri

NIHOMBASHI

Hibi-dōri

TSUKIJI

YŪRAKU-CHŌ

Kasuga-dōri

Hongo-dōri

MITA LINE

Koishikawa Botanical Gardens

Hakusan-dōri Ave.

KŌRAKUEN

MARU-NŌ-UCHI LINE

JIMBO-CHŌ

Jimbo-chō

Iida-bashi

Yasukuni-dōri

IMPERIAL PALACE

Imperial Palace ♦

Uchibori-dōri

Hibiya Park

Chūo-dōri

Yūraku-chō

Ginza

Hibiya-dōri

epa-dōri

Zōshigaya

Shinobazu-dōri

Tōkyō Exwy No.5

ICHIBAN-CHŌ

Yatsuya

Ichigaya

Akasaka-mitsuke

Sotobori-dōri

ASAKASA

Mejiro-dōri

Waseda-dōri

TOEI SHINJUKU LINE

Shinjuku-dōri

Akasaka Palace

Aoyama-dōri

AOYAMA

Aoyama-it-chōme

Takada-no-baba

Shin-Okubo

SHINJUKU

Sendagaya

Shina-no-machi

Tōkyō Exwy No.4

Meiji Jingū Outer Garden

Shinjuku Gyo-en

Meiji-dōri

HARAJUKU

Meiji-Jingū-mae

Okubo

Ome-kaido

Shinjuku

Yoyogi

Meiji Jingū Inner Garden

Yoyogi Kōen

Harajuku

CHIYODA LINE

TOEI SHINJUKU LINE

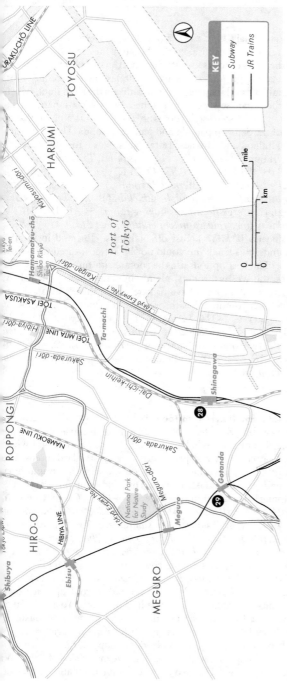

KEY

- - - - Subway
———— JR Trains

0		1 km	
0		1 mile	

ANA Hotel Narita **1**
ANA Hotel Tōkyō **25**
Asakusa View Hotel **3**
Asia Center of Japan **20**
Capitol Tōkyū Hotel **21**
Century Hyatt Hotel **10**
Four Seasons Hotel
Chinzan-sō **7**

Four Seasons Hotel
at Marunouchi **17**
Grand Hyatt Tōkyō at
Roppongi Hills **27**
Hilton Tōkyō **9**
Hotel New Ōtani
Tōkyō and Towers **19**
Hotel Nikkō Winds
Narita **2**

Hotel Okura **26**
Hotel Seiyō Ginza **18**
Hotel Yaesu
Ryūmeikan **15**
Imperial Hotel **22**
Le Meridien Pacific
Tōkyō **28**
Palace Hotel **14**

Park Hyatt Tōkyō **8**
Renaissance Tōkyō Hotel
Ginza Tōbu **24**
Royal Park Hotel **16**
Ryokan Katsutarō **5**
Ryokan Sansuisō **29**
Ryokan Shigetsu **4**
Sawanoya Ryokan **6**

Shinjuku
Washington Hotel **11**
Tōkyō International
Youth Hostel **12**
YMCA Asia
Youth Center **13**
Yoshimizu Ginza **23**

Asakusa

$$$–$$$$ ☒ **Asakusa View Hotel** (浅草ビューホテル). Upscale Western-style accommodations are rare in Asakusa, so the Asakusa View pretty much has this end of the market to itself. Off the smart marble lobby a harpist plays in the tea lounge, and expensive boutiques line the second floor. The communal *hinoki* (Japanese-cypress) baths on the sixth floor, which also houses the Japanese-style tatami suites, overlook a Japanese garden. The best of the Western-style rooms are on the 22nd and 23rd floors, with a view of the Sensō-ji pagoda and temple grounds. There are Chinese, French, Italian, and Japanese restaurants, plus a top-floor lounge with live entertainment. ☒ *3–17–1 Nishi-Asakusa, Taitō-ku, Tōkyō-to 111-8765* ☎ *03/3847–1111* ☒ *03/3842–2117* ⊕ *www.viewhotels.co.jp/asakusa/english* ⊷ *330 Western-style rooms, 7 Japanese-style suites* ⚐ *3 restaurants, coffee shop, pool, health club, Japanese baths, 2 bars, lounge, shops, concierge floor, no-smoking rooms* ▤ *AE, DC, MC, V* Ⓜ *Ginza subway line, Tawara-machi Station (Exit 3).*

★ $$ ☒ **Ryokan Shigetsu** (旅館指月). Just off Nakamise-dōri and inside the Sensō-ji grounds, this small inn could not be better located for a visit to the temple. The best options are the rooms with futon bedding and tatami floors; the Western rooms, plainly but comfortably furnished, are less expensive. All rooms have private baths; there's also a Japanese-style wooden communal bath on the sixth floor with a view of the Sensō-ji pagoda. ☒ *1–31–11 Asakusa, Taitō-ku, Tōkyō-to 111-0032* ☎ *03/3843–2345* ☒ *03/3483–2348* ⊕ *www.roy.hi-ho.ne.jp/shigetsu* ⊷ *14 Western-style rooms, 10 Japanese-style rooms* ⚐ *Restaurant, Japanese baths* ▤ *AE, MC, V* Ⓜ *Ginza subway line, Asakusa Station (Exit 1/Kaminari-mon Exit).*

Ginza

$$$$ ☒ **Renaissance Tōkyō Hotel Ginza Tōbu** (ルネッサンス東京ホテル銀座東武). Relatively reasonable prices, friendly service, and comfortable rooms make the Renaissance something of a bargain for the Ginza area. Blond-wood furniture and pastel quilted bedspreads decorate the standard rooms. The pricier concierge floors have much larger rooms, with such extras as terry robes and hair dryers; breakfast, afternoon tea, and complimentary cocktails in the lounge are part of the package. ☒ *6–13–10 Ginza, Chūō-ku, Tōkyō-to 104-0061* ☎ *03/3546–0111* ☒ *03/3546–8990* ⊕ *http://marriott.com* ⊷ *197 rooms, 9 suites* ⚐ *2 restaurants, coffee shop, room service, minibars, refrigerators, cable TV with movies, hair salon, massage, 2 bars, lounge, dry cleaning, laundry service, concierge floor, business services, travel services, no smoking rooms* ▤ *AE, DC, MC, V* Ⓜ *Hibiya and Asakusa subway lines, Higashi-Ginza Station (Exit A1).*

$$$–$$$$ FodorsChoice ★ ☒ **Yoshimizu Ginza** (銀座吉水). You're expected to fold up your own futon at this modest traditional inn inspired by owner Yoshimi Nakagawa's experience living the simple life at a commune in Woodstock, New York, in the 1970s. The money that isn't spent on service has been spent—with exquisite taste—on simple, natural appointments: wooden floors dyed pale indigo, hand-painted shōji screens, basins of Shigaraki ware in the washrooms. The two stone communal Japanese baths o▸

the ninth floor can be reserved for a private relaxing soak for two. The inn is a few minutes' walk from the Kabuki-za and the fashionable heart of Ginza. Book early. ☒ *3–11–3 Ginza, Chūō-ku, Tōkyō-to 104-0061* ☎ *03/3248–4432* 🖷 *03/3248–4431* ⊕ *www.yoshimizu.com* 📶 *12 Japanese-style rooms without bath* ♿ *2 restaurants, Japanese baths; no room phones, no room TVs, no smoking* ☰ *AE, MC, V* ⏐◎⏐ *BP* Ⓜ *Hibiya subway line, Higashi-Ginza Station (Exit 3 or A2).*

Hakozaki

★ **$$$$**   🖵 **Royal Park Hotel** (ロイヤルパークホテル). The bonus feature of this hotel is its connecting passageway to the Tōkyō City Air Terminal, where you can check in for your flight before boarding the bus to Narita. Pack, ring for the porter, and you won't have to touch your baggage again until it comes off the conveyor belt back home. The comfortable, spacious marble-clad lobby has wood-panel columns and brass trim. Neutral grays and browns decorate the well-proportioned rooms. The best rooms are those on the executive floors (16–18) with a view of the Sumida-gawa, and those on floors 6–8 overlooking the hotel's delightful Japanese garden. ☒ *2–1–1 Nihombashi, Kakigara-chō, Chūō-ku, Tōkyō-to 103-0014* ☎ *03/3667–1111* 🖷 *03/3667–1115* ⊕ *www.rph.co.jp* 📶 *450 rooms, 9 suites* ♿ *7 restaurants, coffee shop, room service, some in-room data ports, minibars, refrigerators, cable TV with movies, 1 bar, lounge, shops, dry cleaning, laundry services, concierge floor, business services, convention center, travel services, no-smoking rooms* ☰ *AE, DC, MC, V* Ⓜ *Hanzō-mon subway line, Suitengū-mae Station (Exit 4).*

Hibiya

$$$$ 🖵 **Imperial Hotel** (帝国ホテル). You can't beat the location of these prestigious quarters: in the heart of central Tōkyō, between the Imperial Palace and Ginza. The finest rooms, on the 30th floor in the New Tower, afford views of the palace grounds. The Old Imperial Bar incorporates elements from the 1922 version of the hotel, which Frank Lloyd Wright designed. The Imperial opened its doors in 1891, and from the outset the hotel has been justly proud of its Western-style facilities and personalized Japanese service. Rooms range from standard doubles to suites that are larger than many homes. ☒ *1–1–1 Uchisaiwai-chō, Chiyoda-ku, Tōkyō-to 100-0011* ☎ *03/3504–1111* 🖷 *03/3581–9146* ⊕ *www.imperialhotel.co.jp* 📶 *1,005 rooms, 54 suites* ♿ *13 restaurants, cable TV with movies, indoor pool, health club, massage, 4 bars, shops, concierge floor, business services, travel services, no-smoking rooms* ☰ *AE, DC, MC, V* Ⓜ *Hibiya subway line, Hibiya Station (Exit 5).*

Higashi-Gotanda

$ 🖵 **Ryokan Sansuisō** (旅館山水荘). Budgeteers appreciate this basic ryokan, a two-story building near Gotanda Station. The proprietor will greet you with a warm smile and a bow and escort you to a small tatami room with a pay TV and a rather noisy heater–air-conditioner mounted on the wall. Some rooms are stuffy, and only two have private baths, but the Sansuisō is clean, easy to find, and only 20 minutes by train from Tōkyō

Station or Ginza. The midnight curfew poses a problem for night owls. The Japan National Tourist Organization can help you make reservations at this Japanese Inn Group property. ⊠ *2–9–5 Higashi-Gotanda, Shinagawa-ku, Tōkyō-to 141-0022* 📞 *03/3441–7475, 03/3201–3331 for Japan National Tourist Organization* 🖷 *03/3449–1944* ⊕ *www.itcj.or.jp/facility/3/facil/313007.html* 🛏 *10 rooms, 2 with bath* ⚷ *Room TVs with movies, Japanese baths* ▤ *AE, V* Ⓜ *Asakusa subway line (Exit A3) and JR Yamanote Line (Higashi-guchi/East Exit), Gotanda Station.*

Kyō-bashi

$$$$ 📺 **Hotel Seiyō Ginza** (ホテル西洋銀座). The grand marble staircase, the thick pile of the carpets, the profusion of cut flowers, the reception staff in coats and tails: all combine to create an atmosphere more like an elegant private club than a hotel. Along with this elegance, location and personalized service are the best reasons to choose the exclusive Seiyō, tucked away on a side street a few minutes from Ginza. Individually decorated rooms have walk-in closets, huge shower stalls, and a direct line to a personal secretary who takes care of your every need. The accommodations, however, are smaller than what you might expect for the price. ⊠ *1–11–2 Ginza, Chūō-ku, Tōkyō-to 104-0061* 📞 *03/3535–1111* 🖷 *03/3535–1110* ⊕ *www.seiyo-ginza.com/* 🛏 *51 rooms, 26 suites* ⚷ *3 restaurants, patisserie, room service, in-room data ports, in-room safes, minibars, refrigerators, cable TV with movies, health club, bar, lounge, babysitting, dry cleaning, laundry service, concierge, business services, convention center, travel services, no-smoking rooms* ▤ *AE, DC, MC, V* Ⓜ *Ginza subway line, Kyō-bashi Station (Exit 2); Yūraku-chō Line, Ginza-Itchōme Station (Exit 7).*

Marunouchi

$$$$ 📺 **Four Seasons Hotel Tokyo at Marunouchi** (フォーシーズンズホテル丸の内東京). The unusual "top-down" design of this ultramodern glass tower means that the first floor is merely a transfer lobby, reception is on the seventh floor, and the guest rooms are on the five floors in between. The muted beige-and-bronze reception area feels like a comfortable private club, with deep-pile carpets, plush brocade sofas, and sumptuous armchairs. Chic black-lacquer doors lead to the spacious guest rooms; beds have brown-leather-covered headboards that continue partway across the ceiling for a canopy effect. Design really *matters* here—but so does high-tech luxury, in touches like plasma-screen TVs and variable lighting. The staff speaks fluent English, and the service is spot-on. ⊠ *1–11–1 Marunouchi, Chiyoda-ku, Tōkyō-to 100-6277* 📞 *03/5222–7222* 🖷 *03/5222–1255* ⊕ *www.fourseasons.com/marunouchi/* 🛏 *48 rooms, 9 suites* ⚷ *Restaurant, room service, in-room data ports, in-room fax, in-room safes, minibars, refrigerators, cable TV with movies, in-room DVD/VCR players, health club, Japanese baths, massage, spa, steam room, bar, lounge, dry cleaning, laundry service, concierge, business services, meeting rooms, no-smoking rooms* ▤ *AE, DC, MC, V* Ⓜ *JR Tōkyō Station (Yaesu South Exit).*

★ **$$$$** 📺 **Palace Hotel** (パレスホテル). The service here is extremely helpful and professional; much of the staff has been with the hotel for more than

10 years. The location is ideal: only a moat separates the hotel from the outer gardens of the Imperial Palace, and Ginza and the financial districts of Marunouchi are both a short taxi or subway ride away. An air of calm conservatism bespeaks the Palace's half century as an accommodation for the well-to-do and well connected. The tasteful, low-key guest rooms are spacious; ask for one on the upper floors, facing the Imperial Palace. ⊠ *1–1–1 Marunouchi, Chiyoda-ku, Tōkyō-to 100-0005* ☎ *03/3211–5211* ⎙ *03/3211–6987* ⊕ *www.palacehotel.co.jp/ english/* ⤴ *384 rooms, 5 suites* ⌂ *7 restaurants, coffee shop, room service, in-room data ports, in-room fax, in-room safes, minibars, refrigerators, cable TV with movies, in-room VCRs, indoor pool, health club, massage, sauna, bar, lounge, shops, dry cleaning, laundry service, concierge, business services, travel services, no-smoking floors* ⊟ *AE, DC, MC, V* Ⓜ *Chiyoda, Marunouchi, Hanzō-mon, Tōzai, and Mita subway lines; Ōte-machi Station (Exit C-13B).*

Nagata-chō

$$$$ 🏨 **Capitol Tōkyū Hotel** (キャピトル東急ホテル). The Capitol was built in 1963, but it feels a bit like a grand hotel of a bygone era and maintains a loyal repeat clientele among foreign business travelers. Traditional touches include an ikebana arrangement dominating the lobby, and an exquisite small garden and fishpond. With two staff members to every guest, the service is excellent. Dark-wood furnishings fill the rooms, but shōji on the windows creates a feeling of soft warmth and light. Request a room overlooking the Hie Jinja shrine. The hotel commands its high prices in part because of its proximity to the National Diet and government offices. ⊠ *2–10–3 Nagata-chō, Chiyoda-ku, Tōkyō-to 100-0014* ☎ *03/3581–4511* ⎙ *03/3581–5822* ⊕ *www.capitoltokyu.com/english* ⤴ *440 rooms, 19 suites* ⌂ *4 restaurants, café, coffee shop, room service, in-room data ports, in-room safes, minibars, refrigerators, cable TV with movies, pool, gym, hair salon, spa, bar, shops, dry cleaning, laundry service, concierge floor, business services, convention center, travel services, no-smoking rooms* ⊟ *AE, DC, MC, V* Ⓜ *Chiyoda and Marunouchi subway lines, Kokkai Gijidō-mae Station (Exit 5); Ginza and Namboku subway lines, Tameike-Sannō Station (Exit 5).*

Nishi-Shinjuku

★ **$$$$** 🏨 **Hilton Tōkyō** (ヒルトン東京). The Hilton, which is a short walk from the megalithic Tōkyō Metropolitan Government Office, is a particular favorite of Western business travelers. When it opened in 1984 it was the largest Hilton in Asia, but opted away from the prevailing atrium style in favor of more guest rooms and banquet facilities; as a result, the lobby is on a comfortable, human scale. A copper-clad spiral staircase reaching to the mezzanine floor above highlights the bar-lounge. Shōji screens instead of curtains bathe the guest rooms in soft, relaxing light. ⊠ *6–6–2 Nishi-Shinjuku, Shinjuku-ku, Tōkyō-to 160-0023* ☎ *03/ 3344–5111, 0120/48–9992 toll-free* ⎙ *03/3342–6094* ⊕ *www.hilton. com* ⤴ *677 rooms, 129 suites* ⌂ *6 restaurants, room service, in-room data ports, in-room fax, some in-room safes, minibars, refrigerators, cable*

TV with movies, 2 tennis courts, pool, gym, hair salon, massage, sauna, bar, cabaret, dance club, shops, babysitting, dry cleaning, laundry service, concierge, business services, travel services, meeting rooms, no-smoking rooms ▭ AE, DC, MC, V Ⓜ *Shinjuku Station (Nishi-guchi/West Exit); Marunouchi subway line, Nishi-Shinjuku Station (Exit C8); Ōedo subway line, Tochō-mae Station (all exits).*

$$$$ 🏨 **Park Hyatt Tōkyō** (パークハイアット東京). An elevator whisks you to the 41st floor, where the hotel—immortalized in the 2003 film *Lost in Translation*—begins with an atrium lounge enclosed on three sides by floor-to-ceiling plate-glass windows. The panorama of Shinjuku spreads out before you. Service is efficient and personal, and the mood of the hotel is contemporary and understated. Guest rooms are large by any standard. King-size beds have Egyptian-cotton sheets and down-feather duvets; other appointments include pale olive-green carpets, black-lacquer cabinets, and huge plasma-screen TVs. Among the hotel's several restaurants is the popular New York Grill, with its open kitchen and steak-and-seafood menu. ✉ *3–7–1–2 Nishi-Shinjuku, Shinjuku-ku, Tōkyō-to 163-1090* ☎ *03/5322–1234* 📠 *03/5322–1288* ⊕ *http://tokyo. park.hyatt.com/* ⇌ *155 rooms, 23 suites* ♨ *3 restaurants, coffee shop, patisserie, room service, in-room data ports, in-room fax, in-room safes, minibars, refrigerators, cable TV with movies, in-room DVD/VCR players, indoor pool, health club, sauna, spa, 2 bars, library, dry cleaning, laundry service, concierge, Internet, business services, convention center, airport shuttle, travel services, no-smoking rooms* ▭ AE, DC, MC, V Ⓜ *Shinjuku Station (Nishi-guchi/West Exit).*

$$$–$$$$ 🏨 **Century Hyatt Hotel** (センチュリーハイアットホテル). The Century has the trademark Hyatt atrium-style lobby: seven stories high, with open-glass elevators soaring upward and three huge chandeliers suspended from above. The rooms are spacious for the price, though unremarkable in design; the best choices are the View Rooms (10th–26th floors), which overlook Shinjuku Kōen (Shinjuku Park). The Hyatt emphasizes its cuisine; at any given time, there's almost sure to be a "gourmet fair" in progress, celebrating the food of one country or another and supervised by visiting celebrity chefs. ✉ *2–7–2 Nishi-Shinjuku, Shinjuku-ku, Tōkyō-to 160-0023* ☎ *03/3349–0111* 📠 *03/3344–5575* ⊕ *http://tokyo. century.hyatt.com/* ⇌ *750 rooms, 16 suites* ♨ *7 restaurants, coffee shop, room service, in-room data ports, in-room safes, minibars, refrigerators, cable TV with movies, indoor pool, gym, hair salon, massage, 2 bars, lounge, shops, dry cleaning, laundry service, concierge floor, business services, convention center, travel services, no-smoking rooms* ▭ AE, DC, MC, V Ⓜ *Shinjuku Station (Nishi-guchi/West Exit).*

$$–$$$ 🏨 **Shinjuku Washington Hotel** (新宿ワシントンホテル). This is the very model of a modern Japanese business hotel, where service is computerized as much as possible and the rooms—utterly devoid of superfluous features—are just about big enough for the furniture and your luggage. The third-floor lobby has an automated check-in and check-out system; you are assigned a room and provided with a plastic card that opens the door and the mini-bar. The clerk at the counter will explain the process, but after that you're on your own. ✉ *3–2–9 Nishi-Shinjuku, Shinjuku-ku, Tōkyō-to 160-0023* ☎ *03/3343–3111* 📠 *03/3340–1804* ⊕ *www.wh-rsv.com/english/shinjuku/*

◻ 1,630 rooms, 3 suites ◻ 4 restaurants, coffee shop, grocery, room service, some in-room data ports, minibars, refrigerators, room TVs with movies, in-room VCRs, massage, bar, no-smoking rooms ▭ AE, DC, MC, V Ⓜ Shinjuku Station (Minami-guchi/South Exit).

Roppongi

$$$$ ▦ **Grand Hyatt Tōkyō at Roppongi Hills** (グランドハイアット東京). The
FodorsChoice Grand Hyatt is a class act—a hotel designed with every imaginable con-
★ venience and comfort. A drawer in the mahogany dresser in each room,
for example, has laptop cables and adaptors. The showers have two delivery systems, one through a luxurious "rain-shower" head affixed to the
ceiling. No expense has been spared on materials, from the Egyptian-cotton bed linens to the red-granite pool in the spa. Rooms are huge, with
high ceilings, black-out blinds, and muted earth tones of brown, beige,
and yellow. Weather permitting, the rooms on the west side on the 10th
floor and higher afford a view of Mt. Fuji. ⊠ *6–10–3 Roppongi, Minato-
ku, Tōkyō-to 106–0032* ☎ *03/4333–1234* 🖷 *03/4333–8123* ⊕ *www.
grandhyatttokyo.com ◻ 361 rooms, 24 suites ◻ 5 restaurants, 2 cafés,
patisserie, room service, in-room data ports, in-room fax, in-room safes,
minibars, refrigerators, cable TV with movies, in-room DVD players, indoor pool, gym, health club, hair salon, Japanese baths, spa, 3 bars, shops,
babysitting, dry cleaning, laundry service, concierge, business services, convention center, airport shuttle, travel services, no-smoking rooms ▭ AE,
DC, MC, V Ⓜ Hibiya subway line, Roppongi Station (Roppongi Hills Exit).*

★ **$$** ▦ **Asia Center of Japan** (アジア会館). Established mainly for Asian stu-
dents and travelers on limited budgets, these accommodations have be-
come generally popular with many international travelers for their good
value and easy access (a 15-minute walk) to the nightlife of Roppongi.
The "semi-doubles" here are really small singles, but twins and doubles
are quite spacious for the price. Appointments are a bit spartan—off-
white walls, mass-market veneer furniture—but the rooms have plenty
of basic amenities like hair dryers, electric kettles, and yukatas. ⊠ *8–10–32
Akasaka, Minato-ku, Tōkyō-to 107-0052* ☎ *03/3402–6111* 🖷 *03/
3402–0738* ⊕ *www.asiacenter.or.jp ◻ 172 rooms, 1 suite ◻ Restau-
rant, in-room data ports, refrigerators, cable TV with movies, massage,
dry cleaning, laundry service, no smoking rooms ▭ AE, MC, V Ⓜ Ginza
and Hanzō-mon subway lines, Aoyama-itchōme Station (Exit 4).*

Sekiguchi

$$$$ ▦ **Four Seasons Hotel Chinzan-sō** (フォーシーズンズホテル椿山荘).Where
FodorsChoice else can you sleep in a million-dollar room? That's about what it cost,
★ on average, to build and furnish each spacious room in this elegant hotel.
The spectacular fifth-floor Conservatory Rooms have bay windows
overlooking private Japanese-garden terraces. The solarium pool, with
its columns, tropical plants, and retractable glass roof, is straight out
of Xanadu. Built on the former estate of an imperial prince, Chinzan-
sō rejoices in one of the most beautiful settings in Tōkyō; in summer
the gardens are famous for their fireflies. Complimentary shuttle ser-
vice connects you to the subway and Tōkyō Station. ⊠ *2–10–8 Sekiguchi,*

Bunkyō-ku, Tōkyō-to 112-0014 ☎ *03/3943–2222* 🖷 *03/3943–2300* ⊕ *www.fourseasons.com/tokyo* 🛏 *283 rooms, 51 suites* ⚭ *4 restaurants, room service, in-room data ports, some in-room faxes, in-room safes, minibars, refrigerators, cable TV with movies, indoor pool, health club, Japanese baths, spa, lounge, shops, babysitting, dry cleaning, laundry service, concierge, business services, convention center, travel services, no-smoking floors* ▤ *AE, DC, MC, V* Ⓜ *Yūraku-chō subway line, Edogawa-bashi Station (Exit 1A).*

Shinagawa

$$$$ 🏨 **Le Meridien Pacific Tōkyō** (ホテルパシフィック東京). Just across the street from JR Shinagawa Station, the Meridien sits on grounds that were once part of an imperial-family estate. The hotel gears much of its marketing effort toward booking banquets, wedding receptions, conventions, and tour groups; rooms are comfortable, but public spaces tend to carry a lot of traffic. The Sky Lounge on the 30th floor affords a fine view of Tōkyō Bay. The entire back wall of the ground-floor lounge is glass, the better to contemplate a Japanese garden, sculpted with rocks and waterfalls. ⊠ *3–13–3 Takanawa, Minato-ku, Tōkyō-to 108-0074* ☎ *03/3445–6711* 🖷 *03/3445–5137* ⊕ *www.lemeridien.com* 🛏 *900 rooms, 40 suites* ⚭ *5 restaurants, coffee shop, grocery, room service, in-room data ports, minibars, refrigerators, cable TV with movies, pool, hair salon, massage, bar, lounge, shops, dry cleaning, laundry service, concierge, business services, convention center, travel services, no-smoking rooms* ▤ *AE, DC, MC, V* Ⓜ *JR Yamanote Line, Shinagawa Station (West Exit).*

Tora-no-mon

$$$$ 🏨 **ANA Hotel Tōkyō** (東京全日空ホテル). The ANA typifies the ziggurat-atrium style that seems to have been a requirement for hotel architecture from the mid-'80s. The reception floor, with its two-story fountain, is clad in enough marble to have depleted an Italian quarry. In general, though, the interior designers have made skillful use of artwork and furnishings to take some of the chill off the hotel's relentless modernism. Guest rooms are airy and spacious. There are Chinese, French, and Japanese restaurants. The Astral Lounge on the top (37th) floor affords a superb view of the city. The hotel is a short walk from the U.S. Embassy. ⊠ *1–12–33 Akasaka, Minato-ku, Tōkyō-to 107-0052* ☎ *03/3505–1111, 0120/02–9501 toll-free* 🖷 *03/3505–1155* ⊕ *www.anahoteltokyo.jp* 🛏 *867 rooms, 16 suites* ⚭ *12 restaurants, cafeteria, coffee shop, food court, room service, in-room data ports, in-room fax, minibars, refrigerators, cable TV with movies, indoor pool, health club, hair salon, massage, sauna, 4 bars, shops, dry cleaning, laundry service, concierge floor, business services, meeting room, travel services, no-smoking floors* ▤ *AE, DC, MC, V* Ⓜ *Ginza and Namboku subway lines, Tameike-Sannō Station (Exit 13); Namboku subway line, Roppongi-itchō Station (Exit 3).*

$$$$
Fodor'sChoice
★
🏨 **Hotel Ōkura** (ホテルオークラ). Year after year, a poll of business travelers ranks the Ōkura among the best hotels in Asia for its exemplary yet unobtrusive service. The hotel opened just before the 1964 Olympics, and, understated in its sophistication, human in its scale, it remains a

favorite of diplomatic visitors. Amenities in the tasteful, spacious rooms include remote-control draperies and terry robes. The odd-number rooms, 871–889 inclusive, overlook a small Japanese landscaped garden. The on-site museum houses fine antique porcelain, mother-of-pearl, and ceramics; tea ceremonies take place here Monday–Saturday 11–4 (¥1,000). The main building is preferable to the south wing, which you reach by an underground shopping arcade. ⊠ *2–10–4 Tora-no-mon, Minato-ku, Tōkyō-to 105-0001* ☎ *03/3582–0111, 0120/00–3751 toll-free* 🖷 *03/3582–3707* ⊕ *www.okura.com/tokyo* ➷ *855 rooms, 47 suites* 🍴 *8 restaurants, cafeteria, coffee shop, room service, in-room data ports, in-room fax, in-room safes, minibars, refrigerators, cable TV with movies, in-room VCRs, indoor pool, health club, spa, 3 bars, shops, dry cleaning, laundry service, concierge, business services, convention center, travel services, no-smoking rooms* ⊟ *AE, DC, MC, V* Ⓜ *Hibiya subway line, Kamiya-chō Station (Exit 3); Ginza subway line, Tora-no-mon Station (Exit 4B).*

Ueno

$ 🈁 **Ryokan Katsutarō** (旅館勝太郎). This small, simple, economical hotel is a five-minute walk from the entrance to Ueno Kōen (Ueno Park) and a 10-minute walk from the Tōkyō National Museum. The quietest rooms are in the back, away from the main street. A simple breakfast of toast, eggs, and coffee is served for only ¥500. To get here, leave the Nezu subway station by Exit 2, cross the road, take the street running northeast, and turn right at the "T" intersection; Ryokan Katsutarō is 25 yards along Dōbutsuen-uramon-dōri, on the left-hand side. ⊠ *4–16–8 Ikenohata, Taitō-ku, Tōkyō-to 110-0008* ☎ *03/3821–9808* 🖷 *03/3891–4789* ⊕ *www.katsutaro.com/katsu-index.html* ➷ *7 Japanese-style rooms, 4 with bath* 🍴 *In-room data ports, Japanese baths; no a/c in some rooms, no TV in some rooms* ⊟ *AE, MC, V* Ⓜ *Chiyoda subway line, Nezu Station (Exit 2).*

Yaesu

★ $$–$$$ 🈁 **Hotel Yaesu Ryūmeikan** (ホテル八重洲龍名館). It's amazing that this ryokan near Tōkyō Station has survived in the heart of the city's financial district, where the price of real estate is astronomical. A friendly, professional staff goes the extra mile to make you feel comfortable; weekday evenings, someone who speaks English is usually on duty. Amenities are few, but for price and location this inn is hard to beat. Room rates include a Japanese-style breakfast; ¥800 per person is deducted from your bill if you'd rather skip it. Checkout is at 10 AM sharp; there's a ¥1,500 surcharge for each hour you overstay. ⊠ *1–3–22 Yaesu, Chūō-ku, Tōkyō-to 103-0028* ☎ *03/3271–0971* 🖷 *03/3271–0977* ⊕ *www.ryumeikan.co.jp/yaesu_e.htm* ➷ *21 Japanese-style rooms, 9 Western-style rooms* 🍴 *2 restaurants, in-room data ports, refrigerators, Japanese baths* ⊟ *AE, MC, V* ⍾ *BP* Ⓜ *JR Line and Marunouchi subway line, Tōkyō Station (Yaesu North Exit); Tōzai subway line, Nihombashi Station (Exit A3).*

Yanaka

★ $ ▣ **Sawanoya Ryokan** (澤の屋旅館). The Shitamachi area is known for its down-to-earth friendliness, which you get in full measure at Sawanoya. This little inn is a family business: everybody pitches in to help you plan excursions and book hotels for the next leg of your journey, and they even organize cultural events in the lobby. The inn is very popular with budget travelers, so reserve well in advance by fax or online. To get here from Nezu Station, walk 300 yards north along Shinobazu-dōri and take the street on the right; Sawanoya is 180 yards ahead on the right. ⊠ *2–3–11 Yanaka, Taitō-ku, Tōkyō-to 110-0001* ☎ *03/3822–2251* 🖷 *03/3822–2252* ⊕ *www.sawanoya.com* ⬮ *12 Japanese-style rooms, 2 with bath* ⟁ *Dining room, in-room data ports, Japanese baths* ▭ *AE, MC, V* Ⓜ *Chiyoda subway line, Nezu Station (Exit 1).*

Hostels & Dormitory Accommodations

$ ▣ **YMCA Asia Youth Center** (YMCAアジア青少年センター). Both men and women can stay here, and all rooms are private and have private baths. The hostel is an eight-minute walk from Suidō-bashi Station. ⊠ *2–5–5 Saragaku, Chiyoda-ku, Tōkyō-to 101-0064* ☎ *03/3233–0611* 🖷 *03/3233–0633* ⊕ *http://ymcajapan.org/ayc* ⬮ *55 rooms* ▭ *MC, V* Ⓜ *JR Mita Line, Suidō-bashi Station.*

¢   ▣ **Tōkyō International Youth Hostel** (東京国際ユースホステル). In typical hostel style, you're required to be off the premises between 10 AM and 3 PM. Less typical is the fact that for an additional ¥1,200 over the standard rate you can eat breakfast and dinner in the hostel cafeteria. TIYH is a few minutes' walk from Iidabashi Station. ⊠ *Central Plaza Bldg., 18th fl., 1–1 Kagura-kashi, Shinjuku-ku, Tōkyō-to 162-0823* ☎ *03/3235–1107* 🖷 *03/3267–4000* ⊕ *www.tokyo-yh.jp/eng/e_top.html* ⬮ *138 bunk beds without bath* ⟁ *Dining room, Japanese baths* ▭ *No credit cards* Ⓜ *JR; Tōzai, Namboku, and Yūraku-chō subway lines: Iidabashi Station (Exit B2b).*

Near Narita Airport

Transportation between Narita Airport and Tōkyō proper takes at least an hour and a half. In heavy traffic a limousine bus or taxi ride can stretch to two hours or more. A sensible strategy for visitors with early-morning flights home would be to spend the night before at one of several hotels near the airport, all of which have courtesy shuttles to the departure terminals; these hotels are also a boon to visitors en route elsewhere with layovers in Narita.

$$$$ ▣ **ANA Hotel Narita** (成田全日空ホテル). This hotel, like many others in the ANA chain, aspires to architecture in the grand style; expect the cost of brass and marble to show up on your bill. The amenities measure up, and the proximity to the airport (about 15 minutes by shuttle bus) makes this a good choice if you're in transit. If you're flying ANA, you can check in for your flight in the lobby. ⊠ *68 Hori-no-uchi, Narita-shi, Chiba-ken 286-0107* ☎ *0476/33–1311, 0120/02–9501 toll-free* 🖷 *0476/33–0244* ⊕ *www.anahotel-narita.com/english* ⬮ *422 rooms* ⟁ *3 restaurants, coffee shop, room service, in-room data ports, mini-*

bars, cable TV with movies, tennis court, indoor pool, gym, sauna, shops, airport shuttle, no-smoking rooms ☰ AE, DC, MC, V.

$$–$$$$ 🏨 **Hotel Nikkō Winds Narita** (ホテル日航ウインズ成田). A regular shuttle bus (at Terminal 1, Bus Stop 14; Terminal 2, Bus Stop 31) makes the 10-minute trip from the airport to the Nikkō Winds, and you can check in for Japan Airlines flights right at the hotel. Basic, cheap furnishings fill the rooms in the main building, and there's barely room to pass between the bed and the dresser en route to the bathroom—but the rooms are thoroughly soundproof. Rooms in the "Executive" building are nicer but pricier. ✉ 560 Tokkō, Narita-shi, Chiba-ken 286-1016 ☎ 0476/33–1111, 0120/58–2586 toll-free 🖷 0476/33–1108 ⊕ www.jalhnn.co.jp/hnn-e 🛏 308 rooms, 9 suites ⚏ 3 restaurants, coffee shop, grocery, room service, in-room data ports, minibars, refrigerators, cable TV with movies, 2 tennis courts, pool, hair salon, massage, lounge, shops, meeting room, airport shuttle, no-smoking rooms ☰ AE, DC, MC, V.

NIGHTLIFE & THE ARTS

Under a rainbow of neon, Tōkyō comes alive at night. This city has more sheer diversity of nightlife than any other Japanese city. It seems as if every neighborhood is packed with secret drinking dens, swank bars, jazz spots, pubs, clubs, hostess bars, and other entertainments. Whether you're a punk rocker, disco diva, or bar-hopper, you'll be in good company if you venture out after dark.

Despite the popularity of *nomunication* (communication through drink), not all of the city's nightlife revolves around Suntory whiskey and Asahi beer. Tōkyō has an incredibly diverse performing-arts scene that spans everything from the traditional arts to Western musicals to avant-garde theater. Japan's own great stage traditions—Kabuki, Nō, Bunraku puppet drama, and various forms of music and dance—take you back in time as they bring to life the histories and folktales of old Japan.

The Arts

An astonishing variety of dance and music, both classical and popular, can be found in Tōkyō, alongside the must-see traditional Japanese arts of Kabuki, Nō, and Bunraku. The city is a proving ground for local talent and a magnet for orchestras and concert soloists from all over the world. Tōkyō also has modern theater—in somewhat limited choices, to be sure, unless you can follow dialogue in Japanese, but Western repertory companies can always find receptive audiences here for plays in English. And it doesn't take long for a hit show from New York or London to open in Tōkyō.

Japan has yet to develop any real strength of its own in ballet and has only just begun to devote serious resources to opera, but for that reason touring companies like the Metropolitan, the Bolshoi, Sadler's Wells, and the Bayerische Staatsoper find Tōkyō a very compelling venue—as well they might when even seats at ¥30,000 or more sell out far in advance. One domestic company that's making a name for itself is the Asami Maki Ballet, whose dancers are known for their technical proficiency and expressiveness; the company often performs at the Tōkyō Metropolitan Festival Hall. Latin dance also has a strong following in Tōkyō, and flamenco heart-throb Joaquin Cortés visits regularly to wide acclaim and packed houses.

One of Tōkyō's best English-language performance guides is *Metropolis,* a free weekly magazine that has up-to-date listings of what's going on in the city; it's available at hotels, book and music stores, some restaurants and cafés, and other locations. Another source, rather less complete, is the *Tour Companion,* a tabloid visitor guide published every two weeks, available free of charge at hotels and at Japan National Tourist Organization offices. For coverage of all aspects of Tōkyō's performance-art scene, visit ⊕ www.artindex.metro.tokyo.jp.

If your hotel cannot help you with concert and performance bookings, call **Ticket Pia** (☎ 03/5237–9999) for assistance in English. Note, however, that this is one of the city's major ticket agencies, and the lines are frequently busy. The **Playguide Agency** (✉ Playguide Bldg., 2–6–4 Ginza, Chūō-ku ☎ 03/3561–8821 🖷 03/3567–0263 Ⓜ Yūraku-chō subway line, Ginza Itchōme Station, Exit 4) sells tickets to cultural events via outlets in most department stores and in other locations throughout the city; you can stop in at the main office and ask for the nearest counter. Note that agencies normally do not have tickets for same-day performances but only for advance booking.

Dance
Traditional Japanese dance, like flower arranging and the tea ceremony, is divided into dozens of styles, ancient of lineage and fiercely proud of their differences from each other. In fact, only the aficionado can really tell them apart. They survive not so much as performing arts but as schools, offering dance as a cultured accomplishment to interested amateurs. At least once a year, teachers and their students in each of these schools hold a recital, so that on any given evening there's very likely to be one somewhere in Tōkyō. Truly professional performances are given at the Kokuritsu Gekijō and the Shimbashi Enbujō; the most important of the classical schools, however, developed as an aspect of Kabuki, and if you attend a play at the Kabuki-za, you are almost guaranteed to see a representative example.

The well-known ballet companies that come to Tōkyō from abroad perform to full houses, usually at the Tōkyō Metropolitan Festival Hall in Ueno. There are now about 15 professional Japanese ballet companies, including the Tōkyō Ballet—which performs at the Tōkyō Metropolitan Festival Hall and regularly tours abroad—but this has yet to become an art form on which Japan has had much of an impact.

Modern dance, on the other hand, is a different story. The modern Japanese dance form known as Butō, in particular, with its contorted and expressive body movements, is acclaimed internationally and domestically. Butō performances are held periodically at a variety of event spaces and small theaters. For details, check with ticket agencies and the local English-language press.

Film

One of the best things about foreign films in Japan is that the distributors invariably add Japanese subtitles rather than dub their offerings. Exceptions include kids' movies and big blockbusters that are released in both versions—if there are two screenings close to each other, that's a sign one may be dubbed. The original soundtrack, of course, may not be all that helpful to you if the film is Polish or Italian, but the majority of first-run foreign films here are made in the United States. Choices range from the usual Hollywood fare to independent movies, but many films take so long to open in Tōkyō that you've probably seen them all already at home. And tickets are expensive: around ¥1,800 for general admission and ¥2,500–¥3,000 for a reserved seat, called a *shitei-seki*. Slightly discounted tickets, usually ¥1,600, can be purchased from the ticket counters found in many department stores.

Unless your Japanese is top-notch, most domestic films will be off-limits, but if you happen to be in town during one of the many film festivals you may be able to catch a screening with English subtitles. Festival season is in the fall, with the Tōkyō International Film Festival taking over the Shibuya district in October and a slew of other more specialized festivals screening more outré fare.

First-run theaters that have new releases, both Japanese and foreign, are clustered for the most part in three areas: Shinjuku, Shibuya, and Yūraku-chō-Hibiya-Ginza. At most of them, the last showing of the evening starts at around 7. This is not the case, however, with the best news on the Tōkyō film scene: the handful of small theaters that take a special interest in classics, revivals, and serious imports. Somewhere on the premises will also be a chrome-and-marble coffee shop, a fashionable little bar, or even a decent restaurant. Most of these small theaters have a midnight show—at least on the weekends.

Bunka-mura. The complex in Shibuya has two movie theaters, a concert auditorium (Orchard Hall), and a performance space (Theater Cocoon); it's the principal venue for many of Tōkyō's film festivals. ⊠ *2–24–1 Dōgen-zaka, Shibuya-ku* ☎ *03/3477–9999* Ⓜ *JR Yamanote Line, Ginza and Hanzō-mon subway lines, and private rail lines; Shibuya Station (Exits 5 and 8 for Hanzō-mon Line, Kita-guchi/North Exit for all others).*

Cine Saison Shibuya. In addition to popular films, this theater occasionally screens recent releases by award-winning directors from such countries as Iran, China, and South Korea. ⊠ *Prime Bldg., 2–29–5 Dōgen-zaka, Shibuya-ku* ☎ *03/3770–1721* Ⓜ *JR Yamanote Line, Shibuya Station (Hachiko Exit).*

Haiyū-za. This is primarily a repertory theater, but on Haiyū-za Talkie Nights it screens notable foreign films. ⊠ *4–9–2 Roppongi, Minato-ku* ☎ *03/3401–4073* Ⓜ *Hibiya subway line, Roppongi Station (Exit 4A).*

Virgin Cinemas. In Roppongi Hills, this complex offers comfort, plus six screens, VIP seats, and late shows on weekends. There are plenty of bars in the area for post-movie discussions. ⊠ *Keyakizaka Complex, 6–10–2 Roppongi, Minato-ku* ☎ *03/5775–6090* Ⓜ *Hibiya and Ōedo subway lines, Roppongi Station (Roppongi Hills Exit).*

Modern Theater

The Shingeki (Modern Theater) movement began in Japan at about the turn of the 20th century, but did not develop a voice of its own here until after World War II. Today it's a lively art, and theaters small and large, in unexpected pockets all over Tōkyō, attest to its vitality.

Most of these performances, however, are in Japanese, for Japanese audiences. You're unlikely to find one with program notes in English to help you follow it. Unless it's a play you already know well, and you're curious to see how it translates, you might do well to think of some other way to spend your evenings out if you don't understand Japanese. Language is less of a barrier, however, to enjoyment of the Takarazuka comedic troupe.

Takarazuka. Japan's own wonderfully goofy all-female troupe was founded in the Ōsaka suburb of Takarazuka in 1913 and has been going strong ever since; today it has not one but five companies, one of them with a permanent home in Tōkyō at the 2,069-seat Tōkyō Takarazuka Theater. Everybody sings; everybody dances; the sets are breathtaking; the costumes are swell. Where else but at the Takarazuka could you see *Gone With the Wind*, sung in Japanese, with a young woman in a mustache and a frock coat playing Rhett Butler? Tickets cost ¥3,800–¥10,000 for regular performances, ¥2,000–¥5,000 for debut performances with the company's budding ingenues. ✉ *1–1–3 Yūraku-chō, Chiyoda-ku* ☎ *03/5251–2001* Ⓜ *JR Yamanote Line, Yūraku-chō Station (Hibiya-guchi Exit); Hibiya subway line, Hibiya Station (Exit A5); Chiyoda and Mita subway line, Hibiya Station (Exit A13).*

Music

Information in English about venues for traditional Japanese music (koto, shamisen, and so forth) can be a bit hard to find; check newspaper listings, particularly the Friday and Saturday editions, for concerts and school recitals. Western music poses no such problem: during the 1980s and early 1990s a considerable number of new concert halls and performance spaces sprang up all over the city, adding to what was already an excellent roster of public auditoriums. The following are a few of the most important.

Casals Hall. The last of the fine small auditoriums built for chamber music before the Japanese bubble economy burst in the early '90s was designed by architect Arata Isozaki—justly famous for the Museum of Contemporary Art in Los Angeles. In addition to chamber music, Casals draws piano, guitar, cello, and voice soloists. ✉ *1–6 Kanda Surugadai, Chiyoda-ku* ☎ *03/3294–1229* Ⓜ *JR Chūō Line and Marunouchi subway line, Ochanomizu Station (Exit 2).*

Nakano Sun Plaza. Everything from rock to Argentine tango music is staged at this hall. ✉ *4–1–1 Nakano, Nakano-ku* ☎ *03/3388–1151* Ⓜ *JR and Tōzai subway lines, Nakano Station (Kita-guchi/North Exit).*

New National Theater and Tōkyō Opera City Concert Hall. With its 1,810-seat main auditorium, this venue nourishes Japan's fledgling efforts to make a name for itself in the world of opera. The Opera City Concert Hall has a massive pipe organ and hosts visiting orchestras and performers.

Large-scale operatic productions such as *Carmen* draw crowds at the New National Theater's Opera House, while the Pit and Playhouse theaters showcase musicals and more intimate dramatic works. Ticket prices range from ¥1,500 to ¥21,000. The complex also includes an art gallery. ☒ *3–20–2 Nishi-Shinjuku, Shinjuku-ku* ☎ *03/5353–0788, 03/5353–9999 for tickets* ⊕ *www.operacity.jp* Ⓜ *Keiō Shin-sen private rail line, Hatsudai Station (Higashi-guchi/East Exit).*

NHK Hall. The home base for the Japan Broadcasting Corporation's NHK Symphony Orchestra is probably the auditorium most familiar to Japanese lovers of classical music, as performances here are routinely rebroadcast on NHK-TV. ☒ *2–2–1 Jinnan, Shibuya-ku* ☎ *03/3465–1751* Ⓜ *JR Yamanote Line, Shibuya Station (Hachiko Exit); Ginza and Hanzō-mon subway lines, Shibuya Station (Exits 6 and 7).*

Suntory Hall. This lavishly appointed concert auditorium in the Ark Hills complex has one of the best locations for theatergoers who want to extend their evening out: there's an abundance of good restaurants and bars nearby. ☒ *1–13–1 Akasaka, Minato-ku* ☎ *03/3505–1001* Ⓜ *Ginza and Namboku subway lines, Tameike-Sannō Station (Exit 13).*

Tōkyō Dome. A 55,000-seat sports arena, the dome hosts the biggest acts from abroad in rock and popular music. ☒ *1–3–61 Kōraku, Bunkyō-ku* ☎ *03/5800–9999* Ⓜ *Marunouchi and Namboku subway lines, Kōraku-en Station (Exit 2); Ōedo and Mita subway lines, Kasuga Station (Exit A2); JR Suidō-bashi Station (Nishi-guchi/West Exit).*

Tōkyō Metropolitan Festival Hall (Tōkyō Bunka Kaikan). In the 1960s and '70s this hall was one of the city's premier showcases for orchestral music and visiting soloists. It still gets major bookings. ☒ *5–45 Ueno Kōen, Taitō-ku* ☎ *03/3828–2111* Ⓜ *JR Yamanote Line, Ueno Station (Kōen-guchi/Park Exit).*

Traditional Theater

BUNRAKU   Bunraku puppet theater is one of Japan's most accessible traditional arts. Incredibly intricate puppets give performances so realistic that you may soon forget they're being guided by black-clad puppet masters. The spiritual center of Bunraku today is Ōsaka, rather than Tōkyō, but there are a number of performances in the small hall of the Kokuritsu Gekijō. The art form has come into vogue with younger audiences, and Bunraku troupes will occasionally perform in trendier locations. Consult *Metropolis* magazine or check with one of the English-speaking ticket agencies for performance schedules.

KABUKI   Kabuki has been pleasing Japanese audiences from all walks of life for more than 300 years. It's the kind of theater—a combination of music, dance, and drama, with spectacular costumes and acrobatics, duels, and quick changes and special effects thrown in—that you can enjoy without understanding a word the actors say.

Fodor'sChoice   **Kabuki-za.** The best place to see Kabuki is at this theater, built especially
★   for this purpose, with its *hanamichi* (runway) passing diagonally through the audience to the revolving stage. Matinees usually begin at 11 and end at 4; evening performances start at 4:30 and end around 9. Reserved seats are expensive and can be hard to come by on short notice (reserve tickets by at least 6 PM the day before you wish to attend). For a mere

¥800 to ¥1,000, however, you can buy an unreserved ticket that allows you to see one act of a play from the topmost gallery. Bring binoculars—the gallery is very far from the stage. You might also want to rent an earphone set (¥650; deposit ¥1,000) to follow the play in English, but for some this is more of an intrusion than a help—and you can't use the set in the topmost galleries. ✉ *4–12–15 Ginza, Chūō-ku* ☎ *03/5565–6000 or 03/3541–3131* ⊕ *www.shochiku.co.jp/play/kabukiza/theater* Ⓜ *Hibiya and Asakusa subway lines, Higashi-Ginza Station (Exit 3).*

Kokuritsu Gekijō. This theater hosts Kabuki companies based elsewhere; it also has a training program for young people who may not have one of the hereditary family connections but want to break into this closely guarded profession. Debut performances, called *kao-mise*, are worth watching to catch the stars of the next generation. Reserved seats are usually ¥1,500–¥9,000. Tickets can be reserved by phone up until the day of the performance by calling the theater box office between 10 and 5. ✉ *4–1 Hayabusa-chō, Chiyoda-ku* ☎ *03/3230–3000* Ⓜ *Hanzō-mon subway line, Hanzō-mon Station (Exit 1).*

Shimbashi Enbujō. Dating to 1925, this theater was built for the geisha of the Shimbashi quarter to present their spring and autumn performances of traditional music and dance. It's a bigger house than the Kabuki-za, and it presents a lot of traditional dance, *kyōgen* (traditional Nō-style comic skits), and conventional Japanese drama as well as Kabuki. Reserved seats commonly run ¥2,100–¥16,800, and there's no gallery. ✉ *6–18–2 Ginza, Chūō-ku* ☎ *03/5565–6000* Ⓜ *Hibiya and Asakusa subway lines, Higashi-Ginza Station (Exit A6).*

NŌ   Performances of Nō, with its slow, ritualized movements and archaic language, are given at various times during the year, generally in the theaters of the individual schools. The schools also often teach their dance and recitation styles to amateurs. Consult the *Tour Companion* listings. Tickets to Takigi Nō (held outdoors in temple courtyards) sell out quickly and are normally available only through the temples.

Kanze Nō-gakudō. Founded in the 14th century, this is among the most important of the Nō family schools in Tōkyō. The current *iemoto* (head) of the school is the 26th in his line. ✉ *1–16–4 Shōtō, Shibuya-ku* ☎ *03/3469–5241* Ⓜ *Ginza and Hanzō-mon subway lines, Shibuya Station (Exit 3A).*

National Nō Theater. This is one of the few public halls to host Nō performances. ✉ *4–18–1 Sendagaya, Shibuya-ku* ☎ *03/3423–1331* Ⓜ *JR Chūō Line, Sendagaya Station (Minami-guchi/South Exit); Ōedo subway line, Kokuritsu-Kyōgijō Station (Exit A4).*

Umewaka Nō-gakuin. Johnny-come-lately in the world of Nō is the Umewaka School, founded in 1921. Classes and performances are held here. ✉ *2–6–14 Higashi-Nakano, Nakano-ku* ☎ *03/3363–7748* Ⓜ *JR Chūō Line, Higashi-Nakano Station (Exit 2); Marunouchi and Ōedo subway lines, Nakano-saka-ue Station (Exit A1).*

RAKUGO   A rakugo comedian sits on a purple cushion, dressed in a kimono, and tells stories that have been handed down for centuries. Using only a few simple props—a fan, a pipe, a handkerchief—the storyteller becomes a whole cast of characters, with all their different voices and facial expressions. There's generally no English interpretation, and the monologues, filled with puns and expressions in dialect, can even be difficult for the Japanese themselves. A performance of rakugo is still worth seeing, however, for a slice of traditional pop culture.

Suzumoto. Built around 1857 and later rebuilt, Suzumoto is the oldest rakugo theater in Tōkyō. It's on Chūō-dōri, a few blocks north of the Ginza Line's Ueno Hirokō-ji stop. Tickets cost ¥2,000, and performances run continually throughout the day 12:20–4:30 and 5:20–9:10. ✉ *2–7–12 Ueno, Taitō-ku* ☎ *03/3834–5906* Ⓜ *Ginza subway line, Ueno Hirokō-ji Station (Exit 3).*

Nightlife

Most bars and clubs in the main entertainment districts have printed price lists, many in English. Drinks generally cost ¥600–¥1,200, although some small exclusive bars and clubs will set you back a lot more. Be wary of establishments without visible price lists. Hostess clubs and small backstreet bars known as "snacks" or "pubs" can be particularly treacherous territory for the unprepared. That drink you've just ordered could set you back a reasonable ¥1,000; you might, on the other hand, have wandered unknowingly into a place that charges you ¥15,000 up front for a whole bottle—and slaps a ¥20,000 cover charge on top. If the bar has hostesses, it's often unclear what the companionship of one will cost you, or whether she is there just for conversation. Ignore the persuasive shills on the streets of Roppongi and Kabuki-chō, who will try to hook you into their establishment. There is, of course, a certain amount of safe ground: hotel lounges, jazz clubs, and cabarets where foreigners come out to play are pretty much the way they are anywhere else. But wandering off the beaten path in Tōkyō can be like shopping for a yacht: if you have to ask how much it costs, you probably can't afford it anyhow.

There are five major districts in Tōkyō that have extensive nightlife, including places that welcome foreigners. The *kinds* of entertainment will not vary much from one to another; the tone, style, and prices will.

Akasaka. Nightlife in Akasaka concentrates mainly on two streets—Tamachi-dōri and Hitotsugi-dōri—and the small alleys connecting them. The area has several cabarets and nightclubs, plus wine bars, coffee shops, late-night restaurants, pubs, and "snacks"—counter bars that will serve (and charge you for) small portions of food with your drinks, whether you order them or not. It's also renowned for its many Korean barbecue restaurants, which tend to be on the pricy side. Akasaka is sophisticated and upscale—which is not surprising for an old geisha district—but not quite as expensive as Ginza and not as popular as Roppongi. Being fairly compact, it makes a convenient venue for testing the waters of Japanese nightlife.

Ginza. This is probably the city's best-known entertainment district, and one of the most—if not *the* most—expensive in the world. It does have affordable restaurants and pubs, but its reputation rests on the exclusive hostess clubs where only the highest of high rollers on corporate expense accounts can take their clients. Many corporations have been taking a harder look at those accounts, however, and Ginza as a nightlife destination has shifted its focus more to affluent young women and trendy couples. Expect to find everything from old-style corporate hangouts and traditional Japanese fare to contemporary dining and tony bars.

Roppongi. At one time Roppongi was the haunt of the rich and the beautiful. Although no longer the unanimous first choice for those seeking a rollicking night on the town, the area remains an indispensable part of the city's nightlife. Sure, the sleaze factor is high—but so are the options. Bars, clubs, cafés, karaoke rooms, restaurants, hostess bars, dinner theater, and comedy acts are all here, and Roppongi is still the part of Tōkyō where Westerners are most likely to feel at home. The 2003 unveiling of the Roppongi Hills complex, with its shops and restaurants, even managed to restore a bit of the old lustre to the area.

Shibuya. Less expensive than Roppongi and not as raunchy as Shinjuku, Shibuya attracts mainly students and young professionals. An up-and-coming neighborhood that is already a center of teen fashion, Shibuya is making a name for itself with a newly vibrant nightlife scene that includes some of Tōkyō's top nightclubs, plus inexpensive bars and restaurants. This is a great place to drink, eat, people-watch, and take in the city's vibrant youth culture.

Shinjuku. Long a favorite drinking spot for artists and businesspeople alike, Shinjuku offers everything from glamorous high-rise bars to sleazy dens. The Golden-Gai area is the haunt of writers, artists, and filmmakers. Nearby Kabuki-chō is the city's wildest nightlife venue—just steer clear of places with English-speaking touts out front and you'll be fine. The 2-chōme area (near Shinjuku Gyo-en National Garden and away from the rowdiness of Kabuki-chō) is a popular nightlife spot for the gay community. Although it's limited to a block or so of small bars and clubs, there is a diverse scene.

Bars

Bandol. This stylish wine bar on Aoyama-dōri has a helpful English-speaking staff and an urbane yet unstuffy clientele. Several dozen vintages from France, Italy, Spain, and New Zealand—most available by the glass—share menu space with reasonably priced Continental cuisine (eight-course dinners for ¥3,900). Weekend brunch is also available. Drinks start at ¥900. ⊠ *2–12–16 Minami-Aoyama, Minato-ku* ☎ *03/5785–3722* ⊙ *Weekdays 6 PM–2 AM, weekends noon–2 AM* Ⓜ *Ginza subway line, Gaien-mae Station (Exit 4).*

D-Zone. Patrons of the D-Zone, part of the Vision Network complex of shops, restaurants, and a gallery space, sport tattoos and neckties in equal measure. The vibe here is inclusive, convivial, and arty, and the terrace restaurant Las Chicas is a popular date spot. The leafy backstreet location, across from the design shop Sputnik Pad, is one of Tōkyō's best. ⊠ *5–47–6 Jingū-mae, Shibuya-ku* ☎ *03/3407–6845* ⊙ *Daily 6 PM–early morning* Ⓜ *Chiyoda, Ginza, and Hanzō-mon subway lines, Omotesandō Station (Exit B2).*

Heartland. Tōkyō's best-looking pickup bar sits in a somewhat disregarded corner of Roppongi Hills, but that doesn't stop the crowd—mostly white-collar *gaijin* (foreign) guys and Japanese women—from spilling out onto the patio. The funky white interior, with its long curving bar and wall-length couch, is done mostly in white, with emerald-green detailing. Drinks start at ¥500. ⊠ *Roppongi Hills West Walk, 1F, 6–10–1 Roppongi, Minato-ku* ☎ *03/5772–7600* ⊙ *Daily 11 AM–5 AM* Ⓜ *Hibiya and Ōedo subway lines, Roppongi Station (Roppongi Hills Exit).*

★ **Montoak.** At the intersection of the Omotesandō high-fashion district and the scruffy strip known as Cat Street, Montoak distills the essence of both neighborhoods into an atmosphere of refined cool. Smoky floor-to-ceiling windows, sleek black couches and cushy armchairs, and a hipper-than-thou clientele that has included the likes of a kimono-clad Sofia Coppola make for a thoroughly appealing scene. The bar food consists of canapés, salads, cheese plates, and the like. ⊠ *6–1–9 Jingū-mae, Shibuya-ku* ☎ *03/5468–5928* ⊙ *Daily 11:30 AM–midnight* Ⓜ *Chiyoda subway line, Meiji Jingū-mae Station (Exit 4).*

Mu-Mu. A sophisticated clientele and a good selection of sake and other kinds of Japanese liquor are the hallmarks of this sleek bar-restaurant in the heart of Ginza. Drinks start at ¥660. ⊠ *Ginza 646 Bldg., 6–4–6 Ginza, Chūō-ku* ☎ *03/3569–0006* ⊙ *Mon.–Sat. 6 PM–4 AM, Sun. 5 PM–10:30 PM* Ⓜ *Ginza, Hibiya, and Marunouchi subway lines, Ginza Station (Exit C3).*

★ **Old Imperial Bar.** Comfortable and sedate, this is the pride of the Imperial Hotel, decorated with elements saved from Frank Lloyd Wright's earlier version of the building—alas, long since torn down. Drinks start at ¥1,000. ⊠ *Imperial Hotel, 1–1–1 Uchisaiwai-chō, Chiyoda-ku* ☎ *03/ 3504–1111* ⊙ *Daily 11:30 AM–midnight* Ⓜ *Hibiya Line, Hibiya Station (Exit 5).*

★ **Sekirei.** Few Tōkyō experiences are more pleasurable than reclining in this outdoor bar on the leafy grounds of the Meiji-Kinenkan complex and watching traditionally garbed *nihon-buyō* dancers perform to the strains of shamisen music. Sekirei serves inexpensive drinks and Japanese- and Western-style food to a mix of after-work types and tourists. Drinks cost less than ¥1,000. ⊠ *2–2–23 Moto-Akasaka, Minato-ku* ☎ *03/ 3746–7723* ⊙ *June–Sept., weekdays 4:30 PM–10:30 PM, weekends 5:30 PM–10:30 PM; dancers perform two or three times nightly at varying times* Ⓜ *JR Chūō Line, Shinanomachi Station.*

Beer Halls & Pubs

Clubhouse. Weekly darts matches and above-average pub food make this Shinjuku sports bar stand out from a crowded field. The clientele, an interesting mix of locals and foreigners, is a bit more restrained than what you'll find at similar venues. ⊠ *3–7–3 Shinjuku, 3F, Shinjuku-ku* ☎ *03/3359–7785* ⊙ *Daily 5 PM–midnight* Ⓜ *Marunouchi subway line, Shinjuku-Sanchōme Station (Exit 3).*

Ginza Lion. This bar, in business since 1899 and occupying the same stately Chūō-dōri location since 1934, is remarkably inexpensive for one of Tōkyō's toniest addresses. Ginza shoppers and office workers alike drop by for beer and ballast—anything from yakitori to spaghetti. Beers start at ¥590. ⊠ *7–9–20 Ginza, Chūō-ku* ☎ *03/3571–2590* ⊙ *Mon.–Sat. 11:30–11* Ⓜ *Ginza, Hibiya, and Marunouchi subway lines, Ginza Station (Exit A3).*

Dance Clubs

Tōkyō's club scene draws internationally renowned DJs who spin all genres and who come for the enthusiastic crowds and the stylish venues. Just about every weekend, a big name will be manning the decks somewhere in town. Tōkyō clubbers tend to be more passionate about their music than they are about cruising. Most nightclubs are not pickup joints or places to preen: instead, it's the music that counts.

Dance clubs in Tōkyō are ephemeral ventures, disappearing fairly regularly only to open again with new identities, stranger names, and different selling points, although the money behind them is usually the same. Even those listed here come with no guarantee they'll be around when you arrive, but if the club you seek is gone, a new and better one may have opened up in its place.

★ **Ageha.** More than a nightclub, Ageha is a bayside venue that has several distinct leisure zones. The cavernous Arena hosts well-known house and techno DJs, the Rose Room plays hip-hop, a summer-only swimming-pool area has reggae, and inside a chill-out tent there's ambient and trance music. After enjoying well-known DJs like Junior Velasquez, who spin until the early hours, the twentysomething crowd watches the sunrise before catching the first train back to town. Free buses to Ageha depart every half hour between 11 PM and 4:30 AM from the Shibuya police station on Roppongi-dōri, a three-minute walk from Shibuya Station (there are also return buses every half hour from 11:30 PM to 5 AM). ✉ *2–2–10 Shin-Kiba, Kotō-ku* ☎ *03/5534–1515* ⊕ *www.ageha.com* 💳 *Around ¥3,500* ⊙ *10 PM–early morning* Ⓜ *Yūraku-chō subway line, Shin-Kiba Station.*

La Fabrique. A continental crowd gathers at the late-night parties at this small, dressy, French restaurant–cum–club in Shibuya's Zero Gate complex. The music is mostly French house. ✉ *B1F, 16–9 Udagawachō, Shibuya-ku* ☎ *03/5428–5100* 💳 *¥3,000–¥3,500* ⊙ *Daily 11 AM–5 AM* Ⓜ *JR Yamanote Line, Ginza and Hanzō-mon subway lines, Shibuya Station (Hachiko Exit for JR and Ginza, Exit 6 for Hanzō-mon Line).*

Lexington Queen. To Tōkyō's hipster club kids, Lexington Queen is something of an embarrassment: the music hasn't really changed since the place opened in 1980. But to visiting movie stars, fashion models, and other members of the international jet set, the Lex is the place to party hard and go wild—and be seen doing it. ✉ *3–13–14 Roppongi, Minato-ku* ☎ *03/3401–1661* ⊕ *www.lexingtonqueen.com* 💳 *Admission varies* ⊙ *Daily 8 PM–5 AM* Ⓜ *Hibiya and Ōedo subway lines, Roppongi Station (Exit 5); Namboku subway line, Roppongi-Itchōme Station (Exit 1).*

911. A great central-Roppongi location and no cover charge make 911 popular as both an early- and late-night singles' spot. Across from the Roi Building, this is a good starting point for a night of bar-hopping. ✉ *3–14–12 Roppongi, B1F, Minato-ku* ☎ *03/5772–8882* ⊙ *Daily 6 PM–6 AM* 💳 *No cover charge* Ⓜ *Hibiya and Ōedo subway lines, Roppongi Station (Exit 3).*

Space Lab Yellow. Yellow, as this club is known, can be counted on for A-list DJs, well-regarded progressive house parties, and the occasional drum 'n' bass event. An international crowd flocks here to dance and lounge late-night in the multilevel, multiroom interior—one of Tōkyō's biggest. ✉ *1–10–11 Nishi-Azabu, Minato-ku* ☎ *03/3479–0690* ⊕ *www. club-yellow.com* ◷ *10 PM–early morning* 💴 *¥3,500–¥4,000* Ⓜ *Chiyoda subway line, Nogizaka Station (Exit 5); Hibiya and Ōedo subway lines, Roppongi Station (Exit 2).*

★ **Womb.** Well-known techno and break-beat DJs make a point of stopping by this Shibuya über club on their way through town. The turntable talent, including the likes of Danny Howells and Richie Hawtin, and four floors of dance and lounge space make Womb Tōkyō's most consistently rewarding club experience. ✉ *2–16 Maruyama-chō, Shibuyaku* ☎ *03/5459–0039* ⊕ *www.womb.co.jp* 💴 *Around ¥3,500* ◷ *Daily 10 PM–early morning* Ⓜ *JR Yamanote Line, Ginza and Hanzō-mon subway lines, Shibuya Station (Hachiko Exit for JR and Ginza, Exit 3a for Hanzō-mon Line).*

Izakaya

Often noisy, bright, and smoky, *Izakaya* (literally "drinking place") are Japanese pubs that can be found on just about every block in Tōkyō. This is where young people start their nights out, office workers gather on their way home, and students take a break to grab a cheap meal and a drink.

Typically, izakaya have a full lineup of cocktails, a good selection of sake, draft beer, and lots of good Japanese and Western food; rarely does anything cost more than ¥1,000. Picture menus make ordering easy, and because most cocktails retain their Western names, communicating drink preferences shouldn't be too difficult.

Amatarō. The Center Gai location of this ubiquitous izakaya chain impresses with a huge, dimly lighted interior. On weekends the crowd is young, boisterous, and fun. ✉ *2–3F Tōkyō Kaikan Bldg., 33–1 Udagawachō, Shibuya-ku* ☎ *03/5784–4660* ◷ *Daily 5 PM–5 AM* Ⓜ *JR Yamanote Line, Ginza and Hanzō-mon subway lines, Shibuya Station (Hachiko Exit for JR and Ginza, Exit 3a for Hanzō-mon Line).*

Takara. This high-class izakaya in the sumptuous Tōkyō International Forum is a favorite with foreigners because of its English-language menu and extensive sake list. ✉ *B1, 3–5–1 Marunouchi, Chiyoda-ku* ☎ *03/5223–9888* ◷ *Weekdays 11:30–2:30 and 5–11, weekends 11:30–3:30 and 5–10* Ⓜ *Yūraku-chō subway line, Yūraku-chō Station (Exit A-4B).*

Watami. One of Tōkyō's big izakaya chains—with a half-dozen branches in the youth entertainment district of Shibuya alone—Watami is popular for its seriously inexpensive menu. Seating at this location ranges from a communal island bar to Western-style tables to more private areas. ✉ *Satose Bldg., 4F, 13–8 Udagawachō, Shibuya-ku* ☎ *03/6415–6516* ◷ *Sun.–Thurs. 5 PM–3 AM, Fri.–Sat. 5 PM–5 AM* Ⓜ *JR Yamanote Line, Ginza and Hanzō-mon subway lines, Shibuya Station (Hachiko Exit for JR and Ginza, Exit 6 for Hanzō-mon Line).*

Jazz Clubs

Tōkyō has one of the best jazz scenes in Asia. The clubs here attract world-class performers and innovative local acts.

Blue Note Tōkyō. The Blue Note sees everyone from the Count Basie Orchestra to Herbie Hancock perform to packed houses. The "Sunday Special" series showcases fresh Japanese talent. Prices here are typically high; expect to pay upwards of ¥13,000 to see acts like Natalie Cole. ✉ 6–3–16 Minami-Aoyama, Minato-ku ☎ 03/5485–0088 ⊙ Shows usually Mon.–Sat. at 7 and 9:30, Sun. at 6:30 and 9 ⊕ www.bluenote. co.jp Ⓜ Chiyoda, Ginza, and Hanzō-mon subway lines, Omotesandō Station (Exit A3).

Shinjuku Pit Inn. This veteran club stages mostly mainstream fare with the odd foray into the avant-garde. Afternoon admission is ¥1,300 weekdays, ¥2,500 weekends; evening entry is typically ¥3,000. Better-known local acts are often a little more. ✉ B1 Accord Shinjuku Bldg., 2–12–4 Shinjuku, Shinjuku-ku ☎ 03/3354–2024 ⊙ Daily, hrs vary Ⓜ Marunouchi subway line, Shinjuku-san-chōme Station.

★ **Sweet Basil 139.** Although it's not related to New York Cityís Sweet Basil, Tōkyō's own jazz hot spot is fast gaining a reputation to rival the famous Greenwich Village venue. An upscale jazz club near Roppongi Crossing, Sweet Basil 139 is renowned for local and international acts that run the musical gamut from smooth jazz and fusion to classical. A large, formal dining area serves Italian dishes that are as good as the jazz. With a spacious interior and standing room for 500 on the main floor, this is one of the largest and most accessible jazz bars in town. Prices range from ¥2,857 to ¥12,000 depending on who's headlining. ✉ 6–7–11 Roppongi, Minato-ku ☎ 03/5474–0139 ⊙ Mon.–Sat. 6 PM–11 PM; shows at 8 ⊕ http://stb139.co.jp Ⓜ Hibiya and Ōedo subway lines, Roppongi Station (Exit 3).

Karaoke

Unlike most karaoke bars in the United States, in which singers perform in front of a crowd of strangers, karaoke in Japan is usually enjoyed by groups of friends or coworkers in the seclusion of private rooms. Basic hourly charges vary but are usually less than ¥1,000. Most establishments have a large selection of English songs, stay open late, and serve inexpensive food and drink.

Big Echo. One of Tōkyō's largest karaoke chains, Big Echo has dozens of locations throughout the city. Cheap hourly rates and late closing times make it popular with youngsters. The Roppongi branch is spread over three floors. ✉ 7–14–12 Roppongi, Minato-ku ☎ 03/5770–7700 ▭ ¥500–¥600 per hr ⊙ Daily 6 PM–5 AM Ⓜ Hibiya and Ōedo subway lines, Roppongi Station (Exit 4).

Pasela. This 10-story entertainment complex on the main Roppongi drag of Gaien-Higashi-dōri has seven floors of karaoke rooms with more than 10,000 foreign-song titles. A Mexican-theme bar and a restaurant are also on the premises. ✉ 5–16–3 Roppongi, Minato-ku ☎ 0120/91–1086 ▭ ¥500 per hr ⊙ Daily 5 PM–10 AM Ⓜ Hibiya and Ōedo subway lines, Roppongi Station (Exit 3).

Shidax. The Shidax chain's corporate headquarters—in an excellent Shibuya location, across from Tower Records—has 130 private karaoke rooms, café, and restaurant. ✉ 1–12–13 Jinnan, Shibuya-ku ☎ 03/5784–8881 ▭ ¥760 per hr ⊙ Daily 11 AM–8 AM Ⓜ JR, Ginza, and Hanzō-mon subway lines, Shibuya Station (Exit 6).

Smash Hits. Smash Hits is an expat favorite, with thousands of English songs and a central performance stage. The cover charge gets you two drinks and no time limit. ✉ *5–2–26 Hiro-o, Shibuya-ku* ☎ *03/3444–0432* 📧 *¥3,000* ⊙ *Mon.–Sat. 7 PM–3 AM* ⊕ *www.smashhits.jp* Ⓜ *Hibiya Line, Hiro-o Station.*

Live Houses

Tōkyō has numerous small music clubs known as "live houses." These basement spots range from the very basic to miniclub venues, and they showcase the best emerging talent on the local scene. Many of the best live houses can be found in the Kichijōji, Koenji, and Nakano areas, although they are tucked away in basements citywide. One of the great things about the live house scene is the variety: a single "amateur night" set can include everything from experimental ethnic dance to thrash rock. Cover charges vary depending on who's performing but are typically ¥3,000–¥5,000.

Manda-la. Relaxed and intimate, this local favorite in Kichijōji attracts an eclectic group of performers. Cover charges range from ¥1,800 to ¥4,000. ✉ *2–8–6 Kichijōji-Minami-chō, Musashino-shi* ☎ *0422/42–1579* ⊙ *6:30 PM to closing time, which varies* Ⓜ *Keiō Inokashira private rail line, JR Chūō and JR Sōbu lines, Kichijōji Station (Kōen-guchi/Park Exit, on Suehiro-dōri).*

Milk. One of the city's larger live houses—it can handle 400 music fans—has three levels and more of a clublike vibe than other venues. Ticket prices are in the ¥2,500–¥3,000 range. ✉ *1–13–3 Nishi-Ebisu, Shibuya-ku* ☎ *03/5458–2826* ⊙ *Weekends 9–early morning* Ⓜ *JR Yamanote Line and Hibiya subway line, Ebisu Station (Nishi-guchi/West Exit).*

Showboat. A small, basic venue that's been going strong for more than a decade, Showboat attracts both amateur and semiprofessional performers. Ticket prices vary by act but are typically around ¥2,000 and often include one drink. ✉ *B1 Oak Bldg. Koenji, 3–17–2 Kita Koenji Suginami-ku* ☎ *03/3337–5745* ⊙ *Daily 6 PM—early morning* Ⓜ *JR Sōbu and JR Chūō lines, Koenji Station (Kita-guchi/North Exit).*

Rooftop Bars

Bellovisto. This 40th-floor lounge bar atop the Cerulean Tower draws a mixed crowd of tourists and local couples who come for the grand views out over Shibuya and beyond. Drinks start at ¥1,000. ✉ *26–1 Sakura-gaoka-chō, Shibuya-ku* ☎ *03/3476–3398* ⊙ *Daily 4 PM–midnight* Ⓜ *JR, Ginza and Hanzō-mon subway lines, Shibuya Station (Minami-guchi/South Exit for JR and Ginza, Exit 8 for Hanzō-mon Line).*

★ **New York Bar.** Even before *Lost in Translation* introduced the Park Hyatt's signature lounge to filmgoers worldwide, New York Bar was a local Tōkyō favorite. All the style you would expect of one of the city's top hotels combined with superior views of Shinjuku's skyscrapers and neon-lighted streets make this one of the city's premier nighttime venues. The quality of the jazz on offer equals that of the view. Drinks start at ¥800, and there's a cover charge of ¥2,000 after 8 PM (7 PM on Sunday). ✉ *Park Hyatt Hotel 52F, 3–7–1–2 Nishi-Shinjuku, Shinjuku-ku*

☏ *03/5322–1234* ⊘ *Sun.–Wed. 5 PM–midnight, Thurs.–Sat. 5 PM–1 AM* Ⓜ *Ōedo subway line, Tochō-mae Station.*

Sorasiso. The Kenji Kumaki–designed interior of this 46th-floor bar-restaurant in Shiodome is almost as impressive as the view out over Tōkyō Bay. Sorasiso attracts a well-heeled crowd. Drinks start at ¥1,000. ✉ *1–8–2 Higashi-Shimbashi, Caretta Shiodome B1F–B2F, Chūō-ku* ☏ *03/6215–8055* ⊘ *Daily 11–11* Ⓜ *Ōedo subway line, Shiodome Station (Exit 7); JR (Shiodome Exit) and Asakusa and Ginza lines (Exit 4), Shimbashi Station.*

SPORTS & THE OUTDOORS

It's fair to say that baseball is as much a national pastime in Japan as it is stateside. If you're a fan—and perhaps even if you aren't—you may want to take in a game in Japan: the way the Japanese have adopted and adapted this Western sport makes it a fascinating and easy-to-grasp microcosm of both their culture and their overall relationship to things Western. The team names alone—the Orix BlueWave and the Hiroshima Carp, for example—have an amusing appeal to Westerners accustomed to such monikers as the Yankees and the Indians, and the fans' cheers are different and chanted more in unison than in U.S. ballparks. Amateur baseball, from high school leagues to corporate teams, has a huge following, and the competition to be a player is fierce, even at the primary-school level. Indeed, sports in general are considered very *kako-ii* ("cool"), especially by young urbanites. Among people in their teens and twenties, there's an active cohort for pretty much any sport you can imagine, from rollerblading to windsurfing, from soccer to squash.

By the time they've joined the workforce and started families, most Japanese have made the transition from participants to fans. Golf remains the game of choice for the aspiring salaryman, but noticeably less so than a generation ago; overpriced and overextended in the boom years of the 1990s, country clubs all over the country are in trouble. But despite the interest in sports and the general notion of fitness, Tōkyō actually has very few green spaces dedicated to active leisure. Every ward maintains at least one substantial sports facility for its own residents, but otherwise fitness is the province of private clubs where memberships are expensive and peak hours are crowded. Besides walking, visitors are mainly limited to their hotel gyms. The few outlets available for participant and spectator sports are listed below.

Baseball

Tōkyō Dome at Kōraku-en is the place to see pro ball in the big city An afternoon in the bleachers, when a despised rival like the Hanshin Tigers are in town from Ōsaka to play the Yomiuri Giants, will give you insights into a Japanese passion like nothing else.

The Japanese baseball season runs between April and October. Same day tickets are hard to come by; try the ticket agency **Playguide** (☏ 03 3561–8821). **Ticket Pia** (☏ 03/5237–9999) handles mainly music and the ater but can also book and sell tickets to sporting events. Depending on the stadium, the date, and the seat location, expect to pay from ¥1,500 to ¥8,000 for an afternoon at the ballpark.

Baseball fans in Tōkyō are blessed with a choice of three home teams. The Yomiuri Giants and the Nippon Ham Fighters both play at the 55,000-seat **Tōkyō Dome**. ⊠ *1–3–61 Kōraku, , Bunkyō Ward* ☎ *03/ 5800–9999* Ⓜ *Marunouchi and Namboku lines, Kōraku-en Station (Exit 2); Ōedo and Toei Mita lines, Kasuga Station (Exit A2); JR Suidō- bashi Station (West Exit).*

The home ground of the Yakult Swallows is **Jingū Baseball Stadium**, in the Outer Gardens of Meiji Jingū. ⊠ *13 Kasumigaoka, Shinjuku Ward* ☎ *03/3404–8999* Ⓜ *Ginza Line, Gaien-mae Station (Exit 2).*

Golf

Golfing can be a daunting prospect for the casual visitor to Tōkyō: The few public courses are far from the city, and booking a tee time on even a week's notice is almost impossible. What you can do, however, if the golf bug is in your blood, is groove your swing at one of the many prac- tice ranges in Tōkyō itself. Most driving ranges are open from 11 AM to 7 or 8 at night and will rent you a club for around ¥200. At **Golf Range Pinflag** (⊠ 1–7–13 Tsukiji, Chūō Ward, ☎ 03/3542–2936 Ⓜ Hibiya sub- way line, Tsukiji Station [Exit 4]), a bucket of 24 balls costs ¥350, and you can generally get a tee without waiting very long. At the **Meguro Gorufu-jō** (⊠ 5–6–22 Kami-Meguro, Meguro Ward ☎ 03/3713–2805 Ⓜ Tōkyū Toyoko private railway line, Nakameguro Station), you buy a prepaid card for ¥2,000, which allows you to hit up to 142 balls.

Running

The venue of choice for runners who work in the central wards of Chūō-ku and Chiyoda-ku is the **Imperial Palace Outer Garden**. Sakurada- mon, the gate at the west end of the park, is the traditional starting point for the 5-km (3-mi) run around the palace—though you can join in any- where along the route. Jogging around the palace is a ritual that begins as early as 6 AM and goes on throughout the day, no matter what the weather. Almost everybody runs the course counterclockwise. Now and then you may spot someone going the opposite way, but freethinking of this sort is frowned upon in Japan.

Soccer

Tōkyō's two teams, FC Tōkyō and Tōkyō Verde, both play at the 50,000-seat **Tōkyō Stadium** in Tama. The season includes two 15-week schedules, one beginning in mid-March and the other in mid-August. Tickets cost ¥1,000–¥6,000 and can be ordered through **Playguide** (☎ 03/3561–8821) or **Ticket Pia** (☎ 0570/029–966), or purchased di- rectly at most Seven-Eleven, Family Mart, or Lawson convenience stores. ⊠ *376–3 Nishi-machi, Chōfu City* ☎ *0424/40–0555* Ⓜ *JR Keiō Line, Tobitakyū Station.*

Sumō

Sumō wrestling dates back some 1,500 years. Originally it was not merely a sport but a religious rite, performed at shrines to entertain the gods that presided over the harvest. Ritual and ceremony are still important elements of sumō matches—contestants in unique regalia, referees in gorgeous costumes, elaborately choreographed openings and closings. To the casual spectator a match itself can look like a mostly naked free-for-all. Stripped down to silk loincloths, the two wrestlers square off in a dirt ring about 15 feet in diameter and charge straight at each other; the first one to step out of the ring or touch the ground with anything but the soles of his feet loses. Other than that, there are no rules—not even weight divisions: a runt of merely 250 pounds can find himself facing an opponent twice his size.

Of the six Grand Tournaments (called *basho*) that take place during the year, Tōkyō hosts three of them: in early January, mid-May, and mid-September. The tournaments take place in the **Kokugikan,** the National Sumō Arena, in the Ryōgoku district on the east side of the Sumida-gawa. Matches go from early afternoon, when the novices wrestle, to the titanic clashes of the upper ranks at around 6 PM. The price of admission buys you a whole day of sumō; the most expensive seats, closest to the ring, are tatami-floor loges for four people, called *sajiki*. The loges are terribly cramped, but the cost (¥9,200–¥11,300 per person) includes all sorts of food and drink and souvenirs, brought around to you by Kokugikan attendants in traditional costume. The cheapest seats cost ¥3,600 for advanced sales, ¥2,100 for same-day box office sales. For same-day box office sales you should line up an hour in advance of the tournament. You can also reserve tickets through **Playguide** (☎ 03/5802–9999) or **Ticket Pia** (☎ 03/5237–9955 or 0570/029–977), or at Seven-Eleven, Family Mart, or Lawson convenience stores. ⊠ *1–3–28 Yokoami, Sumida Ward* ☎ *03/3622–1100* ⊕ *www.sumo.or.jp/eng/ ticket/index.html* Ⓜ *JR Sōbu Line, Ryōgoku Station (West Exit).*

Swimming & Fitness

The vast majority of pools and fitness centers in Tōkyō are for members only. Major international hotels have facilities of their own, but if your accommodations are further downscale, places to swim or work out are harder to find. The fitness center at **Big Box Seibu Sports Plaza Athletic Club** (⊠ 1–35–3 Takadano-baba, Shinjuku Ward ☎ 03/3208–7171) is open to nonmembers for ¥4,000; use of the pool, which is only available on Sunday 10–6, is an additional ¥1,500. The **Clark Hatch Fitness Center** (⊠2–1–3 Azabu-dai, Minato Ward ☎03/3584–4092) has a full array of machines and charges ¥2,600 for nonmembers. It does not have a pool. You don't necessarily have to be a resident to use one of the facilities operated by the various wards of Tōkyō, though the registration formalities can be a hassle (bring your passport or a photo ID). One of the best of these is the **Minato Ward Shiba Pool** (⊠ 2–7–2 Shiba Kōen, Minato Ward ☎ 03/3435–0470), which is open Tuesday–Saturday 9:30–8 and Sunday–Monday 9:30–5. The pool charges only ¥300 for two hours of swimming.

BECOMING A SUMŌ WRESTLER

THE CENTURIES-OLD NATIONAL SPORT OF SUMŌ is not to be taken lightly—as anyone who has ever seen a sumō wrestler will testify. Indeed, sheer weight is almost a prerequisite to success. Contenders in the upper ranks tip the scales at an average of 350 pounds, and there are no upper limits. There are various techniques of pushing, gripping, and throwing in sumō, but the basic rules are very simple: except for hitting below the belt (which is all a sumō wrestler wears), grabbing your opponent by the hair, or striking with a closed fist, almost anything goes. If you get thrown down or forced out of the ring, you lose.

There are no free agents in sumō. To compete, you must belong to a heya (stable) run by a retired wrestler who has purchased that right from the Japan Sumō Association. Sumō is very much a closed world, hierarchical and formal. Youngsters recruited into the sport live in the stable dormitory, doing all the community chores and waiting on their seniors while they learn. When they rise high enough in tournament rankings, they acquire servant-apprentices of their own.

Tournaments and exhibitions are held in different parts of the country at different times, but all stables in the Sumō Association—now some 30 in number—are in Tōkyō. Most are clustered on both sides of the Sumida River near the green-roofed Kokugikan (National Sumō Arena), in the areas called Asakusabashi and Ryōgoku. When wrestlers are in town in January, May, and September, you are likely to see some of them on the streets, cleaving the air like leviathans in their wood clogs and kimonos.

SHOPPING

Horror stories abound about prices in Japan—and some of them are true. Yes, a cup of coffee can cost $10, if you pick the wrong coffee shop. A gift-wrapped melon from a department-store gourmet counter can cost $70. And a taxi ride from the airport to central Tōkyō does cost about $200. But most people take the convenient airport train for $9, and if you shop around, you can find plenty of gifts and souvenirs at fair prices.

Some goods are better bought at home: why go all the way to Tōkyō to buy European designer clothing? Instead, look for items that are Japanese made for Japanese people and sold in stores that do not cater primarily to tourists. Don't pass up the chance to purchase Japanese crafts. Color, balance of form, and superb workmanship make these items exquisite and well worth the price you'll pay. Some can be quite expensive; for example, Japanese lacquerware carries a hefty price tag. But if you like the shiny boxes, bowls, cups, and trays and consider that quality lacquerware is made to last a lifetime, the cost is justified.

Shopping in Japan is an exercise in elegance and refinement. Note the care taken with items after you purchase them, especially in department stores and boutiques. Goods will be wrapped, wrapped again, bagged, and sealed. Sure, the packaging can be excessive—does anybody really need three plastic bags for one croissant?—but such a focus on presentation has deep roots in Japanese culture.

Salespeople are invariably helpful and polite. In the larger stores they greet you with a bow when you arrive, and many of them speak at least enough English to help you find what you're looking for. There's a saying in Japan: *o-kyaku-sama wa kami-sama,* "the customer is a god"— and since the competition for your business is fierce, people do take it to heart.

Stores in Tōkyō generally open at 10 or 11 AM and close at 8 or 9 PM.

Shopping Districts

Akihabara & Jimbō-chō. Akihabara was at one time the only place Tōkyōites would go to buy cutting-edge electronic gadgets, but the area has lost its aura of exclusivity thanks to big discount chains that have sprung up around the city. Still, for its sheer variety of products and for-eigner-friendliness, Akihabara has the newcomers beat—and a visit re-mains essential to any Tōkyō shopping spree. Sales clerks speak English at most of the major shops (and many of the smaller ones), and the big chains offer duty-free and export items. Be sure to poke around the backstreets for smaller stores that sell used and unusual electronic goods. West of Akihabara, in the used-bookstore district of Jimbō-chō, you'll find pretty much whatever you're looking for in dictionaries and art books, rare and out-of-print editions (Western and Japanese), and prints. Ⓜ *For Akihabara: JR Yamanote, Keihin Tōhoku, and Sōbu lines, Akihabara Station (Denki-gai Exit); Hibiya subway line, Akihabara Station. For Jimbō-chō: Hanzō-mon, Shinjuku, and Mita subway lines, Jimbō-chō Station.*

Aoyama. Shopping in Aoyama can empty your wallet in no time: this is where many of the leading Japanese and Western designers have their cash-cow boutiques, and there are lots of elegant and pricey antiques shops on Aoyama's Kotto-dōri. European and American imports will be high, but Japanese designer clothes are usually 30%–40% lower than they are elsewhere. Aoyama tends to be a showcase not merely of high fashion but also of the latest concepts in commercial architecture and interior design. Ⓜ *Chiyoda, Ginza, and Hanzō-mon subway lines, Omotesandō Station (Exits A4, A5, B1, B2, and B3).*

Asakusa. While sightseeing in this area, take time to stroll through its arcades. Many of the goods sold here are the kinds of souvenirs you can find in any tourist trap, but look a little harder and you can find small backstreet shops that have been making beautiful wooden combs, del-icate fans, and other items of fine traditional craftsmanship for gener-ations. Also here are the cookware shops of Kappa-bashi, where you can load up on everything from sushi knives to plastic lobsters. Ⓜ *Asakusa subway line, Asakusa Station (Kaminari-mon Exit); Ginza subway line, Asakusa Station (Exit 1) and Tawara-machi Station (Exit 3).*

SMART SOUVENIRS

ARTICLES MADE OF *WASHI*—hand-molded paper—are among the best buys in Japan. Delicate sheets of almost-transparent stationery, greeting cards, money holders, and wrapping paper are available at traditional crafts stores, stationery stores, and department stores. Small washi-covered boxes (suitable for jewelry and other keepsakes) and pencil cases are also strong candidates for gifts and personal souvenirs.

At first glance, Japanese ceramics may seem priced for a prince's table. Doubtless some are, but if you keep shopping, you can find reasonably priced functional and decorative items that are generally far superior in design to what is available at home. Sale items are often amazingly good bargains. Vases, sake sets consisting of one or two small bottles and a number of cups, and chopstick rests all make good gifts.

Printed fabric, whether by the yard or in the form of finished scarves, napkins, tablecloths, or pillow coverings, is also worth purchasing in Japan. The complexity of the designs and the quality of the printing make the fabric, both silk and cotton, special. Furoshiki—square pieces of cloth used for wrapping, storing, and carrying things—make great wall hangings.

Ginza. This world-renowned entertainment and shopping district dates to the Edo period (1603–1868), when it consisted of long, willow-lined avenues. The willows have long since gone, and the streets are now lined with department stores and boutiques. The exclusive shops in this area—including flagship stores for major jewelers like Tiffany & Co., Harry Winston, and Mikimoto—sell quality merchandise at high prices. Ⓜ *Marunouchi, Ginza, and Hibiya subway lines, Ginza Station (Exits A1–A10); Yūraku-chō subway line, Ginza Itchōme Station; JR Yamanote Line, Yūraku-chō Station.*

Harajuku. The average shopper in Harajuku is under 20; a substantial percentage is under 16. Most stores focus on moderately priced clothing and accessories, with a lot of kitsch mixed in, but there are also several upscale fashion houses in the area—and more on the way. This shopping and residential area extends southeast from Harajuku Station along both sides of Omotesandō and Meiji-dōri; the shops that target the youngest consumers concentrate especially on the narrow street called Takeshita-dōri. Tōkyō's most exciting neighborhood for youth fashion and design lies along the promenade known as Kyū Shibuya-gawa Hodō, commonly referred to as Cat Street. Ⓜ *Chiyoda subway line, Meiji Jingū-mae Station (Exits 1–5); JR Yamanote Line, Harajuku Station.*

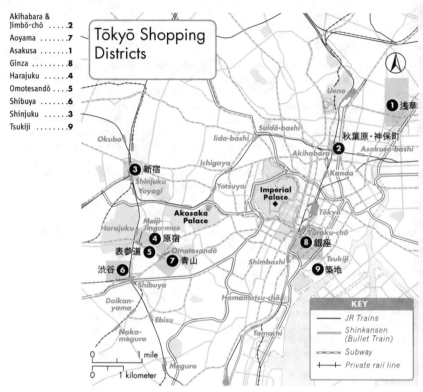

Tōkyō Shopping
Districts

Omotesandō. Known as the Champs-Elysées of Tōkyō, this long, wide avenue running from Aoyama-dōri to Meiji Jingū is lined with cafés and designer boutiques. There are also several antiques and souvenir shops here. Omotesandō is perfect for browsing, window-shopping, and lingering over a café au lait before strolling to your next destination. Ⓜ *Chiyoda, Ginza, and Hanzō-mon lines, Omotesandō Station (Exits A4, A5, B1, B2, and B3).*

Shibuya. This is primarily an entertainment and retail district geared toward teenagers and young adults. The shopping scene in Shibuya caters to these groups with many reasonably priced smaller shops and a few department stores that are casual yet chic. Ⓜ *JR Yamanote Line; Tōkyū and Keiō private rail lines; Ginza and Hanzō-mon subway lines: Shibuya Station (Nishi-guchi/West Exit for JR, Exits 3–8 for subway lines).*

Shinjuku. Shinjuku is not without its honky-tonk and sleaze, but it also has some of the city's most popular department stores. Shinjuku's merchandise reflects the crowds—young, stylish, and hip. Surrounding the station are several discount electronics and home-appliance outlets. Ⓜ *JR Yamanote Line; Odakyū private rail line; Marunouchi, Shinjuku, and Ōedo subway lines: Shinjuku Station.*

Tsukiji. Best known for its daily fish-market auctions, Tsukiji also has a warren of streets that carry useful, everyday items that serve as a window onto the lives of the Japanese. This is a fascinating area to poke around after seeing the fish auction and before stopping in the neighborhood for a fresh-as-can-be sushi lunch. Ⓜ *Ōedo subway line, Tsukiji-shijō Station (Exit A1); Hibiya subway line, Tsukiji Station (Exit 1).*

Shopping Streets & Arcades

Most Japanese villages have pedestrian shopping streets known as *shotengai*, and Tōkyō, a big city made up of smaller neighborhoods, is no different. But you won't find everyday retailers like pharmacies and grocery stores in these areas—Tōkyō's shotengai are thick with boutiques, accessory shops, and cafés. Just like their surrounding neighborhoods, these streets can be classy, trendy, or a bit shabby.

Ame-ya Yoko-chō Market. Everything from fresh fish to cheap import clothing is for sale at this bustling warren of side streets between Okachimachi and Ueno stations. The name of the market is often shortened to Ameyoko. Most shops and stalls are open daily 10–7. ✉ *Ueno 4-chōme, Taitō-ku* Ⓜ *JR Ueno Station (Hirokō-ji Exit), JR Okachi-machi Station (Exit A7).*

International Shopping Arcade. A somewhat ragtag collection of shops in Hibiya, this arcade holds a range of goods, including cameras, electronics, pearls, and kimonos. The shops are duty-free, and most of the sales staff speaks English. It's near the Imperial Hotel. ✉ *1–7–23 Uchisaiwai-chō, Chiyoda-ku* Ⓜ *Chiyoda and Hibiya subway lines, Hibiya Station (Exit A13).*

Kyū Shibuya-gawa Hodō. With its avant-garde crafts stores, funky T-shirt shops, and hipster boutiques, this pedestrian strip, also known as Cat Street, serves as a showcase for Japan's au courant designers and artisans. Cat Street is the place to experience bohemian Tōkyō in all its exuberance. ✉ *Between Jingū-mae 3-chōme and Jingū-mae 6-chōme, Shibuya-ku* Ⓜ *Chiyoda subway line, Meiji Jingū-mae Station (Exits 4 and 5).*

Nishi-Sandō. Kimono and *yukata* (cotton kimono) fabrics, traditional accessories, swords, and festival costumes at very reasonable prices are all for sale at this Asakusa arcade. It runs east of the area's movie theaters, between Rok-ku and the Sensō-ji complex. ✉ *Asakusa 2-chōme, Taitō-ku* Ⓜ *Ginza subway line, Asakusa Station (Exit 1).*

Takeshita-dōri. Teenybopper fashion is all the rage along this Harajuku mainstay, where crowds of high school kids look for the newest addition to their wardrobes. ✉ *Jingū-mae 1-chōme Shibuya-ku* Ⓜ *JR Harajuku Station (Takeshita-dōri Exit).*

Malls & Shopping Centers

Most of these self-contained retail zones carry both foreign and Japanese brands and, like the city's department stores, house cafés, bars, and restaurants. If you don't have the time or energy to dash about Tōkyō in search of the perfect gifts, consider dropping by one of these shopping centers, where you can find a wide selection of merchandise. Most are used to dealing with foreigners.

★ **Axis.** Classy and cutting-edge housewares, fabrics, and ceramics are sold at this multistory design center on the main Roppongi drag of Gaien-Higashi-dōri. Living Motif is a home-furnishings shop with exquisite foreign and Japanese goods. Savoir Vivre has an excellent selection of ceramics. The small Yoshikin sells its own brand of professional-grade cutlery. ⊠ *5–17–1 Roppongi, Minato-ku* ☎ *03/3587–2781* ⊙ *Most shops Mon.–Sat. 11–7* Ⓜ *Hibiya and Ōedo subway lines, Roppongi Station (Exit 3); Namboku subway line, Roppongi Itchōme Station (Exit 1).*

Coredo. Unlike other big stores in the Ginza and Nihombashi areas, this sparkling mall has a contemporary feel thanks to an open layout and extensive use of glass and wood. Housewares, toys, and fashion can all be found here. ⊠ *1–4–1 Nihombashi, Chūō-ku* ☎ *03/3272–4939* ⊙ *Mon.–Sat. 11–9, Sun. 11–8* Ⓜ *Ginza, Tōzai, and Asakusa subway lines, Nihombashi Station (Exit B10).*

Glassarea. Virtually defining Aoyama elegance is this cobblestone shopping center, which draws well-heeled Aoyama housewives to its boutiques, restaurants, and housewares shops. ⊠ *5–4 Minami-Aoyama, Minato-ku* ⊙ *Most shops daily 11–8* Ⓜ *Ginza, Chiyoda, and Hanzō-mon subway lines, Omotesandō Station (Exit B1).*

Roppongi Hills. You could easily spend a whole day exploring the retail areas of Tōkyō's newest minicity, opened in 2003. The shops here emphasize eye-catching design and chi-chi brands. ⊙ *Most shops daily 11–8* Ⓜ *Hibiya and Ōedo subway lines, Roppongi Station (Roppongi Hills Exit).*

Boutiques

Japanese boutiques pay as much attention to interior design as they do to the clothing they sell; like anywhere else, it's the image that moves the merchandise. Although many mainstream Japanese designers are represented in the major upscale department stores, you may enjoy your shopping more in the elegant boutiques of Aoyama and Omotesandō—most of which are within walking distance of one another.

Bape Exclusive Aoyama. Since the late 1990s, no brand has been more coveted by Harajuku scenesters than the A Bathing Ape label—shortened to Bape—from DJ–fashion designer Nigo. At the height of the craze, hopefuls would queue outside Nigo's well-hidden boutiques for the chance to plop down ¥7,000 for a T-shirt festooned with a simian visage or a *Planet of the Apes* quote. Bape has since gone aboveground, with Nigo expanding his business empire to Singapore, Hong Kong, and London. Here in Tōkyō you can see what all the fuss is about at a spacious boutique that houses the Bape Gallery on the second floor. ⊠ *5–5–8 Minami-Aoyama, Minato-ku* ☎ *03/3407–2145* ⊙ *Daily 11–7* Ⓜ *Ginza and Hanzō-mon subway subway lines, Omotesandō Station, (Exit A5).*

Busy Workshop Harajuku. This Harajuku spot sells the trendy Bape clothing line and has an avant-garde interior by noted local designers Wonderwall. ⊠ *B1F, 4–28–22 Jingū-mae, Minato-ku* ☎ *03/5474–0204* ⊙ *Daily 11–7* Ⓜ *Chiyoda line, Meiji-jingū-mae Station (Exit 5); JR Harajuku Station (Takeshita-dori Exit).*

★ **Comme Des Garçons.** Sinuous low walls snake through Rei Kawakubo's flagship store, a minimalist labyrinth that houses the designer's signa-

SHOPPING BLITZ TOUR

TART YOUR DAY, AS SO MANY JAPANESE DO, at the south exit of Shinjuku Station, said to be the busiest in the world. Cross the street (Koshu-kaido) at the light, take a left, and make your way to Takashimaya Times Square, which is the large shopping center off to your right. If you make it to **Takashimaya** when the doors open at 10 AM sharp, you'll receive a formal greeting as you enter this stylish department store with Western and Japanese clothes, jewelry, crafts, and accessories. The back end of the store connects to the housewares-and-hobby emporium **Tōkyū Hands,** a good place to buy talking cigarette lighters and other kitsch keepsakes. Take the escalator to the fifth floor and cross a walkway to **Kinokuniya** bookstore; you'll enter at the English-language section, which has everything from haiku translations to coffee-table tomes on Japanese gardens. Exit the doors near the first-floor elevators, cross the street, and bear right to the taxi stand outside Tōkyū Hands. Take a short cab ride to Harajuku Station; ask the driver to drop you off at **Takeshita-dōri** (at the west end, which is closest to the station), where you can go elbow-to-elbow with Tōkyō's youthful and trendy consumers.

At the east end of Takeshita-dōri, turn right onto Meiji-dōri (it's at the first light). The next big intersection is Omotesandō. Cross it, take a left on the opposite side, and in quick succession you'll come upon **Kiddy Land** (toys), **Fuji-Torii** (antiques), and **Oriental Bazaar** (traditional crafts). Walking farther (southeast) along tree-lined Omotesandō takes you past some of Tōkyō's most exclusive fashion and accessories boutiques. Stop in the basement of the **Hanae Mori Building,** on Omotesandō, for more antiques.

High-fashion heaven continues after you cross the next big intersection at Aoyama-dōri. Don't miss the bizarre **Comme Des Garçons** shop one block farther along on your right. Then take a right (two blocks past Aoyama-dōri) at the stunning, glass-encased Prada building. The side streets here lead to more boutiques (including the first right, where you'll find **Bape Exclusive Aoyama**). After passing the trendy shopping center **Glassarea** on your left, you'll come to "Antiques Road": Kotto-dōri. Home to some of Tōkyō's best antiques dealers, this area also has many cafés and restaurants.

At the intersection of Kotto-dōri and Aoyama-dōri, turn right and head to the Omotesandō subway station. A ¥160 ticket buys you passage on the Ginza subway line to Ginza Station. Take Exit A2 for the main Chūō-dōri thoroughfare and traditional stationer **Kyūkyodō** (on your right as you exit the station). Shop here for washi (paper), calligraphy materials, scrolls, and all manner of decorative paper goods. One block behind Kyūkyodō, between Harumi-dōri and Miyuki-dōri, is the traditional sword shop **Tōken Shibata.** After certifying your samurai credentials, swing back to Chūō-dōri, walk southwest, and get cultured in a different way at **Mikimoto.** Walk farther up the street and duck into the alley behind the Apple Store, where you can shop for traditional clothes at the small kimono store **Tansu-ya.** If you have any leftover energy—or, more importantly, money—you may want to visit the **Matsuya, Wako,** and **Matsuzakaya** department stores, all set around Ginza Station. Or take a break at the second-floor café in **Mitsukoshi,** which affords an excellent view over one of Tōkyō's busiest intersections.

ture clothes, shoes, and accessories. Staff members will do their best to ignore you, but that's no reason to stay away from one of Tōkyō's funkiest retail spaces. ⊠ *5–2–1 Minami-Aoyama, Minato-ku* ☎ *03/3406–3951* ⊙ *Daily 11–8* Ⓜ *Ginza, Chiyoda, and Hanzō-mon subway lines, Omotesandō Station (Exit A5).*

Issey Miyake. The otherworldy creations of internationally renowned designer Miyake are on display at her flagship store in Aoyama, which carries the full Paris line. ⊠ *3–18–11 Minami-Aoyama, Minato-ku* ☎ *03/3423–1407* ⊙ *Daily 11–8* Ⓜ *Ginza, Chiyoda, and Hanzō-mon subway lines, Omotesandō Station (Exit A4).*

10 Corso Como Comme des Garçons. Milanese-lifestyle-guru Carla Sozzani helped create this spacious boutique for designer Rei Kawakubo's Comme des Garçons lines, which include Junya Watanabe menswear and womenswear. Also on offer are Vivienne Westwood and Balenciaga brands, and the staff isn't too busy being hip to help you out. ⊠ *5–3 Minami-Aoyama, Minato-ku* ☎ *03/5774–7800* ⊙ *Daily 11–8* Ⓜ *Ginza, Chiyoda, and Hanzō-mon subway lines, Omotesandō Station (Exit A5).*

Under Cover. This stark shop houses Paris darling Jun Takahashi's cult clothing, with enormously high racks of men's and women's clothing with a tatty punk look. ⊠ *5–3–18 Minami-Aoyama, Minato-ku* ☎ *03/3407–1232* ⊙ *Daily 11–8* Ⓜ *Ginza, Chiyoda, and Hanzō-mon subway lines, Omotesandō Station (Exit A5).*

Y's Roppongi Hills. With its glossy surfaces and spare lines, the interior of this Ron Arad–designed shop on Roppongi's Keyakizaka-dōri serves as a suitable showcase for Yohji Yamamoto's austere fashions. ⊠ *6–12–4 Roppongi, Minato-ku* ☎ *03/5416–3434* ⊙ *Daily 11–9* Ⓜ *Hibiya and Ōedo subway lines, Roppongi Station (Roppongi Hills Exit).*

Department Stores

Most Japanese *depāto* (department stores) are parts of conglomerates that include railways, real estate, and leisure industries. The stores themselves commonly have travel agencies, theaters, and art galleries on the premises, as well as reasonably priced and strategically placed restaurants and cafés.

A visit to a Japanese department store is not merely a shopping excursion—it's a lesson in Japanese culture. Plan to arrive just before it opens: promptly on the hour, immaculately groomed young women face the customers from inside, bow ceremoniously, and unlock the doors. As you walk through the store, all the sales assistants will be standing at attention, in postures of nearly reverent welcome. Notice the uniform angle of incline: many stores have training sessions to teach their new employees the precise and proper degree at which to bend from the waist.

On the top floor of many department stores you'll find gift packages containing Japan's best-loved brands of sake, rice crackers, and other food items. Department stores also typically devote one floor to traditional Japanese crafts, including ceramics, paintings, and lacquerware. If you're pressed for time, these are great places to pick up a variety of souvenirs.

Don't miss the food departments on the lower levels, where you'll encounter an overwhelming selection of Japanese and Western delicacies. No locals in their right minds would shop here regularly for their groceries. A brief exploration, however, will give you a pretty good picture of what people might select for a special occasion—and the price they're prepared to pay for it. Many stalls offer small samples on the counter.

Major department stores accept credit cards and provide shipping services. Some salesclerks speak English. If you're having communication difficulties, someone will eventually come to the rescue. On the first floor you'll invariably find a general information booth with useful maps of the store in English. Some department stores close one or two days a month. To be on the safe side, call ahead.

Ginza/Nihombashi

Matsuya. On the fourth floor, the gleaming Matsuya houses an excellent selection of Japanese fashion, including Issey Miyake, Yohji Yamamoto, and Comme Ça Du Mode. The second-floor Louis Vuitton shop is particularly popular with Tōkyō's brand-obsessed shoppers. ⊠ 3–6–1 *Ginza, Chūō-ku* ☎ *03/3567–1211* ⊘ *Sat.–Thurs. 10–8, Fri. 10–9* Ⓜ *Ginza, Marunouchi, and Hibiya subway lines, Ginza Station (Exits A12 and A13).*

★ **Mitsukoshi.** Founded in 1673 as a dry-goods store, Mitsukoshi later played one of the leading roles in introducing Western merchandise to Japan. It has retained its image of quality and excellence, with a particularly strong representation of Western fashion designers. The store also stocks fine traditional Japanese goods—don't miss the art gallery and the crafts area on the sixth floor. With its own subway stop, bronze lions at the entrance, and an atrium sculpture of the Japanese goddess Magokoro, the remarkable Nihombashi flagship store merits a visit even if you're not planning on buying anything. ⊠ *1–4–1 Nihombashi Muromachi, Chūō-ku* ☎ *03/3241–3311* ⊘ *Daily 10–7:30* Ⓜ *Ginza and Hanzō-mon subway lines, Mitsukoshi-mae Station (Exits A3 and A5)* ⊠ *4–6–16 Ginza, Chūō-ku* ☎ *03/3562–1111* ⊘ *Mon.–Sat. 10–8, Sun 10–7:30* Ⓜ *Ginza, Marunouchi, and Hibiya subway lines, Ginza Station (Exits A6, A7, A8).*

★ **Takashimaya.** In Japanese, *taka* means "high"—a fitting word for this store, which is beloved for its superior quality and prestige. Gift-givers all over Japan seek out this department store; a present that comes in a Takashimaya bag makes a statement regardless of what's inside. The second floor, with shops by Christian Dior, Prada, Chanel, Cartier, and many others, is one of the toniest retail spaces in a shopping district celebrated for its exclusivity. The seventh floor has a complete selection of traditional crafts, antiques, and curios. The lower-level food court carries every gastronomic delight imaginable, from Japanese crackers and green tea to Miyazaki beef and plump melons. ⊠ *2–4–1 Nihombashi, Chūō-ku* ☎ *03/3211–4111* ⊘ *Daily 10–8* Ⓜ *Ginza subway line, Nihombashi Station (Exits B1 and B2)* ⊠ *Takashimaya Times Sq., 5–24–2 Sendagaya, Shibuya-ku* ☎ *03/5361–1111* ⊘ *Daily 10–8* Ⓜ *JR Yamanote Line, Shinjuku Station (Minami-guchi/South Exit).*

Wako. Confining itself to a limited selections of goods at the top end of the market, Wako is particularly known for its glassware, jewelry, and accessories—and for some of the handsomest, most sophisticated window displays in town. ✉ *4–5–11 Ginza, Chūō-ku* ☎ *03/3562–2111* ◷ *Mon.–Sat. 10:30–6* Ⓜ *Ginza, Marunouchi, and Hibiya subway lines, Ginza Station (Exits A9 and A10).*

Ikebukuro & Shibuya

Parco. Parco, owned by the Seibu conglomerate, is actually not one store but four vertical malls filled with small retail shops and boutiques, all in hailing distance of one another in the commercial heart of Shibuya. Parco Part 1 and Part 4 (Quattro) cater to a younger crowd, stocking "generic" unbranded casual clothing, crafts fabrics, and accessories; Quattro even has a club that hosts live music. Part 2 is devoted mainly to interiors and fashion, and Part 3 sells a mixture of men's and women's fashions, tableware, and household furnishings. The nearby Zero Gate complex houses the basement restaurant-nightclub La Fabrique. ✉ *15–1 Udagawa-chō, Shibuya-ku* ☎ *03/3464–5111* ◷ *Parts 1, 2, and 3 daily 10–8:30; Quattro daily 11–9* Ⓜ *Ginza and Hanzō-mon subway lines, Shibuya Station (Exits 6 and 7).*

Seibu. The mammoth main branch of this department store—where even many Japanese customers get lost—is in Ikebukuro. The Shibuya branch, which still carries an impressive array of merchandise, is smaller and more manageable. Seibu has an excellent selection of household goods, from furniture to china and lacquerware, in its stand-alone Loft shops (often next door to Seibu branches, or occasionally within the department store itself). ✉ *1–28–1 Minami Ikebukuro, Toshima-ku* ☎ *03/3981–0111* ◷ *Mon.–Sat. 10–9, Sun. 10–8* Ⓜ *JR, Marunouchi and Yūrakuchō subway lines, Ikebukuro Station (Minami-guchi/South Exit); Seibu Ikebukuro private rail line, Seibu Ikebukuro Station (Seibu Department Store Exit); Tōbu Tōjō private rail line, Tōbu Ikebukuro Station (Minami-guchi/South Exit)* ✉ *21–1 Udagawa-chō, Shibuya-ku* ☎ *03/3462–0111* Ⓜ *JR (Hachiko Exit), Ginza and Hanzō-mon subway lines (Exits 6 and 7), Shibuya Station.*

Shinjuku

Isetan. One of Tōkyō's oldest and largest department stores, Isetan is known for its mix of high-end and affordable fashions. The department store even stocks clothing for women (Clovertown) and men (Supermale) in slightly larger sizes for those not quite petite enough for the standard Japanese range. ✉ *3–14–1 Shinjuku, Shinjuku-ku* ☎ *03/3352–1111* ◷ *Daily 10–8* Ⓜ *JR (Higashi-guchi/East Exit), Marunouchi subway line (Exits B2, B3, B4, and B5), Shinjuku Station.*

Marui. Marui, easily recognized by its red-and-white OI logo, burst onto the department store scene in the 1980s by introducing an in-store credit card—one of the first stores in Japan to do so. Branches typically occupy separate buildings near big stations; there are six big shops in Shinjuku with names like Marui Young, Marui City, and Marui One. Youngsters flock to the stores in search of petite clothing, accessories, and sportswear. The main Shinjuku location, Marui Zacca, carries furniture and products for the home. ✉ *3–1–3 Shinjuku, Shinjuku-ku* ☎ *03/3354–0101* ◷ *Daily 11–8* Ⓜ *JR, Shinjuku Station (Higashi-guchi/East Exit); Marunouchi subway line, Shinjuku San-chōme Station (Exit A1).*

Specialty Stores

Antiques

From ornate *tansu* (traditional chests used to store clothing) to Meiji-era Nō masks, Tōkyō's antiques shops are stocked with fine examples of traditional Japanese craftsmanship. The two best areas for antiques are Nishi-Ogikubo (also known as Nishiogi), which is just outside of Shinjuku, and Aoyama. The elegant shops along Kotto-dōri—Aoyama's "Antiques Road"—are the places to hunt down exquisite ¥100,000 vases and other pricey items. The slapdash array of more than 60 antiques shops in Nishi-Ogikubo has an anything-goes feel. When visiting Nishi-Ogikubo, which you can reach by taking the Sōbu Line to Nishi-Ogikubo Station, your best bet is to pick up the free printed area guide available at the police box outside the train station's north exit. Even though it's mostly in Japanese, the map provides easy-to-follow directions to all stores. Dealers are evenly clustered in each of the four districts around the station, so plan on spending at least half a day in Nishi-Ogikubo if you want to see them all.

Antiquers can also find great buys at Tōkyō's flea markets, which are often held on the grounds of the city's shrines.

★ **Fuji-Torii.** An English-speaking staff, a central Omotesandō location, and antiques ranging from ceramics to swords are the big draws at this shop, in business since 1948. In particular, Fuji-Torii has an excellent selection of folding screens, lacquerware, and *ukiyo-e* (wood-block prints). ☒ *6–1–10 Jingū-mae, Shibuya-ku* ☎ *03/3400-2777* ⊙ *Wed.–Mon. 11–6; closed 3rd Mon. of month* Ⓜ *Chiyoda subway line, Meiji Jingū-mae Station (Exit 4).*

Hanae Mori Building. The basement floor of this Kenzō Tange–designed emporium houses more than a dozen small antiques shops. The emphasis is on European goods, but Japanese offerings include a tasteful sword shop and ceramics dealers. Upstairs, fashion hounds can shop for designs from Hanae Mori, the doyenne of Japanese designers. ☒ *3–6–1 Kita-Aoyama, Minato-ku* ☎ *03/3406-1021* ⊙ *Daily 10:30–7* Ⓜ *Ginza, Chiyoda, and Hanzō-mon subway lines, Omotesandō Station (Exit A1).*

Lee Bong Rae. Stately Korean furniture and ceramics are on offer at this small Aoyama shop just up the road from the designer-housewares store Idee. ☒ *6–2–5 Minami-Aoyama, Minato-ku* ☎ *03/3407-6420* ⊙ *Mon.–Sat. 10–6* Ⓜ *Ginza, Chiyoda, and Hanzō-mon subway lines, Omotesandō Station (Exit B1).*

Morita. This Aoyama shop carries antique and new *mingei* (Japanese folk crafts) in addition to a large stock of textiles from throughout Asia. ☒ *5–12–2 Minami-Aoyama, Minato-ku* ☎ *03/3407-6420* ⊙ *Daily 10–7* Ⓜ *Ginza, Chiyoda, and Hanzō-mon subway lines, Omotesandō Station (Exit B1).*

Tōgō Shrine. One of the city's biggest flea markets—where you can often find antiques—takes place at this shrine near Harajuku's Takeshita-dōri, on the first, fourth, and fifth Sunday of the month from sunrise to sunset. ☒ *1–5 Jingū-mae, Shibuya-ku* ☎ *03/3425-7965* Ⓜ *Chiy-*

oda subway line, Meiji-jingū-mae Station; JR Harajuku Station (Takeshita-dōri Exit).

Yasukuni Jinja. You can search for antiques at the large flea market at Yasukuni, the Shrine of Peace for the Nation, every second and third Sunday of the month from sunrise to sunset. ☒ *3–1 Kudan-Kita, Chiyoda-ku* ☎ *090/2723–0687* Ⓜ *Hanzō-mon and Shinjuku subway lines, Kudanshita Station (Exit 1).*

Books

If you want to read while you're in Tōkyō, it's best to bring your books and magazines with you; foreign titles are often marked up by as much as 300%. All the shops listed below are open daily.

Bookstores of Jimbō-chō. The site of one of the largest concentrations of used bookstores in the world, the Jimbō-chō area is a bibliophile's dream. In the ½-km (¼-mi) strip along Yasukuni-dōri and its side streets you can find centuries-old Japanese prints, vintage manga (sophisticated comic books), and even complete sets of the *Oxford English Dictionary.* Most shops have predominately Japanese-language selections, but almost all stock some foreign titles, with a few devoting major floor space to English books. Kitazawa Shōten, recognizable by its stately entranceway, carries lots of humanities titles. Tokyo Random Walk is the retail outlet of Tuttle Publishing, which puts out books on Japanese language and culture. The large Japanese publisher Sanseido has its flagship store here; the fifth floor sells magazines and postcards in addition to books. The stores in the area are usually open 9 or 9:30 to 5:30 or 6, and many of the smaller shops close on Monday or Sunday. Ⓜ *Mita, Shinjuku, and Hanzō-mon subway lines, Jimbō-chō Station (Exit A5).*

Kinokuniya. The mammoth Kinokuniya bookstore near the south exit of Shinjuku Station devotes most of its fifth floor to English titles, with an excellent selection of travel guides, magazines, and books on Japan. ☒ *Takashimaya Times Sq., 5–24–2 Sendagaya, Shibuya-ku* ☎ *03/5361–3301* ◷ *Daily 10–8* Ⓜ *JR Yamanote Line, Shinjuku Station (Minami-guchi/South Exit).*

Maruzen. There are English titles on the fourth floor, and art books in English and Japanese on the second floor of this well-known bookstore. ☒ *2–3–10 Nihombashi, Chūō-ku* ☎ *03/3272–7211* ◷ *Mon.–Sat. 10–8, Sun. 10–8* Ⓜ *JR Tōkyō Station (Yaesu North Exit 16); Ginza and Tōzai subway lines, Nihombashi Station (Exit B3).*

Tower Records. This branch of the U.S.-based chain carries an eclectic collection of English-language books at more reasonable prices than those of most bookstores in town. It also has the best selection of foreign magazines in Tōkyō. ☒ *1–22–14 Jinnan, Shibuya-ku* ☎ *03/3496–3661* ◷ *Daily 10–11* Ⓜ *JR Yamanote, Hanzō-mon and Ginza subway lines, Shibuya Station (Exit 6).*

Yaesu Book Center. English-language paperbacks, art books, and calendars are available on the seventh floor of this celebrated bookstore. ☒ *2–5–1 Yaesu, Chūō-ku* ☎ *03/3281–1811* ◷ *Mon.–Sat. 10–9, Sun. 10–8* Ⓜ *JR Tōkyō Station (Yaesu South Exit 5).*

Ceramics

The Japanese have been crafting extraordinary pottery for more than 2,000 years, but this art form really began to flourish in the 16th century with the popularity and demand for tea-ceremony utensils. Feudal lords competed for possession of the finest pieces, and distinctive styles of pottery developed in regions all over the country. Some of the more prominent styles are those of the village of Arita in Kyūshū, with painted patterns of flowers and birds; Mashiko, in Tochigi Prefecture, with its rough textures and simple, warm colors; rugged Hagi ware, from the eponymous Western Honshū city; and Kasama, in Ibaraki Prefecture, with glazes made from ash and ground rocks. Tōkyō's specialty shops and department stores carry fairly complete selections of these and other wares.

Noritake. The Akasaka showroom of this internationally renowned brand carries fine china and glassware in a spacious setting. ⊠ *7–8–5 Akasaka, Minato-ku* ☎ *03/3586–0059* ⊙ *Weekdays 10–6* Ⓜ *Chiyoda subway line, Akasaka Station (Exit 7).*

Savoir Vivre. In Roppongi's ultratrendy Axis Building, this store sells contemporary and antique tea sets, cups, bowls, and glassware. ⊠ *Axis Bldg., 3F, 5–17–1 Roppongi, Minato-ku* ☎ *03/3585–7365* ⊙ *Mon.–Sat. 11–7, Sun. 11–6:30* Ⓜ *Hibiya and Ōedo subway lines, Roppongi Station (Exit 3).*

Tsutaya. *Ikebana* (flower arrangement) and *sadō* (tea ceremony) goods are the only items sold at this Kotto-dōri shop, but they come in such stunning variety that a visit is definitely worthwhile. Vases in surprising shapes and traditional ceramic tea sets make for unique souvenirs. ⊠ *5–10–5 Minami-Aoyama, Minato-ku* ☎ *03/3400–3815* ⊙ *Daily 10–6:30* Ⓜ *Ginza, Chiyoda, and Hanzō-mon subway lines, Omotesandō Station (Exit B1).*

Dolls

Many types of traditional dolls are available in Japan, each with its own charm. Kokeshi dolls, which date from the Edo period, are long, cylindrical, painted, and made of wood, with no arms or legs. Daruma, papier-mâché dolls with rounded bottoms and faces, are often painted with amusing expressions. Legend has it they are modeled after a Buddhist priest who remained seated in the lotus position for so long that his arms and legs atrophied. Hakata dolls, from Kyūshū, are ceramic figurines in traditional costume, such as geisha, samurai, or festival dancers.

Kyūgetsu. In business for more than a century, Kyūgetsu sells every kind of doll imaginable. ⊠ *1–20–4 Yanagibashi, Taitō-ku* ☎ *03/3861–5511* ⊙ *Weekdays 9:15–6, weekends 9:15–5:15* Ⓜ *Asakusa subway line, Asakusa-bashi Station (Exit A3).*

Electronics

The area around Akihabara Station has more than 200 stores with discount prices on stereos, digital cameras, PCs, DVD players, and anything else that runs on electricity. The larger shops have sections or floors (or even whole annexes) of goods made for export. Products come with instructions in most major languages, and if you have a tourist visa in your passport, you can purchase them duty-free.

Bic Camera. A large discount-electronics chain in the Odakyū Halc building, Bic Camera has low prices. ☒ *1–5–1 Nishi-Shinjuku, Shinjuku-ku* ☎ *03/5326–1111* ☽ *Daily 11–9* Ⓜ *Marunouchi and Shinjuku subway lines; JR; Keiō Shin-sen and Teitō private rail lines: Shinjuku Station (Nishi-guchi/West Exit).*

LAOX. One of the big Akihabara chains, LAOX has several locations in the area. The "Duty Free Akihabara" branch on the main Chūō-dōri strip carries a full six floors of export models. English-speaking staff members are always on call. ☒ *1–15–3 Soto-Kanda, Chiyoda-ku* ☎ *03/ 3255–5301* ☽ *Daily 10–8* Ⓜ *JR Akihabara Station (Denki-gai Exit).*

Softmap. One Akihabara retailer that actually benefited from the bursting of Japan's economic bubble in the early '90s is Softmap, a used-PC and -software chain with a heavy presence in Tōkyō. Most branches are open daily until 7:30 or 8. ☒ *3–14–10 Soto-Kanda, Chiyoda-ku* ☎ *03/ 3253–3030* ☽ *Daily 11–8* Ⓜ *JR Akihabara Station (Denki-gai Exit).*

☺ **Sony Building.** You can take the latest Sony gadgets for a test drive at this retail and entertainment space in the heart of Ginza. Kids enjoy trying out the latest, not-yet-released PlayStation games, while their parents fiddle with digital cameras and stereos from Japan's electronics leader. ☒ *5–3–1 Ginza, Chūō-ku* ☎ *03/3573–2371* ☽ *Daily 11–7* Ⓜ *Ginza, Hibiya, and Marunouchi subway lines, Ginza Station (Exit B9).*

Yamagiwa. Like LAOX, Yamagiwa has branches and annexes throughout Akihabara, and the upper floors of the main store sell items for foreign markets. ☒ *4–1–1 Soto-Kanda, Chiyoda-ku* ☎ *03/3253–2111* ☽ *Daily 10–8* Ⓜ *JR Akihabara Station (Denki-gai Exit).*

Yodobashi Camera. This discount-electronics superstore near Shinjuku Station carries a selection comparable to Akihabara's big boys. ☒ *1–11–1 Nishi-Shinjuku, Shinjuku-ku* ☎ *03/3346–1010* ☽ *Daily 11–9* Ⓜ *Marunouchi and Shinjuku subway lines; JR; Keiō Shin-sen and Teitō private rail lines: Shinjuku Station (Nishi-guchi/West Exit).*

Folk Crafts

Japanese folk crafts, called mingei—among them bamboo vases and baskets, fabrics, paper boxes, dolls, and toys—achieve a unique beauty in their simple and sturdy designs. Be aware, however, that simple does not mean cheap. Long hours of labor go into these objects, and every year there are fewer craftspeople left, producing their work in smaller and smaller quantities. Include these items in your budget ahead of time: the best—worth every cent—can be fairly expensive.

★ **Bingo-ya.** You may be able to complete all of your souvenir shopping in one trip to this tasteful four-floor shop, which carries traditional handicrafts from all over Japan, including ceramics, toys, lacquerware, Nō masks, fabrics, and lots more. ☒ *10–6 Wakamatsu-chō, Shinjuku-ku* ☎ *03/3202–8778* ☽ *Tues.–Sun. 10–7* Ⓜ *Ōedo subway line, Wakamatsu Kawada Station (Wakamatsu-chō Exit).*

★ **Oriental Bazaar.** The four floors of this popular tourist destination are packed with just about anything you could want as a traditional Japanese (or Chinese or Korean) handicraft souvenir: painted screens, pottery, chopsticks, dolls, and more, all at very reasonable prices. ☒ *5–9–13 Jingū-mae, Shibuya-ku* ☎ *03/3400–3933* ☽ *Fri.–Wed. 10–7* Ⓜ *Chiyoda subway line, Meiji Jingū-mae Station (Exit 4).*

Foodstuffs & Wares

This hybrid category includes everything from crackers and dried seaweed to cast-iron kettles, paper lanterns, and essential food kitsch like plastic sushi sets.

Backstreet Shops of Tsukiji. In Tsukiji, between the Central Wholesale Market and Harumi-dōri, among the many fishmongers you can also find stores selling pickles, tea, crackers, kitchen knives, baskets, and crockery. The area is a real slice of Japanese life. ⊠ *Tsukiji 4-chōme, Chūō-ku* Ⓜ *Ōedo subway line, Tsukiji-shijō Station (Exit A1); Hibiya subway line, Tsukiji Station (Exit 1).*

Tea-Tsu. Some people ascribe Japanese longevity to the beneficial effects of green tea. Tea-Tsu, which has five branches in Tōkyō, sells a variety of leaves in attractive canisters that make unique gifts. The main Aoyama branch also sells tea sets and other ceramics, and the staff will serve you a complimentary cup of *cha* (tea) as you make your selection. ⊠ *3–18–3 Minami-Aoyama, Minato-ku* ☎ *03/5772–2662* ◷ *Tues.–Sat. 11–8* Ⓜ *Ginza, Chiyoda, and Hanzō-mon subway lines, Omotesandō Station (Exit A4).*

Tokiwa-dō. Come here to buy some of Tōkyō's most famous souvenirs: *kaminari okoshi* (thunder crackers), made of rice, millet, sugar, and beans. The shop is on the west side of Asakusa's Thunder God Gate, the Kaminari-mon entrance to Sensō-ji. ⊠ *1–3 Asakusa, Taitō-ku* ☎ *03/3841–5656* ◷ *Daily 9–8:45* Ⓜ *Ginza subway line, Asakusa Station (Exit 1).*

Yamamoto Noriten. The Japanese are resourceful in their uses of products from the sea. Nori, the paper-thin dried seaweed used to wrap maki sushi and *onigiri* (rice balls), is the specialty here. If you plan to bring some home with you, buy unroasted nori and toast it yourself at home; the flavor will be far better than that of the preroasted sheets. ⊠ *1–6–3 Nihombashi Muromachi, Chūō-ku* ☎ *03/3241–0261* ◷ *Daily 9–6:30* Ⓜ *Hanzō-mon and Ginza subway lines, Mitsukoshi-mae Station (Exit A1).*

KAPPA-BASHI A wholesale-restaurant-supply district might not sound like a promising shopping destination, but Kappa-bashi, about a 10-minute walk west of the temples and pagodas of Asakusa, is worth a look. Ceramics, cutlery, cookware, folding lanterns, and even kimonos can all be found here, along with the kitschy plastic food models that appear in restaurant windows throughout Japan. The best strategy is to stroll up and down the 1-km (½-mi) length of Kappa-bashi-dōgu-machi-dōri and visit any shop that looks interesting. Most stores here emphasize function over charm, but some manage to stand out for their stylish spaces as well. Most Kappa-bashi shops are open until 5:30; some close on Sunday. To get here, take the Ginza subway line to Tawara-machi Station.

Kappa-bashi Sōshoku. Come here for *aka-chōchin* (folding red-paper lanterns) like the ones that hang in front of inexpensive bars and restaurants. ⊠ *3–1–1 Matsugaya, Taitō-ku* ☎ *03/3844–1973* ◷ *Mon.–Sat. 9:30–5:30* Ⓜ *Ginza subway line, Tawara-machi Station (Exit 3).*

Kawahara Shōten. The brightly colored bulk packages of rice crackers, shrimp-flavored chips, and other Japanese snacks sold here make offbeat gifts. ⊠ *3–9–2 Nishi-Asakusa, Taitō-ku* ☎ *03/3842–0841* ◷ *Mon.–Sat. 9–5:30* Ⓜ *Ginza subway line, Tawara-machi Station (Exit 3).*

⟳ **Maizuru.** This perennial tourist favorite manufactures the plastic food that's displayed outside almost every Tōkyō restaurant. Ersatz sushi, noodles, and even beer cost just a few hundred yen. You can buy tiny plastic key holders and earrings, or splurge on a whole Pacific lobster, perfect in coloration and detail down to the tiniest spines on its legs. ✉ *1–5–17 Nishi-Asakusa, Taitō-ku* ☎ *03/3843–1686* ⊗ *Daily 9–6* Ⓜ *Ginza subway line, Tawara-machi Station (Exit 3).*

Soi. The selection of lacquerware, ceramics, and antiques sold at this Kappa-bashi shop is modest, but Soi displays the items in a primitivist setting of stone walls and and exposed wood beams, with up-tempo jazz in the background. ✉ *3–17–3 Matsugaya, Taitō-ku* ☎ *03/3843–9555* ⊗ *Daily 10–6* Ⓜ *Ginza subway line, Tawara-machi Station (Exit 3).*

Sōtei Yabukita. In addition to kitchenware, this tasteful shop sells lamps and decorative fountains. ✉ *2–1–12 Matsugaya, Taitō-ku* ☎ *03/ 5828–5082* Ⓜ *Ginza subway line, Tawara-machi Station (Exit 3).*

Housewares

Tōkyōites appreciate fine design, both the kind they can wear and the kind they can display in their homes. This passion is reflected in the exuberance of the city's *zakka* shops—retailers that sell small housewares. The Daikanyama and Aoyama areas positively brim with these stores, but trendy zakka can be found throughout the city.

Idee. Local design giant Teruo Kurosaki's shop, which is just off Kotto-dōri, carries housewares, fabrics, and ceramics by some of Japan's most celebrated young craftspeople. The third-floor café-restaurant is a favorite meeting place of Aoyama creative types. ✉ *6–1–6 Minami-Aoyama, Minato-ku* ☎ *03/3409–6581* ⊗ *Sat.–Thurs. 11–7, Fri. 11–9* Ⓜ *Ginza, Chiyoda, and Hanzō-mon subway lines, Omotesandō Station (Exit B1).*

Nishimura. This Kappa-bashi shop specializes in *noren*—the curtains that shops and restaurants hang to announce they're open. The curtains are typically cotton, linen, or silk, most often dyed to order for individual shops. Nishimura also sells premade noren of an entertaining variety— from white-on-blue landscapes to geisha and sumō wrestlers in polychromatic splendor—for home decorating. They make wonderful wall hangings and dividers. ✉ *1–10–10 Matsugaya, Taitō-ku* ☎ *03/ 3844–9954* ⊗ *Mon.–Sat. 10–5* Ⓜ *Ginza subway line, Tawara-machi Station (Exit 3).*

Sempre. Playful, colorful, and bright describe both the products and the space of this Kotto-dōri housewares dealer. Among the great finds here are interesting tableware, glassware, lamps, office goods, and jewelry. ✉ *5–13–3 Minami-Aoyama, Minato-ku* ☎ *03/5464–5655* ⊗ *Mon.–Sat. 11–8, Sun. 11–7* Ⓜ *Ginza, Chiyoda, and Hanzō-mon subway lines, Omotesandō Station (Exit B1).*

Serendipity. Alessi products and other Western brands are sold at this spacious housewares store in the Coredo shopping center. ✉ *1–4–1 Nihombashi, Chūō-ku* ☎ *03/3272–4939* ⊗ *Mon.–Sat. 11–9, Sun. 11–8* Ⓜ *Ginza, Tōzai, and Asakusa subway lines, Nihombashi Station (Exit B10).*

Sputnik Pad. One of local designer Teruo Kurosaki's shops, Sputnik is Tōkyō's ultimate housewares destination. It carries funky and functional interiors products from big international designers like Marc Newson. Low, a trendy "rice café," is in the basement, and the Vision Network entertainment complex is across the street. ✉ *5–46–14 Jingū-mae, Minato-ku* ☎ *03/6418–1330* ☉ *Daily 11–7* Ⓜ *Ginza, Chiyoda, and Hanzō-mon subway lines, Omotesandō Station (Exit B1).*

☾ **Tōkyū Hands.** Billing itself as a "Creative Lifestyle Store," this do-it-yourself hobby chain stocks an excellent selection of bric-a-brac for the Tōkyō apartment dweller. Tourists find it to be a great spot to pick up inexpensive knickknacks with a Japanese flavor, like toys, picture frames, and kitchen goods. Tōkyū Hands has branches near most big stations. ✉ *Takashimaya Times Sq., 5–24–2 Sendagaya, Shibuya-ku* ☎ *03/5361–3111* ☉ *Daily 10–8* Ⓜ *JR Yamanote Line, Shinjuku Station (Minami-guchi/South Exit).*

Kimonos

Traditional clothing has experienced something of a comeback among Tōkyō's youth, but most Japanese women, unless they work in traditional restaurants, now wear kimonos only on special occasions. Like tuxedos in the United States, they are often rented, not purchased outright, for social events such as weddings or graduations. Kimonos are extremely expensive and difficult to maintain. A wedding kimono, for example, can cost as much as ¥1 million.

Most visitors, naturally unwilling to pay this much for a garment that they probably want to use as a bathrobe or a conversation piece, settle for a secondhand or antique silk kimono. You can pay as little as ¥1,000 in a flea market, but to find one in decent condition you should expect to pay about ¥10,000. However, cotton summer kimonos, called yukata, in a wide variety of colorful and attractive designs, can be bought new for ¥7,000–¥10,000.

Hayashi. This store in the Yūraku-chō International Arcade specializes in ready-made kimonos, sashes, and dyed yukata. ✉ *2–1–1 Yūraku-chō, Chiyoda-ku* ☎ *03/3501–4012* ☉ *Mon.–Sat. 10–7, Sun. 10–6* Ⓜ *Ginza, Hibiya, and Marunouchi subway lines, Ginza Station (Exit C1).*

Kawano Gallery. Kawano, in the high-fashion district of Omotesandō, sells kimonos and kimono fabric in a variety of patterns. ✉ *4–4–9 Jingū-mae, Shibuya-ku* ☎ *03/3470–3305* ☉ *Daily 11–6* Ⓜ *Ginza, Chiyoda, and Hanzō-mon subway lines, Omotesandō Station (Exit A2).*

Tansu-ya. This small but pleasant Ginza shop, part of a chain with locations throughout Japan and abroad, has attractive used kimonos, yukata, and other traditional clothing in many fabrics, colors, and patterns. The helpful staff can acquaint you with the somewhat complicated method of putting on the clothes. ✉ *3–4–5 Ginza, Chūō-ku* ☎ *03/3561–8529* ☉ *Daily 11–8* Ⓜ *Ginza, Hibiya, and Marunouchi subway lines, Ginza Station (Exit A13).*

Lacquerware

For its history, diversity, and fine workmanship, lacquerware rivals ceramics as the traditional Japanese craft nonpareil. One warning: lacquerware thrives on humidity. Cheaper pieces usually have plastic rather than wood underneath. Because these won't shrink and crack in dry climates, they make safer—and no less attractive—buys.

★ **Yamada Heiandō.** With a spacious, airy layout and lovely lacquerware goods, this fashionable Daikanyama shop is a must for souvenir hunters—and anyone else who appreciates fine design. Rice bowls, sushi trays, *bento* lunch boxes, *hashioki* (chopstick rests), and jewelry cases come in traditional blacks and reds, as well as patterns both subtle and bold. Prices are fair—many items cost less than ¥10,000—but these are the kinds of goods for which devotees of Japanese craftsmanship would be willing to pay a lot. ⊠ *Hillside Terrace G Block, 18–12 Sarugakuchō, Shibuya-ku* ☎ *03/3463–5541* ⊗ *Mon.–Sat. 10:30–7, Sun. 10:30–6:30* Ⓜ *Tōkyū Tōyoko line, Daikanyama Station (Komazawa-dōri Exit).*

Miscellaneous

Handmade combs, towels, and cosmetics are other uniquely Japanese treasures to consider picking up while in Tōkyō.

★ **Fuji-ya.** Master textile creator Keiji Kawakami's cotton *tenugui* (teh-*noo*-goo-ee) hand towels are collector's items, often as not framed instead of used as towels. Kawakami is an expert on the hundreds of traditional towel motifs that have come down from the Edo period: geometric patterns, plants and animals, and scenes from Kabuki plays and festivals. When Kawakami feels he has made enough of one pattern of his own design, he destroys the stencil. The shop is near the corner of Dembō-in-dōri on Naka-mise-dōri. ⊠ *2–2–15 Asakusa, Taitō-ku* ☎ *03/3841–2283* ⊗ *Fri.–Wed. 10–6* Ⓜ *Ginza subway line, Asakusa Station (Exit 6).*

Hyaku-suke. This is the last place in Tōkyō to carry government-approved skin cleanser made from powdered nightingale droppings. Ladies of the Edo period—especially the geisha—swore by the cleanser. These days this 100-year-old-plus cosmetics shop sells little of the nightingale powder, but its theatrical makeup for Kabuki actors, geisha, and traditional weddings—as well as unique items like seaweed shampoo, camellia oil, and handcrafted combs and cosmetic brushes—makes it a worthy addition to your Asakusa shopping itinerary. ⊠ *2–2–14 Asakusa, Taitō-ku* ☎ *03/3841–7058* ⊗ *Thurs.–Tues. 10–6* Ⓜ *Ginza subway line, Asakusa Station (Exit 6).*

Jūsan-ya. A shop selling handmade boxwood combs, this business was started in 1736 by a samurai who couldn't support himself as a feudal retainer. It has been in the same family ever since. Jusan-ya is on Shinobazu-dōri, a few doors west of its intersection with Chūō-dōri in Ueno. ⊠ *2–12–21 Ueno, Taitō-ku* ☎ *03/3831–3238* ⊗ *Mon.–Sat. 10–7* Ⓜ *Ginza subway line, Ueno Hirokō-ji Station (Exit 6); JR Ueno Station (Shinobazu Exit).*

Naka-ya. If you want to equip yourself for Sensō-ji's annual Sanja Festival in May, this is the place to come. Best buys here are *sashiko hanten,* which are thick woven firemen's jackets, and *happi* coats, cotton tunics printed in bright colors with Japanese characters. Some items are available in children's sizes. ⊠ *2–2–12 Asakusa, Taitō-ku* ☎ *03/3841–7877* ⊗ *Daily 10–7* Ⓜ *Ginza subway line, Asakusa Station (Exit 6).*

Yono-ya. Traditional Japanese coiffures and wigs are very complicated, and they require a variety of tools to shape them properly. Tatsumi Minekawa, the current master at Yono-ya—the family line goes back 300 years—deftly crafts and decorates very fine boxwood combs. Some combs are carved with auspicious motifs, such as peonies, hollyhocks, or cranes, and all are engraved with the family benchmark. ✉ *1–37–10 Asakusa, Taitō-ku* ☎ *03/3844–1755* ✆ *Daily 10–6; occasionally closed on Wed. or Thurs.* Ⓜ *Ginza subway line, Asakusa Station (Exit 1).*

Paper

What packs light and flat in your suitcase, won't break, doesn't cost much, and makes a great gift? The answer is traditional handmade *washi* (paper), which the Japanese make in thousands of colors, textures, and designs and fashion into an astonishing number of useful and decorative objects.

Kami Hyakka. Operated by the Okura Sankō wholesale paper company, which was founded in the late 19th century, this showroom displays some 512 different types and colors of paper—made primarily for stationery, notes, and cards rather than as crafts material. You can pick up three free samples when you visit. ✉ *2–4–9 Ginza, Chūō-ku* ☎ *03/3538–5025* ✆ *Tues.–Sat. 10:30–7* Ⓜ *Yūraku-chō subway line, Ginza-Itchōme Station (Exit 5); Ginza, Hibiya, and Marunouchi subway lines, Ginza Station (Exit B4).*

Kami-no-Takamura. Specialists in washi and other papers printed in traditional Japanese designs, this shop also carries brushes, inkstones, and other tools for calligraphy. ✉ *1–1–2 Higashi-Ikebukuro, Toshima-ku* ☎ *03/3971–7111* ✆ *Daily 11–6:45* Ⓜ *Ikebukuro Station (Exit 35).*

★ **Kyūkyodō.** Kyūkyodō has been in business since 1663—in Ginza since 1880—selling its wonderful handmade Japanese papers, paper products, incense, brushes, and other materials for calligraphy. ✉ *5–7–4 Ginza, Chūō-ku* ☎ *03/3571–4429* ✆ *Mon.–Sat. 10–7:30, Sun. 11–7* Ⓜ *Ginza, Hibiya, and Marunouchi subway lines, Ginza Station (Exit A2).*

Ōzu Washi. This shop, which was opened in the 17th century, has one of the largest washi showrooms in the city and its own gallery of antique papers. ✉ *2–6–3 Nihombashi-Honchō, Chūō-ku* ☎ *03/3663–8788* ✆ *Mon.–Sat. 10–6* Ⓜ *Ginza subway line, Mitsukoshi-mae Station (Exit A4).*

Pearls

Japan is one of the best places in the world to buy cultured pearls. They will not be inexpensive, but pearls of the same quality cost considerably more elsewhere.

★ **Mikimoto.** Kokichi Mikimoto created his technique for cultured pearls in 1893. Since then his name has been associated with the best quality in the industry. Mikimoto's flagship store in Ginza is less a jewelry shop than a boutique devoted to nature's ready-made gems. ✉ *4–5–5 Ginza, Chūō-ku* ☎ *03/3535–4611* ✆ *Mon.–Sat. 11–7:30, Sun. 11–7; occasionally closed on Wed.* Ⓜ *Ginza, Hibiya, and Marunouchi subway lines, Ginza Station (Exit A9).*

Tasaki Pearl Gallery. Tasaki sells pearls at slightly lower prices than Mikimoto. The store has several showrooms and hosts English-language tours that demonstrate the technique of culturing pearls and explain how to maintain and care for them. ✉ *1–3–3 Akasaka, Minato-ku* ☎ *03/5561–8881* ✆ *Daily 9–6* Ⓜ *Ginza subway line, Tameike-Sannō Station (Exit 9).*

Swords & Knives

Supplying the tools of the trade to samurai and sushi chefs alike, Japanese metalworkers have played a significant role in the nation's military and culinary history. The remarkable knives on offer from the shops below are comparable in both quality and price to the best Western brands. For swords, you can pay thousands of dollars for a good-quality antique, but far more reasonably priced reproductions are available as well. Consult with your airline on how best to transport these items home.

Kiya. Workers shape and hone blades in one corner of this Ginza shop, which carries cutlery, pocketknives, saws, and more. Scissors with handles in the shape of Japanese cranes are among the many unique gift items sold here, and custom-made knives are available on the second floor. ⊠ *1–5–6 Nihombashi-Muromachi, Chūō-ku* ☎ *03/3241–0110* ⊙ *Mon.–Sat. 10–6, Sun. 11:15–5:45* Ⓜ *Ginza subway line, Mitsukoshi-mae Station (Exit A4).*

★ **Nippon Tōken** (Japan Sword). Wannabe samurai can learn how to tell their *toshin* (blades) from their *tsuka* (sword handles) with help from the English-speaking staff at this small shop, which has been open since the Meiji era. Items range from a circa-1390 samurai sword to inexpensive reproductions to armor and masks. ⊠ *3–8–1 Toranomon, Minato-ku* ☎ *03/3434–4321* ⊙ *Weekdays 9:30–6, Sat. 9:30–5* Ⓜ *Hibiya and Ginza subway lines, Toranomon Station (Exit 2).*

Tōken Shibata. A tiny, threadbare shop incongruously situated near Ginza's glittering department stores, Tōken Shibata sells well-worn antique swords. ⊠ *5–6–8 Ginza, Chūō-ku* ☎ *03/3573–2801* ⊙ *Mon.–Sat. 10–6:30* Ⓜ *Ginza, Hibiya, and Marunouchi subway lines, Ginza Station (Exit A1).*

★ **Tsubaya Hōchōten.** Tsubaya sells high-quality cutlery for professionals. Its remarkable selection is designed for every imaginable use, as the art of food presentation in Japan requires a great variety of cutting implements. The best of these carry the Traditional Craft Association seal: hand-forged tools of tempered blue steel, set in handles banded with deer horn to keep the wood from splitting. Be prepared to pay the premium for these items: a cleaver just for slicing soba can cost as much as ¥50,000. ⊠ *3–7–2 Nishi-Asakusa, Taitō-ku* ☎ *03/3845–2005* ⊙ *Mon.–Sat. 9–5:45, Sun. 9–5* Ⓜ *Ginza subway line, Tawara-machi Station (Exit 3).*

Yoshikin. This small shop sells Japan's Global-brand knives, which, thanks to their handiness and maneuverability, have been winning over chefs worldwide at the expense of traditional European cutlers. ⊠ *Axis Bldg., 2F, 5–17–1 Roppongi, Minato-ku* ☎ *03/3568–2336* ⊙ *Mon.–Sat. 11–7* Ⓜ *Hibiya and Ōedo subway lines, Roppongi Station (Exit 3); Namboku subway line, Roppongi Itchōme Station (Exit 1).*

Toys

🕙 **Garage.** A hands-on toy and hobby shop in the sleek Coredo shopping center, Garage carries everything from telescopes to robots. ⊠ *1–4–1 Nihombashi, Chūō-ku* ☎ *03/3272–4939* ⊙ *Mon.–Sat. 11–9, Sun. 11–8* Ⓜ *Ginza, Tōzai, and Asakusa subway lines, Nihombashi Station (Exit B10).*

⏱ **Hakuhinkan.** This is reputedly the largest toy store in Japan, with lots of homegrown-character goods like Hello Kitty in addition to Western products. It's on Chūō-dōri, the main axis of the Ginza shopping area. ✉ *8–8–11 Ginza, Chūō-ku* ☎ *03/3571–8008* ☉ *Daily 11–8* Ⓜ *Ginza and Asakusa subway lines, Shimbashi Station (Exit 1).*

⏱ **Kiddy Land.** Commonly regarded as Tōkyō's best toy store, Kiddy Land also carries kitsch items that draw in Harajuku's teen brigade. ✉ *6–1 Jingū-mae, Shibuya-ku* ☎ *03/3409–3431* ☉ *Daily 11–8* Ⓜ *Chiyoda subway line, Meiji Jingū-mae Station (Exit 4).*

TŌKYŌ A TO Z

To research prices, get advice from other travelers, and book travel arrangements, visit www.fodors.com.

AIR TRAVEL

You can fly nonstop to Tokyo from Chicago, Detroit, New York, Los Angeles, San Francisco, Portland (OR), Seattle, Minneapolis, and Washington D.C. in the United States; from London; from Brisbane, Sydney, and Melbourne in Australia; and from Auckland in New Zealand. Because of the distance, fares to Japan from the United States tend to be expensive, usually between $900 and $1,200 for a seat in coach. But you can get a ticket for as low as $700 from a discount travel Web site, depending on the time of year. For a list of carriers, *see* Air Travel *in* Smart Travel Tips.

AIRPORTS & TRANSFERS

Tōkyō has two airports, Narita and Haneda. Narita, officially the New Tōkyō International Airport in Narita, is 80 km (50 mi) northeast of Tōkyō and serves all international flights, except those operated by (Taiwan's) China Airways, which berths at Haneda. Narita has two fairly well-developed terminals and a central building of shops and restaurants. Traffic in and out of the airport is high, especially during December and August, when millions of Japanese take holidays abroad. Customs clearance delays of an hour or more are not uncommon.

For getting money, there are Citibank ATMs in both terminals. In Terminal 2, the ATM is between the A and B zones for the exits from Customs Clearance to the lobby. To find the ATM in the North Wing of Terminal 1, turn right after you clear Customs and walk down the lobby about 100 yards to the end; the ATM is between the elevator and the escalator. Both terminals also have money exchange counters just inside the customs inspection area and just outside, in the arrivals lobbies. The Japan National Tourism Office (JNTO) Information Center in Terminal No.1 is in the North Wing arrivals lobby, across from the Customs exit; in Terminal No. 2 it's across from the Customs exits, between the A and B Zones.

Haneda Airport, 16 km (10 mi) southwest of Tōkyō, serves all domestic flights, most run by Japan Airlines (JAL) and All Nippon Airways (ANA). ✈ Airport Information **Haneda Airport (HND)** ☎ 03/5757–8111. **Narita Airport (NRT)** ☎ 0476/34–5000.

Directly across from the customs-area exits at both terminals are the ticket counters for buses to Tōkyō. Buses leave from platforms just outside terminal exits, exactly on schedule; the departure time is on the ticket. The Friendly Airport Limousine offers the only shuttle bus service from Narita to Tōkyō. Different buses stop at various major hotels in the $$$$ category and at the JR Tōkyō and Shinjuku train stations; the fare is ¥2,400–¥3,800 ($21–$35), depending on your destination. Even if you're not staying at one of the route's drop-off points, you can take the bus as far as the one closest to your hotel and then use a taxi for the remaining distance. The buses only run every hour or so and the last departure is at 11:30 PM. The trip is scheduled for 70–90 minutes but can take two hours in heavy traffic. A Friendly Airport Limousine bus to the Tōkyō City Air Terminal (TCAT) leaves approximately every 10–20 minutes from 6:55 AM to 11 PM; the fare is ¥2,900 ($26). TCAT is in Nihombashi in north-central Tōkyō, a bit far from most destinations, but from here you can connect directly with Suitengū Station on the Hanzō-mon subway line, then to anywhere in the subway network. A taxi from TCAT to most major hotels will cost about ¥3,000 ($27).

Japan Railways trains stop at both Narita Airport terminals. The fastest and most comfortable is the Narita Limited Express (N'EX), which makes 23 runs a day in each direction. Trains from the airport go directly to the central Tōkyō Station in just under an hour, then continue to Yokohama and Ōfuna. Daily departures begin at 7:43 AM; the last train is at 9:43 PM. The one-way fare is ¥2,940 (¥4,980 for the first-class "Green Car," and ¥5,380 per person for a private compartment that seats four). All seats are reserved, and you'll need to reserve one for yourself in advance, as this train fills quickly. The less elegant *kaisoku* (rapid train) on JR's Narita Line also runs from the airport to Tōkyō Station, by way of Chiba; there are 16 departures daily, starting at 7 AM. The fare to Tōkyō is ¥1,280 (¥2,210 for the Green Car); the ride takes 1 hour and 27 minutes.

The Keisei Skyliner train runs every 20–30 minutes between the airport terminals and Keisei-Ueno Station. The trip takes 57 minutes and costs ¥1,920 ($17). The first Skyliner leaves Narita for Ueno at 9:21 AM, the last at 9:59 PM. There's also an early train from the airport, called the Morning Liner, which leaves at 7:49 AM and costs ¥1,400. From Ueno to Narita, the first Skyliner is at 6:32 AM, the last at 5:21 PM. All Skyliner seats are reserved. It only makes sense to take the Keisei, however, if your final destination is in the Ueno area; otherwise, you must change to the Tōkyō subway system or the Japan Railways loop line at Ueno (the station is adjacent to Keisei-Ueno Station) or take a cab to your hotel.

You can take a taxi from Narita Airport to central Tōkyō, but it'll cost you ¥20,000 (about $180) or more, depending on traffic and where you're going. Private car service is also very expensive; from Narita Airport to the Imperial Hotel downtown, for example, will set you back about ¥35,000.

🚩 **Airport Transport Service Co.** ☎ 03/3665-7232 in Tōkyō, 0476/32-8080 for Terminal 1, 0476/34-6311 for Terminal 2. **IAE Co.** ☎ 0476/32-7954 for Terminal 1, 0476/34-6886 for Terminal 2. **Japan Railways** ☎ 03/3423-0111 for JR East InfoLine ⊙ weekdays 10–6. **Keisei Railway** ☎ 03/3831-0131 for the Ueno information counter, 0476/32-8505 at Narita Airport.

TRANSFERRING FROM HANEDA AIRPORT TO TŌKYŌ The monorail from Haneda Airport to Hamamatsu-chō Station in Tōkyō is the fastest and cheapest way into town; the journey takes about 20 minutes, and trains run approximately every 4 to 5 minutes; the fare is ¥470 ($4). From Hamamatsu-chō Station, change to a JR train or take a taxi to your destination.

A taxi to the center of Tōkyō takes about 40 minutes; the fare is approximately ¥8,000 ($73).

Tōkyō Monorail Co., Ltd. ☎ 03/3434-3171

BOAT & FERRY TRAVEL

The best ride in Tōkyō, hands down, is the *suijō basu* (river bus), operated by the Tōkyō Cruise Ship Company from Hinode Pier, from the mouth of the Sumida-gawa upstream to Asakusa. The glassed-in double-decker boats depart roughly every 20–40 minutes, weekdays 9:45–7:10, weekends and holidays 9:35–7:10 (with extended service to 7:50 July 9–September 23). The trip takes 40 minutes and costs ¥660. The pier is a seven-minute walk from Hamamatsu-chō Station on the JR Yamanote Line.

The Sumida-gawa was once Tōkyō's lifeline, a busy highway for travelers and freight alike. The ferry service dates to 1885. Some people still take it to work, but today most passengers are Japanese tourists. On its way to Asakusa, the boat passes Tsukiji's Central Wholesale Market, the largest wholesale fish and produce market in the world; the old lumberyards and warehouses upstream; and the Kokugikan, with its distinctive green roof, which houses the sumō wrestling arena, the Sumō Museum, and headquarters of the Japan Sumō Association.

Another place to catch the ferry is at the Hama Rikyū Tei-en (Detached Palace Garden: open daily 9–4:30), a 15-minute walk from Ginza. Once part of the imperial estates, the gardens are open to the public for a separate ¥300 entrance fee—which you have to pay even if you are only using the ferry landing. The landing is a short walk to the left as you enter the main gate. Boats depart every 35–45 minutes every weekday 10:25–4:10; the fare between Asakusa and Hama Rikyū is ¥620.

In addition to the ferry to Asakusa, the Tōkyō Cruise Ship Company also operates four other lines from Hinode Pier. The Harbor Cruise Line stern-wheeler makes a 50-minute circuit under the Rainbow Bridge and around the inner harbor. Departures are at 10:30, 12:30, 1:30, and 3:30 (and 4:45 in August). The fare is ¥800. If you visit in August you should definitely opt for the evening cruise; the lights on the Rainbow Bridge and neighboring Odaiba are spectacular. Two lines connect Hinode to Odaiba itself, one at 20-minute intervals from 10:10 to 6:10 to Odaiba Seaside Park and the Museum of Maritime Science at Aomi Terminal (¥400–¥520), the other every 25 minutes from 9 to 5:40 to the shopping/amusement center at Palette Town and on to the Tōkyō Big Sight exhibition grounds at Ariake (¥350). The Kasai Sealife Park Line cruise leaves Hinode hourly from 10 to 4 and travels through the network of artificial islands in the harbor to the beach and aquarium at Kasai

Rinkai Kōen in Chiba; the one-way fare is ¥800. The Canal Cruise Line connects Hinode with Shinagawa Suizokukan aquarium, south along the harborside. There are six departures daily except Tues.) between 10:15 and 4:50; the one-way fare is ¥800.

🚢 **Tōkyō Cruise Ship Company** ✉ 2-7-104 Kaigan, Minato-ku, Hinode Pier ☎ 03/3457-7830 at Hinode, 03/3841-9178 at Asakusa ⊕ http://www.suijobus.co.jp/english/cruise_e/index.html.

BUS TRAVEL

Bus routes in Tōkyō are impossibly complicated. The Tōkyō Municipal Government operates some of the lines; private companies run the rest. There is no telephone number even a native Japanese can call for help. And buses all have tiny seats and low ceilings. Unless you are a true Tōkyō veteran, forget about taking buses.

CAR RENTAL

Congestion, the infrequency of road signs in English, and the difficulty—not to say the expense—of parking make driving in Tōkyō impractical. That said, if you decide to rent a car, the following companies have locations all around Tōkyō and Japan: Budget Rent-A-Car, Dollar Rent-A-Car, Hertz Asia Pacific (Japan), or Nippon Rent-A-Car Service. Be aware that their central business offices close at 6 PM or 7 PM, and that you're not guaranteed to reach anybody who can deal with you in English. Make your reservation via phone or on the Web before you come. With taxes, the cost of a mid-size sedan (1500 cc.) is about ¥12,000 ($110) per day. An international driver's license is required.

You can hire large and comfortable chauffeured cars (the Japanese call them *haiya*) for about ¥5,000 ($46) per hour for a midsize car, up to ¥18,000 ($164) per hour for a Cadillac limousine. Call Hinomaru Limousine. The Imperial, Okura, and Palace hotels also have limousine services.

🚗 Local Agencies **Budget Rent-A-Car** ☎ 0120/15-0801 toll free ⊕ www.budget.com. **Dollar Rent-A-Car** ☎ 0120/11-7801 toll free ⊕ www.dollarcar.com. **Hertz Asia Pacific (Japan) Ltd.** ☎ 03/5401-7651 ⊕ www.hertz.com. **Hinomaru Limousine** ☎ 03/3212-0505 ⊕ www.hinomaru.co.jp. **Nippon Rent-A-Car** ☎ 03/3485-7196.

EMBASSIES & CONSULATES

The following embassies and consulates are open weekdays, with one- to two-hour closings for lunch. Call for exact hours.

🏛 Australia **Australian Embassy and Consulate** ✉ 2-1-14 Mita, Minato-ku. ☎ 03/5232-4111 ⊕ www.australia.or.jp/english Ⓜ Toei Mita Line, Shiba-Kōen Station [Exit A2]; Toei Ōedo and Namboku lines, Azabu-jūban Station [Exits 2 and 4].

🏛 Canada **Canadian Embassy and Consulate** ✉ 7-3-38 Akasaka, Minato-ku ⊕ www.fac-aec.gc.ca ☎ 03/5412-6200 Ⓜ Hanzō-mon and Ginza lines, Aoyama-itchōme Station [Exit 4].

🏛 New Zealand **New Zealand Embassy** ✉ 20-40 Kamiyama-chō, Shubiya-ku ☎ 03/3467-2271 ⊕ www.nzembassy.com Ⓜ Chiyoda Line, Yoyogi-kōen Station [Minami-guchi/South Exit].

🏛 United Kingdom **British Embassy and Consulate** ✉ 1 Ichiban-chō, Chiyoda-ku, Imperial Palace District ☎ 03/5211-1100 ⊕ www.uknow.or.jp Ⓜ Hanzō-mon Line, Hanzō-mon Station [Exit 4].

☷ United States **U.S. Embassy and Consulate** ✉ 1-10-5 Akasaka, Minato-ku, Tora-nomon ☎ 03/3224-500 ⊕ http://tokyo.usembassy.gov/ Ⓜ Namboku Line, Tameike-Sannō Station [Exit 13].

EMERGENCIES

Assistance in English is available 24 hours a day on the Japan Helpline. The Tōkyō English Life Line (TELL) is a telephone service available daily 9 AM–4 PM and 7 PM–11 PM for anyone in distress who cannot communicate in Japanese. The service will relay your emergency to the appropriate Japanese authorities and/or will serve as a counselor. Operators who answer the 119 and 110 hotlines rarely speak English.

☷ Ambulance and Fire ☎ 119. **Police** ☎ 110. **Japan Helpline** ☎ 0120/46-1997 toll free. **Tōkyō English Life Line** (TELL) ☎ 03/5774-0992.

DOCTORS & DENTISTS
The International Catholic Hospital (Seibo Byōin) accepts emergencies and takes regular appointments Monday–Saturday 8 AM–11 AM; outpatient services are closed the third Saturday of the month. The International Clinic also accepts emergencies. Appointments there are taken weekdays 9–noon and 2:30–5 and on Saturday 9–noon. St. Luke's International Hospital is a member of the American Hospital Association and accepts emergencies. Appointments are taken weekdays 8:30 AM–11 AM. The Tōkyō Medical and Surgical Clinic takes appointments weekdays 9–5 and Saturday 9–noon.

The Yamauchi Dental Clinic, a member of the American Dental Association, is open weekdays 9–12:30 and 3–5:30, Saturday 9–noon.

☷ International Catholic Hospital (Seibo Byōin) ✉ 2-5-1 Naka Ochiai, Shinjuku District ☎ 03/3951-1111 Ⓜ Seibu Shinjuku Line, Shimo-Ochiai Station [Nishi-guchi/West Exit]. **International Clinic** ✉ 1-5-9 Azabu-dai, Minato-ku, Roppongi District ☎ 03/3582-2646 or 03/3583-7831 Ⓜ Hibiya Line, Roppongi Station [Exit 3]. **St. Luke's International Hospital** ✉ 9-1 Akashi-chō, Chūō-ku, Tsukiji District ☎ 03/3541-5151 Ⓜ Hibiya Line, Tsukiji Station [Exit 3]; Yūraku-chō Line, Shintomichō Station [Exit 6]. **Tōkyō Medical and Surgical Clinic** ✉ 32 Mori Bldg., 3-4-30 Shiba Kōen Minato-ku ☎ 03/3436-3028 Ⓜ Toei Mita Line, Onarimon Station [Exit A1]; Hibiya Line, Kamiyachō Station [Exit 1]; Toei Ōedo Line, Akabane-bashi Station. **Yamauchi Dental Clinic** ✉ Shirokanedai Gloria Heights, 1st floor, 3-16-10 Shirokanedai Minato-ku ☎ 03/3441-6377 Ⓜ JR Yamanote Line, Meguro Station [Higashi-guchi/East Exit]; Namboku and Toei Mita lines, Shirokanedai Station [Exit 1].

LATE-NIGHT PHARMACIES
No drugstores in Tōkyō are open 24 hours a day. The Koyasu Drug Store in the Hotel Ōkura stocks some non-prescription Western products, and is open Monday–Saturday 8:30–9, Sundays and holidays 10–9. Note that grocery and convenience stores frequently carry such basics as aspirin and ibuprofen.

Nagai Yakkyoku is open daily (except Tues.) 10–7 and will mix a Chinese and/or Japanese herbal medicine for you after a consultation. You can't have a doctor's prescription filled here, but you can find something for a headache or stomach pain. A little English is spoken.

☷ Koyasu Pharmacy ✉ Hotel Ōkura, 2-10-4 Toranomon, Chiyoda-ku ☎ 03/3583-7958 Ⓜ Namboku Line, Tameike-Sannō Station [Exit 13]. **Nagai Yakkyoku** ✉ 1-8-10 Azabu-jūban, Minato-ku. ☎ 03/3583-3889 Ⓜ Namboku and Toei Ōedo subway lines, Azabu-jūban Station [Exit 7].

The Central Lost and Found Office of the metropolitan police is open weekdays only, 8:30–5:15; someone should be able to speak English here. If you leave something on a JR train, report it to the lost-and-found office at any station. You can also call either of the two central JR Lost Property Offices, one at Tōkyō Station (open daily 8:30–8), the other at Ueno Station (open weekdays 10–6, Saturday 10–4). If you leave something on a subway car, contact the Eidan Subways Lost and Found Corner (open weekdays 9:30–7, Saturday 9:30–4). If you leave something in a taxi, contact the Tōkyō Taxi Kindaika Center. The center is open 24 hours, but only Japanese is spoken here.

🚇 **Central Lost and Found Office** ✉ 1-9-11, Kōraku, Bunkyō-ku ☎ 03/3814-4151. **JR Lost Property Office** ✉ Tōkyō Station, Marunouchi ☎ 03/3231-1880 ✉ Ueno Station Ueno ☎ 03/3841-8069. **Eidan Subways Lost and Found Corner** ☎ 03/3834-5577. **Tōkyō Taxi Kindaika Center** ✉ 7-3-3 Minami-Suna, Koto-ku ☎ 03/3648-0300.

MAIL & SHIPPING

Most hotels have stamps and will mail your letters and postcards; they will also give you directions to the nearest post office. The main International Post Office is on the Imperial Palace side of JR Tōkyō Station.

🚇 **International Post Office** ✉ 2-3-3 Ōte-machi, Chiyoda-ku ☎ 03/3241-4891 Ⓜ Tōkyō Station.

MONEY MATTERS

In terms of lodging, food, and transportation (except taxis), Tokyo is about as expensive as New York or Paris. One good way to hold down expenses is to avoid taxis (they tend to get stuck in traffic anyway) and try the efficient, easy-to-use subway system. Restaurants for locals tend to be less expensive than those for tourists, so instead of going to a restaurant with Western-style food and menus in English, go to places where you can rely on your good old index finger to point to the dish you want, and try food that the Japanese eat (⇨ The Discreet Charm of Japanese Cuisine *in* Chapter 15).

Here are some sample prices: a regular cup of coffee costs ¥250–¥600 ($2–$5.50); a bottle of beer, ¥350–¥800 ($3–$7); a 2-km (1-mi) taxi ride, ¥660 ($6); a McDonald's hamburger, ¥84 (75¢); a bowl of noodles, ¥600 ($5.50); an average dinner, ¥2,500 ($22); a double room in Tōkyō, ¥11,000–¥45,000 ($98–$403).

Most hotels will change both traveler's checks and notes into yen. However, their rates are always less favorable than at banks. Because Japan is largely free from street crime, you can safely consider changing even hefty sums into yen at any time; three places that may be familiar to you are American Express International and Citibank. The larger branches of most Japanese banks have foreign exchange counters where you can do this as well; the paperwork will be essentially the same. All major branch offices of the post office have ATM machines that accept Visa, MasterCard, American Express, Diners Club, and Cirrus cards. You can also use cards on the Cirrus network at Citibank ATMs. Banking hours are weekdays 9–3.

🚇 **American Express International** ✉ 4-30-16 Ogikubo, Suginami-ku. ☎ 03/ 3220-6100 Ⓜ JR Chuo Line, Ogikubo Station [Higashi-guchi/East Exit]. **Citibank** ✉ Ōte

Center Bldg. 1F, 1-1-3 Ōte-machi, Chiyoda-ku. ☎ 0120/110-330 toll free for account hold-ers, 03/3215-0051 for other inquiries. Ⓜ Chiyoda, Marunouchi, Hanzō-mon, Tōzai, and Mita subway lines; Ōte-machi Station [Exit C-13B].

SUBWAY TRAVEL

Thirteen subway lines serve Tōkyō; nine of them are operated by the Rapid Transportation Authority (Eidan) and four by the Tōkyō Municipal Authority (Toei). Maps of the system, bilingual signs at entrances, and even the trains are color-coded for easy identification. Japan Travel Phone can provide information in English on subway travel. Subway trains run roughly every five minutes from about 5 AM to midnight; except dur-ing rush hours, the intervals are slightly longer on the newer Toei lines.

The network of interconnections (subway to subway and train to sub-way) is particularly good. One transfer—two at most—will take you in less than an hour to any part of the city you're likely to visit. At some stations—such as Ōte-machi, Ginza, and Iidabashi—long underground passageways connect the various lines, and it does take time to get from one to another. Directions, however, are clearly marked. Less helpful is the system of signs that tell you which of the 15 or 20 exits (exits are often numbered and alphabetized) from a large station will take you above-ground closest to your destination; only a few stations have such signs in English. Exit names or numbers have been included in the text where they'll be most useful. You can also try asking the agent when you turn in your ticket; she or he may understand enough of your question to come back with the exit number and letter (such as A3 or B12), which is all you need.

Subway fares begin at ¥160. Toei trains are generally a bit more expensive than Eidan trains, but both are competitive with JR lines. From Ueno across town to Shibuya on the old Ginza Line (orange), for example, is ¥190; the ride on the JR Yamanote Line will cost you the same. The Eidan (but *not* the Toei) has inaugurated an electronic card of its own, called Metrocard. The denominations are ¥1,000, ¥3,000, and ¥5,000. Automatic card dispensers are installed at some subway stations.

Remember to hold onto your ticket during your trip; you'll need it again to exit the station turnstile.
🔰 **Japan Travel Phone** ☎ 03/3201-3331.

TAXIS

In spite of the introduction of ¥340 initial-fare cabs, Tōkyō taxi fares remain among the highest in the world. Most meters start running at ¥660 and after the first 2 km (1 mi) tick away at the rate of ¥80 every 274 meters (about ⅕ mi). Keep in mind that the ¥340 taxis (which are a very small percentage of those on the street) are only cheaper for trips of 2 km (1 mi) or less; after that the fare catches up with the ¥660 cabs. The ¥340 taxis have a sticker on the left-rear window.

There are also smaller cabs, called *kogata*, that charge ¥640 and then ¥80 per 290 meters (⅕ mi). If your cab is caught in traffic—hardly an uncommon event—the meter registers another ¥80 for every 1½ minutes of immo-bility. Between 11 PM and 5 AM, a 30% surcharge is added to the fare.

You do get very good value for the money, though. Taxis are invariably clean and comfortable. The doors open automatically for you when you get in and out. Drivers take you where you want to go by the shortest route they know and do not expect a tip. Tōkyō cabbies are not, in general, a sociable species (you wouldn't be either if you had to drive for 10–12 hours a day in Tōkyō traffic), but you can always count on a minimum standard of courtesy. And if you forget something in the cab—a camera, a purse—your chances of getting it back are almost 100% (⇨ Lost and Found).

Hailing a taxi during the day is seldom a problem. You would have to be in a very remote part of town to wait more than five minutes for one to pass by. In Ginza, drivers are allowed to pick up passengers only in designated areas; look for short lines of cabs. Elsewhere, you need only step off the curb and raise your arm. If the cab already has a fare, there will be a green light on the dashboard, visible through the windshield; if not, the light will be red.

Night, when everyone's been out drinking and wants a ride home, changes the rules a bit. Don't be astonished if a cab with a red light doesn't stop for you: the driver may have had a radio call, or he may be heading for an area where a long, profitable fare to the suburbs is more likely. (Or the cab driver may simply not feel like coping with a passenger in a foreign language. Refusing a fare is against the law—but it's done all the time.) Between 11 PM and 2 AM on Friday and Saturday nights, you have to be very lucky to get a cab in any of the major entertainment districts; in Ginza it is almost impossible.

TELEPHONES
For directory information on Tōkyō telephone numbers, dial 104; for elsewhere in Japan, dial 105. These services are only in Japanese, but the NTT Information Customer Service Centre, open weekdays 9–5, has service representatives who speak English, French, Spanish, Portuguese, Korean, and Chinese.

🚩 **NTT Information Customer Service Centre** ☎ 0120/36-4463 toll-free.

TOURS
EXCURSIONS   Sunrise Tours, a division of the Japan Travel Bureau, runs a one-day bus tour to Nikkō on Monday, Tuesday, and Friday between April and October, at ¥13,500 (lunch included). Japan Amenity Travel and the Japan Gray Line conduct Mt. Fuji and Hakone tours, with return either by bus or train; one-day trips cost from ¥12,000 to ¥15,000 (lunch included), and two-day tours cost ¥26,500 (meals and accommodation included). Some of these tours include a quick visit to Kamakura. There are also excursions to Kyōto via Shinkansen that cost from ¥49,500 to ¥82,100; you can arrange these Shinkansen tours through Japan Amenity Travel or Japan Gray Line.

ORIENTATION   April–June and mid-September–November, Sunrise Tours conducts a
TOUR   Thursday-morning (8–12:30) "Experience Japanese Culture" bus-and-walking tour (¥7,000), which includes a calligraphy demonstration, a tea ceremony, and a visit to the Edo-Tōkyō Museum. Both Sunrise

Tours and the Japan Gray Line operate a number of other bus excursions around Tōkyō with English-speaking guides. The tours vary with the current demands of the market. Most include the Tōkyō Tower Observatory, the Imperial East Garden, a demonstration of flower arrangement at the Tasaki Pearl Gallery, and/or a Sumida-gawa cruise to Sensō-ji in Asakusa. These are for the most part four-hour morning or afternoon tours; a full-day tour (seven hours) combines most of what is covered in half-day excursions with a tea ceremony at Happō Garden and lunch at the traditional Chinzan-sō restaurant. Costs range from ¥4,000 to ¥12,900. Tours are conducted in large, air-conditioned buses that set out from Hamamatsu-chō Bus Terminal, and there is also free pickup and return from major hotels. (If you travel independently and use the subway, you could probably manage the same full-day itinerary for under ¥3,000, including lunch.)

PERSONAL GUIDES
The Japan Guide Association will introduce you to English-speaking guides. You'll need to negotiate your own itinerary and price with the guide. Assume that the fee will be ¥25,000–¥30,000 for a full eight-hour day. The Japan National Tourist Organization can also put you in touch with various local volunteer groups that conduct tours in English; you need only to pay for the guide's travel expenses, admission fees to cultural sites, and meals if you eat together.

SPECIAL-INTEREST TOURS
You can make online reservations in advance for free weekday tours of parts of the Imperial Palace Grounds with the Imperial Household Agency. The 1¼-hour guided tour (in Japanese, but with a useful pamphlet and audio guide in English) covers 11 of the buildings and sites on the west side of the palace grounds.

Sunrise Tours also offers a "Geisha Night" tour (4:30–7) of Tōkyō on Tuesday and Friday mid-March–November. Dinner is included. Other evening tours include Kabuki drama at the Kabuki-za, and sukiyaki dinner. Prices are ¥5,000–¥9,500, depending on which portions of the tour you select. Sunrise Tours has a free-schedule trip to Tōkyō Disneyland, but this operates only on Tuesday and Friday and works in only one direction: buses pick you up at major hotels but leave you to manage your own way back to Tōkyō at the end of the day. The cost for the trip is ¥9,500.

🛈 Tour Contacts **Imperial Palace Grounds tours** ⊕ http://sankan.kunaicho.go.jp/order/index_EN.html. **Japan Amenity Travel** ✉ 5-13-12 Ginza, Chūō-ku ☎ 03/3542-7200 Ⓜ Hibiya subway line, Higashi-Ginza Station [Exit 4]. **Japan Gray Line** ✉ 3-3-3 Nishi Shimbashi, Minato-ku ☎ 03/3433-5745 Ⓜ JR Yamanote Line, Shimbashi Station [Nishi-guchi/West Exit]. **Japan Guide Association** ☎ 03/3213-2706. **Japan National Tourist Organization** ✉ Tōkyō International Forum B1, 3-5-1 Marunouchi, Chiyoda-ku ☎ 03/3201-3331 Ⓜ Yūraku-chō Line, Yūraku-chō Station [Exit A-4B]. **Sunrise Tours Reservation Center, Japan Travel Bureau** ☎ 03/5620-9500.

TRAIN TRAVEL

The JR Shinkansen (bullet train) and JR express trains on the Tōkaidō Line (to Nagoya, Kyōto, Kōbe, Ōsaka, Hiroshima, and the island of Kyūshū) use Tōkyō Station in central Tōkyō. The JR Shinkansen and express trains on the Tōhoku Line (to Sendai and Morioka) use Ueno Station. JR Shinkansen and express trains on the Jōetsu Line (to Niigata) use both Tōkyō Station and Ueno Station. JR express trains to the Japan Alps (Matsumoto) use Shinjuku Station. The *Hokuriku* Shinkansen travels from Tōkyō Station to Nagano; it uses the Jōetsu Shinkansen tracks to Takasaki, where it branches off for Nagano.

If you buy a Japan Rail Pass for further travel throughout the country, you can use it on all JR trains except the *Nozomi* Shinkansen out of Tōkyō on the Tōkaidō Line. *See* Train Travel *in* Smart Travel Tips A to Z for information on Japanese rail networks and on obtaining JR Passes.

Japan Railways (JR) trains in Tōkyō are color-coded, making it easy to identify the different lines. The Yamanote Line (green or silver with green stripes) makes a 35-km (22-mi) loop around the central-kus of the city in about an hour. The 29 stops include the major hub stations of Tōkyō, Yūraku-chō, Shimbashi, Shinagawa, Shibuya, Shinjuku, and Ueno.

The Chūō Line (orange) runs east to west through the loop from Tōkyō to the distant suburb of Takao. During the day, however, these are limited express trains that don't stop at most of the stations inside the loop. For local cross-town service, which also extends east to neighboring Chiba Prefecture, you have to take the Sōbu Line (yellow).

The Keihin Tōhoku Line (blue) goes north to Ōmiya in Saitama Prefecture and south to Ōfuna in Kanagawa, running parallel to the Yamanote Line between Tabata and Shinagawa. Where they share the loop the two lines usually use the same platform—Yamanote trains on one side and Keihin Tōhoku trains, headed in the same direction, on the other. This requires a little care. Suppose, for example, you want to take the loop line from Yūraku-chō around to Shibuya, and you board a blue train instead of a green one; four stops later, where the lines branch, you'll find yourself on an unexpected trip to Yokohama.

JR Yamanote Line fares start at ¥130; you can get anywhere on the loop for ¥260 or less. Most stations have a chart in English somewhere above the row of ticket vending machines, so you can check the fare to your destination. If not, you can simply buy the cheapest ticket and pay the difference at the other end. In any case, hold on to your ticket: you'll have to turn it in at the exit. Tickets are valid only on the day you buy them, but if you plan to use the JR a lot, you can save time and trouble with an Orange Card, available at any station office. The card is electronically coded; at vending machines with orange panels, you insert the card, punch the cost of the ticket, and that amount is automatically deducted. Orange Cards come in ¥1,000 and ¥3,000 denominations.

Shinjuku, Harajuku, and Shibuya are notorious for the long lines that form at ticket dispensers. If you're using a card, make sure you've lined up at a machine with an orange panel; if you're paying cash and have no change, make sure you've lined up at a machine that will change ¥1,000 note—not all of them do.

Yamanote and Sōbu Line trains begin running about 4:30 AM and stop around 1 AM. The last departures are indicated at each station—but only in Japanese. Bear in mind that 7 AM–9:30 AM and 5 PM–7 PM trains are packed to bursting with commuters; avoid the trains at these times, i possible. During these hours smoking is not allowed in JR stations or on platforms.

ℹ Japan Railways ☎ 03/3423-0111.

TRANSPORTATION AROUND TŌKYŌ

Daunting in its sheer size, Tōkyō is, in fact, an extremely easy city to negotiate. If you have any anxieties about getting from place to place, remind yourself first that a transportation system obliged to cope with 4 or 5 million commuters a day simply *has* to be efficient, extensive, and reasonably easy to understand. Remind yourself also that virtually any place you're likely to go as a visitor is within a 15-minute walk of a train or subway station—and that station stops are always marked in English. Of course there are exceptions to the rule—the system has its flaws. In the outline here you'll find a few things to avoid and also a few pointers that will save you time—and money—as you go.

Excellent maps of the subway system, with major JR lines included as well, are available at any station office free of charge. Hotel kiosks and English-language bookstores stock a wide variety of pocket maps, some of which have suggested walking tours that also mark the locations of JR and subway stations along the way. A bit bulkier to carry around, but by far the best and most detailed resource, is the *Tōkyō City Atlas: A Bilingual Guide* (Kōdansha International, fourth edition; ¥2,100), which contains subway and rail-system guides and area maps. Because all notations are in both English and Japanese, you can always get help on the street, even from people who do not speak your language, just by pointing at your destination.

The standard postal system the Japanese themselves use to indicate addresses in Tōkyō begins with the "ku"—designated by the suffix *-ku* (as in Minato-ku)—followed by the name of the district within the-ku, such as Roppongi or Nishi-Azabu. The district is usually divided into numbered subsections, sometimes designated by the suffix *-chōme*; the subsections can be further divided into units of one or more blocks, each with its own building numbers. Apartment blocks will often have a final set of digits on the address to specify an apartment number. Thus, *Taitō-ku 1–4–301 Asakusa 3-chōme* will be recognizable to the mail carrier as "Apartment No. 301 in Building 4 on the first block of Asakusa subsection No. 3 in Taitō-ku"—but don't count on the driver of a taxi you hail on the other side of the city having the faintest idea how to find it. And don't count on the blocks or the building numbers appearing in any rational geographic order, either. The whole system is impossibly complicated, even for the Japanese. People usually direct each other to some landmark or prominent building in a given neighborhood and muddle on from there. Bear in mind that addresses written in Japanese appear in reverse order, that is, with the postal code, prefecture, and ku, first and the name of the person or establishment last; however, Japanese addresses written in English follow Western order, with the name first and the ward, prefecture, and postal code last. The system used throughout this guide follows the Western order: 1–4–301 Asakusa, 3-chōme, Taitō-ku.

Information on trains is available in English from the JR East InfoLine (weekdays 10–6). The Japan Travel Phone (daily 9–5) provides information in English on all domestic travel, buses, and trains.

🔢 **Japan Travel Phone** ☎ 03/3201-3331, 075/371-5649 for the Kyōto area. **JR East InfoLine** ☎ 03/3423-0111.

VISITOR INFORMATION

The Tourist Information Center (TIC) in the Tōkyō Metropolitan Government Office is an extremely useful source of free maps and brochures. The center also advises on trip planning in Japan. Make a point of dropping by early in your stay in Tōkyō; it's open weekdays 9–5, Saturday 9–noon.

The Asakusa Tourist Information Center, opposite Kaminari-mon, has some English-speaking staff and plenty of maps and brochures; it's open daily 9:30–8.

A taped recording in English about festivals, performances, and other events in the Tōkyō area operates 24 hours a day and is updated weekly. Two free weekly magazines, the *Tour Companion* and *Metropolis,* available at hotels, book and music stores, some restaurants and cafés, and other locations, carry up-to-date announcements of what's going on in the city. The better of the two is *Metropolis,* which breaks its listings down into separate sections for Art & Exhibitions, Movies, TV, Music, and After Dark. *Tōkyō Journal* (¥600), available at newsstands in Narita Airport and at many bookstores that carry English-language books, is a monthly magazine with similar listings. The *Japan Times,* a daily English-language newspaper, is yet another resource for entertainment reviews and schedules.

NTT (Japanese Telephone Corporation) can help you find information (in English), such as telephone numbers, museum openings, and various other information available from its databases. It's open weekdays 9–5.

🔢 Tourist Information **Asakusa Tourist Information Center** ✉ 2-18-9 Kaminari-mon, Taitō-ku ☎ 03/3842-5566 Ⓜ Ginza Line, Asakusa Station [Exit 2]. **Metropolis** ☎ 03/3423-6931 ⊕ www.metropolis.co.jp. **NTT** ☎ 0120/36-4463 toll free. **Tourist Information Center (TIC)** ✉ Tōkyō International Forum, 3-5-1 Marunouchi, Chiyoda-ku ☎ 03/3201-3331 Ⓜ Yūraku-chō Line, Yūraku-chō Station [Exit A-4B].

SIDE TRIPS FROM TŌKYŌ

2

By Jared
Lubarsky

Updated by
Steve Trautlein

NIKKŌ—which means "sunlight"—is the site not simply of the Tokugawa shrine but also of a national park, Nikkō Kokuritsu Kōen, on the heights above it. The centerpiece of the park is Chūzenji-ko, a deep lake some 21 km (13 mi) around, and the 318-ft-high Kegon Falls, Japan's most famous waterfall. "Think nothing splendid," asserts an old Japanese proverb, "until you have seen Nikkō." Whoever said it first might well have been thinking more of the park than of the shrine below.

One caveat: the term "national park" does not quite mean what it does elsewhere in the world. In Japan pristine grandeur is hard to come by; there are few places in this country where intrepid hikers can go to contemplate the beauty of nature for very long in solitude. If a thing's worth seeing, it's worth developing. This world view tends to fill the national parks with bus caravans, ropeways and gondolas, scenic overlooks with coin-fed telescopes, signs that tell you where you may and may not walk, fried-noodle joints and vending machines, and shacks full of kitschy souvenirs. That's true of Nikkō, and it's true as well of Fuji-Hakone-Izu National Park, southwest of Tōkyō, another of Japan's most popular resort areas.

The park's chief attraction is, of course, Fuji-san—spellbinding in its perfect symmetry, immortalized by centuries of poets and artists. South of Mt. Fuji, the Izu Peninsula projects out into the Pacific, with Suruga Bay to the west and Sagami Bay to the east. The beaches and rugged shoreline of Izu, its forests and highland meadows, and its numerous hot-springs inns and resorts (*izu* means "spring") make the region a favorite destination for the Japanese, especially honeymooners.

Kamakura and Yokohama, both close enough to Tōkyō to provide ideal day trips, could not make for more contrasting experiences. Kamakura is an ancient city—the birthplace, one could argue, of the samurai way of life. Its place in Japanese history begins late in the 12th century, when Minamoto no Yoritomo became the country's first shōgun and chose this site, with its rugged hills and narrow passes, as the seat of his military government. The warrior elite of the Kamakura period took much of their ideology—and their aesthetics—from Zen Buddhism, endowing splendid temples that still exist today. A walking tour of Kamakura's Zen temples and Shintō shrines is a must for anyone with a day to spend out of Tōkyō. Yokohama, too, can lay claim to an important place in Japanese history: in 1869, after centuries of isolation, this city became the first important port for trade with the West and the site of the first major foreign settlement. Twice destroyed, the city retains very few remnants of that history, but it remains Japan's largest port and has an international character that rivals—if not surpasses—that of Tōkyō.

See the glossary at the end of this book for definitions of the common Japanese words and suffixes used in this chapter.

About the Restaurants

The local specialty in Nikkō is a kind of bean curd called *yuba*; dozens of restaurants in Nikkō serve it in a variety of dishes you might not have believed possible for so prosaic an ingredient. Other local favorites are

If you have
1 day

If you can afford the time for only one day trip from Tōkyō, make **Kamakura,** the 12th-century military capital of Japan, your destination. The Great Buddha of the Kōtoku-in is but one of the National Treasures of art and architecture here that draw millions of visitors a year. An early morning start by train will allow you to see most of the important sights in a full day and make it back to Tōkyō by late evening. As Kamakura is popular, you can avoid the worst of the crowds by making the trip on a weekday.

If you have
6 days

With six days or more, you can make Tōkyō your home base for a series of side trips. Devote your first day to Kamakura, and return to Tōkyō in the evening. On the second day, take an early train out to **Yokohama,** with its scenic port and Chinatown; overnight back in Tōkyō. Farther off, but an easy train trip, is 🚇 **Nikkō,** where the founder of the Tokugawa shogunal dynasty is enshrined. Tōshō-gū is a monument unlike any other in Japan, and the picturesque Lake Chūzen-ji is in a forest above the shrine. Two full days, with an overnight stay, would allow you an ideal, leisurely exploration of both. End your tour with an overnight trip to 🚇 **Hakone,** with its hiking, hot springs, and close-up view of **Fuji-san** (Mt. Fuji); if you time your trip right, you can even arrange to climb the majestic mountain.

---

soba (buckwheat) and udon (wheat-flour) noodles—both inexpensive, filling, and tasty options for lunch.

Three things about Kamakura make it a good place in which to eat. It's on Sagami Bay, which means that fresh seafood is everywhere; it's a major tourist stop; and it has long been a prestigious place to live among Japan's worldly and well-to-do. On a day trip from Tōkyō, you can feel confident picking a place for lunch almost at random.

Yokohama, as befits a city of more than 3 million people, lacks little in the way of food, from quick-fix lunch counters to elegant dining rooms, and has almost every imaginable cuisine. Your best bet is Chinatown—Japan's largest Chinese community—with more than 100 restaurants representing every regional style.

About the Hotels

Yokohama and Kamakura are treated here as day trips, and as it's unlikely that you'll stay overnight in either city, no accommodations are listed for them. Nikkō is something of a toss-up: you can easily see Tōshō-gū and be back in Tōkyō by evening. But when the weather turns glorious in spring or autumn, why not spend some time in the national park, staying overnight at Chūzenji, and returning to the city the next day? Mt. Fuji and Hakone, on the other hand—and more especially the Izu Peninsula—are pure resort destinations. Staying overnight is an intrinsic part of the experience, and it makes little sense to go without hotel reservations confirmed in advance.

In both Nikkō and the Fuji-Hakone-Izu area, there are modern, Western-style hotels that operate in a fairly standard international style.

More common, however, are the Japanese-style *kankō* (literally, "sight-seeing") hotels and the traditional *ryokan* (inns). The undisputed pleasure of a ryokan is to return to it at the end of a hard day of sightseeing, luxuriate for an hour in a hot bath with your own garden view, put on the *yukata* (sleeping gown) provided for you, and sit down to a catered private dinner party. Kankō hotels do most of their business with big, boisterous tour groups; the turnover of guests is ruthless, and the cost is way out of proportion to the service they provide.

The price categories listed below are for double occupancy, but you'll find that most kankō and ryokan normally quote per-person rates, which include breakfast and dinner. Remember to stipulate whether you want a Japanese or Western breakfast. If you don't want dinner at your hotel, it's usually possible to renegotiate the price, but the management will not be happy about it; the two meals are a fixture of their business. The typical ryokan takes great pride in its cuisine, usually with good reason: the evening meal is an elaborate affair of 10 or more different dishes, based on the fresh produce and specialties of the region, served to you—nay, *orchestrated*—in your room on a wonderful variety of trays and tableware designed to celebrate the season.

WHAT IT COSTS In yen				
$$$$	**$$$**	**$$**	**$**	**¢**
RESTAURANTS over 3,000	2,000–3,000	1,000–2,000	800–1,000	under 800
HOTELS over 22,000	18,000–22,000	12,000–18,000	8,000–12,000	under 8,000

Restaurant prices are per person for a main course at dinner. Hotel price categories reflect the range between the least and most expensive standard double rooms in nonholiday high season, based on the European Plan (with no meals) unless otherwise noted. Taxes (5%) are extra.

NIKKŌ 日光

Nikkō is a popular vacation spot for the Japanese, for good reason: its gorgeous sights include a breathtaking waterfall and one of the country's best-known shrines. In addition, Nikkō combines the rustic charm of a countryside village (complete with wild monkeys that have the run of the place) with a convenient location not far from Tōkyō.

At Nikkō there's a monument to a warlord who was so splendid and powerful that he became a god. In 1600, Ieyasu Tokugawa (1543–1616) won a battle at a place called Seki-ga-hara, in the mountains of south-central Japan, that left him the undisputed ruler of the archipelago. He died 16 years later, but the Tokugawa shogunate would last another 252 years, holding in its sway a peaceful, prosperous, and united country.

The founder of such a dynasty required a fitting resting place. Ieyasu (ee-eh-*ya*-su) had provided for one in his will: a mausoleum at Nikkō, in a forest of tall cedars, where a religious center had been founded more than eight centuries earlier. The year after his death, in accordance with Buddhist custom, he was given a *kaimyō*—an honorific name to bear in the afterlife. Thenceforth, he was Tōshō-Daigongen: the Great Incarnation Who Illuminates the East. The imperial court at Kyōto declared him a god, and his remains were taken in a procession of great pomp and ceremony to be enshrined at Nikkō.

The dynasty he left behind was enormously rich. Ieyasu's personal fief, on the Kantō Plain, was worth 2.5 million *koku* of rice. One koku, in monetary terms, was equivalent to the cost of keeping one retainer in the necessities of life for a year. The shogunate itself, however, was still an uncertainty. It had only recently taken control after more than a century of civil war. The founder's tomb had a political purpose: to inspire awe and to make manifest the power of the Tokugawas. It was Ieyasu's legacy, a statement of his family's right to rule.

Tōshō-gū (東照宮) was built by his grandson, the third shōgun, Iemitsu (it was Iemitsu who established the policy of national isolation, which closed the doors of Japan to the outside world for more than 200 years). The mausoleum and shrine required the labor of 15,000 people for two years (1634–36). Craftsmen and artists of the first rank were assembled from all over the country. Every surface was carved and painted and lacquered in the most intricate detail imaginable. Tōshō-gū shimmers with the reflections of 2,489,000 sheets of gold leaf. Roof beams and rafter ends with dragon heads, lions, and elephants in bas-relief; friezes of phoenixes, wild ducks, and monkeys; inlaid pillars and red-lacquer corridors: Tōshō-gū is everything a 17th-century warlord would consider gorgeous, and the inspiration is very Chinese.

Foreign visitors have differed about the effect Iemitsu achieved. Victorian-era traveler Isabella Bird, who came to Nikkō in 1878, was unrestrained in her enthusiasm. "To pass from court to court," she writes in her *Unbeaten Tracks in Japan,* "is to pass from splendour to splendour; one is almost glad to feel that this is the last, and that the strain on one's capacity for admiration is nearly over." Fosco Mariani, a more recent visitor, felt somewhat different: "You are taken aback," he observes in his *Meeting with Japan* (1959). "You ask yourself whether it is a joke, or a nightmare, or a huge wedding cake, a masterpiece of sugar icing made for some extravagant prince with a perverse, rococo taste, who wished to alarm and entertain his guests." Clearly, it is impossible to feel indifferent about Tōshō-gū. Perhaps, in the end, that is all Ieyasu could ever really have expected.

Exploring Nikkō

The town of Nikkō is essentially one long avenue—Sugi Namiki (Cryptomeria Avenue)—extending for about 2 km (1 mi) from the railway stations to Tōshō-gū. You can easily walk to most places within town. Tourist inns and shops line the street, and if you have time, you might want to make this a leisurely stroll. The antiques shops along the way may turn up interesting—but expensive—pieces like armor fittings, hibachi, pottery, and dolls. The souvenir shops here sell ample selections of local wood carvings.

Buses and taxis can take you from Nikkō to the village of Chūzenji and nearby Lake Chūzenji.

Numbers in the text correspond to numbers in the margin and on the Nikkō Area map.

Tōshō-gū Area

The best way to see the Tōshō-gū precincts is to buy a multiple-entry ticket: ¥1,000 for Rinnō-ji (Rinnō Temple), the Taiyū-in Mausoleum, and Futara-san Jinja (Futara-san Shrine); ¥1,300 for these sights as well as the Sleeping Cat and Ieyasu's tomb at Taiyū-in (separate fees are charged for admission to other sights). There are two places to purchase the multiple-entry ticket: one is at the entrance to Rinnō Temple, in the corner of the parking lot, at the top of the path called the Higashi-sandō (East Approach) that begins across the highway from the Sacred Bridge; the other is at the entrance to Tōshō-gū, at the top of the broad Omote-sandō (Central Approach), which begins about 100 yards farther west.

❶ Built in 1636 for shōguns and imperial messengers visiting the shrine, the original **Sacred Bridge** (Shinkyō, 神橋) was destroyed in a flood; the present red-lacquer wooden structure dates to 1907. Buses leaving from either railway station at Nikkō go straight up the main street to the bridge, opposite the first of the main entrances to Tōshō-gū. The fare is ¥190. The Sacred Bridge is just to the left of a modern bridge, where the road curves and crosses the Daiya-gawa (Daiya River).

❷ A Nikkō landmark, the **Nikkō Kanaya Hotel** (金谷ホテル; ⊠ 1300 Kami Hatsuishi-machi) has been in the same family for more than 100 years. The main building is a delightful, rambling Victorian structure that has hosted royalty and other important personages—as the guest book attests—from around the world. The long driveway that winds up to the hotel at the top of the hill is just below the Sacred Bridge, on the same side of the street.

The **Monument to Masatuna Matsudaira** (松平正綱の杉並木寄進碑)—opposite the Sacred Bridge, at the east entrance to the grounds of Tōshō-gū—pays tribute to one of the two feudal lords charged with the construction of Tōshō-gū. Matsudaira's great contribution was the planting of the wonderful cryptomeria trees (Japanese cedars) surrounding the shrine and along all the approaches to it. The project took 20 years, from 1628 to 1648, and the result was some 36 km (22 mi) of cedar-lined avenues—planted with more than 15,000 trees in all. Fire and time have taken their toll, but thousands of these trees still stand in the shrine precincts, creating a setting of solemn majesty the buildings alone could never have achieved. Thousands more line Route 119 east of Nikkō on the way to Shimo-Imaichi.

★ ❸ **Rinnō-ji** (Rinnō Temple, 輪王寺) belongs to the Tendai sect of Buddhism, the head temple of which is Enryaku-ji, on Mt. Hiei near Kyōto. The main hall of Rinnō Temple, called the **Sanbutsu-dō**, is the largest single building at Tōshō-gū; it enshrines an image of Amida Nyorai, the Buddha of the Western Paradise, flanked on the right by Senju (Thousand-Armed) Kannon, the goddess of mercy, and on the left by Batō-Kannon, re-

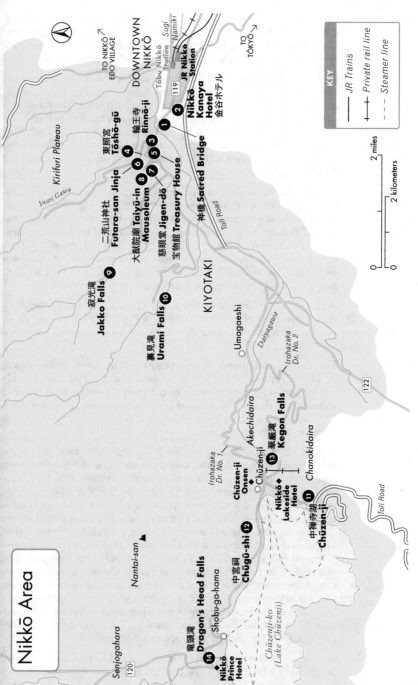

Nikkō Area

TO NIKKŌ
EDO VILLAGE

DOWNTOWN
NIKKŌ

Sugi
Namiki

Tōbu Nikkō
Station

JR Nikko
Station

119

TO
TŌKYŌ

Nikkō
Kanaya
Hotel
金谷ホテル

1
2

輪王寺
Rinnō-ji

3

東照宮
Tōshō-gū

4

5

二荒山神社
Futara-san Jinja

6

8

7

大猷院廟 Taiyū-in
Mausoleum

慈眼堂 Jigen-dō

宝物館 Treasury House

神橋 Sacred Bridge

Toll Road

KIYOTAKI

Inari Gawa

Kirifuri Plateau

寂光滝
Jakko Falls 9

裏見滝
Urami Falls 10

Umagaeshi

Daiyagawa

Irohazaka
Dr. No. 2

Irohazaka
Dr. No. 1

Akechidaira

華厳滝
Kegon Falls

13

Chanokidaira

122

Chūzen-ji
Onsen

Nikkō ◆
Lakeside
Hotel

Chūzen-ji

11

中禅寺湖
Chūzen-ji

中宮祠
Chūgū-shi 12

Nantai-san ▲

Shobu-ga-hama

Senjogahara

120

竜頭滝
Dragon's Head Falls

Nikkō ◆
Prince
Hotel 14

Chūzenji-ko
(Lake Chūzenji)

Toll Road

KEY

———— JR Trains

—+—+— Private rail line

– – – – Steamer line

0 _____ 2 miles

0 _____ 2 kilometers

garded as the protector of animals. These three images are lacquered in gold and date from the early part of the 17th century. The original San-butsu-dō is said to have been built in 848 by the priest Ennin (794–864), also known as Jikaku-Daishi. The present building dates from 1648.

In the southwest corner of the Rinnō Temple compound, behind the abbot's residence, is an especially fine Japanese garden called **Shōyō-en,** created in 1815 and thoughtfully designed to present a different per-spective of its rocks, ponds, and flowering plants from every turn on its path. To the right of the entrance to the garden is the **Treasure Hall** (Hōmotsu-den) of Rinnō Temple, a small museum that displays only a portion of its collection of 6,000 works of lacquerware, painting, and Buddhist sculpture.

Gohōten-dō, in the northeast corner of Rinnō Temple, behind the San-butsu-dō, enshrines three of the Seven Gods of Good Fortune. These three Buddhist deities are derived from Chinese folk mythology: Daikoku-ten and Bishamon-ten, who bring wealth and good harvests, and Ben-zai-ten, patroness of music and the arts. *▦ Rinnō Temple ¥1,000, multiple-entry ticket includes admission to the Taiyū-in Mausoleum and Futara-san Shrine; Shōyō-en and Treasure Hall ¥300 ⊗ Apr.–Oct., daily 8–5, last entry at 4; Nov.–Mar., daily 8–4, last entry at 3.*

❹
Fodor'sChoice
★
With its riot of colors and carvings, inlaid pillars, red-lacquer corridors, and extensive use of gold leaf, **Tōshō-gū** (東照宮), the 17th-century shrine to Ieyasu Tokugawa, is magnificent, astonishing, and never for a mo-ment dull.

The west gate of Rinnō Temple brings you out onto Omote-sandō, which leads uphill to the stone torii of the shrine. The **Five-Story Pagoda** of Tōshō-gū—a reconstruction dating from 1818—is on the left as you approach the shrine. The 12 signs of the zodiac decorate the first story. The black-lacquer doors above each sign bear the three hollyhock leaves of the Tokugawa family crest.

From the torii a flight of stone steps brings you to the front gate of the shrine—the Omote-mon, also called the Nio-mon (Gate of the Deva Kings), with its fearsome pair of red-painted guardian gods. From here the path turns to the left. In the first group of buildings you reach on the left is the **Sacred Stable** (Shinkyū). Housed here is the white horse—symbol of purity—that figures in many of the shrine's ceremonial events. Carvings of pine trees and monkeys adorn the panels over the stable. The second panel from the left is the famous group of three monkeys—"Hear no evil, see no evil, speak no evil"—that has become something of a trademark for Nikkō, reproduced endlessly on souvenirs of every sort. A few steps farther, where the path turns to the right, is a granite font where visitors purify themselves before entering the inner precincts of Tōshō-gū. The **Sutra Library** (Rinzō), just beyond the font, is a repos-itory for some 7,000 Buddhist scriptures, kept in a huge revolving book-case nearly 20 feet high; it's not open to the public.

As you pass under the second (bronze) torii and up the steps, you'll see on the right a belfry and a tall bronze candelabrum; on the left are a drum tower and a bronze revolving lantern. The two works in bronze were presented to the shrine by the Dutch government in the mid-17th century. (Under the policy of national seclusion, only the Dutch retained trading privileges with Japan, and even they were confined to the tiny artificial island of Dejima, in the port of Nagasaki. They regularly sent tokens of their esteem to the shogunate to keep their precarious monopoly.) Behind the drum tower is the **Yakushi-dō**, which enshrines a manifestation of the Buddha as Yakushi Nyorai, the healer of illnesses. The original 17th-century building was famous for a huge India-ink painting on the ceiling of the nave, *The Roaring Dragon,* so named for the rumbling echoes it seemed to emit when visitors clapped their hands beneath it. The painting was by Yasunobu Enshin Kanō (1613–85), from a family of artists that dominated the profession for 400 years. The Yakushi-dō was destroyed by fire in 1961, then rebuilt; the dragon on the ceiling now is by Nampū Katayama (1887–1980).

The centerpiece of Tōshō-gū is the **Gate of Sunlight** (Yomei-mon), at the top of the second flight of stone steps. A designated National Treasure, it's also called the Twilight Gate (Higurashi-mon)—implying that you could spend all day until sunset looking at its richness of detail. And rich it is indeed: dazzling white, 36 feet high, the gate has 12 columns, beams, and roof brackets carved with dragons, lions, clouds, peonies, Chinese sages, and demigods, painted in vivid hues of red, blue, green, and gold. On one of the central columns, there are two carved tigers; the natural grain of the wood is used to bring out the "fur." To the right and left of the Yomei-mon as you enter, there are galleries running east and west for some 700 feet, their paneled fences also carved and painted with pine and plum branches, pheasants, cranes, and wild ducks.

The portable shrines that appear in the annual Tōshō-gū Festival on May 17–18 are kept in the **Shinkōsha**, a storeroom to the left as you come through the Twilight Gate into the heart of the shrine. The paintings on the ceiling, of *tennin* (Buddhist angels) playing harps, are by Ryōtaku Kanō.

The "official" entrance to the Tōshō-gū inner shrine, through which mere mortals may not pass, is the **Chinese Gate** (Kara-mon). Like its counterpart, the Yomei-mon, on the opposite side of the courtyard, the Kara-mon is a National Treasure—and, like the Yomei-mon, carved and painted in elaborate detail with dragons and other auspicious figures. The Main Hall of Tōshō-gū is enclosed by a wall of painted and carved panel screens; opposite the right-hand corner of the wall, facing the shrine, is the **Kitō-den,** a hall where annual prayers were once offered for the peace of the nation. Japanese couples are sometimes married here in traditional Shintō ceremonies.

The **Main Hall** (Hon-den) of Tōshō-gū is the ultimate purpose of the shrine. Here you remove and store your shoes, step up into the shrine, and follow a winding corridor to the Oratory (Hai-den)—the anteroom, resplendent in its lacquered pillars, carved friezes, and coffered ceilings bedecked with dragons. Over the lintels are paintings by Mitsuoki Tosa (1617–91) of the 36 great poets of the Heian period, with their poems in the calligraphy of Emperor Go-Mizuno-o. Deeper yet, at the back of the Oratory, is the Inner Chamber (Nai-jin)—repository of the Sacred Mirror that represents the spirit of the deity enshrined here. To the right is a room that was reserved for members of the three principal branches of the Tokugawa family; the room on the left was for the chief abbot of Rinnō Temple, who was always a prince of the imperial line.

Behind the Inner Chamber is the Innermost Chamber (Nai-Nai-jin). No visitors come this far. Here, in the very heart of Tōshō-gū, is the gold-lacquer shrine where the spirit of Ieyasu resides—along with two other deities, whom the Tokugawas later decided were fit companions.

Recover your shoes and return to the courtyard. Between the Goma-do and the **Kagura-den** (a hall where ceremonial dances are performed to honor the gods) is a passage to the **Gate at the Foot of the Hill** (Sakashita-mon). Above the gateway is another famous symbol of Tōshō-gū, the Sleeping Cat—a small panel said to have been carved by Hidari Jingorō (Jingorō the Left-handed), a late-16th-century master carpenter and sculptor credited with important contributions to numerous Tokugawa-period temples, shrines, and palaces. A separate admission charge (¥520) is levied to go beyond the Sleeping Cat, up the flight of 200 stone steps through a forest of cryptomeria to **Ieyasu's tomb.** The climb is worth making for the view of the Yomei-mon and Kara-mon from above; the tomb itself is unimpressive. 🎫 *Free; Ieyasu's tomb ¥520* ⊙ *Apr.–Oct., daily 8–5; Nov.–Mar., daily 8–4.*

An unhurried visit to the precincts of Tōshō-gū should definitely include
⑤ the **Treasury House** (Hōmotsu-kan, 宝物館), which contains a collection of antiquities from its various shrines and temples. From the west gate of Rinnō Temple, turn left off Omote-sandō, just below the pagoda, onto the cedar-lined avenue to Futara-san Jinja. A minute's walk will bring you to the museum, on the left. 🎫 *¥500* ⊙ *Apr.–Oct., daily 9–5; Nov.–Mar., daily 9–4.*

The holy ground at Nikkō is far older than the Tokugawa dynasty, in whose honor it was improved upon. To the gods enshrined at the 8th-
★ ⑥ century **Futara-san Jinja** (Futara-san Shrine, 二荒山神社), Ieyasu Tokugawa must seem but a callow newcomer. Futara-san is sacred to the Shintō deities Okuni-nushi-no-Mikoto (god of the rice fields, bestower of prosperity), his consort Tagorihime-no-Mikoto, and their son Ajisukitaka-hikone-no-Mikoto. Futara-san actually has three locations: the Hon-sha (Main Shrine), at Tōshō-gū; the Chū-gushi (Middle Shrine), at Chūzenji-ko; and the Okumiya (Inner Shrine), on top of Mt. Nantai.

The bronze torii at the entrance to the shrine leads to the **Chinese Gate** (Kara-mon) and the **Sanctum** (Hon-den)—the present version of which dates from 1619. To the left, in the corner of the enclosure, is an antique bronze lantern, some 7 feet high, under a canopy. Legend has it that the lantern would assume the shape of a goblin at night; the deep nicks in the bronze were inflicted by swordsmen of the Edo period—or guard duty, perhaps, startled into action by a flickering shape in the dark. To get to Futara-san, take the avenue to the left as you're standing before the stone torii at Tōshō-gū and follow it to the end. 🎫 *¥200*

¥1,000 multiple-entry ticket includes admission to Rinnō Temple and Taiyū-in Mausoleum ⊙ Apr.–Oct., daily 8–5; Nov.–Mar., daily 9–4.

❼ Tenkai (1536–1643), the first abbot of Rinnō Temple, has his own place of honor at Tōshō-gū: the **Jigen-dō** (慈眼堂). The hall, which was founded in 848, now holds many of Rinnō Temple's artistic treasures. To reach it, take the path opposite the south entrance to Futara-san Shrine that passes between the two subtemples called Jōgyō-do and Hokke-dō. Connected by a corridor, these two buildings are otherwise known as the Futatsu-dō (Twin Halls) of Rinnō Temple and are designated a National Cultural Property. The path between the Twin Halls leads roughly south and west to the Jigen-dō compound; the hall itself is at the north end of the compound, to the right. At the west end sits the Go-ōden, a shrine to Prince Yoshihisa Kitashirakawa (1847–95), the last of the imperial princes to serve as abbot. Behind it are his tomb and the tombs of his 13 predecessors. ⌨ *Free* ⊙ *Apr.–Nov., daily 8–5; Dec.–Mar., daily 9–4.*

★ **❽** The grandiose **Taiyū-in Mausoleum** (大猷院廟) is the resting place of the third Tokugawa shōgun, Iemitsu (1604–51), who imposed a policy of national isolation on Japan that was to last more than 200 years. Iemitsu, one suspects, had it in mind to upstage his illustrious grandfather; he marked the approach to his own tomb with no fewer than six different decorative gates. The first is another Nio-mon—a Gate of the Deva Kings—like the one at Tōshō-gū. The dragon painted on the ceiling is by Yasunobu Kanō (1613–85). A flight of stone steps leads from here to the second gate, the Niten-mon, a two-story structure protected front and back by carved and painted images of guardian gods. Beyond it, two more flights of steps lead to the middle courtyard. As you climb the last steps to Iemitsu's shrine, you'll pass a bell tower on the right and a drum tower on the left; directly ahead is the third gate, the remarkable **Yasha-mon**, so named for the figures of *yasha* (she-demons) in the four niches. This structure is also known as the Peony Gate (Botan-mon) for the carvings that decorate it.

On the other side of the courtyard is the **Chinese Gate** (Kara-mon), gilded and elaborately carved; beyond it is the **Hai-den,** the shrine's oratory. The Hai-den, too, is richly carved and decorated, with a dragon-covered ceiling. The Chinese lions on the panels at the rear are by two distinguished painters of the Kanō school. From the oratory of the Taiyū-in a connecting passage leads to the **Sanctum** (Hon-den). Designated a National Treasure, it houses a gilded and lacquered Buddhist altar some 9 feet high, decorated with paintings of animals, birds, and flowers, in which resides the object of all this veneration: a seated wooden figure of Iemitsu himself.

As you exit the shrine on the west side, you come to the fifth gate: the **Kōka-mon,** built in the style of the late Ming dynasty of China. The gate is normally closed, but from here another flight of stone steps leads to the sixth and last gate—the cast copper **Inuki-mon,** inscribed with characters in Sanskrit—and Iemitsu's tomb. ⌨ *¥1,000 multiple-entry ticket includes admission to Rinnō Temple and Futara-san Shrine ⊙ Apr.–Oct., daily 8–5; Nov.–Mar., daily 8–4.*

Ⓒ **Nikkō Edo Village** (Nikkō Edo Mura, 日光江戸村), a living-history theme park a short taxi ride from downtown, re-creates an 18th-century Japanese village. The complex includes sculpted gardens with waterfalls and ponds and 22 vintage buildings, where actors in traditional dress stage martial arts exhibitions, historical theatrical performances, and comedy acts. You can even observe Japanese tea ceremony rituals in gorgeous tatami-floored houses, as well as people dressed as geisha and samurai. Strolling stuffed animal characters and acrobatic ninjas keep kids happy. ✉470–2 Egura, Fujiwara-chō, Shiodani-gun ☎0288/77–1777 ☜¥2,300 general admission, plus extra for rides and shows; ¥6,300 unlimited day pass includes rides and shows ◷ Mid-Mar.–Nov., daily 9–5; Dec.–mid-Mar., daily 9:30–4.

To Chūzenji-ko (Lake Chūzenji)

More than 3,900 feet above sea level, at the base of the volcano known as Nantai-san, is Lake Chūzenji, renowned for its clean waters and fresh air. People come to boat and fish on the lake and to enjoy the surrounding scenic woodlands, waterfalls, and hills.

Falling water is one of the special charms of the Nikkō National Park area; people going by bus or car from Tōshō-gū to Lake Chūzenji often **❾** stop off en route to see **Jakkō Falls** (Jakkō-no-taki, 寂光滝), which descend in a series of seven terraced stages, forming a sheet of water about 100 feet high. About 1 km (½ mi) from the shrine precincts, at the Tamozawa bus stop, a narrow road to the right leads to an uphill walk of some 3 km (2 mi) to the falls.

❿ "The water," wrote the great 17th-century poet Bashō about the **Urami Falls** (Urami-no-taki, 裏見滝), "seemed to take a flying leap and drop a hundred feet from the top of a cave into a green pool surrounded by a thousand rocks. One was supposed to inch one's way into the cave and enjoy the falls from behind." It's a steep climb to the cave, which begins at the Arasawa bus stop, with a turn to the right off the Chūzenji road. The falls and the gorge are striking—but you should make the climb only if you have good hiking shoes and are willing to get wet in the process.

The real climb to Lake Chūzenji begins at **Umagaeshi** (literally, "horse return," 馬返し). Here, in the old days, the road became too rough for horse riding, so riders had to alight and proceed on foot. The lake is 4,165 feet above sea level. From Umagaeshi the bus climbs a one-way toll road up the pass; the old road has been widened and is used for the traffic coming down. The two roads are full of steep hairpin turns, and on a clear day the view up and down the valley is magnificent—especially from the halfway point at **Akechi-daira** (Akechi Plain), from which you can see the summit of **Nantai-san** (Mt. Nantai), reaching 8,149 feet. Hiking season lasts from May through mid-October; if you push it, you can make the ascent in about four hours. Wild monkeys make their homes in these mountains, and they've learned the convenience of mooching from visitors along the route. Be careful—they have a way of not taking no for an answer. Umagaeshi is about 10 km (6 mi) from Tōbu Station in Nikkō, or 8 km (5 mi) from Tōshō-gū.

The bus trip from Nikkō to the national park area ends at Chūzenji village, which shares its name with the temple established here in 784. **Chūzenji** (Chūzen Temple, 中禅寺) is a subtemple of Rinnō Temple, at Tōshō-gū. The principal object of worship at Chūzen-ji is the **Tachi-ki Kannon,** a 17-ft-tall standing statue of the Buddhist goddess of mercy, said to have been carved more than 1,000 years ago by the priest Shōdō from the living trunk of a single Judas tree. You reach the temple grounds by turning left (south) as you leave the village of Chūzenji and walking about 1½ km (1 mi) along the eastern shore of the lake. ▨ *¥300* ◷ *Apr.–Oct., daily 8–5; Mar. and Nov., daily 8–4; Dec.–Feb., daily 8–3:30.*

⑫ **Chūgū-shi** (中宮祠), a subshrine of the Futara-san Shrine at Tōshō-gū, is the major religious center on the north side of Lake Chūzenji, about 1½ km (1 mi) west of the village. The **Treasure House** (Hōmotsu-den) contains an interesting historical collection, including swords, lacquerware, and medieval shrine palanquins. ▨ *Shrine free, Treasure House ¥300* ◷ *Apr.–Oct., daily 8–5; Nov.–Mar., daily 9–4.*

Near the bus stop at Chūzenji village is a **gondola** (ゴンドラ; ¥900 roundtrip) to the Chanoki-daira (Chanoki plateau). About 1,000 feet above the lake, it commands a wonderful view of the surrounding area. A few minutes' walk from the gondola terminus is a small botanical garden. ◷ *Daily 8–5.*

⑬ More than anything else, **Kegon Falls** (Kegon-no-taki, 華厳滝), the country's most famous falls, are what draw the crowds of Japanese visitors to Chūzenji. Fed by the eastward flow of the lake, the falls drop 318 feet into a rugged gorge; an elevator (¥530) takes you to an observation platform at the bottom. The volume of water over the falls is carefully regulated, but it's especially impressive after a summer rain or a typhoon. In winter the falls do not freeze completely but form a beautiful cascade of icicles. The elevator is just a few minutes' walk east from the bus stop at Chūzenji village, downhill and off to the right at the far end of the parking lot. ◷ *Daily 8–5.*

Fodor's Choice
★

If you've budgeted an extra day for Nikkō, you might want to consider a walk around the lake. A paved road along the north shore extends for about 8 km (5 mi), one-third of the whole distance, as far as the "beach" at Shōbu-ga-hama. Here, where the road branches off to the ⑭ north for Senjogahara, are the lovely cascades of **Dragon's Head Falls** (Ryūzu-no-taki, 竜頭滝). The falls are less dramatic than Kegon, perhaps, but they're blessed with a charming woodland setting and a rustic coffee shop where you can sit and enjoy the play of the waters as they tumble into the lake. To the left is a steep footpath that continues around the lake to Senju-ga-hama and then to a campsite at Asegata. The path is well marked but can get rough in places. From Asegata it's less than an hour's walk back to Chūzenji village.

Where to Eat

Nikkō

$$$$ ✕ **Gyōshintei** (堯心亭). This is the only restaurant in Nikkō devoted to *shōjin ryōri,* the Buddhist-temple vegetarian fare that evolved centuries

ago into haute cuisine. Gyōshintei is decorated in the style of a *ryōtei* (traditional inn), with all-tatami seating. It differs from a ryōtei in that it has one large, open space where many guests are served at once, rather than a number of rooms for private dining. Dinner is served until 7. ⊠ *2339–1 Sannai, Nikkō* ☎ *0288/53–3751* ▤ *AE, DC, MC, V* ☺ *Closed Thurs.*

$$$–$$$$ ✕ **Fujimoto** (ふじもと). At what may be Nikkō's most formal Western-style restaurant, finer touches include plush carpets, art deco fixtures, stained and frosted glass, a thoughtful wine list, and a maître d' in black tie. The menu combines elements of French and Japanese cooking styles and ingredients; the fillet of beef in mustard sauce is particularly excellent. Fujimoto closes at 7:30, so plan on eating early. ⊠ *2339–1 Sannai, Nikkō* ☎ *0288/53–3754* ▤ *AE, DC, MC, V* ☺ *Closed Fri.*

$$$–$$$$ ✕ **Masudaya** (ゆば亭ますだや). Masudaya started out as a sake maker more than a century ago, but for four generations now it has been the town's best-known restaurant. The specialty is *yuba* (bean curd skin), which the chefs transform, with the help of local vegetables and fresh fish, into sumptuous high cuisine. The building is traditional, with a lovely interior garden; the assembly-line-style service, however, detracts from the ambience. Masudaya serves one nine-course kaiseki-style meal; the kitchen simply stops serving when the food is gone. It's on the main street of Nikkō, halfway between the railway stations and Tōshō-gū. ⊠ *439–2 Ishiya-machi, Nikkō* ☎ *0288/54–2151* ▵ *Reservations essential* ▤ *No credit cards* ☺ *Closed Thurs. No dinner.*

$$$–$$$$ ✕ **Meiji-no-Yakata** (明治の館). Not far from the east entrance to Rinnō Temple, Meiji-no-Yakata is an elegant 19th-century Western-style stone house, originally built as a summer retreat for an American diplomat. The food, too, is Western style; specialties of the house include fresh rainbow trout from Lake Chūzenji, roast lamb with pepper sauce, and melt-in-your-mouth filet mignon made from local Tochigi beef. High ceilings, hardwood floors, and an air of informality make this a very pleasant place to dine. The restaurant closes at 7:30. ⊠ *2339–1 Sannai, Nikkō* ☎ *0288/53–3751* ▤ *AE, DC, MC, V* ☺ *Closed Wed.*

$$–$$$ ✕ **Sawamoto** (澤本). Charcoal-broiled *unagi* (eel) is an acquired taste, and there's no better place in Nikkō to acquire it than at this restaurant. The place is small and unpretentious, with only five plain-wood tables, and service can be lukewarm, but Sawamoto is reliable for a light lunch or dinner of unagi on a bed of rice, served in an elegant lacquered box. Eel is considered a stamina builder: just right for the weary visitor on a hot summer day. Sawamoto closes at 7. ⊠ *Kami Hatsuishi-machi, Nikkō* ☎ *0288/54–0163* ▤ *No credit cards.*

Where to Stay

Nikkō

★ **$$–$$$$** ▥ **Nikkō Kanaya Hotel** (日光金谷ホテル). A little worn around the edges after a century of operation, the Kanaya still has the best location in town: across the street from Tōshō-gū. The hotel is very touristy; daytime visitors browse through the old building and its gift shops. The helpful staff is better at giving area information than the tourist office. The more expensive rooms are spacious and comfortable, with wonderful high ceilings; in the annex the sound of the Daiya-gawa murmuring below the Sacred Bridge lulls you to sleep. Horseback riding and golf are available nearby. ⊠ *1300 Kami Hatsuishi-machi, Nikkō, Tochigi-ken 321-1401* ☏ *0288/54–0001* 📠 *0288/53–2487* ⊕ *www.kanayahotel.co.jp/nkh/index-e.html* ⟿ *77 rooms, 62 with bath* ♨ *2 restaurants, coffee shop, pool, bar* ▤ *AE, DC, MC, V.*

¢ ▣ **Turtle Inn Nikkō** (タートルイン日光). This member of the Japanese Inn Group provides friendly, modest, cost-conscious Western- and Jajpanese-style accommodations with or without a private bath. Simple, cheap breakfasts and dinners are served in the dining room, but you needn't opt for these if you'd rather eat out. Rates go up about 10% in high season (late July and August). To get here, take the bus bound for Chūzenji from either railway station and get off at the Sōgō Kaikan-mae bus stop. The inn is two minutes from the bus stop and within walking distance of Tōshō-gū. ⊠ *2–16 Takumi-chō, Nikkō, Tochigi-ken 321-1433* ☏ *0288/53–3168* 📠 *0288/53–3883* ⟿ *7 Western-style rooms, 3 with bath; 5 Japanese-style rooms without bath* ⊕ *www.turtle-nikko.com* ♨ *Restaurant, Japanese baths, Internet* ▤ *AE, MC, V.*

Chūzenji

$$$$ ▣ **Chūzenji Kanaya** (中禅寺金谷). A boathouse and restaurant on the lake give this branch of the Nikkō Kanaya on the road from the village to Shōbu-ga-hama the air of a private yacht club. Pastel colors decorate the simple, tasteful rooms, which have floor-to-ceiling windows overlooking the lake or grounds. ⊠ *2482 Chū-gushi, Nikkō, Tochigi-ken 321-1661* ☏ *0288/51–0001* 📠 *0288/51–0011* ⊕ *www.kanayahotel.co.jp/ckh/index-e.html* ⟿ *60 rooms, 54 with bath* ♨ *Restaurant, boating, waterskiing, fishing* ▤ *AE, DC, MC, V* ⑩ *MAP.*

$$-$$$ ▣ **Nikkō Lakeside Hotel** (日光レイクサイドホテル). In the village of Chūzenji at the foot of the lake, the Nikkō Lakeside has no particular character, but the views are good and the transportation connections (to buses and excursion boats) are ideal. Prices vary considerably from weekday to weekend and season to season. ⊠ *2482 Chū-gushi, Nikkō, Tochigi-ken 321-1661* ☏ *0288/55–0321* 📠 *0288/55–0771* ⟿ *100 rooms with bath* ♨ *2 restaurants, tennis court, boating, fishing, bicycles, bar* ▤ *AE, DC, MC, V* ⑩ *MAP.*

Shōbu-ga-hama

$$ ▣ **Nikkō Prince Hotel** (日光プリンスホテル). On the shore of Lake Chūzenji, this hotel, part of a large Japanese chain, is within walking distance of the Dragon's Head Falls. With many of its accommodations in two-story maisonettes and rustic detached cottages, the Prince chain markets itself to families and small groups of younger excursionists. The architecture favors high ceilings and wooden beams, with lots of glass in the public areas to take advantage of the view of the lake and Mt. Nantai. ⊠ *Shōbu-ga-hama, Chū-gushi, Nikkō, Tochigi-ken 321-1692* ☏ *0288/55–1111* 📠 *0288/55–0669* ⊕ *www.princehotels.co.jp* ⟿ *60 rooms with bath* ♨ *Restaurant, 2 tennis courts, pool, skiing, bar, lounge* ▤ *AE, DC, MC, V* ⑩ *MAP.*

Nikkō A to Z

To research prices, get advice from other travelers, and book travel arrangements, visit www.fodors.com.

BUS TRAVEL

Local buses leave Tōbu Nikkō Station for Lake Chūzenji, stopping just above the entrance to Tōshō-gū, approximately every 30 minutes from 6:15 AM. The fare to Chūzenji is ¥1,100, and the ride takes about 40 minutes. The last return bus from the lake leaves at 7:39 PM, arriving back at Tōbu Nikkō Station at 9:17 PM.

CAR TRAVEL

It's possible, but unwise, to travel by car from Tōkyō to Nikkō. The trip will take at least three hours, and merely getting from central Tōkyō to the toll-road system can be a nightmare. Coming back, especially on a Saturday or Sunday evening, is even worse. If you absolutely *must* drive, take the Tōkyō Expressway 5 (Ikebukuro Line) north to the Tōkyō Gaikandō, go east on this ring road to the Kawaguchi interchange, and pick up the Tōhoku Expressway northbound. Take the Tōhoku to Utsunomiya and change again at Exit 10 (marked in English) for the Nikkō–Utsunomiya Toll Road, which runs into Nikkō.

TOURS

From Tōkyō, Sunrise Tours operates one-day bus tours to Nikkō, which take you to Tōshō-gū and Lake Chūzenji for ¥13,500 (lunch included). ⚑ **Sunrise Tours** ☎ 03/5796–5454 📠 03/5495–0680 🌐 www.jtb.co.jp/sunrisetour.

TAXIS

Cabs are readily available in Nikkō; the one-way fare from Tōbu Nikkō Station to Chūzenji is about ¥6,000.

TRAIN TRAVEL

The limited express train of the Tōbu Railway has two direct connections from Tōkyō to Nikkō every morning, starting at 7:30 AM from Tōbu Asakusa Station, a minute's walk from the last stop on Tōkyō's Ginza subway line; there are additional trains on weekends, holidays, and in high season. The one-way fare is ¥2,740. All seats are reserved. Bookings are not accepted over the phone; consult your hotel or a travel agent. The trip from Asakusa to the Tōbu Nikkō Station takes about two hours, which is quicker than the JR trains. If you're visiting Nikkō on a day trip, note that the last return trains are at 4:29 PM (direct express) and 7:42 PM (with a transfer at 7:52 at Shimo-Imaichi).

If you have a JR Pass, use JR (Japan Railways) service, which connects Tōkyō and Nikkō, from Ueno Station. Take the Tōhoku–Honsen Line limited express to Utsunomiya (about 1½ hours) and transfer to the train for JR Nikkō Station (45 minutes). The earliest departure from Ueno is at 5:10 AM; the last connection back leaves Nikkō at 8:03 PM and brings you into Ueno at 10:48 PM. (If you're not using the JR Pass, the one-way fare will cost ¥2,520)

More expensive but faster is the Yamabiko train on the north extension of the Shinkansen; the one-way fare, including the surcharge for the express, is ¥5,430. The first one leaves Tōkyō Station at 6:04 AM (or Ueno at 6:10 AM) and takes about 50 minutes to Utsunomiya; change there to the train to Nikkō Station. To return, take the 9:43 PM train from Nikkō to Utsunomiya and catch the last Yamabiko back at 10:53 PM, arriving in Ueno at 11:38 PM.

🚹 Japan Railways ☎ 03/3423-0111 ⊕ www.japanrail.com.

VISITOR INFORMATION

You can do a lot of preplanning for your visit to Nikkō with a stop at the Japan National Tourist Organization office in Tōkyō, where the helpful English-speaking staff will ply you with pamphlets and field your questions about things to see and do. Closer to the source is the Tourist Information and Hospitality Center in Nikkō itself, about halfway up the main street of town between the railway stations and Tōshō-gū, on the left; don't expect too much in the way of help in English, but the center does have a good array of guides to local restaurants and shops, registers of inns and hotels, and mapped-out walking tours.

🚹 Tourist Information **Japan National Tourist Organization** ✉ Tōkyō Kōtsū Kaikan, 10F, 2-10-1 Yūraku-chō, Chiyoda-ku, Tōkyō ☎ 03/3201-3331 ⊕ www.jnto.go.jp Ⓜ JR Yamanote Line [Higashi-guchi/East Exit] and Yūraku-chō subway line [Exit A-8], Yūraku-chō Station. **Nikkō Tourist Information and Hospitality Center** ☎ 0288/54-2496.

KAMAKURA 鎌倉

Kamakura, about 40 km (25 mi) southwest of Tōkyō, is an object lesson in what happens when you set the fox to guard the henhouse.

For the aristocrats of the Heian-era Japan (794–1185), life was defined by the imperial court in Kyōto. Who in their right mind would venture elsewhere? In Kyōto there was grace and beauty and poignant affairs of the heart; everything beyond was howling wilderness. Unfortunately, it was the howling wilderness that had all the estates: the large grants of land, called *shōen,* without which there would be no income to pay for all that grace and beauty. Somebody had to go *out there,* to govern the provinces and collect the rents, to keep the restive local families in line, and to subdue the barbarians at the fringes of the empire. Over time many of the lesser noble families consigned to the provinces began to produce not only good poets and courtiers but also good administrators. To the later dismay of their fellow aristocrats, some of them—with their various clan connections, vassals, and commanders in the field—also turned out to be extremely good fighters.

By the 12th century two clans—the Taira (*ta*-ee-ra) and the Minamoto, themselves both offshoots of the imperial line—had come to dominate the affairs of the Heian court and were at each other's throats in a struggle for supremacy. In 1160 the Taira won a major battle that should have secured their absolute control over Japan, but in the process they made one serious mistake: having killed the Minamoto leader Yoshitomo, they spared his 13-year-old son, Yoritomo, and sent him into exile. Yoritomo bided his time, gathered support against the Taira, and planned his revenge. In 1180 he launched a rebellion and chose Kamakura—a superb natural fortress, surrounded on three sides by hills and guarded on the fourth by the sea—as his base of operations.

The rivalry between the two clans became an all-out war. By 1185 Yoritomo and his half-brother, Yoshitsune, had destroyed the Taira utterly, and the Minamoto were masters of all Japan. In 1192 Yoritomo forced the imperial court to name him shōgun; he was now de facto and de jure the military head of state. The emperor was left as a figurehead in Kyōto, and the little fishing village of Kamakura became—and for 141 years remained—the seat of Japan's first shogunal government.

The Minamoto line came to an end when Yoritomo's two sons were assassinated. Power passed to the Hōjō family, who remained in control, often as regents for figurehead shōguns, for the next 100 years. In 1274 and again in 1281 Japan was invaded by the Mongol armies of China's Yuan dynasty. On both occasions typhoons—the original kamikaze (literally, "divine wind")—destroyed the Mongol fleets, but the Hōjō family was still obliged to reward the various clans that had rallied to the defense of the realm. A number of these clans were unhappy with their portions—and with Hōjō rule in general. The end came suddenly, in 1333, when two vassals assigned to put down a revolt switched sides. The Hōjō regent committed suicide, and the center of power returned to Kyōto.

Kamakura reverted to being a sleepy backwater on the edge of the sea. It remained relatively isolated until the Yokosuka Railway line was built in 1889. After World War II the town began to develop as a residential area for the well-to-do. Nothing secular survives from the days of the Minamoto and Hōjō. As a religious center, however, the town presents an extraordinary legacy. The Bakufu endowed shrines and temples by the score in Kamakura, especially temples of the Rinzai sect of Zen Buddhism. The austerity of Zen, its directness and self-discipline, had a powerful appeal for a warrior class that in some ways imagined itself on perpetual bivouac. Most of those temples and shrines are in settings of remarkable beauty; many are designated National Treasures.

Exploring Kamakura

There are three principal areas in Kamakura, and you can easily get from one to another by train. From Tōkyō head first to Kita-Kamakura for most of the important Zen temples, including Engaku-ji (Engaku Temple) and Kenchō-ji (Kenchō Temple). The second area is downtown Kamakura, with its shops and museums and the venerated shrine Tsuru-ga-oka Hachiman-gū. The third is Hase, to the southwest, a 10-minute train ride from Kamakura on the Enoden Line. Hase's main attractions are the great bronze figure of the Amida Buddha, at Kōtoku-in, and the Kannon Hall of Hase-dera. There's a lot to see in Kamakura, and even to hit just the highlights will take you most of a busy day.

If your time is limited, you may want to visit only Engaku Temple and Tōkei Temple in Kita-Kamakura before riding the train one stop to Kamakura. If not, follow the main road all the way to Tsuru-ga-oka Hachiman-gū and visit four additional temples en route.

Numbers in the text correspond to numbers in the margin and on the Kamakura map.

Kita-Kamakura (North Kamakura)

Hierarchies were important to the Kamakura Shogunate. In the 14th century it established a ranking system called Go-zan (literally, "Five Mountains") for the Zen Buddhist monasteries under its official sponsorship. The largest of the Zen monasteries in Kamakura, **Engaku-ji** (Engaku Temple, 円覚寺), founded in 1282, ranked second in the Five Mountains hierarchy. Here, prayers were to be offered regularly for the prosperity and well-being of the government; Engaku Temple's special role was to pray for the souls of those who died resisting the Mongol invasions in 1274 and 1281. The temple complex once contained as many as 50 buildings. Often damaged in fires and earthquakes, it has been completely restored.

Engaku Temple belongs to the Rinzai sect of Zen Buddhism. Introduced into Japan from China at the beginning of the Kamakura period (1192–1333), the ideas of Zen were quickly embraced by the emerging warrior class. The samurai especially admired the Rinzai sect, with its emphasis on the ascetic life as a path to self-transcendence. The monks of Engaku Temple played an important role as advisers to the shogunate in matters spiritual, artistic, and political. The majestic old cedars of the temple complex bespeak an age when this was both a haven of quietude and a pillar of the state.

Among the National Treasures at Engaku Temple is the **Hall of the Holy Relic of Buddha** (Shari-den), with its remarkable Chinese-inspired thatched roof. Built in 1282, it was destroyed by fire in 1558 but rebuilt in its original form soon after, in 1563. The hall is said to enshrine a tooth of the Gautama Buddha himself, but it's not on display. In fact, except for the first three days of the New Year, you won't be able to go any farther into the hall than the main gate. Such is the case, alas, with much of the Engaku Temple complex: this is still a functioning monastic center, and many of its most impressive buildings are not open to the public. The accessible National Treasure at Engaku Temple is the **the Great Bell** (Ōkane), on the hilltop on the southeast side of the complex. The bell—Kamakura's most famous—was cast in 1301 and stands 8 feet tall. It's rung only on special occasions, such as New Year's Eve. Reaching the bell requires a trek up a long staircase, but once you've made it to the top you can enjoy tea and traditional Japanese sweets at a small outdoor café. The views from here are tremendous.

The two buildings open to the public at Engaku Temple are the **Butsunichi-an,** which has a long ceremonial hall where you can enjoy the Japanese tea ceremony, and the **Ōbai-in.** The latter is the mausoleum of the last three regents of the Kamakura Shogunate: Hōjō Tokimune, who led the defense of Japan against the Mongol invasions; his son Sadatoki; and his grandson Takatoki. Off to the side of the mausoleum is a quiet garden with apricot trees, which bloom in February. As you exit Kita-Kamakura Station, you'll see the stairway to Engaku Temple just in front of you. ✉ *409 Yama-no-uchi* ☎ *0467/22–0478* 🖥 *Engaku Tem-*

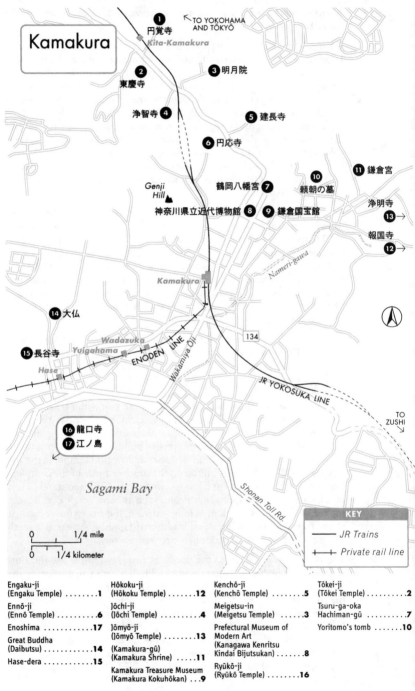

Kamakura

① 円覚寺
Kita-Kamakura
← TO YOKOHAMA
AND TŌKYŌ

③ 明月院

② 東慶寺

浄智寺 ④

⑤ 建長寺

⑥ 円応寺

Genji Hill ▲

鶴岡八幡宮 ⑦

⑩ 頼朝の墓

⑪ 鎌倉宮

浄明寺
⑬ →

神奈川県立近代博物館 ⑧ ⑨ 鎌倉国宝館

報国寺
⑫ →

Nameri-gawa

Kamakura

⑭ 大仏

Wadazuka
Yuigahama

ENODEN LINE

⑮ 長谷寺
Hase

134

Wakamiya-Ōji

JR YOKOSUKA LINE

TO ZUSHI ↘

⑯ 龍口寺
⑰ 江ノ島

Sagami Bay

Shonan Toll Rd.

0 ___ 1/4 mile
0 ___ 1/4 kilometer

KEY
— JR Trains
+—+ *Private rail line*

ple ¥200, Butsunichi-an additional ¥300 ⊘ *Nov.–Mar., daily 8–4; Apr.–Oct., daily 8–5.*

★ ❷ **Tōkei-ji** (Tōkei Temple, 東慶寺), a Zen temple of the Rinzai sect, holds special significance for the study of feminism in medieval Japan. More popularly known as the Enkiri-dera, or Divorce Temple, it was founded in 1285 by the widow of the Hōjō regent Tokimune as a refuge for the victims of unhappy marriages. Under the shogunate, a husband of the warrior class could obtain a divorce simply by sending his wife back to her family. Not so for the wife; no matter what cruel and unusual treatment her husband meted out, she was stuck with him. If she ran away, however, and managed to reach Tōkei Temple without being caught, she could receive sanctuary at the temple and remain there as a nun. After three years (later reduced to two), she was officially declared divorced. The temple survived as a convent through the Meiji Restoration of 1868. The last abbess died in 1902; her headstone is in the cemetery behind the temple, beneath the plum trees that blossom in February. Tōkei Temple was later reestablished as a monastery.

The **Matsugaoka Treasure House** (Matsugaoka Hōzō) of Tōkei Temple displays several Kamakura-period wooden Buddhas, ink paintings, scrolls, and works of calligraphy, some of which have been designated by the government as Important Cultural Objects. The library, called the Matsu-ga-oka Bunko, was established in memory of the great Zen scholar D. T. Suzuki (1870–1966).

Tōkei Temple is on the southwest side of the JR tracks (the side opposite Engaku Temple), less than a five-minute walk south from the station on the main road to Kamakura (Route 21–the Kamakura Kaidō), on the right. ✉ *1367 Yama-no-uchi* ☎ *0467/22–1663* 🏛 *Tōkei Temple ¥ 300, Matsugaoka Treasure House additional ¥300* ⊘ *Tōkei Temple Apr.–Oct., daily 8:30–5; Nov.–Mar., daily 8:30–4. Matsugaoka Treasure House Tues.–Sun. 9:30–3:30.*

❸ In June, when the hydrangeas are in bloom, **Meigetsu-in** (Meigetsu Temple, 明月院) becomes one of the most popular places in Kamakura. The gardens transform into a sea of color—pink, white, and blue—and visitors can number in the thousands. A typical Kamakura light rain shouldn't deter you; it only showcases this incredible floral display to best advantage. From Tōkei Temple walk along Route 21 toward Kamakura for about 20 minutes until you cross the railway tracks; take the immediate left turn onto the narrow side street that doubles back along the tracks. This street bends to the right and follows the course of a little stream called the Meigetsu-gawa to the temple gate. ✉ *189 Yama-no-uchi* ☎ *0467/24–3437* 🏛 *¥300* ⊘ *Apr., May and July–Oct., daily 9–4:30; June, daily 8:30–5; Nov.–Mar., daily 9–4.*

❹ In the Five Mountains hierarchy established by the Kamakura Shogunate for Zen Buddhist monasteries, **Jōchi-ji** (Jōchi Temple, 浄智寺) was ranked fourth. The buildings now in the temple complex are reconstructions; the Great Kantō Earthquake of 1923 destroyed the originals. The garden here is especially fine. Jōchi Temple is on the south side of the railway tracks, a few minutes' walk farther southwest of Tōkei

Temple in the direction of Kamakura. Turn right off the main road (Route 21) and cross over a small bridge; a flight of moss-covered steps leads up to the temple. ✉ *1402 Yama-no-uchi* ☎ *0467/22–3943* 💴 *¥150* 🕙 *Daily 9–4:30.*

★ ❺ Founded in 1250, **Kenchō-ji** (Kenchō Temple, 建長寺) was the foremost of Kamakura's five great Zen temples—and lays claim to being the oldest Zen temple in all of Japan. It was modeled on one of the great Chinese monasteries of the time and built for a distinguished Zen master who had just arrived in Japan from China. Over the centuries, fires and other disasters have taken their toll on Kenchō Temple, and although many buildings have been authentically reconstructed, the temple complex today is half its original size. Near the Main Gate (San-mon) is a **bronze bell** cast in 1255; it's the temple's most important treasure. The Main Gate and the Lecture Hall (Hattō) are the only two structures to have survived the devastating earthquake of 1923. Like Engaku Temple, Kenchō Temple is a functioning temple of the Rinzai sect, where novices train and lay people can come to take part in Zen meditation. The entrance to Kenchō Temple is about halfway along the main road from Kita-Kamakura Station to Tsuru-ga-oka Hachiman-gū, on the left. ✉ *8 Yama-no-uchi* ☎ *0467/22–0981* 💴 *¥300* 🕙 *Daily 8:30–4:30.*

In the feudal period Japan acquired from China a belief in Enma, the lord of hell, who, with his court attendants, judges the souls of the departed and determines their destination in the afterlife. Kamakura's

★ ❻ otherwise-undistinguished **Ennō-ji** (Ennō Temple, 円応寺) houses some remarkable statues of these judges—as grim and merciless a court as you're ever likely to confront. To see them is enough to put you on your best behavior, at least for the rest of your excursion. Ennō Temple is a minute's walk or so from Kenchō Temple, on the opposite (south) side of the main road to Kamakura. A few minutes' walk along the main road to the south will bring you to Tsuru-ga-oka Hachiman-gū in downtown Kamakura. ✉ *1543 Yama-no-uchi* ☎ *0467/25–1095* 💴 *¥200* 🕙 *Mar.–Nov., daily 9–4; Dec.–Feb., daily 9–3:30.*

Kamakura

When the first Kamakura shōgun, Minamoto no Yoritomo, learned he was about to have an heir, he had the tutelary shrine of his family moved to Kamakura from nearby Yui-ga-hama and ordered a stately avenue to be built through the center of his capital from the shrine to the sea. Along this avenue would travel the procession that brought his son—if there were a son—to be presented to the gods. Yoritomo's consort did indeed bear him a son, Yoriie (yo-*ree*-ee-eh), in 1182; Yoriie was brought in great pomp to the shrine and then consecrated to his place in the shogunal succession. Alas, the blessing of the gods did Yoriie little good. He was barely 18 when Yoritomo died, and the regency established by his mother's family, the Hōjō, kept him virtually powerless until 1203, when he was banished and eventually assassinated. The Minamoto were never to hold power again, but Yoriie's memory lives on in the street that his father built for him: Wakamiya Ōji, "the Avenue of the Young Prince."

A bus from Kamakura Station (Sign 5) travels to the sights listed below, with stops at most access roads to the temples and shrines. However, you may want to walk out as far as Hōkoku-ji and take the bus back; it's easier to recognize the end of the line than any of the stops in between. You can also go by taxi to Hōkoku-ji—any cab driver knows the way—and walk the last leg in reverse. In any event, downtown Kamakura is a good place to stop for lunch and shop. Restaurants and shops selling local crafts objects, especially the carved and lacquered woodwork called Kamakura-*bori,* abound on Wakamiya Ōji and the street parallel to it, Komachi-dōri.

★ ❼ The Minamoto shrine, **Tsuru-ga-oka Hachiman-gū** (鶴岡八幡宮), is dedicated to the legendary emperor Ōjin, his wife, and his mother, from whom Minamoto no Yoritomo claimed descent. At the entrance, the small, steeply arched vermilion **Drum Bridge** (Taiko-bashi) crosses a stream between two lotus ponds. The ponds were made to Yoritomo's specifications. His wife, Masako, suggested placing islands in each. In the larger **Genji Pond,** to the right, filled with white lotus flowers, she placed three islands. Genji was another name for the Minamoto clan, and three is an auspicious number. In the smaller **Heike Pond,** to the left, she put four islands. Heike (*heh*-ee-keh) was another name for the rival Taira clan, which the Minamoto had destroyed, and four—homophonous in Japanese with the word for "death"—is very unlucky indeed.

On the far side of the Drum Bridge is the **Mai-den.** This hall is the setting for a story of the Minamoto celebrated in Nō and Kabuki theater. Beyond the Mai-den, a flight of steps leads to the shrine's Main Hall (Hon-dō). To the left of these steps is a ginkgo tree that—according to legend—was witness to a murder that ended the Minamoto line in 1219. From behind this tree, a priest named Kugyō leapt out and beheaded his uncle, the 26-year-old Sanetomo, Yoritomo's second son and the last Minamoto shōgun. The priest was quickly apprehended, but Sanetomo's head was never found. Like all other Shintō shrines, the Main Hall is unadorned; the building itself, an 1828 reconstruction, is not particularly noteworthy.

To reach Tsuru-ga-oka Hachiman-gū from the east side of Kamakura Station, cross the plaza, turn left, and walk north along Wakamiya Ōji. Straight ahead is the first of three arches leading to the shrine, and the shrine itself is at the far end of the street. ⊠ *2–1–31 Yuki-no-shita* ☎ *0467/22–0315* 💷 *Free* ⏱ *Daily 9–4.*

❽ The **Prefectural Museum of Modern Art** (Kanagawa Kenritsu Kindai Bijutsukan, 神奈川県立近代博物館), on the north side of the Heike Pond at Tsuru-ga-oka Hachiman-gū, houses a collection of Japanese oil paintings and watercolors, wood-block prints, and sculpture. ⊠ *2–1–53 Yuki-no-shita* ☎ *0467/22–5000* 💷 *¥800–¥1,200, depending on exhibition* ⏱ *Tues.–Sun. 9:30–4:30.*

❾ The **Kamakura Treasure Museum** (Kamakura Kokuhōkan, 鎌倉国宝館) was built in 1928 as a repository for many of the most important objects belonging to the shrines and temples in the area. The museum, located along the east side of the Tsuru-ga-oka Hachiman-gū shrine precincts, has an especially fine collection of devotional and portrait sculpture in wood from the Kamakura and Muromachi periods; the portrait pieces may be among the most expressive and interesting in all of classical Japanese art. ✉ *2–1–1 Yuki-no-shita* ☎ *0467/22–0753* 💵 *¥300* ⊙ *Tues.–Sun. 9–4.*

The man who put Kamakura on the map, so to speak, chose not to leave it when he died: it's only a short walk from Tsuru-ga-oka Hachiman-gū to the tomb of the man responsible for its construction, Minamoto no Yoritomo. If you've already been to Nikkō and have seen how a later dynasty of shōguns sought to glorify its own memories, you may be surprised at the simplicity of **Yoritomo's tomb** (頼朝の墓). To get here, cross the Drum Bridge at Tsuru-ga-oka Hachiman-gū and turn left. Leave the grounds of the shrine and walk east along the main street (Route 204) that forms the T-intersection at the end of Wakamiya Ōji. A 10-minute walk will bring you to a narrow street on the left—there's a bakery called Bergfeld on the corner—that leads to the tomb, about 100 yards off the street to the north and up a flight of stone steps. 💵 *Free* ⊙ *Daily 9–4.*

Kamakura-gū (Kamakura Shrine, 鎌倉宮) is a Shintō shrine built after the Meiji Restoration of 1868 and dedicated to Prince Morinaga (1308–36), the first son of Emperor Go-Daigo. When Go-Daigo overthrew the Kamakura Shogunate and restored Japan to direct imperial rule, Morinaga—who had been in the priesthood—was appointed supreme commander of his father's forces. The prince lived in turbulent times and died young: when the Ashikaga clan in turn overthrew Go-Daigo's government, Morinaga was taken into exile, held prisoner in a cave behind the present site of Kamakura Shrine, and eventually beheaded. The **Treasure House** (Hōmotsu-den), on the northwest corner of the grounds, next to the shrine's administrative office, is of interest mainly for its collection of paintings depicting the life of Prince Morinaga. To reach Kamakura Shrine, walk from Yoritomo's tomb to Route 204, and turn left; at the next traffic light a narrow street on the left leads off at an angle to the shrine, about five minutes' walk west. ✉ *154 Nikaidō* ☎ *0467/22–0318* 💵 *Kamakura Shrine free, Treasure House ¥300* ⊙ *Daily 9–4.*

Visitors to Kamakura tend to overlook **Hōkoku-ji** (Hōkoku Temple, 報国寺), a lovely little Zen temple of the Rinzai sect that was built in 1334. Over the years it had fallen into disrepair and neglect, until an enterprising priest took over, cleaned up the gardens, and began promoting the temple for meditation sessions, calligraphy exhibitions, and tea ceremonies. Behind the main hall are a thick grove of bamboo and a small tea pavilion—a restful oasis and a fine place to go for *matcha* (tea-ceremony green tea). The temple is about 2 km (1 mi) east on Route 204 from the main entrance to Tsuru-ga-oka Hachiman-gū; turn right at the traffic light by the Hōkoku Temple Iriguchi bus stop and walk about three minutes south to the gate. ✉ *2–7–4 Jōmyō-ji* ☎ *0467/ 22–0762* 💵 *Hōkoku Temple free, bamboo grove ¥200, tea ceremony ¥500* ⊙ *Daily 9–4.*

Jōmyō-ji (Jōmyo Temple, 浄明寺) founded in 1188, is the only one of the Five Mountains Zen monasteries in the eastern part of Kamakura. It lacks the grandeur and scale of the Engaku and Kenchō temples—naturally enough, as it was ranked behind them, in fifth place—but it still merits the status of an Important Cultural Property. To reach it from Hōkoku-ji, cross the main street (Route 204) that brought you the mile or so from Tsuru-ga-oka Hachiman-gū, and take the first narrow street north. The monastery is about 100 yards from the corner. ⊠ *3–8–31 Jōmyō-ji* ☎ *0467/22–2818* ✉ *Jōmyō Temple ¥100, tea ceremony ¥500* ☼ *Daily 9–4:30.*

Hase 長谷

The single biggest attraction in Hase (*"ha-seh"*) is the temple Kōtoku-in's **Great Buddha** (Daibutsu, 大仏)—sharing the honors with Mt. Fuji, perhaps, as the quintessential picture-postcard image of Japan. The statue of the compassionate Amida Buddha sits cross-legged in the temple courtyard, the drapery of his robes flowing in lines reminiscent of ancient Greece, his expression profoundly serene. The 37-foot bronze figure was cast in 1292, three centuries before Europeans reached Japan; the concept of the classical Greek lines in the Buddha's robe must have come over the Silk Route through China during the time of Alexander the Great. The casting was probably first conceived in 1180, by Minamoto no Yoritomo, who wanted a statue to rival the enormous Daibutsu in Nara. Until 1495 the Amida Buddha was housed in a wooden temple, which washed away in a great tidal wave. Since then the loving Buddha has stood exposed, facing the cold winters and hot summers for more than five centuries.

It may seem sacrilegious to walk inside the Great Buddha, but for ¥20 you can enter the figure from a doorway in the right side and explore (until 4:15 PM) his stomach. To reach Kōtoku-in and the Great Buddha, take the Enoden Line from the west side of JR Kamakura Station three stops to Hase. From the east exit, turn right and walk north about 10 minutes on the main street (Route 32). ⊠ *4–2–28 Hase* ☎ *0467/22–0703* ✉ *¥200* ☼ *Apr.–Sept., daily 7–6; Oct.–Mar., daily 7–4:30.*

The only Kamakura temple facing the sea, **Hase-dera** (長谷寺) is one of the most beautiful, and saddest, places of pilgrimage in the city. On a landing partway up the stone steps that lead to the temple grounds are hundreds of small stone images of Jizō, one of the bodhisattvas in the Buddhist pantheon who have deferred their own ascendance into Buddha-hood to guide the souls of others to salvation. Jizō is the savior of children, particularly the souls of the stillborn, aborted, and miscarried; the mothers of these children dress the statues of Jizō in bright red bibs and leave them small offerings of food, heartbreakingly touching acts of prayer.

The **Kannon Hall** (Kannon-do) at Hase-dera enshrines the largest carved-wood statue in Japan: the votive figure of Jūichimen Kannon, the 11-headed goddess of mercy. Standing 30 feet tall, the goddess bears a crown of 10 smaller heads, symbolizing her ability to search out in all directions for those in need of her compassion. No one knows for certain when the figure was carved. According to the temple records, a monk named Tokudō Shōnin carved two images of the Jūichimen Kannon from a huge laurel tree in 721. One was consecrated to the Hase-dera in present-day Nara Prefecture; the other was thrown into the sea in order to go wherever the sea decided that there were souls in need, and that image washed up on shore near Kamakura. Much later, in 1342, Ashikaga Takauji—the first of the 15 Ashikaga shōguns who followed the Kamakura era—had the statue covered with gold leaf.

The **Amida Hall** of Hase-dera enshrines the image of a seated Amida Buddha, who presides over the Western Paradise of the Pure Land. Minamoto no Yoritomo ordered the creation of this statue when he reached the age of 42; popular Japanese belief, adopted from China, holds that your 42nd year is particularly unlucky. Yoritomo's act of piety earned him another 11 years—he was 53 when he was thrown by a horse and died of his injuries. The Buddha is popularly known as the *yakuyoke* (good-luck) Amida, and many visitors—especially students facing entrance exams—make a point of coming here to pray. To the left of the main halls is a small restaurant where you can buy good-luck candy and admire the view of Kamakura Beach and Sagami Bay. To reach Hase-dera from Hase Station, walk north about five minutes on the main street (Route 32) towards Kōtoku-in and the Great Buddha, and look for a signpost to the temple on a side street to the left. ⊠ *3–11–2 Hase* 🕾 *0467/22–6300* 💴 *¥300* ⊙ *Mar.–Sept., daily 8–6; Oct.–Feb., daily 8–5:30.*

Ryūkō-ji & Enoshima　龍口寺

The Kamakura story would not be complete without the tale of Nichiren (1222–82), the monk who founded the only native Japanese sect of Buddhism and who is honored at **Ryūkō-ji** (Ryūkō Temple, 龍口寺). Nichiren's rejection of both Zen and Jōdo (Pure Land) teachings brought him into conflict with the Kamakura Shogunate, and the Hōjō regents sent him into exile on the Izu Peninsula in 1261. Later allowed to return, he continued to preach his own interpretation of the Lotus Sutra—and to assert the "blasphemy" of other Buddhist sects, a stance that finally persuaded the Hōjō regency, in 1271, to condemn him to death. Execution was to take place on a hill to the south of Hase. As the executioner swung his sword, legend has it a lightning bolt struck the blade and snapped it in two. Taken aback, the executioner sat down to collect his wits, and a messenger was sent back to Kamakura to report the event. On his way he met another messenger, who was carrying a writ from the Hōjō regents commuting Nichiren's sentence to exile on the island of Sado-ga-shima.

Followers of Nichiren built Ryūkō Temple in 1337, on the hill where he was to be executed, marking his miraculous deliverance from the headsman. There are other Nichiren temples closer to Kamakura—Myōhon-ji and Ankokuron-ji, for example—but Ryūkō not only has the typical Nichiren-style main hall with gold tassels hanging from its roof but also a beautiful pagoda, built in 1904. To reach it, take the Enoden Line west from Hase to Enoshima—a short, scenic ride that cuts through the hills surrounding Kamakura to the shore. From Enoshima Station walk about 100 yards east, keeping the train tracks on your right, and you'll come to the temple. ⊠ *3–13–37 Katase, Fujisawa* 🕾 *0466/25–7357* 💴 *Free* ⊙ *Daily 6–4.*

The Sagami Bay shore in this area has some of the closest beaches to Tōkyō, and in the hot, humid summer months it seems as though all of the city's teeming millions pour onto these beaches in search of a vacant patch of rather dirty gray sand. Pass up this mob scene and press ❶ on instead to **Enoshima** (江ノ島). The island is only 4 km (2½ mi) around, with a hill in the middle. Partway up the hill is a shrine where the local fisherfolk used to pray for a bountiful catch—before it became a tourist attraction. Once upon a time it was quite a hike up to the shrine; now there's a series of escalators, flanked by the inevitable stalls selling souvenirs and snacks. The island has several cafés and restaurants, and on clear days some of them have spectacular views of Mt. Fuji and the Izu Peninsula. To reach the causeway from Enoshima Station to the island, walk south from the station for about 3 km (2 mi), keeping the Katase-gawa (Katase River) on your right.

To return to Tōkyō from Enoshima, take a train to Shinjuku on the Odakyū Line. From the island walk back across the causeway and take the second bridge over the Katase-gawa. Within five minutes you'll come to Katase-Enoshima Station. Or you can retrace your steps to Kamakura and take the JR Yokosuka Line to Tōkyō Station.

Where to Eat

Kita-Kamakura 北鎌倉

★ $$$–$$$$ ✕ **Hachinoki Kita-Kamakura-ten** (鉢の木北鎌倉店). Traditional *shōjin ryōri* (the vegetarian cuisine of Zen monasteries) is served in this old Japanese house on the Kamakura Kaidō (Route 21) near the entrance to Jōchi Temple. There's some table service, but most seating is in tatami rooms, with beautiful antique wood furnishings. Allow plenty of time; this is not a meal to be hurried through. Meals, which are prix-fixe only, are served Tuesday–Friday 11–2:30, weekends 11–3:30. ✉ *7 Yama-no-uchi, Kamakura* ☎ *0467/22–8719* 🖃 *DC, V* ☾ *Closed Mon. No dinner.*

$$–$$$ ✕ **Kyoraian** (去来庵). A traditional structure houses this restaurant known for its excellent Western-style beef stew. Half the seats are on tatami mats and half are at tables, but all look out on a peaceful patch of greenery. Kyoraian is on the main road from Kita-Kamakura to Kamakura on the left side; it's about halfway between Meigetsu Temple in and Kenchō Temple, up a winding flight of stone steps. Meals are served 11–7:30. ✉ *157 Yamanouchi, Kita-Kamakura* ☎ *0467/22–9835* 🖃 *No credit cards* ☾ *Closed Fri.*

Kamakura 鎌倉

$$–$$$$ ✕ **Tori-ichi** (鳥一). This elegant restaurant serves traditional Japanese kaiseki. In an old country-style building, waitresses in kimonos bring out sumptuous multicourse meals, including one or more subtle-tasting soups, sushi, tempura, grilled fish, and other delicacies. Meals are served Monday and Wednesday–Saturday noon–2 and 5–8, and Sunday 11:30–9. ✉ *7–13 Onari-machi, Kamakura* ☎ *0467/22–1818* 🖃 *No credit cards* ☾ *Closed Tues.*

$–$$$ ✕ **T-Side.** Authentic, inexpensive Indian fare and a second-floor location looking down on Kamakura's main shopping street make this restaurant a popular choice for lunch and dinner. Curries are well done, the various *thali* (sets) are a good value, and the kitchen also serves some Nepalese dishes. T-Side is at the very top of Komachi-dōri, on the left as you enter from Kamakura Station. ⊠ *1–6–2 Komachi, Kamakura* ☎ *0467/24–9572* 🚭 *MC, V.*

¢ **Kaisen Misaki-kō** (海鮮三崎港). This *kaiten-zushi* (sushi served on a conveyor belt that lets you pick the dishes you want) restaurant on Komachi-dōri, Kamakura's main shopping street, serves eye-poppingly large fish portions that hang over the edge of their plates. All the standard sushi creations, from tuna to shrimp to egg, are prepared here for ¥170–¥500. The restaurant is on the right side of the road just as you enter Komachi-dōri from the east exit of Kamakura Station. ⊠ *1–7–1 Komachi, Kamakura* ☎ *0467/22–6228* 🚭 *No credit cards.*

Hase

$$$–$$$$ ✕ **Kaseirō** (華正樓). This establishment, in an old Japanese house on the main street from Hase Station to the Great Buddha at Kōtoku-in, serves the best Chinese food in the city. The dining-room windows look out on a small, restful garden. Meals are served 11–7:30. ⊠ *3–1–14 Hase, Kamakura* ☎ *0467/22–0280* 🚭 *AE, DC, MC, V.*

Kamakura A to Z

To research prices, get advice from other travelers, and book travel arrangements, visit www.fodors.com.

BUS TRAVEL

A bus from Kamakura Station (Sign 5) travels to most of the temples and shrines in the downtown Kamakura area.

TOURS

No bus company in Kamakura conducts guided tours in English. You can, however, take one of the Japanese tours, which depart from Kamakura Station eight times daily, starting at 9 AM; the last tour leaves at 1 PM. Purchase tickets at the bus office to the right of the station. There are two itineraries, each lasting a little less than three hours; tickets, depending on what the tour covers, are ¥2,250 and ¥3,390. These tours are best if you have limited time and would like to hit the major attractions but don't want to linger anywhere or do a lot of walking. Take John Carroll's book *Trails of Two Cities: A Walker's Guide to Yokohama, Kamakura and Vicinity* (Kodansha International, 1994) with you, and you'll have more information at your fingertips than any of your fellow passengers.

On the weekend the Kanagawa Student Guide Federation has a free guide service. Students show you the city in exchange for the chance to practice their English. Arrangements must be made in advance through the Japan National Tourist Organization in Tōkyō. You'll need to be at Kamakura Station between 10 AM and noon.

Sunrise Tours runs daily trips from Tōkyō to Kamakura; these tours are often combined with trips to Hakone. You can book through, and arrange to be picked up at, any of the major hotels. Before you do, however, be certain that the tour covers everything in Kamakura that you want to see, as many include little more than a passing view of the Great Buddha in Hase. Given how easy it is to get around—most sights are within walking distance of each other, and others are short bus or train rides apart—you're better off seeing Kamakura on your own.

🔃 Tour Contacts **Japan National Tourist Organization** ✉ Tōkyō Kōtsū Kaikan, 10F, 2-10-1 Yūraku-chō, Chiyoda-ku, Tōkyō ☎ 03/3201-3331 ⊕ www.jnto.go.jp Ⓜ JR Yamanote Line [Higashi-guchi/East Exit] and Yūraku-chō subway line [Exit A-8], Yūraku-chō Station. **Kanagawa Student Guide Federation** ☎03/3201-3331. **Sunrise Tours** ☎03/5796-5454 🖷 03/5495-0680 ⊕ www.jtb.co.jp/sunrisetour.

TRAIN TRAVEL

Traveling by train is by far the best way to get to Kamakura. Trains run from Tōkyō Station (and Shimbashi Station) every 10–15 minutes during the day. The trip takes 56 minutes to Kita-Kamakura and one hour to Kamakura. Take the JR Yokosuka Line from Track 1 downstairs in Tōkyō Station (Track 1 upstairs is on a different line and does not go to Kamakura). The cost is ¥780 to Kita-Kamakura, ¥890 to Kamakura (or use your JR [Japan Railways] Pass).

Local train service connects Kita-Kamakura, Kamakura, Hase, and Enoshima.

To return to Tōkyō from Enoshima, take a train to Shinjuku on the Odakyū Line. There are 11 express trains daily from here on weekdays, between 8:38 AM and 8:45 PM; 9 trains daily on weekends and national holidays, between 8:39 AM and 8:46 PM; and even more in summer. The express takes about 70 minutes and costs ¥1,220. Or you can retrace your steps to Kamakura and take the JR Yokosuka Line to Tōkyō Station.

🔃 **Japan Railways** ☎ 03/3423-0111 ⊕ www.japanrail.com.

VISITOR INFORMATION

Both Kamakura and Enoshima have their own tourist associations, although it can be problematic getting help in English over the phone. Your best bet is the Kamakura Station Tourist Information Center, which has a useful collection of brochures and maps. And since Kamakura is in Kanagawa Prefecture, visitors heading here from Yokohama can pre-plan their excursion at the Kanagawa Prefectural Tourist Association office in the Silk Center, on the Yamashita Park promenade.

🔃 Tourist Information **Enoshima Tourist Association** ✉ 4-3-17 Kugenuma Kaigan, Fujisawa-shi ☎ 0466/37-4141. **Kamakura Station Tourist Information Center** ✉ 1-1-1 Komachi, Kamakura-shi ☎ 0467/22-3350. **Kamakura Tourist Association** ✉ 1-12 Onari-machi, Kamakura-shi ☎ 0467/23-3050. **Kanagawa Prefectural Tourist Association** ✉ Silk Center 1F, 1 Yamashita-chō, Naka-ku, Yokohama-shi ☎ 045/681-0007 ⊕ www.kanagawa-kankou.or.jp.

YOKOHAMA 横浜

In 1639 the Tokugawa Shogunate adopted a policy of national seclusion that closed Japan to virtually all contact with the outside world. Japan adhered to this policy for more than 200 years, until 1853, when a fleet of four American warships under Commodore Matthew Perry sailed into the bay of Tōkyō (then Edo) and presented the reluctant Japanese with the demands of the U.S. government for the opening of diplomatic and commercial relations. The following year Perry returned and first set foot on Japanese soil at Yokohama—then a small fishing village on the mudflats of the bay, some 20 km (12½ mi) southwest of Tōkyō.

Two years later New York businessman Townsend Harris became America's first diplomatic representative to Japan. In 1858 he was finally able to negotiate a commercial treaty between the two countries; part of the deal designated four locations—one of them Yokohama—as treaty ports. With the agreement signed, Harris lost no time in setting up his residence in Hongaku-ji, in nearby Kanagawa, another of the designated ports. Kanagawa, however, was also one of the 53 relay stations on the Tōkaidō, the highway from Edo to the imperial court in Kyōto, and the presence of foreigners—perceived as unclean barbarians—offended the Japanese elite. Die-hard elements of the warrior class, moreover, wanted Japan to remain in isolation and were willing to give their lives to rid the country of intruders. Unable to protect foreigners in Kanagawa, in 1859 the shogunate created a special settlement in Yokohama for the growing community of merchants, traders, missionaries, and other assorted adventurers drawn to this exotic new land of opportunity.

The foreigners (predominantly Chinese and British, plus a few French, Americans, and Dutch) were confined here to a guarded compound about 5 square km (2 square mi)—placed, in effect, in isolation—but not for long. Within a few short years the shogunal government collapsed, and Japan began to modernize. Western ideas were welcomed, as were Western goods, and the little treaty port became Japan's principal gateway to the outside world. In 1872 Japan's first railway was built, linking Yokohama and Tōkyō. In 1889 Yokohama became a city; by then the population had grown to some 120,000. As the city prospered, so did the international community.

The English enjoyed a special cachet in the new Japan. Was not Britain, too, a small island nation? And did it not do great things in the wide world? These were people from whom they could learn and with whom they could trade, and the Japanese welcomed them in considerable numbers. The British, in turn, helped Japan recover its sovereignty over the original treaty ports, and by the early 1900s Yokohama was the busiest and most modern center of international trade in all of east Asia.

Then Yokohama came tumbling down. On September 1, 1923, the Great Kantō Earthquake devastated the city. The ensuing fires destroyed some 60,000 homes and took more than 40,000 lives. During the six years it took to rebuild the city, many foreign businesses took up quarters elsewhere, primarily in Kōbe and Ōsaka, and did not return.

Over the next 20 years Yokohama continued to grow as an industrial center—until May 29, 1945, when in a span of four hours, some 500 American B-29 bombers leveled nearly half the city and left more than half a million people homeless. When the war ended, what remained became—in effect—the center of the Allied occupation. General Douglas MacArthur set up headquarters here, briefly, before moving to

Tōkyō; the entire port facility and about a quarter of the city remained in the hands of the U.S. military throughout the 1950s.

By the 1970s Yokohama was once more rising from the debris; in 1978 it surpassed Ōsaka as the nation's second-largest city, and the population is now inching up to the 3.5 million mark. Boosted by Japan's postwar economic miracle, Yokohama has extended its urban sprawl north to Tōkyō and south to Kamakura.

The development of air travel and the competition from other ports have changed the city's role in Japan's economy. The great liners that once docked at Yokohama's piers are now but a memory, kept alive by a museum ship and the occasional visit of a luxury vessel on a Pacific cruise. Modern Yokohama thrives instead in its industrial, commercial, and service sectors—and a large percentage of its people commute to work in Tōkyō. Is Yokohama worth a visit? Not, one could argue, at the expense of Nikkō or Kamakura, and not if you are looking for history in the physical fabric of the city: most of Yokohama's late-19th- and early- 20th-century buildings are long gone. In some odd, undefinable way, however, Yokohama is a more *cosmopolitan* city than Tōkyō. The waterfront is fun, and city planners have made an exceptional success of their port redevelopment project. The museums are excellent. And if you spend time enough here, Yokohama can still invoke for you the days when, for intrepid Western travelers, Japan was a new frontier.

Exploring Yokohama

Large as Yokohama is, the central area is very negotiable. As with any other port city, much of what it has to offer centers on the waterfront—in this case, the Bund, on the west side of Tōkyō Bay. The downtown area is called Kannai (literally, "within the checkpoint"); this is where the international community was originally confined by the shogunate. Though the center of interest has expanded to include the waterfront and Ishikawa-chō, to the south, Kannai remains the heart of town.

Think of that heart as two adjacent areas. One is the old district of Kannai, bounded by Basha-michi on the northwest and Nippon-ōdori on the southeast, the Keihin Tōhoku Line tracks on the southwest, and the waterfront on the northeast. This area contains the business offices of modern Yokohama. The other area extends southeast from Nippon-ōdori to the Moto-machi shopping street and the International Cemetery, bordered by Yamashita Kōen and the waterfront to the northeast; in the center is Chinatown, with Ishikawa-chō Station to the southwest. This is the most interesting part of town for tourists.

Numbers in the text correspond to numbers in the margin and on the Yokohama map.

Central Yokohama 横浜市街

Whether you are coming from Tōkyō, Nagoya, or Kamakura, make Ishikawa-chō Station your starting point. Take the south exit from the station and head in the direction of the waterfront. Within a block of
 Ishikawa-chō Station is the beginning of **Moto-machi** (元町), the street that

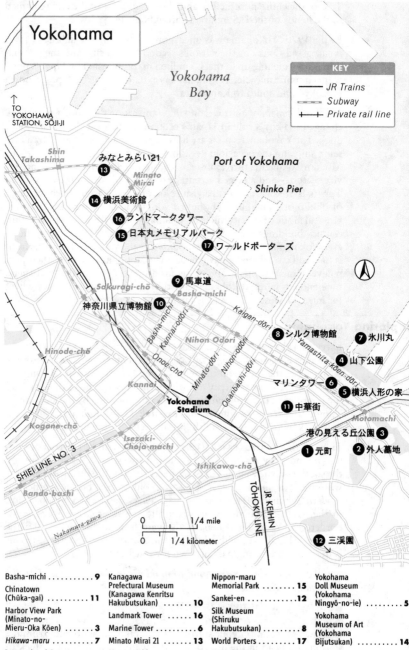

Yokohama

Yokohama Bay

↑
TO
YOKOHAMA
STATION, SŌJI-JI

Shin
Takashima

みなとみらい21

13

Minato
Mirai

Port of Yokohama

Shinko Pier

14 横浜美術館

16 ランドマークタワー

15 日本丸メモリアルパーク

17 ワールドポーターズ

9 馬車道

Sakuragi-chō
Basha-michi

神奈川県立博物館 **10**

Basha-michi
Kannai-odōri

Kaigan-dōri

8 シルク博物館

7 氷川丸

Yamashita-kōen-dōri

Hinode-chō

Nihon Odōri

Nihon-odōri

Minato-dōri

Onoe-chō

4 山下公園

Kannai

Osanbashi-dōri

マリンタワー **6**

5 横浜人形の家

Yokohama
Stadium

11 中華街

Kogane-chō

Motomachi

Isezaki-
Choja-machi

港の見える丘公園 **3**

SHIEI LINE NO. 3

1 元町

2 外人墓地

Ishikawa-chō

Bando-bashi

Nakamura-gawa

0   1/4 mile

0   1/4 kilometer

JR KEIHIN

TŌHOKU LINE

12 三渓園

follows the course of the Nakamura-gawa (Nakamura River) to the harbor. This is where the Japanese set up shop 100 years ago to serve the foreigners living in Kannai. The street is now lined with smart boutiques and jewelry stores that cater to fashionable young Japanese consumers. ⊠ *Naka-ku.*

② The **International Cemetery** (Gaijin Bochi, 外人墓地) is a Yokohama landmark and a reminder of the port city's heritage. It was established in 1854 with a grant of land from the shogunate; the first foreigners to be buried here were Russian sailors assassinated by xenophobes in the early days of the settlement. Most of the 4,500 graves on this hillside are English and American, and about 120 are of the Japanese wives of foreigners; the inscriptions on the crosses and headstones attest to some 40 different nationalities who lived and died in Yokohama. From Moto-machi Plaza, it's a short walk to the north end of the cemetery. ⊠ *Naka-ku.*

③ **Harbor View Park** (Minato-no-Mieru-Oka Kōen, 港の見える丘公園), once the barracks of the British forces in Yokohama, affords a spectacular nighttime view of the waterfront, the floodlighted gardens of Yamashita Park, and the Bay Bridge. The park is the major landmark in this part of the city, known, appropriately enough, as the Bluff (*yamate*). Foreigners were first allowed to build here in 1867, and it has been prime real estate ever since—an enclave of consulates, churches, international schools, private clubs, and palatial Western-style homes. ⊠ *Naka-ku.*

④ **Yamashita Kōen** (Yamashita Park, 山下公園) is perhaps the only positive legacy of the Great Kantō Earthquake of 1923. The debris of the warehouses and other buildings that once stood here was swept away, and the area was made into a 17-acre oasis of green along the waterfront. The fountain, representing the Guardian of the Water, was presented to Yokohama by San Diego, California, one of its sister cities. To get here from Harbor View Park, walk northwest through neighboring French Hill Park and cross the walkway over Moto-machi. Turn right on the other side and walk one block down toward the bay to Yamashita-Kōen-dōri, the promenade along the park. ⊠ *Naka-ku.*

⑤ The **Yokohama Doll Museum** (Yokohama Ningyō-no-ie, 横浜人形の家) houses a collection of some 4,000 dolls from all over the world. In Japanese tradition, dolls are less to play with than to display—either in religious folk customs or as the embodiment of some spiritual quality. The museum is worth a quick visit, with or without a child in tow. It's just across from the southeast end of Yamashita Park, on the left side of the promenade. ⊠ *18 Yamashita-chō, Naka-ku* ☎ *045/671–9361* ☞ *¥300; multiple-entry ticket to museum, Marine Tower, and Hikawa-maru, ¥1,550* ⊗ *Daily 10–6; closed 3rd Mon. of month.*

⑥ For an older generation of Yokohama residents, the 348-ft-high decagonal **Marine Tower** (マリンタワー), which opened in 1961, was the city's landmark structure; civic pride prevented them from admitting that it falls lamentably short of an architectural masterpiece. The tower has a navigational beacon at the 338-ft level and purports to be the tallest lighthouse in the world. At the 328-ft level, an observation gallery provides 360-degree views of the harbor and the city, and on clear days in autumn or winter, you can often see Mt. Fuji in the distance. Marine Tower is in the middle of the second block northwest from the end of Yamashita Park, on the left side of the promenade. ⊠ *15 Yamashita-chō, Naka-ku* ☎ *045/641–7838* ✉ *¥700; multiple-entry ticket to Marine Tower and Hikawa-maru ¥1,300; multiple-entry ticket to Marine Tower, Hikawa-maru, and Yokohama Doll Museum ¥1,550* ☉ *Jan. and Feb., daily 9–7; Mar.–May and Nov. and Dec., daily 9:30–9; June, July and Sept., Oct., daily 9:30–9:30; Aug., daily 9:30–10.*

❼ Moored on the waterfront, more or less in the middle of Yamashita Park, is the ***Hikawa-maru*** (氷川丸), which for 30 years shuttled passengers between Yokohama and Seattle, Washington, making a total of 238 trips. A tour of the ship evokes the time when Yokohama was a great port of call for the transpacific liners. The *Hikawa-maru* has a French restaurant, and in summer there's a beer garden on the upper deck. ⊠ *Naka-ku* ☎ *045/641–4361* ✉ *¥800; multiple-entry ticket to Hikawa-maru and Marine Tower ¥1,300; multiple-entry ticket to Hikawa-maru, Marine Tower, and Yokohama Doll Museum ¥1,550* ☉ *Apr.–June, daily 9:30–7; July and Aug., daily 9:30–7:30; Sept. and Oct., daily 9:30–7; Nov.–Mar., daily 9:30–6:30.*

❽ The **Silk Museum** (Shiruku Hakubutsukan, シルク博物館) pays tribute to the period at the turn of the 20th century when Japan's exports of silk were all shipped out of Yokohama. The museum houses an extensive collection of silk fabrics and an informative exhibit on the silk-making process. In the same building, on the first floor, are the main offices of the Yokohama International Tourist Association and the Kanagawa Prefectural Tourist Association. The museum is at the northwestern end of the Yamashita Park promenade, on the second floor of the Silk Center Building. ⊠ *1 Yamashita-chō, Naka-ku* ☎ *045/641–0841* ✉ *¥300* ☉ *Tues.–Sun. 9–4.*

❾ Running southwest from Shinko Pier to Kannai is **Basha-michi** 馬車道), which literally translates into "Horse-Carriage Street." The street was so named in the 19th century, when it was widened to accommodate the horse-drawn carriages of the city's new European residents. This red-brick thoroughfare and the streets parallel to it have been restored to evoke that past, with faux-antique telephone booths and imitation gas lamps. Here you'll find some of the most elegant coffee shops, patisseries, and boutiques in town. On the block northeast of Kannai Station, as you walk toward the waterfront, is **Kannai Hall** (look for the red-orange abstract sculpture in front), a handsome venue for chamber music, Nō, classical recitals, and occasional performances by such groups as the Peking Opera. If you're planning to stay late in Yokohama, you might want to check out the listings. ⊠ *Naka-ku.*

❿ One of the few buildings in Yokohama to have survived both the Great Kantō Earthquake of 1923 and World War II is the 1904 **Kanagawa Prefectural Museum** (Kanagawa Kenritsu Hakubutsukan, 神奈川県立博物館), a few blocks north of Kannai Station (use Exit 8) on Basha-michi. Most exhibits here have no explanations in English, but the galleries on the third floor showcase some remarkable medieval wooden sculptures (including one of the first Kamakura shōgun, Minamoto no Yoritomo), hanging scrolls, portraits, and armor. ⊠ *5–60 Minami Naka-dōri, Naka-ku* ☎ *045/201–0926* ✉ *¥300, special exhibits ¥800* ⏱ *Tues.–Sun. 9–4:30; closed last Tues. of month and the day after a national holiday.*

★ ⓫ Yokohama's **Chinatown** (Chūka-gai, 中華街) is the largest Chinese settlement in Japan—and easily the city's single most popular tourist attraction, drawing more than 18 million visitors a year. Its narrow streets and alleys are lined with some 350 shops selling foodstuffs, herbal medicines, cookware, toys and ornaments, and clothing and accessories. If China exports it, you'll find it here. Wonderful exotic aromas waft from the spice shops. Even better aromas drift from the quarter's 160-odd restaurants, which serve every major style of Chinese cuisine: this is the best place for lunch in Yokohama. Chinatown is a 10-minute walk southeast of Kannai Station. When you get to Yokohama Stadium, turn left and cut through the municipal park to the top of Nihon-ōdori. Then take a right, and you'll enter Chinatown through the Gembu-mon (North Gate), which leads to the dazzling red-and-gold, 50-ft-high Zenrin-mon (Good Neighbor Gate). ⊠ *Naka-ku.*

Around Yokohama 横浜周辺

★ ⓬ Opened to the public in 1906, **Sankei-en** (三溪園) was once the estate and gardens of Tomitarō Hara, one of Yokohama's wealthiest men, who made his money as a silk merchant before becoming a patron of the arts. On the extensive grounds of the estate he created is a kind of open-air museum of traditional Japanese architecture, some of which was brought here from Kamakura and the western part of the country. Especially noteworthy is **Rinshun-kaku,** a villa built for the Tokugawa clan in 1649. There's also a tea pavilion, Chōshū-kaku, built by the third Tokugawa shōgun, Iemitsu. Other buildings include a small temple transported from Kyōto's famed Daitoku-ji and a farmhouse from the Gifu district in the Japan Alps (around Takayama).

Walking through Sankei-en is especially delightful in spring, when the flowering trees are at their best: plum blossoms in February and cherry blossoms in early April. In June come the irises, followed by the water lilies. In autumn the trees come back into their own with tinted golden leaves. To reach Sankei-en, take the JR Keihin Tōhoku Line to Negishi Station and a local bus from there for the 10-minute trip to the garden. ⊠ *58–1 Honmoku San-no-tani, Naka-ku* ☎ *045/621–0635* ✉ *Inner garden ¥300, outer garden ¥300, farmhouse ¥100* ⏱ *Inner garden daily 9–4, outer garden daily 9–4:30.*

⓭ If you want to see Yokohama urban development at its most self-assertive, **Minato Mirai 21** (みなとみらい21) is a must. The aim of this project, launched in the mid-1980s, was to turn some three-quarters of a square mile of waterfront property, lying east of the JR Negishi Line railroad tracks between the Yokohama and Sakuragi-chō stations, into a model "city of the future." As a hotel, business, international exhibition, and conference center, it's a smashing success. ⊠ *Nishi-ku.*

⓮ Minato Mirai 21 is the site of the **Yokohama Museum of Art** (Yokohama Bijutsukan, 横浜美術館), designed by Kenzō Tange. The 5,000 works in the permanent collection include paintings by both Western and Japanese artists, including Cézanne, Picasso, Braque, Klee, Kandinsky, Ryūsei Kishida, and Taikan Yokoyama. ✉ *3–4–1 Minato Mirai, Nishi-ku* ☎ *045/221–0300* ✉ *¥500* ☉ *Mon.–Wed. and weekends 10–5:30, Fri. 10–7:30; closed day after a national holiday* Ⓜ *JR Line, Sakuragi-chō Station; Minato Mirai Line, Minato Mirai Station.*

On the east side of Minato Mirai 21, where the Ō-oka-gawa (Ō-oka River) ⓯ flows into the bay, is **Nippon-maru Memorial Park** (日本丸メモリアルパーク). The centerpiece of the park is the *Nippon-maru*, a full-rigged three-masted ship popularly called the "Swan of the Pacific." Built in 1930 and now retired from service as a training vessel and an occasional participant in tall-ships festivals, it's open for guided tours. Adjacent to the ship is the **Yokohama Maritime Museum,** a two-story collection of ship models, displays, and archival materials that celebrate the achievements of the Port of Yokohama from its earliest days to the present. ✉ *2–1–1 Minato Mirai, Nishi-ku* ☎ *045/221–0280* ✉ *Ship and museum ¥600* ☉ *Mar.–June and Sept., Oct., daily 10–5; July and Aug., daily 10–6:30; Nov.–Feb., daily 10–4:30; closed day after a national holiday* Ⓜ *JR Line, Sakuragi-chō Station; Minato Mirai Line, Minato Mirai Station.*

☾ ⓰ The 70-story **Landmark Tower** (ランドマークタワー), in Yokohama's Minato Mirai, is Japan's tallest building. The observation deck on the 69th floor has a spectacular view of the city, especially at night; you reach it via a high-speed elevator that carries you up at an ear-popping 45 kph (28 mph). The Yokohama Royal Park Hotel occupies the top 20 stories of the building. On the first level of the Landmark Tower is the **Mitsubishi Minato Mirai Industrial Museum** (みなとみらい技術館), with rocket engines, power plants, a submarine, various gadgets, and displays that simulate piloting helicopters—great fun for kids.

The Landmark Tower complex's **Dockyard Garden,** built in 1896, is a restored dry dock with stepped sides of massive stone blocks. The long, narrow floor of the dock, with its water cascade at one end, makes a wonderful year-round venue for concerts and other events; in summer (July–mid-August), the beer garden installed here is a perfect refuge from the heat. ✉ *3–3–1 Minato Mirai, Nishi-ku* ☎ *045/224–9031* ✉ *Elevator to observation deck ¥1,000, museum ¥500* ☉ *Museum Tues.–Sun. 10–5* Ⓜ *JR Line, Sakuragi-chō Station; Minato Mirai Line, Minato Mirai Station.*

⓱ The **World Porters** (ワールドポーターズ) shopping center, on the opposite side of Yokohama Cosmo World (よこはまコスモワールド), is notable chiefly for its restaurants that overlook the Minato Mirai area. Try arriving at sunset; the spectacular view of twinkling lights and the Landmark Tower, the Ferris wheel, and hotels will occasionally include Mt. Fuji in the background. Walking away from the waterfront area from World Porters will lead to **Aka Renga** (Redbrick Warehouses, 赤レンガ), two more shopping-and-entertainment facilities. ✉ *2–2–1 Shin-minato-chō, Naka-ku* ☎ *045/222–2000* ✉ *Free* ☉ *Daily 10–9, restaurants until 11* Ⓜ *JR Line, Sakuragi-chō Station; Minato Mirai Line, Minato Mirai Station.*

off the beaten path

SŌJI-JI – (総持寺) One of the two major centers of the Sōtō sect of Zen Buddhism, Sōji-ji, in Yokohama's Tsurumi ward, was founded in 1321. The center was moved here from Ishikawa, on the Noto Peninsula (on the Sea of Japan, north of Kanazawa), after a fire in the 19th century. There's also a Sōji-ji monastic complex at Eihei-ji in Fukui Prefecture. The Yokohama Sōji-ji is one of the largest and busiest Buddhist institutions in Japan, with more than 200 monks and novices in residence. The 14th-century patron of Sōji-ji was the emperor Go-Daigo, who overthrew the Kamakura Shogunate; the emperor is buried here, but his mausoleum is off-limits to visitors. However, you can see the **Buddha Hall,** the **Main Hall,** and the **Treasure House.** To get to Sōji-ji, take the JR Keihin Tōhoku Line two stops from Sakuragi-chō to Tsurumi. From the station walk five minutes south (back toward Yokohama), passing Tsurumi University on your right. You'll soon reach the stone lanterns that mark the entrance to the temple complex. ⊠ *2–1–1 Tsurumi, Tsurumi-ku* ☎ *045/581–6021* ⊑ *¥300* ⊗ *Daily dawn–dusk; Treasure House Tues.–Sun. 10–4.*

Where to Eat

$$$$ ✕ **Kaseirō** (華正樓). A smart Chinese restaurant with red carpets and gold-tone walls, Kaseiro serves Beijing cuisine—including, of course, Peking Duck and shark-fin soup—and is the best of its kind in the city. ⊠ *164 Yamashita-chō, Chinatown, Naka-ku* ☎ *045/681–2918* ⌂ *Jacket and tie* ▤ *AE, DC, V.*

$$$$ ✕ **Scandia** (スカンディア). This Scandinavian restaurant near the Silk Center and the business district is known for its smorgasbord. It's popular for business lunches as well as for dinner. Scandia stays open until midnight, later than many other restaurants in the area. ⊠ *1–1 Kaigan-dōri, Naka-ku* ☎ *045/201–2262* ▤ No credit cards ⊗ *No lunch Sun.*

$$$$ ✕ **Seryna** (瀬里奈). The hallmarks of this restaurant are *ishiyaki* steak, which is grilled on a hot stone, and shabu-shabu—thin slices of beef cooked in boiling water at your table and dipped in one of several sauces. "Shabu-shabu," by the way, is onomatapoetic for the sound the beef makes as you swish it through the water with your chopsticks. ⊠ *Shin-Kannai Bldg., B1, 4–45–1 Sumiyoshi-chō, Naka-ku* ☎ *045/681–2727* ▤ *AE, DC, MC, V.*

★ $$$–$$$$ ✕ **Aichiya** (あいちや). One of the specialties at this seafood restaurant is fugu (blowfish)—a delicacy that must be treated with expert care, as chefs must remove organs that contain a deadly toxin before the fish can be consumed. Fugu is served only in winter. The crabs here are also a treat. Aichiya is open 3–10. ⊠ *7–156 Isezaki-chō, Naka-ku* ☎ *045/ 251–4163* ⌂ *Jacket and tie* ▤ No credit cards ⊗ *Closed Mon.*

$$$–$$$$ ✕ **Rinka-en** (隣華苑). If you visit Sankei-en, you might want to have lunch at this traditional country restaurant, which serves kaiseki-style cuisine. The owner is the granddaughter of Hara Tomitaro, who donated the gardens of Sankei-en to the city. Rinka-en is open noon–5:30. ⊠ *Honmoku San-no-tani, Naka-ku* ☎ *045/621–0318* ⌂ *Jacket and tie* ▤ No credit cards ⊗ *Closed Wed. and Aug. No dinner.*

$$–$$$$ ✕ **Rome Station** (ローマステーション). Rome Station, between Chinatown and Yamashita Park, is a popular venue for Italian food. The spaghetti *vongole* (with clam sauce) is particularly good. ✉ *26 Yamashita-chō, Naka-ku* ☎ *045/681–1818* ▭ *No credit cards.*

★ $$–$$$$ ✕ **Winds** (ウインズ). California-influenced cuisine, a spacious dining area, and windows that overlook the Minato Mirai waterfront make this one of Yokohama's finest restaurants. The seafood is particularly good; try the avocado-and-tuna entrée prepared with soy sauce and Japanese basil, or the linguine with sea crab. Winds has an extensive wine list of California labels. ✉ *World Porters, 5F, 2–2–1 Shin-Minato-chō, Nishi-ku* ☎ *045/222–2570* ▭ *AE, MC, V.*

Yokohama A to Z

To research prices, get advice from other travelers, and book travel arrangements, visit www.fodors.com.

AIRPORTS & AIRPORT TRANSFERS

From Narita Airport, a direct limousine-bus service departs once or twice an hour between 6:45 AM and 10:20 PM for Yokohama City Air Terminal (YCAT). The fare is ¥3,500. YCAT is a five-minute taxi ride from Yokohama Station. JR Narita Express trains going on from Tōkyō to Yokohama leave the airport every hour from 8:13 AM to 1:13 PM and 2:43 PM to 9:43 PM. The fare is ¥4,180 (¥6,730 for the first-class Green Car coaches). Or you can take the limousine-bus service from Narita to Tōkyō Station and continue on to Yokohama by train. Either way, the journey will take more than two hours—closer to three, if traffic is heavy.

The Airport Limousine Information Desk phone number provides information in English daily 9–6; you can also get timetables on its Web site. For information in English on Narita Express trains, call the JR Higashi-Nihon Info Line, available daily 10–6.

🚩 **Airport Limousine Information Desk** ☎ 03/3665-7220 ⊕ www.limousinebus.co. jp. **JR Higashi-Nihon Info Line** ☎ 03/3423-0111.

BUS TRAVEL

Most of the things you'll want to see in Yokohama are within easy walking distance of a JR or subway station, but this city is so much more negotiable than Tōkyō that exploring by bus is a viable alternative. Buses, in fact, are the best way to get to Sankei-en. The city map available in the visitor centers in Yokohama and Shin-Yokohama stations has most major bus routes marked on it, and the important stops on the tourist routes are announced in English. The fixed fare is ¥210. One-day passes are also available for ¥600 (contact the tourist office at Yokohama Station for more information).

EMERGENCIES

The Yokohama Police Station has a Foreign Assistance Department.
🚩 **Ambulance or Fire** ☎ 119. **Police** ☎ 110. **Washinzaka Hospital** ✉ 169 Yamate-chō, Naka-ku ☎ 045/623-7688. **Yokohama Police Station** ☎ 045/623-0110.

ENGLISH-LANGUAGE MEDIA

BOOKS Yūrindō has a good selection of popular paperbacks and books on Japan in English. The Minato-Mirai branch is open daily 11–8; the store on Isezaki-chō opens an hour earlier.

🏠 **Yūrindō** ✉ Landmark Plaza 5F, 3-3-1 Minato-Mirai, Nishi-ku ☎ 045/222–5500 ✉ 1-4-1 Isezaki-chō, Naka-ku ☎ 045/261–1231.

SUBWAY TRAVEL

One subway line connects Azamino, Shin-Yokohama, Yokohama, Totsuka, and Shōnandai. The basic fare is ¥200. One-day passes are also available for ¥740. The Minato Mirai Line, a spur of the Tōkyū Toyoko Line, runs from Yokohama Station to all the major points of interest, including Minato Mirai, Chinatown, Yamashita Park, Moto-machi, and Basha-michi. The fare is ¥180–¥200, and one-day unlimited-ride passes are available for ¥450.

TAXIS

There are taxi stands at all the train stations, and you can always flag a cab on the street. Vacant taxis show a red light in the windshield. The basic fare is ¥660 for the first 2 km (1 mi), then ¥80 for every additional 350 meters (⅕ mi). Traffic is heavy in downtown Yokohama, however, and you will often find it faster to walk.

TOURS

Teiki Yūran Bus offers a full-day (9–3:45) sightseeing bus tour that covers the major sights and includes lunch at a Chinese restaurant in Chinatown. The tour is in Japanese only, but pamphlets written in English are available at most sightseeing stops. Buy tickets (¥6,360) at the bus offices at Yokohama Station (east side) and at Kannai Station; the tour departs daily at 9 AM from Bus Stop 14, on the east side of Yokohama Station. A half-day tour is also available, with lunch (9:30–1, ¥3,850) or without (2–5:30, ¥3,000).

The sightseeing boat *Marine Shuttle* makes 40-, 60-, and 90-minute tours of the harbor and bay for ¥900, ¥1,400, and ¥2,000, respectively. Boarding is at the pier at Yamashita Park. Boats depart roughly every hour between 10:20 AM and 6:30 PM. Another boat, the *Marine Rouge,* runs 90-minute tours departing from the pier at 11, 1:30, and 4, and a special two-hour evening tour at 7 (¥2,500).

🏠 Tour Contact **Marine Shuttle** ☎ 045/671–7719.

TRAIN TRAVEL

JR trains from Tōkyō Station leave approximately every 10 minutes, depending on the time of day. Take the Yokosuka, the Tōkaidō, or Keihin Tōhoku Line to Yokohama Station (the Yokosuka and Tōkaidō lines take 30 minutes; the Keihin Tōhoku Line takes 40 minutes). From there the Keihin Tōhoku Line (Platform 3) goes on to Kannai and Ishikawa-chō, Yokohama's business and downtown areas. If you're going directly to downtown Yokohama from Tōkyō, the blue commuter trains of the Keihin Tōhoku Line are best. The private Tōkyū Toyoko Line, which runs from Shibuya Station in Tōkyō directly to Yokohama Station, is a good alternative if you leave from the western part of Tōkyō.

From Nagoya and Points South, the Hikari and Kodama Shinkansen stop at Shin-Yokohama Station, 8 km (5 mi) from the city center. Take the local train from there for the seven-minute ride into town.

Yokohama Station is the hub that links all the train lines and connects them with the city's subway and bus services. Kannai and Ishikawa-chō are the two downtown stations, both on the Keihin Tōhoku Line; trains leave Yokohama Station every two to five minutes from Platform 3. From Sakuragi-chō, Kannai, or Ishikawa-chō, most of Yokohama's points of interest are within easy walking distance; the one notable exception is Sankei-en, which you reach via the JR Keihin Tōhoku Line to Negishi Station and then a local bus.

VISITOR INFORMATION

The Yokohama International Tourist Association arranges visits to the homes of English-speaking Japanese families. These usually last a few hours and are designed to give *gaijin* (foreigners) a glimpse into the Japanese way of life.

The Yokohama Tourist Office, in the central passageway of Yokohama Station, is open daily 9–7 (closed December 28–January 3). A similar office with the same closing times is in Shin-Yokohama Station. The head office of the Yokohama Convention & Visitors Bureau, open weekdays 9–5 (except national holidays and December 29–January 3), is in the Sangyō Bōeki Center Building, across from Yamashita Kōen.

🚉 Tourist Information **Yokohama Convention & Visitors Bureau** ✉ 2 Yamashita-chō, Naka-ku ☎ 045/221–2111. **Yokohama International Tourist Association** ☎ 045/641–4759. **Yokohama Tourist Office** ✉ Yokohama Station, Nishi-ku ☎ 045/441–7300 ✉ Shin-Yokohama Station, Tsurumi-ku ☎ 045/473–2895.

FUJI-HAKONE-IZU NATIONAL PARK 富士箱根伊豆国立公園

Fuji-Hakone-Izu National Park, southwest of Tōkyō between Suruga and Sagami bays, is one of Japan's most popular resort areas. The region's main attraction, of course, is Mt. Fuji, a dormant volcano—it last erupted in 1707—rising to a height of 12,388 feet. The mountain is truly beautiful, utterly captivating in the ways it can change in different light and from different perspectives. Its symmetry and majesty have been immortalized by poets and artists for centuries. Keep in mind that during spring and summer, Mt. Fuji often hides behind a blanket of clouds, to the disappointment of the crowds of tourists who travel to Hakone or the Fuji Five Lakes to see it.

Apart from Mt. Fuji itself, each of the three areas of the park—the Izu Peninsula, Hakone and environs, and the Five Lakes—has its own unique appeal. Izu is defined by its dramatic rugged coastline, beaches, and *onsen* (hot springs). Hakone has mountains, volcanic landscapes, and lake cruises, plus onsen of its own. The Five Lakes form a recreational area with some of the best views of Mt. Fuji. And in each of these areas there are monuments to Japan's past.

Although it's possible to make a grand tour of all three areas at one time, most people make each of them a separate excursion from Tōkyō. Because these are tourist attractions where people are accustomed to foreign visitors, there's always someone to help out in English if you want to explore off the beaten path.

Trains will serve you well in traveling to major points anywhere in the northern areas of the national-park region and down the eastern coast of the Izu Peninsula. For the west coast and central mountains of Izu, there are no train connections; unless you are intrepid enough to rent a car, the only way to get around is by bus.

Numbers in the text correspond to numbers in the margin and on the Fuji-Hakone-Izu National Park map.

Izu Peninsula 伊豆半島

Atami 熱海

❶ *48 min southwest of Tōkyō by Kodama Shinkansen.*

The gateway to the Izu Peninsula is Atami. Most Japanese honeymooners make it no farther into the peninsula than this town on Sagami Bay, so Atami itself has a fair number of hotels and traditional inns. When you arrive, collect a map from the **Atami Tourist Information Office** (熱海市観光協会; ☎ 0557/85–2222) at the train station to guide you to the sights below.

★ The **MOA Museum of Art** (MOA Bijutsukan, MOA 美術館) houses the private collection of the messianic religious leader Mokichi Okada. Okada (1882–1955), who founded a movement called the Sekai Kyūsei Kyō (Religion for the Salvation of the World), also acquired more than 3,000 works of art, dating from the Asuka period (6th and 7th centuries) to the present day. Among these works are several particularly fine *ukiyo-e* (Edo-era wood-block prints) and ceramics. On a hill above the station and set in a garden full of old plum trees and azaleas, the museum also affords a sweeping view over Atami and the bay. ✉ 26–2 Momoyama ☎ 0557/84–2511 ⌨ ¥1,600 ⊗ Fri.–Wed. 9:30–5.

The best time to visit the **Atami Plum Garden** (Atami Bai-en, 熱海梅園) is in late January or early February, when its 850 trees bloom. If you do visit, also stop by the small shrine in the shadow of an enormous old camphor tree: the tree has been designated a National Monument. Atami Bai-en is 15 minutes by bus from Atami or an eight-minute walk from Kinomiya Station, the next stop south of Atami served by local trains.

If you have the time and the inclination for a beach picnic, it's worth taking the 25-minute high-speed ferry (round-trip ¥2,340) from the pier over to **Hatsu-shima** (初島; ☎ 0557/81–0541 for ferry). There are nine departures daily between 7:30 and 5:20. You can easily walk around the island, which is only 4 km (2½ mi) in circumference, in less than two hours. Use of the **Picnic Garden** (open daily 10–3) is free.

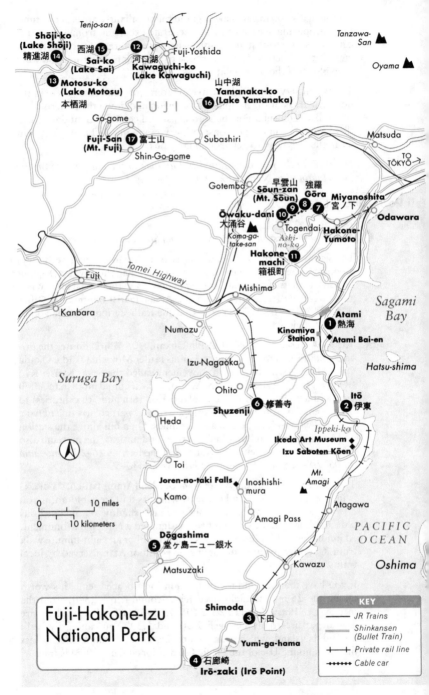

Tenjo-san

Tanzawa-San

Oyama

Shōji-ko (Lake Shōji)
精進湖
西湖 **15**
14
Sai-ko (Lake Sai)
河口湖 **12**
Kawaguchi-ko (Lake Kawaguchi)
Fuji-Yoshida

13
Motosu-ko (Lake Motosu)
本栖湖

山中湖
Yamanaka-ko (Lake Yamanaka)
16

F U J I

Go-gome
Fuji-San 17 富士山 (Mt. Fuji)
Shin-Go-gome

Subashiri

Matsuda

TO TŌKYŌ

早雲山 強羅
Sōun-zan **Gōra**
(Mt. Sōun) **8** **Miyanoshita**
Gotemba **9 7 宮ノ下**

Ōwaku-dani 10
大涌谷 **Hakone-** **Odawara**
Togendai **Yumoto**
Koma-ga- Ashi- **Hakone-machi**
take-san no-ko **箱根町 11**

Fuji
Tomei Highway

Mishima

Kanbara

Numazu

Izu-Nagaoka

Atami 1
熱海
Kinomiya Station
Atami Bai-en

Sagami Bay

Hatsu-shima

Ohito

Suruga Bay

Heda

6 修善寺
Shuzenji

Itō 2
伊東
Ippeki-ko

Ikeda Art Museum
Izu Saboten Kōen

Toi

Joren-no-taki Falls
Inoshishi-mura

Mt. Amagi

Kamo

Amagi Pass

Atagawa

PACIFIC OCEAN

Dōgashima 5
堂ヶ島ニュー銀水

Matsuzaki

Kawazu

Oshima

Shimoda 3 下田

Yumi-ga-hama

4 石廊崎
Irō-zaki (Irō Point)

0   10 miles
0   10 kilometers

Fuji-Hakone-Izu National Park

KEY
— JR Trains
Shinkansen (Bullet Train)
+ + + Private rail line
•••••• Cable car

WHERE TO STAY
★ $$$$
🏠 **Taikansō** (熱海大観荘). The views of the sea must have been the inspiration for Yokoyama Taikan, the Japanese artist who once owned this villa that is now a traditional Japanese inn with exquisite furnishings and individualized service. The prices (¥31,000–¥47,000) are high, but bear in mind that they include a multicourse dinner of great artistry, served in your room, and breakfast the next morning. There are also indoor and outdoor hot-springs baths. The inn is a 10-minute walk from Atami Station. ✉ *7–1 Hayashi-ga-oka-chō, Atami, Shizuoka-ken 413-0031* ☎ *0557/81–8137* 📠 *0557/83–5308* 🌐 *www.atami-taikanso.com* 🛏 *44 Japanese-style rooms with bath* ⌂ *Restaurant, pool, hot springs, sauna, meeting rooms* ▭ *AE, DC, MC, V* ⦿| *MAP.*

$$–$$$$
🏠 **New Fujiya Hotel** (ニュー富士屋ホテル). Only the top rooms have a view of the sea at this modern, inland resort hotel, which makes a useful base for sightseeing. Service is impersonal but professional, and a foreign visitor is no cause for consternation. The hotel is a five-minute taxi ride from Atami Station. ✉ *1–16 Ginza-chō, Atami, Shizuoka-ken 413-0013* ☎ *0557/81–0111* 🛏 *158 Western-style rooms with bath, 158 Japanese-style rooms with bath* ⌂ *3 restaurants, indoor pool, hot springs, bar* ▭ *AE, DC, MC, V.*

Itō 伊東

② *25 min south of Atami by JR local; 1 hr, 40 min southwest of Tōkyō via Atami by Kodama Shinkansen, then JR local.*

There are some 800 thermal springs in the resort area surrounding Itō, 16 km (10 mi) south of Atami. These springs—and the beautiful, rocky, indented coastline nearby—remain the resort's major attractions, although there are plenty of interesting sights here. Some 150 hotels and inns serve the area.

Itō traces its history of association with the West to 1604, when William Adams (1564–1620), the Englishman whose adventures served as the basis for James Clavell's novel *Shōgun,* came ashore.

Four years earlier Adams had beached his disabled Dutch vessel, *De Liefde,* on the shores of Kyūshū and became the first Englishman to set foot on Japan. The authorities, believing that he and his men were Portuguese pirates, put Adams in prison, but he was eventually befriended by the shōgun Ieyasu Tokugawa, who brought him to Edo (present-day Tōkyō) and granted him an estate. Ieyasu appointed Adams his adviser on foreign affairs. The English castaway taught mathematics, geography, gunnery, and navigation to shogunal officials and in 1604 was ordered to build an 80-ton Western-style ship. Pleased with this venture, Ieyasu ordered the construction of a larger oceangoing vessel. These two ships were built at Itō, where Adams lived from 1605 to 1610.

This history was largely forgotten until British Commonwealth occupation forces began coming to Itō for rest and recuperation after World War II. Adams's memory was revived, and since then the Anjin Festival (the Japanese gave Adams the name *anjin,* which means "pilot") has been held in his honor every August. A monument to the Englishman stands at the mouth of the river.

ONSEN

JAPAN'S BIGGEST NATURAL HEADACHE— the slip and slide of vast tectonic plates deep below the archipelago that spawn volcanoes and make earthquakes an everyday fact of life— provides one of Japan's greatest delights as well: thermal baths. Wherever there are volcanic mountains—and Japan is mostly volcanic mountains—you can usually count on drilling or tapping into springs of hot water, rich in all sorts of restorative minerals. Any place where this happens is called, generically, an onsen; any place where lots of spas have tapped these sources, to cash in on the Japanese passion for total immersion, is an onsen chiiki (hot-springs resort area). The Izu Peninsula is particularly rich in onsen. It has, in fact, one-fifth of the 2,300-odd officially recognized hot springs in Japan.

The spas in famous areas like Shuzenji take many forms. The ne plus ultra is that small secluded Japanese inn up in the mountains, where you sleep on futons, in a setting of almost poetic traditional furnishings and design. Such an inn will have for the exclusive use of its guests a rotemburo, an open-air mineral-spring pool, usually in a screened-off nook with a panoramic view. For a room in one of these inns on a weekend or in high season, you often have to book months in advance. (High season is late December to early January, late April to early May, the second and third weeks of August, and the second and third weeks of October.) More typical is the large resort hotel, geared mainly to groups, with one or more large indoor mineral baths of its own. Where whole towns and villages have developed to exploit a local supply of hot water, there will be several of these large hotels, an assortment of smaller inns, and probably a few modest public bathhouses, with no accommodations, where you just pay an entrance fee for a soak of whatever length you wish.

The first challenge in bathing is acknowledging that your Japanese bath mates will stare at your body. Take solace, however, in the fact that their apparent voyeurism most likely stems from curiosity. The second challenge is figuring out what is required of you before you enter the hot pool. Japanese custom dictates that your body must be completely clean before entering a communal pool. So help yourself to the towels, soap, and shampoo set out for this purpose, and grab a bucket and a stool. At one of the shower stations around the edge of the room, crouch on your bucket (or stand if you prefer) and use the handheld showers to wash yourself thoroughly. A head-to-toe twice-over will impress onlookers. Rinse off, and then you may enter the public bath. All you need to do then is lean back, relax, and experience the pleasures of Shintō-style purification—cleanse your body and enlighten your spirit.

Izu Cactus Park (Izu Shaboten Kōen, 伊豆ボテン公園) consists of a series of pyramidal greenhouses that contain 5,000 kinds of cacti from around the world. At the base of Komuro-san (Mt. Komuro), the park is 20 minutes south of Itō Station by bus. ✉ *1317–13 Futo* ☎ *0557/51–5553* 💴 *¥1,800, ¥800 after 5* 🕐 *Mar.–Oct., daily 9–5; Nov.–Feb., daily 9–4.*

The **Ikeda 20th-Century Art Museum** (Ikeda 20-Seiki Bijutsukan, 池田20世紀美術館), at Lake Ippeki, houses works by Picasso, Dalí, Chagall, and Matisse, plus a number of wood-block prints. The museum is a 15-minute walk from Izu Cactus Park. ✉ *614 Totari* ☎ *0557/45–2211* 💴 *¥900* 🕐 *Thurs.–Tues. 10–4:30.*

On the east side of **Komuro-san Kōen** (Mt. Komuro Park, 小室山公園) are 3,000 cherry trees of 35 varieties that bloom at various times throughout the year. A cable car takes you to the top of the mountain. The park is about 20 minutes south of Itō Station by bus. 💴 *Free, round-trip cable car to mountain top ¥400* 🕐 *Daily 9–4.*

en route South of Itō the coastal scenery is lovely—each sweep around a headland reveals another picturesque sight of a rocky, indented shoreline. There are several spa towns en route to Shimoda. Higashi-Izu (East Izu) has numerous hot-springs resorts, of which **Atagawa** (熱川) is the most fashionable. South of Atagawa is **Kawazu** (川津), a place of relative quiet and solitude, with pools in the forested mountainside and waterfalls plunging through lush greenery.

Shimoda 下田
❸ *1 hr south of Itō by Izu Railways.*

Of all the resort towns south of Itō along Izu's eastern coast, none can match the distinction of Shimoda. Shimoda's encounter with the West began when Commodore Matthew Perry, bearing a commission from the U.S. government to open—by force, if necessary—diplomatic relations with Japan, anchored his fleet of black ships off the coast here in 1853. To commemorate the event, the three-day Black Ship Festival (Kurofune Matsuri) is held here every year in mid-May. Shimoda was also the site, in 1856, of the first American consulate.

The **Shimoda tourist office** (下田市観光協会; ☎ 0558/22–1531), in front of the station, has the easiest of the local English itineraries to follow. The 2½-km (1½-mi) tour covers most major sights.

The first American consul to Japan was New York businessman Townsend Harris. Soon after his arrival in Shimoda, Harris asked the Japanese authorities to provide him with a female servant; they sent him a young girl named Saitō Okichi. The arrangement brought her only a new name—Tōjin (the Foreigner's) Okichi—and a tragic end. Harris soon sent her away, compounding poor Okichi's shame and ridicule. She tried and failed to rejoin a former lover, moved to Yokohama, and later returned to Shimoda in an unsuccessful attempt to run a restaurant. Okichi took to drink and drowned herself in 1890. Her tale is recounted in Rei Kimura's biographical novel *Butterfly in the Wind*. **Hōfuku-ji** (宝福寺) was

Okichi's family temple. The museum annex displays a life-size image of her, and just behind the temple is her grave—where incense is still kept burning in her memory. The grave of her lover, Tsurumatsu, is at Tōden-ji, a temple about midway between Hōfuku-ji and Shimoda Station. ✉ *18–26 1-chōme* ☎ *0558/22–0960* 💰 *¥300* 🕐 *Daily 8–5.*

Ryosen-ji (了仙寺) is the temple in which the negotiations took place that led to the United States–Japan Treaty of Amity and Commerce of 1858. The **Treasure Hall** (Hōmotsu-den) contains some personal articles that belonged to Tōjin Okichi. ✉ *3–12–12 Shimoda* ☎ *0558/22–2805* 💰 *Treasure Hall ¥500* 🕐 *Daily 8:30–5.*

WHERE TO STAY

$$–$$$$ 🏨 **Shimoda Prince Hotel** (下田プリンスホテル). This modern V-shape resort hotel faces the Pacific, steps away from a white-sand beach. The decor is more functional than aesthetic, but the panoramic view of the ocean from the picture windows in the dining room makes this one of the best hotels in town. The Prince is just outside Shimoda, 10 minutes by taxi from the station. ✉ *1547–1 Shira-hama, Shimoda, Shizuoka-ken 415-8525* ☎ *0558/22–2111* 🖷 *0558/22–7584* ⊕ *www.princehotels.co.jp* 🛏 *70 Western-style rooms with bath, 6 Japanese-style rooms with bath* 🍴 *2 restaurants, 3 tennis courts, pool, hot springs, sauna, bar, nightclub, shops* 🟰 *AE, DC, MC, V.*

$$–$$$$ 🏨 **Shimoda Tōkyū Hotel** (下田東急ホテル). Perched just above the bay, the Shimoda Tōkyū has impressive views of the Pacific from one side (where rooms cost about 10% more) and mountains from the other. Unlike those at most Japanese resort hotels, the lobby here is full of character and warmth, with an airy layout and floor-to-ceiling windows overlooking the bay. Prices are significantly higher in midsummer. ✉ *5–12–1 Shimoda, Shimoda, Shizuoka-ken 415-8510* ☎ *0558/22–2411* ⊕ *www.tokyuhotels.co.jp* 🛏 *107 Western-style rooms with bath, 8 Japanese-style rooms with bath* 🍴 *3 restaurants, café, pool, hot springs, bar, shops* 🟰 *AE, DC, MC, V.*

¢   **Pension Sakuraya** (ペンション桜家) There are a few Western-style bedrooms at this family-run inn just a few minutes' walk from Shimoda's main beach, but the best lodgings are the Japanese-style corner rooms, which have nice views of the hills surrounding Shimoda. The pleasant Japanese couple who run the pension speak English, and cheap meals are available in the dining room. Sakuraya has a wireless LAN network for PC users. ✉ *2584–20 Shira-hama, Shimoda, Shizuoka-ken 415-0012* ☎ *0558/23–4470* 🖷 *0558/27–2130* 🛏 *4 Western-style rooms with bath, 5 Japanese-style rooms without bath* ⊕ *http://izu-sakuraya.jp/english* 🍴 *Dining room, Japanese baths, laundry facilities, Internet* 🟰 *AE, DC, MC, V.*

 en route   The bus from Shimoda Station stops at **Yumi-ga-hama** (弓ヶ浜), one of the prettiest sandy beaches on the whole Izu Peninsula, before continuing to Irō-zaki, the last stop on the route.

Irō-zaki (Irō Point, 石廊崎)
④ *40 min by bus or boat from Shimoda.*

If you visit Irō-zaki, the southernmost part of the Izu Peninsula, in January, you're in for a special treat: a blanket of daffodils covers the cape.

From the bus stop at the end of the line from Shimoda Station, it's a short walk to the **Irō-zaki Jungle Park** (石廊崎ジャングルパーク), with its 3,000 varieties of colorful tropical plants. Beyond the park you can walk to a lighthouse at the edge of the cliff. ⊠ *546–1 Irō-zaki, Minami-Izu* ☎ *0558/65–0050* 💴 *¥900* ⊘ *Daily 8–5.*

Dōgashima 堂ヶ島

5 *1 hr northwest of Shimoda by bus.*

The sea has eroded the coastal rock formations into fantastic shapes near the little port town of Dōgashima. A **Dōgashima Marine** (堂ヶ島マリン, (☎ 0558/52–0013) sightseeing boat from Dōgashima Pier makes 20-minute runs to see the rocks (¥920). In an excess of kindness, a recorded loudspeaker—which you can safely ignore—recites the name of every rock you pass on the trip.

WHERE TO STAY **$$$$** 🏨 **Dōgashima New Ginsui** (堂ヶ島ニュー銀水). Every guest room overlooks the sea at the New Ginsui, which sits atop cliffs above the water. This is the smartest luxury resort on Izu's west coast. Service is first class, despite its popularity with tour groups. The room rate includes a seafood kaiseki dinner served in your room and a buffet breakfast. ⊠ *2977–1 Nishina, Nishi-Izu-chō, Dōgashima, Shizuoka-ken 410-3514* ☎ *0558/ 52–2211* 🖷 *0558/52–1210* 📡 *90 Japanese-style rooms with bath* ⚕ *Restaurant, 2 pools, hot springs, spa, nightclub, shops, laundry services, concierge, meeting rooms* ☰ *AE, DC, MC, V* ¶❉ *MAP.*

Shuzenji 修善寺

6 *2 hrs north of Shimoda by bus, 32 min south of Mishima by Izu-Hakone Railway.*

Shuzenji—a hot-springs resort in the center of the peninsula, along the valley of the Katsura-gawa (Katsura River)—enjoys a certain historical notoriety as the place where the second Kamakura shōgun, Minamoto no Yoriie, was assassinated early in the 13th century. Don't judge the town by the area around the station; most of the hotels and hot springs are 2 km (1 mi) to the west.

WHERE TO STAY **★ $$$$** 🏨 **Ryokan Sanyōsō** (旅館三養荘). The former villa of the Iwasaki family, founders of the Mitsubishi conglomerate, is as luxurious and beautiful a place to stay as you'll find on the Izu Peninsula. Museum-quality antiques furnish the rooms, the best of which have traditional baths made of fragrant cypress wood and overlooking exquisite little private gardens (note that these high-end rooms cost as much as ¥70,000). Breakfast and dinner, served in your room, are included in the rate. The Sanyōsō is a five-minute taxi ride from Izu-Nagaoka Station. ⊠ *270 Mama-no-ue, Izu-Nagaoka-chō, Shizuoka-ken 410-2204* ☎ *055/9 47–1111* 🖷 *055/947–0610* 📡 *21 Western and Japanese-style rooms with bath* ⚕ *Restaurant, Japanese baths, bar, shops, laundry service, meeting rooms* ☰ *AE, DC, MC, V.*

$$ 🏨 **Kyorai-An Matsushiro-kan** (去来庵 松城館). Although this small family-owned inn five minutes by bus or taxi from Izu-Nagaoka Station is nothing fancy, the owners make you feel like a guest in their home. They also speak some English. Japanese meals are served in a common dining room. Room-only reservations (without meals) are accepted only

on weekdays. ⊠ *55 Kona, Izu-Nagaoka, Shizuoka-ken 410-2201*
☎ *055/948–0072* 🖷 *055/948–4030* 🖙 *16 Japanese-style rooms with
bath* 🍴 *Dining room* 🖃 *AE, DC, MC, V* 🍴 *MAP.*

¢ 🖾 **Goyōkan** (五葉館). This family-run ryokan on Shuzenji's main street
has rooms that look out on the Katsura-gawa, plus gorgeous stone-lined
(for men) and wood-lined (for women) indoor hot springs. The staff speaks
English and can make sightseeing arrangements for you. ⊠ *765–2
Shuzenji-chō, Tagata-gun, Shizuoka-ken 410-24* ☎ *0558/72–2066*
⊕ *www.goyokan.co.jp/english* 🖙 *11 Japanese-style rooms without
bath* 🍴 *Refrigerators, hot springs, sauna* 🖃 *AE, DC, MC, V.*

Hakone 箱根

The national park and resort area of Hakone is a popular day trip from
Tōkyō and a good place for a close-up view of Mt. Fuji (assuming the
mountain is not swathed in clouds, as often happens in summer). Note
that on summer weekends it often seems as though all of Tōkyō has come
out to Hakone with you. Expect long lines at cable cars and traffic jams
everywhere.

You can cover the best of Hakone in a one-day trip out of Tōkyō, but
if you want to try the curative powers of the thermal waters or do some
hiking, then stay overnight. Two of the best areas are around the old
hot-springs resort of Miyanoshita and the western side of Koma-ga-take-
san (Mt. Koma-ga-take).

The typical Hakone route, outlined here, may sound complex, but this
is in fact one excursion from Tōkyō so well defined that you really can't
get lost—no more so, at least, than any of the thousands of Japanese
tourists ahead of and behind you. The first leg of the journey is from
Odawara or Hakone-Yumoto by train and cable car through the mountains to Togendai, on the north shore of Ashi-no-ko (Lake Ashi). The
scenery en route is spectacular, but if you have problems with vertigo
you might be better off on the bus. The long way around, from Odawara
to Togendai by bus, takes about an hour—in heavy traffic, an hour and
a half. The trip over the mountains, on the other hand, will take about
two hours. Credit the difference to the Hakone Tōzan Tetsudō Line—
possibly the slowest train you'll ever ride. Using three switchbacks to
inch its way up the side of the mountain, the train takes 54 minutes to
travel the 16 km (10 mi) from Odawara to Gōra (38 minutes from
Hakone-Yumoto). The steeper it gets, the grander the view.

Trains do not stop at any station en route for any length of time, but
they do run frequently enough to allow you to disembark, visit a sight,
❼ and catch another train. **Miyanoshita** (宮ノ下), the first stop on the train
route from Hakone-Yumoto, is a small but very pleasant and popular
resort. Especially charming is the 19th-century Western-style **Fujiya
Hotel** here. Even if you're not staying at the hotel, drop in for a morning coffee on the first floor overlooking the garden. Before you leave
the hotel, take a peek at the vintage collection of old books and magazines in the library.

★ The **Hakone Open-Air Museum** (Hakone Chōkoku-no-mori Bijutsukan, 箱根彫刻の森美術館) houses an astonishing collection of 19th- and 20th-century Western and Japanese sculpture, most of it on display in a spacious, handsome garden. There are works here by Rodin, Moore, Arp, Calder, Giacometti, Takeshi Shimizu, and Kōtarō Takamura. One section of the garden is devoted to Emilio Greco. Inside are works by Picasso, Léger, and Manzo, among others. The museum is within a minute's walk of Miyanoshita Station; directions are posted in English. ✉ *1121 Mi-no-taira* ☎ *0460/2–1161* ⊕ *www.hakone-oam.or.jp* ☞ *¥1,600* ⊙ *Mar.–Nov., daily 9–5; Dec.–Feb., daily 9–4.*

❽ Gōra (強羅), a small town at the end of the train line from Odawara and the lower end of the Sōun-zan cable car, is a good jumping-off point for hiking and exploring. Ignore the little restaurants and souvenir stands here: get off the train as quickly as you can and make a dash for the cable car at the other end of the station. If you let the rest of the passengers get there before you, and perhaps a tour bus or two, you may stand 45 minutes in line.

❾ The cable car from Gōra up to **Sōun-zan** (Mt. Sōun, 早雲山) departs every 20 minutes and takes 10 minutes (¥410; free with the Hakone Free Pass) to the top. There are four stops en route, and you can get off and re-board the cable car at any one of them if you've paid the full fare. At Kōen-kami, the second stop on the cable car from Gōra, is the **Hakone Museum of Art** (Hakone Bijutsukan), sister institution to the MOA Museum of Art in Atami. The museum houses a modest collection of porcelain and ceramics from China, Korea, and Japan. ✉ *1300 Gōra* ☎ *0460/ 2–2623* ☞ *¥900* ⊙ *Apr.–Nov., Fri.–Wed. 9:30–4:30; Dec.–Mar., Fri.–Wed. 9:30–4.*

★ **❿** At the cable-car terminus of Sōun-zan a gondola swings up over a ridge and crosses the valley called **Ōwaku-dani** (大涌谷) on its way to To-gendai. The landscape here is blasted and desolate, with sulfurous billows of steam escaping through holes from some inferno deep in the earth—yet another reminder that Japan is a chain of volcanic islands. At the top of the ridge is one of the two stations where you can leave the gondola. From the station a ¾-km (½-mi) walking course wanders among the sulfur pits in the valley. Local entrepreneurs make a passable living boiling eggs in these holes and selling them to tourists at exorbitant prices. Just below the station is a restaurant; the food here is truly terrible, but on a clear day the view of Mt. Fuji is perfect. Next to the gondola station is the **Ōwaku-dani Natural History Museum** (Ōwaku-dani Shizen Kagakukan), an uninspired collection of exhibits on the ecosystems and volcanic history of the area, none of which have explanations in English. The museum is open daily 9–4:30; admission is ¥400. Remember that if you get off the gondola here, you—and others in the same situation—will have to wait for someone to make space on a later gondola before you can continue down to Togendai and Ashi-no-ko (but again, the gondolas come by every minute). ✉ *Gondola in same bldg. as cable car terminus at Sōun-zan* ☞ *¥1,330, free with Hakone Free Pass* ⊙ *Gondolas depart every minute.*

From Ōwaku-dani the descent by gondola to Togendai on the shore of **Ashi-no-ko** (Lake Ashi, 芦ノ湖) takes 25 minutes. There's no reason to linger at Togendai; it's only a terminus for buses to Hakone-Yumoto and Odawara and to the resort villages in the northern part of Hakone. Head straight for the pier, a few minutes' walk down the hill, where boats set out on the lake for Hakone-machi. The ride is free with your Hakone Free Pass; otherwise, buy a ticket (¥970) at the office in the terminal. A few ships of conventional design ply the lake; the rest are astonishingly corny Disney knockoffs. One, for example, is rigged like a 17th-century warship. There are departures every 30 minutes, and the cruise to Hakone-machi takes about 30 minutes. With still water and good weather, you'll get a breathtaking reflection of the mountains in the waters of the lake as you go.

⑪ The main attraction in **Hakone-machi** (箱根町) is the **Hakone Barrier** (Hakone Sekisho). In days gone by, the town of Hakone was on the Tōkaidō, the main highway between the imperial court in Kyōto and the shogunate in Edo (present-day Tōkyō). The road was the only feasible passage through this mountainous country. Travelers could scarcely avoid passing through Hakone, which made it an ideal place for a checkpoint to control traffic. The Tokugawa Shogunate built the barrier here in 1618; its most important function was to monitor the *daimyō* (feudal lords) passing through—to keep track, above all, of weapons coming into Edo, and womenfolk coming out.

When Ieyasu Tokugawa came to power, Japan had been through nearly 100 years of bloody struggle among rival coalitions of daimyō. Ieyasu emerged supreme from all this, mainly because some of his opponents had switched sides at the last minute, in the Battle of Sekigahara in 1600. The shōgun was justifiably paranoid about his "loyal" barons—especially those in the outlying domains—so he required the daimyō to live in Edo for periods of time every two years. It was an inspired policy. The rotation system turned the daimyō into absentee landlords, which undercut their bases of power. They had to travel both ways in processions of great pomp and ceremony and maintain homes in the capital befitting their rank—expenses that kept them perennially strapped for cash. When they did return to their own lands, they had to leave their wives behind in Edo, hostages to their good behavior. A noble lady coming through the Hakone Sekisho without an official pass, in short, was a prima facie case of treason.

The checkpoint served the Tokugawa dynasty well for 250 years. It was demolished only when the shogunate fell, in the Meiji Restoration of 1868. An exact replica, with an exhibition hall of period costumes and weapons, was built as a tourist attraction in 1965. The restored barrier is a few minutes' walk from the pier, along the lakeshore in the direction of Moto-Hakone. ⊠ *Ichiban-chō, Hakone-machi* ☎ *0460/3–6635* 🔁 *¥300* ⊙ *Mar.–Nov., daily 9–4:30; Dec.–Feb., daily 9–4.*

Where to Stay

LAKE ASHI   📺 **Hakone Prince Hotel** (箱根プリンスホテル). The location of this resort complex is perfect, with the lake in front and the mountains of Koma-ga-take

★ $$–$$$$

in back. The Hakone Prince draws both tour groups and individual travelers, and it's also a popular venue for business conferences. The main building has both twin rooms and triples; the Japanese-style Ryū-gū-den annex, which overlooks the lake and has its own thermal bath, is superb. The seasonal rustic-style cottages sleep three to four guests. ⊠ *144 Moto-Hakone, Hakone-machi, Ashigarashimo-gun, Kanagawa-ken 250-0522* ☎ *0460/3–1111* 🖷 *0460/3–7616* ⊕ *www.princehotels.co.jp* ⊲ *142 Western-style rooms with bath, 116 Western-style cottages with bath* ⬧ *2 restaurants, coffee shop, dining room, room service, 7 tennis courts, 2 pools, Japanese baths, bar, lounge, shops* ▭ *AE, DC, MC, V* ⫶⊙⫶ *CP.*

MIYANOSHITA
★ $$–$$$$

🏨 **Fujiya Hotel** (富士屋ホテル). Built in 1878, this Western-style hotel with modern additions is showing signs of age, but that somehow adds to its charm. The Fujiya combines the best of traditional Western decor with the exceptional service and hospitality of a fine Japanese inn. There are both Western and Japanese restaurants, and in the gardens behind the hotel is an old imperial villa that serves as a dining room. With its stacks of old books, the library would make a character out of Dickens feel positively at home.Hot-spring water is pumped right into the guest rooms. ⊠ *359 Miyanoshita, Hakone-machi, Kanagawa-ken 250-0522* ☎ *0460/2–2211* 🖷 *0460/2–2210* ⊕ *www.fujiyahotel.co.jp* ⊲ *149 Western-style rooms with bath* ⬧ *3 restaurants, room service, 18-hole golf course, 2 pools, hot springs, bar, convention center, meeting rooms, no-smoking rooms* ▭ *AE, DC, MC, V.*

SENGOKU
¢

🏨 **Fuji-Hakone Guest House** (富士箱根ゲストハウス). A small, family-run Japanese inn, this guesthouse has simple tatami rooms with the bare essentials. The owners, Mr. and Mrs. Takahashi, speak English and are a great help in planning trips off the beaten path. The inn is between Odawara Station and Togendai; take a bus from the station (Lane 4) and get off at the Senkyōro-mae stop. The family also operates the nearby Moto-Hakone Guest House (元箱根ゲストハウス). ⊠ *912 Sengoku-hara, Hakone, Kanagawa-ken 250-0631, 103 Moto-Hakone for Moto-Hakone Guest House* ☎ *0460/4–6577 for Fuji-Hakone, 0460/3–7880 for Moto-Hakone* ⊲ *12 Japanese-style rooms with bath in Fuji-Hakone, 5 Japanese-style rooms without bath in Moto-Hakone* ⬧ *Hot springs, Japanese baths* ▭ *AE, MC, V.*

Fuji Go-ko (Fuji Five Lakes, 富士五湖)

To the north of Mt. Fuji, the Fuji Go-ko area affords an unbeatable view of the mountain on clear days and makes the best base for a climb to the summit. With its various outdoor activities, from skating and fishing in winter to boating and hiking in summer, this is a popular resort area for families and business conferences.

The five lakes are, from the east, Yamanaka-ko, Kawaguchi-ko, Sai-ko, Shōji-ko, and Motosu-ko. Yamanaka and Kawaguchi are the largest and most developed as resort areas, with Kawaguchi more or less the centerpiece of the group. You can visit this area on a day trip from Tōkyō, but unless you want to spend most of it on buses and trains, plan on staying overnight.

12 **Kawaguchi-ko** (Lake Kawaguchi, 河口湖), a 5- to 10-minute walk from Kawaguchi-ko Station, is the most developed of the five lakes, ringed with weekend retreats and vacation lodges—many of them maintained by companies and universities for their employees. Excursion boats depart from a pier here on 30-minute tours of the lake. The promise, not always fulfilled, is to have two views of Mt. Fuji: one of the thing itself and the other inverted in its reflection on the water. A gondola along the shore of Lake Kawaguchi (near the pier) quickly brings you to the top of the 3,622-ft-tall **Tenjō-san** (Mt. Tenjo, 天上山). From the observatory here the whole of Lake Kawaguchi lies before you, and beyond the lake is a classic view of Mt. Fuji.

One of the little oddities at Lake Kawaguchi is the **Fuji Museum** (Fuji Hakubutsukan, 富士博物館). The first floor holds conventional exhibits of local geology and history, but upstairs is an astonishing collection of—for want of a euphemism—phalluses (you must be 18 or older to view the exhibit). Mainly made from wood and stone and carved in every shape and size, these figures played a role in certain local fertility festivals. The museum is on the north shore of the lake, next to the Fuji Lake Hotel. ⊠ *3964 Funatsu, Mizuminako, Kawaguchi-ko-machi* ☎ *0555/ 73–2266* 🎟 *1st fl. ¥200, 1st and 2nd fl. ¥500* ☺ *Mar.–Oct., daily 9–4; Nov.–Feb., Sat.–Thurs. 9–4; closed 3rd Tues. of month.*

☺ The largest of the recreational facilities at Lake Kawaguchi is the **Fuji-kyū Highland** (富士急ハイランド). It has an impressive assortment of rides, roller coasters, and other amusements, but it's probably not worth a visit unless you have children in tow. In winter there's superb skating here, with Mt. Fuji for a backdrop. Fuji-kyū Highland is about 15 minutes' walk east from Kawaguchi-ko Station. ⊠ *5–6–1 Shin Nishi Hara, Fu-jiyoshida-shi* ☎ *0555/23–2111* 🎟 *Full-day pass ¥4,300* ☺ *Weekdays 9–5, weekends 9–8.*

13 Buses from Kawaguchi-ko Station go to all the other lakes. The farthest west is **Motosu-ko** (Lake Motosu, 本栖湖), the deepest and clearest of the Fuji Go-ko, which takes about 50 minutes.

14 Many people consider **Shōji-ko** (Lake Shōji 精進湖), the smallest of the lakes, to be the prettiest—not least because it still has relatively little vacation-house development. The **Shōji Trail** (精進（湖畔）トレイル) leads from Lake Shōji to Mt. Fuji through Aoki-ga-hara (Sea of Trees), a forest with an underlying magnetic lava field that makes compasses go haywire. Any number of people go into Aoki-ga-hara every year and never come out, some of them on purpose—the forest seems to hold a morbid fascination for the Japanese as a place to commit suicide and disappear. If you're planning to climb Mt. Fuji from this trail, go with a guide.

15 **Sai-ko** (Lake Sai, 西湖), between Lakes Shōji and Kawaguchi, is the third-largest lake of the Fuji Go-ko, with only moderate development. From the western shore there is an especially good view of Mt. Fuji. Near Sai-ko there are two natural caves, an ice cave and a wind cave. You can either take a bus or walk to them.

⑯ The largest of the Fuji Go-ko is **Yamanaka-ko** (Lake Yamanaka, 山中湖), 35 minutes by bus to the southeast of Kawaguchi. Lake Yamanaka is the closest lake to the popular trail up Mt. Fuji that starts at Go-gōme, and many climbers use this resort area as a base.

Where to Stay

KAWAGUCHI-KO

$$$–$$$$

🏨 **Fuji View Hotel** (富士ビューホテル). This hotel on Lake Kawaguchi is a little threadbare but comfortable. The terrace lounge affords fine views of the lake and of Mt. Fuji beyond. The staff speaks English and is helpful in planning excursions. Many of the guests are on group excursions and take two meals—dinner and breakfast—in the hotel, but it's possible to opt for the room rate alone. Rates are significantly higher on weekends and in August. ✉ *511 Katsuyama-mura, Fuji-Kawaguchiko-machi, Yamanashi-ken 401-0310* ☎ *0555/83–2211* 📠 *0555/83–2128* ⊕ *www.fujiyahotel.co.jp* ⬤ *40 Western-style rooms with bath, 30 Japanese-style rooms with bath* ⚒ *2 restaurants, 9-hole golf course, 3 tennis courts, hot spring, boating* ▭ *AE, DC, MC, V* ⊙ *MAP.*

YAMANAKA-KO

$$

🏨 **Hotel Mount Fuji** (富士山ホテル). The best resort hotel on Lake Yamanaka, the Mount Fuji has all the facilities for a recreational holiday, and its guest rooms are larger than those at the other hotels on the lake. The lounges are spacious, and they have fine views of the lake and mountain. Rates are about 20% higher on weekends. ✉ *1360-83 Yamanaka, Yamanaka-ko-mura, Yamanashi-ken 403-0017* ☎ *0555/62–2111* ⬤ *153 Western-style rooms with bath, 4 Japanese-style rooms with bath* ⚒ *3 restaurants, 2 tennis courts, pool, hot springs, ice-skating* ▭ *AE, DC, MC, V.*

¢

🏨 **Inn Fujitomita** (旅館ふじとみた) One of the closest lodging options to the Mt. Fuji hiking trails, this inexpensive inn is a launching point for treks around the Fuji Go-ko area. Inn Fujitomita also has a swimming pool and tennis courts. The inn might not be much to look at from the outside, but the interior is spacious and homey. The staff speaks English and can help you plan an itinerary for visiting the area sights. Meals, including vegetarian options, are available at a very low price. Shuttle service is provided from Fuji Yoshida Station and the Lake Yamanaka bus stop. ✉ *13235 Shibokusa, Oshinomura, Minami-Tsuru-gun, Yamanashi-ken 401-105* ☎ *0555/84–3359* ⊕ *www.tim.hi-ho.ne.jp/innfuji/* ⬤ *10 Japanese-style rooms, 3 with bath* ⚒ *Dining room, 3 tennis courts, pool, hot springs, fishing, laundry facilities; no TV in some rooms* ▭ *AE, DC, MC, V.*

Fuji-san (Mt. Fuji, 富士山)

⑰

Fodor'sChoice

★

There are six routes to the summit of the 12,388-ft-high **Fuji-san** (Mt. Fuji 富士山), but only two, both accessible by bus, are recommended: from Go-gōme (Fifth Station), on the north side, and from Shin-Go-gōme (New Fifth Station), on the south. The climb to the summit from Go-gōme takes five hours and is the shortest way up; the descent takes three hours. From Shin-Go-gōme the ascent is slightly longer and stonier, but the way down, via the *sunabashiri* (砂走り), a volcanic sand slide, is faster. The quickest route is to ascend from Go-gōme and descend to Shin-Go-gōme via the sunabashiri.

The Climb

The ultimate experience of climbing Mt. Fuji is to reach the summit just before dawn and to greet the extraordinary sunrise. *Go-raikō* (The Honorable Coming of the Light [here *go* means "honorable"]), as the sunrise is called, has a mystical quality because the reflection shimmers across the sky just before the sun itself appears over the horizon. Mind you, there is no guarantee of seeing it: Mt. Fuji is often cloudy, even in the early morning.

The climb is taxing but not as hard as you might think scaling Japan's highest mountain would be. That said, the air *is* thin, and it *is* humiliating to struggle for the oxygen to take another step while some 83-year-old Japanese grandmother blithely leaves you in her dust (it happens: Japanese grannies are made of sterner stuff than most). Have no fear of losing the trail on either of the two main routes. Just follow the crowd—some 196,000 people make the climb during the official season, July 1–August 26 (outside of this season the weather is highly unpredictable and potentially dangerous, and climbing is strongly discouraged). In all, there are 10 stations to the top; you start at the fifth. There are stalls selling food and drinks along the way, but at exorbitant prices, so bring your own.

Also along the route are dormitory-style huts (about ¥7,000 with two meals, ¥5,000 without meals) where you can catch some sleep. A popular one is at the Hachi-gōme (Eighth Station), from which it's about a 90-minute climb to the top. However, these huts, which are open only in July and August, should be avoided at all costs. The food is vile, there's no fresh water, and the bedding is used by so many people and so seldom properly aired, you'd feel better sleeping on fish skins. Sensible folk leave the Go-gōme at midnight with good flashlights, climb through the night, and get to the summit just before dawn. Camping on the mountain is prohibited.

Be prepared for fickle weather around and atop the mountain. Summer days can be unbearably hot and muggy, and the nights can be a shocking contrast of freezing cold (bring numerous warm layers and be prepared to put them all on). Wear strong hiking shoes. The sun really burns at high altitudes, so wear protective clothing and a hat; gloves are a good idea, too. Use a backpack, as it keeps your hands free and serves a useful function on the way down: instead of returning to Go-gōme, descend to Shin-Go-gōme on the volcanic sand slide called the **sunabashiri** (砂走り)—sit down on your pack, push off, and away you go.

Fuji-Hakone-Izu National Park A to Z

To research prices, get advice from other travelers, and book travel arrangements, visit www.fodors.com.

BUS TRAVEL

Buses connect Tōkyō with the major gateway towns of this region, but except for the trip to Lake Kawaguchi or Mt. Fuji, the price advantage doesn't really offset the comfort and convenience of the trains. If you're interested only in climbing Mt. Fuji, take one of the daily buses directly to Go-gōme from Tōkyō; they run July through August and leave Shinjuku Station at 7:45, 8:45, 10:55, 4:50, 5:50, and 7:30. The last bus allows sufficient time for the tireless to make it to the summit before sunrise. The journey takes about 2 hours and 40 minutes from Shinjuku and costs ¥2,600. Reservations are required; book seats through the Fuji Kyūkō Highway Bus Reservation Center, the Keiō Highway Bus Reservation Center, the Japan Travel Bureau (which should have English-speaking staff), or any major travel agency.

To return from Mt. Fuji to Tōkyō, take an hour-long bus ride from Shin-Go-gōme to Gotemba (¥1,500). From Gotemba take the JR Tōkaidō and Gotemba lines to Tōkyō Station (¥1,890), or take the JR Line from Gotemba to Matsuda (¥480) and change to the private Odakyū Line from Shin-Matsuda to Shinjuku (¥750).

Direct bus service runs daily from Shinjuku Station in Tōkyō to Lake Kawaguchi every hour between 7:10 AM and 8:10 PM (¥1,700). Buses go from Kawaguchi-ko Station to Go-gōme (the fifth station on the climb up Mt. Fuji) in about an hour; there are eight departures a day (9:35, 10:10, 11:10, 12:10, 1:10, 2:10, 3:20, and 5:20) until the climbing season (July and August) starts, when there are 15 departures or more, depending on demand. The cost is ¥1,700.

From Lake Kawaguchi you can also take a bus to Gotemba, then change to another bus for Sengoku; from Sengoku there are frequent buses to Hakone-Yumoto, Togendai, and elsewhere in the Hakone region. On the return trip, three or four buses a day make the two-hour journey from Lake Kawaguchi to Mishima (¥2,130), skirting the western lakes and circling Mt. Fuji; at Mishima you can transfer to the JR Shinkansen Line for Tōkyō or Kyōto. A shorter bus ride (70 minutes, ¥1,470) goes from Lake Kawaguchi to Gotemba with a transfer to the JR local line.

From Lake Kawaguchi you can also connect to the Izu Peninsula. Take the bus to Mishima and from there go by train either to Shuzenji or Atami. From Shimoda, the end of the line on the private Izukyū Railway down the east coast of the Izu Peninsula, you must travel by bus around the southern cape to Dōgashima (¥1,360). From there another bus takes you up the west coast as far as Heda and then turns inland to Shuzenji. From Shimoda, you can also take a bus directly north to Shuzenji through the Amagi Mountains (one departure daily at 10:45 AM, ¥2,180). The Tōkai Bus Company covers the west coast and central mountains of the Izu area well with local service; buses are not especially frequent, but they do provide the useful option of just hopping off and exploring if you happen to see something interesting from the window. Whatever your destination, always check the time of the last departure to make sure that you are not left stranded.

Within the Hakone area, buses run every 15–30 minutes from Hakone-machi to Hakone-Yumoto Station on the private Odakyū Line (40 minutes, ¥930), and Odawara Station (one hour, ¥1,150), where you can take either the Odakyū Romance Car back to Shinjuku Station or

206 < **Side Trips from Tōkyō**

a JR Shinkansen to Tōkyō Station. The buses are covered by the Hakone Free Pass.

🚌 Bus Information **Fuji Kyūkō Highway Bus Reservation Center** ☎ 03/5376-2222. **Keiō Highway Bus Reservation Center** ☎ 03/5376-2222. **Japan Travel Bureau** ☎ 03/3284-7605 ⊕ www.jtb.co.jp/eng. **Tōkai Bus Company** ☎ 0557/36-1112 for main office, 0557/22-2511 Shimoda Information Center.

CAR TRAVEL

Having your own car makes sense only for touring the Izu Peninsula, and only then if you're prepared to cope with less-than-ideal road conditions, lots of traffic (especially on holiday weekends), and the paucity of road markers in English. It takes some effort—but exploring the peninsula *is* a lot easier by car than by public transportation. From Tōkyō take the Tōmei Expressway as far as Ōi-matsuda (about 84 km [52 mi]); then pick up Routes 255 and 135 to Atami (approximately 28 km [17 mi]). From Atami drive another 55 km (34 mi) or so down the east coast of the Izu Peninsula to Shimoda.

One way to save yourself some trouble is to book a car through the Nippon or Toyota rental agency in Tōkyō and arrange to pick it up at the Shimoda branch. You can then simply take a train to Shimoda and use it as a base. From Shimoda you can drive back up the coast to Kawazu (35 minutes) and then to Shuzenji (30 minutes).

🚗 **Nippon Interrent** ☎ 03/3469-0919. **Toyota Rent-a-Car** ☎ 0070/800-0100 toll-free, 03/5954-8008 8 ᴀᴍ-8 ᴘᴍ.

DISCOUNTS & DEALS

For the Hakone area, the best way to get around is with a Hakone Free Pass, issued by the privately owned Odakyū Railways and valid for three days. This coupon ticket (¥5,500 from Shinjuku Station in Tōkyō) covers the train fare to Hakone and allows you to use any mode of transportation in the Hakone area, including the Hakone Tōzan Railway, the Hakone Tōzan bus, the Hakone Ropeway, the Hakone Cruise Boat, and the Sōun-zan cable car.

If you have a JR Pass, it's cheaper to take a Kodama Shinkansen from Tōkyō Station to Odawara and buy the Hakone Free Pass there (¥4,130) for travel within the Hakone region only.

TOURS

Once you are on the Izu Peninsula itself, sightseeing excursions by boat are available from several picturesque small ports. From Dōgashima you can take the Dōgashima Marine short (20 minutes, ¥920) or long (45 minutes, ¥1,240) tours of Izu's rugged west coast. The Fujikyū Kōgyō company operates a daily ferry to Hatsu-shima from Atami (25 minutes, ¥2,340 round-trip) and another to the island from Itō (23 minutes, ¥1,150). Izukyū Marine offers a 40-minute tour (¥1,530) by boat from Shimoda to the coastal rock formations at Irō-zaki.

Sunrise Tours operates a tour to Hakone, including a cruise across Lake Ashi and a trip on the gondola over Ōwaku-dani (¥15,000 includes lunch and return to Tōkyō by Shinkansen; ¥12,000 includes lunch and return to Tōkyō by bus). Sunrise tours depart daily from Tōkyō's Hamamatsu-chō Bus Terminal and some major hotels.

🎫 **Dōgashima Marine** ☎ 0558/52-0013. **Fujikyū Kōgyō** ☎ 0557/81-0541. **Izukyū Marine** ☎ 0558/22-1151. **Sunrise Tours** ☎ 03/5796-5454 🖹 03/5495-0680 🌐 www.jtb.co.jp/sunrisetour.

TRAIN TRAVEL

Trains are by far the easiest and fastest ways to get to the Fuji-Hakone-Izu National Park area. The gateway stations of Atami, Odawara, and Kawaguchi-ko are well served by comfortable express trains from Tōkyō, on both JR and private railway lines. These in turn connect to local trains and buses that can get you anywhere in the region you want to go. Call the JR Higashi-Nihon Info Line (10–6 daily, except December 31–January 3) for assistance in English.

The *Kodama* Shinkansen from Tōkyō to Atami costs ¥3,880 and takes 51 minutes; JR Passes are valid. The JR local from Atami to Itō takes 25 minutes and costs ¥320. Itō and Atami are also served by the JR Odoriko Super Express (not a Shinkansen train). The Tōkyō–Itō run takes 1¾ hours and costs ¥4,190; you can also use a JR Pass. The privately owned Izukyū Railways, on which JR Passes are not valid, makes the Itō–Shimoda run in one hour for ¥1,570.

The Izu–Hakone Railway Line runs from Tōkyō to Mishima (1 hour, 36 minutes; ¥4,090), with a change at Mishima for Shuzenji (31 minutes, ¥500); this is the cheapest option if you don't have a JR Pass. With a JR Pass, a Shinkansen–Izu Line combination will save about 35 minutes and will be the cheapest option. The Tōkyō–Mishima Shinkansen leg (62 minutes) costs ¥4,400; the Mishima–Shuzenji Izu Line leg (31 minutes) costs ¥500.

Trains depart every 12 minutes from Tōkyō's Shinjuku Station for Odawara in the Hakone area. The ¥5,500 Hakone Free Pass, which you can buy at the station, covers the train fare. Reservations are required for the upscale Romance Car, with comfortable seats and big observation windows, to Hakone (an extra ¥870 with Hakone Free Pass). The Romance Car goes one stop beyond Odawara to Hakone-Yumoto; buy tickets at any Odakyū Travel Service counter or major travel agency, or call the Odakyū Reservation Center. Note that beyond Hakone-Yumoto you must use the privately owned Hakone Tōzan Tetsudō Line or buses.

The transportation hub, as well as one of the major resort areas in the Fuji Five Lakes area, is Kawaguchi-ko. Getting there from Tōkyō requires a change of trains at Ōtsuki. The JR Chūō Line Kaiji and Azusa express trains leave Shinjuku Station for Ōtsuki on the half hour from 7 AM to 8 PM (more frequently in the morning) and take approximately one hour. At Ōtsuki, change to the private Fuji-Kyūkō Line for Kawaguchi-ko, which takes another 50 minutes. The total traveling time is about two hours, and you can use your JR Pass as far as Ōtsuki; otherwise, the fare is ¥1,280. The Ōtsuki–Kawaguchi-ko leg costs ¥1,110. Also available are two direct service rapid trains for Kawaguchi-ko that leave Tōkyō in the morning at 6:08 and 7:10 on weekdays, 6:09 and 7:12 on weekends and national holidays.

The Holiday Kaisoku Picnic-gō, available on weekends and national holidays, offers direct express service from Shinjuku, leaving at 8:10 and arriving at Kawaguchi-ko Station at 10:37. From March through August, JR puts on additional weekend express trains for Kawaguchi-ko, but be aware that on some of them only the first three cars go all the way to the lake. Coming back, you have a choice of late-afternoon departures from Kawaguchi-ko that arrive at Shinjuku in the early evening. Check the express timetables before you go; you can also call either the JR Higashi-Nihon Info Line or Fuji-kyūukō Kawaguchi-ko Station for train information.

🚆 Train Information **Fuji-kyūukō Kawaguchi-ko Station (0555/72-0017). Hakone Tōzan Railway** ☎ 0465/24-2115. **Izu-Hakone Railway** ☎ 0465/77-1200. **Izukyū Corporation** ☎ 0557/53-1111 for main office, 0558/22-3202 Izukyū Shimoda Station **JR Higashi-Nihon Info Line** ☎ 03/3423-0111. **Odakyū Reservation Center** ☎ 03/3481-0130.

VISITOR INFORMATION
Few of these visitor centers have staff members who speak fluent English, but you can still pick up local maps and pamphlets, as well as information on low-cost inns, pensions, and guesthouses.

🏛 Tourist Information **Atami Tourist Association** ✉ 12-1 Ginza-chō, Atami-shi ☎ 0557/85-2222. **Fuji-Kawaguchiko Tourist Association** ✉ 890 Funatsu, Kawakuchiko-machi, Minami-Tsurugun ☎ 0555/72-2460. **Hakone-machi Tourist Association** ✉ 698 Yūmoto, Hakone-machi ☎ 0460/5-8911. **Nishi-Izu Tourist Office** ✉ Dogashima, Nishi-Izu-chō, Kamo-gu ☎ 0558/52-1268. **Shimoda Tourist Association** ✉ 1-1 Soto-ga-oka, Shimoda-shi ☎ 0558/22-1531.

NAGOYA, ISE-SHIMA & THE KII PENINSULA

名古屋、伊勢志摩、紀伊半島

3

By John Malloy
Quinn

Updated by
Paul Davidson

JAPAN'S FOURTH-LARGEST CITY, Nagoya purrs along most contentedly, burdened neither by a second-city complex nor by hordes of tourists. Sometimes given a bad rap or dismissed altogether as an unattractive, industry-bent sprawl of concrete, Nagoya in fact has the capacity to pleasantly surprise any visitor who can give it the time.

There is indeed a fair amount of history here, despite the fact that you first notice the bright white skyscrapers sprouting from the ultramodern station—almost a city in itself. An extensive underground network of shopping malls stretches outward in all directions below the wide, clean streets. Prices are very reasonable, and the variety of goods is astounding.

Prosperous locals and comfortable foreign residents alike will tell you that although Nagoya is undeniably a big and hardworking city, it has a certain small-town feel to it. "Stay awhile, and you know *everyone*," they might say. The laid-back and cheerful attitude provides a refreshing contrast to the endless bustle and impersonality of most large cities.

Within two hours' drive of the city you can find Ise-Shima National Park, the revered Grand Shrines of Ise, and the remarkable temple-mountain, Kōya-san. On the untamed Kii Peninsula, steep-walled gorges and forested headlands give way to pristine bays. Fine sandy beaches await in Shirahama, and inland is Yoshino-san, justly famous for its unmatched display of cherry blossoms. Add to all of this the traditional arts of Gifu and Seki, and you have more than enough reasons to visit this corner of Japan.

See the glossary at the end of this book for definitions of the common Japanese words and suffixes used in this chapter.

Exploring Nagoya, Ise-Shima & the Kii Peninsula

After a day or two in Nagoya, take a ride out of the city to see fishing with cormorants in Inuyama, pottery making in Tajimi, and lantern and sword making in Gifu. If you're visiting between March 25 and September 25, 2005, don't miss a visit to the 2005 World Expo in the hills east of Nagoya. For a longer excursion, visit the Grand Shrines of Ise, the Shima Peninsula, and the Kii Peninsula, including Kōya-san and Yoshino-san. A logical place to end your tour is Nara, which is covered in Chapter 6.

About the Restaurants & Hotels

Restaurants in Nagoya and on the peninsulas, except for in the resort areas, are slightly less expensive than in Tokyo. As anywhere in Japan, your cheapest options are the noodle shops, *donburi* (rice bowl) chains, and curry houses. Franchised restaurants tend to have English menus even in smaller towns, but don't expect the staff to know more than a few words in English.

Nagoya has all types of lodging, from *ryokan* (traditional Japanese inns) to efficient business hotels to large luxury palaces. Temples are another lodging option, especially if you are heading to Kōya-san. Furnishings in temples are rather spartan, but sufficient, and the food in temples may be strictly vegetarian. Also note that you may be expected to attend morning prayer service, although you certainly won't be

Nagoya's sights can be seen in a day, and its cosmopolitan atmosphere deserves at least a one-night stay. Tajimi, a major ceramics center, is a short jaunt from the city. The unique tradition of fishing with cormorants may be still observed at Gifu or Inuyama. Kōya-san's mystical temple complex exudes an almost supernatural spirituality, and a visit to nearby Yoshino-san in cherry-blossom season is highly recommended.

Numbers in the text correspond to numbers in the margin and on the Nagoya and the South Gifu-ken, Ise-Shima, and the Kii Peninsula maps.

3

**If you have
3 days**

If you're visiting here between March 25 and September 25, 2005, be sure to visit the **2005 World Expo** in the hill towns east of Nagoya. Take another day to visit 🗺 **Inuyama** ⑩, perhaps stopping in **Tajimi** ⑪ on the way. In Tajimi you can visit the factory outlets, observe some kilns, and even make your own pottery. In Inuyama, see the castle and in the evening enjoy u-kai. Use 🗺 **Nagoya** ① ⌐ – ⑧ as a base and try to allocate half a day to see its most important sights. If you're not going to the Expo or have more time, take a trip to **Kōya-san.**

**If you have
7 days**

Start your trip with a full day and night in 🗺 **Nagoya** ① ⌐ – ⑧, covering the castle, the Tokugawa Art Museum, Atsuta Jingū, and the Noritake China Factory to see the making of porcelain. On the next day go up to 🗺 **Gifu** ⑨ to visit the umbrella- and lantern-making shops. Include the Shangyo Shinko Center in Seki on your tour if sword-making demonstrations are occurring that day—usually the first Sunday of the month—or **Tajimi** ⑪ for some fun with ceramics. The next stop is 🗺 **Inuyama** ⑩ with its original castle and great strolls down by the Kiso-gawa. Enjoy a ceremonial tea at the Jo-an Teahouse. If you're here during u-kai, be sure to take in the spectacle. On the next day return to Nagoya to change trains for **Ise** ⑫ and a visit to venerated Ise Jingū, one of Japan's three most important Shintō shrines. For the fourth night continue out onto the peninsula to **Toba** ⑬, home of Mikimoto pearls, and the fishing town of 🗺 **Kashikojima** ⑭. On your fifth day backtrack north to Taki to pick up the train to 🗺 **Shingū** ⑯, where you can spend the night after taking a river trip through **Doro-kyō** ⑰. If you have time, the falls near **Nachi** ⑱ should not be missed. On Day 6 take a four-hour bus ride north to 🗺 **Yoshino-san** ㉓ first thing in the morning. This is a particularly worthy inclusion at cherry-blossom time, if you can stand crowds or get up early enough the next day to beat them. On Day 7 take a train to Hashimoto and on to 🗺 **Kōya-san** ㉒ and plan to spend the night at a Buddhist temple. From Kōya-san it's easy to reach Kyōto, Nara, and Ōsaka.

**If you have
9 days**

Keep to the seven-day itinerary as far as 🗺 **Kashikojima** ⑭. Then on the way down the peninsula, you could stop for the night in the town of **Owase** ⑮. Or skip Owase and spend the extra time taking in the spectacular sights and sounds of Nachi-no-taki (Nachi Falls), an easy bus ride from **Nachi** ⑱. Just south from there, you can stop off and enjoy one or more of the fine hot springs in the area, such as Katsuura or Yukawa. Continue along the coast of the Kii Peninsula to spend a night or two at the spa and beach resort of 🗺 **Shirahama** ㉑. From there, via Wakayama, go to 🗺 **Kōya-san** ㉒ for a full 24 hours in and around the monasteries. Then go to 🗺 **Yoshino-san** ㉓ for the next night before exiting the region by taking the train to Nara.

pressed into following the faith. In short, staying in a temple can be a fascinating experience. Unless otherwise noted, you can expect to find private baths, air-conditioning, and basic TV in all rooms.

For a short course on accommodations in Japan, *see* Lodging *in* Smart Travel Tips A to Z.

WHAT IT COSTS In yen				
$$$$	$$$	$$	$	¢
RESTAURANTS over 3,000	2,000–3,000	1,000–2,000	800–1,000	under 800
HOTELS over 22,000	18,000–22,000	12,000–18,000	8,000–12,000	under 8,000

Restaurant prices are per person for a main course at dinner. Hotel prices are for a double room with private bath, excluding service and tax.

Timing

Springtime throughout Japan is the most popular season for travel, especially so when cherry trees bloom in early to mid-April. The weather can be sunny and warm but nowhere near as hot as it can get in late July and August. Autumn is another popular season, especially on the Kii Peninsula, where the Pacific Ocean stays warm and the trees turn their fall colors under bright blue skies. Winter can still be quite warm and sunny in coastal Wakayama-ken, and to a lesser extent, in Mie-ken, so don't be overly afraid of visiting at that time, either. If you can visit the area between March 25 and September 25, 2005, you'll have the chance to go to the 2005 World Expo.

NAGOYA 名古屋

By Shinkansen, 1½–2 hrs west of Tōkyō, 1 hr east of Ōsaka, 40 min east of Kyōto.

During the Tokugawa period (1603–1868), Nagoya was already an important stop on the Tōkaidō post road between Kyōto and Edo (Tōkyō). In 1612 Ieyasu Tokugawa established Nagoya town by permitting his ninth son to build a castle. In the shadow of this magnificent fortress, industry and merchant houses sprang up, as did pleasure quarters for samurai. As a result, the town quickly grew in strategic importance. Supported by taxing the rich harvests of the vast surrounding Nōbi plain, the Tokugawa family used the castle as its power center for the next 250 years. By the early 1800s Nagoya's population had grown to around 100,000. Although it was smaller than Edo, where the million-plus population surpassed even that of Paris, Nagoya had become as large as the more established cities of Kanazawa and Sendai.

With the Meiji Restoration in 1868, when Japan began trade with the West in earnest and embraced Western ideas and technology, Nagoya developed rapidly. In 1889, with a population of 157,000, it became a city. When the harbor opened to international shipping in 1907, Nagoya's industrial growth accelerated. By the 1930s it was supporting Japanese expansionism in China with munitions and aircraft. The choice of in-

Castles

Nagoya has a large castle, and although a replica, it's a beautiful one. North of Nagoya, in the town of Inuyama, you can find the genuine ancient article, and its views out over the city and the Kiso-gawa delight those who climb its steep and narrow wooden staircases to the original interior.

Outdoor Activities

Beyond Nagoya many outdoor diversions await. In Gifu city and Inuyama, look for *u-kai,* fishing with cormorants. Gifu's season runs from mid-May to mid-October, and Inuyama's is from June through September. It's great fun if not a particularly active endeavor: the birds are on leashes and do all the work catching the fish. Inuyama also has riverboat rides down the Kiso-gawa. Placid rafting, through steep, green gorges filled with mineral-tinted water, can be done on the Kii Peninsula at Doro-kyō (Doro Gorge). The highest waterfall in Japan is near Nachi. Fine scenery and hiking are possibilities in Owase. For swimming, the most popular beach in the region is at Shirahama, but beautiful bays, lovely beaches, and rocky coves can be found on the Kii Peninsula's entire coast.

3

Shopping

Craftspeople in and around Nagoya produce several unique items, such as cloisonné, *paulownia* (wood chests), and tie-dyed fabrics. Nagoya is home to the world's largest producer of porcelain, Noritake. The nearby towns of Seto and Tajimi have famous ceramics traditions as well—and factory outlets. In Gifu you can buy paper lanterns and umbrellas. In Seki the traditional skill in forging samurai swords is still practiced. Toba, on the Shima-hantō (Shima Peninsula), is where, in 1893, Kōkichi Mikimoto perfected the technique for harvesting pearl-bearing oysters in 1893.

Temples & Shrines

There's no shortage of religious architecture on the Shima and Kii peninsulas, but two Buddhist temple complexes, Kōya-san and Yoshino-san, are exceptional. Kōya-san, founded in 816, is the more popular of the two. To get a real sense of the place, spend a night at one of its temples.

South of Nagoya are the Grand Shrines of Ise. The shrines, rebuilt every 20 years for the last 1,500 years, are among the most sacred in Japan. Nai-kū, the Inner Shrine, is the home of worship to Amaterasu, the sun goddess and highest Shintō deity.

---

dustry was Nagoya's downfall: very little of the city was left standing by the time the Japanese surrendered unconditionally, on August 14, 1945.

Less than two months after the war's end, ambitious and extensive reconstruction plans were laid, and Nagoya began its remarkable comeback as an industrial metropolis. Today the fourth-largest city in Japan, Nagoya bustles with 2.2 million people living in a 520-square-km (200-square-mi) area. Industry is still booming, with shipbuilding, food processing, and the manufacture of textiles, ceramics, machine tools,

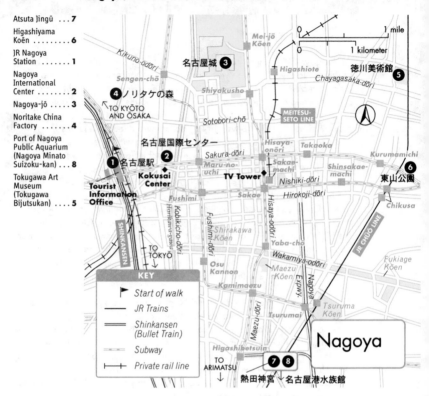

automobiles, railway rolling stock, even aircraft. Nagoya Port sees as much trade as ports in Yokohama and Kōbe.

When they rebuilt Nagoya after the war, urban planners laid down a grid system, with wide avenues intersecting at right angles. Hisaya-odōri, a broad avenue with a park in its 328-ft-wide median, bisects the city. At Nagoya's center, an imposing 590-ft-high television tower (useful for getting your bearings) stands as a symbol of modernity. Nagoya-jō is north of the tower, Atsuta Jingū is to the south, Kenchū-ji is to the east, and the JR station is to the west. The Sakae subway station serves as the center of the downtown commercial area, and a second commercial area is next to the JR station.

1 **JR Nagoya Station** (名古屋駅) is like a small city in itself, with a variety of shops in, under, and around the station complex. Look for the big red question-mark icon to find the **Tourist Information Center** (TIC; ☎ 052/541–4301) in the middle of JR Nagoya Station's central corridor, open daily from 8:30 to 6:45. The **Japan Travel Bureau** (☎ 052/563–0041) also has a branch here. ⊠ *4–6–18 Eki-mae, Nagoya Building 1st fl., Nakamura-ku.*

2 The **Nagoya International Center** (名古屋国際センター), or Kokusai Sentā as it's known locally, is a wise stop on any foreigner's Nagoya itinerary. Venture one stop from the JR station on the Sakura-dōri Subway Line to the Kokusai Sentā Station (or take the seven-minute walk through the underground walkway that follows the line), and the center's friendly, multilingual staff will provide you with a wealth of info on Nagoya. You can also get your hands on brochures in several languages about wherever in Japan you might be heading next. ⊠ *47–1 Sakura-dōri, Nagono 1-chōme, Nakamura-ku* ☎*052/581–0100* ☾ *Tues.–Sat. 9–8:30, Sun. 9–5.*

❸ Originally constructed by Ieyasu Tokugawa for one of his sons in 1612, **Nagoya-jō** (名古屋城) was severely damaged in 1945 and in 1959 was rebuilt of reinforced concrete. The castle as it stands is notable for its impressive size and for the pair of gold-plated dolphins—one male, one female—mounted atop the *tenshukaku* (principal keep). Inside the castle a museum houses collections of armor, paintings, and Tokugawa family treasures salvaged from the original structure. Instead of there being the usual narrow, steep wooden staircases, an elevator whisks you between floors. Inside the east gate of Nagoya-jō, **Ninomaru Tei-en** (Ninomaru Gardens) has a traditional teahouse built of *hinoki* (Japanese cypress), surrounded by peaceful gardens. A traditional tea ceremony costs ¥500.

To get here by bus from Nagoya Station, take the Nishi-ku 2 bus and get off at Nagoya-jō Seimon-mae (Main Gate). By subway, go to the Shiyakusho (City Hall) station on the Meijō Line, which is on the Higashiyama and Sakura-dōri lines from the JR station. Nagoya-jō's east gate is one block north of the subway exit. ☎ *052/231–1700* 🎫 *¥500* ☾ *Daily 9:30–4:30; tenshukaku closes at 4:10.*

❹ Delicate colors and intricate hand-painted designs characterize the china of Noritake, the world's largest manufacturer of porcelain. A free, informative tour of the **Noritake China Factory** (ノリタケの森) is given at 10 and 1 by an English-speaking guide, and a short film about the porcelain is also shown. Make a reservation in advance and allow 1–1½ hours for the tour. If you're interested in watching potters at work, or if you'd like to try making some pottery yourself, head over to the craft center. At the company shop, in front of the north gate, you aren't likely to find any serious bargains, but you may discover pieces not available elsewhere. The factory is a 15-minute walk north of JR Nagoya Station or five minutes from the Kamejima subway station (one stop north of the JR station on the Higashiyama Line) and is closed the second Sunday of each month. ☎ *052/561–7290* 🎫 *Factory free, craft center and museum ¥500* ⊠ *1–36 Mei-eki dōri 3-chōme, north of Kikui-dōri, Noritake-Shin-machi, Nishi-ku* ☎ *052/561–7114 factory, 052/572–5072 shop* ☾ *Factory weekdays 10–4, shop Tues.–Sun. 9–5.*

★ ❺ Because the pieces in the **Tokugawa Art Museum** (Tokugawa Bijutsukan, 徳川美術館) are so valuable, the museum displays only a portion of the more than 20,000 art objects, heirlooms, and furnishings at any one time. Most of the relics were handed down from the Tokugawa family to their descendants, the Owari clan, before becoming a part of the collection. The 12th-century hand scrolls illustrating *The Tale of Genji* have been designated a National Treasure. If you're visiting specifically to see the scrolls, telephone the museum to make sure they are on display. If not, look for the photos and a later incarnation of the scrolls in Room 6 of the museum.

From Sakae Station, take the Meitetsu Seto Line; from Nagoya Station, take either the Meijō Line or the JR Chūō Line to the Ōzone station, from which you can walk about 10 minutes south. Your other option is to catch a bus from the Green No. 7 stop at the Eki-mae bus station (or the Shiyakusho stop across from Nagoya-jō) to the Shindeki bus stop, then walk three minutes north. ⊠ *1017 Tokugawa-chō, Higashi-ku* ☎ *052/935–6262* ☑ *¥1,200* ☺ *Tues.–Sun. 10–5.*

❻ **Higashiyama Kōen** (Higashiyama Park, 東山公園), a huge expanse of green, encompasses a zoo, botanical gardens, amusement park rides, and a sky tower, offering welcome respite (with a view) from city air, traffic, and noise. The food in the tower restaurant is unspectacular, but it's not a bad place to sit and refuel. Best of all, the park is only 16 minutes from Nagoya Station. To get there, take the Higashiyama Line to the Higashiyama-kōen station. ☎ *052/782–2111 zoo and botanical gardens, 052/781–5586 sky tower* ☑ *Zoo and botanical gardens ¥500, sky tower ¥500* ☺ *Zoo and botanical gardens Tues.–Sun. 9–4:30; sky tower Tues.–Sun. 9–9:30; tower restaurant Tues.–Sun. 9–9.*

❼ For 1,700 years a shrine has stood at the site of **Atsuta Jingū** (熱田神宮). After Ise, Atsuta Jingū is the second most important shrine in the country. The **Hōmotsukan** (Treasure House) holds one of the emperor's three imperial regalia—the Kusanagi-no-Tsurugi (Grass-Mowing Sword). Nestled among trees more than 1,000 years old, the shrine is an oasis of tradition in the midst of bustling, modern industrialism. Sixty festivals and 10 religious events are held here each year—check with the tourist office to see what's on when you're coming. From Nagoya Station take the Higashiyama Line east to Sakae Station; then take the Meijō Line south to Jingū-nishi Station. ☎ *052/671–4151* ☑ *Shrine free, Treasure Museum ¥300* ☺ *Daily 9–4; closed last Wed. and Thurs. of month.*

❽ **Port of Nagoya Public Aquarium** (Nagoya-Kō Suizoku-kan, 名古屋港水族館). This is not your average fish tank; practically everything that swims is present. One of the largest in Japan, the aquarium is known especially for its Antarctic Zone. To get here, take the Meijō Line south from Sakae to Nagoya-kō (Nagoya Port). ⊠ *1–3 Minato-machi, Minato-ku* ☎ *052/654–7080* ☑ *¥2,000* ☺ *Apr.–mid-July and Sept.–Nov., Tues.–Sun. 9:30–5:30; mid-July–Aug., Tues.–Sun. 9:30–8; Dec.–Mar., Tues.–Sun. 9:30–5.*

off the beaten path

ARIMATSU CLOTH DYEING VILLAGE (Arimatsu Narumi Shibori Mura, 有松鳴海絞村) – This village once flourished as a *shibori* (tie-dyed cotton) production center, and more than 10 dye houses are still active. At Arimatsu Narumi Shibori Kaikan, you can learn about the history and techniques of the dyeing process and buy exquisite samples of the cloth, which often features striking, alive-looking bright white designs on the deepest indigo. For ¥1,050 you can make your own handkerchief. Arimatsu Station is 25 minutes south of

THE 2005 WORLD EXPOSITION

IFTEEN MILLION VISITORS *are expected to pass through the Aichi region east of Nagoya during the much-anticipated 2005 World Expo, taking place March 25 through September 25. Consisting of landscaped grounds and hundreds of pavilions, the Expo is divided into three major areas in the hill towns of Nagakute, Toyota, and Seto. More than 125 countries, including Cuba, Germany, Iran, South Korea, and Thailand, signed on to participate.*

The pavillions are hosted by countries to showcase exhibits about their particular scientific, technological, social, and cultural advances. In the United States' pavilion, for example, visitors are invited to a watch an audio-visual presentation emceed by Benjamin Franklin, back for his 300th birthday to see what sort of progress America has made. In the Saudi Arabia pavilion, visitors can learn about Islam and the efforts of muslims to promote peace, as well as Saudi Arabian architecture, water

desalinization projects, and the petrochemical industry. In keeping with the theme of the Expo, "Nature's Wisdom," exhibits also look at how progress has interfered with nature and the earth's resources. Each sponsor and participating country examines the ways in which we can protect our environment. The hope is that the Expo will serve as a forum for the meeting of minds and exchange of ideas, fostering communication and cooperation among nations.

One-day adult tickets cost ¥4,100 ($40); substantial discounts are available for kids and for tickets purchased in advance. From Nagoya, train and bus lines connect with the Aichi loop, a 2.6 km (1.6 mi) walkway encircling the site. Environment-friendly trams, gondolas, and hydrogen-powered buses shuttle people between the Expo's main areas. Visit www.expo2005.or.jp for more information.

— *Emmanuelle Alspaugh*

Nagoya on the Meitetsu Nagoya Line. ⊠ *60–1 Arimatsu-hashi Higashi-minami, Midori-ku* ☎ *052/621–0111* ⊠ *Free* ⊙ *Thurs.–Tues. 9–4.*

Hiking

Tado-san Tenbō Course (多度山展望コース). If you seek the refreshment and scenery of a hike—and have four to five hours to spare—consider this 14-km (9-mi) loop up to the green plateau of Tado Sanjō Park, then down through maple-lined Tado-kyō (Tado Gorge). The trail begins as a series of switchbacks to the northwest. From the top of the trail, continue west and downhill to meet and follow the river south and then back east, ending where you started. To get there from JR Nagoya station, take the Kintetsu or JR train southwest to Kuwana Station, and then go north on the local line to Tado Station in neighboring Mie Prefecture. The train ride is 35 minutes. Then walk northwest of Tado Station, cross the river, and head north toward Uga Shrine. ⊠ *Mie-ken, Kuwana-kun, Tado-chō.*

Where to Stay & Eat

Nagoya's hotels are concentrated in three major areas: the district around JR Nagoya Station, downtown, and the Nagoya-jō area.

$$$$ ✕**Kisoji** (木曽路). Come here for reasonably priced (¥4,500) *shabu-shabu*—thinly sliced beef and vegetables boiled in broth at your table. Sushi and sashimi are also on offer, with set courses running from ¥5,000 to ¥7,000. There are Western-style tables and chairs, but waitresses wear kimonos. Private tatami rooms are available by reservation. ⊠ *3–20–15 Nishiki-chō, Naka-ku* ☎ *052/951–3755* ▭ *AE, MC, V.*

★ **$$** ✕**Ibashō** (いば昇). This restaurant serves a specialty of Nagoya, *hitsumabushi*, or local eel, which locals claim is far superior to that of other areas of the country. It really is good, and Westerners who overcome their reservations can taste a true reflection of Japanese culture. At Ibashō, you can try hitsumabushi smothered in miso sause and served in a rice bowl. ⊠ *3–13–22 Nishiki, Naka-ku* ☎ *052/951–1166* ▭ *No credit cards.*

$–$$$ ✕**Jin-maru Nishina** (じんまる Nishina). Locals come here to eat and drink at reasonable prices. Whether you relax at the bar, tatami-seating, or tables, the atmosphere is lively and friendly. Everything from Korean-style kimchi dishes to Taiwan-style noodles is served, along with superb sashimi and draft beers. You can drink all you want for ¥1,500. ⊠ *Tōkyō Kaijō Bldg., 1st fl., 23-34 Sakae 1-chōme, Naka-ku* ☎ *052/203–5885* ▭ *No credit cards.*

$ ✕**Yamamotoya Honke** (山本屋本家). Nothing but *misonikomi-udon*—udon noodles in a hearty, miso-based broth with green onions and mushrooms—is served at this simple restaurant. A big, steaming bowl of this hearty, cold-chasing specialty can be had for just ¥850. ⊠ *3–12–19 Sakae, Naka-ku* ☎ *052/241–5617* ▭ *No credit cards.*

$$$$ 🏨**Nagoya Hilton** (ヒルトン名古屋). Soft live music, which accompanies the nightly dessert buffet, drifts into the cavernous lobby of the Hilton, giving it an intimate feel. Pink granite with gold accents and live trees help fill the space. Light pink, green, and gold decorate the large guest rooms as well, complementing the light-wood furnishings and translucent *shoji* (window screens). Views from the 28th-floor Sky Lounge are magnificent. The staff is friendly and multilingual, and the hotel is only five minutes by taxi from Nagoya Station. ⊠ *3–3 Sakae 1-chōme, Naka-ku, Nagoya, Aichi-ken 460-0008* ☎ *052/212–1111* 🖷 *052/212–1225* ⊕ *www.hilton.com* ⤶ *422 rooms, 28 Western-style and Japanese-style suites* ⚹ *3 restaurants, coffee shop, room service, in-room data ports, minibars, cable TV, tennis court, indoor pool, health club, sauna, shops, laundry services, concierge floor, business services* ▭ *AE, DC, MC, V.*

$$$$
Fodor's Choice
★

🏨**Nagoya Kankō Hotel** (名古屋観光ホテル). The Imperial Family and professional ballplayers are among those regularly served by this, the oldest hotel in Nagoya. A lavish renovation put the well-located, upmarket Nagoya Kankō at the top of the ranks with savvy travelers willing to spend a little extra for lots of class and character. White-brick walls give the lobby a stark, contemporary look tempered by soft-tone carpets and dark-wood furnishings. The breakfast buffet in the tearoom is a particularly good value, at only ¥1,000. ⊠ *19–30 Nishiki 1-chōme, Naka-ku, Nagoya, Aichi-ken 460-8608* ☎ *052/231–7711* 🖷 *052/231–7719* ⊕ *www.nagoyakankohotel.co.jp* ⤶ *375 rooms, 7 suites* ⚹ *5 restaurants, room service, in-room data ports, in-room fax, in-room safes, minibars, cable TV, massage, bar, dry cleaning, laundry services, shops, concierge, business services, parking (fee)* ▭ *AE, DC, MC, V.*

★ **$$$–$$$$** 🏯 **Westin Nagoya Castle** (ホテルキャッスルプラザ). A top-notch, reasonably priced hotel, the Westin has more amenities than most in its price range, including an indoor pool and a fitness center. The Japanese-style rooms are slightly larger than the Western-style rooms, but the latter were renovated in the summer of 2004. The hotel stands at the bank of the Nagoya Castle moat, and your room might overlook the beautiful white castle, which is illuminated at night. Rooms on the other side of the hotel overlook the downtown area. Ten on-site restaurants serve Japanese, Chinese, and various other kinds of food. The hotel is about a 10-minute walk from Nagoya Station. ⊠ *3-19 Hinokuchi-chō, Nishi-ku, Nagoya, Aichi-ken 451-855* ☎ *052/582–2121* 🖷 *052/531–3313* ⊕ *www.westin.com* ⤵ *220 Western-style rooms, 5 suites* ⇩ *3 restaurants, in-room data ports, minibars, cable TV, indoor pool, hair salon, gym, sauna, shop, 2 bars, concierge, business services, meeting rooms, free parking, no-smoking rooms* ▱ *AE, D, DC, MC, V.*

$$ 🏯 **Fushimi Mont Blanc Hotel** (伏見モンブランホテル). Centrally located and comparatively inexpensive, this hotel is a good alternative to the luxury hotels downtown. The rooms are small and simply furnished but not wanting in any of the standard amenities. On the second floor there's a restaurant that serves decent Japanese-style breakfasts and lunches for just ¥700. ⊠ *2-2-26 Sakae, Naka-ku, Nagoya, Aichi-ken 460-0003* ☎ *052/232–1121* 🖷 *052/204–0256* ⇩ *2 restaurants, in-room data ports, refrigerators, meeting rooms* ▱ *AE, DC, MC, V.*

Nightlife

Sakae-chō has a high concentration of restaurants and bars. During the day shoppers and strollers pack its streets, but late at night the area fills mostly with patrons of shady bars called "snacks," places where high fees are charged for women to pour drinks and provide companionship. Unless you've got a lot of cash to burn, avoid such places.

Expats hang out at **Shooter's Sports Bar and Grill** (⊠ Pōla Nagoya Bldg., 2nd fl., 9–26 Sakae 2-chōme, Naka-ku ☎ 052/202–7077). Pool tables and the big-screen TV are the main draws, but special events such as All You Can Drink Night (¥1,500) on Monday and Ladies Night on Wednesday pack them in as well. It's open daily from 11:30 AM to 3 AM. Its location just south of Fushimi subway station Exit No. 5 is not hard to find.

A young crowd gathers at the wild, five-floor **iD Cafe** (⊠ Mitsukoshi Bldg., 1–15 Sakae 3-chōme, Naka-ku ☎ 052/251–0382). On Wednesday night, foreigners showing a valid gaijin card and passport can enter this dance club free, and drinks are only ¥300.

SOUTH GIFU-KEN 南岐阜

Just north of Nagoya, among the foothills of the Hida Sanmyaku (Hida Mountains), old Japan resonates in the area's umbrella, lantern, pottery, and sword makers; in its fishing with cormorants; and in the ancient castle, Inuyama-jō.

Gifu 岐阜

❾ *20 min northwest of Nagoya on the JR Tōkaidō Line or Meitetsu Honsen Line.*

Gifu, known for its paper-lantern and umbrella making, as well as cormorant fishing, is also a center of clothing manufacture, and you can see more than 2,000 wholesale shops within a couple of city blocks as you leave the station. Brightly blooming trees and flowers everywhere attest to the locals' love of color—as do the trains, painted a bright magenta. *Wagasa* (oiled-paper umbrellas) are made in small family-owned shops and can be bought in Gifu's downtown stores. *Chōchin* (paper lanterns) are made locally as well.

If you're interested in the craft of kasa making, visit the **Sakaida Umbrella Company** (境田和傘; ✉ 27 Kanō Nakahiroe-machi ☎ 058/272–3865), an authentic studio and shop 10 minutes on foot southeast of the JR station. It's open weekdays 7–5 except at lunchtime.

To watch chōchin being crafted, head to the **Murase Lantern Company** (村瀬商店; ✉ 23 Imako-machi ☎ 0582/62–0572), north of and next to the city hall. Take the Meitetsu bus (bound for Takatomi) from Shin-Gifu Eki-mae to Shiyakusho-mae. It's open daily from 10 to 5:30.

Fodor'sChoice ★ **U-kai** (鵜飼; ☎ 0582/62–0104 Gifu City U-kai Office, 0582/62–4415 Tourist Information Office), or fishing with cormorants, can be viewed for free from the banks of the Nagara-gawa, just east of Nagara Bridge at around 7:30 PM. Your other option is to buy a ticket for one of approximately 130 boats that ply the waters, each carrying from 10 to 30 spectators. Allow two hours for a u-kai outing: an hour and a half to eat and drink and a half hour to watch the fishing. Boat trips (¥3,300) begin at about 6 PM nightly; reservations, made through Gifu City U-kai Office or Tourist Information Center, are essential. Though you can usually buy food on-board, you're better off bringing your own. There's no fishing on nights during a full moon.

An unusual statue of Buddha (45 feet tall), with a 6-ft-long ear as a symbol of omnipotent wisdom, is housed in **Shōhō-ji** (正法寺). The statue, completed centuries ago, is one of the three largest Buddhas in Japan. It was constructed of pasted-together paper *sutra* (prayers), coated with clay and stucco and then lacquered and gilded; it took 38 years to complete. The orange-and-white temple is 15 minutes by bus from the Gifu JR station. Take Bus 11 (Nagara–Sagiyama) to Gifu Park, walk south along the main road two blocks, then turn right (west); the temple will be on your right. ✉ 8 Daibutsu-chō ☎ 058/264–2760 🎫 ¥150 🕐 Apr.–Nov., daily 8:30–5; Dec.–Mar., daily 9–4.

A major Gifu landmark is **Gifu-jō** (岐阜城). The castle is relatively new (1951), having replaced a 16th-century structure destroyed by an 1891 earthquake. You can either walk—quite a workout—or take the cable car from Gifu Park (¥600 one-way, ¥1050 round-trip). The castle commands a fine view of the city and the surrounding mountains, and the cool breeze is refreshing, especially if you've climbed the hill. There's

CORMORANT FISHING

There's nothing quite like an evening of festive u-kai (cormorant fishing) in Gifu. Fishermen, dressed in traditional reed skirts, glide down the river in their boats. Suspended in front of each boat is a brazier full of burning pinewood that attracts ayu (river smelt) to the surface. U (cormorants), up to 12 per boat, are slipped overboard on leashes to snap up the fish. Because of a small ring around each of the birds' necks, the birds cannot swallow the fish whole. Instead, their long necks expand to hold as many as five wiggling fish. When a bird can't take in another ayu, the fisherman hauls it back to the boat, where it regurgitates its neckful. After many successful hauls, a bird is rewarded with a cut-up fish to swallow. Ayu, which eat only green algae from the rocks, are indeed delicious, and a bucketful of them smells like sliced watermelon.

also a small historical museum in the surrounding park (¥300). ⊠ *Gifu-jō, Ōmiya-chō* ☎ *058/263–4853* ⌖ *¥200* ☉ *Daily 9–5.*

A city **tourist information office** (岐阜観光協会; ☎ 058/262–4415) is at the train station. It's open daily from 10 to 7.

off the beaten path

SANGYŌ SHINKŌ CENTER (Sword Industry Promotion Center, 産業振興センター) – Seki is a traditional center of sword production. A trip to the Shangyo Shinkō Center will help you appreciate the artistry and skill of Japanese swordsmiths. Free demonstrations are held on the first Sunday of the month from March to September and in November and, during the Seki Cutlery Festival, the second weekend in October. The festival is a good time to look for bargains on world-class cutlery. Seki is 30 minutes northeast of Gifu via the Meitetsu Honsen Line. Ask for directions at the station. ⊠ *4–6 Heiwa-dōri, Seki-shi* ☎ *0575/22–3131* ⌖ *Free.*

Where to Stay & Eat

$–$$ Junkissa-u (純喫茶鵜). From wherever you sit in this restaurant you can watch several cormorants strut around the Japanese garden outside, and in Gifu, where there are cormorants, there's ayu (river smelt), which just so happens to be the specialty of this restaurant. The owner boasts of upholding a 1,300-year-old local tradition: that of u-kai fishing, or using cormorants on leashes to catch ayu. And the ayu is prepared in just about every way imaginable. Most popular are the *ayu-no-narezushi*, a kind of reverse sushi with the ayu stuffed full of rice. Ayu and vegetable porridge is another favorite. ⊠ *94–10 Naka-Ukai, Nagara, Gifu-shi* ☎ *058/232–2839* ☰ *No credit cards* ☉ *No dinner.*

★ $$$$ 🏯 Ryokan Sugiyama (杉山旅館). Close to the Nagara River, and embodying a tasteful blend of traditional and modern, Sugiyama is Gifu City's best Japanese inn. The rooms are large with tatami floors and el-

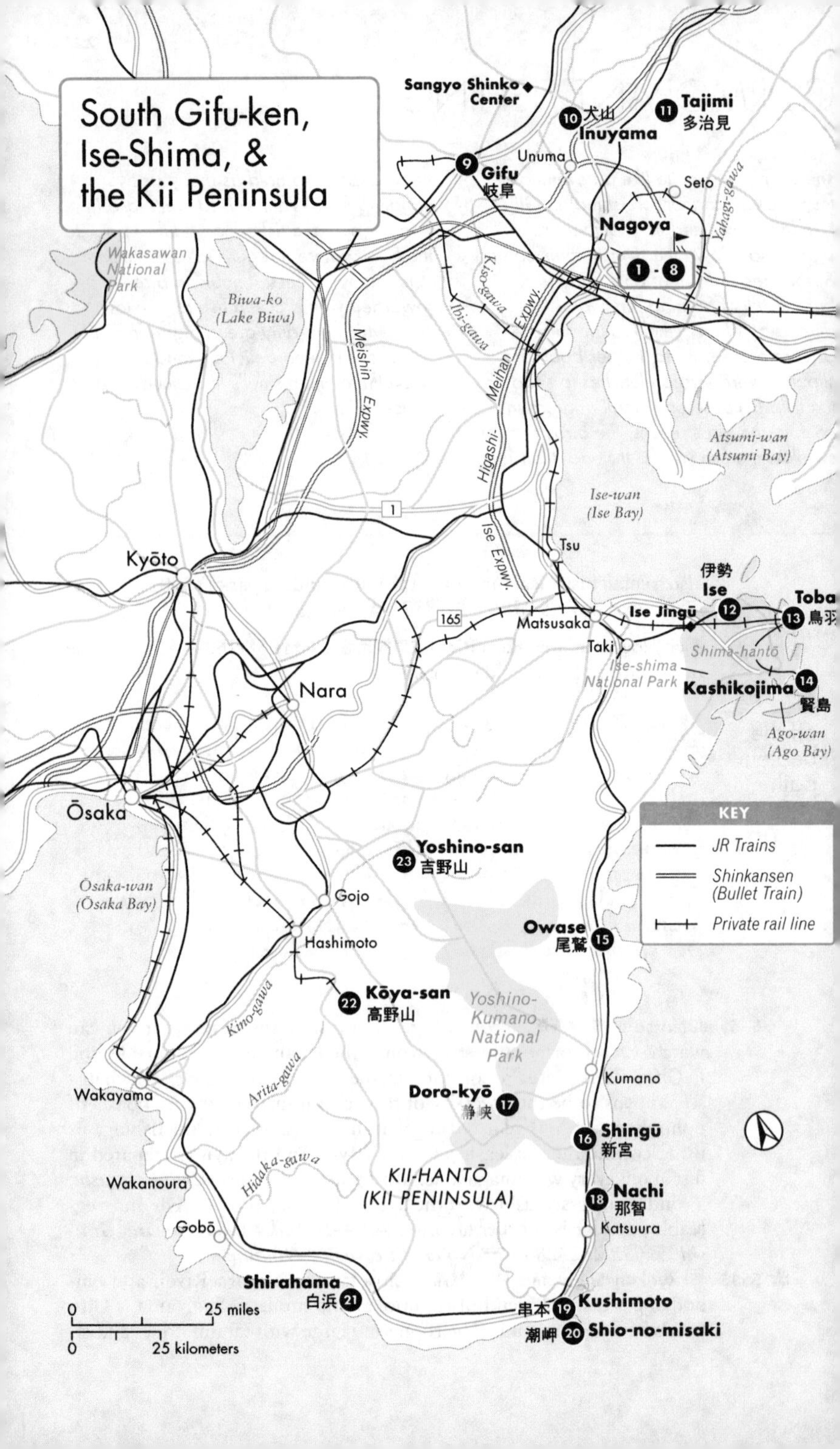
South Gifu-ken, Ise-Shima, & the Kii Peninsula
Sangyo Shinko Center
10 犬山 Inuyama
11 Tajimi 多治見
9 Gifu 岐阜
Unuma
Seto
Nagoya
1 - 8
Yahagi-gawa
Wakasawan National Park
Biwa-ko (Lake Biwa)
Meishin Expwy.
Kiso-gawa
Ibi-gawa
Higashi-Meihan Expwy.
Atsumi-wan (Atsumi Bay)
Ise-wan (Ise Bay)
1
Ise Expwy.
Tsu
Kyōto
伊勢 Ise
12 Ise Jingū
13 Toba 鳥羽
165
Matsusaka
Taki
Shima-hantō
Ise-shima National Park
14 Kashikojima 賢島
Ago-wan (Ago Bay)
Nara
Ōsaka
KEY
JR Trains
Shinkansen (Bullet Train)
Private rail line
23 Yoshino-san 吉野山
Ōsaka-wan (Ōsaka Bay)
Gojo
Hashimoto
15 Owase 尾鷲
22 Kōya-san 高野山
Yoshino-Kumano National Park
Kino-gawa
Kumano
Arita-gawa
Wakayama
17 Doro-kyō 瀞峡
16 Shingū 新宮
Hidaka-gawa
Wakanoura
KII-HANTŌ (KII PENINSULA)
18 Nachi 那智
Katsuura
Gobō
21 Shirahama 白浜
19 串本 Kushimoto
20 潮岬 Shio-no-misaki
0 25 miles
0 25 kilometers

egant shōji doors. The presence of the river adds to the mood of peace and quiet. Very good food, including ayu, is served in the rooms. ⊠ *73–1 Nagara, Gifu-shi, Gifu-ken 502-0071* ☎ *058/231–0161* 🖷 *058/233– 5250* 🖾 *49 rooms* ♨ ☱ *AE* ⍑ *MAP.*

$$$ 🏨 **Hotel 330 Grand Gifu** (ホテル 330 グランデ岐阜). This tall, modern hotel prides itself on its imported American art and furnishings. The place is an outstanding value, with comfortable Western-style rooms, all considerably larger than what you'd find in your average Japanese hotel. A soothing gray and lilac color scheme predominates. Take a room facing Kinkazan Park for excellent views of Gifu Castle and the Nagara River. The restaurant on the first floor offers mostly Western-style food, and has a good an all-you-can-eat breakfast for only ¥1,200. Call ahead and ask about the frequent special offers. To get to the hotel, walk one block north and two blocks west of Gifu Station. ⊠ *5–8 Nagazumi-chō, Gifu-shi, Gifu-ken 500-8175* ☎ *058/267–0330* 🖷 *058/264–1330* 🖾 *147 rooms* ♨ *Restaurant, in-room data ports, cable TV* ☱ *AE, V.*

$–$$ 🏨 **Grand Palais Hotel** (グランパレホテル). This friendly, convenient, and comfortable hotel is directly across from Gifu Station. Rooms are small and simple, but elegant. English speakers work on staff and on-site restaurants serve Western-style, Chinese, Japanese, and Continental menus. ⊠ *8–20 Kogane-machi, Gifu-shi, Gifu-ken 500-8842* ☎ *058/265–4111* 🖷 *058/263–5233* 🖾 *180 Western-style rooms, 1 Japanese-style room* ♨ *4 restaurants, bar, lobby lounge* ☱ *MC, V.*

Inuyama 犬山

🔟 *20 min east of Gifu by Meitetsu Komaki Line, 30 min north of Nagoya by Meitetsu Inuyama Line.*

Like Gifu, Inuyama is a cormorant-fishing town, and as in Gifu, spectator-boat tickets are available from the major hotels. They cost ¥3,300. A pleasant way to see the Kiso-gawa is on a completely tame raft. To travel the hour-long, 13-km (8-mi) river trip (¥3,400), take the train on the Meitetsu Hiromi Line from Inuyama to Nihon-Rhine-Imawatari. Once there, check out several companies before selecting the type of boat you prefer.

If you're headed to Inuyama from Seki, take the JR Line. From Gifu you can take the JR Line, but the privately operated Meitetsu Line is more convenient. If you want to use your JR Pass, take the JR train as far as Unuma and change to the Meitetsu Line for the three-minute last leg to Inuyama. Tajimi and Inuyama are not connected by rail.

★ The origins of Inuyama's most famous sight, **Inuyama-jō** (犬山城), are debated: guidebooks typically state the castle was built in 1440, but local literature, including brochures you can pick up at the castle itself, say its construction was in 1537. Controversy aside, the castle, which is also known as Hakutei-jō, is set on beautiful grounds on a bluff overlooking the Kiso-gawa. Climb up the creaky staircases to the top floor for a great view of the river and hills. From Inuyama-Yūen Eki, walk southwest along the river for 15 minutes. ☎ *0568/61–1711* 🎫 *¥400* 🕐 *Daily 9–4:30.*

The pretty stretch of the **Kiso-gawa** (木曽川) that flows beneath the cliff-top Inuyama-jō has been dubbed the Japanese Rhine. One well-established boating company that offers trips on the Kiso-gawa is **Nippon Rhine Kankō** (日本ライン観光) (☎ 0574/26–2231).

In Uraku-en, the garden of the Meitetsu Inuyama Hotel, the lovely **Jo-an Teahouse** (茶室如庵) is a registered National Treasure. The building was constructed in Kyōto by Grand Master Urakusai Oda in 1618 and moved to its present site in 1971. Tea is served for ¥500, or you can hire the teahouse for your own private ceremony for ¥25,000. It's less than ½ km (¼ mi) from Inuyama-jō. ⊠ *1 Gomon-saki* ☎ *0568/61–4608* 🖃 *Teahouse and gardens ¥1,000* ⊙ *Mar.–Nov., daily 9–5; Dec.–Feb., daily 9–4.*

Hiking

Tsugao-zan (継鹿尾山). A hike to Tsugao-zan will reveal even more of the pleasant scenery near the Inuyama-jō. Start on the riverside trail at the base of Inuyama-jō. Follow the trail east past the Japan Monkey Park, then north to Jakkō-in (built in 654), where the maples blaze in fall. From here you can climb Tsugao-zan or continue northeast to Ōbora Pond and southeast to Zenjino Station, where you can catch the Meitetsu Hiromi Line two stops back to Inuyama Station. The train passes through Zenjino four times an hour. From Inuyama-jō to Zenjino Station is an 8-km (5-mi) hike. Allow 2½ hours from the castle to the top of Tsugao-zan; add another hour if you continue to Zenjino via Ōbora Pond.

Where to Stay

$$$–$$$$ 🏨 **Meitetsu Inuyama Hotel** (名鉄犬山ホテル). This hotel's location on the Kiso-gawa gives it good views and convenience to local sights. Sunny rooms all have nice views; those facing the castle are best. The lobby is bright and lively; the hotel grounds and hot springs are relaxing. ⊠ *107–1 Kita-Koken, Inuyama, Aichi-ken 484-0082* ☎ *0568/61–2211* 🖷 *0568/ 62–5750* 🛏 *92 Western-style rooms, 34 Japanese-style rooms* ⚂ *2 restaurants, hot springs* 🟰 *AE, MC, V.*

Tajimi 多治見

🟕 *26 min from Nagoya on the JR Chūō Line.*

Tajimi has a nearly 2,000-year-old tradition as a ceramics center. Mino Momoyama ceramics, dating from the 16th-century Momoyama period, are legendary, and four major types—Shino, Oribe, Ki-seto, and Seto-guro—are said to be entirely unique to this region. Shino ceramics have a creamy white glaze spotted with dark crimson. Oribe ceramics are a semitranslucent dark green, reflecting the tastes of the 16th-century warrior and tea master Oribe Furuta. Ki-seto pieces, which were popular for the tea ceremony during the Momoyama Period, have a light yellowish brown color. Seto-guro ceramics look as if they were excavated from a meteorite: burned, blistered, black as coal, these often distorted pieces reflect the harsh conditions in which they are fired. They are said to have been a favorite of the famed 16th-century tea master Sen-no-Rikyū. Today, ceramics made in this region are called Mino-yaki and make up about half of the tableware ceramics used in Japan. Industry also uses the ceramics made here—for bricks, tiles, and spark plugs, among other things. There are thousands of kilns in the area, as well as numerous factory outlets where you can choose from an infinite range of types, colors, and prices.

At **Azuchimomoyama** (安土桃山; ⊠ 1–9–17 Higashi-machi ☎ 0572/25–2233), 15 minutes from Tajimi by bus, there's a small ceramics museum as well as a studio where you can take a one-day pottery class. To get here, you can take one of the buses outside Tajimi Station bound for Dachi, Toki Station, or Mizunami Station, and get off at the Higashi-machi stop.

The **Tajimi Tourist Information Center** (多治見観光案内所; ⊠ 2–79–6 Otowa-chō ☎ 0572/24–6460) can help you sort out which ceramic outlets to visit depending on your tastes and budget. It's on the second floor of the building on the right as you exit the front of the station.

ISE-SHIMA NATIONAL PARK 伊勢志摩国立公園

Hanging like a fin underneath central Honshū, the Ise-Shima and Kii peninsulas provide a scenic and sacred counterweight to Japan's over-built industrial corridor. Ise-Shima National Park—which holds the supremely venerated shrines of Ise Jingū—extends from Ise east to Toba (the center of the pearl industry), and south to the indented coastline and pine-clad islands near Kashikojima.

Ise 伊勢

⓬ *80 min south of Nagoya by Kintetsu Limited Express (longer by JR local), 2 hrs east of Kyōto by JR Kyūko Express, 1 hr and 40 min east of Nara by JR, 2 hrs east of Ōsaka by private Kintetsu Line.*

Ise is a small town whose income derives mainly from the pilgrims who visit Ge-kū and Nai-kū, the Outer and Inner shrines, respectively. The most crowded times to visit Ise Jingū are during the Grand Festival, held October 15–17 every year, when thousands come to see the pageantry, and on New Year's Eve and Day, when people come to pray for a good new year.

Fodor'sChoice
★

Astounding as it may be, all of the temple-complex buildings that make up **Ise Jingū** (Grand Shrines of Ise, 伊勢神宮) are rebuilt every 20 years, in accordance with Shintō tradition. To begin a new generational cycle, exact replicas of the previous halls are erected with new wood, using the same centuries-old methods, on adjacent sites. Then the old buildings are dismantled. The main halls you can now see—the 61st set—were completed in 1993 at a cost estimated to be more than ¥4.5 billion.

Deep in a park full of ancient Japanese cedars, **Ge-kū,** which dates from AD 477, is dedicated to Toyouke no Ō-kami, goddess of agriculture. Its buildings are simple, predating the influx of Chinese and Korean influence that swept through the country in the 6th century. Its plain design makes it seem part of the magnificent grounds. It's made from un-painted *hinoki* (cypress), with a fine, closely cropped thatched roof. Again,

ON THE MENU

Local Nagoya dishes include kishimen, white, flat noodles with a velvety smoothness; misonikomi udon, thick noodles cooked in an earthenware pot full of hearty red miso soup with chicken, egg, wood mushrooms, and green onions (you may want to try it with the chili pepper served on the side); hitsumabushi, local eel cooked in miso sauce; and uirō, a sweet cake made of rice powder and sugar, most often eaten during the tea ceremony. The most highly prized food product of the region is the kō-chin, a specially fattened and uniquely tender kind of chicken.

Away from the city, on the Ise Peninsula, lobster is especially fine. On the Kii Peninsula, farmers raise cattle for Matsuzaka beef—the town of Matsuzaka is 90 minutes by train from Nagoya. However, the best beef is typically shipped to Tōkyō, Kyōto, and Ōsaka.

you can see very little of the exterior of Ge-kū—only its roof and glimpses of its walls—and none of its interior. Four fences surround the shrine, and only the imperial family and its envoys may enter.

The same is true for the even more venerated **Nai-kū,** southwest of Ge-kū. Nai-kū is where the Yata-no-Kagami (Sacred Mirror) is kept, one of the three sacred treasures of the imperial regalia. The shrine, said to date from 4 BC, also houses the spirit of the sun goddess Amaterasu, who, according to Japanese mythology, was born of the left eye of Izanagi, one of the first two gods to inhabit the earth. According to legend, Amaterasu was the great-great-grandmother of the first mortal emperor of Japan, Jimmu. Thus, she is revered as the ancestral goddess-mother and guardian deity of Japan. The Inner Shrine's architecture is simple. If you did not know its origin, you would almost think it classically modern. The use of unpainted cypress causes Nai-kū to blend into the ancient forest that circles it.

Both Grand Shrines possess a natural harmony that the more contrived buildings in later Japanese architecture do not. You can see very little of either through the wooden fences surrounding the shrines. But even though shrine sightseeing has certain limits, the reward is in the spiritual aura surrounding Nai-kū and Ge-kū. This condition, where the inner experience is assigned more importance than the physical encounter, is very traditionally Japanese. Entry to the grounds of both shrines, which are open sunrise to sunset, is free.

Where to Stay & Eat

★ $$$$ ✕ **Restaurant Wadakin** (和田金). If you love beef, you may want to make a gustatory pilgrimage to Matsuzaka, a train stop west of Ise. Restaurant Wadakin claims to be the originator of Matsuzaka beef's fame. The cattle are raised with loving care on the restaurant's farm. Sukiyaki or the chef's steak dinner are sure to satisfy your taste buds. ✉ *1878*

Naka-machi, Matsuzaka ☎ *0598/21–1188* ▤ *No credit cards* ⊘ *Closed 4th Tues. of month.*

$ ▥ **Hoshide Ryokan** (星出館). A small Japanese inn in a traditional-style wooden building a short walk from the Ge-kū and the Kintetsu station, Hoshide Ryokan is bare and simple, with a shared Japanese bath, but it has clean tatami rooms and congenial hosts—at a bargain price. Also if you want to explore Ise by bicycle, the hotel rents them for ¥100 a day. ⊠ *2–15–2 Kawasaki, Ise, Mie-ken 516-0009* ☎ *0596/28–2377* 🖷 *0596/27–2830* 🛏 *13 Japanese-style rooms with shared bath* ⚱ *Japanese baths* ▤ *AE, MC, V* ⧉ *MAP.*

Getting Around

To travel to the shrines from Nagoya by JR, change at Taki (two hours from Nagoya) and take the local line to Ise. The fastest and most direct route is on the privately owned Kintetsu Line's Limited Express (¥2,320) to Uji-Yamada. (Ise has two stations five minutes apart, Ise-shi and Uji-Yamada, the main station.)

From either the Kintetsu or JR Ise-shi station it's only a 10-minute walk through town to the Outer Shrine. A frequent shuttle bus makes the 6-km (4-mi) trip between Ge-kū and Nai-kū; a bus also goes directly from the Inner Shrine to Ise Station.

Toba 鳥羽

🔞 *30 min east of Ise by JR train or bus.*

Before Kokichi Mikimoto (1858–1954) perfected a method for cultivating pearls here in 1893, the little treasures were rarely found. *Ama* (female divers)—women were believed to have bigger lungs—would dive all day long, bringing up a thousand oysters, but they wouldn't necessarily find a valuable pearl. Thanks to Mikimoto, the odds have changed slightly. For even after the considerable effort of injecting an irritating substance—rounded muscarine, as it happens, from Iowa—into two-year-old oysters, only one in two bears pearls, and no more than 5% are of gem quality. Because the two-year-old oyster takes three more years to secrete layer after layer of nacre and conchiolin over this implant to form the pearl, these gems remain expensive.

Before pearl-oyster farming, women dove for pearls with more frequency than now. Such a hit-or-miss operation can no longer support them in the face of the larger quantities (and cheaper prices) possible through Mikimoto's research and farming. However, on the outlying islands, women do still dive for abalone, octopus, and edible seaweed.

Toba today is a resort town filled with resort hotels and resort activities.

On Pearl Island, 500 yards southeast from Toba Station, **Mikimoto Pearl Museum** (Mikimoto Shinju no Hakubutsukan, ミキモト真珠の博物館) gives tours, conducted in Japanese, but the guides usually speak some English, and the accompanying film has an English voice-over. A demonstration is also given by female pearl divers. The museum is on the bay between Toba Station and Kintetsu Nakajō Station. ☎ *0599/25–2028* 🎫 *¥1,500* ⊘ *Apr.–Oct., daily 8:30–5; Nov.–Mar., daily 9–4.*

Shima Marine Leisure Cruise boats (志摩マリンレジャー, ☎ 0599/25–3147) make 50-minute tours of the bay (¥1,350) and other ferries go to the outer islands from Ise-wan ferry pier south of the Toba Aquarium.

Where to Stay

Because Toba is very popular and crowded during peak seasons, you might want to consider staying in Kashikojima, 40 minutes away by rail.

$$$$ 🏨 **Toba International Hotel** (鳥羽国際ホテル). Toba's chief resort hotel sits on a bluff overlooking the town and bay. Take a room facing the sea and be sure to get up for the marvelous sunrises. The combination rooms have a Western-style bed and bathroom and a tatami-floor sitting area. Enjoy dinner at the on-site sushi restaurant, which serves local delicacies fresh from the bay. ✉ 1–23–1 Toba, Mie-ken 517-0011 ☎ 0599/25–3121 🖷 0599/25–3139 ⇨ 50 Western-style rooms, 30 Japanese-style rooms, 67 combination rooms ⟡ 2 restaurants, pool, boating, fishing, bar ▭ AE, DC, V.

Getting Around

You can take one of two routes from Ise to Toba: a 45-minute bus ride from near Nai-kū, for ¥980, or the more scenic JR train, for ¥610. Buses run every hour; the last one leaves at 3:56 PM. The bus route follows the Ise-Shima Skyline Drive, which has fine mountainous and wooded scenery.

Kashikojima   賢島

★ ⑭ 50 min south by bus from Toba, 2 hrs south by train on the Kintetsu Line from Nagoya.

The jagged coastline at Ago-wan (Ago Bay) presents a dramatic final view of the Ise Peninsula, and the approach to Kashikojima is very scenic if you go out to the tip of the headland to Goza, through the fishing village of Goza itself, then into the bay on a ferry, past hundreds of rafts from which pearl-bearing oysters are suspended.

Be sure to visit **Daiō** (大王), the fishing village tucked behind a promontory. Standing above the village is a grand lighthouse, the **Anorizaki tōdai** (大王崎灯台), open to visitors daily 9–5 for an entrance fee of ¥80. To reach this towering structure, walk up the narrow street lined with fish stalls at the back of the harbor. From this lighthouse you can see **Anorizaki tōdai** (安乗崎灯台), the oldest (1870) stone lighthouse in Japan, 11 km (7 mi) east. Between the two lighthouses on the curving bay are small fishing villages, coffee shops, and restaurants.

Getting Around

The Kintetsu Line continues from Toba to Kashikojima (about ¥900) on an inland route. There are also two buses a day, at 9:40 and 2:25 (¥1,400). To take a coastal route, get off the train at Ugata and take a bus to Nakiri; then change buses for one to Goza, from which frequent ferries go to Kashikojima. A trip directly to Kashikojima from Nagoya on the Kintetsu rail line costs ¥3,300.

It's possible to follow the coast from Kashikojima to the Kii Peninsula, but there is no train, and in many places the road cuts inland, making the journey long and tedious. From Kashikojima or Toba you are better off taking the Kintetsu Line back to Ise to change to the JR Sangū Line and travel to Taki, where you can change to another JR train to go south to the Kii Peninsula.

Where to Stay

★ **$$$$** ⊡ **Ishiyama-so** (石山荘). On tiny Yokoyama-jima in Ago-wan, this small concrete inn is just a two-minute ferry ride from Kashikojima. Phone ahead, and your hosts will meet you at the quay. The inn is nothing fancy, but it does offer warmth and hospitality, and rooms overlooking the sea. All rooms have private toilets, and four have showers. You'll also find tea sets and Japanese bathrobes in the rooms. Breakfast and dinner, included in the room rate, are served in the communal dining hall. ⊠ *Yokoyama-jima, Kashikojima, Ago-chō, Shima-gun, Mie-ken 517-0502* ☎ *0599/52–1527* 🖷 *0599/52–1240* ✎ *i.i.k-nk@poem.ocn.ne.jp* ◲ *10 rooms, 4 with shower* ↳ *Japanese baths* ⊟ *AE, MC, V* ⏐◯⏐ *MAP.*

★ **$–$$** ⊡ **Daiōsō** (大王荘). This small family-run ryokan has a natural hot spring and a good *izakaya* (traditional-style) restaurant serving two meals a day. The Japanese rooms are slightly cheaper than the Western-style rooms, but all are fairly spartan. Groups receive a per-person discount. ⊠ *244 Namigiri, Shima-gun, Mie-ken 517-0603* ☎ *0599/72–1234* 🖷 *0599/ 72–0489* ◲ *13 rooms, 9 with bath* ↳ *Restaurant, hot springs* ⊟ *AE, DC, MC, V* ⎙ *MAP.*

KII PENINSULA 紀伊半島

Farther down the coast from Ise-Shima, the Kii Peninsula has magnificent marine scenery, coastal fishing villages and resorts, and the remarkable temple-mountain, Kōya-san. Nearby Yoshino-Kumano National Park has pristine gorges, holy mountains, and another large, ancient Buddhist community at Yoshino-san, with its gorgeous hillside sakura flowering in early April.

Owase 尾鷲

⑮ *120 km (72 mi) from Kashikojima, 100 km (60 mi) from Ise.*

The first major town as you head down the coast from Ise-Shima National Park is Owase. The town's harbor is quite beautiful and it's worthwhile to spend the evening and take a walk in nearby **Yakiyama Kōen** (Yakiyama Park, 八鬼山), where pilgrims tread centuries ago on their way to Ise-Shima. Take the Ohara Forest Trail to the rocky waterfalls at **Ayudome no taki,** literally "Waterfalls that Stop River Smelt." Legend has it a giant serpent lay across the river long ago, blocking the fish from swimming downstream.

Where to Stay & Eat

$–$$$ ✗ **Brasserie Couscous** (ブラッスリークスクス). Take a rest and savor some excellent Mediterranean food at Brasserie Couscous. The chef will be happy to show you his fishing trophy photos, the authentic pizza is incredible, and the wine and beer selection is impeccable. Selections start at ¥1,300. ⊠ *2–22 Sakae-chō, Owase-shi* ☎ *05972/3–2586* ⊟ *No credit cards* ☽ *Closed Mon. No lunch.*

$ ▦ **Business Hotel Phoenix** (ビジネスホテルフェニックス). Should you want to stay overnight in Owase, check into the very economical and friendly Hotel Phoenix. A room costs ¥9,800; it's nothing fancy, but it suffices for a quick stopover. The hotel is a five-minute walk from the JR station. ⊠ *5–25 Sakae-chō, Owase-shi, Mie-ken 519-3618* ☎ *0597/22–8111* 🖷 *0597/22–8116* 🛏 *30 rooms* ⌂ *Restaurant* 🖃 *AE, DC, MC, V.*

Shingū 新宮

⑯ *2 hrs south of Taki by JR Limited Express, 2 hrs southwest of Kashiko-jima by the Kintetsu and JR lines, 3½ hrs south of Nagoya by JR.*

Shingū is useful as a jumping-off point for an inland excursion to Doro-kyō. One of the few north–south roads penetrating the Kii Peninsula begins in town and continues inland to Nara by way of Doro-kyō and Gojo. A drive on this winding, steep, narrow road, especially on a bus, warrants a dose of motion-sickness medicine. The mossy canyon walls outside your window, the rushing water far below, and the surrounding luxuriant greenery inspire a deep sense of calm and wonder, but frequent sharp curves provide plenty of adrenaline surges to counteract it.

Where to Stay

$$ ▦ **Shingū-Yū ai Hotel** (新宮ユーアイホテル). Friendly staff, convenience, and fair-size rooms make this a viable option if you're staying overnight in Shingū. It's next to the post office, a five-minute walk from the train station. ⊠ *3–12 I-no-sawa, Shingū-shi, Wakayama-ken 647–0045* ☎ *0735/22–6611* 🖷 *0735/22–4777* 🛏 *82 rooms* ⌂ *Restaurant* 🖃 *AE, DC, MC, V.*

Doro-kyō 瀞峡

⑰ *40 min north of Shingū by JR bus.*

As you travel up the Kumano River from Shingū, the walls of the steep-sided Doro-kyō (Doro Gorge) begin to rise around you. From late May to early June, azaleas line the banks. Farther up, sheer 150-ft cliffs tower above the aquamarine Kumano-gawa, which alternates between rapids and quiet stretches.

The best way to take in this gorge, one of the country's finest, is on a four-hour trip (¥5,100) upriver on a flat-bottomed, fan-driven boat. Outside seats on the boats are the best and usually have odd numbers from 3 to 23 or even numbers from 26 through 48. You can book a trip that includes both bus and boat from the tourist information office in the JR Shingū station plaza, or if you have a JR Pass, save ¥1,120 by taking a 40-minute bus ride from Shingū Station to Shiko, the departure point for the boats going up river.

The boat trip doesn't venture much farther than Doro-hatchō before returning to Shiko. You can, however, hire different boats (two hours round-trip, ¥3,280) to explore the two other gorges and rapids that extend for several miles upstream. From Doro-hatchō (or Shiko) you can take a bus back to Shingū.

Nachi 那智

18 *10 min south of Shingū by JR.*

Nachi-no-taki (那智の滝), said to be the highest waterfall in Japan, has a drop of 430 feet. At the bus stop near the falls, a torii at the top of several stone steps leads down to a paved clearing near the foot of the falls. A 20-minute bus ride (¥600) from the Nachi train station gets you here.

For a view from the top, climb up the path from the bus stop to **Nachi Taisha** (那智大社), one of the three great shrines of the Kii area. Reputed to be 1,400 years old, it's perched just above the waterfall. Next to the shrine is the 1587 Buddhist temple Seiganto-ji, which is the starting point for a 33-temple Kannon pilgrimage through western Honshū.

19 Thirty large, evenly spaced rocks march out into the sea as if following a line from **Kushimoto** (串本) toward Ō-shima, an island 2 km (1 mi) offshore. It was here that the first American set foot on Japanese soil, about 100 years before Perry, although only to replenish his ship's water supply.

20 A couple of miles from Kushimoto, **Shio-no-misaki** (潮岬) is Honshū's southernmost point. It's marked by a white lighthouse stationed high above its rocky cliffs. Adjacent to the lighthouse is a good spot for picnics and walks along the cliff paths. The beach looks inviting, but due to sharp rocks and currents, swimming is not a good idea.

Shirahama 白浜

21 *75 min southeast of Nachi, 3 hrs south of Ōsaka by JR train.*

Rounding the peninsula, 54 km (34 mi) northeast of Kushimoto, Shirahama is considered by the Japanese to be one of the best hot-spring resorts in the country. It does have attractive craggy headlands and coves. One of the peninsula's few wide, sandy beaches is here. The climate, which allows beach days in the winter, does give Shirahama appeal as a base to explore the area. A 17-minute bus ride from the train station gets you to the town.

Along the beach, between stretches of development, **Sandan-beki** (三段壁) is a cliff with caves underneath, which used to be the lair of pirates during the Heian era (794–1185). It costs nothing to stand on the cliff, but to enter the caves below—a sort of museum where you can see the types of attack boats the pirates used—and to view the pirates' old, dark, forbidding Buddhist sanctuary, it'll cost you ¥1,200. The site is open daily from 10 to 5.

Fodor'sChoice ★ Soak in the open-air **Sakino-yu Onsen** (崎の湯温泉) a hollow among the wave-beaten rocks facing the Pacific, where it's said that Emperors Saimei (594–661) and Mommu (683–707) once bathed. It's 1 km (½ mi) south of the main beach, below Hotel Seymor. 🖃 ¥300 ⊗ *Daily, except 4th Wed. of each month, dawn–dusk.*

Where to Stay

$ 🏨 **Shirara Minshuku** (南紀白浜国民民宿しらら). This hotel is right off the beach in Shirahama. All the rooms are simple and Japanese-style, but clean and comfortable. The cafeteria style restaurant on the first floor offers local specialties, including fresh fish brought daily from local fisherman. ✉ *1359 Shirahama-chō, Nishimuro-gun, Wakayama-ken 649–2211* ☎ *0739/42–3655* 🖷 *0739/43–5223* 🛏 *18 Japanese-style rooms* ♨ *Restaurant* 🖃 *AE, V.*

DŌJŌ-JI (道成寺). Between Shirahama and Wakanoura is the famous Dōjō-ji Temple in the town of Gobō. According to legend, Kiyohime, a farmer's daughter, became enamored of a young priest, Anchin, who often passed by her house. One day she blurted out her feelings to him. He, in turn, promised to return that night to see her. However, during the course of the day, the priest had second thoughts and returned to Dōjō-ji. Spurned, Kiyohime became enraged. She turned herself into a dragon and set out in pursuit of Anchin, who, scared out of his wits, hid under the temple bell, which had not yet been suspended. Kiyohime sensed his presence and wrapped her dragon body around the bell. Her fiery breath heated the bell until it became red-hot, and the next morning the charred remains of Anchin were found under the bell.

The most interesting thing about the temple is the legend, but if you want to stop, get off the train at Dōjō-ji Eki, one stop south of Gobō Eki. As at most temples that don't get a lot of tourist traffic, you may wander around outside and onto the porch of Dōjō-ji Temple at any time. ✉ *Gobō, 40 min north of Shirahama by JR.*

KŌYA-SAN & YOSHINO-SAN   高野山と吉野山

Kōya-san   高野山

★ ㉒ *2 hrs east of Wakayama (via Hashimoto) by JR, 90 min west of Ōsaka's Namba Station on the Nankai Dentetsu Line.*

This is the headquarters of the Shingon sect of Buddhism, founded by Kūkai, also known as Kōbō Daishi, in AD 816. Every year about a million visitors pass through Kōya-san's **Dai-mon** (Big Gate, 大門), to enter the great complex of 120 temples, monasteries, schools, and graves on this mesa in the mountains.

If your time is limited, head for **Okuno-in** (奥の院), a memorial park, first. Many Japanese make pilgrimages to the mausoleum of Kōbō Daishi or pay their respects to their ancestors buried here. Try to arrive very early in the morning, before the groups take over, or even better, at dusk, when things get wonderfully spooky.

Exploring this cemetery is like peeking into a lost and mysterious realm. You can almost feel the millions of prayers said here clinging to the gnarled branches of 300-year-old cedar trees reaching into the sky. This *is* a special place. Its old-growth forest is a rarity in Japan, and among the trees are buried some of the country's most prominent families, their graves marked by mossy little pagodas and red- and white-robed stone Buddhas.

You may exit Okuno-in by way of the 2½-km (1½-mi) main walkway, which is lined with tombs, monuments, and statues. More than 100,000 historical figures are honored. The lane exits the cemetery at Ichi-no-hashi-guchi; follow the main street straight ahead to return to the center of town (a 20-minute walk) or wait for the bus that is headed for Kongōbu-ji.

The path from Okuno-in-mae ends at the **Tōrō-dō** (Lantern Hall, 灯籠堂), named after its 11,000 lanterns. Two fires burn in this hall: it's said that one has been alight since 1016, the other since 1088. Behind the hall is the mausoleum of Kōbō Daishi. 🄯 *Free ☉ Lantern Hall Apr.–Oct., daily 8–5; Nov.–Mar., daily 8:30–4:30.*

On the southwestern side of Kōya-san, **Kongōbu-ji** (金剛峰寺) is the chief temple of Shingon Buddhism. Kongōbu-ji was built in 1592 as the family temple of Hideyoshi Toyotomi. It was rebuilt in 1861 and is now the main temple of the Kōya-san community. 🄯 *¥500 ☉ Apr.–Oct., daily 8–5; Nov.–Mar., daily 8:30–4:30.*

The **Danjōgaran** (Sacred Precinct, 壇上伽藍) consists of many halls centered on the **Kompon-daitō** (Great Central Pagoda). This red pagoda, with its interior of brightly colored beams, contains five sitting images of Buddha. Last rebuilt in 1937, the two-story structure stands out due to its unusual style and rich vermilion color. From Kongōbu-ji walk down the temple's main stairs and take the road to the right of the parking lot in front of you; in less than five minutes you will reach Danjogaran. 🄯 *Each building ¥100 ☉ Apr.–Oct., daily 8–5; Nov.–Mar., daily 8:30–4:30.*

The exhibits at **Reihōkan** (Treasure Hall, 霊宝館), given its 5,000 art treasures, continually change. At any given time some of the 180 pieces that have been designated National Treasures will be on display. Among these are *Shaka-nehan-zō*—the scroll of Reclining Image of Shakamuni Buddha on His Last Day—and the exotic *Hachi-dai-doji-zō*—images of the Eight Guardian Deities. The hall is south of Danjogaran across a small path. 🄯 *¥500 ☉ Apr.–Oct., daily 9–5; Nov.–Mar., daily 9–4.*

At the T-junction in the center of town, the **tourist office** (✉ 600 Kōya-san, Kōya-chō, Ito-gun, Wakayama-ken ☎ 0736/56–2616) can be reached by bus for ¥300.

En route from the station to the tourist office, you will pass the **mausoleums** of the first and second Tokugawa shōguns. You may want to walk back and visit these two gilded structures later; they're free, and open daily 9–5.

Where to Stay & Eat

Kōya-san has no modern hotels. However, 53 of the temples do offer Japanese-style accommodations—tatami floors, futon mattresses, and traditional Japanese shared baths. Only a few accept foreign guests. The two meals served are *shōjin ryōri,* vegetarian cuisine that uses locally made tofu. You eat the same food as the priests. The price is around ¥10,000 per person, including meals. You can reserve through Kōya-san Kankō Kyokai, the Nankai Railway Company office in Namba Station (Ōsaka), and the Japan Travel Bureau in most Japanese cities.

If possible, make reservations for temple rooms in advance through **Kōya-san Kankō Kyokai** (Kōya-san Tourism Society, 高野山観光協会; ⊠ Kōya-san, Kōya-machi, Itsu-gun, Wakayama-ken ☎ 0736/56–2616).

¢ 🔲 **Rengejō-in** (蓮華定院). Rengejō-in is an especially lovely temple that is open and friendly to foreigners. Both the head priest and his mother speak English, and they serve excellent vegetarian meals. As in many temples the lodgings are communal and the facilities are sparse, but the experience of staying in one is unforgettable. From the cable car terminus, take the bus and get off at Ishinguchi stop. The drivers and station attendants will help you find Rengejō-in. ⊠ *700 Kōya-san, 648-0211* ☎ *0736/56–2231* 📠 *0736/56–4743* 🛏 *46 rooms* ⚱ *No room phones, no room TVs* 🖃 *No credit cards.*

Getting Around

Depending on where you are coming from, there are many ways to approach Kōya-san. From Wakayama, if you have a JR Pass, you can take the JR Wakayama Line to Hashimoto (80 minutes; ¥820) and change to the Nankai Line for the final 19 km (11½ mi) (40 minutes; ¥430) to Gokuraku-bashi Station, from which the cable car runs (¥380) to the top of Kōya-san. (If you cut across the Yoshino-Kumano National Park by bus from Shingū or Hongu on Route 168, instead of circling the Kii Peninsula, get off the bus at Gojo and backtrack one station on the JR Line to Hashimoto; then take the Nankai Line.)

From Ōsaka you can take the private Nankai Line to reach Kōya-san from Nankai Namba Station, from which a train departs for Kōya-san every 30 minutes. (To reach Namba Station from Shin-Ōsaka Shinkansen Station, use the Midō-suji subway line.) The Ōsaka–Kōya-san journey takes 90 minutes, including the five-minute cable-car ride up to Kōya-san Station, and costs ¥1,230 (try to reserve a seat if you're traveling on a weekend).

By rail, no matter where you start, the last leg of the trip is a five-minute cable-car ride from Gokuraku-bashi Station. JR Passes are not valid for the cable car. The lift will deposit you at the top of 3,000-ft Kōya-san, where you can pick up a map and hop on a bus to the main attractions, which are about 2½ km (1½ mi) from the station and about 5½ km (3½ mi) from each other, on opposite sides of town. Two buses leave the station every 20 or 30 minutes, when the cable car arrives. One goes to Okuno-in Cemetery, on the east end of the main road, and the other goes to the Dai-mon, to the west.

Yoshino-san 吉野山

❷ *3½ hrs east of Kōya-san by cable car, Nankai, JR, and Kintetsu lines; 1 hr south of Nara by JR and private Kintetsu Rail Line.*

Yoshino-san is one of the most beautiful (and crowded) places in Japan to visit during cherry-blossom season. The Sakura Festival, held April 11–12, attracts thousands of visitors. En-no-Ozunu, a 7th-century Buddhist priest who planted the trees and put a curse on anyone who tampered with them, was a skilled gardener. Since he placed the 100,000 trees in four distinct groves in rows up the mountainside, the zone of flowers in full bloom climbs up the slope as the weather warms the trees from bottom to top. As a result, you're virtually guaranteed to see perfect sakura, sometime within a two-week period in mid-April.

Explore the area to see wonderful mountain views and curious temples. The community of temples at Yoshino-san is less impressive than that of Kōya-san, but it's still interesting. Built into the surrounding mountains, shops in Youshino are on the third floor of buildings, and the first and second floors are below the level of the road.

For pilgrims, Sanjo-san is considered the holiest mountain, with two temples at the summit, one of which is dedicated to En-no-Ozunu, the cherry-tree priest who, as you might expect, is revered as something of a saint in the area. Lodging is available at area temples May 8–September 27, and can be booked at the tourist office.

In the middle of the cherry groves is **Kimpusen-ji** (金峰山寺), the main temple of the area. The main hall, Zaō-dō, is said to be the second-largest wooden structure in Japan and also has two superb sculptures of Deva kings at the gate. From the parking lot at Yoshino-san, there's basically only one path: it winds inward, curving along the hill-terrace lined with trees, and is heavily traveled. ☎ *¥350, includes Nyoirin-ji* ⊘ *Daily 9–5.*

Nyoirin-ji (如意輪寺) was founded in the 10th century and is located south of Kimpusen-ji. This is supposedly where the last remaining 143 imperial warriors prayed before going into their final battle for the cause in the 14th century. Behind the temple is the mausoleum of Emperor Go-daigo (1288–1339), who brought down the Kamakura shogunate. ☎ *¥350, includes Kimpusen-ji* ⊘ *Daily 9–5.*

In addition to reserving temple stays, the **tourist office** (✉ Yoshinoyama, Yoshino-machi, Yoshino-gun, Nara-ken ☎ 07463–2–3081) can arrange for accommodations at local *minshuku* (private homes providing lodging and meals for travelers).

Getting Around

From Nara take a JR train to Yoshino-guchi or the Kintetsu Line to Kashihara Jingū-mae Station and connect with a Kintetsu Line train for Yoshino. From Kōya-san return to JR Hashimoto Station; take a train one hour southeast to Yoshino-guchi and then change for the Kintetsu Line to Yoshino. From Ōsaka take a two-hour ride on the Kintetsu Line from Abeno-bashi Station.

NAGOYA, ISE-SHIMA & THE KII PENINSULA A TO Z

To research prices, get advice from other travelers, and book travel arrangements, visit www.fodors.com.

AIR TRAVEL

There are direct overseas flights to Nagoya on Japan Airlines (JAL) from Honolulu, Hong Kong, and Seoul. The major airlines that have routes to Japan have offices in downtown Nagoya.

CARRIERS For domestic travel, Japan Airlines (JAL), All Nippon Airways (ANA), and Japan Air System (JAS) have offices in Nagoya and fly from Nagoya to most major Japanese cities. For other airline phone numbers, *see* Air Travel *in* Smart Travel Tips.

🛈 **All Nippon Airways** ☎ 052/962-6211. **Japan Air System** ☎ 052/201-8111. **Japan Airlines** ☎ 052/563-4141.

AIRPORT & TRANSFER

The Meitetsu Airport Bus makes the 30-minute run between Nagoya's airport and the Meitetsu Bus Center, near Nagoya Station, for ¥870.

🛈 **Komaki Kokusai Kūkō** (Nagoya International Airport) ☎ 0568/29-0765. **Meitetsu Airport Bus** ✉ Nagoya International Airport ☎ 0581/22-3796.

BUS TRAVEL

Buses connect Nagoya with Tōkyō and Kyōto. The bus fare, ¥5,100 and ¥2,500 respectively, is half that of the Shinkansen trains, but the journey by bus takes three times longer.

JR buses crisscross Nagoya, running either north–south or east–west. The basic fare is ¥200, and an unlimited-use bus and subway pass costs ¥850. Route maps are posted, and tickets are available in the train station—follow the signs. Further information on bus and subway travel can be collected at the Tourist Information Office in the center of the station.

CAR TRAVEL

The journey on the expressway to Nagoya from Tōkyō takes about five to six hours; from Kyōto allow 2½ hours. If you're used to high-traffic, high-stress, jam-prone highways that can go from high-speed to a snail's pace in a jiffy—like those of Los Angeles or Denver, for example—you'll be all right.

EMERGENCIES

🛈 **Ambulance** ☎ 119. **Kokusai Central Clinic** ✉ Nagoya International Center Bldg. ☎ 0521/201-5311. **National Nagoya Hospital** ✉ 4-1-1 Sannomaru-ku, Naka-ku, Nagoya ☎ 0521/951-1111. **Police** ☎ 110.

ENGLISH-LANGUAGE MEDIA

BOOKS Maruzen, behind the International Hotel Nagoya downtown, has a broad selection of English-language books.

🛈 Bookstore **Maruzen** ✉ 3-23-3 Nishiki, Naka-ku, Nagoya ☎ 0521/261-2251.

SUBWAYS

Several main subway lines run under Nagoya's major avenues. The Higashiyama Line runs from the north down to JR Nagoya Station and then due east, cutting through the city center at Sakae. The Meijō Line runs north–south, passing through the city center at downtown Sakae. The Tsurumai Line also runs north–south through the city, then turns from the JR station to Sakae to cross the city center. A fourth subway line, the Sakura-dōri, cuts through the city center from the JR station, paralleling the east–west section of the Higashiyama Line. The basic fare, good for three stops, is ¥200. A one-day pass, good for Nagoya's subways (and buses), is ¥850.

TAXIS

Taxis are parked at most major stations, hotels, and wherever there may be pedestrians in need of a lift. You can also wave one over on the street; they are not scarce. The initial fare is ¥610. A ride from Nagoya Station to Nagoya-jō is ¥1,200.

TOURS

The Nagoya Yūran Bus Company runs five different bus tours of the city. The three-hour Panoramic Course tour (¥2,610) includes Nagoya-jō and Atsuta Jingū and has scheduled morning and afternoon departures. A full-day tour (¥6,270) will take you to sights around Nagoya. Trips also run up to Inuyama to watch u-kai (¥7,680 round-trip). These tours have only a Japanese-speaking guide.

You can arrange a full-day tour to Ise and the Mikimoto Pearl Island at Toba from Kyōto or Ōsaka (¥24,800) through Sunrise Tours.

🚌 Tour Contacts **Nagoya Yūran Bus Company** ☎ 052/561-4036. **Sunrise Tours** ☎ 075/361-7241.

TRAIN TRAVEL

Frequent bullet trains run between Tōkyō and Nagoya. The ride takes 1 hour, 52 minutes on the *Hikari* Shinkansen and 2½ hours on the slower *Kodama* Shinkansen and costs ¥ 6,090. JR Passes are not accepted on the ultrafast *Nozomi,* which links Nagoya with Kyōto (43 minutes) and Ōsaka (1 hour). Another option is the less expensive Limited Express trains, which proceed from Nagoya into and across the Japan Alps— to Takayama, Toyama, Matsumoto, and Nagano.

VISITOR INFORMATION

The Nagoya International Center is quite possibly the best-equipped information center in Japan for assisting gaijin. Not only is there an information desk to answer your questions, but there are also audiovisual presentations and an extensive library of English-language newspapers (both Japanese and foreign), magazines, and books. The center also has an English-language telephone hot line available from 9 to 8:30.

The toll-free Japan Travel Phone will answer travel-related questions daily 9–5. Local tourist offices in Ise-Shima and on the Kii Peninsula are located in most train stations.

🚌 Tourist Information **Japan Travel Bureau** ✉ JR Nagoya Station ☎ 0521/563-0041 ✉ 4-6-18 Eki-mae, Nagoya Bldg., 1st fl., Nakamura-ku. **Japan Travel Phone** ☎ 0088-22-4800. **Nagoya Tourist Information Office** ✉ 1-4 Meieki 1-chōme, Nakamura-ku ☎ 052/541-4301 ✉ JR Nagoya Station. **Nagoya International Center** ✉ Nagoya Kokusai Center Bldg., 3rd fl., 1-47-1 Nagono 1-chōme, Nakamura-ku, Nagoya ☎ 052/581-0100 in English.

THE JAPAN ALPS & THE NORTH CHŪBU COAST

日本アルプスと北陸沿岸

4

by John Malloy
Quinn

Revised by
Sarah Richards

SNOW-TOPPED MOUNTAINS, rocky coastal cliffs, open-air hot springs, and superb hiking and skiing make this central alpine region a great escape from Japan's bustling cities. From the traditional villages of Kiso Valley to beautiful Sado Island, this slow-paced region has it all—without the crowds.

Indeed, many traditional villages are virtually untouched by development, while other parts of the country have gone "modern." Towns within the North Chūbu region (Fukui, Ishikawa, Toyama, Niigata, Nagano, and Gifu prefectures) have largely maintained their locally distinctive architecture. In Ogi-machi and Hida Minzoku Mura, sturdy wooden houses with thatched roofs still have open-hearth fireplaces. Famous temples such as Fukui's Zen Eihei-ji, Nagano's Zenkō-ji, and Kanazawa's Nichiren Myōryū-ji, locally called Ninja-dera (Temple of the Ninja), are symbols of the region's important religious history.

Traditional arts are represented in annual events ranging from Sado-ga-shima's solemn performances of *okesa* (folk dances) to the area's riotous festivals like the Seihakusai festival in Nanao on Noto Peninsula. Besides visiting the region's numerous folklore museums, which display Japanese ceramics, pottery, art, and scrolls made over the centuries, you're also welcome to watch craftspeople dye linens, paint silk for kimonos, carve wood, and hand-lacquer objects in workshops and stores.

See the glossary at the end of this book for definitions of the common Japanese words and suffixes used in this chapter.

Exploring the Japan Alps & the North Chūbu Coast

The Japan Alps is not a defined political region; it's a name that refers to the mountains in Chūbu, the Middle District. Chūbu encompasses nine prefectures in the heart of Honshū, three of which—Gifu-ken, Nagano-ken, and Yamanashi-ken—make up the central highlands. Kanazawa, Fukui, and the Noto-hantō, to the northwest, and Niigata and Sado-ga-shima Island, to the northeast, form the neighboring coastal area.

Getting around the Alps is somewhat determined by the valleys and river gorges that run north and south. East–west routes through the mountains are nearly nonexistent, except between Matsumoto and Takayama from May through mid-October. It's easier to get around along the coast and through the foothills of Fukui, Ishikawa, Toyama, and Niigata, except in winter when Fukui gets hit with furious blizzards that can shut down train routes and highways. In Noto-hantō, buses and trains can be relied on for trips to key places, but to really explore the scenery and get a feel for rural life, consider renting a car in Kanazawa or Toyama and making the loop at your own pace.

About the Restaurants & Hotels

The restaurants in this region tend to fall into two categories: casual, inexpensive restaurants serving various types of noodles and international dishes like curry and rice, pasta and sandwiches; or posh traditional Japanese restaurants featuring regional delicacies served in countless elaborate courses.

Accommodations cross the spectrum, from Japanese-style inns to large, modern hotels. Ryokans customarily serve traditional Japanese food, and usually highlight the regional specialties, while hotels in the bigger cities have a variety of Western and Japanese restaurants. Hotels listed in this chapter have private baths, air-conditioning, telephones, and TVs unless stated otherwise. In summer, hotel reservations are advisable—they can be made from any tourist information center in Japan.

WHAT IT COSTS In yen				
	$$$$	$$$	$$	$	¢
RESTAURANTS	over 3,000	2,000–3,000	1,000–2,000	800–1,000	under 800
HOTELS	over 22,000	18,000–22,000	12,000–18,000	8,000–12,000	under 8,000

Restaurant prices are per person for a main course at dinner. Hotel prices are for a double room, excluding service and tax.

Timing

Heavy snow in winter makes getting around the Alps by car difficult or altogether impossible, especially when the road between Takayama and Matsumoto virtually becomes one with the mountain landscape. Unless you've got skiing to do, and a direct route by train to get there, winter is not the best time to explore the area. At the height of summer the Alps and coastal regions become a perfect getaway for those fleeing the stagnant heat of Japan's urban jungles—expect throngs of tourists and lofty prices. May, June, and September are the best times for visiting, when transportation is safe and reliable, and the sights are only mildly peppered with sightseers.

THE JAPAN ALPS

Karuizawa   軽井沢

❶ *66 min by Shinkansen from Tōkyō's Ueno Station.*

Karuizawa's reputation grew by leaps and bounds when Archdeacon A. C. Shaw, an English prelate, built his summer villa here in 1886. The migration of other foreigners to the area sparked the interest of fashionable, affluent Tōkyōites, who soon made it their preferred summer destination. In Kyū-Karuizawa, near the Karuizawa train station, branches of more than 500 trendy boutiques sell, well, the same goods as their flagship stores in Tōkyō. So, unless you've got a cottage in the area, leave the shopping for your time in Tōkyō and partake of the natural scenery. Naka-Karuizawa Station, one stop (five minutes) away on the Shinano Tetsudō line, serves as a gateway to Shiraito and Ryūgaeshi waterfalls, the Yachō wild bird sanctuary, and numerous hiking trails.

Hiking, Biking, & Bird-watching

Asama-san (浅間山), an active volcano of more than 8,000 feet, intermittently threatens to put an end to the whole "Highlands Ginza" scene going on below. If you'd like a view of the glorious Asama-san in its entirety,

To see everything—the Alps, the Noto-hantō (Noto Peninsula), the Chūbu Coast, and Sado-ga-shima—you need about two weeks. Winter weather can slow and sometimes impedes travel (from Matsumoto, Kamikōchi can be reached only between May and October). The region can be reached either from the Nihon-kai coast or the Pacific coast; and indeed we provide itineraries for both travelers coming from the Kantō region (Tōkyō) and for travelers coming from Kansai (Nagoya, Kyōto, and Ōsaka).

To reach the area from Tōkyō, plan to take a Shinkansen to Nagano or Niigata, and an express train to Matsumoto. Kanazawa and other Chūbu coastal destinations are on JR Lines, with connections to Kyōto, Nagoya, and the Shinkansen Line at Maibara.

Numbers in the text correspond to numbers in the margin and on the Japan Alps, Takayama, and Kanazawa maps.

If you have 2 days

From Kansai, head straight to 📷 **Kanazawa** 🔞 ▶–㉞ on the JR Limited Express. Spend the afternoon exploring the structural marvels of the enigmatic Ninja-dera, then pop in for a stroll in either Kenrokuen or Gyokusenen gardens. The next morning, rise early and head for Toyama, where you'll switch to the clunky, one-car train that chugs through the rice paddies and climbs up and down river valleys all the way to 📷 **Takayama** 🔟–⑯. While away the afternoon slipping in and out of traditional Japanese shops and museums in this beautiful mountain town. After a traditional Japanese dinner, head back to Nagoya; skip dinner and bring a snack for the train if you need to get back to Ōsaka (four hours) or Kyōto (both require transfers in Nagoya).

If you're coming from Tōkyō, board the Nagano Shinkansen at Ueno for the short 97-minute ride to **Nagano** ②. Visit Zenkō-ji, and finish up with a lunch of the region's highly acclaimed soba noodles. For the afternoon, you could head to 📷 **Yudanaka Onsen** ③ or 📷 **Kusatsu** ④ to stay in a hot-springs resort for the night, or move west to 📷 **Matsumoto** ⑤. If you choose Matsumoto, spend the latter part of the day taking in the historical sites—Matsumoto-jō and Kaichi Gakkō are must-sees—before retiring for the evening. The next day, begin a superlative day with Japan's biggest wasabi farm, followed by the nation's biggest collection of wood-block prints at the Nihon Ukiyo-e Hakubutsukan. You can catch an early evening express train back to Tōkyō after satisfying your belly in one of the city's popular eateries.

If you have 4 days

From Kansai, head for 📷 **Takayama** ⑧ ▶–⑯ for one or two nights and take a day trip to **Kamikōchi** ⑦. Next, head for 📷 **Matsumoto** ⑤ for another night or two. If you're bound for Nagoya, stop in Nagiso or Nakatsugawa to explore the towns of Tsumago or Magome in the 📷 **Kiso Valley** ⑥. If you're seeking outdoor adventure, you might want to take the time to tour the remote and scenic **Noto-hantō** ㊱ and take a train through Kurobe-kyōkoku, in Toyama-ken, in four days, using 📷 **Kanazawa** 🔞–㉞ as a base.

4

An early start from Tōkyō would afford you the opportunity to zip up to northern ⬚ **Niigata** ㊳ on the Shinkansen, and be relaxing on ⬚ **Sado Island** ㊴–㊷ by lunch time. You can spend the rest of the day exploring all the secluded coves and craggy shores of the island, either by bicycle or bus. The next day, head back to Honshū, taking the ferry from ⬚ **Ogi** ㊶ to Naoetsu port, where you can easily catch a train to ⬚ **Nagano** ➋ (Shinetsu line, 90 minutes). Pause to admire Zenkō-ji before heading to ⬚ **Yudanaka Onsen** ➌ or ⬚ **Kusatsu** ➍ for the night. Spend the last two days in ⬚ **Matsumoto** ➎.

If you have
7 to 9
days

From Kansai, spend your first day in ⬚ **Matsumoto** ➎ ▶ to get a taste of a traditional castle town. On the second day take an excursion to the old post villages of the ⬚ **Kiso Valley** ➏, where you can walk in the footsteps of Edo merchants along the old trading route. On your third day, travel through the mountains to ⬚ **Kamikōchi** ➐, spending the night here. Your next destination will be ⬚ **Takayama** ➑–⓰, where you should set aside at least an entire day to take in some of the city' fabulous architecture and valuable cultural sights. On the sixth day leave the mountains for ⬚ **Kanazawa** ⓲–㉞ and save the last day or two for a trip to the ⬚ **Noto-hantō** ㊱. If you don't linger too long in Kanazawa, you'll have enough time to make it to Mawaki Onsen on the northeastern tip for your last night.

If you're coming from and returning to Tōkyō, consider altering your itinerary slightly. From ⬚ **Matsumoto** ➎ ▶, go through the ⬚ **Kiso Valley** ➏, and make a brief stop in ⬚ **Kamikōchi** ➐ before ending up in ⬚ **Takayama** ➑–⓰ for your fourth night. From here, head over the mountains through the old farm town of **Ogi-machi** ⓱, ending up in ⬚ **Kanazawa** ⓲–㉞ for the night. After paying an early morning visit to the Kenrokuen or Gyokusenen gardens, have lunch in Tatemachi. In the afternoon, follow the coast to **Niigata** ㊳. You can choose to indulge in a coastal meal of seafood and fresh fish in the big city, and retire in one of its many inexpensive business hotels, or take the ferry over to **Sado Island** ㊴–㊷ for some pricier but more interesting accommodations. Spend the last day exploring the isle before ferrying back to Niigata and catching the Shinkansen going south.

---

head to the observation platform at **Usui-tōge** (Usui Pass, 碓氷峠). You can also see neighboring Myogi-san, as well as the whole Yatsugatake, a range of eight volcanic peaks. To get there, walk northeast along shop-filled Karuizawa Ginza street to the end, past Nite-bashi, and follow the trail to the pass. The spectacular view certainly justifies the 1½-hour walk.

Hiking paths at **Shiraito-no-taki and Ryūgaeshi-no-taki** (Shiraito and Ryūgaeshi falls, 白糸の滝 and 竜返しの滝) can get very crowded during the tourist season, but they do make for a pleasant afternoon excursion in the off-season. To get to the trailhead at Mine-no-Chaya, take the bus from Naka-Karuizawa. The ride takes about 25 minutes. From the trailhead it's about a 1½-km (1-mi) hike to Shiraito. From there the trail swings southeast, and 3 km (2 mi) farther are the Ryūgaeshi Falls. For a longer hike, walk back to town via Mikasa village. It'll take you about an hour and 15 minutes. Or catch the bus bound for Karuizawa (10 minutes), which leaves twice hourly from the parking lot.

Yachō-no-mori (Wild Bird Forest, 野鳥の森) is home to about 120 species of birds. You can look closely at the birds' habitat from two observation huts along a 2½-km (1½-mi) forest course. To get to the sanctuary, take a five-minute bus ride from Naka-Karuizawa Station to Nishikuiriguchi, and then walk for 10 minutesup the small road. The narrow entrance is shortly after the café, restaurant, and onsen on the left. Alternatively, you can bike to the mouth of the sanctuary in about 15 minutes. Bikes can be rented at Naka-Karuizawa Station for ¥800 per hour, or ¥2,000 a day.

Where to Stay

$$–$$$ 🏠 **Pension Grasshopper** (ペンショングラスホッパー). This guesthouse offers friendly hospitality and Western-style beds with great views of Asamasan. The English-speaking owner, Kayo Iwasaki, whips up a delicious mix of Japanese and Western fare. If you opt out of the meal plan, the price will be reduced by ¥2,675 per person, but you must specify this at the time of booking. The house is in the suburbs, but the management will transport you to and from the station. ⊠ *5410 Kariyado, Karuizawa-chō, Kitasaku-gun, Nagano-ken 389–0111* ☎ *0267/46–1333* 📠 *0267/46–1099* 🛏 *10 rooms without bath* 🍴 *Dining room, Japanese baths* ▭ *MC, V* 🍽 *EP, MAP.*

Nagano & Environs   長野とその周辺

97 min northwest of Tōkyō's Ueno Station by Shinkansen, 40 min northwest of Karuizawa by Shinkansen, 3 hrs northeast of Nagoya by JR Limited Express.

Nagano   長野

❷ When Nagano (population 300,000) hosted the 1998 XVIII Winter Olympics, a new Shinkansen line was built connecting Tōkyō and Nagano, and new highways were added to handle the increased car and bus traffic. As a result, the somewhat inaccessible Alps region was opened to visitors.

You can pick up a free map of Nagano at the **City Tourist Office** (長野市観光情報センター; ☎026/226–5626 ⊕www.nagano-tabi.net/english), open daily from 9 to 6, inside the JR station.

★ Nagano's unusual **Zenkō-ji** (善光寺) is the final destination for millions of pilgrims each year, the majority of whom are female. Since the 6th century, it has advocated an open-door policy: accepting believers of all religions; admitting women when other temples forbade it; and adhering to no particular sect of Buddhism. As you approach the main hall, do as the pilgrims do and light a few joss sticks, waving the smoke over yourself to bring good fortune and health. Inside, rub the worn wooden statue of the ancient doctor Binzuru (Pindola Bharadvaja in Sanskrit), for relief of aches and pains. A faithful disciple of Buddha, and one of 16 arhats required to uphold the Buddhist law, Binzuru is most famous for stories of his miraculous powers and ability to fly.

Next, summon your courage and explore the pitch-black tunnel in the basement to see if you can find the handlelike latch on the wall, the seizing of which is said to bring enlightenment (eventually). The first Buddhist icon to enter Japan from India (via Korea) in the 6th century is stowed away in the deep recesses of Zenkō-ji, and an exact replica is revealed to the public every seven years. The next opportunity to observe this ceremony, called Gokaichō, will be in April and May of 2010. Hop on Bus 33, 40, or 45 at platform 1 for the 10-minute trip (¥100) through the center of Nagano to the temple gate. ⊠ *Motoyoshi 4–9–1* ☎ *026/234–3591* 🚇 *¥500* 🕙 *Inner sanctuary daily 5:30–4:30.*

Yudanaka Onsen   湯田中温泉

❸ Northeast of Nagano, the Yudanaka Onsen area has hot springs made famous by photographs of snow-covered monkeys huddling in open-air thermal pools to keep warm. Between Yudanaka Onsen and Shibu Spa Resort, there are nine open-air hot springs. The specific onsen where the monkeys come to soak is known as Jigoku-dani (Hell Valley) and is just east of Yudanaka and Shibu. Yudanaka is the last stop on the Nagano Dentetsu Line; the trip from Nagano takes 40 minutes and costs ¥1,230. Several spas string out from here. In its natural aspects, the area is not unlike Yellowstone National Park in the United States, with its bubbling, steaming, sulfurous volcanic vents and pools. However, considerable development including more than 100 inns and hotels, several streets, and shops ends the comparison. The spas are the gateway to Shiga Kōgen (Shiga Heights), site of the Olympic alpine skiing and snowboarding slalom event.

The **Yudanaka Health Center** (湯田中ヘルスケアーセンター) is a public onsen across the Yomase-gawa from the Yudanaka station, and it costs ¥800. Facilities include 10 kinds of mineral baths and a large swimming pool. ⊠ *Shin-Yudanaka Onsen, Yudanakashibu Onsen-gō, Yamanouchi-chō* ☎ *026/933–5888.*

The entire Yudanaka resort area and Shiga Kōgen ski area fall under the jurisdiction of Yamanouchi Town; the **tourist information center** (観光案内センター; ☎ 0269/33–1107, 0269/33–2138 for reservations assistance) is just south of Yudanaka Station.

Kusatsu   草津

★ ❹ The highly touted hot springs at Kusatsu contain sulfur, iron, aluminum, and even trace amounts of arsenic. Just inside the border of Gunma Prefecture, they can be reached in summer by a bus route across Shiga Kōgen from Yudanaka, or by bus from Karuizawa. The *yu-batake* (hot-spring field) gushes 5,000 liters of boiling, sulfur-laden water per minute before it's cooled in seven long wooden boxes and sent on its way to more than 130 ryokans in the village. Beautifully lit up at night, the open field is quite a spectacle.

Netsu-no-yu (Fever Bath. 熱の湯) is the main and often unbearably hot public bath right next door to the yuba-take. Here you can watch one of six daily *yumomi* shows (7 AM, 7:30 AM, 3 PM, 3:35 PM, 4 PM, and 4:35 PM) between April and October, in which locals churn the waters with long wooden planks until the baths have reached a comfortable temperature. Visitors are encouraged to participate. ⊠ *414 Kusatsu-chō* ☎ *0279/88–3613* 🚇 *¥500* 🕙 *Daily 7 AM–10 PM.*

4

Architecture

You may not have heard the name *gassho-zukuri*, but chances are you've seen pictures of these unique cottage homes, found in the mountains of central Japan between Nagoya and Kanazawa. The term gassho-zukuri means "praying hands" and refers to the look of the houses' extremely steep, sloping roofs. Although modern Japanese no longer live in gassho-zukuri houses, several hundred homes have been preserved in historic village settings. These villages, developed in the 1990s, have become increasingly popular tourist destinations, especially for domestic travelers. Of the 150 or so gassho-zukuri that remain, more than half are in the Hida Folk Village in ⇨ Takayama and the Shirakawa-gō Gassho-zukuri Village in ⇨ Ogi-machi.

Festivals

Takayama's biannual festival (April 14–15 and October 9–10) is thought to have originated in the 17th century, possibly from an attempt to appease angry gods in a time of plague. This spectacle transforms the usually quiet town into a rowdy, colorful party scene and culminates in a musical parade of intricately carved and decorated *yatai* (floats) and puppets. Flags and draperies adorn local houses, and at night the yatai are hung with lanterns. Should you plan to attend, book rooms well ahead and expect to pay inflated prices. April's Sannō Matsuri is slightly bigger than October's Hachi-man Matsuri.

During Kanazawa's Hyaku-man-goku Matsuri (June 13–15), parades of people dressed in ancient Kaga costumes march through the city to the sound of folk music. Nō (old-style Japanese theater) performances and singing and dancing in parks add to the contagious atmosphere of merrymaking.

Of the *many* festivals on the Noto-hantō, the impressive ones that attract TV cameras and revelers from far and wide are Nanao's famous Seihakusai festival, a 400-year-old tradition, held May 3–5, and Ishizaki Hoto Matsuri, held the first Saturday of August.

Hiking

The Japan Alps and nearby ranges are a hiker's paradise. Although none of the peaks is more than 11,000 ft, they offer staggering views and a serious workout. The breathtaking Kamikōchi area of Nagano is laced with trails both through and around the snow peaks. Hiking paths and lodges line the wooded banks of the Azusa-gawa. Haku-san, in Ishikawa (accessed from Shiramine), and Tate-yama (from Kurobe-kyōkoku), in Toyama, are two surmountable, sizable peaks ideal for the experienced and prepared hiker. Hidden beneath snow in winter, the highland slopes and valleys come alive with wildflowers in summer.

Hot Springs

Onsen near coastal regions tend to be salty and high in calcium, while those in mountain areas are usually higher in iron and sulfur. Each lays claim to various skin, bone, and mental health benefits, while relaxation and rejuvenation are guaranteed. Mawaki Onsen, in Noto-hantō, overlooks Toyama Bay, while the open-air onsen of Nagano and Gunma, such as Yudanaka or Kusatsu, deliver crisp mountain air and pine-scented breezes.

Skiing Thanks to the 1998 Nagano Winter Olympics, many resorts were upgraded; even expert skiers (and snowboarders) should find something satisfying—if not exhilarating—among the more than 20 resorts. Although the area doesn't get the powdery stuff like you find in Colorado or Hokkaidō, the snow still attracts plenty of outdoor enthusiasts, particularly on weekends. Shiga Kōgen, near Yudanaka, and Happa-one, near Hakuba, are among the best areas.

For a dip in the open air, try the 5,500-square-ft milky bath at **Sai-no-kawara Dai-rotemburo** (西の河原大露天風呂) in the western end of Kusatsu village. Gaze at the pleasant scenery by day, or the twinkling stars overhead after nightfall. The spa is a 15-minute walk west from the Kusatsu bus terminal. ⊠ *521–3 Kusatsu-chō* ☎ *0279/88–6167* 🔁 *¥500* ⊙ *Apr.–Nov., daily 7 AM–8 PM; Dec.–Mar., daily 9 AM–8 PM.*

For more information on local hot springs and accommodations call the **Kusatsu Information Center** (草津観光案内センター; ☎ 0279/88–3642 ⊕ www.kusatsu-onsen.ne.jp/eng/index.html) or consult their excellent Web site, which explains the history of Kusatsu, and provides great resources for planning a trip to the area.

Where to Eat & Stay

\$–\$\$ ✕ **Tomikura-ya** (富蔵家). If you happen to be near Zenkō-ji around lunch time, stop for a meal at this soba shop. Although the interior is simple, the noodles such as *tenzaru* (topped with tempura) for ¥1,375, or *kaki-age* (mixed vegetable fritter) for ¥1,050, are very satisfying. For a lighter mid-afternoon snack, try the interesting *beni-sasazushi* (balls of sticky rice topped with mountain vegetables, walnuts, and miso), which cost ¥315 for two. The small restaurant is one block below the Hotel Fujiya on the same side of Chūō-dōri, and it's open from 11 AM to 5 PM. ⊠ *52 Daimon-chō, Nagano-shi* ☎ *026/231–5320* ▤ *No credit cards* ⊙ *No dinner.*

★ **\$\$\$–\$\$\$\$** 🏨 **Hotel Fujiya** (Gohonjin Fujiya, 御本陣藤屋旅館). The newest part of this famous hotel was rebuilt in 1923, while the rest has been around since the 1660s. During its long life, everyone from feudal lords to celebrities have stayed here—and left autographed plaques—en route to Zenkōji. Tatami rooms vary from small (¥9,450 per person, including meals) to the royal suite (¥28,000 per person, including meals), which has three rooms with sliding doors that open onto a garden. Among the furnishings are antiques and scrolls. Several rooms have private baths, and the shared bath is unusually deep. Fujiya is not sophisticated, but it's wonderfully old-fashioned. No English is spoken, but the family who's been running the hotel since its doors first opened are wonderfully friendly and appreciative of respectful foreigners. It's on Chūō-dōri, two blocks below the temple. ⊠ *80 Daimon-chō, Nagano-shi, Nagano-ken 380-0841* ☎ *026/232–1241* 🖷 *026/232–1243* ⊕ *www.avis.ne.jp/~fuziya* 🛏 *25 rooms, 3 with private bath* ⌂ *Dining room, Japanese baths* ▤ *AE, DC, MC, V* ⊚ *MAP.*

\$\$ ✕🏨 **Nagano Sunroute Hotel** (ホテルサンルート長野). Across from JR Nagano Station, you enter the reception area and tea lounge of this hotel by escalator from the street. A coffee table and two easy chairs are squeezed into each compact and clean Western-style room, which is all you need if you're just passing through en route to other Alps destinations. **Rinsen,** a modern Japanese restaurant off the lobby, has stylish private rooms where you can try curious creations such as cheese tofu (¥630), garlic beef steak (¥987), and chicken with fruit sauce (¥609). ⊠ *1–28–3 Minami-Chitose, Nagano-shi, Nagano-ken 380–0823* ☎ *026/228–2222* 🖷 *026/228–2244* ⊕ *www.sunroute.jp* ⇆ *143 rooms* ⌂ *Restaurant, coffee shop, tea shop, in-room data ports, no-smoking rooms* ⊟ *AE, DC, MC, V.*

★ ¢ 🈁 **Uotoshi Ryokan** (魚敏旅館). This small ryokan in the steamy bath village of Yudanaka has a 24-hour, hot springs–fed *hinoki* (cypress) bathtub. The rooms are rustic and cozy, and not terribly fancy. You can try Japanese archery (*kyūdō*) in the afternoon and look forward to a healthy and delicious dinner of mountain vegetables and Nihon-kai seafood (¥2,520–¥3,680). It's a seven-minute walk from Yudanaka Station, across the Yomase River on the left-hand side. ⊠ *2563 Sano, Yamanouchi-machi, Shimo-Takai-gun, Nagano-ken 381–0402* ☎ *0269/ 33–1215* 🖷 *0269/33–0074* ⊕ *www.avis.ne.jp/~miyasaka* ⇆ *8 Japanese-style rooms without bath* ⌂ *Restaurant, Japanese baths, hot springs* ⊟ *AE, MC, V.*

Matsumoto 松本

▶ ❺ *1 hr southwest of Nagano on JR Shinonoi Line, 2 hrs and 40 min northwest of Tōkyō Shinjuku Station on JR Chūō Line, 2¼ hrs northeast of Nagoya on JR Chūō Line.*

Snowcapped peaks surround Matsumoto on its alpine plateau, where the air is cool and dry. Here an interesting variety of restaurants, shops, and nightlife coexist with one of Japan's oldest castles.

Old Town

To make the most of Matsumoto, pick up a map at the **tourist information center** (松本駅観光案内所 ☎0263/32–2814) at the JR station, and head for the old part of town near the Chitose-bashi Bridge at the end of Honmachi-dōri. *Kura* (warehouses), typical of the early Meiji period and unusual in their use of irregular stone crisscross patterns, adorn the banks of the Metoba River. Matsumoto-jō and the Kaichi School House await on the other side.

★ **Matsumoto-jō** (Matsumoto Castle, 松本城), nicknamed Karasu-jō (Crow Castle) for its black walls, began as a small fortress with moats in 1504. It was remodeled into its current three-turreted form at the turn of the 17th century (1592–1614), just as Japan became a consolidated nation under a central government. The civil wars ended, and the peaceful Edo era began, rendering medieval castles obsolete. Its late construction may explain why the 95-ft-tall *tenshukaku* (stronghold or inner tower) is the oldest surviving tower in Japan—no battles were ever fought here. An exhibit on each floor breaks up the challenging climb (up very steep stairs) to the top. You have to wear the slippers offered to you as you enter, but be forewarned: they make the ascent a little tricky. It's worth the maneuvering, though, because with all those mountains around, the views from the sixth floor are the stuff of postcards.

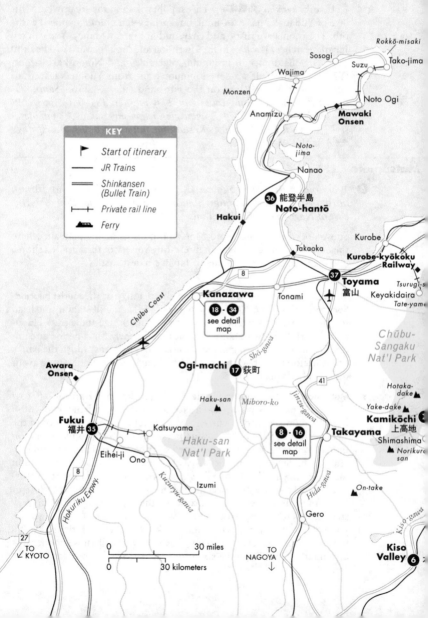

The Japan Alps

NIHON-KAI
(Sea of Japan)

Rokkō-misaki

Sosogi

Wajima   Suzu   Tako-jima

Monzen   Noto Ogi

Anamizu   **Mawaki Onsen**

Noto-jima

Nanao

🏴 36 能登半島
Noto-hantō

Hakui

Kurobe

Takaoka   **Kurobe-kyōkoku Railway**

🏴 37   *Tsurugi-s*
Toyama
富山   Keyakidaira
Kanazawa   Tonami   *Tate-yama*

18 - 34
see detail
map

Chūbu-Sangaku Nat'l Park

Ogi-machi 17 荻町

Awara Onsen

Haku-san   *Miboro-ko*   *Hotaka-dake*

Yake-dake
Kamikōchi
上高地

8 - 16
see detail
map

Fukui
福井 35   Katsuyama

Takayama
Shimashima
Norikura-san

Eihei-ji   Ono   *Haku-san Nat'l Park*

Izumi

On-take

Gero

27
TO
KYOTO

TO
NAGOYA

Kiso Valley 6

KEY

🏴 *Start of itinerary*
— *JR Trains*
= *Shinkansen (Bullet Train)*
+ *Private rail line*
🚢 *Ferry*

Chūbu Coast

Kuzuryu-gawa

Sho-gawa

Jinzu-gawa

Hida-gawa

Kiso-gawa

Hokuriku Expwy.

8

41

0   30 miles
0   30 kilometers

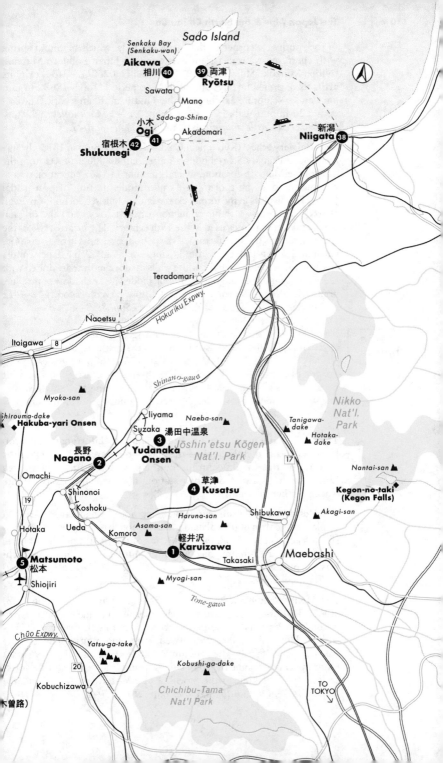

In the southwest corner of the castle grounds, which bloom in spring with cherry trees, azaleas, and wisteria, the **Japan Folklore Museum** (Nihon Minzoku Shiryōkan, 日本民俗資料館; ☎ 0263/32–0133) exhibits artifacts of prefeudal days and of the Edo period (1603–1868). In January an ice-sculpture exhibition is held in the museum's park. The castle is a 20-minute walk from the station. ⊠ *4–1 Marunouchi* ☎ *0263/ 32–2902* 🌊 *Castle and museum ¥520* ⏱ *Daily 8:30–5.*

★ **Kaichi Primary School** (Kyū Kaichi Gakkō, 開智学校). Built in 1873, the former Kaichi Primary School houses more than 80,000 artifacts from the days of the Meiji Restoration, when beginning in 1867 education was to become the unifying tool for the rapid modernization of post-feudal Japan. The displays in the former classrooms include school uniforms, wall charts (used prior to the introduction of textbooks), and the original desks and writing slates used in the 19th century. The bizarre style of the building reflects the architecture of the period: a mishmash of diverse Occidental elements fashioned from Japanese materials. A big, fancy cupola sits atop the shingled roof; the white walls made of mortar are dotted with red, slatted windows; and the front door, hidden in the shadow of the blue, grandiose balcony, is protected by a skillfully carved dragon. ⊠ *2–4–12 Kaichi* ☎ *0263/32–5725* 🌊 *¥300* ⏱ *Tues.–Sun. 8:30–5.*

> **need a break?**
>
> Two blocks before the Chitose-bashi Bridge, which takes you from Hon-machi dōri across the river to the castle, is **Old Rock** (オールドロック; ⊠ 2–3–20 Chūō ☎ 0263/38–0069), a Japanese version of a traditional British pub. Fish-and-chips are ¥780 and draft beer includes Guinness, Kilkenny, Boddingtons, and Stella Artois. Prepare yourself for jovial bartenders and amusing knickknacks.

Museums

The city's museums are west of the JR station. Unfortunately, it's too far to walk, and there's no bus—the only options are a ¥2,000 taxi ride, or a trip on the Kamikōchi train (on the private Matsumoto Dentetsu Line) four stops away to Oniwa Station, from which it's a 10-minute walk to either museum.

The **Matsumoto Folk Craft Museum** (Matsumoto Mingeikan, 松本民芸館) displays more than 600 local, hand-made wood, bamboo, and glass utensils. It's across town from the castle, east of the JR station. To get here, take a taxi or a 15-minute bus ride to the Shimoganai Mingeikan-guchi bus stop. ⊠ *1313–1 Satoyamabe* ☎ *0263/33–1569* 🌊 *¥210* ⏱ *Tues.–Sun. 9–5.*

★ The **Japan Wood-Block Print Museum** (Nihon Ukiyo-e Hakubutsukan, 日本浮世絵博物館) is devoted to the lively, colorful, and widely popular *ukiyo-e* wood-block prints of Edo-period artists, featuring the well-known Hiroshige, Hokusai, and Sharaku. Based on the enormous holdings of the wealthy Sakai family, the museum's 100,000 pieces (displays rotate monthly) contain some of Japan's finest prints and represent the largest collection of its kind in the world. ⊠ *2206–1 Koshiba, Shimadachi* ☎ *0263/47–4440* ⊕ *http://ukiyo-e.co.jp* 🌊 *¥1,000* ⏱ *Tues.–Sun. 10–5.*

The **Japan Judicature Museum** (Shihō Butsukan, 日本司法博物館), next to the Ukiyo-e Hakubutsukan, is Japan's oldest palatial court building and used to house the Matsumoto District Court. Displays pertain to the history of law enforcement from the feudal period to the modern era. ⊠ *2206–1 Shimadachi-Koshiba* ☎ *0263/47–4515* ✒ *¥700* ⊘ *Daily 9–4:30.*

Around Matsumoto

Two more spots of interest, the Daiō horseradish farm and the Rokuzan Art Museum, are 10 stops north of Matsumoto, on the same line, at Hotaka Station. The local train journey will take you through the ravishing beauty of vibrant green fields, apple orchards, and miles upon miles of rice paddies, set against a backdrop of the snowy Alps.

The **Rokuzan Art Museum** (Rokuzan Bijutsukan, 碌山美術館) displays the work of Rokuzan Ogiwara, a master sculptor often referred to as the Rodin of Asia. His works are displayed within an attractive, ivy-covered brick building with a stunning bell tower. The museum is in Hotaka, 10 stops north of Matsumoto Station on the JR Oito Line. From Hotaka Station it's a 10-minute walk to the museum. Ask station attendants to point you in the right direction. ⊠ *5095–1 Ōaza-hotaka* ☎ *0263/82–2094* ✒ *¥700* ⊘ *Apr.–Oct., Tues.–Sun. 9–5; Nov.–Mar., Tues.–Sun. 9–4.*

off the beaten path

DAIŌ WASABI FARM (Daiō Wasabi Nōjo, 大王わさび農場) – At the largest wasabi farm in the country, you can learn about an agricultural technique unique to Japan. The green horseradish roots are cultivated in flat gravel beds irrigated by the melted snow that flows down from the surrounding Alps into the lush Azumino Valley, which extends north from Matsumoto to the Japan Sea. Maintaining a frosty, year-round temperature of 13°C, the mineral water is ideal for the durable wasabi.

If you're feeling adventurous, try some of the farm's products, which range from wasabi cheese and mayonnaise to white wasabi chocolate and ice cream. You can also join one of the 20-minute workshops (¥1,000) to pickle your own horseradish—a "hot" souvenir. Even if you don't like wasabi, you can amble along the paths admiring the vegetation: rows of acadia and poplar trees line the embankments, walnut and plum trees dot the peripheries, and the fields of fresh, green wasabi leaves bloom with white flowers in late spring. The farm is 10 stops (only one if you take the express) north along the JR Ōito Line from platform 6 in Matsumoto Station. To reach the farm you can rent a bike, take a 40-minute walk along a path from the train station (the station attendant will give you directions), or hop in a taxi for about ¥1,170. ⊠ *1692 Hotaka* ☎ *0263/82–8112* ✒ *Free* ⊘ *Daily 10–5:30.*

Where to Eat & Stay

★ ¢ ✕ **Dehli** (デリー). As you open the door to this curry house, savory, mouthwatering smells overwhelm your nose and tease your tastebuds, while an attentive staff welcomes you with a friendly "*irrashaimase*" (welcome!). The house specialty is a fiery Indian-style chicken curry that will send you to spice heaven. Look for the low eaves and black latticework of the traditional building on the south bank of the Metoba River, a five-minute walk east of Chitose-bashi Bridge. The windows are covered with colorful rice paper, and a tiny menu is posted near the door. Catering to a lunchtime crowd, Dehli is open from mid-morning to 6:45 PM. ⊠ *2–4–13 Chūō* ☏ *0263/35–2408* ✆ *Close Wed.*

$–$$
Fodor'sChoice
★
✕ **Kura** (くら). For a surprisingly small number of yen, you can do some serious feasting in this funky 90-year-old Meiji-era warehouse in the center of town. The place serves a full range of sushi and traditional fare: the *aji tataki* (horse-mackerel sashimi) and tempura are particularly tasty. You can't miss with the daily lunch course, either. The owner maintains a stoic face as he expertly prepares your meal, but should his wife spot you relishing the food, you're in for a treat of some downright disarming hospitality—she has an arsenal of potent *ji-zake* (locally brewed sake) and a heart of pure gold. From the station, take a left and turn onto Kōen-dōri. Take a left after Parco department store, and you can see the restaurant's whitewashed facade and curved black eaves on the left. ⊠ *2–2–15 Chūō* ☏ *0263/33–6444* ▤ *AE, MC, V* ✆ *Closed Wed.*

$$$
⊞ **Hotel Buena Vista** (ホテルブエナビスタ). One of Matsumoto's newest and most expensive hotels, the Buena Vista has a glowing marble lobby, a coffeehouse, a café-bar, four restaurants (two Japanese, one Chinese, one French), *and* a sky lounge on the 14th floor called **Monpage.** As the name implies, you can get a great view from the higher floors. Corner rooms with two large picture windows are hot sellers; be sure to request them in advance. Single rooms snugly accommodate a small double bed, while standard doubles and twins have space for a table and chairs. The hotel is four blocks southeast of Matsumoto Station. ⊠ *1–2–1 Hon-jō, Matsumoto, Nagano-ken 390-0814* ☏ *0263/37–0111* 🖷 *0263/37–0666* ⊕ *www.buena-vista.co.jp* 🛏 *200 rooms* ⌂ *5 restaurants, coffee shop, hair salon, massage, bar, no-smoking rooms* ▤ *AE, DC, MC, V.*

$$
⊞ **Hotel New Station** (ホテルニューステーション). Although other good-value business hotels are often rather sterile, this one has a cheerful and attentive staff, and a fun restaurant that serves flavorful freshwater *iwana* (char)—a specialty to the area. Rooms are clean and adequate, but a bit small. To get a "full-size" room by Western standards, request a deluxe twin. There are private baths in every room, as well as shared Japanese baths. To reach the hotel, take a left when you exit the station and walk south for about two minutes. ⊠ *1–1–11 Chūō, Matsumoto, Nagano-ken 390–0811* ☏ *0263/35–3850* 🖷 *0263/35–3851* ⊕ *www.hotel-ns.co.jp/english.html* 🛏 *103 rooms* ⌂ *Restaurant, meeting room, Japanese baths, no-smoking rooms* ▤ *AE, DC, MC, V.*

Nightlife

Off the small park north of the Hotel Buena Vista, **Half Time** (⊠ Takeuchi San-box, 2nd fl., 1–4–10 Fukashi ☏ 0263/36–4985) is a tiny jazz joint that serves tasty cocktails and snacks from 7 PM until well into the wee hours. Owner Akira Shiohara, who is quite a trumpet player, will even join in if you ask him. Two doors down, you can find another bar, **People's** (⊠ Washizawa Building, 2nd fl., 1–4–11 Fukashi ☏ 0263/37–5011), offering cheap Internet access (¥200 per hour), plus beer, cock-

tails, and casual Italian fare. **Monpage** (⊠ 1–2–1 Hon-jō ☎ 0263/
37–0111), the 14th-floor sky lounge of the Buena Vista Hotel, sizzles
nightly with live jazz. The incredible view alone is well worth the cover
(up to ¥2,000). In summer the same price will get you unlimited snacks
and beer from 5:30 to 8:30.

Kiso Valley   木曽谷（木曽路）

★ ❻ *1 hr south of Matsumoto on JR Chūo Line.*

This deep, narrow valley is cut by the Kiso-gawa and enclosed by the
central Alps to the east and the northern Alps to the west. From 1603
to 1867 the area was called Nakasendo (center highway), because it connected western Japan and Kyōto to Edo (present-day Tōkyō).

After the Tōkaidō highway was built along the Pacific coast and the Chūo
train line was constructed to connect Nagoya and Niigata, the 11 old
post villages, where walking travelers and traders once stopped to refresh themselves along the difficult journey, became ghost towns. Two
villages, **Tsumago** and **Magome,** have benefited from recent efforts to
retain the memory of these old settlements. Walking through these preserved, historical areas, you can almost imagine life centuries ago, when
the rustic shops were stocked with supplies instead of souvenirs.

The **Magome Tourist Information Office** (馬籠観光案内所; ☎ 0264/59–2336)
is open from April to November, daily 9 to 5; and from December to
March, Monday to Saturday, 9 to 5. The staff can help you reserve a
hotel room. The **Tsumago Tourist Information Office** (妻籠観光案内所;
☎ 0264/57–3123) has the same hours and services as the Magome
tourist office.

Where to Stay
Be sure to reserve a room in advance, especially for stays on weekends.

★ $$–$$$ ▣ **Hatago Matsushiro-ya** (旅籠松代屋). Tsumago's traditional atmosphere
resonates in this small ryokan, which has been operating as a guesthouse
since 1804. Ten large tatami rooms share a single bath and four immaculately clean old-fashioned pit toilets. Delectable dinners are delicately arranged and served in your room. No English is spoken here, so
a Japanese speaker or someone from the tourist office will need to make
your reservation. The ryokan is closed from Wednesday morning to Thursday morning. ⊠ *807 Azuma-terashita, Minami-Nagiso-machi, Kiso-gun,
Nagano-ken 399–5302* ☎ *0264/57–3022* ⤳ *10 Japanese-style rooms
without bath* ⬧ *Japanese baths; no room phone* ⊟ *No credit cards*
⦿ *MAP.*

$$ ▣ **Onyado Daikichi** (御宿大吉). At this pleasant *minshuku,* windows in
all six tatami rooms face the wooded valley. You can find traditional
shared Japanese baths. At dinner the chef makes good use of the local
specialties, such as horse-meat sashimi, mountain vegetables, and fried
grasshoppers. More familiar dishes are available for the squeamish.
Owner Nobuka-san makes foreign guests feel very welcome, and even
speaks a little English. ⊠ *Tsumago, Nagiso-machi, Kiso-gun, Nagano-
ken 399-5302* ☎ *0264/57–2595* 🖷 *0274/57–2203* ⤳ *6 Japanese-*

style rooms without bath ⚇ *Dining room, Japanese baths* ⊟ *No credit cards* ⍰ *MAP.*

Getting Around

The central valley town of Nagiso is one hour south of Matsumoto on the JR Chūō Line. Tsumago is a 10-minute bus ride (¥240) from JR Nagiso Station. Magome is closer to JR Nakatsugawa Station, which is 12 minutes south on the same line. Both towns are served by buses from the Nagiso and Nakatsugawa stations, so you can take a bus to one village and return from the other. Local buses between Magome and Tsumago are infrequent.

en route

You can make a hike out of your visit by tracing the **old trade route** (旧中仙道) between Magome and Tsumago, which takes about three hours. Although you find people making this trip in both directions—hilly both ways—it's most commonly taken from Magome to Tsumago. Believe it or not, there's a baggage delivery service between the two towns (generally charging ¥500 per bag). Make arrangements at tourist information offices.

To get to Takayama from here, take the 50-minute bus ride from Magome to Gero; then transfer to a JR train for the 45-minute trip to Takayama (¥2,310; one departure per hour). Buses leave three times daily (7:21 AM and 12:05 PM with a change at Sakashita for Gero, or a direct bus at 4 PM); the fare is ¥2,300.

Kamikōchi   上高地

❼ *2 hrs west of Matsumoto by train (Dentetsu Line) and bus, 2 hrs east of Takayama by bus.*

The incomparably scenic route from Matsumoto to Takayama goes over the mountains and through Chūbu-Sangaku National Park (Chūbu-Sangaku Kokuritsu Kōen) via Kamikōchi. Travel on this route is only possible after the last week of April or the first week of May, when the plows have removed the almost 30 feet of snow that accumulate on the road in winter. If you spend the night in Kamikōchi, consider renting a rowboat at Taishō-ike (Taishō Pond)—the view of the snow-covered peaks from the pond is breathtaking.

Hiking

As you approach Kamikōchi, the valley opens onto a row of towering mountains: Oku-Hotaka-san is the highest, at 10,466 feet. Mae-Hotaka-san, at 10,138 feet, is on the left. To the right is Nishi-Hotaka-san, 9,544 feet. The icy waters of the Azusa-gawa flow from the small Taishō Pond at the southeast entrance to the basin.

From the many trails in and around Kamikōchi, you can reach most of the peaks without too much trouble. One easy three-hour walk east starts at **Kappa-bashi** (河童橋), a small suspension bridge over crystal-clear Azusa-gawa, a few minutes northeast of the bus terminal. You will pass the rock sculpture of the British explorer Reverend Walter Weston, who was the first foreigner to ascend these mountains. Continuing on the south side of the river, the trail cuts through pasture to rejoin the river at Myōshin Bridge. Cross here to reach Myōshin-ike (Myōshin Pond). At the edge of the pond sits the small Hotaka Jinja Kappa-bashi (Water Sprite Bridge).

To see the beautiful **Taishō-ike** (Taishō Pond, 大正池), head southeast from Kappa-bashi for a 20-minute walk. You can rent a boat (¥800 per half hour), or continue 90 minutes farther east to **Tokusawa**, an area that has camping grounds and great views of other mountains in the area.

Where to Stay

Hotels and ryokan in Kamikōchi close from mid-November to late April.

$$$$
Fodor'sChoice
★

Imperial Hotel (上高地帝国ホテル). This rustic alpine lodge is owned by Tōkyō's legendary Imperial Hotel, and many of the staff members are borrowed from that establishment for the summer to ensure top-notch service. In the lobby lounge, low wooden beams support the beautifully crafted ceiling, while a central hearth warms the room. The cherry oak furniture and red-velvet rugs on stone floors exude elegance. The guest rooms, decorated in brown tones, have sofas and lots of gorgeous wood-work; some even have balconies. There are Western and Japanese restaurants on the premises. Reservations must be made well in advance. You can see the hotel from Kamikōchi's bus terminal in the center of town. ⊠ *Kamikōchi, Azumi-mura, Minami-Azumi-gun, Nagano-ken 390–1516* ☎ *0263/95–2006, 03/3504–1111 Nov.–Mar., 212/692–9001 in U.S., 0171/355–1775 in U.K.* 🖷 *0263/95–2412* ⊕ *www.imperialhotel.co.jp* 🛏 *75 rooms* ♨ *3 restaurants, bar, lounge* ▤ *AE, DC, MC, V.*

$$$
Taishō-ike Hotel (大正池ホテル). This small mountain resort is perched on the rim of brilliant blue Taishō pond. The lobby, restaurant, and bath have large picture windows providing excellent views of the breathtaking landscape. Opt for the spacious Western-style rooms, with their comfortable beds and soft, puffy quilts. The Japanese rooms are not as nice as in other ryokans. You'll pay ¥3,000–¥5,000 less for rooms at the back, without a view of the water. ⊠ *Kamikōchi, Minami-azumi-gun, Nagano-ken 390–1516* ☎ *0263/95–2301* 🖷 *0263/95–2522* 🛏 *21 Western-style rooms, 6 Japanese-style rooms* ♨ *Restaurant, Japanese baths, shop; no room phones* ▤ *MC, V* ⎹◎⎸ *MAP.*

Getting Around

It takes about two hours to get to Kamikōchi from Matsumoto, and the trip involves taking a ride on both a train and a bus. You pay ¥2,400 for both legs of the trip at the start. Take the Matsumoto Electric Railway from Matsumoto Station to Shin-Shimashima, which is the last stop. There are one or two departures per hour, and the ride takes 30 minutes. At Shin-Shimashima Station, cross the road for the bus to Naka-no-yu and Kamikōchi. You can also take the bus from Matsumoto to Kamikōchi, but there are only two departures per day: at 8:55 AM and 10:15 AM.

Takayama 高山

2 hrs, 10 min north of Nagoya by JR Limited Express, 4 hrs north of Matsumoto by JR via Nagoya, 2 hrs, 20 min by bus from Matsumoto.

Takayama, originally called Hida, is a tranquil town that is imbued with a rare rustic charm owing to hundreds of years of peaceful isolation in the heart of the Hida San-myaku (Hida Mountains, 飛騨山脈). The downtown area is arranged like a museum, where shops and restaurants mingle with museums and inns along traditional rows of wood-lattice buildings. A peculiar-looking ball of cedar leaves suspended outside a storefront indicates a drinking establishment or brewery. Nicknamed "little Kyōto," Takayama can actually be a more rewarding experience, as it boasts fewer crowds and wider streets, not to mention fresh mountain air and gorgeous natural scenery.

Takayama's hugely popular festivals, spring's Sannō Matsuri (April 14–15) and the smaller autumn Hachi-man Matsuri (October 9–10), draw hundreds of thousands of spectators for the parades of floats. Hotels are booked solid during matsuri time, so if you plan to join the festivities, make your reservations several months in advance.

The **Hida Tourist Information Office** (飛騨観光案内所; ☎ 0577/32–5328 🖨 0577/33–5565 ⊕ www.hida.jp/e-taka.htm) in front of the JR station is open from April to October, daily 8:30 to 6:30; and from November to March, daily 8:30 to 5. The staff can provide maps and help you find accommodations, both in town and in the surrounding mountains.

★ ❽ **Takayama Jinya** (Historical Government House, 高山陣屋). This rare collection of stately buildings housed the 25 officials of the Tokugawa shogunate who administered the Hida region for 176 years. Highlights include an original storehouse (1606), which held city taxes in sacks of rice; a torture chamber, curiously translated as the "law court"; and samurai barracks. Free guided tours in English are available upon request and last 30 to 50 minutes. In front of the house you can buy fruit, vegetables, and local crafts at the **Jinya-mae Asa-ichi**, open from April to October, daily 6 to noon, and from November to February, daily 7 to noon. To get here from the JR station, head east on Hirokōji-dōri for a few blocks to the old section of town. Before the bridge, which crosses the small Miya-gawa, turn right, pass another bridge, and the Takayama Jinya will be on your right. ⊠ 1–5 Hachiken-machi ☎ 0577/32–0643 ☞ ¥420 ⊙ Mar.–Oct., daily 8:45–5; Feb.–Mar., daily 8:45–4:30.

❾ The main hall of **Shōren-ji** (照蓮寺) in Shiroyama Kōen (Shiroyama Park) was built in 1504. It was moved here in 1961 from its original site in Shirakawa-gō just before the area was flooded by the Miboro Dam. Beautifully carved, allegedly from the wood of a single cedar tree, this temple is an excellent example of classic Muromachi-period architecture. The temple sits on a hill surrounded by gardens, from where you can see the Takayama skyline and much of the park below. ⊠ Shiroyama Kōen ☎ 0577/32–2052 ☞ ¥200 ⊙ Apr.–Oct., daily 8–5:30; Nov.–Mar., daily 8–5.

❿ The **Archaeology Museum** (Hida Minzoku Kōkokan, 飛騨民族考古館) resides in an old house that once belonged to a physician who served the local daimyō. The mansion has mysterious eccentricities—hanging ceilings, secret windows, and hidden passages—all of which suggest ninja associations. Displays include wall hangings, weaving machines, and other

Hida regional items. ✉ *82 Kamisanno-machi* ☎ *0577/32–1980* 🎟 *¥500* ⊙ *Mar.–Nov., daily 8:30–5:30; Dec.–Feb., daily 9–5.*

⑪ The **San-machi-suji** (三町筋) section of town includes Ichino-machi, Nino-machi, and Sanno-machi streets, which all parallel the Miya-gawa. Most of the old teahouses, inns, dye houses, and sake breweries have been preserved, making this neighborhood somewhat of a vestige of pre-Meiji Japan.

★ **⑫** The **Folk-Craft Museum** (Kusakabe Mingeikan, 日下部民芸館) is in a house from the 1880s that belonged to the Kusakabe family—wealthy traders of the Edo period. The building served as a residence and warehouse, where the handsome interior, with heavy, polished beams and an earthy barren floor, provides an appropriate setting for the Hida folk crafts displayed here. ✉ *1–52 Ōjin-machi* ☎ *0577/32–0072* 🎟 *¥500* ⊙ *Mar.–Nov., daily 8:30–5; Dec.–Feb., Sat.–Thurs. 8:30–4:30.*

⑬ The **Yoshijima-ke** (吉島家) is an elegant merchant house museum that was rebuilt in 1908 but retains the distinctive characteristics of aristocratic houses from the Edo period. It's next door to Folk Craft Museum. ✉ *1–52 Ōjin-machi* ☎ *0577/32–0038* 🎟 *¥500* ⊙ *Mar.–Nov., daily 9–5; Dec.–Feb., Wed.–Mon. 9–4:30.*

★ **⑭** The **Takayama Float Exhibition Hall** (Takayama Yatai Kaikan, 高山屋台会館) is a community center of sorts that displays four of the 11 17th- and 18th-century *yatai* (festival floats) used in Takayama's famous Sannō and Hachiman festivals. More than two centuries ago Japan was ravaged by a wave of the bubonic plague, and yatai were built and paraded through the streets as a way of appeasing the gods. Because this seemed to work in Takayama, locals built bigger, more elaborate yatai to prevent further outbreaks. The delicately etched wooden panels, carved wooden lion head masks for dances, and the elaborate tapestries are all remarkable works of art. Technical wizardry is also involved, as each yatai contains puppets, controlled by rods and wires, that perform amazing feats, as if Olympic gymnasts. ⊠ *178 Sakura-machi* ☎ *0577/32–5100* ⊠ *¥820* ⊗ *Mar.–Nov., daily 8:30–5; Dec.–Feb., daily 9–4:30.*

⑮ **Kokubun-ji** (国分寺) is the city's oldest temple, dating from 1588, and it houses many objects of art, including a precious sword used by the Heike clan. In the Main Hall (built in 1615) sits a figure of Yakushi Nyorai, a Buddha who is purported to ease those struggling with illness. In front of the three-story pagoda is a wooden statue of another esoteric Buddhist figure, Kannon Bosatsu, who reputedly made a vow to hear the voices of all people and immediately grant salvation to those who are suffering. The ginkgo tree standing beside the pagoda is said to be more than 1,200 years old. ⊠ *1–83 Sowa-machi* ☎ *0577/32–1395* ⊠ *¥300* ⊗ *Daily 9–4.*

⑯ **Hida Folk Village** (Hida no Sato, 飛騨の里) is a collection of traditional

Fodor'sChoice ★ farmhouses transplanted here from all over the region. Moving the houses posed few problems because the structural assembly employs ropes rather than nails. Many of the houses are A-frames with thatched roofs called *gasshō-zukuri* (praying hands), so named for their steep triangular shape. Twelve of the buildings are "private houses" displaying folk materials like tableware and weaving tools. Another five houses are folk-craft workshops, with demonstrations of *ichii ittōbori* (wood carving), *Hida-nuri* (Hida lacquering), and other traditional regional arts. To get to Hida Minzoku Mura, walk 20 minutes south from Takayama Station and take a right over the first bridge onto Route 158. Continue west for 20 minutes to the village. You can also take a bus from platform 6, on the left side of the bus terminal. ⊠ *1–590 Kami-Okamoto-chō, 3 km (2 mi) west of Takayama* ☎ *0577/34–4711* ⊠ *¥700* ⊗ *Daily 8:30–5.*

Where to Eat & Stay

★ **$$$$** ✕ **Kakushō** (角正). This restaurant is locally famous for *sansai ryōri,* light meals of mountain vegetables soaked in a rich miso paste and served with freshwater fish that's grilled with salt or soy sauce. Occasionally this delectable treat is served atop a roasted magnolia leaf and called *hōba-miso.* Although there's no dress code per se, you might want to steer toward the semiformal to feel comfortable here. Above all, this is a friendly place, where the owner, Sumitake-san, will happily translate the menu for you. From Miya-gawa, head east on the Sanmachi-dōri, crossing four side streets (including the one running along the river), and take a left at the fifth block. There's no English sign out front, so look

GASSHO-ZUKURI FARMHOUSES

When gassho-zukuri construction reached a height early in the 18th century, there were more than 1,800 of the mountain farmhouses. The sloping gable roofs, achieved by placing wooden beams together at a steep, 60-degree angle, were built to prevent snow from piling up on the house. Large in scale, the open space inside allowed for a multitude of functions: a central hearth sent billows of smoke upward to cure meats and dry food, which were placed on a metal grill suspended from the ceiling; the huge floor space was

used to make gun powder and washi (Japanese paper); and the triangular alcove on top was reserved for silkworm cultivation. Stables were connected to the living space so no one had to go outdoors during the long, cold winter months. Perhaps most intriguing of all, the houses were built without nails. Strips of hazel branches tied the beams together, giving the joints the flexibility literally to sway in the wind.

for a small building with a white *noren* (hanging cloth) in the entrance way. It's directly across from a small pay parking lot. ✉ *2 Babachō-dōri* ☎ *0577/32–0174* ▭ *AE, DC, MC, V.*

$$$$ ✕ **Susaki** (洲さき). Traditional *kaiseki,* carefully prepared and artistically arranged dishes made from only the freshest and highest quality ingredients, are served on beautiful ceramic ware in this restaurant. From the west side of the river, cross the Naka-bashi bridge and you'll find it in the first building on the right. An old navy-blue noren marks the dark entranceway. ✉ *4–14 Shinmei* ☎ *0577/32–0023* ▭ *AE, DC, MC, V.*

★ **$$** ✕ **Suzuya** (寿々や). The secret recipes of this well-known restaurant have been passed down over several generations. The specialty of the house is superb and inexpensive sansai-ryōri, the time-honored mountain cuisine. Suzuya is in a traditional Hida-style house, and the dining room is intimate and wood-beamed. There's an English menu, and the staff is used to serving foreign guests. From the station, turn onto Kokubunji-dōri and take a right after five blocks. ✉ *24 Hanakawa* ☎ *0577/ 32–2484* ▭ *AE, DC, MC, V.*

$$$ ▦ **Hida Plaza Hotel** (ひだホテルプラザ). A cut above most other lodgings in its price range, this is the best international-style hotel in town. Traditional Hida ambience permeates the old wing and beautiful wood is used throughout the hotel's tastefully decorated restaurants. Tatami rooms exude elegance and simplicity, and the western rooms are amazingly large and comfy, with sofas. All rooms have wide-screen TVs, and many have views of the surrounding mountains. Although the newer wing is not nearly as attractive, its rooms are larger. Luxury makes an appearance in the form of mineral baths crafted of fragrant cypress wood. From the station, head north and you will see the hotel on the right. ✉ *2–60 Hanaoka-chō, Takayama, Gifu-ken 506–0009* ☎ *0577/33–4600* ▦ *0577/33–4602* ⤶ *136 Western-style rooms, 89 Japanese-style rooms, 2 suites* ⌂ *4 restaurants, coffee shop, indoor pool, health club, Japanese baths, sauna, dance club, shops* ▭ *AE, DC, MC, V.*

$–$$ ▣ **Minshuku Sōsuke** (民宿惣助). The owner of this private home runs a tight ship and speaks essential English, but don't expect her or her husband to be overly helpful. The shared rooms, baths, and toilets are kept spotless, which is undoubtedly one of the reasons Sōsuke is so popular. Meals are taken at long tables (tatami seating), where you have the opportunity to mingle with other guests. To get here, take a right from the Takayama Station, then another right at the first bridge, and walk seven minutes; it's opposite the enormous Green Hotel. ✉ *1–64 Okamoto-chō, Takayama, Gifu-ken 506–0054* ☎ *0577/32–0818* 🖷 *0577/32–0818* 🛏 *14 rooms without bath* ⚒ *Dining room, Japanese baths, no-smoking rooms; no room phones* ▭ *No credit cards* ⦿ *CP, MAP.*

★ $$ ▣ **Yamakyū** (山久). Cozy, antiques-filled nooks with chairs and coffee tables serve as small lounges in this old Tera-machi minshuku. In the mineral-water baths, a giant waterwheel turns hypnotically as you're lulled by recorded bird songs. Although there's an 11 PM curfew, dinner hours are more flexible than those of the typical minshuku, and the food, of astonishing variety, is superb. Fifteen of the rooms have private toilets. Yamakyū is east of the Enako-gawa, at the very top of San-machi dōri, about a 20-minute walk from Takayama Station. ✉ *58 Tenshō-ji-machi, Takayama, Gifu-ken 506–0832* ☎ *0577/32–3756* 🖷 *0577/35–2350* 🛏 *30 Japanese-style rooms without bath* ⚒ *Dining room, Japanese baths, shop* ▭ *No credit cards* ⦿ *MAP.*

Nightlife

Nightlife in sleepy Takayama revolves around locally produced beer and sake. Open for lunch until 3, and then again at 5:30, **Renga-ya** (レンガ屋; ✉ 3–58–11 Hon-machi ☎0577/36–1339) is a brewery, bar, and restaurant. Head east on Kokubun-ji-dōri and turn left just before the river. It's one block down, on the left. You'll see the brewery at work through the window.

Getting Around

Laid out in a grid pattern, compact Takayama is easy to explore on foot or by bicycle—bikes at the rental shop south of the station cost ¥300 per hour. In San-machi-suji, you can spend ¥3,000 (for two people) and have a 15-minute old-town rickshaw tour. If you just want to pose in one for a photograph, be ready to hand over ¥1,000.

BY BUS   It's easy to get to Takayama by bus from Matsumoto—but only between May and early November—and it costs ¥3,100. A highly recommended detour to Kamikōchi will bring the fare up to ¥6,260.

BY TRAIN   Takayama has connections north to Toyama by JR train (four departures daily). The ride takes about 90 minutes and costs between ¥1,150 and ¥1,620, depending on whether you reserve a seat and whether the train is running express. From Toyama there are trains east to Niigata or west to Kanazawa and the Noto-hantō, via Ogi-machi.

Ogi-machi   荻町

⑰ *2½ hrs northwest of Takayama by bus.*

It's speculated that Ogi-machi, a hamlet nestled deep within Shirakawa-gō village, was originally populated by survivors of the powerful Taira family, who were nearly all killed off in the 12th century by the rival Genji family. The majority of the residents living here still inhabit gasshō-zukuri houses. Both the shape and the materials enable the house to withstand the heavy regional snow, and in summer the straw keeps the houses cool. Household activities center on the *irori* (open hearth), which sends its smoke up through the timbers and thatched roof. Meats and fish are preserved (usually on a metal shelf suspended above the hearth) by the ascending smoke, which also prevents insects and vermin from taking up residence in the straw. Many of these old houses also function as minshuku. To stay in one, you can make reservations through the **Ogi-machi Tourist Office** (荻町観光案内; ⊠ 57 Ogi-machi, Shirakawa-mura ☎ 0576/96–1311), open daily 9–5. It's next to the Gasshō-shuraku bus stop in the center of town.

★ Opposite Ogi-machi, on the banks of the Shō-gawa, is **Shirakawa-gō Gasshō-zukuri Village** (白川郷合掌造り村), an open-air museum with 25 traditional gasshō-zukuri farmhouses. The houses were transplanted from four villages that fell prey to regional modernization when the Miboro Dam was built upriver in 1972. Over the years a colony of artisans has established itself in the village. You can observe the artists creating such folk crafts as weaving, pottery, woodwork, and hand-dyeing in a few of the preserved houses, and many of the finished products are for sale. ⊠ *Ogi-machi, Shirakawa mura, Ogi-machi, Ōno-gun* ☎ *0576/96–1231.*

Getting Around

Although it's more convenient to drive to Ogi-machi, it is possible to get there by public transportation. The train to Ogi-machi departs from Nagoya at 8:40 AM from mid-July to mid-November. The trip takes six hours and costs ¥4,760. You'll also find daily bus service from Ogi-machi to Kanazawa, departing at 2:40 PM. The trip takes two hours and 40 minutes, and costs ¥2,730.

KANAZAWA & THE NORTH CHŪBU COAST

Full of culture, fun, and friendliness, Kanazawa ranks among Japan's best-loved cities. To the east rise snowy mountains, including the revered (and hikeable) Haku-san. To the north stretches the clawlike peninsula of the Noto-hantō, where lush, rolling hills and bountiful rice fields meet scenic coastlines. Farther north along the Nihon-kai are the hardworking industrial capitals of Toyama and Niigata and, offshore, the everlonely former penal colony, Sado-ga-shima.

Kanazawa 金沢

2 hrs northeast of Kyōto, 3 hrs north of Nagoya, 2½ hrs northwest of Takayama, changing trains at Toyama, 3 hrs, 40 min southwest of Niigata—all by JR Limited Express.

Twenty-first century Kanazawa presents an extraordinary union of unblemished old Japan and a modern, trendsetting city. More than 300 years of rich history have been preserved in the earthen walls and flowing canals of Nagamachi, the former samurai quarter west of downtown;

the cluster of Buddhist temples in Tera-machi on the southern bank of the Saigawa River; and the wooden facades of the former geisha district, located north of Asanogawa River. Modern art, fashion, music, and international dining thrive in the downtown core of Kōrinbō, and in the shopping districts of Tatemachi and Katamachi. The Japan Sea gives Kanazawa some of the best seafood in the country and a somewhat dreary climate, similar to Seattle's or Vancouver's. Fortunately the sometimes cold, gray, and wet weather is offset by the overwhelming friendliness of the people.

In the feudal times of the Edo period, the prime rice-growing areas around Kanazawa (known then as the province of Kaga) made the ruling Maeda clan the second wealthiest in the country. Harvests routinely came in at more than *hyaku-man-goku* (1 million *koku,* the Edo-period unit of measurement based on how much rice would feed one person for a year). To the Maedas's credit and to the great benefit of the citizens, much of this wealth was used to fund and encourage various cultural pursuits such as silk dyeing, ceramics, and the production of gold-leaf and lacquerware products—traditions that continue to this day.

This prosperity did not pass unnoticed by the power centers to the east. The possibility of attack by the Edo daimyō inspired the Maeda lords to construct one of the country's most massive castles amid a mazelike network of narrow, winding lanes, making the approach difficult and an invasion nearly impossible. These defensive tactics paid off, and Kanazawa enjoyed some 300 years of peace and prosperity. However, thanks to seven fires over the centuries, all that remains today of the once-mighty Kanazawa-jō are the castle walls and a single, impressive gate. The former castle grounds are now the site of Kanazawa University.

➤ ⓲ The area around the old **Kanazawa-jō** (Kanazawa Castle, 金沢城) is a suitable place to start exploring Kanazawa and its history. Only the **Ishikawa-mon** (Ishikawa Gate) remains intact—its thick mossy stone base is topped with curving black eaves and white lead roof tiles. The tiles could be melted down and molded into ammunition in the case of a prolonged siege. To reach the castle, take any bus (¥200) from Gate 11 at the bus terminal outside the JR station.

★ ⓳ Across the street from the castle remains is Kanazawa's **Kenroku Garden** (Kenrokuen, 兼六園), the largest of the three most famous landscaped gardens in the country (the other two are Mito's Kairaku Garden and Okayama's Kōraku Garden). The Maeda lord Tsunanori began construction of Kenrokuen in 1676, and by the early 1880s it had reached its finest form—25 sprawling acres of skillfully wrought bridges and fountains, ponds and waterfalls. The garden changes with the seasons: spring brings cherry blossoms; brilliant azaleas foretell the arrival of summer; autumn paints the maples deep yellow and red; and in winter the pine trees are strung with long ropes, tied from trunk to bough, for protection against heavy snowfalls. Kenrokuen means "Garden of Six Qualities" (*ken-roku* means "integrated six"), and the garden was so named because it possessed the six superior characteristics judged necessary by

the Chinese Sung Dynasty for the perfect garden: spaciousness, artistic merit, majesty, abundant water, extensive views, and seclusion. Despite the promise of its last attribute, the gardens attract a mad stampede of visitors—herded by megaphone—in cherry-blossom season (mid-April) and Golden Week (late April and early May). Early morning is the only sensible time for a visit, when the grounds are peaceful and relaxing. ✉ *1 Kenroku-chō* ☎ *076/221–5850* 💴 *¥300, free 3rd Sun. of month* 🕐 *Mar.–mid-Oct., daily 7–6; mid-Oct.–Feb., daily 8–4:30.*

⑳ Seisonkaku (Southeast Palace, 成巽閣), in the southeast corner of Kenrokuen, is a retirement manor built in 1863 by one of the Maeda lords for his mother. The exquisite Dutch stained glass embedded in the sliding doors recalls the splendor of the Meiji era, a time when Japan climbed out of its long period of isolation and plunged into a process of rapid Westernization. The building now houses the family heirlooms, which include costumes and furnishings. ☎ *076/221–0580* 💴 *¥600* 🕐 *Thurs.–Tues. 9–5.*

㉑ Gyokusen Garden (Gyokusenen, 玉泉園), a tiny, intimate garden, was built by Kim Yeocheol, who later became Naokata Wakita when he married into the ruling family of Kanazawa. Yeocheol was born the son of a Korean captive brought to Japan by soldiers who had invaded Korea

FodorśChoice
★

in the late 16th century. He grew up in the feudal period and became a wealthy merchant, using his fortune to build this quiet getaway. The garden's intimate tranquillity seems to come from the imaginative and subtle arrangement of moss, maple trees, and small stepping stones by the pond. Two waterfalls that gracefully form the Chinese character for *mizu* (water) feed the pond. The garden is markedly different from the bold strokes of Kenroku Garden. You can have tea here for ¥500. ☎ 076/ 221–0181 ☜ ¥500 ☾ Mid-Mar.–mid-Dec., daily 9–4.

㉒ At the **Prefectural Handicraft Museum** (Kankō Bussankan, 観光物産館), near Gyokusenen, you can see demonstrations of Yūzen dyeing, pottery, and lacquerware production. ☎ 076/224–5511 ☜ ¥700, includes admission to Gyokusenen ☾ Apr.–Oct., daily 9–4:30; Nov.–Mar., Fri.–Wed. 9–4:30.

㉓ The **Ishikawa Prefectural Art Museum** (Ishikawa Kenritsu Bijutsukan, 石川県立美術館) displays the country's best permanent collection of *Kutani-yaki* (colorful overglaze-painted porcelain), dyed fabrics, old Japanese paintings, and various other art objects. ✉ 2–1 Dewa-machi, southwest of Kenrokuen ☎ 076/231–7180 ☜ ¥350 ☾ Daily 9–4:30.

㉔ A narrow path behind the Ishikawa Kenritsu Bijutsukan leads to the **Honda Museum** (Hanrō Honda Zōhinkan, 藩老本多蔵品館). The Honda family members were the key political advisers to the Maeda daimyō, and the museum contains 700 art objects used by the Hondas during their term, including armor, uniforms of the family's personal firefighters, and the trousseaus of the Maeda brides who married into the Honda family. ✉ 3–1 Dewa-machi ☎ 076/261–0500 ☜ ¥500 ☾ Mar.–Oct., Fri.–Wed. 9–4:30.

㉕ **Ōmi-chō Market** (Ōmi-chō Ichiba, 大見町市場／近江町市場), a mazelike warren of fish shops, delights visitors with an astonishing variety of the freshest seafood available in Kanazawa. Look for the appallingly ugly but deliciously buttery *anko* (angler-fish), or the rare and pricey *kegani* (hairy crab) among the variety of sea creatures hauled in from the ocean every morning. If you buy something, the merchant can pack it in ice for you, or show you where to have it cooked at a nearby restaurant. ✉ Ōmi-chō ☎ 076/231–1462 ☾ Mon.–Sat. 9–5.

㉖ Built in 1599, **Oyama Jinja** (尾山神社) was dedicated to Lord Toshiie Maeda, the founder of the Maeda clan. The shrine's unusual three-story gate, **Shin-mon,** was completed in 1875. Previously located atop Mt. Utatsu, it's believed that the square arch containing stained-glass windows once functioned as a lighthouse, guiding ships in from the Japan Sea to the Kanaiwa port, 6 km (4 mi) to the northwest. You're free to walk around the shrine at any time. To get here from the JR station, you can take Bus 30 or 31 from Gate 8. ✉ 11–1 Oyama-chō ☎ 076/ 231–7210 ☜ Free.

㉗ Behind the modern Kōrinbō 109 shopping center, Seseragi-dōri leads to **Naga-machi** (the Samurai District, 長町), where the Maeda clan lived. Narrow, snaking streets are lined with beautiful, golden adobe walls 8 feet high, footed with large stones and topped with black tiles.

A few houses have been carefully restored in the Samurai District, including the **Saihitsuan Yūzen Silk Center** (Kyū-Saihitsuan, 長町友禅館（旧彩筆庵）, where you can watch demonstrations of Yūzen silk painting, a centuries-old technique in which intricate floral designs with delicate white outlines are meticulously painted onto silk used for kimonos. The center is behind the Tōkyū Hotel five blocks southwest of Oyama Jinja. ⊠ *1–3–28 Naga-machi* ☎ *076/264–2811* ☞ *¥500* ⊙ *Fri.–Wed. 9–noon and 1–4:30.*

Nomura-ke (野村家), an elegant house in Naga-machi, was rebuilt more than 100 years ago by an industrialist named Nomura. Visit the Jōdan-no-ma drawing room made of *hinoki* (cypress), with elaborate designs in rosewood and ebony. Then pass through the sliding doors, adorned with the paintings of Sasaki Senkai, of the illustrious Kano school, to a wooden verandah. Rest your feet here, and take in the stunning little garden with weathered lanterns among pine and maple trees, and various shrubs and bonsais. Stepping stones lead to a pond dotted with moss-covered rocks and brilliant orange-flecked carp. In the upstairs tea room you can enjoy a cup of *macha* (green tea) for ¥300 and a bird's-eye view of the gardens. ⊠ *1–3–32 Naga-machi* ☎ *076/221–3553* ☞ *¥500* ⊙ *Apr.–Sept., daily 8:30–5:30; Oct.–Mar., daily 8:30–4:30.*

On the south side of the Sai-gawa is the intriguing and mysterious **Myōryū-ji** (妙立寺). Its popular name, Ninja-dera (Temple of the Ninja), suggests it was a clandestine training center for martial-art masters who crept around in the dead of night, armed with *shuriken* (star-shape blades). In fact the temple was built to provide an escape route for the daimyō in the event of an invasion of the castle. Ninja-dera was built by Toshitsune in 1643, during the tumultuous period of Japanese history when the Tokugawa shogunate was centralizing its power by stealthily knocking off local warlords and eliminating competition. At first glance, it appears a modest yet handsome two-story structure. Inside, however, you find 29 staircases, seven levels, myriad secret passageways and trap doors, a tunnel to the castle hidden beneath the well in the kitchen, and even a *seppuku* room, where the lord could perform an emergency ritual suicide if the assassins penetrated Myōryū-ji. Unfortunately (or fortunately considering all the booby traps), visitors are not permitted to explore the hidden lair alone. You must join a Japanese tour and follow along with your English pamphlet. Call ahead to reserve a time, or show up and register at the front. Lockers are available at ¥100. ⊠ *1–2–12 No-machi* ☎ *076/241–0888* ☞ *¥800* ⊙ *Mar.–Nov., daily 9–4:30; Dec.–Feb., daily 9–4.*

At the **Kutani Pottery Kiln** (Kutani Kōsen Gama, 九谷光仙窯) you can watch artisans making the local Kutani pottery, which is noted for its vibrant color schemes. ⊠ *5–3–3 No-machi* ☎ *076/241–0902* ☞ *Free* ⊙ *Mon.–Sat. 8:30–noon and 1–5, Sun. 8:30–noon.*

In **Nishi-no-Kuruwa** (the Western Pleasure Quarter, 西の郭), the walls no longer confine geisha, but the checkpoint that kept them from skipping town has been preserved. From the JR station take Bus 30, 31, or 32 from Gate 8 to Hirokōji.

③ **Higashi-no-Kuruwa** (the Eastern Pleasure Quarter, 東の郭), near the Asano-gawa, was the high-class entertainment district of Edo-period Kanazawa. Now the pleasures of visiting are limited to viewing quaint old geisha houses recognizable by their wood-slat facades and latticed windows. Many have become tearooms, restaurants, or minshuku, and if you are lucky, you might still see a geisha scuttling to her appointment. Take the JR bus from Kanazawa Station (¥200) to Hachira-chō, just before the Asano-gawa Ōhashi. Cross the bridge and walk northeast into the quarter.

③ One elegant former geisha house in Higashi-no-Kuruwa, **Shima-ke** (志摩家), is open to the public for tours. ⊠ *1–13–21 Higashi-yama* ☎ *076/252–5675* 🎫 *¥400* ⊘ *Tues.–Sun. 9–5.*

Where to Eat & Stay

$$$$ ✕ **Tsubajin** (つば甚). One of Kanazawa's best restaurants for Kaga-ryōri, Tsubajin is actually part of a small, traditional, and expensive ryokan. Try the crab, as well as the house specialty, a chicken stew called *jibuni*. Be forewarned that the extravagant, multicourse set dinners cost more than ¥20,000 per person. Less elaborate yet still expensive lunch sets cost ¥12,000–¥24,000. ⊠ *5–1–8 Tera-machi* ☎ *076/241–2181* 🖎 *Reservations essential* 🚫 *AE, MC, V.*

$$$$ ✕ **Goriya** (ごり屋). The specialty here at one of Kanazawa's oldest restaurants, is the tiny *gori* (a small river fish typically cooked in soy sauce and sugar syrup). More than 200 years old, Goriya achieved notoriety for its fabulous garden on the banks of the Asano-gawa—not for its cooking. You may get the most out of a daytime visit, when lunch is served for around ¥6,000). From Tenjin-bashi walk southeast for 10 minutes; you'll see the restaurant just past the Tokiwa Bridge. The Japanese name is etched into a weathered white stone, and the entrance is nestled in a copse of overgrown shrubbery. ⊠ *60 Tokiwa-chō* ☎ *076/ 252–5596* 🚫 *AE, DC, MC, V.*

★ $$$ ✕ **Kincharyō** (金茶寮). The menu changes seasonally in the showpiece restaurant of the Kanazawa Tōkyū Hotel. The private dining room's ceiling is an impressive piece of delicate craftsmanship; the lacquered, curved countertop of the sushi bar is strikingly beautiful; and in the kitchen, the chef's culinary skill is superb. Dinner courses range from tempura sets (¥4,042–¥8,085) to mixed kaiseki (9 items cost ¥5,775). In spring your meal may include *hotaru-ika* (firefly squid) and *iidako* (baby octopus) no larger than your thumbnail. The lunches and seasonal specials are a real bargain. ⊠ *Kanazawa Tōkyū Hotel, 3rd fl., 2–1–1 Kōrimbo* ☎ *076/231–2411* 🚫 *AE, DC, MC, V.*

★ $$ ✕ **Miyoshian** (三芳庵). Excellent *bentō* (box lunches) and fish and vegetable dinners have been served here for about 100 years in the renowned Kenrokuen garden. Prices are still pretty reasonable, hovering around ¥2,000. ⊠ *1 Kenroku-chō* ☎ *076/221–0127* 🚫 *AE, MC, V* ⊘ *Closed Tues.*

★ $ ✕ **Capricciosa** (カプリチョーザ). Stick to the scrumptious pizza and pasta—including the spicy garlic and the jet-black *ika-sumi* (squid-ink) spaghetti dishes. Skip the puffy calzones—they're just a lot of hot air. The inexpensive house wine is surprisingly delicious, although you'll have to wait for the red to reach room temperature (Japanese restaurants often chill all wines). Capricciosa is across from the McDonald's at the entrance of the Tate-machi shopping street. ⊠ *Tōku Tate-machi Bldg., 1–4–18 Kata-machi* ☎ *076/260–8855* ▭ *No credit cards.*

★ ¢–$ ✕ **Legian** (レギャン). You might be surprised to find a funky Balinese eatery alongside the Sai-gawa. But if you try the *gado-gado* (vegetables in a spicy sauce), *nasi goreng* (Indonesian-style fried rice), or chicken *satay* (grilled on a skewer, with peanut sauce), you'll be very glad you did. Indonesian beer and mango ice cream are also available. Since it's open late (Monday–Thursday until 12:30 AM; Friday and Saturday until 4:30 AM), you might want to hang around after dinner for drinks when things get interesting. From Kata-machi Scramble (the central intersection in this area), turn right just before Sai-gawa bridge, and follow the narrow lane along the river. ⊠ *2–31–30 Kata-machi* ☎ *076/262–6510* ▭ *No credit cards* ⊙ *Closed Wed.*

¢ ✕ **Noda-ya** (野田屋). Slip into this little tea shop for a scoop of delicious *ma-cha sofuto kurīmu* (green tea ice cream), or—oh, yes—a cup of tea. You can sit in the little garden in back or on benches out front where you can watch pedestrian traffic. At the far end of the Tate-machi shopping street, Noda-ya is a little hard to spot, you can find it if you follow your nose—the scent of roasting green tea leaves is heavenly. The shop is open daily from 9 to 8. ⊠ *3 Tate-machi* ☎ *076/22–0982* ▭ *No credit cards.*

★ $$$$ ⊡ **Ryokan Asadaya** (旅館浅田屋). This small ryokan, established during the Meiji Restoration (1867), is the most lavish lodging in Kanazawa. The interior blends traditional elegance with innovative designs—a perfect metaphor for the age of Japan's transition into modernity. Antique furnishings and exquisite scrolls and paintings appear throughout the inn. Superb regional cuisine is served in your room or in the restaurant. ⊠ *23 Jukken-machi, Kanazawa, Ishikawa-ken 920–0906* ☎ *076/232–2228* 🖷 *076/252–4444* ⊕ *www.asadaya.co.jp/asadayaryokan_e.php* ⤴ *5 Japanese-style rooms* ♧ *Restaurant* ▭ *AE* ⃝ *MAP.*

★ $$$$ ⊡ **Hotel Nikkō Kanazawa** (ホテル日航金沢). The exotic lobby of this 30-story hotel is more reminiscent of Singapore than Japan, with its tropical plants, cherry oak slatted doors, and colonial-style furniture—the cushioned rattan chairs are perfect for lounging. A winding staircase curls around a bubbling pond in the middle of the lobby and leads to a European brasserie, Garden House, which serves wonderful coffee and cake. The very colorful and vibrant top-floor lounge, Le Grand Chariot, has panoramic views over Kanazawa, sumptuous French cuisine, and soft piano music. Western-style rooms are decorated with creamy pastels, blond-wood furnishings, and striking views—of the sea, city, or mountains. There is a JAL ticket counter on the premises, and the hotel is connected to the JR station by an underground passageway. The hotel charges ¥2,100 for use of the pool and gym. ⊠ *2–15–1 Hon-machi, Kanazawa, Ishikawa-ken 920-0853* ☎ *076/234–1111* 🖷 *076/234–8802* ⊕ *www.nikkohotels.com* ⤴ *256 rooms, 4 suites* ♧ *4 restaurants, in-room data ports, in-room fax, minibars, cable TV, in-room VCRs, pool, gym, hot tub, sauna, lobby lounge, 2 bars, shops, laundry services, no-smoking rooms, travel services, parking (fee)* ▭ *AE, DC, MC, V.*

$$$$ ⊞ **Kanazawa Tōkyū Hotel** (金沢エクセルホテル東急). In the center of town, just two blocks north of Tate-machi, the reception area of this hotel is on the second floor of the Kōrinbō shopping complex, above the Starbucks. Though the gold enamel on the lacquered pillars seems to have lost some of its lustre, the numerous plants cheer up the lobby. The rooms are Western-style and moderate in size, with pale cream-color walls and black furniture. Kincharyō is a superb Japanese restaurant on-site. ⊠ 2–1–1 Kōrimbo, Kanazawa, Ishikawa-ken 920–0961 ☎ 076/231–2411 🖷 076/263–0154 ⊕ www.tokyuhotels.co.jp 📞 236 rooms ♨ 2 restaurants, in-room data ports, refrigerators, cable TV, hair salon, lounge, shops, meeting room, no-smoking rooms, parking (fee) ▤ AE, DC, MC, V.

$$$ ⊞ **ANA Kanazawa** (金沢全日空ホテル). You enter this hotel to sounds of a cascading waterfall and walk to the check-in counter beneath a glittery, curving chandelier. Rooms are soothing, with wallpaper, fabrics, and furnishings in soft beige tones. The L-shape layout is a welcome change from the usual boxlike plan of most hotel rooms. Of the several restaurants, the penthouse Teppanyaki is the best, with succulent steak lunches (¥2,100–¥2,900) and a panoramic view of the city. Another restaurant, Unkai, serves kaiseki dinners, with excellent sashimi and a view of a miniature version of Kenrokuen. In the summer months an open-air beer garden on the fourth floor offers an all-you-can-eat and drink buffet for ¥5,000. The hotel is adjacent to Kanazawa Station. ⊠ 16–3 Shōwa-chō, Kanazawa, Ishikawa-ken 920–8518 ☎ 076/224–6111, 800/262–4683 from North America 🖷 076/224–6100 ⊕ www.anahotels.com 📞 255 rooms ♨ 5 restaurants, coffee shop, in-room data ports, minibars, cable TV, gym, shops, business services, convention center, meeting rooms, free parking ▤ AE, DC, MC, V.

★ **$$** ⊞ **APA Hotel Eki-mae** (アパホテル金沢駅前). This hotel is so close to the JR station, it's practically inside it. A blue ceiling with sparkling stars watches over a Seattle's Best coffee shop and a modern lobby. Inside your smallish yet stylish room, a charming origami crane perches atop a carefully pressed bath robe. Each room has views over Kanazawa, and the sauna and onsen are free for guests. ⊠ 1–9–28 Hirōka, Kanazawa, Ishikawa-ken 920–0031 ☎ 076/231–8111 🖷 076/231–8112 ⊕ www. apahotel.com 📞 456 rooms ♨ 2 restaurants, coffee shop, refrigerators, massage, sauna, hot springs, no-smoking rooms ▤ AE, DC, MC, V.

$–$$ ⊞ **Kanazawa New Grand Hotel** (金沢ニューグランドホテル). Stepping into this hotel's sleek black-and-cream marble lobby is a refreshing break from the dreary concrete of the busy main drag outside. Beyond the fresh spray of bright flowers, the front desk overflows with attentive staff members, who will bend over backward to accommodate your every need. From the sky lounge, Dichter, and restaurant, Sky Restaurant Roi, which serves some of the city's best contemporary French cuisine, you can watch the sun set and get a great view of Oyama Shrine across the street. The spacious rooms, though far from new, are done in white-and-beige tones, and offer sofas. Japanese-style rooms are slightly larger but furnishings are naturally more sparse. The hotel is a 15 minute walk from the station, if you head down Eki-mae-dōri and take a right on Hikoso-ōdōri. ⊠ 1–50 Takaoka-chō, Kanazawa, Ishikawa-ken 920–0864

☎ *076/233–1311* ☐ *076/233–1591* ⊕ *www.new-grand.co.jp* ↘ *100 Western-style rooms, 2 Japanese-style rooms, 2 suites* ♦ *3 restaurants, coffee shop, shops, no-smoking rooms* ⊟ *AE, DC, MC, V.*

¢ ▥ **Yōgetsu** (陽月). In a century-old geisha house in the Eastern Pleasure Quarter, Yōgetsu is a small, stylish minshuku. The owner is a welcoming hostess, and keeps a neat shared bath. The guest rooms are small and sparsely furnished, but ancient-looking exposed beams add character. ✉ *1–13–22 Higashiyama, Kanazawa, Ishikawa-ken 920–0831* ☎ *076/252–0497* ↘ *5 Japanese-style rooms without bath* ♦ *Dining room, Japanese baths* ⊟ *No credit cards* ¶◉ *MAP.*

Nightlife

All-night fun can be found right in the center of town, and you won't have to burn much money to chase it down. Be warned, these places don't take credit cards.

Free billiard tables make **Apre** (✉ 4th fl., Laporto Bldg., 1–3–9 Katamachi ☎ 076/221–0090) a fun place to hang out on weekends (it's closed Monday). When it opens at 8 PM, the tables fill up, and the action is quite competitive. It's tricky to find, though, so don't hesitate to call for directions. **Pole-Pole** *"po-ray-po-ray"* (✉ 2–31–31 Kata-machi ☎ 076/ 260–1138) is a reggae bar run by the same jolly owner as Legian and is just behind the restaurant. If you want a place to sit, get here before midnight when things really start to get going. The two dark, cramped rooms get so full that the crowd often spills out into the hallway. Pole-Pole is closed on Sunday but open until 5 AM the rest of the week.

Getting Around

Ideal for tourists, the *shū-yū basu* (loop bus), which departs every 15 minutes from 8:30 AM to 9 PM from gate 0 of Kanazawa Station's east exit, delivers you to all the major tourist sites. Stops are announced in English and displayed on a digital board at the front of the bus. A single ride costs ¥200, while the economical day pass is just ¥500. You can purchase the pass from the Hokutetsu bus ticket office in front of Kanazawa Station.

Visitor Information

The **Kanazawa Information Office** (金沢観光情報センター ☎ 076/232–6200 ☐ 076/238–6210) has two desks at the train station and an extremely helpful volunteer staff that will help you find accommodations. It's open daily 9–7; an English speaker is on duty 10–6.

Fukui 福井

❸❺ *40 min southwest of Kanazawa by JR Limited Express, 2 hrs north of Nagoya by JR Limited Express.*

One of the two main Soto Zen temples, **Eihei-ji** (永平寺) is 19 km (12 mi) southeast of Fukui. Founded in 1244, the extensive complex of 70 temple buildings sits on a hillside surrounded by hinoki and *sugi* (cedar) trees hundreds of feet tall, some of which are as old as the original wooden structures. The temple is still active, and there are 200 monks in training at any given time. You can lodge at the temple (for ¥7,000 a night, including two meals) with two weeks' advance notice in writing. If you have the opportunity to stay, arrive by 4 PM to explore the grounds, and then settle in for the night after a delicious feast of traditional Buddhist cuisine. Prepare yourself for a 3 AM wake-up call, and a morning meditation session with the monks, followed by a hearty breakfast. Check out is at 8 AM. The easiest way to get to Eihei-ji from Fukui is by train. ✉ *5–15 Shihi Eiheiji-chō, Yoshida-gun, Fukui 910–1294* ☎ *0776/ 63–3102* 🎫 *Tours ¥500* ⊘ *Daily 5–5.*

Where to Stay

¢–$ 🏨 **Hotel Akebono Bekkan** (ホテルアケボノ別館). Think of this small, two-story wooden hotel as a weekend retreat—the owners can arrange training sessions in Zen meditation and classes in pottery and papermaking. The Akebono Bekkan is actually the annex of a large, modern hotel, the Riverge Akebono, so you can enjoy the best of both worlds: tradition and culture with modern conveniences next door. Both Japanese and Western breakfasts are served, but only Japanese food is available at dinner. All of the small tatami rooms have private toilets, but the bath is shared. The inn is next to Sakura Bridge, a 10-minute walk from Fukui Station. ✉ *3–10–12 Chūō, Fukui-shi, Fukui-ken 910–0006* ☎ *0776/ 22–1000* 🖷 *0776/22–8023* ⊕ *www.riverge.com* ⇌ *10 Japanese-style rooms without bath* ⚭ *Restaurant, Japanese baths* 🖃 *AE, V.*

Noto-hantō (Noto Peninsula, 能登半島)

36 *Nanao, on the east coast of the peninsula, is 52 min northeast from Kanazawa by JR Limited Express. Wajima, on the north coast of Noto-hantō, is 2¼ hrs northeast of Kanazawa by JR Limited Express.*

Thought to be named after an Ainu (indigenous Japanese) word for "nose," the Noto-hantō juts out into the Nihon-kai and shelters the bays of both Nanao and Toyama. Steep, densely forested hills line the west coast, which is wind- and wave-blasted in winter and ruggedly beautiful in other seasons. The eastern shoreline is lapped by calmer waters and has stunning views of Tate-yama (Mt. Tate), the Hida Mountains, and even of some of Nagano's alpine peaks, which are more than 105 km (70 mi) away. This is a good place to explore by car, or even by bicycle. Although the interior routes can be arduous, the coastal roads are relatively flat and good for biking. You can also combine train and bus trips or guided tours, all of which can be arranged in Kanazawa.

The Nanao-sen (Nanao Line) runs from Kanazawa through Nanao and all the way to Wajima, via Anamizu, where it's often necessary to change trains. From Anamizu, the private Noto Line goes northeast to Tako-jima, which is this region's most scenic route. The line to Wajima turns inland after Hakui, however, and misses some of the peninsula's best sights.

A quick sightseeing circuit of the Noto-hantō, from Hakui to Nanao, can be done in six to eight hours, but if your aim is to absorb the peninsula's remarkable scenery, stay two or three days, stopping in Wajima and at one of the minshuku along the coast; arrangements can be made through the tourist information offices in Kanazawa, Nanao, or Wajima.

In **Hakui** (羽咋), a 40-minute train ride away from Kanazawa, you can ride a bicycle along the coastal path as far as beautiful Gan-mon (Sea Gate), some 26 km (16 mi) away, where you can stop for lunch. Just north of Chirihama, a formerly popular and now unkempt beach, the scenery improves. Rent bikes from **Kato Cycle** (加藤サイクル; ☎ 0767/22–0539), across from Joyful Supermarket, west of the JR station in Hakui.

Myōjō-ji 妙成寺 is a temple complex a few miles north by bus from Hakui (buses leave outside the train station). The temple, founded in 1294 and belonging to the Nichiren sect of Buddhism, has an impressive five-story pagoda. Beside the pagoda sits a squat wooden building, which appears from the outside too small to house the very large, colorful Buddhist statue inside. A recorded announcement on the bus tells where to get off for Myōjō-ji. It's a 10-minute walk to the temple from the bus stop. ✉ 1 Yo Taki-tani-machi ☎ 0767/27–1226 ✍ ¥350 ⊙ Daily 8–5.

en route

Although you can take the inland bus route directly north from Hakui to Monzen, the longer (70-minute) bus ride that runs along the coast is highly recommended for its scenic value. It brings you along the 16-km (10-mi) stretch between Fuku-ura and Sekinohana known as the **Noto Seacoast** (Noto-Kongō, 能登金剛), which is noted for fantastic wind- and wave-eroded rocks. There are many different formations, from craggy towers to partly submerged checkerboard-patterned platforms. Among the best is **Gan-mon** (巌門), a rock cut through the center by water. Gan-mon is about 45 minutes north of Hakui and is a stop on tour-bus routes.

The Zen temple complex **Sōji-ji** (總持寺) at Monzen once served as the headquarters of the Soto sect. A fire destroyed most of the buildings in 1818, however, and the sect moved its headquarters to Yokohama. Strolling paths still traverse the grounds, where you can see some spectacular red maples, and an impressive, elaborately carved gate. The Sōji-ji-mae bus stop is directly in front of the temple; use a bus from Monzen Station to reach it. It can also can be accessed from the Anamizu bus station on the Noto Chūō bus bound for Monzen (32 minutes). ✉ 1–18 Monzen, Monzen-chō ☎ 0768/42–0005 ✍ ¥400 ⊙ Daily 8–5.

Only 16 km (10 mi) and one bus stop up the road from Monzen is **Wajima** (輪島). This fishing town at the tip of the peninsula is known not only for its fish but also for its gorgeous lacquerware.

To see how the traditional manufacturing process is carried out, you can visit the **Lacquerware Hall** (Wajima Shikki Kaikan, 輪島漆器会館). The production of a single piece involves more than 20 steps and 100 processes, from wood preparation and linen reinforcement to the application of numerous layers of lacquer, with careful drying and polishing between coats. Wajima Shikki Kaikan is in the center of town on the north side of Route 249, just before Shin-bashi (New Bridge). To get here from the station, turn left when you exit and walk straight (northwest) about four blocks until you hit Route 249. Turn left again—there's a Hokuriku Bank on the corner—and continue southwest along Route 249 for about four blocks. ☎ 0768/22–2155 ✍ ¥200 ⊙ Daily 8:30–5.

The **asa-ichi** (朝市), or morning market, in Wajima is held daily between 8 and 11:30, except on the 10th and 25th of each month. You can buy seafood, fruit, vegetables, local crafts, and lacquerware. Locals advise coming at 11:15, ready to bargain hard. A *yū-ichi* (evening market), a smaller version of the asa-ichi, starts around 3 PM. Almost anyone can point you in the right direction. ✉ *Asa-ichi dōri Kawai-chō* ☎ *0768/22–7653 mornings only.*

need a break?

Missed the morning market? Various sashimi and sushi *teishoku* (sets) are reasonably priced at **Shin-puku** (伸福; ✉ 41 Kawai-chō, Wajima-shi ☎ 0768/22–8133), a small but beautiful sushi bar a 10-minute walk from the train station. To get here from the station, turn left as you exit and walk northwest (left) for about four blocks until you hit the main road, Route 249. Then turn right and walk northeast about three blocks along Route 249. One block past the Cosmo gas station (on the left), you can see Shin-puku on the right.

Wajima's **tourist office** (観光案内センター; ☎ 0768/22–1503), at the station, offers assistance with accommodations, and maps of the area; it's open daily 10–6.

From Wajima an hourly bus runs to **Sosogi** (曽々木), a small village 20 minutes to the northeast, passing the terraced fields of **Senmaida,** where innumerable rice paddies descend from the hills to the edge of the sea.

At Sosogi the road turns inland, and about 8 km (5 mi) farther are two traditional farm manor houses. The **Shimo-Tokikunike** (Shimo-Tokikuni House, 下時国家; ☎ 0768/32–0075 💰 ¥500) is more than 300 years old and is furnished with antiques. Rent a tape recorder at the entrance for an English explanation of each room. The house is open daily from 8:30 to 5. Close by Shimo-Tokikunike is **Kami-Tokikunike** (Kami-Tokikuni House, 上時国家; ☎ 0768/32–0171 💰 ¥500), which took 28 years to build in the early 1800s and remains in near-perfect condition. Each room in this house had a special purpose coinciding with the rigid social hierarchy of 19th-century Japan. Kami-Tokikunike is open daily from 8:30 to 5, until 6 in summer.

en route

You can continue around the peninsula's northern tip by bus—from Sosogi to **Rokkō-zaki** (Cape Rokkō, 禄剛崎), past a small lighthouse, and down to the northern terminus of the Noto Railway Line at Takojima. However, unless you have a car, the views and scenery don't quite justify the infrequency of the public transportation on this particular leg of the peninsula. It's better to take the inland route from Sosogi to Suzu.

The same hourly bus that runs between Wajima and Sosogi continues on to **Suzu** (珠洲) on the *uchi* (inside) coast. Just south of Suzu, near Ukai Station, is an interesting offshore rock formation called **Mitsuke-jima**— look for a huge wedge of rock topped with lush vegetation.

Southeast of Suzu is the superior open-air **Mawaki Onsen** (真脇温泉). Artifacts, including pottery from the *Jōmon* (straw-rope pattern) archaeological period (13,000 BC–300 BC) were found here. Mawaki is also well known for its wonderful hilltop view, which overlooks the rice fields and fishing villages along the edge of Toyama Bay. One bath-and-sauna complex is done in stone, the other in wood; on alternate weeks they open to men and women. A hotel is connected to the bath complex. To get here, it's a bit of a hike up the hill or a short taxi ride from Jōon Mawaki Station on the Noto Line. Mawaki can also be reached in 2¼ hours by car from Kanazawa—along a scenic toll road—or 2½ hours by train (with a change in Wakura). As you make your way south to Mawaki Onsen, there are numerous opportunities for hiking, swimming, and camping. ⊠ 19–39 Mawaki ☏ 0768/62–4567 ⧉ 0768/62–4568 ⧄ ¥450 ⊙ Mon. noon–10, Tues.–Sun. 10–10.

need a break? ★ A terrific brewery and log-cabin-style restaurant called the **Heart and Beer Nihonkai Club** (日本海倶楽部; ⊠ 92 Aza-Tatekabe, Uchiura-machi ☏ 0768/72–8181) is five minutes by taxi from Matsunami Station (on the Noto line). It's operated by two beer masters from eastern Europe in conjunction with an association that helps the disabled. Specials include delicious emu stew (¥1,200), raised on-site, and tasty local Noto beef, along with some very good microbrewed beer (¥460). It's open from Thursday to Tuesday.

Nanao (七尾) is best known for its festivals. **Seihakusai festival,** a 400-year-old tradition held May 3–5, is essentially three days of nonstop partying. Huge (26-ft) 10-ton floats resembling ships called *deka-yama* (big mountains) are paraded through the streets. At midnight the floats become miniature Kabuki stages for dance performances by costumed children. Since Seihakusai festival is celebrated during Golden Week, when almost everyone in Japan enjoys holidays from school and work, it's quite a wild scene. The men pulling the floats are given generous and frequent libations of beer and sake for their efforts, and those in the crowd suffer no shortage of refreshments either. During the day the floats are parked at community centers, where they can be studied more closely. The wheels alone are 6½-ft tall and weigh enough to shake streets and houses as they roll by. On the final day the three deka-yama are gathered together near the wharf for a last celebration and more eating, drinking, and socializing.

During **Ishizaki Hoto Matsuri,** celebrated on the first Saturday of August, many beautiful paper lanterns more than 6 feet tall are carried on platforms and poles by participants delirious with excitement. As with the Seihakusai festival, alcohol plays a major part in this festival, and the proceedings continue long into the night, rain or shine.

Contact the **International Exchange Office** (七尾国際交流協会; ☏ 0767/53–8448 ⧉ 0767/54–8117) in Nanao to get festival details or to arrange for accommodations—or even a home stay.

Takaoka (高岡), the southern gateway to the Noto Peninsula, is not especially worth lingering around, though it does have Japan's third-largest **Daibutsu** (Great Buddha), after those in Kamakura and Nara. It's made of bronze and stands 53 feet high. Also in Takaoka, a 10-minute walk from the station, is **Zuiryū-ji**, a delightful Zen temple that doubles as a youth hostel. A sprawling park, **Kojō-kōen**, not far from the station, is particularly stunning in autumn, with its red-and-silver maples. Takaoka is mostly known for its traditions of copper-, bronze-, and iron-smithing and remains a major bell-casting center.

Where to Stay

$$–$$$$　☒ **Mawaki Pō-re Pō-re** (真脇ポーレポーレ). This interesting little hotel, which is connected to the bath complex at Mawaki, has great views of the sea and surrounding hills. Breakfast is included, and the staff is helpful and friendly. The Western-style rooms are done in blue and purple; the Japanese-style rooms have shōji screens and are slightly larger and brighter. Best of all, you're a minute away from the mineral baths. ☒ *19–110 Aza-Mawaki, Noto-machi, Fugeshi-gun, Ishikawa-ken 927–0562* ☎*0768/62–4700* 🖷*0768/62–4702* ➪*5 Western-style rooms, 5 Japanese-style rooms, 1 suite* ♨ *Restaurant* ▭ *No credit cards.*

Toyama　富山

㊲ *30 min southeast of Takaoka by JR local, 1 hr east of Kanazawa by JR Limited Express, 3 and 4 hrs north of Kyōto and Nagoya, respectively, by JR.*

Busy, industrial Toyama is beautified by Toyama-jōshi Kōen (Toyama Castle Park), a spread of greenery with a reconstructed version of the original (1532) castle.

A slow open-air train called the **Kurobe-kyōkoku Railway** (黒部峡谷鉄道) operates April through November and runs along the river of the deep Kurobe-kyōkoku (Kurobe Gorge) to Keyakidaira. The 20-km (12½-mi), 90-minute ride on the old-fashioned tram chugs past gushing springs and plunging waterfalls, and you might even catch a glimpse of wild monkeys or *serow,* a native type of mountain goat. Bring a windbreaker, even in summer, as it's a cold and humid ride. From June to November, the Kurobe-Kyōkoku trains leave Unazuki for Keyakidaira twice hourly from 7:30 to 3:40 and cost ¥1,440 one way. To get to Unazuki from Toyama Station, take the JR line to Uozu Station and switch to the Chitetsu line (30 minutes).

Walking & Hiking

From Keyakidaira, you can proceed on foot to two rotemburo (open-air spas) nearly 100 years old: **Meiken Onsen** (名剣温泉) is a 10- to 15-minute walk; **Babadani Onsen** (祖母谷温泉), 35 to 40 minutes.

If you're a serious hiker, trails from Keyakidaira can lead you to the peak of **Shirouma-dake** (Mt. Shirouma), more than 9,810 feet high, in several hours. Nearby **Tate-yama** (Mt. Tate) also rewards experienced hikers with stunning views. You can also hike to Kurobe Dam, and to the cable car that leads up to a tunnel through Tate-yama to Murodō. If you have several days to spare, camping gear, and a map of mountain trails and shelters, you can go as far as Hakuba in Nagano.

ON THE MENU

EVERY MICROREGION HAS ITS OWN SPECIALTIES, all of which involve a unique style of preparing the plentiful varieties of fish and seafood from the Nihon-kai. Also, seaweed, like vitamin-rich wakame and kombu, is used frequently, sometimes together with tiny clams called shijimi, in miso soup.

In and around Toyama, spring brings tiny baby squid called hotaru-ika (firefly squid), which are boiled in soy sauce or sake and eaten whole. Try the seasonal ama-ebi (sweet shrimp) and masu-zushi (thinly sliced trout sushi that's been pressed flat). In winter look for various types of delicious crabs, including the red, long-legged beni-zuwaigani.

Fukui also has huge echizen-gani crabs, some 28 inches leg to leg. When boiled with a little salt and dipped in rice vinegar, they're pure heaven. A few exceptional varieties of sole, like wakasa-karei, are slightly dried before grilling. In both Fukui and Ishikawa, restaurants serve echizen-soba (buckwheat noodles, handmade and served with mountain vegetables) with sesame oil and bean paste for dipping, recalling Buddhist vegetarian traditions.

Kanazawa and Noto-hantō's, Kaga-ryōri (Kaga cuisine) is based on seafood, such as tai (sea bream) topped with mountain fern brackens, greens, and mushrooms. At Wajima's early morning fish market (daily except the 10th and 25th of the month), near the tip of Noto-hantō, and at Kanazawa's Omi-chō Market, you can see everything from fresh abalone to seaweed, and it's easy to find some nearby restaurant that will cook it for you.

In Niigata Prefecture, try noppei-jiru, a hot or cold soup with sato-imo (a kind of sweet potato) as its base, and mushrooms, salmon, and a few other local ingredients.

It goes well with hot rice and grilled fish. Wappa–meshi is a hot dish of steamed rice garnished with local ingredients, especially wild vegetables, chicken, fish, and shellfish. In autumn, try kiku-no-ohitashi, a side dish of chrysanthemum petals marinated in vinegar. Like other prefectures on the Nihon-kai coast, Niigata has outstanding fish in winter—buri (yellowtail), flatfish, sole, oysters, abalone, and shrimp. A local specialty is namban ebi, raw shrimp dipped in soy sauce and wasabi. It's butter-tender and especially sweet on Sado-ga-shima. Also on Sado-ga-shima, take advantage of the excellent wakame (seaweed) dishes and sazae-no-tsuboyaki (wreath shellfish) broiled in their shells with a soy or miso sauce.

The area around Matsumoto is known for its wasabi and chilled zarusoba (buckwheat noodles), a refreshing meal on a hot day, especially when accompanied by a frosty mug of beer or a cold glass of locally brewed sake.

In the mountainous areas of Takayama and Nagano, you'll find sansai soba (buckwheat noodles with mountain vegetables) and sansai-ryōri (wild vegetables and mushrooms served in soups or tempura), as well as local river fish such as ayu (smelt) or iwana (char) grilled on a spit with shōyū (soy sauce) or salt. You'll likely also encounter hoba miso, which is a dark, slightly sweet type of miso roasted on a large magnolia leaf.

Nagano is also famous for delicacies such as ba sashi (raw horse meat), sakura nabe (horse meat stew cooked in an earthenware pot), and boiled baby bees. The former two are still very popular; as for the latter, even locals admit they're something of an acquired taste.

For more information on the Kurobe-kyōkoku Railway and hiking or camping in the Keyakidaira area, contact the **tourist information office** (観光案内センター; ☎ 0764/32–9751) in Toyama Station.

The **National Parks Association of Japan** (国立公園協会) in Tōkyō is a good source of help on hiking and camping around Toyama. ✉ *Toranomon Denki Bldg., 4th fl., 2–8–1 Toranomon, Minato-ku, Tōkyō, From Toranomon Station on Ginza subway line, take Exit 2 and walk 2 blocks straight before taking a right. The Toranomon Denki building will be on left side, in the 3rd block* ☎ 03/3502–0488.

Niigata 新潟

38 *3 hrs from Toyama on the JR Hokuriku line, 1½ hrs northwest of Tōkyō's Ueno Station by Shinkansen, 2 hrs, 15 min northwest of Tōkyō on the Toki local line.*

The coast between Kurobe and Niigata is flat and not so interesting. Two towns along the way, Naoetsu and Teradomari, serve as ferry ports to Ogi and Akadomari, respectively, on Sado-ga-shima. Niigata, Japan's major shipping center on the Nihon-kai seacoast, is a good place for replenishing supplies and changing money. The **tourist information office** (観光案内センター; ☎ 025/241–7914) to the left of the station can help you find a hotel and supply city maps and ferry schedules for Sado-ga-shima.

Where to Eat & Stay

$$–$$$ ✕ **Marui** (丸伊). *The* place in Niigata for fresh fish is Marui. For starters, order the *nami nigiri* (standard sushi set) for ¥1,400, plus a bottle of chilled sake; the local Kitayuki brand, for ¥1,260, is a good choice. While savoring these, glance at what your neighbors are ordering and ask for what looks good. You can't go wrong with the freshest fish, abalone, sea urchin, and squid in town—at a reasonable price. Marui closes during mid-afternoon. It's one block off the Furu-machi arcade, around the corner from Inaka-ya. ✉ *8–1411 Higashibori-dōri* ☎ 025/228–0101 ▤ *No credit cards* ☉ *Closed Sun.*

★ $–$$$ ✕ **Inaka-ya** (田舎家). You can find Inaka-ya in the heart of Furu-machi, the local eating and drinking district. The specialty, *wappa-meshi* (rice steamed in a wooden box with toppings of salmon, chicken, or crab), makes an inexpensive and excellent lunch. The *yanagi karei hitohoshi-yaki* (grilled flounder), *nodo-kuro shioyaki* (grilled local whitefish), and *buri teriyaki* (yellowtail) will make your mouth water. Inaka-ya closes between lunch and dinner from 2 to 5. ✉ *1457 Kyūban-chō, Furu-machi-dōri* ☎ 025/223–1266 ⚓ *Reservations not accepted* ▤ *No credit cards.*

$$–$$$$ ▢ **Ōkura Hotel Niigata** (ホテルオークラ新潟). A sophisticated, first-class hotel on the Shinano-gawa, 15 minutes on foot from the station, the Ōkura is one of Niigata's best accommodations. Rooms overlooking Shinano-gawa have the best views. A formal French restaurant in the penthouse looks down on the city and over the Nihon-kai to Sado-ga-shima. Breakfast and lighter meals are served in the Grill Room. ✉ *6–53 Kawabata-chō, Niigata City, Niigata-ken 951-8053* ☎ 025/224–6111 *or 0120/10–0120, toll-free in Japan* ⊟ 025/224–7060 ⊕ *www.okura-*

niigata.com ⤴ *300 Western-style and Japanese-style rooms* ♨ *3 restaurants, shops, business services* ▤ *AE, DC, MC, V.*

$$ 🏨 **Niigata Tōei Hotel** (新潟東映ホテル). For an inexpensive business hotel located a block and a half from the station, this ranks the best. The ninth floor has a Japanese steak house and a lounge that closes unusually early (9 PM). From mid-June to the beginning of September, in the beer garden on the roof, ¥3,500 will get you 100 minutes of all-you-can-eat beer, *chū-hi* (a carbonated mixture of distilled spirits called "shōchū" and fruity flavors), and casual food. From the Bandai exit of Niigata Station, head north on Higashi Ōdōri for three blocks, then take a left. ⊠ *1–6–2 Benten, Niigata 951-0901* ☎ *025/244–7101* 🖷 *025/241–8485* ⤴ *133 rooms* ♨ *2 restaurants, in-room data ports, cable TV, bar, meeting room* ▤ *AE, D, MC, V.*

Sado Island (Sado-ga-shima, 佐渡島)

1 hr by hydrofoil from Niigata, 2½ hrs by car ferry.

Sado is known as much for its unblemished natural scenery as for its melancholy history. Revolutionary intellectuals, such as the Buddhist monk Nichiren, were banished to Sado to endure harsh exile as punishment for treason (read: antigovernment activities). When gold was discovered on Sado during the Edo period (1603–1868), those who occupied the lowest rungs of the social caste system—the homeless and poverty-stricken—were sent to Sado to work as forced laborers in the mines. This long history of hardship has left behind a tradition of soulful ballads and folk dances. Even the bamboo grown on the island is said to be the best for making *shakuhachi,* the flutes that accompany the mournful music.

May through September is the best time to visit Sado. In January and February the weather is bitterly cold and at other times storms can prevent sea and air crossings. Although the island is Japan's fifth largest, it's still relatively small, at 530 square km (331 square mi). Two parallel mountain chains, running along the north and south coasts, are split by a wide plain that encloses the island's principal cities. Despite the more than 1 million tourists who visit the island each year (more than 10 times the number of island inhabitants), the pace of life is slow, even preindustrial. That is the appeal of Sado.

39 Sado's usual port of entry is **Ryōtsu** (両津), the island's largest township. The center of town is on a strip of land that runs between Kamo-ko (Kamo Lake) and the Nihon-kai, with most of the hotels and ryokan on the shore of the lake. Kamo-ko is actually connected to the sea by a small inlet running through the middle of town. Ryōtsu's Ebisu quarter has the island's largest concentration of restaurants and bars.

40 The simplest way to begin exploring Sado is to take the bus from Ryōtsu west to **Aikawa** (相川). Before gold was discovered here in 1601, it was a small town of 10,000 people. The population swelled to 100,000 before the ore was exhausted. Now it's back to a tenth of this size, and tourists coming to see the old gold mine are a major source of the town's income.

Aikawa's **Sado Mine** (Sado Kinzan, 佐渡金山) has been a tourist attraction since operations halted in the 1980s. There are about 325 km (250 mi) of underground tunnels, some running as deep as 1,969 feet beneath sea level; and parts of this extensive digging are open to the public. Robots illustrate to visitors how Edo-period slaves worked in the mine. The robots are, in fact, quite lifelike, and they demonstrate the appalling conditions that were endured by the miners. Sound effects of shovels and pick axes add to the sobering reality. The mine is a tough 40-minute uphill walk or a five-minute taxi ride (about ¥900) from the bus terminal. The walk back is easier. ☎ 0259/74–2389 ☞ ¥700 ⊙ Apr.–Oct., daily 8–5:10; Nov.–Mar., daily 8–sunset.

★ North of Aikawa is **Senkaku Bay** (Senkaku-wan, 尖閣湾), the most dramatic stretch of coastline on Sado-ga-shima.

Information on sightseeing boats is available from **Senkaku Bay Tourism** (Senkaku-wan Kankō, 尖閣湾観光; ☎ 0259/75–2221). From the water you can look back at the fantastic, sea-eroded rock formations and cliffs that rise 60 feet out of the water. You will get off the boat at Senkaku-wan Yuen (Senkaku Bay Park), where you can picnic, stroll, and gaze upon the varied rock formations offshore. From the park, you return by bus from the pier to Aikawa. To reach the bay, take a 15-minute bus ride from Aikawa to Tassha for the 40-minute sightseeing cruise. The one-way cruise-boat runs April–November (¥700, glass-bottom boat ¥850).

The most scenic drive on Sado is the **Ōsado Skyline Drive** (大佐渡スカイライン). No public buses follow this route. You must take either a tour bus from Ryōtsu or a taxi from Aikawa across the skyline drive to Chikuse (¥4,200), where you connect with a public bus either to Ryōtsu or back to Aikawa.

To reach the southwestern tip of Sado, first make your way on a bus to Sawata from Aikawa or Ryōtsu, and then transfer to the bus for Ogi; en route you may want to stop at the town of **Mano** (真野), where the emperor Juntoku (1197–1242) is buried. The **Mano Goryō** (Mano Mausoleum, 真野御陵) and the museum, **Sado Rekishi Densetsukan** (佐渡歴史伝説館), which exhibits some of Emperor Juntoku's personal effects, are located a half-hour's walk from the center of town. There's a sadness to this mausoleum built for a man who spent the latter part of his life in exile on Sado for his unsuccessful attempt to regain power from the tyrannical Kamakura shogunate. Admission to the mausoleum and museum is ¥700; it's open daily April–mid-November, 8–5:30 and December–March, 8:30–5. ✉ 655 Mano, Mano-chō ☎ 0259/55–2525 ☞ ¥700 for mausoleum and museum ⊙ Apr.–Nov., daily 8–5:30; Dec.–Mar., daily 8:30–5.

🔟 The trip from Sawata to **Ogi** (小木) takes 50 minutes, the highlight being the beautiful *benten-iwa* (rock formations), just past Tazawaki. Be sure to take a window seat on the right-hand side of the bus. You can use Ogi as a port for returning to Honshū by ferry (2½ hours to Naoetsu) or on the hydrofoil (1 hour).

Ogi's chief attractions are the **taraibune** (たらい舟), round, tublike boats used for fishing. You can rent one (¥500 for a 30-minute paddle) and with a single oar wind your way around the harbor. Taraibune can also be found in Shukunegi, a more attractive town on the Sawasaki coast, where the water is dotted with rocky islets and the shore is covered with rock lilies in summer.

★ ㊷ **Shukunegi** (宿根木) has become a sleepy backwater town since it stopped building small wooden ships to traverse the waters between Sado and Honshū. It has, however, retained its traditional buildings and simple lifestyle. You can reach Shukunegi from Ogi on a sightseeing boat or by bus. Both take about 20 minutes; consider using the boat at least one way for the view of the cliffs that were created by an earthquake 250 years ago.

Where to Stay

You can make hotel reservations at the information counters of Sado Kisen ship company at Niigata Port or Ryōtsu Port.

$$$$ ▦ **Sado Royal Hotel Manchō** (佐渡ロイヤルホテル万長). This is the best hotel on Sado's west coast. It caters mostly to Japanese tourists and no English is spoken, but the staff makes the few Westerners who come by feel welcome. Be sure to request a room on the sea side for a stunning view of the magnificent blue ocean. Breakfast and dinner are included in the rate. ✉ *58 Shimoto, Aikawa, Sado-ga-shima, Niigata-ken 952-1575* ☎ *0259/74–3221* 📠 *0259/74–3738* 🛏 *90 rooms* ⚲ *Restaurant, Japanese baths* ▤ *DC, V* ⦿ *MAP.*

★ **$** ▦ **Sado Seaside Hotel** (佐渡シーサイドホテル). Twenty minutes on foot from Ryōtsu Port, this is more a friendly inn than a hotel. If you telephone before you catch the ferry from Niigata, the owner will meet you at the dock. He'll be carrying a green Seaside Hotel flag. The rooms and shared baths are spotless. Breakfast is ¥840, and a tasty mélange of regional delicacies for dinner costs ¥1,575. ✉ *80 Sumiyoshi, Ryōtsu, Sado-ga-shima, Niigata-ken 952-0015* ☎ *0259/27–7211* 📠 *0259/27–7213* ⊕ *www2u.biglobe.ne.jp/~sado/englishpage.htm* 🛏 *13 Japanese-style rooms, 5 with bath* ⚲ *Dining room, Japanese baths, laundry service* ▤ *AE, V.*

Getting Around

Check out the island's extensive and up-to-date Web site, www.mijintl.com, for information on ferry schedules, sightseeing routes, and lodging.

BY BUS Frequent bus service is available between major towns on Sado-ga-shima, making movement around the island relatively simple. The 90-minute bus ride from Ryōtsu to Aikawa departs every 30 minutes and costs ¥740. Two-day weekend passes for unlimited bus travel on Saturday and Sunday are ¥2,000 and available at the Ryōtsu and Ogi ports, and in the towns of Sawata and Aikawa. During July and August, a special one-day pass is offered for ¥1,500.

From May through November, there are also four- and eight-hour tours of the island that depart from both Ryōtsu and Ogi. However, these buses seem to have a magnetic attraction to souvenir shops. The best compromise is to use the tour bus for the mountain skyline drive (¥4,030) or the two-day skyline and historic site combined tour (¥7,690), then rent a bike to explore on your own. You can make bus tour reservations directly with the Niigata Kōtsū Regular Sightseeing Bus Center. 🚹 Niigata Kōtsū Regular Sightseeing Bus Center ☎ 0259/52-3200.

BY FERRY Sado Kisen has two main ferry routes, each with both a regular ferry and a hydrofoil service. From Niigata to Ryōtsu the journey takes 2½ hours, with six or seven crossings a day; the one-way fare is ¥2,060 for ordinary second class, ¥3,100 for first class, and ¥6,210 for special class. The jetfoil (¥5,960 one-way, ¥10,730 round-trip) takes one hour, with 10 or 11 crossings daily in summer, 3 in winter, and between 3 and 8 at other times of the year (depending on the weather). The bus from bay No. 6 in front of the JR Niigata Station takes 15 minutes (¥180) to reach the dock for the ferries sailing to Ryōtsu.

Between Ogi and Naoetsu the hydrofoil cost is the same as the Niigata–Ryōtsu crossing, but the Naoetsu ferry terminal is a ¥150 bus ride or ¥900 taxi ride from Naoetsu Station.

Depending on the season, one to three ferries sail between Teradomari (a port between Niigata and Naoetsu) and Akadomari, taking two hours. The fare is ¥1,410 for second class and ¥2,300 for first class. The port is five minutes on foot from the Teradomari bus station, and 10 minutes by bus from the JR train station (take the Teradomari-ko bus). 🚹 Sado Kisen ☎ 025/245-1234 in Niigata.

JAPAN ALPS A TO Z

To research prices, get advice from other travelers, and book travel arrangements, visit www.fodors.com.

AIR TRAVEL

The flight from Tōkyō's Haneda Kūkō to Komatsu Kūkō in Kanazawa takes one hour on Japan Airlines (JAL) or All Nippon Airlines (ANA); allow 40 minutes for the bus transfer to downtown Kanazawa, which costs ¥1,100.

Japan Air System (JAS) offers daily flights between Matsumoto and Fukuoka, Ōsaka, and Sapporo.

ANA has five flights daily between Tōkyō and Toyama. For more details on airlines, *see* Carriers *in* Smart Travel Tips A to Z.

Kyokushin Kōkū (Kyokushin Aviation) has small planes that take 25 minutes to fly from Sado-ga-shima to Niigata; there are five round-trip flights a day in summer and three in winter; the one-way fare is ¥7,350. 🚹 Kyokushin Kōkū ☎ 025/273-0312 in Niigata, 0259/23-5005 in Sado.

CAR RENTAL

Although train and bus travel are more convenient for getting around the region, rental cars are available at all major stations. In Kanazawa, try Nissan Rent-a-Car at the east exit of the train station. In Wajima your best bet is Eki Rent-a-Car at Wajima Station. An economy-size car will cost about ¥8,000 per day, or about ¥50,000 per week. It's best to reserve the car before you leave Tōkyō, Nagoya, or Kyōto, as you won't find many people who speak English in rural Japan. Also keep in mind that most highways require hefty tolls, and the costs can quickly add up.

In winter certain roads through the central Japan Alps are closed. In particular, the main route between Matsumoto and Takayama via Kamikōchi is closed November–April.

🗗 Local Agencies **Eki Rent-a-Car** ✉ Kanazawa Station ☎ 076/265–6659. **Nissan Rent-a-Car** ✉ 14–27 Shōwa-machi, Wajima ☎ 0762/22–0177.

EMERGENCIES
🗗 **Ambulance** ☎ 119. **Police** ☎ 110.

TOURS
The Japan Travel Bureau runs a five-day tour from Tōkyō that departs every Tuesday from April through October 26. The tour goes via Shirakaba-ko to Matsumoto (overnight), to Tsumago and Takayama (overnight), to Kanazawa (overnight), to Awara Onsen (overnight), and ends in Kyōto. The fare is ¥150,000, including four breakfasts and two dinners.

The Kanazawa Hokuriku-Tetsudō Co. has a 6½-hour tour that covers much of the Noto-hantō for ¥7,200, including lunch. The guides speak only Japanese. Tours operate year-round and depart daily at 8:10 AM from Kanazawa Station's east exit.

Contact the Niigata Kōtsū Information Center at the Ryōtsu bus terminal for a tour of Sado-ga-shima. It covers Skyline Drive, where public buses don't run. Tours, from May to November, depart daily from Ryōtsu and cost ¥6,440.

🗗 Tour Contacts **Japan Travel Bureau** ☎ 03/3281–1721. **Hokuriku-Tetsudō Co.** ☎ 076/234–0123. **Niigata Kōtsū Information Center** ☎ 0259/27–3141.

TRAIN TRAVEL
Tōkyō–Nagano Shinkansen service has effectively shortened the distance to the Alps from the east: the trip on the Nagano Shinkansen takes only about 90 minutes. From Kyōto and Nagoya the Alps are three hours away on the Hokuriku and Takayama lines. Unless you are coming from Niigata, you will need to approach Takayama and Kanazawa from the south (connections through Maibara are the speediest) on JR.

TRANSPORTATION AROUND THE JAPAN ALPS
Roads and railways through the Japan Alps follow the valleys. This greatly lengthens trips *around* mountains—as in the four-hour Matsumoto–Takayama ride via Nagoya. Route maps are available for Shinkansen and JR lines at any train station or bookstore. Remember that the last train or bus in the evening may leave as early as 7 PM. Most major train stations have an English-speaking information agent to help you.

Getting around by bus in Japan is not as convenient as by train, but it's not unpleasant, and bus information is easy to come by. Any bus station, which is always adjacent, in front of, or across from the train station, will provide you with maps and schedules. Of course, the local tourist-information office—also always in or near the train station—will help you decipher timetables and fares if you're bewildered.

VISITOR INFORMATION

Offices of the JR Travel Information Center and Japan Travel Bureau are at all major train stations. They can help you book local tours, hotel reservations, and travel tickets. Though you should not assume that English will be spoken, you can usually find someone whose knowledge is sufficient for your basic needs. If you get a map and schedule, you'll be able to get around easily. Where public transportation is infrequent, such as the Noto-hantō and Sado-ga-shima, local tours are available; however, the guides speak only Japanese.

The Japan Travel Phone is a nationwide toll-free service for English-language assistance and travel information, available 9–5 daily. When using a yellow, blue, or green public phone (do not use the red phones; they're for local calls only), insert a ¥10 coin, which will be returned.

The Hida Tourist Information Office, in front of the JR station, is open daily April–October 8:30–6:30, November–March 8:30–5, and serves the Takayama region. The Kanazawa Tourist Information Service is inside the JR station; the Nanao International Exchange Office is in Nanao City Hall, a few minutes' walk east of the station; the Niigata City Tourist Information Center, open daily 8:30–7, is to the left of the JR station exit; the Magome Tourist Information Office is open April–November, daily 8:30–5, and December–March, Monday–Saturday 8:30–5; the Matsumoto City Tourist Information Office is to the right as you exit the JR station; the Karuizawa Station Tourist Office is at the JR station; the Tsumago Tourist Information Office is open daily 9–5; the Wajima Station Tourist Center is in front of the station.

⑦ Tourist Information **Hida Tourist Information Office** ☎ 0577/32-5328. **Japan Travel Phone** ☎ 0120/44-4800. **Kanazawa Tourist Information Service** ☎ 076/232-6200 ☎ 076/238-6210. **Karuizawa Station Tourist Office** ☎ 0267/42-2491. **Magome Tourist Information Office** ☎ 0264/59-2336. **Matsumoto City Tourist Information Office** ☎ 0263/32-2814. **Nanao International Exchange Office** ☎ 0767/53-8448 ☎ 0767/54-8117. **Niigata City Tourist Information Center** ☎ 025/241-7914. **Tsumago Tourist Information Office** ☎ 0264/57-3123. **Wajima Station Tourist Center** ☎ 0768/22-1503 or 0768/22-4277.

KYŌTO 京都

5

By Nigel Fisher
Revised by
Deidre May

KYŌTO'S HISTORY IS FULL OF CONTRADICTIONS: famine and prosperity, war and peace, calamity and tranquillity. Although the city was Japan's capital for more than 10 centuries, the real center of political power was often elsewhere, be it Kamakura (1192–1333) or Edo (1603–1868). Such was Kyōto's decline in the 17th and 18th centuries that when the power of the government was returned from the shōguns to the emperor, he moved his capital and imperial court to Edo, renaming it Tōkyō. Though that move may have pained Kyōto residents, it actually saved the city from destruction. While most major cities in Japan were bombed flat in World War II, Kyōto survived. And where old quarters of Tōkyō have been replaced with characterless modern buildings—a fate that Kyōto has shared in part—much of the city's wooden architecture of the past still stands.

Until 710 Japan's capital was moved to a new location with the accession of each new emperor. When it was decided that the expense of this continuous movement had become overly bloated with the size of the court and the number of administrators, Nara was chosen as the permanent capital. Its life as the capital lasted only 74 years, when Buddhists rallied for, and achieved, tremendous political power. In an effort to thwart them, Emperor Kammu moved the capital in 784 to Nagaoka, leaving the Buddhists behind in their elaborate temples. Within 10 years, Kammu decided that Kyōto (then called Uda) was better suited for his capital. Poets were asked to compose verse about Uda, and invariably they included the phrase *Heian-kyō,* meaning "Capital of Peace," reflecting the hope and desire of the time.

For 1,074 years, Kyōto remained the capital, though at times only in name. From 794 to the end of the 12th century, the city flourished under imperial rule. Japan's culture started to grow independent of Chinese influences and to develop its unique characteristics. Unfortunately, the use of wood for construction, coupled with Japan's two primordial enemies, fire and earthquakes, has destroyed all the buildings from this era, except Byōdō-in in Uji. The short life span of a building in the 11th century is exemplified by the Imperial Palace, which burned down 14 times in 122 years. As if natural disasters were not enough, imperial power waned in the 12th century. There followed a period of shogunal rule, but each shōgun's reign was tenuous. By the 15th century civil wars tore the country apart. Many of Kyōto's buildings were destroyed or looted.

The Ōnin Civil War (1467–77) was particularly devastating for Kyōto. Two feudal lords, Yamana and Hosokawa, disputed who should succeed the reigning shōgun. Yamana camped in the western part of the city with 90,000 troops, and Hosokawa settled in the eastern part with 100,000 troops. Central Kyōto was the battlefield.

Not until the end of the 16th century, when Japan was brought together by the might of Nobunaga Oda and Hideyoshi Toyotomi, did Japan settle down. This period was soon followed by the usurpation of power by Ieyasu Tokugawa, founder of the Tokugawa shogunate, which lasted for the next 264 years. Tokugawa moved the political center of the country to Edo, present-day Tōkyō. Kyōto did remain the imperial capital—

If you have 1 day

Heaven forbid if you have such limited time. Should it be so, start in eastern Kyōto with **Ginkaku-ji** ► for the simplicity of its exterior shape and its gardens. Walk a little way down the **Path of Philosophy** before taking a taxi to **Kiyomizu-dera,** a vast wooden temple built on a hillside.

Next, walk through **Maruyama Kōen** to **Chion-in,** taking special notice of the awesome San-mon at its entrance. From here take a taxi to the **Kyōto Craft Center** to browse through the traditional and regional crafts. You may also want to take a break for lunch here.

Another taxi ride takes you to central Kyōto and **Nijō-jō,** a grandiose statement of Tokugawa military might. Now make tracks for western Kyōto, where you should have time for abbreviated visits to **Kinkaku-ji,** built in 1393, and **Ryōan-ji,** for its soul-searching garden. You can travel between the two on Bus 12. Because you're here so briefly, don't miss an all-out kaiseki dinner for a magical end to the day.

If you have 3 days

Give your first day to visiting the attractions in eastern Kyōto described above, but after **Ginkaku-ji** ► and the **Path of Philosophy,** slip in **Nanzen-ji,** the **Heian Jingū,** and **Sanjūsangen-dō** ► before going on to **Kiyomizu-dera.** On your second day spend the morning in central Kyōto at the **Imperial Palace** and **Nijō-jō.** In the afternoon cover western Kyōto and include **Kinkaku-ji, Ryōan-ji, Ninna-ji,** and **Myōshin-ji.** The morning of the third day take the Hankyū Railway Line from Kyōto's Hankyū Kawara-machi Station to Katsura Station and walk 15 minutes to get to **Katsura Rikyū** (having obtained your permit to do so the morning before). Then return to Kyōto and head to northern Kyōto and **Hiei-zan** to spend a calm afternoon wandering through the temple complex to appreciate the views of Kyōto below. Or get in a little shopping so as not to miss local foods and crafts to stuff into your suitcase.

If you have 6 days

Concentrate on eastern Kyōto for your first day. Then take on the **Imperial Palace** and **Nijō-jō** in central Kyōto the next morning and western Kyōto in the afternoon. On the third day visit the **Katsura Rikyū** in the morning and the sights in Arashiyama in the afternoon. When you come back into central Kyōto, try to visit **Higashi-Hongan-ji.** On the fourth day leave early for northern Kyōto to visit the temples in Ōhara—**Sanzen-in, Jikkō-in,** and **Jakkō-in.** By lunchtime, be at **Hiei-zan** to spend the afternoon on top of the world exploring the temple complexes. On the fifth day head for the **Kyōto Craft Center,** traditional shops, and **Nishiki-kōji** for a few treasures to bring home. Finish off your visit with a day trip to nearby Nara.

the emperor being little more than a figurehead—and the first three Tokugawa shōguns paid homage to it by restoring old temples and building new villas. In the first half of the 17th century, this was yet another show of Tokugawa power. Much of what you see in Kyōto today dates from this period.

Steeped in history and tradition, Kyōto has in many ways been the cradle of Japanese culture, especially with its courtly aesthetic pastimes, such as moon-viewing parties and tea ceremonies. A stroll through Kyōto today is a walk through 11 centuries of Japanese history. Of course the city has been swept into the industrialized, high-tech age along with the rest of Japan—plate-glass windows dominate central Kyōto and parking lots have replaced traditional town houses. Elderly women, however, continue to wear kimonos as they make their way slowly along the canal walkways. Geisha still entertain, albeit at prices out of reach for most visitors. Sixteen hundred temples and several hundred shrines surround central Kyōto. There's rather a lot to see, to say the least, so keep this in mind and don't run yourself ragged. Balance a morning at temples or museums with an afternoon in traditional shops, and a morning at the market with the rest of the day in Arashiyama or at one of the imperial villas.

See the glossary at the end of this book for definitions of the common Japanese words and suffixes used in this chapter.

EXPLORING KYŌTO

Most of Kyōto's interesting sights are north of Kyōto Station. Think of this northern sector as three rectangular areas abutting each other.

The middle rectangle fronts the exit of Kyōto station. This is **central Kyōto.** Here are the hotels, the business district, the Ponto-chō geisha district, and the Kiya-machi entertainment district. Central Kyōto also contains one of the oldest city temples, Tōji; the rebuilt Imperial Palace; and Nijō-jō, the onetime Kyōto abode of the Tokugawa shōguns. **Eastern Kyōto,** Higashiyama, is chockablock with temples and shrines, among them Ginkaku-ji, Heian Jingū, and Kiyomizu-dera. Gion—a traditional shopping neighborhood by day and a geisha entertainment district by night— is also here. You could easily fill two days visiting eastern Kyōto. **Western Kyōto** includes the temples Ryōan-ji and Kinkaku-ji, and Katsura Rikyū, a bit south.

You need three days just to skim over these three areas. However, two other areas have major sights to lure you. West of the western district is **Arashiyama,** with its temple, Tenryū-ji. And north of central Kyōto are **Hiei-zan and the suburb of Ōhara,** where the poignant story of Kenreimonin takes place at Jakkō-in.

Kyōto's sights spread over a wide area, but many of them are clustered together, and you can walk from one to another. Where the sights are not near each other, you can use Kyōto's buses, which run on a grid pattern that's easy to follow. Pick up route maps at the JNTO (Japan National Tourist Organization) office. The following exploring sections keep to the divisions described above so as to allow walking from one sight to another. However, notwithstanding traffic and armed with a bus map, you could cross and recross Kyōto without too much difficulty, stringing together sights of your own choosing.

Unlike other Japanese cities, Kyōto was modeled on the grid pattern of the Chinese city of Xian. Accordingly, addresses in the city are organized

Although Tōkyō has been the imperial capital since 1868, Kyōto—which wore the crown for the 10 centuries before—is still the classic Japanese city. The traditional arts, crafts, customs, language, and literature were all born, raised, and refined here. Kyōto has matchless villas, incomparable gardens, and magnificent temples and shrines. And Kyōto has the most artful Japanese cuisine.

Architecture

No other city in Japan has such a glorious array of religious architecture. Over its 1,200-year history the city has accumulated more than 1,600 Buddhist temples (30 are the headquarters for major sects spread throughout Japan), 200 Shintō shrines, and three imperial palaces. All of these vying for your attention can be a bit daunting, but there are clear standouts, places where you can view the best of Japan's harmonious, graceful architectural styles without having to dash back and forth with a checklist.

5

Gardens

Simplicity and symbolism are the perfected goals of Kyōto's temple gardens. The tea garden at Kinkaku-ji, with stepping stones paving the way through manicured grounds, sets the spirit at rest. The timeless arrangement of the *karesansui* (dry-garden) sand and rocks at Ryōan-ji is an eternal quest for completeness. The tree-shrouded gardens at Jakkō-in feed melancholy.

Matsuri (Festivals)

Kyōto's festival calendar includes five spectacular events: the Aoi (hollyhock), Gion (geisha), Jidai (costume), and the Daimon-ji and Kurama fire matsuri, held between May and October. For more information *see* On the Calendar at the front of this book.

Museums

Kyōto and Tōkyō are rivals for the role of the nation's leading repository of culture. Certainly Kyōto wins hands down for its traditional and courtly treasures. You won't get this feeling from walking the busy, congested streets of modern downtown, but a step into any of the nine major museums, or a walk through the backstreets of the old districts and temple areas will sweep you back to the days of refinement and artistic perfection.

Shopping

Perhaps even more than Tōkyō, Kyōto is *the* Japanese city in which to shop for gifts to take home. As Japan's self-proclaimed cultural capital, Kyōto has no shortage of art and antiques shops. Folk crafts from surrounding regions are brought into town for shops to sell. Secondhand kimonos can be a steal at $50, after image-conscious Japanese discard them for new ones priced in the thousands of dollars. Ceramics and woven bamboo make great souvenirs, and if you're looking for odds and ends, there are always the flea markets.

---

differently than in other parts of the country. Residents will assure you that this makes the city easier to navigate; confounded tourists may disagree. Many of the streets are named and east–west streets are numbered—the *san* in San-jō-dōri, for example, means "three." *Nishi-iru* means "to the west," *higashi-iru*, "to the east." *Agaru* is "to the north"

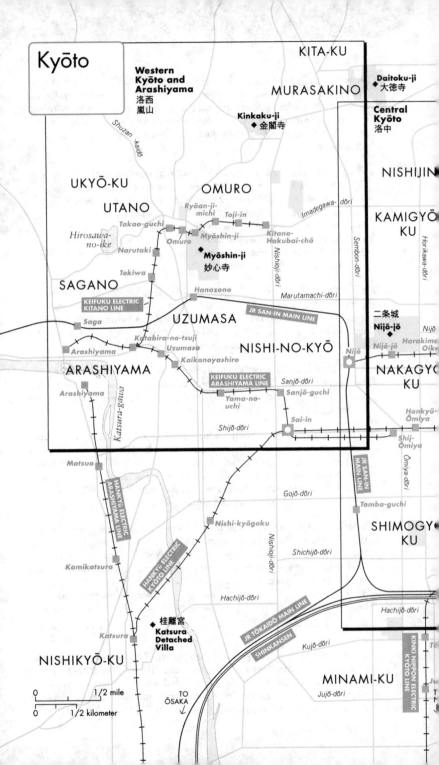

Kyōto

Western Kyōto and Arashiyama
洛西
嵐山

KITA-KU

MURASAKINO

Daitoku-ji
◆ 大徳寺

Kinkaku-ji
◆ 金閣寺

Central Kyōto
洛中

NISHIJIN

UKYŌ-KU

UTANO

OMURO

KAMIGYŌ-KU

Shuzan-kaidō

Ryōan-ji-michi

Tōji-in

Imadegawa-dōri

Takao-guchi

Hirosawa-no-ike

Omuro

Myōshin-ji

Kitano-Hakubai-chō

Sembon-dōri

Horikawa-dōri

Narutaki

◆ **Myōshin-ji**
妙心寺

Nishijōji-dōri

Tokiwa

SAGANO

Hanazono

Marutamachi-dōri

Marutamachi-dōri

KEIFUKU ELECTRIC KITANO LINE

JR SAN-IN MAIN LINE

二条城
Nijō-jō
◆

Nijō

Saga

UZUMASA

NISHI-NO-KYŌ

Nijō-jō

Harakime Oike

Arashiyama

Katabira-no-tsuji

Uzumasa

Nijō

NAKAGYŌ-KU

ARASHIYAMA

Kaikonoyashiro

KEIFUKU ELECTRIC ARASHIYAMA LINE

Sanjō-dōri

Arashiyama

Katsura-gawa

Yama-no-uchi

Sanjō-guchi

Hankyū-Ōmiya

Sai-in

Shijō-dōri

Shijō-Ōmiya

Ōmiya-dōri

Matsuo

JR SAN-IN MAIN LINE

Gojō-dōri

HANKYŪ ELECTRIC ARASHIYAMA LINE

Nishi-kyōgoku

Nishijōji-dōri

Tamba-guchi

SHIMOGYŌ-KU

HANKYŪ ELECTRIC KYŌTO LINE

Shichijō-dōri

Kamikatsura

◆ 桂離宮
Katsura Detached Villa

Hachijō-dōri

Hachijō-dōri

KINKI NIPPON ELECTRIC KYŌTO LINE

Katsura

JR TŌKAIDŌ MAIN LINE

SHINKANSEN

Kujō-dōri

NISHIKYŌ-KU

MINAMI-KU

0 ____ 1/2 mile

0 ____ 1/2 kilometer

TO ŌSAKA
↓

Jujō-dōri

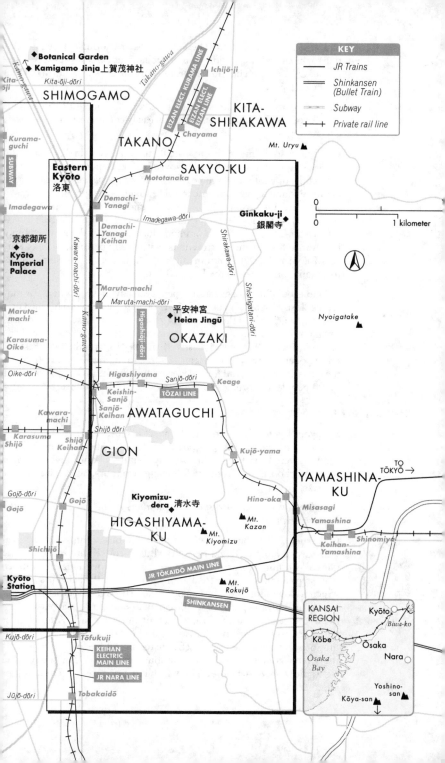

KEY

——————	*JR Trains*
═══════	*Shinkansen (Bullet Train)*
··········	*Subway*
—+—+—+—	*Private rail line*

◆ **Botanical Garden**
◆ **Kamigamo Jinja** 上賀茂神社

Kita-ōji-dōri

SHIMOGAMO

Kita-gawa

Kurama-guchi

SUBWAY

Imadegawa

京都御所
◆ **Kyōto Imperial Palace**

Maruta-machi

Karasuma-Oike

Oike-dōri

Kawara-machi

Karasuma Shijō

Gojō-dōri

Gojō

Shichijō

Kyōto Station

Kujō-dōri

Jūjō-dōri

Eastern Kyōto 洛東

EIZAN ELECT. KURAMA LINE
EIZAN ELECT. EIZAN LINE

Ichijō-ji

Takano-gawa

Chayama

TAKANO

Mototanaka

SAKYO-KU

KITA-SHIRAKAWA

Mt. Uryu ▲

Demachi-Yanagi

Imadegawa-dōri

Demachi-Yanagi Keihan

Ginkaku-ji 銀閣寺 ◆

Shirakawa-dōri

Maruta-machi

Maruta-machi-dōri

Higashiōji-dōri

平安神宮
◆ **Heian Jingū**

OKAZAKI

Shishigatani-dōri

Nyoigatake ▲

Higashiyama

Sanjō-dōri

Keage

Keishin-Sanjō

TŌZAI LINE

Sanjō-Keihan

Shijō dōri

AWATAGUCHI

Kujō-yama

Shijō Keihan

GION

Kawara-machi-dōri

Kamo-gawa

Kiyomizu-dera 清水寺 ◆

HIGASHIYAMA-KU

Mt. Kiyomizu ▲

▲ Mt. Kazan

Hino-oka

YAMASHINA-KU

TO TŌKYŌ →

Misasagi

Yamashina

Keihan-Yamashina

Shinomiya

JR TŌKAIDŌ MAIN LINE

▲ Mt. Rokujō

SHINKANSEN

Tōfukuji

KEIHAN ELECTRIC MAIN LINE

JR NARA LINE

Tobakaidō

0
0   1 kilometer

KANSAI REGION

Kyōto
Biwa-ko

Kōbe

Ōsaka
Nara

Ōsaka Bay

Yoshino-san ▲

Kōya-san ▲

and *sagaru* "to the south." These directions are normally given in relation to the closest intersection. Thus the restaurant Ogawa's address, Kiyamachi, Oike-agaru, Higashi-iru means, "Kiyamachi street, north of Oike on the east side."

Admission to Kyōto sights adds up. Over the course of three days, charges of ¥400–¥600 at each sight can easily come to $100 per person.

Timing

Cherry blossom time in spring (usually the first week in April) and the glorious autumn foliage in early November are remarkable. Except for the depths of winter and the peak of summer in August, when the temperature soars, Kyōto's climate is mild enough—though often rainy, especially mid-June to mid-July—to make sightseeing pleasant for most of the year. In the high season (May–October) the large numbers of visitors to the city can make accommodations scarce, and you must apply in advance to visit those attractions that require permits, such as Katsura Rikyū and the Shūgaku-in imperial villas. You can also expect lines for admission tickets to the Imperial Palace.

Religious buildings are generally open seven days a week, but many museums close Monday. If you're lucky enough to be in Kyōto for the Gion Festival, which is held throughout the month of July, be sure to go downtown on the 17th for the main parade. Two other memorable festivals are Aoi Matsuri (Hollyhock Festival) on May 15, and the Jidai Festival on October 22, which celebrates Kyōto's founding. If you're here for the latter, be sure to head for the Heian Jingū for the procession of about 2,000 people in costumes from every period of Kyōto history.

Eastern Kyōto 洛東

Start your Kyōto odyssey in Higashiyama (literally, "Eastern Mountain"). If you have time to visit only one district, this is the one. These sights can be covered comfortably in two days but if you only have one, then pick and choose sites from the following two tours, according to your interests.

Numbers in the text correspond to numbers in the margin and on the Eastern Kyōto map.

a good walk

NORTHERN HIGASHIYAMA

Ginkaku-ji ❶ ► is one of Kyōto's most famous sights, a wonderful villa turned temple. To get here, take Bus 5 from Kyōto station to the Ginkaku-ji-michi bus stop. When you can tear yourself away, retrace your steps on the entrance road until you reach the **Path of Philosophy** ❷, which follows alongside the canal. At the first large bridge as you walk south, turn off the path, cross the canal, and take the road east to the modest **Hōnen-in** ❸, with its thatched roof and quiet park. After Hōnen-in, return to the Path of Philosophy and continue south. In 15 minutes or so you reach, on your left, the temple **Eikan-dō** ❹. If you cross the street from Eikan-dō and continue south, you can see, on the right, the **Nomura Art Museum** ❺, which has a private collection of Japanese art.

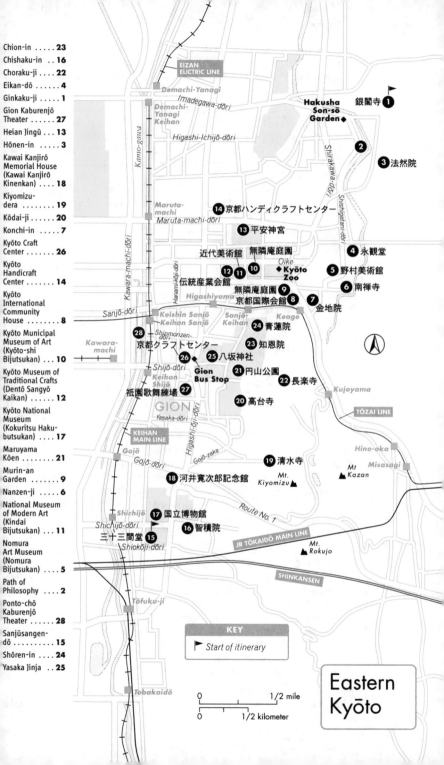

EIZAN
ELECTRIC LINE

Demachi-Yanagi

Imadegawa-dōri

Demachi-
Yanagi
Keihan

Higashi-Ichijō-dōri

Hakusha
Son-sō
Garden ◆

銀閣寺 **1**

2

3 法然院

Kamo-gawa

Kawara-machi-dōri

Shirakawa-dōri

Shishigatani-dōri

Maruta-
machi

14 京都ハンディクラフトセンター

Maruta-machi-dōri

13 平安神宮

4 永観堂

近代美術館

無隣庵庭園

Oike

Kyōto
Zoo ◆

5 野村美術館

12

11

10

伝統産業会館

Hanami-kōji-dōri

Higashiyama

9 無隣庵庭園

京都国際会館

8

7 金地院

6 南禅寺

Sanjō-dōri

Keishin Sanjō

Keihan Sanjō

Sanjō-
Keihan

Keage

24 青蓮院

Kawara-
machi

28

Shimonzen-
dōri

京都クラフトセンター

23 知恩院

26 **25** 八坂神社

Shijō-dōri

Keihan
Shijō

Gion
Bus Stop

21 円山公園

22 長楽寺

TŌZAI LINE

祇園歌舞練場

27

GION

Yasaka-dōri

20 高台寺

Hino-oka

Misasagi

KEIHAN
MAIN LINE

Higashi-ōji-dōri

Gojō

Gojō-dōri

Gojō-zaka

19 清水寺

Mt.
Kiyomizu ▲

Mt
Kazan ▲

18 河井寛次郎記念館

Route No. 1

Shichijō

17 国立博物館

Shichijō-dōri

16 智積院

三十三間堂 **15**

Shiokōji-dōri

JR TŌKAIDŌ MAIN LINE

Mt.
Rokujo ▲

SHINKANSEN

Ponto-chō

Tōfuku-ji

Tobakaido

KEY

▶ Start of itinerary

0   1/2 mile

0   1/2 kilometer

Eastern
Kyōto

If the day is close to an end, walk from the Nomura Art Museum to Heian Jingū and the Kyōto Handicraft Center, on Maruta-machi-dōri behind it. If not, continue this tour, which returns shortly to Heian Jingū.

Walk south from Nomura Art Museum and follow the main path. On your left will be **Nanzen-ji** ⑥, headquarters of the Rinzai sect of Zen Buddhism, with its classic triple gate, San-mon. See also Nanzen-in, a smaller temple within Nanzen-ji. Outside the main gate of Nanzen-ji but still within the complex, take the side street to the left, and you will come to **Konchi-in** ⑦, with its pair of excellent gardens. At the intersection at the foot of the road to Nanzen-ji, you can see the expansive grounds of the **Kyōto International Community House** ⑧, across the street to the left; however, unless you're interested in information about cultural classes, skip a visit to the center. Cross at the traffic light to get to the Meiji-period **Murin-an Garden** ⑨, with an entrance on a side road half a block east. Walk back north toward the canal, turn left and continue to the next right and cross the bridge over the canal. You can see an immense vermilion torii that acts as a distant entry for Heian Jingū. There are two museums flanking the other side of the torii, the **Kyōto Municipal Museum of Art** ⑩ on your right, and the **National Museum of Modern Art** ⑪ on your left. Close by is the **Kyōto Museum of Traditional Crafts** ⑫, which exhibits traditional Kyōto crafts. Pass through the torii to get to the **Heian Jingū** ⑬. After seeing the shrine, you could end your tour by visiting one of these museums or doing a bit of shopping at the **Kyōto Handicraft Center** ⑭. At the intersection of Maruta-machi-dōri and Higashi-ōji-dōri, west of the handicraft center, is the Kumano Jinja-mae bus stop. If you're ready for dinner, you can take Bus 202 or 206 five stops south on Higashi-ōji-dōri to the Gion bus stop; here, some of the city's best restaurants and bars are at your disposal.

SOUTHERN HIGASHIYAMA

Start your exploration of southern Higashiyama by visiting the temple of **Sanjūsangen-dō** ⑮ ▶. You can take Bus 100, 206, or 208 to the Sanjūsangen-dō-mae bus stop. The temple is south of the bus stop, just beyond the Kyōto Park Hotel. You can also take Bus 202 to the Higashiyama-Shichijō bus stop, walk west down Shichijō-dōri, and take the first major street to the left. If you're taking Bus 202 and you plan to see Chishaku-in, go there first—you can avoid doubling back.

From Sanjūsangen-dō retrace your steps back to Shichijō-dōri and take a right. **Chishaku-in** ⑯, famous for its paintings, will be facing you on the other side of Higashi-ōji-dōri. Back across Higashi-ōji-dōri is the prestigious **Kyōto National Museum** ⑰. Just north, less than a five-minute walk along Higashi-ōji-dōri from the museum, is the **Kawai Kanjirō Memorial House** ⑱, which houses the works of renowned potter Kanjirō Kawai. The next place to visit is a very special temple, **Kiyomizu-dera** ⑲. To get there from the museum, cross the major avenue Gojō-dōri and walk north along Higashi-ōji-dōri. The street to the right, Gojō-zaka, leads into Kiyomizu-zaka, which you can take to the temple.

If you take a right halfway down the road (Kiyomizu-zaka) leading from Kiyomizu-dera, you can walk along the **Sannen-zaka and Ninen-zaka** (slopes). Take a left after Ninen-zaka and then an immediate right, and continue walking north. After another five minutes you can see, on the right, **Kōdai-ji** ⑳, a sedate nunnery founded in the early 17th century. Keep heading north; by doing a right–left zigzag at the Maruyama Music Hall, you can get to **Maruyama Kōen** ㉑. The road to the right (east) leads up the mountainside to **Chōraku-ji** ㉒, a temple famous today for the stone lanterns that lead to it. Proceed north through Maruyama Kōen, and you can find **Chion-in** ㉓, headquarters of the Jōdo sect of Buddhism. More paintings by the Kanō school are on view at **Shōren-in** ㉔, a five-minute walk north of Chion-in.

Next turn left (west) on Sanjō-dōri, then left on Higashi-ōji-dōri to reach Shijō-dōri and the **Gion** district, where geisha live and work. At the Gion bus stop, Shijō-dōri goes off to the west. Before going down this street, consider walking up the stairs on the east side into **Yasaka Jinja** ㉕, a shrine that is said to bring good health and wealth. Walk back from Yasaka Jinja, cross Higashi-ōji-dōri, and you are in Gion, on Shijō-dōri. On the right-hand corner is the **Kyōto Craft Center** ㉖, perfect for a quick shopping stop. Shinmonzen-dōri, a street parallel to Shijō-dōri and to the north, is another great place for shopping and browsing. Shijō-dōri itself has interesting, less expensive items.

Off Shijō-dōri, halfway between Higashi-ōji-dōri and the Kamo-gawa, is Hanami-kōji-dōri. The section of this street that runs south of Shijō-dōri (on the right, if you're walking back from the river) will bring you into the heart of the Gion district and the **Gion Kaburenjō Theater** ㉗.

If you continue west on Shijō-dōri, you can cross over the Kamo-gawa. Pontochō-dōri is on the right. Like Gion, this area is known for its nightlife and geisha entertainment. At the north end of Pontochō-dōri, the **Pontochō Kaburenjō Theater** ㉘ puts on geisha performances.

TIMING Both of these walks are long, full-day tours. If you only have time for one day in Higashiyama, visit a selection of sights from both tours. Be sure to include at least one of the gardens and mix major sights with less-visited ones, which tend to be less crowded and more comfortable to visit.

What to See

★ ㉓ **Chion-in** (知恩院). The entrance to the temple is through the 79-ft two-story San-mon and then up a steep flight of stairs. In many people's minds, this is the most daunting temple gate in all of Japan, and it leads to one of Japan's largest temples, the very headquarters of the Jōdo sect of Buddhism, the second-largest Buddhist sect in Japan. On this site Hōnen, the founder of the Jōdo sect, chose to take his leave of this world by fasting to death in 1212. Chion-in was built in 1234. Because of fires and earthquakes, the oldest standing buildings are the Hon-dō (Main Hall, 1633) and the Daihōjō (Abbots' Quarters, 1639). The temple's belfry houses the largest bell in Japan, which was cast in 1633 and requires 17 monks to ring. The corridor behind the Main Hall, which leads to the Assembly Hall, is an *uguisu-bari* (nightingale floor). This type of floor is constructed to "sing" at every footstep to warn the monks of intruders. Walk underneath the corridor to examine the way the boards and nails are placed to create this inventive burglar alarm. From Kyōto station take Bus 206 to the Gion stop. The temple is north of Maruyama Kōen. ⊠ *400 Hayashi-shita-chō 3-chōme, Yamato-ōji, Higashi-hairu, Shimbashi-dōri, Higashiyama-ku* 🖃 *¥400* ⊘ *Mar.–Oct., daily 9–4:30; Nov.–Feb., daily 9–4; not all buildings open to public.*

★ ⑯ **Chishaku-in** (智積院). The major reason for visiting this temple is for its famous paintings, which were executed by Tōhaku Hasegawa and his son Kyūzo—known as the Hasegawa school, rivals of the Kanō school—and are some of the best examples of Momoyama-period art. These paintings were originally created for the sliding screens at Shōun-in, a temple built in 1591 on the same site but no longer in existence. Shōun-in was commissioned by Hideyoshi Toyotomi. When his concubine, Yodogimi, bore him a son in 1589, Hideyoshi named him Tsurumatsu (crane pine), two symbols of longevity. But the child died at age two, and Shōun-in was built for Tsurumatsu's enshrinement. The Hasegawas were commissioned to make the paintings, which were saved from the fires that destroyed Shōun-in and are now on display in the Exhibition Hall of Chishaku-in. Rich in detail and using strong colors on a gold background, they splendidly display the seasons by using the symbols of cherry, maple, pine, and plum trees and autumn grasses.

You may also want to take a few moments in the pond-viewing garden. It has only a vestige of its former glory, but from the temple's veranda you have a pleasing view of the pond and garden. From Kyōto Station take Bus 206 or 208 to the Higashiyama-Shichijō stop. Chishaku-in is on the east side of Higashi-ōji-dōri. ⊠ *Higashiyama-ku* 🖃 *¥350* ⊘ *Daily 9–4:30.*

㉒ **Chōraku-ji** (長楽寺). The procession of stone lanterns along the path gives this temple a modest fame. Although it's a pleasant temple, it may not be worth the hard climb up the mountainside, unless you have plenty of time in Kyōto. Chōraku-ji is east of Maruyama Kōen. ⊠ *Higashiyama-ku* 🖃 *¥400* ⊘ *Daily 9–5.*

★ ④ **Eikan-dō** (永観堂). Officially this temple, founded in 855 by Priest Shinshō, is named Zenrin-ji, but it honors the memory of the 11th-century priest Eikan, and has popularly come to be known as Eikan-dō. He was a man of the people, and he would lead them in a dance in celebration of Amida Buddha. According to tradition, the Amida statue came to life on one occasion and stepped down from his pedestal to join the dancers. Taken aback, Eikan slowed his dancing feet. Amida looked back over his shoulder to reprimand Eikan for slowing his pace. This legend explains why the unusual statue in the Amida-dō has its face turned to the side, as if glancing backward. A climb to the top of the pagoda affords superb views of the grounds below and Kyōto beyond. With colorful maple trees, the grounds are magnificent in autumn. The buildings here are 16th-century reconstructions made after the originals were destroyed in the Ōnin Civil War (1467–77). Eikan-dō is a 15-minute walk south of Hōnen-in on the Path of Philosophy. ⊠ *Higashiyama-ku* 🖃 *¥500* ⊘ *Daily 9–5; last entry at 4:30.*

► ❶ **Ginkaku-ji** (銀閣寺). Ginkaku-ji means "Temple of the Silver Pavilion,"
Fodor'sChoice but the temple is not silver; it was only intended to be. Shōgun Yoshi-
★ masa Ashikaga (1435–90) commissioned this villa for his retirement.
Construction began in the 1460s, but it was not until 1474 that, disil-
lusioned with politics, Ashikaga gave his full attention to the building
of his villa and to romance, moon gazing, and the tea ceremony, which
he helped develop into a high art. Though he never had time to complete the coating of the pavilion with silver foil, he constructed a dozen
or so buildings. Many were designed for cultural pursuits, such as incense and tea ceremonies. On his death, the villa was converted into a
Buddhist temple, as was often the custom during the feudal era. However, with the decline of the Ashikaga family, Ginkaku-ji fell into decline, and many buildings were destroyed.

All that remain today of the original buildings are **Tōgū-dō** (East Seeking Hall) and Ginkaku-ji itself. The four other structures on the grounds
were built in the 17th and 19th centuries. The front room of Tōgu-dō
is where Yoshimasa is thought to have lived, and the statue of the priest
is probably of Yoshimasa himself. The back room, called Dojin-sai
(Comradely Abstinence), became the prototype for traditional tea-ceremony rooms.

Ginkaku-ji is a simple and unadorned two-story building. Its appeal lies
in the serene exterior shape, which combines Chinese elements with the
developing Japanese Muromachi (1333–1568) architecture. The upper
floor contains a gilt image of Kannon (goddess of mercy) said to have
been carved by Unkei, a famous Kamakura-period sculptor; it's not, however ordinarily open to public view.

Ginkaku-ji overlooks the complex **gardens,** attributed to artist and architect Sōami (1465–1523), which consist of two contrasting garden sections that together create a balanced, harmonious result. Adjacent to
the pavilion is a pond garden, with a composition of rocks and plants
designed to afford different perspectives from each viewpoint. The other
garden has two sculpted mounds of sand, the higher one symbolizing,
perhaps, Mt. Fuji. The garden sparkles in the moonlight and has been
aptly named Sea of Silver Sand. The composition of the approach to the
garden is also quite remarkable.

To reach Ginkaku-ji, take Bus 5 from Kyōto Station to the Ginkaku-ji-
michi bus stop. Walk on the street along the canal, going east. Cross a
north–south canal and Hakusha Son-sō Garden on your right; then continue straight and Ginkaku-ji will be in front of you. ⊠ *Ginkaku-ji-chō,
Sakyō-ku* 🎫 *¥500* ☉ *Mid-Mar.–Nov., daily 8:30–5; Dec.–mid-Mar.,
daily 9–4:30.*

**off the
beaten
path**

HAKUSA SON-SŌ GARDEN (白砂村荘庭園)– Coming down the hill
from Ginkaku-ji, a hundred yards before the street crosses a
north–south canal, you can see a small villa with an impeccable
garden. The modest home of the late painter Hashimoto Kansetsu has
an exquisite stone garden and teahouse open to the public. To get
here, take Bus 5 from Kyōto Station to the Ginkaku-ji-michi stop.

Walk east on the street along the canal. Just after the street crosses another canal flowing north–south, Hakusa Son-sō will be on the right. ⊠ *Higashiyama-ku* 🎫 *¥800; with tea and sweets, an extra ¥800* ⊙ *Daily 10–5; last entry at 4:30.*

Fodor's Choice
★

Gion (祇園, ghee-*own*). Arguably Kyōto's most interesting neighborhood, this is the legendary haunt of geisha. In the evening, amid the glow of teahouse and restaurant lanterns, you can see them scurrying about, white faced, on the way to their appointments. In their wake their *maiko* follow—the young apprentice geisha whom you can identify by the longer sleeves of their kimonos.

The heart of the district is on Hanami-kōji-dōri. Heading north, the street intersects with Shinmonzen-dōri, which is famous for its antiques shops and art galleries. Here you can find collectors' items—at collectors' prices—which make for interesting browsing, if not buying. The shops on Shijō-dōri, which parallels Shinmonzen-dōri to the south, carry slightly more affordable paraphernalia of the geisha world, from handcrafted hair ornaments to incense to parasols. ⊠ *Higashiyama-ku.*

need a break?

Kagizen Yoshifusa (鍵善良房) in Gion is reputedly the best *okashi-ya* (confectionery shop) in Kyōto. As you browse through the shops on the north side of Shijō-dōri, west of Hanami-kōji-dōri, look for the store's red *noren* (cloth sign) hanging outside. For a breather and a snack, go to the tearoom at the back, where you can order frothy *matcha* (powdered green tea leaves mixed with water and beaten with a bamboo whisk) and *nama-gashi* (fresh sweets). ⊠ *264 Gion-machi, Kitagawa, Higashiyama-ku* ☎ *075/561–1818* ⊙ *Tues.–Sun. 9–6.*

★ ㉗ **Gion Kaburenjō Theater** (祇園歌舞練場). Because Westerners have little opportunity to enjoy a geisha's performance in a private party setting—which would require a proper recommendation of, and probably the presence of, a geisha's respected client—a popular entertainment during the month of April is the Miyako Odori (Cherry-Blossom Dance), presented at this theater. During the musical presentations, geisha wear their elaborate traditional kimono and makeup. Next door to the theater is **Gion Corner,** where demonstrations of traditional performing arts take place nightly March–November (⇨ Nightlife & the Arts, *below*). ⊠ *Gion Hanami-kōji, Higashiyama-ku* ☎ *075/561–1115.*

⓭ **Heian Jingū** (平安神宮). One of the city's newest historical sites, Heian Jingū was built in 1894 to mark the 1,100th anniversary of the founding of Kyōto. The shrine honors two emperors: Kammu (737–806), who founded the city in 794, and Kōmei (1831–66), the last emperor to live out his reign in Kyōto. The new buildings are for the most part replicas of the old Imperial Palace, at two-thirds the original size. In fact, because the original palace (rebuilt many times) was finally destroyed in 1227, and only scattered pieces of information survive relating to its construction, Heian Jingū should be taken as a Meiji interpretation of the old palace. Still, the dignity and the relative spacing of the **East Hon-**

den and West Hon-den (the Main Halls), and the **Daigoku-den** (Great Hall of State), in which the Heian emperor would issue decrees, conjure up an image of how magnificent the Heian court must have been. During New Year's, kimono-clad and gray-suited Japanese come to pay homage, trampling over the imposing gravel forecourt leading to Daigoku-den.

There are three stroll gardens at Heian Jingū positioned east, west, and north of the shrine itself. They follow the Heian aesthetic of focusing on a large pond, a rare feature at a Shintō shrine. Another notable element is the stepping-stone path that crosses the water—its steps are recycled pillars from a 16th-century bridge that spanned the Kamo-gawa before an earthquake destroyed it.

Spring, with sakura in full bloom, is a superb time to visit. An even better time to see the shrine is during the Jidai Festival, held on October 22, which celebrates the founding of Kyōto. The pageant, a procession of 2,000 people attired in costumes from every period of Kyōto history, winds its way from the original site of the Imperial Palace and ends at the Heian Jingū.

Another choice time to come to the shrine is June 1–2 for **Takigi Nō performances,** so named because they're held at night, in open air, lighted by *takigi* (burning firewood). Performances take place on a stage built before the shrine's Daigoku-den.

From the Dōbutsu-en-mae bus stop, follow the street between the Kyōto Municipal Museum of Art and the National Museum of Modern Art directly to the shrine. Call Tourist Information Center for advance tickets. ⊠ *Okazakinishi Tennō-chō, Sakyō-ku* ☎ *075/371–5649* 🖃 *Garden ¥600; Takigi Nō ¥3,300 at the gate, ¥2,500 in advance* ☉ *Mid-Mar.–Aug., daily 8:30–5:30; Sept., Oct., and early Mar., daily 8:30–5; Nov.–Feb., daily 8:30–4:30.*

❸ **Hōnen-in** (法然院). The walk through the trees leading to the temple is mercifully quiet and comforting, but not many people come to this humble, thatched-roof structure. The temple was built in 1680, on a site that in the 13th century simply consisted of an open-air Amida Buddha statue. Hōnen-in honors the priest Hōnen (1133–1212), the founder of the Jōdo sect, who brought Buddhism down from its lofty peak to the common folk by making the radical claim that all were equal in the eyes of Buddha. Hōnen focused on faith in the Amida Nyorai; he believed that *nembutsu*—"Namu Amida Butsu," the invocation of Amida Buddha—which he is said to have repeated up to 60,000 times a day, and reliance on Amida, the "all-merciful," were the path to salvation. His ideas threatened other sects, especially the Tendai. The established Buddhist powers pressured then-emperor Gotoba to diminish Hōnen's influence over the masses. At about the same time, two of the emperor's concubines became nuns after hearing some of Hōnen's disciples preaching. The incident provided Gotoba with an excuse to decry the Jōdo sect as immoral, with the charge that its priests were seducing noblewomen. Emperor Gotoba had Anraku and Jūren, two of Hōnen's disciples, publicly executed and Hōnen sent into exile. Eventually, in 1211, Hōnen was pardoned and permitted to return to Kyōto, where a year later, at Chion-in, he fasted to death at the age of 79. From the Path of Philosophy, at the first large bridge as you walk south, turn off the path and take the road east. ⊠ *Higashiyama-ku* 🖾 *Free* 🕙 *Daily 7–4.*

⑱ Kawai Kanjirō Memorial House (Kawai Kanjirō Kinenkan, 河井寛次郎記念館). Taking his inspiration from a traditional rural Japanese cottage, Kanjirō Kawai, one of Japan's most renowned potters, designed and lived in this house, now a museum. He was one of the leaders of the Mingei (folk art) movement, which sought to revive interest in traditional folk arts during the 1920s and '30s, when all things Western were in vogue in Japan. On display are some of the artist's personal memorabilia and, of more interest, some of his exquisite works. An admirer of Western, Chinese, and Korean ceramics techniques, Kawai won many awards, including the Grand Prix at the 1937 Paris World Exposition. From Kyōto Station take Bus 206 or 208 to the Sanjūsangen-dō-mae stop and then head east to the end of Shichijō-dōri. The house is a five-minute walk north along Higashi-ōji-dōri. ⊠ *Gojō-zaka, Higashiyama-ku* 🕾 *075/561–3585* 🖾 *¥900* 🕙 *Tues.–Sun. 10–5; when Mon. is national holiday, museum stays open Mon. and closes following day. Closed Aug. 10–20 and Dec. 24–Jan. 7.*

⑲ Kiyomizu-dera (清水寺). Unique Kiyomizu-dera, one of the most visited temples in Kyōto and a prominent feature in the city's skyline, stands out because it's built into a steep hillside, with 139 giant pillars supporting part of its main hall. In the past, people would come here to escape the open political intrigue of Kyōto and to scheme in secrecy.

Fodor'sChoice
★

From the wooden veranda, one of the few temple verandas where you can walk around without removing your shoes, there are fine views of the city and a breathtaking look at the valley below. "Have you the courage to jump from the veranda of Kiyomizu?" is a saying asked when someone sets out on a daring new venture.

Interestingly enough, Kiyomizu-dera does not belong to one of the local Kyōto Buddhist sects but rather to the Hossō sect, which developed in Nara. The temple honors the popular 11-faced Kannon (goddess of mercy), who can bring about easy childbirth. Over time Kiyomizu-dera has become "everyone's temple." You'll see evidence of this throughout the grounds, from the little Jizō Bosatsu statues (representing the god of travel and children) stacked in rows to the many *koma-inu* (mythical guard dogs) marking the pathways, which have been donated by the temple's grateful patrons. The original Kiyomizu-dera was built here in 798, four years after Kyōto was founded; the current structure dates to 1633.

On the north side of the main hall is a small shrine called **Jishu-jinja**, dedicated to Okuni Nushi-no-mikoto, a land-ruling deity also considered to be a powerful matchmaker. Many young people visit the shrine to seek help in finding their life partners. They try to walk between two stones placed 18 meters (59 feet) apart, with their eyes closed. It's said that love will materialize for anyone who can walk in a straight line between the two.

Shops selling souvenirs, religious articles, and ceramics line Kiyomizu-zaka, the street leading to the temple. There are also tea shops where you can sample *yatsuhashi*—doughy, triangular sweets filled with cinnamon-flavor bean paste—a Kyōto specialty. From Kyōto Station take Bus 206 to the Kiyomizu-michi stop. From the Kawai Kanjirō Memorial House cross the major avenue, Gojō-dōri, and walk up Higashi-ōji-dōri. The street to the right, Gojō-zaka, leads into Kiyomizu-zaka, which you'll take to the temple. ⊠ *Kiyomizu 1-chōme, Higashiyama-ku* ☏ *¥300* ☉ *Daily 6–6.*

need a break?

★ On the road to Kiyomizu temple, just south of Ninen-zaka, is a wooden archway covered in *senja-fuda*, adhesive name cards left by pilgrims on the entryways to shrines and temples. The passage under the arch leads to a small courtyard teahouse, **Bun-no-suke Jaya** (文の助茶屋). The specialty here is *amazake*, a sweet, nonalcoholic beverage served with ginger and traditionally enjoyed by nuns. Or you can sip matcha and order fresh Kyōto sweets. The teahouse was founded by Katsura Bun-no-suke, a famous *rakugo* (comic storytelling) artist who's fame waned with the advent of motion pictures. The interior is adorned with an eclectic collection of kites and folk dolls. ⊠ *Kiyomizu 3-chō, Higashiyama-ku* ☏ *075/561–1972* ☉ *Thurs.–Tues. 10–5:30.*

⑳ Kōdai-ji (高台寺). This quiet nunnery established in the early 17th century provides a tranquil alternative to the crowds of nearby Kiyomizu-dera. The temple was built as a memorial to Hideyoshi Toyotomi by his wife, Kita-no-Mandokoro, who lived out her remaining days in the nunnery there. The famous 17th-century landscaper Kobori Enshū designed the gardens, and artists of the Tosa school decorated the ceilings of the Kaisan-dō (Founder's Hall) with raised lacquer and paintings. The teahouse above on the hill, designed by tea master Sen-no-Rikyū, has a unique umbrella-shape bamboo ceiling and a thatched roof. From Kyōto Station take Bus 206 to the Higashiyama-yasui bus stop. ⊠ *Higashiyama* ☏ *¥500* ☉ *Apr.–Nov., daily 9–4:30; Dec.–Mar., daily 9–4.*

★ **❼ Konchi-in** (金地院). The two gardens of this shrine especially merit a visit: famous tea master and landscape designer Kobori Enshū completed them in 1632, under commission by Zen priest Sūden in accordance with the will of Ieyasu Tokugawa. One has a pond in the shape of the Chinese character *kokoro* (heart). The other is a dry garden with a gravel area in the shape of a boat, a large flat worshiping stone, and a backdrop of *o-karikomi* (tightly pruned shrubbery). The two rock groupings in front of a plant-filled mound are in the crane-and-tortoise style. Since ancient times these creatures have been associated with longevity, beauty, and eternal youth. In the feudal eras the symbolism of the crane and the tortoise became very popular with the samurai class, whose profession often left them with only the hope of immortality. Though not on the same grounds as ⇨ **Nanzen-ji,** this temple is in fact part of the Nanzen-ji complex. To get here, leave Nanzen-ji and take the side street to the left. ⊠ *86 Fukuchi-chō, Nanzen-ji, Sakyō-ku* ☏ *¥400* ☉ *Mar.–Nov., daily 8:30–5; Dec.–Feb., daily 8:30–4:30.*

❷❻ **Kyōto Craft Center** (京都クラフトセンター). Kyōto residents come to this collection of stores to shop for fine contemporary and traditional crafts— ceramics, lacquerware, prints, and textiles. You can also purchase moderately priced souvenirs, such as dolls, coasters, bookmarks, and paper products. From Kyōto Station take Bus 206 to the Gion stop. The center is on the corner of Shijō-dōri and Higashi-ōji-dōri. ⊠ *Shijō-dōri, Gion-machi, Higashiyama-ku* ☎ *075/561–9660* ☾ *Thurs.–Tues. 11–7.*

❶❹ **Kyōto Handicraft Center** (京都ハンディクラフトセンター). Seven floors of everything Japanese, from dolls to accessories, is on sale. The center caters to tourists with its English-speaking staff. It's a good place to browse, and the pricing is fairly reasonable. From the Gion bus stop take Bus 202 or 206 five stops north on Higashi-ōji-dōri to the Kumano Jinja-mae bus stop. From Kyōto Station use Bus 206; the center is across Maruta-machi-dōri from the Heian Jingū. ⊠ *Kumano Jinja Higashi, Sakyō-ku* ☎ *075/761–5080* ☾ *Mar.–Nov., daily 9:30–6; Dec.–Feb., daily 9:30–5:30.*

❽ **Kyōto International Community House** (Kyōto Kokusai Koryū Kaikan, 京都国際交流会館). On expansive grounds, the center has library and information facilities, Internet stations, and rental halls for public performances. The bulletin board by the entryway is full of tips on housing opportunities, study, and events in Kyōto. The KICH also offers weekly lessons in tea ceremony, *koto* (a 13-string instrument), calligraphy, and Japanese language at reasonable prices. The book *Easy Living in Kyōto* (available free) gives helpful information for a longer stay. The Community House is just off the intersection at the foot of the road to Nanzen-ji. ⊠ *2–1 Torii-chō, Awata-guchi, Sakyō-ku* ☎ *075/752–3010* ⊠ *Free* ☾ *Tues.–Sun. 9–9; when Mon. is national holiday, Community House stays open Mon. and closes following day.*

❶❶⓪ **Kyōto Municipal Museum of Art** (Kyōto-shi Bijutsukan, 京都市美術館). This space serves mostly as a gallery for traveling shows and local art-society exhibits. It owns a collection of Japanese paintings of the Kyōto school, a selection of which goes on display once a year. From the Dōbutsu-en-mae bus stop, walk down the street that leads to the Heian Jingū. The museum is on the right inside the torii. ⊠ *Enshōji-chō, Okazaki, Sakyō-ku* ☎ *075/771–4107* ⊠ *Depends on exhibition, but usually around ¥1,000* ☾ *Tues.–Sun. 9–5, last entry at 4:30; when Mon. is national holiday, museum stays open Mon. and closes following day.*

❶❷ **Kyōto Museum of Traditional Crafts** (Dentō Sangyō Kaikan, 伝統産業会館). This museum displays a wide array of traditional Kyōto crafts, hosts educational crafts-making demonstrations, and even has a shop where you can pick up crafts souvenirs. In the basement is a model interior of a traditional town house. From the Dōbutsu-en-mae bus stop, head down the street that leads to Heian Jingū. The museum is inside the torii on your left after the National Museum of Modern Art. ⊠ *9–2 Seishōji-chō, Okazaki, Sakyō-ku* ☎ *075/761–3421* ⊠ *Free* ☾ *Tues.–Sun. 9–5; last entry at 4:30.*

❶❼ **Kyōto National Museum** (Kokuritsu Hakubutsukan, 国立博物館). Exhibitions at this prestigious museum change regularly, but you can count on an excellent display of paintings, sculpture, textiles, calligraphy, ceramics, lacquerware, metalwork, and archaeological artifacts from its permanent collection of more than 8,000 works of art. From Kyōto Station take Bus 206 or 208 to the Sanjūsangen-dō-mae stop. The museum is across Higashi-ōji-dōri from Chishaku-in. ⊠ *Yamato-ōji-dōri, Higashiyama-ku* ☎ *075/541–1151* 🎫 *¥420; additional fee for special exhibitions* ⏰ *Tues.–Sun. 9–4:30.*

off the beaten path

KYŌTO ZOO (Dōbutsu-en, 動物園) – The prime reason to stop at the zoo is to entertain your children, if you have any in tow. The zoo has a Children's Corner, where your youngsters can feed the farm animals. It's across from the Dōbutsu-en-mae bus stop, north of Murin-an garden. ⊠ *Hoshōji-chō, Okazaki, Sakyō-ku* ☎ *075/771–0210* 🎫 *¥500* ⏰ *Tues.–Sun. 9–5, winter 9–4:30; when Mon. is national holiday, zoo stays open Mon. and closes following day.*

㉑ Maruyama Kōen (Maruyama Park, 円山公園). You can rest your weary feet at this small park, home to the Maruyama Music Hall. There are usually vendors around to supply refreshment. From Kyōto Station take Bus 206 to the Higashiyama stop; the park is north of Kōdai-ji. ⊠ *Higashiyama-ku.*

❾ Murin-an Garden (無隣庵庭園). The property was once part of Nanzen-ji, but in 1895 it was sold to Duke Yamagata, a former prime minister and advocate of the reforms that followed the Meiji Restoration. Unlike more traditional Japanese gardens, which adopt a more restrained sense of harmony, Murin-an allows more freedom of movement. This is right in step with the Westernizing that the Meiji Restoration brought upon Japan. The garden is south of the Dōbutsu-en-mae bus stop. Enter from the side road on the other side of a canal. ⊠ *Sakyō-ku* 🎫 *¥350* ⏰ *Daily 9–4:30.*

★ ❻ Nanzen-ji (南禅寺). Like the nearby temple of Ginkaku-ji, this former aristocratic retirement villa was turned into a temple on the death of its owner, Emperor Kameyama (1249–1305). The 15th-century Ōnin Civil War demolished the buildings, but some were resurrected during the 16th century. Nanzen-ji has become one of Kyōto's most important temples, in part because it's the headquarters of the Rinzai sect of Zen Buddhism. You enter the temple through the 1628 **San-mon** (Triple Gate), the classic "gateless" gate of Zen Buddhism that symbolizes entrance into the most sacred part of the temple precincts. From the top floor of the gate you can view Kyōto spread out below. Whether or not you ascend the steep steps, give a moment to the statue of Goemon Ishikawa, a Robin Hood–style outlaw of Japan who hid in this gate until his capture.

On through the gate is **Hōjō** (Abbots' Quarters), a National Treasure. Inside, screens with impressive 16th-century paintings divide the chambers. These wall panels of the *Twenty-Four Paragons of Filial Piety and Hermits* were created by Eitoku Kanō (1543–90) of the Kanō school—in effect the Kanō family, because the school consists of eight generations, Eitoku being from the fifth, of one bloodline. Kobori Enshū created the Zen-style garden, commonly called the Leaping Tiger Garden and an excellent example of the karesansui style, attached to the Hōjō. Unusual here, the large rocks are grouped with clipped azaleas, maples, pines, and moss, all positioned against a plain white well behind the raked gravel expanse. The greenery serves to connect the garden quite effectively with the lush forested hillside beyond.

Within Nanzen-ji's 27 pine-tree-covered acres sit several other temples, known more for their gardens than for their buildings. One worth visiting if you have time is **Nanzen-in,** once the temporary abode of Emperor Kameyama. Nanzen-in has a mausoleum and a garden that dates to the 14th century; a small creek passes through it. Nanzen-in is not as famous as other temples, making it a peaceful place to visit. From Nomura Art Museum, walk south along the main pat to Nanzen-ji; the temple complex will be on your left. ⊠ *Sakyō-ku* 🈳 *Main temple building ¥400, entrance to San-mon or Nanzen-in ¥200* 🕙 *Mar.–Nov., daily 8:40–5; Dec.–Feb., daily 8:40–4:30.*

🕦 **National Museum of Modern Art** (Kindai Bijutsukan, 近代美術館). The museum is known for its collection of 20th-century Japanese paintings and its ceramic treasures by Kanjirō Kawai, Rosanjin Kitaōji, Shōji Hamada, and others. Established in 1903, it reopened in 1986 in a building designed by Fumihiko Maki, one of the top contemporary architects in Japan. From the Dōbutsu-en-mae bus stop, walk down the street that leads to the Heian Jingū. The museum is on the left inside the torii. ⊠ *Enshōji-chō, Okazaki, Sakyō-ku* ☎ *075/761–4111* 🈳 *¥420; additional fee for special exhibitions* 🕙 *Tues.–Sun. 9:30–5.*

❺ Nomura Art Museum (Nomura Bijutsukan, 野村美術館). Instead of bequeathing their villas to Buddhist sects, the modern wealthy Japanese tend to donate their art collections to museums, as was the case here. Tokushichi Nomura, founder of the Daiwa Bank and a host of other companies, donated his collection of scrolls, paintings, tea-ceremony utensils, ceramics, and other art objects to establish his namesake museum. The museum is south of Eikan-dō on the west side of the street. ⊠ *61 Shimogawara-chō, Nanzen-ji, Sakyō-ku* ☎ *075/751–0374* 🈳 *¥700* 🕙 *Late Mar.–mid-June and mid-Sept.–early Dec., Tues.–Sun. 10–4:30; last entry at 4.*

❷ Path of Philosophy (Tetsugaku-no-michi, 哲学の道). Cherry trees, which are spectacular in bloom, line this walkway along the canal. It has traditionally been a place for contemplative strolls since a famous scholar, Ikutaro Nishida (1870–1945), took his constitutional here. Now professors and students have to push their way through tourists who take the same stroll and whose interest lies mainly with the path's specialty shops. Along the path are several coffee shops and small restaurants. Omen, one block west of the Path of Philosophy, is an inexpensive, popular restaurant known for its homemade white noodles.

From Kyōto Station take Bus 5 to the Ginkaku-ji-michi bus stop. Walk east on the street that follows the canal. Just after the street crosses a north–south canal, the path begins on your right. ⊠ *Sakyō-ku.*

㉘ Ponto-chō Kaburenjō Theater (先斗町歌舞練場). Like Gion, Ponto-chō is known for its nightlife and geisha entertainment. At the north end of Pontochō-dōri, the Ponto-chō Kaburenjō presents geisha song-and-dance performances in the spring (May 1–24) and autumn (October 15–November 7). The theater sits on the west side of the Kamo-gawa between Sanjō and Shijō streets. ⊠ *Ponto-chō, Sanjō-sagaru, Nakagyō-ku* ☎ *075/221-2025.*

★ ▶ **⑮ Sanjūsangen-dō** (三十三間堂). Everyone knows this temple as Sanjūsangen-dō even though it's officially called Rengeō-in. *Sanjūsan* means "33," which is the number of spaces between the pillars that lead down the temple's narrow, 394-ft-long hall. Enthroned in the middle of the hall is the 6-ft-tall, 1,000-handed Kannon—a National Treasure—carved by Tankei, a sculptor of the Kamakura period (1192–1333). One thousand smaller statues of Kannon surround the large statue, all covered in gold leaf, and in the corridor behind are the 28 guardian deities who protect the Buddhist universe. Notice the frivolous-faced Garuda, a bird that feeds on dragons. Are you wondering about the 33 spaces mentioned earlier? Kannon can assume 33 different shapes on her missions of mercy. Because there are 1,001 statues of Kannon in the hall, 33,033 shapes are possible. People come to the hall to see if they can find the likeness of a loved one (a deceased relative) among the many statues.

From Kyōto Station take Bus 206, 208, or 100 to the Sanjūsangen-dō-mae stop. The temple will be to the south, just beyond the Kyōto Park Hotel. ⊠ *657 Sanjūsangen-dō Mawari-chō, Higashiyama-ku* ☞ *¥600* ◷ *Apr.–mid-Nov., daily 8–5; mid-Nov.–Mar., daily 9–4.*

Sannen-zaka and Ninen-zaka (Sannen and Ninen slopes, 三年坂、二年坂). With their cobbled paths and delightful wooden buildings, these two lovely winding streets are fine examples of Old Kyōto. This area is one of four historic preservation districts in Kyōto, and the shops along the way sell local crafts and wares such as *Kiyomizu-yaki* (Kiyomizu-style pottery), Kyōto dolls, bamboo basketry, rice crackers, and antiques. From Kiyomizu-dera turn right halfway down Kiyomizu-zaka. ⊠ *Higashiyama-ku.*

★ **㉔ Shōren-in** (青蓮院). Paintings by the Kanō school are on view at this temple, a five-minute walk north of Chion-in. Though the temple's present building dates only from 1895, the sliding screens of the Hon-dō (Main Hall) have the works of Motonobu Kanō, second-generation Kanō, and Mitsunobu Kanō of the sixth generation. In the pleasant gardens an immense camphor tree sits at the entrance gate, and azaleas surround a balanced grouping of rocks and plants. It was no doubt more grandiose when artist and architect Sōami designed it in the 16th century, but with the addition of paths through the garden, it's a pleasant place to stroll. Another garden on the east side of the temple is sometimes attributed, probably incorrectly, to Kobori Enshū. Occasionally, koto concerts are held in the evening in the Sōami Garden (check with a Japan Travel Bureau office for concert schedules). From Kyōto Station take Bus 206 to the Higashiyama-Sanjō stop. ⊠ *Higashiyama-ku* ☞ *¥500* ◷ *Daily 9–5.*

㉕ Yasaka Jinja (八坂神社) Your business and health problems might come to a resolution at this Shintō shrine—leave a message for the god of prosperity and good health, to whom Yasaka Jinja is dedicated. Because it's close to the shopping districts, worshippers drop by for quick salvation. Especially at New Year's, Kyōto residents flock here to ask for good fortune in the coming year. From Kyōto Station take Bus 206 or 100 to the Gion bus stop; the shrine is just off Higashi-ōji-dōri. ✉ *625 Gion-machi, Kitagawa, Higashiyama-ku* 🎫 *Free* 🕑 *Daily 24 hrs.*

Western Kyōto & Arashiyama   洛西と嵐山

This tour of western Kyōto begins with the major northern sights, Kitano Tenman-gū first of all. If you're short on time, start instead at Daitoku-ji. Southwest of this group of shrines and temples, Arashiyama is a delightful hillside area along and above the banks of the Ōi-gawa (the local name for the Katsura-gawa as it courses through this area). As in eastern Kyōto, the city's western precincts are filled with remarkable religious architecture, in particular the eye-popping golden Kinkaku-ji and sprawling temple complexes of Daitoku-ji and Myōshin-ji. A visit to both Katsura Rikyū (the tour duration is one hour) and Koizan Saiho-ji are highly recommended, but these sites are a little out of the way, so leave plenty of time to get there. A good time to visit Kitano Tenman-gū is on a market day.

Numbers in the text correspond to numbers in the margin and on the Western Kyōto and Arashiyama map.

a good tour

Start with the Shintō **Kitano Tenman-gū** ❶ ▶, where a flea market is held on the 25th of each month. About a five-minute walk north of Kitano is **Hirano Jinja** ❷, a shrine with wonderful cherry trees in its garden. After visiting the shrine, head for **Daitoku-ji** ❸, a large 24-temple complex. To get there from Hirano Jinja head east to the bus stop at the intersection of Sembon-dōri and Imadegawa-dōri. Climb on Bus 206 and take it north for about 10 minutes. Be sure to see the subtemple, **Daisen-in** ❹, well known for its landscape paintings and for its karesansui garden. Other subtemples to visit if you have time are Kōtō-in and Ryogen-in. To get to the next stop, the impressive **Kinkaku-ji** ❺, hop on Bus 12 west on Kita-ōji-dōri for a 10-minute ride to the Kinkaku-ji-mae stop.

From Kinkaku-ji walk back to the Kinkaku-ji-mae bus stop and take Bus 12 or 59 south for 10 minutes to the Ritsumeikan-daigaku-mae stop. The nearby **Dōmoto Inshō Art Museum** ❻ exhibits works by the 20th-century abstract artist Inshō Dōmoto. When you leave the museum, either get on Bus 12 or 59 or walk for about 10 minutes south; **Ryōan-ji** ❼ will be on your right.

From Ryōan-ji it's about 1½ km (1 mi) farther south on Bus 26 to Myōshin-ji. En route you pass **Ninna-ji** ❽ on the right, a temple that was once the palace of Emperor Uda. From Ninna-ji, take the street veering to the left (southwest); within ¾ km (½ mi) you reach **Myōshin-ji** ❾. Another option from Ryōan-ji is to take Bus 12 or 59 three stops south to Ninna-ji and then change to Bus 8 or 10 to Myōshin-ji. Here you can see Japan's oldest bell. The other (sub-) temple to visit here is Taizō-in, which contains the painting *Four Sages of Mt. Shang,* by Sanraku Kanō. From here you can walk west to Nishiō-dōri to take Bus 203 back down-

Western Kyōto and Arashiyama

0 — 1/2 mile
0 — 1/2 kilometer

④ 大仙院
③ 大徳寺

Kita-ōji-dōri

⑤ 金閣寺

⑥ 堂本印象美術館

⑦ 龍安寺

平野神社 **②**

① 北野天満宮
Kitano Tenmangū-mae

仁和寺 **⑧**

Ryōan-ji-michi *Tōji-in*

Takao-guchi

Kitano-Hakubai-chō

Imadegawa-dōri

Omuro *Myōshin-ji*

Nishiōji-dōri

Sembon-dōri

⑨ 妙心寺

Tokiwa

Hanazono

Marutamachi-dōri

⑭ 竹林

KITANO LINE

JR SAN-IN MAIN LINE

Saga-Eki-mae

⑪ 東映太秦映画村

天龍寺 **⑬**
Saga

Rokuo-in
Kurumazaki

⑩ 広隆寺
Uzumasa

Arisu-gawa

荘 ⑮
Arashiyama

Katabira-no-tsuji

Kaiko-no-yashiro

Nijō

Oi-gawa

▶ **⑫ 渡月橋**

Arashi-yama

KEIFUKU ELECTRIC ARASHIYAMA LINE

Sanjō-guchi *Sanjō-dōri*

Yama-no-uchi

Sai-in

HANKYŪ ELECTRIC ARASHIYAMA LINE

Shijō-dōri

隠山西芳寺 ⑯
桂離宮 ⑰

Katsura-gawa

HANKYŪ ELECTRIC KYŌTO LINE

KEY

▶ *Start of itinerary*

Adashino Nebutsu-ji

Hirosawa-no-ike

Narutaki

Shuzan-kaidō

town, or leave the temple complex by the south side to pick up Bus 61 or 62, which go southwest to **Kōryū-ji** ⑩. For a completely different end to your tour, take a detour to **Uzumasa Movie Village** ⑪ (Japan's equivalent of Universal Studios). It's just north of Kōryū-ji, and a visit will take at least two or three hours.

You're close to the Arashiyama district now and can take the Keifuku Electric Railway Arashiyama Line west to Tenryū-ji Station and the bamboo forest just to the north for a pleasant end to the day. You may get the chance to watch some cormorant fishing on the Ōi-gawa.

If you'd rather head back into central Kyōto, it's easy to do so from Kōryū-ji. Either take the bus (60, 61, 62, or 64) back past the Movie Village to JR Hanazono Station, where the JR San-in Main Line will take you into Kyōto Station, or take the privately owned Keifuku Electric Railway Arashiyama Line east to its last stop at Shijō-Ōmiya. This stop is on Shijō-dōri, from which Bus 201 or 203 can take you to Gion; or take Bus 26 to Kyōto Station.

ARASHIYAMA The pleasure of Arashiyama, the westernmost part of Kyōto, is the same as it has been for centuries. The gentle foothills of the mountains, covered with cherry and maple trees, are splendid, but it's the bamboo forests that really create the atmosphere of untroubled peace. It's no wonder that the aristocracy of feudal Japan came here to escape the famine, riots, and political intrigue that plagued Kyōto with the decline of the Ashikaga shogunate a millennium ago.

The easiest ways to get to Arashiyama are by the JR San-in Main Line from Kyōto Station to Saga Station, or via the Keifuku Electric Railway to Arashiyama Station. South of Arashiyama Station (Saga Station is just north of Arashiyama Station), the Ōi-gawa flows under the **Togetsu-kyō Bridge** ⑫ ▶, where you can watch *ukai* (cormorant fishing) July and August evenings. The first temple to visit is **Tenryū-ji** ⑬— walk north from Arashiyama Station or west from JR Saga Station. One of the best ways to enjoy some contemplative peace is to walk the estate grounds of Denjiro Ōkōchi, a silent-movie actor of samurai films. To reach Ōkōchi's villa, either walk through the temple garden or leave Tenryū-ji and walk north on a narrow street through a **bamboo forest** ⑭, one of the best you can see around Kyōto. The **Ōkōchi Sansō** ⑮ will soon be in front of you. To reach the final two sights on the tour, both south of Arashiyama, you need to take the Hankyū Arashiyama Line; the station is south of the Togetsu-kyō Bridge. Head first to Matsuno Station and the nearby Moss Temple, **Koinzan Saihō-ji** ⑯, popularly known as Kokedera. Note that you need to arrange special permission ahead of time to visit the temple and garden here. The final sight is the imperial villa, **Katsura Rikyū** ⑰, which reaches the heights of cultivated Shoin architecture and garden design. Continue on the Hankyū Arashiyama Line to Katsura Station. You need to make reservations in advance for one of the scheduled guided tours of Katsura. To return to central Kyōto, take the Hankyū Kyōto Line from Katsura Station to one of the central Kyōto Hankyū stations: Hankyū-Ōmiya, Karasuma, or Kawara-machi.

TIMING You need two full days to cover the western Kyōto and Arashiyama sights. If you only have one day, skip a few of the western Kyōto sights in the first walk so you can make your way to Arashiyama in the afternoon. You can see most of Arashiyama in a relaxed morning or afternoon, with the jaunt south to Saihōji and Katsura—where you should plan to spend at least an hour at each location—at the beginning or end of the tour.

What to See in Western Kyōto

★ ❹ **Daisen-in** (大仙院). Of all the subtemples at ⇨ **Daitoku-ji,** Daisen-in is perhaps the best known—in part for its excellent landscape paintings by the renowned Sōami (1465–1523), as well as its karesansui garden, which some attribute to Sōami and others to Kogaku Sōkō (1465–1548) who was the founder of the temple. In the garden, the sand and stone represent the eternal aspects of nature, while the streams suggest the course of life. The single rock, once owned by Shōgun Yoshimasa Ashikaga, may be seen as a ship. *See* Daitoku-ji, *below,* for directions to Daisen-in. ⌧ *Kita-ku* ⌨ *¥400* ☉ *Daily 9–5, 9–4:30 in winter.*

★ ❸ **Daitoku-ji** (大徳寺). The Daitoku-ji complex of the Rinzai sect of Zen Buddhism consists of 24 temples in all, several of which are open to the public. The original temple was founded in 1319 by Priest Daitō Kokushi (1282–1337), but fires during the Ōnin Civil War destroyed it in 1468. Most buildings you see today were built under the patronage of Hideyoshi Toyotomi. However, it's thought that Priest Ikkyū oversaw its development. Ikkyū, known for his rather startling juxtapositions of the sacred and the profane—he was a priest and a poet—is reported to have said, "Brothels are more suitable settings for meditation than temples."

The layout of the temple is straightforward. Running from north to south are the Chokushi-mon (Gate of Imperial Messengers), the San-mon (Triple Gate), the Butsu-den (Buddha Hall), the Hattō (Lecture Hall), and the Hōjō (Abbots' Quarters). The 23 subtemples are on the west side of these main buildings and were donated mainly by the wealthy vassals of Toyotomi.

The **Chokushi-mon** originally served as the south gate of Kyōto's Imperial Palace when it was constructed in 1590. Then Empress Meisho in the mid-17th century bequeathed it to Daitoku-ji. Note the curved-gable style of the gate, typical of the Momoyama period. The **San-mon** is noteworthy for the addition of its third story, designed by tea master Sen-no-Rikyū (1521–91), who is buried in the temple grounds. Three subtemples in the complex are noteworthy: ⇨ **Daisen-in,** Kōtō-in, and Ryogen-in.

The subtemple **Kōtō-in** is famous for its long, maple-tree-lined approach and the single stone lantern that is central to the main garden. The fee is ¥400, and the temple stays open from 9 until 4:30 or 5 (enter 30 minutes before closing).

Ryōgen-in is not as popular as some of the other temples of Daitoku-ji, but it's often quiet and peaceful. The subtemple has five small gardens of moss and stone, one of which, on the north side, is the oldest in Daitoku-ji. The fee is ¥350, and the temple stays open 9–4:30 (enter 30 minutes before closing).

There are several ways to get to the temple from downtown Kyōto. Take the subway north from Kyōto Station to Kita-ōji Station, from which any bus going west along Kita-ōji-dōri will take you to the Daitoku-ji-mae stop. You can also take Bus 12 north up Horikawa-dōri and disembark soon after the bus makes a left on Kita-ōji-dōri. From western Kyōto Bus 204, which runs up Nishi-ōji-dōri, and Bus 206, which runs up Sembon-dōri, will also take you to the temple. ⊠ *Daitoku-ji-chō, Murasakino, Kita-ku* ⊡ *Admission to different temples varies; the average is ¥500* ⊙ *Daily; temple hrs vary between 9 and 4.*

need a break?

Ichiwa (いち和) has been serving tea and *aburi mochi*—skewered rice-flour cakes charcoal-grilled and dipped in sweet miso sauce—since the Heian Era (750 AD–1150 AD). You can enjoy the treats under the eaves of a 17th-century house as you watch visitors on their way to and from Imamiya Shrine. Ichiwa is just outside the shrine, northwest of Daitoku-ji. ⊠ *69 Imamiya-chō, Murasakino, Kita-ku* ☎ *075/ 492–6852* ⊙ *Thurs.–Tues. 10–sunset.*

❻ Dōmoto Inshō Art Museum (Dōmoto Inshō Bijutsukan, 堂本印象美術館). Twentieth-century abstract artist Inshō Dōmoto created the painting and sculpture exhibited here. From the Kinkaku-ji-mae bus stop, take Bus 12 or 59 south for 10 minutes to Ritsumeikan-Daigaku-mae. ⊠ *Kami-Yanagi-chō, Hirano, Kita-ku* ☎ *075/463–1348* ⊡ *¥500* ⊙ *Tues.–Sun. 10–5.*

★ ❷ Hirano Jinja (平野神社). This complex of four shrine buildings dates from the 17th century, but its ancestry is ancient. The shrine was brought from Nagaoka—Japan's capital after Nara and before Kyōto—as one of many shrines used to protect the budding new Heian-kyō, as Kyōto was then called, during its formative years. The buildings are less remarkable than the gardens, with their 80 varieties of cherry trees. Take either Bus 50 or 52 from downtown Kyōto or Kyōto Station. The ride takes a little more than half an hour. The shrine is about a 10-minute walk north of the Kitano Tenman-gū-mae bus stop. ⊠ *Miyamoto-chō 1, Hirano, Kita-ku* ⊡ *Free* ⊙ *Daily 6–5.*

❺ Kinkaku-ji (Temple of the Golden Pavilion, 金閣寺). For a retirement home, Kinkaku-ji is pretty magnificent. Shōgun Yoshimitsu Ashikaga (1358–1409) had it constructed in 1393 for the time when he would quit politics—the following year, in fact—to manage the affairs of state through the new shōgun, his 10-year-old son. On Yoshimitsu's death, his son followed his father's wishes and converted the villa into a temple named Rokuon-ji. The structure sits, following the Shinden style of the Heian period, at the edge of the lake. Pillars support the three-story pavilion, which extends over the pond and is reflected in the calm waters. It's a beautiful sight, designed to suggest an existence somewhere between heaven and earth. To underscore this statement of his prestige and power, the shōgun had the ceiling of the third floor of the pavilion covered in gold leaf. Not only the harmony and balance of the pavilion

Fodor'sChoice ★

and its reflection, but also the richness of color shimmering in the light and in the water, make Kinkaku-ji one of Kyōto's most powerful visions.

In 1950 a student monk with metaphysical aspirations torched Kinkaku-ji, burning it to the ground. (Yukio Mishima's book *Temple of the Golden Pavilion* is a fictional attempt to explore the mind of the student.) Kinkaku-ji was rebuilt in 1955 based on the original design, except that all three stories were covered with gold leaf, in accordance with the shōgun's original intention, instead of only the third-floor ceiling.

Marveling at this pavilion, you might find it difficult to imagine the era in which Shōgun Yoshimitsu Ashikaga lived out his golden years. The country was in turmoil, and Kyōto residents suffered severe famines and plagues—local death tolls sometimes reached 1,000 a day. The temple is a short walk from the Kinkaku-ji-mae bus stop. From Daisen-in the ride on Bus 12 takes about 10 minutes. ⊠ *1 Kinkaku-ji-chō, Kita-ku* 🎫 *¥400* 🕐 *Daily 9–5.*

★ ▶ ❶ **Kitano Tenman-gū** (北野天満宮). This shrine was originally dedicated to Tenjin, the god of thunder. Then, around 942, Michizane Sugawara was enshrined here. In his day, Michizane was a noted poet and politician—until Emperor Go-daigo ascended to the throne. Michizane was accused of treason and sent to exile on Kyūshū, where he died. For decades thereafter Kyōto suffered inexplicable calamities. The answer came in Go-daigo's dream: Michizane's spirit would not rest until he had been pardoned. Because the dream identified Michizane with the god of thunder, Kitano Tenman-gū was dedicated to him. On top of that, Michizane's political rank was posthumously restored. When that was not enough, he was promoted to a higher position and later to prime minister.

Kitano Tenman-gū was also the place where Hideyoshi Toyotomi held an elaborate tea party, inviting the whole of Kyōto to join him—creating a major opportunity for the local aristocracy to show off their finest tea bowls and related paraphernalia. Apart from unifying the warring clans of Japan and attempting to conquer Korea, Toyotomi is remembered in Kyōto as the man responsible for restoring many of the city's temples and shrines during the late 16th century. The shrine's present structure dates from 1607. A large **market** is held on the grounds on the 25th of each month. There are food stalls, and an array of antiques, old kimonos, and other collectibles are sold. Take either Bus 100 or 50 from Kyōto Station and get off at Kitano Tenman-gū-mae. The ride takes a little more than a half hour. ⊠ *Imakoji-agaru, Onmae-dōri, Kamigyō-ku* 🎫 *Shrine free, plum garden ¥500, includes green tea* 🕐 *Shrine Apr.–Oct., daily 5–5; Nov.–Mar, daily 5:30–5:30; plum garden Feb.–Mar., daily 10–4.*

need a break? No trip to Japan is complete without a soak in a hot tub at a local public bath. If you're in western Kyōto in the late afternoon and want to freshen up before dinner, why not drop your inhibitions to experience *skinship*, or the kinship that develops through communal bathing. **Funaoka Onsen** (船岡温泉), on the corner of Sembon and Imadegawa, several blocks north of Kitano Tenman-gū, was established in 1923. The spacious, communal bathing area has been renovated but the changing rooms still have their original wood-relief ceilings and beautiful tiles. There are gender-separate indoor baths, as well as two outdoor baths made of cedar and rock, respectively, that are open to men and women on alternate days. Towels, soap, and shampoo are for sale. ⊠ *Sembon Imadegawa kado, Murosaki no Minami, Funaoka-chō, Kita-ku* ☏ *075/441–3735* 🎫 *¥350* ⊙ *Daily 3 PM–1 AM.*

★ ⑩ **Kōryū-ji** (広隆寺). One of Kyōto's oldest temples, Kōryū-ji was founded in 622 by Kawakatsu Hata in memory of Prince Shōtoku (572–621). Shōtoku, known for issuing the Seventeen-Article Constitution, was the first powerful advocate of Buddhism after it was introduced to Japan in 552. In the Hattō (Lecture Hall) of the main temple stand three statues, each a National Treasure. The center of worship is the seated figure of Buddha, flanked by the figures of the Thousand-Handed Kannon and Fukukenjaku-Kannon. In the Taishi-dō (Prince Hall) there's a wooden statue of Prince Shōtoku, which is thought to have been carved by him personally. Another statue of Shōtoku in this hall was probably made when he was 16 years old.

The numerous works of art in Kōryū-ji's Reihō-den (Treasure House) include many National Treasures. The most famous of all is the **Miroku Bosatsu**, Japan's number one National Treasure. This image of Buddha is the epitome of serenity, and of all the Buddhas in Kyōto, this is perhaps the most captivating. No one knows when it was made, but it's thought to be from the 6th or 7th century, carved, perhaps, by Shōtoku himself.

From Kyōto Station take the JR San-in Main Line to Hanazono Station and then board Bus 61. From Shijō-Ōmiya Station, in central Kyōto, take the Keifuku Electric Arashiyama Line to Uzumasa Station. From central or western Kyōto, take Bus 61, 62, or 63 to the Uzumasa-kōryūji-mae stop. ⊠ *Hachigaoka-chō, Uzumasa, Ukyō-ku* 🎫 *¥600* ⊙ *Mar.–Nov., daily 9–5; Dec.–Feb., daily 9–4:30.*

★ ⑨ **Myōshin-ji** (妙心寺). Japan's oldest bell—cast in 698—hangs in the belfry near the South Gate of this 14th-century temple. When Emperor Hanazono died, his villa was converted into a temple; the work required so many laborers that a complex of buildings was built to house them. In all, there are some 40 structures here, though only four are open to the public. Beware of the dragon on the ceiling of Myōshin-ji's Hattō (Lecture Hall). Known as the "Dragon Glaring in Eight Directions," it looks at you wherever you stand.

Within the complex, the temple **Taizō-in** has a famous painting by Sanraku Kanō called *Four Sages of Mt. Shang*, recalling the four wise men who lived in isolation on a mountain to avoid the reign of destruction. The garden of Taizō-in is gentle and quiet—a good place to revive. The temple structure, originally built in 1404, suffered like the rest of the Myōshin-ji complex in the Ōnin Civil War (1467–77) and had to be rebuilt. Buses 61, 62, and 63 all stop at the Myōshin-ji-mae stop. ⊠ *Ukyō-ku* 🎫 *¥400 for Myōshin-ji; additional ¥400 for Taizō-in* ⊙ *Daily*

9:10–11:50 and 1–4.

⑧ Ninna-ji (仁和寺). The original temple here was once the palace of Emperor Omuro, who started the building's construction in 896. Nothing of that structure remains; the complex of buildings that stands today was rebuilt in the 17th century. There's an attractive five-story pagoda (1637), and the Hon-dō (Main Hall), which was moved from the Imperial Palace, is also worth noting as a National Treasure. The temple's focus of worship is the Amida Buddha. Take either Bus 26 or 59 to the Omuro-ninna-ji stop. ⊠ *Ukyō-ku* ⌧ *¥500* ⏱ *Daily 9–4:30.*

★ ⑦ Ryōan-ji (龍安寺). The garden at Ryōan-ji, rather than the temple, attracts people from all over the world. Knowing that the temple belongs to the Rinzai sect of Zen Buddhism may help you appreciate the austere aesthetics of the garden. It's a karesansui, a dry garden: just 15 rocks arranged in three groupings of seven, five, and three in gravel. From the temple's veranda, the proper viewing place, only 14 rocks can be seen at one time. Move slightly and another rock appears and one of the original 14 disappears. In the Buddhist world the number 15 denotes completeness. You must have a total view of the garden to make it a whole and meaningful experience—and yet, in the conditions of this world, that is not possible.

If possible, visit Ryōan-ji in the early morning before the crowds arrive and disturb the garden's contemplative quality. If you need a moment or two to yourself, head to the small restaurant on the temple grounds near an ancient pond, where you can find solace with an expensive beer if need be. From a southbound 12 or 59 bus, the temple will be on your right. ⊠ *13 Goryōshita-machi, Ryōan-ji, Ukyō-ku* ⌧ *¥500* ⏱ *Mar.–Nov., daily 8–5; Dec.–Feb., daily 8:30–4:30.*

⑪ Uzumasa Movie Village (Uzumasa Eiga Mura, 東映太秦映画村). This is Japan's answer to Hollywood, and had Kyōto been severely damaged in World War II, this would have been the last place to glimpse old Japan, albeit as a reproduction. Traditional country villages, ancient temples, and old-fashioned houses make up the stage sets, and if you're lucky, you may catch a couple of actors dressed as samurai snarling at each other, ready to draw their swords. You can visit the stage sets where popular traditional Japanese television series are filmed, or take in the *Red Shadow* action show, based on a popular TV series derived from a comic book. Also part of Eiga Mura is **Padios**, a small amusement park. Eiga Mura is a fine place to bring young children. For adults, whether it's worth the time depends on your interest in Japanese movies and your willingness to give Eiga Mura the two or three hours it takes to visit. The village is on the 61, 62, and 63 bus routes. ⊠ *10 Higashi-hachi-gaoka-chō, Uzumasa* ☎ *075/881–7716* ⌧ *¥2,200* ⏱ *Mar.–Nov., daily 9–5; Dec.–Feb., daily 9:30–4.*

What to See in Arashiyama

⑭ Bamboo forest (竹林). Dense bamboo forests provide a feeling of composure and tranquillity quite different from the wooded tracts of the Western world. Nowadays they are few and far between. This one, on the way to Ōkōchi Sansō from Tenryū-ji, is a delight. ⊠ *Ukyō-ku.*

⓱ Katsura Rikyū (Katsura Detached Villa, 桂離宮). Built in the 17th century
FodorśChoice for Prince Toshihito, brother of Emperor Go-yōzei, Katsura is beauti-
★ fully set in southwestern Kyōto on the banks of the Katsura-gawa, with
peaceful views of Arashiyama and the Kameyama Hills. Perhaps more
than anywhere else in the area, the setting is the most perfect example
of Japanese integration of nature and architecture.

Here you can find Japan's oldest surviving stroll garden. As is typical
of the period, the garden makes use of a wide variety of styles, with elements of the pond and island, karesansui, and tea gardens, among others.
The garden is a study in the placement of stones and the progressive un-
folding of the views that the Japanese have so artfully mastered in garden design. Look out from the three *shōin* (a style of house that
incorporates alcoves and platforms for the display of personal posses-
sions) and the four rustic tea arbors around the central pond, which have
been strategically placed for optimal vistas. Bridges constructed from
earth, stone, and wood connect five islets in the pond.

An extensive network of varied pathways takes you through a vast
repertoire of Katsura's miniaturizations of landscapes: an encyclopedia
of famous Japanese natural sites and literary references, such as the 11th-
century *Tale of Genji*. These associations might be beyond the average
foreigner's Japanese education, but what certainly isn't is the experience
of the garden that the designer intended for all visitors. Not satisfied to
create simply beautiful pictures, Kobori Enshū focused on the rhythm
within the garden: spaces open then close, are bright then dark; views
are visible and then concealed.

The villa is fairly remote from other historical sites—allow several hours
for a visit. Katsura requires special permission for a visit. Applications
must be made, preferably a day in advance, in person to the **Imperial
Household Agency** (宮内庁; ⊠ Kyōto Gyoen-nai, Kamigyō-ku ☎ 075/
211–1215), open weekdays 8:45–4. You will need your passport to pick
up a permit, and you must be at least 20 years of age. The time of your
tour will be stated, and you must not be late. The tour is in Japanese
only, although a videotape introducing various aspects of the garden in
English is shown in the waiting room before each tour begins.

To reach the villa, take the Hankyū Railway Line from one of the
Hankyū Kyōto Line stations to Katsura Station; then walk 15 minutes
to the villa from the station's east exit or take a taxi for about ¥800.
⊠ *Katsura Shimizu-chō, Ukyō-ku* ☎ *075/211–1215 inquiries only*
🎟 *Free* ⊘ *Tours weekdays at 10, 11, 2, and 3; Sat. tours 1st and 3rd
Sat. of month; every Sat. in Apr., May, Oct., and Nov.*

⓰ Koinzan Saihō-ji (Moss Temple, 供隠山西芳寺). Entrance into the temple
FodorśChoice precincts transports you into an extraordinary sea of green: 120 vari-
★ eties of moss create waves of greens and blues that eddy and swirl gently around Koinzan Saihō-ji's garden and give the temple its popular name,
Kokedera—the Moss Temple. Surrounded by the multihued moss, many
feel the same sense of inner peace that comes from being near water.

The site was originally the villa of Prince Shōtoku (572–621). During the Tempyō era (729–749) the emperor Shōmu charged the priest Gyogi Bosatsu to create 49 temples in the central province, one of which was this temple. The original garden represented Jōdo, the Pure Land, or western paradise of Buddhism. The temple and garden, destroyed many times by fire, lay in disrepair until 1338, when the chief priest of nearby Matsuno-jinja had a revelation here. He convinced Musō Soseki, a distinguished Zen priest of Rinzenji, the head temple of the Rinzai sect of Zen Buddhism, to preside over the temple and convert it from the Jōdo to Zen sect. Soseki, an avid gardener, designed the temple garden on two levels surrounding a pond in the shape of the Chinese character for heart. Present-day visitors are grateful for his efforts. The garden is entirely covered with moss and provides a unique setting for a contemplative walk. May and June, when colors are brightest due to heavy rains, are the best times to see the garden.

Another interesting aspect to your temple visit is the obligatory *sha-kyō*, writing of sutras. Before viewing the garden, you enter the temple and take a seat at a small, lacquered writing table where you'll be provided with a brush, ink, and a thin sheet of paper with Chinese characters in light gray. After rubbing your ink stick on the ink stone, dip the tip of your brush in the ink and trace over the characters. A priest explains in Japanese the temple history and the sutra you are writing. If time is limited you don't have to write the entire sutra; when the priest has ended his explanation, simply place what you have written on a table before the altar and proceed to the garden.

To gain admission send a stamped, self-addressed postcard to: Saihō-ji Temple, 56 Matsuno Jinjatani-chō, Nishikyō-ku, Kyōto 615-8286. Include the date and time you would like to visit. You can write in English, and the response will also be in English. The postcard must reach the temple at least five days prior to your visit. It's also possible to arrange a visit through the Tourist Information Center. To reach the temple, take the Hankyū Line from Arashiyama to Matsuno Station. ☒ ¥3,000; *have exact change.*

⑮ Ōkōchi Sansō (大河内山荘). Walk the estate grounds of Ōkōchi's Mountain Villa to breathe in some contemplative peace—Denjirō Ōkōchi, a renowned silent-movie actor of samurai films, chose this location for his home because of the superb views of Arashiyama and Kyōto. Admission to the villa includes tea and cake to enjoy while you absorb nature's pleasures. ☒ *8 Tabuchiyama-chō, Ogurayama, Saga, Ukyō-ku* ☎ *075/872–2233* ☒ *¥900* ⊘ *Daily 9–5.*

off the beaten path

ADASHINO NEMBUTSU-JI (化野念仏寺)–If you're in no rush to leave Saga Arashiyama, after Ōkōchi Sansō, continue walking along the country lane past Nison-in for about half an hour. Along the way you'll come across souvenir shops and noodle restaurants. Eventually you climb a small hill up to an unusual temple: Adashino Nembutsu-ji. Here about 8,000 stone Buddhas are packed together like a silent congregation. Their enshrinement is believed to honor the destitute whose remains were abandoned in the Adashino area from the Heian to the Edo periods. The main hall, built in 1712, contains a statue of Amida Buddha carved by Tankei, a sculptor famous in the Kamakura Era (1185–1333). On August 23 and 24, at a Buddhist ceremony called Sentō-kuyō, more than 1,000 candles are lit for the repose of the spirits of ancestors. A stirring time to be on this hillside is in late afternoon, when the shadows beneath the effigies lengthen. You can get back to Arashiyama or Kyōto stations on Bus 72 from the Toriimoto stop. ⊠ *17 Adashino-chō, Toriimoto, Ukyō-ku* ☎ *075/ 861-2221* ✆ *¥500* ⊙ *Mar.–Nov., daily 9–4:30; Dec.–Feb., daily 9–4.*

★ ⓭ **Tenryū-ji** (天龍寺) For good reason is this known as the Temple of the Heavenly Dragon: Emperor Go-Daigo, who had successfully brought an end to the Kamakura shogunate, was unable to hold on to his power and was forced from his throne by Takauji Ashikaga. After Go-Daigo died, Takauji had twinges of conscience. That's when Priest Musō Sōseki had a dream in which a golden dragon rose from the nearby Ōi-gawa. He told the shōgun about his dream and interpreted it to mean the spirit of Go-Daigo was not at peace. Worried that this was an ill omen, Takauji built Tenryū-ji in 1339 on the same spot where Go-Daigo had his favorite villa. Apparently that appeased the spirit of the late emperor. In the Hattō (Lecture Hall), where today's monks meditate, a huge "cloud dragon" is painted on the ceiling. The temple was often ravaged by fire, and the current buildings are as recent as 1900; the painting of the dragon was rendered by 20th-century artist Shōnen Suzuki.

The **Sōgenchi garden** of Tenryū-ji, however, dates from the 14th century and is one of the most notable in Kyōto. Musō Soseki, an influential Zen monk and skillful garden designer, created the garden to resemble Mt. Hōrai in China. It is famed for the arrangement of vertical stones in its large pond and for its role as one of the first gardens to use "borrowed scenery," incorporating the mountains in the distance into the design of the garden.

If you visit Tenryū-ji at lunchtime, consider purchasing a ticket for Zen cuisine served at **Shigetsu** (篩月; ☎ 075/882–9725) within the temple precinct. The ¥3,500 price includes lunch in the large dining area overlooking a garden, as well as admission to the garden itself. Here you can experience the Zen monk's philosophy of "eating to live" rather than "living to eat." While you won't be partaking of the monk's daily helping of gruel, a salted plum, and pickled radishes, you will get to try Zen cuisine prepared for festival days. The meal includes sesame tofu served over top-quality soy sauce, a variety of fresh boiled vegetables, miso soup, and rice. The *tenzo,* a monk specially trained to prepare Zen cuisine, creates a multicourse meal that achieves the harmony of the six basic flavors—bitter, sour, sweet, salty, light, and hot—required to enable the monks to practice Zen with the least hindrance to body and mind. It's an experience not to be missed. Though advance reservations are not required for the ¥3,500 course, there are more elaborate courses for ¥5,500 and ¥7,500 that do require reservations; ask someone at your hotel or at the Tourist Information Center to make a reservation for you. Take the JR San-in Main Line from Kyōto Station to Saga Station or the Keifuku Electric Railway to Arashiyama Station. From Saga Station walk west; from Arashiyama Station walk north. ✉ *68 Susuki-no-bamba-chō, Saga-Tenryū-ji, Ukyō-ku* 🏯 *Garden ¥500; ¥100 additional to enter temple building* ◷ *Apr.–Oct., daily 8:30–5:30; Nov.–Mar., daily 8:30–5.*

▶ ⑫ **Togetsu-kyō Bridge** (Togetsu-kyō-bashi, 渡月橋). Spanning the Ōi-gawa, the bridge is a popular spot from which you can watch ukai during the evening in July and August. Fisherfolk use cormorants to scoop up small sweet fish, which are attracted to the light of the flaming torches hung over the boats. The cormorants would swallow the fish for themselves, of course, but small rings around their necks prevent this. After about five fish, the cormorant has more than his gullet can hold. Then the fisherman pulls the bird back on a string, makes the bird regurgitate his catch, and sends him back for more. The best way to watch this spectacle is to join one of the charter passenger boats. Make a reservation using the number below, call the **Japan Travel Bureau** (☎ 075/361–7241), or use your hotel information desk. Take the JR San-in Main Line from Kyōto Station to Saga Station or the Keifuku Electric Railway to Arashiyama Station. The bridge is south of both ekis. *Reservations* ✉ *Arashiyama Tsusen, 14–4 Nakaoshita-chō, Arashiyama, Nishikyō-ku* ☎ *075/861–0223 or 075/861–0302* 💴 *¥1,400.*

Central & Southern Kyōto 洛中と洛南

Central Kyōto can be explored after eastern and western Kyōto. If your hotel is in this area, you may prefer to see these sights individually rather than combining them into a single itinerary. Treat sights south of Kyōto Station the same way, choosing the most interesting for a morning or afternoon venture. The two major sights in central Kyōto are Nijō-jō and the Kyōto Gosho, the castle and the Imperial Palace. The latter requires permission, and you must join a guided tour. The most interesting southern Kyōto sights are Tōfuku-ji and Byōdō-in and the tea-producing Uji-shi.

Numbers in the text correspond to numbers in the margin and on the Central Kyōto map.

a good tour

The easiest ways to reach the **Kyōto Imperial Palace** ① ▶ are to take the subway to Imadegawa or to take a bus to the Karasuma-Imadegawa stop. You can join the tour of the palace at the Seisho-mon entrance on Karasuma-dōri. You can easily combine Kyōto Gosho with **Nijō-jō** ②, Kyōto residence of the Tokugawa shogunate, on the same trip. Take the Karasuma subway line from Imadegawa Station toward Kyōto Station to Ōike (two stops) and change to the Tōzai subway line. Board the car heading for Nijō and get off at the next stop, Nijō-jō-mae.

For an excursion into the culture of the tea ceremony, make your way west to the **Raku Art Museum** ③, a museum that displays the Raku family's tea bowls. For another change of pace, visit the Nishijin silk-weaving district, north of the Raku Art Museum on Horikawa-dōri at the corner of Imadegawa-dōri. At the **Nishijin Textile Center** ④ you can watch demonstrations. The Raku Art Museum and the Nishijin Textile Center are both roughly halfway between the Gosho and Nijō-jō.

Buses 9, 12, 50, and 52 run up and down Horikawa-dōri past these two sights.

From the museum, the textile center, or Nijō-jō, take Bus 9 south on Horikawa-dōri. Disembark at the Nishi-Hongan-ji-mae bus stop. Across from the temple, on the fifth floor of the Izutsu Building at the intersection of Horikawa and Shin-Hanaya-chō, is the **Kyōto Costume Museum** ⑤, which has clothes that were worn from the pre-Nara era, before 710, to the Meiji period, post-1868. The most famous temples in the area are nearby **Nishi-Hongan-ji** ⑥ and **Higashi-Hongan-ji** ⑦. Higashi-Hongan-ji is the second-largest wooden structure in Japan. Nishi-Hongan-ji has interesting art objects, but the temple proper requires special permission to enter.

From Nishi-Hongan-ji it's a 10-minute walk southeast to **Kyōto Station**. Take some time to look around the station building—it's a sight in its own right. If you still have time, visit **Tō-ji** ⑧, one of Kyōto's oldest temples, southwest of the station. It holds a flea market on the 21st of each month. The best way here is to leave Nishi-Hongan-ji by the west exit and take Bus 207 south on Ōmiya-dōri. Get off at the Tō-ji-Higashimon-mae bus stop, and Tō-ji will be across the street. From Kyōto Station, Tō-ji is a 10-minute walk southwest; or you can take the Kintetsu Kyōto Line to Tō-ji Station and walk west for 5 minutes.

Points of interest south of Kyōto Station require individual trips, returning back to the station after each visit. **Byōdō-in**, a former 10th-century residence turned temple, is in Uji, a famous tea-producing area where you can taste the finest green tea. **Daigo-ji**, in the Yamashina suburb southeast of Kyōto, is a charming 9th-century temple with a five-story pagoda. To reach Daigo-ji, take the Tōzai subway line to Daigo Station. **Tōfuku-ji**, a Zen temple of the Rinzai sect, ranks as one of the most important Zen temples in Kyōto. It's on the Bus 208 route from Kyōto Station; or it's a 15-minute walk from Tōfuku-ji Station on the JR Nara Line or the Keihan Main Line. You may want to combine a visit here with a stop at the **Fushimi-Inari Taisha**, farther south. This shrine is one of Kyōto's oldest and most revered. Fushimi-Inari Taisha is a three-minute walk from the JR Nara Line's Fushimi-Inari Station.

TIMING The temples and shrines in southern Kyōto are a distance from one another, so traveling time can eat into your day. But central Kyōto's sights are fairly close to each other and quickly accessible by bus or taxi. A morning would be mostly taken up with the Imperial Palace and Nijō-jō. Remember that the Imperial Palace is closed Saturday afternoon and Sunday, and also all day on the second and fourth Saturday of the month in winter and summer.

What to See

★ **Byōdō-in** (平等院). South of Kyōto in Uji-shi, this temple was originally the villa of a 10th-century member of the influential Fujiwara family. The Amida-dō, also called the Phoenix Hall, was built in the 11th century by the Fujiwaras and is still considered one of Japan's most beautiful religious buildings—something of an architectural folly—where heaven is brought close to earth. Jōchō, one of Japan's most famous 11th-

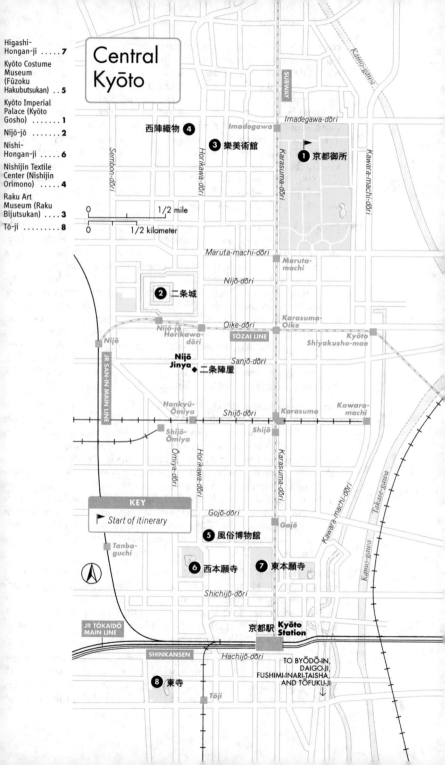

Central Kyōto

西陣織物 ❹

❸ 樂美術館

❶ 京都御所

0 ━━━━ 1/2 mile

0 ━━━━ 1/2 kilometer

Imadegawa

Imadegawa-dōri

SUBWAY

Sembon-dōri

Horikawa-dōri

Karasuma-dōri

Kawara-machi-dōri

Kamo-gawa

Maruta-machi-dōri

Maruta-machi

❷ 二条城

Nijō-dōri

Oike-dōri

Nijō-jō Horikawa-dōri

Nijō

TŌZAI LINE

Karasuma-Oike

Kyōto Shiyakusho-mae

JR SAN-IN MAIN LINE

Nijō Jinya ◆ 二条陣屋

Sanjō-dōri

Hankyū-Ōmiya

Shijō-dōri

Karasuma

Kawara-machi

Shijō-Ōmiya

Shijō

Ōmiya-dōri

Horikawa-dōri

Karasuma-dōri

KEY

▶ *Start of itinerary*

Gojō-dōri

Gojō

Takase-gawa

Tanba-guchi

❺ 風俗博物館

❻ 西本願寺

❼ 東本願寺

Kawara-machi-dōri

Kamo-gawa

Shichijō-dōri

JR TŌKAIDŌ MAIN LINE

京都駅 **Kyōto Station**

SHINKANSEN

Hachijō-dōri

TO BYŌDŌ-IN,
DAIGO-JI,
FUSHIMI-INARI-TAISHA,
AND TŌFUKU-JI
↓

❽ 東寺

Tō-ji

century sculptors, crafted a magnificent statue of a seated Buddha here. Uji itself is a famous tea-producing district, and the slope up to the temple is lined with shops where you can sample the finest green tea and pick up a small package to take home. It's possible to set up a visit to a tea farm through the Kyōto tourist information center. The shrines and temples surrounding the Uji River are also pleasant to explore. For more about Uji consider reading the famous 11th-century novel, *The Tale of Genji*; the last 10 chapters are set in the area. To get to Uji, take the JR Nara line to Uji Station. Byōdō-in is a 12-minute walk east toward the river from the station. ⊠ *Ujirenge, Uji-shi* ☎ *0774/21–2861* 🖃 *¥500; additional ¥300 for Phoenix Hall* ☉ *Temple Mar.–Nov., daily 8:30–5:30; Dec.–Feb., daily 9–4:30; Phoenix Hall Mar.–Nov., daily 9–5; Dec.–Feb., daily 9–4.*

★ **Daigo-ji** (醍醐寺). This temple was founded in 874, and over the succeeding centuries, other buildings were added and its gardens expanded. Its five-story pagoda, which dates from 951, is reputed to be the oldest existing structure in Kyōto. By the late 16th century the temple had begun to decline in importance and showed signs of neglect. Then Hideyoshi Toyotomi paid a visit one April, when the temple's famous cherry trees were in blossom. Hideyoshi ordered the temple restored. The smaller **Sambō-in** houses paintings by the Kanō school. From the temple you can continue up the mountain (about an hour's hike) to several subtemples. At the top, on a clear day, it's possible to make out the Ōsaka skyline in the far distance. To reach Daigo-ji, in the southeast suburb of Yamashina, take the Tōzai subway line to Daigo Station. ⊠ *22 Higashi Ōji-chō, Fushimi-ku* 🖃 *¥500* ☉ *Mar.–Oct., daily 9–5; Nov.–Feb., daily 9–4.*

★ **Fushimi-Inari Taisha** (伏見稲荷大社). One of Kyōto's oldest and most revered shrines, the Fushimi-Inari honors the goddesses of agriculture (rice and rice wine) and prosperity. It also serves as the headquarters for all the 40,000 shrines representing Inari. The shrine is noted for its bronze foxes and for some 10,000 small torii, donated by the thankful, which stretch up the hill behind the structure. If possible, visit near dusk—you'll be among the only people wandering through the tunnels of torii in the quiet woods, a nearly mystical experience as daylight fades. Take the JR Nara Line to Fushimi-Inari Station, from which it's a three-minute walk to the shrine. From Tōfuku-ji join the JR train at Tōfuku-ji Station and go one stop south, toward Nara. ⊠ *68 Fukakusa Yabu-no-uchi-chō, Fushimi-ku* 🖃 *Free* ☉ *Daily sunrise–sunset.*

★ ❼ **Higashi-Hongan-ji** (東本願寺). Until the early 17th century Higashi-Hongan-ji and Nishi-Hongan-ji were one temple. Then Ieyasu Tokugawa took advantage of a rift within the Jōdo Shinshu sect of Buddhism and, to diminish its power, split it apart into two different factions. The original faction has the west temple, Nishi-Hongan-ji, and the latter faction the eastern temple, Higashi-Hongan-ji.

The rebuilt (1895) structure of Higashi-Hongan-ji is the second-largest wooden structure in Japan, after Nara's Daibutsu-den. The **Daishi-dō**, a double-roofed structure, is admirable for its curving, swooping lines. Inside are portraits of all the head abbots of the Jōdo Shinshu sect, but unfortunately, it contains fewer historical objects of interest than does its rival, Nishi-Hongan-ji. From Kyōto Station walk 500 yards northwest; from the costume museum walk south on Horikawa-dōri. ⊠ *Shichijō-agaru, Karasuma-dōri, Shimogyō-ku* ☞ *Free* ⊙ *Mar.–Oct., daily 5:50–5:30; Nov.–Feb., daily 6:20–4:30.*

★ ❺ **Kyōto Costume Museum** (Fūzoku Hakubutsukan, 風俗博物館). It's well worth a stop here to marvel at the range of fashion, which starts in the pre-Nara era and works its way up through various historical eras to the Meiji period. The museum is one of the best of its kind, and in its own way gives an account of the history of Japan. Exhibitions, which change twice a year, highlight a specific period in Japanese history. From the Raku Museum, the Nishijin Textile Center, or Nijō-jō, take Bus 9 south on Horikawa-dōri. Disembark at the Nishi-Hongan-ji-mae bus stop. The museum is on the fifth floor of the Izutsu Building, which is at the intersection of Horikawa and Shin-Hanaya-chō, north of the temple on the other side of the street. ⊠ *Izutsu Bldg., Shimogyō-ku* ☎ *075/342–5345* ☞ *¥400* ⊙ *Oct. 9–Sept. 2, Mon.–Sat. 9–5* ⊙ *Closed Apr. 1–8, July 1–8, and Dec. 23–Jan. 6.*

▶ ❶ **Kyōto Imperial Palace** (Kyōto Gosho, 京都御所). The present palace, a third-generation construction, was completed in 1855, so it has housed only two emperors, one of whom was the young emperor Meiji before he moved his imperial household to Tōkyō. The original, built for Emperor Kammu to the west of the present site, burned down in 1788. A new palace, modeled after the original, then went up on the present site, but it, too, ended in flames. The Gosho itself is a large but simple wooden building that can hardly be described as palatial. On the one-hour tour you'll only have a chance for a brief glimpse of the Shishin-den—the hall where the inauguration of emperors and other important imperial ceremonies take place—and a visit to the gardens. Though a trip to the Imperial Palace is on most people's agenda and though it fills a fair amount of space in downtown Kyōto, it holds somewhat less interest than do some of the older historic sites.

Guided tours start at the Seisho-mon entrance. You must arrive at the Imperial Palace before 9:40 AM for the one-hour 10 AM guided tour in English. Present yourself, along with your passport, at the office of the **Kunaichō** (Imperial Household Agency) in the palace grounds. For the 2 PM guided tour in English, arrive by 1:40 PM. The Kunaichō office is closed on weekends, so visit in advance to arrange a Saturday tour. To get to the palace, take the Karasuma Line of the subway in the direction of Kokusaikaikan. Get off at Imadegawa Station, and use the Number 6 Exit. Cross the street and turn right. Enter the palace through the Inui Go-mon on your left. ⊠ *Kunaichō, Kyōto Gyoen-nai, Kamigyō-ku* ☎ *075/211–1215 information only* ☞ *Free* ⊙ *Office weekdays 8:45–noon and 1–4; tours weekdays at 10 AM and 2 PM; Sat. tours on 1st and 3rd Sat. of month; every Sat. in Apr., May, Oct. and Nov.*

Kyōto Station (京都駅). Kyōto's train station, opened in 1997, is more than just the city's central point of arrival and departure: its impressive marble-and-glass structure makes it as significant a building as any of

Kyōto's ancient treasures. Hiroshi Hara's modern design was at first controversial, but his use of space and lighting—and the sheer enormity of the final product—eventually won over most of its opponents. The station houses a hotel, a theater, a department store, and dozens of shops and restaurants with great views of the city from the 16th floor. ✉ *Shimogyō-ku.*

2 **Nijō-jō** (二条城). Nijō Castle was the local Kyōto address for the Tokugawa shogunate. Dominating central Kyōto, it's an intrusion, both politically and artistically. The man who built the castle in 1603, Ieyasu Tokugawa, did so to emphasize that political power had been completely removed from the emperor and that he alone determined the destiny of Japan. Accordingly, Tokugawa built and decorated his castle with such ostentation as to make the populace cower in the face of his wealth and power. This kind of display was antithetical to the refined restraint of Kyōto's aristocracy.

FodorsChoice
★

Ieyasu Tokugawa had risen to power through skillful political maneuvers and treachery. His military might was unassailable, and that's probably why his Kyōto castle had relatively modest exterior defenses. However, as he well knew, defense against treachery is never certain. The interior of the castle was built with that in mind. Each building had concealed rooms where bodyguards could maintain a watchful eye for potential assassins, and the corridors had built-in "nightingale" floors, so no one could walk in the building without making noise. Rooms were locked only from the inside, thus no one from the outer rooms could gain access to the inner rooms without someone admitting them. The outer rooms were kept for visitors of low rank and were adorned with garish paintings that would impress them. The inner rooms were for the important lords, whom the shōgun would impress with the refined, tasteful paintings of the Kanō school.

The opulence and grandeur of the castle were, in many ways, a snub to the emperor. They relegated the emperor and his palace to insignificance and the Tokugawa family even appointed a governor to manage the emperor and the imperial family. The Tokugawa shōguns were rarely in Kyōto. Ieyasu stayed in the castle three times, the second shōgun twice, including the time in 1626 when Emperor Gomizuno-o was granted an audience. After that, for the next 224 years, no Tokugawa shōgun visited Kyōto and the castle started to fall into disrepair and neglect. Only when the Tokugawa shogunate was under pressure from a failing economy, and international pressure developed to open Japan to trade, did the 14th shōgun Iemochi Tokugawa (1846–66), come to Kyōto to confer with the emperor. The emperor told the shōgun to rid Japan of foreigners, but Iemochi did not have the strength. As the shōgun's power continued to wane, the 15th and last shōgun, Yoshinobu Tokugawa (1837–1913), spent most of his time in Nijō-jō. Here he resigned, and the imperial decree was issued that abolished the shogunate after 264 years of rule.

After the Meiji Restoration in 1868, Nijō-jō became the Kyōto prefectural office until 1884; during that time it suffered from acts of vandalism. Since 1939 the castle has belonged to the city of Kyōto, and considerable restoration work has taken place.

You enter the castle through the impressive **Kara-mon** (Chinese Gate). Notice that you must turn right and left at sharp angles to make this entrance—a common attribute of Japanese castles, designed to slow the advance of any attacker. From the Kara-mon, the carriageway leads to the **Ni-no-maru Goten** (Second Inner Palace), whose five buildings are divided into many chambers. The outer buildings were for visits by men of lowly rank, the inner ones for those of higher rank. The most notable room, the **Ōhiroma** (Great Hall), is easy to recognize. In the room, costumed figures reconstruct the occasion when Keiki Tokugawa returned the power of government to the emperor. This spacious hall was where, in the early 17th century, the shōgun would sit on a raised throne to greet important visitors seated below him. The sliding screens of this room have magnificent paintings of forest scenes.

Even more impressive than the palace itself is its garden, created by landscape designer Kobori Enshū shortly before Emperor Gomizuno-o's visit in 1626. Notice the crane-and-tortoise islands flanking the center island (called the Land of Paradise). The symbolic meaning is clear: strength and longevity. The garden was originally designed with no deciduous trees, for the shōgun did not wish to be reminded of the transitory nature of life by autumn's falling leaves.

The other major building on the grounds is the **Hon-maru Palace**, a replacement of the original, which burned down in the 18th century. It's not normally open to the public. To reach the castle, take the bus or subway to Nijō-jō-mae. ⊠ *Horikawa Nishi-Iru, Nijō-dōri, Nakagyō-ku* ☎ *075/841–0096* ⤳ *¥600* ☉ *Daily 8:45–5; last entry at 4.*

need a break?

After your visit to Nijō-jō take a break at the traditional Japanese candy store **Mukashi Natsukashi** (昔なつ菓子), on the corner of Ōmiya-dōri, three blocks west of the intersection of Horikawa-dōri and Oike-dōri. Browse through the quaint candy store, grab a cold drink from a cedar bucket filled with cold water, and try the specialty of the house, *dorobo* (a molasses-covered rice-flour crispy snack). You can rest on the bench outside the shop while sampling your wares. ⊠ *Oshikoji-dōri, Ōmiya-dōri, Nakagyō-ku* ☎ *075/841–4464.*

off the beaten path

NIJŌ JINYA (二条陣屋)– A short walk south of Nijō-jō is the less visited Nijō Jinya, a former merchant house built in the 17th century. The house later became an inn for traveling *daimyo*, or feudal lords. When Kyōto was the seat of the imperial crown, Nijō Jinya served as a safe venue for the daimyo to conduct secret meetings. The house is crammed with built-in safeguards against attack, including hidden staircases, secret passageways, and hallways that are too narrow to allow the wielding of a sword. Since the hour-long tour through the warren of rooms is in Japanese, it is recommended that you hire a translator. The staff at the **Utano Hostel** (宇多野ユースホステル; ☎ 075/462–2288) can make arrangements for a translator if you call at least three days in advance. Ask your concierge to call Nijō Jinya to make a reservation for you to tour the house. ⊠ *Sembon Ōmiya-chō, Nakagyō-ku* ☎ *075/841–0972* ⤳ *¥1,000* ☉ *Tours daily 10–4.*

★ ❻ **Nishi-Hongan-ji** (西本願寺). The marvelous artifacts at this temple were confiscated by Ieyasu Tokugawa from Hideyoshi Toyotomi's Jurakudai Palace, in Kyōto, and from Fushimi-jō, in southern Kyōto. He had the buildings dismantled in an attempt to erase the memory of his predecessor.

Hideyoshi Toyotomi was quite a man. Though most of the initial work of unifying Japan was accomplished by the warrior Nobunaga Oda (he was ambushed a year after defeating the monks on Hiei-zan), it was Hideyoshi who completed the job. Not only did he end civil strife, he also restored the arts. For a brief time (1582–98), Japan entered one of the most colorful periods of its history. How Hideyoshi achieved his feats is not exactly known. He was brought up as a farmer's son, and his nickname was Saru-san (Mr. Monkey) because he was small and ugly. According to one legend—probably started by Hideyoshi himself—he was the son of the emperor's concubine. She had been much admired by a man to whom the emperor owed a favor, so the emperor gave the concubine to him. Unknown to either of the men, she was soon pregnant with Hideyoshi. Whatever his origins (he changed his name frequently), he brought peace to Japan after decades of civil war.

Because much of what was dear to Hideyoshi Toyotomi was destroyed by the Tokugawas, it's only at Nishi-Hongan-ji that you can see the artistic works closely associated with his personal life, including the great **Kara-mon** (Chinese Gate) and the **Daisho-in,** both brought from Fushimi-jō, and the **Nō stage** from Jurakudai Palace.

Nishi-Hongan-ji is on Horikawa-dōri, a couple of blocks north of Shichijō-dōri. Visits to some of the buildings are permitted four times a day by permission from the temple office. Phone for an appointment once you arrive in Kyōto; if you don't speak Japanese, you may want to ask your hotel to place the call for you. Tours of Daisho-in (in Japanese) are given occasionally throughout the year. ⊠ *Shichijō-agaru, Horikawa-dōri, Shimogyō-ku* ☎ *075/371–5181* ⊟ *Free* ☉ *Mar., Apr., Sept., and Oct., daily 5:30–5:30; May–Aug., daily 5:30 AM–6 PM; Nov.–Feb., daily 6–5.*

❹ **Nishijin Textile Center** (Nishijin Orimono, 西陣織物). The Nishijin district still hangs on to the artistic thread of traditional Japanese silk weaving. The Nishijin Textile Center hosts demonstrations of age-old weaving techniques and presents fashion shows and special exhibitions. On the mezzanine you can buy kimonos and gift items, such as *happi* (workmen's) coats and silk purses. The center is on the 9 and 12 bus routes, north of the Raku Art Museum, at the corner of Horikawa-dōri and Imadegawa-dōri. ⊠ *Horikawa-dōri, Imadegawa-Minami-Iru, Kamigyō-ku* ☎ *075/451–9231* ⊟ *Free, kimono show ¥600* ☉ *Daily 9–5* ☉ *Closed Aug. 13–15, Dec. 29–Jan. 15.*

❸ **Raku Art Museum** (Raku Bijutsukan, 樂美術館). Any serious collector of tea-ceremony artifacts is likely to have a Raku bowl in his or her collection. Here you can find tea bowls made by members of the Raku family, whose roots can be traced to the 16th century. As a potter's term in the West, *raku* refers to a low-temperature firing technique, but the word originated with this family, who made exquisite tea bowls for use in the shōgun's tea ceremonies. The museum is to the east of Horikawa-dōri, two blocks south of Imadegawa-dōri; take Bus 9 or 12 to Ichi-jō-modōri-bashi. ⊠ *Aburakōji, Nakadachuri-agaru, Kamigyō-ku* ☎ *075/414–0304* ✉ *¥700–¥1,000, depending on exhibition* ⊗ *Tues.–Sun. 10–4:30.*

★ **Tōfuku-ji** (東福寺). In all, two dozen subtemples and the main temple compose the complex of this Rinzai-sect Zen temple, established in 1236, which ranks as one of the most important in Kyōto, along with the Myōshin-ji and Daitoku-ji. Autumn is an especially fine time for visiting, when the burnished colors of the maple trees add to the pleasure of the gardens. There are at least three ways to get to Tōfuku-ji, which is southeast of Kyōto Station: Bus 208 from Kyōto Station, a JR train on the Nara Line to Tōfuku-ji Station, or a Keihan Line train to Tōfuku-ji Station. From the trains, it's a 15-minute walk to the temple. Consider combining a visit here with one to Fushimi-Inari Taisha, farther south. ⊠ *Hon-machi 15-chōme, Higashiyama-ku* ☎ *075/561–0087* ⊕ *www.tofukuji.jp/english.html* ✉ *¥400* ⊗ *Daily 9–4.*

❽ **Tō-ji** (東寺). Established by imperial edict in 796 and called Kyō-ō-gokoku-ji, Tō-ji was built to guard the city. It was one of the only two temples that Emperor Kammu permitted to be built in the city—he had had enough of the powerful Buddhists during his days in Nara. The temple was later given to Priest Kūkai (Kōbō Daishi), who founded the Shingon sect of Buddhism. Tō-ji became one of Kyōto's most important temples.

Fires and battles during the 16th century destroyed the temple buildings, but many were rebuilt, including the Kon-dō (Main Hall) in 1603. The Kō-dō (Lecture Hall), on the other hand, has managed to survive the ravages of war since it was built in 1491. Inside this hall are 15 original statues of Buddhist gods that were carved in the 8th and 9th centuries. Perhaps Tōji's most eye-catching building is the 180-ft, five-story pagoda, reconstructed in 1695.

An interesting time to visit the temple is on the 21st of each month, when a market, known locally as Kōbō-san, is held. Antique kimonos, fans, and other artifacts can sometimes be found at bargain prices if you know your way around the savvy dealers. A smaller antiques market is held on the first Sunday of the month. From Kyōto Station take the Kintetsu Kyōto Line one stop to Tō-ji Station or walk 10 minutes west from the central exit of JR Kyōto Station. Bus 207 also runs past Tō-ji: either south from Gion, then west; or west from Karasuma-dōri along Shijō-dōri, then south. Get off at the Tō-ji-Higashimon-mae stop. ⊠ *1 Kujō-chō, Minami-ku* ✉ *Main buildings ¥500, grounds free* ⊗ *Mar. 20–Sept. 19, daily 9–5; Sept. 20–Mar. 19, daily 9–4:30.*

Northern Kyōto   洛北

Hiei-zan and Ōhara are the focal points in the northern suburbs of Kyōto. Ōhara was for several centuries a sleepy Kyōto backwater surrounded by mountains. Although it's now catching up with the times, it still has a feeling of old Japan, with several temples that deserve visits. Hiei-zan is a fount of Kyōto history. On its flanks Saichō founded Enryaku-ji and with it the vital Tendai sect of Buddhism. It's an essential Kyōto site, and walking on forested slopes among its 70-odd temples is a good reason to make the trek to Hiei-zan.

Since Hiei-zan and Ōhara both require a fair amount of walking, consider combining Hiei-zan with a visit to the Shūgaku-in Imperial Villa, saving Ōhara for another day. If you enjoy walking a lot, however, a visit to Hiei-zan and Ōhara on the same day is quite feasible.

a good tour

To get to Ōhara, take private Kyōto Line Bus 17 or 18 from Kyōto Station and get out at the Ōhara bus stop. The trip takes 90 minutes and costs ¥480. From the bus station, walk northeast for about seven minutes along the signposted road to **Sanzen-in,** a small Tendai-sect temple on delightful grounds with a remarkable carved Amida Buddha. Two hundred yards from Sanzen-in sits the quiet **Jikkō-in,** where you can drink traditional matcha. On the other side of Ōhara and the Takano-gawa is **Jakkō-in,** a romantic temple full of pathos and a sanctuary for nuns. To get here, return to the Ōhara bus stop and walk 20 minutes north up the road.

From the bus stop you can take Kyōto Line Bus 16, 17, or 18 down the main highway, Route 367, to the Yase Yūen-chi bus stop in **Hiei-zan.** Or you can take the same bus to the Shūgaku-in Rikyū-michi bus stop and make the 15-minute walk to the **Shūgaku-in Imperial Villa,** which consists of a complex of three palaces. If you are heading for Hiei-zan, once you get off the bus you can see the entrance to the cable car on your left. It departs every 30 minutes, and you can transfer to the ropeway at Hiei for the remaining distance to the top. At the summit is an observatory with panoramic views of the mountains and of Biwa-ko (Lake Biwa). From the observatory, a mountain path leads to **Enryaku-ji,** an important center of Buddhism. The walk takes about 30 minutes. To return you can either take Bus 5 to Kyōto Station or take the Keifuku Eizan train to Demachi-Yanagi Station, just north of Imadegawa-dōri. Alternatively, Keihan Bus 83 leaves from the bus stop near Enryaku-ji and takes a scenic route that meanders down the mountain, arriving at Sanjō Keihan about 50 minutes later.

One final sight, closer to central Kyōto, is **Kamigamo Jinja,** built by the ancient local ruling family Kamo. It's near the end of the Bus 9 route north from Kyōto Station by the Kamigamo-Misonobashi stop.

TIMING It's best to make this a day trip to allow for unhurried exploration of Ōhara and on Hiei-zan. If you're booked on a tour to the Shūgaku-in Imperial Villa on the same day then you'll probably only have time to explore either Ōhara or Hiei-zan.

What to See

★ **Hiei-zan and Enryaku-ji** (比叡山延暦寺). From the observatory at the top of Hiei-zan, a serpentine mountain path leads to Enryaku-ji, which remains a vital center of Buddhism. At one time it consisted of 3,000 buildings and had its own standing army. That was its downfall. Enryaku-ji really began in 788. Emperor Kammu, the founding father of Kyōto, requested Priest Saichō (767–822) to establish a temple on Hiei-zan to protect the area (including Nagaoka, then the capital) from the evil spirits. Demons and evil spirits were thought to come from the northeast, and Hiei-zan was a natural barrier between the fledgling city and the northeastern Kin-mon (Devil's Gate), where devils were said to pass. The temple's monks were to serve as lookouts and, through their faith, keep evil at bay.

The temple grew, and because police were not allowed on its mountaintop sanctuary, criminals flocked here, ostensibly to seek salvation. By the 11th century the temple had formed its own army to secure order on its estate. In time this army grew and became stronger than that of most other feudal lords, and the power of Enryaku-ji came to threaten Kyōto. No imperial army could manage a war without the support of Enryaku-ji, and when there was no war, Enryaku-ji's armies would burn and slaughter monks of rival Buddhist sects. Not until the 16th century was there a force strong enough to sustain an assault on the temple. With accusations that the monks had concubines and never read the sutras, Nobunaga Oda (1534–82), the general who unified Japan by ending more than a century of civil strife, attacked the monastery in 1571 to rid it of its evil. In the battle, monks were killed, and most of the buildings were destroyed. Structures standing today were built in the 17th century.

Enryaku-ji has three main precincts: the Eastern Precinct, where the main building in the complex, the **Kompon Chū-dō**, stands; the Western Precinct, with the oldest building, the **Shaka-dō**; and the Yokawa district, a few miles north. The Kompon Chū-dō dates from 1642, and its dark, cavernous interior quickly conveys the sense of mysticism for which the esoteric Tendai sect is known. Giant pillars and a coffered ceiling shelter the central altar, which is surrounded by religious images and sacred objects. The ornate lanterns that hang before the altar are said to have been lighted by Saichō himself centuries ago.

The Western precinct is where Saichō founded his temple and where he is buried. An incense burner wafts smoke before his tomb, which lies in a small hollow. The peaceful atmosphere of the cedar trees surrounding the main structures—Jōdo-in, Ninai-dō, and Shaka-dō—suggests the life of a Tendai Buddhist monk, who devotes himself to the esoteric. Enryaku-ji is still an important training ground for Buddhism, on a par with the temples at Kōya-san. The value of coming here is in experiencing Enryaku-ji's pervasive aura of spiritual profundity rather than its particular buildings. Though the temple complex is only a 20th of its original size, the magnitude of the place and the commitment to esoterica pursued here are awesome.

Take Kyōto Line Bus 16, 17, or 18 up the main highway, Route 367, to the Yase Yuenchi bus stop, next to Yase Yuen Station. You can see the entrance to the cable car on your left. It departs every 30 minutes, and you can transfer to the ropeway at Hiei for the remaining ride to the summit, where an observatory affords panoramic views of the mountains and of Biwa-ko. *Enryaku-ji* ⊠ *4220 Sakamoto-hon-machi, Ōtsu-shi,* ☎ *Enryaku-ji ¥800; Hiei-zan cable car ¥530, ropeway ¥310*

⊗ *Enryaku-ji Mar.–Nov., daily 8:30–4:30; Dec.–Feb., daily 9–4. Hiei-zan ropeway Apr.–Sept., daily 9–6; Oct.–Mar., daily 9–5; mid-July–late Aug., observatory stays open until 9.*

Jakkō-in (寂光院). In April 1185 the Taira clan met its end in a naval battle against the Minamoto clan. For two years Yoshitsune Minamoto had been gaining the upper hand in the battles. In this one, the Minamotos slaughtered the Tairas, turning the Seto Nai-kai (Inland Sea) red with Taira blood. Recognizing that all was lost, the Taira women drowned themselves, taking with them the young infant emperor Antoku. His mother, Kenreimon-in, too, leaped into the sea, but Minamoto soldiers snagged her hair with a grappling hook and hauled her back on board their ship. She was the sole surviving member of the Taira clan and, at 29, she was a beautiful woman.

Taken back to Kyōto, Kenreimon-in shaved her head and became a nun. First, she had a small hut at Chōraku-ji in eastern Kyōto, and when that collapsed in an earthquake she was accepted at Jakkō-in. She lived in solitude in a 10-ft-square cell made of brushwood and thatch for 27 years, until death erased her memories and with her the Taira. Ask for directions to her mausoleum, higher up the hill away from the throng of visitors.

When Kenreimon-in came to Jakkō-in, it was far removed from Kyōto. Now Kyōto's sprawl reaches this far and beyond, but the temple, hidden in trees, is still a place of solitude and a sanctuary for nuns. From Kyōto Station take Kyōto Line Bus 17 or 18 for a 90-minute ride and get out at the Ōhara bus stop; the fare is ¥480. Walk 20 minutes or so along the road leading to the northwest. ⊠ *Sakyō-ku* 🎟 *¥500* ⊗ *Mar.–Jan., daily 9–5; Dec.–Feb., daily 9–4:30.*

★ **Jikkō-in** (実光院). At this small, little-frequented temple you can sit, relax, and have a taste of the powdered matcha of the tea ceremony. To enter, ring the gong on the outside of the gate and then wander through the carefully cultivated garden. Take Kyōto Line Bus 17 or 18 for 90 minutes from Kyōto Station; the fare is ¥580. From the Ōhara bus stop, walk northeast for about seven minutes along the signposted road. Jikkō-in is 200 yards from Sanzen-in. ⊠ *Sakyō-ku* 🎟 *¥500* ⊗ *Daily 9–5.*

Kamigamo Jinja (上賀茂神社) The Kamo family built Kamigamo and its sister shrine, Shimogamo Jinja (farther south on the Kamo-gawa), in the 8th century. Such is Kamo's fame that even the river that flows by the shrine and through the center of Kyōto bears his name. Kamigamo has always been associated with Wakeikazuchi, a god of thunder, rain, and fertility. Now the shrine is famous for its Aoi (Hollyhock) Festival, which started in the 6th century when people thought that the Kamigamo deities were angry at being neglected. Held every May 15, the festival consists of 500 people wearing Heian-period costumes riding on horseback or in ox-drawn carriages from the Imperial Palace to Shimogamo and then to Kamigamo. To get to the shrine, take Bus 9 north from Kyōto Station or from a stop on Horikawa-dōri. Or take the subway north to Kitayama Station, from which the shrine is 20 minutes on foot northwest. ⊠ *Motoyama, Kamigamo, Sakyō-ku* 🎟 *Free* ⊗ *Daily 9–4:30.*

Miho Museum (Miho Bijutsukan, ミホミュージアム). Built in and around a mountaintop and thoughtfully landscaped—its wooded setting in the hills of Shigariki north of Kyōto is part of the experience of a visit here— the I. M. Pei–designed Miho Museum houses the remarkable Shumei family collection of traditional Japanese art and Asian and Western antiquities. An Egyptian falcon-headed deity, a Roman fresco, a Chinese tea bowl, and a Japanese Bosatsu (Buddha) are among the superb pieces here. A restaurant on-site sells bentō with organic ingredients, and a tearoom serves Japanese and Western beverages and desserts. From Kyōto Station take the JR Tōkaidō Line (¥230 to Ishiyama Station, 15 minutes; from there the bus to the museum will take 50 minutes. There are only two buses a day, at 9:10 AM and 11:55 AM during the week; bus service is extended on weekends and public holidays. ⊠ *300 Momodani, Shigariki, Shiga-ken* ☎ *0748/82–3411* 🖅 *¥1,000* ☺ *Mid-Mar.–mid-June and Sept.–mid-Dec., Tues.–Sun. 10–5; last entry at 4.*

★ **Sanzen-in** (三千院). This small temple of the Tendai sect was founded by a renowned priest, Dengyō-Daishi (767–822). The Hon-dō (Main Hall) was built by Priest Eshin (942–1017), who probably carved the temple's Amida Buddha—though some say it was carved 100 years after Eshin's death. Flanked by two disciples, Daiseishi and Kannon, the statue is a remarkable piece of work, because rather than representing the bountiful Amida, it displays much more the omnipotence of Amida. Although Eshin was not a master sculptor, this statue possibly reflects his belief that, contrary to the prevailing belief of the Heian aristocracy that salvation could be achieved through one's own actions, salvation could be achieved only through Amida's limitless mercy. The statue is in the Main Hall. Unusual for a Buddhist temple, Sanzen-in faces east, not south. Note its ceiling, on which a painting depicts the descent of Amida, accompanied by 25 bodhisattvas, to welcome the believer.

The grounds are also delightful. Full of maple trees and moss, the gardens are serene in any season. During autumn the colors are magnificent, and the approach to the temple up a gentle slope enhances the anticipation for the burned gold trees guarding the old, weathered temple. Snow cover in winter is also magical. Take Kyōto Line Bus 17 or 18 north for 90 minutes from Kyōto Station to Ōhara; the fare is ¥580. From the Ōhara bus station walk northeast for about seven minutes along the signposted road. ⊠ *Raigōin-chō, Ōhara, Sakyō-ku* 🖅 *¥600* ☺ *Mar.–Nov., daily 8:30–4:30; Dec.–Feb., daily 8:30–4.*

★ **Shūgaku-in Imperial Villa** (Shūgaku-in Rikyū, 修学院離宮). Three palaces make up this villa complex with pleasant grounds. The Upper and Lower villas were built in the 17th century by the Tokugawa family to entertain the emperor; the Upper Villa provides nice views. The Middle Villa was added later as a palace home for Princess Bunke, daughter of Emperor Go-mizunoo. The villa was transformed into a temple when Princess Bunke decided that a nun's life was her calling.

Special permission is required to visit the villa from the Imperial Household Agency, preferably a day in advance (⇨ Kyōto Gosho *in* Central & Southern Kyōto, *above*). From Hiei-zan take the Eizan Railway from

Yase Yuen Station to Shūgaku-in Station. The villa is a 15-minute walk from there. From downtown Kyōto the trip takes an hour on Bus 5 from Kyōto Station. Or take the 20-minute ride north on a Keifuku Eizan Line train from the Demachi-Yanagi terminus, which is just northeast of the intersection of Imadegawa-dōri and the Kamo-gawa. ⊠ *Yabusoe Shūgaku-in, Sakyō-ku* ⌨ *Free* ☉ *Tours, in Japanese only, weekdays at 9, 10, 11, 1:30, and 3; Sat. tours on 1st and 3rd Sat. of month; every Sat. Apr.–May and Oct.–Nov.*

WHERE TO EAT

Most of Kyōto's restaurants accept credit cards; however, some of the finest traditional restaurants do not, so it's wise to check ahead, especially since traditional *kaiseki ryōri* (a Japanese meal of several exquisite courses that include only the freshest seasonal ingredients cooked lightly and served on complimentary ceramics) can be quite expensive. Customarily, people dine early in Kyōto, between 7 PM and 8 PM, so most restaurants, apart from hotel restaurants and bars, close around 9 PM. The average Japanese businessman wears a suit and tie to dinner—no matter how casual the restaurant. Young people tend to dress more informally. Many Kyōto restaurants do have English-speakers on staff, if it turns out that you need assistance making reservations.

Apart from the restaurants listed below, Kyōto has plenty of the quasi-Western–style budget chain restaurants found all over Japan. These places, which serve sandwiches and salads, gratins, curried rice, and spaghetti, are easy to locate along Kawara-machi-dōri downtown; most have plastic food models in the window to which you can point if spoken language fails you.

For more on Japanese cuisine, *see* Chapter 15 *and* Eating & Drinking *in* Smart Travel Tips A to Z.

WHAT IT COSTS In yen				
	$$$$	$$$	$$	$	¢
AT DINNER	over 3,000	2,000–3,000	1,000–2,000	800–1,000	under 800

Prices are per person for a main course.

Eastern Kyōto

Indonesian

$$ ✕ **Café Carinho** (カフェカリーニョ). By day this friendly café serves Brazilian coffee, Montréal-style bagels (made from Canadian stone-ground flour), and ¥1,000 lunch specials with choices like chickpea hamburgers. At night chef Déjan Alakhan conjures up a range of Indonesian curries, satays, and desserts flavored with exotic spices. The café has a small veranda and is decorated in cheerful red and green tones. From Ginkaku-ji, it's a 15-minute walk west down Imadegawa-dōri. ⊠ *1148 Nishida-chō, Imadegawa-dōri, Sakyō-ku* ☎ *075/752–3636* 🚫 *No credit cards* ☉ *Closed Mon.*

ON THE MENU

PARIS EAST IS A DIFFICULT EPITHET FOR KYŌTO TO LIVE UP TO, but in many ways the elegant sister cities do seem to be of the same flesh and blood—not least in that both serve up their nation's haute cuisine. The presence of the imperial court was the original inspiration for Kyōto's exclusive yusoku ryōri. Once presented on lacquered pedestals to the emperor himself, it's now offered at but one restaurant in the city, Mankamerō.

The experience not to miss in Kyōto is kaiseki ryōri, the elegant full-course meal that was originally intended to be served with the tea ceremony. All the senses are engaged in this culinary event: the scent and flavor of the freshest ingredients at the peak of season; the visual delight of a continuous procession of porcelain dishes and lacquered bowls, each a different shape and size, gracefully adorned with an appropriately shaped morsel of fish or vegetable; the textures of foods unknown and exotic, presented in sequence to prevent boredom; the sound of water in a stone basin outside in the garden. Even the atmosphere of the room enhances the experience: a hanging scroll displayed in the alcove and a carefully crafted flower arrangement evoke the season and accent the restrained appointments of the tatami room. Kaiseki ryōri is often costly yet always unforgettable.

For an initiation or a reasonably priced sample, the kaiseki bentō (box lunch) served by many ryōtei (high-class Japanese restaurants) is a good place to start. Box lunches are so popular in Kyōto that restaurants compete to make their bentō unique, exquisite, and delicious.

Because it's a two-day journey from the sea, Kyōto is historically more famous for ingenious ways of serving preserved fish—dried, salted, or pickled—than for its raw-fish dishes, though with modern transport have come good sushi shops. Compared with the style of cooking elsewhere in Japan, Kyōto-ryōri (Kyōto cuisine) is lighter and more delicate, stressing the natural flavor of ingredients over enhancement with heavy sauces and broths. Obanzai (Kyōto home cooking) is served at many restaurants at reasonable cost. Organic food is the latest trend, and in some more eclectic restaurants chefs are experimenting with traditional cuisine to create fresh, new, and unexpected dishes, while retaining the light and subtle flavors. Tsukemono (pickled vegetables) and wagashi (traditional sweets) are two other local specialties; they make excellent souvenirs. Food shops are often kept just as they were a century ago—well worth the trip if only to browse.

Kyōto is also the home of shōjin ryōri, the Zen vegetarian-style cooking, best sampled on the grounds of one of the city's Zen temples, such as Tenryū-ji in Arashiyama. Local delicacies like fu (glutinous wheat cakes) and yuba (soy-milk skimmings) have found their way into the mainstream of Kyōto ryōri but were originally devised to provide protein in the traditional Buddhist diet.

Kyōto is famed throughout Japan for the best in traditional Japanese cuisine, and although the city has been slower to pick up on international cuisines, it does have a few fine European and Asian restaurants.

Japanese

$$$$ ✕ **Ashiya Steak House** (あしや). A short walk from the Gion district, famous for its teahouses and geisha, Ashiya Steak House is the best place in Kyōto to enjoy "a good steak . . . a real martini . . . and the essence of traditional Japan," in the words of owner Bob Strickland and his wife, Tokiko. While you're seated at a *kotatsu* (recessed hearth), your *teppanyaki* dinner of the finest Ōmi beefsteak, grilled and sliced in style, will be prepared as you watch. Cocktails, domestic and imported wines, and beer are available, as well as an impressive selection of sake. You can take cocktails in the art gallery upstairs, which has a display of traditional and contemporary arts and crafts. Set steak dinners include an appetizer, soup, salad, and rice; and the price increases depending the size of your steak. ✉ *172–13 4-chōme, Kiyomizu, Higashiyama-ku* ☎ *075/541–7961* ⌚ *Reservations essential* 🖃 *AE, DC, V* ⊘ *Closed Mon. No lunch.*

★ $$$$ ✕ **Minokō** (美濃幸). The specialty at this former villa on the eastern fringe of Gion is *cha-kaiseki* cuisine—elegant multicourse meals that evoke the rituals of formal tea ceremonies. Upon arriving, you'll be led by Mrs. Yoshida, the gracious hostess, to a quiet room that overlooks a tea garden with stone lanterns and a trickling stream. Meanwhile, Mr. Yoshida oversees every detail in the preparation of your meal. Not only are the secrets for creating subtle flavors preserved and passed down by kaiseki's master chefs but also the knowledge of the harvest and spawning cycles of plants and animals. In summer, eggs are not used here because this is believed to be strenuous for the hens—an example of Minokō's approach to harmonious living. At lunchtime an informal box lunch called *chabako-bentō* is served for ¥6,000; it includes frothy matcha and a sweet. One of the curious turtles may leave the pond and come closer to watch you dine. ✉ *480 Kiyoi-chō, Shimogowara-dōri, Gion, Higashiyama-ku* ☎ *075/561–0328* ⌚ *Reservations essential* 🏛 *Jacket and tie* 🖃 *DC, MC, V* ⊘ *Closed 2nd and 4th Wed. of each month.*

★ $$$$ ✕ **Rokusei Nishimise** (六盛). Few restaurants in Kyōto have matched Rokusei Nishimise's magical combination of traditional cuisine and contemporary setting. Formal kaiseki dishes are served (as they have been since 1899) in a setting of polished marble floors and manicured interior-garden niches. Popular ¥3,500 *te-oke bentō* lunches—a collage of flavors and colors presented on a handmade cypress-wood serving tray—can be enjoyed at tables that overlook a tree-lined canal, where brilliant azaleas bloom in May. Rokusei also serves a different exquisite multicourse meal each month for ¥10,000. A three-minute after-dinner walk will bring you to the turn-of-the-20th-century gardens of the Heian Jingū. ✉ *71 Nishitennō-chō, Okazaki, Sakyō-ku* ☎ *075/751–6171* ⌚ *Reservations essential* 🖃 *AE, DC, V* ⊘ *Closed Mon.*

$$$$ ✕ **Yagembori** (やげんぼり). North of Shijō-dōri in the heart of Kyōto's still-thriving geisha district, this restaurant is in a teahouse a few steps down a cobbled path from the romantic Shira-kawa, a small tributary of the Kamo-gawa. The *o-makase* meal is an elegant sampler of Kyōto's finest kaiseki cuisine, with local delicacies presented on handmade ceramics. The *shabu-shabu* (thinly sliced beef, dipped briefly into hot stock) and *suppon* (turtle dishes) are excellent. Don't miss the *hōba miso*—bean paste

Fodor'sChoice
★

with *kinoko* mushrooms and green onions, which are wrapped in a giant oak leaf and grilled at your table—on the à la carte menu. A cheaper option is the excellent box lunch for ¥2,500. ⊠ *Sueyoshi-chō, Kiridoshi-kado, Gion, Higashiyama-ku* ☎ *075/551–3331* ☐ *AE, DC, V.*

$$$–$$$$ ✕ **Matsuno** (松乃). Eel may not sound very appetizing at first, but the appeal of *unagi* is slightly more obvious. Once most visitors taste the succulent broiled fish served in its own special sweet sauce, they don't feel so squeamish. Two doors down from the Kabuki theater Minami-za, Matsuno specializes in serving unagi to an after-theater crowd in simple but elegant surroundings. ⊠ *Minamiza-higashi 4-ken-me, Shijō-dōri, Higashiyama-ku* ☎ *075/561–2786* ☐ *MC, V* ⊙ *Closed Thurs.*

$$$–$$$$ ✕ **Nontaro** (呑太呂). This sushi restaurant in the heart of the geisha district has been serving visitors to Gion for more than 40 years. You can order sushi à la carte or choose one of the *omakase* (chef's choice) selections. If you're in the mood for something different, try the *kokesushi*—a giant sushi roll. ⊠ *Hanamikō-ji Shijō-agaru, Higashiyama-ku* ☎ *075/561–3189* ⌣ *Reservations essential* ☐ *AE, DC, MC, V* ⊙ *Closed Sun.*

★ **$$$–$$$$** ✕ **Oishinbo** (祇園おいしんぼ). In the hub of old Gion is a surprisingly reasonable restaurant where you can leisurely sample *obanzai*, classic home-style Kyōto cooking. Organic shiitake mushrooms star in many of the dishes, which range from tofu gluten steaks to duck carpaccio. Trust the chef and order one of the set menus; these consist of many seasonal delights complemented by a glass of Seishū oishinbo, the raw house sake. Tatami-matted rooms on the first floor overlook a small *tsuboniwa* (small courtyard garden). ⊠ *Hanamikōji-sagaru, Futatsuji-me Higashi-iru, Higashiyama-ku* ☎ *075/532–2285* ⌣ *Reservations essential* ⌂ *Jacket required* ☐ *AE, D, DC, MC, V.*

★ **$$$–$$$$** ✕ **Omen** (おめん). Just south of Ginkaku-ji, this is one of the best places to stop for an inexpensive home-style lunch before proceeding down the old canal—the walkway beneath the cherry trees known as the Path of Philosophy—on the way to Nanzen-ji. Omen is also the name of the house specialty: thick white noodles brought to your table in a basket with a bowl of hot broth and a platter of seasonal, organic vegetables, which are added to the broth a little at a time and sprinkled with roasted sesame seeds. Another famed Kyōto dish, *saba* (salted mackerel) sushi is also served. Like the food, the restaurant is country style, with a choice of counter stools, tables and chairs, or tatami mats. The waiters dress in *happi* coats and headbands; the atmosphere is lively and comfortable. Reservations are accepted only on weekdays. ⊠ *74 Ishi-bashi-chō, Jōdo-ji, Sakyō-ku* ☎ *075/771–8994* ⊕ *www.omen.co.jp* ☐ *No credit cards* ⊙ *Closed Thurs.*

$$$ ✕ **Hanbei Fu** (半兵衛麸). *Fu* (wheat gluten) and *yuba* (soy milk skimmings) historically have been important sources of protein in the Japanese diet, which was largely vegetarian until the 20th century. This 18th-century establishment in a 19th-century house is an excellent place to sample the versatility of both ingredients, which can be grilled, baked, used in tempura, or warmed in soup. ⊠ *Minamizume, Goshō Bridge E, Higashiyama-ku* ☎ *075/525–0008* ⌣ *Reservations essential* ☐ *D, V* ⊙ *No dinner.*

★ **$$** ✕ **Café Peace** (カフェピース). Delicious all-vegetarian cuisine featuring soy-based dishes is the main draw here. Choose between several kinds of

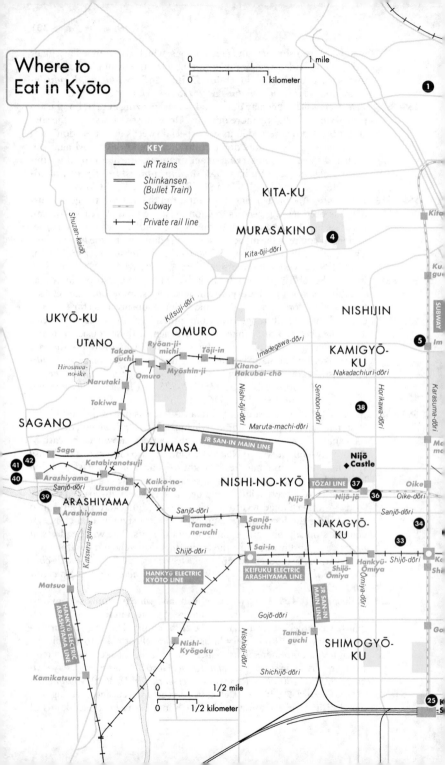

Where to Eat in Kyōto

KEY
—— JR Trains
═══ Shinkansen (Bullet Train)
╌╌╌ Subway
+—+ Private rail line

0 ———— 1 mile
0 ———— 1 kilometer

❶

Shuzan-kaidō

KITA-KU

MURASAKINO ❹

Kita-ōji-dōri

Kita

Ku gue

NISHIJIN

UKYŌ-KU

UTANO

OMURO

Kitsuji-dōri

Ryōan-ji-michi   Tōji-in

Takao-guchi

Imadegawa-dōri

KAMIGYŌ-KU ❺ Im

Hirosawa-no-ike

Omuro   Myōshin-ji

Kitano-Hakubai-chō

Nakadachiuri-dōri

Narutaki

Nishi-ōji-dōri

Sembon-dōri

Horikawa-dōri

Karasuma-dōri

SUBWAY

Tokiwa

❸❽

Maruta-machi-dōri

Ma ma

SAGANO

Saga

Katabiranotsuji

UZUMASA

JR SAN-IN MAIN LINE

Nijō Castle ◆

❹❷

Kaiko-no-yashiro

NISHI-NO-KYŌ

TŌZAI LINE ❸❼

Oike

❹❶

Arashiyama

Uzumasa

Sanjō-dōri

Nijō ❸❻ Oike-dōri

❹❷

ARASHIYAMA

Arashiyama

Yama-no-uchi

Sanjō-guchi

Sanjō-dōri

NAKAGYŌ-KU

Sanjō-dōri ❸❹

Hozu-gawa

Sai-in

Shijō-dōri

❸❸

Matsuo

HANKYŪ ELECTRIC KYŌTO LINE

KEIFUKU ELECTRIC ARASHIYAMA LINE

Hankyū-Ōmiya

Shijō-Ōmiya

Shijō-dōri

Ke Shi

Ōmiya-dōri

JR SAN-IN MAIN LINE

HANKYŪ ELECTRIC ARASHIYAMA LINE

Gojō-dōri

Nishi-Kyōgoku

Nishijō-dōri

Tamba-guchi

SHIMOGYŌ-KU

Ga

Kamikatsura

Shichijō-dōri

0 ———— 1/2 mile
0 ———— 1/2 kilometer

❷❺ K S

homemade soup, spring rolls, noodle dishes, and curries. Meat lovers have sworn that the sweet-and-sour "pork" tastes like the real thing. The staff here is hip, environmentally aware, and anti–animal testing. The restaurant has a great view of the mountains from its third floor vantage point, on the corner of Higashioji and Imadegawa. ✉ *3F Domus Hyakumanben Bldg., Higashiōji dōri, Sakyō-ku* ☎ *075/707–6856* ⊟ *No credit cards* ◷ *Closed Sun.*

★ ¢ ✕ **Rakushō** (洛匠). Flowering plum trees, azaleas, irises, camellias, and maple trees take seasonal turns adding color to this tea shop in a former villa. En route from Maruyama Kōen to Kiyomizu-dera, this is a pleasant place to enjoy a bowl of frothy matcha or freshly brewed coffee while gazing over the elaborately landscaped garden. You can order *warabi mochi,* rice-flour dumplings with the consistency of Jell-O, rolled in sweetened soya bean powder. Rakushō closes at 6 PM. ✉ *Kōdai-ji Kitamon-mae-dōri, Washio-chō, Higashiyama-ku* ☎ *075/561–6892* ⌚ *Reservations not accepted* ⊟ *No credit cards* ◷ *Closed 4 days a month, call ahead.*

Western Kyōto

Japanese

★ $$$$ ✕ **Kitchō** (吉兆). What Maxim's is to Paris, Kitchō is to Kyōto—classic cuisine, an unparalleled traditional atmosphere, exclusive elegance. Lunch here starts at ¥45,000, dinner at ¥50,000, making this perhaps the world's most expensive restaurant. Although there are 20 other branches (all run by members of the original founder's family), this one has a truly stunning location, in the foothills of Arashiyama's mountains and beside the Ōi River. Here you can experience the full sensory delight of formal kaiseki cuisine; only the finest ingredients are used, and meals are served on exquisite antique porcelain in an elegant dining room. The chefs here aim to compose *ichigo-ichi* (once in a lifetime) experiences by never serving exactly the same meal twice. Expect to spend a minimum of two hours here. Kitchō takes last orders for dinner at 7. ✉ *58 Susuki-no-bamba-chō, Tenryū-ji, Saga, Ukyō-ku* ☎ *075/881–1101* ⌚ *Reservations essential* ⌂ *Jacket and tie* ⊟ *AE, DC, MC, V* ◷ *Closed Wed.*

★ $$$$ ✕ **Nishiki** (錦). On an island in the middle of the Ōi-gawa, and surrounded by the densely forested Arashiyama, Nishiki offers one of the most memorable lunches in Kyōto. Called the *oshukuzen-bentō* lunch, it allows you to sample seven courses of delicious, beautifully prepared kaiseki cuisine, and for a very reasonable price (¥4,400). Served in an elegant tiered lacquer box, and using only the finest seasonal ingredients, this lunch rivals other meals that are three times the price. A summer lunch might include a course of *kamo-nasu,* the prized Kyōto eggplant, served *dengaku-*style—smothered in sweet miso sauce. The top layer of the box might be covered with a miniature bamboo trellis in which are nestled tiny porcelain cups the shape of morning glories, each filled with a different appetizer—perhaps sea urchin or sprigs of spinach in sesame sauce. The last dinner order is taken at 7:30. ✉ *Nakanoshima Kōen-guchi, Arashiyama, Ukyō-ku* ☎ *075/871–8888* ⌚ *Reservations essential* ⊟ *DC, MC, V* ◷ *Closed Tues.*

★ **$$$–$$$$** ✕ **Sagano** (嵯峨野). Amid Arashiyama's lush, green bamboo forests, this quiet retreat serves one of the finest meals of *yudōfu* (cubes of bean curd simmered in broth) in Kyōto. The meal, which is the same for lunch and dinner, includes such local delicacies as tempura and *aburage* (deep-fried tofu) with black sesame seeds and some seasonally changing dishes. You can take a seat at the sunken counter, where waitresses in kimonos will prepare the meal in front of you—with a backdrop of antique wood-block prints on folding screens—or walk out through the garden to private, Japanese-style rooms in the back. If weather permits, you can dine on low tables in the courtyard garden beneath towering bamboo. Reservations are a good idea year-round, and particularly during fall foliage season, when the maple trees of Arashiyama are stunning. Arrive before 5:30 for dinner in the tatami rooms, before 6:30 for counter service. ⊠ *45 Susuki-no-bamba-chō, Saga, Tenryū-ji, Ukyō-ku* ☎ *075/861–0277* ▭ *No credit cards.*

Spanish

$$$–$$$$ ✕ **Bodegon** (ボデゴン). A white-walled, tile-floored, wrought-iron, and blown-glass Spanish restaurant in Arashiyama is about as rare (and welcome) as decent paella in a neighborhood famous for its tofu. Bodegon sits unobtrusively along the main street that runs through the center of this scenic district, combining Spanish fare and wine with Kyōto hospitality. A wildly popular tourist area in daylight, Arashiyama rolls up its sidewalks after dark, so Bodegon is a good place to escape the crowds downtown in the evening after other places close. ⊠ *1 Susuki-no-bamba-chō, Saga, Tenryū-ji, Ukyō-ku* ☎*075/872–9652* ▭*MC, V* ☉*Closed Thurs.*

Central Kyōto

Coffee Shops

$–$$ ✕ **Inoda** (イノダ). One of Kyōto's oldest and best-loved *kissaten* (coffee shops), this century-old establishment is hidden down a side street in the center of town. The turn-of-the-20th-century Western-style brick buildings along Sanjō-dōri nearby are part of a historic preservation district, and Inoda's original old shop blends well with its surroundings. Floor-to-ceiling glass windows overlook an interior garden, and the place even has some stained-glass windows and a pair of witty resident parrots. The coffee is excellent with a range of prim, white-bread sandwiches, cakes, and meat loaf. Inoda closes at 6 PM. ⊠ *Sakai-machi-dōri, Sanjō-sagaru, Nakagyō-ku* ☎ *075/221–0507* ⌦ *Reservations not accepted* ▭ *No credit cards.*

¢–$$ ✕ **Café Sarasa** (カフェさらさ). In an area where trendy new designer stores recycle old kimonos and rub shoulders with traditional art supply shops, there's a lovely old café where you can sip the largest café au lait in Kyōto. The exposed beams and mud walls of this Edo-era house lend the café woodsy charm. The laid-back eatery serves light meals—try the Okinawa-style fried rice with vegetable and tofu, or the Vietnamese-style pancakes. Café Sarasa is three blocks west of Teramachi-dōri and a little south of Sanjō. Look out for a tiny bicycle shop and head up the stairs to the left of it. ⊠ *2F Wood-Inn, 534 Asakuchi-chō, Tominokōji-dori, Sanjō-agaru, Nakagyō-ku* ☎ *075/212–2310* ▭ *No credit cards.*

French

★ $$$$ ✕ **Natsuka** (ナツカ). This fine French restaurant overlooks the Kamo River. The Japanese proprietors learned their trade in Paris, and delicious dishes such as roasted sea bream with saffron, beef fillet with mushroom sauce, and conger eel with fruit salad bear testament to their culinary education. The dessert tray, loaded with pastries and other baked goods, is also sumptuous. The last dinner order is taken at 8. ⊠ *Ponto-chō, Shijō-agaru, Higashi-gawa, Nakagyō-ku* ☎ *075/255–2105* ⌱ *Reservations essential* ▤ *MC* ◷ *Closed Wed.*

★ $$$$ ✕ **Ogawa** (おがわ). The best in Kyōto-style nouvelle cuisine is served in this intimate spot across from the Takase canal. Finding a seat at the counter or upstairs in the wood-panel dining room is as difficult as getting tickets for opening night at the opera—but the food is worth the wait. With particularly Japanese sensitivity to the best ingredients only in the peak of the season, proprietor Ogawa promises never to bore by serving the same meal twice. *Ayu*, a popular local river fish, is served in summer, salmon in fall, crab in winter, shrimp in spring. The marvelous desserts might include fresh papaya sherbet or mango mousse with mint sauce. The set meals are spectacular, but you can also opt for an hors d'oeuvres selection of three dishes, such as oyster gratin, crab and scallop stew, and *matsutake* (wild mushroom) tempura. ⊠ *Kiya-machi Oike-agaru Higashi-Iru, Nakagyō-ku* ☎ *075/256–2203* ⌱ *Reservations essential* ⌂ *Jacket and tie* ▤ *AE, DC, MC, V* ◷ *Closed Tues.*

Indian

$$$–$$$$ ✕ **Ashoka** (アショカ). One of the first international restaurants to open its doors in this capital of culinary daintiness, Ashoka offers a dazzling *Thali* dinner, including about 10 small plates. Consisting of several curries, along with rice and tandoori dishes, this meal should only be ordered if you're very hungry. Red carpets, carved screens, brass lanterns, and tuxedoed waiters set the mood, and diners wear everything from denim to silk. The last dinner order is taken at 9 PM, 8:30 PM on Sunday. ⊠ *Kikusui Bldg., 3rd fl., Tera-machi-dōri, Shijō-agaru, Nakagyō-ku* ☎ *075/241–1318* ▤ *AE, DC, MC, V* ◷ *Closed 2nd Tues. of month.*

Italian

★ $$$–$$$$ ✕ **Cucina Il Viale** (イルヴィアーレ). The signature dish here is handmade pasta served with an electric-pink tomato sauce that's bound to make the most travel-weary sourpusses smile. Rounding out the menu are antipasti such as Kyōto vegetables served with fine Italian ham; and main dishes like ultratender pork steak, and grilled fish in balsamic vinegar with a hint of orange. Espresso and decadent desserts are also served; the litchi mousse alone is worth the visit. While you wait for your food to arrive, you can watch the two chef-owners working their culinary magic behind the counter. ⊠ *Horikawa, Oike Nishi-iru, Nakagyō-ku* ☎ *075/812–2366* ⌱ *Reservations essential* ▤ *AE, V* ◷ *Closed Mon. No lunch Tues.*

$$ ✕ **Capricciosa** (カプリチョーザ). A convenient location under Kyōto Station, a casual atmosphere, and huge bowls of steaming spaghetti make this unpretentious Italian restaurant (part of a nationwide chain), a popular spot. The pasta dishes are large enough to share, and the pizzas are

a good value. Capricciosa has two more branches, on Kawara-machi-dōri in the Opa department store and in the Vox building. ☒ *Kyōto Station basement, Porta Restaurant Zone, Shimogyō-ku* ☏ *075/343–3499* ▭ *No credit cards* ⊗ *Closed 3rd Tues. of month.*

Japanese

$$$$
Fodor'sChoice
★

✕ **Mankamerō** (萬亀楼). Established in 1716, Mankamerō is the only restaurant in Kyōto that offers formal *yusoku ryōri,* the type of cuisine once served to members of the imperial court. A specially appointed—and ceremonially dressed—chef prepares the food using utensils made only for this type of cuisine. A dramatic dish is the "dismembered" fish; the chef elaborately arranges each part of the fish, which is then served to you on a series of pedestal trays. Prices are also quite elaborate—up to ¥30,000 per person for the full yusoku ryōri repertoire—though a wonderful *take-kago bentō* (lunch served in a bamboo basket) is within reach of wealthy commoners at ¥6,500. Mankamerō is on the west side of Inokuma-dōri north of Demizu-dōri. It closes at 8 PM. ☒ *Inokuma-dōri, Demizu-agaru, Kamigyō-ku* ☏ *075/441–5020* ☞ *Reservations essential* 🏛 *Jacket and tie* ▭ *AE, DC, MC, V* ⊗ *Closed once a month, call ahead.*

★ $$$$

✕ **Mishima-tei** (三嶋亭). This is really the one choice for *sukiyaki* (stir-fried beef, vegetables, and noodles) in Kyōto. In the heart of the downtown shopping district, Kyōto housewives line up out front to pay premium prices for Mishima-tei's high-quality beef, sold by the kilogram over the counter at the meat shop downstairs. Mishima-tei was established in 1904, and climbing the staircase of this traditional wood-frame restaurant with its turn-of-the-20th-century atmosphere is like journeying into the past. Down the long dark corridors with polished wood floors, kimono-clad servers bustle about with trays of beef and refills of sake to dozens of private tatami-mat rooms. Ask for a room that faces the central courtyard garden for the best view. Plan on dining by 7, as the service—and the preparation of your food—can be rushed toward the end of the evening. ☒ *Tera-machi, Sanjō-sagaru, Higashi-Iru, Nakagyō-ku* ☏ *075/221–0003* ☞ *Reservations essential* ▭ *AE, DC, MC, V* ⊗ *Closed Wed.*

$$$$

✕ **Mukadeya** (百足屋). *Obanzai*—Kyōto home-style cooking is served in this sophisticated, refurbished old villa. Several dainty morsels like bonito sashimi and pumpkin with gingery ground chicken are artfully laid out on lacquer trays. Unlike many traditional houses, where winding corridors lead to small interior rooms, here the open-plan renovation and dark stone-tile *genkan* (foyer) adds a feel of expansiveness. ☒ *381 Mukadeya-chō, Shinmachi-dōri, Nishiki-agaru, Nakagyō-ku* ☏ *075/256–9393* ☞ *Reservations essential* 🏛 *Jacket and tie* ▭ *AE, MC, V* ⊗ *Closed Wed.*

$$$$

✕ **Ōmi.** The Ebisugawa-tei annex to the Fujita Hotel is a restored Meiji-era villa that also houses this excellent steak restaurant. The specialty is the celebrated beer-fed and hand-massaged Ōmi beef. You'll be ushered through corridors to the dining room and seated around a *hori-hotatsu,* a recessed grill, with counter seating in a pristine tatami room. There's also an excellent seafood platter to choose from and a good lunch set menu on weekends. After your meal, you can stop in at the basement bar of the Fujita Hotel for a drink beside the beautiful duck pond and waterfall. ✉ *Fujita Hotel, Nijō-dōri, Kiya-machi Kado, Nakagyō-ku* ☎ *075/222–1511* 🍴 *Reservations essential* 🏛 *Jacket and tie* 🍴 *AE, DC, MC, V* ⊘ *No lunch weekdays.*

$$$$ ✕🏠 **Yoshikawa** (吉川). Adjacent to the well-reputed inn of the same name, this restaurant serves full-course kaiseki ryōri dinners (¥12,000) that include a lavish selection of sashimi, soup, rice, vegetables, baked fish, and tempura, the specialty of the house. Or you can try the tempura dinners (¥6,000), which include 13 different pieces of fish, meat, and vegetable tempura, plus rice and soup. Dinner is served in a tatami room. A better value is the ¥2,000 lunch served at the counter, where you can watch the chef fry up your meal. Tempura should be light and crisp—best right from the pot—and for this Yoshikawa is famous. English is spoken, and last orders are taken by 8:30. ✉ *Tomino-kōji, Oike-sagaru, Nakagyō-ku* ☎ *075/221–5544 or 075/221–0052* 🍴 *Reservations essential* 🏛 *Jacket and tie* 🍴 *AE, DC, MC, V* ⊘ *Closed Sun.*

$$$ ✕ **Shinsen-en Heihachi** (神泉苑 平八). When you order a pot-for-two of Japan's fattest *udon* (wheat noodles) here, and look out over the remnants of Kyōto's first Imperial Palace garden, you'll be doing the Japanese equivalent of munching a hot dog while gazing at the White House Rose Garden. When Emperor Kammu established Heian-kyō in 794, he built a 33-acre Sacred Spring Garden containing pleasure pavilions for moon-viewing and other pastimes, of which a pond with vermilion bridge and some small shrines remain today. The hotpot dinners are very popular, so it's best to book ahead. ✉ *Nijō-jō Minami-gawa, Nakagyō-ku* ☎ *075/841–0811* 🍴 *AE, MC, V.*

$$$ ✕ **Ōiwa** (大岩). Ōiwa, which is at the head of the Takase-gawa canal, serves *kushikatsu*—skewered meats and vegetables battered, deep-fried, and then dipped in a variety of sauces. The building is actually a *kura*, or treasure house. Kuras were traditionally separate from the main house and made of thicker walls covered in white plaster to protect valuables from fire. This particular kura once belonged to a kimono merchant family, and it's one of the first in Kyōto to have been turned into a restaurant. The Japanese chef trained in one of the finest French restaurants in Tōkyō, and his version of kushikatsu (usually considered a working man's snack with beer) has an unpretentious elegance. Order by the skewer or ask for the *o-makase* set course. ✉ *Kiya-machi-dōri, Nijō-sagaru, Nakagyō-ku* ☎ *075/231–7667* 🍴 *No credit cards* ⊘ *Closed Wed.*

$$–$$$ ✕ **Karyō-an** (迦陵庵). A little north of Sanjo, on the third floor of a narrow building, Karyō-an is an unpretentious, pine-finished *izakaya* (pub) with seating along the open hearth or charcoal grill. Some of the ingredients are on display and you can watch the chef as he grills chicken, fish, vegetables and other Kyōto specialties like *nama fu* (fresh wheat gluten), and then passes them to you on a giant wooden paddle. If you're having trouble choosing what to order, ask for the *omakase* (chef's special). ✉ *3rd fl., Yurika Bldg., Kiyamachi-dōri, Sanjō-agaru, Nakagyō-ku* ☎ *075/212–7099* 🍴 *AE, DC, MC, V* ⊘ *No lunch.*

$$–$$$ ✕ **Yamatomi** (山とみ). *Yuka*, the outdoor dining platforms that extend onto the banks of the Kamogawa River, first appeared in the late 16th century. A summer meal under the stars with a breeze off the river in this lively open setting can be an unforgettable experience. Although most of the restaurants with yuka are pricey, Yamatomi offers more than 100 dishes of traditional Japanese food on an à la carte menu with reasonable prices. Set menus start at ¥6,000. ⊠ *Higashigawa-dōri, Shijō-agaru, Nabeya-chō, Nakagyō-ku* ☎ *075/221–3268* 🍽 *AE, DC, MC, V* ☺ *Closed Tues.*

★ $$ ✕ **Daikokuya** (大黒屋). If you're shopping downtown and want a quick meal, stop in at Daikokuya for a soba dish or *domburi,* a bowl of rice with your choice of toppings. The *oyako domburi,* rice with egg and chicken—*oyako* means "parent and child"—is the best choice. The buckwheat for the soba is ground in-house on an antique stone mill powered by a wooden waterwheel. Fresh noodles are also served with exceedingly delicate, light, and crunchy tempura. Both tatami and table-and-chair seating arrangements are available. You can recognize Daikokuya by the big red lantern outside the door. ⊠ *281 Minami-kurumaya-chō, Takoyakushi, Kiya-machi Nishi-Iru, Nakagyō-ku* ☎ *075/221–2818* 🖎 *Reservations not accepted* 🍽 *AE, D, MC, V* ☺ *Closed Tues.*

¢–$$ ✕ **Tagoto** (本家田毎). One of the best noodle shops in the downtown area, this place has been serving soup with homemade soba for more than 100 years in the same location (on the north side of the covered Sanjō Arcade). That said, the dining area has been thoroughly modernized with natural woods, *shōji* (rice-paper) windows, tatami mats, and a pretty interior garden. Tagoto serves both thin soba and thick white udon noodle dishes with a variety of ingredients, such as shrimp tempura and baked eel, hot or cold to suit the season. It's half a block west of Kawara-machi-dōri. ⊠ *Sanjō-dōri, Tera-machi Higashi-Iru, Nakagyō-ku* ☎ *075/221–3030* 🖎 *Reservations not accepted* 🍽 *AE, DC, MC, V.*

Korean

$$ ✕ **Kicchan** (きっちゃん). Spicy Korean food has long been favored in Japan, and at this cheerful renovated *machiya* (Japanese town house), you can sample this spicy fare while listening to the loud bantering between chef and waiters. Many dishes here are made with the chili condiment *kimchee.* And one popular choice is actually Japanese: *okonomiyaki* is a thick pancake with vegetables and meat or seafood, topped with a dark sauce. ⊠ *Rokkaku-dōri, Muromachi-nishi-iru, Nakagyō-ku* ☎ *075/241–3390* 🍽 *No credit cards* ☺ *No lunch.*

Thai

$$$$ ✕ **E-san** (E-さん). Only a stone's throw away from Kyōto's Imperial Palace, this restaurant, with its elephant carvings and Thai music playing in the background, feels a million miles from Japan. E-san's popular lunch buffet is filling and a good value at ¥1,200; dinner prices start at ¥6,000. If the food is too spicy for your taste, order a bowl of delicious sweet-potato ice cream to cool down. ⊠ *Imadegawa-dōri, Kamigyō-ku* ☎ *075/441–6199* 🍽 *MC, V.*

Vietnamese

$$–$$$ ✕ **Tiêm ân Hu'o'ng Viêt** (テイエム・フォーン・ヴィエット). Tucked away in a small street north of Karasuma Oike, this delightful eatery has green walls and dark Vietnamese furnishings. Order several dishes to share, and be sure to try the *Ban Xeo,* a huge pancake that you assemble yourself with vegetables, shrimp, and fragrant herbs and then dip into a spicy

sauce. ✉ *Oshikōji-dōri, Karasama Oike-agaru, Nakagyō-ku* ☎ *075/253–1828* ▭ *No credit cards* ⊘ *Closed Tues.*

Northern Kyōto

Japanese

★ $$$$ ✗ **Heihachi-Jaya** (平八茶屋). A bit off the beaten path in the northeastern corner of Kyōto, along the old road to the Sea of Japan, this roadside inn has provided comfort to many a weary traveler during its 400-year history. Heihachi-Jaya hugs the levee of the Takano-gawa and is surrounded by maple trees in a quiet garden with a stream. Apart from the excellent full-course kaiseki dinner, the famed duck hotpot on offer in winter, and the delicious *mugitoro bentō* (a boxed lunch of mountain-potato salad served with barley rice), what makes this restaurant special is its clay sauna. Called a *kamaburo*, the sauna is a mound-shape clay steam bath heated from beneath the floor by a pinewood fire. Have a bath and sauna, change into a cotton kimono if you wish, and retire to the dining room (or to a private room) for a *very* relaxing meal. An unforgettable way to round off a day of exploring Hiei-zan and Ōhara. Heihachi-Jaya closes at 9 PM. ✉ *8–1 Kawagishi-chō, Yamabana, Sakyō-ku* ☎ *075/781–5008* ✑ *Reservations essential* ▭ *AE, DC, MC, V.*

★ $$$–$$$$ ✗ **Izusen** (泉仙). In the garden of Daiji-in, a subtemple of Daitoku-ji, this restaurant specializes in shōjin ryōri, vegetarian Zen cuisine. Lunches are presented in sets of red-lacquer bowls of diminishing sizes, each one fitting inside the next as the meal is completed. Two Kyōto specialties *fu* (wheat gluten) and *yuba* (soy milk skimmings), are served in a multitude of inventive forms—in soups and sauces that prove vegetarian cuisine to be as exciting as anything with meat. You can dine in tatami-mat rooms, and in warm weather on low tables outside in the temple garden. Reservations are recommended in spring and fall. Izusen closes at 4 PM. ✉ *4 Daitoku-ji-chō, Murasakino, Kita-ku* ☎ *075/491–666?* ▭ *No credit cards.*

$$$–$$$$ ✗ **Sagenta** (左源太). Discovering the town of Kibune is one of the best parts of summer in Kyōto. A bump-and-rumble train ride into the mountains north of Kyōto on the nostalgic little Eizan train leaves you on
Fodor'sChoice a mountain road that winds along a stream for about 2 km (1.2 mi)
★ to Kibune. This road is lined with restaurants that place dining platforms across the stream in summer. Sagenta is the last of these restaurants, at the very top of the slope, and it serves kaiseki lunches year-round, as well as one-pot *nabe* (stew) dishes in fall and winter. A popular summertime specialty is *nagashi-somen* or chilled noodles that flow down a bamboo spout from the kitchen to a boat-shape trough; you catch the noodles from the trough as they float past, dip them in a sauce, and eat them with mushrooms, seasonal green vegetables, and shrimp. To get there take the Eizan Electric Railway on the Kurama Line from Demachiyanagi Station to Kibuneguchi Station, and then walk up the hill for 30 minutes or arrange for the restaurant shuttle bus to pick you up. ✉ *76 Kibune-chō, Kurama, Sakyō-ku* ☎ *075/741–2244* ✑ *Reservations essential* ▭ *AE, DC, MC, V* ⊘ *Closed periodically in winter.*

★ **$–$$$** ✕ **Azekura** (愛染倉). On the northern outskirts of Kyōto, not far from Kamigamo Jinja, Azekura serves home-style buckwheat noodles under the giant wooden beams of a 300-year-old sake warehouse. Originally built in Nara, the warehouse was moved here more than 25 years ago by kimono merchant Mikio Ichida, who also maintains a textile exhibition hall, a small museum, and a weavers' workshop within the walls of this former samurai estate. Have lunch on low stools around a small charcoal brazier or on tatami next to a window overlooking the garden and waterwheel outside. The soba noodles at Azekura have a heartier country flavor than you can find in most of the other noodle shops in town. This is a perfect place to stop while exploring the Shake-machi district around the shrine, an area in which priests and farmers have lived for more than 10 centuries. Azekura closes at 5 PM. ✉ *30 Okamoto-chō, Kamigamo, Kita-ku* ☎ *075/701–0161* ⌨ *Reservations not accepted* 🚫 *No credit cards* ⊘ *Closed Mon. No dinner.*

WHERE TO STAY

Kyōto is a tourist city, and its hotel rooms, often designed merely as places to rest at night, are small by international standards. Service in this city is impeccable; the information desks are well stocked and concierges or guest-relations managers are often available in the lobby to respond to your needs.

No other Japanese city can compete with Kyōto for style and grace. For the ultimate experience of Kyōto hospitality, you'll want to stay in a traditional ryokan, like Ryokan Yachiyo. Though often costly, a night in a ryokan guarantees you beautiful traditional Japanese surroundings, excellent service, and elegant meals. Unfortunately, ryokan owners do not always welcome foreign guests. This is because most foreigners do not understand the customs of traditional inns and are inclined to commit gaffes, such as forgetting to remove bathroom slippers. If you have your heart set on staying in a ryokan, *see* the Ryokan Etiquette box in this chapter to find out what's expected. Then have a Japanese person make the reservation for you; the ryokan will be more inclined to accept their request.

You can assume all hotel rooms have private bathrooms, air-conditioning, telephones, and televisions, unless noted otherwise. In expensive ($$$–$$$$) and moderately priced ($$) lodgings, rooms come with a hot-water thermos and tea bags or instant coffee, as well as *yukata* (cotton kimonos).

Book your stay at least a month in advance, or as early as three months ahead if you're traveling during peak spring and autumn seasons or around important Japanese holidays and festivals. Hotels in Kyōto often offer considerable discounts in summer. Keep in mind the following festival dates when making reservations: May 15, July 16–17, August 16, and October 22. Rooms will be scarce at these times.

For a short course on accommodations in Japan, *see* Lodging *in* Smart Travel Tips A to Z.

WHAT IT COSTS In yen				
$$$$	$$$	$$	$	¢
FOR 2 PEOPLE	over 22,000	18,000–22,000	12,000–18,000	8,000–12,000	under 8,000

Price categories reflect the range between the least and most expensive standard double rooms in nonholiday high season, based on the European Plan (with no meals) unless otherwise noted. Taxes (5%) and service charges are extra.

Central Kyōto

$$$$
Fodor'sChoice
★

Tawaraya (俵屋). The most famous of Kyōto's inns, this is where royalty, presidents, and dictators stay when they visit Kyōto. Celebrity guests have included Keanu Reeves and Steven Spielberg. Tawaraya was founded more than 300 years ago and is currently run by the 11th generation of the Okazaki family. The hotel's hallmark is its subdued beauty, sense of tradition, impeccable service, and splendid gardens. An example of the hotel's legendary hospitality: a piano was installed for Leonard Bernstein in a flash. Each room is unique, furnished with superb antiques from the Okazaki family collection, and the private baths are made from cedar. You can also be assured of modern comforts, like air-conditioning and Internet access. Reservations are accepted a year in advance. Dinner, costing ¥12,000 to ¥60,000, should be ordered a day in advance. ⊠ Fuyachō-Aneyakōji-agaru, Nakagyō-ku, Kyōto-shi 604-8094 ☎ 075/211–5566 ☐ 075/211–2204 ➪ 18 Japanese-style rooms ♢ In-room data ports, cable TV, laundry services, free parking ☐ AE, DC, V ⑪ EP.

$$$–$$$$
Hiiragiya (柊家旅館). For more than 150 years the Nishimura family has been welcoming dignitaries and celebrities to this elegant inn. Founded in 1818 to accommodate provincial lords visiting the capital, the inn has welcomed Charlie Chaplin, Elizabeth Taylor, and Yukio Mishima in addition to its 19th-century samurai visitors. The inn is representative of Kyōto itself in the way it skillfully combines ancient and modern. Where else could you find cedar baths with chrome taps? And look out for the lacquered gourd designed by the present owner's greatgrandfather. Not only does it turn on the lights, but it allows you to open and close the curtains by remote control. Rooms in the newer annex generally cost less than in the original building. ⊠ Nakahakusan-chō, Fuyachō-Anekōji-agaru, Nakagyō-ku, Kyōto-shi 604-8094 ☎ 075/221–1136 ☐ 075/221–1139 ⊕ www.hiiragiya.co.jp ➪ 33 Japanese-style rooms, 28 with bath ♢ Laundry facilities, concierge, Internet, free parking ☐ AE, DC, MC, V.

$$$$
Yoshikawa (吉川). This quiet, unpretentious, traditional inn is within walking distance of the downtown shopping area. Opened in the 1950s, the layout is in the sukiya-zukuri style: traditional Japanese architecture surrounded by a landscaped garden. Each tastefully decorated room has a cypress-wood bath. The room rate includes two excellent meals, which makes it more affordable than some of the more famous ryokan. Guests are served kaiseki ryōri, including tempura, in their rooms. ⊠ Tomino-kōji, Oike-sagaru, Nakagyō-ku, 604-8093 ☎ 075/221–5544 or 075/221–0052 ☐ 075/221–6805 ⊕ www.kyoto-yoshikawa.

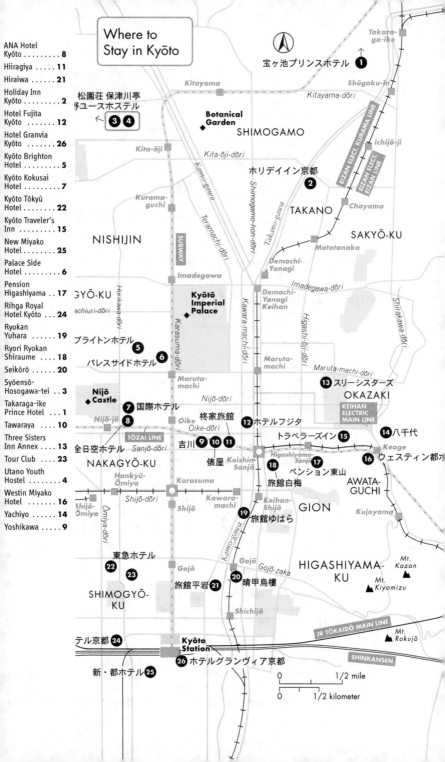

Where to Stay in Kyōto

co.jp ➷ *9 Japanese-style rooms* ☾ *Restaurant, in-room data ports, free parking* ▤ *AE, DC, MC, V* ¶⦿¶ *MAP.*

$$$$
Fodor'sChoice
★

▦ **Kyōto Brighton Hotel** (京都ブライトンホテル). The Brighton, on a quiet side street close to the Imperial Palace, is unquestionably the city's best top-end Western-style hotel. Its simple, clean design gives it an airy and spacious quality lacking in most other Kyōto hotels. Hallways circle a central atrium with glass elevators, and plants hang from the banisters of every floor. A full-service concierge desk caters to your every need. Rooms are large by Japanese standards, with separate seating areas that include a couch and TV. Forever updating and upgrading its facilities, the hotel installed a water-purification system in 2004 to keep the PH balance just right. Be sure to visit the restaurant, Hotaru, whose resident chef won the renowned (and nationally televised) Iron Chef contest for his inventive cuisine. ✉ *Nakadachiuri, Shin-machi-dōri, Kamigyō-ku, Kyōto-shi 602-8071* ☎ *075/441–4411, 800/223–6800 in U.S., 0800/181–123 in U.K.* 🖷 *075/431–2360* ⊕ *www.brightonhotels. co.jp* ➷ *183 rooms, 2 suites* ☾ *5 restaurants, cable TV, pool, hair salon, 2 bars, shops, business services, no-smoking floors* ▤ *AE, DC, MC, V.*

$$$–$$$$
▦ **Hotel Fujita Kyōto** (ホテルフジタ京都). In the light of a full moon, the waterfall in the garden sparkles while waterfowl play. The lobby is narrow and long, with comfortable gray armchairs against a fading red carpeting. The Fujita has Japanese and Scandinavian decor throughout, and 18 rooms have Japanese-style furnishings. The two main restaurants are a kaiseki dining room and a steak house with counter and table service. Not far from the nightlife center of Gion, this pleasant yet pricey hotel is along the Kamo-gawa. ✉ *Nishizume, Nijō-Ōhashi, Kamo-gawa, Nakagyō-ku, Kyōto-shi 604-0902* ☎ *075/222–1511* 🖷 *075/256–4561* ⊕ *www.fujita-kyoto.com* ➷ *171 Western-style rooms, 18 Japanese-style rooms* ☾ *6 restaurants, hair salon, bar, shops* ▤ *AE, DC, MC, V.*

★ **$$$–$$$$**
▦ **Hotel Granvia Kyōto** (ホテルグランヴィア京都). Elements of traditional Japanese interior design—dark wood, clean lines, and subdued beige tones—are combined with ultramodern touches—dark marble, quirky geometrical floor lamps (in the lobby)—at this hotel inside the Kyōto Station building. Rooms are spacious; a standard double room has two double beds, a desk, a little sitting area, and the best combination of Western- and Japanese-style bathrooms. The showerhead is mounted on the wall next to the bathtub, allowing guests to shower outside the tub and then relax in the tub as the Japanese do. Take some time to walk between the north and south towers along the glassed walkway. On the 15th floor, the sky lounge has a panoramic view of the city. As in most hotels there's a charge (¥1,000) to use the pool and gym; and no children are admitted to either. ✉ *Karasuma, Oshikoji-dori-sagaru, Shimogyō-ku, Kyōto-shi 600-8216* ☎ *075/344–8888* 🖷 *075/344–4400* ⊕ *www.granvia-kyoto.co.jp* ➷ *539 rooms* ☾ *15 restaurants, indoor pool, health club, hair salon, shops, business services* ▤ *AE, DC, MC, V.*

$$$$
▦ **Kyōto Tōkyū Hotel** (京都東急ホテル). The pillared main entrance, entrance hall, and lobby are expansive, and the courtyard, with its reflecting pool and waterfall, is a good attempt to add some drama to this otherwise ordinary redbrick chain hotel. Rooms have slightly dated furnish-

ings but are well maintained, comfortable, and spacious by Japanese standards. A shuttle bus can take you Itami Airport for ¥1,300. ⊠ *580 Kakimoto-chō, Gojō-sagaru, Horikawa-dōri, Shimogyō-ku,, Kyōto-shi 600-8519* ☎ *075/341–2411* 🖷 *075/341–2488* ⊕ *www.tokyuhotel.com* 📮 *432 rooms* ⚐ *3 restaurants, hair salon, 2 bars, shops, travel services, Internet* 🖃 *AE, DC, MC, V.*

★ **$$$** 🏨 **New Miyako Hotel** (新・都ホテル). The 10-story white edifice has two protruding wings with landscaping and street lamps reminiscent of a hotel in the United States. Its location on the south side of Kyōto Station makes it attractive if you're planning train trips from the city. A friendly guest-relations manager on hand in the bright marble lobby can help you plan your day. ⊠ *17 Nishi-Kujōin-chō, Minami-ku, Kyōto-shi 601-8412* ☎ *075/661–7111* 🖷 *075/661–7135* ⊕ *www.miyakohotels. ne.jp/newmiyako* 📮 *710 Western-style rooms, 4 Japanese-style rooms* ⚐ *7 restaurants, tea shop, in-room data ports, cable TV, hair salon, bar, shops, business services* 🖃 *AE, DC, MC, V.*

$$–$$$ 🏨 **Kyōto Kokusai Hotel** (京都国際ホテル). Across the street from Nijō-jō, Kokusai provides excellent views of the castle from the rooftop lounge and rooms on the west side, and is only a few yards from the entrance to the Nijō-jō-mae stop on the Tōzai subway line. Perhaps the best reason to choose this hotel is the Lounge Miyabi, where you can look out through large glass windows into a beautiful courtyard garden. A stage with a thatched roof and lacquered flooring floats on the garden's pond. In the daytime you can relax with matcha and a sweet while watching a single swan swim gracefully on the pond. At night, have your picture taken with a maiko. Then take your seat either inside or outside to watch her perform two dances. Pictures are taken every night from 7 to 7:20, and the performance lasts from 7:20 to 7:40. Beds swathed in golden silken duvets grace the large double rooms. Japanese-style paper screens shade the windows. Family rooms are available. ⊠ *Nijō-eki-mae, Horikawa-dori, Nakagyō-ku, Kyōto-shi 604-8502* ☎ *075/222–1111* 🖷 *075/231–9381* ⊕ *www.kyoto-kokusai.com* 📮 *277 rooms* ⚐ *5 restaurants, bar, 2 lounges, shops* 🖃 *AE, DC, MC, V.*

$$$ 🏨 **Rihga Royal Hotel Kyōto** (リーガロイヤルホテル京都). The rooms at this well-established chain hotel vary in price according to size, but even the smallest rooms don't seem claustrophobic thanks to the delicate shōji doors. Family rooms for four people are available. On the 14th floor is Kyōto's only revolving restaurant, which offers splendid views of the city. There's also a branch of the famous western Kyōto restaurant, Kitchō, on the premises. The hotel is a five-minute walk from Kyōto Station, and a shuttle bus leaves the Hachijō Exit every 15 minutes. There's a ¥1,050 charge to use the pool and sauna. ⊠ *Horikawa-Shiokōji, Shimogyō-ku, Kyōto-shi 600-8327* ☎ *075/341–1121, 800/877–7107 in U.S.* 🖷 *075/341–3073* ⊕ *www.rihga.com* 📮 *494 rooms* ⚐ *6 restaurants, coffee shop, snack bar, indoor pool, hair salon, sauna, 3 bars, shops, karaoke box, travel services, no-smoking rooms* 🖃 *AE, DC, MC, V.*

$$–$$$ 🏨 **ANA Hotel Kyōto** (京都全日空ホテル). The best thing about this hotel is its location, directly across from Nijō-jō. If your room faces the castle rather than another high-rise, you can be assured that you are indeed in Kyōto. The roof garden has spectacular 360-degree views of the city and surrounding mountains, and even from the lobby you can look out onto a pretty scene: a delicate waterfall cascading into a courtyard pond. The rooms are a bit snug, but with all this beauty around you, you may not spend much time in them. There are French, Chinese, and Japanese restaurants. ⊠ *Nijō-jō-mae, Horikawa-dōri, Nakagyō-ku, Kyōto-shi 604-0055* ☎ *075/231–1155* 🖷 *075/231–5333* ⊕ *www.anahkyoto.com* ⬐ *303 rooms* ⌂ *7 restaurants, indoor pool, health club, 1 bar, shops* ▤ *AE, DC, MC, V.*

$ 🏠 **Hiraiwa** (旅館平岩). Imagine the ambience of a friendly Western-style youth hostel with tatami-mat rooms, and you have the Hiraiwa ryokan, a member of the hospitable and economical Japanese Inn Group. To be a member, inns must have English-speaking staff and provide clean comfortable accommodations. Hiraiwa is the most popular of these inns in Kyōto; it's a great place to meet fellow travelers from around the world. Rules and regulations governing your stay are posted on the walls. Guests are welcome to eat with the owners in the small kitchen. The inn has shared toilets and showers. ⊠ *314 Hayao-chō, Kaminoguchi-agaru, Ninomiya-chō-dōri, Shimogyō-ku, Kyōto-shi 600-8114* ☎ *075/351–6748* ⊕ *www2.odn.ne.jp/hiraiwa* ⬐ *21 Japanese-style rooms without bath* ⌂ *Japanese baths; no room TVs, no room phones* ▤ *AE, MC, V.*

★ ¢ 🏠 **Palace Side Hotel** (パレスサイドホテル). A budget traveler's dream, this hotel is centrally located, on the east side of the Imperial Palace, and it has excellent facilities, including a communal kitchen, laundry room, and two meeting rooms. Guest rooms are tiny, of course, but they are spotless and perfectly acceptable. Larger family rooms are available, and there are discounts for stays longer than three nights. Masseurs that specialize in Thai massage are on hand to bring you pain relief and relaxation. Breakfast is ¥1,050 per person, and you can eat at outdoor tables. ⊠ *Karasuma-dōri, Shimō-dachiuri-agaru, Kamigyō-ku 602-8011* ☎ *075/ 415–8887* 🖷 *075/415–8889* ⊕ *www.palacesidehotel.co.jp* ⬐ *120 rooms* ⌂ *Restaurant, some kitchenettes, Internet, parking (fee)* ▤ *AE, DC, MC, V.*

¢ 🏠 **Tour Club.** Tatami mats cover the floors, Japanese paintings are on the walls, and there's even a pretty little garden in this hotel, formerly an apartment building. The rooms are small flatlets with futons, kettles, and private bathrooms. The communal kitchen, living room, laundry room, and Internet station encourage you to meet other guests and talk to the staff, who all speak English and can provide sightseeing advice. Tea and coffee are always available for free, and there are bikes for rent. Tour Club is a 10-minute walk from Kyōto Station. ⊠ *362 Momiji-chō, Kitakōji-agaru, Higashinakasuji-dōri, Shimogyō-ku, 600-8345* ☎ *075/353–6968* ⊕ *www.kyotojp.com* ⬐ *11 rooms, 2 dormitories* ⌂ *Internet; no room TVs, no room phones* ▤ *No credit cards.*

Eastern Kyōto

★ $$$$ 🏠 **Ryori Ryokan Shiraume** (旅館白梅). The White Plum Inn is reached by crossing a small footbridge over a tiny canal in one of the old pleasure quarters of Gion. Before the war this was a famous *o-chaya,* or teahouse where geisha parties were often held. Rooms are all different sizes, and the best one, at the end of the downstairs corridor, overlooks a tsuboniwa small courtyard garden. Breakfast and dinner are included, though it's possible to arrange a stay without meals. Shinbashi-dōri is a gorgeous location not much changed in 140 years and the accommodating owner, a former flight attendant, speaks English. ⊠ *Gionmachi, Shirakawa-hotori, Shinbashi-dōri, Higashiyama-ku, Kyōto-shi 605-0080* ☎ *075/561–1459* ⤵ *8 Japanese-style rooms without bath* ♨ *Japanese baths* ⊟ *AE, DC, MC, V* ⦿ *MAP.*

★ **$$$$** ⊡ **Seikōrō** (晴鴨楼). This lovely inn, established in 1831, is a short walk from busy Gojō Station, a convenience that makes it popular among both gaijin and Japanese. A local resident who speaks English fluently manages the ryokan. Among the interesting decor are Western antiques that mysteriously blend in quite well with the otherwise traditional setting. When you return to Seikōrō after a day of sightseeing, you may get the distinct feeling that you're returning to your Japanese home. No meals are included in the rate. ⊠ *Toiya-machi-dōri, Gojō-sagaru, Higashiyama-ku, Kyōto-shi 605-0907* ☎ *075/561–0771* ⤶ *075/541–5481* ⤵ *23 Japanese-style rooms* ⊟ *AE, DC, MC, V.*

$$$$ ⊡ **Yachiyo** (八千代). Carefully shaped bushes, pine trees, and rocks surround the woodwork and low-hanging tiled eaves of the special entrance to this ryokan, and the sidewalk from the gate curves into the doorway. Yachiyo is less expensive than its brethren in the deluxe category but nevertheless provides fine attentive care. Perhaps the biggest draw of the inn is its proximity to Nanzen-ji, one of the most appealing temples in Kyōto. Rooms without private baths are much less expensive than rooms that overlook the garden. Breakfast and dinner are included in the rates, but you can negotiate lower rates by choosing not to dine here. ⊠ *34 Nanzen-ji-fukuchi-chō, Sakyō-ku, Kyōto-shi 606-8435* ☎ *075/771–4148* ⤶ *075/771–4140* ⊕ *www.ryokan-yachiyo.com* ⤵ *25 rooms, 20 with bath* ♨ *Restaurant, Japanese baths* ⊟ *AE, DC, MC, V* ⦿ *MAP.*

$$$–$$$$
Fodor's Choice
★
⊡ **Westin Miyako Hotel** (ウェスティン都ホテル). The Miyako, grande dame of Kyōto hotels, first opened in the early 1900s and underwent its most recent renovation in 2001. Perched atop Mt. Kacho near the Eastern temples, the hotel has a walking trail, several Japanese gardens, and indoor and outdoor pools (free for guests). Twenty Japanese-style rooms in two annexes retain the feel of a traditional ryokan. Western-style rooms in the south wing are large and tastefully furnished. Other Western-style rooms that were not renovated in 2001 are smaller and tired but less expensive. A free shuttle bus runs to the station via the downtown shopping district, a 20 minute ride. ⊠ *Sanjō-Keage, Higashiyama-ku, Kyōto-shi 605-0052* ☎ *075/771–7111* ⤶ *075/751–2490* ⊕ *www. westinmiyako-kyoto.com* ⤵ *300 Western-style rooms, 20 Japanese-style rooms* ♨ *8 restaurants, coffee shop, 2 pools, gym, 2 bars, shops, business services* ⊟ *AE, DC, MC, V.*

$$ ⊡ **Holiday Inn Kyōto** (ホリデイイン京都). This member of the American chain is in a residential area surrounded by small modern houses, occasionally interrupted by large traditional estates. A free shuttle bus makes the 30-minute run to and from Kyōto Station every 90 minutes. Eastern and northern Kyōto sites are within a few miles of the hotel, but it takes a 15-minute taxi ride to get downtown. The Holiday Inn has the best sports facilities of any hotel in Kyōto but will charge you ¥3,200

RYOKAN ETIQUETTE

UPON ENTERING, *take off your shoes, as you would do in a Japanese household, and put on the slippers that are provided in the entryway. A maid, after bowing to welcome you, will escort you to your room, which will have tatami (straw mats) on the floor and will probably be partitioned off with shōji (sliding paper-paneled walls). Remove your slippers before entering your room; you should not step on the tatami with either shoes or slippers. The room will have little furniture or decoration—perhaps one small low table and cushions on the tatami, with a long, simple scroll on the wall. Often the rooms overlook a garden.*

Plan to arrive in the late afternoon, as is the custom. After relaxing with a cup of green tea, have a long, hot bath. In ryokan with thermal pools, you can take to the waters anytime, although the doors to the pool are usually locked from 11 PM to 6 AM. In ryokan without thermal baths or private baths in guest rooms, guests must stagger visits to the one or two public baths. Typically the maid will ask what time you would like your bath and fit you into a schedule. In Japanese baths, washing and soaking are separate functions: wash and rinse off entirely, and then get in the tub. Be sure to keep all soap out of the tub. Because other guests will be using the same bathwater after you, it is important to observe this custom. After your bath, change into a yukata, a simple cotton kimono, provided in your room. Don't worry about walking around in what is essentially a robe—all other guests will be doing the same.

Dinner, included in the price, is served in your room at smaller and more personal ryokan; at larger ryokan, especially the newer ones, meals will be in the dining room. After you are finished, a maid will discreetly come in, clear away the dishes, and lay out your futon. In Japan futon means bedding, and this consists of a thin cotton mattress and a heavy, thick comforter. In summer the comforter is replaced with a thinner quilt. The small, hard pillow is filled with grain. The less expensive ryokan (under ¥7,000 for one) have become slightly lackadaisical in changing the sheet cover over the quilt with each new guest; feel free to complain (in as inoffensive a way as possible, of course, so as not to shame the proprietor). In the morning a maid will gently wake you, clear away the futon, and bring in your Japanese-style breakfast. If you are not fond of Japanese breakfasts, which often consist of fish, pickled vegetables, and rice, the staff will usually be able to rustle up some coffee and toast.

Because most ryokan staffs are small and dedicated, it is important to be considerate and understanding of their somewhat rigid schedules. Guests are expected to arrive in the late afternoon and eat around 6. Usually the doors to the inn are locked at 10, so plan for early evenings. Breakfast is served around 8, and checkout is at 10.

Bear in mind that not all inns are willing to accept foreign guests because of language and cultural barriers. Also, top-level ryokan expect even new Japanese guests to have introductions and references from a respected client of the inn, which means that you, too, might need an introduction from a Japanese for very top-level ryokan. On the other side of this issue, inns that do accept foreigners without introduction sometimes treat them as cash cows, which means giving you cursory service and a lesser room. When you reserve a room, try to have a Japanese make the call for you, or you can do it yourself if you know Japanese; this will convey the idea that you understand the customs of staying in a traditional inn.

per day to use them, including the pool. ⊠ *36 Nishihiraki-chō, Takano, Sakyō-ku, Kyōto-shi 606-8103* ☎ *075/721–3131* 🖷 *075/781–6178* ⊕ *www.hi-kyoto.co.jp* 🛏 *150 rooms* ♨ *3 restaurants, coffee shop, tennis court, indoor pool, gym, sauna, 2 bars, shops, laundry services, business services, free parking* ▤ *AE, DC, MC, V.*

$$ 🖼 **Kyōto Traveler's Inn** (京都トラベラーズイン). This no-frills modern inn is in the perfect spot for sightseeing, with Heian Jingū, Nanzen-ji, and the museums in Okazaki Park minutes away on foot. Its Western-style and Japanese-style rooms are plain and small but clean and practical; all have a private bath and toilet. Ask for a room with a view (most don't have one). Because of its location, size, and price, the hotel often hosts large travel groups. Head for the coffee shop on the first floor to look out over the river and plot your course for the day. In contrast to some of Kyōto's other budget inns, this one imposes no curfew. ⊠ *Heian Jingū Torii-mae, Okazaki, Sakyō-ku, Kyōto-shi 606-8344* ☎ *075/771–0225* ⊕ *www.kid97.co.jp/traveler.html* 🛏 *40 Western-style rooms, 38 Japanese-style rooms* ♨ *Coffee shop, meeting room, parking (fee)* ▤ *AE, MC, V* ¶◯∦ *EP.*

$$ 🖼 **Pension Higashiyama** (ペンション東山). About a kilometer from downtown and close to the major temples along the eastern foothills, this tiny pension overlooks the lovely Shira-kawa Canal, south of Sanjō-dōri. The pension has created a friendly atmosphere for families on a budget and is accustomed to gaijin. Several rooms have tatami and three rooms have a private baths. The curfew is 11:30 PM. ⊠ *474–23 Umemiya-chō, Shirakawa-suji, Sanjō-sagaru, Higashiyama-ku, Kyōto-shi 605-0061* ☎ *075/ 882–1181* ⊕ *www.kid97.co.jp/st-kyoto* 🛏 *15 rooms, 3 with bath* ♨ *Dining room* ▤ *AE* ¶◯∦ *EP.*

$$ 🖼 **Three Sisters Inn Annex** (Rakutō-sō Bekkan, スリーシスターズ洛東荘別館). A traditional inn popular with gaijin for decades, the annex—which is nicer than the main branch—sits on the northeast edge of Heian Jingū, down a trellised path that hides it from the street. This is a quiet and friendly place, and a good introduction to inn customs because the management is accustomed to foreign guests. On the down side, the rooms could use refurbishment, and the doors close at 11:30 PM sharp. Some rooms have baths and overlook the garden. ⊠ *Heian Jingū, Higashi-kita-kado, Sakyō-ku, Kyōto-shi 606-8322* ☎ *075/761–6333* 🖷 *075/761–6335* 🛏 *12 rooms, 3 with bath* ♨ *Dining room, Japanese baths* ▤ *AE, DC.*

$–$$ 🖼 **Ryokan Yuhara** (旅館ゆはら). Yuhara draws repeat visitors wishing to save a few yen while exploring Kyōto. The friendliness of the staff more than compensates for the spartan amenities. Especially rewarding is a springtime stay, when the cherry trees are in full bloom along the Takasegawa, which the inn overlooks. This is a 15-minute walk from Gion and Ponto-chō. No meals are served and baths are communal. ⊠ *188 Kagiya-chō, Shomen-agaru, Kiya-machi-dōri, Higashiyama-ku, Kyōto-shi 605-0909* ☎ *075/371–9583* 🛏 *8 Japanese-style rooms* ♨ *Japanese baths* ▤ *No credit cards.*

Northern Kyōto

★ **$$$–$$$$** 🖼 **Takaraga-ike Prince Hotel** (宝ヶ池プリンスホテル). Although some distance north of the center, this deluxe hotel is close to the Kokusaikaikan subway station and is especially convenient for the nearby International Conference Hall. Its unusual doughnut-shape design provides each room with a view of the surrounding mountains and forests. Inside corridors overlook an inner garden. The tasteful spacious guest rooms are decorated with colors that complement the greenery of the outside views, and all have beds that are probably the largest you can find in Japan. Details include impressive chandeliers all around the building, Miró prints hanging in every suite, and an authentic teahouse beside a pond. Demonstrations of the tea ceremony can be arranged on request. The hotel offers discounts in summer; check out the Web site for special packages. Breakfast is buffet style. ⊠ *Takaraga-ike, Sakyō-ku, Kyōto-shi 606-8505* ☎ *075/712–1111, 800/542–8686 in U.S.* 🖷 *075/ 712–7677* ⊕ *www2.princehotels.co.jp* ⇨ *322 rooms* ♨ *3 restaurants, tea shop, 2 bars, Internet* ▭ *AE, DC, MC, V* ⊙I *BP.*

Western Kyōto

$$$$ ☒ **Syōensō-Hosogawa-tei** (松園荘 保津川亭). In the *onsen* (hot springs) village of Yunohana in the mountains of Tamba northwest of Kyōto, this hotel allows you to soak in your own *rotemburo* (outdoor bath) overlooking a private garden. If you're feeling adventurous you can get into the full swing of an onsen visit by joining other guests in one of the communal baths (separated by gender). The building itself looks like something out of *The Twilight Zone,* but the *machiya* (layers of sliding paper screens) facade of the lobby and the steps bordered on one side by a gently sloping waterfall suggest Old Kyōto. A kaiseki dinner is prepared with seasonal favorites, including Tamba boar in winter. An overnight stay at the hotel complements a trip to Arashiyama. For ¥600 you can take the scenic Sagano Torokko train, which leaves Saga Torokko Station in Arashiyama six minutes before the hour for the 20-minute ride to Kameoka, where Yunohana is located. Call ahead to ask the hotel shuttle bus to meet you at the station. To return to Arashiyama, take the Hosogawa-kudari boat the next day. Alternatively, you can take the JR line between Kameoka and Kyōto stations. ⊠ *Kameoka City, Yunohana-onsen, 621-0034* ☎ *0771/22–0903* 🖷 *0771/23–6572* ⊕ *www. syoenso.com* ⇨ *56 Japanese-style rooms, 7 with bath* ♨ *Restaurant, sauna, 2 lounges, shops, hot springs* ▭ *AE, MC, V* ⊙I *MAP.*

$ ☒ **Utano Youth Hostel** (宇多野ユースホステル). If you like the onsen feel without the onsen price, try the Utano, which provides a communal, indoor hot-spring bath. Near Kinkaku-ji and Ryōan-ji, the hostel is convenient for sightseeing in Arashiyama and western Kyōto. There are double rooms and dormitory-style rooms with bunk beds for up to eight people. Some have televisions. Sip tea or coffee with the other guests every night from 10 to 10:30. The friendly staff speaks English. Dinner and breakfast are served for a nominal additional fee, and you can even rent a bicycle here for ¥600 a day. Internet access is available. ⊠ *29 Nakayama-chō, Uzumasa, Ukyō-ku, Kyōto-shi 6160-8191* ☎ *075/ 462–2288* 🖷 *075/462–2289* ⊕ *http://web.kyoto-inet.or.jp/org/utano-yh.* ⇨ *25 rooms without bath* ♨ *Cafeteria, tennis court, bicycles, laundry facilities, hot springs, Japanese baths* ▭ *AE, MC, V.*

NIGHTLIFE & THE ARTS

The Arts

Kyōto is quickly following Tōkyō and Ōsaka on domestic and international performing artists' circuits. The city has hosted the likes of Bruce Springsteen, but it's better known for its traditional performances—dance and Kabuki and Nō theater. All dialogue at theaters is in Japanese, of course. *See also* Chapter 16 for descriptions of Japanese performing arts.

Information on performances is available from a number of sources; the most convenient is your hotel concierge or guest-relations manager, who may even have a few tickets on hand, so don't hesitate to ask. For further information on Kyōto's arts scene check the music and theater sections of the monthly magazine *Kansai Time Out,* at bookshops for ¥300; you can also find information on the Web site www.kto.co.jp. Another source is the *Kyōto Visitor's Guide,* which devotes a few pages to "This Month's Theater." Look at the festival listings for temple and shrine performances. It's available free from the Kyōto Tourist Information Center on the 9th floor of the Kyōto Station building. It's strongly suggested that you stop by the TIC if you're interested in the performing arts in Kyōto, but if you don't have time to visit in person, you can call.

Gion Corner

Some call it a tourist trap, but for others it's a comprehensive introduction to Japanese performing arts. The one-hour show combines court music and dance, ancient comic plays, Kyōto-style dance performed by *maiko* (apprentice geisha), and puppet drama. Segments are also offered on the tea ceremony, flower arrangement, and koto music.

Before attending a show, walk around Gion and Ponto-chō. You're likely to see beautifully dressed geisha and maiko making their way to work. It's permissible to take their picture—"*Shashin o totte mō ii desu ka?*" is the polite way to ask—but as they have strict appointments, don't delay them.

An even less expensive introduction to geisha arts can be had at the **Kyōto Kokusai Hotel** (⊠ Horikawa, Nijō-jō-mae, Kamigyō-ku ☎ 075/222–1111), which has free maiko dance performances in its first-floor lounge every evening from 7:20 to 7:40. The hotel is opposite Nijō-jō.

For tickets to Gion Corner contact your hotel concierge or call the theater directly. The show costs ¥2,800—a bargain considering that it would usually cost 10 times as much to watch maiko and geisha perform. Two performances are held nightly at 7:40 and 8:40 March–November. No performances are offered August 16. ⊠ *Yasaka Hall, 1st fl., Gion, Higashiyama-ku* ☎ *075/561–1119.*

Seasonal Dances

In the **Miyako Odori** in April, and the **Kamo-gawa Odori** in May and October, geisha and maiko dances and songs pay tribute to the seasonal splendor of spring and fall. The stage settings are spectacular.

Tickets to performances at the **Gion Kaburenjō Theater** (✉ Gion Hanami kōji, Higashiyama-ku ☎ 075/561–1115) cost ¥1,900, ¥3,800, and ¥4,300. Tickets at the **Ponto-chō Kaburenjō Theater** (✉ Ponto-chō, Sanjō sagaru, Nakagyō-ku ☎ 075/221–2025) cost ¥1,650 to ¥3,800.

Kabuki

Kabuki has found quite a following in the United States due to tours by Japanese Kabuki troupes in Washington, D.C., New York, and a few other cities. Kabuki is faster paced than Nō, but a single performance can easily take half a day. Devoted followers pack bentō and sit patiently through the entire performance, mesmerized by each movement of the performers.

For a first-timer, however, the music and unique intonations of Kabuki might be a bit of an overload. Unless you're captured by the Kabuki spirit, don't spend more than an hour or two at Kyōto's famed **Minami-za** (✉ Shijō Kamo-gawa, Higashiyama-ku ☎ 075/561–1155), the oldest theater in Japan. Beautifully renovated, it hosts a variety of performances year-round. Top Kabuki stars from around the country make guest appearances during the annual monthlong **Kaomise** (Face Showing) Kabuki Festival, in December. Tickets range from ¥4,000 to ¥9,000.

Nō

A form of traditional theater, Nō is more ritualistic and sophisticated than Kabuki. Some understanding of the plot of each play is necessary to enjoy a performance, which is generally slow moving and solemnly chanted. The carved masks used by the main actors express a whole range of emotions, though the mask itself may appear expressionless until the actor "brings it to life." Nō performances are held year-round and range from ¥4,000 to ¥6,000. Particularly memorable are outdoor performances of Nō, especially **Takigi Nō**, held outdoors by firelight on the nights of June 1–2 in the precincts of the Heian Jingū. For more information about the performances, contact the tourist information center.

Kanze Kaikan Nō Theater. This is the older of Kyōto's two Nō theaters, and it sometimes hosts Nō orientation talks. The theater does not offer programs in English. ✉ *44 Enshōji-chō, Okazaki, Sakyō-ku ☎ 075/ 771–6114.*

Shin Kongo Nō Theater. ✉ *Karasuma-dōri, Ichijō-sagaru, Kamigyō-ku ☎ 075/441–7222.*

Nightlife

Though Kyōto's nightlife is more sedate than Ōsaka's, the areas around the old geisha quarters downtown thrive with nightclubs and bars. The Kiya-machi area along the small canal near Ponto-chō is as close to a consolidated nightlife area as you'll get in Kyōto. It's full of small watering holes with red lanterns (indicating inexpensive places) or small neon signs in front. It's also fun to walk around the Gion and Ponto-chō areas to try to catch a glimpse of a geisha or maiko stealing down an alleyway on her way to or from an appointment.

Café Independents. As its name suggests, this bar hosts a spectrum of indie rock, jazz, and blues artists, making it a good place to tap into the underground music scene. Trestle tables line the graffiti-covered walls of this basement venue. ⊠ *1928 Bldg., Sanjō-dōri, Nakagyō-ku* ☎ *075/255–4312.*

Le Club Jazz. You can hear live jazz, blues, and soul gigs on Tuesday, jam sessions every night from Thursday to Monday. There's a ¥2,000 cover charge including two drinks on weekends. ⊠ *Sanjō Arimoto Bldg., 2nd fl., Sanjō-Gokōmachi Nishi-Iru, Kamigyō-ku* ☎ *075/211–5800.*

Live Spot Rag. A more sophisticated dinner and jazz bar north of Sanjō-dōri, Live Spot Rag has cover charges starting from ¥2,000 for its live sessions that run from 7 to 11 nightly. Reserving a table is recommended. ⊠ *Kyōto Empire Bldg., 5th fl., Kiya-machi, Kamigyō-ku* ☎ *075/241–0446.*

Mamma Zappa. An arty crowd munches on Indonesian food while sipping cocktails at this bar. David Bowie came in for a drink at Mamma Zappa while visiting Kyōto. ⊠ *Takoyakushi-dōri, off Kawara-machi-dōri, south of Maruzen, Nakagyō-ku* ☎ *075/255–4437.*

Sesamo. Worn leather chairs line the counter of this stylish bar and restaurant. Flamenco guitar and jazz musicians play on Friday and Saturday. You can order tapas with your rioja, and as in Madrid, you can stay late. ⊠ *Ebisukaikan, Kawara-machi, Sanjo-agaru, Nakagyō-ku* ☎ *075/251–0858.*

★ **Tadg's Irish Pub.** North of the Minamiza Theatre in Gion, this convivial pub entertains patrons with Irish music and sporting events on TV. The menu offers classic fish-and-chips, plus Irish stew and a beef and Guiness pie. ⊠ *236 Ōtobiru 2F, Nijuichiken-chō, Yamato-ōji, Kawabata Shijō-agaru, Higashiyama-ku* ☎ *075/525–0680* ⊕ *www.tadgspub.com.*

★ **Taku Taku.** This bar is an enduring live music venue tending toward rock and blues. You can find it in an old *kura,* or storehouse, in the backstreets southwest of the Takashimaya department store. ⊠ *Tominokōji-dōri, Bukkōji-sagaru, Shimogyō-ku* ☎ *075/351–1321.*

Tranq Room. With ambient lighting and cream vinyl sofas (autographed by Vincent Gallo), Tanq Room takes a stab at Japanese minimalism then adds a modern twist. It's a good place to relax over a cocktail and snacks. The music ranges from world to funk. ⊠ *162–2 Shinnyo-chō, Shirakawa-dōri, Jōdo-ji, Sakyō-ku* ☎ *075/762–4888.*

Yoramu. Israeli sake aficionado Yoram has an extensive range of the delicate rice wine, from unfiltered to aged, fruity to dry, all available by the glass. A tasting set of three kinds of sake starts at ¥900. The dishes on the menu have all been chosen to complement the drink. The cozy bar is south of Nijō-dōri, east of Higashino-tōin-dōri. ⊠ *Nijō-dōri, Nakagyō-ku* ☎ *075/213–1512.*

★ **Metro.** One of the best clubs in Kansai, Metro has an extremely wide range of regular events, from salsa to reggae, as well as frequent guest appearances by famous DJs from Tōkyō and abroad. ⊠ *Ebisu Bldg.,*

2nd fl., 82 Shimotsutsumi-chō, Maruta-machi-sagaru, Kawabata-dōri, Sakyō-ku ☎ 075/752–4765.

SPORTS & THE OUTDOORS

Biking

Bicycling is a fine way to get around Kyōto, and you can have a bicycle delivered anywhere in the city from **Kyoto Tour Cycling Project** (KCTP ✉ 552–13 Higashi-Aburanokōji-chō, Aburanokōji-dōri, Shiokō-ji-sagaru, Shimogyō-ku ☎ 075/354–3636 ⊕ www.kctp.net). Rentals start at ¥1,000 (¥1,500 for a mountain bike) per day and include a map of suggested routes. KCTP also offers reduced weekly rentals and bike tours. **Rental Cycle Yasumoto Kawabata** (✉ Kawabata-dōri, just north of Sanjō-dōri, Higashiyama-ku ☎ 075/751–0595) rents bikes downtown for ¥1,000 per day from Monday to Saturday, 9 to 5.

Boating

You can rent a rowboat in Arashiyama and row on the Ōi-gawa while enjoying a view of the mountains. **Arashiyama Tsūsen** (✉ 14-4 Nakaoshita-chō, Arashiyama, Nishigyō-ku ☎ 075/861–0223), near Togetsu-kyō Bridge, rents rowboats for ¥1,400 an hour.

Martial Arts

If you're interested in or practice a martial art, such as *kyūdō* (Japanese archery) and *kendō* (Japanese fencing), request a list of *dojos* that can be visited from the **Kyōto Tourist Information Center** (✉ 9F JR Kyōto Station building, Kyōto International Prefectural Center, Karasuma-dōri, Shimogyō-ku ☎ 075/344–3300 ⊕ www.kyoto-kankou.or.jp).

Running & Walking

Broad pathways along the banks of the **Kamo-gawa,** from Kita-ōji-dōri in the north to Shijō-dōri in the south, accommodate joggers, walkers, and occasionally groups practicing tai chi.

Swimming

Pool admissions are pricey in Kyōto and require some travel. The Kyōto Tourist Information Center can provide a list of pools open to the public.

One of the cheaper options is **Fushimikō Kōen** (✉ Yoshijima, Hanaidō-chō, Fushimi-ku ☎ 075/611–7081), which has an outdoor pool open from late July to the end of August and an indoor pool open year-round. Both are closed Tuesday. The cost to swim is ¥600 for adults and ¥450 for children, and the park is a short walk from Keihan Chūshojima.

From May to September, try the indoor **Kyōto Aquarena** (✉ 61 Dango-den-chō, Tokudaiji, Nishikyōgoku, Ukyō-ku ☎ 075/315–4800). It's open Wednesday through Sunday until 9 PM, and the cost is ¥800 for adults and ¥400 for children. The Aquarena is a five-minute walk from Hankyū Nishikyōgoku Station.

SHOPPING

Most shops slide their doors open at 10, and many shopkeepers partake of the morning ritual of sweeping and watering the entrance to welcome the morning's first customers. Shops lock up at 6 or 7 in the evening. Stores often close sporadically once or twice a month, so it's a good idea to call in advance if you're making a special trip. As Sunday is a big shopping day for the Japanese, most stores remain open.

The traditional greeting of a shopkeeper to a customer is *o-ideyasu* (Kyōto-ben, the Kyōto dialect for "honored to have you here"), voiced in a lilting Kyōto dialect with the required bowing of the head. When a customer makes a purchase, the shopkeeper will respond with *o-okini* ("thank you" in Kyōto-ben), a smile, and a bow. Take notice of the careful effort and adroitness with which purchases are wrapped; it's an art in itself. American Express, MasterCard, Visa, and traveler's checks are widely accepted.

If you plan to make shopping one of your prime pursuits in Kyōto, look for a copy of Diane Durston's thorough *Old Kyōto: A Guide to Traditional Shops, Restaurants, and Inns* (Kodansha America, 1986). The free monthly *Kyoto Visitor's Guide* is an excellent up-to-date resource.

Shopping Districts

Compared with sprawling Tōkyō, Kyōto is compact and relatively easy to navigate. Major shops line both sides of **Shijō-dōri,** which runs east–west, and **Kawara-machi-dōri,** which runs north–south. Concentrate on Shijō-dōri between Yasaka Jinja and Karasuma Station as well as Kawara-machi-dōri between Sanjō-dōri and Shijō-dōri.

Some of modern Kyōto's shopping districts are to be found underground. **Porta,** under Kyōto Station, hosts more than 200 shops and restaurants in a sprawling subterranean arcade.

Roads leading to Kiyomizu-dera run uphill, yet you may hardly notice the steepness for all of the alluring shops that line the way. Be sure to peek in for unique gifts. Food shops offer sample morsels, and tea shops serve complimentary cups of tea.

Shin-Kyōgoku, a covered arcade running between Teramachi-dōri and Kawara-machi-dōri, is another general-purpose shopping area with many souvenir shops.

Crafts Centers

The **Kyōto Craft Center,** on Shijō-dōri in Gion, has two floors of contemporary and traditional crafts for sale in a modern setting. More than 100 crafts studios are represented, giving a diversity to the products for sale. ⊠ *Shijō-dōri, Gion-machi, Higashiyama-ku* ☎ *075/561–9660* ☉ *Thurs.–Tues. 11–7.*

★ The **Kyōto Handicraft Center** is a seven-story shopping emporium with a vast selection of crafts, including cloisonné and pearl jewelry, porcelain, lacquerware, woodblock prints, kimonos, and much more. It's a good place to compare prices and grab last-minute souvenirs. ⊠ *Kumano*

Jinja Higashi, Sakyō-ku ☎ *075/761–5080* ☉ *Feb.–Dec., daily 9:30–6; Jan., daily 9:30–5:30.*

Depāto

Kyōto *depāto* (department stores) are small in comparison to their mammoth counterparts in Tōkyō and Ōsaka. They still carry a wide range of goods and are great places for one-stop souvenir shopping. Wandering around the food halls (in all but Hankyū) is also a good way to build up an appetite. Prices drop dramatically during end-of-season sales. Note that all the stores close irregularly for a few days each month. You can call at the beginning of the month to find out about scheduled closures.

Daimaru mainly appeals to a more expensive and conservative taste and is on the main Shijō-dōri shopping avenue. Its basement food hall is the best in town. ✉ *Shijō-Karasuma, Shimogyō-ku* ☎ *075/211–8111* ☉ *Daily 10–7:30.*

Hankyū, directly across from Takashimaya on Kawara-machi-dōri, has two restaurant floors. Window displays show the type of food served, and prices are clearly marked. ✉ *Shijō-kawara-machi, Shimogyō-ku* ☎ *075/223–2288* ☉ *Daily 10–7:30.*

Isetan, in the Kyōto Station building, has 13 floors, including a restaurant floor, a cosmetics floor, an amusement arcade, and an art gallery. It closes periodically on Tuesday. ✉ *Karasuma-dōri, Shimogyō-ku* ☎ *075/352–1111* ☉ *Daily 10–7:30.*

Kintetsu is on Karasuma-dōri, the avenue leading north from Kyōto Station. Like Isetan, it carries several foreign labels, like Gap, plus trendy Japanese labels popular with the younger set. ✉ *Karasuma-dōri, Shimogyō-ku* ☎ *075/361–1111* ☉ *Daily 10–7:30.*

Takashimaya, on Kawara-machi-dōri, is Japan's most established and sophisticated depāto, with designer and luxury goods at matching prices. You'll find accommodating English-speaking salespeople and a convenient money-exchange counter. ✉ *Shijō-kawara-machi, Shimogyō-ku* ☎ *075/221–8811* ☉ *Daily 10–7:30.*

Markets

Contact the **Kyōto Tourist Information Center** (✉ 9F JR Kyōto Station building, Kyōto International Prefectural Center, Karasuma-dōri, Shimogyō-ku ☎ 075/344–3300 ⊕ www.kyoto-kankou.or.jp) for information about seasonal antiques fairs, usually held in May, June, and October.

Kyōto has a wonderful food market, **Nishiki-kōji,** which is north of Shijō-dōri and branches off from the Teramachi-dōri covered arcade in central Kyōto. Look for delicious grilled fish dipped in soy for a tasty snack or fresh Kyotō sweets. Try to avoid the market in late afternoon, when housewives come to do their daily shopping. The market is long and narrow; in a sizable crowd there's always the possibility of being pushed into the display of fresh fish. ✉ *Nishiki-kōji-dōri, Nakagyō-ku.*

Temple Markets

Several temple markets take place in Kyōto each month. These are great places to pick up bargain kimonos or unusual souvenirs. They're also some of the best spots for people-watching.

The largest and most famous temple market is the one at **Tō-ji** (⇨ Central & Southern Kyōto), which takes place on the 21st of each month. Hundreds of stalls display fans, kimonos, antiques, and trinkets, which attract many collectors. The temple also hosts a smaller market on the first Sunday of the month. ⊠ *1 Kujō-chō, Minami-ku.*

The flea market at **Kitano Tenman-gū** (⇨ Western Kyōto) is held on the 25th of each month. ⊠ *Imakoji-agaru, Onmae-dori, Kamigyō-ku.*

A market specializing in homemade goods is held at **Chion-in** on the 15th of each month. To get to the Chion-ji market, take Bus 206 from Kyōto Station to Hyakumanben. ⊠ *400 Hayashi-shita-chō 3-chōme, Yamato-ōji, Higashi-hairu, Shimbashi-dōri, Higashiyama-ku.*

Traditional Items & Gift Ideas

Art & Antiques

Nawate-dōri between Shijō-dōri and Sanjō-dōri is noted for fine antique textiles, ceramics, and paintings. ⊠ *Higashiyama-ku.*

Shinmonzen-dōri holds the key to shopping for art and antiques in Kyōto. It's an unpretentious little street of two-story wooden buildings between Higashi-ōji-dōri and Hanami-kōji-dōri, just north of Gion. What gives the street away as a treasure trove are the large credit-card signs jutting out from the shops. There are no fewer than 17 shops specializing in scrolls, *netsuke* (small carved figures to attach to Japanese clothing), lacquerware, bronze, wood-block prints, paintings, and antiques. Shop with confidence, because shopkeepers are trustworthy and goods are authentic. Pick up a copy of the pamphlet *Shinmonzen Street Shopping Guide* from your hotel or from the Tourist Information Center. ⊠ *Higashiyama-ku.*

Tera-machi-dōri between Oike-dōri and Maruta-machi is known for antiques of all kinds and tea-ceremony utensils. ⊠ *Nakagyō-ku.*

Bamboo

The Japanese wish their sons and daughters to be as strong and flexible as bamboo. Around many Japanese houses are small bamboo groves, for the deep-rooted plant withstands earthquakes. On the other hand, bamboo is so flexible it can bend into innumerable shapes. Bamboo groves flourish on the hillsides surrounding Kyōto. The wood is carefully cut and dried for several months before being stripped and woven into baskets and vases.

Kagoshin has been in operation since 1862. Basket weavers here use more than 50 varieties of bamboo in intricate designs. ⊠ *Ōhashi-higashi, Sanjō-dōri, Higashiyama-ku* ☎ *075/771–0209* ⊙ *Mon.–Sat. 9–6.*

Ceramics

Asahi-do, in the heart of the pottery district near Kiyomizu-dera, specializes in Kyōto-style hand-painted porcelain, and offers the widest selection of any pottery store in the area. ⊠ *1–280 Kiyomizu, Higashiyama-ku* ☎ *075/531–2181* ⊙ *Daily 9–6.*

Tachikichi, on Shijō-dōri west of Kawara-machi, has five floors full of contemporary and antique ceramics. One floor is an art gallery that hosts exhibits of very fine ceramics by Japanese and international artists. In business since 1872, Tachikichi has a reputation for excellent quality. ⊠ *Shijō-dōri, Tominokōji, Nakagyō-ku* ☎ *075/211–3143* ⊙ *Thurs.–Tues. 10–7.*

Dolls

Ningyō were first used in Japan in the purification rites associated with the Doll Festival, an annual family-oriented event on March 3. Kyōto ningyō are made with fine detail and embellishment.

Nakanishi Toku Shōten has old museum-quality dolls. The owner, Mr. Nakanishi, turned his extensive doll collection into the shop two decades ago and has since been educating customers with his vast knowledge of the doll trade. ⊠ *359 Moto-chō, Yamato-ōji Higashi-Iru, Furumonzen-dōri, Higashiyama-ku* ☎ *075/561–7309* ⊙ *Daily 10–5.*

Folk Crafts

For many, the prize souvenir of a visit to Kyōto is the **shuinchō,** a booklet usually no larger than 4 by 6 inches. It's most often covered with brocade, and the blank sheets of heavyweight paper inside continuously fold out. You can find them at gift stores or at temples for as little as ¥1,000 and use them as "passports" to collect ink stamps from places you visit while in Japan. Stamps and stamp pads are ubiquitous in Japan—at sights, train stations, and some restaurants. Most ink stamping will be done for free; at temples, monks will write calligraphy over the stamp for a small fee.

Kuraya Hashimoto has one of the best collections of antique and newly forged swords and will ship them for you. ⊠ *Nishihorikawa-dōri, Oike-agaru, southeast corner of Nijō-jō, Nakagyō-ku* ☎ *075/821–2791* ⊕ *www.japansword.com* ⊙ *Thurs.–Tues. 10–6.*

At **Ryūshido** you can stock up on calligraphy and *sumi* supplies, including writing brushes, ink sticks, ink stones, paper, paperweights, and water stoppers. ⊠ *Nijō-agaru, Tera-machi-dōri, north of Nijō, Kamigyō-ku* ☎ *075/252–4120* ⊙ *Daily 10–6.*

Yamato Mingei-ten, next to the Maruzen Bookstore downtown, has an ever-changing selection of folk crafts, including ceramics, metalwork, paper, lacquerware, and textiles from all over Japan. ⊠ *Kawara-machi, Takoyakushi-agaru, Nakagyō-ku* ☎ *075/221–2641* ⊙ *Wed.–Mon. 10–8:30.*

Novelty Gift shop

Loft has five floors jam-packed with kitsch, from beauty products to anime merchandise. Kids and teenagers love browsing here, and you're sure

KYŌTO CRAFTS

TEMPLES, SHRINES, GARDENS, *and the quintessential elements of Japanese culture are all part of Kyōto's appeal, but you can't take them home with you. You can, however, pack up a few* omiyage *(mementos)—the take-home gifts for which this city is famous. The ancient craftsmen of Kyōto served the imperial court for more than 1,000 years, and the prefix kyō- before a craft is synonymous with fine craftsmanship. The wares you can find in Kyōto are, for their superb artistry and refinement, among the world's finest.*

Kyō-ningyō, *exquisite display dolls, have been made in Kyōto since the 9th century. Constructed of wood coated with white shell paste and clothed in elaborate, miniature patterned-silk brocades, Kyōto dolls are considered the finest in Japan. Kyōto is also known for fine ceramic dolls and* Kyō-gangu, *its local varieties of folk toys.*

Kyō-sensu *are embellished folding fans used as accoutrements in Nō theater, tea ceremonies, and Japanese dance. They also have a practical use—to keep you cool. Unlike other Japanese crafts, which have their origin in Tang dynasty China, the folding fan originated in Kyōto.*

Kyō-shikki *refers to Kyōto lacquerware, which also has its roots in the 9th century. The making of lacquerware, adopted from the Chinese, is a delicate process requiring patience and skill. Finished lacquerware products range from furniture to spoons and bowls, which are carved from cypress, cedar, or horse-chestnut wood. These pieces have a brilliant luster; some designs are decorated with gold leaf and inlaid mother-of-pearl.*

Kyō-yaki *is the general term applied to ceramics made in local kilns; the most popular ware is from Kyōto's Kiyomizu district. Often colorfully hand-painted in blue, red, and green on white, these elegantly shaped teacups, bowls, and vases are thrown on potters' wheels located in the Kiyomizu district and in Kiyomizu-danchi in Yamashina. Streets leading up to Kiyomizu-dera—Chawan-zaka, Sannen-zaka, and Ninen-zaka—are sprinkled with kyō-yaki shops.*

Kyō-yuzen *is a paste-resist silk-dyeing technique developed by 17th-century dyer Yūzen Miyazaki. Fantastic designs are created on plain white silk pieces through the process of either tegaki yūzen (hand-painting) or kata yūzen (stenciling).*

Nishijin-ori *is the weaving of silk. Nishijin refers to a Kyōto district producing the best silk textiles in all of Japan, which are used to make kimonos. Walk along the narrow backstreets of Nishijin and listen to the persistently rhythmic looms.*

to find some unusual souvenirs and gifts. ☒ *Kawara-machi-nishi, Tako-yakushi-dōri, Nakagyō-ku* ☏ *075/255–6210* ☺ *Daily 11–9.*

Kimonos & Accessories

Shimmering new silk kimonos can cost more than ¥1,000,000—they are art objects, as well as couture—while equally stunning old silk kimonos can cost less than ¥3,000. You can find used kimonos at some local end-of-the-month temple markets.

Aizen Kōbō, two blocks west of the textile center on Imadegawa-dōri and a block south, specializes in the finest handwoven and hand-dyed indigo textiles. Unlike chemical dyes, pure Japanese indigo dye with its famed rich color may soften but will never fade. The shop is in a traditional weaving family home, and the friendly owners will show you their many dyed and woven goods, including garments designed by Hisako Utsuki, the owner's wife. ☒ *Ōmiya Nishi-Iru, Nakasuji-dōri, Kamigyō-ku* ☏ *075/441–0355* ⊕ *http://web.kyoto-inet.or.jp/people/aizen* ☺ *Mon.–Sat. 9–5:30.*

Jūsan-ya has been selling *tsugekushi* (boxwood combs) for more than 60 years. *Kanzashi,* the hair ornaments worn with kimonos, are also available. ☒ *Shinkyōgoku Higashi-Iru, Shijō-dōri, Shimogyō-ku* ☏ *075/221–2008* ☺ *Daily 10–6.*

Umbrellas protect kimonos from the scorching sun or pelting rain. Head for **Kasagen** to purchase authentic oiled-paper umbrellas. The shop has been around since 1861, and its umbrellas are guaranteed to last for years. ☒ *284 Gion-machi, Kita-gawa, Higashiyama-ku* ☏ *075/561–2832* ☺ *Daily 10–9.*

The most famous fan shop in all of Kyōto is **Miyawaki Baisen-an,** in business since 1823. It delights customers not only with its fine collection of lacquered, scented, painted, and paper fans but also with the old-world atmosphere that emanates from the building that houses the shop. ☒ *Tominokōji Nishi-Iru, Rokkaku-dōri, Nakagyō-ku* ☏ *075/221–0181* ☺ *Daily 9–6.*

The **Nishijin Textile Center** (⇨ Central & Southern Kyōto, *above*) provides an orientation on silk-weaving techniques. ☒ *Horikawa-dōri, Imadegawa-Minami-Iru, Kamigyō-ku* ☏ *075/451–9231* ☒ *Free* ☺ *Daily 9–5.*

Visit **Takumi** for kimono accessories like obis, handbags, and *furoshiki* (gift-wrapping cloth). ☒ *Sanjō-sagaru, Kawara-machi-dōri, Nakagyō-ku* ☏ *075/221–2278* ☺ *Daily 10:30–9.*

Lacquerware

Monju sells authentic lacquered trays, bowls, incense holders, and tea containers. Unlike the inexpensive, plastic, faux lacquerware sold at some souvenir shops, real lacquerware has a wooden base, which is then coated with natural lacquer made from the Asian sumac tree. Gold-and-silver powder is used in the more lavish *maki-e* lacquerware. You can even buy chopsticks with their own carrying case to use instead of the disposable ones so often supplied in restaurants. This shop is on Shijō street in Gion. ☒ *Hanamikōji Higashi-iru, Shijō-dōri, Higashiyama-ku* ☏ *075/525–1617* ☺ *Fri.–Wed. 10.30–7.30.*

KYŌTO A TO Z

To research prices, get advice from other travelers, and book travel arrangements, visit www.fodors.com.

AIRPORTS & TRANSFERS

The closest international airport to Kyōto is Kansai International Airport (KIX), near Ōsaka. KIX does have domestic flights, particularly to major cities, but the majority of internal air traffic uses Ōsaka's Itami Airport. Flight time between Tōkyō and Ōsaka is about 70 minutes.

⚑ **Itami Airport** ☎ 06/6856-6781. **Kansai International Airport** ☎ 0724/55-2500.

AIRPORT TRANSFERS From KIX to Kyōto Station, take the JR Haruka Limited Express, which departs every 30 minutes to make the 75-minute run and costs ¥3,490 including charges for a reserved seat; or use a JR Pass. From Itami, buses depart for Kyōto approximately every 20 minutes from 8:10 AM to 9:20 PM. Some stop at major hotels, but most go straight to Kyōto Station. The trip takes from 55 to 90 minutes and costs ¥1,280 or ¥1,370, depending on the Kyōto destination.

Taxis cost more than ¥10,000 from KIX and Itami to Kyōto.

⚑ **JR Haruka Limited Express** ⬤ JR West, Kyōto Station building, Karasuma-dōri ☎ 075/691-1000

BIKE TRAVEL

Kyōto's sights are fairly close together, and being mostly flat the city is an excellent place to bicycle around. *See* Biking under Sports & the Outdoors for rental shops.

BUS TRAVEL

A network of bus routes covers the entire city. Most city buses run 7 AM–9 PM daily, but a few start as early as 5:30 AM and run until 11 PM. The main bus terminals are Kyōto Station, Keihan Sanjō Station, Karasuma-Kitao-ji, and at the Shijō-dōri–Karasuma-dōri intersection. Many city buses do not have signs in English, so you need to know the bus number. Because you will probably ride the bus at least once in Kyōto, try to pick up a bus map early in your stay from the Kyōtō Tourist Information Center.

At each bus stop a guidepost indicates the stop name, the bus route, and the bus-route number. Because the information at most guideposts is only in Japanese (except for the route number, which is given as an Arabic numeral), you are advised to ask your hotel clerk beforehand to write down your destination in Japanese, along with the route number, to show to the bus driver and fellow passengers; this will allow the driver and others to help you if you get lost. You might also ask your hotel clerk beforehand how many stops your ride will take.

Within the city the standard fare is ¥220, which you pay before leaving the bus; outside the city limits the fare varies according to distance. Several special transportation passes are available, including the following: a one-day city bus pass for ¥500; a multiday discount bus pass that provides ¥2,250 worth of riding for ¥2,000; and the *torafika kyō* pass, which provides ¥3,300 worth of transport via city bus or subway for ¥3,000.

Additionally, you can purchase combination one-day (¥1,200) or two-day (¥2,000) passes that cover travel on city buses, the subway, and private Kyōto Line buses, with restrictions on some routes. The ¥3,000 *surutto Kansai,* a versatile multiday pass, covers transportation on city buses, the subway, and all the major Kansai railways except the JR line. All of these passes are sold at travel agencies, main bus terminals, and information centers in Kyōto Station.

You can use a JR Pass on the local bus that travels between Kyōto Station and Takao (in northwestern Kyōto), passing close to Nijō Station.

CONSULATES
The nearest American, Canadian, and British consulates are in Ōsaka.

EMERGENCIES
The Sakabe Clinic has 24-hour emergency facilities.

🗐 Doctors **Daiichi Sekijūji** (Red Cross Hospital) ✉ Higashiyama Hon-machi, Higashiyama-ku ☎ 075/561-1121. **Daini Sekijūji Byōin** (2nd Red Cross Hospital) ✉ Kamanza-dōri, Maruta-machi-agaru, Kamigyō-ku ☎ 075/231-5171. **Japan Baptist Hospital** ✉ Kita-Shirakawa, Yamanomoto-chō, Sakyō-ku ☎ 075/781-5191. **Sakabe Clinic** ✉ 435 Yamamoto-chō, Gokō-machi, Nijō-sagaru, Nakagyō-ku ☎ 075/231-1624.
🗐 Emergency Services **Ambulance** ☎ 119. **Police** ☎ 110.

ENGLISH-LANGUAGE MEDIA
BOOKS Izumiya Book Center, across from Kyōto Station on the Shinkansen side, devotes a large corner to English-language books. Maruzen Kyōto has the city's broadest selection of books. Nearby, Media Shop carries a wide range of coffee-table books and titles on art and architecture in English and Japanese.

🗐 Bookstores **Izumiya Book Center** ✉ Avanti Bldg., 6th fl., Minami-ku ☎ 075/671-8987. **Maruzen Kyōto** ✉ 296 Kawara-machi-dōri, Nakagyō-ku ☎ 075/241-2169. **Media Shop** ✉ Vox Bldg., 1st fl., Kawara-machi, San-jō, Nakagyō-ku ☎ 075/255-0783.

NEWSPAPERS & Established in 1977, the monthly *Kansai Time Out* publishes comprehensive events listings for Kōbe, Kyōto, Nara, and Ōsaka. It costs ¥300 and is available in major hotels and bookshops throughout the region.

INTERNET CAFÉS
At the Kyōto Tourist Information Center in the station building, you can use the Internet for ¥100 per 15 minutes. Yū Yū Kūkan Internet Cafe has both Macs and PCs and is open 24 hours daily. A free drink is included when you pay ¥500 for one hour of Internet use. Each additional quarter-hour costs ¥100. At c.coquet, on the southeast corner of the Imperial Palace grounds, you can surf on an iBook for free with one drink or food order. The interior is white with pale mint tones, a dreamy space in which to order a meal or latte. It's open from Friday to Wednesday, 9 to 10. On the south end of Shinkyōgo-ku arcade is Fujiyama, the haunt of *manga otaku* (computer geeks). Once you complete the obligatory membership form for ¥300, you can use the Internet for ¥200 per 30 minutes. It's open daily from 9 to 9.

🗐 **Kyōto Tourist Information Center** ✉ 9F JR Kyōto Station building, Kyōto International Prefectural Center, Karasuma-dōri, Shimogyō-ku ☎ 075/344-3300 ⊕ www.

kyoto-kankou.or.jp. **Yū Yū Kūkan Internet cafe** ✉ 3F Wao Cube, 448 southeast corner of Karasuma-dōri and Gojō-dōri,Shimogyō-ku ☎075/354–3900. **c.coquet** ✉Okazaki bldg., at Imadegawa-dōri and Teramachi-dōri, Nakagyō-ku ☎ 075/212–0882. **Fujiyama Café** ✉3rd Bldg., 557 Kyōto-shochiku, Nakanomachi, Shinkyōgo-ku, Shijō-agaru, Nagakyō-ku ☎ 075/221–2494.

SIGHTSEEING TOURS

EXCURSIONS Hozugawa Yūsen organizes excursions down a 15-km (9-mi) stretch (about 90 minutes) of the Hozu Rapids in flat-bottom boats, from Kameoka to Arashiyama, which cost ¥3,900. Sunrise Tours, a subsidiary of Japan Travel Bureau, conducts full- and half-day tours to Nara and Ōsaka. An afternoon tour to Nara costs ¥6,300. Morning and afternoon trips to Ōsaka, for ¥8,900 and ¥6,200, respectively, are not worth the cost, especially if you have a JR Pass.

🔳 **Hozugawa Yūsen** ☎ 0771/22–5846. **Sunrise Tours** ☎ 075/341–1413.

ORIENTATION TOURS Sunrise Tours organizes half-day morning and afternoon deluxe coach tours highlighting different city attractions. Pickup service is provided from major hotels. A ¥5,300 morning tour commonly covers Nijō-jō, Kinkaku-ji, Kyōto Imperial Palace, Higashi-Hongan-ji, and the Kyōto Handicraft Center. A ¥5,300 afternoon tour includes the Heian Jingū, Sanjūsangen-dō, and Kiyomizu-dera. An ¥11,200 full-day tour covers all the above sights and includes lunch.

🔳 **Sunrise Tours** ☎ 075/341–1413 ⊕ jtb.co.jp/sunrisetour/kyoto.

SPECIAL-INTEREST TOURS There are several private companies offering guided tours of Kyōto. Joe Okada of Kyōto Specialist Guide Group will tailor a tour to fit your interests and budget. Your Japan Speciality Services is run by the editor-in-chief of the Kyōto Visitor's Guide, Ian Roepke, and offers half-day or full-day tours of Kyōto, including both familiar sights and lesser-known backstreet views. If you would like a seasoned guide to shed insight into the mysterious world of the geisha, Peter MacIntosh of Kyōto Sights and Nights takes both morning and evening walks through the old teahouse districts of Gion. Private tours are more expensive than group tours. Volunteer guides can be requested by calling Utano Youth Hostel. Bookings must be made three days in advance. The Kyōto International Community House can arrange home visits.

🔳 **ISC** ✉ Utano Youth Hostel, Ukyō-ku ☎ 075/462–2288. **Kyōto International Community House** ✉ 2-1 Torii-chō, Awata-guchi, Sakyō-ku ☎ 075/752–3010. **Kyoto Sights and Nights** ☎ 090/5169–1654 ⊕ www.kyotosightsandnights.com. **Kyōto Specialist Guide Group** ✉ 1137 Amarube-shimo, Maizuru-shi ☎ 0773/64–0033. **Your Japan Speciality Services** ☎ 090/5642–4724 ⊕ www.kyoto-tokyo-private-tours.com.

WALKING TOURS The Japan National Tourist Office (JNTO) publishes pamphlets with descriptions of five walking tours, including maps. The tours range in length from about 40 to 80 minutes. Pick up the pamphlets at the Kyōto Tourist Information Center in the Kyōto Station building.

Personable Kyōto-ite Johnnie Hajime Hirooka conducts walking tours of Kyōto, in English, that leave from Kyōto Station at 10:15 AM from Monday to Thursday, early March through late November, rain or shine. Itineraries vary—he often takes people to sights they might not otherwise see. Walks take four hours and cost ¥2,000 per person, ¥3,000 per couple.

⊠ **Johnnie Hajime Hirooka** ☎☐ 075/622–6803. **Kyōto Tourist Information Center**
⊠ 9F JR Kyōto Station building, Kyōto International Prefectural Center, Karasuma-dōri, Shimogyō-ku ☎ 075/344–3300 ⊕ www.kyoto-kankou.or.jp.

SUBWAY TRAVEL

Kyōto has a 26-station subway system. The Karasuma Line runs north to south from Kokusai Kaikan to Takeda. The Tōzai Line runs between Nijō in the west and Daigo in the east. Purchase tickets at the vending machines in stations before boarding. Fares increase with distance traveled and begin at ¥200. Service runs 5:30 AM–11:30 PM. Discounted passes are available for tourists (⇨ Bus Travel, *above*).

TAXIS

Taxis are readily available in Kyōto. Fares for smaller-size cabs start at ¥650 for the first 2 km (1 mi), with a cost of ¥90 for each additional ⅔ km (⅓ mi). Many taxi companies provide guided tours of the city, priced per hour or per route. Keihan Taxi has four-hour tours from ¥14,600 per car; MK Taxi runs similar tours for ¥16,600. There are fixed fares for some sightseeing services that start and end at Kyōto Station. A 7½-hour tour of the city's major sights will cost ¥26,000 with any of 17 taxi companies, including Keihan Taxi and MK Taxi.

⊠ **Keihan Taxi** ☎ 0120/113–103. **MK Taxi** ☎ 075/721–2237.

TRAIN TRAVEL

Frequent daily Shinkansen run between Tōkyō and Kyōto (2 hours, 40 minutes). The one-way fare, including charges for a reserved seat, is ¥13,220. Train service between Ōsaka and Kyōto (30 minutes) costs ¥540 one-way. From Shin-Ōsaka Station you can take the Shinkansen and be in Kyōto in 15 minutes; tickets cost ¥1,380. You may use a Japan Rail Pass on the Hikari and Kodama Shinkansen.

The Keihan and the Hankyū limited express trains (40 minutes each) are less expensive than the JR, unless you have a JR Pass. The one-way Ōsaka–Kyōto fare is ¥400 or ¥460 on the Keihan Line and ¥390 on the Hankyū Line. They depart every 15 minutes from Ōsaka's Yodoyabashi and Umeda stations respectively.

In Kyōto the Keihan Line from Ōsaka is partly underground (from Shichijō Station to Demachi-Yanagi Station) and extends all the way up the east bank of the Kamo-gawa to Imadegawa-dōri. At Imadegawa-dōri a passage connects the Keihan Line with the Eizan Railway's Demachi-Yanagi Station. The Eizan has two lines, the Kurama Line, running north to Kurama, and the Eizan Line, running northeast to Yase. The Hankyū Line, which runs to the Katsura Rikyū, connects with the subway at Karasuma Station. From Shijō-Ōmiya Station the Keifuku Arashiyama Line runs to western Kyōto. JR also runs to western Kyōto on the San-in Main Line.

VISITOR INFORMATION

The Kyōto Tourist Information Center is on the ninth floor of the Kyōto Station building, in the Kyōto International Prefectural Center. To get there, take the south elevator from the second floor of Isetan department store. The counter may be small but commendable assistance comes from a friendly, knowledgeable staff. The office is open daily 10 to 6 and closed the second and fourth Tuesday of each month.

The Japan Travel Bureau (JTB) and Keihan Travel Agency provide information on tours, such as the Sunrise Tours JTB offers; conferences and symposiums; and obtaining Japan Rail Passes. The JTB Web site lists contact numbers outside of Japan.

🖉 **Japan Travel Bureau** ✉ Kyōto eki-mae, Shiokōji Karasuma Higashi-Iru, Shimogyō-ku ☎ 075/361-7241 ⊕ www.jtb.co.jp/eng. **Keihan Travel Agency** ✉ 12 Mori-chō, Fushimi-ku ☎ 075/602-8162. **Kyōto Tourist Information Center** ✉ 9F JR Kyōto Station building, Kyōto International Prefectural Center, Karasuma-dōri, Shimogyō-ku ☎ 075/344-3300 ⊕ www.kyoto-kankou.or.jp.

NARA 奈良

6

Revised by
Justin Ellis

THE ANCIENT CITY OF NARA was founded in 710 by Emperor Kammu—thus predates Kyōto—and it was the first Japanese capital to remain in one place over a long period of time. Until then capitals had been established in new locations with each successive ruler. The founding of Nara, then known as Heijō-Kyō, occurred during a period when Japan's politics, arts, architecture, and religion were being heavily influenced by China. Also at this time the Japanese began using and incorporating *kanji,* Chinese characters, in their writing system.

Introduced from China in the 6th century, Buddhism flourished in Nara and enjoyed the official favor of rulers and the aristocracy, even as it coexisted with well-established Shintō beliefs. Many of Nara's Buddhist temples and monasteries were built by emperors and noble families, while other temples were transferred to Nara from former capitals. At its peak during the 8th century, Nara was said to have had as many as 50 pagodas. The grandest of the Buddhist temples built in this era was Tōdai-ji, which Emperor Shōmu intended to serve as a central monastery for all other provincial monasteries. The emperor, who saw much to emulate in Chinese culture, also hoped that religion could help to consolidate Japan. He established Tōdai-ji not only for spiritual purposes but as a symbol of a united Japan.

In 794 Kyōto became Japan's capital, and Nara lost its status as a city of political consequence. The move proved beneficial for Nara's many venerable buildings and temples, however, which remained essentially untouched by the ravages of civil wars that later damaged Kyōto. Of the surviving temples, Kōfuku-ji recalls the power of the Fujiwara clan in the 7th century. Its close connection with Kasuga Taisha, the Fujiwara family shrine, exemplifies the peaceful coexistence of Buddhism and Shintoism. And, both Tōdai-ji and Tōshōdai-ji demonstrate how pervasively and consistently Buddhism has influenced Japanese life.

See the glossary at the end of this book for definitions of the common Japanese words and suffixes used in this chapter.

EXPLORING NARA

In the 8th century Nara was planned as a rectangular city with checkerboard streets, modeled after the Chinese city of Ch'ang-an. Its well-organized layout has endured, and today Nara is still extremely easy to navigate. It's also one of the greenest of Japanese cities. Much of what you'll come to Nara to see will be in picturesque Nara Kōen (Nara Park), such as the Tōdai-ji Temple complex and Great Buddha statue. Other major temples in western Nara, such as Hōryū-ji, Yakushi-ji, and Tōshōdai-ji, are all on one bus route. And you should save a couple of hours to wander in the historic backstreets of Nara-machi, the old Edo-period residential and commercial district.

Nara-Kōen 奈良公園

It's a singular pleasure to wander around lush, green Nara Kōen (Nara Park) and its ponds as you stroll from temple to temple. Nara Kōen is inhabited by some 1,000 tame, if at times aggressive, deer, which roam freely around the various temples and shrines. They are considered to be divine messengers and are particularly friendly when you feed them deer crackers, which you can buy at stalls in the park.

Tōdai-ji Temple Complex 東大寺

It's hard to say which is the most magnificent Buddhist temple in Nara, but resplendent Tōdai-ji in Nara Kōen is certainly a contender. The temple complex was conceived by Emperor Shōmu in the 8th century as the seat of authority for Buddhist Japan. It was completed in 752, and even though the imperial household later left Nara, Tōdai-ji remained the symbol of Buddhist authority. An earthquake damaged it in 855, and in 1180 the temple was burned to the ground. Its reconstruction met a similar fate during the 16th-century civil wars. A century later only the central buildings were rebuilt; these are what remain today. Among the structures, the Daibutsu-den is the grandest, with its huge beams that seem to converge somewhere in infinity.

a good walk

To get to Tōdai-ji, board Bus 2 from the front of either the JR or Kintetsu Nara station, and get off at Daibutsu-den. Cross the street to reach the path that leads to the Tōdai-ji complex.

You can also walk from Kintetsu Nara Station to Tōdai-ji in about 15 minutes. To do this, walk east from the station on Noboriōji-dōri, the avenue that runs parallel to the station. In Nara Kōen turn left onto the pedestrians-only street, lined with souvenir stalls and small restaurants, that leads to Tōdai-ji. You can also walk from the JR station along Sanjo-dōri and turn left up Yasuragi-no-michi to Noboriōji-dōri. From here you can walk east as from Kintetsu Nara Station, but the route is longer and passes through the less attractive modern sections of town.

As you walk along the path leading to the temple complex, you pass through the impressive dark wooden front gate known as **Nandai-mon** ❶ ▶, supported by 18 large wooden pillars.

Continue straight to the main buildings of the Tōdai-ji temple complex. The Daibutsu-den entrance is in front of you, but first you may wish to visit the small temple on the left, **Kaidan-in** ❷, guarded by four ferocious-looking statues. From Kaidan-in, return to the **Daibutsu-den** ❸, purportedly the largest wooden structure in the world. The Daibutsu, Nara's famous statue of Buddha, is inside.

As you exit the Daibutsu-den, turn left and walk up the winding path to the left of the torii. Turn right, ascend the stone staircase, go straight and then veer left on the slope lined with stone lanterns. On your left, on top of the slope, you come to the **Ni-gatsu-dō** ❹, which has expansive views of Nara Kōen. Return along the same incline that led to Ni-gatsu-dō and turn left. The wooden structure on your left is **San-gatsu-dō** ❺, the oldest Tōdai-ji building. The entrance is on the right side as you face the building.

A good place to take a break or to have lunch is the street at the base of Wakakusa-yama (Wakakusa Mountain). From San-gatsu-dō, walk south, passing Tamukeyama-hachimangu Shrine, to get to Wakakusa-yama.

Most people visit Nara on a hurried day trip from Kyōto, missing the best that Nara has to offer—generous hospitality and a relaxed pace along with classical architecture and delicious food. To really appreciate Nara at a reasonable pace allow yourself at least two days—one for central Nara and another for western Nara.

Numbers in the text correspond to numbers in the margin and on the Nara map.

6

If you have 1 day

If you do have just a day, start with the sights around Nara Kōen, such as Tōdai-ji and its **Daibutsu-den** ③, **Kōfuku-ji** ⑩ with its five-story pagoda, and **Kasuga Taisha** ⑥. Have lunch near Wakakusa-yama or in **Nara-machi** ⑪ and leave the afternoon to see western Nara's **Hōryū-ji** ⑮, the oldest remaining temple complex in all of Japan.

If you have 2 days

If you have two days in Nara, you can focus on Nara Kōen and Nara-machi on Day 1, and set aside Day 2 for the temples of Western Nara. Spend the morning of Day 2 at **Hōryu-ji** ⑮ and **Chūgū-ji** ⑯, and the afternoon at **Yakushi-ji** ⑰ and **Tōshōdai-ji** ⑲. There are some noodle shops in front of the Hōryū-ji complex or you can enjoy a leisurely lunch at Ban Kio restaurant in front of Yakushi-ji.

If you have 3 days

Three days in Nara will enable you to see all the city's sights and enjoy Nara's easygoing pace. On the first and second days you can explore all the temples and shrines in Nara Kōen and spend a full morning or afternoon shopping and strolling through the streets of Nara-machi. On the third day visit Western Nara.

TIMING All of these sites are close together, making this a leisurely walk of about three hours, allowing for time to stop and feed the deer.

WHAT TO SEE ③ **Fodor's**Choice ★

Daibutsu-den (Hall of the Great Buddha, 大仏殿). This white, elegant, austere building, its wooden beams darkened with age, is an impressive sight. A pair of gilt ornaments decorates the roof ridge. These are called *kutsu-gata* (shoe-shape) because they resemble footwear and were once believed to ward off fire. Unfortunately, they didn't prevent the original building from burning. The current Daibutsu-den was restored in 1709 at two-thirds its original scale. At 157 ft tall and 187 ft long, it's still considered the largest wooden structure in the world.

Inside Daibutsu-den is the **Daibutsu**, a 53-ft bronze statue of the Buddha that is perhaps the most famous sight in Nara. The Daibutsu was originally commissioned by Emperor Shōmu in 743. After numerous unsuccessful castings, this figure was finally made in 749. A statue of this scale had never before been cast in Japan, and it was hoped that it would serve as a symbol to unite the country. The Daibutsu was dedicated in 752 in a grand ceremony attended by then-retired Emperor Shōmu, the imperial court, and 10,000 priests and nuns.

Behind the Daibutsu to the right, look for a large wooden pillar with a hole at its base. You can see many Japanese visitors attempting to crawl through the opening, which is barely large enough for a child. Local tradition has it that those who pass through the opening will find their way to an afterlife paradise. Children in particular love darting in and out and watching adults suffer the indignity of barely squeezing through. Behind the Daibutsu, to the left, is a model of the original Tōdai-ji. ⊠ *Tōdai-ji Temple Complex, Nara Kōen* 🎫 *¥500* ⊙ *Jan., Feb., Nov., and Dec., daily 8–4:30; Mar., daily 8–5; Apr.–Sept., daily 7:30–5:30; Oct., daily 7:30–5.*

❷ **Kaidan-in** (戒壇院). Inside this small temple are clay statues of the Four Heavenly Guardians, depicted in full armor, wielding weapons and displaying fierce expressions. *Kaidan* is a Buddhist word for the terrace on which priests are ordained; the Chinese Buddhist Ganjin (688–763) administered many induction ceremonies of Japanese Buddhists here. The original temple was destroyed repeatedly by fire; the current structure dates to 1731. Kaidan-in is in northwestern Nara Kōen, west of Daibutsu-den. ⊠ *Tōdai-ji Temple Complex, Nara Kōen* 🎫 *¥500* ⊙ *Apr.–Sept., daily 7:30–5:30; Oct., daily 7:30–5; Nov.–Feb., daily 8–4:30; Mar, daily 8–5.*

▶ ❶ **Nandai-mon** (Great Southern Gate, 南大門). The impressive Tōdai-ji Gate, standing over the path to the temple, is supported by 18 large wooden pillars, each 62 ft high and nearly 3⅓ ft in diameter. The original gate was destroyed in a typhoon in 962 and rebuilt in 1199. Two outer niches on either side of the gate contain wooden figures of Deva kings, who guard the great Buddha within. They are the work of master sculptor Unkei, of the Kamakura period (1185–1335). In the inner niches are a pair of stone *koma-inu* (Korean dogs), mythical guardians that ward off evil.

❹ **Ni-gatsu-dō** (Second Month Temple, 二月堂). Named for the religious ritual that used to be performed here each February, Ni-gatsu-dō was founded in 752. It houses some important images of the Buddha that are, alas, not on display to the public. Still, its hilltop location and veranda afford a breathtaking view of Nara Kōen. ⊠ *Tōdai-ji Temple Complex, Nara Kōen* 🎫 *Free* ⊙ *Jan., Feb., Nov., and Dec., daily 8–4:30; Mar., daily 8–5; Apr.–Sept., daily 7:30–5:30; Oct., daily 7:30–5:30.*

❺ **San-gatsu-dō** (Third Month Temple, 三月堂). Founded in 733, this temple, which takes its name from a March ritual, is the oldest original building in the Tōdai-ji complex. As you enter, to your left are some benches covered with tatami mats, where you can sit and contemplate the 1,200-year-old National Treasures that crowd the small room. The principal image is the lacquer statue of Fukūkensaku Kannon, the goddess of mercy, whose diadem is encrusted with thousands of pearls and gemstones. The two clay *bosatsu* (bodhisattvas) statues on either side of her, the Gakkō (Moonlight) and the Nikkō (Sunlight), are considered fine examples of the Nara (or Tenpyo) period, the height of classic Japanese sculpture. ⊠ *Tōdai-ji Temple Complex, Nara Kōen* 🎫 *¥500* ⊙ *Jan., Feb., Nov., and Dec., daily 8–4:30; Mar., daily 8–5; Apr.–Sept., daily 7:30–5:30; Oct., daily 7:30–5.*

6

Architecture

Nara's temples and shrines are among the oldest wooden structures in the world—unlike the replicas found elsewhere in Japan. Paradoxically, the large concentration of old buildings here is somewhat due to their neglect as the city's sociopolitical importance diminished. Crafted in the Chinese style when Buddhism was first imported to Japan, they're a snapshot of Old Japan that represents the spirit of newly born imperial and religious institutions.

Hospitality & Tranquillity

Nara is known for the unaffected, generous hospitality of its people. One of the great pleasures of a trip to Nara is taking a leisurely meal in one of its kaiseki restaurants, some of which are close to 400 years old. In ryokans you are encouraged to relax and wind down with a cup of tea and a hot bath. Nara's small-town feel also makes travelers feel welcome. You'll see mostly residents on the quiet streets, and except during holidays and on some weekends, few visitors stay overnight. Nara might not have the volume of sacred sights that Kyōto has—or all of its concrete and steel—but Nara's shrines, parks, and kaiseki restaurants are among the country's finest. That this quiet old city exists in the midst of Japan's overbuilt industrial corridor makes its understated tranquillity all the more precious.

Shopping

Alongside the merchants' houses and traditional restaurants of Nara-machi's narrow backstreets, just south of Sarusawa-ike, old wooden shops sell the crafts for which Nara is famous: *fude* (foo-deh, handmade brushes) and *sumi* (ink sticks) for calligraphy and ink painting, Nara dolls carved in wood, and Nara *sarashi-jofu*—fine handwoven, sun-bleached linen.

Elsewhere in Nara Kōen

a good walk

From the base of Wakakusa-yama, continue south past all the restaurants and shops. At the end of the street you can see stone steps. Descend these and cross a small bridge over a stream; then walk for about 10 minutes along the path that leads into shady and peaceful woods. At its end, turn left up the staircase to **Kasuga Taisha** ⑥ ▶ at the top.

Leaving Kasuga Taisha, walk south down the path lined with stone lanterns past the Kasuga-Wakamiya Shrine. Continue on this wooded path until you reach a paved road. Cross the road and take the first right onto a residential street with many traditional Japanese houses. Take the first left and follow it south about 300 ft, until it curves to the right and leads you directly to **Shin-Yakushi-ji** ⑦, founded in 747. Of the many original buildings that once stood here, only the Main Hall remains. For a glimpse of seldom-visited rural Japan through photographs, head for the **Nara City Museum of Photography** ⑧, a modern structure discreetly hidden under a traditional tiled roof. As you leave the temple, the museum is to your immediate right.

Nara

TO KYOTO ↑

TO KYOTO ↑

TO OSAKA ←

Yamato-Saidaiji Station

KINTETSU RAILROAD/NARA LINE

JR NARA LINE

Minakuni-ike Pond

Umunabe-ike Pond

Ichijo-dōri

44

Shin Omiya Station

Nara Prefectural Museum ♦

369

Noboriōji-dōri

24

Nara City Tourist Center ♦

Kintetsu Nara Station

10 興福寺

Amagatsuji Station

Akishino-gawa

JR Nara Station

754

Sanjo-dōri
Sarusawa-ike Pond

11 古梅園

12 遊中川

Nara-machi

TO OSAKA ←

Tomio-gawa

奈良町資料館 **13**

14 赤膚焼

Nishinokyō Station **18**

17

18 唐招提寺

0 — 1 mile

0 — 1 kilometer

JR Kyobate Station

Nishinakyō Station

Tomio-gawa

17 薬師寺

Akishino-gawa

Yamato-Koizumi Station

15 **16** 中宮寺

15 · 16 see detail map

法隆寺

Nishimeihan Expwy.

Hirahata Station

TO HORYUJI ↓

TO SAKURAI ↓

TO TENRI ↓

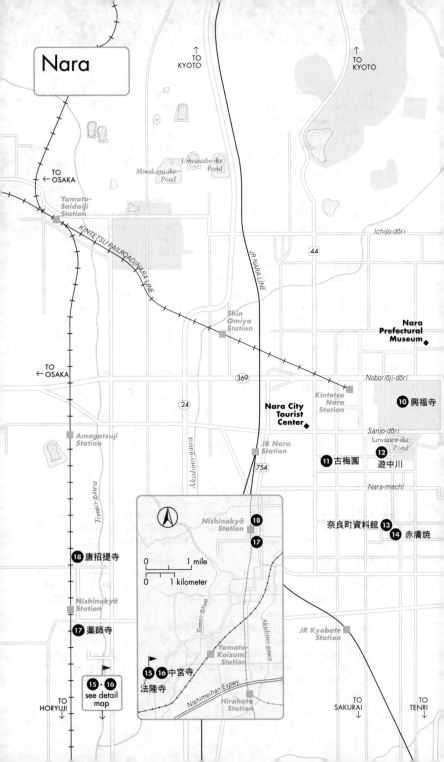

Tōdai-ji Temple Complex

Elsewere in Nara Kōen

Nara-machi

Western Nara

From the museum retrace your steps past Shin-Yakushi-ji to the residential street you walked down earlier. Turn left onto this street and walk to the major intersection at the end of it. Across the street you see a bus stop, where you can board Bus 1 back to the Daibutsu-den stop. Or if you've got a second wind, visit **Nara National Museum** ⑨ via Bus 1 and the Kokuritsu Hakubutsukan stop, in front of the museum. Leaving the west exit of the east wing of the museum, walk west along the path for about five minutes to the **Kōfuku-ji** ⑩ complex, which once contained 175 buildings; fewer than a dozen remain. The most eye-catching structure is the Five-Story Pagoda. There are good restaurants within minutes of the Kōfuku-ji Pagoda complex.

Before continuing to western Nara and Hōryū-ji, take some time out from temple viewing to walk through the old neighborhood of **Nara-machi** ⑪–⑭, just south of Sarusawa-ike.

TIMING | From Kasuga Taisha to Shin-Yakushi-ji it's a pleasant half-hour walk through a small forest. It should take another half hour to get back to the city. Allow a good three or four hours to see everything on this walk, including Nara-machi. On a hot summer day it's best to leave early in the morning and have lunch in Nara-Kōen or Nara-machi. At other times of the year you could go in the late morning or early afternoon.

WHAT TO SEE
★ ▶ ❻

Kasuga Taisha (春日大社). Kasuga is famous for the more than 2,000 stone lanterns that line the major pathways that lead to it, all of which are lighted three times a year on special festival days (February 2 and August 14–15). Kasuga was founded in 768 as a tutelary shrine for the Fujiwaras, a prominent feudal family. For centuries, according to Shintō custom, the shrine was reconstructed every 20 years on its original design. Many Shintō shrines, like the famous Ise Jingū in Mie Prefecture, are rebuilt in this way, not merely to renew the materials but also to purify the site. It's said that Kasuga Taisha has been rebuilt more than 50 times; its current incarnation dates to 1893. After you pass through the torii, the first wooden structure you'll see is the **Hai-den** (Offering Hall); to its left is the **Naorai-den** (Entertainment Hall). To the left of Naorai-den are the four **Hon-den** (Main Shrines). They are designated as National Treasures, all built in the same Kasuga style and painted vermilion and green—a striking contrast to the dark wooden exterior of most other Nara temples.

To get to Kasuga Taisha, walk east on Sanjo-dōri, Nara's main street. You can find the shrine just past the Manyo Botanical Garden, at the western end of Nara Kōen. ✉ *160 Kasuga-no-chō, Nara-shi* ☎ *0742/ 22–7788* 🏛 *Kasuga Shrine Museum ¥420; shrine's outer courtyard free; inner precincts with 4 Hon-den structures and gardens ¥500* ☉ *Museum daily 9–4; inner precincts Jan., Feb., and Dec., daily 7–4:30; Mar. and Nov., daily 7–5; Apr., daily 6:30–5:30; May–Sept., daily 6:30–6; Oct., daily 6:30–5:30.*

❿ **Kōfuku-ji** (興福寺). The main attraction at Kōfuku-ji is the first-rate collection of Buddhist statues in the **Great Eastern Hall** (Tōkondō). The current hall is a reconstruction dating from the 15th-century. Originally built to speed the recovery of the ailing empress Genshō it's dominated by a statue of Yakushi Nyorai (Physician of the Soul), and is flanked by Four Heavenly Kings and Twelve Heavenly Generals. In contrast to the highly stylized and enlightened Yakushi Nyorai, the seated figure to the left of it is a statue of a mortal, Yuima Koji.

Additionally, Kōfuku-ji's two magnificent pagodas are considered the most important temple structures from the period when Nara was the capital of Japan, because they were supposed to have held the relics, such as a bone or a tooth, of the Buddha. The **Five-Story Pagoda**, at 164 ft, is the second-tallest in Japan. Built in 1426, it's an exact replica of the original pagoda built here in 730 by Empress Kōmyō, which burned to the ground. It currently houses four Buddha triad statues (Buddha and two attendants), enshrined around the central pillar. The **Three-Story Pagoda** was built in 1114 and is renowned for its graceful lines and fine proportions. This pagoda is home to four paintings on wood depicting 1,000 images of each of the Buddhas enshrined in the Five Story Pagoda.

Ironically, the unattractive, modern **Kokuhōkan** (National Treasure House) has the largest and most varied collection of National Treasure sculpture and other works of art. The most famous is a statue of Ashura, one of Buddha's eight protectors, with three heads and six arms.

Kōfuku-ji was originally founded in 669 in Kyōto by the Fujiwara family. After Nara became the capital, Kōfuku-ji was moved to its current location in 710. It was an important temple encompassing 175 buildings, of which fewer than a dozen remain. The history of Kōfuku-ji reflects the intense relationship between Buddhism and Shintoism in Japan. In 937 a Kōfuku-ji monk had a dream in which the Shintō deity Kasuga appeared in the form of a Buddha, asking to become a protector of the temple. In 947 a number of Kōfuku-ji monks held a Buddhist ceremony at the Shintō Kasuga Taisha to mark the merging of the Buddhist temple with the Shintō shrine.

Kōfuku-ji is a five-minute walk west of Nara Kokuritsu Hakubutsukan in the central part of Nara Kōen, and it's an easy 15-minute walk from the JR or Kintetsu station. ⊠ *48 Noboriōji-chō, Nara Shi* ☎ *0742/ 22–7755* ✉ *Great Eastern Hall ¥500, National Treasure House ¥500* ☉ *Daily 9–5.*

❾ **Nara National Museum** (Nara Kokuritsu Hakubutsukan, 奈良国立博物館). The East Wing, built in 1973, has many examples of calligraphy, paintings, and sculpture. The West Wing, built in 1895, displays objects of archaeological interest. During the driest days of November, the Shōsō-in Repository (closed to the public), behind the Tōdai-ji, displays some of its magnificent collection here. ⊠ *50 Noboriōji-chō* ☎ *0742/22–7771* ✉ *¥420* ☉ *Tues.–Sun., daily 9:30-5; enter by 4:30.*

❽ **Nara City Museum of Photography** (Nara-shi Shashin Bijutsukan, 奈良市写真美術館). Through the evocative postwar photography of Irie Taikichi, who documented the people and ways of the rural, preindustrial Yamato area around Nara, you can experience a way of life that has all but vanished from contemporary Japan. Other exhibits, usually related to Nara's history and culture, are regularly on display in the un-

CloseUp

THE BURNING OF
WAKAKUSA MOUNTAIN

EACH JANUARY 15, *15 priests set Wakakusa-yama's (若草山) dry grass afire while fireworks illuminate Kōfuku-ji's Five-Story Pagoda in one of the most photographed rites in Japan. The ritual is undoubtedly a grand spectacle, though its origins are unclear. Some believe that it commemorates the resolution of a boundary dispute between the monks and priests of Tōdai-ji, Kasuga Taisha, and Kōfuku-ji. Others hold to the more mundane belief that the fire was originally lit by farmers at different times of the year to reduce insect numbers, and that the burning became an annual tradition for fear of Tōdai-ji catching fire and burning down.*

The ritual and its accompanying festival offer a rare opportunity to see Nara's streets crowded with people in the evening. Year-round, the street at the base of Wakakusa-yama is a good place to have a cup of coffee, a snack, or even lunch when you are visiting the sights of Nara Kōen. The restaurants facing the hill serve standard lunch sets and noodle dishes.

derground exhibition space. The museum is just west of Shin-Yakushi-ji. ☒ 600–1 Takabatake-chō ☎ 0742/22–9811 ☜ ¥500 ☉ Daily 9:30–5; last entry at 4:30.

★ **❼ Shin-Yakushi-ji** (新薬師寺). This temple was founded in 747 by Empress Kōmyō (701–760) as a prayer requesting the recovery of her sick husband, Emperor Shōmu. Most of the temple buildings were destroyed over the years; only the Main Hall, which houses many fine objects of the Nara period, still exists. In the center of the hall is a wood statue of Yakushi Nyorai, the Physician of the Soul. Surrounding this statue are 12 clay images of the Twelve Divine Generals who protected Yakushi. Eleven of these figures are originals. The generals stand in threatening poses, bearing spears, swords, and other weapons, and display terrifying expressions. ☒ 1289 Takabatake-chō ☜ ¥600 ☉ Daily 9–5.

Nara-machi   奈良町

This neighborhood is a maze of narrow residential streets lined with traditional houses and old shops, many of which deal in Nara's renowned arts and crafts. A signboard map on the southwest edge of Sarusawa-ike shows the way to all the important shops, museums, and galleries.

Whether you go on foot or by bicycle, Nara-machi can offer a change of pace from ordinary sightseeing, and local residents are willing to point you in the right direction.

We've noted usual store hours, but be aware that these stores may close irregularly. You can try calling ahead to find out if they're open, but you may not find someone who speaks English. But you'll likely enjoy walking in Nara-machi even if you find some shops are closed.

⑭ **Akahadayaki** (赤膚焼). A potter's wheel can be seen from the window of Akahadayaki, where beautiful ceramic candle holders illuminate rooms with leaf and geometric patterns. ⊠ *18 Shibashinya-chō* ☎ *0742/23–3110* ⊘ *Thurs.–Tues. 10:30–5.*

⑪ **Kobaien** (古梅園). For 400 years Kobaien has made fine ink sticks for calligraphy and ink painting. From October to April, make an appointment here to watch the actual production of the ink sticks. ⊠ *7 Tsubakii-chō* ☎ *0742/23–2965* ⊘ *Weekdays 9–5.*

⑬ **Nara-machi Historical Library and Information Center** (Nara-machi Shiryōkan, 奈良町資料館). Gango-ji temple is Nara-machi's focal point, and near it is this little museum, with Buddhist statuary and other artwork. Here you can also buy *migawarizaru* or "substitute monkeys," red cloth monkeys on pieces of rope that are meant to ward off illness. Families often have one monkey per family member, and each monkey is supposed to suffer illness and accidents for its owner, keeping its owner healthy. ⊠ *12 Shibashinya-chō* ☎ *0742/22–5509* ⊘ *Tues.–Sun. 10–4.*

⑫ **"Yū" Nakagawa** (遊中川). For the best of local goods, you'll want to visit this store, which specializes in handwoven, sun-bleached linen textiles, a Nara specialty known as *sarashi-jofu*. ⊠ *31–1 Genrin-in chō* ☎ *0742/22–1322* ⊘ *Daily 11–6.*

Western Nara   奈良西部

Of the four major temples on the western outskirts of Nara, Hōryū-ji is the most famous. It should be one of the places you visit if you have just one day in Nara. If you're in Nara for two days, you may want to spend the second day exploring the rest of western Nara.

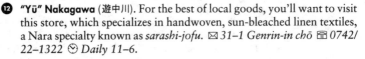

a good tour

It's easy to get to the four major temples on the outskirts of Nara from JR Nara Station or Kintetsu Nara Station. Bus 97 stops at Hōryū-ji, Chūgū-ji, Yakushi-ji, and Tōshōdai-ji returning along the same route. It takes 50 minutes and costs ¥760. If you're only going to Hōryū-ji, it's quicker and more pleasant to take the JR train on the Kansai Main Line to Hōryū-ji Station (¥210); from here the temple is a short shuttle-bus ride or a 15-minute walk. **Hōryū-ji** ⑮ ▶ is the most remarkable temple in western Nara, and its complex contains buildings that are among the oldest wooden structures in the world.

A path of carefully raked pebbles behind Hōryū-ji's eastern precinct leads to the quiet nunnery of **Chūgū-ji** ⑯, home to a graceful statue of Buddha that dates from the Asuka period (552–645). If you are pressed for time, you might want to skip this temple.

Get back on Bus 97 in the direction from which you came and get off at Yakushi-ji-mae. **Yakushi-ji** ⑰ was founded in 680 and moved to its current location in 718. As you enter the temple grounds, on your right you'll see the East Pagoda, which dates to 1285. The West Tower, to your left, was built in 1981. The new vermilion building in the center is Yakushi-ji's Kon-dō.

From the back gate of Yakushi-ji it's a 10-minute walk to the 8th-century temple **Tōshōdai-ji** ⑱ down the "Path of History," lined with clay-wall houses, gardens, restaurants, and small shops selling antiques, crafts, and *nara-zuke* (vegetables pickled in sake). You can pass through the Nandai-mon to enter the temple complex. The first building, the Kon-dō, is under restoration until 2009, however the rest of the temple complex is still open to the public. Outside, and behind the Kon-dō, is Tōshōdai-ji's Daikō-dō, once the Nara Imperial Court's assembly hall. When you leave Tōshōdai-ji, you can take Bus 63 back to Kintetsu Nara Station or JR Nara Station; the bus stop is in front of the temple.

TIMING At a leisurely pace, you can visit one or two temples in an afternoon—Hōryū-ji should be one of them—but you'll need a full day's exploration of western Nara to see some of Japan's finest religious architecture.

What to See

⑯ **Chūgū-ji** (中宮寺). Chūgū-ji was originally the home of Prince Shōtoku's mother in the 6th century. When she died, it became a temple dedicated to her memory. Today this quiet nunnery houses a graceful wooden image of the Miroku Bodhisattva, the Buddha of the Future. The statue dates from the Asuka period (552–645), and its gentle countenance has made it famous as an ageless view of hope. Also of interest here is the oldest example of embroidery in Japan, which also dates from the Asuka period. The framed cloth depicts Tenjukoku (Land of Heavenly Longevity). In front of the temple is a small, carefully tended pond with a rock garden emerging from just below the surface.

From the JR or Kintetsu station, take Bus 97, which stops at all the Western temples. From Hōryū-ji, the path at the rear of the temple's eastern precinct takes you to Chūgū-ji. ✉ 1–2 1-Chōme Ikaruga-chō, Hōryū-ji, Kita Ikoma-gun, Nara-ken ☎ 0745/75–2106 🗺 ¥500 ⊙ Daily 9–4:30; Oct.–Mar., daily 9–4.

▶ ⑮ **Hōryū-ji** (法隆寺). This is the most captivating of the temples in western
FodorśChoice Nara. Hōryū-ji was founded in 607 by Prince Shōtoku (573–621), and
★ its original wooden buildings are among the world's most ancient. The first gate you pass through at Hōryū-ji is **Nandai-mon,** which was rebuilt in 1438 and is therefore a young 500 years old. Remarkably, the second gate, **Chū-mon** (Middle Gate), is the 607 original—almost 1,400 years old. Unlike most other Japanese gates, which are supported by two pillars at the ends, this gate is supported by central pillars. Note their unusual entastic (curved outward in the center) shape, which is an architectural technique used in ancient Greece that traveled as far as Japan. Entastic pillars are found in Japan only in the 7th-century structures of Nara.

After passing through the gates, you enter the temple's western precincts. The first building on the right is the **Kon-dō** (Main Hall), a two-story reproduction of the original 7th-century hall, which displays Buddhist images and objects dating from as far back as the Asuka period (552–645). The five-story pagoda to its left was disassembled in World War II to protect it from air raids, after which it was reconstructed in its original form, with the same materials used in 607. Behind the pagoda is the **Daikō-dō** (Lecture Hall), destroyed by fire and rebuilt in 990. Inside is a statue of Yakushi Nyorai (Physician of the Soul) carved from a camphor tree.

From the Daikō-dō, walk back past the Kon-dō and Chū-mon; then turn left and walk past the pond on your right. You come to two concrete buildings known as the **Daihōzō-den** (Great Treasure Hall), which display statues, sculptures, ancient Buddhist religious articles, and brocades. Of particular interest is a miniature shrine that belonged to Lady Tachibana, mother of Empress Kōmyō. The shrine is about 2½ ft tall; the Buddha inside is about 20 inches tall.

Tōdai-mon (Great East Gate) opens onto Hōryū-ji's eastern grounds. The octagonal **Yumedono** (Hall of Dreams) was so named because Prince Shōtoku used to meditate in it.

To get here, take a JR Kansai Main Line train to Hōryū-ji Station (¥210). The temple is a short shuttle ride or a 15-minute walk. Alternatively, Bus 97 or 60 to Hōryū-ji is a 50-minute ride from the JR Nara station and Kintetsu Nara Station (¥760). The Hōryūji-mae bus stop is in front of the temple. ⊠ *1–1 Ikaruga-chō, Hōryū-ji, Ikoma-gun, Nara-ken* ☎ *0745/75-2555* ☜ *¥1,000* ⊙ *Feb. 22–Nov. 3, daily 8–5; Nov. 4–Feb. 21, daily 8–4:30; last entry 30 min before closing.*

⑱ Tōshōdai-ji (唐招提寺). The main entrance to this temple is brazenly called the "Path of History," since in Nara's imperial days dignitaries and priests trod this route; today it's lined with clay-wall houses, gardens, and small shops selling antiques, crafts, and nara-zuke, a popular local specialty. Tōshōdai-ji was built in 751 for Ganjin, a Chinese priest who traveled to Japan at the invitation of Emperor Shōmu. At this time, Japanese priests had never received formal instruction from a Buddhist priest. The invitation was extended by two Japanese priests who had traveled to China in search of a Buddhist willing to undertake the arduous and perilous journey to Japan.

On Ganjin's first journey, some of his disciples betrayed him. His second journey resulted in a shipwreck. During the third trip his ship was blown off course, and on his fourth trip he was refused permission to leave China by government officials. Before his next attempt, he contracted an eye disease that left him blind. He persevered, nevertheless, and finally reached Japan in 750. Ganjin shared his knowledge of Buddhism with his adopted country and served as a teacher to many Japanese priests as well as Emperor Shōmu. He is also remembered for bringing the first sampling of sugar to Japan. Every June 6, to commemorate his birthday, the **Miei-dō**, in the back of the temple grounds displays a lacquer statue of Ganjin that dates from 763.

The temple's entrance, the **Nandai-mon** (Great South Gate), is supported by entastic pillars like those in the Chū-mon of Hōryū-ji. Beyond Nandai-mon, the **Kon-dō** (Main Hall) is a superb example of classic Nara architecture; it's due to be under restoration until 2009. Inside the hall is a lacquer statue of Vairocana Buddha, the same incarnation of Buddha that's enshrined at Tōdai-ji. The halo surrounding him was originally covered with 1,000 Buddhas—only 864 remain. In back of the Kon-dō sits the **Daikō-dō** (Lecture Hall), formerly an assembly hall of the Nara Imperial Court. It's the only remaining example of Nara palace architecture.

Tōshōdai-ji is a 10-minute walk from the rear gate of Yakushi-ji along the Path of History. From central Nara or Hōryū-ji, take Bus 97 to the stop in front of Tōshōdai-ji. ✉ 13–46 Gojo-chō, Nara-shi ☎ 0742/33–7900 💷 ¥600 ⊙ Daily 8:30–5.

★ ⓱ **Yakushi-ji** (薬師寺). Officially named one of the Seven Great Temples of Nara, Yakushi-ji was founded in 680 and moved to its current location in 718. Yakushi-ji's **East Pagoda** dates from 1285 and has such an interesting asymmetrical shape that it inspired Boston Museum of Fine Arts curator Ernest Fenollosa (1853–1908), an early Western specialist in Japanese art, to remark that it was as beautiful as "frozen music." Although it appears to have six stories, in fact it has only three—three roofs with smaller ones attached underneath. The **West Tower** was built in 1981, and the central **Kon-dō** (Main Hall) was rebuilt in 1976 and painted a garish vermilion. These newer buildings are not nearly as attractive as the older structures, and they look out of place in the otherwise appealing temple complex. However, they do house important works of Buddhist art dating as far back as the 8th century.

From central Nara take either the Kintetsu Line train, changing at Saidaiji to Nishinokyo, or Bus 97 to Yakushi-ji; from Hōryū-ji or Chūgū-ji, take Bus 97 to Yakushi-ji-mae. ✉ 457 Nishinokyo-chō, Nara-shi ☎ 0742/33–6001 💷 ¥800 ⊙ Daily 8:30–5.

WHERE TO EAT

It's a mistake to visit Nara without experiencing an elegant Japanese meal in a traditional kaiseki restaurant—even if you're just here for the day. The thoughtfully prepared food here is remarkably good. If you don't have time for dinner, at least have a leisurely lunch.

Traditional restaurants are often small and tend to have limited menus with set courses. Also, restaurants tend to close early, at around 10 PM, taking last orders at around 9. Because some places don't have English-speaking staff or English menus, ask someone from your hotel to help make your arrangements. Alternatively, and much simpler, consider staying in a *ryokan* (traditional inn), where a kaiseki dinner is included in the room rate.

Small restaurants and izakaya are dispersed throughout the maze of streets that make up Nara-machi. Unless you know a few words of Japanese, you may need to point to an appetizing dish that another diner is enjoying. Remember that each time you point it may be interpreted as placing an order and add ¥500–¥800 to your bill. Expect to pay about ¥750 for a large bottle of beer.

For more on Japanese cuisine, *see* Chapter 14 *and* Dining *in* Smart Travel Tips A to Z.

	WHAT IT COSTS In yen				
	$$$$	$$$	$$	$	¢
AT DINNER	over 3,000	2,000–3,000	1,000–2,000	800–1,000	under 800

Prices are per person for a main course.

Nara Kōen Area

★ **$$$$** ✕**Onjaku** (温石). Hidden down a quiet street just south of Ara-ike in Nara Kōen is this intimate restaurant serving exquisitely presented traditional kaiseki meals. Inside the faded wooden exterior walls, a common architectural motif in Nara, you can sit at a rustic counter or in one of two serene tatami rooms. Choose from one of the two set meals on offer. This is definitely a place to linger and be spoiled. ⊠ *1043 Kita-temma-chō* ☎ *0742/26–4762* ⌂ *Reservations essential* ☰ *No credit cards* ☼ *Closed Tues.*

★ **$$$$** ✕**Tsukihitei** (月日亭). Deep in the forest behind Kasuga Taisha, Tsukihitei is the perfect setting for kaiseki. From the walk up a wooded path to the tranquillity of your own tatami room, everything is conducive to experiencing the beautiful presentation and delicate flavors. When reserving a table, enlist the help of a good Japanese speaker to select a set meal for you as well, and then allow yourself to be regaled. The lunch sets run from ¥10,000 to ¥15,000. ⊠ *158 Kasugano-chō* ☎ *0742/26–2021* ⌂ *Reservations essential* ☰ *AE, DC, M, V.*

★ **$$$$** ✕**Uma no Me** (馬の目). In a little 1920s farmhouse just north of Ara-ike pond in Nara Kōen, this delightful restaurant with dark beams and pottery-lined walls serves delicious home-style cooking. Everything is prepared from scratch in the time-honored way. Highly recommended is the ¥3,500 lunch course with seasonal vegetables, melt-in-your-mouth tofu, and succulent fried fish. As there's only one set meal, ordering is no problem. ⊠ *1158 Takabatake-chō* ☎ *0742/23–7784* ☰ *No credit cards* ☼ *Closed Thurs.*

★ **$$$$** ✕**Yanagi-ja-ya** (柳茶屋). Though the building is unassuming from the outside, once you enter the revered old Yanagi-ja-ya you're transported to a bygone age. In a secluded tatami room overlooking a garden, you'll be served elegantly simple bento meals of sashimi, stewed vegetables, and tofu in black-lacquer boxes. Lunch runs ¥4,000–¥6,000. There are two branches: the original shop on the north bank of Sarusawa-ike and another just east of Kōfuku-ji. *Original* ⊠ *49 Noboriōji-chō* ☎ *0742/22–7460* ☼ *Closed Wed.* ⊠ *48 Teraoji-chō* ☎ *0742/22–7560* ☼ *Closed Mon.* ⌂ *Reservations essential* ☰ *No credit cards.*

$$–$$$$ ✕**Tō-no-chaya** (塔の茶屋). One of Nara's most distinctive meals is *chagayu* (green tea–flavored rice porridge). During the day Tō-no-chaya serves a light meal of this special dish, with sashimi and vegetables, plus a few

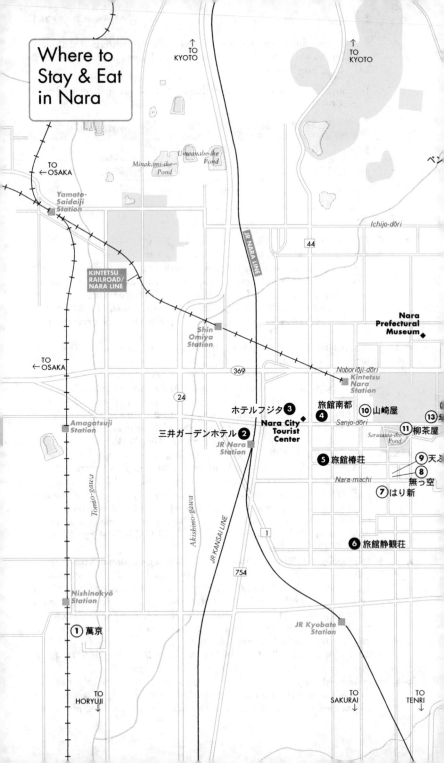

Where to Stay & Eat in Nara

↑ TO KYOTO

↑ TO KYOTO

ペン

TO ←OSAKA

Yamato-Saidaiji Station

Minakami-ike Pond

Umeanabe-ike Pond

Ichijo-dōri

JR NARA LINE

44

KINTETSU RAILROAD/ NARA LINE

Nara Prefectural Museum ◆

Shin Omiya Station

Noboriōji-dōri

Kintetsu Nara Station

TO ←OSAKA

369

24

ホテルフジタ **3**

旅館南都 **4**

10 山崎屋

13

Sanjo-dōri

Nara City Tourist Center

Sarusawa-ike Pond

11 柳茶屋

Amagatsuji Station

三井ガーデンホテル **2**

JR Nara Station

5 旅館椿荘

9 天ぷ

8

無っ空

Nara-machi

7 はり新

Tomio-gawa

Akishino-gawa

JR KANSAI LINE

1

6 旅館静観荘

754

Nishinokyō Station

JR Kyobate Station

1 萬京

TO HORYUJI ↓

TO SAKURAI ↓

TO TENRI ↓

ON THE MENU

Nara's specialty, like Kyōto's, is kaiseki, a carefully prepared and aesthetically arranged 7- to 12-course set meal using the freshest ingredients. Simpler set meals might include tempura and soba (buckwheat noodles). One popular local dish, cha-gayu, rice porridge flavored with green tea and served with seasonal vegetables, is known for its healthfulness. Both local wisdom—which attributes Nara's low rate of stomach cancer to cha-gayu—and Western doctors have

acknowledged its benefits. Often with traditional meals you'll be served nara-zuke, tangy vegetables pickled in sake, as a side dish.

sweetened rice cakes for dessert. The restaurant was named Tō-no-chaya, which means "tearoom of the pagoda," because you can see the Five-Story Pagoda of Kōfuku-ji from here. Bento-box meals are served 11:30–4. You must reserve ahead for cha-gayu in the evenings. ⊠ 47 Noborioji-chō ☎ 0742/22–4348 ⊟ No credit cards ⊘ Closed Tues.

$$–$$$$ ✕ **Yamazakiya** (山崎屋). Pungent nara-zuke will lure you off the street into this well known shop and adjoining restaurant. Inside you can watch white-capped staff members busily preparing packages of pickles that you can try with cha-gayu or a meal of tempura. The menus are on display, keeping ordering simple, and this is a good place to take a break from the crowds on Higashi-mukō-dori, the main shopping street. Nara Kintetsu Station and Nara Kōen are within a five-minute walk. ⊠ 5 Minami-chō ☎ 0742/22–8039 ⊟ No credit cards ⊘ Closed Mon.

Nara-machi

$$$–$$$$ ✕ **Harishin** (はり新). Because this Nara-machi restaurant is traditional and quite rustic, you sit in either a large tatami room overlooking a garden or around a large irori (hearth). The Kamitsumichi bento, with a selection of sashimi, tofu, fried shrimp, vegetables, and homemade plum liqueur, is a bargain at ¥2,500. From the southwest corner of Sarusawa-ike, head south into Nara-machi. Harishin is on your right shortly after crossing the main road. Smoking is not permitted at lunchtime. ⊠ 15 Nakashinya-chō ☎ 0742/22–2669 ⊟ AE, D, MC, V ⊘ Closed Mon.

$$–$$$ ✕ **Tempura Asuka** (天ぷら飛鳥). If you choose from the selection of set meals, make sure you pick one with tempura—the house specialty, of course. Other fare ranges from a light tempura-soba lunch to an elaborate kaiseki dinner. Lunch options start at only ¥1,000. As with other less formal Nara-machi restaurants, you can sit at the counter, at a table over-

looking the garden, or in a tatami room. ⊠ *11 Shōnami-chō* ☎ *0742/ 26–4308* 🖃 *AE, DC, MC, V* ☯ *Closed Mon.*

$$ ✕ **Muku** (無っ空). Housed in a former artisan's home full of antiques and pottery, this lunch-only restaurant is a delight. The daily lunch course (there's only one) consists of healthful home-style dishes with *genmai* (brown rice), tofu, and seasonal vegetables. At ¥1,000, it's an excellent value. Seating is at cozy tables on tatami mats. Walk south from the south-west corner of Sarusawa-ike into Nara-machi. Muku is the last build-ing on your left before the first major road. It's open 1–6. ⊠ *22–3 Shōnami-chō* ☎ *0742/25–5140* ⚑ *Reservations not accepted* 🖃 *No credit cards* ☯ *Closed Mon.–Wed. No dinner.*

Western Nara

$$$–$$$$ ✕ **Van Kio** (萬京). This large, well-established restaurant just south of Yakushi-ji's south gate is famous for its *suien mushi* (hot-stone steam cuisine). Other specialties from the extensive menu (in English) include the *tamatebako* set meal, in which chicken and vegetables are sealed in earthenware, baked, and then opened before you with some fanfare. From the sumptuous dining room you look out onto a garden where concerts occasionally take place. The restaurant stays open all day. ⊠ *410 Rokujo-chō* ☎ *0742/33–8942* 🖃 *MC, V* ☯ *Closed Mon.*

WHERE TO STAY

Nara has accommodations in every style and price range, and because most people treat the city as a day-trip destination, at night the quiet streets are the domain of Nara's residents. If you stay over, you have a chance to stroll undisturbed beside the ponds and on temple grounds. All lodgings have air-conditioning, televisions, and communal baths un-less noted otherwise. Note that some ryokans close on Sunday nights. Hotels in Central Nara around the main railway stations tend to be nois-ier than those closer to Nara Kōen and in Nara-machi.

For a short course on accommodations in Japan, *see* Lodging *in* Smart Travel Tips A to Z.

WHAT IT COSTS In yen				
$$$$	**$$$**	**$$**	**$**	**¢**
FOR 2 PEOPLE over 22,000	18,000–22,00 0	12,000–18,000	8,000–12,000	under 8,000

Price categories are assigned based on rack rates in high season, based on the European Plan (with no meals) unless otherwise noted. Tax (5%) and service charges are extra.

Nara Kōen Area

$$$$ 🏠 **Edo-San** (江戸三). Individual cottages, some thatched, make up this ryokan in the greenery of Nara Kōen. Deer may wander to your door from the park. A kaiseki dinner, served in your cottage, is included in the price. There's a communal bath. The one drawback is its proximity to a rather noisy, major road. ⊠ *1167 Takabatake-chō, Nara-shi, Nara-ken 630-8103* ☎ *0742/26–2662* 🖷 *0742/26–2663* ⊕ *www. edosan.jp* ➷ *10 Japanese-style cottages* ⚒ *Massage, free parking* ⊟ *AE, DC, MC, V* ¶◎¶ *MAP*.

★ **$$$$** 🏠 **Kankasō** (観鹿荘). At once exquisitely refined and delightfully friendly, Kankasō exemplifies the best of Japanese hospitality. Beautiful gardens surround this intimate ryokan near Tōdai-ji, and inside, carefully arranged flowers adorn the alcove. Each room is tastefully decorated with scrolls and pottery. Although the building has been renovated extensively over the centuries, a testament to its longevity is its 1,200-year-old central beam. The communal baths look out onto the gardens. A delicious kaiseki dinner is included, as is breakfast. ⊠ *10 Kasugano-chō, Nara-shi, Nara-ken 630-8212* ☎ *0742/26–1128* 🖷 *0742/26–1301* ➷ *9 Japanese-style rooms* ⚒ *In-room safes, refrigerators, massage, gift shop, dry cleaning, free parking* ⊟ *MC, V* ¶◎¶ *MAP*.

$$$$ 🏠 **Nara Kikusuirō** (菊水楼). It's understandable that this historic, grand old ryokan just south of Kōfuku-ji is often the choice of visiting royalty and dignitaries. Built in the Meiji era, the inn has rooms lavishly furnished with antiques; the gardens are immaculately kept with a stunning variety of plants and flowers. Service is thorough and attentive. Room rates, which start at ¥70,000, include a superb kaiseki dinner. In the morning you can choose either a Western or Japanese breakfast, also included in the price. ⊠ *1130 Takabatake-chō, Nara-shi, Nara-ken 630-8301* ☎ *0742/23–2001* 🖷 *0742/26–0025* ➷ *20 Japanese-style rooms, 14 with bath; 1 suite* ⚒ *In-room fans, in-room safes, massage, shop, free parking* ⊟ *D, MC, V* ¶◎¶ *MAP*.

$$$$ 🏠 **Nara Hotel** (奈良ホテル). Overlooking several temples, this establishment is itself a site of historical and architectural interest. Built in 1909, it has a graceful tiled roof and a magnificent lobby with high wooden ceilings. It's no wonder the emperor and his family stay here when visiting Nara. Although most rooms have a good view of the temples, those in the new wing are not as interesting as the turn-of-the-20th-century-style rooms in the old wing. Dining is a special event in the superb, old-fashioned Edwardian-style room—mostly Japanese fare is served, but there are a few Western choices as well. ⊠ *1096 Takabatake-chō, Nara-shi, Nara-ken 630-8301* ☎ *0742/26–3300* 🖷 *0742/23–5252* ⊕ *www. narahotel.co.jp* ➷ *132 rooms, 3 suites* ⚒ *Restaurant, tea shop, in-room data ports, minibars, massage, bar, lobby lounge, laundry service, free parking* ⊟ *AE, D, MC, V*.

FodorsChoice
★

$$ 🏠 **Pension Nara Club** (ペンション奈良倶楽部). On a quiet street behind Tōdai-ji, this small family-run establishment is reminiscent of a European hotel. The plainly decorated rooms have simple, dark-wood furniture and private bathrooms. The surrounding neighborhood is pleasant to stroll through, and you can avoid crowds and noise altogether. A meal plan is available. ⊠ *21 Mikado-chō, Nara-shi, Nara-ken 630-8204* ☎ *0742/22–3450* 🖷 *0742/22–3490* ⊕ *www.naraclub. com* ➷ *8 rooms* ⚒ *Restaurant, massage, free parking, no-smoking rooms* ⊟ *AE, V*.

Central Nara

Hotels in Central Nara are near JR Nara Station and Kintetsu Nara Station.

$$$–$$$$ ⬜ **Tsubakisō** (旅館椿荘). Friendly service and an intimate garden make for a relaxed stay in this quiet mix of old and new. Rooms in the newer wing have suites with private baths, while rooms in the old wing share a communal bath. A cha-gayu breakfast is served in the dining room overlooking the garden. Prices include a kaiseki dinner and breakfast, and there are reduced prices for longer stays. ⊠ *35 Tsubai-chō, Nara-shi, Nara-ken 630-8343* ☎ *0742/22–5330* 🖷 *0742/27–3811* 🛏 *7 Japanese-style rooms, 3 with bath* ⚄ *In-room data ports in some rooms, minibars, parking (fee)* ⊟ *A, MC, V* ⦿ *MAP.*

$$–$$$ ⬜ **Hotel Fujita Nara** (ホテルフジタ奈良). Centrally situated between JR Nara Station and Nara Kōen, this modern hotel has simple rooms in light shades. Rates run ¥20,000–¥22,000 in peak season (April, October, and November) but drop considerably to ¥10,000–¥15,000 the rest of the year. The restaurant, Hanakagami, serves Japanese cuisine. ⊠ *47–1 Shimo Sanjo-chō, Nara-shi, Nara-ken 630-8236* ☎ *0742/23–8111* 🖷 *0742/22–0255* ⊕ *www.fujita-nara.com* 🛏 *115 rooms, 3 suites* ⚄ *Restaurant, massage, bar, lobby lounge, some free parking, no-smoking rooms* ⊟ *AE, DC, MC, V.*

$$ ⬜ **Mitsui Garden Hotel** (三井ガーデンホテル奈良). Nara's largest hotel sets out to provide comfort at reasonable rates. Rooms have large windows and are generally quite bright, but the stock furnishings are somewhat soulless. The hotel is atop a shopping arcade next to Nara JR Station, convenient for travelers who need to make an early departure. It's also close to downtown restaurants. All rooms have private baths and there's a communal bath as well. ⊠ *8–1 Sanjohommachi, Nara-shi, Nara-ken 630-8122* ☎ *0742/35–8831* 🖷 *0742/35–6868* ⊕ *www.gardenhotels.co.jp* 🛏 *330 rooms, 1 suite* ⚄ *Restaurant, café, some in-room data ports, refrigerators, massage, shop, dry cleaning, Japanese baths, laundry service, meeting rooms, parking (fee), no-smoking rooms* ⊟ *AE, D, MC, V.*

$$ ⬜ **Ryokan Nanto** (旅館南都). The quietest ryokan on the city side of Nara Kōen, Nanto has simple airy rooms and friendly service. Most rooms have toilets, some have baths, and there are large rooms for families and small groups. A Japanese bento breakfast is included. ⊠ *29 Kamisanjo-chō, Nara-shi, Nara-ken, 630-8228* ☎ *0742/22–3497* 🖷 *0742/23–0882* ⊕ *www.basho.net/nanto* 🛏 *13 Japanese-style rooms, 3 with bath* ⚄ *Dining room, lobby lounge, massage, parking (fee)* ⊟ *D, MC, V* ⦿ *CP.*

Nara-machi

$ ⬜ **Ryokan Seikansō** (旅館静観荘). Of the many inexpensive, small ryokans in Nara-machi, this friendly, family-run establishment is the pick of the bunch for its spotlessness and attentive service at a good price. The quiet neighborhood contributes to the inn's relaxed atmosphere. Simple rooms overlook a large central garden. It's very popular with international and domestic travelers, so it's best to book a room far in advance. ⊠ *29 Higashikitsuji-chō, Nara-shi, Nara-ken 630-8327* ☎ *0742/22–2670*

🕿 0742/22–2670 🛏 9 *Japanese-style rooms* 🅿 *Free parking; no a/c* 💳 *AE, MC, V.*

NARA A TO Z

To research prices, get advice from other travelers, and book travel arrangements, visit www.fodors.com.

AIRPORTS & TRANSFERS
The nearest airports are in Ōsaka. All international and a few domestic flights use Kansai International Airport (KIX). Most domestic flights use Itami Airport. The hourly airport limousine bus from KIX takes 90 minutes and costs ¥1,800. From Itami, buses leave hourly, take 55 minutes, and cost ¥1,440.

BIKE TRAVEL
Because Nara is a small city with relatively flat roads, biking is a good way to get around. You can rent a bicycle from Kintetsu Sunflower. The cost is ¥900 for the day (until 5); on weekends it's ¥1,000. Ask the Nara City Tourist Information Office, in Kintetsu Nara Station, for further information or directions. Some hotels also rent bicycles.
🚲 Bike Rentals **Kintetsu Sunflower** ⊠ On Konishi-dōri, near Kintetsu Nara Station 🕿 0742/24-3528.

BUS TRAVEL
The most economical way to explore Nara is by bus. Two local routes circle the main sites (Tōdai-ji, Kasuga Taisha, and Shin-Yakushi-ji) in the central and eastern parts of the city: Bus 1 runs counterclockwise, and Bus 2 runs clockwise. This urban loop line costs ¥180. Both stop at JR Nara Station and Kintetsu Nara Station. Bus 97 west to Hōryū-ji (with stops at Tōshōdai-ji and Yakushi-ji) takes about 50 minutes and costs ¥760; you can catch it in front of either station. Pick up a bus map at the Nara City Tourist Center.

EMBASSIES & CONSULATES
The nearest U.S., U.K., and Canadian consulates are in Ōsaka; the nearest Australian and New Zealand embassies are in Tōkyō (⇨ Embassies *in* Smart Travel Tips).

EMERGENCIES
🚑 **Ambulance** 🕿 119. **Nara National Hospital** 🕿 0742/24-1251. **Kintetsu Nara police station** 🕿 0742/22-5612. **Police** 🕿 110.

TAXIS
The rate is ¥610 for the first 1½ km (1 mi) and ¥90 for each additional 1,300 ft. From Kintetsu Nara Station to Kasuga Taisha it's about ¥900; to Hōryū-ji, about ¥5,000.

TOURS
The Japan Travel Bureau conducts daily tours of Nara in English. The five-hour (¥6,300) tour departs from Kyōto at 1:40. Reservations must be made one day in advance.

The Student Guide Service and the YMCA Guide Service are free and depart from the JR Nara Station information center and Kintetsu Nara Station. Guides are friendly and helpful, though not always fluent in English. And because they're volunteers, it's best to call in advance to determine availability.

The Japan National Tourist Office (JNTO) publishes the leaflet "Walking Tour Courses in Nara," for a self-guided two-hour tour of Nara Kōen and several nearby temples and shrines; other tours start with a bus ride from the city center. There's no JNTO office in Nara; *see* Visitor Information *in* Smart Travel Tips A to Z for addresses elsewhere in Japan.
🚹 **Japan Travel Bureau** ☎ 075/341-1413. **Student Guide Service** ✉ Sarusawa Tourist Information Center, 49 Nobori Ōji-chō, north side of Sarusawa-ike ☎ 0742/26-4753. **YMCA Guide Service** ✉ Kasuga Taisha ☎ 0742/45-5920.

TRAIN TRAVEL
From Kyōto, the private Kintetsu Railway's Limited Express trains (¥1,110) leave every half hour for the 33-minute trip to Nara. Three JR trains from Kyōto run every hour. The express takes 45 minutes; the two locals take 70 minutes. All JR trains cost ¥740 without a JR Pass (⇨ Train Travel in Smart Travel Tips A to Z).

From Ōsaka's Kintetsu Namba Station, Nara is a 31-minute ride on a Limited Express (¥1,040). Trains leave every hour. Ordinary Express trains (¥540) leave every 20 minutes, and the trip takes 35 minutes. The JR Line from Tennō-ji Station takes 50 minutes and costs ¥450; from JR Namba it costs ¥540 and takes 40 minutes; from Ōsaka Station it takes one hour and costs ¥780.

From Kōbe, take the JR Tōkaidō Line rapid train from San-no-miya Station to Ōsaka and transfer to one of the trains listed above.

Both JR Nara Station and Kintetsu Nara Station are close to major sights. Because these sights are concentrated in the western part of the city, you'll do much of your sightseeing on foot. One exception is Hōryū-ji, which is best accessed by a JR train from JR Nara Station. The ride to Hōryū-ji Station takes 11 minutes and costs ¥210.

VISITOR INFORMATION
The Nara City Tourist Information Office is on the first floor of Kintetsu Nara Station and is open daily 9–5.

A city information window, open daily 9–5, can be found at JR Nara Station—and its staff is always helpful.

Nara City Tourist Center is open daily 9–9, but the English-speaking staff is only on duty until 7 PM. The center is a 10-minute walk from both Kintetsu Nara Station and JR Nara Station and has free maps, sightseeing information in English, a souvenir corner, and a lounge where you can rest and plan your day.
🚹 Tourist Information **City Information Window** ✉ JR Nara Station, 1 Banchi Sanjō, Hon-machi, Nara-shi ☎ 0742/22-9821. **Nara City Tourist Center** ✉ 23-4 Kami-sanjo-chō, Nara-shi ☎ 0742/22-3900. **Nara City Tourist Information Office** ✉ Kintetsu Nara Station, 29 Nakamachi, Higashi-muki, Nara-shi ☎ 0742/24-4858.

ŌSAKA 大阪

7

By Nigel Fisher

Updated by
Dominic
Al-Badri

JAPAN'S SECOND CITY in terms of industry, commerce, and technology, Ōsaka is known for its dynamic spirit, superb restaurants, and Bunraku puppet theater. It's not a window to Japan's past—go to Kyōto and Nara for that—but a storefront display of what moves the country today.

Anyone older than 70 in Japan remembers Ōsaka as an exotic maze of crisscrossing waterways that provided transportation for the booming merchant trade. All but a few of the canals and nearly all of the traditional wooden buildings were destroyed by the bombings of World War II. Architecturally, the city has leapt into the future with such buildings as the Imperial Hotel on the bank of the Yodo-gawa (Yodo River), the inverted U-shape of the Umeda Sky Building, and the enormous Ferris wheel on top of the HEP Five complex. The city is working hard to restore some of the beauty that was lost, with a strong movement for establishing green natural areas.

Ōsaka is still a merchant city, with many streets devoted to wholesale commerce. For example, medical and pharmaceutical companies congregate in Dosho-machi, and fireworks and toys are found in Matcha-machi-suji, which is also famous for shopping. Head to Umeda, Shin-Sai-bashi, or Namba for the greatest concentration of department stores, movie theaters, and restaurants. The city's nightlife is also legendary. Be sure to stroll through the Dōtombori-dōri area, beside Dōtom-bori-gawa (Dōtombori River), which has more nightclubs and bars per square foot than any other part of town. Although Ōsaka may not have many sights of historical interest, it's a good, central starting point for trips to Nara, Kyōto, Kōya-san (Mt. Koya), and Kōbe.

See the glossary at the end of this book for definitions of the common Japanese words and suffixes used in this chapter.

EXPLORING ŌSAKA

Ōsaka is divided into 26 wards, and though the official city population is only 2.6 million, if you were to include the rest of Ōsaka Prefecture, this number would jump to nearly 9 million. Central Ōsaka is predominantly a business district, with some shopping and entertainment. The JR Kanjō-sen (Loop Line) circles the city center. Ōsaka Station, the primary train station for the city, is at the north end of this loop. In front of Ōsaka Station, to the east of Hankyū Umeda Station, is the center of Kita-ku (Kita Ward), one of Ōsaka's major shopping areas. Although ultramodern skyscrapers soar above the streets, Umeda Chika Center is an underground maze of malls, crowded with dozens of restaurants, shops that carry the latest fashions, and department stores that sell every modern gadget.

If you continue south, you come to two rivers, Dōjima-gawa and Tosa-bori-gawa, with the Naka-no-shima (Inner Island) separating them. Here's Ōsaka's oldest park, which is home to many of the city's cultural and administrative institutions, including the Bank of Japan and the Municipal Art Museum of Asian Ceramics.

South of these rivers and Naka-no-shima are the Minami and Shin-Sai-bashi districts, though the boundary between the two is hard to distinguish. Shin-Sai-bashi was once Ōsaka's most expensive shopping street, but with the downturn in the economy in the 1990s it has become less exclusive, especially at its southern end. Nearby Amerika Mura, with its cubbyhole-size fashion outlets, and Yōroppa Mura, with continental boutiques, appeal to young Ōsaka trendsetters. Minami-ku has a wonderful assortment of bars and restaurants, especially on Dōtombori-dōri. The National Bunraku Theater is also close by, a few blocks southeast, near the Nippon-bashi subway station.

If you come by train you're likely to arrive by Shinkansen at Shin-Ōsaka Station. Three kilometers (2 mi) north of Ōsaka Station, the main railway station, amid some of the city's most modern architecture, Shin-Ōsaka is close to Senri Expo Park. To get to the city center from Shin-Ōsaka Station, take either the Midō-suji subway line to Umeda or, if you have a Japan Rail Pass, the JR Kōbe Line to Ōsaka Station. The Umeda subway station and Ōsaka Station are next to each other, on the edge of central Ōsaka.

Timing

Spring and fall, with their crisp air, are the best seasons to visit. Ōsaka can become very hot and humid in summer, and winter can get a bit chilly.

a good tour

Start your exploration of Ōsaka with the city's major landmark, **Ōsaka-jō** ❶ ▶, the castle that Hideyoshi Toyotomi built in the late 16th century. You can easily reach it by taking the Loop Line from JR Ōsaka Station to Ōsaka-jō Kōen Station, from which it's a 10-minute walk uphill through the park.

Leave the castle and, facing north, walk down the hill past Ōsaka-jō Hōru (Ōsaka-jō Hall), which is used for sports competitions and concerts, and cross the overpass near the Aqua Liner water-bus pier. On Sunday afternoons this area hosts amateur bands, each with its own gaggle of adoring fans. Enthusiasm and fashionable outfits make up for the often rudimentary music skills. On the other side of Hirano-gawa (Hirano River) are the Hotel New Ōtani and Ōsaka Business Park, full of modern, high-rise office blocks. The two mighty skyscrapers you see within the business park are the Twin 21 Towers, a symbol of Japan's rush into the 21st century.

Next, stop in to see the ceramics exhibits of **Municipal Art Museum of Asian Ceramics** ❷, on the eastern end of Naka-no-shima, the island in Nakano-shima Kōen. To get here from Ōsaka Business Park, walk northeast for five minutes to Kyōbashi Station and take the Keihan Line to the Yodoya-bashi stop. The museum is a five-minute walk away. Ōsaka Festival Hall, which is considered the city's best concert hall, and part of the Ōsaka University campus are also on the island.

From here it's a 15-minute walk up to the city's Umeda district, home to JR Ōsaka Station, three of the city's department stores, and the **HEP Five** ❸ shopping plaza, complete with a giant Ferris wheel on its roof.

Take the Midō-suji subway line from Yodoya-bashi to Shin-Sai-bashi Station. When you emerge, you're on **Midō-suji** ❹. Shin-Sai-bashi and Ebisu-bashi-suji, which run parallel to Midō-suji, are two of Ōsaka's

Ōsaka is known for its dynamism, and you can enjoy the fruits of this energy in a couple of days. If you stay longer, use Ōsaka as a base to explore the surrounding Kansai region—Kyōto, Nara, and Kōbe are each 30 minutes away by train. Ōsaka is also the most convenient jumping-off point for a trip to the mountainside monasteries of Kōya-san, two hours away on the Nankai private rail line.

Numbers in the text correspond to numbers in the margin and on the Ōsaka map.

7

If you have
1 day

Twenty-four hours in Ōsaka will give you a chance to catch many of the city's major sights. **Ōsaka-jō** ① ▶, Ōsaka's majestic castle, should be first on your list. Then head south to **Tennō-ji Kōen** ⑨, a park that contains the **Municipal Museum of Fine Art** ⑩ and its collection of classical Japanese art. Nearby **Shitennō-ji** ⑫, also known as Tennō-ji, is the oldest Buddhist temple in Japan. In the afternoon head to **Den Den Town** ⑧ to browse through the gadget stores or to **Yōroppa Mura** ⑥ and **Amerika Mura** ⑤ for fashion. At the end of the day, **Dōtombori-dōri** ⑦ is the place to go for dinner and nightlife.

If you have
2 days

With two full days in Ōsaka, you can cover all the city's major sights. To the above day-in-town suggestions, add **Sumiyoshi Taisha** ⑬, one of the three most famous shrines in Japan, **Senri Expo Park** ⑮ and its museums, the **Municipal Art Museum of Asian Ceramics** ② in Naka-no-shima Kōen, and the shops on **Midō-suji** ④. Plan to catch a performance at the National Bunraku Theater late in the afternoon. To wrap up your stay, instead of heading to Dōtombori-dōri after dark, go to central Ōsaka.

---

best shopping and entertainment streets. West of Midō-suji, **Amerika Mura** ⑤—America Village—is a group of streets with trendy clothing shops, music stores, and nightclubs. East of Midō-suji, **Yōroppa Mura** ⑥— Europe Village—has numerous stylish European boutiques, but is less well defined than its American cousin.

Walk south on Midō-suji and cross Dōtombori-gawa to **Dōtombori-dōri** ⑦, a broad cross street that runs alongside the canal. The street and the area around it are filled with bars, restaurants, and nightclubs.

At the far southern end of Midō-suji are the Kabuki-za and the Takashimaya department stores. From Namba Station (the subway station, not Nankai Namba Station, the train station) on Dōtombori-dōri, take the Sennichi-mae subway line one stop east to Nippon-bashi Station. Nearby is **Den Den Town** ⑧, *the* place to go for discounted electronics. While you're in the area, try to attend an afternoon performance at the National Bunraku Theater (afternoon performances are usually held at 4 PM). Exit 7 leads from the station to right outside the theater.

Now head to the east end of Den Den Town for **Tennō-ji Kōen** ⑨ and its peaceful ponds and gardens. In the park, consider visiting the **Municipal**

Museum of Fine Art ⑩, with its ancient and modern art and ancient pottery and artifacts. Rest a while in the adjacent **Keitaku-en** ⑪, a calming garden with cherry trees and azaleas around a pond. Your next stop is north of Tennō-ji Kōen at **Shitennō-ji** ⑫, usually referred to as Tennō-ji. Founded in 593, though resurrected many a time, it's said to be the oldest Buddhist temple in Japan.

To supplement or substitute sights on the tour above, keep in mind the following. At the southern reaches of Ōsaka is one of the three most famous shrines in Japan, **Sumiyoshi Taisha** ⑬. In the Nankō port area is the **Ōsaka Aquarium** ⑭, the country's finest aquarium. In the city's northern quarters are **Senri Expo Park** ⑮ and its four museums. Two are particularly worth your time: **Japan Folk Art Museum** ⑯, for its outstanding traditional regional handicrafts, and **National Museum of Ethnology** ⑰, for its exhibits on comparative cultures of the world.

Film buffs and amusement-park fans may want to add a day to enjoy the attractions of **Universal Studios Japan** ⑱.

Timing

Most museums are closed Monday. One notable exception is Senri Expo Park, which closes along with its museums Wednesday instead. Museums stay open on Monday national holidays, closing the following day instead. Likewise, Senri Expo Park stays open on Wednesday holidays, closing Thursday instead.

What to See

North of Chūō-dōri

Hattori Ryokuchi Kōen (服部緑地公園). The main appeal of this park is the open-air **Museum of Old Japanese Farmhouses** (Nihon Minka Shūraku Hakubutsukan), which has full-size replicas of traditional rural buildings from all over the country. Also here are horseback-riding facilities, tennis courts, a youth hostel, a swimming pool, and an open-air stage, which hosts concerts and other events in the summer. Take the Midō-suji subway line from Umeda to Ryokuchi Kōen Station. The park is a 10-minute walk away. ⊠ *1–1 Hattori Ryokuchi, Toyonaka-shi* ☎ *06/6862–4946 park office, 06/6862–3137 museum* ⊡ *Park free, museum ¥500* ☉ *Apr.–Oct., daily 10–5, last entry at 4:30; Nov.–Mar., daily 10–4:30, last entry at 4.*

❸ **HEP Five** (ヘップファイブ). With its 11 floors of restaurants, shops, and entertainment facilities, HEP Five (the acronym *HEP* is short for Hankyū Entertainment Plaza) appears to be just another enormous shopping palace in Ōsaka's already world-class collection. What makes HEP Five special, though, is the enormous Ferris wheel on its roof, which at its apex is a good 40 feet taller than the Statue of Liberty. It's a very popular place for young couples—the most popular date spot in the city, in fact—so expect a wait to ride the wheel on weekends. ⊠ *Kita-ku, 3 min north of Hankyū Umeda terminus* ☎ *06/6366–3636* ⊡ *Ferris wheel ¥500* ☉ *Hrs vary.*

⑯ **Japan Folk Art Museum** (Nihon Mingei-kan, 日本民芸館). Exhibiting many outstanding examples of traditional regional handicrafts, this museum in Senri Expo Park is one of the best places in all Japan to see ceram-

7

Ōsakan Cuisine

Ōsakans are passionate about food. As the old saying goes, *Ōsaka wa kuida-ore*—Ōsaka people squander their money on food. They expect the restaurants they frequent to use the freshest ingredients available—a reasonable conceit that developed over centuries of reliance on the nearby Seto Inland Sea, which allowed all classes easy access to fresh seafood. Ōsakans continue to have discriminating palates and demand their money's worth. Prices in Ōsaka, both for food and lodging, are generally a better value than in Kyōto.

Ōsakan cuisine is flavored with a soy sauce that is lighter in color, milder in flavor, and saltier in content than the soy used in Tōkyō. One local delicacy is *okonomiyaki*, grilled pancakes filled with cabbage, mountain yams, pork, shrimp, and other ingredients. *Ōsaka-zushi* (Ōsaka-style sushi), made in wooden molds, has a distinctive square shape. *Unagi* (eel) prepared in several styles remains a popular local dish; grilled unagi is often eaten in summer for quick energy. *Fugu* (blowfish) served boiled or raw is a winter delicacy that is less expensive in Ōsaka than in other Japanese cities.

The thick white noodles known as *udon* are a Japanese staple, but Ōsakans are particularly fond of *kitsune* udon, a local dish now popular throughout the nation in which the noodles are served with fried tofu known as *abura-age*. Another Ōsaka invention is *takoyaki*, griddle-cooked dumplings with bits of octopus, green onions, and ginger smothered in a delicious sauce. Sold by street vendors in Dōtombori, these tasty snacks also appear at every festival and street market in Kansai.

Puppet Theater

Ōsaka is the home of Bunraku (puppet drama), which originated during the Heian period (794–1192). In the late 17th and early 18th centuries the genius of local playwright Chikamatsu distilled Bunraku as an art form. Bunraku puppets are about two-thirds human size. Three puppeteers move the puppets, and they are completely visible to the audience. These master puppeteers not only skillfully manipulate the puppets' arms and legs but also roll the eyes and move the lips so that the puppets express fear, joy, and sadness. A typical play deals with themes of tragic love or stories based on historical events. At the National Bunraku Theater, the story is chanted in song by a *jōruri*, who is accompanied by ballad music played on a three-stringed instrument, the shamisen. Although you may not understand the words, the tone of the music will set an appropriate mood of pathos.

Also, perhaps out of rivalry with Tōkyō, the city has renovated an old theater and incorporated technological innovations that are better than those found in the capital. The Shōchiku-za Kabuki Theater puts on Kabuki in addition to modern plays and variety shows.

ics, textiles, wooden crafts, and bamboo ware and to familiarize yourself with Japanese handicrafts. ☒ *10–5 Bampaku Kōen, Senri Expo Park, Senri, Suita-shi* ☎ *06/6877–1971* 🎟 *¥700* ⏱ *Thurs.–Tues. 10–5; last entry at 4:30.*

Minō Kōen (箕面公園). Ōsakans come here in autumn to admire the dazzling fall foliage, especially the maple trees, whose leaves turn brilliant crimson. The path along the river leads to the Minō-no-taki (Minō Waterfall). Monkeys reside here in a protected habitat, which is always open and free to the public. ☒ *Minō, 30 min from Hankyū Umeda Station on Minō subway line, north of Minō Station* 🎟 *Free.*

Mint Museum (Zōhei, 造幣博物館). Part of the Ministry of Finance, this money museum exhibits some 16,000 examples of Japanese and foreign currencies. Also on display are Olympic medals, prehistoric currency, and ancient Japanese gold coins. Part of the Mint Bureau's grounds are open to the public for a short period during the cherry-blossom season (usually April); during this time you can stroll on a blossoms-shaded path along the Yodo-gawa. The Zohei is a 15-minute walk east of Minami-Mori-machi Station on the Tani-machi subway line. ☒ *1–1–79 Tenma, Kita-ku* ☎ *06/6351–8509* ⊕ *www.mint.go.jp* 🎟 *Free* ⏱ *Weekdays 9–4:30; last entry at 4.*

★ ❷ **Municipal Art Museum of Asian Ceramics** (Ōsaka Shiritsu Tōyō Jiki Bijutsukan, 大阪市立東洋陶磁美術館). This world-class museum within Naka-no-shima Kōen, the city's oldest park (opened in 1891), houses about 1,000 pieces of Chinese, Korean, and Japanese ceramics. The collection, rated as one of the finest in the world, includes 14 works that have been designated National Treasures or Important Cultural Properties. The work comes mostly from the priceless Ataka collection, which belonged to a wealthy industrialist and was donated to the museum by the giant Sumitomo Group conglomerate. To get here take the Sakai-suji subway line to Kita-hama or the Midō-suji subway line to Yodoya-bashi and walk north across the Tosabori-gawa to the museum. ☒ *1–1 Naka-no-shima, Kita-ku* ☎ *06/6223–0055* 🎟 *¥500* ⏱ *Tues.–Sun. 9:30–5; last entry at 4:30.*

❶⑦ **National Museum of Ethnology** (Kokuritsu Minzokugaku Hakubutsukan, 国立民族学博物館). Within this modern black-and-silver building are regional exhibits on world cultures, including good displays on the Ainu (the original inhabitants of Japan) and other aspects of Japanese culture. Automatic audiovisual equipment, called Videotheque, provides close-up views of customs of the peoples of the world. An English pamphlet that comes with your admission ticket explains these fascinating displays. Comprehensive information sheets explaining all the sections of the museum are also available on request. The museum is on the east side of the main road that runs north–south through Senri Expo Park. ☒ *Senri Expo Park, Senri, Suita-shi* ☎ *06/6876–2151* ⊕ *www.minpaku. ac.jp/english/* 🎟 *¥420* ⏱ *Thurs.–Tues. 10–5; last entry at 4:30.*

Fodor'sChoice ★ ❶④ **Ōsaka Aquarium** (Kaiyūkan, 海遊館). Widely regarded as the nation's best aquarium, this unusual red, gray, and blue building is one of the biggest aquariums in the world. More than 11,000 tons of water—the

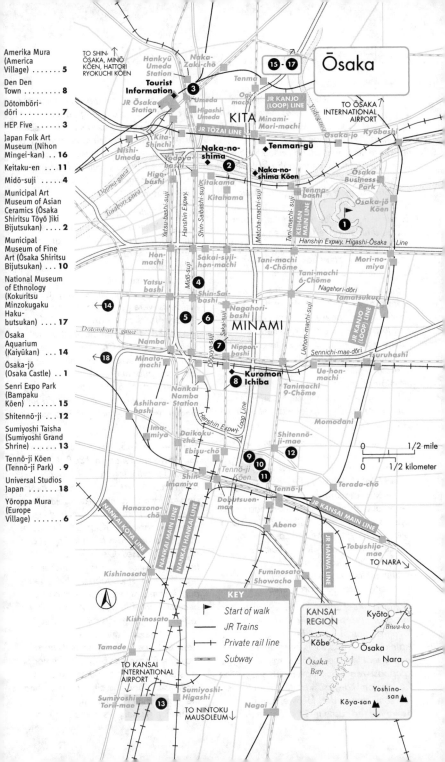

Ōsaka

KITA

MINAMI

Tourist Information

TO SHIN-ŌSAKA, MINŌ KŌEN, HATTORI RYOKUCHI KŌEN

TO ŌSAKA INTERNATIONAL AIRPORT

TO NARA

TO KANSAI INTERNATIONAL AIRPORT

TO NINTOKU MAUSOLEUM

Hankyū Umeda Station
Naka-Zaki-chō
Tenma
Ogi-machi
JR KANJO (LOOP) LINE
JR Ōsaka Station
Umeda
Higashi-Umeda
Minami-Mori-machi
Ōsaka-jo
Kyobashi
Yodogawa
JR TŌZAI LINE
Kita-Shinchi
Nishi-Umeda
Yodoya-bashi
Naka-no-shima
Tenman-gū
Osaka Business Park
Higo-bashi
Naka-no-shima Kōen
Tenma-bashi
Ōsaka-jō Kōen
Dojima-gawa
Kitakama
Kitahama
Tosabori-gawa
Hanshin Expwy. Higashi-Ōsaka Line
KEIHAN MAIN LINE
Hon-machi
Sakai-suji-hon-machi
Tani-machi 4-Chōme
Mori-no-miya
Yatsu-bashi
Tani-machi 6-Chōme
Nagahori-dōri
Shin-Sai-bashi
Nagahori-bashi
Tamatsukuri
Dōtombori-gawa
Namba
Nippon-bashi
Sennichi-mae-dōri
Tsuruhashi
Minato-machi
Kuromon Ichiba
Ue-hon-machi
Nankai Namba Station
Tanimachi 9-Chōme
Ashihara-bashi
Ima-miya
Daikoku-chō
Momodani
Ebisu-chō
Shitennō-ji-mae
Shin-Imamiya
Tennō-ji Kōen
Tennō-ji
Terada-chō
Hanazono-chō
Dōbutsuen-mae
Abeno
JR KANSAI MAIN LINE
JR HANWA LINE
Tobushio-mae
Kishinosato
Fuminosato
Showacho
Kishinosato
Tamade
Sumiyoshi-Higashi
Sumiyoshi Torii-mae
Nagai
NANKAI KOYA LINE
NANKAI MAIN LINE
NANKAI HANKAI LINE
Loop Line
Hanshin Expwy.
Yatsu-bashi-suji
Shin-Saibashi-suji
Midō-suji
Sakai-suji
Hanshin Expwy.
Matcha-machi-suji
Tani-machi-suji
Uehon-machi-suji

KANSAI REGION
Kyōto
Biwa-ko
Kōbe
Ōsaka
Nara
Ōsaka Bay
Yoshino-san
Kōya-san

0 — 1/2 mile
0 — 1/2 kilometer

CloseUp

A SHORT HISTORY OF ŌSAKA

Ō SAKA BEGAN EXPANDING *as a trading center at the end of the 16th century. But until the Meiji Restoration in 1868, the* merchant class was at the bottom of the social hierarchy, even though plenty of merchants were among the richest people in Japan. Denied the usual aristocratic cultural pursuits, merchants sought and developed their pleasures in the theater and in dining. Indeed, it's often said that many a successful Ōsaka businessperson has eventually gone bankrupt by spending too much on eating.

In the 4th and 5th centuries, the Ōsaka-Nara region was the center of the developing Japanese (Yamato) nation. It was through Ōsaka that knowledge and culture from mainland Asia filtered into the fledgling Japanese society. During the 5th and 6th centuries, several emperors maintained an imperial court in Ōsaka, but the city lost its political importance after a permanent capital was set up in Nara in 694.

For the next several hundred years, Ōsaka, then known as Naniwa, was just another backwater port on the Seto Nai-kai (Seto Inland Sea). At the end of the 16th century, however, Hideyoshi Toyotomi (1536–98), the great warrior and statesman, had one of Japan's most majestic castles built in Ōsaka following his successful unification of Japan. The castle took three years to complete. Hideyoshi encouraged merchants from around the country to set up their businesses in the city, which soon prospered.

Not long after Hideyoshi died, Ieyasu Tokugawa usurped power from the Toyotomi clan in 1603. But the clan maintained Ōsaka as its base. In 1614 Ieyasu sent his troops from Kyōto to Ōsaka to oppose rebellious movements supporting the Toyotomis. Ieyasu's army defeated the Toyotomi clan and its followers and destroyed the castle in 1615. Even though the Tokugawa shogunate eventually rebuilt the castle, Ōsaka once again found itself at a distance from Japan's political scene. Ōsaka's merchants, left to themselves far from the shōgun's administrative center in Edo—now Tōkyō—continued to prosper, and they channeled products from the hinterland to Kyōto and Edo.

During this time of economic growth, some of Japan's business dynasties were founded, whose names still reign today—Sumitomo, Marubeni, Sanwa, and Daiwa. Their growing wealth gave them the means to pursue culture, and by the end of the Genroku era (17th century), Ōsaka's residents were giving patronage to such literary giants as the dramatist Chikamatsu (1653–1724) and the novelist Saikaku Ihara (1642–93). Chikamatsu's genius as a playwright elevated Bunraku, traditional Japanese puppet drama, to a dignified dramatic art. Also at this time, Ōsakan merchants' patronage of comic Kabuki theater helped the form grow to maturity.

With the opening of Japan to Western commerce in 1853 and the end of the Tokugawa shogunate in 1868, Ōsaka stepped into the forefront of Japan's commerce. At first Yokohama was the major port for Japan's foreign trade, but after the Great Kantō Earthquake leveled it in 1923, foreigners looked to Kōbe and Ōsaka as alternative gateways for their import and export businesses. Ōsaka's merchant heritage positioned it well for industrial growth—iron, steel, fabrics, ships, heavy and light machinery, and chemicals all became part of its output. As a result, the region today accounts for 25% of Japan's industrial product and 40% of the nation's exports. Since the building of its harbor facilities, Ōsaka has become a major port in its own right, and it relies less on the facilities in Kōbe; the city's ferry terminal is the largest in the country, handling nearly 60 million passengers a year.

largest volume in an aquarium worldwide—hold a multitude of sea creatures, including whale sharks, king penguins, giant spider crabs, jellyfish, and sea otters. There are 15 different re-created environments to stroll through, including regions representing the rivers and streams of Japanese and Ecuadorian forests, the icy waters around Antarctica, the dark depths of the Japan Sea, and the volcanically active Pacific Ring of Fire. To get here, take the Chūō subway line to Ōsaka-kō Station; the aquarium is a five-minute walk from the station. ⊠ *1–1–10 Kaigandōri, Minato-ku* ☎ *06/6576–5501* ⊕ *www.kaiyukan.com/eng/index.htm* ☞ *¥2,000* ۞ *Tues.–Sun. 10–8; last entry at 7.*

▶ ❶ **Ōsaka-jō** (Ōsaka Castle, 大阪城). Ōsaka's castle, one of Hideyoshi Toyotomi's finest buildings, is without doubt the city's most famous sight.
Fodor's Choice The first stones were laid in 1583, and for the next three years as many
★ as 100,000 workers labored to build a majestic and impregnable castle. Note the thickness and the height of the walls. In order to demonstrate their loyalty to Hideyoshi, the feudal lords from the provinces were requested to contribute immense granite rocks. The largest piece of stone is said to have been donated by Hideyoshi's general, Kiyomasa Katō (1562–1611), who had it brought from Shōdo-shima (Shōdo Island), off Shikoku. Known as Higo-Ishi, the rock measured a gigantic 19 feet high and 47 feet wide.

Hideyoshi was showing off with this castle. He had united Japan after a period of devastating civil wars, and he wanted to secure his western flanks. He also wanted to establish Ōsaka as a merchant town that could distribute the produce from the surrounding wealthy territories. The castle was intended to demonstrate Hideyoshi's power and commitment to Ōsaka in order to attract merchants from all over Japan.

Hideyoshi's plan succeeded, but within two years of his death in 1598, Ieyasu Tokugawa, an executor of Hideyoshi's will, took power and got rid of Hideyoshi's son's guardians. However, it was not until 1614 that Ieyasu sent his armies to defeat the Toyotomi family and their allies. In 1615 the castle was destroyed.

During a 10-year period the Tokugawa shogunate rebuilt the castle according to original plans, and this version stood from 1629 until 1868, when the Tokugawa shogunate's power came to an end. Rather than let the castle fall into the hands of the forces of the Meiji Restoration, Tokugawa troops burned it. In 1931 the present five-story (eight stories inside) *tenshukaku* (stronghold) was built in ferroconcrete for the prestige of the city. An exact replica of the original, though marginally smaller in scale, it stands 189 feet high and has 46-ft-high stone walls. At night, when illuminated, it becomes a brilliant backdrop to the city.

Inside the castle there's a museum with artifacts of the Toyotomi family and historical objects relating to Ōsaka prior to the Tokugawa shogunate. Unless you are a Hideyoshi fan, these exhibits are of marginal interest. The castle's magnificent exterior and the impressive view from the eighth floor of the tenshukaku are the reasons to see Ōsaka-jō. If you plan ahead, and get lucky, you might catch the cherry blossoms (usually April) and **Nishi-no-maru Teien** (Nishi-no-maru Garden) at its best.

From Ōsaka-jō Kōen-mae Station it's about a 10-minute walk up the hill to the castle. You can also take the Tani-machi subway line from Higashi-Umeda Station (just southeast of Ōsaka Station) to Tani-machi 4-chōme Station. From here it's a 15-minute walk. ⊠ *1–1 Ōsaka-jō, Chūō-ku* ☎ *06/6941–3044* 🖭 *Castle ¥600, garden additional ¥210* ☾ *Sept.–mid-July, daily 9–5, last entry at 4:30; mid-July–Aug., daily 9–8:30, last entry at 8.*

❶ **Senri Expo Park** (Bampaku Kōen, 万博公園). On the former site of Expo '70—one of the defining events in Ōsaka's postwar history—this 647-acre park contains sports facilities, an enormous statue by Okamoto Taro called the *Tower of the Sun,* a garden with two teahouses, other gardens, a vast amusement park called Expo Land that's popular with families and young couples, the ⇨ **National Museum of Ethnology,** the ⇨ **Japan Folk Art Museum,** and two other smaller museums. To get to the park, take the Midō-suji subway line to Senri-Chūō Station (20 minutes from Umeda); then take the Expo Land bus to Nihon Teien-mae Station (30 minutes) or the monorail to Bampaku Kōen-mae (10 minutes). ⊠ *Senri, Suita-shi* ☎ *06/6877–0560 for Expo Land* 🖭 *Gardens ¥150–¥310 each, Expo Land ¥1,100; other facilities vary* ☾ *Mar.–late Dec., Thurs.–Tues. 9–5.*

Tenman-gū (天満宮). This 10th-century shrine is the main site of the annual **Tenjin Matsuri,** held July 24 and 25, one of the three largest and most enthusiastically celebrated festivals in Japan. During the festival, dozens of floats are paraded through the streets, and more than 100 vessels, lighted by lanterns, sail along the canals amid a dazzling display of fireworks. A renowned scholar of the 9th century, Michizane Sugawara, is enshrined at Tenman-gū; he's now considered the god of academics. Tenman-gū is a short walk from either JR Enman-gū Station or Minami-Mori-machi Station on the Tani-machi-suji subway line. ⊠ *2–1–8 Tenjin-bashi, Kita-ku* ☎ *06/6353–0025* 🖭 *Free* ☾ *Apr.–Sept., daily 5:30 AM–sunset; Oct.–Mar., daily 6 AM–sunset.*

☾ ❶ **Universal Studios Japan** (ユニバーサルスタジオジャパン). The 140-acre Universal Studios Japan (USJ) combines the most popular rides and shows from Universal's Hollywood and Florida movie-studio theme parks with special attractions designed specifically for Japan. Popular rides include those based on Hollywood films such as *Jurassic Park, Spider-Man,* and *E.T.* The Japan-only Snoopy attraction appeals to the local infatuation with all things cute. Numerous restaurants and food outlets abound throughout the park, and the road from the JR Universal City Station is lined with well-known names such as Hard Rock Cafe and Bubba Gump Shrimp, local fast-food chain Mos Burger, and Ganko Sushi.

Tickets can be bought at numerous locations throughout the city, including branches of Lawson convenience stores and at larger JR stations, as well as at USJ itself. However, due to high demand on weekends and during holiday periods, tickets must be bought in advance and are not available at the gate. The park is easily reached by direct train from JR Ōsaka Station (about 20 minutes) or by changing to a shuttle train at JR Nishi-kujo Station on the Loop Line. ⊠ *2–1–33 Sakurajima, Kono-hana-ku* ☎ *06/4790–7000* ⊕ *www.usj.co.jp* 🖭 *¥5,500* ☾ *Daily 10–10.*

South of Chūō-dōri

⑤ Amerika Mura (America Village, アメリカ村). Though it takes its name from the original shops that opened up here selling cheap American fashions and accessories, Ame-Mura (*ah*-meh *moo*-ra), as it's called, is now a bustling district full of trendy clothing shops, record stores, bars, cafés, and clubs that cater to teenagers and young adults. Shops are jammed on top of each other, and it's virtually impossible to walk on the streets weekends. For a glimpse of the variety of styles and fashions prevalent among urban youth, Ame-Mura is *the* place to go in Ōsaka. ⊠ *On west side of Midō-suji, 6 blocks south of Shin-Sai-bashi Station, Chūō-ku.*

⑧ Den Den Town (でんでんタウン). Ōsaka's equivalent of Tōkyō's Akihabara district may not be quite as large as its cousin, but it still offers plenty of specialty shops for gadget fans. All the latest electronic wonders— video games, calculators, computers, cameras, CD players—are discounted here. "Den Den" is a takeoff on the word *denki,* which means electricity. ⊠ *2 blocks east of Namba Station, Naniwa-ku.*

★ ⑦ Dōtombori-dōri (道頓堀通り). The good life of Dōtombori's restaurants and bars lures flocks of Ōsakans here to forget their daily toils. The street— a virtual feast for neonophiles—runs alongside Dōtombori-gawa, and it's the best place to stroll in the evening for a glimpse of Ōsaka nightlife. Look for the giant, undulating Kani Dōraku crab sign, a local landmark. Movie fans may be interested to know that parts of *Black Rain,* starring Michael Douglas and Andy Garcia, were filmed in the immediate area. Ebisu-bashi, the main bridge spanning the river, is a popular gathering spot for young sports fans when major events take place; the atmosphere can get quite lively. The more exuberant fans dive in—much to the annoyance of the police. ⊠ *From Umeda, take Midō-suji subway line to Namba and walk north 2 blocks up Midō-suji; or walk south from Yōroppa Mura 5 blocks on Midō-suji and cross Dōtombori-gawa, Chūō-ku.*

Fujii-dera (藤井寺). An 8th-century, 1,000-handed, seated statue of Kannon, the goddess of mercy, is the main object of worship at this temple. The statue is a National Treasure, the oldest Buddhist sculpture of its kind, and it's only on view on the 18th of each month. To get here, take the Midō-suji subway line to Tennō-ji Station; then transfer to the Kintetsu Minami–Ōsaka Line and take it to Fujii-dera Station. The temple is a few minutes' walk away. ⊠ *1–16–21 Fujii-dera, Fujii-dera-shi* ☎ *0729/38–0005* 🎟 *Free* ☉ *Statue on view 18th of month.*

⑪ Keitaku-en (慶沢園). This garden, originally constructed in 1908 as a circular garden, was given to the city by the late Baron Sumitomo. Its cherry trees and azaleas surrounding a pond are lovely when in bloom. The garden offers a welcome respite from the city. Keitaku-en is adjacent to Shiritsu Bijutsukan in Tennō-ji Kōen. ⊠ *Tennō-ji-ku* 🎟 *Included in Tennō-ji Kōen admission* ☉ *Tues.–Sun. 9:30–4:30; last entry at 4.*

④ Midō-suji (御堂筋). With its many shops, this is one of Ōsaka's major boulevards, with the Midō-suji subway running underneath it. Shin-Sai-bashi and Ebisu-bashi-suji parallel Midō-suji and are two of Ōsaka's best shopping and entertainment streets, though they are not quite as fashionable as they once were. If you're in town on the second Sunday in

October, try to catch the annual Midō-suji Parade, with its colorful procession of floats and musicians. The Shin-Sai-bashi stop on the Midō-suji subway line is in the heart of the city's shopping districts. ⊠ *Chūo-ku.*

⑩ Municipal Museum of Fine Art (Ōsaka Shiritsu Bijutsukan, 大阪市立美術館). The building might not be terribly impressive—it was taken over by the Japanese Army during World War II and then by occupation forces after the war—but the exceptional collection of 12th- to 14th-century classical Japanese art is. Other collections include the works of Edo-period artist Ogata Korin, some modern art, more than 3,000 examples of modern lacquerware, and a collection of Chinese paintings and artifacts, including several Important Cultural Properties. To get here, take the Loop Line or the Midō-suji subway line to Tennō-ji Station, or the Tani-machi subway to Shitennō-ji-mae. The museum is in Tennō-ji Kōen, southwest of Shitennō-ji. ⊠ *1–82 Chausuyama-chō, Tennō-ji-ku* ☎ *06/6771–4874* ☞ *¥300* ⊙ *Tues.–Sun. 9:30–5; last entry at 4:30.*

Nintoku Mausoleum (仁徳陵). The 4th-century mausoleum of Emperor Nintoku is in the city of Sakai, southeast of Ōsaka. The mausoleum was built on an even larger scale than that of the pyramids of Egypt—archaeologists calculate that the central mound of this site covers 1.3 million square feet. Construction took more than 20 years and required a total workforce of about 800,000 laborers. Surrounding the emperor's burial place are three moats and pine, cedar, and cypress trees. You can walk around the outer moat to get an idea of the size of the mausoleum and the grounds. However, entry into the mausoleum is not allowed. From Tennō-ji Station, take the JR Hanwa Line to Mozu Station (a half-hour ride). From there the mausoleum is a five-minute walk. ⊠ *7 Daisen-chō, Sakai-shi* ☎ *0722/41–0002.*

⑫ Shitennō-ji (Shitennō Temple, 四天王寺). Tennō-ji, as this temple is popularly known, is one of the most important historical sights in Ōsaka. Architecturally, it's gone through the wringer, having been destroyed by fire many times. The last reconstruction of the Main Hall (Kon-dō), Taishi-den, and the five-story pagoda in 1965 has maintained the original design and adhered to the traditional mathematical alignment. What has managed to survive from earlier times is the 1294 stone torii that stands at the main entrance. (Torii are rarely used at Buddhist temples.)

Shitennō-ji claims to be the oldest temple in Japan. Outdating Hōryū-ji in Nara (607), it was founded in 593. The founder, Umayado no Mikoto (573–621), posthumously known as Prince Shōtoku (Shōtoku Taishi), is considered one of early Japan's most enlightened rulers for his furthering of Buddhism and his political acumen. He was made regent over his aunt, Suiko, and set about instituting reforms and establishing Buddhism as the state religion. Buddhism had been introduced to Japan from China and Korea in the early 500s, but it was seen as a threat to the aristocracy, which claimed prestige and power based upon its godlike ancestry. Prince Shōtoku recognized both the power of Buddhism and its potential as a tool for the state. His swords and a copy of the *Hokkekyō Lotus Sutra,* written during the Heian period (897–1192), used to be stored at Shitennō-ji. Now they're kept in the Tōkyō National Museum. On the 21st of every month, the temple has a flea market that sells antiques and baubles; go in the morning for a feeling of old, pre-prosperity Japan.

Three train lines will take you near Shitennō-ji. The Tani-machi-suji subway line's Shitennō-ji-mae Station is closest both to the temple and the temple park. The Loop Line's Tennō-ji Station is several blocks south of the temple. The Midō-suji subway line also has a Tennō-ji stop, which is next to the JR station. ✉ *1–11–18 Shitennō-ji, Tennō-ji-ku* ☏ *06/6771–0066* 🔊 *¥200* ⊙ *Apr.–Sept., daily 8:30–4:30; Oct.–Mar., daily 8:30–4.*

⑬ **Sumiyoshi Taisha** (Sumiyoshi Grand Shrine, 住吉大社). Most extant Shintō shrines in Japan were built after the 8th century and were heavily influenced by Buddhist architecture. Sumiyoshi Taisha, however, is one of three shrines built prior to the arrival of Buddhism in Japan (the other two are the great Ise Jingū and Izumo Taisha near Matsue). Of the three ancient shrines, only Sumiyoshi has a Japanese cypress structure that's painted vermilion; the other two have a natural wood finish. According to Shintō custom, shrines were torn down and rebuilt at set intervals to the exact specifications of the original. Sumiyoshi, which, incidentally, is also the name given to the style of architecture of this shrine, was last replaced in 1810.

Sumiyoshi Taisha honors the goddess of sea voyages, Sumiyoshi, and, according to legend, was founded by Empress Jingū in 211 to express her gratitude for her safe return from a voyage to Korea. In those days the shrine faced the sea rather than the urban sprawl that now surrounds it. On the shrine's grounds are many stone lanterns donated by sailors and shipowners as dedications to Sumiyoshi and other Shintō deities that guard the voyages of seafarers. Note the arched bridge, said to have been given by Yodogimi, the consort of Hideyoshi Toyotomi, who bore him a son.

Every June 14, starting at 1 PM, a very colorful rice-planting festival takes place here, with various traditional folk performances and processions. Sumiyoshi Matsuri, one of the city's largest and liveliest festivals, is held from July 30 to August 1. A crowd of rowdy young men carries a 2-ton portable shrine from Sumiyoshi Taisha to Yamato-gawa and back; this event is followed by an all-night street bazaar. To reach the shrine, take the 20-minute ride south on the Nankai Main Line from Nankai Namba Station to Sumiyoshi Kōen Station. ✉ *2–9–89 Sumiyoshi, Sumiyoshi-ku* ☏ *06/6672–0753* 🔊 *Free* ⊙ *Apr.–Oct., daily 6–5; Nov.–Mar., daily 6:30–5.*

⑨ **Tennō-ji Kōen** (Tennō-ji Park, 天王寺公園). This park contains not only the ⇨ **Municipal Museum of Fine Art** and the garden of ⇨ **Keitaku-en**, but also the **Tennō-ji Botanical Gardens** (Tennō-ji Shokubutsuen). Also within the park is a prehistoric burial mound, **Chausuyama Kofun,** that was the site of Ieyasu Tokugawa's camp during the siege of Ōsaka-jō in 1614–15. Take the Loop Line from Ōsaka Station to Tennō-ji Station. The park is on the left side of the road going north to Shitennō-ji. ✉ *6–74 Chausuyama-chō, Tennō-ji-ku* ☏ *06/6771–8401* 🔊 *¥150, park only* ⊙ *Tues.–Sun. 9:30–4:30; last entry at 4.*

⑥ **Yōroppa Mura** (Europe Village, ヨーロッパ村). With its cobbled sidewalks and European-style cafés meant to re-create the atmosphere of a continental city, this neighborhood was initially touted as a more refined and cosmopolitan area than Amerika Mura. It hardly resembles a European city nowadays, and younger people tend not to use the term "Yōroppa Mura" (referring to it, instead, as the Shin-Sai-bashi area), but it's still an important shopping area. Many of Japan's top department stores, such as the Loft and Daimaru, have branches here. At the north end, Sony Tower has imported goodies for sale and the latest technological wonders on display. ☒ *East side of Midō-suji, 6 blocks south of Midō-suji subway line's Shin-Sai-bashi Station, Chūō-ku.*

WHERE TO EAT

Food of all kinds is available in Ōsaka, with the notable exception of good Middle Eastern and Mediterranean cooking. If you feel like you're in a Japanese food rut, this is the place to get out of it. Or if you just can't get enough of Japanese food, Ōsakan cuisine won't disappoint.

Surrounding Ōsaka Station are a number of self-proclaimed "gourmet palaces," each with several floors of restaurants. Exploring them can be fun. Head for restaurants in the Hankyū Grand Building, the Hankyū Samban-gai (in the basement below Hankyū Station), and Acty Ōsaka (in front of JR Ōsaka Station). Most large department stores also house scores of good restaurants, notably the Daimaru in front of JR Ōsaka Station.

Ōsaka's shopping arcades and underground shopping areas abound with affordable restaurants and coffee shops, but when in doubt, head to Dōtombori-dori and Soemon-chō (so-eh-mon cho-oh), two areas along Dōtombori-gawa that spill over with restaurants and bars. Kita-shinchi, in south Kita-ku, is the city's most exclusive dining quarter—the local equivalent of Tōkyō's Ginza.

WHAT IT COSTS In yen				
$$$$	$$$	$$	$	¢
AT DINNER	over 3,000	2,000–3,000	1,000–2,000	800–1,000	under 800

Prices are per person for a main course.

North of Chūō-dōri

★ **$$$$** ✕ **Checkers** (チェッカーズ). One of Ōsaka's best deals can be found in the comfortable, casual setting of the Hilton's ever-popular buffet-style restaurant. The buffet's theme changes regularly, ranging from Asian to Californian, but there's always a wide assortment of hot and cold dishes as well as a fine selection of desserts. The wine list is a little limited, however. ☒ *Hilton Ōsaka, 8–8 Umeda 1-chōme, Kita-ku* ☎ *06/6347–711.* ▤ *AE, DC, MC, V.*

★ **$$$$** ✕ **La Baie** (ラベ). The city's premier hotel restaurant serves innovative and extremely good Franco-Japanese fusion food. The wood-panel La Baie is more akin to a British-country-house dining room than a formal hotel restaurant—smart but relaxed. Service is impeccable, and the wines are specially chosen to complement each of the four full-course menus avail able. ✉ *Ritz-Carlton Ōsaka, 2–5–25 Umeda, Kita-ku* ☎ *06/6343–7020* ☆ *Reservations essential* 🎩 *Jacket and tie* 💳 *AE, DC, MC, V.*

$$$–$$$$ ✕ **Kani Dōraku** (かに道楽). This branch of the famed Dōtombori-dōri restaurant also serves crab dishes at fairly reasonable prices. For lunch, a crab set, with large portions of crab, will run around ¥4,000; crab for dinner will cost more than ¥6,000. English-language menus are available. Reserve ahead on weekends. ✉ *Sonezaki Shinchi 1–6–7, Kita-ku,* ☎ *06/6344–5091* 💳 *AE, DC, MC, V.*

$$–$$$ ✕ **Benten Bekkan** (弁天別館). All of the seafood served at this vast restaurant is brought in directly from Hokkaidō, Japan's northernmost island, and prepared in the style of that region. Diners flock here for the wonderful crab *nabe* (hot pot), but the poached salmon and squid noodle dishes are also excellent. If you're dining in a group (four or more), order one of the big nabe set courses, starting at ¥3,800. Sake buffs appreciate the good selection of Hokkaidō *jizake* (regional sake). ✉ *6–9 Dōyama-chō, Kita-ku* ☎ *06/6361–5155* 💳 *AE, DC, MC, V* ◷ *Closed Mon.*

$$–$$$
Fodor'sChoice
★
✕ **Mimiu** (美々卯). Udon-*suki*—thick, noodle stew with Chinese cabbage, clams, eel, yams, shiitake mushrooms, *mitsuba* (greens), and other seasonal ingredients simmered in a pot over a burner at your table—was born here. Indeed, so successful has the recipe become that there are now branches of Mimiu throughout the city—another convenient location is on the 10th floor of the Hanshin department store, opposite JR Ōsaka Station. ✉ *6–18 Hirano-machi, 4-chōme, near Hon-machi subway station, Chūō-ku* ☎ *06/6231–5770* ☆ *Reservations not accepted* 💳 *V* ◷ *Closed Sun.* ✉ *Hanshin department store, 1–13–13 Umeda, Kita-ku* ☎ *06/6345–6648* 💳 *V* ☆ *Reservations not accepted.*

$$–$$$ ✕ **Osteria Gaudente** (オステリアガウダンテ). Relatively authentic decor, attentive waiters, and its popularity with the younger set—especially at lunchtime—make Gaudente an agreeable Italian option. The fish dishes are particularly good, and set dinner menus change daily, depending on what delicacies the chef unearths at the Ōsaka central fish market each morning. Lunch courses offer great value. Reservations are essential in the evening. ✉ *Dai-yon Bldg., B1 fl., Ōsaka Eki-mae-dōri, 1–11–4 Umeda, Kita-ku* ☎ *06/6344–8685* 💳 *AE, DC, MC, V.*

¢–$$$ ✕ **Kantipur** (カンティプール).The *dhal baat* (soup made from rice and lentils) and chicken curries prepared at this Nepalese restaurant are tasty without being particularly spicy, and the lunchtime portions are generous. Though not strictly from Nepal, the restaurant's specialty is the Tibetan hot pot known as *gyakok*: meat, shrimp, cottage cheese, and vegetables in a rich, buttery broth. The restaurant is divided into two halves, with the semi-outdoor, faux terrace section being the nicer location if the weather is good; it also allows you to watch the chefs hard at work baking the fresh nan in the oven. ✉ *7–13 Kurosaki-chō, Kita-ku* ☎ *06/6359–3884* 💳 *AE, DC, MC, V.*

$$ ✕ **Madonna** (まどんな). Restaurants that prepare the local dish okonomiyaki can be found throughout the city, but those served here are outstanding. Often mistakenly called "Japanese pizza," okonomiyaki are really pancakes made of cabbage and mountain yams and filled with ingredients like bacon or shrimp. Try the *yakitsubo*, a sample of five mini okonomiyaki, to experience different flavors. ✉ *Hilton Plaza, B2 fl., 1–8–16 Umeda, Kita-ku* ☎ *06/6347–7371* 💳 *No credit cards.*

$$ ✕ **Mami** (まみ). One of the main gathering spots for Ōsaka's Thai community, Mami serves authentic Thai cuisine. The narrow restaurant, in a slightly seedy part of town, is nothing to look at from the outside, and inside it's crammed with small tables and Thai Tourist Authority posters and beer advertisements. Still, the language most overheard is Thai, which gives you the sensation of being in a Bangkok eatery. The *tom yum kung* (spicy Thai soup) and *gaeng kiow wahn* (spicy green-curry chicken, beef, or shrimp) are excellent. It's a good option for fish lovers. ⊠ *10–4 Togano-chō, Kita-ku* ☎ *06/6314–2392* 🖃 *MC, V.*

$–$$ ✕ **Radish** (らでぃっしゅ). This tiny basement restaurant serving *katei ryori* (homestyle cooking) has built up a solid reputation almost solely by word of mouth. It's next to the Kita-Shinchi entertainment district and has seating for only 28 people, so getting a table can require a lot of patience. It's well worth the effort, though, for such excellent dishes as pumpkin gratin and potato *manju* (steamed bun). Many dishes have a strong vegetable base. A wide selection of regional sake and an always-joyous and busy atmosphere make this a good place to kick back and relax. ⊠ *Fujimoto Bldg. B1F, 1–1–44 Sonezaki Kita-Shinchi, Kita-ku* ☎ *06/6348–0044* 🔊 *Reservations not accepted* 🖃 *AE, DC, MC, V.*

¢–$$ ✕ **Gataro** (がたろ). Hidden away in the warren of restaurants under the Hankyu railway terminus is this intimate, high-class *izakaya* (Japanese-style pub-restaurant) with a long, U-shape wooden counter and three small tables. If you sit at the counter you can watch the food being prepared—perhaps a grilled fish being given a finishing touch with a handheld blowtorch. Dishes include deep-fried squid, white *sōmen* (thin wheat noodles) with raw *nagaimo* (long potato), and seasonal *anago tenpura* (eel tempura). There's no English menu, but an extensive jizake selection and a friendly staff more than compensate. ⊠ *Kappa Yokochō-nai, Shibata 1–7–2, Kita-ku* ☎ *06/6373–1484* 🖃 *V.*

¢–$$ ✕ **Los Inkas** (ロスインカス). Hugely popular with the local Latin community, Los Inkas is always busy, and the up-tempo music adds to the convivial atmosphere, making it a good restaurant for a party. Many of the dishes are Peruvian, though other Latin cuisines, including the usual Mexican dishes, are represented. Menu highlights include *ceviche mixto* (shrimp, octopus, and fish marinated in lime juice and spices) and *lomo saltado* (beef, vegetables, and french fries sautéed together). A tiny stage at the far end of the restaurant hosts live music performances (weekends), and there's a small counter bar. ⊠ *2F Kodama Leisure Bldg., 1–14 Dōyama-chō, Kita-ku* ☎ *06/6365–5190* 🖃 *No credit cards* ⊘ *Closed Mon.*

South of Chūō-dōri

★ $$$$ ✕ **Ume no Hana** (梅の花). Healthful prix-fixe, multicourse menus of tofu-based cuisine—particularly refreshing on hot summer days—are the specialty here. This is a good spot to take a break from shopping in Shin-Sai-Bashi, and if you come in the day you can order one of the cheaper lunch sets. The private dining rooms are decorated in a traditional Japanese style with pottery and ikebana artfully displayed. Reserve ahead on weekends and in the evenings. ⊠ *Shin-sai-bashi OPA Bldg., 11th fl., 1–4–3 Nishi-Shin-sai-bashi, Chūō-ku* ☎ *06/6258–3766* 🖃 *AE, DC, MC, V.*

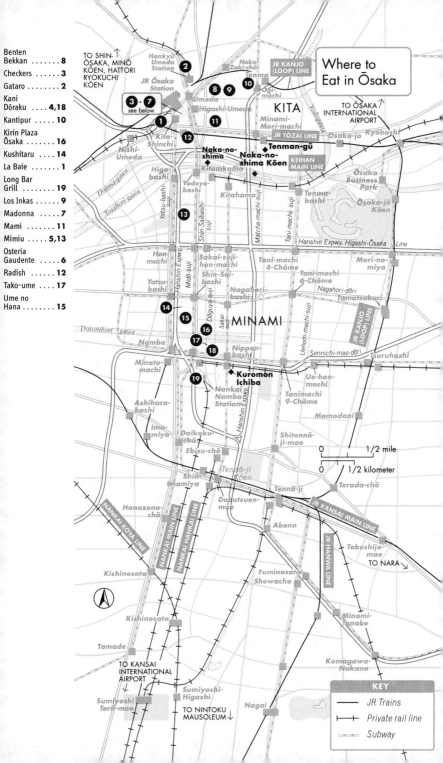

Where to Eat in Ōsaka

TO SHIN-
ŌSAKA, MINŌ
KŌEN, HATTORI
RYOKUCHI
KŌEN

Hankyū
Umeda
Station

JR Ōsaka
Station

3 - 7
see below

Naka-
Zaki-chō

JR KANJO
(LOOP) LINE

Tenma

Ōgi-
machi

Umeda

Higashi-Umeda

KITA

TO ŌSAKA
INTERNATIONAL
AIRPORT

Minami-
Mori-machi

Kita-
Shinchi

JR TŌZAI LINE

Osaka-jo

Kyōbashi

Nishi-
Umeda

Naka-no-
shima

Naka-no-
shima Kōen

Tenman-gū

KEIHAN
MAIN LINE

Ōsaka
Business
Park

Higo-
bashi

Kitahama

Ōsaka-jō
Kōen

Yodoya-
bashi

Kitahama

Matcha-machi-suji

Tenma-
bashi

Dojima-gawa

Tosabori-gawa

Yatsu-bashi-suji

Shin-Saibashi-suji

Tani-machi-suji

Hanshin Expwy. Higashi-Ōsaka   Line

Mori-no-
miya

Hon-
machi

Sakai-suji-
hon-machi

Tani-machi
4-Chōme

Shin-Sai-
bashi

Tani-machi
6-Chōme

Yatsu-
bashi

Nagahori-
bashi

Nagahori-dōri

Tamatsukuri

MINAMI

Dōtombori   gawa

Namba

Sakai-suji

JR KANJO
(LOOP) LINE

Hanshin Expwy.

Midō-suji

Dōguya-suji

Nippon-
bashi

Uehon-machi-suji

Sennichi-mae-dōri

Tsuruhashi

Minato-
machi

**Kuromon
Ichiba**

Ue-hon-
machi

Ashihara-
bashi

Nankai
Namba Station

Tanimachi
9-Chōme

Momodani

Ima-
miya

Daikoku-
chō

Hanshin Expwy.

Ebisu-chō

Shitennō-
ji-mae

0   1/2 mile

0   1/2 kilometer

Shin-
Imamiya

Tennō-ji
Kōen

Tennō-ji

Terada-chō

Hanazono-
chō

NANKAI KOYA LINE

NANKAI MAIN LINE

NANKAI HANKAI LINE

Dōbutsuen-
mae

Abeno

JR KANSAI MAIN LINE

JR HANWA LINE

TO NARA

Kishinosato

Fuminosato
Showacho

Tobushijo-
mae

Kishinosato

Minami-
Tanabe

Tamade

Komagawa-
Nakano

TO KANSAI
INTERNATIONAL
AIRPORT

Sumiyoshi-
Higashi

TO NINTOKU
MAUSOLEUM

Nagai

Sumiyoshi
Torii-mae

KEY

—   JR Trains

+   Private rail line

=   Subway

$$$–$$$$ ✕ **Kani Dōraku** (かに道楽). The most famous restaurant on Dōtombori-dōri—the enormous mechanical crab is a local landmark—Kani Dōraku is noted for fine crab dishes at fairly reasonable prices. For lunch, a crab set, with large portions of crab, will run around ¥4,000; crab for dinner will cost more than ¥6,000. There's another branch in Umeda, and both have English-language menus. Reserve ahead on weekends. ✉ *1–6–18 Dōtombori, Chūo-ku* ☎ *06/6211–8975* ▤ *AE, DC, MC, V.*

★ $$$–$$$$ ✕ **Long Bar Grill** (ロングバーグリル). Adding class and style to the city's hotel-restaurant scene is this grill in the Swissôtel Nankai Ōsaka. The heavy French cutlery, Mark Rothko lithographs, and dark-red upholstery are as exciting as the contemporary food. Locally raised Ōmi beef, Hiroshima oysters, and salmon loin flown in from Scotland—after having been hand-smoked in the Catskills—are among the items on the menu. ✉ *Swissôtel Nankai Ōsaka, 1–60 Namba 5-chōme, Chūo-ku* ☎ *06/6646–5126* ☞ *Reservations essential* ▤ *AE, DC, MC, V.*

$$–$$$$ ✕ **Kushitaru** (串樽). Specializing in dinners served piping hot on skewers, this restaurant behind the Hotel Nikkō is an Ōsaka favorite. Possible selections include *tsukune* (chicken meatballs), celery with sea eel, quail egg with half beak, and oysters with bacon. Of the two dining rooms, the one upstairs is a throwback to the 1970s, with period furniture and music. Although there's no English menu, Kushitaru is well worth a visit. ✉ *Sander Bldg., 13–5 Nishi-Shin-Sai-bashi 1-chōme, Unagidani, Chūo-ku* ☎ *06/6281–0365* ▤ *AE, DC, MC, V* ⊘ *Closed Sun.*

★ $$ ✕ **Tako-ume** (たこ梅). Take a rest from the glitter of Dōtombori nightlife at this 200-year-old dining spot, which specializes in *oden*—a mixture of vegetables, fish cakes, hard-boiled eggs, and fried tofu, cooked in a broth they say has been simmering here in the same pot for the past 30 years. A hot Chinese mustard dip is mixed with sweet miso—a house recipe. Sake is poured from pewter jugs that were handmade in Ōsaka. This is one of Ōsaka's most famous establishments. Reserve ahead on weekends. ✉ *1–1–8 Dōtombori, Chūo-ku* ☎ *06/6211–0321* ▤ *No credit cards* ⊘ *Closed Wed.*

$–$$ ✕ **Kirin Plaza Ōsaka** (キリンプラザ大阪). Designed by Shin Takamatsu, one of Japan's most controversial architects, this branch of the Kirin City beer-hall chain has a working microbrewery in full view on the open-plan ground floor. It's inside the Kirin Plaza Building (a complex that also hosts contemporary art exhibitions). The restaurant, on the third floor, serves mixed Japanese and Western dishes such as avocado tempura and hot salads. ✉ *Kirin Plaza Bldg., 3rd fl., 7–2 Soemon-chō, Chūo-ku* ☎ *06/6212–6572* ▤ *V.*

WHERE TO STAY

Ōsaka is known more as a business than a tourist destination. But the city has modern accommodations for almost every taste, from first-class hotels to more modest business hotels, which are rarely distinctive. Guest quarters have become increasingly stylish at the top-end hotels, though Japanese designers of mid-range lodgings are more concerned with efficiency than elegance. You'll often encounter individual attention from a solicitous staff no matter where you stay.

A hotel room in Ōsaka costs less than one of comparable size in Tōkyō. And Ōsaka has more hotels to choose from than nearby Kyōto, which is important to keep in mind during peak tourist seasons. There's currently a glut of rooms at the top end of the market, which means you can find discounts if you book online at hotel Web sites. Because Ōsaka hotels offer much the same in room size and facilities within a given price range, it's wise to choose accommodations based on location rather than amenities.

	WHAT IT COSTS In yen				
	$$$$	$$$	$$	$	¢
FOR 2 PEOPLE	over 22,000	18,000–22,000	12,000–18,000	8,000–12,000	under 8,000

Price categories are assigned based on the range between the least and most expensive standard double rooms in nonholiday high season, based on the European Plan (with no meals) unless otherwise noted. Taxes (5%–15%) are extra.

North of Chūō-dōri

$$$$ 🏨 **ANA Hotel Ōsaka** (大阪全日空ホテル). The ANA, one of Ōsaka's oldest deluxe hotels, overlooks the city's picturesque Naka-no-shima Kōen. Though showing its age a little, the 24-story building remains a handsome white-tile structure, with some unusual architectural features—including great fluted columns in the lobby. There's also an enclosed courtyard with trees. The main bar is a throwback to a 1950s English gentleman's club. Guest rooms are done in pastel shades and have travertine baths. Each room is furnished with twin or double beds; some come with pull-out sofas. ✉ 1–3–1 Dojimahama, Kita-ku, Ōsaka 530-0004 ☎ 06/6347–1112, 800/262–4683 for U.S reservations, 0171/995–8211 for U.K. reservations 🖷 06/6347–9208 ⊕ www.anahtlosaka.co.jp/english ⇆ 500 rooms ⚐ 5 restaurants, coffee shop, in-room data ports, minibars, refrigerators, cable TV with movies, indoor pool, health club, massage, sauna, business services, meeting rooms, parking (fee) ▤ AE, DC, MC, V.

★ $$$$ 🏨 **Hotel New Ōtani Ōsaka** (ホテルニューオータニ大阪). Such amenities as indoor and outdoor pools, a rooftop garden, tennis courts, and a sparkling marble atrium lobby make this a popular lodging choice for Japanese and Westerners alike. The modern rooms, large by Japanese standards, afford handsome views of Ōsaka-jō and the Neya-gawa (Neya River). Rooms have light color schemes, twin or double beds, dining tables, and nice bathrooms. A large selection of bars and restaurants provides enough diversity to suit almost any taste. Indeed, the New Ōtani is like a minicity within the Ōsaka Business Park. ✉ 4–1 Shiromi 1-chōme, Chūō-ku, Ōsaka 540-0001 ☎ 06/6941–1111 🖷 06/6941–9769 ⊕ www. osaka.newotani.co.jp ⇆ 559 rooms ⚐ 12 restaurants, in-room data ports, minibars, refrigerators, cable TV with movies, indoor-outdoor pool, 2 tennis courts, health club, hair salon, bicycles, 3 bars, Internet, business services, meeting rooms, parking (fee) ▤ AE, DC, MC, V.

$$$$ 🏨 **Imperial Hotel** (帝国ホテル). The old Frank Lloyd Wright–designed Imperial Hotel in Tōkyō was the inspiration for this riverfront hotel, one of only two hotels in Ōsaka allowed to receive official state guests (the other is the Rihga Royal Hotel). The service here is excellent. Elegant and understated furnishings fill the rooms, and high ceilings meet the

sky through great picture windows showcasing city views. Imperial Tower rooms include separate concierge service, as well as special floor keys for added privacy and security. ⊠ *8–50 Temmabashi 1-chōme, Kita-ku, Ōsaka 530-0042* ☎ *06/6881–1111, 800/223–6800 in U.S, 0800/181–123 in U.K.* 🖷 *06/6881–4111* ⊕ *www.imperialhotel.co.jp* 📑 *390 rooms* ♧ *7 restaurants, 2 coffee shops, in-room data ports, in-room fax, cable TV with movies, 3 tennis courts, health club, sauna, squash, 2 bars, shops, concierge, business services, parking (fee)* 🖿 *AE, DC, MC, V.*

$$$$ 🏨 **Hotel New Hankyū and Hotel New Hankyū Annex** (新阪急ホテル大阪・新阪急ホテル大阪アネックス). The single rooms here are not enormous but are cozy in Japanese fashion. This very convenient hotel complex is in Umeda, close to many restaurants and shopping outlets. The 17-story Annex, a block from the main hotel, offers a buffet breakfast and a fitness club with an indoor pool (you have access if you stay in either building). Japanese, French, Chinese, and steak restaurants are in the main building. ⊠ *1–1–35 Shibata, Kita-ku, Ōsaka 530-8310* ☎ *06/6372–5101* 🖷 *06/6374–6885* ⊕ *http://hotel.newhankyu.co.jp/welcome-e.html* 📑 *1,224 rooms* ♧ *5 restaurants, tea shop, in-room data ports, indoor pool, health club, Japanese baths, sauna, bar, lounge* 🖿 *AE, DC, MC, V.*

$$$$ 🏨 **Rihga Grand Hotel** (リーガグランドホテル). A sister to the Rihga Royal, the Grand is a lively first-class commercial hotel with free shuttle service every few minutes to the Yodoya-bashi subway station. Everything here is neat and clean. The staff is large and hardworking, housekeeping is efficient, and the rooms are bigger than average for Japanese accommodations. The decor is somewhat dated but in good repair. ⊠ *2–3–18 Naka-no-shima, Kita-ku, Ōsaka 530-0005* ☎ *06/6202–1212* 🖷 *06/6227–5054* ⊕ *www.rihga.com/osgrand* 📑 *346 rooms* ♧ *3 restaurants, cable TV, shops, Internet, business services, meeting rooms* 🖿 *AE, DC, MC, V.*

$$–$$$$ 🏨 **Rihga Royal Hotel** (リーガロイヤルホテル). A veritable city within a city built in the 1930s, the Royal encompasses more than 20 restaurants, bars, and karaoke rooms, and no fewer than 60 shops—in addition to nearly 1,000 rooms. Standard rooms are spacious and well equipped, with, among other things, in-room data ports, comfortable armchairs, and plenty of closet space. A stay in the VIP tower allows you free access to the swimming club's two sun-roof pools (other guests pay ¥2,000). ⊠ *5–3–68 Naka-no-shima, Kita-ku, Ōsaka 530-0005* ☎ *06/6448–1121* 🖷 *06/6448–4414* ⊕ *www.rihga.com* 📑 *980 rooms* ♧ *20 restaurants, in-room data ports, cable TV with movies, 3 pools (1 indoor), health club, hair salon, massage, sauna, steam room, 2 bars, shops, babysitting, concierge, business services* 🖿 *AE, DC, MC, V.*

$$$$ 🏨 **Ritz-Carlton Ōsaka** (リッツカールトン大阪). Smaller than Ōsaka's other

FodorsChoice ★ top hotels, the Ritz-Carlton manages to combine a homey feel and old-world European elegance into the city's most luxurious hotel. King-size beds with goose-down pillows and plenty of dark-wood furnishings fill the guest rooms, and the well-appointed bathrooms have plush bathrobes and towels. Stay on a Club floor to have the use of a special lounge, as well as free use of the hotel's fitness center. All this comes, of course, at a price—the Ritz-Carlton is also Ōsaka's most expensive hotel. ⊠ *2–5–25 Umeda, Kita-ku, Ōsaka 530-0001* ☎ *06/6343–7000, 800/241–3333 in U.S.* 🖷 *06/6343–7001* ⊕ *www.ritzcarlton.com* 📑 *292 rooms* ♧ *5*

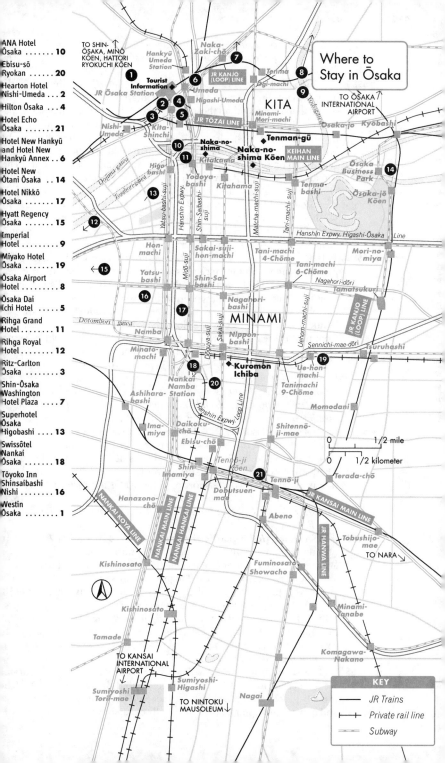

ANA Hotel
Ōsaka **10**

Ebisu-sō
Ryokan **20**

Hearton Hotel
Nishi-Umeda . . . **2**

Hilton Ōsaka . . . **4**

Hotel Echo
Ōsaka **21**

Hotel New Hankyū
and Hotel New
Hankyū Annex . . **6**

Hotel New
Ōtani Ōsaka . . **14**

Hotel Nikkō
Ōsaka **17**

Hyatt Regency
Ōsaka **15**

Imperial
Hotel **9**

Miyako Hotel
Ōsaka **19**

Ōsaka Airport
Hotel **8**

Ōsaka Dai
Ichi Hotel **5**

Rihga Grand
Hotel **11**

Rihga Royal
Hotel **12**

Ritz-Carlton
Ōsaka **3**

Shin-Ōsaka
Washington
Hotel Plaza **7**

Superhotel
Ōsaka
Higobashi **13**

Swissôtel
Nankai
Ōsaka **18**

Tōyoko Inn
Shinsaibashi
Nishi **16**

Westin
Ōsaka **1**

Where to Stay in Ōsaka

TO SHIN-
ŌSAKA, MINŌ ↑
KŌEN, HATTORI
RYOKUCHI KŌEN

Hankyū
Umeda
Station

Naka-
Zaki-chō

Tourist
Information

JR Ōsaka Station

JR KANJO
(LOOP LINE)

Tenma

TO ŌSAKA ↑
INTERNATIONAL
AIRPORT

Umeda

Ōgi-machi

Higashi-Umeda

Nishi-
Umeda

KITA

Minami-
Mori-machi

Kita-
Shinchi

JR TŌZAI LINE

Osakajo
Kyōbashi

Naka-no-
shima

Naka-no-
shima Kōen

Tenman-gū

KEIHAN
MAIN LINE

Ōsaka
Business
Park

Dojima-gawa

Higo-
bashi

Kitahama

Yodoya-
bashi

Tenma-
bashi

Ōsaka-jō
Kōen

Tosabori-gawa

Kitahama

Yatsu-bashi-suji

Hanshin Expwy.

Shin-Saibashi-suji

Matcha-machi-suji

Tani-machi-suji

Hanshin Expwy. Higashi-Ōsaka Line

Hon-
machi

Sakai-suji-
hon-machi

Tani-machi
4-Chōme

Mori-no-
miya

Midō-suji

Tani-machi
6-Chōme

Nagahori-dōri

Tamatsukuri

Yatsu-
bashi

Shin-Sai-
bashi

Nagahori-
bashi

MINAMI

Uehon-machi-suji

JR KANJO
(LOOP LINE)

Dōtombori-gawa

Namba

Nippon-
bashi

Dōguya-suji

Sakai-suji

Sennichi-mae-dōri

Tsuruhashi

Minato-
machi

Kuromon
Ichiba

Ue-hon-
machi

Nankai
Namba
Station

Hanshin Expwy. Loop Line

Tanimachi
9-Chōme

Ashihara-
bashi

Momodani

Ima-
miya

Daikoku-
chō

Shitennō-
ji-mae

Ebisu-chō

Tennō-ji
Kōen

0   1/2 mile

0   1/2 kilometer

Shin-
Imamiya

Dōbutsuen-
mae

Tennō-ji

Terada-chō

NANKAI KOYA LINE

NANKAI MAIN LINE

NANKAI NANKAI LINE

Abeno

JR KANSAI MAIN LINE

Hanazono-
chō

JR HANNA LINE

Tobushijo-
mae

TO NARA

Kishinosato

Fuminosato
Showacho

Kishinosato

Minami-
Tanabe

Tamade

Komagawa-
Nakano

TO KANSAI
INTERNATIONAL
AIRPORT ↓

Sumiyoshi
Torii-mae

Sumiyoshi-
Higashi

Nagai

TO NINTOKU
MAUSOLEUM ↓

KEY

— JR Trains

⊢——⊢ Private rail line

═══ Subway

restaurants, coffee shop, in-room data ports, cable TV with movies, pool, health club, bar, concierge floor, business services, free parking ▭ *AE, DC, MC, V.*

\$\$\$\$ ⊡ **Westin Ōsaka** (ウェスティンホテル大阪). Though its location is slightly inconvenient, the Westin has a good reputation and provides standard rooms that are larger than those at the Ritz-Carlton. Wooden desks, comfortable chairs, and large beds fill the European-style rooms. Guests staying in Executive rooms have the use of a lounge with free drinks and breakfast. The hotel abuts the Umeda Sky Building, so make sure you get a room on the opposite side if you want a good view of the city. The Amadeus serves innovative dishes. A shuttle bus runs to and from JR Ōsaka Station. ✉ *1–1–20 Ōyodo Naka, Kita-ku, Ōsaka 531-0076* ☎ *06/6440–1111* 🖷 *06/6440–1100* ⊕ *www.starwood.com/westin* 🛏 *304 rooms* ♧ *4 restaurants, café, coffee shop, in-room data ports, cable TV with movies, indoor pool, health club, massage, sauna, shops, business services, parking (fee)* ▭ *AE, DC, MC, V.*

★ **\$\$\$–\$\$\$\$** ⊡ **Hilton Ōsaka** (ヒルトン大阪). Glitz and glitter draw both tourists and expense-accounters to the Hilton Ōsaka, the city's most convenient hotel, across from JR Ōsaka Station in the heart of the business district. It's a typical Western-style hotel, replete with marble and brass. The high-ceiling lobby is dramatic and stylish, and the hotel's arcade contains designer boutiques. The three executive floors have a lounge for complimentary Continental breakfasts and evening cocktails. Checkers, which serves various buffet dinners, is among its 11 restaurants. ✉ *8–8 Umeda 1-chōme, Kita-ku, Ōsaka 530-0001* ☎ *06/6347–7111* 🖷 *06/6347–7001* ⊕ *www.hilton.co.jp/osaka* 🛏 *525 rooms* ♧ *11 restaurants, café, coffee shop, in-room data ports, minibars, refrigerators, cable TV with movies, 2 tennis courts, indoor pool, health club, massage, sauna, shops, business services, meeting rooms, parking (fee)* ▭ *AE, DC, MC, V.*

\$\$–\$\$\$\$ ⊡ **Ōsaka Airport Hotel** (大阪エアポートホテル). This is *the* place if you have an early flight out of Ōsaka's domestic airport, the confusingly named Ōsaka International Airport: it's right inside the terminal building. These are hardly the most luxurious rooms for the price, but the location is a lifesaver if you're short on time. ✉ *Ōsaka Airport Bldg., 3rd fl., Toyonaka-shi, Ōsaka 560-0036* ☎ *06/6855–4621* 🖷 *06/6855–4620* 🛏 *105 rooms* ♧ *2 restaurants, cable TV with movies, 2 bars, shops* ▭ *AE, DC, MC, V.*

\$\$\$ ⊡ **Shin-Ōsaka Washington Hotel Plaza** (新大阪ワシントンホテルプラザ). Part of a no-nonsense chain of business hotels throughout the country, the Washington is the smartest of its kind. Rooms are not large, but are clean and comfortable. Among the highlights here are some no-smoking rooms and a lively Japanese-style pub in the basement. It's convenient to the JR Shin-Ōsaka Station, from which the Shinkansen arrives and departs. ✉ *5–5–15 Nishi-Nakajima, Yodogawa-ku, Ōsaka 532-0011* ☎ *06/6302 7007* 🖷 *06/6303 8111* ⊕ *http://shinosaka.wh-at.com* 🛏 *490 rooms* ♧ *4 restaurants, in-room data ports, refrigerators, cable TV, parking (fee), no-smoking rooms* ▭ *AE, DC, MC, V.*

\$\$ ⊡ **Ōsaka Dai Ichi Hotel** (大阪第一ホテル). As Japan's first cylindrical skyscraper—known as the Maru-Biru (Round Building)—the Dai Ichi is easily picked out of the Ōsaka cityscape. The rooms are wedge shape, and half are small singles that are usually occupied on weekdays by businesspeople. The hotel has a coffee shop, open around-the-clock, and an underground shopping arcade. It's conveniently across from Ōsaka Station and next to the Hilton Ōsaka. ✉ *1–9–20 Umeda, Kita-ku, Ōsaka 530-0001* ☎ *06/6341–4411* 📠 *06/6341–4930* 🌐 *www.daiichihotels.com* 🛏 *478 rooms* 🍴 *6 restaurants, in-room data ports, refrigerators, bar, shops* 🚪 *AE, DC, MC, V.*

$–$$ 🏨 **Hearton Hotel Nishi-Umeda** (ハートンホテル西梅田). Clean, efficient, and with a good location a few minutes' walk from JR Ōsaka Station, the Hearton is popular with domestic and foreign travelers alike. Unless you're really on a budget, however, opt for one of the larger twin rooms, as the smaller rooms are barely big enough for you to swing the proverbial cat. ✉ *3–3–55 Umeda, Kita-ku, Ōsaka 530-0001* ☎ *06/6342–1111* 📠 *06/6342–1122* 🌐 *www.hearton.co.jp/english* 🛏 *471 rooms* 🍴 *Restaurant, coffee shop, refrigerators, cable TV with movies, dry cleaning, parking (fee)* 🚪 *AE, DC, MC, V.*

$ 🏨 **Superhotel Ōsaka Higobashi** (スーパーホテル大阪肥後橋). Don't expect much in the way of innovative interior design at this Superhotel, a member of the hugely popular nationwide chain of business hotels. There are just two set prices, for singles or doubles. ✉ *1–20–1 Edo-bori, Nishi-ku, Ōsaka 550-0002* ☎ *06/6448–9000* 📠 *06/6448–2400* 🛏 *80 rooms* 🍴 *No room phones* 🚪 *No credit cards.*

South of Chūō-dōri

$$$$ 🏨 **Hotel Nikkō Ōsaka** (ホテル日航大阪). An impressive and rather striking white tower in the colorful Shin-Sai-bashi Station area, the Nikkō is within easy reach of Ōsaka's nightlife. The atmosphere here is lively, even exciting: as you enter, you may be greeted by a doorman in top hat and tails. Some rooms have contemporary furnishings with Japanese touches and traditional light decor. Higher-price rooms come with expensive furniture, thick carpets, and bedside controls, and the tiled baths on executive floors are particularly well appointed. Note that standard rooms are on the small side. The bars and restaurants are varied, and service here is an art. ✉ *1–3–3 Nishi-Shin-Sai-bashi, Chūō-ku, Ōsaka 542-0086* ☎ *06/6244–1111* 📠 *06/6245–2432* 🌐 *www.hno.co.jp* 🛏 *640 rooms* 🍴 *3 restaurants, coffee shop, minibars, refrigerators, cable TV with movies, 3 bars, shops, Internet, business services, meeting rooms, parking (fee)* 🚪 *AE, DC, MC, V.*

$$$$ 🏨 **Hyatt Regency Ōsaka** (ハイアットリージェンシー大阪). If you're going to the Universal Studios Japan theme park, the Hyatt, in the Nankō development area, is quite convenient, and Kansai International Airport is a 45-minute bus ride away. The hotel is, however, a 20-minute subway ride away from the city center. Modern comforts abound: guest rooms are spacious, especially deluxe doubles and junior suites, which are larger than the typical Japanese apartment. Some rooms on the upper floors have grand views of Ōsaka Bay. ✉ *1–13 Nankō-Kita, Suminoe-ku, Ōsaka 559-0034* ☎ *06/6612–1234, 800/233–1234 in U.S., 0171/580–8197 in U.K.* 📠 *06/6614–7800* 🌐 *www.hyattregencyosaka.com* 🛏 *500 rooms* 🍴 *12 restaurants, minibars, refrigerators, cable TV with movies, indoor-outdoor pool, health club, massage, sauna, spa, 3 bars, Internet, business services, meeting rooms, free parking* 🚪 *AE, DC, MC, V.*

$$$$ 🏨 **Miyako Hotel Ōsaka** (都ホテル大阪). Guest rooms at the Miyako, a practical, well-appointed hotel, are modern and inviting, and some have extras such as dining tables. Public rooms are impressive, too, particularly the two-story lobby with marble columns and pastel color schemes. Executive rooms occupy two floors and have plusher appointments. Trains for Nara and Kyōto on the private Kintetsu Line leave from the next-door Ue-hon-machi Station. The National Bunraku Theater and Shitennō-ji are also fairly close. ✉ *6–1–55 Ue-hon-machi, Tennō-ji-ku, Ōsaka 543-0001* ☎ *06/6773–1111, 800/333–3333 in U.S., 0800/37–4411 in U.K.* 🖷 *06/6773–3322* ⊕ *www.miyakohotels.ne.jp/osaka/english* ⇦ *58 rooms* ⚘ *12 restaurants, 2 coffee shops, in-room data ports, cable TV, indoor pool, health club, racquetball, 2 bars, lounge, shops, concierge floor, airport shuttle* ▭ *AE, DC, MC, V.*

$$$$ 🏨 **Swissôtel Nankai Ōsaka** (スイスホテル南海大阪). With understated contemporary art, European-style furnishings, and warm shades of beige, the standard rooms at this high-end hotel, a member of the Raffles International Group, are some of the best in the city. The Executive Club offers additional privacy and a private lounge for breakfast, cocktails, and nightcaps. Be sure to have a drink in Tavola 36, the hotel's top-floor Italian sky lounge, complete with a DJ booth. ✉ *1–60 Namba 5-chōme, Chūō-ku, Ōsaka 542-0076* ☎ *06/6646–1111* 🖷 *06/6648–0331* ⊕ *www.swissotel-osaka.co.jp* ⇦ *535 rooms, 11 Western-style suites, 2 Japanese-style suites* ⚘ *11 restaurants, in-room data ports, cable TV with movies, indoor pool, health club, hot tub, massage, sauna, shops, concierge floor* ▭ *AE, DC, MC, V.*

$$ 🏨 **Hotel Echo Ōsaka** (ホテルエコーオーサカ). If you're seeking good, moderately priced accommodations, the Echo Ōsaka is a solid choice. The hotel is neat and clean, if nothing more, and has an accommodating young staff. The plain rooms have basic furnishings (including double or twin beds), uncoordinated carpeting, and small baths. It's near the JR Tennō-ji station, though far from other major parts of the city. ✉ *1–4–7 Abeno-suji, Abeno-ku, Ōsaka 545-0052* ☎ *06/6633–1141* 🖷 *06/6633–3845* ⇦ *84 rooms* ⚘ *2 restaurants, coffee shop, bar* ▭ *AE, DC, MC, V.*

$ 🏨 **Ebisu-sō Ryokan** (えびす荘旅館). Ōsaka's only member of the inexpensive Japanese Inn Group is a partly wooden structure with 15 Japanese-style rooms. It's a very basic, no-frills operation, with traditional shared baths and no restaurant, though there are plenty nearby. Close to the electrical-appliance and computer center of Den Den Town and the National Theater, Ebisu-sō Ryokan is a five-minute walk from Ebisu-chō Station on the Sakai-suji subway line. ✉ *1–7–33 Nippon-bashi-nishi, Naniwa-ku, Ōsaka 556-0004* ☎ *06/6643–4861* ⇦ *15 Japanese-style rooms without bath* ⚘ *Japanese baths* ▭ *AE, MC, V.*

¢–$ 🏨 **Tōyoko Inn Shinsaibashi Nishi** (東横イン心斎橋西). A 10-minute walk west of Shin-Sai-Bashi subway station and close to the heart of the city's nightlife is this good-value, clean, comfortable business hotel. It's part of a nationwide chain that's very popular with Japanese business travelers. Ask for a no-smoking room if you'd rather not be assaulted by the smell of stale cigarettes, however. ✉ *1–9–22 Kita-Horie, Nishi-ku, Ōsaka 550-0014* ☎ *06/6536–1045* 🖷 *06/6536–1046* ⊕ *www.toyoko-inn.com/eng* ⇦ *135 rooms* ⚘ *In-room data ports, refrigerators, room TVs with movies, Internet, no-smoking rooms* ▭ *AE, DC, V* ❑ *CP.*

NIGHTLIFE & THE ARTS

The Arts

National Bunraku Theater. Ōsakans have helped make Bunraku a sophisticated art form—so a performance of this puppet drama here is a must. The theater is active in January, March, April, June, July, August, and November, and each run starts on the third of the month and lasts about three weeks. The Ōsaka tourist offices will have the current schedule, which is also printed in *Kansai Time Out* and the quarterly tourist booklet, *Meet Ōsaka*. Tickets are ¥4,400 and ¥5,600; performances usually begin at 11 AM and 4 PM. From the Namba subway station, take the Sennichi-mae subway line one stop east to Nippon-bashi Station. Exit 7 will bring you right outside the theater. ✉ *12–10 Nippon-bashi 1-chōme, Chūō-ku* ☎ *06/6212–2531* ⊕ *www.osaka.isp.ntt-west.co.jp.*

Shōchiku-za Kabuki Theater. Ōsaka's Kabuki theater, built in 1923 as Japan's first Western-style theater, rivals even Tōkyō's Kabuki-za. Technology has been cleverly incorporated into Shōchiku-za alongside traditional theater design. The house hosts Kabuki for about half the year, with major performances most months. The rest of the year it hosts musicals and other concerts. Tickets range in price from ¥4,000 to ¥20,000. ✉ *1–9–19 Dōtombori, Chūō-ku* ☎ *06/6214–2211, 06/6214–2200 for reservations.*

Nightlife

Ōsaka has as diverse a nightlife scene as Tōkyō. The Kita (North) area surrounds JR Umeda Station; and the Minami (South) area is between the Shin-Sai-bashi and Namba districts and includes part of Chūō-ku (Central Ward). Many Japanese refer to Minami as being "for kids," but there are still plenty of good restaurants and drinking spots for more seasoned bon vivants. Ōsaka's hip young things hang out in Amerika Mura, in the southern part of Chūō-ku, with its innumerable bars and clubs. Kita draws a slightly more adult crowd, including lots of businesspeople.

Bars

Pig & Whistle. This minichain of English-style pubs is a mainstay of foreign bars, with two of its three locations in Ōsaka. Fish-and-chips (what else?) is served alongside Guinness, bottled beers, and a good selection of spirits. These places are packed on weekends. *Kita:* ✉ *Ohatsutenjin Bldg., basement, 2–5 Sonezaki, Kita-ku* ☎ *06/6361–3198* ✉ *Minami:* ✉ *ACROSS Bldg., 2nd fl., 6–14 Shin-Sai-bashi-suji 2-chōme, Chūō-ku* ☎ *06/6213–6911.*

Sam & Dave. The most popular international hotspots in town have to be the two main branches of this large-scale bar-cum-disco. Both branches draw a young Japanese crowd as well as expats, and they're always busy, especially weekends, when there's sometimes a cover charge of ¥1,000. *Kita:* ✉ *4–15–19 Nishi-Tenma, Kita-ku* ☎ *06/6365–1688* ✉ *Minami:* ✉ *1–21–19 Shimanouchi, Chūō-ku* ☎ *06/6251–5333.*

Tocca a Te. If you want a quiet drink during the week, this artsy spot is a good choice. With an event hall as well as a bar, Tocca a Te stages club nights as well as salsa evenings and film nights. It can get busy on the weekend, but the high ceilings mean it never feels cramped. ✉ 2–2–1. *Sonezaki, Kita-ku* ☎ 06/6365–5808.

Dance Clubs

Club Joule. Club Joule caters to R&B and hip-hop fans during the week and house and techno clubbers on weekends. A café-style seating area upstairs is a good place to recuperate between dances—or an ideal location for those who'd rather just watch the action. ✉ *Brutus Bldg. 2nd and 3rd fl., 2–11–30 Nishi-Shin-sai-bashi, Chūō-ku* ☎ 06/6214–1223

Club Karma. If you're looking for serious techno or all-night dancing this is the place. Club Karma hosts all-night drum 'n' bass/techno events on weekends and on nights before national holidays (cover from ¥2,500). On nonevent nights it's a stylish bar serving good food to hip music. ✉ *Kasai Bldg., 1st fl., 1–5–18 Sonezaki-shinchi, Kita-ku* ☎ 06/6344–6181.

Mother Hall. Mother Hall doesn't host club events every night, but when it does, they're packed. This is a large-scale club–event hall that can accommodate up to 1,500 people for trance, house, and other kinds of music. ✉ *B1 Swing Yoshimoto Bldg., 12–35 Namba, Chūō-ku* ☎ 06/4397–9061.

Underlounge. In Minami, this is the city's slickest and most modern dance club, with a state-of-the-art sound system and regular appearances by big-name international DJs. ✉ *634 Bldg., B1 fl., 2–7–11 Nishi-Shin-sai-bashi, Chūō-ku* ☎ 06/6214–3322.

Jazz

Blue Note. Jazz fans should head to Umeda and this high-end club where the cream of the international and national jazz scenes plays two sets nightly. Tickets aren't cheap, however: expect to pay anywhere from ¥5,000 to ¥12,000. ✉ *B1 fl., Ax Bldg., 2–3–21 Sonezaki Shinchi, Kita-ku* ☎ 06/6342–7722.

Mr. Kelly's. This club, on the ground floor of the Sun Garden Hotel, regularly features a jazz trio plus a guest vocalist. The cover charge is usually ¥1,500. ✉ *1F Sun Garden Dōjima, 2–4–1 Sonezaki Shinchi, Kita-ku* ☎ 06/6342–5821.

Rock & Alternative

Bears. A tiny basement, full when more than 70 people are present, this is the single most interesting venue for live music in the city. It's ground zero for the region's avant-garde musical underground, including such performers as Haco and Empty Orchestra. Events tend to start and finish early, so get here by 6:30. There's something on every evening. ✉ *B1 fl., Shin-Nihon Namba Bldg., 3–14–5 Namba-naka, Naniwa-ku* ☎ 06/6649–5564.

Club Quattro. Up-and-coming Japanese rock bands and popular (and more expensive) Western bands play here, and there's something going on almost every night. The sound system is excellent. ✉ *Shin-Sai-bashi Parco Bldg., 8th fl., Shin-sai-bashi-suji 1–9–1, Chūō-ku* ☎ 06/6281–8181.

Fandango. This club hosts a range of lesser-known punk, guitar-pop, and hard-rock bands, both local and from overseas. ⊠ *1–17–27 Jūsō-Honmachi, Yodogawa-ku* ☎ *06/6308–1621.*

SPORTS & THE OUTDOORS

Baseball

Ōsaka Dōmu (Ōsaka Dome). For a taste of Japanese *bēsubōru* (baseball), head to this futuristic stadium where the local Kintetsu Buffaloes square off against national rivals. Tickets can be had for as little as ¥1,600. Buy them at the gate, at branches of Lawson convenience store in the city, or by telephone from Ticket Pia. ⊠ *Taishō-ku, Next to Ōsaka Dōmu-mae Chiyozaki subway station on Nagahori Tsurumi-ryokuchi line* ☎ *06/6363–9999 Ticket Pia.*

Jogging

With its extensive grounds, **Ōsaka-jō Kōen** (Ōsaka Castle Park) is the best place to jog in the city. ⊠ *Next to JR Ōsaka-jō Kōen-mae Station, Chūō-ku.*

Skating

Ōsaka Pool Skating Rink is a world-class skating facility open November to March, daily from 9 to 9. It's easily accessible, near JR Ashiobashi Station on the Loop Line, and costs ¥1,400. ⊠ *3–1–20 Tanaka, Minato-ku* ☎ *06/6571–2010.*

Soccer

Two J. League soccer teams, Gamba Ōsaka and Cerezo Ōsaka, play in Ōsaka. Tickets are reasonably priced, starting at ¥1,500 for adults, and the season runs from March to November. J. League games rarely sell out, as the stadiums are very big.

The Gamba Ōsaka play at **Bampaku EXPO Memorial Stadium** (⊠ 5–2 Senri Bampaku Kōen, Suita-shi ☎ 06/6202–5201) in the north of the city. Access is via the Ōsaka Monorail to Kōen Higashi-guchi Station. The Cerezo Ōsaka play at the **Nagai Stadium** (⊠ 2–2–19 Nagai-Higashi, Sumiyoshi-ku ☎ 06/6692–9011) in south Ōsaka, close to Nagai Station on the JR Hanwa Line or Midō-suji subway line.

Sumō

Ōsaka is one of Japan's centers for sumō wrestling, in which athletes weighing from 198 to 352 pounds battle to throw an opponent to the floor or out of the ring.

From the second Sunday through the fourth Sunday in March, one of Japan's six sumō tournaments takes place in the **Ōsaka Furitsu Taiikukaikan** *(Ōsaka Prefectural Gymnasium)*. Most seats, known as *masu-seki,* are prebooked before the tournament begins, but standing-room tickets (¥1,000) and a limited number of seats (¥3,000) are available on the day of the event. The ticket office opens at 9 AM, and you're advised to get in line as early as possible. The stadium is a 10-minute walk from Namba Station. ⊠ *3–4–36 Namba-naka, Naniwa-ku* ☎ *06/6631–0120.*

Swimming

If you're not staying in one of the high-end hotels with a swimming pool, you have a few other options. **Ōgimachi Pool** (⊠ Ōgimachi Kōen, Kita-ku ☎ 06/6383–8911) is a modern affair close to JR Tenma Station, one stop from JR Ōsaka. It's closed Wednesday. **Ōsaka Pool** (⊠ 3–1–20 Tanaka, Minato-ku ☎ 06/6571–2010), closed Monday, is near JR Ashiobashi Station on the Loop Line. The 50-meter, 10-lane swimming pool was designed with an eye toward the city's (unsuccessful) bid to host the 2008 Olympics.

Tennis

At **Hattori Ryokuchi Kōen,** no reservation is necessary for tennis (¥610–¥710) during the week; for weekend play at this park you must reserve in advance. ⊠ 1–1 Hattori Ryokuchi, Toyonaka-shi ☎ 06/ 6862–4946.

SHOPPING

Ōsaka is known for its vast underground shopping malls, which, even to the long-term resident, are notoriously difficult to navigate, especially the ones underneath JR Ōsaka Station. Seemingly the human equivalent of rabbit warrens, the various shopping malls merge with one another along ill-defined boundaries, but the wealth of shops makes strolling a pleasure, especially if it's raining or if you're seeking respite from the heat of summer. Everything from cafés and Italian restaurants to secondhand CD shops, fashionable clothing boutiques, and discount ticket outlets can be found underground. A good place to start exploring these malls is from JR Ōsaka Station in the northern part of the city or from Namba subway station in the south. Signage is in both English and Japanese in many places, and if you're ever not quite sure of your bearings, all you have to do is pop up to ground level, like some sort of urban submariner.

In addition to Ōsaka's numerous shopping arcades and underground malls, there are specialized wholesale areas throughout the city, many of which have a few retail shops and are worth a visit. One such area is **Dōguya-suji,** just east of Nankai Namba Station and the Takashimaya department store. This street is lined with shops selling nothing but kitchen utensils—all sorts of pots, pans, and glassware are piled to the rafters. Though most customers are in the restaurant trade, plenty of laypeople shop here, too. Feel free to wander around: there's no pressure to buy anything. A trip here could be combined with a visit to nearby Den Den Town, known for its electronic goods. Also in this neighborhood, east of the main entrance to Dōguya-suji, is **Kuromon Ichiba,** the famous market district where chefs select the treats—fruits, vegetables, meat, and much more—for meals due to be served at restaurants the length and breadth of the city that evening.

Department Stores

All major Japanese *depāto* (department stores) are represented in Ōsaka. Some of them, like Hankyū and Kintetsu, are headquartered here.

They're open 10–7, but close on Wednesday or Thursday. The following are some of Ōsaka's leading depātos. Note that the food hall in the basement of Hanshin is widely regarded as the city's best. **Daimaru** (✉ 1–7–1 Shin-Sai-bashi-suji, Chūō-ku ☎ 06/6343–1231). **Hankyū** (✉ 8–7 Kakuta-chō, Kita-ku ☎ 06/6361–1381). **Hanshin** (✉ 1–13–13 Umeda, Kita-ku ☎ 06/6345–1201). **Kintetsu** (✉ 1–1–43 Abeno-suji, Abeno-ku ☎ 06/6624–1111 ✉ 6–1–55 Ue-hon-machi, Tennō-ji-ku ☎ 06/6775–1111). **Matsuzakaya** (✉ 1–1 Tenma-bashi Kyo-machi, Chūō-ku ☎ 06/6943–1111). **Mitsukoshi** (✉ 7–5 Korai-bashi 1-chōme, Chūō-ku ☎ 06/6203–1331). **Takashimaya** (✉ 5–1–5 Namba, Chūō-ku ☎ 06/6631–1101).

Crafts

At one time famous for its traditional crafts—particularly its *karaki-sashimono* (ornately carved furniture), its fine Naniwa Suzuki pewter-ware, and its *uchihamono* (Sakai cutlery)—Ōsaka lost much of its traditional industry during World War II. The simplest way to find Ōsakan crafts is to visit one of the major department stores, many of which carry a selection of locally made wares.

Nihon Kōgeikan Mingei Fukyubu (Japan Folkcraft Collection). Folk crafts from all over the country, including ceramics, basketry, paper goods, folk toys, and textiles, are sold at this store near the Umeshin East Hotel in the popular gallery district, within walking distance of the U.S. consulate. It's open Monday–Saturday 10–5:30. ✉ *4–7–15 Nishi-Tenma, Kita-ku* ☎ *06/6362–9501.*

Electronics

Though some Japanese electronic goods may be cheaper in the United States than in Japan due to discounting policies, bear in mind that many of the latest electronics products are released on the Japanese market from 6 to 12 months before they reach shops in the West.

Den Den Town. This district has about 300 retail shops that specialize in electronics products, as well as stores selling cameras and watches. Shops are open 10–7 daily. Take your passport, and make your purchases in stores with signs that say TAX FREE in order to qualify for a 5% discount. The area is near Ebisu-chō Station on the Sakai-suji subway line (Exit 1 or 2), and Nippon-bashi Station on the Sakai-suji and Sennichi-mae subway lines (Exit 5 or 10).

Sofmap. A large-scale specialist computer and digital-camera shop, Sofmap also deals in secondhand products and has an on-site computer-repair clinic. Head here if your laptop suddenly breaks down, or if you're after cheap hardware components. It's near the west end of JR Ōsaka Station and is open daily 11–9:30. ✉ *3–2–135 Umeda, Kita-ku* ☎ *06/4797–4300.*

Yodobashi Camera. If you haven't got time to spend exploring Den Den Town, this enormous electronics department store in Umeda is the place to head. Prices are reasonable, and the selection is very good. Don't be put off by the name: they sell far more than just cameras. On the north side of JR Ōsaka Station, opposite the Hotel New Hankyū, the store is impossible to miss. Fashion outlets and numerous restaurants round out the complex. It's open daily 9:30–9. ✉ *1–1 Ōfuka-chō, Kita-ku* ☎ *06/ 4802–1010.*

ŌSAKA A TO Z

To research prices, get advice from other travelers, and book travel arrangements, visit www.fodors.com.

AIR TRAVEL

International carriers flying into Ōsaka include Air Canada and Northwest Airlines from North America, and Japan Airlines from the United Kingdom. Flights from Tōkyō, which operate frequently throughout the day, take 65 minutes. Japan Airlines (JAL) and All Nippon Airways (ANA) have domestic flights to major cities.

🛫 Carriers **Air Canada** ☎ 0120/048–048. **All Nippon Airways** ☎ 0120/02–9222. **Japan Airlines** ☎ 0120/255–931 international, 0120/25–5971 domestic. **Northwest Airlines** ☎ 0120/120–747.

AIRPORTS & TRANSFERS

All international flights arrive at Kansai International Airport (KIX), which also handles connecting domestic flights to major Japanese cities. The airport, constructed on reclaimed land in Ōsaka Bay, is laid out vertically—the buildings, not the runways. The first floor is for international arrivals, the second floor is for domestic departures and arrivals, the third floor has shops and restaurants, and the fourth floor is for international departures.

About 60% of domestic flights still use Ōsaka's old airport, confusingly called Ōsaka International Airport; it's more commonly known as Itami Airport, Itami being the name of the city it's located in, a half hour or so northwest of Ōsaka. Flights from Tōkyō, which operate frequently throughout the day, take 65 minutes.

TRANSFERS   KIX was designed to serve the entire Kansai region (Kōbe, Kyōto, and Nara), not just Ōsaka, so there's good train service out of the airport. There are four main access routes to Ōsaka: to Shin-Ōsaka take the JR Kansai Airport Express Haruka for the 45-minute run (¥3,180); to Tennō-ji Station, the same JR train will take about 29 minutes (¥2,470); to JR Kyō-bashi Station take the Kansai Airport Rapid train for a 70-minute run (¥1,160); and, to Nankai Namba Station take the private Nankai Rapid Limited Express for a 29-minute trip (¥1,390). There is no English-language hot line for JR schedules, but tourist information offices and hotel staff should be able to help.

The airport is not that large: as soon as you come out through customs you are in the arrivals lobby, where you'll find English-language tourist information and direct access to limousine buses. Airport bus limousine service runs between KIX and many of Ōsaka's downtown hotels. The very comfortable bus takes about 60 minutes and costs ¥1,300–¥1,800.

Buses from Itami Airport operate at intervals of 15 minutes to one hour, daily 6 AM–9 PM, and take passengers to seven locations in Ōsaka: Shin-Ōsaka Station, Umeda, Namba (near the Nikkō and Holiday Inn hotels), Ue-hon-machi, Abeno, Sakai-higashi, and Ōsaka Business Park (near the New Ōtani Hotel). Buses take 25–50 minutes, depending on the destination, and cost ¥490–¥620. Schedules, with exact times and fares, are available at the information counter at the airport.

Taxis to the city from Kansai International Airport are prohibitively expensive; between Itami Airport and hotels in central Ōsaka, taxis cost approximately ¥7,500 and take about 40 minutes.

BUS TRAVEL

Economical one-day transportation passes for Ōsaka are valid on bus lines as well as subway routes, and the service operates throughout the day and evening. These passes cost ¥850 and are available at the commuter ticket windows in major subway stations and at the Japan Travel Bureau office in Ōsaka Station. However, bus travel is a challenge best left to local residents or those fluent in Japanese.

BUSINESS ASSISTANCE

Contact Information Service System Co., Ltd., for business-related assistance, including quick-print business cards and interpreting. For laptop repair, try Sofmap.

Information Service System Co., Ltd. ⊠ Hotel Nikkō Ōsaka, 1-3-3 Nishi-Shin-Sai-bashi, Chūō-ku ☎ 06/6245-4015. **Sofmap** ⊠ 3-2-135 Umeda, Kita-ku ☎ 06/4797-4300.

CONSULATES

Canada ⊠ 2-2-3 Nishi-Shin-Sai-bashi, Chūō-ku ☎ 06/6212-4910. **U.K.** ⊠ Seiko Ōsaka Bldg., 19th fl., 35-1 Bakuro-machi, Chūō-ku ☎ 06/6281-1616. **U.S.** ⊠ 2-11-5 Nishi-Tenma, Kita-ku ☎ 06/6315-5900.

EMERGENCIES

For medical advice in English, call the AMDA International Medical Center Kansai.

Doctors & Hospitals AMDA International Medical Center Kansai ☎ 06/6636-2333. **Sumitomo Hospital** ⊠ 2-2 Naka-no-shima 5-chōme, Kita-ku ☎ 06/6443-1261. **Tane General Hospital** ⊠ 1-2-31 Sakai-gawa, Nishi-ku ☎ 06/6581-1071. **Yodo-gawa Christian Hospital** ⊠ 9-26 Awaji 2-chōme, Higashi, Yodo-gawa-ku ☎ 06/6322-2250.

Emergency Services Ambulance ☎ 119. **Metropolitan Police Office Service** ☎ 06/6943-1234. **Police** ☎ 110.

ENGLISH-LANGUAGE MEDIA

BOOKS Kinokuniya Book Store is open daily 10–9, except for the third Wednesday of the month. It's across the street from the Midō-suji entrance of Ōsaka Station in the Hankyū Station complex. Maruzen sells English-language books and is open daily 10–8 on Shin-sai-bashi-suji, north of Shin-sai-bashi subway station.

Kinokuniya Book Store ⊠ Hankyū Samban-gai 1-1-3, Shibata, Kita-ku ☎ 06/6372-5821. **Maruzen** ⊠ 3-3-2 Bakuromachi, Chūō-ku ☎ 06/6251-2700.

NEWSPAPERS & Established in 1977, *Kansai Time Out* (⊕ www.kto.co.jp) is a monthly
MAGAZINES publication listing all sorts of events in Kōbe, Kyōto, Nara, and Ōsaka. There are also topical articles written for travelers and residents. It costs ¥300 and is available at all major hotels and bookshops throughout the region.

SIGHTSEEING TOURS

The Aqua Liner runs a 60-minute tour (¥1,600–¥1,880) through Ōsaka's waterways, departing daily every hour from 10 to 4 from April to September. There are also evening tours from 6 to 7 on Friday, Saturday, Sunday, and national holidays departing from three piers, at Ōsaka-jō, Tenma-bashi, and Yodoya-bashi. These are the only tours of Ōsaka conducted in both Japanese and English.

Japan Travel Bureau Sunrise Tours runs afternoon tours daily to Kyōto (¥8,000) and Nara (¥9,000). Pickup service is available at several hotels.

Japan's Home Visit System, which enables foreign visitors to meet local people in their homes for a few hours and learn more about the Japanese lifestyle, is available in Ōsaka. Apply in advance through the Ōsaka Tourist Information Center at either JR Shin-Ōsaka Station or JR Ōsaka Station.

🏢 **Aqua Liner** ☎ 06/6942–5511. **Japan Travel Bureau Sunrise Tours** ☎ 03/5796–5454. **Ōsaka Tourist Information Center** ✉ JR Shin-Ōsaka Station, Higashi-Yodo-gawa-ku ☎ 06/6305–3311 ✉ JR Ōsaka Station, Kita-ku ☎ 06/6345–2189.

SUBWAYS

Ōsaka's fast, efficient subway system offers the most convenient means of exploring the city—complicated bus routes display no signs in English, and taxis, while plentiful, are costly. There are seven lines, of which Midō-suji is the main one; it runs between Shin-Ōsaka and Umeda in 6 minutes, Shin-Ōsaka and Shin-Sai-bashi in 12 minutes, Shin-Ōsaka and Namba in 14 minutes, and Shin-Ōsaka and Tennō-ji in 20 minutes.

A very useful subway map of Ōsaka is available in city tourist offices, most hotels, and from the Japan National Tourist Organization in the United States or in Tōkyō (⇨ Visitor Information *in* Smart Travel Tips A to Z).

Adding to the efficiency of the subway system is the JR Loop Line, which circles the city aboveground and intersects with all subway lines. Fares range from ¥120 to ¥190, or you can use your JR Pass.

FARES & SCHEDULES   Subways run from early morning until nearly midnight at intervals of three to five minutes. Fares begin at ¥200 and are determined by the distance traveled. You can purchase a one-day pass (¥850)—which provides unlimited municipal transportation on subways, the New Tram (a tram line that runs to the port area), and city buses—at the commuter ticket windows in major subway stations and at the Japan Travel Bureau office in Ōsaka Station.

TAXIS

You'll have no problem hailing taxis on the street or at taxi stands. (A red light in the lower left corner of the windshield indicates availability.) The problem is moving in Ōsaka's heavy traffic. Fares are metered at ¥550–¥640 for the first 2 km (1 mi), plus ¥90 for each additional 500 yards. Few taxi drivers speak English, so it's advisable to have your address written in Japanese characters to show to the driver. It's not customary to tip, and many taxis now accept credit cards. Late at night, generally after midnight, there's a 20% surcharge. Some taxis offer 50% discounts on fares that are more than ¥5,000.

TELEPHONES
🗂 Directory & Operator Assistance **Directory assistance in English** ☎ 0120/364-463.

TRAIN TRAVEL
Hikari Shinkansen trains from Tōkyō's Tōkyō Station to Shin-Ōsaka Station take about three hours and cost ¥13,950. You can use a JR Pass for the *Hikari* but not for the faster *Nozomi* Shinkansen trains, which cost ¥14,720 and are about 30 minutes faster. Shin-Ōsaka Station, on the north side of Shin-Yodo-gawa, is linked to the city center by the JR Kōbe Line and the Midō-suji subway line. On either line the ride, which takes 6–20 minutes, depending on your mid-city destination, costs ¥180–¥230. Train schedule and fare information can be obtained at the Travel Service Center in Shin-Ōsaka Station. A taxi from Shin-Ōsaka Station to central Ōsaka costs ¥1,500–¥2,700.

The JR Loop Line circles the city aboveground and intersects with all of Ōsaka's subway lines. Fares range from ¥120 to ¥190, or you can use your JR Pass.

TRAVEL AGENCIES
Academy Travel and No. 1 Travel sell cheap air tickets, and staff members are well versed in English.
🗂 **Academy Travel** ✉ Takada II, 4th fl., 2-6-8 Jūsō Higashi, Yodo-gawa-ku ☎ 06/6303-3538. **No. 1 Travel** ✉ Nisshin Bldg., 11th fl., 8-8 Taiyūji-chō, Kita-ku ☎ 06/6363-4489.

VISITOR INFORMATION
The main Ōsaka Tourist Information Center, open daily 8–8 and closed December 31–January 3, is on the east side of the main exit of JR Shin-Ōsaka Station. There's another location at the Midō-suji gate of JR Ōsaka Station, open daily from 8 to 8 and closed December 31–January 4. A small branch on the first floor of the passenger terminal building in Kansai International Airport is open daily 9–9.

Japan Travel Phone, available daily 9–5, provides free tourist information in English.
🗂 Tourist Information **Japan Travel Phone** ☎ 0088/22-4800. **Ōsaka Tourist Information Center** ✉ JR Shin-Ōsaka Station, Higashi-Yodo-gawa-ku ☎ 06/6305-3311 ✉ JR Ōsaka Station, Kita-ku ☎ 06/6345-2189 ✉ Kansai International Airport ☎ 0724/56-6025.

KŌBE 神戸

By Nigel Fisher

Revised by
Dominic
Al-Badri

LONG A POPULAR CHOICE OF RESIDENCE FOR MANY WESTERNERS, Kōbe is known throughout Japan as one of the country's most international cities, in part due to its busy, prosperous harbor. In the 12th century the Taira family moved the capital from Kyōto to Fukuhara, the western part of modern Kōbe, with the hope of increasing Japan's international trade. Fukuhara remained the capital for a mere six months, although its port, known as Hyōgo, continued to flourish. When Japan reestablished trade with the West in 1868, after a long period of isolationism, the more remote port of Kōbe was opened for international traffic, while the port of Hyōgo was reserved for domestic shipping. Within a few years, Kōbe, slightly northeast of Hyōgo, eclipsed it in importance. Kōbe's port now handles more than 2 million containers a year and about 10,000 ships.

A century of exposure to international cultures has left its mark on Kōbe, a sophisticated and cosmopolitan city. Of its population of 1.5 million, some 70,000 residents are *gaijin* (foreigners). Most are Chinese or Korean, but a noticeable European contingent also lives and works in Kōbe. Over the years foreign merchants, traders, and sailors have settled in the hills above the port area, and more recently on the man-made Rokkō Island in the city's eastern precincts. Western-style houses built in the late 19th century are still inhabited by Kōbe's foreign population, although others have been opened to the public as buildings of historical interest. So don't come to Kōbe looking for traditional Japan. Instead, visit to experience a new, diverse Japan in a cosmopolitan setting with excellent shopping and international cuisines.

In the decade since the Great Hanshin earthquake, which struck in January 1995 killing more than 5,000 people and destroying some 100,000 buildings, Kōbe has all but fully recovered. Indeed, the only cultural attractions completely wiped out were the half-dozen or so 19th-century sake breweries that had been converted into museums.

Plans for a domestic airport to be built on a man-made island continue apace, even though some 300,000 signatures were collected protesting that it was an unnecessary waste of taxpayers' money. Kōbe Kūkō (Kōbe Airport) is due for completion in mid-2005 and remains a controversial topic among the city's residents.

See the glossary at the end of this book for definitions of the common Japanese words and suffixes used in this chapter.

EXPLORING KŌBE

Kōbe is a hill-and-harbor town that brings to mind San Francisco. Downtown Kōbe, the site of most businesses, is near the harbor. The rest of Kōbe is built on slopes that extend as far as the base of Rokkō-san (Mount Rokkō). In the middle of the harbor is the man-made Pōto Airando (Port Island), which has conference centers, an amusement park, and the Portopia Hotel. The island is linked with downtown by a fully computerized monorail—with no human conductor. The major nightlife area, Ikuta (a part of the Kitano area), is just north of San-no-miya Station.

What to See

Downtown Kōbe & Port Island

▶ ⓫ **Great Hanshin-Awaji Earthquake Memorial** (Hanshin Awaji Daishinsai
Fodor'sChoice Kinen, 人と防災未来センター). Part of the Disaster Reduction and Human
★ Renovation Institution, this is a memorial to the 5,273 people who lost
their lives in the 1995 earthquake. Both the on-site Disaster Reduction
Museum and Human Renovation Museums have plenty of photographs,
hi-tech multimedia displays, a re-created postquake street scene, and film
screenings, a number of which are in English. English guide booklets
are also available. The institution is 10 minutes' walk from the south
exit of JR Nada Station, one stop east of JR San-no-miya Station.
✉ 1–5–2 Wakinohama Kaigan-dōri, Chūō-ku ☎ 078/262–5050 ⊕ www.
dri.ne.jp ✎ ¥500 per museum, ¥800 for both ⊙ Daily 9:30–5:30.

⓬ **Hyōgo Prefectural Museum of Art** (Hyōgo Kenritsu Bijutsukan,
Fodor'sChoice 兵庫県立美術館). Designed by internationally acclaimed architect Tadao
★ Andō, the prefecture's leading art museum is a striking concrete structure with a commanding waterfront presence. The museum has a collection of 7,000 works of art, including some by local artists and some
by foreigners such as sculptors Henry Moore and Auguste Rodin. Two
memorial rooms are dedicated to noted 20th-century painters of the so-
called "Western-style" school of Japanese art, Ryōhei Koiso and Heizō
Kanayama. The museum is 10 minutes' walk from the south exit of JR
Nada Station, one stop east of JR San-no-miya Station. Combining a
visit here with a trip to the nearby Great Hanshin-Awaji Earthquake
Memorial is a good way to spend the afternoon. ✉ 1–1–1 Wakinohama
Kaigan-dōri, Chūō-ku ☎ 078/262–0901 ⊕ www.artm.pref.hyogo.jp
✎ ¥500 ⊙ Daily 10–6.

❹ **Ikuta Jinja** (生田神社). The entrance to this Shintō shrine is through an
impressive orange torii, which was rebuilt after the 1995 earthquake.
According to legend, the shrine was founded by Empress Jingū in the
3rd century and therefore is one of the oldest in Japan. It's in the heart
of the city, about 450 yards west of San-no-miya Station, and a short
visit makes a nice change from the busy surrounding streets. ✉ 1–2–1
Shimoyamate-dōri Chūō-ku.

★ ▶ ❶ **Kōbe City Museum** (Kōbe Shiritsu Hakubutsukan, 神戸市立博物館). For a
look into Kōbe's history, especially the foreign settlement of the late 19th
century, spend an hour in this well-organized museum. You can find a
model of the old foreign concession, plus memorabilia and three rooms
from a turn-of-the-20th-century Western house. The museum also has
a famous collection of Namban art: prints, screens, and paintings by
Japanese artists of the late 16th to 17th centuries depicting foreigners
in Japanese settings from that period. (Originally referring to Portuguese
sailors, *namban* now refers to any Western thing or person from the time
of first contact between Japan and the West.) The museum also stages
exhibitions of international art.

From San-no-miya Station, walk south on Flower Road to Higashi-
Yuenchi Kōen. Walk through the park to the Kōbe Minato post office,

A stroll around the Kitano area punctuated by a café stop and a great dinner is time well spent. You can see Kōbe's main sights in a one-day excursion from Ōsaka or Kyōto, including a stop on your way down the San-yō Coast. With a second day in Kōbe you can make a side trip to Rokkō-san and Arima Onsen.

Except for during the cold days of winter and the humid days of mid-summer, Kōbe enjoys a mild climate tempered by the Seto Nai-kai. Spring, especially at cherry-blossom time, and autumn are the optimal seasons to visit Kōbe, as well as most of the rest of Japan.

8

Numbers in the text correspond to numbers in the margin and on the Kōbe map.

If you have
1 day

A good place to start your visit to Kōbe is the **Kōbe City Museum ①** ▶, where you can take in the history of the town, including memorabilia from the heyday of the old foreign settlement. To get to the museum, walk south down Flower Road from San-no-miya Station, past the Flower Clock and City Hall, to Higashi-Yuenchi Kōen. Walk through the park to the Kōbe Minato post office, across the street on the west side. Walk east on the road in front of the post office toward the Oriental Hotel. Turn left at the corner in front of the hotel; the museum is in the old Bank of Tōkyō building, at the end of the block.

From here, continue on toward the water and stop into Meriken Park and the **Kōbe Maritime Museum ③**, with its exhibits of ships and all things nautical. Return to San-no-miya Station, browsing through **Nankin-machi** (Chinatown) **②** and the Moto-machi and San-no-miya shopping arcades if time permits. Once back at San-no-miya Station, begin your tour of the northern district by crossing the street that runs along the tracks and turning left at the first main intersection to see the classic outline of the orange torii at **Ikuta Jinja ④**. The road that runs up the right side of the shrine leads up the slope to Nakayamate-dōri. Cross the avenue and continue up the slope. Turn right at the corner of Yamamoto-dōri, a road lined with high-fashion boutiques and restaurants. Turn left at Kitano-zaka, which leads to **Kitano-chō,** an area where Western traders and businessmen have lived since the late 19th century. Many of the older ijinkan have been turned into museums. Continue up the slope from Nakayamate-dōri. At the first intersection after Yamamoto-dōri (nicknamed Ijinkan-dōri), just past Rin's Gallery, which is filled with boutiques of Japan's top designers, turn right and walk east to visit the 1907 **Eikoku-kan ⑤**.

Three ijinkan in the Kitano-ku area are publicly owned. **Rhein-no-Yakata ⑥**, opposite Eikoku-kan, has a German-style coffee shop inside. Near Kitano Tenman Jinja at the top of the hill is the **Kazami-dori-no-Yakata ⑦**, made famous on a national TV series some years ago. Continue back down the slope via Kitano-zaka toward San-no-miya Station and turn right on Yamamoto-dōri. One ijinkan house not to miss is the 1869 **Choueke Yashiki ⑧**, full of interesting turn-of-the-20th-century items. Return to San-no-miya Station and walk to the **Portliner ⑨** platform, and take the automated train to the consumer diversions on **Port Island** (Pōto Airando) **⑩**.

If you have
2 days

On your second day, take a trip to the city's eastern districts. From JR San-no-miya, take a local train one stop to JR Nada Station. From here walk south for 10 minutes until you come to the HAT (Happy Active Town) district. The two main sights in HAT are the **Great Hanshin-Awaji Earthquake Memorial** ⑪ ☞ and the nearby **Hyogo Prefectural Museum of Art** ⑫. With an early start, you'd be able to see them both in the morning, and then enjoy a light lunch at the art museum's very good café. After lunch, head back to JR San-no-miya Station and change to the adjoining Hankyū San-no-miya Station. Here, catch a local train heading east to Hankyū Rokkō Station. The journey over **Rokkō-san** and descent into the resort town of **Arima Onsen** ⑭ offers wonderful views. After a refreshing soak in the town's famous hot baths, the return trip to San-no-miya should see you back in the center of town just in time for a hearty dinner of Kōbe beef.

---

across the street on the west side. Walk east on the road in front of the post office toward the Oriental Hotel. Turn left at the corner in front of the hotel, and the City Museum is in the old Bank of Tōkyō building, at the end of the block. ⊠ *24 Kyō-machi, Chūō-ku* ☏ *078/391–0035* 🖾 *¥200; more for special exhibitions* ⊙ *Tues.–Sun. 10–5.*

❸ **Kōbe Maritime Museum** (Kōbe Kaiyō Hakubutsukan, 神戸海洋博物館). This museum in Meriken Kōen displays models of all kinds of vessels, from ancient designs to modern hydrofoils. Look for the Oshoro Maru model—it was one of Japan's earliest sailing ships and is adorned with pearls, rubies, gold, and silver. On the first floor is a model of the HMS *Rodney*, the British flagship that led a 12-ship flotilla into Kōbe Harbor on January 1, 1868—the date that marked the official opening of Japan after 250 years of isolationism. In contrast to all of this backward looking, the *Submarine Travel 2090* puts you in the center of a biosphere on the sea floor. The museum has a dramatic, prowlike roof best appreciated from the top of Port Tower, on the nearby Port Island. ⊠ *2 Meriken Kōen, Hatoba-chō, Chūō-ku* ☏ *078/391–6751* 🖾 *¥600, ¥900 including admission to Port Tower* ⊙ *Tues.–Sun. 10–5.*

❷ **Nankin-machi** (Chinatown, 南京町). Centered at Daimaru Depāto, Kōbe's Chinatown is where Japanese come to buy souvenirs and try out Chinese restaurants. To find Nankin-machi from Moto-machi Station, walk on the port side and enter the neighborhood through the large, fake marble gate.

❿ **Port Island** (Pōto Airando, ポートアイランド). The degree to which Kōbe has been internationalized is reflected in the Japanese name for this piece of landfill: Pōto Airando is a wholesale borrowing from English pronounced Japanese-style to sound like Port Island. The Portliner monorail's Shimin Hiroba Station is right in the heart of the island's futuristic complex, with parks, hotels, restaurants, and fashion boutiques to explore. Although many buildings were destroyed in the 1995 earthquake, Port Island is likely to see more development after the 2005 opening of the new airport on another man-made island just south of Pōto Airando.

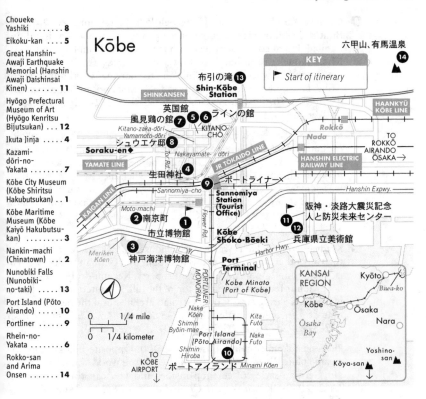

9 Portliner ポートライナー This digitally driven monorail departs from San-no-miya Station every six minutes from 6:05 AM until 11:40 PM on its loop to and around Port Island, with eight stops along the way. The ride affords a close-up view of Kōbe Harbor, and a second line is due to extend south to Kōbe Airport in 2005. ☞ *¥480 round-trip.*

Kitano-chō 北野町

★ In the area known as **Kitano**, wealthy foreigners in the late 19th century set up residences, bringing to Japan Western-style domestic architecture, referred to in Kōbe as ijinkan. The district is extremely popular with young Japanese tourists, who enjoy the opportunity of seeing old-fashioned Western houses, which are rare in Japan. The curious mélange of Japanese and Western Victorian and Gothic architecture makes for an interesting walk in the hills of this neighborhood. Some residences are still inhabited by Westerners, but more than a dozen 19th-century ijinkan in Kitano-chō are open to the public. Seeing all of them can get repetitious.

To get to Kitano-chō to see the ijinkan, take a 15-minute walk north along Kitano-zaka-dōri from San-no-miya Station or a 10-minute walk west along Kitano-dōri from Shin-Kōbe Station. Yamamoto-dōri (nicknamed Ijinkan-dōri) is Kitano's main street, and the ijinkan are on the small side streets ascending the hill.

★ ❽ **Choueke Yashiki** (Choueke ["choo-eh-keh"] Mansion, シュウエケ邸). Built in 1889, this is the only house open to the public that is still inhabited. It's filled to the rafters with memorabilia from East and West. Mrs. Choueke is on hand to show you her treasures, which include many namban wood-block prints, and to share her vast knowledge of Kōbe. Her ijinkan is not to be missed. ✉ *Yamamoto-dōri, street also known as Ijinkan-dōri, Chūō-ku* 📞 *078/221–3209* 💴 *¥500* 🕙 *Wed.–Mon. 9–5.*

❺ **Eikoku-kan** ("*eh*-ee-ko *koo*-kan," English House, 英国館). This typical old-fashioned Western house—with Union Jacks draped outside—was constructed in 1907 by an Englishman named Baker and served as a makeshift hospital during World War II, when the city's main hospital was damaged in an air attack. It's currently a house museum, furnished in period style and complete with an authentic black taxi from London in the driveway. ✉ *2–3–16 Kitano-dōri, Chūō-ku* 📞 *078/241–2338* 💴 *¥700* 🕙 *Daily 9–5.*

❼ **Kazami-dori-no-Yakata** (Weathercock House, 風見鶏の館). More elaborate than any other Kōbe ijinkan, this one, built by a German trader in 1910, is listed as an Important Cultural Property. Kazami-dori-no-Yakata is near Kitano Tenman Jinja at the top of the hill. The interior of this building reflects various traditional German architectural themes, including that of a medieval castle. ✉ *3–13–3 Kitano-dōri, Chūō-ku* 📞 *078/242–3223* 💴 *Free* 🕙 *Wed.–Mon. 10–5.*

❻ **Rhein-no-Yakata** (Rhein House, ラインの館). Opposite Eikoku-kan, the cream-colore Rhein-no-Yakata, built just before World War I, has a pleasant German-style coffee shop inside, and you can tour the house. ✉ *2–10–24 Kitano-dōri, Chūō-ku* 📞 *078/222–3403* 💴 *Free* 🕙 *Fri.–Wed. 10–5.*

Elsewhere in Kōbe

⓭ **Nunobiki Falls** (Nunobiki-no-taki, 布引の滝). A quiet side trip from the city is the 20-minute walk up the hill behind Shin-Kōbe Station to Nunobiki Falls, whose beauty has been referred to in Japanese literature since the 10th century. The four cascades of varying heights are collectively known as one of the three greatest falls in Japan. Signs give directions to the falls from the station and the adjoining OPA shopping mall. ✉ *Chūō-ku.*

⓮ **Rokkō-san and Arima Onsen** (六甲山、有馬温泉). A cable car climbs this, the highest peak in the Rokkō Mountains, which form a backdrop to Kōbe. Some of the most exciting views are en route, so have your camera ready. Once at the top in the cool mountain air—a delight in summer—you get a staggering view of the city and the Seto Nai-kai. On the mountain are various recreational areas, including the oldest golf course in Japan, designed in 1903 by resident English merchant Arthur H. Gloom, and the summer houses of some of Kōbe's wealthier residents.

To get to Rokkō-san, take the Hankyū Kōbe Line from Hankyū San-no-miya Station to Hankyū Rokkō Station (¥180). From there take either a taxi or a bus to Rokkō Cable-shita Station. A funicular railway trav-

Kōbe Beef

All over the world, the name Kōbe is synonymous with superb beef. Tender, tasty, and extremely expensive, Kōbe beef is a delicacy that steak lovers should not miss. Raised in the nearby Tajima area of Hyōgo Prefecture, Kōbe cows are fed beer and massaged regularly to improve the quality of their meat and give it its signature, fat-marbled texture. Although many people know and love Kōbe beef, most don't know that beef was introduced to Kōbe by Westerners in the late 19th century. Eventually, the Japanese took over the management of the cattle and improved and refined the process. The beef is always served as steak, and depending on the restaurant, the steaks may be accompanied with a Western-style selection of vegetables, like potatoes and carrots, or with fried vegetables prepared Japanese-style, including mushrooms, beansprouts, and cabbage. Most of the best beef restaurants are located in the central Chūō-ku district, and it's also on the menu at the top-class hotels.

Hiking

Kōbe is a long, narrow city with a backdrop of beautiful mountains. Hiking is a popular pastime among locals, and there are two easily accessible starting points for leisurely hikes. One is Shin-Kōbe Station, from which you can take a short climb up to the Nunobiki Falls. Rokkō-san is also good for a day's hiking; from Hankyū Kōbe Line Rokkō Station you can take a bus or taxi to Rokkō Cable Shita cable-car station. From here you can either hike all the way up the mountain or take the cable-car part of the way. You may see wild boar, which are harmless if not provoked, in the forested mountains.

---

els up the mountain to Rokkō-sanjo Station (¥570). You can either return to Kōbe by the cable car or go directly back on the Kōbe Dentetsu (electric railway; ¥650), which uses Shin-kaichi Station, two stops west of Kōbe's Moto-machi Station. Or take the Kōbe Dentetsu to Tanigami Station and change for the subway back to San-no-miya (¥900).

Even before Nara became the capital in the 7th century, **Arima Onsen** had established itself as a place to take the thermal waters. The hot spring's fame reached a high point when Hideyoshi Toyotomi took the waters here in the late 16th century. Arima is on the north slope of Rokkō-san and is a maze of tiny streets still lined with traditional houses. Some 30 ryokan have established themselves, using the thermal waters' reputed curative powers to attract guests. Although the water gushes up freely from springs, some ryokan charge as much as ¥10,000, for use of their baths. Go instead to the public bath, **Arima Onsen Kaikan** (有馬温泉会館), in the center of the village near the bus terminal. Here ¥520 gets you entrance and a soak in the steaming waters. Arima Onsen Kaikan is open daily 8 AM–10 PM (closed the first and third Tuesday of the month). A cable car continues after Rokkō-sanjo Station over the mountain's crest at Country Station before traversing a beautiful valley to Arima Onsen (¥1,460 one-way, ¥2,640 round-trip).

WHERE TO EAT

There are many international cuisines available in Kōbe, especially examples from Southeast Asia. The place to look for restaurants is north of San-no-miya Station in the Kitano area, especially the main street, Kitano-zaka, and the Tor Road area between JR San-no-miya Station and JR Moto-machi Station. Port Island also has a reputation for good restaurants of various cuisines—look near the Portopia Hotel.

WHAT IT COSTS In yen					
	$$$$	**$$$**	**$$**	**$**	**¢**
AT DINNER	over 3,000	2,000–3,000	1,000–2,000	800–1,000	under 800

Prices are per person for a main course.

$$$$ ✕**Aragawa** (あら皮). Japan's first steak house is famed for its superb hand-
Fodor'sChoice fed Kōbe beef, all of it from one farm in the nearby city of Sanda. The
★ melt-in-your-mouth *sumiyaki* (charcoal-broiled) steak is worth its weight
in yen—and it's only served with mustard and pepper. (Don't even
think about asking for other condiments.) Dark-wood paneling and a
lovely chandelier give the dining room a European feel. Aragawa is considered *the* place for Kōbe beef, and, accordingly, an evening here is the
ultimate splurge—be prepared to spend ¥20,000 for your main course.
✉ *2–15–18 Nakayamate-dōri, Chūō-ku* ☎ *078/221–8547* ⓜ *Jacket and
tie* ▭ *AE, DC, MC, V.*

$$$$ ✕**Tōtenkaku** (東天閣). This restaurant has been famous among Kōbe residents since 1945 for its Peking duck, flown in fresh from China, but
the building itself is worth the proverbial cost of admission. Built at the
turn of the 20th century, Tōtenkaku is located in one of Kōbe's ijinkan,
the F. Bishop House. You can keep the price down by ordering one of
the Chinese noodle specialties to fill you up, or by going at lunchtime
when you can have a filling set meal for just ¥1,800. ✉ *3–14–18 Yamamoto-dōri, Chūō-ku* ☎ *078/231–1351* ▭ *AE, DC, MC, V.*

$$$$ ✕**Wakkoku** (和黒). If you want to try Kōbe beef without spending a bun-
dle, come at lunchtime to this smart but plain restaurant on the third
floor of the shopping plaza underneath the Oriental Hotel, across from
Shin-Kōbe Station. Don't be distracted by the other restaurants on this
floor—Wakkoku is the best choice. Prices at lunchtime—count on
¥3,000 for Kōbe beef—are lower than they are at dinner. ✉ *Kitano-chō
1-chōme, Chūō-ku* ☎ *078/262–2838* ▭ *AE, DC, V.*

$$$$ ✕**A-1.** For affordable Kōbe beef in the neighborhood north of Hankyū
San-no-miya Station, come to A-1. The *teppan* (broiled on a hot plate)
steak is served on a hot grill with a special spice-and-wine marinade that
is as memorable as the garlicky crisp-fried potatoes. Right across from
the Washington Hotel, A-1 has a relaxed and friendly atmosphere.
✉ *Lighthouse Bldg., ground floor, 2–2–9 Shimoyamate-dōri, Chūō-ku*
☎ *078/331–8676* ▭ *No credit cards* ☉ *Closed Tues.*

★ **$$$$** ✕**Ōishi** (大西). This popular restaurant has a well-deserved reputation,
both among Japanese locals and long-time foreign residents, for serving fine Kōbe beef. There's nothing pretentious about the restaurant—

Restaurants

Hotels

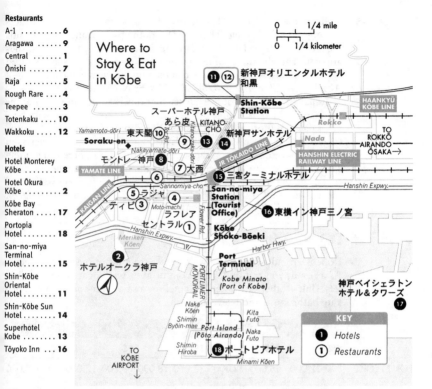

the counter is one enormous hot plate around which all the diners sit. Steaks are cooked up in the middle by master chefs, and then brought over and placed in front of you. Baseball players and sumō wrestlers are among the celebrity diners. ⊠ *3F Yūberu Bldg., 1–4–6 Nakayamate-dōri, Chūō-ku* ☎ *078/332–4029* ▭ *No credit cards* ☉ *Closed Mon.*

$$ ✕ **Central** (セントラル). You can expect fast, friendly service at this Italian-Japanese café popular with the stylish twentysomething set. A filling spaghetti prix-fixe lunch can be had for under ¥1,000, though dinner can stretch to double that. Central is often busy with local office workers at lunchtime, so arrive early or expect to wait. A decent wine list and good music—usually jazz—make it a good spot for an early evening cocktail as well. ⊠ *104 Edomachi-chō, Chūō-ku* ☎ *078/325–2033* ▭ *No credit cards.*

★ **$$** ✕ **Raja** (ラジャ). This small, unassuming place near Moto-machi Station was opened by a former chef of Gaylord, the city's premier Indian restaurant prior to the 1995 earthquake. Raja serves home-style Indian food, with spicy curries, top-notch tandoori, and excellent saffron rice. The dining room is simple and functional, with a few prints on the walls and Indian music. ⊠ *Sanonatsu Bldg., basement, 2–7–4 Sakae-machi, Chūō-ku* ☎ *078/332–5253* ▭ *AE, DC, V.*

★ **$–$$** ✕ **Rough Rare** (ラフレア). This funky, laid-back, two-story café attracts a young, stylish clientele. There's a DJ booth upstairs, and on weekends the tables are cleared away for dancing. Pasta, burgers, and curry dishes are typical at lunchtime, while Japanese-style tapas dishes, such as sliced eggplant in miso sauce, are more common on the evening menu. ⊠ *18–2 Akashi-chō, Chūō-ku* ☎ *078/333–0808* ▤ *No credit cards.*

★ **¢–$$** ✕ **Teepee** (ティピ). The only evidence that this is an Italian restaurant is the menu, which lists some of the best pizzas in town, along with pastas, salads, and other Italian dishes. You can eat inside or out on the large balcony, where a teepee stands near a wood-fired pizza oven. Neil Young is as often as not on the stereo, and the atmosphere is definitely casual. Teepee is more spacious than is the norm for Japanese restaurants, and the staff are in no hurry to move you on after you've finished eating—unusual in Japan. ⊠ *KCS Bldg., 3Ft, 1–2–26 Sakae-machi, Chūō-ku* ☎ *078/327–7177* ▤ *MC, V.*

WHERE TO STAY

Kōbe is an industrialized city that caters to a lot of business travelers. As a result, you can find many comfortable, well-located business hotels. Unless otherwise noted, all hotel rooms have air-conditioning, private bathrooms, and televisions.

WHAT IT COSTS In yen				
$$$$	**$$$**	**$$**	**$**	**¢**
FOR 2 PEOPLE over 22,000	18,000–22,000	12,000–18,000	8,000–12,000	under 8,000

Price categories are assigned based on the range between the least and most expensive standard double rooms in nonholiday high season, based on the European Plan (with no meals) unless otherwise noted. Taxes (5%-15%) are extra.

$$$$ ▦ **Kōbe Bay Sheraton** (神戸ベイシェラトンホテル&タワーズ). The city's most international hotel is ideally located for business travelers—on the man-made Rokkō Airando (Rokkō Island), Kōbe's commercial center. Rooms are comfortable and have interesting views of the surrounding commercial and industrial areas, and service is of the highest order. However, unless you're on business, there's little to see or do on Rokkō Island, which makes this less than convenient as a base for sightseeing. On the other hand, the hotel has a free shuttle bus to Universal Studios Japan in Ōsaka. ⊠ *2–13 Koyo-chō-naka, Higashi-nada-ku, Kōbe-shi, Hyōgo-ken 658-0032* ☎ *078/857–7000* ▤ *078/857–7041* ⊕ *www. sheraton-kobe.co.jp* ⋈ *276 rooms ♨ 4 restaurants, coffee shop, room service, minibars, cable TV, pool, tennis court, gym, sports bar, shops* ▤ *AE, DC, MC, V.*

★ **$$$–$$$$** ▦ **Hotel Ōkura Kōbe** (ホテルオークラ神戸). A 35-story hotel on the wharf in Meriken Kōen, this is one of the city's best. Beautifully furnished, the property lives up to the Ōkura chain's worldwide reputation for excellence. Rooms were done by David Hicks, who has designed interiors for the British royal family. The hotel has a well-equipped health club and stunning views of the bay from the Emerald Restaurant. ⊠ *Meriken*

Kōen, 2–1 Hatoba-chō, Chūō-ku, Kōbe-shi, Hyōgo-ken 650-8560 ☎ *078/333–0111* 🖷 *078/333–6673* ⊕ *www.kobe.hotelokura.co.jp* 🛏 *489 rooms* ♤ *5 restaurants, coffee shop, room service, in-room data ports, minibars, cable TV, indoor pool, gym, 2 bars* ⊟ *AE, DC, MC, V.*

$$$–$$$$ 🏨 **Hotel Monterey Kōbe** (ホテルモントレー神戸). With its marvelous Mediterranean-style courtyard fountains and European furnishings, the Hotel Monterey takes you off Kōbe's busy streets and into modern Italy. It was modeled after a monastery in Florence. Twin rooms are standard size; duplex (maisonette) rooms come with a carpeted bedroom upstairs and a small lounge area with a tiled floor. The on-site Japanese restaurant recalls the 1920s Taisho Period. ✉ *2–11–13 Shimoyamate-dōri, Chūō-ku, Kōbe-shi, Hyōgo-ken 650-0011* ☎ *078/392–7111* 🖷 *078/322–2899* 🛏 *164 rooms* ♤ *Restaurant, room service, in-room data ports, cable TV, pool, gym, hot tub, bar* ⊟ *AE, DC, MC, V.*

$$$–$$$$ 🏨 **Portopia Hotel** (ポートピアホテル). A dazzling modern hotel with every facility imaginable, the Portopia suffers from its location on the manmade Port Island. Spacious rooms overlook the port, and the restaurants and lounges on the top floors have panoramic views of Rokkō-san and Ōsaka Bay. Ask for a room in the south wing if you want a balcony and ocean view. Because of its location, the hotel can only be reached by the Portliner monorail or by taxi, but it will be convenient to the new Kōbe Airport, due to open on another island in 2005. This inconvenience is countered by the fact that everything from food—Chinese, Japanese, and French—to clothing is available inside the hotel. ✉ *6–10–1 Minatojima Naka-machi, Chūō-ku, Kōbe-shi, Hyōgo-ken 650-0046* ☎ *078/302–0111* 🖷 *078/302–6877* ⊕ *www.portopia.co.jp* 🛏 *761 rooms* ♤ *3 restaurants, coffee shop, room service, in-room data ports, cable TV, tennis court, 2 pools (1 indoor), health club, hair salon, sauna, shops* ⊟ *AE, DC, MC, V.*

$$$ 🏨 **Shin-Kōbe Oriental Hotel** (新神戸オリエンタルホテル). The tallest build-
Fodor's Choice ing in Kōbe, this architecturally stunning luxury hotel viewed from
★ downtown at night appears as a brightly lit needle-thin tower jutting into the sky. Guest rooms, with marble-tile bathrooms, are neatly decorated in pastel fabrics and furnished with a desk, a coffee table, and two reading chairs. Corner rooms on higher floors have superb views over Kōbe. Beneath the lobby are five floors of shops and restaurants. The hotel was acquired by Morgan Stanley in 2003. It faces JR Shin-Kōbe Station, where the Shinkansen arrives, and is three minutes from downtown by subway. Several hiking trails pass very close to the hotel. ✉ *Kitano-chō 1-chōme, Chūō-ku, Kōbe-shi, Hyōgo-ken 650-0002,* ☎ *078/291–1121* 🖷 *078/291–1154* ⊕ *www.orientalhotel.co.jp* 🛏 *600 rooms* ♤ *5 restaurants, room service, in-room data ports, minibars, cable TV, indoor pool, gym, hair salon, sauna, shops* ⊟ *AE, DC, MC, V.*

$$ 🏨 **San-no-miya Terminal Hotel** (三宮ターミナルホテル). In the terminal building above JR San-no-miya Station, this hotel is extremely convenient, particularly if you need to catch an early train. The rooms are large for the price and are clean and pleasant, but the hotel itself doesn't have much in the way of facilities. However, you'll find shops and restaurants in the station complex. Views from the upper floors have views of Ōsaka Bay. ⊠ *8 Kumoi-dōri, Chūō-ku, Kōbe-shi, Hyōgo-ken 651-0096* ☎ *078/291–0001* 🖷 *078/291–0020* ⊕ *www.sth-hotel.co.jp* 🛏 *190 rooms* ⚇ *In-room data ports, cable TV* ⊟ *AE, DC, MC, V.*

$ 🏨 **Shin-Kōbe Sun Hotel** (新神戸サンホテル). Built in the early boom years after World War II, this old-fashioned business hotel could do with a renovation. Although the rooms are tired, the hotel has a nice, large, Japanese-style public bath, and the staff is very friendly. The hotel is halfway between JR Shin-Kōbe Station and JR San-no-miya Station. ⊠ *2–1–9 Nunobiki-chō, Chūō-ku, Kōbe-shi, Hyōgo-ken 651-0097* ☎ *078/272–1080* 🖷 *078/272–1088* 🛏 *125 rooms* ⚇ *Restaurant, refrigerators, cable TV, Japanese bath, no-smoking rooms* ⊟ *AE, DC, V* ⦿ *CP.*

¢ 🏨 **Superhotel Kōbe** (スーパーホテル神戸). This member of the popular nationwide chain of business hotels opened in 2002. Rooms are built according to a formula, and there are just two set prices, for singles and doubles. The bathrooms are tiny and you can't expect much in the way of interior design, but you will get a clean space with a comfortable bed in central Kōbe, halfway between the city's two main train stations, San-no-miya and Shin-Kōbe. ⊠ *2–1–11 Kanō-chō, Chūō-ku,, Kōbe-shi, Hyōgo-ken 650-0001* ☎ *078/261–9000* 🖷 *078/261–9090* 🛏 *80 rooms* ⚇ *No room phones* ⊟ *No credit cards.*

¢ 🏨 **Tōyoko Inn** (東横イン神戸三ノ宮). Part of a nationwide chain, this high-rise hotel offers small and bland but clean rooms at excellent rates. Be sure to ask for a no-smoking room if you want a fresh-smelling environment. Rooms on higher floors have slightly better views of the mountains to the north. The hotel is a 10-minute walk east of the city's main San-no-miya district. ⊠ *2–2–2 Gokō-dōri, Chūō-ku, Kōbe-shi, Hyōgo-ken 651-0087* ☎ *078/271–1045* 🖷 *078/271–1046* ⊕ *www.toyoko-inn.com* 🛏 *95 rooms* ⚇ *In-room data ports, in-room safes, refrigerators, cable TV, massage, business services, free parking, no-smoking rooms* ⊟ *AE, DC, V* ⦿ *CP.*

NIGHTLIFE

Although Kōbe doesn't have as diverse a nightlife scene as Ōsaka does, its compactness is an advantage—virtually all of the best bars are within walking distance of each other. Kōbe is also regarded as the center of Japan's thriving jazz scene.

Becak. An Indonesian-theme bar just around the corner from the Washington Hotel, Becak serves decent food alongside beer and cocktails. Dance music events are scheduled on Friday and Saturday nights, when the bar stays open until the first morning trains start running. ⊠ *4F, 2–15–12 Shimoyamate-dōri* ☎ *078/392–5232.*

Sone. The city's most famous jazz club (indeed, one of the most famous in the whole country), Sone is run by the family of that name. There are four sets of live music every night, starting at 6:50, and the action often centers around a piano trio with rotating guest vocalists. There's a cover charge of about ¥700, depending on the night and the music ⊠ *1–24–10 Nakayamate-dōri* ☎ *078/221–2055.*

Ryan's. One of the most popular Western-style watering holes in Kōbe, Ryan's is a lively place that attracts a youngish crowd. ✉ *Rondo Bldg., 7th fl., north side of San-no-miya Station* ☎ *078/391–6902.*

Polo Dog. The bar serves reasonable meals, including burgers, salads, and excellent garlic french fries, and is tastefully arrayed with '50s and '60s Americana. ✉ *K Bldg., 2nd fl., 1–3–21 Sannomiya-chō* ☎ *078/331–3944.*

SHOPPING

Kōbe is a shopper's paradise. Unlike shops in Tōkyō, Ōsaka, and other places in Japan, which are scattered all over the city, most of the shopping districts in Kōbe are in clusters, so you can cover a lot of ground with ease.

Major Shopping Districts

Kōbe's historic shopping area is known as **Moto-machi,** and it extends west for 2 km (1 mi) from JR Moto-machi Station. Much of the district is under a covered arcade, which starts opposite the Daimaru department store. Stores here sell everything from antiques to cameras and electronics.

Nearly connected to the Moto-machi arcade, extending from the department store Sogō to the Moto-machi area for 1 km (½ mi), is the **San-no-miya Center Gai** arcade. Because it's right next to San-no-miya Station, this is a good place for a quick bite to eat. Next to Sogō is a branch of the Loft department store, home to all sorts of crafts and hip lifestyle accessories spread over four floors. The building also houses a branch of the Kinokuniya bookstore chain, with a small selection of English-language books.

Kōbe's trendy crowd tends to shop in the exclusive stores on **Tor Road,** which stretches north–south on a slope lined with trees. Fashionable boutiques featuring Japanese designers and imported goods alternate with chic cafés and restaurants. The side streets are well worth exploring as well, especially on the west side in the Tor West district.

Specialty Stores

Harishin. For antiques, try Harishin, open since 1881. You can find it on the west side of the Moto-machi arcade. ✉ *3–10–3 Moto-machi-dōri, Moto-machi* ☎ *078/331–2516* ☉ *Daily 10–6.*

Naniwa-ya. This shop sells excellent Japanese lacquerware at reasonable prices and has been in operation since before World War I. ✉ *3–8 Moto-machi-dōri 4-chōme, Moto-machi* ☎ *078/341–6367* ☉ *Daily 10–6.*

Sakae-ya. Traditional Japanese dolls of all shapes and colors are sold at this Moto-machi shop. ✉ *8–5 Moto-machi-dōri 5-chōme, Moto-machi* ☎ *078/341–1307* ☉ *Daily 10–6.*

Tasaki Shinju. The famous pearl company on Port Island has a museum and demonstration hall along with its retail pearl shop. ✉ *Tasaki*

Bldg., 6–3–2 Minatojima, Naka-machi, Port Island ☎ 078/303–7667
⊙ *Daily 10–6.*

Santica Town. This underground shopping mall, with 120 shops and 30
restaurants, extends for several blocks beneath Flower Road south from
San-no-miya Station. It's closed the third Wednesday of the month.
✉ *1–10–1 Sannomiya, Chūō-ku, Kōbe-shi, Hyōgo-ken 650-0021* ☎ 078/
291–0001 ⊙ *Daily 10–8.*

KŌBE A TO Z

*To research prices, get advice from other travelers, and book travel ar-
rangements, visit www.fodors.com.*

AIRPORTS & TRANSFERS
Kansai International Airport (KIX) south of Ōsaka handles the region's
international flights as well as some domestic flights to and from Japan's
larger cities. Most domestic flights still fly out of Ōsaka International
Airport, approximately 40 minutes away from Kōbe in the city of Itami.

AIRPORT TRANSFERS · Excellent public transport from the airports makes using taxis impractical. From KIX take the JR Kansai Airport Express Haruka to Shin-
Ōsaka and change to the JR Tōkaidō Line for Kōbe's JR San-no-miya
Station, a 75-minute (¥3,520) trip. For a quicker trip, ignore the train
and take the comfortable limousine bus (70 minutes; ¥1,800), which
drops you off in front of San-no-miya Station.

From Ōsaka International Airport, buses to San-no-miya Station leave
from a stand between the airport's two terminals approximately every
20 minutes, 7:45 AM–9:10 PM. The trip takes about 40 minutes (¥1,020).

BUS TRAVEL
City bus service is frequent and efficient, though it might be somewhat
confusing to first-timers. At each stop a pole displays a route chart of
official stops; the names of stops are spelled out in Roman letters. Enter
at the rear or center of the bus; pay your fare with exact change as you
leave at the front. The fare is ¥200, regardless of the distance. A special city loop bus that looks like a trolley and has a wood interior with
brass fittings stops at 15 major sights on its 12½-km (7½-mi), 80-
minute run between Nakatottei Tsutsumi (Nakatottei Pier) and Shin-
Kōbe. The buses operate at 16- to 20-minute intervals and cost ¥250
per ride or ¥650 for a day pass, which you can purchase on the bus or
at the Kōbe Information Center. (LOOP BUS signs in English indicate stops
along the route.) Service runs 9:30–4:25 weekdays, 9:30–5:25 weekends and holidays.

EMERGENCIES
Daimaru Depāto has a pharmacy that's a three-minute walk from JR
Moto-machi Station.
🏥 Doctors **Kōbe Adventist Hospital** ✉ 4-1 Arinodai 8-chōme, Kita-ku ☎ 078/981-
0161. **Kōbe Kaisei Hospital** ✉ 3-11-15 Shinohara-Kita-machi, Nada-ku ☎ 078/871-5201.
🏥 Emergency Services **Ambulance** ☎ 119. **Police** ☎ 110.
🏥 Pharmacy **Daimaru Depāto** ✉ 40 Akashi-chō, Chūō-ku ☎ 078/331-8121.

ENGLISH-LANGUAGE MEDIA

Kansai Time Out (www.kto.co.jp) is a monthly publication listing all sorts of events in Kōbe, Kyōto, Nara, and Ōsaka. There are also topical articles written for travelers and residents. It costs ¥300 and is available at all major hotels and bookshops throughout the region.

Kinokuniya stocks a small selection of new English-language novels as well as guidebooks, books on Japan, and Japanese study guides. Those looking for a wider selection of English reading material should head to Wantage Books, the only second-hand English-language bookshop in the Kansai region.

🖪 Bookstores **Kinokuniya** ⊠ 8-1-8 Onoe-dōri ☎ 078/265-1607. **Wantage Books** ⊠ 1-1-13 Ikuta-chō ☎ 078/232-4517.

SUBWAY TRAVEL

Kōbe's main subway line runs from Tanigami in the far north of the city, and passes through Shin-Kōbe and San-no-miya Stations before continuing west to the outskirts of town. Another line runs along the coast from San-no-miya and links up with the main line at Shin-Nagata Station. Fares start at ¥180 and are determined by destination. The San-no-miya–Shin-Kōbe trip costs ¥200.

TAXIS

Taxis are plentiful; hail them on the street or at taxi stands. Fares start around ¥550 for the first 2 km (1 mi) and go up ¥90 for each additional ½ km (¼ mi). Late at night, generally after midnight, there is a 20% surcharge. Some taxis offer 50% discounts on fares over ¥5,000.

TOURS

All year-round, the City Transport Bureau has several half-day and full-day tours of major attractions in and around the city. The tours are conducted in Japanese, but they do provide an overview of Kōbe. Buses depart from the south side of the Kōbe Kotsu Center Building, near San-no-miya Station. Information and tickets, which start at ¥2,700, can be obtained at the Shi-nai Teiki Kankō Annaisho (Sightseeing Bus Tour Information Office), on the second floor of the Kōbe Kotsu Center Building. The buses leave from the San-no-miya Bus Terminal, to the east of JR San-no-miya Station.

Authorized taxi services also run tours (¥4,200 per hour) that cover 11 different routes and take from two to five hours. Reserve at the Kōbe Tourist Information Center (also known as "Hello Kōbe"), close to the west exit of JR San-no-miya Station.

🖪 **Kōbe Tourist Information Center** ☎ 078/322-0220. **Shi-nai Teiki Kankō Annaisho** ☎ 078/231-4898.

TRAIN TRAVEL

The Hikari Shinkansen runs between Tōkyō and Shin-Kōbe Station in about 3½ hours. If you don't have a JR Pass, the fare is ¥14,470. The trip between Ōsaka Station and Kōbe's San-no-miya Station takes 20 minutes on the JR Tōkaidō Line rapid train, which leaves at 15-minute intervals throughout the day; without a JR Pass the fare is ¥390. The Hankyū and Hanshin private lines run between Ōsaka and Kōbe for ¥310.

The Portliner is a computerized monorail that serves Port Island. Its central station is connected to JR San-no-miya Station; the ride from the station to Port Island takes about 10 minutes (¥480 round-trip).

Within Kōbe, Japan Rails and the Hankyū and Hanshin lines run parallel from east to west and are easy to negotiate. San-no-miya and Moto-machi are the principal downtown stations. Purchase tickets from a vending machine; you surrender them upon passing through the turnstile at your destination station. Fares depend on your destination.

VISITOR INFORMATION

The Kōbe Information Center, by the west exit of JR San-no-miya Station, is open daily 9–7. You can pick up a free detailed map of the city in English. The tourist information center has another branch at JR Shin-Kōbe Station, open daily 10–6.

The Japan Travel Bureau can arrange for hotel reservations, train tickets, package tours, and more throughout the country and abroad. The Japan Travel Phone, available daily 9–5, provides free information in English on all of Japan.

🏛 Tourist Information **Japan Travel Bureau** ✉ JR San-no-miya Station ☎ 078/231-4118. **Japan Travel Phone** ☎ 0088/22-4800. **Kōbe Information Center** ✉ JR San-no-miya Station ☎ 078/322-0220 ✉ Shin-Kōbe Station ☎ 078/241-9550. **Kōbe Tourist Information Center** ✉ At the west exit of JR San-no-miya Station ☎ 078/271-2401.

WESTERN HONSHŪ 西本州

9

By John Malloy
Quinn

THE TWO COASTS OF WESTERN HONSHŪ, separated by a long east–west range of mountains called the Chūgoku San-chi, reveal two very different experiences of Japan. The south side, San-yō, faces the Inland Sea and is the more populated and industrial of the two. The north side, San-in, faces the Japan Sea and is much more rural.

A visit to San-yō would be incomplete without a visit to Miyajima, the small island off Hiroshima world famous for its vermilion floating torii, and Kurashiki, with its willow-lined canals and quaint old warehouses. In Okayama, Kōrakuen is one of Japan's time-honored Top Three gardens. And no one should miss Himeji's graceful castle.

The San-in coast provides a more quintessentially Japanese experience, due in part to the isolation of the region. Traditional customs, such as the crafting of ceramics in the town of Hagi, remain at the core of many people's lives here. Charming fishing villages and rocky, unpolluted bays speckle the entire coastline. Matsue, with its lovely canals and spectacular sunsets over Lake Shinji, is one of Japan's most likeable cities. Inland, tiny mountain towns like Tsuwano are blessed with some of the freshest air and sweetest water you'll find anywhere.

See the glossary at the end of this book for definitions of the common Japanese words and suffixes used in this chapter.

Exploring Western Honshū

This chapter sketches an itinerary from Ōsaka down the San-yō coast, stopping at Himeji, Okayama, Kurashiki, Hiroshima, and Miyajima before reaching Shin Yamaguchi. The route then cuts north through rugged mountains to reach Hagi and begins an exploration of the San-in coast north- and eastward, taking in the scenic and cultural highlights of Tsuwano and Matsue along the way. The final leg is an easy return to Himeji by veering south from Tottori.

Numbers in the text correspond to numbers in the margin and on the Western Honshū, Hiroshima, and Hagi maps.

About the Restaurants

Western Honshū is one of the best regions in which to sample local Japanese seafood, thanks to regional specialties from the Nihon-kai and Seto Nai-kai. Oysters in Hiroshima and sashimi and sushi on the San-in coast are superb. Matsue's proximity to the water makes a variety of both freshwater and saltwater fish available and allows for truly delicious eating experiences.

Most reasonably priced restaurants will have a visual display of the menu in the window. On this basis, you can decide what you want before you enter. If you cannot order in Japanese and no English is spoken, after you secure a table, lead the waiter to the window display and point.

For more details on Japanese cuisine, *see* Chapter 15.

About the Hotels

Accommodations cover a broad spectrum, from pensions and *min-shuku* (private residences that rent rooms) to large, modern resort ho-

The Shinkansen makes traveling the San-yō a breeze. The highlights of the San-in are inconvenient by comparison, but with careful planning, can be just as fully enjoyed.

If you have 2 days

You have three options, and each would give you a bit of old and new Japan. You can cover ⚹ **Hiroshima** ④–⑭ the first day and strike out for either ⚹ **Hagi** ⑯–㉖ or ⚹ **Tsuwano** ㉗ the second. Another choice is to spend a day and night in ⚹ **Kurashiki** ③ and continue to ⚹ **Hiroshima** ④–⑭. You could also do a leisurely two-day visit to ⚹ **Matsue** ㉙, with a jaunt over to **Izumo Taisha** ㉘.

If you have 4 days

You could cover either coast quite thoroughly, or a bit of both, in four days. For San-yō, start by taking in the fantastic castle at **Himeji** ①, then go to ⚹ **Okayama** ② for a look at the lovely garden and castle there, and the next day head to traditional ⚹ **Kurashiki** ③. ⚹ **Hiroshima** ④–⑭ deserves at least a full day. The fourth day is good for a visit to ⚹ **Miyajima** ⑮, spending a romantic night there on the island after the day-trippers leave, or returning for the frenzied nightlife of the city.

A four-day San-in trip could start at either end, east or west. Begin at the sand dunes of **Tottori** ㉚, reaching historic ⚹ **Matsue** ㉙ by nightfall. The next few days could be spent between **Izumo Taisha** ㉘, Japan's oldest and most venerated shrine, and the precious gems of ⚹ **Tsuwano** ㉗ and ⚹ **Hagi** ⑯–㉖. Of course, you could also do it in reverse. Another option might be to spend a couple days on each coast, in ⚹ **Matsue** ㉙ and ⚹ **Kurashiki** ③, since train routes connect them through the nearby hubs of Yonago in the north and Okayama in the south.

If you have 7 to 10 days

You can cover much of Western Honshu well in a week or so. Start with **Himeji** ① and a night in ⚹ **Okayama** ②. Spend the next day strolling in the famous park and admiring the black castle. Head to ⚹ **Kurashiki** ③ for a night or two of time-travel under the willows by the old canals. Strike out for a day or two in ⚹ **Hiroshima** ④–⑭, where you can cry cathartic tears about the past in the Peace Memorial Park and then embrace the future amid the lively environs of Nagarekawa and Shintenchi. Visit picturesque ⚹ **Miyajima** ⑮. Make your way over the impressive mountains to the remote and breathtaking vistas (and seafood!) of ⚹ **Hagi** ⑯–㉖, either staying there awhile or moving on to the indescribable mountain-valley hamlet of ⚹ **Tsuwano** ㉗. When you're ready, make your way to ⚹ **Matsue** ㉙ and **Izumo Taisha** ㉘, and/or **Tottori** ㉚ before zipping back down through gorgeous, thickly wooded hills to **Okayama** ②.

tels that have little character but all the facilities of an international hotel. Large city and resort hotels have Western as well as Japanese restaurants. In summer hotel reservations are highly advised.

Unless otherwise noted, rooms have private baths, air-conditioning, and basic TV service. For a short course on accommodations in Japan, *see* Lodging *in* Smart Travel Tips A to Z.

WHAT IT COSTS In yen					
	$$$$	**$$$**	**$$**	**$**	**¢**
RESTAURANTS	over 3,000	2,000–3,000	1,000–2,000	800–1,000	under 800
HOTELS	over 22,000	18,000–22,000	12,000–18,000	8,000–12,000	under 8,000

Restaurant prices are per person for a main course at dinner. Hotel prices are for a double room with private bath, excluding service and tax.

Timing

The San-yō is said to be the sunniest region in Japan, and almost anytime is a good time to visit. The northern shore gets a stronger dose of winter than the southern, but the San-in coast does have a beautiful, long spring. Though like most of Japan, it can get muggy by midsummer, the wind off the Nihon-kai manages to cool the coast. Summer festivals and autumn colors are spectacular and attract large numbers of tourists, so be prepared and reserve well ahead.

THE SAN-YŌ REGION 山陽地方

The stretch of coastline from Ōsaka to Hiroshima is well developed, and you can't really see much of the Seto Nai-kai from the train, but all it takes are small, convenient detours from the main corridor to put you in touch with some of the unique beauty the region has to offer.

Himeji 姫路

▶ ❶ *35 min west of Shin-Ōsaka; 50 min west of Kyōto; 3 hrs, 45 min west of Tōkyō by Shinkansen.*

Himeji is served by Shinkansen, with trains arriving and departing every 15 minutes during the day. The Shinkansen to Okayama, farther west, arrives and departs every hour during the day. Himeji's **Tourist Information Office** (姫路駅観光案内所; ☎ 0792/85–3792), to the right of the station's north exit, open 9 to 5 daily, is staffed with friendly bilingual people 10 to 3 and lends out free bicycles 9 to 4.

Fodor'sChoice You can see **Himeji-jō** (姫路城), also known as Shirasagi-jō (White Egret
★ Castle), as soon as you exit the station. Universally loved, it dazzles the city from atop a nearby hill. A visit to Himeji-jō could well be one of the high points of your trip to Japan, especially if you can manage to see the brilliantly lighted white castle soaring above cherry blossoms or pine branches at night. Thanks to frequent rail service, it should be easy to hop off, visit the castle, and jump on another train two hours later.

Himeji-jō could be regarded as medieval Japan's crowning achievement of castle design and construction. It arrived at its present state of perfection after many transformations, however. It was first a fortress in the year 1333 and was transformed into a castle in 1346. Radically enlarged by Terumasa Ikeda in the period 1601–1610, it has remained essentially the same ever since, surviving numerous wars and—perhaps even more miraculously—never once falling victim to the scourge of fire.

Culture As much as or more than in any other region, cultural events are part of daily life in Western Honshū. The pottery centers of Bizen and Hagi host numerous annual ceramics festivals, which are not only educational but make great shopping opportunities as well. Arts and music are of prime importance in Kurashiki, and exhibits and concerts take place regularly. Hiroshima has an international element that leavens all that happens there. Second only to Ise Jingū in importance, the shrine at Izumo provides many Japanese with a firm foundation in their culture.

Sports & the Outdoors The Seto Nai-kai and the San-in seascapes are impressive. The San-in coast is perfect for bicycling—the scenery changes frequently enough to sustain interest, and the air is clean and cool. Tottori with its dunes and beaches is a magnet for surfers and parachute-jumpers. Matsue is a haven for water-sport enthusiasts. Mount Daisen offers good hiking and climbing, and many ski areas, including some quite near Hiroshima, offer decent snow sports in winter.

9

The five-story, six-floor main *tenshukaku* (stronghold) stands more than 100 feet high and is built into a 50-ft-high stone foundation. Surrounding this main tenshukaku are three smaller ones; all four are connected by covered passageways. Attackers would have had to cross three moats, penetrate the outer walls, and then withstand withering attack from the four towers and the more than 30 other buildings within. It was an impregnable fortress then, and its grace and grand proportions still inspire awe. Filmmaker Akira Kurosawa used Himeji-jō's exterior and the castle's grounds in his 1985 movie *Ran*.

Although not completely necessary for getting around or understanding the features of this amazing castle, informative, detailed free guided tours in English are occasionally available; try calling ahead to see if you can arrange to meet one at the gate. Tours usually take 90 minutes.

From the central north exit of JR Himeji Station, the castle is a 15- to 20-minute walk or a 5-minute bus ride (¥170); also, bicycles are available free at the Tourist Info Office next door. The bus departs from the station plaza, on your left as you exit. ☎ *0792/85–1146* ☞*¥600; ¥640 combined with ticket to enter adjacent park* ☉ *Daily 9–5, grounds until 6.*

Easy to visit in the vicinity of the castle (walk five minutes north) is the **Hyōgo Prefectural Museum of History** (Hyōgo-Ken Rekishi Hakubutsu Kan, 兵庫県立歴史博物館), which not only details the history of Himeji-jō but of other castles in Japan and all over the world. There are exhibits of prehistoric bones found in the area, and a room where from one to three times a day a volunteer is allowed to try on some samurai armor or a traditional kimono, which with its 12 layers is a sort of armor itself. Architect Kenzo Tange designed the plain-fronted, postmodern building. ✉ *68 Hon-machi* ☎ *0792/88–9011* ☞*¥200* ☉ *Tues.–Sun. 10–4:30.*

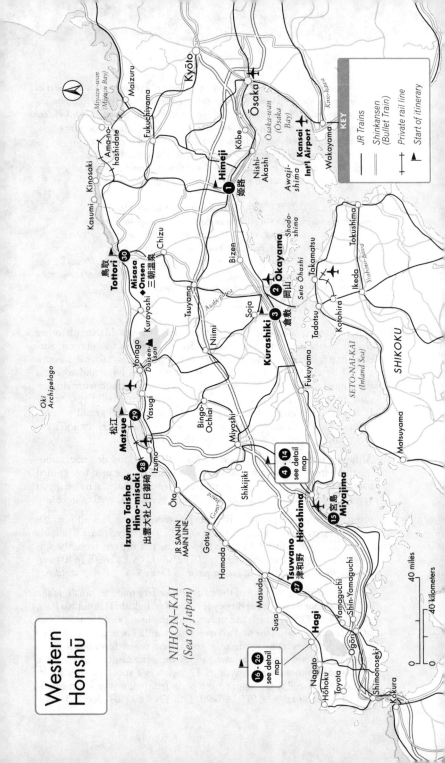

Western Honshū

KEY

	JR Trains
	Shinkansen (Bullet Train)
	Private rail line
▲	Start of itinerary

NIHON-KAI
(Sea of Japan)

SETO-NAI-KAI
(Inland Sea)

SHIKOKU

Oki Archipelago

Miyazu-wan (Miyazu Bay)

Osaka-wan (Osaka Bay)

Kyōto

Ōsaka

Kōbe

Nishi-Akashi

Himeji 姫路 ❶

Kansai Int'l Airport

Wakayama

Kino-kawa

Maizuru

Fukuchiyama

Ama-no-hashidate

Kinosaki

Kasumi

Chizu

鳥取 **Tottori** ❸⓪

Misasa Onsen 三朝温泉 ◆

Kurayoshi

Tsuyama

Bizen

Okayama 岡山 ❷

Sōja

Kurashiki 倉敷 ❸

Niimi

Daisen-zan

Yonago

Yasugi

Matsue 松江 ❷⑨

Izumo

Izumo Taisha & Hino-misaki 出雲大社と日御碕 ❷⑧

Bingo-Ochiai

Miyoshi

Shikijiki

Ōta

Gōnō-gawa

Gotsu

JR SANIN MAIN LINE

Hamada

Masuda

Susa

Nagato

Hōhoku

Toyota

Shin-Yamaguchi

Yamaguchi

Ogōri

Shimonoseki

Kokura

Hagi ⑯ - ㉖ see detail map ▲

Tsuwano 津和野 ㉗

Hiroshima

Miyajima 宮島 ❹❺

❹ · ⑭ see detail map

Fukuyama

Tadotsu

Takamatsu

Kotohira

Ikeda

Tokushima

Matsuyama

Shodo-shima

Awaji-shima

Seto Ōhashi

Yoshino-gawa

Asahi-gawa

Saba

40 miles

40 kilometers

The small **Himeji Museum of Literature** (Himeji Bungaku Kan, 姫路文学館), which is dedicated to the work of Himeji's men and women of letters (including philosopher Tetsuro Watsuji), is more celebrated for its unique exterior than for the memorabilia within. Designed by renowned architect Tadao Andō, the museum makes use of Andō's trademark reinforced concrete and is a minimalist masterpiece in the shadow of the mighty Himeji-jō. ⊠ *84 Yamanoi-chō,* ☎ *0792/93–8228* 💴 *¥300* ☉ *June–Aug., Tues.–Sun. 10–6; Sept.–May, Tues.–Sun. 10–5.*

If you're interested in getting out onto the Seto Nai-kai, you can take the 1-hour, 40-minute ferry trip to **Shōdo-shima** (小豆島), near Shikoku. Kansai Kyūko (Express) Ferry Himeji Branch ferries depart from Himeji Port. However, there are even shorter sea crossings to Shōdo-shima from Okayama if you're headed there next. ⊠ *Himeji Port* ☎ *0792/34–7100, 0120/80–6161 toll-free* 💴 *¥1,320* ☉ *1 trip per hr, but not on the hr.*

Okayama   岡山

❷ *30 min west of Himeji; 1 hr west of Ōsaka; 3 hrs 17 min west of Tokyo by Shinkansen.*

Okayama is a pleasant, cosmopolitan town famous for its black castle and spacious garden. The thickly forested, wonderfully sculpted mountains in the interior of the prefecture are among the country's most beautiful as well. Okayama claims to have the most sunny days in Japan, and if the weather's nice you may want to hop on one of the frequent streetcars plying Momotaro-dōri, the main boulevard heading east from the Shinkansen station (¥100); ride three stops east; and walk southeast to the castle, park, and museums. For ¥530, you can buy a combined park-castle ticket.

The Shinkansen station makes Okayama an attractive base for visiting the quaint charms of Kurashiki—only a 12-minute local-JR-train hop to the west. The city is the best departure point for Shōdo-shima (near Shikoku) if you're coming from Ōsaka or Hiroshima, and is also a fine gateway to the remote and beautiful realm of Matsue, 2 hours, 40 minutes by JR train to the northwest. Twenty-three ferries a day make the 40-minute run from Okayama Port to Shōdo-shima. From JR Okayama Station, it takes 45 minutes on Bus 12 to reach the port.

Should you need a map of Okayama or city information, head to the **Tourist Information Office** (岡山市観光案内所; ☎ 086/222–2912), open daily 9–6, in the JR station.

★ **Kōraku Garden** (Kōrakuen, 後楽園) is a fine garden for strolling, with charming tea arbors, green lawns, ponds, and hills that were laid out three centuries ago on the banks of the Asahi-gawa. The maple, apricot, and cherry trees give the 28-acre park plenty of flowers and shade. Kōrakuen's riverside setting, with Okayama-jō in the background, is delightful. The garden's popularity increases in peak season (April through August), but this is perhaps the most spacious park in Japan, so don't be put off from seeing it. Bus 20 (¥160) from Platform 2 in front of the

JR station goes directly to Kōrakuen. ✉ *1–5 Korakuen* ☎ *086/272–1148* 🎟 *¥350* ⏰ *Apr.–Sept., daily 7:30–6; Oct.–Mar., daily 8–5.*

Painted black, **Okayama-jō** (岡山城) is known as U-jō (Crow Castle). Though the castle was built in the 16th century, only the "moon-viewing" outlying tower survived World War II. A ferroconcrete replica was painstakingly constructed in 1966. The middle floors now house objects that represent the region's history, including a nice collection of armor and swords. Unlike many other castles with great views from the top, this one has an elevator to take you the six floors up. Less than a five-minute walk across the bridge brings you from the south exit of Kōrakuen to the castle, and there are also various boats for rent on the attractive river below. ✉ *2–3–1 Marunouchi* ☎ *086/225–2096* 🎟 *¥300* ⏰ *Daily 9–5.*

The **Museum of Oriental Art** (Orient Bijutsukan, 岡山市立オリエント美術館) has a Parthenon-like temple front and 2,000 items on display inside. Its special exhibits, which show how Middle Eastern art reached Japan via the Silk Road, range from Persian glass goblets and mirrors to stringed instruments. To reach the museum from the JR station, take the streetcar (¥140) bound for Higashiyama directly north for 10 minutes. The museum is across Asahi-gawa from Kōrakuen (about a 10-minute walk). ☎ *086/232–3636* 🎟 *¥300* ⏰ *Tues.–Sun. 9–5.*

Where to Stay

$$$$ 🏨 **Hotel Granvia Okayama** (ホテルグランヴィア岡山). This large, luxurious hotel makes a superb, comfortable base for exploring the area. The lobby is done in white marble and wood paneling, and, like the bilingual staff, exudes a bright, cheery confidence. The rooms are spacious and have a fair share of opulence. It's connected to the JR Okayama Station—stay on the second (Shinkansen) level and follow the signs toward the south end. ✉ *1–5 Ekimoto-chō, Okayama-shi, Okayama-ken 700-8515* ☎ *086/234–7000* 🖷 *086/234–7099* 🛏 *323 Western-style rooms, 3 Western-style suites, 2 Japanese-style suites* 🍴 *7 restaurants, coffee shop, bar, shops* 🖃 *AE, DC, MC, V.*

Kurashiki   倉敷

▶ ★ ❸ *3 hrs 17 min west of Tokyo or 1½ hrs west of Ōsaka by Shinkansen to Okayama, then 12 min by local train.*

Few places make you feel as if you're back in Old Japan as Kurashiki can. From the 17th through the 19th centuries, this vital shipping port supplied the metropolis of Ōsaka with cotton, textiles, sugar, and rice. Those days are long past, but Kurashiki lives on, thriving on the income from more than 4 million visitors a year. Most come as day-trippers, to stroll around the old town, locally called Bikan. Southeast of the station it's an area of canals, bridges, shops, restaurants, ryokans, and museums.

You can see most of Kurashiki's sights in a half-day or so, but it's worth staying longer, perhaps in a rustic ryokan, to fully appreciate the place. The white stucco walls of the old warehouses are accented smartly with charred pine-plank paneling and/or random groupings of leaden-gray burnt-brown, and carbon-black tiles crisscrossed with raised diagonals of stark white mortar. The sight of the structures lining willow-shaded canals and cobblestone streets can transport you to an entirely different frame of time and mind.

Virtually the entire town shuts down on Monday. Some lodgings actually boot out their guests for that day and night, so inquire ahead and plan accordingly.

Ōhara Art Museum (Ōhara Bijutsukan, 大原美術館), in the old town, is one of the finest museums in Japan and should not be missed. Founder Magosaburo Ōhara built this Parthenon-style building to house a superb collection of Western art that includes works by El Greco, Corot, Manet, Monet, Rodin, Gauguin, Picasso, Toulouse-Lautrec, and many others. Two wings exhibit Japanese paintings, tapestries, wood-block prints, and pottery—including works by such greats as Shoji Hamada and Bernard Leach–as well as both modern and ancient Asian art. ✉ *1–15–Chūō* ☎ *086/422–0005* 💴 *¥1,000* ⊙ *Tues.–Sun. 9–5.*

In four converted granaries that still have their Edo-period white walls and black-tile roofs, the **Kurashiki Folk Craft Museum** (Kurashiki Mingeikan, 倉敷民芸館) houses some 4,000 folk-craft objects, including ceramics, rugs, wood carvings, and bamboo wares from all over the world. ✉ *1–4–11 Chūō* ☎ *086/422–1637* 💴 *¥700* ⊙ *Mar.–Nov., Tues.–Sun. 9–5; Dec.–Feb., Tues.–Sun. 9–4:15.*

The **Japan Rural Toy Museum** (Nihon Kyōdo Gangukan, 日本郷土玩具館) is one of the two top toy museums in Japan and is more worthwhile if you can find a Japanese to show you around and explain the stories behind the toys. It displays some 40,000 toys from all regions of the country and has one room devoted to foreign toys. The toy museum is on the north bank of the Kurashiki-gawa. ✉ *1–4–16 Chūō* ☎ *086/422–8058* 💴 *¥310* ⊙ *Daily 8–5.*

Ivy Square (アイビースクエア) is an ivy-covered complex that used to be a weaving mill. Artfully renovated, it contains the Ivy Hotel, several boutiques, three museums, a restaurant, and, in the central courtyard, a summer beer garden. The most interesting of the museums in the complex, **Kurabō Kinen Butsukan** (Kurabō Memorial Hall) is devoted to the history of spinning and textiles, an industry that helped build Kurashiki. The other two are the **Torajiro Kajima Kinen Butsukan** (Torajiro Kajima Memorial Hall), which has Western and Asian art, and the **Ivy Gakkan** (Ivy Academic Hall), an educational museum that uses reproductions to explain Western art to the Japanese. Ivy Square is across the bridge from Chūō-dōri and up an alleyway. 💴 *Kurabō ¥350, all 3 museums ¥600* ⊙ *Tues.–Sun. 9–5.*

Kanryū-ji and Achi Jinja (観龍寺と阿智神社), a temple and a shrine, stand atop the only real hill in Old Kurashiki and provide an excellent view of the town. You can see the hill straight ahead when you exit the Ōhara Art Museum. A short, easy walk takes you to the summit. 💴 *Free* ⊙ *Daily 9–5.*

Kurashiki Tourist Information Office (倉敷観光案内所; ☎ 086/426–8681), inside the station across from the turnstiles, is staffed with amicable locals who can give you useful maps and information. There's also another office in the Bikan district, on the first bend of the canal, on the right a block past the Ōhara Museum of Art (☎ 086/422–0542); both offices are open daily 9–5.

Where to Stay & Eat

$–$$$$ ✕ **Kiyū-tei** (亀遊亭). For the best grilled steak in town, come to this attractive restaurant where chefs work over the fires cooking your steak to order. The entrance to the restaurant is through a courtyard across from the entrance to the Ōhara Museum. ⊠ *1–2–20 Chūō* ☎ *086/ 422–5140* 🖿 *AE, DC, MC, V* 🕙 *Closed Mon.*

$–$$$ ✕ **Hamayoshi** (浜吉). Only three tables and a counter bar make up this personable restaurant specializing in fish from the Seto Nai-kai. Sushi is just one option; another is *mamakari,* a kind of vinegared sashimi that's sliced from a small fish caught in the Inland Sea. Other delicacies are *shako-ebi,* a type of spiny prawn, and lightly grilled *anago,* or sea-eel. No English is spoken, but the owner will help you order and instruct you on how to enjoy the chef's delicacies. Hamayoshi is on the main street leading from the station, just before the Kurashiki Kokusai Hotel. ⊠ *Achi 2–19–30* ☎ *086/421–3430* 🖿 *No credit cards* 🕙 *Closed Mon.*

¢–$ ✕ **KuShuKuShu (9494)** (くしゅくしゅ). Cool music and loud laughter can be heard coming from this place when all else on the streets is locked up tight. An eclectic mix of traditional white stucco, black wooden beams, bright lights, and Western jazz makes this a great place to unwind with stylish locals. Scores of tasty à la carte snacks, such as grilled meats or cheese and salami plates, and low-price beer add to the fun. It's tucked along the east side of the covered Ebisu-dōri shopping arcade halfway between the station and Kanryu-ji. ⊠ *Achi 2–16–41* ☎ *086/421–0949* 🖿 *No credit cards* 🕙 *No lunch.*

$$$–$$$$ ✕🛏 **Ryokan Kurashiki** (旅館倉敷). If you're an open-minded sort, you simply could not pick a better place in which to let go and submit to the ritual pleasures sought by wealthy Japanese holiday-makers at traditional ryokan 300 years ago. It's not for everyone—to the uninitiated time-traveler full-on ryokan service can feel intimidatingly intrusive and overattentive. The primary task at hand here is to deliver an exquisite display of hospitality and grace, and it's achieved within labyrinthine lodgings patched together from three ancient rice-and-sugar warehouses along the most picturesque bend of Kurashiki's old canal. The delectable multicourse meals (also available to nonguests) are alone worth the trip. Some English is spoken, but for navigation of the deeper intricacies, a command of Japanese brings incalculable reward here. Next door is a delightful coffee shop, Coffee Kan, run by the owner's daughter. ⊠ *4–1 Hon-machi, Kurashiki, Okayama-ken 710-0054* ☎ *086/422–0730* 🖷 *086/422–0990* 🛏 *18 rooms, 9 with bath* ⚭ *Restaurant, Japanese baths* 🖿 *AE, DC, MC, V* 🍴 *MAP.*

Fodor's Choice
★

$$$–$$$$ 🛏 **Ryokan Tsurugata** (旅館鶴形). A 250-year-old merchant's mansion and a converted rice-and-sugar storehouse make up this ryokan with Edo-era character. Rooms are on the cozy side, but bonus points are the fragrant wooden bathtubs and the hotel's location directly across the bridge from the art museum. The suite overlooking the garden is especially fine. Some English is spoken. ⊠ *1–3–15 Chūō, Kurashiki, Okayama-*

ken 710-0046 ☎ 086/424–1635 🖷 086/424–1650 ⇨ 13 *Japanese-style rooms* ♨ *Japanese baths* 🖃 *AE, DC, MC, V* ⦿I *MAP.*

$$–$$$ 🏨 **Kurashiki Kokusai Hotel** (倉敷国際ホテル). Perhaps the best Western-style hotel in town welcomes you with a lobby paved with black tile and hung with dramatic Japanese wood-block prints. Ask for a room in the newer annex at the back of the building overlooking a garden. The location of the Kokusai is ideal—a 10-minute walk on the main road leading from the station and just around the corner from the old town and the Ōhara Museum. 🖂 *1–1–44 Chūō, Kurashiki, Okayama-ken 710-0046* ☎ *086/ 422–5141* 🖷 *086/422–5192* ⇨ *106 Western-style rooms, 4 Japanese-style rooms* ♨ *Restaurant, bar, shop, free parking* 🖃 *AE, DC, MC, V.*

$$ 🏨 **Kamoi** (民宿カモ井). This delightfully antique hostelry is the best bargain in Kurashiki. An eight-minute walk from the Ōhara Art Museum, this minshuku is next to Achi Jinja. The rooms are simple and the food is good—a multicourse breakfast (Western- or Japanese-style) and dinner are available. Note that in true Kurashiki fashion, the entire place is shut down (after checkout time) on Monday; guests must leave the premises for that day and night. 🖂 *1–24 Hon-machi, Kurashiki, Okayama-ken 710-0054* ☎ *086/422–4898* 🖷 *086/427–7615* ⇨ *17 Japanese-style rooms without baths* ♨ *Japanese baths* 🖃 *No credit cards* ⦿I *MAP* ⊙ *Closed Mon.*

Hiroshima   広島

➤ *1 hr 45 min west of Ōsaka; 3 hrs 53 min from Tokyo by Shinkansen*

On August 6, 1945, at 8:15 in the morning, a fire almost as hot as the sun glowed for only an instant above the center of Hiroshima. In an instant, half the city was leveled, the rest set ablaze. A half-hour later rain fell, bringing only misery instead of relief; it bore radioactive fallout destined to kill many that the white-hot flash and 1,000-mph shock wave had spared. All told, more than 140,000 people died when the United States dropped an atomic bomb on Hiroshima.

That terrible day in Hiroshima saw the first of only two full-scale nuclear attacks ever launched. The use of the bomb at the end of World War II remains controversial to this day, but many authorities still assert that it may have saved lives in the long run, given the proven ruthlessness and desperation of the Japanese Imperial Army at that stage in the war. Hiroshima in particular was a legitimate target, as the Imperial Army had commandeered the city's castle to serve as its headquarters. Unfortunately, in its attempt to hide behind the facade of a historic national treasure the Army put the citizens of Hiroshima in harm's way. Also killed in the fission blast were some 10,000 hapless Korean prisoners whom the Japanese Army was using as laborers.

In modern Hiroshima, only one original site bears witness to that mind-boggling release of atomic energy in the middle of the 20th century: the A-Bomb Dome. But it's fairly easy to forget the past, for this metropolis has zealously embraced the future. The A-Bomb Dome is surrounded at a respectful distance by a vibrant, entirely rebuilt city, and only a short walk to the east you can get an invigorating dose of celebratory nightlife.

There are two **Tourist Information Offices** (広島市観光案内所; ☎ 082/261–1877 south exit, 082/263–6822 Shinkansen north exit ⊙ Daily 9–5:30) at JR Hiroshima Station: one at the south exit for downtown, and one at the north exit for the Shinkansen. Both provide free maps and brochures as well as help in securing accommodations. The main tourist office, **Hiroshima City Tourist Association** (☎ 082/247–6738 ⊙ Apr.–Sept., daily 9:30–6, Oct.–Mar., daily 8:30–5) is in the Peace Memorial Park, next to the Motoyasu fork of the river, between the Children's Peace Memorial and the Flame of Peace. Also in the park, in the southwest corner between the Ōta River and the Peace Memorial Museum, is the **International Conference Center Hiroshima** (☎ 082/247–9715 ⊙ May–Nov., daily 9–7, Dec.–Apr., daily 10–6), which offers ample useful English information.

Peace Memorial Park Area

The **Peace Memorial Park** (Heiwa Kinen Kōen, 平和記念資料館) contains the key World War II sights in Hiroshima. It sits in the northern point of the triangle formed by two of Hiroshima's rivers, the Ōta-gawa (also called Hon-kawa) and Motoyasu-gawa. You can walk there in about 20 minutes from Hiroshima Station, or take Streetcar 2 or 6 to the Gembaku-Dōmu-mae stop and cross over Motoyasu-gawa on the Aioi-bashi. In the middle of the bridge is the entrance to the park, and in the park en route from the bridge to Peace Memorial Museum are statues and monuments. Head straight for the museum (it's about a 10-minute walk from the bridge); you can linger at the monuments on your way back. A less dramatic approach from Hiroshima Station is to take the Hiroshima Bus Company's red-and-white Bus 24 to Heiwa Kōen, only a two-minute walk from the museum, or to take Streetcar 1 to Chūden-mae for a five-minute walk to the museum.

❹ The **A-Bomb Dome** (Gembaku Dōmu, 原爆ドーム) is a poignant symbol of man's apparently incurable tendency toward destruction. The half-shattered skeleton of the city's old Industrial Promotion Hall—the sole structural ruin of World War II left erect in the city—stands in stark contrast to the new Hiroshima, which hums and throbs not far away. Despite its location almost directly below the 1945 blast, the building did not completely collapse. Eerie, twisted, and charred, the sturdy structure of iron and concrete has stood basically untouched since that horrible morning, forever left darkly brooding next to the river. If you come here at dusk, the sad old building's foreboding appearance and derelict pose can be absolutely overwhelming. At any time of day, a visit to A-Bomb Dome is a sobering reminder of the imbecilic folly of war, particularly atomic war. Perhaps unexpectedly, the A-Bomb Dome is outside the official boundaries of the Peace Memorial Park, just to the northeast. To get here, take Streetcar 2 or 6 from Hiroshima Station to the Gembaku-Dōmu-mae stop. ⊠ *Heiwa Kinen Kōen.*

FodorsChoice
★

❺ A visit to the disturbing and educational **Peace Memorial Museum** (Heiwa Kinen Shiryōkan, 平和記念資料館) may be too intense an experience for some to stomach. Through exhibits of models, charred fragments of clothing, melted ceramic tiles, lunch boxes, and watches—and hideously surreal photographs—Hiroshima's story of death and destruction is told. Nothing can quite recapture the horror wrought by an atomic chain re-

action, but the ineffably sad heat-ray-photographed human shadow permanently imprinted on granite steps and the Dalí-esque watch forever stopped at 8:15 do leave a lasting impression. Most exhibits have brief explanations in English. However, more detailed information is available on audiocassettes, which you can rent for ¥150. ⊠ *Heiwa Kinen Kōen* ☎ 082/241–4004 ≊ *¥50* ⊘ *Apr.–July, daily 9–5:30; Aug. 1–15, daily 8:30–6:30; Aug. 16–Nov., daily 8:30–5:30; Dec.–Mar., daily 9–4:30.*

⑥ The **Memorial Cenotaph** (Gembaku Shibotsusha Irei-hi, 原爆死没者慰霊碑), designed by Japanese architect Kenzō Tange, resembles the primitive A-frame houses of Japan's earliest inhabitants. Buried inside is a chest containing the names of those who died in the destruction brought down by the atomic bomb. On the exterior is the inscription (translated), REST IN PEACE, FOR THE ERROR SHALL NOT BE REPEATED. The cenotaph stand before the north side of the Heiwa Kinen Shiryōkan. ⊠ *Heiwa Kinen Kōen.*

⑦ The **Flame of Peace** (Heiwa no Tomoshibi, 平和の灯) burns behind the Memorial Cenotaph. The flame will be extinguished only when all atomic weapons are banished. In the meantime, every August 6 there is a solemn commemoration in which the citizens of Hiroshima float paper lanterns on the city's rivers for the repose of the souls of the atomic-bomb victims. ⊠ *Heiwa Kinen Kōen.*

8 Opened in 2002, the **Hiroshima National Peace Memorial Hall for the Atomic Bomb Victims** (Kokuritsu Hiroshima Hibakusha Tsuito Heiwa Kinen-kan, 原爆死没者追悼平和祈念館) is a worthwhile stop where you can learn about many of the known victims of the atomic devastation. In addition to the seemingly endless archives of names, there's a vast collection of victims' photos that lends immediacy and intimacy to one of the most shocking moments in history. Disturbing first-hand accounts and memoirs of survivors are also available for viewing. ⊠ *1–6 Naka-jima-chō, Heiwa Kinen Kōen, Hiroshima, 730-0811* ☎ *082/543–6271* 🖷 *082/543–6273* 🖭 *Free* ⊙ *Apr.–July, daily 9–6; Aug. 1–15, daily 8:30–7; Aug. 16–Nov., daily 8:30–6; Dec.–Mar., daily 9–5.*

9 Pause before the **Children's Peace Monument** (Kodomo no Hiewa Kinen-hi, 原爆の子像) before you leave the park. Many visitors consider this the most profound memorial in Peace Memorial Park. The figure is of a Sadako, a young girl who at age 10 developed leukemia as a result of exposure to atomic radiation. Her will to live was strong, and she believed that if she could fold 1,000 paper *senbazuru* (cranes)—a Japanese symbol of good fortune and longevity—her illness would be cured. She died before finishing the thousand, and her schoolmates finished the job for her. But her story, which has become a folktale of sorts, inspired a nationwide paper-crane folding effort among schoolchildren that continues to this day. The colorful chains of paper cranes—delivered daily from schools all over the world—are visually striking. ⊠ *Heiwa Kinen Kōen.*

Elsewhere in Hiroshima

10 Around **Hon-dōri** (本道り), Hiroshima's central district, hundreds of shopkeepers sell their wares. Take the tram that runs from the main station to stop T-31 (Hon-dōri), or simply walk east across the north bridge out of Peace Park. The big department stores are at the east end of the arcade, near the Hatchobori streetcar stop: Sogō (closed Tuesday) is open from 10 to 8; Fukuya (closed Wednesday) and Tenmaya (closed Thursday) are open from 10 to 7:30; and Mitsukoshi (closed Monday) is open from 10 to 7. Many restaurants, including a big, gorgeous bakery of the popular Andersen's chain (one block down on the right from T-31), and a range of modern hotels are also found here. ⊠ *Hon-dōri.*

11 **Hiroshima-jō** (広島城) was originally built by Terumoto Mōri on the Ōtagawa delta in 1589. He gave the surrounding flatlands the name *Hiro-Shima,* meaning wide island, and it stuck. By using the castle as headquarters in World War II, the Japanese army made it one of the legitimate targets of the bomb, and it was destroyed in 1945. In 1958 the five-story tenshukaku was rebuilt to its original specifications. Inside, a Hiroshima historical museum has exhibits from Japan's feudal Edo Period (17th–19th centuries). It's a 15-minute walk north from the A-Bomb Dome. ⊠ *21–1 Motomachi, Naka-ku* ☎ *082/221–7512* 🖭 *Castle and museum* ¥320 ⊙ *Apr.–Sept., daily 9–5:30; Oct.–Mar., daily 9–4:30.*

12 The garden laid out in 1630 by Lord Naga-akira Asano, **Shukkei-en** (縮景園), resembles a famed scenic lake in Hangzhou, China. Streams and islets wind their way between the sculpted pine trees. Small bridges cross the waters, which are filled with colorful carp, a fish venerated for its long life. Shukkei-en is east of Hiroshima-jō castle on the banks of the Kyō-bashi-gawa. Return to the JR station on Streetcar 9; at the end of the line transfer to Streetcar 1, 2, or 6. If you purchase a combined ticket (¥600) for the garden and the Prefectural Art Museum, you must visit the museum first and enter the garden from the museum. ⊠ *2–11 Kamiya-chō, Naka-ku, 730-0014* ☎ *082/221–3620* ☜¥*250* ◎ *Apr.–Sept., daily 9–6; Oct.–Mar., daily 9–5.*

❸ **Hiroshima Prefectural Art Museum** (Hirsohima Kenritsu Bijutsukan, 広島県立美術館), next to the Shukkei Garden, is a visual treat. Standouts include two particularly surrealistic pieces; one, a typically fantastical piece by Salvador Dali, and the other, Ikuo Hirayama's *Holocaust at Hiroshima,* inspired by actual events. Hirayama, who became one of Japan's most highly acclaimed artists, was a junior high school student at the time the A-bomb was dropped. ⊠ *Moto-mach, Naka-ku* ☎ *082/ 222–5346* ☜¥*500; museum and park ¥600* ◎ *Tues.–Sun. 10–6.*

🜄 ❹ The **Hiroshima Science and Cultural Museum for Children** (Kodomo Bunka Kagakukan, 子供文化科学館) is a hands-on museum. The happiness of the youngsters here can dispel some of the depression that a visit to the Peace Memorial Park is bound to cause. To get here, leave the park via Aioi-bashi at the North Entrance and walk north and east, keeping the river on your left and the baseball stadium on your right. There's a planetarium next door. ⊠ *5-83 Moto-machi, Naka-ku* ☎ *082/222–5346* ☜ *Center free, planetarium ¥440* ◎ *Tues.–Sun. 9–5.*

Where to Stay & Eat

★ **$$$$** ✕ **Kakifune Kanawa** (Kanawa Oyster Boat, かき船かなわ). Hiroshima is known for its oysters. Kanawa, on a barge moored on the Motoyasu-gawa, near the Peace Memorial Park, is Hiroshima's most famous oyster restaurant. *Kaiseki ryōri* (Japanese haute cuisine) is also a top draw. Dining is on tatami mats, with river views. ⊠ *3-1 Chisaki Ohtemachi, moored on river at Heiwa-bashi, Naka-ku, 730-0051* ☎ *082/241–7416* ⊟ *AE, DC, MC, V* ◎ *Closed Sun. Apr.–Sept., 1st and 3rd Sun. Oct.–Mar.*

★ **$$$$** ✕ **Mitaki-sō Ryokan** (三滝荘). For a kaiseki lunch or an elaborate kaiseki dinner in a private tatami room, Mitakiso Ryokan is superb. You needn't stay at the ryokan in order to enjoy its cuisine; it's an excellent place to entertain Japanese guests. (If you do stay, it's worth going all out and choosing a room with sliding doors onto the private garden.) ⊠ *1–7 Mitaki-machi, Nishi-ku, 733-0005* ☎ *082/237–1402* ⊞ *082/237–1403* ⊲ *Reservations essential* ⊟ *AE, MC, V.*

$–$$$ ✕ **Suishin** (酔心). Famous for its sashimi and sushi, this restaurant serves the freshest fish from the Seto Nai-kai—globefish, oysters, and eel, to name but a few. If you don't like raw fish, try the rockfish grilled with soy sauce. Suishin has an English-language menu. It's a plain and simple place with a counter bar and four tables. ⊠ *6–7 Tate-machi, Naka-ku* ☎ *082/247–4411* ⊟ *AE, DC, MC, V* ◎ *Closed Wed.*

★ **$–$$** ✕ **Sawadee** (サワデイ). A tiny but wonderful Thai restaurant, Sawadee serves up some of the finest green curry and *tom yum kung* (a delicious soup of coconut milk, chilies, lemongrass, and seafood) this side of the Chao Praya. Be forewarned that if you tell the Thai cook you like it hot, she will make you sweat. ✉ *4–6 Fukuru-machi, 3rd fl., Naka-ku* ☎ *082/243–0084* ▤ *AE, DC, MC, V* ⊘ *Closed Mon.*

¢–$$ ✕ **Okonomi Mura** (Village of Okonomiyaki, お好み村). In this enclave there are 20 shops serving *okonomi-yaki*, literally, "as you like it." Okonomi-yaki is best described as an everything omelet—a crepe of sorts topped with noodles, bits of shrimp, pork, squid, or chicken, cabbage, and bean sprouts. Different areas of Japan make different kinds of okonomi-yaki; in Hiroshima the ingredients are layered rather than mixed. Seating in these shops, many of which are open late, is either at a wide counter in front of a grill or at a table with its own grill. The complex is near the Hon-dōri shopping area, just west of Chūō-dōri. ✉ *Shintenchi Plaza, 5–13 Shintenchi, 2nd–4th fls., Naka-ku* ▤ *No credit cards.*

★ $$$$ 🏨 **ANA Hotel Hiroshima** (広島全日空ホテル). With a look updated in 2004, the ANA Hotel strives to remain one of the very best. Rooms are pink and gray, with small baths. The Unkai restaurant, on the fifth floor, has good Japanese food and a view onto a garden of dwarf trees, rocks, and a pond with colorful carp. The hotel is in a great location, within walking distance of the Peace Museum as well as the incredible nightlife of Nagarekawa. ✉ *7–20 Naka-machi, Naka-ku, Hiroshima, Hiroshima-ken 730-0037* ☎ *082/241–1111* 🖷 *082/241–9123* ⬎ *427 Western-style rooms, 4 Japanese-style rooms* ⚏ *5 restaurants, indoor pool, health club, sauna, beer garden (May–Aug.), shops* ▤ *AE, DC, MC, V.*

$$$–$$$$ 🏨 **Hiroshima Prince** (広島プリンスホテル). The hotel's location beside Motoujina Park, on the tip of a peninsula jutting into Hiroshima Bay, assures peace and quiet. All the rooms overlook the Seto Nai-kai and are done up in relaxing hues of blue and violet. For a beer with a view, take the elevator to the 23rd-floor lounge. The hotel is 15–20 minutes by taxi from Hiroshima's JR station, and from the pier behind the hotel you can hop a fast ferry to Miyajima (32 minutes; ¥1,460 each way). Tickets are sold in the travel agency off the lobby. You can also get here via Bus 21 from the train station. ✉ *23–1 Motoujina-machi, Minami-ku, Hiroshima, Hiroshima-ken 734-8543* ☎ *082/256–1111* 🖷 *082/256–1134* ⬎ *550 rooms* ⚏ *4 restaurants, pool, bowling, bar, shops, travel services* ▤ *AE, DC, MC, V.*

$$ 🏨 **Hiroshima Central Hotel** (広島セントラルホテル). Experience a great bargain at this hotel. The building stands along the Kyobashi River and the pastel-color rooms are fine enough. Rooms are equipped with trouser presses, and public areas include a vending machine corner and a business corner. The hotel's location is central, only a 2-minute taxi ride or a 15-minute walk from Hiroshima Station. ✉ *1–8–Ginzan-chō, Naka-ku, Hiroshima, Hiroshima-ken 730-0022* ☎ *082/243–2222* 🖷 *082/243–9001* ⬎ *136 Western-style rooms* ⚏ *Restaurant, in-room data ports* ▤ *AE, DC, MC, V* ⊙ *EP, MAP.*

$–$$ 🏨 **Rijyo Kaikan** (Kenmin Bunka Center, 鯉城会館 (県民文化センター)). For a no-nonsense place to stay close to Peace Memorial Park, this accommodation is the best value in Hiroshima. It's run as a business hotel for government workers, with small rooms and tiny bathrooms. The rooms are cheerful, though, and the bathtubs are deep enough for a good soak. Check-in is not until 4 PM, and six-months' advance reservations are recommended. ✉ *1–5–3 Ohtemachi, Naka-ku, Hiroshima,*

Hiroshima-ken 730-0051 ☎ *082/245–2322* 🖷 *082/245–2315* 🛏 *50 Western-style rooms* ⛨ *3 restaurants* ☰ *MC, V* ⭐ *EP, MAP.*

Nightlife

Shin-tenchi and Nagarekawa are entertainment districts east of the Hon-dōri shopping district. This side of Hiroshima offers some of Japan's hottest nightlife. The following are but a couple of reliable options; in truth, you could probably drop into any one of the hundreds of night spots in the area and have the time of your life, bopping and talking until half-past sunrise with sociable locals and fellow gaijin alike.

In Nagarekawa, the rooftop **Live Cafe Jive** (⊠ Carp Bldg., 5th fl., 2–16 Nagarekawa, Naka-ku ☎ 082/246–2949) has live jazz, blues, rock or pop Monday through Saturday—all easily heard from down in the street. Stop in for a drink, and you may find it hard to leave.

Rock rules at **MAC** (☎082/243–0343 ⊠6–18 Nagarekawa-chō, 2F, Naka-ku), home to some of the most loyal and friendly customers in the land. From a librarylike ladder-and-shelf setup that houses the impressive tune collection, the DJs will get down whatever you may request and slap it on the turntable for you. Wear your dancing shoes and be ready to rock 'til sunup. The place is upstairs on a side street, halfway between the Ritz movie theater (on Nagarekawa Street) and Chūō Street. Look for the simple sign with the silver letters "MAC" suspended above the open outdoor stairway. Don't be shy about calling for directions; the fantastic crew speaks English.

Getting Around

The streetcar (tram) is the easiest form of transport in Hiroshima. Enter the tram from its middle door and take a ticket. Pay the driver at the front door when you leave. All fares within the city limits are ¥150. A one-day pass is ¥600, available for purchase at the platform outside JR Hiroshima Station. There are seven streetcar lines; four of them either depart from the JR station or make it their terminus. Stops are announced by a tape recording, and each stop has a sign in *rōmaji* posted on the platform. Buses also ply Hiroshima's streets; the basic fare is ¥180. In-formation in English can be gathered at the Hiroshima Station Tourist Info Center.

Taxis can be hailed throughout the city. The initial fare for small taxis is ¥570 (¥620 for larger taxis) for the first 1½ km (1 mi), then ¥70 for every 300 meters (335 yards).

Hiroshima is Western Honshū's major city, and it's a major terminus for the JR Shinkansen trains; several Shinkansen end their runs at Hi-roshima rather than continuing to Hakata on Kyūshū. During the day Shinkansen arrive and depart for Okayama, Ōsaka, Kyōto, and Tōkyō approximately every 30 minutes, and about every hour for Hakata. From Tōkyō, travel time is 3 hours, 37 minutes, and unless you have a Japan Rail pass, the fare is ¥18,050. Hiroshima Station also serves as the hub for JR express and local trains traveling along the San-yō Line. There are also two trains a day that link Hiroshima to Matsue, on the north-ern shore (the Nihon-kai coast) of Western Honshū.

Tours

A number of sightseeing tours are available, including tours of Hiroshima and cruises on the Seto Nai-kai, in particular to Miyajima, the island with the famous sea-bound torii.

To arrange for a sightseeing taxi ahead of time, telephone the **Hiroshima Station Tourist Information Center** (広島駅観光案内所; ☎ 082/261–1877). A two-hour tour is approximately ¥8,400. Because these taxi drivers are not guides, you should rent a taped recording describing key sights in English. These special taxis can be picked up from a special depot in front of Hiroshima Station at the Shinkansen entrance.

A 4-hour, 40-minute tour of the city's major sights operated by **Hiroshima Bus Company** (広島バス; ☎082/243–7207 ☎082/243–0272) costs ¥3,510. An eight-hour tour of both the city and Miyajima costs ¥9,470. You depart from in front of Hiroshima Station's Shinkansen entrance. All tours are in Japanese, but the sights visited are gaijin-friendly.

Hiroshima Peace Culture Foundation International Relations and Cooperation Division (広島平和文化センター国際交流・協力課; ☎ 082/242–8879 ☎ 082/242–7452) has a home-visit program. To make arrangements, go the day before you wish to visit a Japanese home to the International Center on the ground floor of the International Conference Center in Peace Memorial Park. Although not required, bringing along an inexpensive gift such as flowers or treats from your home country will ensure a successful beginning for your visit.

The **Seto Nai-kai Kisen Company** (瀬戸内海汽船会社; ☎ 082/255–1212 ☎ 082/505–0134) operates several cruises on the Seto Nai-kai. Its cruise boat, the *Southern Cross,* operates a 7¼-hour trip (9:30–4:45) daily, March–November, which takes in Etajima, Ondo-no-Seto, Kure-wan (Kure [*koo*-reh] Bay), and Ōmishima (¥4,500–¥6,500 includes lunch and soft drinks). There are also a variety of river cruises, one of which includes dinner (¥6,000–¥10,000). Tours are in Japanese only.

Miyajima 宮島

⑮ *20 min southwest of Hiroshima by ferry.*

Not far from Hirsohima lies Miyajima, site of one of Japan's traditionally noted Top Three scenic attractions. The island's easily recognizable majestic vermilion torii, made of stout, rot-resistant camphor tree trunks, is famed for the illusion it gives of "floating" over the water. Although most of the time it actually presides over drab, tidal mudflats, time your visit right—for when the tide is in (check with tourist offices and hotel front desks)—and a nice view of the torii can make your whole Japan trip click into perfect focus.

Landward of the famous red sea-gate is the elegant shrine called Itsukushima Jinja. These environs are the site of the annual June Kangen-sai Matsuri (Kangen-en Festival), when three stately barges bearing a portable shrine, priests, and musicians cross the bay, followed by a fleet of decorated boats.

To get to the shrine, and to the places where you can photograph the torii, head to the right from the pier, on the path that leads through the terribly touristy village, which is crowded with restaurants, hotels, and souvenir shops. As you pass through the park, expect to be greeted by herds of fearless deer.

★ **Ō-torii** (大鳥居), 500 feet from the shore, at an entrance to the cove where the shrine stands, rises 53 feet out of the water, making it one of the tallest torii in Japan. Built with trunks of ancient trees in 1875, it has become a national symbol. As the sun sets over the Seto Nai-kai, the gate and its reflection are an unforgettable sight. At low tide neither the torii nor the shrine appears to rest on the water at all but, instead, stand looking rather forlorn above the mud and sand flats. Most hotels and ferry operators have tide charts you can check to maximize your photo opportunities.

Itsukushima Jinja (厳島神社) was founded in 593 and dedicated to the three daughters of Susano-o-no-Mikoto, the Shintō god of the moon and the oceans. The shrine has been continually repaired and rebuilt, and the present structure is thought to be a 16th-century copy of 12th-century buildings. Most of the shrine is closed to the public, but you can walk around its deck, which provides gorgeous views of the torii. ☞ *¥300, combined ticket with Hōmotsukan ¥500* ☉ *Mar.–Oct., daily 6:30–6; Nov.–Feb., daily 6:30–5:30.*

The **Hōmotsukan** (Treasure House, 宝物館) at Itsukushima Jinja is a must-see. Because the victor of every battle that took place on the Seto Nai-kai throughout Japan's long history saw fit to offer his gratitude to the gods by giving gifts to Itsukushima Jinja, the Hōmotsukan is rich with art objects, 246 of which have been designated as either National Treasures or Important Cultural Properties. It's across from Itsukushima Jinja's exit. ☞ *¥300, combined ticket with Itsukushima Jinja ¥500* ☉ *Daily 8:30–5.*

Atop a small hill overlooking Itsukushima Jinja, **Go-jū-no-tō** (Five-Storied Pagoda, 五重の塔) dates to 1407. If you climb up the steps to this building for a closer look, you can access a small street on the other side (away from the shrine) as a shortcut back to the village.

Senjōkaku (Hall of One Thousand Mats, 千畳閣), dedicated by Hideyoshi Toyotomi in 1587, has rice scoops attached to the walls, symbols of the soldiers who died fighting for Japan's expansionism. It's next to the Five-Storied Pagoda. Most often, you'll only be able to view Senjōkaku's exterior, but if you're lucky a door may be open.

Many people spend only a half day on Miyajima, but if you have more time to enjoy its beauty, take a stroll through **Momijidani Kōen** (Red Maple Valley Park, 紅葉谷公園), inland from Itsukushima Jinja. Here in the park you can board the gondola that takes you a mile up to nearly the summit of **Misen-dake** (Mt. Misen). A short hike takes you from the upper cable car terminus to the top of the mountain, where you can take in views of the Seto Nai-kai and Hiroshima beyond. ☞ *Cable car ¥900 one-way, ¥1,500 round-trip; park free.*

Where to Stay & Eat

$$–$$$$　✕🏠 **Iwasō Ryokan** (岩惣). For tradition and elegance, this is the best Japanese inn on the island. Older rooms are full of character, those in the newer wing less so. Two cottages on the grounds have suites superbly decorated with antiques. Prices vary according to the size of your room, its view, and the kaiseki dinner you select, so be sure to specify what you want when you reserve. Breakfast (Western style if you ask) and dinner are usually included. Nonguests are welcome to dine here. ✉ *345 Miyajima-chō, Hiroshima, Hiroshima-ken 739-0500* ☎ *0829/44–2233* 🖷 *0829/44–2230* 🛏 *42 Japanese-style rooms, 33 with bath* ♨ *Japanese baths, restaurant* ▭ *AE, DC, V* 🍽 *EP, MAP.*

$$$–$$$$　🏠 **Jūkei-sō Ryokan** (聚景荘). This modest family ryokan makes a pleasant home away from home. It's to the east of the ferry pier, away from the town and shrine, which might be a bit inconvenient, but the owner, who speaks English, can arrange to pick you up on arrival. ✉ *50 Miyajima-chō, Hiroshima, Hiroshima-ken 739-0533* ☎ *0829/44–0300* 🖷 *0829/44–0388* 🛏 *12 Japanese-style rooms* ♨ *Japanese baths, outdoor bath, restaurant* ▭ *AE, DC, MC, V.*

Getting Around

The easiest, least expensive way to Miyajima is to take the commuter train on the JR San-yō Line from Hiroshima Station to Miyajima-guchi Station. From Miyajima-guchi Station a three-minute walk takes you to the pier from which ferries depart for Miyajima. The train takes about 25 minutes and departs from Hiroshima every 15–20 minutes. The first train leaves Hiroshima at 5:55 AM; the last ferry returns from Miyajima at 10:05 PM. There are two boats, one of which belongs to Japan Rail: your JR Pass is valid on this boat only. The one-way cost for the train and ferry, without a JR Pass, is ¥560. There are also eight direct ferries (¥1,440 one-way, ¥2,800 round-trip) daily from Hiroshima Ujina Port, next to the Prince Hotel, that make the 32-minute trip. Allow a minimum of three hours for the major sights of Miyajima, one hour or so to have a stroll and get some photos of Ō-torii and the shrine.

THE SAN-IN REGION　山陰地方

In dramatic contrast to the modern urbanization of the San-yō coast, the north coast of Western Honshū has remained relatively free of power lines, skyscrapers, concrete corporate housing blocks, and traffic jams. Thanks to the rugged mountains that make transport from the populous south slow, expensive, and infrequent, there are (except at holiday times) also few tourists, so if you are looking for adventure in a "real Japan" setting, you have come to the right place.

The JR San-in Main Line from Shimonoseki to Kyōto is the second-longest in Japan, at 680 km (422 mi). It has the most stations of any line, which means plenty of stops and longer traveling times. Only two Limited Express trains a day cover the Shimonoseki–Kyōto route in either direction. Local trains and buses run frequently between major towns on the San-in coast but still nowhere near as often or as quickly as in San-yō. Keep this in mind when you make your plans, so you can actually enjoy the deliciously slower pace of the region.

Hagi   萩

3½ hrs north of Shin-Yamaguchi by JR train, 1½ hrs by JR bus; 2½ hrs north of Shin-Yamaguchi by JR Yamaguchi Line only; 2 hrs northeast of Shimonoseki by JR Limited Express.

The sleepy, historic town of Hagi is almost entirely surrounded by a moat formed by two forks of the Abu-gawa—the south fork, Abu-gawa, and the north fork, Matsumoto-gawa. Backing the town are waves of evocative, shadowy, symmetrical mountains, and before it lies a clean, jewel-blue sea.

Although its castle was razed in 1874 as a feudal relic, Hagi is rich with history and retains the atmosphere of a traditional castle town. From 1865 to 1867 the city was of critical importance in the movement to restore power to the emperor. Hagi can also claim credit for supplying much of the intellectual framework for the new Japan: Japan's first prime minister, Hirobumi Ito (1841–1909), was born and educated here.

Hagi claims distinction beyond the realm of politics too. It's famous for Hagi-yaki, a pottery with soft colors and milky, translucent glazes ranging from beige to pink. There are conflicting theories regarding the notch commonly found on the base of each piece: the first is that it's a tradition going back to when the artists defaced their work deliberately so they could own it, for if it was "perfect" it was destined to belong to the samurai class; the second theory is that the notch serves to let water vapor pass from under the base during firing, lessening the risk of deformation.

Hagi-yaki got its start in a rather shameful way. In the 16th century a Mōri general brought home with him many captive Korean potters, (perhaps his only consolation for a miserable and failed attempt at invasion), who created it for their new masters under duress. In a typical effort to whitewash the dark stains of history, some government tourist information sources actually claimed that these Korean potters were "*invited* to Japan by the fiefdom." In any case, eye-pleasing Hagi-yaki has since become second to Raku-yaki as the most esteemed pottery in Japan, and therefore does not come cheaply. The Hagi-yaki Festival takes place yearly, May 1–5.

The **City Tourist Office** (萩市観光課 ✉ 495–4 Emukai, Hagi-shi, 758-0053 ☎ 0838/25–3131) is downtown in city hall, virtually in the center of the island that is Hagi. There's a lot more to do in and around this beautiful town than you might think, as the staff here will be happy to show you. City information is also available from helpful staff at the **Hagi City Tourist Bureau** (萩市観光協会; ☎ 0838/25–1750 or 0838/25–3145) next to Hagi Station. For local information at Higashi-Hagi Station try **Hagi Ryokan Kyōdō-kumiai** (萩旅館協同組合; ☎ 0838/22–7599 🖷 0838/ 24–2202). Its main business is booking accommodations, but its English-speaking owner is a helpful adviser to tourists and dispenses official guide maps. The agency is in the Rainbow Building to the left of the station, in the first office on the left side of the shopping arcade.

Central Hagi

▶ **16** The second-floor **Ishii Tea-Bowl Museum** (Ishii Chawan Bijutsukan, 石井茶碗美術館) displays a small collection of rare antique tea bowls produced in Hagi. Also in this prized collection are Korean celadon tea bowls made during the Koryo dynasty (916–1392). For connoisseurs this museum is a pleasure, but if you are short on time, you may want to skip it. From Higashi-Hagi Station, cross the bridge over the Matsumoto-gawa and, keeping right, continue on the street until you reach the Hagi Grand Hotel. Turn left here, walk seven blocks, and then turn right. Walk straight for at least 10 minutes until you reach a curve. Take the first right after the curve; the museum is on the left. ⊠ *33–3 Minamihuruhagi-chō, Hagi, Yamaguchi-ken, 758-0077* ☎ *0838/22–1211* 💰 *¥1,000* 🕐 *Open 9–noon and 1–5* 🕐 *Closed Tues.*

17 **Tamachi Mall** (田町商店街) is the busiest street in Hagi, with some 130 shops selling local products from Yamaguchi Prefecture. Two stores worth noting are **Harada Chōjuen** and **Miwa Seigadō.** The latter is at the top end of Tamachi, past the San Marco restaurant. Another gallery and store is **Saito-an,** in which both masters and "unknown" potters display their works for sale. Prices range from ¥500 for a small sake cup to ¥250,000 for a tea bowl by such "Living National Treasure" potters as Miwa Kyūsetsu. Tamachi Mall is six blocks southwest from the Hagi Grand Hotel, across the Matsumoto-gawa from Higashi-Hagi Station.

18 The **Tera-machi** (寺町) section of town has about 10 17th-century temples to explore, and each has something of interest, from the old wooden temple of **Hōfuku-ji,** with its bibbed statues of Jizō, guardian deity of children, to **Kaichō-ji,** with its two-story gate and veranda around the Main Hall's second floor. From the top of Tamachi Mall, a right turn toward the sea will take you to Tera-machi.

19 The **Kumaya Art Museum** (Kumaya Bijutsukan, 熊谷美術館) was once the home of a wealthy merchant, and the warehouse has been made into a museum of art objects and antiques. Of special note are the scrolls, paintings, a screen from the Kanō school, and a collection of ceramics, which include some of the first Hagi-yaki produced. To get here, take a left after Kaichō-ji, and the museum will be on the left at the large metal gate. ⊠ *47 Imauonotana-machi, Hagi, Yamaguchi-ken, 758-0052* ☎ *0838/22–7547* 💰 *¥700* 🕐 *Daily 9–5.*

20 The **Kikuya-ke Jūtaku** (Kikuya House, 菊屋家住宅), built in 1604, was once the home of the chief merchant family to the Mōri clan. Though the Kikuya were only traders, their connections allowed them to live ostentatiously. To get here from the Kumaya Art Museum, take the next left (south and away from the sea); it's not far after the turn. ⊠ *1–1 Gofuku-machi, Jōka-machi district* ☎ *0838/25–8282* 💰 *¥500* 🕐 *Daily 9–5.*

Elsewhere in Hagi

21 **Shizuki Kōen** (指月公園), bounded on three sides by the sea, surrounds 475-foot Shizuki-yama, at the western end of Hagi. The park contains the ruins of Hagi-jō, Mōri House, and Hana-no-e Teahouse.

Hagi-jō (萩城) was destroyed around 1874 as a symbol of backward ways by the hell-bent-for-progress Meiji Restoration. The walls and moats are

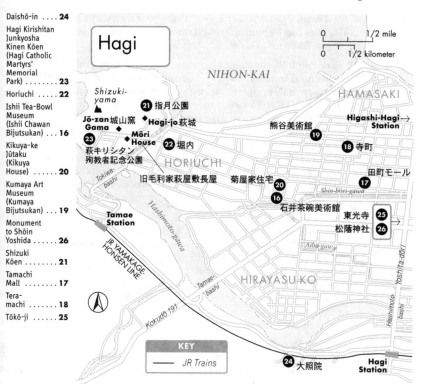

Hagi

NIHON-KAI

HAMASAKI

⑳ 指月公園

Shizuki-yama

Jō-zan 城山窯 Gama ◆ ◆Hagi-jo 萩城

熊谷美術館 ⑲

Higashi-Hagi → Station

◆Mōri House

㉓ 萩キリシタン 殉教者記念公園

㉒ 堀内

HORIUCHI

⑱ 寺町

田町モール

旧毛利家萩屋敷長屋 菊屋家住宅

⑳

Shin-bori-gawa

⑰

Tamae Station

⑯

石井茶碗美術館

東光寺 ㉕ →

松蔭神社 ㉖

JR YAMAKAGE HONSEN LINE

'Aibu-gawa'

HIRAYASU-KO

Yoshita-dōri

Hashimoto-bashi

Tamae-bashi

KEY
—— JR Trains

Kokudō 191

㉔ 大照院

Hagi Station

all that remain of the old castle. On the grounds you can find **Shizuki-yama Jinja,** a shrine with a rustic feel, built in 1879. From the top of the castle walls there is a panoramic view of Hagi, the bay, and the surrounding mountains.

Mōri House (旧毛利家萩屋敷長屋) is a long, narrow building that was home to samurai foot soldiers in the late 18th century. Rooms in the house are sparely decorated and lie in a straight line, one next to the other. This peculiar arrangement allowed the soldiers to assemble in rank at a moment's notice.

★ The **Hana-no-e Teahouse** (花江茶亭) is set amid peaceful gardens and greenery. The attendants will make the classic, slightly bitter-tasting *matcha* (¥500.) for you while you meditate. ⊠ *Ō-aza Horiuchi* ☎ *0838/ 25–1826* ¥210, *includes admission to Hagi-jō grounds, Mōri House, and Hana-no-e Teahouse* ⊗ *Apr.–Oct., daily 8–6:30; Nov.–Feb., daily 8:30–4:30; Mar. daily 8:30–6.*

Stop in at **Jō-zan Gama** (Jō-zan Kiln, 城山窯), near Shizuki Kōen; your admission ticket from the park allows entry here as well. Browse through the Hagi-yaki and, if finances allow, purchase some of the magnificent work. Most of the time you will be welcome to enter the studios and see the kilns (across the street from the shop) where the pieces are made and fired. Classes or a chance to make your own may also be available. Bicycles can be rented through this outfit as well. ⊠ *Hagi-jo-ato, Horiuchi* ☎ *0838/25–1666* ⊙ *Daily 8–5.*

㉒ Horiuchi (堀内), the samurai section of town, has several interesting architectural features. To get here from Shizuki Kōen, recross the canal (on the middle bridge) to the east side and head back toward downtown. The tomb of **Tenju-in** is a memorial to Terumoto Mōri, who early in the 16th century founded the tenacious clan that ruled the Choshu area for 13 generations. Next you come to the **Outer Gate of Mōri;** the **Toida Masuda House Walls** are on your right as you head south. Dating to the 18th century, these are the longest mud walls in the area, and for a moment they can thrust you back in time. At the next chance, turn right and head west to check out the ancient, wooden **Fukuhara Gate.**

㉓ Hagi Kirishitan Junkyosha Kinen Kōen (Hagi Catholic Martyrs' Memorial Park, 萩キリシタン殉教者記念公園), south of Shizuki Kōen and Jō-zan Kiln, is a graveyard where some Christians exiled to Hagi around 1868 for torture are buried. Government officials who were perfectly content to worship the sun, and who offered loyalty only to those who employed and paid them, were confounded by the Christians' devotion to an unseen deity. They resorted to unspeakable cruelty in their efforts to weaken and disperse the believers. Before outcry from the international community forced an end to the killing, many Japanese Christians died for their unfashionable faith.

Outer Precincts

㉔ The first two Mōri generations are buried at **Daishō-in** (大照院), whose temple was founded in 1691. Thereafter, even-numbered generations are buried at Daishō-in, odd-numbered generations at Tōkō-ji. When Hidehari Mōri died, seven of his principal retainers and one of the retainers' servants followed him in death, dutifully committing ritual suicide. Aghast, the Tokugawa shogunate promptly declared such extreme demonstrations of loyalty illegal. Future generations of Mōri retainers donated lanterns instead, and the path leading to the main hall of Daishō-in is lined with more than 600 of them. In May the wisteria blossoms are an eyeful. Another special time to visit is August 13–15, when all the lanterns are lighted for Obon, the Buddhist festival of the dead.

Daishō-in is on the southern outskirts of Hagi, 650 yards west of JR Hagi Station. You can take a train from Higashi-Hagi Station to Hagi Station or take a bus south to the Hagi-station-mae bus stop. From Shizuki Kōen, Daishō-in is about 20 minutes by bicycle: ride across the canal that marks the boundary of Shizuki Kōen and follow it south to the Tokiwa-bashi. Once over the Hashimoto-gawa, take the main road that follows the river upstream. Daishō-in is on the right, across the JR San-in Main Line tracks. ☎ *0838/22–2134* ⊠ *¥200* ⊙ *Daily 8–5.*

㉕ The grounds of **Tōkō-ji** (東光寺) contain one of the two Mōri family cemeteries. Directly east of Matsumoto-bashi, the temple was founded by the Zen priest Domio in 1691. It's here that he (and every succeeding odd-numbered generation of the Mōri family) is buried. On August 15, during the Obon festival, all 500 stone lanterns lining the mossy lanes are lighted.

If you're coming from Daishō-in, the other Mōri family cemetery, take the train from Hagi Station to Higashi-Hagi Station, and then walk south to Matsumoto-bashi and turn left to cross the river. If you have a bicycle, return to Hashimoto-gawa, follow it upstream to Hashimoto-bashi, and then head into central Hagi. At the Bōchō Bus Center, turn right and cross Matsumoto-bashi over the river. ✉ *Ō-aza Higashi* ☎ *0838/26–1052* 💴 *¥200* ⏰ *Daily 8:30–5.*

㉖ The **Monument to Shōin Yoshida** (松蔭神社) (1830–59) commemorates the life of a young teacher and important revolutionary who, with the coming of Commodore Matthew Perry's black ships in 1853, recognized the need for Japan to tear down the walls of feudalism and embrace at least a few Western ideas. Yoshida was captured by the shogunate and kept under house arrest. When he went so far as to suggest introducing democratic elements into the government he was executed, an act that inflamed and united the antishogunate elements of the entire Chōshū Province (now Yamaguchi Prefecture). The monument is a short walk southwest of Tōkō-ji on the loop road.

Where to Stay & Eat

$$$–$$$$ ✕ **Nakamura** (中村). Set-menu courses here might include sashimi, baked fish, fish grilled in soy sauce, mountain vegetables, miso soup, and steamed rice. Nakamura has tatami and Western seating but no English-language menu. You can select your food from the window display. ✉ *Furu-Hagi-chō* ☎ *0838/22–6619* 🍽 *Reservations not accepted* 🚫 *No credit cards.*

$$–$$$$ ✕ **Chiyo.** Local sea delicacies are served, such as sashimi and sushi, in classically elegant surroundings. Dining here, you have views of a small garden. ✉ *20–4 Ima-Furu-Hagi* ☎ *0838/22–1128* 🚫 *No credit cards* ⏰ *Closed Sun.*

$$–$$$$ ✕ **Hyakuman-goku** (百万国). The San-in coast has some of the best seafood
FodorsChoice in the world, and there's no finer or more enjoyable place in Hagi to
★ try it. Most of the fish is served as sashimi, but a few items are lightly grilled, and the crabs are boiled. Absolutely the best *uni* (sea urchin) in the world is served here—don't even think of dunking it in soy sauce! The *maguro* (tuna) melts in your mouth. These and more local wonders are part of the very reasonably priced *sashimi-teishoku* (raw fish set). The 100-year-old building itself is a visual treat. Ask the master to open the upper-level wooden shutters from behind the cash register, using an interesting and complicated series of pulleys and ropes. ✉ *Shimo Goken-machi* ☎ *0838/22–2136* 🚫 *No credit cards.*

$–$$ ✕ **Fujita-ya** (藤田屋). This is a casual restaurant, full of color, where locals come for handmade *soba* (thin wheat noodles) and hot tempura served on handmade cypress trays. ✉ *Kumagai-chō* ☎ *0838/22–1086* 🚫 *No credit cards* ⏰ *Closed 2nd and 4th Wed. of month.*

$$$$ 🏨 **Hagi Royal Hotel** (萩ロイヤルホテル). In the Rainbow Building above JR Higashi-Hagi Station, this former business hotel has become a ryokan. Guest rooms are on the small side for the money, but they are clean and comfortable. ✉ *3000–5 Chintō, Hagi, Yamaguchi-ken 758-*

0026 ☎ 0838/25–9595 🖷 0838/25–8434 ⇨ 51 *Japanese-style rooms,*
4 Western-style rooms ▭ *AE, DC, MC, V.*

★ $$$$ 🏨 **Hokumon Yashiki** (北門屋敷). An elegant ryokan with luxurious rooms,
the Hokumon Yashiki has gracious, refined service that makes you feel
pampered in a style to which the ruling Mōri clan were surely accustomed. Meals are served in your room. The inn overlooks a garden in
the samurai section of town, near the castle grounds. ⊠ *210 Horiuchi,*
Hagi, Yamaguchi-ken 758-0057 ☎ *0838/22–7251* 🖷 *0838/25–8144*
⇨ *42 Japanese-style rooms without baths, 5 Western-style rooms*
♨ *Japanese baths* ▭ *No credit cards* ❙◎❙ *MAP.*

$$–$$$ 🏨 **Hagi Grand Hotel** (萩グランドホテル). Its decidedly 1960s-style rooftop
lookout-lounge might make you either smile or cringe, but convenience
to JR Higashi-Hagi Station makes this the most desirable international-
style hotel in Hagi. The staff are helpful, and guest rooms, half of which
are Western style, are relatively spacious. There are Japanese- and Western-style restaurants on-site. ⊠ *25 Kohagi-chō:, Hagi, Yamaguchi-ken*
758-0026 ☎ *0838/25–1211* 🖷 *0838/25–4422* ⇨ *190 rooms* ♨ *2*
restaurants, shops, travel services, hot springs, outdoor Japanese baths
▭ *AE, DC, MC, V.*

Getting Around

The most convenient way to get to Hagi is by crossing the mountains
from the San-yō town of Shin-Yamaguchi, at which the Hiroshima–Hakata
Shinkansen stops. From there, you can take a Super Oki train to Masuda, where there always seems to be a long layover, and then the San-
in Line train to Hagi, for a total time of four hours and cost of ¥4,600.
The Yamaguchi Line to Masuda is an hour slower but saves ¥1,000. The
ideal way to explore Hagi is by bicycle, and there are many outlets where
you can rent a bike for ¥1,000 per day. Try the shop across from the
Rainbow Building, left of the station plaza. As an alternative, you can
hire a "sightseeing taxi" (¥4,300 per hour); it takes about three hours
to complete a hurried city tour.

The **Bōchō Bus Company** (☎ 0838/25–3131) has a sightseeing bus tour
(Japanese-speaking guides only) that departs from the Bōchō Bus Center on the eastern edge of the central city. Fares start at ¥2,810; lunch
is an additional ¥1,200; the 8:35 AM tour from Higashi-Hagi is the
best deal.

Tsuwano 津和野

㉗ *1 hr, 20 min northeast of Hagi; 1 hr northeast of Ogōri by JR Yamaguchi*
Fodor'sChoice *Line. (Ogōri is 1 hr west of Hiroshima by Shinkansen.)*
★

This hauntingly beautiful mountain town may well be the most picturesque
hamlet in all Japan. If you catch it on a clear day, the view from the old
castle ruins can simply take your breath away. Even if skies are not blue,
the mist often seen hanging among the trees and ridges here only adds
to the romantic appeal of the place. The stucco-and-tile walls can be
reminiscent of those in Hagi and Kurashiki, and the clear carp- and iris-
filled streams running beside the streets can thrill even tired, jaded travelers, making for pleasant strolls or bike rides. Note that many sights

listed below are oriented along just such a street, Tono-machi-dōri, which begins two blocks east and slightly south of the station.

Tsuwano's **Tourist Information Office** (津和野町観光協会; ☎ 0856/72–1771) is inside the Photograph Gallery to the right of the railway station. It's open daily 9–5, has free brochures, and staff members will help you reserve accommodations. As with most places in town, little or no English is spoken here.

The **Katorikku Kyōkai** (Catholic church, カトリック教会; ☎ 08567/2–0251), built in 1931, is unusual for its tatami floors. It's a replica of a church in Ōura, Nagasaki, and is set among trees next to the road and a stream. Masses are Monday–Wednesday and Friday and Saturday at 6:30 AM and Sunday at 9 AM. Doors are left open until 5. To get there from the station, cross the street that runs in front of the Tourist Information Center and take the one that heads diagonally away from the station. In two blocks, turn right onto Tonomachi-dōri. Follow it for four blocks, and you can see the church on the left before the street crosses the Tsuwano-gawa.

Built in the Edo Period, the **Shiryōkan** (資料館) was originally a feudal school where the sons of samurai would train in the arts of manhood. Today, in its fencing hall, there's a folk-craft museum. It's a few steps past the Catholic church on the left side of Tono-machi-dōri. ☎ 08567/ 2–1000 🈺 ¥200 ☉ Daily 8:30–5.

The **Kyōdōkan** (教堂館) is a museum with a collection of exhibits that recount regional history, including information about the exiled Christians. Past the Catholic church, on Tono-machi-dōri, the road crosses the Tsuwano-gawa. Kyōdōkan is on the other side of the river. 🈺 ¥350 ☉ Daily 8:30–5.

The **Taikodani Inari Jinja** (Taiko Valley Inari Shrine, 太鼓谷稲荷神社) is one of the five most revered Inari shrines in Japan. Inari shrines, of which there are thousands scattered around the country, are connected with the fox, a Shintō symbol of luck and cleverness. To get here from the station, follow the delightful Tono-machi-dōri past the Katorikku Kyōkai (Catholic church), but before crossing the river turn right onto the small lane. The lane leads to the tunnel-like approach to the shrine, along which you pass under numerous red torii—1,174 of them—to reach the structure high on a cliffside. You can opt out of the long walking ascent under the torii by taking a bus that follows another road; the Tourist Information Office can help you with this. **Yasaka Jinja** is another shrine on the site, where every July 20, 24, and 27 the Heron Dance Festival is held.

From the castle ruins of **Tsuwano-jō** (津和野城), the panoramic view of the sleeping volcano, Aono-yama, the surrounding ridges, and the valley below is positively awe-inspiring. To get here, you can hike a trail from Taiko-dani Inari Jinja or take a chairlift from the area below the Inari shrine for ¥450, round-trip. The chairlift takes 5 minutes, and from there it's about a 10-minute hike to the castle foundations. Like Hagi-jō, Tsuwano Castle was a casualty of the Meiji Restoration in the late 19th century.

The **Old House of Ōgai Mori** (森鴎外旧宅・森鴎外記念館) is worth a visit. Ōgai Mori (1862–1922) was one of the prominent literary figures in the Meiji Restoration, and lived here until he was 11. From Tsuwano Station, it's a rather long walk 12 blocks south along the main road, or take the bus and get off at Ōgai Kyūkyo-mae; a six-minute ride. ☎ 08567/ 2-3210 ☜ ¥500 ☉ *Tues.–Sun. 9–5* ☉ *Closed Mon.*

The **Sekishūkan** (石洲館) displays *washi,* Japanese handmade paper. There are demonstrations of papermaking, as well as a display of Iwami-style paper. On the second floor there are displays of washi from other regions of Japan. If you have not seen the process of creating handmade paper, this is a good museum to visit. It's next door to the Old House of Ōgai Mori. ☜ *¥500* ☉ *Daily 9–5.*

A surprising local find is Tsuwano's **Katsushika Hokusai Art Museum** (Katsushika Hokusai Bijutsukan, 葛飾北斎美術館), a block from the train station. Katsushika Hokusai (1760–1849) was the famous *ukiyo-e* (floating world) painter from the end of the Tokugawa era who influenced future generations of painters in Japan and overseas. This museum exhibits his wood-block prints, books, and paintings, and was founded here because his original sketchbook was discovered here. ☎ 0856/72–1850 ☜ ¥500 ☉ *Daily 9:30–5.*

Tsuwano has put its geothermal gifts to good use at the spa at **Nagomi-no-Sato** (津和野温泉なごみの里). Inside and out, the tubs give you great views of the surrounding gumdrop-shape volcanic peaks marching into the distance. Delightfully fragrant *hinoki* (Japanese cypress, a type of redwood) is all around you here, and its scent fills the air. The wood's color contrasts with earth-tone tiles, and the water's temperature is just right for the interminable soaking of your travelers' aches. It's a bit west of everything else in town, across the river from the Washibara Hachiman-gū (a shrine where traditional horseback archery contests are held every April 2), but still not too far to get to by rented bike (and well worth getting to in any case). There's also a decent restaurant and a gift shop full of local specialties, from crafts and green tea to strong, excellent Tsuwano sake. ⊠ 257–Ō-aza Washibara ☎ 0856/72–4122, 0120–26–4753 toll-free ☜ ¥500 ☉ *Hot springs daily 10–8, except 2nd and 4th Thurs. of month; restaurant daily 10–8, except 1st and 3rd Thurs.*

off the beaten path

OTOMETŌGE MARIA SEIDŌ – (乙女峠マリア聖堂) Between 1868 and 1870, in an effort to disperse Christian strongholds and cause them extreme hardship—and in the hope that the believers would recant their faith—the Tokugawa shogunate sent 153 Christians from Nagasaki to Tsuwano, where they were imprisoned and tortured. Many gave in to the torture, but in the end 36 held firm and died for their faith. Otometōge Maria Seidō (St. Mary's Chapel at the Pass of the Virgin) was built in 1951 to commemorate them, and the plight of the 36 martyrs is portrayed in the stained-glass windows. The chapel is a pleasant 1-km (½-mi) walk from Tsuwano Station. Go right out of the station, make another right at the first street (which leads to Yōmei-ji), and just after crossing the tracks, turn right again and walk up the hill. Every May 3 a procession begins at the church in town and ends in the courtyard of the chapel, where a large outdoor mass is held.

Where to Stay & Eat

$$$–$$$$ ✕ **Yūki** (遊亀). Carp dishes (such as carp sashimi and carp miso soup) and mountain vegetables are what made Yūki's reputation. The dining room has traditional beams and a stream running through the center of it. There are sunken pits for your feet under the low tables. It's best to come early, as Yuki often closes around 7 PM. ✉ *271–4 Hon-chō-dōri* ☎ *0856/72–0162* ⊟ *No credit cards* ☉ *Closed Thurs.*

★ **¢–$$** ✕ **Aoki** (あおき). An old-fashioned, rustic sushi restaurant, Aoki has reasonable prices and a cheerful staff. It's also within walking distance of Tsuwano Station. Try the *jyo-nigiri* (deluxe sushi set). That and a frosty mug of beer set you back only ¥1,900. ✉ *Takaoka-dōri* ☎ *0856/72–0444* ⊟ *No credit cards* ☉ *Closed Thurs.*

★ **$$$** ▥ **Tsuwano Lodge** (津和野ロッジ). Kick back and relax in style at this jewel of a spot tucked in along the way to the Washibara Hachiman-gū shrine. The owners are friendly, the rooms are basic but clean and tasteful, and the food is diverse and prepared with flair. Perhaps best of all, there's a *rotemburo* (outside bath) full of sulfur-laden water—good for the skin, hair, and nails—to die for. As in the rest of this region, little English is spoken here. ✉ *Rte. 345, Washibara, Tsuwano-chō, Kanoashi-gun, Shimane-ken 699-5613* ☎ *0856/72–1683* ◨ *0856/72–2880* ⏦ *8 Japanese-style rooms without baths* ⚲ *Dining room, Japanese baths* ⊟ *No credit cards* ❙⊙❙ *EP, MAP.*

★ **$$** ▥ **Wakasagi-no-Yado** (民宿若さぎの宿). Despite the limited English of the family that runs this small inn, the staff is eager to help overseas tourists and will meet you at Tsuwano Station, an eight-minute walk away. Typical of minshuku, there's a common bath. A Japanese and Western breakfast is served, included in the rates. ✉ *Mōri, Tsuwano-chō, Kanoashi-gun, Shimane-ken 699-0056* ☎☎ *0856/72–1146* ⏦ *8 Japanese-style rooms without bath* ⚲ *Japanese baths* ⊟ *No credit cards* ❙⊙❙ *BP.*

Getting Around

JR train routes from Hagi to Tsuwano involve layovers in Masuda. To use a JR Pass without going through Masuda, you could take a JR bus from Iwakuni (west of Hiroshima and site of a famous five-arch bridge); this takes two hours. An attractive option is to get to Ogōri (which is not far from Hiroshima on the Shinkansen line); from there, it's an hour to Tsuwano by JR train.

You can take a bus from Hagi's **Bōchō Bus Center** (☎ 0856/72–0272) directly to Tsuwano, a trip that takes 1 hour, 20 minutes (¥2,080). **Iwami Kotsu** (☎ 0856/24–0085) has a Hiroshima–Tsuwano bus route (you change at Nichihara). The ride takes a total of three hours and costs ¥3,550.

In Tsuwano all sights are within easy walking distance. You can rent a bicycle from one of the four shops near the station plaza (two hours ¥500; all day is ¥800).

Izumo Taisha & Hino-misaki 出雲大社と日御碕

㉘ *3 hrs 10 min northwest of Okayama by hourly JR Limited Express; 3 hrs, 22 min northeast of Tsuwano on the JR San-in Line Oki Limited Express; 1 hr west of Matsue by Ichibata Dentetsu (electric railway); 40 min west of Matsue by JR Kunibiki Limited Express*

Although **Izumo Taisha** (出雲大社) is Japan's oldest Shintō shrine, the *hon-den* (main building) you can see dates from 1744, and most of the other buildings from 1874. The architectural style, with its projecting, saddled crests, and ornamental roof fixtures resembling crossed swords, is said to be unique to the Izumo region, but some similarities with Ise Jingū on the Kii Peninsula can be noted. The taisha is dedicated to a male god, Ōkuninushi, known in mythology as the creator of the land and god of marriage and fortune. Unlike at other shrines, here instead of clapping twice, you should clap four times—twice for yourself, and twice for your current or future partner.

On either side of the compound there are two rectangular buildings that are believed to house the Shintō gods during the 10th lunar month of each year. Accordingly, in the rest of Japan, the lunar October is referred to as Kaminazuki, "month without gods," while in Izumo, October is called Kamiarizuki, "month with gods." The shrine is a five-minute walk north, to the right along the main street, from Izumo Taisha-mae Station. ⊠ *Izumo Taisha, Izumo-shi* ☎ *0853/53–2298* ⊠ *Free* ⊗ *Daily 8:30–5:30.*

From its perch 208 feet above the sea, **Hino-misaki Tō-dai** (Cape Hino Lighthouse, 日御碕灯台) towers another 145 feet. Its height makes for stunning views of the San-in coast and, in fine weather, the Oki Islands. The lighthouse is open to the public for a fee of ¥150, daily 8:30–4 from April to September (from 9 AM the rest of year). To get to Hino-misaki take a bus (hourly) from the Ichibata bus terminal at Ichihata Izumo Taisha-mae Station for the 25-minute ride (¥1,150).

Next to Hino-misaki Tō-dai are **Hino-misaki Jinja** (日御碕神社), a pair of shrines dedicated to the goddesses Amaterasu and Susonō. Brightly painted on the outside, the shrines have colorful murals inside. ⊠ *Free* ⊗ *Daily 9–5.*

Getting Around

From Tsuwano, the ride to Izumo Taisha is 3 hours, 22 minutes on the JR San-in Line Oki Limited Express and then local trains, and costs ¥6,030. It's also a 3-hour 10-minute train ride from Okayama, and costs ¥6,710.

To go from Matsue Onsen to Taisha, the location of Izumo Taisha, takes one hour on the Ichibata Dentetsu (electric railway, ¥790), leaving from Matsue Onsen Station. You need to change trains at Kawato Station for the final leg to Izumo Taisha-mae Station. You can also get there by taking the JR train from Matsue Station to Izumo, then transferring to the JR Taisha Line and taking that to Taisha Station, where you can either take a 5-minute bus ride to Taisha-mae Station or walk to the shrine in about 20 minutes.

Matsue 松江

⏵ ㉙ *2½ hrs northeast of Tsuwano by Super Oki Express; 2 hrs, 27 min north-*
Fodor'sChoice *west of Okayama by JR Yakumo Limited Express.*
★

Matsue, a city blessed with natural and man-made beauty, elegance, history, and an abundance of delicious food, lies at the point where the lake named Shinji-ko empties into the lagoon called Nakaumi-ko, which connects directly with the sea. This makes Matsue a seafood-lover's paradise, bursting with fish from the Nihon-kai and delicacies such as eel, shrimp, shellfish, carp, sea bass, smelt, clams, and whitebait from Shinji-ko. The water also blesses the city with a lovely network of canals.

It's easy to argue that Matsue has it all: in addition to scenic and culinary treasures, Matsue also has some of the country's most welcoming people. All three assets help make this remote realm a traveler's favorite.

★ Start a tour of Matsue at **Matsue-jō** (松江城) and spacious, meditative **Jōzen Kōen**, the castle park. Constructed entirely of pine, the castle was completed in 1611 and partially reconstructed in 1642, and it was neither ransacked nor burned during the Tokugawa shogunate.

Built by the daimyō of Izumo, Yoshiharu Horio, for protection, Matsue-jō is a beautiful structure as well. Its tenshukaku, at 98 feet, is said to be the second-tallest among originals still standing in Japan. Camouflaged among the surrounding trees, Matsue-jō seems almost spooky at times. Note the overhanging eaves above the top floor, designed to cut down glare that might have prevented spotting an attacking force. The castle is fabulously preserved, with six interior levels belied by a facade that suggests only five. The lower floors exhibit a collection of samurai swords and armor. The long climb to the castle's uppermost floor is worth it—the view encompasses the city, Shinji-ko lake, the Shimane Peninsula, and the distant mountains.

The castle and park lie a nice stroll northwest from the station, but if you're not up for it, there's an amazing choice of buses—none of which are run by JR, however. The cheapest and best option is to take the Lake-line Bus from Terminal 7 in front of the station and get off at Ote-mae. The fare is only ¥100. ☎ 0852/21–4030 🖃 ¥550 🕙 Apr.–Sept., daily 8:30–6; Oct.–Mar., 8:30–4:30.

Also within the park, the **Matsue Cultural Museum** (Matsue Kyōdokan, 松江郷土館) displays art, folk craft, and implements used during the first three imperial eras after the fall of the Tokugawa shogunate. The Kyōdōkan is in the two-story, white Western-style building just south of the castle. ☎ 0852/22–3958 🖃 Free 🕙 Daily 8:30–5.

Meimei-an Teahouse (明々庵) was built in 1779 and is one of the best-preserved teahouses of the period. For ¥300 you can take in a fine view of Matsue-jō, and for ¥360 more, you get tea and a sweet. To get here, leave Shiroyama Kōen, the castle park, at its east exit and follow the moat going north; at the top of the park a road leads to the right, northwest of the castle. The teahouse is a short climb up this road. ⊠ Kita-hori-chō ☎ 0852/21–9863 🕙 Daily 9–5.

Samurai Mansion (Buke Yashiki, 武家屋敷), built in 1730, belonged to the well-to-do Shiomi family, chief retainers to the daimyō. Note the separate servant quarters, a shed for the palanquin, and slats in the walls to allow cooling breezes to flow through the rooms. Buke Yashiki is on the main road at the base of the side street on which Meimei-an Teahouse is located (keep the castle moat on your left). ⊠ 305 Kitahori-

chō ☎ 0852/22–2243 🎫 ¥300 ☉ *Apr.–Sept., daily 8:30–6; Oct.–Mar., daily 8:30–4:30.*

Tanabe Art Museum (Tanabe Bijutsukan, 田部美術館), dedicated mainly to objects of the tea ceremony, exhibits beautiful ceramics and tea sets from the region. The museum is next to Buke Yashiki. ☎ 0852/26–2211 🎫 ¥500, varies with exhibit ☉ Tues.–Sun. 9–4:30.

The **Lafcadio Hearn Residence** (Koizumi Yakumo Kyūkyo, 小泉八雲旧宅), next to the Tanabe Bijutsukan, has remained unchanged since the famous writer left Matsue for Tōkyō in 1891. Born of an Irish father and a Greek mother, Lafcadio Hearn (1850–1904) spent his early years in Europe, then moved to the United States to become a journalist. In 1890 he traveled to Japan and began teaching in Matsue, where he met and married a samurai's daughter. Later he became a Japanese citizen, taking the name Koizumi Yakumo. He spent only 15 months in Matsue, but it was here that he became fascinated with Japan. ☎ 0852/23–0714 🎫 ¥250 ☉ Daily 9–4:30.

The **Lafcadio Hearn Memorial Hall** (Koizumi Yakumo Kinenkan, 小泉八雲記念館) contains a good collection of the author's manuscripts and other artifacts that reflect his life in Japan. It's adjacent to Koizumi Yakumo Kyūkyo. Two minutes from the Memorial Hall is the Hearn Kyūkyo bus stop, where you can catch a bus back to the center of town and the station. ☎ 0852/21–2147 🎫 ¥300 ☉ Apr.–Sept., daily 8:30–6; Oct.–Mar., daily 8:30–4:30.

When dusk rolls around, position yourself for a good view of the sunset over **Shinji-ko** (宍道湖). You can watch it from Shinjiko Ōhashi, the town's westernmost bridge, but the best spot is south of the bridge along the road, at water level in **Shiragata Kōen**, the narrow lakeside park just west of the NHK Building and the hospital. This is a fabulous place to kick back and enjoy some carry-out sushi.

Where to Stay & Eat

$$–$$$
Fodor'sChoice
★

✕ **Kawakyō** (川京). This is the best place in town to try the seven famous delicacies from Shinji-ko: *suzuki* (or *hosho-yaki*), sea bass wrapped in *washi* (paper) and steam-baked over hot coals; *unagi* (freshwater eel) split, broiled, and basted in sweet soy sauce; *shirao*, a small whitefish often served as sashimi or cooked in vinegar-miso; *amasagi* (smelt), teriyaki-grilled or cooked in tempura; *shijimi*, small black-shelled clams served in miso or other soup; *koi*, string-bound, washi-wrapped, steam-baked carp; and *moroge-ebi*, steamed shrimp. Especially good here is the hosho-yaki. The folks who run the place are amazingly outgoing, as is the regular crowd. Don't forget to ask for one of the delicious *jizake* (locally made sake) samplers. Reservations are a good idea. Kawakyō is less than a block west of the Washington Hotel (north of the river). ✉ 65 Suetsugu Honmachi ☎ 0852/22–1312 ▭ No credit cards ☉ Closed Sun. No lunch.

★ $–$$

✕ **Yakumo-an** (八雲庵). This traditional house is a lovely setting in which to enjoy the best soba in town. A colorful garden surrounds the dining area. Recommended dishes include the *sanshurui soba* (three kinds of soba) for ¥750. Take the top dish and, leaving the garnishes in, pour the broth into it; then dunk the three different dishes of noodles. Drink the leftover broth, too; it's full of B vitamins and good for you. ⊠ *Just west of Tanabe Bijutsukan, north of castle* ☏ *0852/22–2400* ▭ *No credit cards.*

¢ ✕ **Daikichi** (大吉). For having fun and socializing with locals, this *yakitori* (grill) bar with counter service offers an evening's entertainment, good grilled chicken, and flowing sake. The owner speaks English and welcomes foreigners. The place is easily recognized by its red lanterns outside. ⊠ *Asahi-machi* ☏ *0852/31–8308* ▭ *No credit cards* ☽ *No lunch.*

$$$$ ✕▣ **Minami-kan** (皆美館). An elegant and prestigious ryokan, Minami-kan is known for its refined service and tasteful furnishings. It also has the best restaurant in Matsue for kaiseki, cooked on hot stones, and *taimeshi* (sea bream with rice). Even if you do not stay here, you can make dinner reservations. ⊠ *14 Suetsugu, Hon-machi, Matsue, Shimane-ken 690-0816* ☏ *0852/21–5131* 🖷 *0852/26–0351* ➳ *9 Japanese-style rooms* ♨ *Restaurant, Japanese baths* ▭ *DC, MC, V* ⵙⵡ *EP, MAP.*

$$–$$$$ ▣ **Hotel Ichibata** (ホテル一畑). In the Matsue Onsen section of town, fronting Shinji-ko, the Ichibata has well-known thermal waters and some great views. All rooms are large, but only Japanese-style rooms face the lake. The view of the sunsets from the top-floor lounge is stunning, but beware the drink prices. The hotel is a 20-minute bus ride from the station or a 10-minute, ¥1,000 taxi ride. ⊠ *30 Chidōri-chō, Matsue, Shimane-ken 690-0876* ☏ *0852/22–0188* 🖷 *0852/22–0230* ➳ *71 Japanese-style rooms, 71 Western-style rooms* ♨ *3 restaurants, beer garden, hot springs* ▭ *AE, DC, MC, V.*

$$ ▣ **Matsue Washington Hotel** (松江ワシントンホテル). The best thing about the Washington is its location: a short walk away are a pedestrian mall lined with shops, Shinji-ko, and Matsue-jō. The rooms are modern, with basic chain-hotel-style furnishings in muted pastels and cream. Although they're not especially large, they are quite satisfactory and a good value. The coffee shop on the ground floor serves a decent breakfast buffet and light meals. There is also a more formal restaurant serving Western and Chinese fare. ⊠ *2–22 Higashi Hon-machi, Matsue, Shimane-ken 690-0842* ☏ *0852/22–4111* 🖷 *0852/22–4120* ➳ *158 rooms* ♨ *2 restaurants, coffee shop* ▭ *AE, DC, MC, V.*

★ $–$$ ▣ **Ryokan Terazuya** (旅館寺津屋). By all means treat yourself to a stay here. The vivacious family that runs this riverside ryokan has maintained a tradition of heart-warming hospitality since 1893. Every room is air-conditioned, and the location is perfect for watching those incomparable Shinji-ko sunsets. The food is superb and of an astounding variety—virtually all the local seafood and vegetable specialties are on offer, both raw and cooked, and served with a smile. English is spoken, and if you're interested, your hosts may demonstrate sushi-making and the tea ceremony. ⊠ *60–3 Tenjin-machi, Matsue, Shimane-ken 690-0064* ☏ *0852/21–3480* 🖷 *0852/21–3422* ➳ *9 Japanese-style rooms without baths* ♨ *Japanese baths* ▭ *No credit cards* ⵙⵡ *EP, MAP.*

Nightlife

Among Matsue's multiple nightspots there is one standout.

Filaments (⊠ *5 Hakkenya-chō* ☏ *0852/24–8984*), an upstairs place, hops all night long—every night. Osamu-san, the hip yet down-to-earth proprietor, speaks English, and his collection of music will amaze anyone. The drinks are good and cheap (from ¥500), and tasty food is served too, at prices from ¥650 to ¥1,000. Filaments is just south of the river near the second of the four main bridges.

Getting Around

Most sights in Matsue are within walking distance of each other. Where they are not, the buses fill in. The bus station faces the train station.

To arrange for a Goodwill Guide, contact the **Matsue Tourist Information Office** (松江国際観光案内所; ⊠ 665 Asahi-machi ☎ 0852/21–4034 🖷 0852/27–2598) a day in advance. English-speaking volunteers show you around the city or escort you to Izumo Taisha. There's no charge for the service, though you should pay your guide's expenses, including lunch. The office is in JR Matsue Station and open daily 9–6. You can also collect free maps and brochures here.

en route

A couple of stops between Matsue and Tottori are worth considering. In the town of Yasugi is the **Adachi Bijutsukan** (Adachi Museum of Art, 足立美術館), which exhibits the works of both past and contemporary Japanese artists and has an inspiring series of gardens. ⊠ 320 Furukawa-chō, Yasugi, Shimane-ken ☎ 0854/28–7111 💰 ¥2,200, half price if you show your passport ⊙ Daily 9–4:30.

Daisen (Mt. Daisen, 大山), popular with hikers—and skiers in winter—is a steep, ancient volcanic cone that locals liken to Mt. Fuji. On the slopes above the town of Daisen there's an 8th-century Tendai sect temple, **Daisen-ji** (大山寺). The peak can be climbed in about seven hours (round-trip) from here. If it's clear, you can even see the island of Shikoku from the top. Though not actually very high (1,729 meters), Daisen looks quite spectacular, rising virtually straight up from sea-level within a very short distance. **Dōmyō-in** (洞明院; ☎ 0859/52–2038) is a subtemple that offers lodging. Subtemple **Renjō-in** (蓮浄院; ☎ 0859/52–2506) has accommodations you can rent. Buses leave Yonago, in Tottori-ken, every hour for the 50-minute ride to Daisen (¥730).

Near Yonago is the largest flower park in the country, the 124-acre **Hana-Kairō** (Flower Gallery, 花回廊). Here 750,000 flowers bloom each year. It's a half-hour bus ride from Yonago JR Station, or you can take the Hakubi Line train to Hōkimizuguchi Station and a five-minute taxi ride from there. ⊠ Kaiken-machi, Tsuru 110, Nishi-haku-gun, Tottori-ken ☎ 0859/48–3030 💰 Apr.–Nov. ¥1,000, Dec.–Mar. ¥700 ⊙ Apr.–Nov., daily 9–5; Dec.–Mar., daily 9–4:30.

Up the coast from Mt. Daisen, toward Tottori, **Misasa Onsen** (三朝温泉) is a famous 1,000-year-old hot-spring resort claiming the highest radium-content waters (reputed to have strong curative powers) in the country. It's a 20-minute bus ride from Kurayoshi Station.

Tottori 鳥取

➤ ㉚ *1 hr 22 min east of Matsue by JR Super Oki Express, 1 hr 25 min north-west of Himeji by direct JR Super Hakuto Express, 2 hrs 18 min north-west of Ōsaka by Super Hakuto.*

Although not really worth a special trip, if you're passing through Tottori you should by all means visit the famous *sakyū* (sand dunes) on the coast north of the city. Other attractions, all within about 1 km (½ mi) of Tottori Station, include the ruins of a castle and a few small museums: the Watanabe Bijutsukan (Watanabe Art Museum), the Kenritsu Hakubutsukan (Tottori Prefectural Museum), and the Mingei Bijutsukan (Folk Craft Museum). There's a hot spring only five minutes from the station.

The **sakyū** (砂丘) stretch along the shore for about 16 km (10 mi); some of the crests rise 300 feet or more. Climb to the top of one and watch the sea in the foreground with the green, mist-covered hills behind. *Woman in the Dunes,* Kobo Abe's haunting story about a bug collector who himself becomes trapped in a sandpit, like a bug, is set here.

Tourists and surfers come for the miles of fine beaches and waves in summertime, and parachute-jumpers like to leap from the top of the highest dune, riding the breeze and landing just in front of the ocean far below. First thing in the morning or late in the day you don't have to walk far to escape the crowds if you're seeking solitude. You can also rent a bicycle from the Cycling Terminal at Kodomo-no-kuni, near the entrance to the dunes. Ride east to the Uradome ("oo-ra-*do*-meh") Seashore and follow the roads next to the sand.

To get to the dunes, take Bus 20, 24, 25, or 26 from Gate 3 at the bus terminal in front of the JR station for the 20-minute ride (¥330) north.

The **City Tourist Information Office** (観光案内所; ☎ 0857/26–0756) and the Tourist Information booth at the station (☎ 0857/22–3318), both open 9:30–6:30 daily, can help with lodging or travel questions.

Where to Stay

$$$–$$$$ 🏨 **New Ōtani** (ニューオータニ). This tall red-concrete building across from the JR station and next to the Daimaru department store is the most modern hotel in town. The bright lobby, with white and pink marble, green-and-white-striped chairs, and light-wood paneling, is gorgeous. The guest rooms on higher floors have views over Tottori; be sure to request one on the west side. ⊠ *2–153 Ima-machi, Tottori-shi, Tottori-ken 680-0822* ☎ *0857/23–1111* 🖷 *0857/23–0979* 🛏 *138 rooms* 🍴 *5 restaurants* 🖃 *AE, DC, MC, V.*

$$ 🏨 **Tottori Washington Hotel Plaza** (鳥取ワシントンホテルプラザ). On your right as you exit the station, this tall white hotel offers good value. All of the pastel-color rooms are spacious and look out on the Chūgoku Sanchi-chi (Chūgoku Mountains) and/or the Nihon-kai. ⊠ *102 Higashi Honji-chō, Tottori-shi, Tottori-ken 680-0835* ☎ *0857/27–8111* 🖷 *0857/27–8125* 🛏 *156 rooms* 🍴 *2 restaurants* 🖃 *AE, DC, MC, V.*

WESTERN HONSHŪ A TO Z

To research prices, get advice from other travelers, and book travel arrangements, visit www.fodors.com.

AIRPORTS

Hiroshima Kūkō is the major airport for this region, with many daily flights to Haneda Kūkō in Tōkyō and direct daily flights to Kagoshima, Okinawa, Sendai, and Sapporo. There are connections with many major Asian cities as well. Other airports in Western Honshū—at Izumo, Tottori, and Yonago—have daily flights to Tōkyō. JAS and ANA fly out of Iwami Airport, which serves Hagi, Tsuwano, and Masuda, to Tōkyō and Ōsaka. For airline phone numbers, *see* Air Travel *in* Smart Travel Tips A to Z.

Seven daily flights connect Hiroshima and Tōkyō's Haneda Kūkō, and there are flights to Kagoshima, on Kyūshū, and to Sapporo, on Hokkaidō. There are also many flights to Singapore, Hong Kong, Seoul, and other regional hubs.

BOAT & FERRY TRAVEL

Hiroshima is a ferry hub. Seto Nai-kai Kisen Company runs eight boats daily to Miyajima (¥1,460 one-way, ¥2,800 round-trip). Two important connections are to and from Matsuyama on Shikoku—16 hydrofoil ferries a day take one hour (¥6,000), and 12 regular ferries a day take three hours (¥4,340 first class, ¥2,170 second class); and to and from Beppu on Kyūshū; one daily, ¥8,500, 3 hours.

🚢 Boat & Ferry Information **Seto Nai-kai Kisen Company** ✉ 12–23 Ujinakaigan 1-chōme, Minami-ku, Hiroshima ☎ 082/253–1212 🖷 082/505–0134.

EMERGENCIES

🚑 **Ambulance** ☎ 119. **Police** ☎ 110.

TRAIN TRAVEL

By far the easiest way to travel to Western Honshū and along its southern shore is by Shinkansen from Tōkyō, Kyōto, and Ōsaka. Major Shinkansen stops are Himeji, Okayama, and Hiroshima. It takes approximately 4 hours on the Shinkansen to travel to Hiroshima from Tōkyō; 1 hour, 45 minutes from Ōsaka (times vary depending on which stops trains make). To cover the length of the San-yō coast from Ōsaka to Shimonoseki takes 3 hours, 25 minutes.

JR express trains run along the San-yō and San-in coasts, making a loop beginning and ending in Kyōto. Crossing from one coast to the other in Western Honshū requires traveling fairly slowly through the mountains. Several train lines link the cities on the northern Nihon-kai coast to Okayama, Hiroshima, and Shin-Yamaguchi on the southern.

TRANSPORTATION AROUND WESTERN HONSHŪ

Except for the short crossing to Miyajima from Hiroshima, traveling through San-yō means hopping on and off JR's Shinkansen and local trains on the main railway line that follows the southern shore of Western Honshū between Ōsaka and Shimonoseki. Local buses or streetcars are the best way to get around major cities. If you know a little Japanese, can handle both middle-of-nowhere navigation and hectic urban traffic situations, and are traveling with one or more other people (the highway tolls and gas equal the train fare for one), you might consider renting a car and exploring Western Honshū at your own pace.

A few train routes cross the mountains to cities on either coast. The major connecting ones are between Himeji or Okayama and Tottori, and between Shin-Yamaguchi and Tsuwano, Hagi, or Matsue.

JR and Bōchō bus lines also run over the mountains. It's important to call ahead and reserve seats for these buses. Local tourist information offices will help reserve tickets for non-Japanese speakers.

VISITOR INFORMATION

Most major towns or sightseeing destinations have tourist information centers that offer free maps and brochures. They will also help you secure accommodations.

The Japan Travel Bureau (JTB) has offices at every JR station in each of the major cities and can assist with local tours, hotel reservations, and ticketing. Except for JTB's Hiroshima office, you should not assume that any English will be spoken beyond the essentials.

The Japan Travel Phone, a nationwide service for English-language assistance and travel information, is available seven days a week from 9 to 5. Dial toll-free from outside Tōkyō or Kyōto. When using a gray, blue, or green public phone, insert a ¥10 coin or telephone card before dialing, your cost will be refunded when you hang up.

🚪 Tourist Information **Hagi City Information Office** ☎ 0838/25-3138. **Hagi City Tourist Association** ☎ 0838/25-1750 or 0838/25-3145. **Hiroshima City Tourist Office** ☎ 082/247-6738. **Hiroshima Prefectural Tourist Office** ☎ 082/228-9907. **Hiroshima Tourist Information Office** ☎ 082/249-9329. **Japan Travel Bureau Hiroshima** ☎ 082/261-4131. **Japan Travel Phone** ☎ 0120/44-4800 or 0088/22-4800. **Matsue Tourism Association** ☎ 0852/27-5843. **Matsue Tourist Information Office** ☎ 0852/27-4034. **Miyajima Tourist Association** ☎ 0829/44-2011. **Okayama Prefectural Tourist Office** ☎ 086/224-2111. **Okayama Tourist Association** ☎ 086/256-2000. **Okayama Tourist Information Office** ☎ 086/222-2912.

SHIKOKU 四国

10

By Nigel Fisher
& Simon
Richmond

Updated by
Paul Davidson

THE SMALLEST OF JAPAN'S FOUR MAIN ISLANDS, Shikoku rests neatly beneath western Honshū, a comfortable distance across the famed Seto Nai-kai (Inland Sea). Rugged east–west mountain ranges halve Shikoku, where you will be treated more as a welcome foreign emissary than as an income-bearing tourist.

Until the 21st century, Japanese and international vacationers left Shikoku off their itineraries, perhaps because the ferry ride across the Seto Nai-kai discouraged most people. Since 10 bridges were completed in 1999, however, the Shimanami Kaidō (Shimanami Sea Road) leapfrogs across seven islands and carries the Nishi-seto Expressway from Onomichi, in Hiroshima Prefecture, to Imabari, on Shikoku's northwest coast. The Akashi Kaikyō Ōhashi—the longest suspension bridge in the world (it's 3,910 meters or 2.43 miles long)—joins Shikoku to Honshū via Awaji-shima, an island to the west of Tokushima. At night the lights of the bridge, which change color according to the season, resemble a necklace strung across the water, thus the nickname "Pearl Bridge." Shikoku is also linked to Honshū via the Seto Ōhashi, a 12-km-long (7½-mi-long) series of six bridge spans that connect the islands in great arching leaps. Driving across it you can get off on the various small islands with lookout areas and souvenir shops.

Otherwise, the train from Okayama will whisk you across the Seto Nai-kai in 15 minutes, before turning east to Takamatsu and Tokushima, west to Matsuyama, or south to Kōchi. These four cities are the capitals of the four prefectures—Kagawa, Tokushima, Kōchi, and Ehime—which explains the island's name: *shi* (four) *koku* (countries).

The rugged heart of Shikoku consists of mountain ranges that run from east to west, dividing the island in two. The northern half, which faces the Seto Nai-kai, has a dry climate, with only modest autumn rains during typhoon season. The southern half, which faces the Pacific, is more likely to have ocean storms sweep in, bringing rain throughout the year. With its shores washed by the warm waters of the Kuroshio (Black Current), it has a warmer climate and especially mild winters. The mountain ranges of the interior are formidable, achieving heights up to 6,400 feet, and are cut by wondrous gorges and valleys. In these valleys are small farming villages that have remained almost unchanged since the Edo period (1603–1868).

Although Shikoku has been part of Japan's political and cultural development since the Heian period (794–1192), the island maintains a certain independence from mainstream Japan. Some factories litter the northern coast, but to a great extent Shikoku has been spared the ugliness of Japan's industrialization. The island is still considered by many Japanese as a rural backwater where pilgrims follow the route of the 88 sacred temples.

The Buddhist saint Kōbō Daishi was born on Shikoku in 774, and it was he who founded the Shingon sect of Buddhism that became popular in the shōgun eras. (During the Tokugawa shogunate, travel was restricted, except for pilgrimages.) Pilgrims visit the 88 temples to honor the priest, and by doing so, they can be released from having to go through the cycle of rebirth. Many Japanese wait until they retire to make this pilgrimage, in part because the time is right and in part because it takes two months on foot—the traditional way to visit all the temples. Most of today's more numerous pilgrims scoot around by bus in 13 days.

Towns large and small all over Shikoku have constructed tourist attractions, such as Uzu-no-michi in Naruto, and American-style outlet malls in order to attract busloads from other parts of Japan. In spite of increased development, however, the island continues to be known as a place of abundant natural beauty and traditional ways.

Exploring Shikoku

With more than just a couple of days, you can take in the island's mountainous interior, the sun-kissed city of Kōchi with its castle and rugged coastline, and Uwajima, another castle town with interesting shrines. Two weeks would easily allow you to add Shikoku's other major sights, including Tokushima as a base from which you can search out traditional handicrafts, and a trip out to Shōdo-shima, the second-largest island in the Seto Nai-kai.

Numbers in the text correspond to numbers in the margin and on the Shikoku map.

About the Restaurants

The delight of Shikoku is the number of small Japanese restaurants that serve the freshest fish, either caught in the Seto Nai-kai or in the Pacific. You will know that the seafood is fresh because it's often killed in front of you—or because it arrives still wriggling on the plate. Each of Shikoku's main cities has lively entertainment districts where you will have no problem finding a range of other cuisines, if Japanese food does not appeal. Outside the main cities, make sure you eat earlier in the evening: few places remain open after 8:30.

About the Hotels

Accommodations on Shikoku range from pensions and *minshuku* (rooms for rent in private homes) to large, modern resort hotels that have little character but all the facilities of an international hotel. Unless otherwise noted, all hotel rooms have private baths, phones, and air-conditioning. Large city and resort hotels serve Western and Japanese food. During summer and major Japanese holiday periods, such as Golden Week in late spring, reservations are essential.

For a short course on accommodations in Japan, *see* Lodging *in* Smart Travel Tips A to Z.

WHAT IT COSTS In yen				
$$$$	**$$$**	**$$**	**$**	**¢**
RESTAURANTS over 3,000	2,000–3,000	1,000–2,000	800–1,000	under 800
HOTELS over 22,000	18,000–22,000	12,000–18,000	8,000–12,000	under 8,000

Restaurant prices are per person for a main course at dinner. Hotel prices are for a double room with private bath, excluding service and tax.

If you have
2 days

Spend a day in 🖼 **Takamatsu** ❶ ⌐ strolling around Ritsurin Kōen and then go on to **Kotohira** ❹ and its much-revered Kotohira-gū (Kotohira Shrine). From here the obvious choice is to travel west along the northern coast to 🖼 **Matsuyama** ❿ for its castle and justly famous Dōgo Onsen. From Matsuyama you can take a hydrofoil to Hiroshima. Alternatives include a visit to **Yashima** ❷ for Shikoku Mura, a collection of traditional Edo-period houses, and the highland plateau, which provides a stunning view of the Seto Nai-kai; a trip out to Naruto Kaikyō to see the whirlpools; or a trip to 🖼 **Tokushima** ❺ to take part in making traditional crafts.

10

If you have
4 days

In addition, or as an alternative, to the sights around 🖼 **Takamatsu** ❶ ⌐, take a day trip to **Shōdo-shima** ❸, a rural island in the Seto Nai-kai. A more adventurous option is to head for the mountainous interior after checking out **Kotohira** ❹ and stop off at **Ōboke Koboke** ❻, where you can inspect the gorge from a boat. If you start off early enough, you should be able to make 🖼 **Kōchi** ❼ for the night. Spend the third day at Kōchi's castle and nearby Katsura-hama (Katsura Beach) before heading across to 🖼 **Matsuyama** ❿.

If you have
7 days

You can see all of Shikoku's major sights in a week by spending two nights in 🖼 **Takamatsu** ❶ ⌐; a night each in 🖼 **Kōchi** ❼ and 🖼 **Uwajima** ❾, for its castle and fertility shrine; and the final two nights in 🖼 **Matsuyama** ❿. As an alternative, you could use Matsuyama as a base for forays out to Uwajima and the islands along the **Shimanami Kaidō** ⓫. Or you could strike out from Kōchi for either of the rugged capes, **Ashizuri-misaki** ❽ or Muroto.

Timing

In winter only the snowbound valleys and hills of the interior are difficult to negotiate. In February crimson camellias bloom along the south coast of the island, particularly at Ashizuri-misaki. April is the only month in which Kabuki plays are performed in Kotohira, at Kompira Ō-Shibai, the oldest such theater in Japan. June is the time to head for Ritsurin Kōen to see its ponds filled with purple and white irises, although at any time of the year there are flashes of color in the garden. In summer head for the cool of the mountains or stay by the coast and its sea breezes. Dance festivals run in late summer, the Awa Odori from August 12 to 15. The bullfights in Uwajima are held on January 2, the third Sunday in March, the second Sunday in April, July 24, August 14, and the third Sunday in November. Plan to be in Kōchi on a Sunday for antiques and farm produce.

TAKAMATSU & EASTERN SHIKOKU

Takamatsu   高松

⌐ ❶ *1 hr from Okayama by JR.*

Sprawling, prosperous Takamatsu is the first stop for most people visiting Shikoku. Come here to stroll in the gardens of Ritsurin Kōen—the city's major landmark after wholesale destruction of Takamatsu during World War II—and to admire the Seto Nai-kai panorama from Yashima plateau. Many ferries still call at Takamatsu from Honshū—and the central port area has been redeveloped—but because of the Seto Ōhashi, you are most likely to come by train, bus, or car.

The **Takamatsu Information Office** (高松インフォメーションプラザ, ☎ 087/ 851–2009) is just outside the JR station. The maps and brochures are limited to Kagawa Prefecture, of which Takamatsu is the capital. If you need information on the entire island, make sure that you visit the Tourist Information Center in Tōkyō or Kyōto before you set out for Shikoku. A bus tour (Japanese-speaking guide only) departs at 8:45 AM from the Takamatsu-Chikkō Bus Station (near the JR station) and covers Ritsurin Kōen, Kotohira, and other sights. The tour takes about 8 hours, 45 minutes.

★ Once the summer retreat of the Matsudaira clan, **Ritsurin Kōen** (Ritsurin Park, 栗林公園) is the number one attraction in Takamatsu. The gardens—for there are actually two: the northern Hokutei and the southern Nantei—were completed in the late 17th century after 100 years of careful planning, landscaping, and cultivation. The Hokutei is more modern and has wide expanses of lawns, in addition to an exhibition hall that displays and sells local products from Kagawa Prefecture, including wood carvings, masks, kites, and umbrellas.

Ritsurin's real gem is the Nantei section of the park, which follows a classical Japanese design. The southern garden's six ponds and 13 scenic mounds are arranged to frame a new view or angle to hold your attention at virtually every step on the intersecting paths. You cannot hurry through: each rock, each tree shape, each pond rippling with multicolor carp—and in turn the reflections of the water and the shadows of the trees—beckons. The teahouse, Kikugetsutei, looks as if it's floating on water. Here you can sip *sencha* (green tea; ¥510) and muse on the serene harmony of the occasion, or experience *matcha* (powdered tea-ceremony green tea; ¥710) just as the lords of Matsudaira did in previous centuries. Combination tickets for the gardens and tea are ¥880 (sencha) and ¥1,080 (matcha). The teahouse is open from 9 to 4.

The **Sanuki Folk Art Museum** (Sanuki Mingeikan), next to the park office, is also worth a visit for its interesting displays of local handicraft and folk crafts. It's open Thursday through Tuesday from 8:45 to 4:30 and Wednesday until 4; admission is free.

To get to Ritsurin Kōen, which is at the far end of Chūō-dōri, take a 10-minute ride (¥220) on any bus that leaves from in front of the Grand Hotel, stop No. 2. (The bus makes a short detour from the main avenue to include a bus depot on its route. Don't disembark from the bus until it rejoins the main avenue—Chūō-dōri—and travels two more stops.) Or take the JR train toward Tokushima and disembark five minutes later at the second stop, Ritsurin Kōen Kita Guchi. ☎ 087/833-7411 ⬚ ¥400 ☼ June–Aug., daily 7–sunset; Sept.–May, daily 7–5.

Tamamo-jō (玉藻城（高松城）), built in 1588, was once the home of the Matsudaira clan, which ruled Takamatsu during the Edo period. All that is

10

Local Traditions

Geographical isolation has allowed Shikoku to preserve more of its traditional arts and culture than other parts of Japan have. You can learn about pottery and indigo dyeing near Matsuyama and Tokushima and even try your hand at *washi* (papermaking) close to Kōchi and Tokushima. The performing arts are represented by *ningyō joruri* puppet shows in Tokushima, and Kabuki at Uchiko and Kotohira, which has the oldest Kabuki stage in Japan. In country towns like Kotohira, Uwajima, and Uchiko, narrow streets and well-preserved old wooden houses are a delight. And there are late-summer dance festivals in Kōchi, Naruto, Takamatsu, and the most famous of all—perhaps in all of Japan—Tokushima's Awa Odori.

Sports & the Outdoors

The dramatic interior of Shikoku, especially around Ōboke-kyōkoku and Iya-dani (Iya Valley), is great for hiking and cycling. On the southern coast of the island, the rocky capes, Ashizuri and Muroto, lapped by the unimpeded Pacific Ocean, are favored by Japan's surfing fraternity. Takamatsu, with its excellent Ritsurin Kōen, one of the best traditional gardens in Japan, and Matsuyama, with Dogo Onsen—a 2,000-year-old hot-spring resort—are particularly worth visiting.

---

left of the castle in Tamamo Kōen are a few turrets and the inner section of its three-ring moat, but the surrounding park, with the Seto Nai-kai in the background, makes it a pleasant place to relax while waiting for a train or ferry. The park's entrance is beside the Chikkō terminus for the Kotoden tram network at the top of Chūō-dōri, where the JR station and main ferry pier are located. ☎ 087/851–1521 🖀 ¥200 ⊗ *West Gate daily 9–sunset, East Gate daily 9–6.*

The department stores, shops, and restaurants of the city's **covered shopping arcades** (アーケード) are 300 yards down Chūō-dōri from the JR station on the left-hand side. The east–west Hyōgo-machi arcade is intersected by the Marugama-machi arcade running north–south (parallel to Chūō-dōri). The small streets off the arcades are crowded with bars, cabarets, and smaller restaurants.

The studio of the late Japanese-American sculptor Isamu Noguchi (1904–88) has been converted into **Isamu Noguchi Garden Museum** (Isamu Noguchi Teien Hakubutsukan, イサム・ノグチ庭園美術館), which is in Mure, a 20-minute drive from Takamatsu. The museum stores about 150 complete and incomplete works and has an exquisite Japanese garden carved by the master out of a hill. Noguchi was originally attracted to the area by the local high-quality granite and other stone materials he found there. Reservations are required for viewing the collection. Take a JR train to Yashima Station (15 minutes). From there, it's a seven-minute taxi ride to the museum. ⊠ 3–5–19 Mure, Mure-chō ☎ 087/870–1500 🖷 087/845–0505 🖀 ¥2,100 ⊗ *Tues., Thurs., and Sat. at 10, 1, and 3 by appointment.*

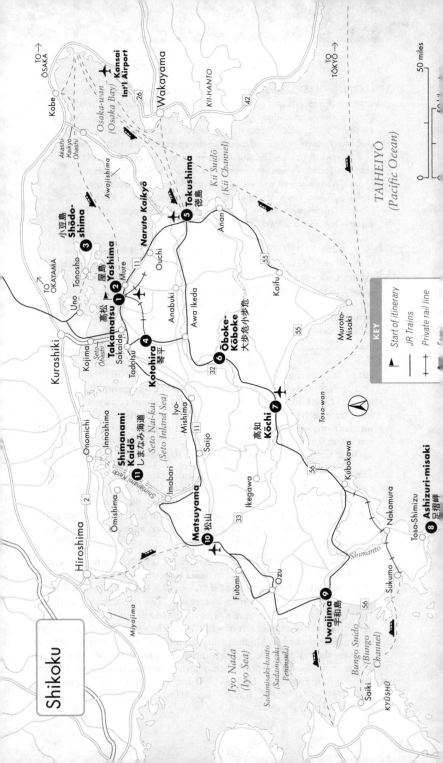

Shikoku

TO ŌSAKA →

Kobe

TO ŌSAKA →

Kansai Int'l Airport

26

Wakayama

KII-HANTŌ

42

Osaka-wan (Osaka Bay)

Akashi Kaikyō Ōhashi

Awajishima

Kii Suidō (Kii Channel)

TAIHEIYŌ (Pacific Ocean)

50 miles

50 km

小豆島 Shōdo-shima

③

Naruto Kaikyō

Tokushima 徳島

⑤

OKAYAMA

Tonosho

屋島 Yashima

Mure

Ouchi

Anan

Uno

高松 Takamatsu

① ②

11

Anabuki

Awa Ikeda

Kaifu

55

Kurashiki

Kojima

Seto-Ōhashi

Sakaide

Tadotsu

琴平 Kotohira

④

32

大歩危小歩危 Ōboke-Kōboke

⑥

55

Muroto-Misaki

Iyo-Mishima

Shimanami Kaidō しまなみ海道

⑪

Seto Nai-kai (Seto Inland Sea)

11

高知 Kōchi

⑦

Tosa-wan

Hiroshima

Ōnomichi

Innoshima

Saijo

KEY

△ Start of itinerary

— JR Trains

+++ Private rail line

2

Ōmishima

33

Ikegawa

Kubokawa

56

Miyajima

Imabari

松山 Matsuyama

⑩

Tosa-Shimizu

Nakamura

足摺岬 Ashizuri-misaki

⑧

Futami

Ōzu

Shimanto

Sukumo

56

Iyo Nada (Iyo Sea)

宇和島 Uwajima

⑨

56

Sadamisaki-hantō (Sadamisaki Peninsula)

Saiki

Bungo Suidō (Bungo Channel)

KYŪSHŪ

TO TŌKYŌ →

Where to Stay & Eat

$$$ ✕ **Tenyasu** (天安). This charming restaurant specializing in tempura has been in business for more than 50 years. From the outside the restaurant looks like a traditional Japanese house; inside there's seating at a long, circular counter and at low tables on a tatami floor. The second floor has private rooms for bigger parties. You can choose from several set menus of shrimp, fresh local fish, or vegetable tempura, or let the chef select for you. For something different, try the *tencha,* a bowl of rice topped with shrimp tempura and soaked in green tea. ⊠ *2–5 Hyakken-chō* ☎ *087/821–7634* ▭ *AE, DC, MC, V.*

$$–$$$ ✕ **Tenkatsu** (天勝). This classy restaurant serves all manner of fish dishes, from succulent sushi to steaming *nabe* (one-pot) stews, at the far west end of the Hyōgo-machi shopping arcade. Elegant kimono-clad waitresses pad silently between tatami rooms and a jet-black counter bar that surrounds a central sunken pool where the fish swim until their number is up. ⊠ *Nishizumi Hiroba, Hyōgo-machi* ☎ *087/821–5380* ▭ *AE, DC, MC, V.*

$$–$$$ ✕ **Teuchi-soba Sugitei** (手打ちそば杉亭). Homemade soba noodles are the specialty at this wood and tatami restaurant. The chef makes all of the noodles himself each day and serves seasonal variations of soba dishes. Try to make it for lunch, because the restaurant stays open no later than 7 PM and it closes as soon as the chef runs out of noodles. The restaurant is about a three-minute walk from Busshōzan Station on the Kototden tram line. ⊠ *1867–5 Tahi Kamichō* ☎ *087/888–5785* ▭ *No credit cards.*

¢–$ ✕ **Ikkaku** (一鶴). This ultramodern restaurant off the Marugmae-machi shopping street might not look like much from the outside, but once you sit down in its stylish, brightly lit interior, the reason for the lines of people waiting for a table becomes clear. The food—spicy barbecued chicken accompanied by raw cabbage leaves and served on shiny platters—is delicious. Side dishes are available, and it would be an oversight not to have a glass of the restaurant's own brewed beer. You can find Ikkaku next to the Starbucks. ⊠ *Fesuta II, 5F Kajiya-chō* ☎ *087/823–3711* ▭ *No credit cards.*

$$$–$$$$ ✕▭ **Kiyomi Lodge** (喜代美山荘). Built in 1951 on a hillside overlooking Takamatsu City, this hotel has one of the best restaurants in town as well as a lovely hot spring. All of the rooms are Japanese-style and include breakfast and an elegant dinner. **Hanajukai Onsen** (花樹海温泉) on the roof offers some spectacular views of the both the city and Seto Naikai, as well as Yashima in the distance. ⊠ *3–5–10 Nishitakara-chō, Takamatsu, Kagawa-ken 760-004* ☎ *087/861–5580* 🖷 *087/834–9912* ⟿ *48 Japanese-style rooms* ⟐ *Restaurant, cable TV, hot spring* ▭ *AE, DC, MC, V* ❢❢ MAP.

★ $ ▭ **Hotel Kawaroku/Her-Stage** (川六ホテル／エルステージ). The hotel was built in 1877, destroyed during World War II, and rebuilt on the same spot in the center of town. A more recent annex, with the strange name "Her-Stage," is a business hotel with all Western-style rooms. The hotel's location and price make it one of the best values in Takamatsu. ⊠ *1–2 Hyakken-chō, Takamatsu, Kagawa-ken 760-8691* ☎ *087/ 821–5666* 🖷 *0878/21–7301* ⊕ *www.kawaroku.co.jp* ⟿ *Kawaroku, 21*

Western-style rooms, 49 Japanese-style rooms; Her-Stage, 140 Western style rooms ዼ Restaurant, cable TV, Japanese baths ▱ AE, V.

Yashima   屋島

❷ *20 min by JR or Kotoden tram from Takamatsu.*

Once an island, Yashima is now connected to Shikoku by a narrow strip of land. Its tabletop plateau, standing nearly 1,000 feet above Seto Nai-kai, is an easy half-day trip from Takamatsu. This was the battle site where the Minamoto clan finally defeated the Taira family in 1185, allowing Yoritomo Minamoto to establish Japan's first shogunate in Kamakura, southwest of what is now Tōkyō.

★ Easily the most interesting sight in the area, **Shikoku Mura** (四国村) is an open-air village museum. Similar to Hida Village near Takayama in the Japan Alps, Shikoku Mura has 21 houses that have been relocated from around Shikoku to represent what rural life was like during the Edo period and earlier, 200–300 years ago. The village may be artificial, but in this age, in which ferroconcrete has replaced so much of old Japan, Shikoku Mura provides an opportunity to see traditional thatch-roof farmhouses, a papermaking workshop, a ceremonial teahouse, a rural Kabuki stage, and other buildings used in earlier times. ☎ 087/843–311 ⊠ ¥800 ⊙ Apr.–Oct., daily 8:30–5; Nov.–Mar., daily 8:30–4:30.

Ascend to the top of Yashima for the expansive vista from the **plateau** over the Seto Nai-kai and Shōdo-shima. A five-minute walk west of Shikoku Mura's entrance is a cable car that takes five minutes to climb to the top of the plateau; it costs ¥700 one-way, ¥1,300 round-trip and runs from 8:35 to 5:35.

Near the upper terminus for the cable car on Yashima Plateau, **Yashima-ji** (屋島寺), originally constructed in 754, is the 84th of the 88 temples in the sacred pilgrimage. The temple's museum contains some interesting screens and pottery and a mixed bag of relics of the battle between the Minamoto and Taira clans. The shrine is free and can be seen at any time. ☎ 087/841–9418 ⊠ Museum ¥500 ⊙ Museum daily 9–4:30.

Getting Around

Local JR trains from Takamatsu Station run at least every hour to Yashima Station, from which it is a 10-minute walk north to Shikoku Mura. You can also take the Kotoden tram from the Chikko terminal (across from the JR station). These run 10 times a day; the tourist office can supply a schedule. Kotoden Yashima Station is only a couple minutes' walk from both Shikoku Mura (to the east) and the Yashima cable car station (directly north).

Shōdo-shima   小豆島

★ ❸ *35 min north of Takamatsu by hydrofoil, 1 hr by ferry.*

For something of a rural escape, take a ferry out to the principle town of Tonoshō on Shōdo-shima, the second-largest island in the Seto Nai-kai. Shōdo's craggy mountains are spectacular, and its seacoasts equal so for the contrast of ruggedness with sandy beaches. The island is also the site of quarries from which the stone used to build the original Ōsaka-jō was cut.

The **Port of Tonoshō Visitor Center** (Shodo-shima bus Company, 小豆島バス; ☎ 0879/62–1205), near the ferry terminal, can provide bus information and maps.

Inland, the 6-km by 4-km (3½-mi by 2½-mi) **Kankakei-kyōkoku** (寒霞渓峡谷) is hemmed in by a wall of mountainous peaks with weather-eroded rocks. The thick maple and pine forest lining the gorge is splashed with color in autumn; in spring the profusion of azaleas makes for an equally colorful spectacle. Walks among the rocks and along the stream are excellent. If you'd rather not hike, you can reach the summit on an aerial tramway (¥700 one-way, ¥1,250 round-trip) that travels frighteningly close to the cliffs' walls. Kankakei is an hour by bus from Tonoshō, including a change at Chōshikei O-saru no Kuni (¥610).

The water-carved walls of **Chōshikei-kyōkoku** (Chōshikei Gorge, 銚子渓峡谷), 25 minutes by bus from Tonoshō, extend along the upper stream of the Dempo-gawa (Dempo River). The gorge is home to 700 wild monkeys at **Chōshikei Monkey Land** (Chōshikei O-saru no Kuni, 銚子渓お猿の国; ⊠ Kagawa-ken, Tonoshō-chō ☎ 0879/62–0768), where you can pet and feed the monkeys for ¥370. The gorge and animal park, which is open daily 8–5, are a 40-minute bus ride from Tonoshō Port.

You can rent motorized bicycles for ¥3,000 a day, including insurance, from **Ryobi Rent-a-Bike** (☎ 0879/62–6578) near Tonoshō's pier, open daily 8:30–5.

Where to Stay & Eat

$$ ✕ **Yosakoi** (よさこい). This restaurant close to Tonoshō Port serves thin somen noodles with hot or cold dipping sauce, depending on the season. Sashimi, tempura, and other Japanese delicacies are also on the menu. Yosakoi caters to group tours, so lunchtime may be noisy. ⊠ *228–14 Tonoshō-kō-mae, Tonoshō-chō* ☎ *0879/62–1666* ▭ *No credit cards.*

$ ▦ **Kokumin Shukusha Shōdoshima** (国民宿舎小豆島). On the bus route west to Kami-no-ura, this inn sits on a plateau with a view of the Seto Nai-kai and Shikoku's distant mountains. The tatami rooms are large and decorated in brown and beige. The Western-style rooms, while not as spacious, all have separate sitting areas. A cafeteria serves food cooked with locally produced olive oil. Best of all is the hot spring, which overlooks the channel islands. ⊠ *1500–4 Ikeda, Ikeda-chō, Shōdo-gun 761–4432* ☎ *0879/75–1115* 🖷 *0879/75–1116* ➦ *20 Japanese-style rooms, 9 Western-style rooms* ⚫ *Cafeteria, hot spring* ▭ *MC, V* ⊡ *MAP.*

$$$$ ▦ **Mari** (真里). Built in the 1930s and renovated in 2002, Mari is an elegant, family-run lodge near the Sakade Wan (Sakade Bay), on the south side of the island. Each room is decorated in its own unique way, with traditional Japanese elements such as tatami floors and shōji doors mixed with modern lighting and high ceilings. The rooms are named after characters in Japanese script, and each has its own traditional Japanese bath. To get here from Tonoshō, take the Shōdoshima bus in the direction of Sakate-kō. It's a 30 minute ride to Mari. ⊠ *Nai-kaichō,*

Shōyūzō-dōri, Shōdogun 761–4421 ☎ *0879/82–0086* 🖷 *0879/82–643.*
🖙 *7 Japanese-style rooms* ♿ ▭ *AE, DC, MC, V.*

Getting Around

To get to Tonoshō, the island's largest port and town, from Takamats◄
Pier, there are two options: a ferry (¥510) and a hydrofoil (¥1,000). There'
also a hydrofoil to Shōdo-shima (40 minutes; ¥1,600) from Okayam◄
Port (take Bus 12 from JR Okayama Station to Okayama Port) and ◄
regular ferry from Himeji Port (1 hour, 40 minutes; ¥1,300).

Sightseeing buses depart from Tonoshō to all island sights; public buse
cover the island efficiently and thoroughly.

Kotohira 琴平

❹ *55 min by JR or Kotoden tram from Takamatsu.*

★ Visit Kotohira to climb the 785 steps to its shrine **Kotohira-g◄**
(琴平宮、金毘羅宮). Fondly known as Kompira-san, the shrine may no
be quite as important as the Grand Shrines at Ise or Izumo Taisha nea
Matsue, but it's one of Japan's oldest and most stately. It's also one o
the most popular: 4 million pilgrims pay their respects each year.

Founded in the 11th century and built on the slopes of Zōzu-zan, Koto◄
hira-gū is dedicated to Omono-nushi-no-Mikoto (also called Kompira)
the guardian god of the sea and patron of seafarers. Traditionally, fish
ermen and sailors would visit the shrine and solicit divine assurance fo◄
a safe sea passage. However, their monopoly on seeking the aid of Kom◄
pira has ended, as his role has expanded to include all travelers, includ◄
ing tourists.

To reach the main gate of the shrine, you have to mount 365 granit◄
steps, which are flanked with souvenir stands. Beyond the main gate
the souvenir stands are replaced by stone lanterns, and the climb be
comes a solemn, spiritual exercise. Just before the second torii is the shrine'
Relic Museum (hōmotsu-kan), with a rather dry display of sculpture
scrolls, and, despite their potentially interesting Buddhist origins, N◄
masks. It's open daily 9–4, and the entrance fee is ¥200.

The next important building, on your right, is the 1659 **Sho-in** (formerl◄
a reception hall), its interior covered in delicate screen paintings by th
famous 18th-century landscape artist Ōkyo Maruyama (1733–95). Th◄
Sho-in is open daily 9–4, and the entrance fee is ¥200.

Onward and forever upward, the intricate carvings of animals grac◄
the facade of **Asahi-no-Yashiro** (formerly the main shrine; the name mean
that it's the first building to receive light when the sun comes up in th
morning). At the next landing you'll finally be at the main shrine, ◄
complex of buildings that was rebuilt 100 years ago. Aside from th◄
sense of accomplishment in making the climb, the views over Takamats◄
and the Seto Nai-kai to the north and the mountain ranges of Shikok◄
to the south justify the effort, even more, perhaps, than a visit to th
shrine itself.

Allow a total of 1½ hours from the time you start your ascent up the granite stairs until you return. Just as the feudal lords once did, you may hire a palanquin to porter you up and down; the fee is ¥5,000 up, ¥3,000 down, ¥6,500 round-trip. Riding in a palanquin certainly saves the calf muscles, but the motion and narrow confines are not exactly comfortable.

Kanamaru-za (金丸座)—the oldest Kabuki theater in Japan—hosts performances only in April, but throughout the year the theater is open for viewing. Because it was built in 1835, one of the interesting aspects is how the theater managed its special effects without electricity. Eight men in harness, for example, rotate the stage. Within the revolving stage are two trap lifts. The larger one is used for quick changes in stage props, the smaller one for lifting actors up to floor level. Equally fascinating are the sets of sliding *shōji* (screens) used to adjust the amount of daylight filtering onto the stage. The theater is exceptionally large and was moved from the overcrowded center of Kotohira to Kotohira Kōen and restored in 1975. It's a 10-minute walk from Kotohira Station, near the first flight of steps leading to Kotohira-gū. ☎ 0877/73–3846 ⊠ ¥300 ⊙ *Daily 9–5.*

Where to Stay & Eat

¢ ✕ **Tanuki-ya** (狸屋). This noodle shop on the pilgrim's path to Kotohira Shrine offers several kinds of udon noodles, each served with different toppings, such as fried mushrooms, sliced beef, and *sansai* ("edible mountain plants"). You'll find both Western-style seating and low-lying Japanese tables on tatami mats. If you're traveling in a group, or if you're just really, really hungry, try the *kazoku udon* (family udon), a mass of noodles served in a tub for ¥2,200. ⊠ *700–8 Kotohira-chō* ☎ *0877/73–2409* ⊙ *Daily 9–5* ☰ *No credit cards.*

$$ ☒ **Toramaru Ryokan** (虎丸旅館). Standing on the 92nd step of Kotohira-gū, this inn is a convenient place to stay the night for visitors to the shrine. The tatami-floor rooms are spacious and elegantly decorated with ink paintings and ikebana flowers. Each room has a private bath, and the hotel also has a large marble hot bath (free for guests; ¥900 nonguests). You can order lavish in-room meals that usually include seafood from the Seto Nai-kai. ⊠ *1017 Kotohira-chō, 766-0001* ☎ *0877/75–2161* ↪ *16 Japanese-style rooms* ♨ *Japanese baths* ☰ *AE, DC, MC, V.*

Getting Around

From JR Kotohira Station it's an eight-minute walk to the steps of Kotohira-gū. There's a cloakroom to the left of the JR station (¥200), which is open daily 6:30 AM–9 PM. Even if you're only visiting for the day, travel lightly—small packs become very heavy while you're mounting the 785 stairs to the shrine. The Kotoden tram runs every half hour between Kawara-machi Station in Takamatsu and Kotoden Station in Kotohira.

From Kotohira Station, trains continue south to Kōchi, the principal city of Shikoku's south coast. If you aren't heading south to the coast, you can return to the north coast of Shikoku and travel west to Matsuyama, or change at Awa Ikeda for the branch line east to Tokushima.

Tokushima 徳島

❺ *1 hr, 10 min by JR from Takamatsu and from Awa Ikeda.*

If you decide to visit Tokushima, count yourself among the few foreigners who do. Between August 12 and 15 you can witness one of the liveliest, most humor-filled festivals in Japan, Awa Odori. At other times of the year, come to Tokushima for the opportunity to watch and participate in local traditional Japanese crafts, such as papermaking, indigo dyeing, and pot making. Although the city is quite modern, its small scale and well-designed riverside walkways make it a pleasant place to spend a day.

For brochures and other information in English, **Tokushima Prefecture International Exchange Association** (TOPIA ⊠ Clement Plaza, 6th fl. ☎ 088/656–3303) is just outside Tokushima Station and is open daily 10–6.

★ The **Awa Odori** (阿波おどり) dance festival is an occasion for the Japanese to relax. Prizes are even given to the "Biggest Fool" in the parades, and foreigners are welcome to compete for these awards. Make sure you reserve accommodations well in advance, since more than a million people pack the city during the four-day event.

At **ASTY Tokushima** (アスティとくしま), a state-of-the-art tourist facility, the **Tokushima Taikenkan** has a 360-degree cinema in which you can find yourself at the center of the Awa Odori festival. After the film you can learn the dance routines from immaculately dressed women. Simulated bus, bike, and windsurfing rides take you on a virtual tour through the prefecture. The *ningyō jōruri* (*"neen*-gyo jo-*roo*-ree," puppet) section has displays and daily shows. Also inside ASTY there's a large shopping area where you can make *washi* (handmade Japanese paper), practice indigo dyeing, and watch many other local crafts being made, including ningyō joruri. A conference hall and restaurants are on-site. ASTY Tokushima is a 15-minute walk from Tokushima Station. 🎫 ¥910 ⊙ *Daily 9–4:30.*

Tokushima Chūō Kōen (徳島中央公園) is a pretty park on the site where the first lord of Tokushima, Hachisuka Iemasa, built his fortress in 1586 (his family lived in it for the next 280 years). In 1896 the castle was destroyed; all that remains are a few stone walls, moats, and a beautiful formal garden that has been designated a National Scenic Spot. The **Tokushima Castle Museum** (Tokushima-jō Hakubutsukan), built in 1992, is not out of place amid these refined surroundings. Displays relate to the Hachisuka clan and give a good idea of what the castle looked like. The park is five minutes east of the JR station on foot. ☎ 088/621–5295 🎫 *Museum ¥200* ⊙ *Museum Tues.–Sun. 9:30–4:30.*

At each ebb and flow of the tide in the **Naruto Kaikyō** (Naruto Straits, 鳴門海峡), the currents rush through this narrow passage to form hundreds of foaming whirlpools of various sizes—some giant. One hour on either side of the tidal change, the Awa-no-Naruto whirlpools are at their fiercest, below the beginning of the long Naruto Ōhashi (Naruto Suspension Bridge), which crosses the straits to Awaji-shima. To get here, take yellow Bus 1 from JR Tokushima Station Plaza to Seto Nai-kai Koku-ritsu Kōen (Seto Inland Sea National Park), of which the Naruto whirlpools are a part.

You can see the Awa-no-Naruto whirlpools from **Uzu-no-michi** (渦の道), a walkway recently constructed along the girders of Naruto Ōhashi. Panes of glass in the floor of the Observation Room permit a pulse-quickening look at the whirlpools 149 feet below. From the station it's a 15-minute walk to the bridge; the bus fare is ¥690. ☎ 088/683–6262 ⊠ ¥500 ⊙ Tues.–Sun. 9:30–5:30.

For a close encounter with the swirling waters of Naruto Kaikyō, hop aboard a sightseeing boat operated by **Naruto Kankō-Kisen** (鳴門観光汽船; ☎ 088/687–0101). The 40-minute cruise costs ¥1,530 and the dock is a five-minute walk downhill from the Seto Inland Sea National Park.

When the Japanese captured the German settlements in Qingdao, China, during World War I, a thousand POWs were brought to Naruto and kept here from 1917 to 1920, when they were sent back to Germany. Colonel Matsue, the camp director during these years, operated a highly humane administration that allowed soldiers to interact with townspeople and to engage in athletic, creative, and intellectual pursuits. In the spirit of international friendship, the **Naruto German House** (Naruto Doitsu-kan, 鳴門市ドイツ館) was built on the site of the POW camp. Here you can see photos and other memorabilia, as well as dioramas depicting the soldiers' daily lives. The museum is a 30-minute bus ride from the Naruto JR Station. You can also take a JR train on the Takamatsu-Tokushima line and get off at Bando Station. ⊠ 55–2 Higashi-yamada, Ōasa-chō, Naruto-shi ☎ 088/689–0099 ⊠ ¥400 ⊙ Tues.–Sun. 9:30–4:30.

Natural indigo dyeing in Tokushima dates back at least 400 years: learn about the local craft at the informative **House of Indigo** (Ai-no-Yakata, 藍の館), where minidioramas show the coloring process and examples of blue-patterned cloth. You can wander around the old buildings of the complex and try your hand at dyeing (¥ 500). A handkerchief costs ¥500, a T-shirt ¥2,800. The museum is 30 minutes by bus from JR Tokushima Station (get off at Higashi Nakatomi). ☎ 088/692–6317 ⊠ ¥300 ⊙ Daily 9–5.

At the **Hall of Awa Handmade Paper** (Awa Washi Dentō Sangyō Kai-kan, 阿波和紙伝統産業会館) you might be able to meet "Prefectural Intangible Cultural Asset" Minoru Fujimori—a genial, gray-haired expert in the art of papermaking. The hall holds exhibitions, a shop where its multicolor products are sold, and a huge work space in which you can try your hand at making washi postcards ¥500. Take the JR Tokushima main line west to Yamakawa Station; the hall is then a 15-minute walk south. ☎ 0883/42–6120 ⊠ ¥300 ⊙ Tues.–Sun. 9–5.

Where to Stay & Eat

A variety of reasonably priced restaurants serve Indian, Chinese, French, and Japanese cuisine on the fifth floor of **Tokushima Clement Plaza** (徳島クレメントプラザ), above Tokushima Station.

$$–$$$$ ✕ **Tensaku** (天作). This restaurant is known for its tempura, fish salad, rice balls, and dumplings, all made from sardines. Local specialties such as Naruto sea bream and Awa steak are also on the menu. The seafood sampler, with a selection of fish fresh from the Seto Nai-kai, is pricey but worthwhile. ✉ *3–7–2 Ichiban-chō, 2nd fl. of Daidō Seimei Bldg.* ☎ *088/623–3736* ▭ *MC, V.*

¢–$ ✕ **Tōfuya** (十ふ屋). Japanese lights and ikebana flowers decorate this restaurant, which specializes in tofu dishes. Try the spicy bean curd or the tofu sashimi for something different. Omnivores will find meat and seafood dishes too. ✉ *2–9 Tomida-chō, Akutifai Bldg., 3rd fl.* ☎ *088/624–1028* ▭ *No credit cards.*

$$$$ ✕▣ **Tokushima Grand Hotel Kairakuen** (徳島グランドホテル偕楽園). Built in 1914, this ryokan underwent a renovation in 2000 to make it one of the most comfortable and charming hotels in Tokushima. It stands against the protected parkland at the foot of Mt. Bizan, overlooking the downtown area. The lobby opens up to a traditional Japanese garden with goldfish ponds and moss-covered stones. The Japanese-style rooms are bright and pristine, with tatami floors. There are also larger rooms with Western-style beds and Japanese-style sitting areas. Two meals are included; for dinner you can choose from three different Japanese set menus or two Western set menus, all offering a lavish assortment of dishes. ✉ *1–8 Iga-chō, Tokushima, Tokushima-ken 770-0831* ☎ *088/623–3333* 🖷 *088/622–7426* 🛏 *55 Western-style rooms, 23 Japanese-style rooms* ♨ *Japanese baths, hot springs* ▭ *AE, MC, V* ⊘| *MAP.*

$ ✕▣ **Hotel Marston Green** (ホテルマーストングリーン). A business hotel five minutes' walk from Tokushima Station, the Marston Green is a reasonably priced alternative to the city's expensive resort hotels. The Western-style rooms are slightly faded but they offer a bit more space than your average Japanese business hotel. Meals are not included in the room price, but a Continental breakfast, including Italian pastries, can be had for ¥800 at the restaurant on the first floor. ✉ *1–12 Ryōgoku Honchō, Tokushima, Tokushima-ken 770-0843* ☎ *088/654–1777* 🖷 *088/652–8104* 🛏 *99 rooms* ♨ *Restaurant, Japanese baths* ▭ *AE, DC, MC, V.*

Getting Around

Trains arrive at Tokushima Station from Takamatsu and Kōchi via the Dosan and Tokushima lines. City and prefectural buses depart from outside Clement Plaza. For the airport, take the bus from platform 2. Tokushima is also connected by bus to Kansai International Airport, Kyōto, Ōsaka, and Tōkyō.

Ōboke Koboke   大歩危小歩危

★ ❻ *50 min by JR from Kotohira.*

On the way south to Kōchi, explore the area around **Ōboke Koboke** (大歩危小歩危), where the road and rail lines south from Awa Ikeda follow the valleys, cut deep by swift-flowing rivers. The earth is red and rich, the foliage lush and verdant. It's an area of scenic beauty that lends

ON THE MENU

Takamatsu and Kōchi are the best places to eat seafood, especially Kōchi, which specializes in Tosa ryōri (Tosa is the old name for Kōchi, and ryōri means cooking), which are bonito dishes tataki style: tender fresh fish steaks seared lightly over a fire of pine needles and served with garlic-flavor soy sauce. In Matsuyama the local specialty is ikezukuri, a live fish with its meat cut into strips. In Tokushima try kaizoku ryōri (pirate's cuisine), in which you grill seafood on your own earthenware brazier. Also consider ordering what the chef recommends.

Noodle restaurants abound too: in Takamatsu you should try sanuki udon (a thick noodle slightly firmer in texture and more elastic than udon served elsewhere in Japan), while in Matsuyama go for sōmen (thin wheat noodles usually served cold), which traditionally come in five colors.

itself to exploration by car, though once you are off the main roads a little knowledge of Japanese will help your navigation. You can also take a boat trip down the river from near Ōboke Station; check with the tourist section of the town hall in Awa Ikeda.

off the beaten path

KAZURA-BASHI – (かずら橋) In the heart of the mountains, this 50-yard-long bridge made of vines and bamboo spans the Iyadanikei-kyōkoku (Iyadanikei Gorge). For ¥500 you can walk across; it's safe, since the bridge is remade every three years and is strung through with steel cables. The bridge is a 20-minute bus ride from Ōboke Station and is open during daylight hours.

Where to Stay & Eat

$$$ ✕ ⊞ **Hotel Ōbokekyō-mannaka** (ホテル大歩危峡まんなか). The only thing to do in Ōboke Koboke after the sun goes down is sit in an onsen, a particularly attractive option if you've spent the day walking along the riverbank. This hotel has the best onsen around, and the views of the river and gorge from the bath are beautiful. The rooms are simply functional, but what they lack in charm is made up by the spectacular scenery and the hotel's seasonal dinner menu of freshwater fish and local produce. ✉ *Sanjō-chō, Ōboke, Tokushima 779–5451* ☎ *0883/84–1216* 🖷 *0883/84–1218* 🛏 *30 rooms* ⌕ *Restaurant, hot springs* ▭ *AE, V.*

Getting Around

To get here, take the branch rail line that runs from Tokushima to Kōchi or the main line that runs from Okayama on Honshū to Kōchi via Kotohira. The jumping-off point is Awa Ikeda, an unremarkable town at the head of the gorge. Very infrequent buses run from Awa Ikeda and Ōboke to Kazura-bashi, so be sure to check the schedule for the return bus before leaving.

Kōchi 高知

❼ *50 min by JR from Ōboke Koboke, 2 hrs by JR from Kotohira.*

On the balmy southern coast of Shikoku, Kōchi is a relaxed city with a cosmopolitan atmosphere, enhanced by its trundling trams and the swaying palms that line the streets. The prefecture is reputed to be one of the poorest in Japan, with residents relying on fishing and agriculture for their living. However, perhaps because of its warm climate, the people of Kōchi are full of humor. Even their local folk songs poke fun at life, for example, "On Harimaya-bashi, people saw a Buddhist priest buy a hairpin. . . ." Priests in those days were forbidden to love women, and they shaved their heads—so it's implied in the lyrics that some naughty business must have been afoot.

Except for Kōchi-jō and Kenritsu Bijutsukan, Kōchi is not architecturally inspired, but it's friendly and fun-loving. People congregate every evening in the compact downtown area. Several downtown streets closed to traffic form shopping arcades.

Fodor'sChoice
★

Kōchi-jō (高知城) dominates the town, and is the only castle in Japan still to have both its tenshukaku and its daimyō's residence intact. The donjon—its stone foundation seemingly merging into the cliff face—admittedly was rebuilt in 1753, but it faithfully reflects the original (1601–03). The donjon has the old style of watchtower design, and, by climbing up to its top floor you can appreciate its purpose—the view is encompassing, and splendid. The daimyō's residence, **Kaitoku-kan,** is southwest of the tenshukaku. The formal main room is laid out in Shoin style, which is known for its decorative alcove, staggered shelves, ornate doors, tatami-covered floors, and shōji screens reinforced with wooden lattices. The easiest way to get here is to hop on a green Yosakoe Gurarin Bus in front of Kōchi Station. The fare is ¥100. ⊠ *1–2–1 Marunouchi* ☎ *088/872–2776* ☞ *¥400* ⊙ *Daily 9–5; last entry at 4:30.*

The main collection of **Kōchi Prefectural Museum** (Kenritsu Bijutsukan, 県立美術館), a spacious two-story facility, includes modern Japanese and Western art. One room is dedicated to works by Marc Chagall. Take any tram from Harimaya-bashi bound for Kenritsu Bijutsukan-dōri, a 15-minute ride. ☎ *0888/66–8000* ☞ *¥350* ⊙ *Tues.–Sun. 9–4:30.*

Should you be in town on a Sunday morning, go to the approximately 650 stalls at the **Nichiyō-ichi** (Sunday open-air market, 日曜市). Farmers have been bringing their produce to sell here for 300 years. You might see the incredibly long-tailed (more than 20 feet) Onagadori roosters, for which Kōchi is known. The market runs from the main gate of Kōchi-jō for 1 km (½ mi) along Ōtetsuji-dōri.

In summer Kōchi-ites flock to **Katsura-hama** (桂浜), 13 km (8 mi) southeast of town. The beach consists of gravelly white sand, but the swimming is good, and there are scenic rock formations offshore.

On the headland above Katsura-hama is the architecturally dazzling **Sakamoto Ryoma Kinen-kan** (Sakamoto Ryoma Memorial Museum, 坂本龍馬記念館), built in memory of local hero Ryoma, a progressive samurai who helped bring about the Meiji Restoration of the 19th century. It's open daily 9–4:30; entry costs ¥400.

If you prefer to spend an afternoon amid lawns and greenery, take a bus to Godai-san and **Godai-san Kōen** (五台山公園), designed to have something in bloom all year. Inside the park, visit **Chikurin-ji,** a temple with an impressive five-story pagoda, which is in fact a fairly uncommon sight in Japan. This structure compares to those of Kyōto, and the people from Kōchi say it's more magnificent. Belonging to the Shingon sect of Buddhism, the temple was founded in 724 and is the 31st temple in Shikoku's sequence of 88 sacred temples. The bus to Godai-san Kōen departs from the Toden stop, next to Seibu department store on Harimaya-bashi. The ride costs ¥300 and takes 20 minutes. Entrance into the gardens and museum costs ¥400.

Near Chikurin-ji in Godai-san Kōen, **Makino Botanical Garden** (Makino Shokubutsuen, 牧野植物園) was built to honor the botanist Dr. Tomitaro Makino (1862–1957). The greenhouse has a collection of more than 1,000 plants. ☎ *088/882–2601* 🎫 *¥500* 🕐 *Daily 9–5.*

Half-day and full-day sightseeing tours of Kōchi and environs are offered by **Kochi-ken Kotsu** (高知県交通; ✉ 70 Banchi, Iku ☎ 088/845–1607) and leave from the JR bus terminal at Kōchi Station at 8:30 AM and 1:50 PM.

off the beaten path

MUROTO POINT (Muroto Misaki, 室戸岬) – The road east (there's no train line) follows a rugged shoreline cut by frequent inlets and indentations. Most of the coast consists of a series of 100- to 300-foot terraces. Continuous wave action, generated by the Kuroshio (Black Current), has shaped these terraces. The result is a surreal coastline of rocks, surf, and steep precipices. It's about a 2½-hour drive along the coast road out to the cape, a popular sightseeing and surfing spot, where the sea crashes against the cliffs and there are black-sand beaches.

Where to Stay & Eat

$$–$$$$ ✕ **Tosahan** (土佐藩). This branch of a famous local chain serving Tosa specialties is decorated like a farmhouse, with dark wooden beams and red paper lanterns. A picture menu and plastic food displays in the window help you select a meal. Seafood *nabe* (stews) cooked at the table and *tataki* (finely chopped pieces of fish) are particularly good bets. Tosahan is easy to find at the start of the Obiya-machi shopping arcade, close by Harimaya-bashi. ✉ *1–2–2 Obiya-machi Arcade* ☎ *088/821–0002* 🖃 *AE, DC, MC, V.*

$$–$$$$ ✕ **Tosa Ryōori Tsukasa Kōchi Honten** (土佐料理　司高知本店). *Katsuo-tataki* (seared and finely sliced bonito) from Tosa Bay is one of Kōchi's delicacies and this restaurant does it better than just about any other. Meals are served in several small portions on Japanese porcelain dishes. The whale meat hot pot, though politically incorrect, is a popular choice with the local crowd. ✉ *1–2–15 Harimaya-chō* ☎ *088/873–4351* 🖃 *AE, DC, MC, V.*

$$$$ 🏠 **Jōseikan** (城西館). A rather monumental exterior masks a more restrained, airy lobby and a small central garden in this elegant Japanese-

style hotel, which has hosted the emperor on his visits to Kōchi. Tatami suites are immaculate, and the sauna and bath (¥1000 for nonguests) on the eighth floor have a spectacular night view of Kōchi-jō. The ryokan is close to the castle, two stops west of Harimaya-bashi by tram. ⊠ *2–5–34 Kami-machi, Kōchi-shi, Kōchi-ken 780-0901* ☎ *088/875–0111* 🖷 *088/824–0557* ⊕ *www.jyoseikan.co.jp* ⤴ *72 Japanese-style rooms* ⌾ *Restaurant, coffee shop* ⊟ *AE, DC, MC, V.*

★ **$$$–$$$$** 🖭 **Hotel Shin-Hankyu** (新阪急ホテル). Within sight of Kōchi-jō, the Shin-Hankyu is indisputably the best hotel in Kōchi. The ground floor has a modern, open-plan lobby, with a lounge away from the reception area and a small cake-and-tea shop to the side. On the second floor are several excellent restaurants that serve Japanese, Chinese, and French fare. Spacious guest rooms, most of which are Western style, are pleasantly decorated with light pastel furnishings, and the staff is extremely helpful to foreign guests. ⊠ *4–2–50 Hon-machi, Kōchi-shi, Kōchi-ken 780-0870* ☎ *088/873–1111* 🖷 *088/873–1145* ⊕ *hotel.newhankyu.co.jp* ⤴ *238 Western-style rooms, 4 Japanese-style rooms* ⌾ *4 restaurants, pool, health club, bar, meeting rooms, no-smoking rooms* ⊟ *AE, DC, MC, V.*

$$ 🖭 **Washington Hotel** (ワシントンホテル). Part of a nationwide chain of business hotels, this establishment has a prime position on the street leading to Kōchi-jō, on which the Sunday market is held. There's a small restaurant, and rooms are a good size for this kind of lodging. It's a 15-minute walk from the JR station. ⊠ *1–8–25 Otetsuji, Kōchi-shi, Kōchi-ken 780-0842* ☎ *088/823–6111* 🖷 *0888/25–2737* ⤴ *172 rooms* ⌾ *Restaurant* ⊟ *AE, V.*

Getting Around

Kōchi Station is a 10-minute walk from the city center at Harimaya-bashi. The tram system, which starts directly opposite the station, costs a flat ¥180. A taxi ride from Kōchi Station to downtown is about ¥550.

If you want direct Matsuyama–Kōchi transportation, take the three-hour JR bus from Kōchi Station (there's no direct train). The fare is covered by the JR Pass. For the Kōchi–Uwajima train trip you will need to change at Kubokawa, where you must pick up a branch line.

WESTERN SHIKOKU

Ashizuri-misaki (Cape Ashizuri, 足摺岬)

★ **⑧** *2½ hrs by JR from Kōchi to Nakamura, 1 hr by bus from Nakamura.*

Part of Ashizuri National Park (Ashizuri Kokuritsu Kōen), at the southwestern tip of Shikoku, this is wonderfully wild country—with a skyline-drive road running down the cape's middle. Keep in mind that the Kubokawa–Nakamura leg of the journey is on the private Kuroshio Tetsudō Line (¥210, not covered by the JR Pass). At Nakamura Station, continue by bus to Ashizuri-misaki—you might have to change buses at Tosa Shimizu. Buses also run from Kōchi Station to Ashizuri-misaki.

At the tip of Ashizuri-misaki are a lighthouse and **Kongōfuku-ji** (金剛福寺), 38th of Shikoku's 88 sacred temples. Its origins go back 1,100 years, although what you see was rebuilt 300 years ago.

Exhibits in **John Mung House** (ジョン万ハウス) tell the story of Nakahama Manjiro's extraordinary life. In 1841 the 14-year-old Manjiro, who hailed from Ashizuri, was shipwrecked on a remote Pacific island. He was eventually rescued by an American whaling ship. The ship's captain, John Whitfield, took a shine to Manjiro and nicknamed him John Mung. The boy stayed with the whaling crew for years and eventually settled in Bedford, Massachusetts, where Whitfield educated him. Mung's fluency in English lead him to play a pivotal role in negotiating the opening of Japan to the world after Commodore Perry's Black Ships arrived in 1853. ✉ *Ashizuri-misaki, Tosa Shimizu-shi* ☎ *0880/88–1136* 💰 *¥300* 🕐 *9–4.*

en route

Returning from Ashizuri-misaki, you can follow the coastline west to Sukumo or return to Nakamura for a bus there (1 hour; ¥1,100). Change buses to continue north to Uwajima, the terminal for JR rail lines running between Matsuyama and Kōchi. Four ferries a day (2½ hours; ¥1,650) sail from Sukumo for Saiki, on Kyūshū.

Uwajima 宇和島

❾ *4½ hrs by bus from Ashizuri-misaki, 3½ hrs by JR from Kōchi.*

Like Kōchi, Uwajima contains one of Japan's 12 extant feudal castles. This agreeable, peaceful town is famous for its bullfights sans matador and its fertility shrine.

Uwajima's **Warei-Taisai** (和霊大祭) is celebrated every July 23–24 with a parade of *mikoshi* (portable shrines), decorated fishing boats, and two giant *ushi-oni* (demon bulls). The climax is a mock battle in the local river between the teams carrying the bulls.

Uwajima-jō (宇和島城), a compact, friendly castle, is free of the usual defensive structures, such as a stone drop. The first castle on-site was torn down and replaced with this updated version in 1665—suggesting that by the end of the 17th century, war (at least the kind fought around castles) was a thing of the past. It's a 10-minute walk south of Uwajima Station. 💰 *¥200* 🕐 *Daily 9–5.*

Most people come to Uwajima for the **tōgyū** (闘牛), a sport in which two bulls lock horns and, like sumō wrestlers, try to push each other out of the ring. Though there are very similar bouts in the Oki Islands, Uwajima claims that these bullfights are a unique tradition dating back 400 years—an obvious tourism ploy. There are six tournaments a year: January 2, the third Sunday in March, the first Sunday in April, July 24, August 14, and the second Sunday in November. The stadium is at the foot of Maru-yama, a 30-minute walk from Uwajima Station.

The **Tourist Information Centre** (宇和島観光協会; ☎ 0895/22–3934), opposite Uwajima Station, is open daily 9–5.

Getting Around

JR trains connect Uwajima with Kōchi and Matsuyama. Ferries depart from Uwajima for Usuki, two JR train stops from Beppu on Kyūshū, and cost about ¥2,200.

Matsuyama 松山

🔟 *30 min by JR from Uchiko, 3 hrs west of Takamatsu by JR, 1 hr south of Hiroshima by fast boat, 3 hrs by ferry.*

Shikoku's largest city, Matsuyama bristles with industry: from chemicals to wood pulp and textiles to porcelain. Most of its appeal is in its famous literary associations, its castle, and the spas of Dōgo Onsen. Matsuyama was the home of Masaoka Shiki, one of Japan's most famous haiku poets, and city officials encourage its residents to continue the haiku tradition.

The **City Tourist Information Office** (松山市観光案内所; ⊠ Matsuyama Station ☎ 089/931–3914), open from Monday to Saturday, 8:30–5, provides maps and brochures. **Ehime Prefectural International Centre** (Kōryū Kyōkai Ehime-ken Kokusai Sentā, 愛媛県国際交流協; ☎ 089/917–5678), on the south side of Katsu-yama below the castle, has information in English on the rest of the prefecture and on the city's efforts to encourage haiku poetry.

Matsuyama-jō (松山城)—the third such feudal castle in Shikoku to have survived intact, though barely—is on top of Katsu-yama, right in the center of the city. Originally constructed in 1603, the castle burned down in 1779 and was rebuilt in 1835 with the addition of a major three-story tenshukaku and three lesser ones. The lesser ones succumbed to fire again after a U.S. bomb attack in 1945, but all have been reconstructed. The main donjon now serves as a museum for feudal armor and swords owned by the Matsudaira clan, the daimyō family that lorded over Matsuyama and Takamatsu throughout the Edo period.

Ninomaru Shiseki Teien (松山二之丸史跡庭園), an agreeable park on the west side of the hill, includes the grounds of the former outworks of the castle. You can either walk through Ninomaru Shiseki Teien and up the hill to get to the castle, or take a cable car or chairlift to the castle from Ōkaidō, the shopping street on the east side of the hill. ⊠ *5 Maru-no-uchi, Matsuyama-shi* ☎ *089/921–2000* 🖃 *Castle ¥500; park ¥100; cable car ¥210 one-way, ¥400 round-trip* 🕙 *Castle Tues.–Sun. 9–4:30, park Tues.–Sun. 9–5.*

Downtown Matsuyama revolves around the **covered shopping arcade** (アーケード), at the foot of the castle grounds, and is best reached by taking Tram 5 (fare ¥170) from the plaza in front of Matsuyama Station.

★ Rather than staying downtown in Matsuyama, consider spending the night at **Dōgo Onsen** (道後温泉). With a history that is said to stretch back for more than two millennia, Dōgo Onsen is one of Japan's oldest hot-spring resort areas. It hasn't outlived its popularity, either. More than 60 ryokan and hotels, old and new, operate here, and most now have their own thermal waters. Dōgo Onsen is 18 minutes away from Matsuyama on Tram 5, which you can take from Matsuyama Station or catch downtown at the stop in front of the ANA Hotel (Trams 3, 5, and 6).

At the turn of the last century, bathing was done at public bathhouses, and the grandest of them all was—as it still is today—**Dōgo Onsen Honkan** (道後温泉本館; ⊠ Dōgo Yu-no-machi ☎ 089/921–5141) the municipal bathhouse. Bathing is a social pastime in Japan, and to stay in the area and not socialize at the municipal bathhouse is to miss the delight of this spa town. The grand, three-story, castlelike wooden building was built in 1894, and with its sliding panels, tatami floors, and shōji screens it looks like an old-fashioned pleasure palace. In many ways it is. More than 2,000 bathers come each day for a healthy scrub and soak. Many pay extra to lounge around after their bath, drinking tea in the communal lounge or private rooms. Even if you decide not to pay for a private room, make sure you visit the third floor to see the Botchan Room, named after the comic novel by local writer Natsume Sōseki.

There are different price levels of enjoyment: a basic bath is ¥300; a bath, rented *yukata* (cotton robe), tea and snack, and access to the communal tatami lounge are ¥620; access to a smaller lounge and bath area away from the hoi polloi is ¥980; and a private tatami room is ¥1,240. A separate wing was built in 1899 for imperial soaking. It's no longer used, but for ¥210 you can follow a guide through this royal bathhouse daily from 6:30 AM to 9 PM. The baths are open 6:30 AM–11 PM.

Where to Stay & Eat

$$$$ ✕ **Kawasemi** (川瀬見). At this modern interpreter of traditional *kaiseki ryōri* (a style of food and service that's a traditional art) you can sit at tables or on tatami in private booths and savor delicate morsels of marinated seafood or slivers of poached fish and vegetables artfully arranged in a mound, surrounded by a savory coulis. A slightly gloomy interior, decorated in minimalist black and grays, has seasonal flower arrangements, which add splashes of color. The restaurant is on the second floor, two streets east of Ōkaidō—look for a purple sign with CLUB on it in English. Lunches cost about ¥1,000. ⊠ *2–5–18 Niban-chō* ☎ *089/ 933–9697* 🖃 *AE, MC, V.*

¢ ✕ **Kotori** (ことり). This popular restaurant has been around since 1949, serving hot-pot udon noodles topped with fish, clams, and vegetables. The menu is limited to noodles and inari-sushi (fried tofu sushi) but taste them and you'll know why people line up to eat this restaurant's udon before they run out for the day. ⊠ *3–7–2 Kanaderi-chō* ☎ *089/932– 3003* 🖃 *No credit cards.*

$$$$ 🏨 **ANA Hotel Matsuyama** (松山全日空ホテル). The best international hotel downtown, the ANA is five minutes on foot from the cable car to Matsuyama-jō, and Tram 5 out to Dogo Onsen stops out front. Guest rooms are well maintained, reasonably spacious, and fully equipped, with everything from bathrobes to hair dryers. Ask for a room on the 11th or 12th floor that overlooks the Bansuiso Mansion, an imitation French château (housing the missable Prefectural Museum Annex), which is floodlighted at night. The hotel has shopping arcades, several restaurants, and a rooftop beer garden. ⊠ *3–2–1 Ichiban-chō, Matsuyama, Ehime-ken 790-8520* ☎ *089/933–5511* 🖷 *089/921–6053* 🌐 *www.anahotels.com* 🛏 *327 rooms* ⚙ *4 restaurants, hair salon, beer garden* 🖃 *AE, DC, V.*

$$$$ 🏨 **Funaya Ryokan** (ふなや旅館). The best Japanese inn in Dōgo Onsen, this is where the imperial family stays when it comes to take the waters. The ryokan has a long history—the original structure dates back to 1626, but the present building was constructed in 1963 and has some

Western-style rooms. The finest rooms look out on the garden. Breakfast and dinner are included in the rate. ⊠ *1–33 Dōgo Yu-no-machi, Matsuyama, Ehime-ken 790-9842* ☎ *089/947–0278* 🖷 *089/943–2139* ➥ *28 Japanese-style rooms, 26 Western-style rooms* ⌣ *Pool, hot springs, sauna* 🖃 *AE, DC, MC, V* ⦿ *MAP.*

Getting Around

Frequent JR train service runs between Matsuyama and Takamatsu, and high-speed boat service and ferry service can shuttle you between Matsuyama and Hiroshima.

Shimanami Kaidō   しまなみ海道

⓫ *40 minutes from Matsuyama via train or bus*

Fodor'sChoice
★

The Shimanami Kaidō (Shimanami Sea Road), finished in 1999, is a series of 10 bridges connecting several islands between the town of Imabari in Ehime Prefecture and the town of Onomichi in Hiroshima Prefecture. Whereas in the past the only way to visit these islands was by ferry or airplane, you can now drive, cycle, or simply walk over the network of suspension bridges to any of the eight large islands in the straits between Shikoku and Honshū. Buses also travel along the Shimanami Kaidō from Imabari to Onomichi in Hiroshimi. Without stopping, the trip takes about 1½ hours.

Ōmishima   大三島

The third island along the Shimanami Sea Road from Imabari-shi, Ōmishima is home to **Ōyamazumi Jinja** (Ōyamazumi Shrine, 大山祇神社). In the 8th century warriors and royalty made pilgrimages to the shrine to offer prayers to the sea and war gods. Victors often left their armor and weapons by way of thanks for divine assistance in battle. The shrine's museum now preserves these artifacts, many of which are entered in the list of recognized national treasures. ⊠ *3327 Miya-ura, Ōshima-chō* ☎ *0897/82–0032* 🖾 *Museum, ¥1,000* ⊗ *Daily 8:30–4:30.*

Innoshima   因島

This is the fifth major island from Imabari-shi and the second from Onomichi in Hiroshima Prefecture. It also has the only castle built by a naval admiral in Japan. **Innoshima Suigun-jō** (Innoshima Naval Fortress, 因島水軍城), built during the Muro-machi period by Admiral Murakami sits atop a small hill overlooking the Seto Nai-kai. A small museum provides information on Murakami's voyages and military exploits, some of which took him as far as China and Southeast Asia. ⊠ *3228–2 Chūatsu-chō, Innoshima* ☎ *08452/4–0936* 🖾 *¥310* ⊗ *Daily 8:30–4:30.*

Getting Around

BY BIKE   If the weather is good, the best way to travel between the islands is by bicycle. It'll take you 3 to 4 hours to bike between Imabari and Onomichi. **Sunrise Itoyama** (サンライズ糸山; ⊠ *2–8–1 Sunaba-chō, Imabari-shi* ☎ *0898/41–3196*) has rental bikes for ¥500 a day plus a ¥1,000 refundable deposit. The shop is open from May to September, daily 8–8, and from October to March, daily 8–5. **Yoshiumi Rental Cycle Terminal** (吉海レンタサイクルターミナル; ⊠1042–8 Kurana, Yoshiumi-chō ☎0897/84–3233) on Ōshima, the first island from Imabari-shi, rents bikes for about ¥500 per day. The shop is open from April to September, daily 8–8, and from October to March, daily 8–5.

BY BUS **Shimanami Liner** (☎ 0898/25–4873) travels over the Shimanami Kaidō in about 1½ hours. There are six departures per weekend day (three on weekdays) between 9 AM and 8 PM. The trip costs ¥2200.

SHIKOKU A TO Z

To research prices, get advice from other travelers, and book travel arrangements, visit www.fodors.com.

AIR TRAVEL

All Nippon Airways and Japan Airlines provide domestic flights to and from Shikoku's four airports. Takamatsu is served by 7 daily flights from Tōkyō and by 10 daily flights from Ōsaka; Tokushima by 5 daily from Tōkyō and 10 from Ōsaka; Kōchi by 5 daily from Tōkyō and 23 from Ōsaka; and Matsuyama by 6 daily from Tōkyō and 6 from Ōsaka.

🛪 Carriers **All Nippon Airways (ANA)** ☎ 800/235-9262 in U.S. and Canada, 0120/ 02-9222 in Japan ⊕ www.anaskyweb.com or www.ana.co.jp. **Japan Airlines (JAL)** ☎ 800/525-3663 in U.S. and Canada, 0120/255-971 in Japan ⊕ www.jal.co.jp.

BOAT & FERRY TRAVEL

The Kansai Kisen (Kansai Steamship) to Takamatsu takes 5½ hours from Ōsaka's Bentenfuto Pier and 4½ hours from Kōbe's Naka-Tottei Pier. The boat leaves Ōsaka at 8:30 AM and 2:20 PM and Kōbe at 9:50 AM and 3:40 PM. It arrives at Takamatsu at 2 PM and 8:10 PM. From Ōsaka, the cost is ¥2,500 and up; it's slightly less from Kōbe.

Nankai Tokushima Shuttle Line provides ferry connections between Tokushima and Kansai International Airport via Wakayama. The journey takes about two hours and costs ¥3,390 one-way, ¥5,400 round-trip.

To Kōchi from Tōkyō a ship operated by Blue Highway Line departs at 7:40 PM, stops in Katsura, Wakayama Prefecture, at 8:50 AM, and arrives in Kōchi at 5 AM.

Hourly high-speed boat service by Ishizaki Kisen takes one hour to travel between Matsuyama and Hiroshima (¥5,700). Ferry service by Seto Naikai Kisen (three hours) costs ¥4,260 for first class, ¥2,130 for second class.

🛥 **Blue Highway Line** ☎ 0888/31-0520 Japanese only. **Ishizaki Kisen** ☎ 089/953-1003. **Kansai Kisen** ☎ 06/573-0530 Japanese only. **Nankai Tokushima Shuttle Line** ☎ 088/664-3330 Japanese only. **Seto Nai-kai Kisen** ☎ 082/253-1212.

CAR TRAVEL

Because traffic is light, the scenery marvelous, and the distances relatively short, Shikoku is one region in Japan where renting a car makes sense. (Remember that an international driver's license is required.) Budget Rent-a-Car has rental offices in Matsuyama, Takamatsu, and Kōchi, as do other car-rental agencies.

🚗 **Budget Rent-a-Car** ✉ Kūko-dori 1-13-6, Matsuyama ☎ 089/973-0543 ✉ Nishinomaru-chō 2-20, Takamatsu ☎ 087/851-6543 ✉ Kitahon-machi 4-chōme 6-48, Kōchi ☎ 088/884-0543.

EMERGENCIES
🛈 **Ambulance** ☎ 119. **Police** ☎ 110.

TRAIN TRAVEL
To get to Shikoku, take the JR Hikari Shinkansen to Okayama (four hours from Tōkyō; one hour from Ōsaka), then transfer to the JR Limited Express for either Takamatsu (one hour) or Matsuyama or Kōchi (three hours).

You can also get to Matsuyama by taking the JR Shinkansen to Hiroshima (5 hours, 10 minutes from Tōkyō; 2 hours, 20 minutes from Kyōto). From Hiroshima's Ujina Port, the ferry takes three hours to cross the Seto Nai-kai to Matsuyama; the high-speed boat takes one hour.

All major towns on Shikoku are connected either by JR express and local trains or by bus. Because of the lower population density on Shikoku, transportation is not so frequent as on the southern coast of Honshū. So before you step off a train or bus, find out how long it will be before the next one departs for your next destination.

The main routes are from Takamatsu to Matsuyama by train (2 hours, 45 minutes); from Takamatsu to Kōchi by train (3 hours), from Takamatsu to Tokushima (90 minutes); from Matsuyama to Kōchi by JR bus (approximately 3 hours, 15 minutes); from Matsuyama to Uwajima by train (three hours); and from Kōchi to Nakamura by train (two hours).

VISITOR INFORMATION
Major tourist information centers are located at each of Shikoku's main cities: Takamatsu, Kōchi, Matsuyama, and Tokushima.

A nationwide service for English-language assistance or travel information is available daily 9–5. Throughout Shikoku, dial the hot line toll-free for information on western Japan. When using a yellow, blue, or green public phone (do not use red phones), insert a ¥10 coin, which will be returned.

🛈 Tourist Information **English-language hot line** ☎ 0120/444-800 or 0088/224-800. **Kōchi** ☎ 088/882-1634. **Matsuyama** ☎ 089/931-3914. **Takamatsu** ☎ 087/851-2009. **Tokushima** ☎ 088/656-3303.

KYŪSHŪ 九州

By Nigel Fisher
& Simon
Richmond

Updated by
Sarah Richards

THE SERENE ISLAND OF KYŪSHŪ, which hangs like a tail off the south end of Honshū, has a balmy climate, lush green countryside, soothing hot springs, and awesome volcanic formations. Its cities are generous with greenery and filled with sights of historical and cultural significance.

Archaeological evidence indicates that Kyūshū was the earliest inhabited island in the archipelago of Japan. Here the early roots of Japanese civilization—rice, pottery, and tools—were cultivated during the Yayoi period (250 BC–AD 300). Japanese scholars from Kyūshū ventured into the Asian continent during the 5th and 6th centuries and brought back religious and legal theories. Soldiers returned with Korean ceramics—and the artisans with the skills to make ceramics—in the early 17th century. Western scholarship, religion, and cuisine also found their way to Japan through the ports of Kyūshū.

Encounters with foreigners fill the pages of the island's extraordinary history. In the mid-16th century fleets of European merchants and missionaries began arriving at Nagasaki's port, only to be expelled shortly thereafter in 1639 by the ruling shōgun, Iemitsu Tokugawa (1604–51). Only the mercantile Chinese and nonproselytizing Dutch were permitted to stay—under close surveillance. For 200 years Dejima, a small island in Nagasaki Harbor, remained the only point of contact between Japan and the West. When Japan emerged from its isolation in the mid-19th century, foreigners once again flooded into the ports of Kyūshū, eager to take advantage of an unexploited market. Evidence of the successive waves of immigrants is still apparent in Nagasaki: restored Catholic churches and European colonial mansions dot the hills of this cosmopolitan city, and the stories of the Chinese and Dutch live on in their restored downtown settlements.

This is a land marked by both the soothing and wrathful extremities of Japan's fascinating geology. Spa resorts and peaceful mountain retreats abound in Beppu and Yufuin, cities built on lava fields, and underground mineral springs. Farther south, in Mt. Aso National Park and the city of Kagoshima, volcanic formations grow into monolithic monsters, coughing and spluttering with rage, and shattering the silence of the beautiful scenery.

See the glossary at the end of this book for definitions of the common Japanese words and suffixes used in this chapter.

Exploring Kyūshū

The conventional route for touring Kyūshū starts in the north with Fukuoka and moves counterclockwise to Nagasaki on the west coast, west to the central city of Kumamoto, south to the city of Kagoshima, and northeast to Aso-san (Mt. Aso) and the hot-springs resorts of Beppu and Yufuin. Circling the island will take you past rich green rice fields, smoking volcanoes, and magical views of the ocean.

About the Restaurants

Fresh fish is served just about everywhere on Kyūshū. Western-style restaurants, on the other hand, are limited to bigger cities like Fukuoka, Ku-

You can cover the island's must-see sights in a brief tour from Nagasaki to Beppu via Mt. Aso. Express trains and buses will be your principle mode of transport.

Numbers in the text correspond to numbers in the margin and on the Kyūshū and Nagasaki maps.

If you have **2 days**

With only two days, spend your time in 🗺 **Nagasaki** ④–⑩ ⧫, enjoying the city's rich history, cultural gems, and culinary treats. Make sure your stay includes a visit to Glover Garden, with its Western-style houses and great views of Nagasaki, and a day trip to Unzen, a barren landscape punctuated by seething cauldrons of scalding-hot mineral water.

If you have **4 days**

Spend your first few hours peeling away the layers of intricate Canal City, Kyūshū's largest entertainment center, in the heart of 🗺 **Fukuoka** ① ⧫. In the morning, leave the concrete jungle behind and discover the island's richest cultural and historical attractions in 🗺 **Nagasaki** ④–⑩. Overnight here and catch the morning train for 🗺 **Aso-san** ⑬ for an afternoon of rigorous mountain climbing or a bird's-eye view of the bubbling blue caldera lake from the comfort of a helicopter. Settle down for the evening in one of the provincial inns tucked away in the folds of sprawling Mt. Aso National Park. End your trip with an indulgent visit to the hot springs of kitschy 🗺 **Beppu** ⑭ or quieter 🗺 **Yufuin** ⑮.

If you have **7 days**

You can cover all of Kyūshū's major points in a week without running yourself ragged. Spend your first day and night in 🗺 **Fukuoka** ① ⧫ and then move on to 🗺 **Nagasaki** ④–⑩ for a day and a half of easygoing exploring. From here it's a four-hour bus ride to 🗺 **Kumamoto** ⑪. Be sure to break up the trip with a visit to the barren landscape of Unzen. Spend the night and next day delving into Kumamoto's feudal past before heading south to Sakurajima, the active volcano near 🗺 **Kagoshima** ⑫. The hot sands of nearby Sunamushi Kaikan, at the southern tip of Kyūshū, are well worth the hour-long train journey from Kagoshima. On your way back north, stop at 🗺 **Aso-san** ⑬ for an afternoon of challenging hiking up Nakadake or a quiet picnic in the green pastures of Kusasenri. Try the kitschy hot-springs experience of 🗺 **Beppu** ⑭, or, for something more elegant, spend the night in a rustic ryokan in 🗺 **Yufuin** ⑮. Save the last few hours for the mysterious Buddhist carvings in Usuki before leaving this enchanting island.

mamoto, and Nagasaki. In addition to regional favorites, an interesting snack called *onsen tamago,* eggs boiled black by sulphurous hot springs, can be found all over this volcanic island.

About the Hotels

You can find the usual American hotel chains, with all the familiar extras, in Fukuoka and Nagasaki. The rural areas surrounding Aso and Kagoshima have inns with stunning views of the surrounding peaks. Beppu and Yufuin hotels and *ryokan* (traditional inns) are equipped with natural hot-springs water, a welcome extravagance after an exhausting day of sightseeing. All hotel rooms have private baths, basic television service, and air-conditioning unless otherwise noted.

Reservations are essential during the long national holidays—Golden Week (late April–early May), Obon (mid-August), and New Year's (first week of January)—when hordes of Japanese tourists flock to the island.

	WHAT IT COSTS In yen				
	$$$$	$$$	$$	$	¢
RESTAURANTS	over 3,000	2,000–3,000	1,000–2,000	800–1,000	under 800
HOTELS	over 22,000	18,000–22,000	12,000–18,000	8,000–12,000	under 8,000

Restaurant prices are per person for a main course at dinner. Hotel prices are for a double room, excluding 5% tax and tip.

Timing

Kyūshū is at its most beautiful in early spring when the greenery is richest, and temperatures are pleasantly warm. May and June tend to be wet and muggy; July and August are usually hot and sticky. Autumn colors are rich, particularly in the north, and they arrive in late October or early November. The mountains of central Kyūshū see a spattering of snow around January or February, and the migration of Siberian cranes adds drama to the gentle winter landscape.

FUKUOKA & NORTHERN KYŪSHŪ 福岡と北九州

Too small to have a cosmopolitan appeal yet too large to be considered quaint, bustling Fukuoka is nonetheless an ideal place to while away a few hours en route to other locations, or to spend a few days experiencing the sights and smells of Kyūshū. Among its cultural highlights are two major festivals and the Hakata Machiya Folk Museum. The lively nightlife districts, Nakasu and Tenjin, smile at each other over the banks of the Naka-gawa (Naka River).

Southwest of Fukuoka are the hot springs of Takeo Onsen and the small village of Arita, known for its fine pottery.

Fukuoka 福岡

▶ **❶** *1½ hrs west of Tōkyō by plane; by Shinkansen, 5 hrs west of Tōkyō or 2½ hrs west of Ōsaka.*

Fukuoka was originally a castle town founded at the end of the 16th century, while the nearby district of Hakata emerged as the leading commercial center of the region. In 1889 the two districts were officially merged under the name Fukuoka, but the historical names are still used. The Naka-gawa is the dividing line of the city, with everything west of the river known as Fukuoka and everything east of the river still known as Hakata.

Flattened during World War II bombing raids, Fukuoka emerged from its rubble on a new, efficient grid plan with wide tree-lined avenues.

Ceramics & Porcelain

In the early 17th century, when Kyūshū warlords unsuccessfully invaded Korea, they retreated with several kidnapped artisans in tow. These skilled craftspeople were forced to produce ceramic objects for the feudal government in Arita, where precious kaolin clay had been excavated. The result was a fine porcelain known for its colorful glazes. The Dutch East India Company initiated the sale of Japanese pottery to the European market, spreading the fame of this art form. The original kilns in Arita and nearby Ōkawachi-yama continue to produce exquisite pieces of art for the emperor and other dignitaries, as well as for common folk.

11

Onsen (Hot Springs)

Kyūshū is a center of one of Japan's national pastimes: bathing, particularly in *onsen*, or natural hot springs. Pleasure-seekers flock to Kyūshū from every corner of the country to soak in the thousands of natural springs that bubble out of this volcanic island. Many of these springs are surrounded by resorts ranging from massive Western-style hotels to small humble inns, all with at least one indoor communal bath that uses the hot-springs water. The finer establishments also have *rotemburo* (open-air hot-springs baths), where you can soak outdoors, even in the midst of a snowy winter landscape.

Outdoor Activities

Beyond the major cities, the nature of Kyūshū is dramatic, with mountains, valleys, forests, and seascapes, all with great walking and cycling routes. Mt. Aso National Park in particular is appealing to hikers, who climb the volcanic cones and meander through the rolling green pastures surrounding the caldera.

Fukuoka's comprehensive subway system connects all the downtown attractions and has an extension to the international airport. In addition to the subway, an inexpensive bus operates throughout the city center.

The **Fukuoka International Association** (福岡国際交流協会; ☒ Rainbow Plaza, IMS, 8th fl., 1–7–11 Tenjin, Chūō-ku ☎ 092/733–2220) is a good source of information for both travelers and residents of Fukuoka. The English-speaking staff is very helpful, and English-language newspapers and periodicals are available for visitors to read. **Japan Travel Bureau** (☒ Yamato Seimei Kaikan Bldg., 1–14–4 Tenjin, Chūō-ku ☎ 092/731–5221) offers domestic and international travel services.

After studying religion and culture for several years in China, the monk Eisai (1141–1215) introduced Zen Buddhism to Japan (he is also said to have brought the first tea seeds from China to Japan). Upon his return, Eisai established **Shōfuku-ji** (正福寺); the inscription on the main gate by Emperor Gotoba confirms that this is the site of Japan's first Zen temple. Note the bronze bell in the belfry, designated an Important Cultural Property by the Japanese government. The temple is a 15-minute walk northwest from Hakata Station, or a five-minute Nishitetsu bus ride from the station to the nearby Oku-no-dō stop (you can pick up

Kyūshū

NIHON-KAI
(Sea of Japan)

HONSHŪ

Ikishima

Hakata-wan
(Hakata Bay)

Shimonoseki

Kokura

SETO NAI-KAI
(Inland Sea)

Fukuoka
福岡 **①** ✈

Karatsu

Ōkawachi-Yanaa

Tōsu

湯布院
Yufuin

別府
Beppu

Beppu-wan
(Beppu Bay)

Imari

Saga

Hita

⑮

⑭ ✈

②③ Arita 有田

Kurume

Kurokawa
Onsen

Ōita

Usuki

Sasebo

**② Takeo
Onsen**
武雄温泉

Ariake-kai
(Ariake
Bay)

3

Aso
National
Park

Trans-Kyushu Hwy.

Ōmura-wan
(Ōmura
Bay)

Shimabara

⑬ Aso-San 阿蘇山
(Mt. Aso)

④ · ⑩
see detail
map

Nagasaki

Unzen

Shimabara
Peninsula

⑪ Kumamoto
熊本

KYŪSHŪ MTS.

Gokasegawa

Nobeōka

Misumi

Yatsushiro

Kamijima

Shimojima

Yatsushirokai
(Yatsushiro Bay)

Hitoyoshi

Kirishima-
Yaku
National
Park

Miyazaki

✈

✈

Miyakonojo

鹿児島
Kagoshima

⑫

Mt.
Sakurajima

Kagoshima-wan
(Kagoshima
Bay)

Makurazaki

Ibusuki

**Sunamushi
Kaikan**

Yamagawa

Sata

TAIHEIYŌ
(Pacific Ocean)

Tanegashima

KEY

⚐ *Start of itinerary*

— *JR Trains*

═ *Shinkansen
(Bullet Train)*

┼ *Private rail line*

Yakushima

0 _____ 40 miles
0 _____ 40 kilometers

the bus on the main road in front of Hakata Station's west exit). ✉ *6–1 Gokushō-machi, Hakata-ku* ☎ *092/291–0775* 💳 *Free* 🕐 *Daily 9–5.*

Kushida Jinja (櫛田神社), founded in 757, hosts the biggest festival in Fukuoka: the **Hakata Gion Yamagasa.** Elaborate portable shrines decorated with pictures of Hakata ningyō, the feudal castle Hakata-jō, and other images of cultural and historical significance are paraded throughout the city and raced on the last day. The days leading up to the festival are full of elaborate preparations, including full dress rehearsals. The festivities kick off on July 1 and end with a climatic finale on the 15th at 4:59 AM. ✉ *1–41 Kawabata-chō, Hakata-ku* ☎ *092/291–2951* 💳 *Free* 🕐 *Daily 9–5.*

If you visit Fukuoka at the beginning of January, don't miss the exciting **Tamaseseri Festival** at **Hakozakigū Jinja** (箱崎宮). Two teams—one representing the sea, the other land—of brave young men in loincloths fight for a wooden ball, each member atop his partner's shoulders. If the "sea" team wins, good fishing is predicted for the year. A "land" victory forecasts a plentiful harvest. Though not particularly interesting in itself, the shrine is a handsome wooden building with a lovely stone torii. To get here take the Hakozaki subway line to Hakozaki Miya-mae Station. ✉ *1–22–1 Hakozaki, Higashi-ku* ☎ *092/641–7431* 💳 *Free* 🕐 *Daily 9–5.*

Three Meiji-era merchant residences house the **Hakata Machiya Folk Museum** (Hakata Machiya Furusato-kan, 博多町家ふるさと館). The museum highlights the lifestyles of early-20th-century Hakata artisans and the art of traditional doll making. The gift shop sells handicrafts and old-fashioned toys. It's across the street from Kushida Jinja. ✉ *6–10 Reisen-machi, Hakata-ku* ☎ *092/281–7761* 💳 *¥200* 🕐 *Daily 10–5:30.*

The lake at **Ōhori Kōen** (大濠公園) was once part of a moat surrounding Fukuoka's castle, of which little remains. In early April the northern part of the park is graced with the pink and white flowers of 2,600 cherry-blossom trees. You can enjoy a leisurely 1-mi walk around the perimeter of the lake, or see what's biting in the designated fishing area in the park's southern section. Also within the park are the **Fukuoka City Modern Art Gallery,** which houses a few works by Salvador Dalí, and a traditional sculpted Japanese **garden** across from the gallery. From Hakata Station, take the subway to Ōhori Kōen Station; it's a 20-minute ride. ✉ *Chūō-ku* ☎ *092/741–2004* 💳 *Park free, museum ¥270, garden ¥240* 🕐 *Museum and garden Tues.–Sun. 9–5.*

A "city within a city," the impressive **Canal City** (キャナルシティ) entertainment complex combines the futuristic grandeur of glass and steel with the tranquillity of a flowing artificial canal. Inside are restaurants and cafés, shops, hotels, cinemas, theaters, and an entertainment stage on the first floor that is visible from the dozens of balconies that swell out from alternating concave and convex levels. The maze of bridges connecting each section of this bright-red trendy hotspot can be confusing, but you can pick up an English map at one of the information counters. To get here, follow the road leading from the west exit of Hakata Station; it's a 15-minute walk. ✉ *1–2 Sumiyoshi, Hakata-ku* ☎ *092/ 282–2525* ⊕ *www.canalcity.co.jp/english.*

Where to Stay & Eat

If you're having trouble deciding where to eat, you can always try one of the 64 restaurants and cafés at Canal City.

★ $$$ ✕ **Bassin** (バサン). Earthy wooden counters and floors complement small linen-covered chairs, sheer curtains, and art deco lamps on the first floor of this showcase of modern Japanese interior design. Dark-wood furniture set against cream-color brick walls creates a stark and alluring contrast in the main dining room. As a starter, try the garden salad with a tangy roasted-seaweed dressing or the creamy marinated tofu; unique main dishes include grilled chicken in a burdock sauce, and boiled turtle meat with summer vegetables. Elaborate Japanese courses run ¥3,500–¥7,000. ⊠ *Plaza Hotel Tenjin, 1–9–63 Daimyō, Chūō-ku* ☎ *092/739–3210* ⊟ *AE, DC, MC, V.*

★ ¢ ✕ **Deko** (デコ). The central tables of this cheerful bar are Japanese style, positioned above sunken floors for increased leg comfort; there are also tables and chairs at the back of the pub. Deko has no English menu, but the daily special is usually a good bet. The salmon-and-basil spring rolls, and the dumplings flavored with *shiso* (Japanese basil) are excellent starters. It's between the Hakata train station and Yakuin subway station on Sumiyoshi-dōri. ⊠ *1–24–22 Takasago, Rasa Bldg., B1, Chūō-ku* ☎ *092/526–7070* ⊟ *AE, DC, MC, V.*

¢ ✕ **Ganso-Akanoren Ramen** (元祖赤のれんラーメン). Owner Tsuda-san, who learned the culinary art of ramen in China, runs this casual joint, a favorite among Fukuoka folks. His ramen recipe combines extra-thin noodles and secret spices, which create a unique golden-color dish. Take the West 2 Exit from Tenjin Station; the restaurant is south of the big department store Elgara. ⊠ *5–24–26 Watanabe-dōri, Chūō-ku* ☎ *092/741–0267* ⊟ *No credit cards.*

¢ ✕ **Umauma** (うま馬). This is a popular and inexpensive place to sample a staple of Fukuoka fare: the Chinese-influenced dish tonkatsu ramen. For ¥580 you can dive into this bowl of thin noodles in a steamy pork-based soup garnished with chopped onions, slivers of ginger, and slices of meat. If you have any room left, try the excellent cheese dumplings. It's one block south of Bassin restaurant. ⊠ *Kotani Bldg. 2F, 1–11–15 Daimyō, Chūō-ku* ☎ *092/738–5811* ⊟ *AE, DC, MC, V.*

★ $$$–$$$$ ▥ **Hotel Il Palazzo** (ホテルイルパラツォ). Classic Italian design meets postmodernism in Fukuoka's chicest lodging, a tall box-shape building with red columns intersected by green horizontal bars. The Western-style guest rooms are bathed in soft, dim lighting and have sleek modern furniture and rich deep-pile carpets. Muted lights in the restaurant cast dramatic shadows across the walls. It's a 10-minute walk from the Nakasu-Kawabata subway station and very hard to miss. ⊠ *3–13–1 Haruyoshi, Chūō-ku, Fukuoka, Fukuoka-ken 810-0003* ☎ *092/716–3333* 🖷 *092/724–3330* ⇥ *53 Western-style rooms, 9 Japanese-style rooms* ⌂ *Restaurant, café, 2 bars* ⊟ *AE, DC, MC, V.*

$$ ▥ **Hakata Tōkyū Inn** (博多東急ホテル). Among the upscale Western hotels clustered downtown around the Naka-gawa, this is the most economical choice. Free satellite TV and large picture windows compensate for the small size of the rooms. If the savory snacks of the street stalls across the river don't appeal for dinner, you can always drop by the hotel's

ON THE MENU

THE MOST CELEBRATED DISH *in Fukuoka is tonkotsu rāmen, a strongly flavored pork-based soup with noodles, scallions, and strips of roasted pork. Wherever you are on Kyūshū, ramen can never be too far, but within Fukuoka it's particularly popular in the street stalls of Nakasu and the casual restaurants of Daimyō.*

Popular in Nagasaki, shippoku consists of elaborately prepared dishes that harmoniously blend the flavors of Asia and Europe—not surprising given the city's multicultural history. Served Chinese style at a round table and custom-tailored for large groups, shippoku is never a solitary affair. Another Nagasaki favorite, champon, consists of Chinese-style noodles, vegetables, and shellfish in a thick soup. Sara udon, created with the same ingredients, is fried instead of boiled.

Basashi (horse meat)—served roasted, fried, or raw—is a Kumamoto specialty. An easier-to-swallow delicacy is karashi renkon: slices of lotus root bathed in spicy curry and deep-fried. Compared to the subdued taste of most Japanese dishes, these foods attest to the bolder, more reckless flavors of the region.

In Kagoshima, don't pass up a chance to try satsuma-age, a fried fish cake stuffed with ingredients like garlic, cheese, meat, potato, or burdock root. Imo-shōchū, a spirit distilled from sweet potatoes, helps wash down these little goodies.

In Beppu most people tend to dine in their ryokans, where the culinary focus is always fresh fish and seafood. One particularly popular dish is fugu, or blowfish; yes, it's potentially poisonous, but only licensed chefs may prepare it.

bar-grill, Sora, on the top floor; the views from here of the Nakasu district are stunning. Head east from Exit 16 of the Tenjin subway station; take your first left, and you'll see the hotel on the right side. ✉ *1–16–1 Tenjin, Chūō-ku, Fukuoka, Fukuoka-ken 810-8584* ☎ *092/781–7111* 🖷 *092/781–7198* ⊕ *www.tokyuhotels.co.jp/en* ⇗ *217 rooms* ⏚ *Restaurant, in-room data ports, refrigerators, cable TV, bar, no-smoking rooms* ▭ *AE, DC, MC, V.*

★ $$ 🏨 **Hyatt Regency and Grand Hyatt** (ハイアットリージェンシー福岡 グランドハイアット福岡). There are two Hyatts in Fukuoka: the Hyatt Regency, near the station (on the Shinkansen side), and the Grand Hyatt in the Canal City entertainment complex. The Hyatt Regency attracts business travelers looking for efficient service and comfortable guest rooms. Those craving more extravagance and sophistication gravitate toward the Grand Hyatt. Its impressive lobby of rising square windows overlooks the architectural wonder of Canal City. Huge pillars, winding staircases, and sleek restaurants mark the entrance of this stylish hotel. The tasteful understated rooms peer out over either Canal City or the Nakagawa. *Hyatt Regency* ✉ *2–14–1 Hakata Eki-higashi, Hakata-ku, Fukuoka, Fukuoka-ken 812-0013* ☎ *092/412–1234* 🖷 *092/414–2490* ⊕ *www.fukuoka.regency.hyatt.com* ⇗ *248 rooms* ⏚ *2 restaurants,* *café, minibars, bar, shops, concierge floor, no-smoking rooms* ▱ *AE, DC, MC, V* ✉ *Grand Hyatt* ✉ *1–2–82 Sumiyoshi, Canal City, Hakata-ku, Fukuoka, Fukuoka-ken 812-0018* ☎ *092/282–1234* 🗟 *092/282–2817* ⊕ *www.fukuoka.grand.hyatt.com* 📞 *356 rooms, 14 suites* 👌 *4 restaurants, in-room data ports, minibars, pool, health club, hair salon, 2 bars, no-smoking rooms* ▱ *AE, DC, MC, V.*

¢ 🏨 **Hakata JBB Hotel** (博多JBBホテル). The lowest rates in the Hakata Station area can be found at this hotel, which shares the block with the Hakata Machiya Folk Museum. The Western-style rooms are modest, and the friendly owner, Mr. Yamada, speaks English. Follow the street from Exit 2 of the Gion subway station (one stop north of Hakata Station) and turn left at the first block. ✉ *6–5–1 Reisen-machi, Hakata-ku, Fukuoka, Fukuoka-ken 812-0039* ☎🗟 *092/263–8300* ⊕ *www5.ocn.ne.jp/~yamada1/index-english.htm* 📞 *45 rooms* ▱ *No credit cards.*

Nightlife

A lively nightlife scene dominates the Nakasu and Tenjin areas, which run along the Naka-gawa (Nakasu on the east side of the river, and Tenjin on the west side). Street stalls known as *yatai,* serving everything from Chinese dumplings to fried squid and skewered chicken, creep along the river on the Nakasu side; most stalls are only big enough for four or five customers to huddle together, but the intimacy creates warmth and coziness.

The classy **BaccuhsBassin** (バキュースバサン; ✉ Plaza Hotel Tenjin, 1–9–63 Daimyō, Chūō-ku ☎ 092/739–3210), on the top floor of Bassin restaurant, serves original cocktails, imported and domestic beers, and more than 150 types of sake. For a breathtaking view of Nakasu, join the quiet older crowd at **Sora** (ソラ; ✉ 1–16–1 Tenjin, Chūō-ku ☎ 092/781–7111), in the Hakata Tōkyū Inn. You can enjoy cocktails and innovative French cuisine with your view.

Jazz aficionados head to the polished **Blue Note Bar** (福岡ブルーノート; ✉ Chūō-ku Tenjin 2–7–6 ☎ 092/715–6666), in the basement of the Dada building, for nightly live performances. The cover varies. It's west of Iwataya department store.

The DJs at **Club Vibe** (クラブバイブ; ✉ Chūō-ku Tenjin 3–2–13 ☎ 092/716–2030), on the third floor of the Tenjin Center Building, play hip-hop, reggae, and R&B until 6 AM, so you can dance the night away or watch others tear up the floor. Admission is free except Friday (¥1,000) and Saturday (¥2,000) nights, when the cover charge includes one free drink for women. From Tenjin Station's West Exit 12, head north past Futata Fashion Store, take your first left, and then your second right.

Shopping

Fukuoka is known for two traditional folk crafts: Hakata *ningyō* (dolls) and Hakata obi (kimono sashes). Made of fired clay and hand-painted with bright colors and distinctive expressions, Hakata ningyō are primarily ornamental figures representing children, women, samurai, and geisha. For local girls, the purchase of their first Hakata obi marks their transition into adulthood. The obi are made of a local silk that has a slightly coarse texture; other products made of this silk, such as bags and purses, make excellent souvenirs.

The seventh floor of the department store **Iwataya** (岩田屋デパート; ⊠ 2–11–1 Tenjin, Chūō-ku ☎ 092/721–1111) carries the most complete selection of local merchandise, including Hakata ningyō, Hakata silk, and pottery. Expect mobs of Japanese shoppers every day of the week. You can head to the two basement levels of the main building for free food samples, or check out the restaurants on the 7th and 8th floors of the annex (known as the *shinkan*). From the Tenjin subway station, take Exit W-5 and follow the road straight for two blocks. Traditional Edo-style restaurants and shops selling quaint souvenirs line the **Kawabata Shopping Arcade** (Kawabata Shōtengai, 川端商店街), stretching along the Naka-gawa from the Nakasu-Kawabata subway station to Canal City.

Getting Around

BY AIR Fukuoka Airport is Kyūshū's only international airport. It's just two stops away from Fukuoka's Hakata train station on the Kūkō subway line, which means you can get from the airport to downtown within three minutes.

All Nippon Airways (ANA), Japan Airlines (JAL), and Skymark Airlines (SKY) fly the 1½-hour route to Fukuoka Airport from Tōkyō's Haneda Airport. JAL also flies once daily (1¾ hours) between Tōkyō's Narita International Airport and Fukuoka Airport. ANA and JAL have 12 direct flights (1¼ hours) between Ōsaka and Fukuoka. *See* Smart Travel Tips for airline phone numbers.

BY BUS A low-cost bus (¥100) operates in the city center of Fukuoka. Most city buses leave from **Hakata Kōtsū Bus Center** (☎ 092/431–1171), just across the street from Hakata Station, and from Tenjin Bus Center.

The **Kyūshū Kyūkō Bus Company** (☎ 092/734–2500 or 092/771–2961) makes the two-hour trip between Fukuoka's Tenjin Bus Center and Nagasaki. Frequent buses make the four-hour trip between Fukuoka (departing from Hakata Kōtsū Bus Center and Tenjin Bus Center) and Kagoshima.

Sightseeing buses leave from **Tenjin Bus Center** (☎ 092/734–2500 or 092/771–2961) and from Hakata Kōtsū Bus Center. Very few tours are given in English, so it's best to ask at your hotel or the tourist information office for recommended tours. A four-hour tour costs approximately ¥2,400.

BY SUBWAY Fukuoka's two major transportation hubs are Hakata Station and Tenjin, the terminal station for both subway lines. The Kūkō Line runs downtown through Tenjin to Hakata Station and Fukuoka Airport, and the Hakozaki Line runs from downtown toward the bay. Fares start at ¥200.

BY TRAIN JR *Hikari* Shinkansen trains travel between Tōkyō and Hakata Station in Fukuoka (5½ hours) via Ōsaka and Hiroshima. The regular nonreserved fare is ¥21,210 (free for JR Pass holders), and there are 15 daily runs. Regular JR express trains also travel this route but take twice as long.

Takeo Onsen & Arita 武雄温泉、有田

1 hr southwest of Fukuoka by JR, 1½ hr north of Nagasaki by JR.

❷ According to folklore, **Takeo Onsen** (武雄温泉) dates to the 3rd century AD, when the semilegendary Empress Jingū stopped here to recover from childbirth on her way home from invading Korea. She reportedly tapped the mineral spring, causing the hot waters to bubble to the surface, when she drove her walking stick in between two rocks to steady herself. There are several public baths, with both indoor and outdoor tubs, where you can take the waters; head west from the train station and enter the hot-springs area through the large Chinese-style vermilion gate—the symbol of the town. Three lofty camphor trees, all more than 3,000 years old and designated National Natural Monuments, can be seen at Takeo Onsen.

❸ The small village of **Arita** (有田) has one main street, which is lined with family-owned pottery shops—each with its own kiln passed down from generation to generation. The highly esteemed porcelain is known for its brightly colored glazes and exceptional durability. The prices increase with quality, but you can get a beautiful handmade teacup for around ¥1,800, or a set of five cups and a teapot for ¥10,000. Once a year, from April 29 to May 5, there's a large pottery fair, during which all merchandise goes on sale. Arita is about 20 minutes by local train from Takeo Onsen.

For more information on local pottery, contact the **Arita town office** (有田町役場; ✉ 2–8–1 Iwatanigawauchi ☎ 0955/43–5068).

off the beaten path

ŌKAWACHI-YAMA (大川内山) A 20-minute local train ride from Arita brings you to this town in the shadows of three towering mountains peaks. Porcelain pottery was first produced here by Ri Sampei, a Korean captive brought to Japan in the 17th century. The clandestine techniques of feudal-era craftsmanship were guarded here, earning Ōkawachi-yama the nickname "the village of the secret kilns."

Where to Eat

¢ ✕ **Muraichi-ban** (村一番). The centerpiece of this restaurant is a large open kitchen where cooks energetically fillet fish and stir-fry noodles. Eat at the counter to watch this performance or, if you don't want distractions, sit in one of the booths around the edge of the dining room. Bric-a-brac hangs from the wood-beamed ceilings, and posters on the walls add to the playful ambience of this local pub. The menu includes the likes of sashimi, grilled fish, yakitori, and omelets. ✉ 7283 Ōaza Takeo, Takeo-chō ☎ 0954/23–4995 ▭ *No credit cards.*

NAGASAKI 長崎

▶ *2 hrs southwest of Fukuoka by JR, 1½ hrs south of Takeo Onsen by JR.*

A colorful city surrounding a pleasant natural harbor, Nagasaki climbs up the sides of a narrow valley. The bay, now dominated by Mitsubishi cranes and shipyards, was once the most culturally significant port in Japan.

In 1639, fearful of foreign political interference, Shōgun Iemitsu Tokugawa's government closed all Japanese ports to outsiders. By the following year, the last of the remaining Portuguese and Spanish missionaries
had been expelled. A spattering of Chinese traders was permitted to stay
in Nagasaki, though the traders were restricted to their own settlement
in the city. Additionally, the Protestant Dutch traders, considered less
disruptive than other Europeans, were allowed to remain within the confines of Dejima, a small man-made island in Nagasaki Harbor. Through
this extremely limited contact, knowledge from the external world continued to seep into Japanese society, albeit at a slow and controlled rate.
Japan reopened its doors to the West at the beginning of the Meiji era
(1868–1912), and foreigners began to pour into Japan once again.

After more than two centuries of mercantile importance, Nagasaki had
sunk into relative obscurity until World War II, when an atomic bomb
devastated the city in 1945. Although the bomb destroyed one-third of
the city, enough has remained to testify to Nagasaki's unique foreign
history. Nineteenth-century European-style houses, the restored buildings of Dejima, Chinese temples, and Christian churches all speak elo-
quently of this city's past.

Exploring Nagasaki

Nagasaki is small enough to cover on foot if you have the energy to attack some of the inclines. Most of the interesting sights, restaurants, and
shopping areas are south of Nagasaki Station. Peace Park and the
Atomic Bomb Museum are to the north.

The **City Tourist Information Center** (長崎市観光案内所; ⊠ Nagasaki Station,
1–1 Onoue-machi ☎ 095/823–3631 ⊕ www1.city.nagasaki.nagasaki.jp)
provides English maps and brochures; it's open daily 8 to 7. The **Nagasaki
Prefecture Tourist Office** (長崎県観光連盟; ⊠ Nagasaki Ken-ei Bus Terminal
Bldg., 2nd fl., 3–1 Daikoku-machi ☎ 095/826–9407) is across the street
from Nagasaki Station. Use the pedestrian bridge on the second floor of
the train station to reach it. English travel information for the entire prefecture, including maps and bus schedules, is available daily 9 to 5:30.

❹ **Heiwa Kōen** (Peace Park, 平和公園) was built at the epicenter of the August 9, 1945, atomic blast. In a blinding flash, an area of 6.7 square km
(2.59 square mi) was obliterated, 74,884 people were killed, and another 74,909 were injured. With cold precision, a black pillar marks the
exact center of the blast. At the other end of the park is a 32-ft-tall statue
of a man with one arm pointing horizontally (symbolizing world peace),
the other pointing toward the sky (indicating the harm of nuclear
power). Every year on August 9 there is an anti-nuclear-war demonstration
here. From Nagasaki Station, take either Streetcar 1 or 3 for the 10-minute
ride to the Matsuya-machi stop. 🚶 *Free* ☉ *Daily 9–6.*

❺ The architecture of the **Atomic Bomb Museum** (Gembaku Shiryōkan,
原爆資料館) literally steers you spiraling downward into a collection of
video testimonies, interactive TV displays, and hands-on exhibits that
demonstrate the devastating effects of the nuclear bomb. A section pays
tribute to the foreign bomb victims, including the interned Allied POWs

and Korean slave laborers. Audio tours are available in English. To get to the museum, take Streetcar 1 from Nagasaki Station to the Hamaguchi stop. ⊠ *7–8 Hirano-machi* ☎ *095/844–1231* ⊕ *www1.city.nagasaki.nagasaki.jp* ⊡ *¥200, audio tour ¥150* ⊙ *Daily 8:30–5:30.*

❻ When the government expelled foreigners from Japan in the mid-17th century, Dutch traders were the only Westerners allowed to maintain contact. They were relegated to the artificial island of **Dejima** (出島), a post of the former Dutch East India Company in Nagasaki Harbor. The original island has been absorbed into downtown Nagasaki owing to a series of land-reclamation projects. You can view exhibitions and films in five buildings here, part of a reconstruction plan that will continue until 2010. The current displays afford fascinating insights into the lifestyles and trading practices of the Dutch during Japan's 220-year period of isolation. Take Streetcar 1 to the Dejima stop. ⊠ *6–3 Dejima-machi* ☎ *095/821–7200* ⊡ *¥300* ⊙ *Daily 9–5.*

❼ **Oranda-zaka** (Holland Slope, オランダ坂) is a cobblestone incline with wooden houses built by Dutch residents who moved into Nagasaki in the late 19th century, following the end of Japan's self-imposed isolation. Black-and-white Meiji-period photographs hang on the buildings, which house shops and tearooms that are open in summer. To get here, follow the street on the southeast side of the Chinese Mansion.

❽ The **Chinese Mansion** (Kōshibyō, 孔子廟), a bright-red Confucian shrine, was built in 1893 by the Chinese residents of Nagasaki. English explanations provide a worthwhile introduction to the Chinese influence on Nagasaki, and the small museum here displays artifacts on loan from Beijing's National Museum of Chinese History and the Palace Museum of Historical Treasures. The building stands on the property of the Chinese government, which is administered by the Chinese consulate in Tōkyō. The closest streetcar stop is Ishi-bashi; look for the signs leading to the shrine. ☎ *095/824–4022* ⊡ *¥525* ⊙ *Daily 8:30–5.*

❾
Fodor'sChoice
★
Glover Garden (Glover-en, グラバー園) contains an impressive collection of 19th-century Western houses, some in their original location, others transplanted from around the city. Wooden verandas, Greco-Roman porticos and arches, and other random elements of European architecture adorn the bases of these houses, which are crowned with Japanese-style roofs. The result is a fascinating fusion of styles. All of the buildings and furnishings are important relics, but the main attraction is the former mansion (1863) of Thomas Glover, a prominent Scottish merchant who contributed tremendously to the modernization of Japan by introducing the first steam locomotive and industrialized coal mine. The story for Giacomo Puccini's opera *Madame Butterfly* was allegedly set here, and the main character was rumored to be based on Glover's Japanese wife. Escalators whisk you up the steep hillside to the gardens. Be sure to pause and admire the breathtaking views of Nagasaki and the harbor. Take Streetcar 5 to Ōura Tenshudo-shita and follow the signs. ☎ *0958/22–8223* ⊡ *¥600* ⊙ *Oct.–July, daily 8–6; Aug. and Sept., daily 8–6.*

❿ **Ōura Catholic Church** (Ōura Tenshu-dō, 大浦天主堂) was constructed in 1865 to commemorate the death of 26 Christians who were crucified

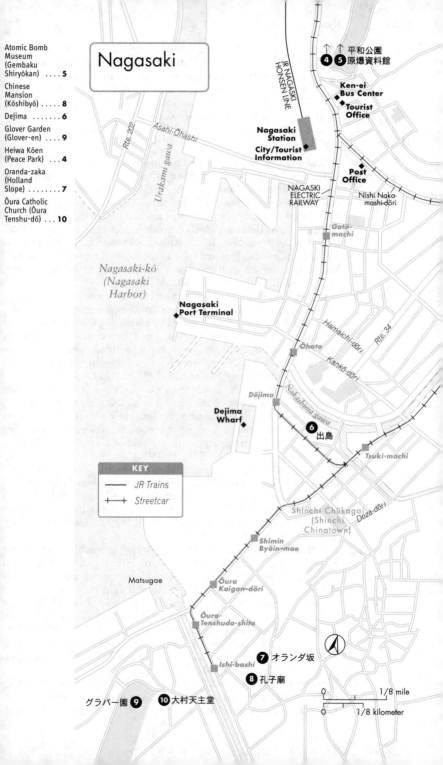

in 1597—victims of the fierce shōgun Hideyoshi Toyotomi's intolerant religious laws. It's the oldest Gothic-style building in Japan, and contains beautiful stained-glass windows imported from France. Below the entrance to Glover Garden, the church is a five-minute walk from the Ōura Tenshu-dō-shita streetcar stop.   ☎ 0958/23–2628 ✍ ¥300 ⊙ Mar.–Nov., daily 8–6; Dec.–Feb., daily 8:30–5.

Where to Stay & Eat

$$$$ ✕ **Kagetsu** (花月). Nagasaki's most prestigious restaurant is this quiet hill-
Fodor'sChoice top establishment. Dishes are served as kaiseki (Kyōto-style multicourse
★ meals) or shippoku, elaborate dishes that blend Asian and European elements. Lunch runs from ¥5,200 to ¥10,500; multicourse dinners start
at ¥11,000. The interior wooden beams date to 1618, when Kagetsu
reputedly operated as a high-class brothel. According to another local
legend, Meiji Restoration leader Ryōma Sakamoto became engaged in
a brawl while dining here and took a chunk out of a wooden pillar with
his sword, leaving a gash that is still visible today. ⊠ 2–1 Maruyama-
chō ☎ 095/822–0191 ⊟ DC, MC, V.

★ **¢–$$$** ✕ **Dejima Wharf** (出島ワーフ). Warm nights draw crowds to the outdoor
terraces of this trendy two-story wooden complex on the pier next to
Nagasaki Port. You'll find a sprawl of tantalizing seafood restaurants
downstairs; a quiet pub serving basic pasta dishes, pizza, and cocktails
at the north end of the second floor; and a family restaurant with burg-
ers and Japanese noodle and rice dishes on the south end of the second
floor. ⊠ Dejima Wharf ☎ 095/828–3939 ⊟ AE, DC, MC, V.

¢–$$ ✕ **Kōzanrō** (江山楼). Of the Chinese restaurants in Nagasaki's compact
Chinatown, this is one of the best known. Although its reputation is
grander than its cooking, Kōzanrō is a fun, lively restaurant. Dishes run
the gamut from champon (Chinese-style noodles and vegetables in a soup)
to gyōza (fried meat dumplings) to sweet-and-sour pork. ⊠ 12–2
Shinchi-machi ☎ 095/821–3735 ⊟ MC, V.

$ ✕ **Karuda** (カルダ). For authentic Italian cuisine, try this restaurant serv-
ing 50 varieties of pizza and 20 different pasta dishes. Rustic wooden
tables upstairs peer out over the narrow streets below. Takeout is also
available. From the Shian-bashi tram stop head two blocks north into
the arcade and another two blocks east. ⊠ 1–20 Kajiya-machi ☎ 095/
826–1302 ⊟ No credit cards.

★ **$$$$** ✕▢ **Hotel New Nagasaki** (ホテルニュー長崎). The marble lobby is light
and refreshing, and the French restaurant, Hydrangea, has the airy feel
of a conservatory. The 13th-floor Steak House specializes in the famous
succulent beef from Gotō Island. The standard twin rooms are the
largest in the city, with enough space for a couple of easy chairs and a
table. This hotel is just a two-minute walk from Nagasaki Station.
⊠ 14–5 Daikoku-machi, Nagasaki-shi, Nagasaki-ken 850-0057 ☎ 095/
826–8000 🖷 095/823–2000 ⊕ www.newnaga.com ✍ 145 rooms ♤ 8
restaurants, some in-room data ports, cable TV, indoor pool, gym,
sauna, shops ⊟ AE, DC, MC, V.

$$$$ ▢ **Nagasaki Prince Hotel** (長崎プリンスホテル). The interior of the city's grandest accommodation (and one of the most expensive) is a convincing imitation of a fine European hotel. The long rectangular lobby shimmers with

glass and marble, but is softened by natural elements like ponds, rocks, and wood. Guest rooms, decorated in pastels, provide all the amenities of a first-class hotel. The Prince is at the Takara-machi tram stop, or you can reach it in a 10-minute walk north from Nagasaki Station. ✉ *2–26 Takara-machi, Nagasaki-shi, Nagasaki-ken 850-0045* ☎ *095/821–1111* 🖷 *095/823–4309* ⊕ *www.princejapan.com/NagasakiPrinceHotel* 🛏 *183 rooms* ♨ *5 restaurants, room service, hair salon, concierge, meeting rooms, no-smoking rooms* ▭ *AE, DC, MC, V.*

★ **$$$$** 🏨 **Sakamoto-ya** (坂本屋). Established in 1895 in a wooden building that reflects the simple elegance of Japanese architecture, this ryokan seems to have changed very little from its founding days. The inn is very small, but offers extremely personalized service and cedar Japanese baths. The cost of the rooms varies according to size and location, but charges always include breakfast and dinner. The restaurant specializes in shippoku. ✉ *2–13 Kanaya-machi, Nagasaki-shi, Nagasaki-ken 850-0037* ☎ *095/826–8211* 🖷 *095/825–5944* 🛏 *14 Japanese-style rooms* ♨ *Restaurant, Japanese baths* ▭ *AE, DC, MC, V* ❘⊚❘ *MAP.*

$
Fodor's Choice
★
🏨 **Holiday Inn Nagasaki** (ホリデーイン長崎). If you're seeking affordability and a prime location—with a bit of style and sophistication—thrown in, this is the place. Leather chairs and vintage sofas, antique telephones, and dark oil paintings in the lobby are reminiscent of an old-fashioned European drawing room. Free English newspapers are available at the entrance, and the hotel staff provides friendly advice in perfect English. Rooms are comfortably spacious, with writing desks and large drawers. Look for the familiar sign on Kankō-dōri, the busy, main strip of downtown Nagasaki, at the Shian-bashi tram stop. ✉ *6–24 Dōza-machi, Nagasaki-shi, Nagasaki-ken 850-0841* ☎ *095/828–1234* 🖷 *095/ 828–0178* ⊕ *www.ichotelsgroup.com* 🛏 *87 rooms, 6 suites* ♨ *Restaurant, room service, refrigerators, lounge, car rental, no-smoking rooms* ▭ *AE, DC, MC, V.*

¢–$ 🏨 **Hotel WingPort** (ホテルウィングポート). PC rentals and in-room Internet access make the WingPort especially popular with business travelers. Guest quarters are a bit small, but the hotel is just a two-minute walk from Nagasaki Station (across the pedestrian bridge on the narrow road past the convenience store). ✉ *9–2 Daikoku-machi, Nagasaki-shi, Nagasaki-ken 850-0057* ☎ *095/833–2800* 🖷 *095/833–2801* 🛏 *200 rooms* ♨ *Restaurant, in-room data ports* ▭ *AE, DC, MC, V.*

Shopping

Castella cake, the first baked good in Japan, was introduced by the Portuguese. This sweet sponge cake has become *the* souvenir of Nagasaki, and can be found in every sweet shop and souvenir store in town. Creative variations on the original—including green tea, chocolate, and cheese versions—are quickly gaining in popularity.

The bakery **Fukusaya** (福砂屋; ✉ *3–1 Funadaiku-machi* ☎ *095/821–2938*) has been in business since the beginning of the Meiji period. When you say "castella," most people think of this famous shop and its distinctive yellow packaging. There are two satellite shops in the shopping complex at Nagasaki Station.

Not far from Dejima, **Hamano-machi** (浜野町) is the major shopping district in downtown Nagasaki. This covered arcade stretches over four blocks and contains numerous department stores, cake shops, cafés, pharmacies, and fashion boutiques.

Glass Road 1571 (グラスロード1571; ⊠ 2–11 Minami-yamate-machi ☎ 095/822–1571), near Ōura Catholic Church, sells Nagasaki glassware, an art form introduced by the Europeans during the Tokugawa period. Prices ranges from ¥250 to ¥100,000.

Getting Around

BY AIR   Nagasaki Airport is approximately one hour by bus or car from Nagasaki. A regular shuttle bus travels between Nagasaki Airport and Nagasaki Station in 55 minutes and costs ¥1,200. All Nippon Airways and Japan Airlines fly daily from Haneda Airport in Tōkyō to Nagasaki Airport (1¾ hours). From Ōsaka the flights are about 1¼ hours. *See* Smart Travel Tips for airline phone numbers and Web sites.

BY BOAT   One-hour **cruises** (☎ 095/824–0088) of Nagasaki Harbor depart from Nagasaki-kō (Nagasaki Port) at 10:30, noon, 1:30, 3, and 4:30; the cost is ¥1,200.

BY BUS   The **Kyūshū Kyūkō Bus Company** (☎ 092/734–2500) runs buses between Fukuoka's Tenjin Bus Center and **Nagasaki's bus terminal** (⊠ 3–1 Daikoku-machi ☎ 095/826–6221); the trip takes two hours. From Nagasaki it's a two-hour trip to Unzen (¥1,900), on the Shimabara Peninsula, and a three-hour trip to Kumamoto (¥3,600) on the **Nagasaki Ken-ei Bus** (☎ 095/823–6155).

BY RICKSHAW   A few privately run rickshaws hang out on the streets of Chinatown, advertising a friendly, comfortable alternative to touring the city on foot. The minimum cost is ¥1,000 per person, and you can call ahead to arrange a pickup at your hotel.

BY STREETCAR   Nagasaki's streetcar system is the most convenient mode of transportation in the city, as stops are posted in English and lines extend to every attraction in town. You can purchase a one-day streetcar pass (¥500) at tourist offices and major hotels. Otherwise, pay ¥100 as you get off the streetcar. If you wish to transfer from one streetcar to another, take a *norikae kippu* (transfer ticket) from the driver of the first streetcar.

BY TRAIN   The JR Nagasaki Line Limited Express train from Fukuoka's Hakata Station to **Nagasaki Station** (⊠ 1–1 Onoue-machi, Nagasaki-shi ☎ 095/826–4336) takes two hours. To get to Kumamoto from Nagasaki, take the Kamome Line to Tosu Station (two hours) and switch to the Kagoshima Main Line (one hour).

en route   The bus from Nagasaki to Kumamoto passes through the site of an infamous 17th-century battleground: Shimabara Peninsula. In 1637 disgruntled samurai, poor peasants, and religious zealots rose up against the oppressive feudal system; the revolt was quelled, but some 37,000 people lost their lives. **Unzen,** a town built in the shadow of Unzen-dake (Mt. Unzen, 雲仙) in the middle of the peninsula, abounds with underground sulphur springs and steam vents, geological phenomena referred to as *jigoku* (the hells). High-pressure steam shrieks from the fumaroles, and puffs of yellow sulphurous smoke put on quite a performance. In an attempt to purge Japan of evangelical influences, feudal armies once massacred Christians in these scalding pits. The two-hour bus ride from Nagasaki Ken-ei Bus Terminal (¥1,900) drops you at the northern end of Unzen's only street. Head east and follow the signs for the hells. You can soak in thermal baths in the Tudor-style **Unzen Spa House** (雲仙スパハウス; ✉ across from post office ☎ 095/573–3131). It's open daily 11–7 and costs ¥800. If you have a lot of time to spend in the Unzen area, you may want to hike or take the cable-car ride up **Fugen-dake** (Mt. Fugen, 普賢岳) for rewarding views and lush foliage.

KUMAMOTO 熊本

⑪ *1½ hrs south of Fukuoka by JR Limited Express.*

Kumamoto was an important center of power during the Tokugawa shogunate (1603–1868) and the civil wars of 1868–1877. The castle and gardens of Suizen-ji Kōen date from this period and are among the most famous historical sights in Japan.

Exploring Kumamoto

Very little surrounds the JR Kumamoto Station, a rare sight in Japanese cities. Most shops, restaurants, hotels, and attractions are downtown, squeezed in between the Tsuboi and Shira rivers, huddling under the protective shadow of the castle.

The **City Tourist Information Office** (観光案内所; ✉ JR Kumamoto Station, 3-15-1 Kasuga ☎ 096/352–3743 ⊕ www.city.kumamoto.kumamoto. jp), open daily 9 to 5, can provide maps and information in English. And the city's Web site has good descriptions of major sights.

★ The towering **Kumamoto Castle** (Kumamoto-jō, 熊本城) was completed in 1607 under the auspices of Kiyomasa Katō, the area's *daimyō*, or feudal lord. Graceful black-and-white curved roofs sit atop a wide stone base with *mushagaeshi*: massive, concave defensive walls that prevented intruders from scaling the castle. Seemingly impregnable, the castle lay under siege for 57 consecutive days during the Satsuma Rebellion of 1877—an uprising of disenchanted samurai enraged over their diminishing status and wealth under the imperial Meiji government. The samurai fought valiantly, but it was a swift victory for the imperial army, which was trained in European military techniques and armed with modern Western guns. The castle was seriously damaged in the battle, and the costly reconstruction of all 49 turrets, 18 turret gates, and 29 gates didn't occur until 1960. Exhibits inside include samurai armor and swords that evoke images of the fiercely loyal warriors dressed in full regalia and charging into battle. The top floor commands an excellent view of Kumamoto. To get to the castle, board Streetcar 2, get off at the Kumamoto-jō-mae stop, and walk up the tree-lined slope. Volunteer guides conduct tours in English, or you can take a self-guided audiocassette tour for ¥300. ☎ 096/352–5900 🎫 ¥500; ¥640 for combined admission to castle and Hosokawa Mansion; purchase ticket at castle ⊙ Apr.–Oct., daily 8:30–5:30; Nov.–Mar., daily 8:30–4:30.

The **Hosokawa Mansion** (Kyū-Hosokawa Gyōbutei, 旧細川刑部邸) was built in 1646 for the Hosokawa family, who came into power after the death of the daimyō Kato in 1611. Now it stands as a rare example of a high-ranking samurai residence. English-speaking guides lead a detailed tour, pointing out fascinating architectural features such as hidden doors and booby traps. To get here, follow the signs from the main castle entrance. ✉ 3–1 Furukyō-machi ☎ 096/352–6522 🎫 ¥300; ¥640 for combined admission to mansion and Kumamoto Castle; purchase ticket at castle ⊙ Apr.–Oct., Tues.–Sun. 8:30–5:30; Nov.–Mar., Tues.–Sun. 8:30–4:30.

In the late 16th century, Kiyomasa Katō built **Honmyō-ji** (Honmyō Temple, 本妙寺), which is today the Kyūshū headquarters of the Nichiren sect of Buddhism. Katō's mausoleum is here, perched at the top of a steep flight of stairs and eye level with the *tenshukaku* (stronghold) of his castle. The small adjacent museum contains Katō's personal effects, but is of marginal interest. Instead, check out the view of Kumamoto from the observatory on top. Follow the signs from the Honmyōji-mae streetcar station. 🎫 ¥300 ⊙ Tues.–Sun. 9–4:30.

Created in the mid-17th century, **Suizen-ji Kōen** (Suijzen-ji Park, 水前寺公園） was originally part of the sprawling villa of the ruling Hosokawa family. A portion of the garden re-creates the 53 stations of the Tōkaidō— the old post road stretching between Edo (present-day Tōkyō) and Kyōto—and its prominent features, Biwa-ko (Lake Biwa) and Fuji-san (Mt. Fuji). The ruling aristocracy would come to this quiet retreat to practice the tea ceremony and gaze at the expertly sculpted landscape. Also on the grounds is Izumi Jinja (Izumi Shrine), which houses the tombs of several eminent Hosokawa clan members. To get to the park, take Streetcar 2 or 3 east from the castle to the Suizen-ji Kōen-mae stop. 🎫 ¥400 ⊙ Mar.–Nov., daily 7:30–6; Dec.–Feb., daily 8:30–5.

need a break?

Near the pond in Suizen-ji Kōen, stop at the celebrated **old-fashioned teahouse** (Kokin Denju no Ma, 古今伝授の間) to enjoy green tea and a small sweet while appreciating the exquisite view of the gardens. Originally a part of the Imperial Palace in Kyōtō, this thatched house was moved here in 1912.

Where to Stay & Eat

$$$$ ✕ **Loire** (ロワール). Prix-fixe French dinners are served at this elegant, spacious restaurant on the 11th floor of the Kumamoto Castle Hotel. Windows provide a dramatic view of the castle, which is flooded in pale-green light at night. ✉ 4–2 Jōtō-machi ☎ 096/326–3311 ☰ AE, DC, MC, V.

$ ✕ **Aoyagi** (青柳). When you enter, a Japanese woman clad in a beautiful kimono will softly shuffle over to greet you. You can sit at the sushi counter and admire the skilled chefs hard at work, or at one of the cozy Japanese-style booths. The extensive menu includes regional favorites—basashi (raw horse meat) and karashi renkon (lotus root fried in a spicy batter)—in addition to sushi, salads, and tofu dishes. Near the Shiyakusho-mae streetcar stop, the restaurant is tucked away behind the Daiei department store. ⊠ *1–2–10 Shimotori-chō* ☎ *096/353–0311* ▤ *AE, DC, V.*

$$$ 🏨 **Hotel New Ōtani Kumamoto** (ホテルニューオータニ熊本). Weary travelers welcome the sight of this sleek chain hotel just outside Kumamoto Station. Although smaller than its big-city counterparts, this branch offers all the same fine services and amenities. ⊠ *1–13–1 Kasuga, Kumamoto-shi, Kumamoto-ken 860-0047* ☎ *096/326–1111* 🖨 *096/326–0800* ⊕ *www.newotani.co.jp/en* ➘ *130 rooms* ♨ *4 restaurants, room service, sauna, piano bar* ▤ *AE, DC, MC, V.*

★ ¢–$$$ 🏨 **Ark Hotel Kumamoto** (アークホテル熊本). The modern lobby of this hotel has wooden floors, massive skylights, and picture windows overlooking an unexpected courtyard of bamboo groves. The location, just across from the moat of Kumamoto Castle, is excellent; be sure to request a room with a view, which is well worth the extra ¥1,000–¥1,500. ⊠ *5–16 Jōtō-machi, Kumamoto-shi, Kumamoto-ken 862-0846* ☎ *096/351–2222* 🖨 *096/326–0909* ➘ *222 rooms* ♨ *2 restaurants* ▤ *AE, DC, MC, V.*

$ 🏨 **Fujie Hotel** (藤江ホテル). The foyer of this business hotel has free Internet access and comfortable couches that face the delicate garden outside. Service is personable and friendly, and breakfast is available for ¥945. You can choose from Western-style single rooms or Japanese-style doubles. Look for the bright entrance on the main street leading away from Kumamoto Station. ⊠ *2–2–35 Kasuga, Kumamoto-shi, Kumamoto-ken 860-0047* ☎ *096/353–1101* 🖨 *096/322–2671* ➘ *4 Western-style rooms, 43 Japanese-style rooms* ♨ *Restaurant, Internet* ▤ *AE, DC, MC, V.*

$ 🏨 **Tōyoko Inn Karashima Kōen** (東横イン唐島公園). This immaculate, inexpensive hotel built in 2003 offers a rare bonus: a free in-room movie channel in the otherwise no-frills Western-style rooms. Be sure to ask for the complimentary Japanese breakfast—rice ball, miso soup, and coffee—before you head out in the morning. To get here take the streetcar to Karashima-chō. ⊠ *1–24 Konyaima-machi, Kumamoto-shi, Kumamoto-ken, 860-0012* ☎ *096/322–1045* 🖨 *096/322–2045* ⊕ *www.toyoko-inn.com* ➘ *153 rooms* ♨ *Restaurant, cable TV, laundry facilities, Internet, no-smoking rooms* ▤ *AE, DC, MC, V* ⎮◉⎮ *CP.*

Shopping

Kumamoto's most famous product is *higo zōgan*, black steel delicately inlaid with silver and gold. A form of metalwork originally employed in the decoration of swords, scabbards, and gun stocks of the Hosokawa clan, it is now used to make fashionable jewelry.

Dentō Kōgei-kan (伝統工芸館; Kumamoto Traditional Crafts Center; ⊠ 3–35 Chiba-jō ☎ 096/324–4930), open Tuesday–Sunday 9–5, is the best place in the city to buy regional handicrafts. It's in a redbrick building across from the Akazumon entrance to the castle. The **Shimotōri-Kamitōri Shōtengai** (下通・上通アーケード) arcade, which marks the commercial center of Kumamoto, sells everything from toothpaste and underwear to local crafts. It's near Kumamoto Castle; the Tōrichō-Suji bus and streetcar stops bisect the arcade.

Getting Around

BY AIR   The Kyūshū Sankō bus makes the 50-minute run from Kumamoto Airport to JR Kumamoto Station for ¥670. Flights on All Nippon Airways and Sky Net Asia (SNA) connect Tōkyō's Haneda Airport with Kumamoto Airport (1¼ hours). ANA flies the hour-long route from Ōsaka's Itami Airport eight times a day. *See* Smart Travel Tips for airline phone numbers and Web sites.

BY BUS   The Nagasaki Ken-ei Bus from Nagasaki Ken-ei Bus Terminal costs ¥3,600 and takes three hours to **Kumamoto City Kōtsū Center** (✉ 3–10 Sakuramachi ☎ 096/354–6411). Before reaching Kumamoto the bus stops in Unzen (¥1,900, two hours). **Sankō buses** (☎ 096/355–2525) leaving from Kumamoto City Kōtsū Center make the three-hour trip to Kagoshima.

BY STREETCAR   Two streetcar lines (Nos. 2 and 3) connect the major areas of the city. Grab a ticket from the automatic dispenser when you board the streetcar and pay as you get off. A fare chart is posted at the front, to the left of the driver. From the Kumamoto Eki-mae streetcar stop in front of the train station, it's a 10-minute ride downtown (¥150). One-day travel passes, good for use on streetcars and municipal *shiei* (buses), are available for ¥500 from the City Tourist Information Office.

BY TRAIN   The Tsubame, JR's Limited Express from Fukuoka's Hakata Station, stops at **Kumamoto Station** (✉ 3–15–1 Kasuga ☎ 096/211–2406) en route to southern Kyūshū. The trip from Fukuoka takes 1¼ hours and costs ¥3,940. From Nagasaki, take JR to Tosu and change to the train for Kumamoto (2¾ hours, ¥7,170).

KAGOSHIMA 鹿児島

⑫ *1¼ hrs south of Kumamoto by Shinkansen, 2¼ hrs south of Fukuoka by JR.*

The attractions of this sultry southern city, where palm trees sway against the backdrop of smoky Mt. Sakurajima, used to be too remote for travelers on a tight schedule. Now, the superfast Shinkansen train whisks you from Kumamoto to southern Kyūshū in just one hour.

Exploring Kagoshima

The heart of the city lies in Tenmonkan-dōri, the downtown shopping-arcade area located between two JR stations: Chūō Kagoshima Station, to the west, and Kagoshima Station, to the northeast.

The **Chūō Kagoshima Station Tourist Office** (中央駅総合観光案内所; ✉ 1–1 Chūō-machi ☎ 099/253–2500) is a short walk north of the station's east exit. There's always at least one English-speaking person on hand to help you make hotel reservations. You can also pick up an excellent English map here. It's open daily 8:30–6.

Across the sparkling waters of Kinkō Bay rises the magnificent volcano
★ **Sakurajima** (桜島), which has been spewing thick plumes of smoke almost
continuously since its massive eruption in 1955. The volcano also experiences occasional explosive burps that light up the sky with fireworks
and cover Kagoshima in a blanket of ash. Because of its striking resemblance to Pearl Harbor in Hawaii, the Kinkō Bay area was the primary
location used for training Japanese fighter pilots in the months leading
up to the surprise attack on the United States on December 7th, 1942.
If the stunning view of Sakurajima across the bay fails to satisfy your curiosity, you may want to hop aboard the **24-hour ferry,** which will bring
you face to face with the fiery monster. Ferries leave Kagoshima for Sakurajima Port every 10–15 minutes, with fewer connections after 10 PM.
The ride costs ¥150 each way and takes 15 minutes. It's possible to pick
up a 3-hour **kankō bus** (観光バス; ☎ 099/293–2525) tour of the volcano
from Sakurajima Port; tours depart daily at 9:30 AM and 1:30 PM and
cost ¥1,700. ✉ *Kagoshima Port, 4–1 Shinmachi, Honkō* ☎ *099/223–
7271* ✉ *Sakurajima Port, 61–4 Sakurajima-Yokoyama-chō* ☎ *099/
293–2525.*

**off the
beaten
path**

SUNAMUSHI KAIKAN – (砂蒸し会館) For an unforgettable afternoon
of relaxation, head to the geothermal sands of this seaside resort on
the southern tip of the Satsuma Peninsula. You can purchase tickets
and rent towels and robes on the second floor of the main building
before heading out to the sandy beach. Stake out a spot with a nice
view of the ocean, and wait for an assistant to flip-flop over and bury
you alive with her shovel. Aside from providing health benefits, the
stimulating experience is an ancient form of therapeutic treatment—
guaranteed to cleanse your pores and soften even the toughest skin.
Take the one-hour trip south to Ibusuki on the Ibusuki-Makurazaki
train line. ✉ *5–25–18 Yū-no-hama, Ibusuki-shi* ✉ *¥900, including
towel and robe rental* ⊘ *Daily 8:30–noon and 1–8:30.*

Where to Stay & Eat

★ **$$$** ✕ **Kumasotei** (熊襲亭). Behind the austere entrance is a cheerful labyrinth
of private and semiprivate Japanese-style rooms. The English menu, with
photographs of the food, lists set meals ranging from ¥3,150 to ¥5,250.
Even the smallest set includes samples of all the local specialties: *kibi-
nago* (raw herring), satsuma-age (fish cakes filled with potato or bur-
dock root), *kurobuta-no-tonkotsu* (pork chops marinated in sake, ginger,
and brown sugar, and sautéed with radish and bamboo). Larger courses
come with additional meat and tempura dishes. From the Tenmonkan-
dōri streetcar stop, walk four blocks north through the covered arcade
and turn left; the restaurant will be on the right. ✉ *6–10 Higashi Sen-
goku-chō* ☎ *099/222–6356* ☰ *AE, DC, MC, V.*

$$ ✕ **Amami Restaurant Keihan** (奄美レストランけいはん). This restaurant specializes in *keihan,* a dish from the southern Kyūshū island of Amami
Oshima. Sliced chicken, cooked egg, strips of dried seaweed, green
onions, and mushrooms are meticulously arranged on a circular platter and served with bowls of rice and broth. Place the meat and veg-

etables on the rice, add a little wasabi, and douse the mixture with the broth to create a hearty, flavorful feast. From the Tenmonkan-dōri streetcar stop, head north, take the first right, and walk two blocks. After crossing the big road, Tengoku-dōri, turn right at the first block. ✉ *Yamahira Bldg. 2F, 5–19 Naka-chō* ☎ *099/223–2855* �__ *AE, DC, V* ☺ *Closed 3rd Tues. of month.*

$$ 🏨 **Furusato Kankō Hotel** (ふるさと観光ホテル). The outdoor onsen of this
FodorsChoice Sakurajima hotel affords a superb view of the Pacific Ocean. If you pre-
★ fer a swim, head to the small sea-water pool near the beach or the heated indoor lap pool. The slight alkalinity of the waters here is said to soothe burns, cuts, rashes, and other skin ailments. Unlimited use of the onsen, pools, and meditation room are included in the rate, as well as two meals. Every room has a view of the water; five have miniature gardens. A free shuttle (15 minutes) runs every half hour between the hotel and the Sakurajima ferry port. ✉ *1076–1 Furusato-chō, Kagoshima-shi, Kagoshima-ken 891-1592* ☎ *099/221–3111* 🖷 *099/ 221–2345* 🛏 *40 Japanese-style rooms* ⚟ *Restaurant, pool, hot springs, bar* 🚪 *AE, DC, MC, V* 🍴 *MAP.*

$$ 🏨 **Kinkō Kōgen Hotel** (錦江高原ホテル). The highlight of this hotel is the "panorama onsen": an unadorned outdoor bath with stunning views of Kinkō-wan (Kinkō Bay) and the Sakurajima volcano. Containing sodium and chlorides, the spring water is said to provide relief from rheumatism, nervous disorders, and shoulder pain. Double rooms come with sofas; the Japanese-Western combination rooms for fami-lies have spacious tatami sitting rooms. Among the eateries here are a family restaurant with a Western buffet, a pricey Japanese restau-rant, a cozy dark tea lounge serving coffee and cake; and a summer-only beer garden overlooking Sakurajima. Room and meal charges are half price for children. ✉ *3273 Shimo-fukumoto-machi, Kagoshima-shi, Kagoshima-ken 891-0144* ☎ *099/262–2111* 🖷 *099/262–2198* 🛏 *14 combination rooms, 9 Western-style twin rooms, 1 suite* ⚟ *3 restaurants, tea shop, 3 tennis courts, hot springs, massage, beer gar-den* 🚪 *AE, DC, MC, V* 🍴 *BP.*

$ 🏨 **Urban Port Hotel** (アーバンポートホテル). This jazzed-up, good-value busi-ness hotel offers many extras, including a gallery displaying paintings by local artists. The hotel's best feature is convenience: within a 10-minute walk are the Kagoshima train station, Tenmonkan nightlife district, Saku-rajima ferry port, and Kagoshima market. ✉ *15–1 Ogawa-chō, Kagoshima-shi, Kagoshima-ken 892-0817* ☎ *099/239–4111* 🖷 *099/239–4112* 🛏 *102 rooms* ⚟ *Restaurant, pool, health club, massage, no-smoking rooms* 🚪 *AE, MC, V.*

Getting Around

BY AIR The flight between Tōkyō's Haneda Airport and Kagoshima Airport lasts 1¾ hours. From Ōsaka the flight takes about 1¼ hours. The **Airport Limou-sine** (☎ 099/256–2151) picks up passengers every 10 minutes (until 9 PM) at bus stop No. 2 outside the Kagoshima Airport. The 55-minute trip to Chūō Kagoshima Station costs ¥1,200.

BY BUS   Frequent buses make the four-hour trip from Fukuoka (departing from Hakata Kōtsū Bus Center and Tenjin Bus Center) to **Chūō Kagoshima Station** (⊠ 1–1 Chūo-chō ☎ 099/256–1585). **Sankō buses** (☎ 096/355–2525) leave from Kumamoto City Kōtsū Center and take three hours to get to Kagoshima.

Kagoshima-shi Transportation Office (⊠ Sakurajima Port ☎ 099/293–2525) offers tours of the Sakurajima-volcano area that include lava outcrops and Yunohira Observatory (Yunohira Tenbōsho). From Sakurajima Port, follow the English signs for the tours on the first floor. Tours (¥1,700) depart twice daily at 9:30 AM and 1:30 PM and last 3 hours; they're in Japanese, but English tapes are available.

BY FERRY   The **24-hour ferry** (⊠ Kagoshima Port, 4–1 Shinmachi, Honkō ☎ 099/223–7271 ⊠ Sakurajima Port, 61–4 Sakurajima-Yokoyama-chō ☎ 099/293–2525) connects Kagoshima with Sakurajima Port, from which you can visit the Sakurajima volcano. Ferries depart every 10 to 15 minutes, with fewer connections after 10 PM. The one-way fare is ¥150, and the trip takes 15 minutes.

BY STREETCAR   The easiest way to get around Kagoshima is by streetcar. A ¥160 fare will take you anywhere on the network. One-day travel passes for unlimited rides on streetcars and municipal buses cost ¥600. You can buy one at the Chūō Kagoshima Station Tourist Office, on a bus, or on a streetcar.

BY TRAIN   The JR Limited Express Tsubame, which becomes the Kyūshū Shinkansen in Shin-Yatsushiro, arrives at **Chūō Kagoshima Station** (⊠ 1–1 Chūo-chō ☎ 099/256–1585) from Fukuoka's Hakata Station in 2¼ hours and from Kumamoto in 1¼ hours.

ASO-SAN (MT. ASO, 阿蘇山)

⑬ *2 ¾ hrs northeast of Kagoshima by JR or 1 hr east of Kumamoto by JR, then 40 min by bus.*

Aso-san sits on top of the world's largest caldera—measuring 18 km (11 mi) by 24 km (15 mi)—formed after a series of eruptions around 100,000 years ago. The crater area, officially named the Aso-Kujū (Mt. Aso National Park), contains five volcanic cones, one of which is still active. The road leading to the park passes through the splendor of rural Kyūshū: cows and horses grazing in wide open pastures and farmers bent over rice fields. Surrounding the peaks, the emerald-green pastures that nourish Aso's many dairy cows and ranch cattle thrive off the fertile soil of volcanic ash. This serene imagery dramatically transforms as you draw near the furrowed walls of the active volcanic peak, Nakadake, which exhales angry yellow clouds laced with malodorous gases.

Mt. Aso National Park is an excellent stopover on the way to Beppu or Yufuin from western Kyūshū. If you want to spend more time in the park, you can stay in one of the many mountain pensions clustered in the southern half. Stop by the **Aso Station Information Center** (阿蘇駅インフォメーションセンター; ⊠ JR Aso Station ☎ 0967/34–0751) to get your bearings.

Exploring Aso-san

Fodor'sChoice
★

The one active volcano, **Nakadake** (中岳), is reason enough to visit Mt. Aso National Park. From the inside of the crater, which is 1,968 feet across and 525 feet deep, a churning lake bubbles and spits scalding steam. Nakadake can be reached from the **Aso Nishi cable car** (⊠ Furubōchū, Aso-chō ☎ 0967/34–0411) at Asosan-jō. The cable car (¥410 one-way) takes you to the top of the crater in four minutes, weather and volcano conditions permitting. You can either descend the same way or walk down along a path that leads you back to the cable car station in about 20 minutes.

Because of the death of two tourists from gaseous emissions in 1997, the local authorities regularly suspend Nakadake cable-car service and close hiking trails at the slightest sign of danger. In these cases, you can often still take a helicopter tour for a view of the volcano; the choppers park in the fields off the road leading from Kusasenri to the cable-car station.

Kusasenri (草千里) is the base for all Aso activities. Skip the overpriced restaurants and coffee shops in the rest area and head across the street to the sprawling green meadows, which are perfect for a picnic or a scenic walk. Horses and cows roam freely, as do young couples and kids. Expect to find the fields packed during holidays, and only mildly populated the rest of the year. From the JR Aso Station, it's a 35-minute bus ride on the Kyūshū Sankō line to Kusasenri.

Most hiking trails originate in Kusasenri. The easiest loop, 5½ km (3½ mi) around the base of Kijimadake crater, takes one hour and provides splendid views of the surrounding peaks and fields. Ambitious hikers can choose from several trails of various lengths and intensities in the area. Be sure to pick up the *Aso Trekking Route Map* and inquire about current hiking conditions at the information center in JR Aso Station or at Kusasenri.

To observe live footage of the volcanic activity from a distance, stop by the **Aso Volcano Museum** (Aso Kazan Hakubutsukan, 阿蘇火山博物館) at the Kusasenri parking and rest area. The museum also has exhibits about the natural history of Aso-san and information on other active volcanoes around the world. ⊠ *Kusasenri Aso-chō* ☎ *0967/34–2111* ⊞ *¥840* ⊙ *Daily 9–5.*

Where to Stay

$$$–$$$$ ☒ **Aso Prince Hotel** (阿蘇プリンスホテル). Tucked away at the base of Nakadake, this hotel overlooks two courses designed by golf legend Arnold Palmer. The indoor baths, tennis courts, and hotel grounds are all immaculately maintained, and even the driveway running through the golf course is a work of art. ⊠ *Akamizu, Komezuka Onsen, Aso-chō, Aso-gun, Kumamoto-ken 869-2232* ☎ *0967/35–2111* ⊟ *0967/35–1124* ⊷ *180 rooms* ⌂ *Restaurant, 2 golf courses, 6 tennis courts, Japanese baths, massage, horseback riding, bar, shops* ⊟ *AE, DC, MC, V.*

★ $$$ ☒ **Yamaguchi Ryokan** (山口旅館). From the outdoor baths of this rustic ryokan built in the late 19th century you can watch gentle streams of water meander down the rocky cliffs of the green mountainside. Two meals are included, and dinner is served in your Japanese-style room. The lobby, with its high wood-beam ceiling and toasty old-fashioned furnace, is a cozy place to enjoy a cup of tea or coffee. From Kumamoto, take the JR Hōhi Line to Tateno and switch to the Minami Aso Tetsudō Line. ⊠ *2331 Kawayō, Chōyō-mura, Aso-gun, Kumamoto-ken 860-1404* ☎ *0967/67–0006* 📠 *0967/67–1694* 🛏 *35 Japanese-style rooms* ♨ *Hot springs* 🖃 *AE, DC, MC, V* ❘⊙❘ *MAP.*

\$\$ 🖼 **Pension Angelica** (ペンションアンジェリカ). The main appeal of this country manor is the hospitality of the friendly Tatsuji family, who fill their lovely inn with warm smiles. White lacy bedspreads decorate the bright guest rooms, which have tall windows overlooking well-maintained lawns, rose bushes, and colorful flowers. Appetizing fragrances emanate from the kitchen, where the chef whips up Mediterranean dishes. At the crafts classes here you can learn to make *washi* (Japanese paper) or clay figurines. From Kumamoto, take the JR Hōhi Line to Tateno and switch to the Minami Aso Tetsudō Line. Get off at Takamori and call the pension, which will have someone pick you up. ⊠ *1800 Shirakawa, Hakusai-mura, Aso-gun, Kumamoto-ken 869–1502* ☎📠 *0967/62–2223* ⊕ *www5.ocn.ne.jp/~angelica* 🛏 *7 rooms, 2 with bath* ♨ *Restaurant, Japanese baths, bar, lounge, no-smoking rooms* 🖃 *No credit cards* ❘⊙❘ *MAP.*

*Fodor's*Choice
★

\$ 🖼 **Pension Okanoie** (ペンションおかの家). The friendly owner of this small retreat in Pension Nombiri Village will be happy to pick you up at the station or drive you to the cable car. The Western-style rooms come with small bath-showers, and there are two larger (family-size) mineral baths available (use the OCCUPIED sign for privacy). Rates are for bed and breakfast, but you can also arrange to have a nice Western-style dinner and spend a quiet evening working on the locally crafted wooden puzzles while chatting with the owner. It's not far from Tateno Station (on the JR Hōhi Line). ⊠ *4732–10 Kawayō, Chōyō-mura, Aso-gun, Kumamoto-ken 869-1404* ☎ *0967/67–1818* 📠 *0967/67–2156* ⊕ *www.asopension. com/okanoie* 🛏 *10 rooms* ♨ *Japanese baths, no-smoking rooms* 🖃 *No credit cards* ❘⊙❘ *CP.*

Getting Around

BY BUS **Kyūshū Sankō and Kumakita Sankō buses** (☎ 096/355–2525 or 0968/857–1000) make frequent runs between Kumamoto City Kōtsū Center, the Aso Nishi cable-car station at Asosan-jō, and Kurokawa Onsen. The Kyūshū bus continues from Kurokawa Onsen to Yufuin and Beppu.

BY HELICOPTER Even when the Nakadake crater is too active to ascend on foot, private helicopter companies are permitted to fly in the area. The flights afford a view of the caldera's fiery blue lake and expose you to the intense heat and strong sulphur smell. This adrenaline rush costs about ¥5,000. Look for the helicopters in the fields off the road leading from Kusasenri to the cable-car station.

BY TRAIN The JR Hōhi Line runs between Kumamoto Station and **JR Aso Station** (⊠ Kurokawa, Aso-chō ☎ 0967/34–0101) in 56 minutes. From JR Aso Station you must board a bus (40 minutes; ¥620) to get to the Aso Nishi cable-car station at Asosan-jō. It's better to begin your trip early in the day, because the last buses for the cable-car station leave mid-afternoon. The JR Hōhi Main Line also travels on from JR Aso Station to Beppu.

> **en route**
>
> The enchanting village of **Kurokawa Onsen** (黒川温泉) is nestled in the mountains between Aso-san and Yufuin in Mt. Aso National Park. Those who make the effort to visit this tranquil hot-springs retreat, accessible by bus from Mt. Aso, are rewarded by the soothing sounds of trickling water and the pleasant scents of nearby forests. Book well in advance to stay the night, or buy a day pass (¥1,200) for entrance to three baths of your choice in any of the rustic inns. Reservations can be made through the Aso Station Information Center.

BEPPU & YUFUIN   別府と湯布院

For centuries Beppu's onsen have been used as health curatives by Japanese seeking treatment for various ailments. It's said that the hot mineral waters of Beppu's 2,849 different springs can cure arthritis, bronchitis, rheumatism, and more after just one week of frequent bathing. With a carefree atmosphere and attractions that are especially appealing to children and retired couples, Beppu remains a top vacation spot for Japanese. Garish popular culture also thrives here, in the form of neon signs, amusement centers, and souvenir shops.

Having developed more recently than Beppu, Yufuin has suffered from fewer of the pitfalls of modern tourism. This small town has blossomed into a quieter, more sedate getaway than Beppu, albeit at inflated prices. Unadorned natural baths can be found here, as well as a thriving arts-and-crafts industry. To experience the region in its entirety, visit both Beppu and Yufuin—buses between the two resort towns run frequently and take just over an hour.

Beppu   別府

⑭ *2 hrs northeast of Aso-san by JR, 1 hr, 50 min southeast of Fukuoka by JR, 4 ¼ hrs northeast of Kagoshima by Shinkansen and JR express.*

Mentioning Beppu outside Kyūshū usually invokes a smile, maybe even a giggle. The comical image of this celebrated hot-springs town has become synonymous with overindulgence and absurdity. Although much of the city has been overwhelmed by colossal bathing pleasure parks and garish pachinko halls, Beppu offers a multilayered experience for those willing to embrace—or venture beyond—the kitsch and neon. Foray into old Beppu by relaxing in the hot sands of Takegawara Onsen, a 100-year-old public bath, or spend the night at a friendly *minshuku* (a private house that takes in guests). You can idle away afternoons bath-hopping in the Beppu Station area; spend evenings wandering around the Kannawa area, a neighborhood in northern Beppu; and join fellow travelers, clad in *yukata* (cotton bathrobes) and geta (wooden sandals), for a night out on the town Beppu style.

The **Beppu Foreign Tourist Information Service** (別府外国人観光客案内所; ✉ Beppu Station, 12–13 Eki-mae ☎ 0977/23–1119 🖶 0977/21–6220) is open Monday through Saturday 9 to 5. In addition to offering useful maps and guides, the office of enthusiastic volunteers can help with local and long-distance transportation information and reservations for hotels and restaurants.

A landmark in Beppu, **Takegawara Onsen** (竹瓦温泉) is a classic example of handsome, unembellished, wooden late-Edo-period architecture. The building dates to 1879 (it was rebuilt in 1938), which may explain why the facilities look a little rough around the edges. Nevertheless, 10 minutes in the hot sands promote rejuvenation and improved circulation. Down the street from Nogamihonkan Ryokan, the onsen is a 10-minute walk from Beppu Station. Be sure to bring a bathing towel; the tiny rentals will barely cover your face. ⊠ *16–23 Moto-machi* ☎ *0977/23–1585* 💴 *¥780* ☉ *Daily 8 AM–9:30 PM.*

★ In Kannawa visit the **Jigoku Meguri** (Hells Circuit, 地獄めぐり) for nine types of natural springs; they're not for bathing, but are fascinating to observe. The most remarkable are Monk's Hell (Oni-ishi Bōzu Jigoku), with bubbling mud springs; Sea Hell (Umi Jigoku), with water the color of the ocean; Blood Pond Hell (Chi-no-ike Jigoku), a boiling spring with gurgling red water; and the Cyclone Hell (Tatsumaki Jigoku), a geyser that erupts every 25 minutes. Pick up a map of the Hells at Beppu Station before you board the bus for Kannawa (departing every 15 minutes). Six of the eight Hells are within easy walking distance of each other, but you might want to take another bus to the Blood Pond Hell and the Cyclone Hell. ☎ *0977/66–1577* 💴 *¥400 per spring, ¥2,000 for combined ticket to all springs* ☉ *Daily 8–5.*

☺ Packed with all the frills and fanfare of a hedonistic heaven, the spectacular **Suginoi Palace** (スギノイパレス) offers a crash course in Japanese commercial tourism. From the opulent outdoor baths of **Tanayu,** flirt with panoramic views of Beppu while soaking in soothing Jacuzzis and reclining "sleeping" tubs, complete with wooden headrests. For separate admission you can entertain yourself in **AquaBeat,** a water park with water slides and wave pools, a batting cage, and virtual golf. Suginoi Palace also includes bowling alleys and a synthetic ice rink (plastic, not ice). ⊠ *1 Kankai-ji* ☎ *0977/24–1160* 💴 *Tanayu ¥2,000, AquaBeat ¥2,800* ☉ *Tanayu daily 9 AM–11 PM, AquaBeat daily 9–6, 7 on holidays.*

☺ Approximately 1,900 monkeys roam free in three distinct packs at **Mt. Takasaki Monkey Park** (Takasaki-yama Shizen Dōbutsuen, 高崎山自然動物園). Once a menace to local farmers, the monkeys are now fed several times daily in the park area, where they playfully chase tourists—hold on to your lunch. Buses headed for Ōita and stopping at Mt. Takasaki leave frequently from Beppu Station and Kitahama Bus Station; the trip takes about 15 minutes. ⊠ *3098–1 Kanzaki, Oita-shi* ☎ *097/532–5010* 💴 *¥500* ☉ *Daily 8:30–5.*

off the beaten path

USUKI –(臼杵) Over a period of 150 years beginning in the 12th century, the 60 stone figures of the Buddha at Usuki on Kyūshū's east coast were elaborately carved from a rocky cliff. Most impressive is the fine detailing of the 16-ft-tall Dainichi, the principal figure in Shingon (an esoteric sect of Japanese Buddhism). English pamphlets are available, and the souvenir shop sells delicious ginger-flavor *senbei* (rice crackers). Keep an eye out for wildlife—snakes love to lurk around the footpaths. Take the JR express from Beppu to Usuki Station (¥1,510) and catch the bus bound for Usuki-no-Sekibutsu (¥300, departs seven times daily). ⊠ *Usuki* 🖾 *¥530* ⊙ *Daily 8:30–5:30.*

Where to Stay & Eat

¢–$$$ ✕ **Fugumatsu** (ふぐ松). In winter the specialty of the house is the infamous fugu (blowfish), which leaves you with a slight tingling sensation on your lips and an amazing story to tell your friends back home. The main summer dish is *karei*, a type of flatfish caught only in Beppu Bay. It's one block north of the Tokiwa department store and one block from the bay. ⊠ *3–6–14 Kitahama* 🕿 *0977/21–1717* 🖃 *No credit cards.*

¢–$$ ✕ **Jin** (陣). For cold refreshing beer and sake and inexpensive, robust, home-style *izakaya* (Japanese-style pub) cuisine such as yakitori and grilled seafood, try this spot near the station. You can sit either at wooden tables or bar seats overlooking dinner: rows of fresh fish on crushed ice. The mood is jovial, and the staff is friendly. Jin is easy to find: walk from the JR station on the right side of Eki-mae-dōri and toward the bay; it's just before the T-junction and across from the Tokiwa department store. ⊠ *1–15–7 Eki-mae-dōri* 🕿 *0977/21–1768* 🖃 *No credit cards.*

$$$$ 🏨 **Suginoi Hotel** (杉乃井ホテル).This is more than a hotel: it's a lavish resort and getaway. Beppu's most illustrious lodging sits atop a hillside, offering a panoramic view of the city and the ocean below. Most of the indoor and outdoor hot springs also have lovely views. Rooms range from simple Western-style twins to large, combination Japanese-Western-style rooms. It's connected to Suginoi Palace, and entrance is free for hotel guests after 5 PM. ⊠ *1 Kankai-ji, Beppu-shi, Ōita-ken 874–0822* 🕿 *0977/24–1141* 🖨 *0977/21–0010* ⊕ *www.suginoi-hotel.com/index e.html* 🍃 *111 Western-style rooms, 34 Japanese-style rooms, 403 combination rooms* ⟁ *4 restaurants, 2 cafés, hair salon, hot springs, 3 bars, shops* 🖃 *AE, DC, MC, V.*

$ 🏨 **Nogamihonkan Ryokan** (野上本館旅館). At this inn conveniently located in the downtown shopping area, a few blocks from Beppu Station, all of the rooms are Japanese-style and spacious enough to accommodate up to four people. If you don't have a room with your own private Japanese bath, you can make a reservation for the hotel facilities when you check in. Full-course dinners (¥4,000), tempura dinners (¥2,500), and Japanese- or Western-style breakfast (¥1,000) are available. The lobby has free 24-hour Internet access and complimentary coffee. ⊠*1–12–1 Kitahama, Beppu-shi, Ōita-ken 874-0920* 🕿 *0977/22–1334* 🖨 *0977/22–1336* ⊕ *www008 upp.so-net.ne.jp/yuke-c/english.html* 🍃 *24 Japanese-style rooms, 19 with bath* ⟁ *Japanese baths, Internet* 🖃 *MC, V* 🍴 *EP, MAP.*

★ $ 🏨 **Sakaeya** (サカエ家). A traditional old wooden building houses this gem, a minshuku with surprisingly low rates. Meals are prepared in backyard ovens, which are heated by underground springs. If you opt out of the meal plan, you're still permitted to store groceries in your room refrigerator and use the outdoor ovens. Reserve ahead, and be sure to ask for a room in the minshuku—unless you prefer to stay at the pricier ryokan next door. To reach the inn, take any bus for Kannawa from Beppu Station (a 30-minute ride), and get off at Kamenoi Bus Center

✉ *Ida 2 kumi, Ida, Kannawa, Beppu-shi, Ōita-ken 874-0046* ☎ *0977/ 66–6234* 🖷 *0977/66–6235* 🖙 *10 Japanese-style rooms without bath* ♨ *Refrigerators, Japanese baths* 🖃 *No credit cards* 🍴 *EP, MAP.*

Yufuin   湯布院

★ ⑮   *1¼ hrs by bus or 1 hr by JR west of Beppu, 1 hr west of Ōita by JR, 2 hrs southeast of Fukuoka by JR.*

Hidden in the shadow of majestic Yufudake is this tranquil village resembling a checkered quilt. Chunks of dense forest mingle with quiet clusters of galleries, local crafts shops, and rustic lodgings. Most of the year this is a relatively peaceful area, though the sleepy village wakes up in July and August for the arrival of national music and film festivals.

To enjoy the best of Yufuin in a day, start by picking up an English map at the **Yufuin Tourist Information Office** (由布院温泉観光案内所 ✉ Yufuin Station, 8–2 Kawakita ☎ 0977/84–2446), open daily 9 to 5. For more detailed information, visit the **main tourist center** (✉ 2863 Kawakami ☎ 0977/85–4464), also open daily 9 to 5 and located five minutes from the station on foot. Bicycles can be rented from either office.

From Yufuin Station take the five-minute taxi ride north to **Kūsō-no-Mori** (空想の森)—a collection of art galleries tucked into the mountainside of Yufudake. Work your way south back toward the train station via the **Yu-no-tsu** neighborhood—a long shopping street lined with traditional Japanese wooden buildings—where you can mill in and out of artsy craft shops and souvenir stalls, or rest your feet in one of the many coffee shops or tearooms. If you visit during winter you can admire the spellbinding effect of steam rising from the surface of **Kinrin-ko** (Lake Kinrin, 金鱗湖), a thermal lake in the east end of town. Warm up with a dip in one of the bathhouses along the shores.

On most days an artist is painting at the large wooden table in the center of the **Yutaka Isozaki Gallery** (由夛加磯崎ギャラリー). Small cards with inspirational messages and illustrations such as persimmons and wildflowers make original souvenirs (¥300–¥2,000). For a unique memento of old Japan you can sift through clothing made from antique kimonos at the rear of the gallery or piles of antique cotton and silk textiles in **Folk Art Gallery Itoguruma** (フォークアートギャラリー糸車), the little shop to the right of the entrance. ✉ *1266–21 Kawakami* ☎ *0977/85–4750* ⊙ *Daily 9–6.*

At the **Kyūshū Yufuin Folk Crafts Museum** (Kyūshū Yufuin Mingei Mura, 湯布院民芸村) local artisans turn out traditional crafts such as blown glass, toys, and steel blades. ✉ *1542–1 Kawakami* ☎ *0977/85–2288* 🎫 *¥650* ⊙ *Daily 8:30–5:30.*

> **need a break?**
>
> **Tenjōsajiki Coffeeshop** (天井桟敷; ✉ 2633–1 Kawakami ☎ 0977/ 85–2866), in the Kamenoi Bessō Ryokan complex, makes a sumptuous wild-strawberry ice cream. The establishment becomes a bar in the evening. **Tearoom Nicol** (ティールームニコル; ✉ 2731 Kawakami ☎ 0977/84–2158), at Tamanoyu Ryokan, serves a flat homemade apple pie slathered in a succulent apricot sauce (¥300).

Where to Stay & Eat

★ **$$$$** ✕ **Budōya** (葡萄屋). Originally a sanatorium for Zen Buddhist monks, this restaurant retains an air of solemnity and quiet elegance. The first level greets you with stone floors, thick wooden tables, and walls of windows overlooking a thicket of wildflowers and tall grass; the private rooms upstairs have tatami floors and bamboo-mat ceilings. For lunch try the *amiyaki* course (¥6,000), with charcoal-grilled beef, seasonal vegetables, and homemade *kabosu* (citrus) sherbet. Another good choice is *ki*, a course with fresh tofu and vegetable dishes, soup, and sherbet (¥2,500). ⊠ *Kawakami* ☎ 0977/84–4918 ▭ *AE, DC, MC, V.*

$$$ ▥ **Onyado Yufu Ryōchiku** (御宿由府両築). In winter, warm yourself by the *irori* (sunken hearth) in the lobby of this inn built in 1925. The only baths here are "family-style," meaning you may reserve one for private use along with the members of your party. Breakfast and dinner are included and are served in your room. The inn is among the shops and galleries near Lake Kinrin. ⊠ *1097–1 Kawakami, Yufuin-chō Ōita-gun, Ōita-ken 879-5102* ☎ *0977/85–2526* 🖷 *0977/85–4466* ➘ *8 Japanese-style rooms without bath* ♨ *Japanese baths, hot springs* ▭ *MC, V* ◍ *MAP.*

$$ ▥ **Pension Momotaro** (ペンション桃太郎). The owners of this pension go out of their way to make you feel at home—they'll even take you to the station when you depart. Both Western-style and Japanese-style rooms are available in the main building, and there are four A-frame chalets on the premises. Rates include breakfast; add ¥2,000 per person for dinner. ⊠ *1839–1 Kawakami, Yufuin-chō, Ōita-gun, Ōita-ken 879-5102* ☎ *0977/85–2187* 🖷 *0977/85–4002* ➘ *6 Western-style rooms, 3 Japanese-style rooms, 4 chalets* ♨ *Dining room, hot springs* ▭ *No credit cards* ◍ *BP, MAP.*

★ **$** ▥ **Oyado Sansuisō** (御宿山翠荘). Cedar walls fill the steamy indoor bath with a rich earthy scent, while the peaceful dribbling of the cascading rock waterfall in the background eases the mind. The waters here are renowned for relieving chronic muscle aches and skin disorders. For an extra ¥3,000 you can enjoy two meals cooked by the hot waters of the underground springs. Dark-wood furniture and tatami floors decorate the spacious Japanese-style rooms. From the station, take a right at the Kamenoi bus terminal, walk east, and take the first left and then the first right. ⊠ *Yufuin-chō, 1203–5 Kawakami, Ōita-gun, Ōita-ken, 879-5102* ☎ *0977/28–8748* 🖷 *0977/28–8757* ➘ *4 Japanese-style rooms without bath, 1 Western-style room without bath* ♨ *Pool, tennis court, hot springs, Japanese baths, bar* ▭ *No credit cards* ◍ *EP, MAP.*

Getting Around

BY AIR The closest airport to Beppu and Yufuin is **Ōita Airport** (⊠ 3600 Itohara, Musashi-machi, Higashi Kunisaki-gun ☎ 0978/67–1174). The flight to Ōita Airport from Tōkyō's Haneda Airport takes 1½ hours; the flight from Ōsaka's Itami Airport takes one hour. **Ōita Kōtsu Bus Company** (☎ 097/534–7455) runs the hourly airport shuttle to the Kitahama Bus Station in Beppu. The trip takes about 45 minutes and costs ¥1,450. Reservations are not required. From Beppu, take a local bus or JR train to Yufuin.

BY BUS   The *Kujūgō*, run by **Kyūshū Ōdan Teiki Kankō Bus** (☎ 096/355–2525) travels between Kumamoto and Beppu three times times daily (8:40 AM, 9:50 AM, and 2:30 PM) on the Trans-Kyūshū Highway, stopping in Yufuin. The one-way fare is ¥3,450 from Kumamoto to Yufuin (3¾ hours) and ¥3,850 to Beppu (4½ hours).

City buses can take you to most place of interest in Beppu. Destinations are usually written in English on the bus directories. The main terminal, **Kitahama Bus Station** (✉ 2–10–4 Kitahama, Beppu-shi ☎ 0977/23–0141), is down the road from the Beppu station. Ask at the Foreign Tourist Information Service in the train station for a one-day pass, a good buy at ¥900.

Regular bus service between Beppu and Yufuin costs ¥980. It's best to walk or take a taxi from the **Yufuin Bus Terminal** (✉ 3–1 Kawakita, Yufuin-chō ☎ 0977/85–3048) to the sights, as local bus service does not travel through the village.

Kamenoi Bus (☎ 0977/23–5170) runs several sightseeing tours that leave from Beppu Station and Kitahama Bus Station. For example, there are eight tours of the Hells Circuit in Beppu daily, which take about 2½ hours each and cost ¥3,850 including entrance fees. No English-speaking guides are available, but the sights are self-explanatory.

A sightseeing bus, **Kyūshū Sankō** (☎ 096/325–0100), makes a four-hour scenic trip (¥3,790) that starts at Fugen-dake and Shimabara, then ferries across Ariake Bay to Kumamoto-kō (Kumamoto Port) before ending the journey at Kumamoto City Kōtsū Center.

BY FERRY   Three ferries connect Beppu with Matsuyama and Ōsaka on the **Kansai Kisen Line** (☎ 0977/22–1311 in Beppu, 06/6613–1571 in Ōsaka, 089/951–0167 in Matsuyama). Direct Beppu–Ōsaka ferries depart at 7 PM and arrive at 6:20 AM; Ōsaka–Beppu ferries depart at 6:50 PM and arrive at 6:20 AM. Second-class tickets cost ¥7,400; reservations are necessary only for first class (¥14,400–¥22,300). Ferries bound for Beppu depart from Matsuyama Port at 6:15 AM and 6:40 AM and arrive four hours later. Ferries on the reverse route depart from Beppu at 4 PM and arrive six hours later in Matsuyama. Second-class seats cost ¥2,600; reserved first-class tickets are ¥8,100.

BY TAXI   Most taxi drivers in the area do not speak English but will probably understand your attempts to convey a message. Hiring a taxi for two hours to visit the Hells Circuit in Beppu would cost approximately ¥8,000.

BY TRAIN

The JR Hōhi Main Line travels between Kumamoto and **Beppu Station** (✉ 12–13 Eki-mae ☎ 0977/22–0585), stopping at Aso-san. The JR Nichirin Limited Express runs more than 10 times daily (two hours) between Beppu and Hakata Station in Fukuoka. JR Yufugō and Yufuin-no-Mori express trains run six times daily between Fukuoka's Hakata Station and **Yufuin Station** (✉ 8–2 Kawakita ☎ 0977/84–2021), but only Yufugō trains are covered on the JR rail pass.

KYŪSHŪ A TO Z

To research prices, get advice from other travelers, and book travel ar-rangements, visit www.fodors.com.

CONSULATES

🛈 Australia **Australian Consulate** ✉ 7F Tenjin Twin Bldg., 1-6-8 Tenjin, Chūō-ku, Fukuoka ☎ 092/734-5505.

🛈 Canada **Canadian Consulate** ✉ 4-8-28 Watanabe-dōri, Chūō-ku, Fukuoka ☎ 092/752-6055.

🛈 United States **U.S. Consulate** ✉ 2-5-26 Ōhori, Chūō-ku, Fukuoka ☎ 092/751-9331.

EMERGENCIES

🛈 Emergency Services **Ambulance** ☎ 119. **Police** ☎ 110.

🛈 Hospital **Fukuoka Nakagawa Hospital** ✉ 17-17 Mukaishin-machi 2-chōme, Minami-ku, Fukuoka ☎ 092/565-3531. **Kagoshima City Hospital** ✉ 20-17 Kajiya-chō ☎ 099/224-2101. **Kumamoto Chūō Hospital** ✉ 96 Tamukae ☎ 096/370-3111. **Nagasaki University Hospital** ✉ 7-1 Sakamoto-machi 1-chōme ☎ 095/847-2111. **Nakamura Hospital** ✉ 8-24 Akiba-chō, Beppu-shi ☎ 0977/23-3121.

OKINAWA 沖縄

BEST BEACH
Maehama on Miyako-jima ⇨*p.553*

DIVERS' CHOICE
Manta Way ⇨*p.563*

JUNGLE CRUISE
Urauchi-gawa river trip ⇨*p.564*

STATE-OF-THE-ART SHARK TANK
Churaumi Aquarium ⇨*p.551*

BEST PUB MEAL
Rafute and cold Orion beer at Gōya
on Miyako-jima ⇨*p.555*

PRETTIEST BALCONIES
Hotel Sun Palace in Naha ⇨*p.548*

LIVELIEST MARKETS
Ichiba-dōri and Heiwa-dōri arcades ⇨*p.544*

By John Malloy Quinn

OKINAWA LITERALLY MEANS "ROPE (ALONG THE) OPEN SEA," a name that fits this chain of 100-plus coral-fringed, subtropical islands stretching more than 700 km (435 mi) into the Pacific Ocean. The main group of islands extends from 200 km (125 mi) southwest of Kyūshū to within 100 km (62 mi) of Taiwan.

Once part of the ancient seafaring kingdom of Ryūkyū, the islands were ruled by the local Shō Dynasty, based in Shuri near the present-day capital of Naha, from the 15th century until the early 17th century. During this time the indigenous Ryūkyūans enjoyed great prosperity due to a favorable climate and thriving trade with China. Ryūkyū lacquerware and textiles were exchanged for Chinese pottery and herbs, and spices from Southeast Asia.

Ryūkyū successfully navigated the straits between Chinese and Japanese domination until 1609, when the capital was invaded and conquered by the powerful Shimazu clan from Kyūshū. From this moment forward, island inhabitants were required to pay taxes to Japan.

In the late 1870s the Meiji government took control and renamed the islands Okinawa Prefecture. Over time, the Ryūkyūan language was replaced with Japanese, and the two cultures were firmly and purposely integrated. The Meiji government instituted major tax and land-distribution reforms, and eventually introduced military conscription. Despite rapid industrialization in Japan, Okinawa has remained the poorest prefecture.

Although hundreds of miles from the main Japanese islands, Okinawa bore the brunt of the final years of World War II. Haplessly squeezed between the advancing American forces and the Japanese army, Okinawa lost as many as 100,000 native civilians. Following Japan's defeat, and continuing today, the islands are host to the majority of U.S. troops protecting this corner of the Pacific region. There remains a peculiar irony here: although the presence of the U.S. military here is controversial, it undeniably provides a tremendous monetary boost to an otherwise very poor region.

Tourism and other industries have not easily taken root in Okinawa, partly because of the archipelago's isolation. Yet Okinawa has long been known as Japan's Hawaii, with gorgeous beaches, a warm climate—the average yearly temperature is 72°—and open-hearted, friendly locals. Among the most unforgettable experiences of a trip to Okinawa, especially the southern islands, is spectacular diving and snorkeling—and even some jungle-trekking, all within a few hours of Tōkyō.

See the glossary at the end of this book for definitions of the common Japanese words and suffixes, such as -hama (beach), used in this chapter.

Exploring Okinawa

Naha Airport works well as an entry point. The town of Naha itself is worth one day, as are the main island and the Kerama Islands nearby, but if you have four days or more you'll want to focus most of your trip on exploring the southern islands of Miyako, Ishigaki, and lush, prim-

Numbers in the text correspond to numbers in the margin and on the Okinawa map.

12

If you have
3 days

Spend your first day in **Naha ❶** and explore cosmopolitan, frenetic Kokusai-dōri; wander among the exotic fish and pig-parts on display in the Heiwa-dōri market; then admire the pottery in the district of Tsuboya. Save time to ride the monorail to the end of the line and marvel at the unique Ryūkyū style and grace of Shuri-jō. On your second day make your way up the coast to the Motobu Peninsula and the amazing **Churaumi Aquarium ❺**, or head down to the various battle sites and **war memorials** in the south of the island. On your third day, hop over to the lovely **Kerama Islands ❻-❽** for some snorkeling and time at the beach.

If you have
5 days

Spend the first two days exploring **Naha ❶** and either the **war memorials** or the **Kerama Islands ❻-❽** offshore. On the third day, take a flight down to the fabulous white sands of either **Miyako-jima** or **Ishigaki-jima** if you like mountains, for some relaxing snorkel-therapy and other outdoor pursuits.

If you have
7 to 10 days

Now you have some time to do a serious exploration of the region. After a couple of days based in **Naha ❶**, fly down to **Ishigaki-jima.** For the next few days explore the various islets around Ishigaki-jima, including **Taketomi-jima, Kohama-jima ㉗**, and **Kuroshima-jima ㉘**. Be sure to reserve two days at the end of your trip to visit the fabled, jungle island of **Iriomote-jima** and either **Hateruma-jima ㉚**, Japan's southernmost reach, where the water is clearer than glass and gets frighteningly deep in a hurry, or **Yonaguni-jima**, at Japan's western end, where wild ponies roam, giant moths flap about like white bats at night, and mysterious Atlantis-like ruins lie on the seabed just off the southern shore.

itive Iriomote-jima. It's in the south that you can find the best beaches, reef diving, and exotic culture of the region.

From Naha Airport you can travel the 5 km (3 mi) into town via a convenient monorail system. There are frequent, regularly scheduled flights and ferries to the southern islands.

About the Restaurants

You can find nearly every kind of cuisine in Okinawa, from American standbys like burgers to tiny traditional noodle shacks and cheap, smoky taverns. There are also trendy, upscale establishments of every sort, especially in the cities and resort hotels. In most cases, perhaps due to the large and lingering American military presence, someone nearby will probably speak at least a little English.

About the Hotels

Accommodations in Naha have range from a youth hostel and cheap hotels to luxurious, internationally known resorts. Note that rooms may be scarce and outrageously expensive around New Year's, Golden Week

(April 29 to May 5), and in August, especially during the Obōn holiday mid-month.

For a short course on accommodations in Japan, *see* Lodging *in* SmarTravel Tips A to Z.

	$$$$	$$$	$$	$	¢
WHAT IT COSTS In yen					
RESTAURANTS	over 3,000	2,000–3,000	1,000–2,000	800–1,000	under 800
HOTELS	over 22,000	18,000–22,000	12,000–18,000	8,000–12,000	under 8,000

Restaurant prices are per person for a main course at dinner. Hotel prices are for double room with private bath, excluding service and 5% tax.

Timing

Okinawa enjoys winters most folks just dream about. Temperatures in January average 60°. Some travelers who come to Okinawa for its fantastic diving prefer the winter months, believing the water to be even more transparent than usual. Winter is also the off-season, when Okinawa has fewer crowds and cheaper prices. From early February to the end of March whale watching is a popular activity, especially on Zamami Island, easily reached on a day trip from Naha's port.

May and June are the rainiest months—avoid a trip to Okinawa during this time. In July, when rains taper off—though squalls can blow up at any time—and temperatures average 82°, the prices go way up as well. August sees the worst of the heat, crowding, and prices.

September through October is typhoon season, when, as the locals say, "the weather is . . . well, it's up to God." Although you may get lucky and have glorious, perfect weather, you would be wise to leave some extra days at both ends of any trips planned during this time to allow for possible flight or ferry cancellations due to high winds or heavy rainfall. On November 1–3, Shuri-jō (Shuri Castle) hosts a festival showcasing court dances, traditional music, and a big parade.

OKINAWA HONTŌ 沖縄本島

2½ hrs from Tōkyō by air, 2 hrs from Osaka by air; 44–48 hrs from Tōkyō by ferry, 34–40 hrs from Osaka by ferry.

Okinawa Hontō, the largest and most populous island of the Nansei (Southwest) group, is usually just referred to as Okinawa. The capital of the prefecture is here in the city of Naha.

Although Okinawa Hontō is not endowed with as many pristine reefs and primitive landscapes as the islands farther south, there are some lovely beaches (and expensive resorts) on its northern shores between Moon Beach and Inbu Beach, and fine diving off the somewhat more rocky Motobu Peninsula. Also, the nearby Kerama Islands are rugged and within easy reach.

12

Beaches

If you love beaches, you could hardly choose a better destination than Okinawa. Almost all the beaches here are heaped with generous helpings of white sand made of pulverized coral that is soft and small-grained up at the tide line and loose and large-grained near and under the water. The sand on some beaches, such as those on Taketomi and one or two on Iriomote, is actually made from the tiny, dried, and sun-bleached, star-shape skeletons of dead aquatic critters; this sand is called *hoshi-suna* (star-sand).

Some say the best beaches are on Miyako-jima, some say they're on islands in the Keramas, and others argue for the beaches of Ishigaki, Taketomi, or Hateruma-jima. The truth is quite simple: virtually anywhere you go in Okinawa, you can find world-class beaches. Even Hontō (the main island) has some nice ones, especially to the north, and a few on Miyako-jima can actually rival or beat anything in the Caribbean.

Diving

For intrepid and veteran divers, Okinawa offers some of the world's best diving experiences, especially in the waters off the southern islands of Miyako-jima, Ishigaki-jima, and Iriomote-jima. You can find healthy coral, an impressive number and variety of fish and mollusks, and clear warm water of every shade, from deep violet-blue to emerald-green. Atop a ridge that divides some of the deepest waters of the globe, the Okinawan islands are surrounded by nutrient-rich currents and the creatures that follow them. For example, in the unique Manta Way, entire schools of spooky-looking but harmless giant manta rays glide in formation, scooping loads of plankton into their maws. Divers are practically certain to see them in abundance in late spring, especially in the stretch of sea between Iriomote and Kohama.

Ideally, those interested in diving will have completed their open-water training and received certification in their home country. You can learn to dive in Okinawa, but you need to know a fair amount of Japanese. If you've made the decision to dive, rest assured that the waters are safe, and there are scores of diving outfitters on all the islands.

Jungle-Island Exploration

If you're tired of beach life, or if beaches really aren't your thing; and if it does not impress you that people come from around the world to see Okinawa's undersea wonders; and if you're the kind of person who doesn't mind a few days without every modern convenience; and if instead of scaring you it thrills you that you that you may be sharing muck and weeds with deadly snakes and slimy leeches, then, chances are, Iriomote-jima is the place for you. With languid rivers winding through mangroves and vines, waterfalls that attract swimmers and butterflies alike, and jungle trails that may or may not take you to the other side of the island before night falls and the bats begin to flutter, how could an adventurer like you be disappointed? Iriomote is the kind of place you go to if you want to test your mettle before auditioning for *Survivor*. Just remember to pack a knife, a compass, a camera, a journal, some yen, swamp-strength bug repellent, a snake-bite and first-aid kit, salt or a flame source to fight off the leeches, and, of course, plenty of food and water.

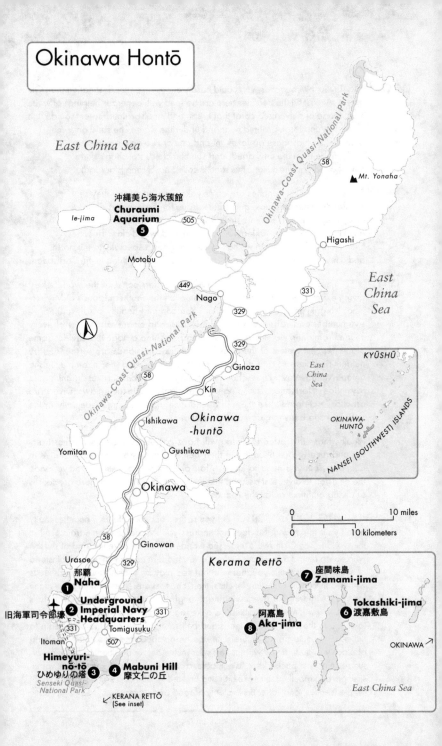

Okinawa Hontō

East China Sea

Ie-jima

Okinawa-Coast Quasi-National Park

▲ Mt. Yonaha

(58)

Higashi

East China Sea

沖縄美ら海水族館
Churaumi Aquarium
❺

(505)

Motobu

(449)

Nago

(331)

(329)

(329)

Ginoza

Kin

Okinawa-huntō

Ishikawa

Okinawa-Coast Quasi-National Park

(58)

Yomitan

Gushikawa

Okinawa

Ginowan

(58)

Urasoe

那覇
❶ Naha

旧海軍司令部壕
❷ Underground Imperial Navy Headquarters

(329)

(331)

Tomigusuku

Itoman

(507)

Himeyuri-nō-tō
ひめゆりの塔
❸

❹ Mabuni Hill
摩文仁の丘

Senseki Quasi-National Park

↙ KERANA RETTŌ (See inset)

Inset (top right):

KYŪSHŪ

East China Sea

OKINAWA-HUNTŌ

NANSEI (SOUTHWEST) ISLANDS

Scale:
0 ———— 10 miles
0 ———— 10 kilometers

Inset (bottom right): Kerama Rettō

座間味島
❼ Zamami-jima

阿嘉島
❽ Aka-jima

Tokashiki-jima ❻
渡嘉敷島

OKINAWA ↗

East China Sea

LEGEND OF THE SHIISĀ

A popular Okinawan legend tells of an angry and vicious dragon that once besieged the islands. One day the desperate islanders placed a shiisa statue that belonged to a local boy on the beach just as the monster was approaching. The tiny lion roared and out leapt a living lion large enough to fight and drown the dragon. Its body was changed into a new string of offshore islands, and afterward there were no more attacks.

To this day, homes and businesses often display two shiisā lions—one with its mouth open to scare off evil spirits and the other with its mouth closed to keep in good spirits. The lions are thought of as good-luck talismans, and they are popular keepsakes sold by dozens of souvenir shops on Kokusai-dōri in Naha.

Southern Okinawa Hontō has a great number of historically significant sights and war memorials related to the devastating Battle of Okinawa (1945). About 50,000 American troops are also based on this island, and they toss lifesaving amounts of money into the mix that is modern Okinawa.

Naha   那覇

❶ The modern capital city of Naha, population 307,000, is the main entry point for travelers to Okinawa. With Naha so well-connected to islands farther south, you are at the gateway to some amazing diving, beach, and jungle experiences. Since Naha has few compelling sights of its own, there's no reason to linger for more than a couple of days.

The main and most worthy sight in Naha, which was also the ancient Ryūkyū capital, is the wonderfully reconstructed Shuri-jō, a World Heritage Site. A strong pottery tradition also exists here, and there are many shops that specialize in that craft, as well as textile arts. There are some lively interesting markets worth exploring in town, and Naha is home to the highest concentration and largest variety of dining and drinking establishments to be found in the prefecture.

The people of Naha are friendly and outgoing, and eager to see that foreigners are enjoying their time here. Don't be surprised if the old gentleman who sits next to you on the monorail turns and strikes up a conversation, and does his level best to make sure you've got all the information and advice you might need.

Kokusai-dōri (国際通り). "International Street" runs for exactly a mile from the center of town out toward Shuri-jō. A lively street lined with endless shops, Kokusai-dōri is always abuzz with shoppers, revelers, and tourists. There are salsa dance-bars, American-style steak-and-lobster restaurants, even Starbucks coffee shops. The souvenir shops sell everything from snake-skin banjos and ceramic *shiisa* (lion figurines) to jugs of awamori (rice liquor).

You'll see all types of people, too—tattooed and pierced adolescents in baggy clothes; short-skirted high-school girls eating ice cream while talking on their mobile phones; gaggles of smartly dressed office ladies on tour from Tōkyō or Ōsaka and ready to spend their bonuses in record time; American GIs looking for diversion from life on the bases; and milling packs of staggering salarymen, singing badly on their way to the next karaoke bar. Follow the crowds. Something interesting is bound to happen.

To get to the main stretch, walk one block south of the Kenchō-mae monorail station, past the post office and Kumoji Palette shopping center, then turn left. For maps and additional sightseeing information, stop into the **Okinawa Tourist Information Center** (那覇市観光案内所 ; ⊠ Okie Ōdōri at Ichiba-dōri ☎ 098/868–4887).

★ **Ichiba-dōri and Heiwa-dōri shopping arcades**(市場通りと平和通り). About halfway up Kokusai-dōri, on the right, just past the building called Opa, and roughly across from the large Mitsukoshi department store, is a set of streets definitely worth a visit. The first of these shopping arcades is called Ichiba-dōri, and the next one to the right is called Heiwa-dōri. Both are lined with funky, hole-in-the-wall eateries and bars; shops selling discount clothing, hardware, and gadgets; drugstores peddling the latest health-craze tonics and remedies; and, best of all, the numerous first-floor entrances and exits into the sometimes shocking and always entertaining **markets.** Here ghoulish pressed, pickled, and smoked pigs' faces stare down like Halloween masks from hooks everywhere, and all those rainbow-color fish you can see darting about the reefs are resting on ice, about to be converted into sushi, sashimi, or grillable fillets. Tropical fruit and lengths of sugarcane are ready to be sliced or juiced on the spot, and any kind or quantity of meat and vegetable is available for buying or ogling. A foray into Naha's labyrinthine markets is a treat for the senses, and they're mostly air-conditioned, so you can escape for a chill-session when it's unbearably muggy out on the streets.

★ **Shuri-jō** (首里城). Shuri Castle is a bit east of the center, and though a reconstruction is a beautiful, unique one. The original 15th-century castle was once part of a sprawling estate: the Ryūkyū royal compound. During World War II the Japanese Imperial Army made the complex their headquarters and it was completely destroyed in the Battle of Okinawa. The superbly reconstructed castle and main buildings demonstrate the strong Chinese influence in the Ryūkyū style. Bright red walls and roof tiles contrast with the gray-white stone blocks of the massive outer walls. In the 5,000-square-ft central courtyard the rows of red-and-white tiles are said to indicate where the various ranks of officials lined up for ceremonies. Nearby are high-walled, narrow streets with original paving stones from the 1500s. Shuri-jō is a 15-minute walk from Shuri Station, the last stop on the monorail; follow the signs from the station. ⊠ *1–2 Kinjo-chō, Shuri* ☎ *098/886–2020* ⊠ *¥800* ◷ *Mar.–Nov., daily 9–5:30, Dec.–Feb., daily 9–5.*

OKINAWAN ARTS

Foreign influences, especially from the main Japanese islands and China, can be seen in the architecture of the region; for example, in the imported stone-cutting skills and arch work used in the construction of the exquisite Chinese-style Shuri Castle, among other structures.

Okinawan textiles also bear resemblances to both Chinese and Japanese styles; yet, in addition, the sharp observer will notice Southeast Asian traces; for example, in the bingata (stencil-dyed fabric) and kasuri (ikat fabric), which resembles the weavings of Indonesia.

Likewise, the music of Okinawa owes much to Chinese influence. In the early 15th century the three-string Chinese sangen was introduced to the Ryūkyūs. The sangen eventually developed into the samisen, which subsequently entered the main islands of Japan, thus beginning a profound musical transformation that is still reverberating in Japanese music today.

Tsuboya pottery district (壺屋). More than 300 years of ceramic tradition are celebrated in this potters' paradise, where nearly 20 workshops still crank out the goods. Legend has it that the guru of aluminosilicates himself, famous Japanese potter Hamada Shōji, lurked about here in the 1920s and '30s and came away with inspiration for his work. As you wander, notice the bits of broken pottery randomly, whimsically jammed into walls in Gaudi-esque embellishment. Most of the workshops are open to visitors, so you can observe the various stages of pottery-making, and then purchase the finished wares. Popular items include wedge-shape soy-sauce or oil decanters and shiisa lions of all sizes and colors.

The small **Tsuboya Pottery Museum** (Tsuboya Yakimono Hakubut-sukan, 壺屋焼物博物館; ⊠ 1–9–32 Tsuboya ☎ 098/862–3761) has exhibits that illustrate the history of earthenware production in the region, including representative pieces from all periods. There's even a reproduction of the interior of a traditional Okinawan house, showing Tsubo-yaki tableware and kitchen utensils. The museum is open Tuesday through Sunday, from 10 to 6, and admission costs ¥315. There are no English explanations, and you can admire the entire collection in about an hour. Next to the museum is an intact 19th-century climbing kiln, called a *nobori-gama*.

To get to the pottery district, walk east on Heiwa-dōri until it turns into Yachimun-dōri. ⊠ *Between Yachimun-dōri and Rte. 330.*

Where to Eat

In Naha you have plenty of choices at mealtimes. You can do as the Japanese tourists do and head for a steak house, where you can feast on the cheapest steaks in Japan; or follow the locals and pig out on pork in all its myriad forms and dishes.

★ $$$$ ✕ **Sam's Anchor Inn** (サムズアンカーイン). Done up in a nautical theme, with friendly waitresses in sailor uniforms, Sam's is lively and always crowded. Hungry, steak-loving GIs are regulars. Sam's is a bit pricier than many places on bustling Kokusai-dōri, but it delivers good, hearty set meals of steak and seafood. If you've got the appetite, don't miss the steak-and-lobster combo. Lunches are an excellent value, with set meals for less than ¥3,000. From the Kencho-mae monorail station, take a right on the busy Kencho-mae-dōri, then go left at the next street, which is Kokusai-dōri. Walk two blocks, and you can see Sam's on the left. ⊠ *3–3–18 Kumoji, 2F* ☎ *098/862–9090* ⊟ *AE, MC, V.*

¢–$$ ✕ **Helios Pub** (ヘリオスパブ). A microbrewery and pub, Helios serves up four tasty brews along with tempting snacks like tender oxtails stewed in black beer, a goya champur omelet with rice, and herb-seasoned bratwurst sausages. Wood floors and beams and brick pillars form the backdrop for hanging sheaves of barley. From Kencho-mae Station, cross Kencho-mae-dōri, go right one block, then turn left at Kokusai-dōri. It's 8½ blocks up, on the left side. ⊠ *1–2–25 Makishi* ☎ *098/863–7227* ⊟ *D, MC, V.*

★ ¢–$ ✕ **Gosso Gozzo** (ごっそごっつぉ). Entering here you step across flat stones with water running between them, then go past vats of steaming tofu to take a seat in the dark and appropriately ancient-looking dining room. Choose from an Okinawan menu that includes pickled pigs' ears; various forms of tofu (one is as old and stinky as blue cheese); and umi-budo, or sea grapes, a type of sea vegetable netted and plucked from an aquarium on the bar. Or try the sliced octopus served in creamy, sweet-and-sour dill-weed sauce. To drink, order the delicious, locally made Ni-heide beer or the smooth local sake, called *nama genshu*. Gosso Gozzo is only a couple of blocks from the Kencho-mae monorail station. From the station, cross the busy street and follow the canal until you get to Lawson's convenience store, then turn right. Take the first left onto a tiny side street, and it's on the left side in the middle of the block. ⊠ *3–12–18 Kumoji* ☎ *098/860–5211* ⊟ *No credit cards* ☺ *No lunch.*

¢ ✕ **Tacos-ya** (タコス屋). Among the funky, little, hole-in-the-wall eateries on busy Kokusai-dōri, Tacos-ya is a perfect place to make a pit stop for lunch. It serves tiny, tasty tacos that are unbelievably cheap, and the taco-rice—spicy ground beef, shredded lettuce, and diced tomatoes on rice—is a filling delight for only ¥550. And where else in Japan can you get a chilled Corona for only ¥400? ⊠ *2–18–13 Matsuo* ☎ *098/862–6080* ⊟ *No credit cards.*

Where to Stay

$$$$ ⊡ **Okinawa Harbor View Hotel** (沖縄ハーバービューホテル). One of Naha's finest, this spiffy ANA-operated hotel caters to the higher-end market. Rooms are classy and elegant, with cream walls and blue, gray, or egg-plant carpets. Picture windows and several lamps keep the rooms cozy and bright. The restaurants serve meals starting at ¥2,000, and you can head to the rooftop bar for a before- or after-dinner cocktail. The near-est monorail stop is the Asahibashi Station; from there head southeast on Tsubokawa-dōri to the third major intersection, then turn left. ⊠ *2–46 Izumizaki, Naha 900–0021* ☎ *098/853–2111* 🖷 *098/835–1776* ⊕ *www.harborview.co.jp* ⇝ *368 rooms* ♨ *4 restaurants, pool, hair salon, massage, sauna, bar, lobby lounge, laundry services, shop, business services, convention center, meeting rooms* ⊟ *AE, D, DC, V.*

ON THE MENU

KINAWANS ARE AMONG the longest-lived people on earth, and few experts would disagree that diet must be a contributing factor. The islands abound in fresh seafood and vegetables, from the exotic, colorful, delicious fish called goma-aigo, found in the waters off Ishigaki-jima, to the bitter gourds known as goya, which are ubiquitous in the region and reputed to be chock-full of antioxidants and toning agents.

You'll soon note that the food in Okinawa is far more adventurous than in the rest of Japan. Southeast Asian and Chinese flavors are incorporated into many dishes. Although beef is fairly cheap and popular among travelers from other parts of Japan, the natives are more fond of pork, and you'd probably have to go deep into the Black Forest or the Ozarks to find people getting as much mileage out of their beloved dead swine. In the markets you can find pressed pigs' faces hanging on hooks, with face parts sold as snacks; and in restaurants you can see sliced marinated pig ears, smoked pig tongue, and pig feet of every variety and flavor. You can also find thick, fatty, melt-in-your mouth chunks of meat floating in bowls of sōki soba (thin, white noodles in a hearty broth).

On the outer islands, goat or sea-snake stew is sometimes served. Although you might be averse to eating such fare, don't miss a chance to try the delectable rafutē: slabs of pork bacon that have been slow-cooked in a mix of awamori (rice liquor), soy sauce, locally grown brown sugar, and ginger root.

Okinawa loves blending things, and goya champur is a stir-fried dish of bitter gourd, meat, and vegetables. The word "champur" is Malay–Indonesian for "mix." The locals are so fond of this word and its implications (even if unaware of its origins) that they proudly refer to the entire mélange that is Okinawa culture as "chanpuru." Taco rice is a weird but delicious mix of Tex-Mex–style seasoned ground beef and shredded lettuce, onion, and tomato, served on top of white Japanese rice, usually with spicy salsa on top of it all. Taco rice is said to have been made popular by GIs after World War II.

Spice freaks can indulge in the local hot sauce, kure-gusu, a gasoline-color, magma-flavor liquid that is the result of cramming as many red chili peppers as can fit into a small bottle full of high-octane awamori. Go ahead, fire a squirt or two into your noodles or onto your plate of goya champur.

Among interesting delicacies from the sea, you might see umi-budo (sea grapes) on a menu. These are a type of seaweed that squirt and crunch in the mouth like caviar, but with a much less fishy taste.

As for drinks, the locals are fond of awamori, distilled to three levels of potency: strong (25%–30% alcohol), stronger (40%–50%), and downright deadly (60%). Most locals drink it straight up or on the rocks, then remain silent until they are able to speak again. For the less intrepid, awamori blends well with just about anything. You may even get curious and want to try the bizarre "healthy liver tonic drink": awamori mixed with water and ukon (turmeric powder) over ice. Whether or not it really does prevent hangovers or cleanse the blood and liver, it tastes just medicinal enough to win over most skeptics.

The local beer, Orion, is good, but quite light; for those wanting more flavor, there are some tasty microbrews available in Naha.

For dessert, you may be offered fresh-squeezed sugarcane juice, purple sweet-potato ice cream, or a kind of limeadelike fruit juice called shikuwasā. Don't hesitate to try anything—it's all good!

$–$$ ⊞ **Hotel Sun Palace** (ホテルサンパレス). An earth-tone tile exterior and rounded, bougainvillea-filled balconies greet you as you approach this appealing riverside hotel. Inside, the rooms are not overly attractive but quite acceptable. However, it's the reasonable prices, good service, and convenient location that make the Sun Palace an excellent choice for a stay in Naha. From the Kencho-mae monorail station, cross the bridge spanning the Kumoji River, then turn right. ⊠ *2–5–1 Kumoji, Naha 900-0015* ☎ *098/863–4181* ⊕ *www.palace-okinawa.com* 🖷 *098/861–1313* ➷ *67 Western-style, 8 Japanese-style rooms* ⌂ *Restaurant, in-room data ports, shop* ⊟ *D, MC, V.*

$–$$ ⊞ **Roynet Hotel Naha Kumoji** (ロイネットホテル那覇久茂地). Opened in April 2004, the Roynet offers crisp, new rooms and facilities on 10 floors. As in many chain hotels, the rooms are a bit cramped and they don't have much character, but each has a large square window and a writing desk. You can rent a PC for ¥800 a night, a color printer for ¥500. The hotel is four blocks from the Miebashi monorail station. ⊠ *2–23–12 Kumoji, Naha 900-0015* ☎ *098/869–0077* 🖷 *098/862–0088* ⊕ *www. roynet.co.jp/naha* ➷ *239 rooms* ⌂ *Restaurant, in-room data ports, Internet, business services* ⊟ *MC, V.*

¢ ⊞ **Hyper Hotel Naha** (ハイパーホテル那覇). It's nothing fancy and the rooms are small, but the Hyper Hotel is a good value for travelers on a tight budget. Beds are wider than in most business hotels, and there are desks in each room. Family rooms with a raised bunk bed are available. It's five minutes by taxi from the airport, along Route 221, across from the big Jusco department store. ⊠ *5–11–1 Kanagusuku, Naha 901-0155* ☎ *098/840–1000* 🖷 *098/858–1001* ➷ *89 rooms* ⌂ *Restaurant, laundry service, business services, Internet* ⊟ *MC, V* ⦿ *CP.*

Nightlife

For nightlife in Naha, you need only follow the crowds up and down Kokusai-dōri, or duck into side streets on a whim and give someplace a try. There's something for everyone, and at all hours. Folks are friendly, the draft-beer mugs are big, and the prices are tame by Tōkyō standards.

Rock in Okinawa (⊠ 3–11–2 Makishi ☎ 098/861–6394) hosts live rock shows nearly every night of the year. It's open from 7 PM to 7 AM nightly, and the cover charge is generally ¥1,000 to ¥2,000. Rock in Okinawa is on Kokusai-dōri near the Heiwa-dōri arcade and the Kokusai shopping center.

Club Cielo (⊠ 1–1–1 Matsuo, 6F ☎ 098/861–9955) is an upscale, rooftop, strut-your-stuff dance club, where it behooves you to dress well. Patrons are allowed entrance only between 9 PM and midnight, although the party never stops. Cover charges range from ¥1,500 to ¥2,000. Club Cielo is in the Best Denki Building on Kokusai-dōri, diagonally across from the Palette Kumoji shopping center.

Getting Around

The downtown area can be easily covered on foot, and if you get tired it's easy to flag down a taxi. Just remember to keep a card or matchbook with the name of your hotel on it to show the driver. To get to Shuri Castle, take the monorail.

BY AIR There are no direct nonmilitary flights to Okinawa from the United States. International air connections are available from Taipei, Taiwan; from Hong Kong and Shanghai, China; and from Seoul, Korea. Domestic flights from mainland Japan to Okinawa include those from Kagoshima (1 hour 20 minutes; ¥22,000 one-way) and Fukuoka (1 hour 35 minutes; ¥22,000) in Kyūshū, from Tōkyō (2 hours 30 minutes; ¥35,000), from Ōsaka (2 hours; ¥28,500), and from Nagoya (2 hours 15 minutes; ¥32,500).

Japan TransOcean Air (JTA ☎ 0120/25–5971 ⊕ www.japanair.com), an arm of Japan Airlines, flies to Naha from several Japanese cities. **ANK** (☎ 0120/02–9222), a regional arm of All Nippon Airways, offers similar flights.

Naha's monorail system makes it easy and cheap to get to downtown Naha from the airport, and most hotels are near monorail stops. If traffic is moving, a taxi will cost around ¥1,500 and take about 15 minutes between the airport and downtown.

BY CAR Roads are paved and fairly smooth in Naha, but they are often heavily congested, especially at rush hour. Outside of town, things open up and driving is almost normal, except that you drive on the left side, and signage, even when in English, can be downright confusing. For those keen on driving in Okinawa, there's a handy and in-depth English reference available at the airport and bookstores in Okinawa and Tōkyō called *Okinawa by Road* (Kume Publishing Co.). For a vehicle, contact **Kūko Rent-a-Car** (⊠ 1–1 Yamashita-chō, Naha ☎ 098/859–1111).

BY MONORAIL Naha's main points of interest are conveniently and cheaply connected by its excellent monorail. Trains begin running at 6 AM, and the last trains in each direction depart at 11:30 PM. Buses in Naha are slow and therefore not recommended.

BY TAXI Taxis are everywhere and easy to flag down in Naha. Fares start at ¥550. You can arrange for basic transport or tours in English through **Okinawa Prefectural Taxi Association** (☎ 098/855–1344). Tours of the Shuri Castle area take four hours and cost ¥12,000 and up, depending on the type of car you reserve. **Naha Kojin (taxi cooperative)** (☎ 098/868–1145) offers tours similar to those by the Okinawa Taxi Association.

The War Memorials

On April 1, 1945, within a month of taking Iwō-jima at a heavy cost, American forces came ashore at Kadena and set about the daunting task of capturing Okinawa. The unfortunate Okinawan civilians were shown no mercy by the retreating Imperial Army, and were in fact routinely killed by Japanese soldiers for their hiding places and food as the battle lengthened and grew in intensity. Ironically, the civilians who survived were led to believe that their fate would be even worse at the hands of the advancing Americans, and consequently many committed suicide. By the time the last of the Japanese commanders had killed themselves in lieu of surrender, some 200,000 people had lost their lives, half of them Okinawan civilians. A number of memorials dedicated to victims of war stand on Okinawa Hantō and most are in the south.

② **Underground Imperial Navy Headquarters** (Kyū Kaigun Shireibugō, 旧海軍司令部壕). The cold, clammy confines of the tunnels here are where things came to a dramatic end for Admiral Ōta and 174 of his men on June 13, 1945. He and six of his top officers shot themselves to escape capture or death by American forces. The grenade blasts that killed the rest of Ōta's men left visible shrapnel damage on the walls. An information desk has pamphlets in English, but the staff is unlikely to speak a language other than Japanese. The site is 25 minutes from the Naha Bus Terminal via buses No. 33, 46, or 101 (¥220). Get off at the Tomigusuku-Jōshi Kōen-mae (Tomigusuku Castle Park) bus stop, and walk 10 minutes uphill to the ticket gate. ⊠ *236 Aza Tomishiro, Tomishiro-shi* ▨ *¥420* ☎ *098/850–4055* ✆ *Daily 8:30–5.*

❸ **Himeyuri-nō-tō** (ひめゆりの塔). It was here on June 19, 1945, that more than 200 high-school students, mostly girls, and their teachers committed mass suicide rather than submit to the encroaching American army. The women had been recruited to help the Imperial Army in war efforts but were left to fend for themselves during the Japanese retreat. Fearing they would suffer a worse fate if captured, they chose to kill themselves. Adjacent to the site, there is the **Himeyuri Peace Prayer & Memorial Museum.** Himeyuri-no-tō is 60 minutes from Naha via bus No. 32 or 89 (¥550), with a change in Itoman to bus No. 82 (¥270). Buses depart hourly and continue on to Mabuni Hill after Himeyuri-no-tō. ☎ *No phone.*

❹ **Mabuni Hill** (Mabuni-no-Oka, 摩文仁の丘). Mabuni Hill and its monuments overlook a gorgeous, grassy view now, but in late spring and early summer of 1945 it was the site of the worst battle of World War II in Japan, where the remainder of the Imperial Army was cornered and vanquished. Tens of thousands of soldiers on both sides died here, and an unspeakable number of civilians as well. Rows of inscribed stone tablets scattered about the hillside list the name of every person who died in the Battle of Okinawa: Japanese soldiers, civilians, and, in a rather controversial move for Japan, American soldiers as well. The nearby **Peace Memorial Hall** (Heiwa Kinen Shiryōkan) is presided over by a large Buddha statue in a white tower. You can find pamphlets in English, and the location of any name listed on the tablets can be accessed via a computer directory. Mabuni Hill is about 80 minutes from Naha via bus No. 32 or 89 (¥870) and No. 82. ⊠ *448–2 Mabuni, Itoman-shi* ☎ *098/ 997–3011* ▨ *¥500* ✆ *Tues.–Sun. 9–5.*

Getting Around

Since public buses are infrequent and bus tours are in Japanese, the best ways to get to the war memorials and other sights outside of Naha are by renting a car or hiring a taxi with an English-speaking driver.

BY BUS Public buses depart from the Naha bus terminal downtown at the south end of Kokusai-dōri. To get to the war memorials from Naha, take buses No. 32 or 89 to Itoman (¥550, 40 minutes). At Itoman, change to the infrequent—only one or two per hour—bus No. 82, which will take you to Himeyuri-no-tō (¥270) in about 20 minutes, then on to Mabuni Hill (¥320) in 10 more minutes.

A guided bus tour of the war memorials can be arranged via your hotel, the tourism bureau, or any travel agency along Kokusai-dōri, but you are basically paying for transportation because tours are conducted in Japanese. The **Ryūkyū Bus** (☎ 098/863–3636) offers six-hour tours departing from various points in downtown Naha at 10 AM and 1 PM. Tours cost ¥4,800 including one meal. The buses stop at the Underground Navy Headquarters, Himeyuri-no-tō, and Mabuni Hill, as well as one of the largest caves in Asia, and you're also given the chance to do some souvenir shopping.

BY CAR   Driving a car within Naha is not recommended because of poor signage and bad traffic, but the intrepid will not be too uncomfortable driving outside of town. A good map is indispensable. You can buy a road map at bookstores in Naha or at the airport. You'll also need an international driver's license, which must be accompanied by your home country's valid license. There are several car-rental agencies at the airport as well as downtown, all charging more or less ¥5,000 per day. Be sure to book your car ahead of time.

🗐 **Japaren** ☎ 098/861-3900. **Nippon** ☎ 098/868-4554. **Orion Rent-A-Car** ☎ 098/867-0082. **Toyota** ☎ 098/857-0100

BY TAXI   You can hire a taxi with an English-speaking driver for about ¥18,000 for six hours. Book one day ahead via the front desk of your hotel, the tourist information office, or by calling the **Okinawa Prefectural Taxi Association** (☎ 098/855–1344). **Naha Kojin (taxi cooperative)** (☎ 098/868–1145) offers tours similar to those by the Okinawa Taxi Association.

Elsewhere on Okinawa Hontō

Scattered along the west coast of Okinawa Hontō north of Naha, there are some flashy beach resorts usually booked solid with package-tour travelers from Tōkyō or Ōsaka: Sunset Mihama, Moon Beach, Manza Beach, Emerald Beach, and Okuma Beach, listed from south to north. Although pleasant enough, the beaches at these resorts are nowhere near as beautiful as those on the southern islands of Miyako-jima and Ishigaki-jima, and on the Kerama Islands. The impressive Churaumi Aquarium, however, with its 7-meter (22½-ft) whale sharks and fleet of giant manta rays, is well worth visiting.

★ ☺ ❺ **Churaumi Aquarium** (Churaumi Suizokukan, 沖縄美ら海水族館). This $150 million aquarium is one of the world's best and largest. Opened in 2002, the Churaumi features a unique 7,500-ton, 10-meter- (30-ft-) deep tank big enough to give play space to a trio of whale sharks, four giant mantas, and schools of tuna, grouper, and other fish from the nutrient-rich Kuroshio (Black Current), which flows past Okinawa. It's the world's first tank deep enough to allow the viewing of whale sharks feeding in their natural, vertical position. Other tanks hold dangerous sharks, a pioneering coral-breeding experiment, deep-water species, and more. Churaumi means "beautiful sea" in the regional dialect, and Okinawans certainly do have something to be proud about here.

To get here, take bus No. 20 or 120 from Naha Terminal to Nago (¥1,740; 2 hours, 20 minutes). In Nago, change to bus No. 65 or 70 to Kinenkōenmae and get off at the south or central gates of the Ocean Expo Park (¥790, 65 minutes). ⊠ *424 Ishikawa, Motobu-chō* ☏ *098/048–3748* ⊕ *www.chample.tv/churaumi/index_en.html* ✉ *¥1,800* ☉ *Dec.–Feb., daily 9–4; Mar.–July 19, daily 9–5; July 20–Aug., daily 8:30–6:30; Sept.–Nov., daily 9–5.*

KERAMA RETTŌ 慶良間列島

35 km (22 mi) west of Naha by ferry

The Kerama Islands have many pristine beaches despite their proximity to Naha, and divers rate the coral and clear water off their coasts highly. There are three main islands in the group: Takashiki, Zamami, and Aka-jima, plus many more small uninhabited islets. You can experience the best of the Keramas in a day trip or two from Naha. Eating and drinking establishments are scattered over all three of the main islands, so you won't go hungry or thirsty as you explore.

DIVING **Fathoms Diving** (☏ 090/8766–0868 mobile), run by an American expat, former U.S. military man Richard Ruth, offers guided diving trips from Naha out to the Keramas.

Tokashiki-jima 渡嘉敷島

 The largest of the Kerama Islands, and the closest one to Okinawa Hontō, Tokashiki-jima gets the most tourist traffic from Naha. There are two lovely beaches with clean, white sand on the west side: Tokashiki Beach, in the center of the coast, and Aharen Beach, toward the south.

Zamami-jima 座間味島

❼ At the harbor, you can duck into the **tourist information office** (座間味村観光案内所; ☏ 098/987–2277) in the cluster of buildings to the left of the ferry exit for information in English on boat tours, bike rentals, and diving outfitters. The tourist office is open daily 8:30–5.

SNORKELING For great snorkeling, it's hard to beat **Furuzamami Beach** (古座間味ビーチ), a short walk south of the harbor and village. In summer you can find snorkel rentals and showers. There's also a restaurant, and shuttle buses run to and from the pier and other beaches.

WHALE WATCHING Winter whale watching on Zamami-jima is a popular Okinawan pastime. Late January through March is the prime whale-watching season, and during those months you can join two-hour boat tours for ¥5,000. Weather permitting, the **Zamami Whale Watching Association** (座間味村ホエールウォッチング協会; ☏ 098/987–2277) sends out boats from Zamami port daily at 10:30 AM. From land, the north shore gives you the best chance of seeing whale-tails and fin-slapping humpback antics—bring your best binoculars.

Aka-jima 阿嘉島

❽ Aka-jima doesn't get much traffic yet, but most travelers who make it here won't say that's a bad thing! Beautiful and quiet **Nishibama Beach** (北浜ビーチ), near the northern tip of the island, offers good snorkeling and diving, with equipment rental locations. To get there from the pier, walk over the hill to the east. The gently sloping beach west of the pier is also pretty, and there are places to eat and rent snorkel gear.

Getting Around

From Naha's Tomari Port, you can catch ferries to all three of the main islands. The Ferry Kerama reaches Tokashiki-jima in 70 minutes. The fare is ¥1,360 and there are generally two departures daily. Call **Tokashiki-son Renrakusho** (☎ 098/868–7541) to confirm schedules.

To get to Zamami-jima you have two choices: the high-speed Queen Zamami ferry reaches the island in 55 minutes, stopping at Aka-jima along the way. The fare is ¥2,750 per person, and there are two or three departures daily. The slower Zamami-maru ferry reaches the island in two hours, and makes one run daily, also via Aka-jima. The fare is ¥1,860. Call **Zamami-son Renrakusho** (☎ 098/868–4567) for schedules.

Once you're on one of the islands, you can rent bicycles or scooters from vendors at the piers. You can also walk to many places of interest. Bicycles rent for about ¥500 per hour, scooters ¥3,000 per day. Zamami-jima also has a car-rental agency, **Zamami Rent-a-Car** (☎ 098/987–3250), extending from the jetty at the east end of the village. Prices range from ¥3,000 an hour to ¥8,000 a day.

MIYAKO-SHOTŌ 宮古諸島

300 km (186 mi) southwest of Okinawa Hontō

For those seeking it, some intensive beach-therapy can be engaged in here. In the southwest corner of the main island, Miyako-jima, is Maehama, perhaps Japan's finest beach, and across the bridge on the adjacent tiny island of Kurima-jima lies the gorgeous, secluded beach Nagama-hama. Throughout the Miyako islands you can find stark white sand and emerald, turquoise, and cobalt waters. If you're traveling to Miyako-jima in July or August, or during a Japanese holiday, be sure to book your lodging ahead of time.

Hirara 平良

❾ On the main island of Miyako-jima, sprawling, unremarkable Hirara doesn't have many sights but offers plenty of budget accommodations. Whether you arrive by plane or ferry, stop in at the **tourist information desk** (宮古観光協会; ☎ 098/072–0899 airport, 098/073–1881 ferry), open daily 9–5, for help on travel, tour, and lodging arrangements.

DIVING & SNORKELING **The Goodfellas Club** (☎ 098/073–5483) on Route 390 just east of Route 192 in south Hirara offers diving trips in the waters around Miyako-jima. You can rent or buy snorkeling equipment at one of the many shops in Hirara or near the beaches.

Beaches

⓬ **Boraga Beach** (保良泉ビーチ). Here, on the southern shore of the island, a swimming pool filled with water from a cold natural spring is next to some nice stretches of beach. Snorkel gear and kayak rental are arranged through the pool complex, which includes a refreshment stand.

❿ **Maehama Beach** (前浜ビーチ). Maehama, or as you may see on local signs, Yonaha Maehama, is regarded by many as Japan's best beach, and it truly does live up to its reputation. Pure white sand stretches for

FodorsChoice
★

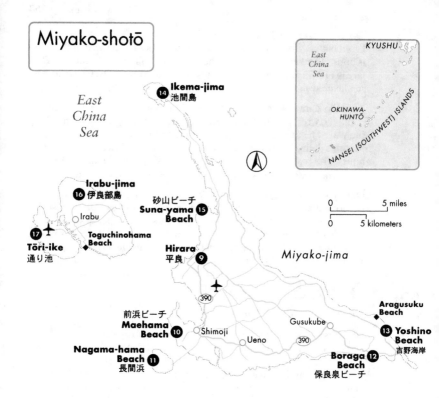

Miyako-shotō

East
China
Sea

Ikema-jima
池間島 ⑭

Irabu-jima
⑯ 伊良部島

○ Irabu

砂山ビーチ
**Suna-yama
Beach** ⑮

✈ ⑰
Tōri-ike
通り池

**Toguchinohama
Beach** ◆

Hirara
平良
⑨

Miyako-jima

East
China
Sea

KYUSHU

OKINAWA-
HUNTŌ

NANSEI (SOUTHWEST) ISLANDS

0   5 miles

0   5 kilometers

✈ 390

前浜ビーチ
**Maehama
Beach** ⑩

○ Shimoji

○ Ueno

Gusukube

**Aragusuku
Beach** ◆

⑬ **Yoshino
Beach**
吉野海岸

**Nagama-hama
Beach** ⑪
長間浜

**Boraga
Beach** ⑫
保良泉ビーチ

390

miles on a smooth, shallow shelf that extends straight and far into the warm, clear water. Eventually the sand gives way to forests and canyons of coral that provide shelter and playgrounds for beautiful, luminescent aquatic creatures. A tiny slice of Maehama can keep you entertained all day, but it actually stretches for 7 km (4.4 mi). You can find a marina and water-sports equipment rentals at the Tokyu Resort. The beach is 25 minutes from Hirara via bus.

⑪ **Nagama-hama Beach** (長間浜). A lovely and often deserted beach on the west side of tiny Kurima-jima, Nagama-hama can be reached via the bridge just southeast of Maehama. This is a fantastic place to spend the day snorkeling and picnicking on the fine white sand.

⑮ **Suna-yama Beach** (砂山ビーチ). This beach centers around an enormous sand dune (*suna-yama* means "sand mountain") out of which juts a marvelously rugged and picturesque natural stone arch. The snorkeling is just as good here as at Maehama, and the beach is only a few kilometers (15 minutes by bus) north of Hirara.

off the
beaten
path

HIGASHI-HENNA MISAKI (Cape Higashi-henna, 東平安名崎) – If you happen to be in the scenic southern corner of Miyako-jima and you have a couple of hours to spare, take a leisurely walk out to see the surreal landscape on this cape. A twisty, narrow road atop a spine of rock leads through a thatch of green grass out to a lonely, perfectly lovely lighthouse. In all seasons, the 2-km (1.2-mi) peninsula retains an impressive, end-of-the-earth-feeling; and in spring the ground is covered with trumpet lilies. The transparent water is too shallow and the shore is too rocky for safe snorkeling, but the multicolor coral below can be viewed from above. Allow about one hour to walk from the Bora bus stop at Boraga Beach. If you rented a scooter in Hiraga, you can ride right out to the end of the road next to the lighthouse.

⑬ Yoshino Beach (吉野海岸). The water of this beach is said to have the highest concentration of colorful fish in all of Miyako-shotō; needless to say, it's an awesome spot to snorkel. The beach is just north of Higashi-henna-misaki.

⑭ Ikema-jima (池間島). Connected to the northwestern corner of Miyako-jima by a bridge, this small island, ringed with a scenic coastal road, has some fine views both above and below the surface of the sea. Many postcards of the area feature a distinctive rock formation shaped like a whale tail poised as if ready to slap the water not far from shore here. The island is 35 minutes by bus from Hirara.

⑯ Irabu-jima (伊良部島). This small, rural island, only a 15-minute boat ride (¥410) from Hirara port, has two more gorgeous and secluded beaches: **Toguchi-no-hama** (渡口の浜) and **Sawada-no-hama** (佐和田の浜).

⑰ Tōri-ike (通り池). Travel even farther, across one of the several small bridges from Irabu-jima to Shimoji-jima, and proceed to its west side, beyond the oversize runway where ANA sometimes trains its jumbo-jet pilots to take off and land the unbelievably noisy things, and you can check out Tōri-ike, a deep, mysteriously dark cenote connected by underwater caverns to the sea. It's a justifiably famous and popular spot for diving.

Where to Stay & Eat

★ ¢–$ ✕ **Gōya** (郷家). The wooden walls of this rustic establishment are full of alcoves holding treasures and knickknacks of all sorts, from dolls to farm implements to ancient jugs of fresh awamori. Raised tatami-style rooms, partially enclosed by wooden walls, offer intimate dining and drinking experiences, while the beer hall–style central area in front of the stage makes socializing easy. There's live music nightly, and cheap, filling, delicious food. Tasty gōya chips, melt-in-your-mouth rafute (bacon slow-cooked in a mix of awamori, soy sauce, brown sugar, and ginger root), and garlicky *gyoza* (fried meat dumplings) should be accompanied by large mugs of icy cold Orion beer. Gōya is 10 minutes from downtown Hirara by taxi. ⊠ *570–2 Nishizato, Hirara, Miyako-jima, Rte. 78 just past Rte. 390* ☎ *098/074–2358* ⊟ *No credit cards* ⊘ *Closed Wed. No lunch.*

$ ✕ **Chūzan** (中山). This simple, local tavern serves inexpensive Okinawa favorites, such as gōya champur; Korean-style *bibimbap*, a delicious, tangy, healthy dish of kimchi, bean sprouts, spinach, and other vegetables stirred into rice; and a plate of *katsuo* (bonito) sashimi that's big enough for two or three people. A couple of blocks east from the port, it's on the left side of McCrum-dōri before it meets Route 83. ⊠ *McCrum-dōri, Hirara, Miyako-jima* ☎ *098/073–1959* 🚫 *No credit cards* ⊘ *No lunch.*

$$$$ 🏨 **Hotel Atoll Emerald** (ホテルアトールエメラルド). Every room at this contemporary high-rise hotel next to the pier has a view of the ocean. The Atoll Emerald is the nicest and most convenient hotel in downtown Hirara. The rooms are large and well decorated in blue, brown, and beige. Each has a big picture window, and corner deluxe rooms have windows in two walls. Suites are enormous, with L-shape sectional sofas. ⊠ *108–7 Shimozato, Hirara, Miyako-jima, 906-0013* ☎ *098/073–9800* 🖷 *098/ 073–0303* ⊕ *www.atollemerald.jp* ➦ *133 Western-style rooms, 4 Japanese-style rooms, 4 Western-style suites* ◇ *4 restaurants, pool, hair salon, sauna (men only), bar, lobby lounge, shops, laundry facilities, business services, convention center* 🖃 *AE, D, MC, V.*

$$$$ 🏨 **Miyakojima Tōkyū Resort** (宮古島東急リゾート). One of Japan's finest ho-
Fodor'sChoice tels—regally situated on Japan's finest beach—the Miyakojima Tōkyū
★   Resort delivers everything you could want from a beach vacation and more. Rooms are spacious and beautiful (and newer in the Coral Wing), and most are graced with superb views over one of the most incredible beach scenes in the world. Significant discounts can be had by booking air–hotel packages through any major travel agency. ⊠ *914 Yonaha, Shimoji-chō, Miyako-jima, 906-0305* ☎ *098/076–2109* 🖷 *098/076–6781* ⊕ *www.tokyuhotels.co.jp* ➦ *205 Western-style rooms, 40 Japanese-style rooms, 3 Western-style suites* ◇ *5 restaurants, tennis courts, 2 pools, boating, marina, fishing, dive shop, snorkeling gear, windsurfing, jet skiing, waterskiing, bicycles, bar, video game room, shop, laundry services, business services, convention center* 🖃 *AE, D, MC, V* ❍ *BP.*

$-$$ 🏨 **Miyako Central Hotel** (ミヤコセントラルホテル). On Route 78 a few blocks from the pier, this tidy, narrow, eight-story hotel caters well to those on a tight budget. It's within walking distance of downtown, near the bus depot, ferry port, and car-rental agencies, so you easily can get an early start on your touring. Several nightspots are also within walking distance. ⊠ *225 Nishizato, Hirara, Miyako-jima 906-0012* ☎ *098/ 073–2002* 🖷 *098/073–5884* ⊕ *www.cosmos.ne.jp/~mcentral* ➦ *62 rooms* ◇ *Restaurant, meeting room* 🖃 *AE, V.*

Nightlife

Miyako-jima has a notoriously hard-drinking nightlife. It has been boasted that there are more bars per person here than in any other part of the country, which, given the Japanese fondness for drinking, likely means that Miyako-jima has one of the highest concentration of bars in the world. You can find countless nightspots in Hirara, especially in the blocks just east of the piers.

Bar Alchemist (⊠ 215-3 Shimozato, Hirara ☎ 090/4582–4278) is a friendly bar with a piano, a telescope, and an endearing, eccentric owner. It's a couple of blocks south of the ferry terminal on the seafront road, upstairs above the A Dish restaurant. It's closed on Monday, but other nights you might find live music.

South Park (⊠ 638–Shimozato, Hirara ☎ 098/073–7980) bills itself as an "American shot bar." Cocktails are only ¥700, and shots begin at ¥600. All in all, this isn't a bad spot to watch sports on the huge TV.

South Park is a bit of a hike east of the piers near where Route 243 crosses Route 190. From the post office downtown walk south five blocks then east for two blocks. It's closed Monday; the rest of the week it opens at 6 PM.

Getting Around

The best ways to get around the island are by taxi or scooter.

BY AIR **Japan TransOcean Air** (JTA ☎ 0120/25–5971 ⊕ www.japanair.com), an arm of Japan Airlines, operates flights to Miyako-jima from Naha, Ishigaki-jima (another Okinawan island), Tōkyō, Ōsaka, and Fukuoka. **ANK** (☎ 0120/02–9222), a regional arm of All Nippon Airways, offers similar flights. From Naha there are up to 11 flights daily; the trip takes just 45 minutes, and a one-way ticket costs ¥14,500. From Tōkyō's Haneda Airport there are two 3-hour flights per day, and a ticket costs ¥46,800. From Ōsaka, there's one 2½-hour flight per day, and a ticket costs ¥42,000. From Ishigaki-jima, there are two half-hour flights per day, costing ¥9,500.

The best way to travel the 3 km (2 mi) from the airport to Hirara is by taxi (about ¥1,300).

BY BUS Buses on Miyako-jima depart from two different terminals in Hirara and travel the coastal roads around the island. Buses to the north of the island and Ikema-jima (35 minutes from Hirara) depart from the Yachiyo bus station, a few blocks north of the central post office along Route 83. Buses heading south to Maehama (25 minutes from Hirara) and Cape Higashi-henna (50 minutes from Hirara) depart from the Miyako Kyōei terminal, about a kilometer east of the downtown post office on Mc-Crum-dōri. Buses run daily every couple of hours from morning to early evening.

BY CAR If you want to rent a car, it's essential that you reserve in advance. **Nippon Rent-a-Car** (☎ 098/072–0919, 0120/17–0919 toll-free), near the airport, will arrange to pick you up on arrival at the airport or ferry terminal. Rates average around ¥5,500–¥6,000 per day. Although following the coastal roads is straightforward enough, be warned that driving in the interior of Miyako-jima requires more time and patience, and should not be attempted after dark. Signage is confusing, and the endless sugarcane fields all look the same.

BY FERRY Ferries from Naha reach Miyako-jima in 8¼ hours, and a one-way ticket costs about ¥5,000. Some ferries then go on to Ishigaki-jima, an additional five-hour, ¥2,700 trip. All trips take place overnight and require at least two weeks' advance booking. Two companies run these routes, but not daily, so you need to check the schedules. **Arimura Sangyō** (☎ 098/860–1980, 03/3562–2091 in Tōkyō) runs ferries 8 to 10 times a month. **R.K.K.** (☎ 098/868–1126, 03/3281–1831 in Tōkyō) runs ferries five times a month, and the trips may take up to 10 hours. From the ferry terminal, taxi fare to central Hirara runs about ¥500.

From Hirara Port, ferries also make day trips to nearby Irabu-jima, Shimoji-jima, Tarama-jima, and Minna-jima, where you can find lovely beaches and fabulous snorkeling opportunities. Tickets for these trips can be bought at the agencies inside the Hirara ferry terminal. Schedules vary, but boats generally leave every half hour for the 10-minute trip to Irabu-jima (¥410). Boats to the other islands depart less often.

BY SCOOTER
Miyako-jima is just big enough to make bicycling in the heat and humidity not such a good idea. Perhaps the best and easiest option for getting around the island is by scooter (¥3,000–¥4,000 per day) or motorbike (¥6,500 per day). **Nippon Rent-a-Car** (☎ 098/072–0919, 0120/17–0919 toll-free) rents motorbikes, and you can arrange to be dropped at your hotel as well.

BY TAXI
Taxi use on Miyako-jima is convenient and reasonable. Just raise your hand to flag one down. A taxi for the 10-km (6.2-mi) trip to Maehama Beach should cost ¥5,000 or less. **Miyako Taxi** (☎ 098/072–4123) has English-speaking drivers. Rates for all-day hire vary, so check with your hotel or the tourist information offices in advance.

YAEYAMA-SHOTŌ 八重山諸島

430 km (267 mi) southwest of Okinawa Hontō

A hundred kilometers (62 mi) southwest of Miyako-jima is the first of a string of lush, mountainous islands called the Yaeyama-shotō (Manifold Mountain Islands) that stretch nearly to Taiwan. If you make it down here you'll be spoiled by the choices of adventures that await you. On the jungled, swampy, and mysterious Iriomote-jima you can find a fascinating national park above ground and unsurpassed diving and manta-viewing opportunities offshore. Ishigaki-jima has the highest mountain (526 meters [1,725 ft]) in Okinawa, and more lovely beaches. On the minuscule island of Taketomi-jima there's an adorable, traditional, Ryūkyū-style village where time seems to have stopped and no one's keen to start it again. Still other choices include remote Hateruma-jima, Japan's southernmost point, and Yonaguni-jima, Japan's westernmost point.

Ishigaki-jima 石垣島

Ishigaki-jima, the main island of and gateway to the entire Yaeyama region, is known for its black-pearl industry, pineapples, white-sand beaches, and emerald waters. It's also the only island in the Yaeyama chain with a sizable town. Unlike Hirara on Miyako-jima, Ishigaki is not sprawling, and it's easy to explore on foot. Consisting of a harbor—with great connections to the rest of the Yaeyamas and, occasionally, even Taiwan—and a couple of main streets lined with shops, diving outfitters, hotels, bars, and restaurants, downtown Ishigaki is a place you can scout out in about an hour or two.

The **tourist information office** (石垣市観光協会; ☎ 098/082–2809) is in the complex of municipal buildings next to the library (which has free Internet access) and across from Shinei Kōen, a few blocks east of the long-distance ferry terminal and a few blocks west of the bus terminal. It's open Tuesday through Saturday from 8:30 to 5, and some English is spoken. Inside you can get loads of pamphlets in English about Ishigaki-jima and the rest of the islands, plus maps and lists of dive shops and sights to see.

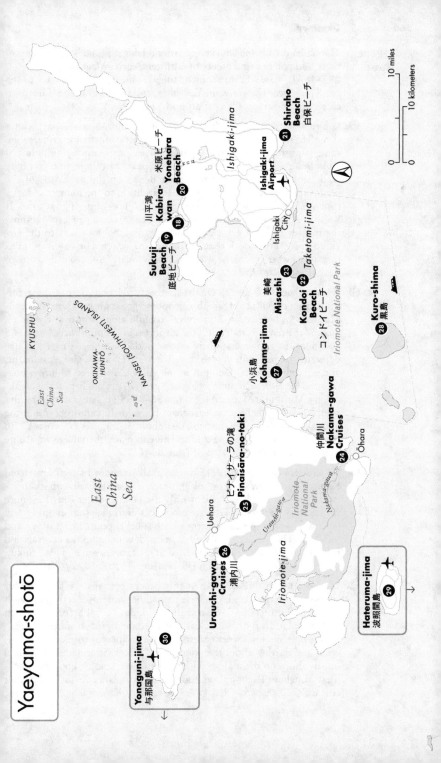

The scuba diving and snorkeling around Ishigaki-jima is absolutely superb, and you can find plenty of outfitters, such as **Tom Sawyer** (☎ 098/083–4677), based in downtown Ishigaki-shi. Popular trips are to the coral reefs near Kabira-wan, Yonehara, and Cape Hirakubo. Lunch-inclusive outings typically cost around ¥12,000.

⑱ Kabira-wan (Kabira Bay, 川平湾). This beautiful, sheltered bay, with a complete spectrum of greens and blues contrasting against fine, white sand, is at the center of the Japanese black-pearl cultivation industry. Swimming is discouraged (due to the pearl farming), but you may walk along the road over to **Sukuji Beach** on the back side of the peninsula for a swim and snorkel. In addition to the numerous tacky tourist shops and eateries, there are many glass-bottom boat tours at Kabira. A 30-minute ride costs about ¥1,000. You can avoid joining the masses and still get a good view by making your way to the elevated observation deck that overhangs the water. The bay is 30 minutes northwest by car or 40 minutes by bus(¥580) from downtown Ishigaki. ✉ *Rte. 207 off Rte. 79.*

㉑ Shiraho Beach (白保ビーチ). On the southeast corner of Ishigaki-jima, offshore from the village of Shiraho, lie submerged some very rare and beautiful reefs of blue coral. A proposal to build an airport over the beach has so far been rejected, but if the airport is ever built the reefs will end up under the runway, so there's some added incentive to see this underwater garden while you're here. There are many lodging, restaurant, and equipment-rental facilities in the village. You need to hire a boat (around ¥2,000, including snorkeling gear) to get safely past the breakers; try **Minshuku Maezato** (☎ 098/086–8065); it's next to the Shiraho post office. A bus heading east from Ishigaki-shi can drop you at the Shōgaku-mae bus stop; the trip takes about 30 minutes and costs ¥350. If you're driving or taking a taxi, you can reach the village via Route 390. ✉ *10 km (6.2 mi) east of Ishigaki-shi.*

⑲ Sukuji Beach (底地ビーチ). A 15-minute walk or about 1 km (0.6 mi) from Kabira Bay, lovely, shallow Sukuji Beach will startle you with its amazing variety of reef life. Perhaps only the Great Barrier Reef has more giant clams, and here many are embedded into the coral in only a few meters of water, so nearly anyone with snorkel gear can get down and see them. This area is fairly well developed, with equipment rentals and resorts, and there's a new Club Med at the far western end of it. Sukuji is 30–35 minutes by car from Ishigaki-shi. ✉ *Rte. 207 off Rte. 79.*

⑳ Yonehara Beach (米原ビーチ). At this beach, perhaps the best one for snorkeling on the island, you have to waddle with fins (get the kind with decent heel protection) over a shelf of old, dead coral before you reach a spectacular drop-off with clear water fading off into a startling abyss. Beyond the shelf is a world crowded with multicolor tropical fish, hovering and darting about the young coral below. Snorkel gear is rented out by shops on the main road, and there are camping and toilet facilities. Yonehara is about one hour north from Ishigaki-shi by bus at a cost of ¥720. ✉ *Rte. 79, 5 km (3 mi) east of Kabira-wan.*

Where to Stay & Eat

Considering the town's size, Ishigaki has a fairly wide choice of accommodations, and the tourist information office can help you make reservations.

$–$$$ ✕ **Sushi Bar Tatsu** (たつ). Some of the best fish you're ever likely to taste swims just offshore, and a fair portion of it ends up on plates in this lively, Hawaiian-style restaurant. The sushi master in fact once lived in Hawaii. Recommended for sushi or sashimi is a local rainbow-color fish called *goma-aigo*; its firm and tasty flesh will make an addict out of you. Tatsu is at the corner of Shiyakusho-dōri and Shimin-kaikan-dōri, three blocks northwest of Shimei Kōen. ✉ *10–28 Shinei-chō, Ishigaki-shi* ☱ *No credit cards* ☾ *Closed Sun.*

$–$$ ✕ **Iso** (磯). Near the harbor and behind the post office, this traditional Okinawan café serves local cuisine at reasonable prices. Most dishes are based on pork. The lunch special is only ¥600. ✉ *9 Ōkawa, Ishigaki-shi* ☎ *098/082–7721* ☱ *No credit cards.*

$$$$ ⊟ **Hotel Miyahira** (ホテルミヤヒラ). Not far from the piers and main downtown streets, the Miyahira is an upscale standby with a squat, orange-tile, Ryūkyū-style exterior and lots of shiisa lions around for good measure. The interior is done in a comfortable Western style. Breakfast is available for ¥400; for the dinner plan, add ¥2,100. ✉ *4–9 Misaki-chō, Ishigaki-shi 907-0012* ☎ *098/082–6111* 🖷 *098/083–3236* ⊕ *www.miyahira.co.jp* ⤳ *158 Western-style rooms* ⚥ *6 restaurants, pool, Internet, car rental* ☱ *AE, MC, V* ⦿ *EP, MAP.*

$$$$ ⊟ **Ishigaki Grand Hotel** (石垣グランドホテル). This hotel in a spot next to the pier has a bright, attractive lobby and a friendly, helpful staff. Breakfast is included, and dinners from ¥980 can be arranged. Rooms are simple but clean and sufficiently appointed. Suites are much larger than standard rooms. ✉ *1 Tonoshiro, Ishigaki-shi 907-0004* ☎ *098/082–6161* 🖷 *098/082–2981* ⊕ *www.ishigaki-grand-hotel.com* ⤳ *64 Western-style rooms and suites, 10 Japanese-style rooms and suites* ⚥ *2 restaurants, Japanese baths, sauna* ☱ *AE, MC, V* ⦿ *CP.*

¢–$ ⊟ **Hyper Hotel Ishigaki** (ハイパーホテル石垣). A member of the Hyper chain, this hotel offers wider-than-standard beds and fluffy duvets as well as a good location a block or so east of the ferry dock. Best of all, the prices are unbeatable for a reputable establishment with Western-style rooms that include all of the basic amenities. It's an especially good choice for families or groups, as a third person in one room costs only ¥1,000 more. ✉ *1–2–3 Yashima-chō, Ishigaki-shi 907-0011* ☎ *098/082–2000* 🖷 *098/082–3933* ⊕ *www.hyper-ishigaki.co.jp* ⤳ *94 rooms* ⚥ *Laundry facilities* ☱ *MC, V* ⦿ *CP.*

Getting Around

The best way to get to the island is by air, and the best ways to get around are by car and scooter.

BY AIR Ishigaki-jima is 55 minutes from Naha, 3 hours from Ōsaka, and 3½ hours from Tōkyō by plane. One-way tickets cost ¥19,000, ¥41,500, and ¥50,000, respectively. Both **JTA** (☎0120/25–5971) and **ANK** (☎0120/02–9222) airlines fly here.

BY BICYCLE &   **Ai-Ai** (☎ 098/083–9530), at the corner of Yui-dōri, one block northeast
SCOOTER   of the post office on Sanbashi-dōri, rents bikes and scooters.

BY CAR   Ishigaki-jima has a couple of buses that circulate along the coastal
roads, but the service is too infrequent to be convenient. Consider renting a car to explore the island. **Toyota** (☎ 098/082–0100) and **Nippon
Rent-a-Car** (☎ 098/082–3629) have branches at the airport. **Nissan Rent-
a-Car** (☎ 098/083–0024) is to the left of the bus station on Sanbashi-
dōri, near the piers and fish market.

BY FERRY   **Arimura Sangyō** (☎ 098/860–1980, 03/3562–2091 in Tōkyō) runs ferries from Naha to Ishigaki-jima via Miyako-jima 12–15 times per month
and tickets cost ¥5,860. **R.K.K.** (☎ 098/868–1126, 03/3281–1831 in
Tōkyō) runs ferries between Naha, Miyako-jima, and Ishigaki-jima five
times a month. The trip from Naha to Ishigaki runs 13–16 hours and
costs ¥6,360–¥14,620.

Several ferries depart daily from the town Ishigaki to the surrounding
islands, including Iriomote-jima, Taketomi-jima, and Kuro-shima.

Taketomi-jima   竹富島

8 km (5 mi) west of Ishigaki-jima

On tiny Taketomi-jima you can imagine you are on a distant planet. Cute,
compact houses with red-tile roofs and white coral-block walls sit contentedly amidst a riot of greenery and blossoms. Even the sand is unique
here—the star-shape grains are actually the dried calcinous skeletons of
tiny aquatic creatures. Only 300 folks call this speck home, but since
it's only a 10-minute ride from Ishigaki-jima, boatloads of people visit
each day. Ferries leave on the half hour and the trip costs ¥580 each
way. Once you're on the islet you can wander around, swim, and snorkel
in the clear, shallow water. Flat, less than a mile across at its widest point,
and with a circumference of less than 9 km (6 mi), it's perfect for a bicycling tour.

There's a **visitor center,** a block east of the ferry pier. Little or no English
is spoken, but you can pick up a map of the island.

㉒ **Kondoi Beach** (コンドイビーチ). Perhaps the best beach on tiny Taketomi,
Kondoi is a prime spot to examine the island's famous star sand. Signs
tell you not to take any, but someone is making money selling tons of
it at the shops. There are views of the islands of Iriomote, Kohama, and
Kuroshima. Kondoi-misaki (Cape Kondoi) is a 30- to 40-minute walk
from the ferry pier, halfway down the west coast of the island.

㉓ **Misashi** (美崎). The water around the northern tip of the island is the
best for snorkeling. Offshore rocky outcrops attract and shelter colorful gatherings of undersea critters. Walk northwest for 20 minutes along
the beach or road from the ferry terminal; like anything else on tiny Taketomi, it's not far.

Where to Stay & Eat
After the last ferry back to Ishigaki-jima departs, Taketomi once more
becomes an intimate little community on the edge of the earth. The lodg-

ings here are not at all sophisticated, but a night on quiet Taketomi is an unforgettable experience. The inns serve dinner, and there are a couple of small restaurants within a block of the pier. There's even a pub, called Chirorin-mura, a block south of the Unbufuru lookout, at the southern end of the tiny village.

¢ ✕🖼 **Nohara-sō** (のはら荘). A very informal place to stay, Nohara-sō is about good food and super-friendly service. It's only a block or so east of the pier, just past the visitor center. Two meals and the use of snorkeling gear is included in the rates. ⊠ *Taketomi-chō* ☎ *098/085–2252* ⚪ *No room phones, no room TVs* ↩ *7 Japanese-style rooms without bath* ⚪ *No room phones, no room TVs* ☰ *No credit cards* ¶◎ *MAP.*

¢ ✕🖼 **Minshuku Izumiya** (民宿泉屋). Popular for its lovely flower garden, this inn offers meals as part of the package. Those seeking more privacy can rent the separate traditional-style house across the sandy lane. ⊠ *Taketomi-chō* ☎ *098/085–2250* ↩ *7 Japanese-style rooms without bath, villa* ⚪ *No room phones, no room TVs* ☰ *No credit cards* ¶◎ *MAP.*

Iriomote-jima 西表島

30 km (19 mi) west of Ishigaki-jima

You might not expect Japan to have a remote pocket of subtropical rain forest, but then again, Japan is nothing if not full of the unexpected. Arguably the most secluded and unexplored region in the country, Iriomote-jima is an adventure-lover's paradise. You can see flora and fauna here that you won't find elsewhere, such as the *yamaneko,* a lynx-like wildcat; knobby-kneed trees called *sakishima suōnoki*; deadly vipers called *habu*; murky, jungle-lined river systems like mini-Amazons; and leeches lurking among the weeds.

Only about 2,000 people live on Iriomote, most along the northeast coastal road. Much of the island is a protected national park, and there are no roads at all heading into the interior. The entire southwest third of the island is isolated and wild, with not even a coastal road and almost no settlements.

There's a **tourist information center** (西表島観光センター; ☎ 098/082–9836), staffed part time, in Funaura next to the ferry pier. Although the staff won't speak much or any English, they can provide you with information on the few hostels and inns in and between the towns of Funaura and Uehara, on the northern coast, and near the remote southern port of Ōhara. They can also point you in the right direction if you want to hire a dive outfitter, or rent a bike, scooter, or car and driver.

Note that there are no money-withdrawal facilities on Iriomote-jima, so be sure to arrive with enough money to last your entire stay.

★ **Manta Way.** One of earth's rarest spectacles can be observed in the famous Manta Way, the nickname for the straits between the east coast of Iriomote-jima and the neighboring Kohama-jima. Here the straits' gentle but scary-looking namesake creatures often cruise in vast fleets, gracefully flapping along and feeding on plankton. April to June is the best time for manta watching. Farther out, experienced divers can explore pinnacles of coral jutting up from the deep blue. Any of the min-shuku or hostels on Iriomote can help arrange transport and dives.

㉔ Nakama-gawa Cruises (仲間川遊覧船; 0980/85–5304). The second-longest river on the island can be explored via cruises that depart from the port of Ōhara, take about an hour, and cost ¥1,260. The trips offer you an Amazon-like experience with fewer tourists than at the Urauchi-gawa up north.

㉕ Pinaisāra-no-taki (ピナイサーラの滝). These waterfalls, the tallest in the prefecture, can sometimes be seen from boats coming into Funaura. To get to the best viewpoints you can either take a kayak or wade through the lagoon, depending on the tide, and climb a path to the top of the falls. Beware of leeches and especially the poisonous *habu* (water moccasins). A film cannister of salt will save you from an attack of thirsty leeches; make plenty of noise to frighten away the snakes. The best option is to hire a local guide, such as Mr. Susumu Murata at ☎ 098/085–6425.

★ ㉖ Urauchi-gawa Cruises (内浦川遊覧船). A boat tour along this river is the sole reason many day-trippers come to the island, and though touristy, it's worthwhile. Boat operators wait for at least four riders, then for ¥1,500 per person they take you upriver as far as possible. You then disembark and continue along a footpath to the waterfalls known as Mariudo-no-taki and Kanpirē-no-taki, where there are many suitable swimming spots, and lots of butterflies swarming in the mists. Allow about three hours for the round-trip. Kayak rentals can also be negotiated from the boat operators. The first boats depart at 9 AM and the last depart at 4 PM. Since this is the most popular activity for visitors to Iriomote-jima, you'll find plenty of boats as well as frequent buses to Urauchibashi, the mouth of the river, 20 minutes west of Funaura.

A 15-km (9.3-mi) **cross-island trail** connects the falls of the Urauchi-gawa to a point near Ōhara, but this hike is a serious and rigorous undertaking. End to end, the hike will take 6–8 hours and should not be attempted if you're alone or unprepared.

Getting Around

Ferries from Ishigaki-jima to the port of Funaura, in north–central Iriomote-jima, take about 40 minutes. There are nine sailings daily, and the fare is ¥2,000.

Bus service connects Funaura with the towns of Ōhara and Shirahama at the end of the 60 km (37 mi) coastal road, for ¥1,050. Buses run only twice daily and take about 80 minutes each way.

Kohama-jima & Kuro-shima   小浜島と黒島

㉗ Between Iriomote-jima and Taketomi-jima lies the small island of **Kohama-jima** (小浜島). There a few places to stay, but most people visit on a short day trip from Ishigaki-jima. High-speed boats from Kohama to Ishigaki are frequent, cost ¥1,050, and take only 30 minutes. The most popular activities are diving along Manta Way, and biking around to the beaches. Bikes can be rented near the dock.

㉘ Due south of Kohama-jima is the tiny island of **Kuro-shima** (黒島), also blessed with fabulous diving. Chances are high you'll come across some

Napoleon fish (reputed to be highly poisonous) among the colorful canyons of coral offshore. There's good snorkeling at Nishi-no-hama, just east of where the boat lets you off, and another beach with a U-shape reef is at the south end of the island. Bikes are available at the pier for the 3 km (2 mi) zigzag ride. In addition to great diving and snorkeling, the island is famous for raising the bulls used in Okinawa Hontō's unusual form of bullfighting called tōgyū. Like Kohama, Kuro-shima has a few inns, but since boats (¥1,150) from Ishigaki are fairly frequent and take only 30 minutes, most visitors make the crossing for a day trip.

Hateruma-jima & Yonaguni-jima 小浜島と黒島

29 **Hateruma-jima** (波照間島), Japan's southernmost point, is surrounded by some of the clearest water on the planet. Here coral shelves drop away into a vertiginous indigo, and underwater visibility nears the edge of human vision. Just west of the pier at the amazing, gorgeous Nishi-no-hama, or Nishi Beach, you can find a sort of a snorkel-swim park. Facilities include bathrooms and a campground.

The island is only 5 km (3 mi) long, and rented bikes and scooters are the best way to get around. Speedboats from Ishigaki-jima to Hateruma-jima depart three times daily and the one-hour trip costs ¥3,050 one-way; buy tickets at the counter inside Ishigaki's ferry terminal.

The latest buzz in these far reaches of the realm has to do with a mysterious and huge carved-rock staircase or pyramid found in the 1980s on
30 the seabed in the waters off **Yonaguni-jima** (与那国島), Japan's westernmost point. Some experts claim that the rocks are far too straight and true of edge and corner to be explained as nature's handiwork, and they believe that the rocks are actually the ruins of some great ancient civilization, and may be up to 10,000 years old. Although the investigation is ongoing, and the final ruling still very much out, the site has become popular among divers, especially since schools of photogenic hammerhead sharks often invade the area in winter. Marlin fishing here is also highly rated.

Yonaguni-jima is also known for wonders above ground: unusually shaped rock formations, the world's largest species of moth (bigger than a hand in wingspan), and wild Yonaguni ponies.

To get to Yonaguni-jima, you can fly via JTA from Ishigaki-jima in 30 minutes for ¥10,000. There are two flights per day. Twice a week there's also ferry service, but the trip take 4½ hours. A one-way ticket costs ¥3,700.

Where to Stay

$$ **Hotel Irifune** (ホテル入船). This hotel in the main village of Sonai, on Yonaguni's north coast, is a good lodging option. It's nothing to rave about, but the management offers guided dive expeditions, and at ¥14,000 for two in a Western-style room with private bath, including meals, the price is right. Also, there are a few Japanese-style rooms with shared bath, and these run ¥12,000 for two. *Sonai* ☎ *0980/87-2311* *8 Western-style rooms, 3 Japanese-style rooms without bath* *No credit cards* *MAP.*

OKINAWA A TO Z

To research prices, get advice from other travelers, and book travel arrangements, visit www.fodors.com.

FERRY TRAVEL
Ferries are best used for travel between a main island and surrounding islets, rather than for travel from one main island to another (except Iriomote-jima and Ishigaki-jima, which are closer together).

🚩 Arimura Sangyō ☎ 098/860-1980. R.K.K. ☎ 098/868-1126.

EMERGENCIES
🚩 Adventist Medical Center ✉ 868 Kouchi, Nishihara-chō ☎ 098/946-2833. Police ☎ 110 Urasoe Sōgō Byōin (General Hospital) ✉ 4-16-1 Iso, Urasoe-shi ☎ 098/878-0231. U.S. Naval Hospital ✉ Camp Lester, Bldg. 6000 ☎ 098/643-7509.

ENGLISH-LANGUAGE MEDIA
The U.S. Armed Forces Radio Network at 648 on the AM dial broadcasts the news, a lot of cheesy infomercials, and a little music.

For a small selection of books, magazines, and newspapers, visit the bookshop on the seventh floor of the Palette Kumoji department store, at the bottom of Kokusai-dōri in Naha.

TOURS
Tours abound in Okinawa, though all are in Japanese. Any travel agency along Kokusai-dōri can book a tour for you, and your hotel should be able to arrange them as well.

🚩 Tour Contacts Naha Kōtsū ☎ 098/868-7149. Chūbū Kankō Bus Charter only ☎ 098/937-7858.

VISITOR INFORMATION
🚩 Tourist Information Okinawa Prefectural Government Tourism and Resort Bureau ✉ 1-2-2 Izumizaki, Naha 900-8570 ☎ 098/866-2764. Naha Airport Information Desk ☎ 098/857-6884. Okinawa Tourist Information Office ✉ Kokusai-dōri ☎ 098/868-4887.

TŌHOKU 東北

13

By James M.
Vardaman Jr.

IT'S A SHAME that so few foreign travelers venture farther above Tōkyō than the monument town of Nikkō, because Tōhoku, comprising the six prefectures of northern Honshū, has an appealing combination of country charm, coastal and mountain scenery, old villages, and revered temples. For a long time the area was known as Michinoku—the "end of the road" or "backcountry"—and it retains the spirit of Matsuo Bashō's 17th-century poetic travel journal, *Narrow Road to the North*. Many Japanese still hold that image of remote rusticity, with the result that Tōhoku is one of the least-visited areas in modern Japan.

In a nation where politeness is paramount, the people in Tōhoku are friendlier than their more urbanized compatriots. With the exception of Sendai, Tōhoku's cities are small, and the fast pace of city life is foreign to their residents. Bullet-train lines extend only halfway into the region, and most of the people of Tōhoku live their lives with less of the post-modern intensity than is the norm in the southern two-thirds of Honshū.

Tōhoku's six largest cities are prefectural capitals, and they have the amenities of any international community. With the exception of Sendai, however, these cities don't have many sights to explore. In hopes of attracting tourists, they have modern complexes that serve as giant souvenir shops, museums, and information centers in one, but these aren't what you would come halfway around the world to see.

Instead, come to see the traditional ways and folk arts that are still alive in the north, along with the independence of spirit that locals share with people in Hokkaidō, even farther north. In the Tōno Valley people still live in the traditional northern Japan *magariya* (L-shape farmhouses), and the old people still know the stories of mystical creatures and how place-names came into being. The architecture of the *bushi* (warrior class) residences is preserved in Kakunodate, and its people continue to make traditional folk crafts from cherrywood and bark.

Ruggedness is a feature of the landscape here, be it the windblown slopes of Tappi-zaki (Cape Tappi) or Zaō-san's huddled "ice monster" trees, which get covered with airborne crystals. In the midst of the mountains are the verdant calm of Towada-ko (Lake Towada) and the gurgling Oirase-kyōkoku (Oirase Gorge), where the gentle passage of water replaces the violence of volcanic eruptions.

See the glossary at the end of this book for definitions of the common Japanese words and suffixes used in this chapter.

Exploring Tōhoku

The mountains that rise on the spine of Honshū run north all the way through Tōhoku. Most of the island's trains and highways travel north–south on either side of the mountains. Thus, when taking the major roads or railway trunk lines, you tend to miss some of the grandest mountain scenery. This chapter, laid out as an itinerary up the Pacific side of Tōhoku's spine and down the Nihon-kai (Sea of Japan) side, takes in the best of Tōhoku, using the JR trains as much as possible, but covering more remote areas as well. If you plan to cross north into Hokkaidō

Numbers in the text correspond to numbers in the margin and on the Tōhoku map.

13

If you have 3 days

In 🖼 **Sendai** ⑤ ⌐, start at Aoba Castle, and then walk down to the Sendai Municipal Museum for a visual and historical overview of the city. From there stroll along the Hirose-gawa (Hirose River) to Zuihō-den, the extravagant mausoleums of the Date leaders. Spend the afternoon at 🖼 **Yamadera** ⑦, climbing to the top of the mountainside temple for spectacular views of the town and the Yamagata Basin; spend the night in Yamadera (perhaps at nearby Sakunami Onsen) or return to Sendai. The next day travel to 🖼 **Matsu-shima** ⑥, relaxing on the ferry that travels through the islets of the bay to Matsu-shima itself. Spend the night in Matsu-shima or return to Sendai. On the third day take the train north for a day outdoors in one of two areas. See the gorge known as **Gembikei-kyōkoku** ⑩ and then continue to Mōtsu-ji in **Hiraizumi** ⑪. From there wander along the fields to Chūson-ji and Konjiki-dō. Or, if you pick **Tōno** ⑫ instead, get an early start in order to have a full afternoon to cover the distances around town. See Kappa-buchi, a small riverside pool of local lore, and then, for a look at farm life, the Denshō-en folk museum. On foot or by bicycle, this will take the afternoon. If you go by taxi, also go up the mountainside to see the 500 Disciples of Buddha, carved on moss-covered boulders.

If you have 5 days

One five-day approach to Tōhoku would include two days for 🖼 **Sendai** ⑤ ⌐, another day for an excursion to the temple of **Yamadera** ⑦ or the temples and gorges in and around **Hiraizumi** ⑪, then the final two days for the rural splendor of 🖼 **Tōno** ⑫. As an alternative, you could head farther north: two days in 🖼 **Sendai** ⑤ and either **Yamadera** ⑦ or **Matsu-shima** ⑥; a third day in **Hiraizumi** ⑪, ending for the night in 🖼 **Morioka** ⑬, a busy city known for its ironware; then the last two days taking in the scenery at the lake known as 🖼 **Towada-ko** ⑰. Spend the night in the Towada-ko area at the resort of Yasumi-ya, taking a morning hike before moving on.

If you have 7 days

With a week to take in Tōhoku's natural beauty, start in 🖼 **Sendai** ⑤ ⌐; then take a second-day jaunt west for a climb up **Yamadera** ⑦ and a relaxing bath in the open-air hot springs at Sakunami Onsen. From there return to JR Sendai Station and transfer to the train out to 🖼 **Matsu-shima** ⑥; on the way, stop off in Hon-Shiogama to see the Shiogama Jinja. Spend the night in Matsu-shima or return to Sendai. On the third day head north to 🖼 **Tōno** ⑫ for a day of strolling between sights. On the fourth day take it easy in 🖼 **Morioka** ⑬ and enjoy some of the best Tōhoku cooking at dinner. On the fifth day head by bus to 🖼 **Towada-ko** ⑰ and take on the 9-km (5½-mi) trail that parallels the Oirase-kyōkoku before spending the night at nearby Yasumi-ya. The next day take the bus to the castle town of 🖼 **Hirosaki** ⑱. On the seventh day head south, with seaside stops either at the Oga-hantō (Oga Peninsula), **Akita** ⑳, or the delightful traditional town of **Kakunodate** ⑮.

from Aomori, consider heading down the quieter west coast of Tōhoku on the way back.

Keep in mind that Shinkansen lines don't go any farther north than the inland city of Yamagata, the west-coast city of Akita (via Morioka), and Hachinohe, on the northeast coast. Buses take over, and travel slows beyond these points—which is part of what Tōhoku is all about. That said, using a combination of trains and buses, most of Tōhoku's hinterland is easily accessible, except in heavy winter snows.

About the Hotels & Restaurants

The restaurants in the region serve the freshest of fish in sushi and sashimi as well as wild vegetables and mushrooms in season.

Tōhoku has a broad spectrum of accommodations, from inns and *minshuku* (private homes that accept lodging guests) to large modern hotels. Many accommodations are contemporary, utilitarian, and functional, with little local character. Higher prices tend to mean larger lobby areas and guest rooms. As in other regions of the country, cities and towns have Western-style rooms, while in smaller towns and villages most lodging is Japanese-style. All large city and resort hotels serve Western and Japanese food. In summer hotel reservations are advised.

WHAT IT COSTS In yen				
$$$$	**$$$**	**$$**	**$**	**¢**
RESTAURANTS over 3,000	2,000–3,000	1,000–2,000	800–1,000	under 800
HOTELS over 22,000	18,000–22,000	12,000–18,000	8,000–12,000	under 8,000

Restaurant prices are per person for a main course at dinner. Hotel prices are for a double room with private bath, excluding service and 5% tax.

Timing

Tōhoku's climate is similar to that of New England. Winters are cold, and in the mountains snow blocks some of the minor roads. At the same time, snow rarely falls in Sendai and Matsu-shima and along the Pacific coast, and temperatures rarely dip below freezing. Spring and autumn are the most colorful seasons. Summer is refreshingly cool, and as a result attracts Japanese tourists escaping the heat and humidity of Tōkyō and points south.

If your timing is perfect, you can see all of Tōhoku's big summer festivals, starting with Hirosaki's Neputa Festival (August 1–7), Aomori's Nebuta (August 3–7), Akita's Kantō (August 5–7), and Sendai's Tanabata (August 6–8). The festivals are very popular and very crowded. All of Tōhoku's energy is released in colorful parades of lanterns and floats and wild dancing. Reserve at least several weeks in advance for hotels and trains.

SOUTH TŌHOKU 南東北

Fukushima Prefecture, in southern Tōhoku, is tamer both in scenery and in attitude than the rest of Tōhoku. Nonetheless, there are lakes, hot springs, and traces of traditional Japanese life that are worth seeing.

Mountains, Lakes & Hot Springs
In a country that is split by mountains top to bottom, Tōhoku, because of its relative emptiness, is one of the best places in Japan to take in its rugged landscapes. Deep volcanic lakes such as Towada-ko and a slew of onsen resorts such as Nyūtō Onsen are classic Japanese escapes. Good hiking spots include Zaō-san, Haguro-san, Yamadera, Hachiman-tai Kōgen, and Oirase-kyōkoku.

Rural Landscapes
With sophisticated metropolises like Tōkyō and Ōsaka, Japan, like the rest of the modernized world, has turned its back on rural living. But Tōhoku still retains patches of agrarian life, with its rice fields and clear streams. If farmhouses and agricultural areas hold some appeal, visit the Tōno Basin near Morioka to see traditional magariya: L-shape farmhouses in which the stables are attached to the living quarters.

13

Bandai Kōgen   磐梯高原

❶ *30 min northwest of JR Inawashiro Station by bus.*

Fukushima was the first region in northern Honshū to become a popular resort area for Japanese families, especially around the tableland known as Bandai Kōgen, or the Bandai Plateau. The volcano Bandai-san erupted in 1888 and in 15 short minutes wiped out more than 40 small villages, killing 477 people and resculpting the landscape. The eruption dammed several streams to form hundreds of lakes, the largest of which is Hibara-ko, with its crooked shoreline and numerous islets. Bandai Kōgen is also the name for the tourist center at Hibara-ko, where Japanese vacationers disperse to their campgrounds, bungalows, or modern *ryokan* (traditional inns).

Though the Bandai Kōgen area is somewhat spoiled by hordes of tourists, a particularly pleasant walk, the Go-shiki-numa Trail, meanders past the dozen or more tiny lakes (ponds, really) that are collec-
★ tively called **Go-shiki-numa** (Five-Color Lakes, 五色沼), because each throws off a different color. The trail begins across from the Bandai Kōgen bus station and runs in the opposite direction from Hibara-ko; the round-trip takes two hours. There are other lake and mountain trails in the area as well.

Inawashiro-ko (猪苗代湖) is Japan's third-largest lake, and the town of Inawashiro is on its northern shore. Unlike Tōhoku's other large lakes, Towada-ko and Tazawa-ko, Inawashiro-ko is not a caldera lake but instead is formed by streams. So its flat surrounding shore isn't exactly spectacular, though the scenery is pretty enough as far as Japanese beaches go. Kitschy, swan-shape sightseeing boats cruise the waters.

Hideyo Noguchi's Birthplace and Memorial Museum (Noguchi Hideyo Kinen-kan, 野口秀世記念館) honors the life of Noguchi (1876–1928) and

ON THE MENU

Tōhoku is famous for its clean water and its rice, and these two ingredients are made into delicious sake throughout the region. Sansai (wild vegetables) and mushrooms appear in an amazing variety of dishes, as do river fish (mostly carp and sweetfish). Along the coast you can find squid so fresh it's translucent, along with uni (sea urchin) so delectable it can convert even the squeamish.

In Sendai look for Sendai miso—the heartier red northern version of the staple

fermented soybean paste—in soups, and grilled gyūtan (beef tongue), for which locals stand in line. Akita's kiritampo is boiled rice that's pounded into cakes, molded on sticks, and grilled; simmered in broth with chicken and vegetables it becomes kiritampo-nabe. Aomori and Iwate's apples often appear in the form of desserts and juice.

his research of yellow fever, which eventually killed him in Africa. It's 10 minutes by bus from Inawashiro Station. ☎ *0242/65–2319* ✆ *¥500* ☉ *Apr.–Oct., daily 8:30–4:15; Nov.–early Dec. and late Dec.–Mar., daily 9–4.*

Where to Stay

$$$$ ⊞ **Ura-Bandai Royal Hotel** (裏磐梯ロイヤルホテル). A comfortable resort hotel with a magnificent setting, the Royal also has seven restaurants, including traditional Japanese, *robatayaki* (grill), sushi, and French. Don't miss the rare blueberry cheesecake served in the coffee shop. Rooms come with two meals, served in the main dining room, or you can opt out of the meal plan. In the back garden behind the hotel there's a path leading around a small lake, and the west entrance of the Go-shiki-numa Trail is nearby. ⊠ *1093 Hibara Kengamine, Kita-Shiobara Mura, Yama-gun, Fukushima-ken 969-2701* ☎ *0241/32–3111* 🖷 *0241/32–3130* ✍ *227 Western-style and Japanese-style rooms with bath* ♨ *6 restaurants, coffee shop, lake* ⊟ *AE, DC, MC, V* ◉| *EP, MAP.*

$$ ⊞ **Pension Heidi** (ペンションハイジ). Rooms are simple but comfortable, but the location (within walking distance of the Kengamine intersection at Ura-Bandai) is convenient, but what wins return visits and two-night stays is the food—very few pensions in Japan offer this level of cuisine in an area so delightful for hiking. And, so guests won't get bored, the chef alternates nightly between French and Chinese cooking. Breakfast and dinner are included in the price. The manager is very helpful. ⊠ *1093 Ura-Bandai Kengamine, Kita-Shiobara Mura, Yama-gun, Fukushima-ken 969-2701* ☎ *0241/32–2008* 🖷 *0241/32–3456* ✍ *10 rooms, 2 with bath; no a/c, no room TVs* ⊟ *AE, DC, MC, V* ◉| *MAP.*

Kitakata　喜多方

★ ❷ *1 hr 50 min northwest of Kōriyama by JR.*

Mud-wall *kura* can be seen all over Japan, but Kitakata is unique in having more than 2,600 of them. A kura is a thick-walled, tile-roofed storehouse that's usually two stories high and has small windows with thick shutters at the top—which can be quickly shut and sealed with mud when there's danger of fire. Kura are not only simple places to store rice, miso, soy sauce, sake, fertilizer, and charcoal: they're also status symbols of the local merchants. In the past the kura fascination spread so much that shops, homes, and inns were built in this architectural style as people tried to outdo their neighbors. You can quickly use up a couple of rolls of film taking photographs of the many different kura—some are of black-and-white plaster, some simply of mud, some with bricks, and some with thatched roofs or tiles. You can pick up a kura walking-tour map of the town at the tourist office in the train station. If you're short on time, head to the area northeast of the station, which has a selection of storehouses, including **Kai Shōten** (甲斐商店), a black kura storefront of an old miso and soy-sauce factory.

Kitakata is also known for its ramen, and several tourism-conscious entrepreneurs have combined the town's two big attractions by converting storehouses into ramen shops. The town also has a kura-shape carriage, towed by a brawny cart horse, in which you can ride if the spirit of Japanese kitsch moves you.

The **Kitakata tourist office** (観光案内所; ⊠ JR Kitakata Station ☎ 0241/22–2233) has a kura walking-tour map of the city; it's open Monday–Saturday 8:30–5 and Sunday 10–5.

Kai Honke Kura Zashiki (甲斐本家蔵座敷) an elaborate mansion that took seven years to build, provides an example of how efficient and beautiful the kura were in times past. ⊠ *1-4611 Aza* ☎ *0241/22–0001* 💴 *¥400* ⊙ *Daily 9–5.*

Aizu Lacquer Museum (Aizu Urushi Bijutsu Hakubutsukan, 会津うるし美術博物館) displays elegant local lacquer products from trays and bowls to tables. ⊠ *4095 Higashi-machi* ☎ *0241/24–4151* 💴 *¥300* ⊙ *Apr.–Nov., daily 9–5; Dec.–Mar., daily 9–4.*

Yamatogawa Sake Brewery (大和川酒蔵北方風土館) consists of seven kura, one of which serves as a small museum to display old methods of sake production. The other buildings are still used for making sake. After a dutiful tour, you're offered the pleasurable reward of tasting different types of sake. The brewery is across the center of town from the Aizu Lacquer Museum. ⊠ *4761 Aza Teramachi* 💴 *Free* ⊙ *Daily 9–4:30.*

Aizu-Wakamatsu　会津若松

❸ *20 min south of Kitakata by JR, 70 min west of Kōriyama by JR.*

As the locus of a tragic, if partly misconceived, event in the course of the Meiji overthrow of Japan's feudal shogunate in the mid-1800s,

Aizu-Wakamatsu has a couple of relevant sights. But the compelling story of the Byakkotai far outshines the town itself.

Every Japanese knows this story, so it bears telling. In 1868, 20 young warriors, known as Byakkotai (White Tigers), had been fighting pro-Restoration forces outside the city when they were sent back to Tsuruga Castle to aid in its defense. The boys arrived on a nearby hillside, Iimoriyama. To their horror, they saw smoke rise from the castle and mistakenly believed the castle to be overrun by the enemy. As good samurai, all 20 boys began a mass suicide ritual. One boy was saved before he bled to death. For a samurai this was a curse. He spent the rest of his life with a livid scar and the shame of having failed to live up to the samurai code. Ironically, the castle had not at that point fallen into enemy hands, and the fighting continued for another month—indeed, had they lived, the Byakkotai might have helped to turn the battle in their side's favor. On the hill next to their graves there now stands the **Byakkotai Monument** (白虎隊士自刃の地), built in remembrance of the 19 who died. A festival is held in memory of the Byakkotai September 23–24 at Iimoriyama. The small Byakkotai Kinenen museum and a hexagonal Buddhist temple, Sazaedō, are also here. The monument is reached by a 10-minute bus ride from the station. ☞ ¥400 ⊙ *Apr.–June and 2nd wk of July–Nov., daily 8–5; 2nd wk of Dec.–Mar., daily 8:30–4.*

Tsuruga Castle (Tsuruga-jō, 鶴ヶ城) was the most powerful stronghold of the northeast during the shōgun period. The Aizu clan was closely linked to the ruling family in Edo and remained classically loyal until the end. When the imperial forces of the Meiji Restoration pressed home their successful attack in 1868, that loyalty caused the castle, which had stood for five centuries, to be partly burned down, along with most of the city's buildings. The new government destroyed the castle completely in 1874. The five-story structure was rebuilt in 1965 as a museum and is said to look like its original, but without the presence it must have had in 1868, when the 19 Byakkotai committed ritual suicide. From the JR station plaza, take a bus from Gate 14 or 15, but check with the information booth first. The bus loops around the city past the castle and the Byakkotai Monument. ☞ ¥500 ⊙ *Daily 8:30–5; last entry at 4:30.*

★ The **Aizu Samurai Residence** (Aizu Buke Yashiki, 会津武家屋敷), to the east of the castle, is an excellent reproduction of a wealthy samurai's manor home. The 38-room house gives an idea of how well one could have lived during the shōgun period. A museum on the grounds displays Aizu craft, culture, and history, and there are several other old or reconstructed buildings in addition to the manor house. To get here take the Higashiyama bus from the JR station. ✉ *1 Innai, Ōaza Ishiyama Aza, Higashiyama-machi* ☏ *0242/28–2525* ☞ *¥850* ⊙ *Apr.–Nov., daily 8:30–5; Dec.–Mar., daily 9–4:30.*

The **Aizu-Wakamatsu tourist office** (観光案内所; ☏ *0242/24–3000*) is in the center of town. The **JR information and reservation office** (JRみどりの窓口; ✉ Aizu-Wakamatsu Station ☏ *0242/32–0688*) distributes a free English-language map and leaflets about the area.

Higashiyama Onsen 東山温泉

❹ *30 min from Aizu-Wakamatsu by bus.*

Higashiyama Onsen, a spa town with several modern ryokan, makes a good base for visiting Aizu-Wakamatsu, especially if you enjoy hot mineral baths. The village's scenic location and its shambles of older houses deserve better than the new and monstrous-looking ryokan that have supplanted most of the old. Nevertheless, Higashiyama is a spa town and a pleasant place to stay. The village is in a gorge, and the bus route terminates at the bottom end of the village. Most ryokan will send a car for you so you don't have to hike up the narrow village street.

Where to Stay

$$–$$$ 🏨 **Mukaitaki Ryokan** (向瀧旅館). This is the one ryokan in Higashiyama Onsen that retains a traditional ambience, thanks to its plank floors, shōji screens, and screen prints. English is spoken, and rooms can be reserved until 9:30 PM, though the place is open 24 hours a day. The inn serves Japanese food only. ✉ *200 Kawamukai, Yumoto-aza, Higashiyama-machi, Oaza, Aizu-Wakamatsu, Fukushima-ken 965-0814* ☎ *0242/27–7501* ⟳*25 Japanese-style rooms with bath* ♨ *Japanese baths* 🛏 *AE, DC, MC, V* ¶ *MAP.*

Getting Around South Tohoku

By Bus

Buses connect from JR Inawashiro Station and Hideyo Noguchi's Birthplace and Memorial Museum to the Bandai-Kōgen stop in 30 minutes. From the city of Fukushima buses depart from near the Shinkansen station daily between April 22 and November 5 and travel the Bandai-Azuma Skyline Drive to Bandai-Kōgen, offering splendid views of mountains by climbing up through Jōdodaira Pass at 5,214 feet. The whole mountain resort is, in fact, crisscrossed by five scenic toll roads. All sightseeing buses and local Inawashiro buses arrive at the Bandai-Kōgen bus stop.

To get to Higashiyama Onsen from Aizu-Wakamatsu, take the bus from Platform 4 at JR Aizu-Wakamatsu Station for the 20-minute ride, which costs ¥310.

By Train

JR Kōriyama Station is on the Tōhoku Shinkansen line, providing access north to Sendai and south to Tōkyō. Trains also run west from here to Niigata. From the station in Kōriyama you can take local trains to Kitakata, Aizu-Wakamatsu, and Inawashiro-ko (from which you can take a bus to Bandai Kōgen). What you will lose in backtracking to Kōriyama (before traveling to other parts of Tōhoku) you will make up in reduced travel time and more interesting sights.

Train routes also run south from Aizu-Wakamatsu to Nikkō.

SENDAI 仙台

▶ ❺ *By Shinkansen, 40 min north of Kōriyama, 2 hrs north of Tōkyō.*

With a population of more than 1 million, Sendai is the largest city between Tōkyō and Sapporo, the northern island of Hokkaidō's major city. Because American firebombs left virtually nothing unscorched by the end of World War II, it's a very modern city. The buildings that replaced the old ones are not particularly attractive, but Sendai is an open city with a generous planting of trees that justifies its nickname "Morino-Miyako": the City of Trees. With eight colleges and universities, including the prestigious Tōhoku University, the city has intentionally developed an international outlook and appeal. This has attracted many foreigners to take up residency. Sendai's old customs and modern attitudes make it a comfortable base from which to explore Tōhoku. And unlike other urban centers in Tōhoku, Sendai has a larger number of sights worth visiting, and you can easily spend a day looking around.

The city's origins can largely be traced to a fantastic historic figure, Masamune Date (1567–1636). Affectionately called the "one-eyed dragon" for his valor in battle and the loss of an eye from smallpox when he was a child, Masamune Date established a dynasty here that maintained its position as one of the three most powerful *daimyō* (feudal lord) families during the shōgun period. In addition to his military skills and progressive administration—he constructed a canal linking two rivers, thus improving the transport of rice—he was also an artist and a scholar open to new ideas.

Exploring Sendai

Sendai is easy to navigate—a good thing, since public transportation here is not so good—and even the major streets have signs in *rōmaji* (Japanese words rendered in roman letters). The downtown, an easy walk from the train station, is compact, with modern hotels, department stores with fashionable international clothing, numerous Japanese and Western restaurants, and hundreds of small specialty shops. Three broad avenues—Aoba-dōri, Hirose-dōri, and Jōzen-ji-dōri—and the Chūō-dōri shopping arcade head out from the station area toward Aoba Castle and cut through the heart of downtown, where they are bisected by the wide shopping arcade of Ichiban-chō. Between these two malls and extending farther east are narrow streets, packing in the 3,000 to 4,000 bars, tea shops, and restaurants that make up Sendai's entertainment area.

The **Sendai tourist information office** (仙台市総合観光案内所; ☎ 022/222–4069) on the second floor of Sendai JR Station has essential maps with bus routes to help you get to the main sights in and around Sendai. **Sendai International Center** (仙台国際センター; ☎ 022/224–1919 hot line, 022/265–2471 general assistance) is across the street from the Sendai Municipal Museum; this has more English information than the office in the train station, which makes it a good stop before you cross Hirose-gawa on your way to Zuihō-den. The office also operates an English-language hot line to answer questions about the city and prefecture.

THE TANABATA FESTIVAL

CloseUp

Sendai's major festival is Tanabata, held August 6–8. Although similar festivals are held throughout Japan (usually on July 7; the Sendai dates in August are in keeping with the lunar calendar), the festival at Sendai is the largest, swelling the city to three times its normal size with Japanese tourists. The celebration stems from a poignant Chinese legend of a weaver girl and her boyfriend, a herdsman, represented by the stars Vega and Altair, respectively. Their excessive love for each other caused them to become idle, and the irate king of heaven exiled the two lovers to opposite sides of the Milky Way galaxy. However, he permitted them to meet one day a year—and that day is now celebrated as Tanabata. Among the highlights of the festival are fireworks and a theatrical stage performance of the young lovers' anguish. For the festival, locals decorate houses and streets with colorful paper and bamboo streamers fluttering from poles.

To get an overview of the city and save yourself an uphill hike, take a bus up Aoba-yama to **Aoba Castle** (Aoba-jō, 青葉城). There never was a traditional military stronghold, but the grand building that once stood here was the Date clan's residence for 266 years. Because it sat 433 feet above the city on Aoba-yama and was protected by the Tatsunokuchi-kyōkoku (Tatsunokuchi Gorge) to the south, even without a traditional castle the site was considered impregnable when the first structure went up in 1602. The later castle was destroyed during the Meiji Restoration. The outer gates managed to survive another 70 years, until World War II firebombs destroyed them in 1945. The rather grandiose, heavy, and cumbersome **Gokoku Jinja** (Gokoku Shrine) is the main feature of the area where the castle stood. Near the observation terrace is an equestrian statue of the city's founder, Date Masamune, who looks out over the city with his one good eye. On a clear day you can see the Pacific Ocean on the horizon to the right. Take a bus from Stop No. 9 in front of JR Sendai Station, or ride the Sendai Loopletourist bus to get here. ✉ *Free* ⊙ *Daily dawn–dusk.*

The **Sendai Municipal Museum** (Sendai-shi Hakubutsukan, 仙台市博物館), at the foot of the hill beneath Aoba Castle, does a nice job of presenting the history of the Date family and the city. The café on the second floor is a good place to get refreshments before the walk to the mausoleums of Zuihō-den. ✉ *26 Kawauchi* ☎ *022/225–3075* ✉ *¥400* ⊙ *Tues.–Sun. 9–4:30, last entry at 4:15; closed last day of each month, the day following special exhibits, and national holidays.*

★ **Zuihō-den** (瑞鳳殿), the mausoleum of Masamune Date, burned during the firebombing in 1945 but was reconstructed in a five-year period beginning in 1974. During the excavation, Masamune Date's well-preserved remains were found and have been reinterred in what appears to be a perfect replica of the original hall. Two other mausoleums for the remains of the second (Tadamune Date) and third (Tsunamune Date) lords of Sendai were also reconstructed. These mausoleums, which cost in excess of ¥800 million to rebuild, are astounding in their craftsmanship and authenticity in the architectural style of the Momoyama period (16th century). Each mausoleum is the size of a small temple, and their exteriors are inlaid with figures of people, birds, and flowers in natural colors, all sheltered by elaborate curving roofs. Gold leaf is used extravagantly on the pillars and in the eaves of the roofs, creating a golden aura. To get here take Bus 11 from JR Sendai Station to the Otamaya-bashi Zuihō-den stop. The mausoleum is a short walk up the hill. If you're heading here from Aoba Castle, it's a 30-minute walk down Aoba-yama and across the Hirose-gawa (Hirose River). ☎ 022/262–6250 ⛩ ¥550 🕙 *Feb.–Nov., daily 9–4:30; Dec.–Jan., daily 9–4.*

Ōsaki Hachiman Jinja (大崎八幡神社) was one of the few historic buildings in Sendai to survive World War II. Built in Yonezawa in 1527, the shrine was later moved to Toda-gun. Date Masamune liked it, and in 1607 had it moved from its second site to be rebuilt in Sendai. Its free-flowing architectural form has a naturalness similar to that of buildings in Nikkō, and its rich black-lacquer main building more than justifies its designation as a National Treasure. In the northwest section of the city, the shrine is about 10 minutes from downtown or Aoba-yama by taxi and 15 minutes from the Zuihō-den area. You can also take Bus 15 from JR Sendai Station for ¥220. ⛩ *Free* 🕙 *Daily dawn–dusk.*

★ Peace fills the Zen garden at **Rinnō-ji** (Rinnō Temple, 輪王寺). A small stream leads the eye to the garden's focal point: the lotus-filled pond. Waving, undulating hummocks covered with clusters of bamboo flow around the pool. In June the garden is a blaze of color, with irises everywhere, but there are so many visitors that Rinnō-ji loses the tranquillity it has at other times of the year. The temple is a 20-minute walk from Ōsaki Hachiman Jinja, northwest of the city center. Use Bus 24 if you are coming here directly from JR Sendai Station. ⛩ *¥300* 🕙 *Daily 8–5.*

The top three floors of the 30-story **SS 30 Building** (SS30ビル; ⊠ 4–6–1 Chūō) are reserved for restaurants and viewing galleries. If you want a bird's-eye view of the city, you can't get any higher. At night, riding up in the outside elevator, with the city lights descending below, is quite a thrill.

Where to Eat

The main cluster of restaurants is on the parallel streets Ichiban-chō, Inari-kōji, and Kokubun-chō. Most places display their menus in their windows, along with the prices for each dish. Also, in the JR station there are tempting arrays of prepared foods and numerous restaurants in the underground mall called Restaurant Avenue.

$$$–$$$$ ✕ **Gintanabe Bekkan** (銀たなべ別館). A favorite with locals, this is the place for fish in any form—sashimi, fried, boiled, baked, or grilled. You can sit at the counter and order one item at a time, or in the back where complete courses are available, with the catch of the day brought in from Pacific fishing ports. The sashimi *moriawase* (assorted sashimi) at ¥4,000 is an excellent selection for two people. From the Ichiban-chō exit of Mitsukoshi department store, turn left, take a right at the first narrow street, walk two short blocks, turn left, and walk 50 yards. It's the restaurant with the tub-shape fish tank. ✉ *2–9–34 Kokubun-chō* ☎ *022/227–3478* 🖃 *AE, DC, MC, V* ✆ *No lunch.*

$$$–$$$$ ✕ **Jirai-ya** (地雷也). A curtain next to a big red paper lantern leads to this Sendai gem. Chef Itaru Watanabe keeps a sharp eye on the grill, where *kinki* (deepwater white fish) are prepared to go with sansai—vegetable tempura in spring and mushrooms in autumn. Try *kinoko-jiru* (mushroom soup), a local dish popular at picnics in autumn. The ingredients are all fresh, and the warm atmosphere makes this a local favorite. It's just off Ichiban-chō, near Hirose-dōri. ✉ *2–1–15 Kokubun-chō* ☎ *022/261–2164* 🖃 *MC, V* ✆ *Closed Sun.*

★ **$$$–$$$$** ✕ **Santarō** (三太郎). Known especially for delicious tempura, Santarō also serves shabu-shabu—thin slices of Sendai beef briefly simmered in broth—as well as sukiyaki, fugu (blowfish), and kaiseki (Kyōto-style set meals). Tempura courses start at ¥4,000; sukiyaki and shabu-shabu courses start at ¥5,000. To enjoy the refined atmosphere at a lower price, try weekday lunch specials for ¥1,000–¥3,000. The restaurant is just off Bansui-dōri several blocks south of Jōzen-ji-dōri. ✉ *1–20 Tachi-machi* ☎ *022/224–1671* 🖃 *AE, DC, MC, V* ✆ *Closed mid-Aug.*

$$–$$$$ ✕ **Kaki-toku** (かき徳). Matsu-shima Bay is famous for its *kaki* (oysters), and even when the mollusks are unavailable locally, this shop brings in the best available. In business for more than 70 years, the place specializes in raw oysters, vinegar oysters, and fried oysters. If you're not crazy about oysters, you can always dine on steak or another entrée while your friends revel in their shellfish. ✉ *4–9–1 Ichiban-chō* ☎ *022/222–0785* 🖃 *AE, DC, MC, V* ✆ *Closed Mon.*

★ **$$** ✕ **Aji Tasuke** (味太助). This small shop, with a counter and several tables that seat no more than 30, is a local institution that serves delicious Japanese meals at inexpensive prices, beating similar shops hands-down. A ¥1,450 *shokuji* (meal) will get you the full set of grilled beef tongue and pickled cabbage, oxtail soup, and a bowl of barley mixed with rice. From the Ichiban-chō exit of Mitsukoshi department store turn left, walk to the first narrow street, turn right, and turn left at the next corner; Aji Tasuke will be 50 yards ahead on the left next to a small shrine. ✉ *4–4–13 Ichiban-chō* ☎ *022/225–4641* 🖃 *No credit cards* ✆ *Closed Tues.*

Where to Stay

$$$$ 🏨 **Hotel Metropolitan Sendai** (ホテルメトロポリタン仙台). This upscale business hotel adjacent to the railway station has reasonably large Western-style guest rooms decorated in light colors. The 21st-floor Sky Lounge restaurant offers the best city view—and French food to go with it. Simpler fare at more reasonable prices is available in the coffee shop. ✉ *1–1–1 Chūō, Aoba-ku, Sendai, Miyagi-ken 980-8477* ☎ *022/268–2525* 🖷 *022/268–2521* 🌐 *www.jrhotelgroup.com/eng/hotel/* 🛏 *300 rooms with bath* ⚒ *5 restaurants, coffee shop, indoor pool, gym* 🖃 *AE, DC, MC, V.*

★ **$$$$** 🏨 **Sendai Kokusai Hotel** (仙台国際ホテル). The newest of Sendai's hotels, the Kokusai immediately won attention as the town's leading hotel upon its completion. The lobby glistens with marble and stainless steel, guest rooms are furnished in light pastels, and larger rooms have stucco arches to exaggerate their size. Fresh flowers add a touch of color. The hotel restaurants serve French, Chinese, and Japanese fare. Next to the SS 30 complex, the hotel is a short walk from downtown. ⊠ *4–6–1 Chūō, Aoba-ku, Sendai, Miyagi-ken 980-0021* ☎ *022/268–1112* 🖷 *022/268–1113* ⊕ *www.tobu-skh.co.jp/english/english.htm* ➪ *234 rooms with bath* ⌂ *11 restaurants, coffee shop, cable TV, bar, shop, business services, meeting rooms* ⊟ *AE, DC, MC, V* ⍩ *BP.*

$ ▦ **Hotel Shōwa** (松島ホテル昭和). A five-minute walk from JR Sendai Station, this business hotel is convenient for sightseeing and getting to the best downtown restaurants. The simple, clean rooms come at a reasonable price. From the station walk to the Chūō-dōri arcade and turn left. In the second block on the right, take one flight up to the hotel entrance. ⊠ *2–6–8 Chūō, Aoba-ku, Sendai, Miyagi-ken 980-0021* ☎ *022/224–1211* 🖷 *022/224–1214* ➪ *117 rooms with bath* ⊟ *AE, DC, MC, V.*

Shopping

Ideal for shopping, bustling downtown Sendai is compact, and many of the stores and small shops are in or connected to the two main shopping arcades, Ichiban-chō and Chūō-dōri. Sendai is the unofficial capital of the Tōhoku region, and you can find many of the regional crafts here, including cherry-bark letter boxes and *washi* (handmade paper), which are made outside Miyagi Prefecture.

Shimanuki (⊠ 3–1–17 Ichiban-chō ☎ 022/223–2370) is tops for folk crafts from around Tōhoku. It's open daily 10:30–7:30.

en route

On your way to Matsu-shima by JR train you may want to stop in Hon-Shiogama to see its shrine, **Shiogama Jinja** (塩釜神社)—supposedly the home of guardian deities who look after mariners and expectant mothers—and views of the bay. The town has little appeal aside from the shrine, but its buildings, with bright orange-red exteriors and simple natural-wood interiors, are worth seeing. To reach the shrine, turn left from Hon-Shiogama Station and walk for about 10 minutes. Be warned that after passing through the main entrance you have to clamber up 202 stone steps. Shiogama Jinja is the main building of the complex, and the second one you come to. **Shiwahiko Jinja** (志波彦神社) is the first; admission here is free. On the grounds is a 500-year-old Japanese holly tree, easily identified by the crowds taking photographs of themselves standing before it. A modern building in the complex houses swords, armor, and religious articles on its first floor and exhibits about fishing and salt manufacturing on its second. 🎟 *¥200* ⊗ *Apr.–Nov., daily 8–5; Dec.–Mar., daily 9–4.*

Getting Around Sendai

By Air

Sendai has fives daily flights from Ōsaka International Airport (also known as Itami Airport) by All Nippon Airways. There are also flights from Fukuoka, Nagoya, Hiroshima, and to Sapporo's Chitose Airport.

Yamagata has one flight daily from Tōkyō's Haneda Airport by All Nippon Airways and four flights daily from Ōsaka International Airport by JAL. There are also two flights from Fukuoka and one flight from Sapporo.

For airline phone numbers, *see* Air Travel *in* Smart Travel Tips A to Z.

By Bus

The **Tōhoku Kyūkō Express night bus** (☎ 03/3529–0321 in Tōkyō, 022/262–7031 in Sendai) from Tōkyō to Sendai is inexpensive (¥6,210) and takes approximately six hours. There are five departures leaving Tōkyō Station (Yaesu-guchi side) between 11 PM and midnight. The bus from Sendai departs from the train station at 11 PM and arrives in Tōkyō at 5 AM. Reservations are required for all buses. You can buy a ticket right at the bus stop.

Within Sendai, city buses will work for sightseeing, but it's advisable to consult the bus and subway information office, near the subway station in front of the JR station, beforehand. Here you can pick up English-language brochures that tell you about bus departure points, stops, and fares for each of the major sights.

Your best choice for transportation within Sendai, however, is the Sendai Loople, a limited-access bus that looks like one of the streetcars that ran through the city until the 1970s. The bus stops at Zuihō-den (20 minutes from the station) and Aoba Castle (30 minutes) and returns to the station in about an hour. A day pass costs only ¥600; buses depart from the west exit of JR Sendai Station every half hour from 9–4.

By Subway

The Sendai subway awkwardly runs north–south only, and its stations are far from the most interesting sights. A new east–west subway line is planned, which may improve the situation. There's a subway information office near the subway station in front of the JR station.

By Train

From Tōkyō, the *Hayate* Shinkansen and the slower *Yamabiko* Shinkansen run to Sendai; the trip takes 2–2⅓ hours.

For the 25-minute trip from Sendai to Hon-Shiogama Station and the Shiogama Jinja, take the JR Sensstation Line. Its platforms are reached from the JR Sendai Station basement. The same train goes on to Matsushima Kaigan Station, five minutes away. Fares from Sendai are ¥320 to Hon-Shiogama and ¥400 to Matsu-shima Kaigan.

A local train from Sendai makes the 100-minute run to Hiraizumi.

The Yamagata Shinkansen takes slightly less than three hours to get to Yamagata from Tōkyō. There's also direct train service on the JR Senzan Line from Sendai (about an hour). From west-coast towns, travel times to Yamagata by JR are as follows: 3½ hours from Niigata (Yonesaka Line), 2 hours, 20 minutes from Tsuruoka (Uetsu and Riku-u Sai lines), three hours from Akita (Ōu Line). The Tazawa-ko and Ōu lines (connecting in Ōmagari) provide access from Morioka in central Tōhoku.

To get to Yamadera, take the Senzan Line from Sendai (50 minutes) or Yamagata (20 minutes). Sakunami Onsen is 40 minutes from Yamagata on the JR Senzan Line.

SIDE TRIPS FROM SENDAI

Matsu-shima　松島

❻ *30 min northeast of Sendai by JR.*

The Japanese have named three places as their Three Big Scenic Wonders: Ama-no-hashidate, on the Sea of Japan in Western Honshū; Miyajima, in Hiroshima Bay; and Matsu-shima Bay. Hands down, Matsu-shima and its bay are the most popular coastal resort destinations in Tōhoku. Matsu-shima owes its distinction to the Japanese infatuation with oddly shaped rocks, which the bay has in abundance. Counts vary, but there are about 250 small, pine-clad islands scattered in the bay. Some are mere rocks with barely enough room for a couple of trees; others are large enough to shelter a few families. Each of the islets has a unique shape. Several have tunnels large enough to pass through in a rowboat. Its mass appeal aside, the bay is beautiful indeed, and it makes for a pleasant day's excursion from Sendai. You can either go directly to Matsu-shima by train or opt for the scenic route by sea from Shiogama. The key sights are within easy walking distance of each other. For maps and brochures, visit the tourist office at the end of the Matsushite Kaigan Pier.

At the behest of Masamune Date, the small temple of **Godai-dō** (五大堂) was constructed in 1609 on a tiny islet connected to the shore by two small arched bridges. Weathered by the sea and salt air, the small building's paint has peeled off, giving it an intimacy often lacking in other temples. Animals are carved in the timbers beneath the temple roof and among the complex supporting beams. The interior is open to the public only during special ceremonies held once every 33 years, and the next opening is scheduled for 2006. The temple is just to the right as you step off the boat on the pier in Matsu-shima.

★ **Zuigan-ji** (瑞巌寺), Matsu-shima's main temple, dates from 828, but the present structure was built on Masamune Date's orders in 1609. Designated a National Treasure, Zuigan-ji is the most representative Zen temple in the Tōhoku region. The main hall is a large wooden structure with ornately carved wood panels and paintings (faded with age) from the 17th century. Surrounding the temple are natural caves filled with Buddhist statues and memorial tablets that novices carved from the rock face as part of their training. The grounds surrounding the temple are full of trees, including two plum trees brought back from Korea in 1592 by Masamune Date after an unsuccessful military foray. Zuigan-ji is down the street from Godai-dō, across Route 45 and the central park. ⌨ ¥700 ☽ *Apr.–Sept., daily 8:30–5; Oct.–Mar., daily 9–4.*

For a glimpse at how people looked and dressed during Date Masamune's time, visit the wax museum, **Michinoku Date Masamune Historical Museum** (Michinoku Date Masamune Rekishi-kan, みちのく伊達政宗歴史館). With life-size figures, the museum displays scenes from the feudal period—battles, tea ceremonies, and processions. ⊠ *13–13 Fugendo (Rte. 45); from Zuigan-ji, turn left and walk back toward the bay* ☎ *022/354–4131* 🎫 *¥1,000* ⊙ *Apr.–Nov., daily 8:30–5; Dec.–Mar., daily 9–4:30.*

★ **Kanrantei** (観瀾亭), translated as "Water Viewing Pavilion," was originally part of Fushimi-Momoyama Castle in Kyōto. When the castle was demolished, the pavilion was moved to Edo (Tōkyō) before being shifted again by Date Tadamune—the great Masamune's eldest son—to its present location in Matsu-shima. Here the Date family held their tea parties for the next 270 years. The **Matsu-shima Museum** (Matsu-shima Hakubutsukan), next to Kanrantei, houses a full collection of the Date family's armor, swords, pikes, and more genteel artifacts, including lacquerware. Kanrantei is on the south side of the harbor opposite Godai-dō. 🎫 *¥200* ⊙ *Apr.–Oct., daily 8–5; Nov.–Mar., daily 9–4:30.*

From Godai-dō it's a short walk across the 250-yard pedestrian bridge near the Matsu-shima Century Hotel to the islet of **Fukurajima** (福浦島). For the ¥200 toll you can walk away from the crowds to enjoy a picnic in the park here while looking out across the bay.

Throughout the year, **sightseeing ferries** (観光船) leave from Shiogama for Matsu-shima. Whether you catch the gaudy Chinese dragon ferry or one that is less ostentatious, the route through the bay will be the same. So will the incessant and distracting loudspeaker naming (in Japanese) the islands. The first 10 minutes of the hour-long trip are dismal. Don't fret! Shiogama's ugly port and the oil refinery on the promontory soon give way to the beauty of Matsu-shima Bay and its islands. The dock is to the right (seaward side) of Hon-Shiogama Station. ☎ *022/354–2232* 🎫 *¥1,420 one-way* ⊙ *Daily 9–3; ferries depart every 30 min Apr.–Nov., every hr Dec.–Mar.*

Where to Stay

$$$$ 🏨 **Hotel Ichinobo** (ホテル一の坊). This elegant, pricey resort hotel has a large garden consisting of a small man-made island, which is connected by bridges and is lighted up at night. All rooms overlook the bay and are spacious; the hotel's facilities are attractively designed. ⊠ *1–4 Takagi Aza Hama, Matsu-shima-chō, Miyagi-ken 981-0215* ☎ *022/353–3333* 🖷 *022/353–3339* 🛏 *20 Western-style rooms with bath, 104 Japanese-style rooms with bath* ♨ *Restaurant, coffee shop, pool* ⊟ *AE, DC, MC, V.*

★ **$$$$**   🏨 **Matsu-shima Century Hotel** (松島センチュリーホテル). With an excellent view of the water, this luxury hotel in the heart of Matsu-shima sits right on the bay. Many rooms are lavish, and the food is excellent; meals include the best ingredients from the coastline and the deep Pacific. ⊠ *8 Sensui Aza Matsu-shima, Matsu-shima-chō, Miyagi-ken 981-0213* ☎ *022/354–4111* 🖷 *022/354–4191* 🛏 *192 Western-style and Japanese-style rooms with bath* ♨ *2 restaurants, coffee shop, pool* ⊟ *AE, DC, MC, V.*

Yamadera   山寺

❼ *By JR, 50 min west of Sendai.*

This village, more formally known as Risshaku-ji, makes a delightful day trip from Sendai.

Built 1,100 years ago, Yamadera's complex of temples with steeply pitched slate roofs on the slopes of **Hōju-san** (Mt. Hōju, 宝珠山) is the largest one of the Tendai sect in northern Japan. It attracts some 700,000 pilgrims a year. To get here, walk through the village, cross the bridge, and turn right. Just inside the entrance is **Kompon Chū-dō,** the temple where the sacred Flame of Belief has been burning constantly for 1,000 years, aside from one interruption: in 1521 a local lord called Tendo Yorinaga ransacked the complex and extinguished the flame, so that a replacement had to be brought from the original sacred fire at Mt. Hiei in Kyōto.

Near Kompon Chū-dō there's a statue of the Japanese poet **Matsuo Bashō** (1644–94), who wrote extensively of his wanderings throughout Japan in 17-syllable haiku. The path here continues up 1,015 well-tended steps; the best views are from the **Niō-mon.** The ascent is relatively easy, but the path can be crowded in summer and treacherous with snow in winter.

Finally, after a steep ascent you reach **Oku-no-in,** a hall at the summit dedicated to the temple founder, Jikaku Daishi. After your descent, on the way back to the station, grab a snack at the shop to the right of the bridge, where you can sit and look out over the river. You should allow two hours for the climb up and back down. ￥300 *Daily dawn–dusk.*

The train from Sendai to Yamadera passes through **Sakunami Onsen** (作並温泉). Within the Sendai city limits (40 minutes by train from the main station), the town and its hot springs are close enough to make it an alternative spot to overnight.

Where to Stay

$$$$ **Iwamatsu Ryokan** (岩松旅館). Though called an inn, Iwamatsu is more of a hotel with full amenities. It stands alongside a cascade, and the rooms look out on trees and the stream. The original open-air bath is covered with a wooden roof, but it's at river level, allowing views of spring leaves, autumn foliage, or winter snow. Dinner is Japanese, with several local specialties. Breakfast is a buffet with a large selection of Japanese and Western foods. The inn has shuttle-bus service from JR Sakunami Station, and regular bus service from JR Sendai Station stops in front of the inn. ⊠ *16 Sakunami Motoki, Aoba-ku, Sendai-shi, Miyagi-ken 989-3431* ☎ *022/395–2211* ⬢ *022/395–2020* ⬢ *102 Japanese-style rooms with bath* ⬢ *Restaurant, tea shop, dance club, hot springs* ⬢ *AE, MC, V* ⬢ *MAP.*

Yamagata   山形

8 *20 min southwest of Yamadera, 1 hr west of Sendai by JR.*

Yamagata, with a population of 240,000, is the capital of the prefecture of the same name. It's a friendly town that's working to improve its appeal to travelers. Yamagata Prefecture, incidentally, has at least one onsen in each of its 44 municipalities—the only 100% thermal Japanese prefecture. You can pick up free maps and brochures from the **Yamagata tourist information office** (山形駅観光案内所; ☎ 023–631–7865) opposite the ticket turnstiles inside Yamagata JR Station; it's open weekdays 10–6, weekends 10–5.

At the **Hana-gasa Festival**(花笠まつり; August 5–7), some 10,000 dancers from the entire area dance their way through the streets in traditional costume and *hana-gasa,* hats so named for the safflowers used to decorate them. Floats are interspersed among the dancers, and stalls provide food and refreshments.

Most people come to Yamagata for **Zaō-san** (Mt. Zaō, 蔵王山), where nearly 1.4 million alpine enthusiasts ski its 14 slopes between December and April. In summer hikers come, though in smaller numbers, to walk among the colored rocks and take in **Zaō Okama**, a caldera lake with a diameter of nearly 1,200 feet. Cable cars leave from **Zaō Onsen**, the mountain's resort town: one climbs 1,562 feet from the base lodge, which is 2,805 feet above sea level; another makes the final ascent, an additional 1,083 feet. Even nonskiers make the wintertime trip to see the *juhyō,* a phenomenon caused by heavy snow on the conifers: layer after layer of snow covers the fir trees, creating weird cylindrical figures that look like fairy-tale monsters. Zaō Onsen is 19 km (12 mi) from Yamagata Station, a 45-minute trip by bus. In winter there are direct buses between Tōkyō and Zaō Onsen.

If you're interested in pottery, take a trip to **Hirashimizu** (平清水) on the outskirts of the city. This small enclave of traditional buildings and farmhouses is a step back in time and a sharp contrast to the modern urban sprawl of Yamagata. About six pottery families live here, each with its own kiln, each specializing in a particular style. Two of them, the Shichiemon and Heikichi, offer pottery lessons, and participants can have the results fired and then, two to four weeks later, mailed back home. The best-known pottery is that of the Seiryū-gama (Seiryū kiln), which has been exhibited in America and Europe; the prices are high. The potteries are generally open daily 9–3, but keep irregular holidays, so it's best to check with the tourist information office (観光案内所) at the train station. From Bus Stop 5, in front of JR Yamagata Station, take a bus for Geijutsu Kōka Daigaku, a 15-minute ride (¥210); you can also take a taxi for about ¥2,000.

Where to Stay & Eat

$$$–$$$$ ✕ **Sagorō** (佐五郎). Sukiyaki, shabu-shabu, and good steaks: this stylish restaurant serves excellent Yonezawa beef. Although the set courses of the above are pricey, a plate of *shōga-yaki* (beef grilled in ginger sauce; ¥1,700), *oshinko moriawase* (pickled vegetables; ¥700), rice, and soup make a delicious, fairly reasonable meal. Look for the black bull on the sign above the street and take the stairs up one flight. ⊠ *1–6–10 Kasumi-chō* ☎ *023/631–3560* ▭ *No credit cards* ◷ *Closed Sun.*

$$–$$$ ✕ **Mimasu** (三桝). The highlights of this restaurant are good sushi, tempura, and *donburi*—bowls with cutlets, tempura, and chicken placed on top of rice. Lunch specials include *danjurō bentō,* a filling assortment of seasonal vegetables and fish. Within Nanoka-machi, Mimasu is a short walk from the Yamagata Washington Hotel. ⊠ *2–3–7 Nanoka-machi* ☎ *023/632–1252* ▭ *No credit cards* ◷ *Closed 2nd Wed. of month.*

¢–$$ ✕ **Shōjiya** (庄司屋). Yamagata is famous for soba, and this fine shop is one of the best places to try the thin brown buckwheat noodles. For lunch or a light dinner, try the simple *kake* soba (served in a hot broth; ¥650).

tempura soba (with tempura; ¥1,300), or *nameko* soba (with mushrooms; ¥900). For a full meal, consider *aimori itaten,* a course consisting of two different types of noodles and sauces (¥2,000). The staff speaks no English, but the menu has the complete selection in photographs. It's a 10-minute walk from the JR station. ⊠ *14–28 Saiwai-chō* ☎ *023/622–1380* ▤ *No credit cards* ⊘ *Closed Mon.*

$$ 🏨 **Hotel Metropolitan Yamagata** (ホテルメトロポリタン山形). Leave through the train-station exit, walk to the right a few paces, and you have arrived. With a modern lobby and spacious rooms, this is the best hotel in Yamagata. It's also within easy walking distance of downtown restaurants. ⊠ *1–1–1 Kasumi-chō, Yamagata, Yamagata-ken 990-0039* ☎ *023/628–1111* 🖷 *012/628–1166* ⊕ *www.jrhotelgroup.com/eng/hotel/* ⤶ *116 rooms with bath* ♨ *3 restaurants* ▤ *AE, DC, V.*

$$ 🏨 **Yamagata Washington Hotel** (山形ワシントンホテル). This downtown Yamagata business hotel, a short taxi ride from the station, is smart and efficient and has a friendly staff. The coffee shop is on the ground floor, the reception area and a Japanese restaurant are on the next floor, and guest rooms are above, from the third to the eighth floor. The rooms are compact, and the bathrooms are the prefabricated plastic units typical of many moderately priced hotels in Japan. ⊠ *1–4–31 Nanoka-machi, Yamagata, Yamagata-ken 990-0042* ☎ *023/625–1111* 🖷 *023/624–1512* ⤶ *223 rooms with bath* ♨ *Restaurant, coffee shop* ▤ *AE, DC, MC, V.*

The Gorges & Hiraizumi 峡谷と平泉

35 min north of Sendai (via Ichinoseki) by Shinkansen, 95 min by JR local.

East of Ichinoseki, the Iwai-gawa (Iwai River) flows through the naturally carved Geibikei-kyōkoku, and you can either walk along the banks or travel upstream and take a boat through the gorge. Another gorge, Gembikei-kyōkoku, is west of Ichinoseki, and its proximity to the temples of Hiraizumi makes these two places a good combination for a full-day outing.

❾ Flat-bottom boats, poled by two boatmen, ply the river for a 90-minute round-trip through **Geibikei** (Geibikei Gorge, 猊鼻渓). The waters are peaceful and slow moving, relentlessly washing their way through silver-streaked cliffs. The high point of the trip is reaching the depths of the gorge, faced with 300-foot cliffs. Coming back downstream would be an anticlimax if it were not for the boatmen, who, with little to do but steer the boat, sing traditional songs. The boat trip costs ¥1,500. From Sendai you can head east to Geibikei by changing to the Ōfunato Line for a 30-minute ride to Higashiyama. But the direct route is only about 21 km (13 mi), so a taxi (about ¥2,000) is much more convenient. There's little other than Geibikei to see along this route.

★ ❿ **Gembikei** (Gembikei Gorge, 厳美渓), at 1,000 yards long and less than 20 feet deep, may be small, but it has all the features of the world's best gorges. Once, rushing water carved its path into solid rock; now it's quiet. Because of its small scale, you can walk its entire length and appreciate every detail of its web of sculpted patterns; look for the circular holes (called Jacob wells) scoured into the rock side. To get to Gembikei, take a taxi west (10 minutes) from Ichinoseki, or take an Iwate-ken Kōtsu bus (22 minutes) from the Ichinoseki train station to the end of the line. If you're going to Mōtsu-ji and Hiraizumi from here, you're best off taking a taxi the 1½ km (1 mi).

⑪ In the 12th century **Hiraizumi** (平泉) came close to mirroring Kyōto as a cultural center. Hiraizumi was the family seat of the Fujiwara clan, which for three generations dedicated itself to promoting peace and the arts. The fourth-generation lord became power hungry, however, and his ambition wiped out the dynasty. Little remains of the efflorescence of the first three generations of the Fujiwara clan, but what does—in particular Chūson-ji and the golden Konjiki-dō—is a tribute to Japan's past. From Hiraizumi Station you can walk to the two major temples. If time is short and you plan to limit your sightseeing outside of Sendai to Mōtsu-ji and Chūson-ji, just take the local train from Sendai for the 100-minute run to Hiraizumi.

Maps are available at the **Hiraizumi tourist office** (観光案内所; ☎ 0191/46–2110), on your right as you leave JR Hiraizumi Station; it's open April–October, daily 8:30–5, and November–March, daily 8:30–4:30.

During the time of the Fujiwara clan, **Mōtsū-ji** (毛越寺) was the most venerated temple in northern Honshū. The complex consisted of 40 temples and some 500 lodgings. Eight centuries later, only the foundations remain. The current buildings, including the local youth hostel, are of more recent vintage. The Heian-period Jōdo (paradise-style) gardens, however, which were laid out according to the Buddhist principle in fashion some 700 years ago, have survived in good condition. The gardens are especially beautiful during the **Ayame (Iris) Festival,** from June 20 through July 10. The **Hiraizumi Museum,** with artifacts of the Fujiwara family, is beside the garden. To get to Mōtsu-ji, walk 1,000 yards up the street that leads directly away from JR Hiraizumi Station. *Gardens and museum ¥500 ☉ May–Oct., daily 8:30–5; Nov.–Apr., daily 8:30–4:30.*

The temple of **Chūson-ji** (中尊寺), set amid thick woods, was founded by the Fujiwara family in 1105. At that time there were more than 40 buildings. In Chūson-ji's heyday the number reached 300. Unfortunately for the northern Fujiwara dream, war and a tremendous fire in 1337 destroyed all but two halls, Konjiki-dō and Kyōzō. The other buildings in the complex are reconstructions from the Edo period.

The small but magnificent **Konjiki-dō** (Golden Hall) is considered one of Japan's most historic temples. Indeed, it was the first of Japan's National Treasures to be so designated. Konjiki-dō's exterior is black lacquer, and the interior is paneled with mother-of-pearl and gold leaf. In the Naijin (Inner Chamber) are three altars, each with 11 statues of Buddhist deities. The remains of the three rulers of the Fujiwara family—Kiyohira, Motohira, and Hidehira—are beneath the central altar.

Of the two original buildings, **Kyōzō** is the less interesting. It once housed the greatest collection of Buddhist sutras, but fire destroyed many of them, and the remainder have been removed to the **Sankōzō Museum,** next door.

To commemorate the grandeur that once was, two festivals are held every year—the spring and autumn **Fujiwara festivals** (May 1–5 and November 1–3). Costumed warriors line the temple slope on horseback. To get to Chūson-ji, you can walk along a narrow road from Mōtsū-ji (30 minutes), take a taxi, or walk or take a short bus ride from the JR station. *Chūson-ji and Sankōzō Museum ¥800 ☉ Apr.–Oct., daily 8–5; Nov.–Mar., daily 8:30–4:30; last entry 30 min before closing time.*

NORTHERN TŌHOKU   北東北   ⑬

The northern reaches of Tōhoku are distinguished by rugged people and rugged geography that makes for spectacular natural beauty—from rocky cliffs along the ocean to volcanic peaks inland. The Tōno Basin's farmland and the Pacific coastline to the east are easy to reach by train. The national parks of the central highlands are among the best places to view autumn foliage in late September. Oddly enough, Morioka is still considered a castle town, even though its castle was destroyed in the mid-1800s. However, the town still does make its revered *Nambu-tetsu* (Nambu ironware).

Tōno   遠野

⑫ *2 hrs north of Sendai by Shinkansen to Shin-Hanamaki and then local train east to Tōno.*

The people of Tōno like their old ways. The town itself is not particularly remarkable, but the Tōno Basin has old buildings and historical remains that transport you back to Old Japan. Allow a day or two for a turn through this traditional pastoral corner of Japan. Tōno is rich in traditional ways and folklore, and the coast is an ever-changing landscape of cliffs, rock formations, and small coves. To make the most of the Tōno experience, consider reading Kunio Yanagita's *Tōno Monogatari,* translated into English by Robert Morse as *The Legends of Tōno.*

In a peaceful wooded area above the Atago Jinja (Atago Shrine) southwest of downtown are the **500 Disciples of Buddha** (Go-hyaku Rakan, 五百羅漢). Carved on boulders in a shallow ravine, these images were created by a priest who wanted to appease the spirits of the quarter of Tōno's inhabitants who starved to death in the two-year famine of 1754–55.

Along the valley on either side of Tōno there are several magariya: L-shape, thatched-roof, Nambu-style farmhouses. A good representative is **Chiba-ke Magariya** (千葉家曲がり家), 13 km (8 mi) west of the JR station. Families live in the long side of the L, and horses are kept in the short side.

North of Tōno, **Fukusen-ji** (Fukusen Temple, 福泉寺) contains Japan's tallest wooden Kannon (Goddess of Mercy). The 56-ft-tall statue was created by the priest Yūzen Suriishi to boost morale after World War II. There are few sign markers, so ask for directions once you get to this tiny village. ✉ *Matsuzaki-chō Komagi* ☎ *0198/62–3822* 💴 *¥300* 🕐 *Apr.–Sept., daily 8–5; Oct.–Dec., daily 8–4; Jan.–Mar., Sun. 8–5.*

A long taxi ride northeast of town will take you to a **suisha** (water mill, 水車), one of the few working mills left in Japan—this is not a museum piece.

Kappa-buchi (河童淵), which is a reasonable bike or taxi ride northeast of town, is a pool in a stream where *kappa,* supernatural amphibious creatures, supposedly live. They are said to drag people, horses, and cows into the water and to impregnate young girls, who then give birth to demi-kappas. The site is along the edge of the grounds of Jōken-ji (Jōken Temple), 6 km (3¾ mi) from the station, which is about as far as you need to go to see interesting countryside.

At **Denshō-en** (伝承園), a Japanese folk-village museum, you can see a good Nambu magariya, complete with barn, storehouse, mill, and bathhouse. Be sure to go in the room at the back to see the **oshirasama**, 1,000 small carved sticks upon which are placed votive clothes. These small god figures are said to represent the god of silkworm cultivation—who is able to predict the future. The museum is about 6½ km (4 mi) northeast of Tōno Station. ☎ *0198/62–8655* 💴 *¥310* 🕐 *Daily 9–4:30; closed last day of month.*

Where to Stay

$$$$ 🏨 **Minshuku Magariya** (民宿曲がり家). A highlight if you're planning to overnight in Tōno, this L-shape farmhouse has been converted into a family-run hotel—without the animals. Two meals including fish, chicken, and wild-vegetable dishes are served, and after dinner one of the local elder ladies often tells folktales (in Japanese). Surrounded by fields 7 km (4¼ mi) west of town, Magariya is best reached by a taxi from the station in Tōno, unless you prefer the 20-minute walk from the nearest bus stop. ✉ *30–58–3 Niisato, Ayaori-chō, Tōno-shi, Iwate-ken 028-0531* ☎ *0198/62–4564* 🛏 *16 rooms with bath* ♨ *No a/c, no room TVs* ▭ *No credit cards* 🍴 *MAP.*

★ **$$**   🏨 **Forukurōro Tōno** (フォルクローロ遠野). If you decide to walk or bike around the sights of this small town, this bed-and-breakfast above JR Tōno Station is a fine choice. With comfortable beds, simple but clean rooms, and a very friendly staff, it's reliable and convenient for the price—and easy to manage even if you don't speak Japanese. Reservations are advised, but if you arrive in town without a place to stay, check here first. ✉ *5–7 Shinkoku-chō, Tōno-shi, Iwate-ken 028-0522* ☎ *0198/62–0700* 🖨 *0198/62–0800* 🛏 *18 rooms with bath* ♨ *Japanese bath* ▭ *AE, MC, V* 🍴 *CP.*

$$ 🏨 **Fukuzansō Inn** (福山荘). Highly polished creaky floors characterize this friendly old-fashioned ryokan a five-minute walk from JR Tōno Station. Rooms, which share a Japanese-style bath, have a dressing room–closet area and a small enclosed balcony with table and chairs. Breakfast is served downstairs for ¥1,000 per person. No English is spoken, but the hospitable staff is all smiles and will lend you a bike for sightseeing. Fukuzansō is open 24 hours a day, 365 days a year. ✉ *5–30 Chūō-dōri, Tōno-shi, Iwate-ken 028-0523* ☎ *0198/62–4120, 0120/48–8588 toll-free* 🛏 *18 rooms without bath* ♨ *Japanese bath* ▭ *V* 🍴 *EP.*

Getting Around

To get to the Tōno Basin from Sendai or Hiraizumi, take the Shinkansen to Shin-Hanamaki Station and then board a local eastbound JR train; the entire trip should take about two hours.

Distances between Tōno's sights are too far to walk. Unless you have a car, plan to rent a bicycle from a hotel, bicycle shop, or even the Tōno tourist office. A sightseeing taxi is a convenient way to see the faraway places, and even if the driver waits for you here and there, you can see a lot in one hour, which will cost about ¥6,000.

Morioka 盛岡

13 *By Shinkansen, 45 min north of Ichinoseki, 50–100 min north of Sendai.*

Morioka is a busy commercial and industrial city ringed by mountains. Westerners are often pleased by the generous amount of information written in English—on street signs and on the destination boards in the bus terminal, for example. Aside from horses—Morioka was a center of horse breeding—the major attraction of the city is Nambu-tetsu. The range of ironware articles, from small wind bells to elaborate statues, is vast, but the most popular items are *Nambu-tetsu-bin* (heavy iron kettles), which come in all shapes, weights, and sizes. Dozens of shops throughout the city sell Nambu-tetsu, but the main shopping streets are Saien-dōri and Ō-dōri, which pass Iwate Kōen (Iwate Park).

If you get to town on June 15, stay around the front of the station around 12:30. That's when the parade of grandly decorated, bell-clad horses passes by during the festival called **Chagu-chagu Umakko** (チャグチャグ馬っ子). The horses parade through the streets between 9:30 and 1:30, so just look for people gathering.

The Morioka tourist office, **Kankō Center** (観光センター; ☎019/625–2090), in the Train Square lounge on the south end of the second floor of JR Morioka Station, has useful maps and other information on Morioka and Iwate Prefecture. The office can also help arrange accommodations. It's open daily 9–5:30.

Morioka had a fine castle built by the 26th Lord of Nambu in 1597, but it was destroyed in the Meiji Restoration, and all that remains of it are ruins. The site is now **Iwate Kōen** (Iwate Park, 岩手公園), the focus of town and the place to escape the congestion of traffic and people in downtown Morioka. To reach the park from JR Morioka Station, cross Kai-un-bashi and walk straight down the middle of the three roads when the road forks.

Gozaku (ござ九), across from Iwate Park, is the most interesting place to browse for Nambu-tetsu: this area of small shops looks much as it did a century ago. To get to Gozaku from the park, cross the Naka-no-hashi bridge and take the first main street on the left. A short way down, just past Hotel Saitō, are the large Nambu Iron Shop and the narrow streets of the Gozaku section on your left. Beyond Gozaku is another bridge, Yonoji-hashi. On the street corner is a very Western-looking fire station, built in the 1920s and still in operation.

Not far from Gozaku is **Kami-no-hashi** (上の橋), one of the few decorated bridges in Japan. Eight specially crafted bronze railings were commissioned in 1609, and 10 bronze posts added two years later.

Whether you just want to wander around town between train connections or are in Morioka overnight, don't miss a visit to **Kōgensha** (光原社), a shop specializing in quality folk crafts like lacquerware, kites, dyed fabrics, and pottery. The main shop is composed of several small buildings along a courtyard. You can walk through the courtyard to a relaxing *kissaten* (coffee shop) and farther to the river. Along the wall to the left are poems by Kenji Miyazawa. To get to Kōgensha from Morioka Station, walk left to the stoplight in front of the Hotel Metropolitan Morioka, turn right, and cross the river on Asahi-bashi. Take the first left into an artistically designed street that leads to the main shop 50 yards down on the left and a branch shop across the street that sells basketry and wooden bowls. ⊠ *2–18 Zaimoku-chō* ☎ *019/622–2894* ⊘ *Daily 10–6; closed the 15th of each month and several days in mid-Aug.*

Where to Stay & Eat

★ **$$$–$$$$** ✕ **Banya Nagasawa** (番屋ながさわ). Everyone in town recommends this shop for yellowtail, grilled shellfish such as scallops and abalone, mushrooms in the fall, local wild vegetables in spring, and its own original sake. To reach Banya Nagasawa from the train station, follow Ō-dori to the Iwate Bank and turn right at the statue of Takuboku Ishikawa. The restaurant is 2 ½ blocks ahead on the right, across from the Hotel New Carina. From the station you could also follow Saien-dōri to the Saien police box and turn left; the restaurant will be on your left. ⊠ *1–11–23 Saien* ☎ *019/622–6152* ▭ *MC, V* ⊘ *Closed Sun. and mid-Aug.*

★ **$$$** ✕ **Nambu Doburoku-ya** (南部どぶろく家). For local Tōhoku food and atmosphere, this is the place to visit. The milky-looking sake served in huge bowls here is *doburoku*, at one time the moonshine of Tōhoku farmers. To go with a bowl of doburoku (¥600), try the *hyakushō* (farmer) course (¥3,000), which includes stewed meat, fresh squid, grilled fish, tofu, and soup. ⊠ *2–6–21 Ō-dori* ☎ *019/622–9212* ▭ *No credit cards* ⊘ *Closed Mon. and mid-Aug.*

★ **$$–$$$** ✕ **Azumaya** (東家). Hearty soba comes from northern Japanese grain, and Azumaya is Morioka's place to eat these noodles. *Wanko* soba courses, all the soba you can eat, start at ¥2,500, and a delicious tempura soba is only ¥1,200. The *maneki-neko* (decorative beckoning cats) are mascots to ensure that customers will come again and again, and they seem to be doing their job. Azumaya is in Gozaku, 10 minutes from the train station by taxi. ⊠ *1–8–3 Naka-no-hashi-dōri* ☎ *019/622–2252* ▭ *No credit cards* ⊘ *Closed 1st and 3rd Tues. of month.*

$$ 🏨 **Hotel Metropolitan Morioka** (ホテルメトロポリタン盛岡). Both wings of this hotel have an English-speaking staff, restaurants, and a bar. Just to the left of the station plaza, the older wing provides clean utilitarian rooms and good service. From the old wing, cross the street facing the hotel and walk one block to the new wing, where the rooms are larger and average ¥2,000 more. As a guest you can use the Central Fitness Club facilities for ¥575, including a 25-meter pool, weight machines, a sauna, and a Jacuzzi. ⊠ *1–44 Morioka Eki-mae-dōri, new wing: 2–27 Morioka Eki-mae Kita-dōri, Morioka, Iwate-ken 020-0034* ☎ *019/625–1211* 🖷 *019/625–1210* ⊕ *www.jrhotelgroup.com/eng/hotel/* ⇗ *134 rooms with bath in old wing, 121 rooms with bath in new wing* ⌂ *5 restaurants, 2 bars, meeting rooms* ▤ *AE, DC, MC, V.*

$ 🏠 **Ryokan Kumagai** (旅館熊ヶ井). A two-story wooden building houses this simple hostelry, a member of the affordable Japanese Inn Group, with basic tatami rooms. There's a small dining area where Japanese and Western breakfasts and Japanese dinners are optional. In traditional style, no rooms have private baths. Located between the station and center city, the inn is a 10-minute walk from JR Morioka Station—cross the river and walk along Kaiun-bashi-dōri two blocks and turn right (a gas station is on the left and a bank on the right). Cross over one block, and the ryokan is on the left. ⊠ *3–2–5 Ōsawakawara, Morioka, Iwate-ken 020-0025* ☎ *019/651–3020* 🖷 *019/626–0096* ⇗ *11 Japanese-style rooms without bath* ⌂ *Dining room, Japanese baths* ▤ *AE, MC, V* ¶⊙ *EP or MAP.*

Getting Around

BY AIR Morioka (whose Hanamaki Airport is 50 minutes by bus from downtown) has three flights from Ōsaka International Airport by JAL. There are also flights to Nagoya, Fukuoka, and Sapporo's Chitose Airport. For airline phone numbers, *see Air Travel in Smart Travel Tips A to Z.*

BY BUS To get to downtown Morioka from the JR Morioka Station, take Bus 5 or 6 from the terminal in front of the station. There's also a convenient loop bus for tourists called Denden-mushi, which goes to Gozaku, departing every 20 minutes 9–6 from Bus Stop 15 or 16 in front of JR Morioka Station (¥100 for one ride, ¥300 for the day pass).

April 20–November 23, the **Iwate Kankō Bus Company** (岩手観光バス; ☎ 019/651–3355) runs a morning and afternoon half-day tour of Morioka with Japanese-speaking guides. The 10:30–12:55 tour costs ¥2,000, and the 1:45–5 tour costs ¥2,500. All departures are from JR Morioka Station.

BY TRAIN From Tōkyō, the *Hayate* Shinkansen and the slower *Yamabiko* Shinkansen run to Morioka; the trip takes 2¾–3½ hours.

Tazawa-ko & Kakunodate 田沢湖と角館

The lake area of Tazawa-ko (Lake Tazawa) and the traditional town of Kakunodate make for good side trips into Tōhoku's rugged interior from either Morioka or the west-coast city of Akita. For a little thermal relaxation, head to the old spa town of Nyūtō Onsen, just north of Lake Tazawa.

Tazawa-ko 田沢湖

★ ⓮ *40 min west of Morioka, 70 min east of Akita by JR Express.*

With a depth of 1,390 feet, Tazawa-ko (Lake Tazawa) is Japan's deepest lake. Its blue waters are too alkaline to support any fish. Like most of Japan's other lakes, Tazawa sits in a volcanic cone, its shape a classic caldera. The clear waters and forested slopes create a mystical quality that appeals so much to the Japanese. According to legend, the great beauty from Akita, Takko Hime, sleeps in the water's deep as a dragon. The lake never freezes over in winter because Takko Hime and her dragon husband churn the water with their passionate lovemaking. Or, perhaps, as scientists say, the water doesn't freeze because of a freshwater source that enters the bottom of the lake. In winter the Tazawa area is a popular and picturesque skiing destination, with the lake visible from the ski slopes.

A 15-minute bus ride (¥350) from the JR Tazawa-ko Station gets you to the Tazawa-ko-han center on the lakeshore. A 30-minute bus ride from JR Tazawa-ko Station via Tazawa-ko-han takes you up to Tazawa-ko Kōgen northeast of Tazawa-ko for ¥580. The journey affords spectacular views of the lake, showing off the full dimensions of its caldera shape. A boat takes 40-minute cruises on the lake from late April to November (¥1,170). There's also regular bus service around the lake (halfway around in winter), and bicycles are available for rent at the Tazawa-ko-han bus terminal. If you go by bike, you can take more time to appreciate the beauty of Takko Hime, whose bronze statue is on the western shore.

The **Tazawa-ko tourist information office** (田沢湖観光情報センター; ☎ 0187/43–2111) to the left of the JR Tazawa-ko Station has maps and bus schedules; it's open daily 8:30–5:15.

Nyūtō Onsen (乳頭温泉), accessible by bus from Tazawak-ko, is a collection of small, unspoiled, mountain hot-spring spas in some of the few traditional spa villages left in Tōhoku. Most of these villages have only one inn, so it's advisable to arrange accommodations before you arrive if you plan to stay the night.

Komaga-take (Mt. Komaga, 駒ヶ岳) stands a few miles east of Lake Tazawa. At 5,370 feet, it's the highest mountain in the area—and it's one of the easiest to climb. Between June and October a bus from Tazawa-ko Station runs up to the eighth station, from which it takes an hour to hike to the summit. You can walk through clusters of alpine flowers if you hike in June or July.

WHERE TO STAY   Nyūtō Onsen consists of six small spa villages, each with an inn, all generally within the same price range (¥20,000–¥30,000). Only Japanese-style rooms are available, and you must take your meals on-site. No Western credit cards are accepted.

Kaniba Onsen (蟹場温泉; ☎ 0187/46–2021). **Kuro-yu Onsen** (黒湯温泉; ☎ 0187/46–2214). **Magoroku Onsen** (孫六温泉; ☎ 0187/46–2224). **Ōgama Onsen** (大釜温泉; ☎ 0187/46–2438). **Taeno-yu Onsen** (妙乃湯温泉; ☎ 0187/46–2740). **Tsuro-no-yu Onsen** (鶴の湯温泉; ☎ 0187/46–2139).

$$$–$$$$ 🏨 **Tazawa-ko Prince** (田沢湖プリンスホテル). A modern white hotel on the edge of the lake, the Tazawa-ko Prince has views of the water as well as Mt. Komaga. Choose from rooms that are large with a lake view, small with a lake view, or small with a mountain view. In addition to the main dining room, there is a garden room down near the lake. ✉ Nishiki-mura, Semboku-gun, Akita-ken 014-0511 ☎ 0187/47–2211 🖷 0187/47–2211 ⚐ Dining room, lake, boating, recreation room, shops ⇨ 128 rooms with bath ▭ AE, DC, MC, V.

Kakunodate　角館

 ★ *16 min southwest of Tazawa-ko by JR.*

The small and delightful town of Kakunodate was founded in 1620 by the local lord, and it has remained an outpost of traditional Japan that, with cause, claims to be Tōhoku's "little Kyōto." The whole town is full of weeping cherry trees, more than 400 of them, and they are direct descendants of those imported from Kyōto three centuries ago. A number of them form a 2-km-long (1¼-mi-long) "tunnel" along the banks of Hinokinai-gawa (Hinokinai River).

Within a 15-minute walk northwest from the station are several well-preserved samurai houses that date to the founding of the town in the 17th century. The most renowned of these is **Aoyagi-ke** (青柳家), with its sod-turf roof. The cherry tree in Aoyagi's garden is nearly three centuries old. ☒ *¥500* ⏱ *Apr.–Nov., daily 8:30–5; Dec.–Mar., daily 9–4.*

If you have time, visit **Denshō House** (Aoyagi-ke Denshōkan, 伝承館), a hall in front of a cluster of samurai houses that serves as a museum and a workshop for cherry-bark handicrafts. ☒ *10–1 Omote Shimo-chō* ☎ *0187/54–1700* ☒ *¥300* ⏱ *Apr.–Nov., daily 9–5; Dec.–Mar., Fri.–Wed. 9–4:30.*

WHERE TO STAY　☒ **Forukurōro Kakunodate** (フォルクローロ角館). The JR people have con-
$$　verted part of Kakunodate Station into an inexpensive B&B with clean rooms with private baths. A simple buffet breakfast and unbeatable convenience are included in a low price. It's only 6 feet from the station exit. ☒ *14 Nakasugasawa, Iwaze-aza, Kakunodate-machi, Akita-ken 014-0314* ☎ *0187/53–2070* ☒ *0187/53–2118* ⬎ *26 rooms with bath* ▭ *MC, V* ⏐☺⏐ *CP.*

Getting Around

JR Express trains run from Morioka (40 minutes) and Akita (70 minutes) to JR Tazawa-ko Station; local trains then run southwest to Kakunodate.

Towada–Hachiman-tai National Park　十和田八幡平国立公園

★ *2 hrs northwest of Morioka by JR and bus.*

From Morioka the main railway line runs north to Aomori via Hachinohe, circumventing Tōhoku's rugged interior, Hachiman-tai Kōgen. The mountains of Towada–Hachiman-tai National Park afford sweeping panoramas over the park's gorges and valleys—which form wrinkles in which locals seek shelter during the region's harsh winters—crystal-clear lakes like Towada-ko, gnarled and windswept trees, volcanic mountain cones, and the ubiquitous hot springs. Winter weather conditions are not conducive to extensive traveling, so if you plan to travel at this time, be sure to check beforehand which bus services are running and which roads are open.

Hachiman-tai Kōgen

 Higashi-Hachiman-tai (東八幡平), on the Hachiman-tai Kōgen (Hachiman-tai Plateau), is the resort town where hikers and skiers begin their ascent into the upper reaches of the mountains. The village of **Pūtaro Mura** (プータロ村) consists of log cabins with private thermal pools. In this part of the park you can either bring in your own food and cook in your cabin or eat in the attached restaurant. A few miles from Pūtaro Mura is **Gozaisho Onsen** (御在所温泉), a popular spa resort that can be a useful overnight stop.

Matsu-kawa Onsen (松川温泉) is noted for its pure waters. This spa town is on the backside of Mt. Iwate, amid the eerie barrenness left by the volcano's eruption in 1719. To get here follow the left-hand fork of the road that leads from Higashi-Hachiman-tai.

The **Aspite Line** (アスピーテライン), a 27-km-long (17-mi-long) scenic toll road running west of Morioka, skirts the flanks of Chausu-san (Mt. Chausu; 5,177 feet) and Hachiman-tai-san (Mt. Hachiman-tai; 5,295 feet). Each turn reveals another view of evergreen-clad slopes and alpine flowers. The entrance to the Aspite Line is past Gozaisho Onsen; it's closed November–April.

From the Hachiman-tai-chōjō bus stop off the Aspite Line it's a 20-minute walk up a path to **Hachiman-numa** (Hachiman Marsh, 八幡沼), originally a crater lake of a volcano. There's a paved esplanade around the crater, and in July and August alpine wildflowers are in peak bloom.

Tōshichi Onsen (藤七温泉), a year-round spa town—elevation 4,593 feet at the foot of Mokko-san, off the Aspite Line—is a popular spring skiing resort. On the north side of Tōshichi is **Hōraikyō**, a natural garden with dwarf pine trees and alpine plants scattered among strange rock formations. In early October the autumn colors are fantastic.

Goshogake Onsen (後生掛温泉), noted for its abundance of hot water, is just before the western end of the Aspite Line. This is a good place to overnight, especially if you want to try *ondo-ru* (Korean-style) steam baths and box-type steam baths where only your head protrudes. Just outside Goshogake is a mile-long nature trail highlighting the volcanic phenomena of the area, including *doro-kazan* (muddy volcanoes) and *oyu-numa* (hot-water swamps). After Goshogake Onsen, the toll road joins Route 341; a left turn leads south to Lake Tazawa. A right turn at the junction heads north for an hour's bus journey to the town of Hachiman-tai, where you can rejoin the JR Hanawa Line either to return to Ōbuke and Morioka or to travel north toward Towada-ko and Aomori.

WHERE TO STAY

$$$–$$$$
🏠 **Kyōun-sō Inn** (峡雲荘). It's just the essentials at this little two-story wooden inn: small tatami rooms and traditional shared bathroom facilities. Meals are served in a communal room. Open-air hot springs are nearby, and the owners are always delighted to have a Westerner stay ✉ *Matsu-kawa Onsen, Matsuo-Mura, Iwate-gun, Iwate-ken 028-7302* ☎ *0195/78–2256* 🖷 *0195/78–2818* ➤ *18 Japanese-style rooms without bath* ♨ *Dining room, Japanese baths; no a/c* ☰ AE, MC, V ⟡ MAP.

$$$
🏠 **Matsu-kawa-sō** (松川荘). Rejuvenating spa waters and a rustic flair make this ryokan a popular lodging. It's simple, clean, and traditional with highly polished wooden floors. Two meals are included, though

you can opt out of the meal plan. ⊠ *Matsu-kawa Onsen, Matsuo-mura, Iwate-gun, Iwate-ken 028-7302* ☎ *0195/78–2255* 🛏 *62 Japanese-style rooms with bath* ⚒ *Dining room, hot springs; no a/c* ⊟ *No credit cards* ⦿ *EP, MAP.*

$$ ⊡ **Pūtaro** (プータロ). If you're looking for a place to relax and hike, this is a good base. These cabins sleep anywhere from 2 to 12 in connecting rooms. The theme is do-it-yourself: basic cooking utensils are provided, and there's a food store. There's also an athletic course with ropes and bridges. Reservations are strongly advised. ⊠ *Hachiman-tai Onsen, Matsuo-Mura Iwate-gun, Iwate-ken 028-7302* ☎ *0195/78–2277* 📠 *0195/78–3283* 🛏 *66 cabins* ⚒ *Grocery, kitchenettes, miniature golf, 6 tennis courts; no a/c in some cabins* ⊟ *MC, V.*

Towada-ko 十和田湖

⑰ The area around **Towada-ko** (Lake Towada) is one of the most popular resorts in northern Tōhoku—almost crushingly so in autumn. If you choose one lake to visit, this should be it. The caldera lake fills a volcanic cone to depths of 1,096 feet, making it the third-deepest in Japan. The lake had no fish in it until Sadayuki Wainaistocked it with trout in 1903. The town of Towada-minami (Towada South) is 20 minutes north of Hachiman-tai on the JR Hanawa Line. From here buses leave on the hour to Lake Towada; the bus fare is ¥1,110.

The road to Lake Towada snakes over **Hakka-tōge** (Hakka Pass, 発荷峠), which has some of the best views over the lake. Following a series of switchbacks, the road descends to circle the lakeshore, though the bus from Towada-Minami goes only part of the way around it.

At the village resort of **Yasumi-ya** (休屋)—the word *yasumi* means "holiday"—pleasure boats run across the lake to the village of Nenokuchi. The one-hour trip on the boat (¥1,320) covers the most scenic parts of the lake. Boats run every 30 minutes from mid-April to early November, less frequently until January 31, then not at all until mid-April.

You can rent a bike at Yasumi-ya and Nenokuchi, but you're better off on foot. First, walk along the lakeside at Yasumi-ya, especially to the right from the sightseeing boat pier. Go at least as far as the statue of two women, and if you are a rock-hopper continue on up the trail to the end of the peninsula. A short walk inland from the statue will take you to the impressively carved, weather-beaten shrine **Towada Jinja.** Regular bus service from Yasumi-ya to Nenokuchi and beyond takes about 25 minutes.

An excellent choice for a walk is to the **Oirase-kyōkoku** (Oirase [oh-*ee*-ra-seh] Gorge, 奥入瀬峡谷), northeast of the lake at Nenokuchi. The carefully tended trail along the gorge follows the stream for a total of 9 km (5½ mi; about 2 hours and 40 minutes). A two-lane road parallels the river; from it you can catch a bus at intervals of about 2 km (1 mi). The first stop is a 20-minute walk from the lake, and the second is another 50 minutes. Buses along the trail go north to Aomori and south to Nenokuchi and Yasumi-ya. Don't miss this easy trail, for it passes through one of the most pristine areas of Tōhoku. Be prepared for rain, take a map of the river and bus stops, and find out the bus schedule before you start out—and don't be daunted by the crowds of tourists, especially in autumn.

WHERE TO STAY
★ $$–$$$$

🏠 **Towada Kankō Hotel** (十和田観光ホテル). Yasumi-ya is dominated by old hotels that cater to busloads of tourists and high-school excursions, but this hotel makes a sophisticated base for enjoying the lake, which is steps away. Western-style rooms have comfortable beds and a separate tatami area. Kaiseki-style Japanese dinner is served in your room and includes kiritampo-nabe (stew made of grilled rice, fish, mushrooms, and wild vegetables); Japanese breakfast is served in the dining room. ⊠ *Towada-ko, Yasumi-ya, Aomori-ken 018-5501* ☎ *0176/75–2111* 🖷 *0176/75–2327* 🛏 *72 rooms with bath* ♨ *Dining room, café, hot springs, bar* 🖃 *AE, DC, MC, V* ⑪ *MAP.*

Getting Around

There are two ways to get from Morioka to Hachiman-tai Kōgen: take the JR Hanawa Line for a 43-minute ride to Ōbuke, 19 km (12 mi) from the plateau. From there continue by bus 50 minutes to Higashi-Hachiman-tai. The faster way of reaching Higashi-Hachiman-tai is to take one of the seven daily buses directly from Morioka (1 hour, 50 minutes; from the Number 4 bus stop in front of the JR station); the fare is ¥1,090. The last stop on the bus is Hachiman-tai Kankō Hotel. Change buses in town for Matsu-kawa Onsen. There's also bus service from Morioka to Tōshichi Onsen and Goshogake Onsen.

From Higashi-Hachiman-tai there are 10 daily buses north to Towada-minami, from which you can take a bus to Lake Towada or connect in Ōdate to Hirosaki and Aomori. Wherever you go from here, the total travel time will be less than a day, but you should plan on spending at least one night en route to take in the remarkable scenery.

Hirosaki 弘前

★ ⑱ *1 hr, 40 min north of Towada-minami by JR; 2 hrs, 20 min northwest of Morioka by express bus, 4 hrs by JR.*

Hirosaki is one of northern Tōhoku's friendliest and most attractive cities. Its major, and really only, sight is Hirosaki Castle, but the town has an intimacy that makes it appealing. Though the city is compact and walkable, finding your bearings in the ancient castle town might be difficult. Hirosaki's streets were designed to disorient invaders before they could get to the battlements. So pick up a map at the tourist information office.

The first week of August the city outdoes itself with its famous **Neputa Festival** (ねぷた祭り; August 1–7). Each night floats follow different routes through town, displaying scenes from Japanese and Chinese mythology on huge fanlike paintings that have faces on both sides. With lights inside the faces, the streets become an illuminated dreamscape: just follow the throb of the 12-foot-diameter drums.

The **Hirosaki Sightseeing Information Center** (弘前観光館; ☎0172/37–5501), south of the castle grounds, displays local industry, crafts, and regional art and provides tourist information; it's open dailyand is free. The **Hi-**

rosaki tourist information office (弘前市観光案内所; ☎ 0172/32–0524) is on the right side of the train station as you exit; it's open January 4–March, daily 8–5, and April–December 28, daily 8:45–6.

Hirosaki Castle (Hirosaki-jō, 弘前城) is a pleasant change from the admirable castle replicas throughout Japan: this is the original building, completed in 1611. The castle is perfectly proportioned in its compactness and is guarded by moats. The gates in the outlying grounds are also original. When the more than 5,000 *someiyoshino*, or cherry trees, blossom (a festival takes place around April 25–May 5) or the maples turn red in autumn (there's a festival late October–mid-November), the setting is marvelous. Winter snows mirror the castle's whiteness and give the grounds a sense of stillness and peace. A snow-lantern festival with illuminated ice sculpture is held in early February. The castle is on the northwest side of town, across the river. ☒ *Grounds free, castle ¥300* ☉ *Grounds daily 7 AM–9 PM; castle Apr.–Oct., daily 9–5.*

On the northeast corner of the castle grounds, **Tsugaru-han Neputa Mura** (津軽藩ねぷた村) is an exhibit of the giant drums and floats used in the Neputa Festival. If you miss the real thing, come here to see the 39-ft fan-shape floats lighted from within. In the workshop you can paint your own traditional kite, paper-and-frame goldfish, and *kokeshi* (traditional wooden doll) and take them home as souvenirs. ☎ 0172/39–1511 ☒ *¥500* ☉ *Apr.–Nov., daily 9–5; Dec.–Mar., daily 9–4.*

Where to Stay & Eat

$$$–$$$$ ✕ **Cartie** (カルティエ). A relaxed, attractive restaurant serving French cuisine at fairly reasonable prices (especially at lunch), Cartie is a real find. The pasta lunch and daily specials range from ¥1,200 to ¥1,500, and dinner costs anywhere from ¥2,500 to ¥3,500. Light meals, as well as cake and desserts, are served on the terrace throughout the day, and the neighboring bakery provides the French bread and desserts for the restaurant. It's a short taxi ride from JR Hirosaki Station. ☒ *3–17–1 Miyakawa* ☎ *0172/37–5010* ☰ *DC, MC, V.*

$$$ ✕ **Anzu** (杏). At this Japanese restaurant, performances of live shamisen (a three-string banjolike instrument) music take place evenings at 7, 9, and 10:30. Arrive an hour early to sit on cushions on the floor, in typical local style, and enjoy a menu of seasonal vegetables, sashimi, grilled scallops, grilled fish and rice, and soup for a reasonable ¥3,000. ☒ *44–1 Oyakata* ☎ *0172/32–6684* ☰ *No credit cards.*

$$$ ✕ **Yamauta** (山唄). Hirosaki's most interesting eatery is a five-minute walk past City Hirosaki Hotel from the train station. Yamauta serves sashimi, grilled fish, yakitori, and other grilled meat for ¥380–¥2,700 and has live shamisen music every hour. The restaurant gets its musical character from its owner, who was once national shamisen champion and now uses the premises as a school for aspiring shamisen artists. Yamauta is closed one day a month, but the day varies. ☒ *1–2–7 Ō-machi* ☎ *0172/ 36–1835* ☰ *No credit cards.*

$$–$$$$ ▦ **Hotel New Castle** (ホテルニューキャッスル). This smart business hotel near Hirosaki Castle is notable for its friendly staff rather than for its amenities. The restaurants here serve formal and elegant Japanese meals. ☒ *24–1 Kamisayashi-machi, Hirosaki, Aomori-ken 036-8354* ☎ *0172/*

36–1211 🖨 *0172/36–1210* 🛏 *59 Western-style and Japanese-style rooms with bath* ♨ *2 restaurants* ▤ *AE, DC, MC, V.*

$$–$$$ 🏨 **City Hirosaki Hotel** (シティ弘前ホテル). Just to the left as you exit JR Hirosaki Station, this modern efficient hotel is very well situated, and the atmosphere is excellent. Off the second-floor lobby is the Japanese restaurant Kazahana, which serves attractive lunches for ¥1,800. The top-floor La Contre-haut, a French restaurant, is slightly overpriced, but the food is good. The Repos Lounge is a pleasant place to contemplate sightseeing plans. ✉ *1–1–2 Ō-machi, Hirosaki, Aomori-ken 036-8004* ☎ *0172/37–0109* 🖨 *0172/37–1229* 🌐 *www.tokyuhotels.co.jp/en* 🛏 *141 rooms with bath* ♨ *2 restaurants, tea shop, bar* ▤ *AE, DC, MC, V.*

Nightlife

If you want to explore Hirosaki's nightlife, look for Kaji-machi, the small entertainment area just beyond the river as you head toward the castle, south of the two main streets, Chūō-dōri and Dote-machi. If you're baffled by the town's complex layout, simply mention the name of the area to any local, and you'll be directed to its clutter of narrow streets. There are plenty of places to dine, from *izakaya* (Japanese-style pubs) to restaurants with picture menus in their windows. And there are coffeehouses, *nomi-ya* (bars), and more expensive clubs.

Getting Around

The express train from Morioka to Hirosaki takes slightly less than 2½ hours; local trains take four hours.

Aomori   青森

⑲ *40 min by JR local from Hirosaki; 2 hrs, 10 min by JR express from Morioka.*

Aomori is another of Tōhoku's prefectural capitals that have more appeal to their residents than to travelers. Foreign visitors used to stop here while waiting for the ferry to cross to Hokkaidō. Now you can transfer to an express train and ride through the Seikan Undersea Tunnel—about 54 km (33½ mi) long, with approximately 24 km (15 mi) of it deep under the Tsugaru Kaikyo (Tsugaru Straits)—to Hokkaidō. The Seikan Tunnel was the world's longest undersea tunnel until the Channel Tunnel linking Britain and France opened in 1994.

The **Aomori tourist information center** (青森市観光案内所; ☎ 017/723–4670) is at the JR Aomori Station. English maps and brochures for the city and prefecture are available here, and you can also apply for the discount Welcome Aomori Card. It's open daily 8:30–5:30.

Aomori's main event is its **Nebuta Festival** (ねぶた祭り; August 3–7), not to be confused with Hirosaki's Neputa Festival (residents of both places get greatly irritated when they are). Though both are held in early August—and both have large, illuminated floats paraded through the streets at night because of an ancient mythology to do with a battle fought by the Tsugaru clan—there are important differences. Hirosaki's festival is rooted in the period before the battle and has a somber atmosphere, with slowly beating drums. Aomori's festival celebrates the postbattle victory and is thus noisier and livelier. Although spectators in Hirosaki can only watch, at Aomori you can participate if you are willing to jump, yell, and generally shed your inhibitions.

If you can't visit during the Nebuta Festival, you might want to head to the **Nebuta Museum** (Nebuta-no-Sato, ねぶたの里), in the southeast part of town, where 10 of the figures used in Aomori's festival are stored and displayed. To get here take the JR bus toward Lake Towada from Bus Stop 8 or 9 (30 minutes; ¥450), right outside the train station. ☎ *017/ 738–1230* 💴 *¥630* ⊙ *July–Sept., daily 9–8 (closed during Nebuta Festival in early Aug.); mid-Apr.–June, Oct., and Nov., daily 9–5:30.*

The **Sannai Maruyama Historical Site** (三内丸山遺跡) dates back 5,000-plus years to Japan's Jōmon period. Discovered in the early 1990s while land was being cleared for a proposed sports complex (since relocated), this was quickly recognized as a large, immensely important archaeological site for Japan's early history. There are reconstructions of Jōmon buildings, and an exhibition hall displays clay figurines, lacquerware, and other items unearthed here. Volunteer guides offer tours in Japanese every two hours. The site is accessible from Bus Stop 2 at JR Aomori Station (35 minutes; ¥330). ☎ *017/766–8282 Japanese only* ⊕ *http://sannaimaruyama.pref.aomori.jp/english/main.html* 💴 *Free* ⊙ *Apr.–Aug., daily 9–7; Sept.–Mar., daily 9–5.*

Munakata Shikō Kinen-kan (棟方志功記念館), a museum dedicated to native son Shikō Munakata (1903–75), displays the wood-block prints, paintings, and calligraphy of this internationally known artist. The building itself is constructed in the attractive, rough-hewn, wooden *azekura* style. Take a bus from Bus Stop 2 at the JR station in the direction of Tsutsumi and get off at Shimin Bunka Kaikan-mae (15 minutes). Then walk back to the crossing and take a left. The museum is on the left. ☎ *017/777–4567* 💴 *¥500* ⊙ *Apr.–Oct., Tues.–Sun. 9:30–5; Nov.–Mar., Tues.–Sun. 9:30–4.*

The **Aomori Prefectural Museum** (Aomori Kenritsu Kyōdo-kan, 青森県立郷土館) displays folk crafts and archaeological artifacts. It's a 10-minute bus ride (¥160) from Bus Stop 4 at JR Aomori Station or a 20-minute walk. ⊠ *2-8-14 Honchō* ☎ *017/777–1585* 💴 *¥310* ⊙ *Apr.–Sept., Tues.–Sun. 9:30–4:30; Oct.–Mar., Tues.–Sun. 9:30–4.*

The **Museum of Folk Art** (Keiko-kan, 稽古館) has a large display of local crafts, including fine examples of *tsugaru-nuri* (lacquerware), which achieves its hardness from 48 coats of lacquer. Dolls representing the Haneto dancing girls of the Nebuta Festival are also on display. The museum is 25 minutes away from the JR station by bus (¥290; board at Bus Stop 3) on a busy highway of malls, arcades, and giant pachinko (a kind of gambling played on upright pinball-like machines) parlors, which makes it easy to miss. Watch for the Sanwa complex on your right, and get off the bus three sets of traffic lights later; the museum is tucked away on the right side. ⊠ *207-1 Aza Tamagawa, Ōaza Hamada* ☎ *017/ 739–6422* 💴 *Free* ⊙ *Daily 9–4:30; last entry at 4.*

For a quick overview of Aomori, you can head up the **ASPAM Building** (Asupamu Biru, アスパムビル), 10 minutes' walk from the JR station down by the waterfront, where the Hokkaidō ferryboats used to dock. The 15-story ultramodern facility is easy to recognize by its pyramid shape. An outside elevator whisks you 13 floors up to an enclosed observation deck, which stays open after the lower floors are closed. There are several restaurants and exhibits on Aomori's tourist attractions and crafts inside the building. Though the staff speaks little English, a tourist information desk in the entrance lobby is very helpful in supplying details of the prefecture's attractions. *¥800; deck only, ¥400 ☉ Daily 9 AM–10 PM; closed every 4th Mon. and the last Mon.–Wed. in Jan.*

For local flavor, head to the **Auga** complex and its lower-level market, where fish, shellfish, preserved seaweed, smoked fish eggs, and other marine products are hawked by hundreds of shopkeepers. It's one block east of JR Aomori Station, across from the Aomori Grand Hotel, in a modern building complex with distinctive crimson pillars. ☉ *Daily 5 AM–6:30 PM.*

off the beaten path

TAPPI-ZAKI (Cape Tappi, 竜飛崎**)** – Northwest of Aomori is the cape on the Tsugaru Kaikyo (Tsugaru Straits) under which the JR Seikan Undersea Tunnel connects Honshū with Hokkaidō. Tappi is the perfect place to enjoy sea urchin fresh from the sea, stroll along steep Nihon-kai cliffs, climb the stairs off National Highway 339 to a windswept lighthouse, observe the power-generating Wind Park turbo fans, and generally get away from it all. Several JR trains per day on the Tsugaru Line pass through Kanita to Mimmaya (1 hour, 40 minutes; ¥1,100), where you change to a bus that goes on to Tappi (30 minutes; ¥200). There are minshuku with minimal facilities for an overnight stay, but you may prefer to return to the Aomori area.

OSORE-ZAN (恐山**)** – Aomori Prefecture possesses a great deal of natural beauty. If you have a day to spare, consider heading to this mountaintop in the center of the **Shimokita-hantō** (Shimokita Peninsula, 下北半), the ax-shape piece of land that juts from Aomori's northeastern corner. Osore-zan's temple, **Entsū-ji** (円通寺), is dedicated to the spirits of dead children. The atmosphere of otherworldliness is heightened by its setting: the surrounding peaks, the neighboring dead lake, the steam from the hot springs, the desolate grounds that have been whitened by sulfuric rock, and the distinct sulfur smell that hangs in the air. Even eerier are some of the visitors: crows often come to feed on the crackers and candles left at the shrines by mourning parents, and blind women gather at the site in late July to offer their services as mediums for contacting the dead. The trip to Osore-zan takes a little more than three hours. From JR Aomori Station take the train to Shimokita Station (¥1890), transfer by bus to Mutsu Terminal (¥140), then take another bus to Osore-zan (¥750).

Where to Stay & Eat

$$–$$$$ ╳ **Hide-zushi** (秀寿司). You're in a major seafood city, and if you want the very best available, this is the place to eat. Excellent service, bright surroundings, and sea urchin, salmon roe, scallops, squid, tuna, and crab

make a visit here worthwhile. ⊠ *1–5 Tsutsumi-machi* ☎ *017/722–8888* ▤ *AE, MC, V* ⊘ *Closed Sun.*

$$–$$$$ ╳ **Nishimura** (西むら). It'd be hard to walk out of this Japanese restaurant hungry: the *danna* course (¥3,000), for example, includes abalone and sea-urchin soup, seaweed and fish, an all-marine hot pot, and fried eggplant. From JR Aomori Station walk one block east on Shinmachi-dōri, and take the first left. Nishimura will be two blocks ahead on your right. ⊠ *1–5–19 Yasukata* ☎ *017/773–2880* ▤ *AE, MC, V* ⊘ *Closed Sun.*

$$–$$$ 🏨 **Aomori Grand Hotel** (青森グランドホテル).This hotel close to the train station is the best place in town for an overnight stay. The lounge for morning coffee has superbly comfortable armchairs, and the Continental Bellevue Restaurant (on the 12th floor) is an enjoyable place to spend an evening. Guest rooms tend to be small. ⊠ *1–1–23 Shin-machi, Aomori-shi, Aomori-ken 030-0801* ☎ *017/723–1011* 🖷 *017/734–0505* ⮑ *140 Western-style and Japanese-style rooms with bath* ⌂ *Restaurant* ▤ *AE, DC, MC, V.*

¢ 🏨 **Daini Ryokan** (大二旅館). The proprietor keeps this spacious inn neat and warmly welcomes foreign visitors. Guests take turns using the communal bath and private shower facilities. Long-term rates are also available, making this a good base for exploring. Prices are minutely higher in winter due to heating costs. From the JR station, turn right and walk one block to Nikoniko-dōri. Turn left and take the third narrow right. The inn is on the right. ⊠ *1–7–8 Furu-machi, Aomori-shi, Aomori-ken 030–0862* ☎ *017/722–3037* ⮑ *19 rooms without bath* ⌂ *Japanese baths* ▤ *No credit cards.*

Getting Around

BY AIR   Aomori has six daily flights from Tōkyō's Haneda Airport by JAL and one by All Nippon Airways. Aomori also has two JAL flights from Nagoya, two from Ōsaka, and two from Sapporo's Chitose Airport. For airline phone numbers, *see* Air Travel *in* Smart Travel Tips A to Z.

BY TRAIN   From Hirosaki it's a 40-minute trip by JR local train to Aomori.

| en route |

Between Aomori and Akita, the train goes back through Hirosaki and past the 5,331-ft-high **Iwaki-san** (Mt. Iwaki, 岩木山), which dominates the countryside. A bus from Hirosaki travels to the foot of this mountain (40 minutes), from which you can take a sightseeing bus up the Iwaki Skyline toll road (open late April–late October) to the eighth station. The final ascent, with the reward of a 360-degree view, is by a five-minute cable car, followed by a 30-minute walk to the summit.

South of Mt. Iwaki, straddling Aomori Prefecture's border with Akita, are the **Shirakami Sanmyaku** (Shirakami Mountains, 白神山脈), site of the world's largest virgin beechwood forest. This is one of Japan's entries on UNESCO's list of World Heritage Sites. Access to the mountains is provided by just a few minor roads on their Aomori and Akita flanks, and the area is great for adventurous hiking. Once you're back on the train, soon after Hirosaki and Iwaki-san, the mountains give way to the rice fields and flat plains that surround Akita.

TŌHOKU WEST COAST 東北西海岸

The "backside" of Tōhoku bears the brunt of Siberian cold fronts, and the rugged mountains provide the base of the esoteric religious practices of Shugendō, a sect founded about 1,400 years ago that combines Buddhism and Shintō.

Akita 秋田

20 *2½ hrs southwest of Aomori by JR express, 4 hrs, 15 min northwest of Tōkyō by Shinkansen.*

Akita, another prefectural capital (population 300,000), is a relaxing city, though not one loaded with sights to see. The surrounding countryside is said to grow the best rice and have the purest water in Japan—the combination produces excellent dry sake.

The major draw here is the famous **Kantō Festival** (August 3–6), during which young men balance a 36-ft-long bamboo pole that supports as many as 46 lighted paper lanterns on its eight crossbars and weighs up to 110 pounds.

The **Akita tourist information office** (秋田市観光案内所; ☎ 018/832–7941) next to the entrance to the Shinkansen tracks at the station has English language pamphlets.

Senshū Kōen (千秋公園), once the site of the now-ruined Kubota Castle, is a pleasant green haven, with cherry blossoms and azaleas adding color in season. It's a 10-minute walk west of the train station on Hiroko-ji dōri.

The **Hirano Masakichi Museum of Art** (Hirano Masakichi Bijutsukan 平野政吉美術館) has a noted collection of paintings by Tsuguji Fujita (1886–1968), as well as works by Vincent van Gogh and Paul Cézanne. The most eye-catching work is Fujita's *Events in Akita*, in which three of the local festivals are merged to form a single scene: rendered on a monstrous piece of canvas measuring 11 feet by 66 feet. It took Fujita just 15 days to complete the painting, and he later bragged that the feat would never be bettered. The building itself is architecturally interesting for its copper-cover Japanese-palace-style roof, which slopes down and rolls outside at the edges. ⊠ *3–7 Meitoku-chō* ☎ *018/833–5809* 🖼 *¥610* ⊙ *Early Jan.–Apr. and Oct.–late Dec., Tues.–Sun. 10–5 May–Sept., Tues.–Sun. 10–5:30; last entry 30 min before closing.*

For regional arts and crafts and more information about the prefecture, visit the 12-story **Atorion Building** (アトリオンビル), a two-minute walk south from the park on the other side of Hirokō-ji (Hirokō Temple). The **Akita Marugoto Plaza** (秋田まるごとプラザ; ☎ 018/836–7835) on the first floor is the prefectural information center, open daily 9–7. The same floor houses a concert hall and the **Akita Senshu Museum of Art** (¥600), which displays the work of local artists as well as oil paintings by Okada Kenzō, who achieved some fame in New York after World War II. The museum is open daily 10–6. A large shop in the basement (open daily 10–7) sells local crafts and souvenirs.

The avenue known as **Kawabata-dōri** (川反通り) is where everyone comes in the evening to sample the regional hot-pot dishes *shottsuru-nabe* (salted-sandfish stew) and kiritampo-nabe, drink *ji-zake* (locally brewed sake), and find entertainment at one of the many bars. It's six blocks west of the Atorion Building, across the Asahi-gawa (Asahi River) and slightly to the south.

The **Oga-hantō** (Oga Peninsula, 男鹿半島) coastline is indented by strange rock formations and reefs, its mountains are clad with Akita cedar, and its hills are carpeted with grasses. At the neck of the peninsula, the summit of Kampu-san (Kampu-san) affords a panoramic view extending as far as Akita city. Nearby, the town of Oga hosts a strange custom each December 31: men dressed in ferocious demon masks and coats of straw, carrying buckets and huge knives, go from home to home issuing dire warnings against any loafers and good-for-nothings in the households. This ritual is reenacted for the public at the **Namahage Sedo Matsuri** (Namahage Sedo Festival) on February 13–15 on the grounds of the local Shinzan Jinja (Shinzan Shrine).

Where to Stay & Eat

\$\$–\$\$\$\$ ✕**Hinaiya** (比内や). The restaurant is named for the local breed of chicken that goes into *Hinai-jidōri* kiritampo-nabe, a hot pot made with kiritampo, rice that's cooked, pasted onto skewers, then grilled over a charcoal fire. This rice is then simmered in a pot with chicken broth, seasonal vegetables, burdock, leeks, and mushrooms (¥1,800). To get to Hinaiya, which is in the heart of the Kawabata entertainment district, walk one block from the river on Suzuran-dōri; it's on the second floor. ✉ *4–2–2 Ō-machi* ☎ *018/823–1718* ⊟ *DC, MC, V.*

\$\$\$ ✕**Dai-ichi Kaikan** (第一会館). The third-floor restaurant of this complex specializes in Akita cuisine such as kiritampo-nabe: ¥2,000 for just the hot pot alone or ¥3,500 for the full-course. The *inaniwa gozen* is a tray with chicken, dried ray, seaweed, wild vegetables, noodles, and *tsukemono* (pickled vegetables). Try it even if you have never seen many of the ingredients before. ✉ *5–1–17 Kawabata* ☎ *018/823–4141* ⊟ *MC, V.*

★ \$\$\$–\$\$\$\$ ▦**Akita Castle Hotel** (秋田キャッスルホテル). Opposite the moat and a 15-minute walk from the train station, this hotel has the best location in town, plus the most professional service and well-maintained rooms. The Western-style doubles are spacious, and the three Japanese-style rooms are even more commodious. Both the bar and the French restaurant overlook the park, and there are Japanese and Chinese restaurants on-site as well. ✉ *1–3–5 Naka-dōri, Akita-shi, Akita-ken 010-0001* ☎ *018/834–1141* 🖷 *018/834–5588* 🛏 *179 Western-style rooms with bath, 3 Japanese-style rooms with bath* ♨ *3 restaurants, bar* ⊟ *AE, DC, MC, V.*

\$\$–\$\$\$ ▦**Akita View Hotel** (秋田ビューホテル).The rooms are clean and fresh at the largest hotel in Akita. On the right side of Seibu department store, it's convenient to shopping. A three-minute walk will bring you to JR station, and a 10-minute walk will bring you to the entertainment district. The staff will be happy to give you advice on what to see and do in the city and prefecture. ✉ *2–6 Naka-dōri, Akita-shi, Akita-ken 010-0001* ☎ *018/832–1111* 🖷 *018/832–0037* 🛏 *192 rooms with bath* ♨ *2 restaurants, coffee shop, indoor pool, gym, bar, shops* ⊟ *AE, DC, MC, V.*

$ ⌂ **Kohama Ryokan** (小浜旅館). This small inn is friendly, homey, and priced right. It's only a five-minute walk to the left of the square in front of JR Akita Station. The Japanese-style dinner incorporates fresh local seafood and is a bargain at ¥2,000; breakfast goes for ¥1,000. The ryokan has traditional shared baths. ⌂ *6–19–6 Naka-dōri, Akita-shi, Akita-ken 010-0001* ☎ *018/832–5739* 🖷 *018/832–5845* ⤴ *13 Japanese-style rooms without bath* ⌂ *Japanese baths; no a/c, no room TVs* 🖃 *AE, MC, V.*

Getting Around

BY AIR JAL flies to Akita four times daily from Tōkyō's Haneda Airport, once daily from Ōsaka International Airport, and twice daily from Sapporo's Chitose Airport. For airline phone numbers, *see* Air Travel *in* Smart Travel Tips A to Z.

BY TRAIN Akita is connected to Tōkyō by the Akita Shinkansen Ko-machi trains; the trip to Tōkyō takes slightly less than four hours, and to Sendai 2¼ hours. There are five trains a day between Akita and Niigata; the trip takes about 3¾ hours. The trip to Aomori takes about three hours.

Tsuruoka & Haguro-san   鶴岡と羽黒山

2½ hrs south of Akita by JR.

South of Akita along the Nihon-kai coast there are small fishing villages, notable only because few foreigners, not to mention Japanese, stop here. ㉑ The one exception is **Tsuruoka** (鶴岡), the town that serves as the gateway to Haguro-san, the most accessible of the three sacred mountains of the Dewa-san range. All three mountains are deemed holy by the *yama-bushi*, the popular name given to members of the Shugendō sect.

㉒ The climb up **Haguro-san** (Mt. Haguro, 羽黒山) begins in Haguro Center at **Zaishin Gate** (Zaishin-mon), then up the 2,446 stone steps to the summit. The rigorous ascent follows avenues of 300-year-old cedar trees with shafts of sunlight filtering through, the occasional waterfall, tiny shrines, and a tea shop halfway up. Running alongside the steps is a trail of rock carvings depicting sake cups, gourds, lotus cups, and more. According to legend, the lucky pilgrim who locates all 33 of the carvings will have a wish granted. This climb is the main draw to Haguro-san, and you should allow several hours to complete it. At the summit, the thatch-roof shrine **Dewa Sanzan Jinja** serves as the focus of the mountain-worship of Shugendō, and you may happen upon one of the many festivals and ceremonies held throughout the year. A bus runs to Haguro Center from JR Tsuroka Station; many of the buses go all the way up to the summit as well. If you decide to skip the climb or have climbed up the mountain from Haguro Center and don't want to hike back down, the bus is an alternative to consider.

Where to Stay & Eat

There are two options for spending the night around Tsuruoka: you can stay in town or at the mountain summit at the Sai-kan, which is attached by a long stairway to the Dewa Sanzan Jinja.

$$–$$$ ✕ **Kanazawa-ya** (金沢屋). Ten minutes on foot from JR Tsuruoka Station, there's an excellent place to eat soba—the *tenzaru* (tempura served with cold soba noodles) and *kamo nanba* soba (duck meat with soba in hot broth) in particular are superb. From the station walk straight to the corner at Marica and Mister Donut, turn left, and walk past the highway. Kanazawa-ya is on the left. ⊠ *3–48 Daihōji-machi, Tsuruoka* ☎ *0235/24–7208* ▤ *No credit cards* ☉ *Closed Wed.*

\$\$ ⌗ **Dewa Sanzan Jinja Hajuro-san Sai-kan** (出羽三山神社羽黒山・斉館). This facility, connected to Dewa Sanzan Jinja by a long stairway, provides an excellent alternative to the city accommodations because you can enjoy the shrine and scenery at the summit after the tourists have gone. The large tatami-mat rooms can be separated by *fusuma* (sliding paper doors on wood frames) to make smaller guest rooms. Meals—made of wild vegetables, tofu, fish, and other local products—are also served in these rooms after the bedding (futon) is put away. The place is jam-packed at festival times, but because Sai-kan can handle 300 guests, one more person can almost always squeeze in. ⊠ *Tōge, Haguro-machi, Higashi Tagawa-gun, Yamagata-ken 997-0211* ☎ *0235/62–2357* 🖷 *0235/62–2352* 🛏 *300 futons* ⌂ *No room phones, no a/c, no room TVs* ▤ *No credit cards* ℐ◉ *MAP.*

\$\$ ⌗ **Tōkyō Dai-ichi Hotel Tsuruoka** (東京第一ホテル鶴岡). The facilities are utilitarian but pleasant enough at this standard business hotel in Tsuruoka. It's a few minutes' walk from JR Tsuruoka Station and next to the Shōnai Kōtsū Mall bus terminal, from which buses depart for Haguro-san. ⊠ *2–10 Nishiki-machi, Tsuruoka-shi, Yamagata-ken 997-0031* ☎ *0235/ 24–7611* 🖷 *0235/24–7621* ⊕ *www.daiichihotels.com/hotel/tsuruoka/* 🛏 *124 rooms with bath* ⌂ *4 restaurants, Japanese baths, bar, meeting rooms* ▤ *AE, MC, V.*

Getting Around

From Tsuruoka, it's easiest to get to Haguro Center by bus (55 minutes), either from Bus Stop 2, in front of JR Tsuruoka Station, or from Stop 5, at Shōkō Mall; there are four departures in winter and at least hourly departures in summer. A fare of ¥680 will take you from the station to lodgings run by yama-bushi in the village at the entrance to the peak itself. Most buses from Tsuruoka to Haguro Center continue to the summit, Haguro-san-chō, which is not much farther, but the fare jumps to ¥990 (because it covers a toll charge for use of a private road).

Daily flights connect Shōnai Airport in Sakata, near Tsuruoka and Haguro-san, with Tōkyō, Ōsaka, Sapporo, and other cities in Japan. For airline phone numbers, *see* Air Travel *in* Smart Travel Tips A to Z.

TŌHOKU A TO Z

To research prices, get advice from other travelers, and book travel arrangements, visit www.fodors.com.

BUS TRAVEL

Buses take over where trains do not run, and in most instances they depart from JR train stations. You should be able to find someone at the train station to direct you to the appropriate bus.

CAR RENTAL

All major towns have car-rental agencies. Hertz is the one most frequently represented. Note that maps are not provided by car-rental agencies; be sure to obtain bilingual maps in Tōkyō or Sendai.

🖉 Agency **Hertz Domestic Reservation Center** ☎ 0120/48-9882 toll-free in Japan ⊕ www.hertz.com.

CAR TRAVEL

Although a car can be handy in certain areas, the cost of gas, tolls, and car rental makes driving expensive. Additionally, except on the Tōhoku Expressway, which links Tōkyō with Aomori, few road signs are in romaji. However, major roads have route numbers. If you're going to drive, be sure to obtain a road map in which the towns are written in romaji and kanji.

Note that it's also considerably slower to drive than to ride on the Shinkansen. The approximate driving times from Tōkyō (assuming you can clear the metropolitan area in two hours) are five hours to Fukushima, six hours to Sendai, 8–10 hours to Morioka, and 10–11 hours to Aomori.

DISCOUNTS & DEALS

Aomori has an excellent way for *gaijin* (foreginers) staying in Japan one year or less to see the sights of the prefecture: the Aomori Welcome Card, which gets you discounts on public buses (50%), hotels (10%), and museums (discount varies). The card is available upon presentation of your passport, after filling out a short application form. Inquire at the JNTO office in Tōkyō, the information office at JR Aomori Station, or at Aomori Airport.

EMERGENCIES

🖉 **Ambulance** ☎ 119. **Police** ☎ 110.

TOURS

Roads trace the Oga-hantō coastline, but public transportation is infrequent. The easiest way to tour the peninsula, which is 45 km (28 mi) northwest of Akita, is by using Akita Chūō Kōtsū bus lines (秋田中央交通). Full-day tours in Japanese cost ¥5,000 (not including meals); they depart from JR Akita Station from July to early November.

In summer the local Japan Travel Bureau at the train station in each major tourist area, or at major hotels, can make arrangements for scenic bus tours. The offices in Tōkyō, Kyōto, and Sendai arrange tours, some in English.

🖉 **Akita Chūō Kōtsū bus lines** ☎ 018/823-4890. **Japan Travel Bureau** ☎ 03/5796-5454 in Tōkyō, 075/371-7891 in Kyōto, 022/221-4422 in Sendai.

TRAIN TRAVEL

The most efficient way to get to Tōhoku from Tōkyō is on the Tōhoku Shinkansen trains, all of which the JR Pass covers. The *Hayate,* which makes the fewest stops, and the slower *Yamabiko* Shinkansen run to Sendai, Morioka, and Hachinohe; the *Tsubasa* runs to Yamagata; and the *Komachi* goes to Akita. North of Hachinohe, conventional trains continue on to Aomori (an additional 70 minutes).

On the west coast, Niigata is connected to Tōkyō's Ueno Station by the *Jōetsu* Shinkansen, which at its fastest makes the run in two hours.

Elsewhere in Tōhoku, JR local trains are slower and less frequent (every two hours rather than every hour during the day) when they cross the region's mountainous spine. Most railways are owned by Japan Railways, so your JR Pass will work. Be aware that most trains stop running before midnight.

VISITOR INFORMATION

Japan Travel Bureau, a worldwide tourist agency, has offices at every JR station in each of the prefectural capitals and can assist in many areas, including hotel reservations and ticketing for onward travel. Individual towns and prefectural governments have their own offices that provide local information. The largest and most helpful tourist centers, which provide information on all of Tōhoku, are at the Sendai and Morioka stations.

Within Tōkyō, each prefecture has an information center with some English brochures and maps.

The nationwide Japan Travel Phone service for English-language assistance or travel information is available daily 9–5. Dial toll-free for information on eastern Japan. When using a yellow, blue, or green public phone (do not use the red phones, which are for local calls only), insert a ¥10 coin, which will be returned. There are different numbers for callers in Tōkyō and Kyōto, and in those cities the service costs ¥10 per three minutes.

🚩 Tourist Information **Aomori Prefecture Tourist Information Center** ☎ 017/734–9386. **Fukushima Prefecture Tourist Information Center** ☎ 0245/21–3811. **Japan Travel Phone** ☎ 0088/22–4800, 03/3503–4400 in Tōkyō, 075/344–3300 in Kyōto. **JNTO Tourist Information Center in Tōkyo (TIC)** ✉ Tōkyō International Forum, 3-5-1 Marunouchi, Chiyoda-ku ☎ 03/3201–3331 Ⓜ Yūraku-chō Line, Yūraku-chō station [Exit A-4B]. **Prefecture information offices in Tōkyō** ☎ 03/3211–1775 for Akita ☎ 03/5276–1788 for Aomori ☎ 03/3524–8282 for Iwate ☎ 03/3504–8713 for Yamagata. **Tōno tourist office** ☎ 0198/62–1333.

HOKKAIDŌ 北海道

14

By Nigel Fisher

Updated by
Amanda
Harlow

HOKKAIDŌ IS JAPAN UNTAMED. Its cities and towns are outposts of modern urban humanity, which is kept at bay by wild mountains, virgin forests, sapphire lakes, and surf-beaten shores. This is Japan's last frontier, and the attitudes of the inhabitants are akin to those of the pioneers of the American West—or any other last places.

One of the delights of traveling through Hokkaidō is meeting the people, who are known as Dosanko, after the sturdy draft horse native to the area. Since virtually all the Japanese on this island are descended from "immigrants to a new frontier," they are less traditional and more open-minded. They have a great attachment to their island. Hokkaidō consistently ranks at the top of surveys on where Japanese would most like to live.

Hokkaidō as we know it was born during the Meiji Restoration (1868–1912), a time when the Japanese government turned to the West for new ideas. This island looked to America and Europe as models of modern development. In the 1870s some 63 foreign experts came here, including an American architect who designed the prefecture's principal city, Sapporo. Around the same time, agricultural experts from abroad were brought in to introduce dry farming as a substitute for rice, which would not grow in the severe winter climate until hardy varieties were developed, which didn't happen until much later. This history of cooperation has left Dosanko with a peculiar fondness for Europeans. In Sapporo, Westerners are warmly received. In the countryside Dosanko are shy—but hardly timid—in coming to the aid of Westerners.

Because Hokkaidō consists more of countryside than of cities—which implies language barriers that are more often than not bridged by the friendliness of locals—the number of gaijin (foreigners) who come here has traditionally been small, compared to the many Japanese from elsewhere in the country who come for winter skiing and summer hiking. Tour groups from other Asian countries and Australian skiers make up the bulk of the foreign visitors. Sapporo's Chitose Airport has flights to Asian cities such as Seoul, Taipei, and Hong Kong, so most travelers from outside Asia have a domestic transfer to reach Hokkaidō. Because this is Japan's northernmost and least-developed island, it's easy to romanticize it as a largely uncharted territory. That is mostly untrue, as road and rail networks crisscross the island. Of course, wild beauty and open space still abound—from volcanic mountains and lakes to the marshlands of the red-crested *tanchō-zuru* (red-crested crane), to the ice floes of the Ohotsuku-kai (Sea of Okhotsk) to the northerly isolation of the Rishiri and Rebun islands.

See the glossary at the end of this book for definitions of the common Japanese words and suffixes used in this chapter.

Exploring Hokkaidō

With little visible past and cities that are relatively new, Hokkaidō has few temples, shrines, and castles. But the island is a geological wonderland: lava-seared mountains hide deeply carved ravines; hot springs, gushers, and steaming mud pools boil out of the ground; and crystal-clear caldera lakes fill the seemingly bottomless cones of volcanoes. Half of Hokkaidō is covered in forest. Wild, rugged coastlines hold back the sea, and all around the prefecture, islands surface offshore. Some are volcanic peaks poking out of the ocean, and others were formed eons ago by the crunching of the earth's crust. The remnants of Hokkaidō's bear population, believed to number about 2,000, still roam the forests, snagging rabbits and scooping up fish from mountain streams, and deer wander the pastures, stealing food from cows. Hokkaidō's native crane, the tanchō-zuru, is especially magnificent, with a red-cap head and a white body trimmed with black feathers. Look for it on the ¥1,000 note and in the marshes of Kushiro, east of Sapporo on the Pacific coast.

About the Restaurants

Eat at local Japanese restaurants as often as possible to experience one of the true joys of Hokkaidō, the regional food, which includes delicious seafood and lamb. Many reasonably priced restaurants have a visual display of their menu in the window, which allows you to decide what you want before you enter. If you cannot order in Japanese and no English is spoken, lead the waiter to the window display and point, or try sketching for your server the Japanese character for the dish you want.

Eki-ben—the classic box lunch—is a must in Hokkaidō. Pick one up in JR Hakodate Station: the local *nishin-migaki-bentō* consists of nishin (herring) boiled in a sweet, spicy sauce until the bones are soft enough to eat. At Mori Station, about an hour's drive north of Hakodate, you can try a different well-known Eki-ben, *ika-meshi,* a box lunch made by stuffing a whole *ika* (squid) with rice and cooking it in a sweet, spicy sauce. Each meal includes two or three ika.

About the Hotels

Accommodations in Hokkaidō tend to consist of modern, characterless hotels built for Japanese tour groups. Large, sparsely furnished sitting areas and lobbies are the norm, with the scenery as the only distinguishing element. Invariably, prices depend on views, and the size of public areas and guest rooms. Unless otherwise noted, all rooms have private bathrooms. Room air-conditioning is unusual, apart from large hotels, but the cool Hokkaidō summers render it unnecessary. As tourism in Hokkaidō grows, more attractive and comfortable hotels are appearing. Guesthouses, known as *pensions,* are a cheaper, friendlier option, although booking in Japanese is usually necessary and dinner reservations are required. Youth hostels are also a good option; in the towns and cities they are often clean and modern, and in the national parks they are excellent touring bases. (See *Lodging* in Hokkaidō A to Z.)

Outside Sapporo and Hokkaidō's industrial and commercial cities, hot-spring hotels charge on a per-person basis including two meals and excluding service and tax. In those cases, the rates listed below are for two people with two meals each, and the Modified American Plan (MAP) is noted in the service information. If you don't want dinner, it's usually possible to renegotiate the price. Isolated resort areas may offer the limited choice of dining at your hotel or risking the local equivalent of fast food: ramen or Japanese-style curry.

Hokkaidō's expansiveness is daunting. Fortunately, the main sights—calderas, remote onsen, craggy coasts, dramatic climate—are everywhere. Rather than rushing to see everything, consider balancing the natural with the urban, the inland with the coastal, and figure in the seasonality of sights and activities more heavily than you would elsewhere in Japan. The historically minded should focus on the major cities of southern Hokkaidō. Wilderness lovers should venture east and center.

Numbers in the text correspond to numbers in the margin and on the Hokkaidō map.

If you have 3 days

Three days is just enough to take in a slice of southern Hokkaidō. Fly into Chitose Kūkō, outside 🗺 **Sapporo** ▶ ② – ⑬, and spend a day touring the city, finishing with the neon thrill of the Susukino nightlife district. The next day, head south and east by JR to Tomikawa and then take the Dōnan Bus service up to the Ainu village of **Nibutani** ⑲, backtracking to 🗺 **Shikotsu-ko** ⑳ for the night. That will position you for a final day around the caldera lake, either soaking in the scenery or going for a morning hike up the volcanic cones of Eniwa-dake or Tarumae-zan. Or, instead of two days between Nibutani and Shikotsu-ko, you could head west and south for 🗺 **Niseko** ⑮ and a day's hiking or skiing. Overnight there and return to Sapporo on the third day on a coastal circuit around rocky Shakotan-hantō, stopping in **Otaru** ⑭ for its rustic charm and peerless sushi.

If you have 5 days

Five days will allow a more in-depth tour of southern Hokkaidō or, if you skip Sapporo entirely, a dash around the central and eastern parts of the island. For the southern option, spend your first day in 🗺 **Hakodate** ▶ ① or 🗺 **Sapporo** ② – ⑬; then make a thorough loop through the active volcanic areas of **Shikotsu-Tōya National Park** ⑰ – ⑳, detouring east to **Nibutani** ⑲ for its Ainu village. You could otherwise spend the last four days passing through 🗺 **Otaru** ⑭, then around the Shakotan-hantō on the way down to **Niseko** ⑮ for hiking or an adventure-company trip with English-speaking guides.

If you have 7 days

With a week, you can give yourself time in 🗺 **Sapporo** ▶ ② – ⑬ or 🗺 **Hakodate** ① and one or two of the farther-flung parks. Skip the areas south of Sapporo and make your way through 🗺 **Asahikawa** ㉕ to the gorges and onsen of 🗺 **Daisetsu-zan National Park** ㉖ or the northern cape's **Wakkanai** ㉗, **Rebun Island** ㉘, and 🗺 **Rishiri Island** ㉙. It takes two days of travel round-trip to reach these islands—unless you fly—but the tiny fishing villages, fresh seafood, great hiking, and volcanic scenery will make for a singular experience of Japan. Or, head east through Asahikawa and Daisetsu-zan National Park to 🗺 **Abashiri** ㉑ to see the wonders of the Ohotsuku-kai and 🗺 **Akan National Park** ㉓. Take five days or more to see all of eastern Hokkaidō, including a venture into the end-of-the-world wilds of **Shiretoko National Park** ㉒ and a stop at **Kushiro Marsh** ㉔ to see the rare and beautiful tanchō-zuru.

WHAT IT COSTS In yen				
$$$$	**$$$**	**$$**	**$**	**¢**
RESTAURANTS over 3,000	2,000–3,000	1,000–2,000	800–1,000	under 800
HOTELS over 22,000	18,000–22,000	12,000–18,000	8,000–12,000	under 8,000

Restaurant prices are per person for a main course at dinner. Hotel prices are for a double room, excluding service and 5% tax.

Timing

Hokkaidō has Japan's most dramatic seasons. Festivals predominate in summer and winter. May and early summer bring lilacs and alpine flowers. The cherry trees in Hokkaidō are the last to offer up *sakura* (cherry blossoms) in Japan, in late April and early May. Gloriously refreshing weather from May to October lures Japanese drowning in the muggy air of Honshū. Hotel accommodations become relatively difficult to find in summer, and the scenic areas become crowded with tour groups and Japanese families. September brings brief but spectacular golden foliage, reaching a peak in early October. Fall is as brief as it is crisp and striking, giving way to chilly drizzle in November and early December—times to avoid. Winter makes travel more difficult (some minor roads are closed), and especially on the east coast, weather is frigid. It's no less beautiful a time, however, with crisp white snow covering everything and ice floes crowding the Ohotsuku-kai. If you're here during the second week in February, don't miss the dazzling Snow Festival in Sapporo.

HAKODATE 函館

 ❶ *3 hrs north from Tōkyō to Morioka by JR Shinkansen, then 2 or 3 hrs north from Morioka to Aomori by JR Limited Express, then 2½ hrs north to Hakodate by JR Rapid via the Seikan Tunnel.*

Traveling by train from Honshū into Hokkaidō, you come first to Hakodate. As one of the first three Japanese ports that the Meiji government opened up to international trade in 1859, it has the most extensive bricks-and-mortar history of any Hokkaidō city, and apart from the listed sights has many wonderful decaying buildings, which are best appreciated by hiking the slopes of the historic Moto-machi area. Heritage information boards in English are plentiful.

For maps and a hotel list in English, stop at the **Hakodate City Tourist Information Center** (函館市駅前観光案内所; ☎ 0138/23–5440) inside the station building. It's open April–October, daily 9–7, and November–March, daily 9–5.

The Moto-machi Museums 元町博物館

A cluster of old buildings with definite European- and American-style architecture stands at the foot of Hakodate-yama (Mount Hakodate), and inside you'll find the Moto-machi museums. Admission to one museum costs ¥300, or pay ¥840 for all four. They're open from April to October, daily 9 to 7; and from November to March, daily 9 to 5.

British Consulate Building (Kyū Igirisu Ryōji-kan, 旧イギリス領事館). Formerly the headquarters of the British Consulate in Hakodate, this at-

Skiing

Powder snow makes Hokkaidō arguably the best skiing and snowboarding destination in Japan. Australian winter sports fans join thousands of Japanese in Hokkaidō's mountains from late November to early May, and the snowboarders outnumber the skiers.

The big areas are Niseko and Rusutsu, two hours west of Sapporo; Kokusai and Kiroro, one hour west of Sapporo; and Furano, Tomamu, and Sahoro, two hours east of Sapporo. Courses are well maintained and lifts are generally modern and fast, with no drag lifts to flummox beginners. Ski patrols are becoming less strict about off-course skiing, and the backcountry possibilities are wondrous.

14

Many ski schools and the adventure tour companies in Niseko have English-speaking guides and teachers. A day's lift pass averages ¥4,500, but ski packages that include bus transportation are a better option and often include lunch and/or hot-spring tickets, too. Hotels and sports shops in Sapporo have lift discount coupons, too, so nobody actually pays the full rate for a lift ticket.

Reservations for short ski tours to Hokkaidō from Tōkyō or Ōsaka usually have to be made a week in advance. On weekends there may be 20-minute waits for the lifts, but only in the January 1–4 period are waits any longer. Equipment and wear can be rented at the resorts, but call ahead to check availability of larger boot sizes. Hokkaidō is home to Everest skier Yuichiro Miura as well as many of the Japanese Olympic ski jumpers and mogul experts. International ski and boarding events are sometimes held at Hokkaidō resorts.

Hiking

Hokkaidō's mountains and lakes are challenging hiking destinations, and the support network of maps, signs, public transport, and lodging is improving as more non-Japanese join the mainly middle-age and elderly local hikers. The national parks provide the most dramatic scenery, with peaks such as the 6,870-ft Asahidake in the Daisetsu-zan range and the 5,967-ft Yōtei-zan near Niseko, but there are many shorter, easier hikes nearer cities and towns. Trails are not marked in English, so hikers should carry Japanese maps for cross-referencing. Check with tourist offices for up-to-date maps and information. Plaza i in Sapporo sells inexpensive trekking and onsen guides.

Hokkaidō's most dangerous wildlife are brown bears, particularly in spring and early summer. Hikers should learn the Japanese character for "bear" and take note of information on signs at trailheads. No local hiker sets out without a bear bell attached to his or her backpack, to give bears warning that a human is in their area. Bear sightings are most likely in Shiretoko in eastern Hokkaidō, but dog walkers in suburban parks near Sapporo have had some early morning encounters. Anyone encountering a fellow human on the trail should offer a cheerful *konichiwa!* (hello!) in greeting.

↑
TO
SAKHALIN
ISLAND

30 **Sōya-misaki**
宗谷岬

礼文島
Rebun Island **28**

Kafuka

Oshidomari

27 **Wakkanai** 稚内

Kutcharo-ko

Hama Tonbetsu

Kutsugata

29 **Rishiri Island** 利尻島

Horonobe

Esashi

238

KITAMI

Okoppe

Monb

NIHON-KAI
(Sea of Japan)

Tomamae

Nayoro

Takinoue

MTNS.

Kamikaw

Teshio-dake

Rumoi

旭川
Asahikawa

25

Asahi-dake

Sōun-ky

Dais

Mashike

Daisetsu-zan National Park 大雪山

26

Shirogane Onsen

Nukabira

Shakotan-misaki

Yobetsu

Kamui-misaki

Tomaru Tōge

Ishikara-wan

Furubira

小樽
Otaru

2 - **13**
see detail map

Furano

Tokachi-dake

Shikaribetsu-ko

Yoichi

14

Yūbari-doke

Kamoenai

Tengu-yama

Shakotan-hantō

Kutchan

16

Iwanai

5

Jōzankei Onsen 定山渓温泉

Sapporo

Iwamizawa

Obihi

Niseko
ニセコ

15

Yotei-zan

Shikotsu-Tōya National Park

20 **Shikotsu-ko** 支笏湖

Chitose

19 **Nibutani**
二風谷

HIDAKA RANGE

Tōya-ko Onsen 洞爺湖温泉

17

Tomakomai

Oshamambe

Noboribetsu 登別温泉 **Onsen**

18

Shiraoi

Tomikawa

Hire

Ar
da

Noboribetsu

Oshima-hantō

Uchiura-wan

Muroran

5

Komaga-dake

Esashi

Hakodate
函館

1

Matsumae Castle

Tsugaru Kaikyo
(Tsugaru Straits)

Fukushima

TO
AOMORI
↓

Seikan Tunnel

HONSHŪ

KEY	
⚐	*Start of itinerary*
—	*JR Trains*
🚢	*Ferry*

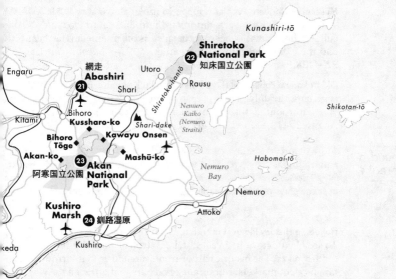

Hokkaidō

OHOTSUKU-KAI
(Sea of Okhotsk)

Kunashiri-tō

Shiretoko National Park
知床国立公園 **22**

Engaru

網走
Abashiri 21

Utoro

Shari

Shiretoko-hantō

Rausu

Nemuro Kaikō (Nemuro Straits)

Shikotan-tō

Kitami

Bihoro

Kussharo-ko

Bihoro Tōge

▲ *Shari-dake*

Kawayu Onsen

Habomai-tō

Akan-ko

23

Mashū-ko

Akan National Park
阿寒国立公園

Nemuro Bay

Nemuro

Kushiro Marsh
24 釧路湿原

Attoko

...keda

Kushiro

TAIHEIYŌ
(Pacific Ocean)

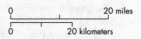

0   20 miles
0   20 kilometers

tractive building is now a museum devoted to the opening of the port in the 19th century. Actually, the quaint English information handout and the coffee shop, which serves tea and scones, are more interesting than the sparsely furnished rooms. ✉ *33–14 Moto-machi* ☎ *0138/ 27–8159.*

Hakodate City Museum of Literature (Hakodate-shi Bungaku-kan, 函館市文学館). The city's most noted writers are profiled here, and some of the information is in English. None of the writers are household names in the West, but the museum is pleasant and has a photographic display of the "eight most beautiful scenes in Hakodate"—more evidence of the Japanese mania for cataloging and ranking everything. The museum is downhill from the Russian Orthodox Church. ✉ *22–5 Suehiro-chō* ☎ *0138/22–9014.*

Museum of Northern Peoples (Hoppo Minzoku Shiryō-kan, 北方民族資料館). This museum gives a straightforward introduction to Hokkaidō's Ainu culture, though it's not nearly as detailed as other museums farther north, and the exhibitions are rather spartan. ✉ *21–7 Suehiro-chō* ☎ *0138/ 22–4128.*

Old Hakodate Public Hall (Kyū Hakodate-ku Kokaido, 旧函館区公会堂). This is perhaps the only place in Japan where you can see the Emperor's private bathroom, dating from when the Taishō Emperor stayed here in August 1911. ✉ *11–13 Moto-machi* ☎ *0138/22–1001.*

need a break? More than 100 kimono-clad dolls watch guests with their coffees, teas, and traditional desserts in the tiny, two-room **Kitchen and Cafe Hana** (キッチン＆カフェ華; ✉ *2–21 Funami-chō* ☎ *0138–24–4700*), in a house near the gates of the Old Public Hall. Shoes off at the door please.

Elsewhere in Hakodate

Hakodate History Plaza (Hakodate Histori Puraza, 函館ヒストリープラザ). To see Hakodate at its liveliest, take a stroll around this restored 19th-century plaza. The historic harbor-front warehouses that surround it contain modern markets, restaurants, and bars that attract a thriving local trade. The bars close at 10:30 PM. ✉ *14–16 Suehiro-chō, about 750 feet northwest of Jūji-gai streetcar stop* ☎ *0138/23–0350.*

Hakodate Russian Orthodox Church (Harisutosu Sei Kyōkai, 函館ハリストス正教会). This beautiful white church is Hakodate's most exotic attraction. It dates from 1859, when it served as the first Russian consulate in the city. After a 1907 fire, it was rebuilt in Byzantine style in 1916. A large-scale restoration project was completed in 1989. To get here from the JR station, take Streetcar 5 to the Suehiro-chō stop and walk 10 minutes toward Hakodate-yama. ✉ *3–13 Moto-machi* ☎ *0138/23–7387.*

Goryōkaku Fort (五稜郭). North of the city center is this Western-style fort completed in 1864. Its design is unusual, especially the five-pointed-star shape, which enabled its defenders to rake any attackers with murderous cross fire. In spite of all that protection, the Tokugawa shogunate was unable to hold out against the forces of the Meiji Restoration, and its walls were breached. Nothing of the interior castle remains, but there's a small museum with relics from the battle. The fort area is now a park with some 4,000 cherry trees, which, when they bloom in late April, make the stopover in Hakodate worthwhile. An observation tower in the park, at ¥630 admission, is not worth the climb. Take Bus 12, 20, 30, or 27–1 from JR Hakodate Station's Gate B, or Streetcar 2 or 5 to the Goryōkaku Kōen-mae stop. From either stop it's a 10-minute walk to the fort. ☒ *Free* ⊙ *Late Apr.–late Oct., daily 8–7; late Oct.–late Apr., daily 9–6.*

Hakodate-yama (Mount Hakodate, 函館山). Jutting out from the city like a spur, this volcanic mountain rises to a height of 1,100 feet. Views of the city from its summit are especially good at night, with the darkness of the Tsugaru Kaikyō on one side and the brilliant city lights accenting the small isthmus that connects the peak to the downtown. You can take a 30-minute bus ride to the top of Hakodate-yama from the JR station from late April through October, or for a more interesting trip, hop on Streetcar 2 or 5 to the Jūji-gai stop and then walk about seven minutesto the cable car for the three-minute ride up the mountain. ☒ *Cable car ¥640 one-way, ¥1,160 round-trip* ⊙ *Cable car late Apr.–early May and late July–late Aug., daily 9 AM–10 PM; early May–late July and late Aug–Oct., daily 10–10; Nov.–late Apr., daily 10–9.*

off the beaten path

MATSUMAE CASTLE (Matsumae-jo, 松前城) — West of Hakodate are fishing villages and sweeping coastal vistas, now a backwater to Hokkaidō's more popular areas farther north—but the center of military and economic power from the 17th century until 1868. Matsumae Castle, the seat of power for 15 generations of samurai, is now just a small rebuilt fortress tower overlooking the sea. The museum inside has paintings and armor from its exciting past. The surrounding temples and shrines, which escaped war and Meiji-era destruction, are older and full of atmosphere. Matsumae has 8,000 cherry trees and is best avoided in the early May tourist season. If you're not driving, you can get to Matsumae via a 3½-hour bus ride (¥2,000) from Hakodate. ☒ *248 Fukuyama, Matsumae* ☏ *01394/2–2275* ☒ *Castle grounds ¥310, museum ¥210* ⊙ *Apr.–Dec., daily 9–5.*

Where to Stay & Eat

$$–$$$ ✕ **Gotōken** (五島軒). Good curries, borsht, and crab croquettes compete with the bland surroundings at this Hakodate institution, which has been serving pricy foreign foods since 1879. Splurge on lobster or try the duck curry served with a tray of pickles, raisins, and peanuts. An extensive menu in English and proximity to the sights make it a good lunch stop, but savvy diners are likely to be otherwise unimpressed with this dated so-called "foreign experience." It does continue to wow the locals, however. Dinner is served in the more ornate formal restaurant. ☒ *4–5 Suehiro-chō* ☏ *0138/23–1106* ☐ *AE, MC, V.*

¢–$$ ✕ **Hakodate Beer Hall** (函館ビアホール). This seaside hall in Hakodate History Plaza serves seafood specialties, such as squid, octopus, and tofu *shabu shabu* (cooked at the table by dipping in boiling water and then into a sauce) for ¥1,300 and three local brews (wheat beer, ale, and the slightly more bitter "alt" beer). Its spaciousness and conviviality are typical of Hokkaidō and favored by domestic travelers. ⊠ *5–22 Ote-machi,* ☎ *0138/23–8000* ⊟ *AE, V.*

¢ ✗ **Lucky Pierrot** (ラッキーピエロ). Hakodate's most famous burger shop serves up 15 kinds—including a squid burger—and a range of curries, too. There are a few seats inside; most customers take out. The shop made news when it was chosen to supply hamburgers to a local high school, and there are now franchises all over town. The original shop is next to Hakodate History Plaza. ⊠ *23–18 Suehiro-chō* ☎ *0138/ 26–2099* ⊟ *No credit cards.*

$$$–$$$$ ✗🏨 **Hakodate Kokusai Hotel** (函館国際ホテル). This bustling modern hotel occupies three buildings just a short walk away from the station/morning market area and the History Plaza warehouses. Standard rooms in pastel shades have views of the waterside highway or city. *Tennpan* chefs slice and dice in Vue Mer on the top floor. If you're coming from Sapporo, check with Japan Rail about rail–hotel combination packages for good deals at this hotel. ⊠ *5–10 Ohtemachi, Hakodate 040-0064* ☎ *0138/23–5151* 🖷 *0138/23–0239* ⊕ *www.hakodate.ne.jp/kokusaihotel* 🛏 *304 Western-style rooms, 6 Japanese-style rooms* ☼ *4 restaurants, room service, minibars, cable TV, hair salon, 3 bars, shop, laundry service, free parking* ⊟ *AE, MC, V.*

$$–$$$$ 🏨 **Harborview Hotel** (ハーバービューホテル). Proximity to the station and the morning fish market makes this a convenient place to stay. A pleasant coffee lounge and a bar that attracts a sociable crowd are in the lobby. Standard Western-style rooms are furnished in light blue or peach—not particularly attractive, but comfortable enough for a night. ⊠ *14–10 Wakamatsu-chō, Hakodate 040-0063* ☎ *0138/22–0111* 🖷 *0138/ 23–0154* 🛏 *200 Western-style rooms* ☼ *3 restaurants, coffee shop, bar* ⊟ *AE, DC, MC, V.*

$$$ 🏨 **Pension Kokian** (ペンション古稀庵). A hundred-year-old former seaweed shop with a modern annex just behind the waterfront warehouses offers small Western motel-style rooms, each with sink units and use of shared bath–toilets. The traditional restaurant in the old building serves the best of the morning's catch. ⊠ *13–2 Suehiro-chō, Hakodate 040-0053* ☎ *0138/26–5753* 🖷 *0138/22–2710* ⊕ *www.hakodate.or.jp/hotel/kokian* 🛏 *17 Western-style rooms* ☼ *Restaurant, bar; no a/c* ⊟ *AE, DC, V.*

$ 🏨 **Eiley's** (エイリーズ). An Irish bar with small, clean guest rooms one block back from the History Plaza, this former bank hall has been transformed with salmon pink walls, dart boards, table soccer, and bar stools. Several of the small, plain rooms (all have private baths) are singles, making this a good place for solo travelers to network. ⊠ *23–9 Suehiro-chō, Hakodate 040-0053* ☎ *0138/22–8884* 🖷 *0138/22–8884* ⊕ *http://stay.eileys.co.jp* 🛏 *20 Western-style rooms, 1 Japanese-style room* ☼ *Restaurant, bar; no room phones, no room TVs* ⊟ *V* ⦿*CP.*

★ ¢–$ 🏨 **Pension Puppy Tail** (ペンションパピーテール). Decoupage decorations and garlands of silk flowers overwhelm, but the family welcome is big at this three-decades-old business a 10-minute walk north of the station on Route 5. Rooms in the new annex have private bathrooms. The owner, Fukui-san, speaks English and can pick guests up from the station. Breakfast (¥1,000) and dinner (¥2,000) should be reserved the day before. Faxed reservations are best. The kitschy name? The Fukui family thought their red setter's tail looked like the Hakodate part of the Hokkaidō map. ⊠ *30–16 Wakamatsu-chō, Hakodate 040-0063* ☎ *0138/23–5858* 📠 *0138/26–8239* ⊕ *www.p-puppytail.com* ➦ *6 Western-style rooms, 13 Japanese-style rooms* ♦ *Dining room, Japanese baths* ⊟ *No credit cards.*

Getting Around

The cost of travel on streetcars ranges from ¥200 to ¥250 and on the municipal buses from ¥200 to ¥260. You can buy a one-day bus and streetcar pass (¥1,000), and borrow an audio city-walking guide (deposit ¥500) from the tourist center.

Hokuto Kōtsū (☎ 0138/57–7555), a bus company, runs 4½-hour sightseeing tours of the city (in Japanese), leaving from JR Hakodate Station and covering most of the city sights for ¥4,000.

SAPPORO 札幌

3½ hrs north of Hakodate by JR.

Sapporo is both Hokkaidō's capital and the island's premier city. With 1.8 million inhabitants, it's four times larger than Asahikawa, the prefecture's next-largest city. And it continues to expand as Hokkaidō's unemployed from the economically depressed farms in the central plains and industrial and fishing towns on the coast migrate to Sapporo for work. Though it's a large city, it's not confusing or congested. In 1870 the governor of Hokkaidō visited President Grant in the United States and requested that American advisers come to Hokkaidō to help design the capital on the site of an Ainu village. (The name *Sapporo* is derived from a combination of Ainu words meaning "a river running along a reed-filled plain.") As a result, Sapporo was built on a 330-ft grid system with wide avenues and parks. It's not the exotic and cultural city you expect to find in Japan and is distinctly lacking in pre-Meiji historic sights. On the other hand, you can walk the sidewalks without being swept away in a surge of humanity.

By hosting the 1972 Winter Olympic Games, Sapporo relaunched itself as an international city and took on a cosmopolitan attitude. Developers built plenty of hotels and restaurants that are still up and running. Banks here are used to traveler's checks, and there's always someone on hand to help you out in English. Ultimately, though, Sapporo is best to use as a base from which to make excursions into the wild, dramatic countryside. If you want to explore the city, a day, perhaps two at most, will do.

Numbers in the text correspond to numbers in the margin and on the Sapporo map.

a good walk

Most comforting about Sapporo is the simplicity of the city's layout. East–west streets are called *jō*, and those running north–south are *chōme*. They are numbered consecutively, and each block is approximately 100 yards square. The cardinal points are used more often than elsewhere in Japan. North, south, east, and west are *kita, minami, higashi,* and *nishi,* respectively. Ōdōri Park divides the city in half north–south, and the Sosei-gawa separates east from west. Thus, the address Kita 1–jō Nishi 2 means one block north of Ōdōri Park and two blocks west of the Sosei River, putting you at the Clock Tower.

A good place to start out on foot is **JR Tower Observatory** ➤ ❷, 524 feet above Sapporo Station and with panoramic views all over the cityscape and the mountains beyond. At the base of the tower, near the south (west) station exit is the tourist information office. From the base of the tower start walking down Eki-mae-dōri, which is the main street running from the station, through the city center and Susukino to Nakajima Park in the south.

Two blocks south of the station, turn right to see the large, redbrick **Old Hokkaidō Government Building** ❸. A few blocks farther west behind various modern municipal offices are the **Botanical Gardens** ❹, with a profusion of northern plants and greenhouses.

Return to Eki-mae-dōri, via the **Sapporo Grand Hotel** ❺, with its small lobby exhibition about famous guests who have stayed there. Cross to the east side of Eki-mae-dōri and continue for one block to see Japanese visitors posing for pictures in front of Sapporo's landmark **Clock Tower** ❻, and pick up sightseeing information across the street from the downtown office of **Plaza i** ❼, or upstairs in the same building at the international meeting lounge and noticeboards of **Sapporo International Communication Plaza** ❽.

Walk south again one block to the greenery and flowerbeds of **Odōri Kōen** ❾ (Odōri Park) where shoppers and office workers sit with their lunchboxes and Sapporo's youth entertain with hip-hop, skateboarding, and guitars. At the eastern end is the TV Tower and 11 blocks west is a 1920s European-style building, now the City Document Museum, which started life as the Sapporo Court of Appeals.

The Odōri shopping area is south of the park. Dive down any of the more than 20 subway entrances to find Sapporo's subterranean shopping streets, such as **The Downtown Underground** ❿, perfect for shopping in winter. Also protected from the weather is the covered arcade **Tanuki Mall** ⓫, with its discount clothing stores and souvenir shops. At the eastern end of the arcade, across the small river, domestic tourists are paying extortionate prices for souvenirs at the fish market, **Nijō-ichiba** ⓬.

The downtown shopping area extends four blocks south from Odōri Park to the three-lane Route 36. South of this is the entertainment area **Susukino**, which comes alive around 7 PM as mini-skirted or kimonoed bar hostesses head in for work and attractions are promoted by the orange-haired, blacksuited touts who hover at intersections.

A 15-minute walk down Eki-mae-dōri south of Susukino, or one stop on the subway, lies the beautiful **Nakajima Park** ⓭ with its lakes, gardens, and two national cultural treasures: the tiny 17th-century Hassōan Teahouse, and the blue and white, Western-style Hoheikan. One block east of the park is the broad Tōyohira River where Sapporites go for dog walking, tennis, and weekend barbecues.

The other sights listed below are best reached by city sightseeing loop bus, subway, taxi, or bicycle rickshaw. Head to Susukino after 7 PM, when the street scene starts to pick up.

TIMING   You can see the sights downtown on foot in about 2½ hours, not including time spent meandering, looking into museums, shopping, and dining. In winter you can use the underground malls to cover large areas of downtown. Using the Odōri subway station as your center point, you can walk east to the TV Tower and the shopping center Sapporo Factory, or head south to get to the Susukino subway station without venturing out into the snow.

What to See

❹ **Botanical Gardens** (Shokubutsu-en, 札幌植物園). With more than 5,000 plant varieties, the Shokubutsu-en makes for a cool retreat in the summer, both for its green space and its shade. ⊠ *Kita 3-jō Nishi 8, Chūo-ku* 🚇 *May–Oct. gardens and greenhouse ¥400; Nov.–Apr. gardens free, greenhouse ¥110* 🕐 *Apr.–Sept., daily 9–4; Oct.–Nov., daily 9–3:30; Dec.–Mar., weekdays 9–5.*

❻ **Clock Tower** (Tokeidai, 時計台). This is Sapporo's most identifiable landmark. It was built in 1878 in Russian style, and a clock from Boston was added three years later. Other than being on every Sapporo travel brochure, it's rather ordinary. Inside the building a museum recounts the local history of Sapporo and includes displays on the tower and photos from Sapporo's early history. ⊠ *Kita 1-jō Nishi 2, Chūo-ku* 🚇 *¥200* 🕐 *Tues.–Sat. 9–5.*

10 **The Downtown Underground** (Chikagai, 地下街). Sapporo's subterranean promenades make perfectly protected shopping routes during the harsh winters. The passages form a "T" of shops and restaurants, intersecting at the Ōdōri subway station where the Namboku and Tōzai subway lines cross. Pole Town is the T's vertical leg, extending north all the way from beneath the clock in the middle of the Susukino crossing. Aurora Town, the east–west cap to the T, runs from below the TV Tower to Nishi 5-chōe.

★ ▶ **2** **JR Tower Observatory** (JRタワー展望台). Hokkaido's newest man-made viewpoint is atop Sapporo Station. It rises to 567 feet and from the observation floor at 524 feet has views of the coast, the Daisetsu mountains, and the downtown grid. You can get almost the same view (south only) for free from the 36th floor, reached via the JR Tower Hotel Nikko. ⊠ *JR Sapporo Station, Stellar Place 6th fl.,* ☎ *011/209–5500* 💴 *¥900* ⊙ *10 AM–11 PM.*

13 **Nakajima Kōen** (Nakajima Park, 中島公園). Some historic sites, along with a small lake for boating (¥600 for 40 minutes) and Japanese and Western gardens, make this city park worth a visit.

One of Nakajima Park's national cultural treasures is the 17th-century **Hassō-an Teahouse** (八窓庵), harmoniously surrounded by a Japanese garden on the west side of the park. The small hut is less impressive than its setting. 💴 *Free* ⊙ *May–Oct., daily 9–4.*

The other cultural treasure in Nakajima Kōen is **Hōheikan** (豊平館), a stately Western-style building originally constructed as an imperial guest house. The empty interior, which is hired out for lunch parties, does not offer much to visit, but the blue-and-white exterior makes a grand sight—especially when the cherry blossoms are out. 💴 *Free* ⊙ *Daily 9–5.*

12 **Nijō-ichiba Market** (二条市場). Gleaming piles of crab and fish, packs of seaweed, and hustling vendors are all photo opportunities at Sapporo's one-block fish market. Actual purchases are better made in supermarkets or department stores with less-inflated prices—but free tastings are worth the five-minute walk across the river behind the TV Tower. ⊠ *Minami 3, Higashi 1, Chūo-ku.*

9 **Ōdōri Kōen** (Ōdōri Park, 大通公園). This 345-foot-wide, east–west avenue park bisects the city center. It's a good place to people-watch in summer, when office workers buy lunch from various food vendors and take in the sun, so long absent during the winter months. Various events are held here in succession from June through August; in February the park displays large, lifelike snow sculptures that the Japanese Self-Defense Forces create for the Sapporo Snow Festival, which has made the city famous. ⊠ *Ōdōri.*

3 **Old Hokkaidō Government Building** (Hokkaidō Kyū Honchōsha, 北海道旧本庁舎). The grandest structure in Hokkaidō, this Western-style building was erected in 1888 and now contains rather dry exhibits about the early development of Hokkaidō. Its nickname, *Aka Renga*, means "Ol' Redbrick." It's just northwest of the Grand Hotel in a complex of municipal buildings and is closed the third Thursday of every month. ⌧ *Kita 2–jō at Nishi 5* ☎ *011/231–4111* 📧 *Free* 🕐 *Apr.–Sept., weekdays 9–5; Oct.–Mar., weekdays 9–5.*

❼ Plaza i (プラザi). English-speaking staff members at the Ōdōri or JR station desks are extremely helpful in distributing free brochures, maps, and flyers on current happenings in town and will send and receive faxes. They can assist with accommodations throughout the area. The "Hokkaidō Trekking and Onsen Guide" and the "Hokkaidō Camping Guide" at ¥400 and hiking map booklets at ¥100 each are excellent English-language information. ⌧ *Kita 1-jō Nishi 3, JR Sapporo Station, south exit (west), Chūō-ku, Ōdōri; Station* ☎ *011/211–3678 or 011/209–5030* 🖨 *011/219–0020 or 011/209–5021* ⊕ *www.plaza-sapporo. or.jp* 🕐 *Daily 9–5:30.*

❺ Sapporo Grand Hotel (札幌グランドホテル). Classical European architecture appears so out of place in Japan, especially in modern Sapporo, that the columns and majestic lobby of the Sapporo Grand make it even more of a landmark than the Clock Tower. The hotel has a bustling café looking out on the street, and a lobby display of its famous guests and the food they ate, such as the Tiffin Menu for the New York Yankees in '55. ⌧ *Kita 1-jō Nishi 4, Chūō-ku, Ōdōri Station area* ☎ *011/261–3311.*

❽ Sapporo International Communication Plaza (Sapporo Kokusai Kōryū Puraza, 札幌国際プラザ). Established to facilitate commercial and cultural relations with the world beyond Japan, this center is the best place for getting suggestions on travel in Hokkaidō and for meeting other people who speak English. It's also a useful place to have something translated from Japanese into English. The center has a salon with books, newspapers, and brochures in English and is meant for informal socializing. Ask foreign residents and Japanese about their favorite restaurants and nightspots. For up-to-date information on local cultural events, pick up a free copy of *What's On in Sapporo* and *Xene* at the salon information counter. The Clock Tower faces the building. ⌧ *3rd fl., Kita 1-jō Nishi 3, Chūō-ku, Ōdōri* ☎ *011/221–2105* 🕐 *Mon.–Sat. 9–5:30.*

Sapporo JR Station Area. The mundane business of buying a rail ticket is almost hidden within a shopping metropolis of glass and concrete. The south side of the station complex has: Daimaru, a department store; Stellar Place, a 10-floor mall; Cinema Frontier, a 12-screen multiplex; an observation deck in the tower; a hotel; and three major electronics stores. There's even a Gothic castle–theme wedding hall. Shopping is mainly clothes for the young and slim, but dining options include 22 restaurants on Stellar Place's sixth and ninth floors (open until 11 PM). In the basement, Sony Plaza has plenty of American candies for any travelers not getting their required sugar-fix from Japanese chocolate. ⌧ *Bordered by Kita 7–jō, Nishi 4, and Kita 5–jō, and Nishi 1.*

⓫ Tanuki Mall (Tanuki Kōji, 狸小路). A *tanuki* is a raccoon dog, which in Japanese mythology is known for its cunning and libidinous nature. The Tanuki Kōji covered arcade got its name because the place used to be frequented by prostitutes, who displayed similar characteristics when it came to relieving their clients of cash. Now it's the arcade's merchants who are so eager to lighten the wallets of passersby. Its sides are crowded with small shops selling clothing, footwear, electronics, records, and, inevitably, Ainu-inspired souvenirs of Hokkaidō. Tanuki Kōji has considerably lower prices than the area's department stores. It's also the place to find Hokkaidō specialties—from melon confections to dried salmon and seaweed—which are good presents for Japanese friends on Honshū. ⊠ *Minami 3-jō, extending from Nishi 1 to 7, Chūō-ku.*

Elsewhere in Sapporo

★ **Historical Museum of Hokkaidō** (Kaitaku Kinenkan, 開拓記念館). Exhibits here range from ancient bones to cultural artifacts, early home appliances, and the propaganda materials created to persuade mainland settlers to head north. The drawback is the location, about 10 km (6 mi) outside Sapporo. Japan Rail buses depart Tuesday through Friday at 9, 9:30, and 10 AM from Sapporo Station for the ¥230, one-hour trip. Alternatively, take a 10-minute taxi ride from Shin–Sapporo Station. ⊠ *Konopporo, Atsubetsu-chō, Atsubetsu-ku* ☎ *011/898–0456* ⊠ ¥300 ☽ *Tues.–Sat. 9:30–4:30.*

★ ☽ **Historical Village of Hokkaidō** (Kaitaku-no-mura, 北海道開拓の村). More than 60 old buildings from all over Hokkaidō have been brought together to form this reconstructed village, and an excellent English guidebook helps you understand farm and village life 100 years ago. The centerpiece is the former Sapporo railway station, a glorious red-and-white edifice that served as the city's gateway from 1908 to 1952. In winter, horse-drawn sleighs tour the village. The entrance gate to the village is a five-minute walk from the Historical Museum. ⊠ *1–50–1 Konopporo, Atsubetsu-chō, Atsubetsu-ku* ☎ *011/898–2692* ⊠ ¥610 ☽ *Tues.–Sun. 9:30–4:30.*

Hokkaidō Shrine (Hokkaidō Jingu, 北海道神宮). Hidden away in the forests of Maruyama Park, the 1871 Shintō shrine is home to three gods deemed helpful in Hokkaidō's development: the gods for land and nature, for land development, and for healing. The main courtyard is open until 5 PM daily, and apart from small children and newlyweds, new cars can be seen getting blessed by the priests. In May this is Sapporo's main *hanami* (cherry blossom) party venue. It's a 15-minute walk from Maruyama subway station. ⊠ *Maruyama Kōen, Chūō-ku.*

Hokkaidō University (Hokkaidō Daigaku, 北海道大学). The beautiful, manicured grounds of Hokkaidō University, with its stately 19th-century buildings, are worth the 10-minute walk, or five-minute bicycle rickshaw ride, to the campus from the station. The school was founded in 1878, and the Clock Tower downtown was the original student drill-training hall. A bust honors Dr. William S. Clark, the school's first president and a central figure in Hokkaidō's development. The main gate is about 200 yards north of Sapporo Station; ask at the guardhouse for an English map and guide. ⊠ *Kita 8–jō to Kita-18-jō, Nishi 5, Kita-ku.*

off the beaten path

MOIWA-YAMA (Moiwa Mountain, 藻岩山) – A pleasant escape into the greenery around Sapporo city, the 45-minute hike to the top of this 1,742-ft hill is easy enough for local elementary kids to be taken here on excursions in early summer (be prepared to say *"hello!"* hundreds of times if you see children). The trail is guarded by many

SAPPORO FESTIVALS

ONE OF JAPAN'S BEST-KNOWN ANNUAL EVENTS, *held for a week beginning February 5 or 6, the* **Sapporo Snow Festival** *is the greatest of its kind. More than 300 lifelike ice sculptures, as large as 130 feet tall by 50 feet deep by 80 feet wide, are created each year. Recent memorable statues included baseball star Matsui, cavorting whales, dinosaurs, and world-famous buildings such as the Taj Mahal.*

The festival began in 1950 with six statues that were commissioned by the local government to entertain Sapporo citizens, depressed by the aftermath of the war and the long winter nights. Now the event is so large that the sculptures must be spread around three different sections of the city: Ōdōri Kōen, Makomanai, and Susukino. Besides sculptures of all sizes, you'll find ice slides for children. International teams of amateur and professional ice sculptors hired by major local businesses have four days to sculpt their creations as everyone looks on. Judges award prizes for the best sculptures toward the end of the festival. Although statues are roped off, taking photographs is no problem.

The festival attracts more than 2 million visitors each year, so book accommodations well in advance. The week before the festival is a good alternative visiting time, because you can see the statues taking shape and accommodations are easier to find.

During the **Yosakoi Festival** *every June, Sapporo's streets become the stage for one giant community dance festival, Japan's version of Carnaval. More than 40,000 performers go wild in brightly colored costumes and face paint as they run, jump, and chant their way through the city streets. Dance teams wave flags and snap naruko (wooden clappers) in the wakes of giant trucks mounted with powerful sound systems and taiko drummers in loincloths. Ticketed seats are available in stands lining the route in Ōdōri Kōen and at an outdoor stage, but they aren't necessary—most people just perch wherever they can get a vantage point. Dance teams also perform in Susukino at night. Yosakoi is far more exciting than the traditional bon ōdōri community dancing—a boisterous Japanese take on hip-hop crossed with aerobics.*

The Yosakoi Festival was started in 1992 and is based on the Koichi Festival in Shikoku. Dancers perform to music based on soran, a Hokkaidō fisherman's folk song. Yosakoi usually starts the second week of June, and the main events take place over a long weekend. More than 1.5 million spectators and participants come for the fun, so hotels are generally packed full.

jizō, Buddhist stone statues that are often dressed in red woolly caps and garish shirts donated by grateful supporters. From the top are views out to the sea, the UFO-like stadium used for the Soccer World Cup matches, and the city's surprisingly rural suburbs. Two restaurants and a shop sell sustenance for the hike down. The nearest trailhead to downtown is from behind the Jikeikai Hospital at Minami 13. Take a Rōpu-way sen bus from near Maruyama Bus terminal and get off at the Jikeikai stop. A cable car also reaches the top for ¥1,000 (round-trip). The cable car station is five-minutes' walk from the Rōpu-way Iriguchi stop on the city streetcar, ¥170 from either the Ōdōri or Susukino terminals.

Sapporo Beer Garden and Museum (Sapporō Biiru-en, 札幌ビール園＆博物館). During the day, free tours through the redbrick museum will acquaint you with the history and the modern brewing technology of Hokkaidō's most famous product. Museum reservations are required; request a guide who speaks some English. But the real fun of coming here is the huge beer garden and the cavernous, three-tier beer hall. Most of the action occurs during the evening in the hall, which is similar in atmosphere to a German beer hall. It was a German, after all, who, upon finding wild hops growing on Hokkaidō, taught locals how to make beer. Instead of bratwurst, however, the beer garden's *Jingisukan* ("Ghengis Kahn" or griddle-cooked lamb) is the highlight.

In summer the beer garden is a gathering place day and evening, good for seeing and meeting the Japanese at play. The *tabe-nomi-hodai* (all you can eat and drink) menu means mugs of lager downed with gusto amid exclamations of *"Kampai!"*—"Bottoms up!" Around February, snow sculptures and igloos festoon the site. The beer garden is on the Factory Line circular bus route, or a ¥1,000 taxi ride from downtown ⊠ *Kita 7-jō Higashi 9, Higashi-ku,* ☎ *011/731–4368 museum, 011/742–1531 restaurant* ⊠ *Free* ⊙ *Museum Sept.–May, daily 9–5; June–Aug., daily 8:40–6, last entry 80 min before closing; beer garden May–Sept. daily 11–9:30; Oct.–Apr., daily 11–8:45.*

Sapporo Factory (サッポロファクトリー). A soaring glass roof 275 feet above an indoor garden and shopping mall creates an oasis of greenery when all is snowy outside. The complex occupies several buildings— including the old Sapporo Beer brewery, which retains its distinctive red brick and chimney. Among the venues are a 1,500-seat beer restaurant, a wine cellar containing some 2,000 varieties of wine, an IMAX theater, and 11 movie theaters. ⊠ *Kita 2-jō Higashi 4, Chūō-ku* ⊙ *Store daily 10–8; restaurants daily 11–10, except Nutberry Club, 11 AM–3 AM.*

Sapporo Winter Sports Museum (札幌ウィンタースポーツミュージアム). Leap off a ski jump on a simulator or try your skills at ice hockey or curling at Sapporo's newest museum near the Olympic Ōkura Jump. The enormous slope is visible from downtown, and the views from the competitors' chairlift are chilling. Take a 15-minute bus ride from Maruyama Bus Terminal, City Bus Nishi 14 (¥200). ⊠ *1274 Miyanomori, Chūō-ku* ☎ *011/641–1972* ⊠ *¥600* ⊙ *May–Oct., daily 9–6; Nov.–Apr., daily 9:30–5.*

Where to Eat

Most of Sapporo's restaurants, whatever the culinary origin, use visual displays for their menus. The greatest concentration of restaurants for nighttime dining is in the entertainment district of Susukino; daytime key locations are the downtown department stores and at the JR station. Formal dining rooms and/or coffee shops in all the major hotels serve Continental food. Invariably, the food will be French-inspired and expensive. Most larger hotels also have at least one Japanese restaurant and a Chinese restaurant.

Hokkaidō is known for its ramen, and Sapporo for its miso ramen. The city has more than 1,000 ramen shops, so it won't be hard to find a noodle lunch. For a truly Japanese dining experience, head to the **Ramen Yoko-chō** (ラーメン横丁) area, a small alley that has as many as three dozen tiny ramen shops with counter service. You'll need to get in and out in less than five minutes, and the next customer will be standing behind you waiting for your seat. The alley runs perpendicular to Susukino-dōri, or Route 36.

To eat cheaply and without the pressure of the next ramen-shop customer looking over your shoulder, you might try one of the large *iza-kaya* (restaurant–bars) in **Susukino,** many of which have gaijin-friendly menus with pictures.

$$$$ ✕ **Chanko Kita-no-Fuji** (ちゃんこ北の富士). Ever wonder how sumō wrestlers bulk into fighting form? Find the answer here: *chanko nabe,* a hot pot of meat or seafood and vegetables. The restaurant's colorful replica of a sumō ring contributes to the lively atmosphere. The downside is rushed service and dingy tableside ambience. Reservations are strongly recommended, especially in winter—chanko season. ⊠ *Susukino Plaza Bldg., Minami 7-jō Nishi 4, 1st fl., Chūo-ku* ☎ *011/512–5484* ⌖ *Reservations essential* ⊟ *AE, DC, V.*

★ **$$$–$$$$** ✕ **Kani Honke** (かに本家). A crab-eating heaven, this restaurant serves raw, steamed, boiled, and baked crustaceans from the Hokkaidō (or Russian) seas. The waitress will tell you whether the *ke-gani* (hairy crab), *taraba* (king crab), or *tzuwai-kani* (snow crab) is in season. The menu is in English and has photographs, so it's easy to choose from the set dinners, which start at ¥2,000. Wooden beams, tatami mats, and traditional decorations provide an authentic setting for the feast. There are two restaurants, one near the station and the other in Susukino. ⊠ *Station branch, Kita 3, Nishi 2* ☎ *011/222–0018* ⊠ *Susukino, Minami 6, Nishi 4* ☎ *011/551–0018* ⊟ *AE, DC, MC, V.*

$$$–$$$$ ✕ **Daruma** (だるま). Below the sign with a roly-poly red doll, this 40-year-old establishment serves the freshest Jingisukan (¥700 a plate). At the end of the meal, you're given hot tea to mix with the dipping sauce remaining from your meat. You drink the tea and sauce together: Delicious! Be sure to wear your least favorite clothes, store your coat in one of the lockers, and don a paper bib. ⊠ *Crystal Bldg., Minami 5 Nishi 4, Chūo-ku* ☎ *011/552–6013* ⌖ *Reservations not accepted* ⊟ *No credit cards* ⊗ *Closed Mon.* ⊠ *Noguchi Bldg., Minami 6 Nishi 4,*

Susukino ☎ 011/533–8929 ⚉ *Reservations not accepted* 🗏 *No credit cards* ⊘ *Closed Tues.*

★ $$$–$$$$ ✕ **Sushi-zen** (すし善). The fresh fish here is so good that even sushi novices may fall in love with it. Sushi-zen is an empire with three restaurants and a delivery service. To taste the best at bargain prices, time your visit to the Maruyama branch for the third Wednesday of every month—when the trainee chefs' sushi is available for ¥200 a piece. ✉ *Kita 1 Nishi 27, Maruyama, Chūō-ku* ☎ 011/644–0071 ✉ *109 Bldg., Minami 4 Nishi 5, Chūō-ku* ☎ 011/521–0070 ✉ *Minami 7 Nishi 4, Chūō-ku* ☎ 011/531–0069 🗏 *AE, DC MC, V* ⊘ *Closed Wed.*

★ $$$ ✕ **Sapporo Beer Garden** (サッポロビール園). All the beer you can drink in 100 minutes is included in the set dinners at this restaurant on the northeast side of the station. Jingisukan is a popular option, but other Japanese dishes are available, too. The atmosphere is festive in both the garden and in the cavernous halls of the old brewery, where you can also find a small museum. ✉ *Kita 7-jō Higashi 9, Higashi-ku* ☎ 011/742–1531 🗏 *AE, DC, MC, V.*

★ $$ ✕ **The Buffet** (ザ・ブッフェ). This restaurant is a serious contender for top place in Sapporo's highly competitive lunch-buffet wars. You can choose from a daunting, 70-dish spread of good-quality hot dishes from three cuisines, with more vegetables than usual and great desserts. At the top of Daimaru department store, the restaurant offers good views over the south side of the station. Avoiding the noon–1 lunchtime lines is easy, because lunch is served until 5 PM. From 5:30 PM a quieter dinner buffet starts. The basic lunch is ¥1,490, and dinner is ¥2,079. ✉ *Daimaru department store, 8th fl., JR Sapporo Station* ☎ 011/828–1263 ⚲ *No smoking* 🗏 *MC, V.*

¢–$$ ✕ **Zazi** (ザジ). A casual downtown coffee shop with an English menu, this hangout is popular with students and ex-pat customers. Favorites include the Power Lunch (¥1,000 for two fried eggs, sausages, potatoes, salad, and bread), generous spaghetti plates, one-pot stews for ¥630, and homemade cakes. Upstairs is more spacious, although you may have to share one of the large tables. Only one cook is working hard in the kitchen, so don't expect a speedy lunch. The restaurant opens at 10 AM. ✉ *Minami 2-jō, Nishi 5, Chūō-ku* ☎ 011/221–0074 🗏 *No credit cards.*

Where to Stay

★ $$$$ ✕🏨 **JR Tower Hotel Nikko Sapporo** (JRタワーホテル日航). Sapporo's skyscraper over the station puts the city at your feet from small, elegant rooms that look north to the university or south over downtown. Corner room prices buy more space, but not much view improvement. Tanchō and Sky J (¥2,000 lunch buffet) on the 35th floor serve delicately arranged Japanese food and Continental cooking. Japanese chef Mikuni has a French restaurant and coffee shop in the Nikko, too. ✉ *Sapporo Station JR Tower, Kita 5 Nishi 2, Chūō-ku, Sapporo 060-0005* ☎ 0120/58–2586 *or* 011/251–2222 🖷 011/251–6370 ⊕ *www.nikkohotels.com* ⚲ *350 Western-style rooms* ⚐ *3 restaurants, café, patisserie, hair salon, hot spring, massage, sauna, bar, Internet* 🗏 *AE, DC, MC, V.*

$$$$ 🏨 **Keio Plaza Hotel Sapporo** (京王プラザホテル札幌). The proximity of government offices and the university ensure a constant bustle around this

ON THE MENU

HOKKAIDŌ IS KNOWN FOR ITS SEAFOOD—*the prefecture's name means "the Road to the Northern Sea."* Shake *(salmon),* ika *(squid),* uni *(sea urchin),* nishin *(herring),* and kai *(shellfish) are abundant, but the real treat is the fat, sweet scallop,* kaibashira, *collected from northernmost Wakkanai. The other great favorite is* crab, *which comes in three varieties:* ke-gani *(hairy crab),* taraba-gani *(king crab),* and Nemuro's celebrated hanasaki-gani *(spiny king crab).*

ingisukan is thinly sliced mutton cooked on a dome-shape griddle. The name comes from the griddle's resemblance to helmets worn by Mongolian cavalry under Genghis Khan. Vegetables—usually onions, green peppers, and cabbage—are added to the sizzling mutton, and the whole mix is dipped in a tangy brown sauce. Ramen is extremely popular and inexpensive. Local residents favor miso ramen, which uses a less delicate variety of fermented soybean paste than does miso soup. Ramen with shio (salt) or shōyu (soy sauce) soup base is also widely available.

large modern hotel near the station. The staff is friendly, though, and can find an English speaker if required. The rooms are very spacious for a Japanese hotel. The Jurin coffee shop, which stays open until 2 AM, is a haven for jet-lagged travelers. You can also find an izakaya and sushi bar, a tea lounge, and a delicatessen. ☒ *Kita 5-jō Nishi 7, Chūō-ku, Sapporo 060-0005* ☎ *011/271–0111* 🖷 *011/221–5450* ⊕ *www.keioplaza-sapporo.co.jp* 🛏 *525 Western-style rooms* ♨ *7 restaurants, coffee shop, patisserie, tea shop, indoor pool, health club, 2 bars, Internet, car rental, travel services, no-smoking rooms* ▤ *AE, DC, MC, V.*

★ **$$$$** 🏨 **Sapporo Grand Hotel** (札幌グランドホテル). Built in 1934, Sapporo's oldest Western-style lodging retains the traditions of a great European hotel. Service is first-rate. Rooms in the newer annex have a fresher, more modern look than those in the older wing. The hotel's restaurants—Japanese, Chinese, French, and a pub—are more lively than you might expect from Sapporo's oldest hotel. For a less expensive meal in the opulent surroundings, it's worth checking out the lunch specials. The Grand is also keeping up with the times—machines to make prints from digital camera pictures are in the lobby. ☒ *Kita 1-jō Nishi 4, Chūō-ku, Sapporo 060-0001* ☎ *011/261–3311* 🖷 *011/231–0388* ⊕ *www.mitsuikanko.co.jp/sgh* 🛏 *560 Western-style rooms* ♨ *9 restaurants,* coffee shop, room service, in-room safes, minibars, cable TV, shops, Internet, travel services, no-smoking rooms ⊟ AE, DC, MC, V.

★ **$$$–$$$$** 🏨 **Hotel Ōkura** (ホテルオークラ). Right in the shopping heart of the city, one block from the Ōdōri subway station and the park, this stylish, friendly hotel has spacious rooms in browns and creams. Rooms have lighting and interior blinds that set a Japanese mood missing in many large hotels—plus modern necessities such as CNN. Dining highlights include quality Cantonese dishes in Toh-Li—the ¥3,700 lunch sets for couples are a good way to dine economically, and the ¥3,600 afternoon tea centers around your very own cake stand of goodies. Reservations 24 hours in advance are essential for the tea. ⊠ *Nishi 5 Minami 1, Chūō-ku, Sapporo 060-0061* ☎ *011/221–2333* 🖷 *011/221–0819* ⊕ *www.hotelokura.co.jp/sapporo* 🛏 *147 Western-style rooms* ♻ *3 restaurants, coffee shop, cable TV, hair salon, bar, shop, Internet, no-smoking floor* ⊟ *AE, DC, MC, V.*

$$$ 🏨 **Nakamuraya Ryokan** (中村屋旅館). This inn near the botanical gardens dates from 1898—ancient for Sapporo—though the current building is more recent. The six tatami-mat rooms seem larger because of their spacious cupboards, built-in minibars, and wide window shelf. Rooms have tiny private bathrooms. The staff is welcoming to foreign guests, particularly if you're carrying this guidebook. The large communal bath is a welcome comfort in winter. The Japanese dinner (included, along with breakfast, in the rate) is expansive, with a selection of fresh seafood from local waters. ⊠ *Kita 3-jō Nishi 7, Chūō-ku, Sapporo 060-0003* ☎ *011/241–2111* 🖷 *011/241–2118* 🛏 *29 Japanese-style rooms* ♻ *Restaurant, minibars, Japanese baths* ⊟ *AE, MC, V* ⦿ *MAP.*

$ 🏨 **Hotel Maki** (ホテル牧). A family hotel, Maki offers a change of style from the sterility of big city hotels, and the Inada family speaks a little English. Half the rooms have baths; all have toilets and washbasins. There's also a general bath. The hotel is a favorite with out-of-town sports teams, who wolf down the extensive Japanese-style breakfast available for ¥900. It's in a quiet area just five streetcar stops from Susukino or 10 minutes from Horohirabashi subway station. ⊠ *1–20 Minami 13 Nishi 7, Chūō-ku, Sapporo 064-0913* ☎ *011/521–1930* 🖷 *011/531–6747* 🛏 *15 Japanese-style rooms* ♻ *Dining room, Japanese baths; no a/c* ⊟ *No credit cards* ⦿ *MAP.*

Nightlife

★ **Susukino** (すすきの), Sapporo's entertainment district, is a night owl's paradise, with more than 5,000 bars, nightclubs, and restaurants providing bacchanalian delights, Japanese style. The compact area, illuminated with lanterns and flashing signs, is mind-boggling, and in itself justifies an overnight stay in Sapporo. Most bars remain open until the wee hours, some as late as 5 AM, though restaurants often close before midnight. Susukino is bounded by Minami 3-jō, Minami 7-jō, Nishi 2-chōme, and Nishi 6-chōme. The seedier alleys are mostly west of Station-mae-dōri, but all of Susukino is safe.

Make sure that you know what kind of bar you're going into before you enter. There are several kinds: clubs stocked with hostesses who make small talk (¥5,000 and up per hour, proving that talk is *not* cheap);

sunakku bars (the word sounds like "snack," which translates into fewer hostesses and expensive *ōdoburu*—hors d'oeuvres); izakaya, for both Japanese and Western food and drink; bars with entertainment, either karaoke or live music; and "soapland" and *herusu* (health) massage parlors, which are generally off-limits to non-Japanese without an introduction. If at all possible, go to the clubs and *sunakku* with a Japanese-speaking acquaintance. Signs that say NO CHARGE only mean that there's no charge to be seated; you should beware of hidden extras. Many bars add on all sorts of strange charges for peanuts, female companionship, song, cold water, hand towel, etc. The term "free drink" refers to an all-you-can-drink special that does cost money.

On the Ōdōri side of the road dividing Susukino and Ōdōri is beer bar **Slainte** (スランチェ; ✉ Playtown Fuji Bldg., 8th fl., Minami 3-jō Nishi 3, Ōdōri ☎ 011/222–6801), with 13 seats at a quiet counter bar. You can find Japanese and foreign beers on tap, and 12 kinds of Irish whiskey. Slainte is open every evening from 5 to midnight. At **Saloon Maco** (✉ Asano Bldg., 2nd fl., Minami 3-jō Nishi 4, Ōdōri ☎ 011/222–4828), Stetson-wearing Japanese staff (and drinkers) sing country and pop karaoke, fortified by a generous no-time-limit *nomi-hodai* (all-you-can-drink plan) for ¥2,000. Pasta and salad dishes go for under ¥1,000. Look behind the JRA building to find this bar.

Powerful British rock and roll is played in five nightly sets by bar owner Kazuaki and his band at **Brits Beat Club** (✉ Green Bldg. No. 4, 2nd fl., Minami 5-jō Nishi 3, Susukino ☎ 011/531–8808 ⊕ www.brits.jp). The small bar serves cheap Brit fare, such as fish-and-chips and cottage pie, while Kazu and the guys play everything from Beatles to Blur. There's a ¥2,100 cover charge, and the bar is open nightly from 8 PM to 4 AM.

On Susukino's main street, drinkers perch on high bar stools to check out the action through the big windows at **Rad Brothers** (✉ Minami 7 jō Nishi 3 ☎ 011/561–3601). Weekend dancers and drinkers head for **Booty** (✉ Minami 8-jō Nishi 4, ☎ 011/521–2336 ⊕ www.booty-disco.com). The big armchairs and sofas on the second floor offer a respite from the exertions downstairs, where French owner DJ Sebastien and others stir up a sweaty, sexy scene. Booty is open Friday and Saturday nights. If you're looking for a quiet drinking spot and good tacos, try **Viva** (✉ Minami 7-jō Nishi 4, ☎ 011/532–1349), open nightly from 7 PM until 1 AM.

Sapporo A to Z

AIR TRAVEL

There are no nonstop flights from the United States to Hokkaidō. Passengers arriving in Japan on international flights with All Nippon Airways (ANA) and Japan Airlines (JAL) can get domestic discounted connections to Chitose. The Hokkaidō-based Air Do (rhymes with "who") often has the least expensive flights between Tōkyō and Sapporo. The company No. 1 Travel caters to the travel needs of foreigners in Japan and can offer good deals on domestic travel.

🛈 Airlines & Contacts **Air Do** ☎ 011/200–7333. **Japan Air System** ☎ 0120/711–283 international, 0120/511–283 domestic. **Japan Airlines** ☎ 0120/255–931 international, 0120/

255–971, 011/232–3690 domestic. **Japan Travel Bureau** ☎ 011/241–6201. **No. 1 Travel** ☎ 011/251–3314 or 03/3205–6073 🖷 011/251–4607 ⊕ www.no1-travel.com.

AIRPORTS & TRANSFERS

Sapporo's New Chitose Airport (Shin-Chitose Kūkō), 40 km (25 mi) south of the city, is Hokkaidō's main airport. More than 30 domestic routes link Chitose to the rest of Japan, and flights from Chitose to other parts of Asia are increasing.

🛈 Airport Information New Chitose Airport ☎ 0123/23–0111.

AIRPORT TRANSFERS   Japan Railways (JR) runs every 20 minutes or so between the airport terminal and downtown Sapporo. (Shin-Chitose Kūkō Station is the final eastbound stop from Sapporo; do not get off at the Chitose or Minami Chitose stations if you want the airport.) The trip is usually made by rapid transit train (¥1,040, 40 minutes). Hokuto Bus runs a shuttle bus (¥820) that connects with ANA flights at Chitose and its hotel, the ANA Zennikku, in Sapporo, first stopping at the Renaissance and Sunroute hotels. Chūō Bus (¥820) runs a shuttle between the airport and Sapporo's Grand Hotel, also stopping at Ōdōri Kōen, JR Sapporo Station, and the Korakuen, Royton, and Keio Plaza hotels. These buses reach the airport in under an hour, though you should allow more time in winter. Taxis are available, but ridiculously expensive.

🛈 Hukuto Bus ☎ 011/377–3855.

BUS TRAVEL

Local bus fares begin at ¥200. Buses follow the grid system and run until shortly after 11 PM. There are no English schedules for buses in Sapporo, and bus-stand information is all in Japanese. However, two circular routes connect many of the main sites. The Factory Line—bus stops are confusingly marked "Sapporo Walk"—connects downtown shops, the train station, the fish market, Sapporo Factory, and the Sapporo Beer Garden. The Sansaku or Stroller Bus (May to October only) connects downtown with Maruyama Park and Ōkurayama Jump Hill. Rides on both cost ¥200 each time or ¥750 for a day pass. In summer, a ¥1,200 day pass gives unlimited rides on both circular bus lines as well as a one-way ticket to Shin-Chitose Airport. Tickets are available on the buses or from Chūō Bus counter at the JR station or bus terminal.

🛈 Bus Information Chūō Bus ☎ 011/231–0500.

CAR TRAVEL

Driving is the best way to see Hokkaidō, because the distances are vast and public transport is patchy. Fortunately, major road signs are in English as well as Japanese. Small cars can be rented for about ¥6,000 a day. Alternatively, travel by train first and then rent a car from near the station for local exploring. Beware of police speed traps, as Hokkaidō's roads are straight and empty, and it's easy to go over the 50 kph to 60 kph (31 mph to 37 mph) limits in rural areas.

Sapporo has two expressways. The Dō Expressway heads southeast to Chitose, then the main route veers southwest to hug Hokkaidō's underside as far as Oshamanbe, while a very underused branch—an infamous Hokkaidō white-elephant government project—goes east to near

Yubari. The Sasson Expressway links Otaru to the west with Asahikawa in the northeast.

ROAD CONDITIONS Information on road conditions is available during the winter. It's only in Japanese, however, so if you're not conversant, ask the staff at your hotel or Plaza i to place the call for you.

🔲 **Plaza i** ☎ 011/211-3678. **Road Conditions** ☎ 011/281-6511.

CONSULATE

🔲 **U.S. Consulate** ⊠ Kita 1-jō Nishi 28, Chuo-ku, Maruyama Park, Sapporo ☎ 011/641-1115.

EMERGENCIES

🔲 **Ambulance** ☎ 119. **Hokkaidō University Hospital** ⊠ Kita 14-jō Nishi 5, Sapporo ☎ 011/716-1161. **Nighttime Emergency Hospital** ⊠ Ōdōri Nishi 16, Ōdōri, Sapporo ☎ 011/641-4316. **Police** ☎ 110. **Sapporo City General Hospital** ⊠ Kita 11-jō Nishi 13, Sōen Station, Sapporo ☎ 011/726-2211.

ENGLISH-LANGUAGE MEDIA

BOOKS Outside Sapporo, finding English-language books is difficult, so you may want to browse in Sapporo's two largest bookstores: Kinokuniya and Maruzen. Sprawling Tower Records sells magazines in Japanese and in English to trend-hungry young locals. More reasonable prices can be found at New Day Books, where long-time residents Terry and Kathleen Riggins have hundreds of second-hand titles.

🔲 **Kinokuniya** ⊠ Dai-ni Yūraku Bldg., 2nd fl., Minami 1-jō Nishi 1, Ōdōri, Sapporo ☎ 011/231-2131. **Maruzen** ⊠ Minami 1-jō Nishi 3, 4th fl., Ōdōri, Sapporo ☎ 011/241-7251. **New Day Books** ⊠ Sanyu Bldg., 3F, Minami 2-jō Nishi 5, Ōdōri, Sapporo ☎ 011/223-6819. **Tower Records** ⊠ Pivot Bldg., 7th fl., Minami 2-jō Nishi 4, Ōdōri, Sapporo ☎ 011/241-3851.

STREETCARS

Sapporo has a streetcar service with a flat fare of ¥170. However, it's confined to a single line connecting Susukino with Moiwa-yama in the city's southwest corner—well away from most of the sights mentioned in this section—and has remained in business more because of public affection than profitability. In an effort to scrape a little more money out of the service, the city has made its streetcars available to be rented out for parties, and you may see the vehicles trundling across town with a crowd of revelers on board.

SUBWAYS

Sapporo's subway is a pleasure. Trains have rubber wheels that run quietly, and most signs include English. There are three lines. The Namboku Line runs south from JR Sapporo Station past Susukino to Nakajima Kōen; the Tōzai Line bisects the city from east to west. These two cross at Ōdōri Station. The third, the Tōhō Line, enters central Sapporo from the southeast of the city, then parallels the Namboku Line from Ōdōri Station to the JR station before branching off into the northeastern suburbs.

The basic fare, covering a distance of about three stations, is ¥200. A one-day open ticket (*ichi-nichi-ken*) for ¥1,000 provides unlimited access to the subway, bus, and streetcar (¥800 for the subway alone); a ¥700 Eco-ticket (*ekokippu*), intended to encourage residents to leave their cars at home for the day, covers the same three types of public transport on the 5th and 20th of every month. These tickets are available at any subway station and at the Ōdōri Station Underground Commuters' Ticket Office, open weekdays 8:30–7, weekends 10–5:30. Prepaid cards (available for ¥1,000, ¥3,000, ¥5,000, and ¥10,000 at vending machines) automatically debit the appropriate amount when you've reached your destination and give you a 10% discount. Trains stop running at midnight.

TAXIS

Taxi meters start at ¥550 or ¥600, depending on the company. Check the basic fare, which is posted on the door, before you get in. An average fare, such as from the JR station to Susukino, runs about ¥800 ($7).

TRAIN TRAVEL

All JR trains arrive at the central station, on the north side of downtown Sapporo. Trains depart for Honshū about every two hours. The route sometimes involves a change of trains in Hakodate. As many as six trains per hour run to and from Otaru and east. Every half hour from 7 AM to 10 PM there are trains north to Asahikawa.

TRANSPORTATION AROUND SAPPORO

Sapporo is a walking city with wide sidewalks; it's easy to find your way around. The International Information Corner (⇨ Visitor Information at Sapporo Station or opposite Tokei-dai has city maps, and most hotels have a smaller map marking their locations and major points of interest. The finest map is in *Travelers' Sapporo,* a free brochure available at all of the tourist offices and at the Ōdōri subway station. Give your tired feet a break by taking one of the bicycle rickshaws (¥500 for 10 minutes, ¥3,000 for one hour) that can be picked up near Ōdōri Kōen.

VISITOR INFORMATION

The most helpful places for information on Sapporo and Hokkaidō in general are the International Information Corner, open daily from 9 to 5 except the second and fourth Wednesday of the month (second Wednesday only January, February, and July–September), at the southwest exit of the JR station; and the Sapporo International Communication Plaza's tourist office, Plaza i, opposite Tokei-dai, which is open daily from 9 to 5:30.

Look for copies of the magazine *Xene* in hotels and bookstores for its listings of local and Hokkaidō-wide events and festivals, as well as coupons and articles. *What's On in Sapporo* informs readers of local events. You'll find it at Plaza i.

🚺 Tourist Information **Kokusai Jōhō** (International Information Corner) ⊠ Sapporo Station ☎ 011/209-5030. **Plaza i** ⊠ MN Bldg., Kita 1-jō Nishi 3, Ōdōri, Sapporo ☎ 011/211-3678.

OTARU & NISEKO 小樽とニセコ

West of Sapporo, the small port city of Otaru faces out to the Japan Sea. Its historic canal and commercial quarter are worth seeing in a day trip from Sapporo, and Otaru is easily reached by rail. Over the mountains in the hinterland lies the Niseko area, where the perfect cone-shape

Mount Yōtei—Hokkaidō's Fuji—is surrounded by a farming region dotted with villages and hot springs. In winter this is one of Japan's leading ski areas, while from May to October outdoor enthusiasts enjoy river rafting and hiking. Niseko is best experienced by car over two or three days.

Otaru   小樽

★ ⑭ *50 min west of Sapporo by JR, 40 km (25 mi) west of Sapporo by car.*

Otaru is known for its Meiji-era canal as well as its stone and wood warehouses, and the commercial buildings on what was once dubbed the Wall Street of the North. Its image as a charming port city and romantic weekend retreat from Sapporo has made Otaru a popular spot for domestic tourists; gaijin are usually less impressed with the single canal and its adjacent tourist strip. Walk away from the main drag, however, and you can find quaint neighborhoods to explore and interesting buildings to see. In contrast to modern Sapporo, Otaru is a quieter, less touristy base for a Hokkaidō stay. One black mark—Otaru gained infamy as the home of Yunohana Onsen in Temiya, which tried to ban foreign bathers and subsequently got hit by a lawsuit brought on by local foreign residents.

The **Otaru tourist office** (小樽駅観光案内所; ☎ 0134/29–1333) is to the left of the ticket gates inside the station. It's open daily 9–6, but as it shares office space with the JR travel office, the staff is somewhat harried. You can get more attention at the **Unga Plaza tourist office** (運河プラザ観光案内所; ☎ 0134/33–1661), by the canal. From the station, walk straight down the main street for about eight minutes; the office is in the stone buildings on the left before the canal.

You can find the canal and **Sakai-machi Street Historic District** (堺町本通り) sandwiched between a contemporary shopping area and a busy port about 10 minutes' walk downhill from the station. A one-day pass ¥750 on the replica trolley car bus is a useful energy-saver; and sun-burned rickshaw runners offer tours starting at ¥3,000 for two people. A 20-minute, ¥200 bus ride from the station (Bus No. 3) to the Otaru Aquarium area, which includes a rocky peninsula and historic fishing houses, is a good way to start your sightseeing. Alternatively, rent a bicycle (about ¥400 an hour) three blocks south of the station.

In the port you'll see Russian ships and ferries from Niigata, plus sightseeing boats in summer. The Russian presence is quite noticeable in Otaru—one telephone booth even has a helpful area code list for sailors calling home.

Otaru City Museum (Otaru Hakubutsukan, 小樽博物館). In a former warehouse, this museum combines natural history exhibits with displays about the town's development since the 19th century. It's in the same building as the Unga Plaza tourist office, eight minutes on foot south of the JR station. ✉ *2–1–20 Ironai* ☎ *0134/33–2439* 🎫 *¥100* 🕘 *Daily 9:30–5.*

☺ **Otaru Aquarium** (Otaru Suizokukan, 小樽水族館). Hokkaidō's only worthwhile aquarium is on a stunning, windy peninsula 3 km (2 mi) from downtown. There are 20,000 fish and mammals in the collection and some of the tanks are at sea level. Highlights include a marine mammal show with a cast of dolphins and seals, plus penguins. ✉ *3–303*

Shukutsu ☎ 0134/33–1400 💳 ¥1,300 🕙 *Apr.–Oct., daily 9–5; Nov.–Mar., daily 9–4.*

★ **Herring Mansion** (Nishin Mansion, 錬御殿). Herring fishermen ate, slept, and dreamt of riches in this 1897 home of a fishery boss, which now contains artifacts and photographic memories of the herring heyday. ☒ 3–228 *Shukutsu* ☎ 0134/22–1038 💳 ¥200 🕙 *Apr.–Nov., daily 9–5.*

Aoyama Villa (Aoyama Bettei, 旧青山別邸). Gorgeous painted sliding doors and lacquered floors testify to the huge wealth that could be made from herring. It's all on show at this villa built around 1917 by the Chief Imperial carpenter in a sumptuousness rare in Hokkaidō. Gyokudo Kawai, a master artist, and 10 followers created many of the sliding-door paintings and calligraphies. Take bus No. 3 from the station to the Shukutsu 3-chōme bus stop, then walk up the hill for about 10 minutes. ☒ *Shukutsu 3–63* ☎ 0134/24–0024 💳 ¥1,000 🕙 *Apr.–Oct., daily 9–6; Nov.–Mar., daily 9–5.*

🕙 **Goblin Hall** (Tengu-no-yakata, 天狗の館). You can come nose to nose with a *tengu* (long-nose goblin) at this small museum. It contains hundreds of goblin masks and is incongruously situated alongside a room detailing Japanese success in various Winter Olympics. To get to Tengu-no-yakata, take a 15-minute Chuo Bus ride from Otaru Station to the Tengu-yama Ropeway and then ride the cable car (¥1,000) to the top of the mountain. ☒ *Tengu-yama, Otaru* ☎ 0134/33–7381 💳 *Free* 🕙 *Daily 10–5.*

Where to Stay & Eat

$$–$$$$ ✕ **Uomaru** (魚○ (うおまる)). Barbecue your own fish and vegetables on table-top charcoal burners in a former canal-side warehouse. The wood and stone interior has both Western-style and Japanese-style tables. The *hokkai marugoto sumbiyaki* (pick-of-Hokkaidō charcoal grill) sets include varying combinations of crab, squid, shrimp, scallops, and vegetables. Raw fish and salmon roe side dishes cost ¥3,150–¥5,250. ☒ *5–4 Minato-machi* ☎ 0134/31–2255 🟰 *MC, V,.*

$$ ✕ **Kita Hōru** (北ホール). You probably won't be able to write postcards in the gloom here, but chances are you won't want to. Oil lamps and their reflection off the glassware lining the walls are the only source of illumination in this cavernous dining room, an 1891 former herring warehouse with heavy, circular tables and beer-barrel seating. Fish and rice dishes are the mainstay, or you can order coffee and cakes from the slightly atmosphere-jarring self-service machine at the entrance. ☒ *7–26 Sakai-machi* ☎ 0134/33–1993 🟰 *No credit cards.*

¢–$ ✕ **Sakaiya** (さかい家). Traditional desserts and light meals, including vegetables in cheese sauce and various soups, are served in Sakaya, a 1907 fancy-goods store. The dining room is resplendent in dark woods and 100-year-old, double-glazed windows. A 3-ton safe with triple doors is the centerpiece of the room. Try *macha-kintoki*, a bowl of azuki beans and sweet rice dumplings, topped with green-tea ice cream, for ¥630. ☒ *4–4 Sakai-machi* ☎ 0134/29–0105 🟰 *No credit cards.*

¢ ✕ **Kita-no Ice Cream** (北のアイスクリーム). Beer ice cream anyone? Maybe you'd prefer sake ice cream—or squid, cherry blossom, or pumpkin? This Otaru institution serves up 20 varieties from a shop in an 1892 warehouse in an alleyway one block from the canal. ⊠ *Ironai 1-chōe* ☎ *0134/23–8983* ▤ *No credit cards.*

★ $$$–$$$$ ▦ **Authent Hotel** (オーセントホテル). In the heart of the downtown shopping area, a former department store has new life as an elegant city-center hotel. Cream upholstery and yellow walls in the lobby are echoed in the rooms, which have larger-than-usual bathrooms. Kaio is a small *teppanyaki* restaurant, and the 11th-floor piano bar has city views from the curved front of the building. ⊠ *15–1, Inaho 2, Otaru 047-0032* ☎ *0134/ 24–8100* 🖷 *0134/27–8118* ⊕ *www.authent.co.jp* 🛏 *190 Western-style rooms, 5 Japanese-style rooms* ♻ *3 restaurants, café, Japanese baths, bar, piano bar, 2 shops, Internet, no-smoking rooms* ▤ *AE, DC, MC, V.*

★ $$$–$$$$ ✕▦ **Otaru Hilton** (小樽ヒルトン). The 18 floors of this hotel rise above the redbrick WingBay complex, one of the largest shopping malls in Japan, with numerous shops, seven movie theaters, a hot spring, and restaurants galore. There's even a Ferris wheel outside. Otherwise the location is unattractive, however; the hotel is between the railroad and a harbor wall, 15 minuteson foot from the historic district. Western-style rooms, in calming golds, blues, and browns, have large twin or double beds, and most overlook the marina. Amenities include CNN, excellent meals by guest chefs from other hotels in the group (the on-site Marina Restaurant is a favorite with local foodies), and a trolley stop just outside. Early booking and a best-rate guarantee can produce competitive rates, depending on the season. ⊠ *11–3 Otaru Chikkō, Otaru 047-0008* ☎ *0134/21–3111, 0120/48–9852 toll-free* 🖷 *0134/21–3322* ⊕ *www. hilton.com* 🛏 *289 Western-style rooms* ♻ *3 restaurants, café, patisserie, cable TV, 2 bars, Internet, no-smoking floors* ▤ *AE, DC, MC, V.*

¢–$$ ▦ **Hotel 1-2-3** (ホテル 1・2・3). The ghosts of bankers past are still a presence in this 1923 converted bank building, where former offices make small bedrooms. Pricier rooms are more spacious, and family rooms have large shelf-beds. The reception desk is closed from 10 AM to 3 PM. Room 109 in the basement was actually a vault, complete with a set of non-operational iron doors. The hotel is one block away from the canal. ⊠ *1–3–1 Ironai, Otaru 047-0031* ☎ *0134/31–3939* 🖷 *0134/31–5995* ⊕ *www.hotel1-2-3.co.jp/hotel/otaru* 🛏 *58 Japanese-style rooms* ♻ *Coffee shop, fans, shop, laundry facilities, no-smoking rooms; no room phones* ▤ *AE, MC, V* ⃝ *CP.*

$$ ▦ **Cottage Sakanoue-kan Hirao** (コテージ坂の上館ひらお). One large room sleeps up to five people at this homey, family-run operation. With its net curtains, big beds, and stained glass, the cottage offers a vaguely Russian experience in the heart of Otaru. The Hirao family built the cottage in their garden as an extension of their own home, and the large room has sofas, a table, and a small kitchenette for basic cooking. There's a private bathroom and a separate entrance for guests. The bay windows overlook the harbor. No meals are offered, and no English is spoken, but the family is welcoming to foreign guests. The cottage is a short walk up the hill behind the Steam Clock. ⊠ *3–10 Sumiyoshi-chō, Otaru 047-0015* ☎ *0134/ 33–9151* 🛏 *1 room* ♻ *Refrigerator, microwave* ▤ *No credit cards.*

Getting Around

Otaru makes a good base for touring around Hokkaidō by car. **Toyota Car Rental** (☎ 0134/27–0100), open daily 8 AM to 8 PM, is near Otaru

Station. **Nippon Rentacar** (☎ 0134/32–0919), open daily 8:30 AM to 7 PM, is downtown. Neither agency has an English-speaking staff, so ask the tourist office or your hotel to help with reservations.

> **off the beaten path**
>
> Northwest of Otaru the **SHAKOTAN-HANTŌ** (Shakotan Peninsula, 積丹半島) – juts out into the ocean, separated from the waves by a dramatic coastline of mysterious rock formations, plunging cliffs, and hidden beaches. The small fruit-growing town of **Yoichi** (余市) is the gateway to the peninsula and **Route 229** (国道229号) then circles the coast via the two capes, Shakotan-misaki and Kamui-misaki. The most dramatic scenery is near **Yobetsu** (余別). Inland volcanic peaks such as Shakotan-dake (4,258 ft/1,297 meters) have hiking trails that leading to spectacular views. You can tour the peninsula by car in about four hours, but be careful: in summer the narrow road is very busy with day-trippers from Sapporo seeking sand and camping space.

Niseko ニセコ

★ **⑮** *2 hrs, 10 min southwest of Otaru by JR.*

For the best skiing in Hokkaidō, and perhaps in all Japan, head for Niseko as over 50,000 Australian powderhounds do every winter. The skiing is on Mt. Annupuri, and the whole surrounding area has hot springs, farms, artists' workshops, and hiking trails. Outdoor adventure companies run by Australian and Canadian ex-pats offer year-round thrills, including rafting (the best season is April to May), backcountry skiing, mountain biking, and bungee jumping. The Niseko area is hands-down the best place to discover the Hokkaidō countryside, and it's easy to find an English-speaking guide if you want one.

The town of Kutchan is the gateway to the Niseko area and is served by trains from Sapporo. From Kutchan you can switch to trains heading for the villages of Hirafu or Niseko, where many pensions and hotels offer pick-up services from the stations. The best hotels and almost all of the adventure companies are at Hirafu village.

To the right of the ticket gate at the JR Kutchan Station is the excellent **Kutchan Tourist Association Tourist Office** (Kutchan Kankō Kyōkai no Kankō Annai-sho; 倶知安観光協会の観光案内所; ⌧ Minami 1-jō Nishi 4 chōme, Kutchan-chō ☎ 0136/22–5151). The **Niseko Tourism Office** (ニセコ町観光案内所; ⌧ JR Niseko Station ☎ 0136/44–2468 ⊕ www. niseko.gr.jp) also offers maps and information.

Hiking

Kutchan has a sleepy charm, but the real action is on **Yōtei-zan** (Mt. Yotei; 羊蹄山). Climbing this Fuji look-alike takes four hours. Two trails lead up the mountain: the more challenging **Hirafu Course** and the easier but still arduous **Makkari Course**. Regardless of your approach, you're bound to be taken by the wildflowers in summer, as well as the elderly Japanese chomping on bamboo shoots that grow wild on the hills. A hut at the top provides crude lodging if you decide to hike up to see the next day's sunrise. To get to the trails, take the bus from JR Kutchan Station 20 min utes to Yotei To-zan-guchi (hiking trail entrance) for the Hirafu Course or 40 minutes to the Yotei Shinzan Kōen stop for the Makkari Course.

Skiing

From November to May, skiers and snowboarders enjoy 61 courses covering 47 km (30 mi) of powder in the Niseko area. There are five ski resorts, but the big three are Grand Hirafu, Higashiyama, and Annupuri. You can ski them all with a Niseko All-Mountain Pass costing ¥4,800 for one day or ¥8,800 for two days. Yotei-zan provides a dramatic backdrop for everyone's photographs if the weather is clear. Nondrivers coming from Sapporo can buy package ski tours, including lunch and transportation by bus, for about ¥4,500. You can book tours at almost any city hotel. If you're driving to Niseko, check Sapporo convenience stores for discount lift tickets.

Annupuri Resort (ニセコアンヌプリ国際スキー場 ☎ 0136/58–2080) has wide, gently sloping runs that are great for beginners and shaky intermediates. Day passes cost ¥4,400. **Higashiyama Resort** (ニセコ東山スキー場 ☎ 0136/44–1111), based at the Prince Hotel, has a super-fast cable car that takes you to beautifully designed forested courses. You descend through the trees to the mountain base. Day passes cost ¥4,000. **Grand Hirafu** (グラン・ヒラフ ☎ 0136/22–0109) is the largest of the Niseko ski resorts, with 34 courses, 27% of which are classed "expert." The longest run is more than 5 km (3 mi) long. After fresh snowfall there's a rush to be first up the mountain for the beautiful powder at the top off-piste areas. A day pass costs ¥4,900. Check out www.niseko.ne.jp, www.grandhirafu.jp and www.snowjapan.com for snow reports and other information on skiing in Niseko.

Outfitters

Niseko Adventure Centre (ニセコアドベンチャーセンター; ☎ 0136/23–2093 ⊕ www.nac-web.com) is the oldest adventure company in the area, in operation since 1994. In addition to river trips, mountain biking, and winter sports, the center has an indoor rock-climbing wall at its base. After all that exertion, kick back and relax at the on-site JoJo's bar and café. **Niseko Outdoor Adventure Sports Club** (ニセコアウトドアアドベンチャースポーツクラブ; ☎ 0136/23–1688 ⊕ www.noasc.com) sponsors river activities, and, for height lovers, bungee jumping, bridge swinging, mountain boarding, and ice climbing. Its POW POW bar and café provides the après-adventure venue for tall tales of derring-do. **Scott Adventures** (スコットアドベンチャー; ☎ 0136/21–3333 ⊕ www.sas-net.com) rafting trips are popular with domestic school groups. The company also arranges hot-air ballooning, fishing, snowshoeing, and dogsled riding with a team of huskies.

Where to Stay & Eat

¢–$$ ✕ **Genten** (玄天). Powerhounds and adventurers flock to this funky restaurant and bar in a Mongolian tent. You can choose from a variety of Asian dishes, including Thai curries, Vietnamese soups, and Chinese stir-fries. Genten is a good place to meet local ex-pats, and the full-moon party nights are a Niseko institution. It's between the Hirafu and Higashiyama ski areas. ⊠ 63–25 Aza Kabayama, Niseko ☎ 0163/23–3154 ▭ No credit cards.

¢–$$ ✕ **Izakiya Bang Bang** (居酒屋ばんばん). *Yakitori* (sizzling meats on wood skewers) and other Hokkaidō favorites, such as salmon and herring, keep company with imports like spare ribs and tacos on the menu here. Your dining neighbors may become tomorrow's skiing or adventure-tour buddies, and the staff of your pension probably enjoys their evenings off here. In the heart of Hirafu Village, Izakiya Bang Bang is definitely the place to be. English translations on are the menu. ⊠ *188–27 Aza Yamada, Hirafu* ☎ *0136/22–4292* ⊕ *www.niseko.or.jp/bangbang* ▭ *MC, V* ☽ *Closed Wed. No lunch.*

$$$–$$$$ ▨ **Niseko Higashiyama Prince Hotel** (ニセコ東山プリンスホテル). This posh mountain ski resort at the foot of Mt. Annapuri is busy year-round. During ski season, a six-person ski lift right outside the hotel can take you to the top of the slopes. In summer the curved white tower stands out amidst the three golf courses that surround it. Views from the spacious, standard rooms are impressive. Consider the spa package, which includes a room, breakfast, and unlimited use of the hot springs for about ¥10,000 per person, depending on the season. Dinners cost ¥3,500 extra. ⊠ *Higashiyama Onsen, Niseko 048-1592* ☎ *0136/44–1111* ▣ *0136/44–3224* ⊕ *www.princehotels.co.jp* ⇥ *706 Western-style rooms* ♨ *6 restaurants, 3 18-hole golf courses, 23 tennis courts, downhill skiing, 3 bars, shops* ▭ *AE, MC, V.*

$ ▨ **Grand Papa** (グランパパ). In keeping with Niseko's rather wishful claim to be the St. Moritz of Asia, this Alpine-style pension in Hirafu village has lots of dark wood and red carpeting. The owners are exceptionally friendly and hospitable. Nikawara-san is a woodcut artist and alpenhorn player, and his wife Yoko used to be a British Airways flight attendant. Rooms are simple, and only three have small bathrooms. You can walk to Yukou hot spring (¥600) in just three minutes. After a winter dinner of Swiss cheese fondue, retire to Grand Papa's snug bar. ⊠ *163 Hirafu, Niseko 044-0081* ☎ *0136/23–2244* ▣ *0136/23–2255* ⇥ *17 Western-style rooms, 3 with bath; 2 Japanese-style rooms without bath* ♨ *Dining room, hot springs, mountain bikes, bar, Internet* ▭ *No credit cards* ⦿ *BP.*

¢–$ ▨ **Ryū's Inn** (リューズイン). A tiny, simply furnished house in the middle of the fields near the Higashiyama ski area, this is the place to stay if you want to be adopted by owners Ryū and Eriko Yasui. Ryū, who once worked in London's Dorchester Hotel, is a passionate Niseko promoter and he'll drive you to his favorite hot springs, recommend restaurants, and tell you about Niseko's craft workshops. Dinners are by reservation and there is a shared bathroom. ⊠ *744–2 Soga, Niseko 048-1522* ☎ *0136/44–3265* ⊕ *www.niseko.gr.jp* ⇥ *4 Western-style rooms with shared bath* ♨ *Dining room, Japanese baths, ski storage, bar, free parking; no a/c, no room phones, no room TVs* ▭ *AE, MC, V* ⦿ *BP.*

Getting Around

Niseko is a 2½-hour drive from New Chitose Airport. From November to May, public buses run from the airport to the Niseko ski resorts several times per day. In July and August, Chuō bus company has two buses a day. The one-way trip costs ¥2,300.

From Sapporo, you can drive to Niseko in about two hours. You can also go by rail; trains depart hourly for Kutchan, and the trip takes about two hours and costs ¥1,790. You may have to change trains in Otaru. From Kutchan there are seven train services a day to the Hirafu and Niseko villages, where you'll find most of the guesthouses and hotels. Hotel staff are quite willing to pick up guests at the stations, and most are happy to drive guests to the trailheads and ski lifts too. Or, take the train to Niseko and rent a car once you get there. **Nippon Rental Car** (✉ 247–7 Aza-Soga ☎ 0136/43–2929) is open from April to October, daily 9 to 6; and from November to March, daily 9 to 5. **Mazda Rent-A-Car 9–5** (✉ 74–4 Aza-Honchō ☎ 0136/44–1188) is open daily from 9 to 5. Both agencies are a five-minute walk from the station.

Jōzankei Onsen 定山渓温泉

16 *40 min southeast of Tengu-dake by car, 1 hr west of Sapporo by bus.*

Because Jōzankei is actually within Sapporo city limits, weekend day-trippers crowd in. The resort town itself is wedged in a small valley in the foothills beneath the mountains of Shikotsu-Tōya National Park. Were it not for the modern, square-block hotels, the village would be beautiful. New developments have nearly spoiled the area, but there are a few curiosities that still warrant a quick day-trip from Sapporo.

The House of Secret Treasures (Hihō-kan, 秘宝館). One of the most un-usual museums in Hokkaidō attests to Japan's legacy of peasant frank-ness about things sexual. The coyly named museum is devoted to Japan's tradition of erotica and sexual folk culture, including phallic and yonic objects formerly related to fertility rites. The museum is by the huge statue of a crying Kannon, the Buddhist goddess of mercy. ✉ *Rte. 230, Higashi 2-chōme, Jōzankei* ☎ *011/598–4141* 💴 *¥1,500* 🕐 *Daily 10–8.*

Hotel Sansui (ホテル山水). The coed, open-air hot springs at this modern hotel in the village center overlook the gorge. Plastic modesty wraps called *yugi* are available at the front desk. Nonguest bathing times are on week-days noon to 7 and weekends noon to 3. ✉ *Higashi 3-chōme, Jōzankei* ☎ *011/598–2301* 💴 *¥600.*

Hōheikyō Onsen (豊平峡温泉). For a rustic hot-spring experience, head to this onsen 1 km (½ mi) southwest of Jōzankei. There are no resort ho-tels to spoil the view from the rotemburo (outdoor bath), which is stud-ded with rock islands and a working waterwheel. This is an onsen as it should be. As is the norm in Japan, there are separate baths for men and women. Leave Jōzankei on Route 230 west, and take the first left at the sign that shows a turbaned man (the hot spring also has a very good Indian restaurant; ask about the onsen-dinner package). The onsen is on the left in a ramshackle building. ✉ *680-banchi, Minami-ku, Jōzankei* ☎ *011/598–2410* 💴 *¥1,000* 🕐 *Onsen daily 10 AM–midnight, restaurant daily 11 AM–10 PM.*

SHIKOTSU-TŌYA NATIONAL PARK 支笏・洞爺国立公園

Mountains, forests, refreshing caldera lakes, hot-spring resorts, and vol-canoes—all are virtually in Sapporo's backyard in this national park.

For a quick tour of the area, plan two days by car and three by public transport.

Tōya-ko   洞爺湖

★ *2½ hrs southwest of Sapporo by bus.*

Hokkaidō's most recently active volcanic area is centered at Tōya-ko (Lake Tōya), a vast volcanic crater, now the sight of a popular resort. The crater's rim dominates the skyline from whichever direction you approach, and steam from the surrounding volcanoes drifts out across the surrounding farmland. There are two ways to drive there from Sapporo: Route 230 leads directly to the lakeside and its attractions, but for the most scenic approach, turn off Route 230 about 11 km (7 miles) after the amusement park at Rusutsu and follow signs for Toya Mura.

⑰ Tōya-ko Onsen (洞爺湖温泉). A spa town on the southwestern edge of Tōya-ko, this is the chief holiday center for this part of Shikotsu-Tōya Park. Consequently, it's loaded with hotels, inns, and souvenir shops. The hotels are open all year, but the busiest time is from June through August. Japanese families come in droves for hiking, trout fishing, boating on the lake, and enjoying the curative waters of the hot springs. A nightly fireworks show in summer gathers everyone at the border of the lake.

Volcanic Science Museum (Abuta Kazan Kagaku-kan, 虻田町立火山科学館). At lunchtime on March 28, 2000, **Usu-zan** erupted for the first time in 23 years. A 10,500-foot-high cloud of ash and smoke exploded over the resort. Approximately 16,000 people were evacuated, and for three months life in the town came to a stop while vulcanologists and government members debated the unpredictably of volcanoes. By July 2000 the resort was back in business, encompassing the still-smoking craters in its midst. Today you can still see buildings and street signs marooned in solidified mudflows. The volcanic activity of the entire area is chronicled at this museum in Japanese, but with plenty of dramatic photographs and artifacts, including the remains of cars and household effects. Stop in to watch the 15-minute video, which plays 11 times per day. The museum is on the second floor of the Dōnan bus terminal in the center of Tōya-ko Onsen. ☎ *0142/75–4400* 🎟 *¥600* ⊙ *Daily 9–5.*

off the beaten path

SHŌWA SHIN-ZAN –(昭和新山) A few minutes' drive east from Tōya-ko Onsen, the name means "new mountain of the Shōwa era." Japan's newest volcano, it made its appearance in 1943, surprising everyone, but no one more than the farmer who watched it emerge from his wheat field. In the course of two years, it grew steadily until it reached its present height of 1,312 feet. A cable-car ride up the eastern flank of the mountain costs ¥600 and is open daily from 9 to 5. If you're short of time, the Nishiyama Craters are generally more interesting.

Hiking

★ **Nishiyama Crater Trail** (西山火口群散策路). Five years after the volcanic eruption of 2000, you can still see steaming hillsides, solidified mudflows, and crumpled buildings, including a fire station that was built just one year before the eruption. Buses from Tōya Station to the onsen stop at the trailhead. From there, 3,960 feet of walkways wind up into the hills. The trail is accessible from the coast or from the lakeside just above the village. ⊠ *3–4–5 Takashaga-dori, between Abuta and Tōya-ko* ✉ *Free* ⊙ *Apr.–Nov., daily.*

Where to Stay & Eat

$$–$$$ ✕ **Biyōtei** (びようてい). A European-style restaurant in the heart of the village, Biyōtei has a stone floor, low beams, log table legs, and a garden full of gnomes. The menu is in English, and the sizzling hamburger platters are the best choices. ⊠ *38 Rte. 2, Tōya-ko Onsen* ☎ *0142/75–2311* 🖃 *No credit cards.*

$$$$ ✕⊡ **The Windsor Hotel** (ザ・ウィンザーホテル) Visible from miles around—

Fodor'sChoice the hotel looks like a giant luxury cruise ship perched on the rim of the

★ Tōya volcano—the Windsor is the best hotel in Hokkaidō for location and service. The blue rooms have views of the lake and Tōya-ko Onsen's volcanic activity, while the rust-color rooms look out to the sea. French chef Michel Bras uses Hokkaidō fish, meats, and vegetables in his only restaurant outside of France. The simple, 14-table room has wooden floors and wicker chairs overlooking the lake. Unusual in Japan, the Windsor asks guests to refrain from smoking in all restaurants and most rooms. Foreign staff speak English, French, and Japanese. ⊠ *Shimizu, Abuta-chō 049-5722* ☎ *0120/29–0500 or 0142/73–1111* 🖷 *0142/73–1210* ⊕ *www.windsor-hotels.co.jp* ⇨ *395 Western-style rooms, 3 Japanese-style rooms* ⚒ *14 restaurants, patisserie, cable TV, 2 18-hole golf courses, 3 tennis courts, indoor pool, gym, Japanese baths, sauna, spa, mountain bikes, downhill skiing, 2 bars, piano bar, shops, baby-sitting, Internet, business services, meeting rooms, airport shuttle, helipad* 🖃 *AE, D, DC, MC, V.*

$$$ ⊡ **Hotel Grand Tōya** (ホテルグランド洞爺). This hotel is faded rather than grand, but it's as close as you can stay to the volcanic craters. You are literally steps from the lakeside promenade, and in summer you can watch kimono-clad revelers go by. Although no English is spoken, the staff is welcoming. Meals are served in the rooms, all of which have small, private bathrooms. ⊠ *32 Tōya-ko Onsen, Abuta-chō 049-5721* ☎ *0142/75–2288* 🖷 *0142/75–3434* ⇨ *35 Western-style rooms, 4 Japanese-style rooms* ⚒ *Lobby lounge, shop* 🖃 *No credit cards* ⍓ *MAP.*

★ ¢–$ ⊡ **Pension Ohno** (ペンションおおの). A family-run guesthouse next to the Lakeside Park bus stop, ½ km (¼ mi) east of Tōya-ko Onsen, Pension Ohno is a calm alternative to the lodgings in the bustling, touristy village. Cozy rooms have large beds and private bathrooms; the small on-site hot spring is open round-the-clock. Your meals might include salmon or beef. No English is spoken. ⊠ *56–2 Aza Sobetsu-chō Onsen-chō, Abuta-chō 052-0103* ☎ *0142/75–4128* 🖷 *0142/75–3880* ⇨ *11 Western-style rooms* ⚒ *Restaurant, hot spring* 🖃 *MC, V* ⍓ *MAP.*

Getting Around

BY CAR The drive from Sapporo to Tōya-ko via Jōzankei is easy. Take the road that runs along the west side of the Botanical Gardens; it's a straight run to Jōzankei, less than an hour south of the city. There are sufficient signs in *rōmaji* (Japanese written in Roman script) throughout this area to give you directional confidence, and the route number—230—is frequently displayed.

BY BUS   Direct buses from Sapporo to Tōya-ko Onsen via Nakayama Tōge take 2½ hours (¥2,700). **Jōtetsu Bus** (☎ 011/572–3131) runs between Sapporo and Tōya-ko Onsen; reservations are necessary. **Dōnan Bus** (☎ 011/261–3601) makes the Sapporo to Tōya-ko Onsen trip daily.

BY TRAIN   Tōya-ko Onsen is on the JR Sapporo–Hakodate Line. Disembark from the train at JR Tōya Station for a 15-minute bus ride to the lake.

Noboribetsu Onsen   登別温泉

⑱ *1 hr, 20 min east of Tōya-ko by bus; 1 hr, 40 min south of Sapporo by bus.*

Noboribetsu Onsen is the most famous spa in Hokkaidō, perhaps even in all of Japan. It's said that some 34,300 gallons of geothermally heated water are pumped out every hour, making it the most prodigious hot spring in Asia. Its 11 types of water are said to cure ailments ranging from rheumatism to diabetes to menopause.

Noboribetsu Onsen is also a tourist town, so expect masses of hotels and souvenir shops. Although the modern hotel architecture is decidedly unattractive and out of tune with the mountain and forest surroundings, the village is not without charm. A stream runs through it, the main thoroughfare is cobblestone, and clouds of steam billow from every street grate in winter. Most hotels in Noboribetsu Onsen have their own baths, and the grandest of all are those at the Dai-ichi Takimotokan. You can get more for your yen if you arrange a tour from Sapporo through your hotel or the Plaza i tourist office.

Whatever you do, don't confuse Noboribetsu Onsen with Noboribetsu, a city on the coast that is 13 minutes by bus from its namesake spa town. Noboribetsu is an ugly industrial city on the JR Muroran Line. In fact, the whole coastal area from Date to Tomakomai is an industrial eyesore, worsened by a sagging regional economy. Noboribetsu city is one hour south of Sapporo by JR Limited Express. From the JR station in Noboribetsu, a shuttle bus serves Noboribetsu Onsen.

★ ☺ **Valley of Hell** (Jigokudani, 地獄谷). In this volcanic crater that looks like a bow-shape valley, boiling water spurts out of thousands of holes, sounding like the heartbeat of the earth itself—although, because of its strong sulfur smell, you could describe it differently. Whereas hot springs elsewhere in Japan—Unzen on Kyūshū is a notable example—were used to dispose of zealous foreign missionaries during the equally zealous periods of xenophobia, the natural cauldrons here were once favored by suicidal natives. Moms shouldn't worry, though; the walkways to photo-op points have handrails and are actually very safe. Admission is free.

Where to Stay & Eat

$–$$ ✕🏠 **Dai-ichi Takimoto-kan** (第一滝本館). More than 1,000 guests a night enjoy the 12 different thermal pools in this prime example of a Japanese mass-tourism venue. It's like a giant youth hostel and always fully booked. One indication of the size of the place is the English-language map available at the reception desk to help you negotiate the labyrinth of buildings and passageways. A vast dining room, the Attaka-tei, serves average Japanese and Western food, including a suitably sprawling dinner buffet of 75 dishes. Nonguests can bathe for ¥2,000 (¥3,000 on weekends. ✉ *55 Noboribetsu Onsen, Noboribetsu 059-0551* ☎ *0143/84–2111* 🖷 *0143/84–2202* ⊕ *www.takimotokan.co.jp* ↘ *393 Western-style rooms, 8 Japanese-style rooms* ⚸ *3 restaurants, dining room, room service, indoor pool, hot spring, 3 bars, dance club, pub, video game room, shops, laundry service* ▭ *AE, DC, MC, V* ⏐◯⏐ *MAP.*

★ **$$–$$$$** 🏠 **Noboribetsu Manseikaku Hotel** (登別万世閣ホテル). An outdoor hot spring and Japanese haute cuisine—*kaiseki ryōri*—are the attractions at this Japanese-style inn. Except between 2 PM and 4 PM, use of the baths is restricted to guests. The charge for nonguests is ¥1,000. ✉ *21 Noboribetsu Onsen, Noboribetsu 059-0551* ☎ *0143/84–3500* ↘ *19 Western-style rooms, 175 Japanese-style rooms* ⚸ *Dining room, hot spring* ▭ *AE, DC, MC, V* ⏐◯⏐ *MAP.*

¢–$ 🏠 **Pension Utopia** (ペンションユートピア). Guests with musical ability are welcome to play any of the many instruments at this modern, family-run guesthouse on the main road between the coastal highway and Noboribetsu Onsen. Large bedrooms with big, springy beds and an outdoor hot spring beckon at the end of the day. No English is spoken, but the owners are *gaijin*-friendly in part because there are two foreigners in the extended family. ✉ *166–2 Naka Noboribetsu, Noboribetsu 059-0463* ☎ *0143/83–1878* ↘ *6 Western-style rooms with bath, 4 Japanese-style rooms without bath* ⚸ *Dining room, hot spring* ▭ *No credit cards* ⏐◯⏐ *BP, MAP.*

Getting Around

From June to late October three buses per day make the 1¼-hour run between Tōya-ko Onsen and Noboribetsu Onsen; only one bus runs per day the rest of the year (¥1,530; reservations necessary). Heavy snow keeps the road closed until spring. To get to Noboribetsu Onsen by train, take the JR Sapporo–Hakodate Line, disembark at Noboribetsu, and then get on the Donan Bus (a 20-minute ride) to the spa town.

Dōnan Bus (☎ 011/261–3601) travels from Sapporo to Noboribetsu Onsen; the trip takes 100 minutes by expressway (¥1,900; reservations advised).

Nibutani　二風谷

★ ⑲ *45 min east of Tomakomai by bus, 2 hrs southeast of Sapporo by car.*

Nibutani is one of the very last places in Hokkaidō with a sizable Ainu population—or at least part-Ainu, as there are very few pure-blooded Ainu left at all. The tiny village has only two museums and a handful of souvenir shops—and it's a long way from Sapporo—but it's where you can find the best collection of Ainu art and artifacts in Hokkaidō.

The surrounding hills and spacious horse ranches make Nibutani a beguiling place to visit in summer, though it has been spoiled somewhat by the building of a dam that put part of the area under water. Unfortunately, much of the lost land was of spiritual or economic value to the local Ainu. In 1997 Japanese authorities finally passed a law recognizing Ainu culture and protecting the remainder of their land.

Nibutani Ainu Culture Museum (Nibutani Ainu Bunka Hakubutsukan, 二風谷アイヌ文化博物館). Although this museum is an excellent resource for information about the Ainu, it's sadly unknown to many Japanese. Ainu artifacts, such as shoes of salmon skin, water containers made from animal bladders, and heavy blue-and-black embroidered coats are on display, as well as implements used in *iyomante,* a ritual in which the Ainu sent the spirit of the bear back to heaven. A brief bilingual pamphlet is available, and some translated booklets are on sale. A selection of videos lets you listen to eerie traditional Ainu chants and songs. ⊠ *Off Rte. 237, Nibutani 55, Biratori-chō* ☎ *01457–2–2892* 🖾 *¥400, ¥700 joint ticket with Kayano Shigeru Nibutani Ainu Archive* ☉ *Mid-Jan.–mid-Dec., Tues.–Sun. 9:30–4:30.*

Kayano Shigeru Nibutani Ainu Archive (Kayano Shigeru Nibutani Shirrō-kan, 萱野茂二風谷アイヌ資料館). This museum puts a spotlight on artifacts, particularly Ainu clothing and items used in sacred rites, collected by prominent Ainu activist Shigeru Kayano, who was a member of Japan's House of Councillors from 1994 to 1998. He has traveled extensively and the archive contains presents to the Ainu from other indigenous peoples. In 2001 Kayano set up the only Ainu-language radio station, which broadcasts once a month. The museum is across the main road from the Culture Museum. ⊠ *Nibutani 54, Biratori-chō* ☎ *01457/ 2–3215* 🖾 *¥400, ¥700 joint ticket with Nibutani Ainu Culture Museum* ☉ *Mid-Jan.–mid-Dec., Tues.–Sun. 9:30–4:30.*

Getting Around

Nibutani is hard to get to by public transport. The best way to reach it from Sapporo is to go by train to Tomakomai, and then by bus to Nibutani. There's also a small railway line between Tomakomai and Tomikawa, and to the right of the JR station in Tomikawa you can catch a bus to Nibutani. Don't make the mistake of getting off the bus too early at Biratori.

Shikotsu-ko 支笏湖

⓴ *50 min south of Sapporo by bus, 2¼ hrs west of Nibutani by bus via Tomakomai.*

Shikotsu-ko is the deepest lake in Hokkaidō—outfathomed only by Honshū's Tazawa-ko as the deepest in all of Japan. Swimmers should remember that although the beach shelves gently for 35 feet, it drops suddenly to an eventual depth of 1,191 feet. The lake's shape is that of a classic caldera, except that the rise of two volcanoes crumbled its peripheral walls on both north and south shores. Both the southern volcano, **Tarumae-zan,** and its northern counterpart, **Eniwa-dake,** remain active. They have fine hikes and summits with superb views of the lake, Eniwa-dake being the more challenging climb.

Where to Stay & Eat

★ $$–$$$ ✕🛏 **Marukoma Onsen Ryokan** (丸駒温泉旅館). The lakeside sun deck and hot-spring baths at this small hotel are perfect for some quiet contemplation. The hotel building is just a concrete box, but the location, down in the woods off the main A453 road, is stunning. If you get a

HOKKAIDŌ'S FIRST INHABITANTS

HOKKAIDŌ WAS NOT EVEN MENTIONED IN BOOKS UNTIL THE 7TH CENTURY. For the next millennium it was written off as the place of the "hairy Ainu." The Ainu, indigenous inhabitants of Japan—possibly related to ethnic groups that originally populated Siberia—were always thought of as the inferior race by the Yamato, who arrived in Japan from the south via Kyūshū and founded Japan's imperial house. As the Yamato spread and expanded their empire from Kyūshū through Honshū, the peace-loving Ainu retreated north to Hokkaidō. There they lived, supporting themselves with their traditional pursuits of hunting and fishing. By the 16th century the Yamato had established themselves in the southern tip of Hokkaidō, and they soon began to make incursions into the island's interior.

With the Meiji Restoration in 1868, Japan changed its policy toward Hokkaidō and opened it up as the new frontier to be colonized by the Yamato Japanese. The Tōkyō government encouraged immigration from the rest of Japan but made no provision for the Ainu people. Indeed, the Ainu were given no choice but to assimilate themselves into the life and culture of the colonizers. Consequently, Ainu culture went into a sudden and terminal decline—so much so that academics have been known to write off the Ainu as a "doomed" or even "extinct" race.

But since the 1980s there has been something of a revival in Ainu culture and activism. The number of full-blooded Ainu might be very small, but 24,000 people believe themselves to possess enough of the bloodline to have officially declared themselves "Ainu." Similarly, though the Ainu language has virtually disappeared as a native tongue, many people have begun to study it in a burgeoning number of college and evening courses. Ainu

activism, meanwhile, received a boost when the United Nations made 1993 the Year of Indigenous Peoples, and the Ainu scored a propaganda victory in 1994 when their leading activist, Shigeru Kayano, was elected to Japan's House of Councillors—the first Ainu to reach such a prominent position. In May 1997 the national government passed belated legislation acknowledging the existence of Ainu and requiring local and national government to respect their dignity as a distinct race by promoting Ainu culture and traditions. The act stopped short of designating Ainu as an indigenous ethnic group though, following concerns about aboriginal rights to land and natural resources, and critics say it also fails to address racial discrimination, as well as economic and education disadvantages. Sadly, little of the progress may be obvious to visitors who head for Hokkaidō's (reconstructed) Ainu villages, many of which are tourist traps and poor reflections of actual or historic Ainu life.

room facing the lake and mountains beyond, you are in for a magical evening. Dinner is served in the tatami-floor guest rooms, which have basic, modern, light-wood furnishings. You can catch a bus to Shikotsu-kohan from Sapporo for ¥1,300. Call the ryokan in advance, and they'll pick you up from the village. Nonguests can bathe here daily from 10 AM to 3 PM for ¥1,000, and there are private hot-spring rooms available for ¥2,500. ⊠ *Poropinai, Banga-ichi, Chitose-shi 066-0287* ☎ *0123/25–2341* 🖃 *1 Western-style room and 60 Japanese-style rooms without bath* ⸝ *Restaurant, coffee shop, Japanese baths, hot spring, bar, recreation room* 🖃 *AE, DC, MC, V* ⦿ *MAP*.

Getting Around

To reach Shikotsu-ko from Nibutani, take the expressway to Tomakomai and follow Route 276 to Shikotsu Onsen, or follow Route 453 south from Sapporo. You can also take a train to JR Tomakomai Station, from which Shikotsu-ko is a 40-minute bus ride.

From Shikotsu-ko you could return to Tomakomai by bus and take the JR train back westward in the direction of Hakodate, or take a bus to Chitose Kūkō, then the JR back to Sapporo.

EASTERN HOKKAIDŌ　東北海道

Abashiri, on the Ohotsuku-kai (Sea of Okhotsk), makes a good base from which to head south to explore the mysterious lakes of Akan National Park, east out to the mountains and coastal scenery of Shiretoko National Park. The great wetland breeding grounds of the striking and endangered *tanchō-zuru* (red-crested crane) are 1½ hours south of Akan-kohan, just off the A240 to Kushiro.

Abashiri　網走

㉑ *5½ hrs east of Sapporo via Asahikawa by JR Limited Express.*

In the shadow of Tento-zan, Abashiri is the principle Ohotsuku-kai town, but it's quite small. In winter, *ryūhyō* (ice floes) jam up on its shores and stretch out to sea as far as the eye can see.

Some staff members at the **Abashiri tourist office** (網走市観光協会; ☎ 0152/43–4261 ⊕ www2s.biglobe.ne.jp/~abashiri/e/index_e.html), adjoining the JR station, speak English. This is where to find information about transportation and lodging in the area.

Two pleasure boats leave from **Aurora Terminal** (オーロラターミナル; ☎ 0152/43–6000) at the east end of the port. The *Aurora 1* and the *Aurora 2* give you a chance to inspect the ryūhyō at close range from mid-January to mid-April, for ¥3,000.

Abashiri Municipal Museum (Abashiri Kyōdo Hakubutsukan 網走郷土博物館). The Ainu are not the only indigenous Japanese people. Another nationality, the Moyoro, lived in Japan before the Ainu. They are believed to have come to an end in the 9th century. Anthropological evidence, such as bones and domestic tools, found in the Moyoro Shell Mound on Hokkaidō's east coast, is exhibited here. A good collection of Ainu artifacts, including clothes and hunting implements, is also on display. The museum is across the railroad tracks to the south of downtown, in Katsura-gaokaen (Katsura-gaoka Park), two minutes on foot from Abashiri Shogakko (elementary school). ⊠ *1–3 Katsura-machi 1-chōme, Abashiri-shi* ☎ *0152/43–3090* ✑ *¥100* ⊙ *May–Oct., daily 9–5; Nov.–Apr., Tues.–Sat. 9–4.*

Hokkaidō Museum of Northern Peoples (Hoppo Minzoku Hakubutsukan, 北方民族博物館). Here you can find artifacts, such as kitchen implements, clothes, and hunting snares and nets, depicting the lifestyles of various indigenous cultures from northern Japan, the neighboring Russian island of Sakhalin, and the northern parts of America and Eurasia. The Ainu, Inuit, and Lapps are among the nationalities in the spotlight here. If the museum's layout seems a little bizarre, it's because the building was designed to resemble a flying swan. The museum is 5 km (3 mi)—a 10-minute drive—from JR Abashiri Station on the Dōdo Taikan Yama Kōen-sen, a local road. ☎ *0152/45–3888* ✑ *¥250* ⊙ *Tues.–Sun. 9:30–4:30.*

★ ⌚ **Prison Museum** (Abashiri Kangokuku Hakbutsukan, 網走監獄博物館). A prison until 1984, this park museum traces the history of convict labor, which was used to develop the region. Only the most heinous criminals were banished to this forbidding northern outpost, the Alcatraz of Japan. The cells, watch towers, and prison farm buildings show how stark and monotonous life was for inmates, relieved only by strictly restricted bathhouse visits. There's little information in English, but anguished-looking mannequins bring it all to life. ⊠ *1–1 Yobito* ☎ *0152/ 45–2411* ⊕ *www.ryuhyo.com/kangoku2* ✑ *¥1,050* ⊙ *Apr.–Oct., daily 8–6; Nov.–Mar., daily 9–5.*

Where to Stay & Eat

$–$$ ✕ **Nakazushi** (中鮨). Rotarian Kanio Nakano presides over the Ohotsuku-kai's freshest catch in a small restaurant that has been in the same family for more than 40 years. Depending on the season, Nakano-san has salmon roe on rice, sea urchin, and the famous Abashiri scallop. The whaling fleet goes out on "research" in spring and fall from Abashiri, under Japanese interpretation of IWC rules, so *tsuchi-kujira* (Baird's Beaked Whale) is sometimes on the menu. Nakano-san doesn't speak English, but he's aware of the whale-meat debate and can make substitutions if you let him know your no-whale preference through gestures. ⊠ *Minami 2-jō Nishi 2, Abashiri* ☎ *0152/43–3447* ▭ *No credit cards.*

★ **$$–$$$$** ⌂ **Hotel Abashiri-ko-so** (ホテル網走湖荘). On the shores of Lake Abashiri, a few kilometers from town, this is the usual, vast, impersonal resort hotel. But the staff is friendly, and just outside the doors at sunrise or sunset you can enjoy the peace of the lake with its water birds, flowers, and mist. The combination rooms have raised beds but tatami sitting areas. Reservations can be made in English via the Web site. ⊠ *Abashiri Kohan Onsen, Abashiri 099-2421* ☎ *0152/48–2245* 🖷 *0152/48–2828* ⊕ *ww6.et.tiki.ne.jp/~abashirikoso/indexE.html* ⇥ *37 Western-style rooms, 20 Japanese-style rooms, 100 combination rooms* ⌛ *3 restaurants, hot spring, sauna, 2 bars, shops* ▭ *AE, MC, V* ⌾ *MAP.*

$$–$$$ ▣ **Abashiri Central Hotel** (網走セントラルホテル). Luxurious from the moment you enter the green-and-cream lobby area, this downtown hotel seems a world away from small-town Abashiri. Rooms in yellows and blues overlook a main road out front or parking at the back. Fish from the local icy waters feature big in the Grand Glacier restaurant, which serves Japanese, Chinese, and French food in style. The weekday lunch buffet at ¥1,000 is a good value. English speakers are on staff. ⊠ 7, *Minami 2-jo Nishi 3, Abashiri 093-0012* ☎ *0152/44–5151* 🖷 *0152/43–5177* ☟ *94 Western-style rooms, 2 Japanese-style rooms* ☖ *Restaurant, bar, café.*

$ ▣ **Hotel Sun Abashiri** (ホテルサン網走). A large, mauve, Western-style house, this hotel has small bedrooms and a genteel dining room. It's popular with local business travelers year-round. You can pre-order meals at the hotel, or head to the family-friendly steak house across the street. ⊠ *3–8 Shinmachi 2-chōme, Abashiri, 093-0046* ☎ *0152/43–3155* 🖷 *0152/43–3108* ☟ *35 Western-style rooms* ☖ *Dining room* ▤ *No credit cards.*

¢–$ ▣ **Abashiri Ryūhyō-no-oka Youth Hostel** (網走流氷の丘ユースホステル). Panoramic sea views are yours to enjoy at this hostel atop a green bluff. The cheerful touring base is a 10-minute bus ride north from town (last bus 5 PM) and a 10-minute steep walk from the bus stop. Once you get there, you'll receive a genuine welcome and an invitation to relax in the small, shared Japanese bath. Breakfast costs ¥600, and dinner ¥1,000. ⊠ *22–6 Aza Meiji, Abashiri 093-0085* ☎ *0152/43–8558* ☟ *6 bunk-bed rooms, 1 Japanese-style room* ☖ *Dining room, Japanese bath; no room phones, no room TVs* ▤ *No credit cards.*

Getting Around

The significant distance from Sapporo to Abashiri makes it advisable to take a train out, then rent a car or take a bus to get to the surrounding parks and towns. Coastal Highway 238 skirts Saroma-ko between Mombetsu and Abashiri.

A single bus runs to all of the worthwhile sights in Abashiri. A day-pass costs ¥900, and the bus departs hourly from **JR Abashiri Station** (⊠ Shinmachi 2-chōme 2-banchi).

Shiretoko National Park   知床国立公園

★ ㉒ *45 min by train to JR Shari Station, then 45 min east of Abashiri by bus.*

For decades a combination of remoteness, changeable weather, somewhat difficult roads, and a healthy local bear population kept this park largely off the tourist map. Since the peninsula is being considered for UNESCO World Heritage Site designation, however, and Japanese TV programs and guidebooks have trumpeted it as "the last wilderness in Japan," the park has become a more mainstream destination. Indeed, it can feel like every rental car in Hokkaidō is here during the summer school holidays. The last stretch of the peninsular road is now closed to all vehicles except park tour buses in the high season. If you visit outside of the summer crush—June and September are good times—Shiretoko is a remarkable, untouched pocket of wilderness in a heavily industrialized and technologically advanced nation. Read *Audrey Hepburn's Neck* (1996, Simon & Schuster, Inc.), a novel by Alan Brown, for a tale of a 20th-century childhood on Shiretoko.

You enter Shiretoko National Park at Utoro, where the **Shiretoko Sightseeing Boat** (知床観光船; ☎ 01522/4–2147 or 0152/43–6000) runs out to the cape from late April to late October. Catch the boat from the *fune noriba* (boat pier), about a 10-minute walk from the Utoro Onsen bus terminal. It departs five times daily (less in winter) and costs ¥2,700 for a 90-minute tour, ¥6,000 for a 3¾-hour excursion. As the boat skirts the shore and rounds the cape's tip, the views are impressive, with 600-ft cliffs breaking straight out of the sea and rugged mountains inland.

Shiretoko Nature Center (Shiretoko Shizen Centā, 知床自然センター). Stop by the park's main office to talk to rangers about the season's flora and fauna, and to get advice about exploring the peaks. The center is a few kilometers out of Utoro, where Route 334 starts to climb across the peninsula. ⊠ *531 Aza Iwa-Ubetsu, Shari-chō* ☎ *01522/4–2114* ◷ *May–Oct., daily 8–5; Nov.–Apr., daily 9–4.*

☺ **Kamuiwakka Onsen** (カムイワッカ温泉). *Kamui* means "spirit" or "god"
Fodor'sChoice in the Ainu language, and there's certainly something wondrous, if not
★ other-worldly, about this tumbling, hot river on the north shore under Iō-zan (Mt. Iō). Water rushes down the mountain through a series of falls and pools, creating a rotemburo with an ocean view. The pools are free—just strip and hop in. But between July 28 and August 29 the road is closed to private vehicles and you have to use the Shari Bus service from Uturo village or the Nature Center to the onsen.

The **Shari Bus** (斜里バス; ☎ 01522/3–3145) runs every 20 minutes from the Shiretoko Nature Center to the rotemburo at Kamuiwakka Onsen, with a stop near the Five Lakes hiking area. The ride takes about an hour and costs ¥900 from Utoro village, ¥590 from the nature center.

Shiretoko Go-ko (Five Lakes, 知床五湖). Twenty minutes east of Utoro by car, a collection of small lakes cling like dewdrops on a precipice above the ocean, giving hikers fantastic views.

Getting Around

Frequent train service runs from Sapporo to Abashiri and on to Shari. To get to Shiretoko National Park, travel southeast of Abashiri on the Kanno Line beyond Hama-Koshimizu. Shari is the end of the line and the jumping-off point for Utoro, the gateway to the peninsula and park. Most proper roads end about halfway along the peninsula. The final road terminates at Aidomari, with 30 km (19 mi) remaining before Shiretoko's tip. Bus service is erratic, and winter closes most of the area off to wheeled vehicles. To get to the park by public transport (available in summer only), take the 55-minute bus ride from Shari to Utoro.

Highway 244 heads east to Shari, from which 334 heads on to the Shiretoko-hantō until it dead-ends in the wilds of the national park.

Akan National Park   阿寒国立公園

㉓ *2 hrs southeast of Mombetsu by car.*

Like Shikotsu-Tōya National Park, this national park has some of Hokkaidō's most scenic lakes and mountains. And although the mountains are not as high as those in Daisetsu-zan National Park, they are no less imposing. In addition, Akan has three major lakes, each of which has a distinctive character. And, crucial to the success of any resort in Japan, the park has an abundance of thermal springs.

★ **Akan-ko** (Lake Akan, 阿寒湖). Smoking volcanoes Me-Akan and O-Akan (Mr. and Mrs. Akan) watch over this beautiful mountain lake, but Akan-ko is best known for its much smaller roommates. *Marimo* are very rare spherical colonies of green algae that may be as small as a Ping-Pong ball or as large as a soccer ball (the latter taking up to 500 years to form). The only other areas marimo can be found are in Yamanaka-ko (Lake Yamanaka), near Fuji-san, and in a few lakes in North America, Siberia, and Switzerland. These strange plants act much like submarines, photosynthesizing by absorbing carbon dioxide from the water and then rising to the surface, where they exhale oxygen and sink. They also serve as weather indicators, rising closer to the surface when bright sunshine increases their photosynthesis but less so in inclement weather, when light levels drop.

A popular sport from January to March is skating between the *wakasagi* (pond smelt) fishermen. The wakasagi are hooked from ice holes and laid on the ice in order to freeze immediately. Their freshness makes them popular minced and eaten raw, though some people prefer to fry them. Grilled wakasagi often appears on the winter menus of Hokkaidō izakayas.

Akan-kohan (阿寒湖畔). The resort area of the park, this small village has expanded around the lake as new hotels go up. As in so much of Hokkaidō, these hotels are not very attractive. The key is to obtain a room over the lake so you're looking at nature and not architectural calamities. The village center is cluttered with kitschy souvenir shops displaying endless rows of carved bears, made by Ainu residents of the village. The bear features heavily in traditional Ainu spiritual life.

★ **Mashū-ko** (Lake Mashū, 摩周湖). Hokkaidō's mystery lake is ringed by 656-ft-high rock walls, and, curiously, no water has been found either to enter or leave the lake, so what goes on in its 695-ft depths is anybody's guess. Perhaps that mystery and the dark blue water combine to exert a strange, hypnotic effect on visitors, causing them to stare endlessly down from the cliffs into the lake, said to be clear to a depth of 115 ft. These cliff sides are incredibly steep and have few or no footholds, so forego the pleasure of inspecting the pristine water up close. Instead take in the lake from its two observation spots on the west rim.

Kussharo-ko (Lake Kussharo, 屈斜路湖). Once Akan National Park's largest lake had a nearly perfect caldera shape, but other volcanoes have since sprung up and caused its shores to become flat and less dramatic. It is, however, an ideal area for camping and boating, and is popular with families on vacation. There are also a couple of natural hot springs that can be used free of charge. One other tourist attraction has been enthusiastically promoted in recent years—perhaps with an eye on the profits being made on the shores of Scotland's Loch Ness—"Kusshie," a creature said to inhabit the lake's depths.

Bird-Watching

★ ㉔ **Kushiro Marsh** (Kushiro Shitsugen, 釧路湿原). Graceful red-crested cranes preen and breed in protected Kushiro Marsh, which constitutes 60% of Japan's marshland and is a good place to observe the birds. These rare cranes, whose feathers were thought to bring good luck, were ruthlessly hunted at the beginning of the 20th century and were even believed to be extinct until a handful of survivors were discovered in 1924. They have slowly regenerated and now number about 650. The crane—long-legged, long-billed, with a white body trimmed in black and a scarlet cap on its head—is a symbol of long life and happiness. Legends hold that the birds live 1,000 years, and they have made it to a rather impressive 80 years of age in captivity. They pair for life, which has also made them the symbol of an ideal couple, and they are frequently cited in Japanese wedding speeches. In March or April females lay two eggs. The male and female play an equal role in looking after the eggs and, later, the chicks.

It's difficult to recommend a trip to see the cranes in the wild in summer; the birds are busy rearing their chicks and go deep into the swamps, where you can see them only through binoculars. November to March is the best season for wild-crane watching. If you visit in summer, the best places to see the birds up close are the few captivity centers in the area. The **Akan International Crane Center** (Akan Kokusai Tsuru Centa) and the adjoining **Crane Home** (Tancho-no-Sato; ⊠ 23–40 Akan-chō ☎ 0154/66–4011) are both about one hour south of Lake Akan, near the Tancho-zuru bus stop on the Akan-kohan–to–Kushiro bus route. Here you can watch a feeding and visit the center's units for egg hatching, chick rearing, and bird medical care.

Where to Stay & Eat

$ ╳🏠 **Minshuku Yamaguchi** (民宿山口). The mynah bird, Tarō, may screech a welcome as you enter this small home with its slightly faded rooms and mineral-stained shared baths. The owners don't speak English but are proud to welcome foreign guests. Japanese meals include tempura made from local fish, such as wakasagi, and mountain vegetables. Look for the impressive flower display out front, just past the Ainu village end of the town. ⊠ 5–3–2 Akan-ko Onsen, Akan-chō 085-0467 ☎ 0154/ 67–2555 ⭗ 10 Japanese-style rooms without bath △ Dining room, hot spring, Japanese baths; no room phones ☰ No credit cards ⓘⓞⓘ MAP.

★ $–$$$ 🏠 **New Akan Hotel** (ニュー阿寒ホテル). The prestigious New Akan tends toward sterility and vastness, but it does have an ideal location on Akan-ko, and the roof-top pool and hot springs are sensational. Its newer annex is called Shangri-La; the original hotel is the Crystal Wing. The Western-style rooms are simply furnished in crisp white, and the Japanese-style rooms can accommodate up to five people. Despite the hotel's size, there are only a few English speakers on staff. ⊠ Akan-ko Onsen,

Akan-chō 085-0467 ☏ *0154/67–2121* 🖷 *0154/67–3339* ⊕ *www. newakanhotel.co.jp/english* 🛏 *75 Western-style rooms, 295 Japanese-style rooms* ☆ *2 restaurants, tea shop, outdoor pool, hot springs, bar, shops* 🖃 *AE, DC, MC, V* ⵙ *MAP.*

Getting Around

There are buses to Akan-ko from Kushiro airport and station. You can also catch a bus from Akan-ko to Abashiri if you change buses in Bihoro. By car from Kitami, west of Abashiri, a road heads south to the small town of Tsubetsu, where it joins Route 240, entering Akan National Park near Akan-ko. From the southern part of Daisetsu-zan National Park at Nukabira, a road to Kamishihoro continues to Ashoro, which connects with Route 241; this runs directly to Akan.

CENTRAL & NORTHERN HOKKAIDŌ 道央と道北

Taking in Japan's largest national park, its northernmost points, and the island's highest mountain, this area is one of superlatives. Make the breathtaking Daisetsu-zan range in central Hokkaidō your first priority, and if you have plenty of time, take the trek to Sōya-misaki, the northern cape in Japan, and the stark beauty of the Rishiri and Rebun islands.

Asahikawa 旭川

❷❺ *1½ hrs northwest of Sapporo by tollway, 1 hr, 20 min by train.*

Asahikawa, Hokkaidō's second-largest city, is the principal entrance to Daisetsu-zan National Park. The city is vast and sprawling—361,000 people reside in an area of 750 square km (465 square mi)—even though the first pioneers didn't establish a base here until 1885. Cosmopolitan it is not. The endless suburbs can be depressing, but the downtown center contains several international accommodations, including the sparkling Palace Hotel; a pedestrian shopping mall, the first car-free outdoor mall in Japan; and a slew of restaurants, izakaya, and bars.

Asahikawa's major attractions are the Ainu Memorial Hall and the Ice Festival—held in February, this is Asahikawa's smaller version of Sapporo's Snow Festival (200 sculptures, compared with the 300 at Sapporo). Here, the celebration has the feeling of a country fair.

Kawamura Kaneto Ainu Memorial Hall (Kawamura Kaneto Ainu Kinen-kan, 川村兼人アイヌ記念館). A reasonably good Ainu museum, if slightly ramshackle. However, like the Kayano Shigeru Ainu Shiryō-kan in Nibu-tani, it does have the moral advantage of being run by a genuine Ainu, a man named Kaneto Kawamura, whose family has lived in the Asahikawa area for seven generations. There's a feeling that the museum really does exist to educate people about Ainu culture. To get here, take Bus 24 (¥170) from bus Platform 14, which is two blocks north of the JR station, and get off at Ainu Kinenkan-mae. ⊠ *11 Hokumon-chō* ☏ *0166/51–2461* 🎫 *¥500* ⏱ *July and Aug., daily 8–6; Sept.–June, daily 9–5.*

☸ **Asahiyama Zoo** (あさひやま動物園). Animals appear up-close and personal at the well-designed Asahiyama Zoo, which underwent major refurbishments in 2003. The polar bear swimming pool and the daily penguin walk are big attractions. Take the bus from stand No. 5 in front of Asahikawa Station. ⊠ *Kuranuma, Higashi-Asahikawa-chō* ☎ *0166/ 36–1104* ☑ *¥580* ⊙ *Apr. 29–Oct. 22, daily 9:30–5:15; Nov. 3–Mar. 31, Fri.–Tues. 9:30–5:15.*

Where to Stay & Eat

Far from the sea and from Hokkaidō's breadbaskets, Asahikawa is not known for its cuisine, with two notable exceptions: ramen and *tonkatsu* (breaded, deep-fried pork cutlet). Asahikawa ramen features a distinctively salty pork broth prized by ramen connoisseurs. Several noodle shops pepper the area around the station.

$–$$ ✕ **Tonkatsu Isen** (とんかつ井泉). This chain is famous for tonkatsu; a full-course meal will set you back about ¥1,200. Non-meat eaters can choose seafood, such as oysters. The chain's many branches include a gaijin-friendly one three minutes from the station on foot. ⊠ *2-jō 7-chōme* ☎ *0166/26–7363* ▤ *AE, V.*

¢–$$ ✕ **The Den** (ザ・デン). Barman Mark cooks up burgers, Thai curry, and Tex-Mex at this friendly expat hang out. It's a good place to make foreign contacts north of Sapporo. You can find 12 different kinds of beer from around the globe, plus a pool table, live music, and parties (Halloween costume competition, anyone?). The bar closes at 1 AM most nights, and at 3 AM on Friday and Saturday. The Den is a three-minute walk from the station. Look for the big lit-up sign near the Okuno department store. ⊠ *Yoshitake 2 Bldg. (2F), 2-jō 7-chome,* ☎ *0166/27–0999* ⊕ *www.thedenasahikawa.com* ▤ *MC, V* ⊙ *No lunch.*

$$ ⌸ **Asahikawa Terminal Hotel** (旭川ターミナルホテル). Although the rooms in this tower are not big, they are bright and tastefully furnished. The location can't be beat—the hotel is connected to the railway station, which makes sense since both are operated by JR Hokkaidō. Fukutsuru-teii, a restaurant on the sixth floor, offers standard Japanese fare with set courses from ¥1,500. The Orion Café serves light meals and drinks. ⊠ *Miyashita-dōri 7-chōme, Asahikawa 070-0030* ☎ *0166/24–0111* ⊟ *0166/21-2133* ▱ *155 Western-style rooms, 4 Japanese-style rooms* ♨ *3 restaurants, tea shop, bar* ▤ *AE, DC, MC, V.*

$–$$ ⌸ **Toyo Hotel** (東洋ホテル). The understated lobby here makes for a hotel more appealing inside than out. Small rooms are decorated in clean whites and grays. No English is spoken; the Toyo is used to serving Japanese guests, but the staff is friendly and helpful to Westerners. A Japanese restaurant on the ground floor offers meals priced from ¥2,500 to ¥3,500. Anjou restaurant serves French fare with meals priced from ¥4,000 to ¥9,000. ⊠ *7-jō 7-chōme, Asahikawa 070-0037* ☎ *0166/22–7575* ⊟ *0116/23–1733* ▱ *104 Japanese-style rooms* ♨ *2 restaurants* ▤ *AE, DC, MC, V.*

Daisetsu-zan National Park   大雪山国立公園

㉖ *50 min east of Asahikawa by car.*

Fodor's Choice
★

The geographical center of Hokkaidō and the largest of Japan's national parks, Daisetsu-zan contains the very essence of rugged Hokkaidō: vast plains, soaring mountain peaks, hidden gorges, cascading waterfalls, wildflowers, forests, hiking trails, wilderness, and, of course, onsen. Daisetsu-zan, which means great snow mountains, refers to the park's five major peaks, whose combined altitudes approach 6,560 feet. Their presence dominates the area and channels human access into the park: only a few roads pass through. The rest dead-end in formidable terrain.

★ **Souun-kyo** (Sōun-kyo Gorge, 層雲峡). As you follow the main route through the park, the first place to go is this 24-km (15-mi) ravine extending into the park from its northeast entrance. For an 8-km (5-mi) stretch, sheer cliff walls rise on both sides of the canyon as the road winds into the mountains. In winter and early spring, foreboding stone spires loom as if in judgment; in other seasons they thrust through glorious foliage. Sōun-kyo Onsen is at the halfway point of the ravine.

Ugly resort hotels diminish the gorge's impact. Sōun-kyo Onsen is another unfortunate example of how natural splendor can be abused. Resting precariously on the walls of the gorge are grocery stores, houses, inns, and the inevitable souvenir shops that make up the village of Sōun-kyo. Activities take place in resort hotels, not in the village, and during the day most people are out on trails hiking through the park. One popular, if easy, trip combines a seven-minute gondola ride (¥1,600 round-trip) with a 15-minute chairlift ride (¥600 round-trip) up Kuro-dake for great views of Daisetsu-zan. For even finer views, including one of Sōun-kyo, take the hour's walk to the very top. In July and August alpine wildflowers cover the mountain.

On the west side of the park, two **spa towns** serve as hiking centers in summer and ski resorts in winter. **Shirogane Onsen**, at 2,461 ft, has had especially good skiing since its mountain, Tokachi-dake, erupted in 1962, creating a superb ski bowl. It erupted again in 1988. At **Asahi-dake Onsen**, you can take a cable car up Asahi-dake, Hokkaidō's highest mountain, to an altitude of 5,250 ft, and hike for two hours to the 7,513-ft summit. In late spring and early summer the slopes are carpeted with alpine flowers. Serious skiers come here for Japan's longest ski season.

Where to Stay & Eat

For good or ill, you have no option but to lodge at **Sōun-kyo Onsen** (層雲峡温泉) if you want to stay in the northern part of the park. Rates tend to be 20% lower in winter. Because Sōun-kyo's hotels are almost exclusively ryokan, where meals are included, other dining opportunities in town are limited.

$$-$$$$ ✕🏨 **Chōyōtei** (朝陽亭). Perched on a bluff halfway up the side of the gorge, this hotel has the best views of any hotel in the park. Unfortunately, the hotel itself is an eyesore and spoils some of Sōun-kyo's beauty. Although it's cold and sterile, and it bustles with the tour group masses, the hotel has sumptuous baths. Rooms that face the gorge merit the price, but rooms at the back overlook a parking lot. Dinner is in the huge buffet restaurant, or you can make reservations for a traditional *kaiseki* dinner (¥21,000 for two people) in a smaller restaurant. ⊠ *Sōun-kyo Onsen Kamikawa 078-1701* ☎ *01658/5–3241* ➳ *5 Western-style rooms, 257 Japanese-style rooms* ⬧ *3 restaurants, minibars, hot springs, bar, recreation room, video game room, shops* ▭ *AE, DC, MC, V* ⫟❙ *MAP.*

$$–$$$ ✕▦ **Yamanoue** (山の上). This friendly modern guesthouse is in the center of the village's flower-filled pedestrian area. The owner is a keen fisherman, so dinners often include freshwater fish, plus a wild mushroom soup served from the giant cauldron in the dining room. Sake liquors made from fruits such as mountain grape may enhance (or hinder) the next day's hiking power. Clean tatami rooms are upstairs with shared washing areas. Use of the hot spring next door is free. ✉ *Sōun-kyo Onsen, Kamikawa 078-1701* ☎ *01658/5–3206* 🖷 *01658/5–3207* 🛏 *14 Japanese-style rooms without bath* ⚒ *Dining room, hot spring, Japanese baths* ▭ *MC, V* ⦿ *MAP.*

¢ ▦ **Sōun-kyo Youth Hostel** (層雲峡ユースホステル). Nestled between the big hotels—but at a fraction of the price and with a more personal welcome—this 40-year-old hostel is a good base for mountain hiking. Dorm rooms have eight wide bunk beds, and there are tatami or bunk-bed family rooms. Small Japanese baths. Mountain boot rental. The hostel is closed from October to May. ✉ *Sōun-kyo Onsen, Kamikawa 078-1701* ☎ *01658/ 5–3418* 🖷 *01658/5–3186* 🛏 *12 rooms* ⚒ *Dining room, Japanese baths, Internet; no room phones, no room TVs* ▭ *No credit cards.*

Getting Around

Sōun-kyō is two hours southeast of Asahikawa by car. You can catch a bus directly to Sōun-kyō Onsen (¥1,900) from in front of Asahikawa's JR station. If you are using a JR Pass, you can save money by taking the train to Kamikawa Station and transferring to the Dohoku Bus for the 30-minute run to Sōun-kyō. Bicycles can be rented for ¥1,000 a day in the village at the Northern Hotel.

Visitor Information

The **Sōun-kyō tourist office** (層雲峡観光案内所; ☎ 01658/5–3350), in the bus terminal, provides hiking maps and information on sightseeing and lodging. English is spoken here.

The Northern Cape　道北

Wakkanai is 5¾ hrs north of Sapporo by JR Limited Express, 1 hr north of Okadama Airport, or ¾ hr north from New Chitose Airport.

㉗ **Wakkanai** (稚内) is a working-class town that subsists on farming the scrubland and fishing the cold waters for Alaska pollack and Atka mackerel when the sea is not packed with ice floes. It's an isolated outpost of humanity: winter nights are long, and in summer there's a feeling of poetic solitude that comes from the eerie quality of the northern lights. From Wakkanai Park, on a ridge west of the city, there's a commanding view of Sakhalin, an island taken over by the Russians at the end of World War II. Several monuments in this park are dedicated to the days when Sakhalin was part of Japan. One commemorates nine female telephone operators who committed suicide at their post office in Maoka (on Sakhalin) when the island was taken by the Russians.

Few travelers come as far as Wakkanai for the town itself. You're likely to do the same and stick around only long enough to catch one of the ferries that make the daily crossing to Rebun-tō and to Rishiri-tō. The main attraction of these islands is the hiking and the short flower season: if you have limited time in Hokkaidō, Daisetsuzan and Shiretoko offer similar experiences closer to Sapporo.

 Rebun Island (Rebun-tō, 礼文島) is the older of two Nihon-kai islands created by an upward thrust of the earth's crust. The long, narrow island is oriented on a north–south axis. Along the east coast there are numerous fishing villages where men bring their catch, some of which is made into *nukabokke* (pollack covered in rice-bran paste), while women rake in edible yellow-green kelp, often used for soup broth, from the shore. Fleets of uni boats fish just offshore; prickly sea urchin are spotted through bottomless boxes held over the side of the boat and then raked in.

On the west coast, cliffs stave off the surging waters of the Nihon-kai. Inland, during the short summer months, wild alpine flowers, 300 species in all, blanket the mountain meadows. Momo-iwa, or Peach Rock, is an 820-ft-high mound 2 km (1 mi) west of the ferry landing. Here the wildflowers are in such profusion in mid-June that you almost fear to walk, for each step seems to crush a dozen of the delicate blossoms, including the white-pointed *usuyo-kiso,* which is found only on Rebun. Its name roughly translates as "dusting of snow."

Buses stop at the trailhead to the **Kitosu Course** (midway down the eastern side of the island) and the **Nairo Course** (10 km [6 mi] north). Bamboo and low-lying pines predominate. Leave 1¼ hours to cover the 4½-km (3-mi) loop to the top of 1,600-ft Rebun-dake, which overlooks rolling hills and the ocean beyond. Another hike, the **Eight-Hour Course,** covers the island from top to bottom on the west coast, passing along the way cliffs, waterfalls, and tiny seasonal villages. Buses also go to Sukotan-misaki, a lovely cape on the west side of the island with a cove that is popular with anglers. Be warned that, apart from Kafuka, there are no restaurants on the island, and village shops tend to be in the front room of a home and hard to spot.

★ ㉙ **Rishiri Island** (Rishiri-tō, 利尻島). The island is the result of a submarine volcano whose cone now towers 5,640 feet out of the water. The scenery is wilder than on Rebun-tō, and, though it's a larger island, Rishiri-tō has fewer inhabitants. The ruggedness of the terrain makes it harder to support life and figures for hardier climbing—sometimes too hardy: the Oniwaki Course was closed after a climber suffered a fatal misstep. The intermediate **Kutsugata Course** (four hours to the top), on the west side of the island, will take you past patches of wildflowers, including the buttercup-like *botan kimbai,* vibrant purple *hakusan chidori,* and numerous bird species.

To get the lay of the island, it's a good idea to take one of the regularly scheduled buses, which make a complete circle in two hours. From May through November there are six a day between 6:30 AM and 4:40 PM, which go both clockwise and counterclockwise.

㉚ **Sōya-misaki** (Cape Sōya, 宗谷岬). At the northernmost limit of Japan, mountains push out into the sea toward Russia's Sakhalin Island across the frigid waters. This lonely but significant spot is the site of several monuments marking the end of Japan's territory, as well as a memorial to the Korean airliner downed by the Soviet military north of here in

1982. A public bus makes the hour-long run between Wakkanai and Cape Sōya six times a day.

Where to Stay & Eat

¢–$$$ ✗ **Sakatsubo** (さかつぼ). Famous for sea urchin, this restaurant serves a variety called *bafun* (literally, "horse turd"). Despite its inauspicious name, it's prized and is served as *domburi* (over steamed rice) or even *uni-ramen* (with noodles). The *unigiri* (sea urchin-filled rice balls) go for ¥400. ⊠ *Kafuka, Rebun-chō* ☎ *01638/6–1894* ▭ *No credit cards* ☉ *No dinner.*

$$$–$$$$ ▦ **Hera-san no Ie** (ヘラさんの家). Hera's House, as the name translates, typifies the warm, casual atmosphere that makes Hokkaidō so loved by Japanese hippies. Mr. Hera refuses to use artificial or frozen foods for the two meals that come with the Japanese-style rooms, and he welcomes travelers from every nation. Bicycles are available for rent. The house is at the entrance to the Peshi-misaki hiking trail. ⊠ *Oshitomari, Rishiri-Fuji-chō, 097-0400* ☎ *01638/2–2361* ◩ *9 Western-style rooms, 3 Japanese-style rooms without bath* ♨ *Dining room; no a/c* ▭ *No credit cards* †○† *MAP.*

$$$ ▦ **Pension Ūnii** (ペンション・うーにー). This sky-blue building is at the top of the cliffs above the village, and although no English is spoken, the family is welcoming to foreigners. Rooms have private bathrooms, and the two meals included in the rate feature ingredients that were swimming only hours earlier. Gargantuan dinners alternate from Western-style to Japanese-style for guests who stay more than one night, although it's possible that only the cutlery–chopsticks switch will give a clue as to which is which. ⊠ *Kafuka-Irifune, Rebun-chō, 097-1201* ☎ *01638/ 6–1541* ◩ *9 Western-style rooms, 1 Japanese-style room* ♨ *Dining room* ▭ *No credit cards* †○† *MAP.*

Getting Around

From June through August, Air Nippon flies from Shin-Chitose Airport directly to Rishiri Airport on Rishiri-tō. Check the departure board for local weather conditions, and if the flights to the island are delayed, try to reimburse your ticket and go by ferry instead. Buses meet the planes and take passengers into town; otherwise a taxi for the 25-minute journey will cost about ¥2,000.

Higashi-Nihon Ferry (☎ 0162/23–3780) has boats that make the daily two-hour crossing to Rebun-tō and the one-hour, 40-minute crossing to Rishiri-tō. In summer there are four or five daily ferries, in winter two. Fares to Rebun are ¥3,780 for first class and ¥2,100 second class. Fares to Rishiri are ¥3,360 and ¥1,880. A ferry between the two islands costs ¥730.

HOKKAIDŌ A TO Z

To research prices, get advice from other travelers, and book travel arrangements, visit www.fodors.com.

AIR TRAVEL

Japan Airlines (JAL), Japan Air System (JAS), and All Nippon Airways (ANA) link Hokkaidō to Honshū by direct flights from Tōkyō's Haneda

Kūkō to Hakodate, Sapporo (New Chitose Airport), Asahikawa Airport, Abashiri (Memambetsu Airport), Nemuro (Nakashibetsu Airport), and Kushiro Airport. There are also two flights a day from Tōkyō's Narita International Airport. Many other major cities on Honshū have flights to Sapporo, as do several places in the Asian and Pacific region.

The cost by air from Tōkyō to Sapporo can be as low as ¥12,000, compared with ¥22,430 by train. Fly–stay packages from Tōkyō offer excellent deals for short trips. Some air travelers arriving in Japan on European flights can, with a change of planes at Tōkyō, fly at no extra charge to Sapporo. If you're flying from overseas to Sapporo via Tōkyō, book the domestic portion when you buy your international ticket; otherwise you will have to fork out for what is, per mile, one of the most expensive domestic tickets in the world. Some fledgling Japanese airlines, including Air Dō (rhymes with "who"), are starting to rectify this situation.

The two domestic airlines—Japan Air System (JAS) and All Nippon Airways (ANA)—have local companies connecting Sapporo with Hakodate, Kushiro, Wakkanai, and the smaller Memambetsu, Naka-Shibetsu, and Ohotsuku-Mombetsu airports in eastern Hokkaidō. Hokkaidō Air System is part of JAS. Air Hokkaidō and Air Nippon are part of ANA. There's also daily service between Wakkanai and both Rebun and Rishiri islands. Because of the potential for weather and other delays in Hokkaidō, always check flights before you get to Sapporo.

Air Hokkaidō and Air Nippon 🕾 0120/029-222. **Hokkaidō Air System** 🕾 0120/ 511-283.

BOAT & FERRY TRAVEL

This is the least expensive form of travel to Hokkaidō. First-class fares are typically somewhat more than double the second-class rate. From Tōkyō the luxury ferryboat *Sabrina Blue Zephyr* sails three or four times weekly to Kushiro (32 hours) and is operated by the Kinkai Yūsen Company, with rates of ¥9,400.

Higashi Nihon Ferry's express *Unicorn* makes two round-trips daily from Aomori to Hakodate. The express ferry takes two hours (to the train's 2½) but costs only ¥1,420 second class. Higashi-nihon boats also make the journey from Hachinohe to Tomakomai in nine hours (¥3,970); from Hachinohe to Muroran in eight hours (¥3,970); from Sendai to Tomakomai in 16½ hours (¥9,020); and from Aomori to Muroran in seven hours (¥3,460).

Shin Nihon Ferry travels from Niigata to Otaru in 18 hours (¥5,250). Taiheiyo Ferry routes include Sendai to Tomakomai (18 hours, ¥7,600) and Nagoya to Tomakomai (36 hours, ¥10,200).

Higashi Nihon Ferry 🕾 0177/82-3631 in Aomori, 0138/42-6251 in Hakodate, 0178/ 28-3985 in Hachinohe, 0144/34-5261 in Tomakomai, 0143/34-5261 in Muroran, 022/25-7221 in Sendai. **Kinkai Yūsen Company** 🕾 0154/52-4890. **Shin Nihon Ferry** 🕾 025/273-2171 in Niigata, 0134/22-6191 in Otaru. **Taiheiyō Ferry** 🕾 022/25-7221 in Sendai, 052/ 203-0227 in Nagoya.

BUS TRAVEL

Buses cover most of the major routes through the scenic areas, and all the excursions in this chapter may be accomplished by bus. There's no English-language telephone service for buses in Hokkaidō, although Chuo Bus has an English brochure for Japanese-speaking tours out of Sapporo. Plaza i in Sapporo will supply bus route and schedule information and make telephone bookings if required.

CAR RENTAL

Cars are easy to rent. Orix Rent-a-Car has offices in central Sapporo, at Chitose Airport, and at major JR stations in Hakodate and Asahikawa. For the most part, the Japanese are cautious drivers, though a combination of wide straight roads, light traffic, treacherous weather conditions, and Honshū visitors' unfamiliarity with all of the above gives Hokkaidō the worst traffic fatality figures in Japan. However, Dosanko, the area residents, are extremely helpful in giving instructions and directions to Western travelers. The limitation to renting a car is the expense. A day's rental is about ¥11,000 (not including tax), including 220 free km (132 mi), after which you are charged ¥20 per km (½ mi).

Local Agency Orix Rent-a-Car ✉ Minami 4 Nishi 1, Chūō-ku, Sapporo ☎ 011/241-0543.

EMERGENCIES

Ambulance ☎ 119. **Police** ☎ 110.

LODGING

Plaza i in Sapporo can help with telephone reservations for lodgings throughout Hokkaidō and also publishes an excellent camping guide. The Hokkaidō Youth Hostel Association Web site also has information in English.

Plaza i ☎ 011/211-3678. **Hokkaidō Youth Hostel Association** ☎ 011/825-3389 ⊕ www.youthhostel.or.jp/English.

TOURS

The Japan Travel Bureau runs tours of Hokkaidō from Tōkyō, lasting from a few to several days. These include airfare, hotel, and meals and stop at major cities and scenic areas. Bookings should be made at least 10 days in advance. Although your guide may speak some English, the tours are geared to domestic travelers and are conducted in Japanese.

Japan Travel Bureau ☎ 03/5620-9500 in Tōkyō.

TRAIN TRAVEL

With the 55-km (34-mi) Seikan Tunnel permitting train travel between Hokkaidō and Honshū, the train journey from Tōkyō to Sapporo can take as little as 10 hours. This trip involves a combination of the Shinkansen train to Morioka (2½ hours), the northernmost point on the Tōhoku Shinkansen Line, and a change to an express train for the remaining journey to Hakodate (4 hours, 20 minutes) and then on to Sapporo (3¼ hours). The JR Pass covers this route (the cost is ¥22,430 without the pass). The Hokutosei sleeper train provides greater comfort if not speed. It makes the voyage in 17 hours and eliminates the need to change trains. The fare is ¥23,520 (¥9,450 for JR Pass holders). Forget about local trains from Tōkyō (¥14,070); the combined travel time to Sapporo is 30 hours, not including the required overnight stop in Aomori. Travelers with more time than cash would do better on the ferry.

Japan Railways (JR) has routes connecting most of the major cities. For the most part, trains travel on less scenic routes and are simply efficient means to reach the areas that you want to explore. Bus routes pass through the more scenic areas.

Japan Rail's English-language information line provides price and schedule information for JR lines nationwide.

🚉 Train Information **Japan Railway Information Line** ☎ 03/3423-0111.

TRANSPORTATION AROUND HOKKAIDŌ

The best way for foreign visitors to explore is by car. Most car-rental companies offer the option of having different pick-up and drop-off locations and will meet customers from train, ferries, and local flights. Long-distance buses are a good way to cut some driving miles off a Hokkaidō journey, but check that the service will use the expressways and is not stopping at every village.

VISITOR INFORMATION

The Hokkaidō Tourist Association has an office in Tōkyō, on the second floor of the Kokusai Kankō Kaikan Building, near the Yaesu exit of Tōkyō Station. The Japan National Tourist Organization's Tourist Information Center (TIC) in Tōkyō has free maps and brochures on Hokkaidō. Within Hokkaidō, the best place for travel information is Sapporo.

Important regional tourist information centers are in Akan-ko, Noboribetsu Onsen, Sōun-kyō Onsen, and Tōya-ko.

There are bus and train travel information centers at all the major train stations.

Japan Travel Phone, the toll-free nationwide service for English-language assistance or travel information, is available from 9 to 5, seven days a week. You may see pamphlets listing other numbers for different areas of Japan; however, these numbers have been consolidated into one toll-free number.

🚉 Tourist Information **Hokkaidō Tourist Association** ✉ 1-8-3 Marunōchi, Chiyoda-ku, Tōkyō ☎ 03/3214-2481. **Japan Travel Phone** ☎ 0088/22-4800. **Regional Tourist Information Centers** ☎ 0154/67-2254 in Akan-ko, 0143/84-3311 in Noboribetsu Onsen, 01658/5-1811 in Sōun-kyō Onsen, 01427/5-2446 in Tōya-ko. **Tourist Information Center (TIC)** ✉ Tōkyō International Forum Bldg., Fl. B-1, 3-5-1 Marunōchi, Chiyoda-ku, Tōkyō ☎ 03/3201-3331.

THE DISCREET CHARM OF JAPANESE CUISINE

EAVE BEHIND THE HUMIDITY OF JAPAN IN SUMMER and part the crisp linen curtain of the neighborhood *sushi-ya* some hot night in mid-July. Enter a world of white cypress and chilled sea urchin, where a welcome *oshibori* (hot towel for cleaning your hands) awaits and a master chef stands at your beck and call. A cup of tea to begin, a tiny mound of ginger to freshen the palate, and you're ready to choose from the colorful array of fresh seafood on ice inside a glass case before you. Bite-size morsels arrive in friendly pairs, along with a glass of ice-cold beer. The young apprentice runs up and down, making sure everyone has tea—and anything else that might be needed. The chef has trained for years in his art, and he's proud, in his stoic way, to demonstrate it. The *o-tsukuri* (a kind of sashimi) you've ordered arrives; today the thinly sliced raw tuna comes in the shape of a rose. The fourth round you order brings with it an unexpected ribbon of cucumber, sliced with a razor-sharp sushi knife into sections that expand like an accordion. The chef's made your day . . .

Red-paper lanterns dangling in the dark above 1,000 tiny food stalls on the backstreets of Tōkyō . . . To the weary Japanese salaryman on his way home from the office, these *akachōchin* (red lanterns) are a prescription for the best kind of therapy known for the "Subterranean Homesick Blues," Japanese style: one last belly-warming bottle of sake, a nerve-soothing platter of grilled chicken wings, and perhaps a few words of wisdom for the road. Without these nocturnal way stations, many a fuzzy-eyed urban refugee would never survive that rumbling, fluorescent nightmare known as the last train home.

And where would half of Japan's night-owl college students be if not for the local *shokudō,* as the neighborhood not-so-greasy spoon is known? Separated at last from mother's protective guidance (and therefore without a clue as to how to boil an egg or heat a bowl of soup), the male contingent of young lodging-house boarders put their lives in the hands of the old couple who run the neighborhood café. Bent furtively over a platter of *karē-raisu* (curry and rice) or *tonkatsu teishoku* (pork cutlet set meal), these ravenous young men thumb through their baseball comics each night, still on the road to recovery from a childhood spent memorizing mathematical formulas and English phrases they hope they'll never have to use.

Down a dimly lighted backstreet not two blocks away, a geisha in all her elaborate finery walks her last silk-suited customer out to his chauffeur-driven limousine. He has spent the evening being pampered, feasted, and fan-danced in the rarefied air of one of Tōkyō's finest *ryōtei.* (You must be invited to these exclusive eateries—or be a regular patron, introduced by another regular patron who vouched for your reputation with his own.) There have been the most restrained of traditional dances, some shamisen playing—an oh-so-tastefully suggestive tête-à-tête. The customer has been drinking the very finest sake, accompanied by a succession of exquisitely presented hors d'oeuvres—what amounts to a seven-course meal in the end is the formal Japanese haute cuisine known as *kaiseki.* If it were not for his company's expense account, by now he would have spent the average man's monthly salary. Luckily for him, he's not the average man.

On a stool now, under the flimsy awning of a street stall, shielded from the wind and rain by flapping tarps, heated only by a portable kerosene stove and the steam from a vat of boiling noodles, you'll find neither tourist nor ptomaine. Here sits the everyday workingman, glass of *shōchū* (a strong liquor made from sweet potatoes) in sun-baked hand, arguing over the Tigers' chances of winning the Japan Series as he zealously slurps down a bowl of hot noodle soup sprinkled with red-pepper sauce—more atmosphere and livelier company than you're likely to find anywhere else in Japan. The *yatai-san,* as these inimitable street vendors are known, are an amiable, if disappearing, breed.

Somewhere between the street stalls and the exclusive ryōtei, a vast culinary world exists in Japan. Tiny, over-the-counter restaurants, each with its own specialty—from familiar favorites, such as tempura, sukiyaki, or sushi to exotic delicacies, like *unagi* (eel) or *fugu* (blowfish)—inhabit every city side street. Comfortable, country-style restaurants abound, serving a variety of different *nabemono*, the one-pot stew dishes cooked right at your table. There are also lively neighborhood *robatayaki* grills, where cooks in happi coats wield skewered bits of meat, seafood, and vegetables over a hot charcoal grill as you watch.

A dozen years ago, sukiyaki and tempura were exotic enough for most Western travelers. Those were the days when raw fish was still something a traveler needed fortitude to try. But with *soba* (buckwheat noodle) shops and sushi bars popping up everywhere from Los Angeles to Paris, it seems that—at long last—the joy of Japanese cooking has found its way westward.

There *is* something special, however, about visiting the tiger in his lair—something no tame circus cat could ever match. Although tours to famous temples and scenic places can provide important historical and cultural background material, there's nothing like a meal in a local restaurant—be it under the tarps of the liveliest street stall or within the quiet recesses of an elegant Japanese inn—for a taste of the real Japan. Approaching a platter of fresh sashimi in Tōkyō is like devouring a hot dog smothered in mustard and onions in Yankee Stadium. There's nothing like it in the world.

The Essentials of a Japanese Meal

The basic formula for a traditional Japanese meal is deceptively simple. It starts with soup, followed by raw fish, then the entrée (grilled, steamed, simmered, or fried fish, chicken, or vegetables), and ends with rice and pickles, with perhaps some fresh fruit for dessert, and a cup of green tea. It's as simple as that—almost.

An exploration of any cuisine should begin at the beginning, with a basic knowledge of what it is you're eating: rice, of course—the traditional staple; and seafood—grilled, steamed, fried, stewed, or raw; chicken, pork, or beef, at times—in that order of frequency; a wide variety of vegetables (wild and cultivated), steamed, sautéed, blanched, or pickled, perhaps—but never overcooked; soybeans in every form imaginable, from tofu to soy sauce; and seaweed, in and around lots of things.

The basics are just that. But there are, admittedly, a few twists to the story. Beyond the raw fish, it's the incredible variety of vegetation used in Japanese cooking that still surprises the Western palate: *take-no-ko* (bamboo shoots), *renkon* (lotus root), and the treasured *matsutake* mushrooms (which grow wild in jealously guarded forest hideaways and sometimes sell for more than $60 apiece), to name a few.

Tangy garnishes, both wild and domestic, such as *kinome* (leaves of the Japanese prickly ash pepper tree), *mitsuba* (trefoil, of the parsley family), and *shiso* (a member of the mint family), are used as a foil for oily foods. The more familiar-sounding ingredients, such as sesame and ginger, appear in abundance, as do the less familiar—*wasabi* (Japanese horseradish), *yuri-ne* (lily bulbs), *ginnan* (ginko nuts), and *daikon* (gigantic white radishes). Exotic? Perhaps, but delicious, and nothing here bites back. Simple? Yes, if you understand a few of the ground rules.

Absolute freshness is first. According to world-renowned Japanese chef Shizuo Tsuji, soup and raw fish are the two test pieces of Japanese cuisine. Freshness is the criterion for both: "I can tell at a glance by the texture of their skins—like the bloom of youth on a young girl—whether the fish is really fresh," Tsuji says in *The Art of Japanese Cooking*. A comparison as startling, perhaps, as it is revealing. To a Japanese chef, freshness is an unparalleled virtue, and much of a chef's reputation relies on the ability to obtain the finest ingredients at the peak of season: fish brought in from the sea this morning (not yesterday) and vegetables from the earth (not the hothouse), if at all possible.

Simplicity is next. Rather than embellishing foods with heavy spices and rich sauces, the Japanese chef prefers flavors au naturel. Flavors are enhanced, not elaborated, accented rather than concealed. Without a heavy dill sauce, fish is permitted a degree of natural fishiness—a garnish of fresh red ginger will be provided to offset the flavor rather than to disguise it.

The third prerequisite is beauty. Simple, natural foods must appeal to the eye as well as to the palate. Green peppers on a vermilion dish, perhaps, or an egg custard in a blue bowl. Rectangular dishes for a round eggplant. So important is the seasonal element in Japanese cooking that maple leaves and pine needles will be used to accent an autumn dish. Or two small summer delicacies, a pair of freshwater *ayu* fish, will be grilled with a purposeful twist to their tails to make them "swim" across a crystal platter and thereby suggest the coolness of a mountain stream on a hot August night.

Mood can make or break the entire meal, and the Japanese connoisseur will go to great lengths to find the perfect yakitori stand—a smoky, lively place—an environment appropriate to the occasion, offering a night of grilled chicken, cold beer, and camaraderie.

Atmosphere depends as much on the company as it does on the lighting or the color of the drapes. In Japan this seems to hold particularly true. The popularity of a particular *nomiya*, or bar, depends entirely on the affability of the *mama-san*, that long-suffering lady who's been listening to your troubles for years. In fancier places, mood becomes a fancier problem, to the point of quibbling over the proper amount of "water music" trickling in the basin outside your private room.

Culture: The Main Course

Sipping coffee at a sidewalk café on the Left Bank, you begin to feel what it means to be a Parisian. Slurping noodles on tatami in a neighborhood soba shop overlooking a tiny interior garden, you start to understand what it's like to live in Japan. Food, no matter which country you're in, has much to say about the culture as a whole.

Beyond the natural dictates of climate and geography, Japanese food has its roots in the centuries-old cuisine of the imperial court, which was imported from China— a religiously formal style of meal called *yusoku ryōri*. It was prepared only by specially appointed chefs, who had the status of priests in the service of the emperor, in a culinary ritual that is now nearly a lost art. Although it was never popularly served in centuries past (a modified version can still be found in Kyōto), much of the ceremony and careful attention to detail of yusoku ryōri are reflected today in the formal kaiseki meal.

Kaiseki Ryōri: Japanese Haute Cuisine

Kaiseki refers to the most elegant of all styles of Japanese food available today, and *ryōri* means cuisine. Rooted in the banquet feasts of the aristocracy, by the late 16th century it had developed into a meal to accompany ceremonial tea. The word *kaiseki* refers to a heated stone (*seki*) that Buddhist monks placed inside the folds (*kai*) of their kimonos to keep off the biting cold in the unheated temple halls where they slept and meditated.

Cha-kaiseki, as the formal meal served with tea (*cha*) is called, is intended to take the edge off your hunger at the beginning of a formal tea ceremony and to counterbalance the astringent character of the thick green tea. In the tea ceremony balance—and the sense of calmness and well-being it inspires—is the keynote.

The formula for the basic Japanese meal derived originally from the rules governing formal kaiseki—not too large a portion, just enough; not too spicy, but perhaps with a savory sprig of trefoil to offset the bland tofu. A grilled dish is served before a steamed one; a steamed dish before a simmered one; a square plate is used for a round food; a bright green maple leaf is placed to one side to herald the arrival of spring.

Kaiseki ryōri appeals to all the senses at once. An atmosphere is created in which the meal is to be experienced. The poem in calligraphy on a hanging scroll and the flowers in the alcove set the seasonal theme, a motif picked up in the pattern of the dishware chosen for the evening. The colors and shapes of the vessels complement the foods served on them. The visual harmony presented is as vital as the balance and variety of flavors of the foods themselves, for which the ultimate criterion is freshness. The finest ryōtei will never serve a fish or vegetable out of its proper season—no matter how marvelous a winter melon today's modern greenhouses can guarantee. Melons are for rejoicing in the summer's bounty . . . period.

Kaiseki ryōri found its way out of the formal tearooms and into a much earthier realm of the senses when it became the fashionable snack with sake in the teahouses of the geisha quarters during the 17th and 18th centuries. Not only the atmosphere but the Chinese characters used to write the word *kaiseki* are different in this context; they refer to aristocratic "banquet seats." And banquets they are. To partake in the most exclusive of these evenings in a teahouse in Kyōto still requires a personal introduction and a great deal of money, though these days many traditional restaurants serve elegant kaiseki meals (without the geisha) at much more reasonable prices.

One excellent way to experience this incomparable cuisine on a budget is to visit a kaiseki restaurant at lunchtime. Many of them offer *kaiseki bentō* lunches at a fraction of the dinner price, exquisitely presented in lacquered boxes, as a sampler of their full-course evening meal.

Shōjin Ryōri: Zen-Style Vegetarian Cuisine

Shōjin ryōri is the Zen-style vegetarian cuisine. Traditional Japanese cuisine emphasizes the natural flavor of the freshest ingredients in season, without the embellishment of heavy spices and rich sauces. This probably developed out of the Zen belief in the importance of simplicity and austerity as paths to enlightenment. Protein is provided by an almost limitless number of dishes made from soybeans—such as *yu-dōfu,* or boiled bean curd, and *yuba,* sheets of pure protein skimmed from vats of steaming soy milk. The variety and visual beauty of a full-course shōjin ryōri meal offer new dimensions in dining to the vegetarian gourmet. *Goma-dōfu,* or sesame-flavored bean curd, for example, is a delicious taste treat, as is *nasu-dengaku,* grilled eggplant covered with a sweet *miso* sauce.

There are many fine restaurants—particularly in the Kyōto area—that specialize in shōjin ryōri, but it's best to seek out one of the many temples throughout Japan that open their doors to visitors; here you can try these special meals within the actual temple halls, which often overlook a traditional garden.

Sushi, Sukiyaki, Tempura & Nabemono: A Comfortable Middle Ground

Leaving the rarefied atmosphere of teahouses and temples behind, an entire realm of more down-to-earth gastronomic pleasures waits to be explored. Sushi, sukiyaki, and tempura are probably the three most commonly known Japanese dishes in the Western world. Restaurants serving these dishes are to be found in abundance in every major hotel in Japan. It is best, however, to try each of these in a place that specializes in just one.

An old Japanese proverb says *"Mochi wa mochi-ya"*—if you want rice cakes, go to a rice-cake shop. The same goes for sushi. Sushi chefs undergo a lengthy apprenticeship, and the trade is considered an art form. Possessing the discipline of a judo player, the *itamae-san* (or, "man before . . . or behind . . . the counter," depending on your point of view) at a sushi-ya is a real master. Every neighborhood has its own sushi shop, and everyone you meet has his or her own secret little place to go for sushi.

The Central Wholesale Market district in Tōkyō is so popular for its sushi shops that you usually have to wait in line for a seat at the counter. Some are quite expensive, while others are relatively cheap. "Know before you go" is the best policy; "Ask before you eat" is next. Among the dozens types of sushi available, some of the most popular are *maguro* (tuna), *ebi* (shrimp), *hamachi* (yellowtail), *uni* (sea urchin), *anago* (conger eel), *tako* (octopus), *awabi* (abalone), and *akagai* (red shellfish). The day's selection is usually displayed in a glass case at the counter, which enables you to point at whatever catches your eye.

Tempura, the battered and deep-fried fish and vegetable dish, is almost certain to taste better at a small shop that serves nothing else. The difficulties of preparing this seemingly simple dish lie in achieving the proper consistency of the batter and the right temperature and freshness of the oil in which it is fried.

Sukiyaki is the popular beef dish that is sautéed with vegetables in an iron skillet at the table. The tenderness of the beef is the determining factor here, and many of the best sukiyaki houses also run their own butcher shops so that they can control the quality of the beef they serve. Although beef did not become a part of the Japanese diet until the turn of the 20th century, the Japanese are justifiably proud of their notorious beer-fed and hand-massaged beef (e.g., the famous Matsuzaka beef from Kōbe and the equally delicious Ōmi beef from Shiga Prefecture).

Shabu-shabu is another possibility, though this dish has become more popular with tourists than with the Japanese. It's similar to sukiyaki in that it is prepared at the table with a combination of vegetables, but it differs in that shabu-shabu is swished briefly in boiling water, while sukiyaki is sautéed in oil and, usually, a slightly sweetened soy sauce. The word *shabu-shabu* actually refers to this swishing sound.

Nabemono, or one-pot dishes, are not as familiar to Westerners as the three mentioned above, but the possibilities are endless, and nothing tastes better on a cold winter's night. Simmered in a light, fish-based broth, these stews can be made of almost anything: chicken (*tori-nabe*), oysters (*kaki-nabe*), or the sumō wrestler's favorite, the hearty *chanko-nabe* . . .with something in it for everyone. Nabemono is a popular family or party dish. The restaurants specializing in nabemono often have a casual, country atmosphere.

Bentō, Soba, Udon & Robatayaki: Feasting on a Budget

Tales of unsuspecting tourists swallowed up by money-gobbling monsters disguised as quaint little restaurants on the back-streets of Japan's major cities abound. There are, however, many wonderful little places that provide excellent meals and thoughtful service—and have no intention of straining anyone's budget. To find them, you must not be afraid to venture outside your hotel lobby or worry that the dining spot has no menu in English. Many restaurants have menus posted out front that clearly state the full price you can expect to pay (some do add a 10% tax, and possibly a service charge, so ask in advance).

Here are a few suggestions for Japanese meals that do not cost a fortune and are usually a lot more fun than relying on the familiar but unexciting international fast-food chains for quick meals on a budget: *bentō* (box) lunches, *soba* or *udon* (noodle) dishes, and the faithful neighborhood *robatayaki* (grills), ad infinitum.

The Bentō. This is the traditional Japanese box lunch, available for takeout everywhere and usually comparatively inexpensive. It can be purchased in the morning to be taken along and eaten later, either outdoors or on the train as you travel between cities. The bentō consists of rice, pickles, grilled fish or meat, and vegetables, in an almost limitless variety of combinations to suit the season. The basement levels of most major department stores sell beautifully prepared bentō to go. In fact, a department-store basement is a great place to sample and purchase the whole range of foods offered in Japan: among the things available are French bread, imported cheeses, traditional bean cakes, chocolate bonbons, barbecued chicken, grilled eel, roasted peanuts, fresh vegetables, potato salads, pickled bamboo shoots, and smoked salmon.

The o-bentō (the o is honorific) in its most elaborate incarnation is served in gorgeous, multilayer lacquered boxes as an accompaniment to outdoor tea ceremonies or for flower-viewing parties held in spring. Exquisite bentō-bako (lunch boxes) made in the Edo period (1603–1868) can be found in museums and antiques shops. They are inlaid with mother-of-pearl and delicately hand-painted in gold. A wide variety of sizes and shapes of bentō boxes are still handmade in major cities and small villages throughout Japan in both formal and informal styles. They make excellent souvenirs.

A major benefit to the bentō is its portability. Sightseeing can take you down many an unexpected path, and if you bring your own bentō you won't need to worry about finding an appropriate place to stop for a bite to eat. No vacationing Japanese family would ever be without one tucked carefully inside their rucksacks right beside the thermos bottle of tea. If they do somehow run out of time to prepare one in advance—no problem—there are hundreds of wonderful options in the form of the beloved eki-ben (train-station box lunch).

Each whistle-stop in Japan takes great pride in the uniqueness and flavor of the special box lunches, featuring the local delicacy, sold right at the station or from vendors inside the trains. The pursuit of the eki-ben has become a national pastime in this nation in love with its trains. Entire books have been written in Japanese explaining the features of every different eki-ben available along the 26,000 km (16,120 mi) of railways in the country. This is one of the best ways to sample the different styles of regional cooking in Japan and is highly recommended to any traveler who plans to spend time on the Japan Railway trains.

Soba and Udon. Soba and udon (noodle) dishes are another lifesaving treat for stomachs (and wallets) unaccustomed to exotic flavors (and prices). Small shops serving soba (thin, brown buckwheat noodle) and udon (thick, white-wheat noodle) dishes in a variety of combinations can be found in every neighborhood in the country. Both can be ordered plain (ask for o-soba or o-udon), in a lightly seasoned broth flavored with bonito and soy sauce, or in combination with things like tempura shrimp (tempura soba or udon) or chicken (tori-namban soba or udon). For a refreshing change in summer, try zaru soba, cold noodles to be dipped in a tangy soy sauce. Nabeyaki-udon is a hearty winter dish of udon noodles, assorted vegetables, and egg served in the pot in which it was cooked.

Robatayaki. Perhaps the most exuberant of inexpensive options is the robatayaki (grill). Beer mug in hand, elbow to elbow at the counter of one of these popular neighborhood grills—that is the best way to relax and join in with the local fun. You'll find no pretenses here—just a wide variety of plain, good food (as much or as little as you want) with the proper amount of alcohol to get things rolling.

Robata means fireside, and the style of cooking is reminiscent of old-fashioned Japanese farmhouse meals cooked over a charcoal fire in an open hearth. It's easy to order at a robatayaki shop because the selection of food to be grilled is lined up behind glass at the counter. Fish, meat, vegetables, tofu—take your pick. Some popular choices are yaki-zakana (grilled fish), particularly karei-shio-yaki (salted and grilled flounder) and *asari saka-mushi* (clams simmered in sake). Try the grilled Japanese shiitake mushrooms, *shishi-tō* (green peppers), and the *hiyayakko* (chilled tofu sprinkled with bonito flakes, diced green onions, and soy sauce). Yakitori can be ordered in most robatayaki shops, though many inexpensive drinking places specialize in this popular barbecued chicken dish.

The budget dining possibilities in Japan don't stop there. **Okonomiyaki** is another choice. Somewhat misleadingly called the Japanese pancake, it is actually a mixture of vegetables, meat, and seafood in an egg-and-flour batter grilled at your table, much better with beer than with butter. It's most popular for lunch or as an after-movie snack.

Another is **kushi-age**, skewered bits of meat, seafood, and vegetables battered, dipped in bread crumbs, and deep-fried. There are many small restaurants serving only kushi-age at a counter, and many of the robatayaki serve it as a side dish. It's also a popular drinking snack.

Oden, a winter favorite, is another inexpensive meal. A variety of meats and vegetables slowly simmered in vats, it goes well with beer or sake. This, too, may be ordered piece by piece (*ippin*) from the assortment you see steaming away behind the counter or *moriawase*, in which case the cook will serve you up an assortment.

Beer, Wine, Sake & Spirits

Japan has four large breweries, Asahi, Kirin, Sapporo, and Suntory. Asahi and Kirin are the two heavyweights, constantly battling for the much coveted title of "Japan's No. 1 Brewery," but many beer fans rate Suntory's Malts brand and Sapporo's Yebisu brand as the tastiest brews in the land. Since a change in the law in the early 1990s, an increasing number of microbreweries have sprung up across Japan, but locally produced brews can still be hard to find, even when you know they exist.

Japan produces a small amount of domestic wine, but imports far more from both the Old and New Worlds. Wine is easy to find in neighborhood liquor shops and 24-hour convenience stores, but department stores boast the best selections.

Shōchū, a liquor made from grain and particularly associated with the southern island of Kyūshū, is drunk either on the rocks or mixed with water, hot or cold. Sometimes a wedge of lemon or a small pickled apricot, known as *umeboshi,* is added as well.

Japan's number one alcoholic beverage is *sake* (pronounced *sa*-kay), the "beverage of the samurai," as one brewery puts it. There are more than 2,000 different brands of sake produced throughout Japan. Like other kinds of wine, sake comes in sweet (*amakuchi*) and dry (*karakuchi*) varieties; these are graded *tokkyū* (superior class), *ikkyū* (first class), and *nikkyū* (second class) and are priced accordingly. (Connoisseurs say this ranking is for tax purposes and is not necessarily a true indication of quality.)

Best drunk at room temperature (*nurukan*) so as not to alter the flavor, sake is also served heated (*atsukan*) or with ice (*rokku de*). It's poured from *tokkuri* (small ceramic vessels) into tiny cups called *choko*. The diminutive size of these cups shouldn't mislead you into thinking you can't drink too much. The custom of making sure that your companion's cup never runs dry often leads the novice astray.

Junmaishu is the term for pure rice wine, a blend of rice, yeast, and water to which no extra alcohol has been added. Junmaishu has the strongest and most distinctive flavor, compared with various other methods of brewing and is preferred by the sake *tsū*, as connoisseurs are known.

Apart from the *nomiya* (bars) and restaurants, the place to sample sake is the *izakaya,* a drinking establishment that serves only sake, usually dozens of different kinds, including a selection of *jizake,* the kind produced in limited quantities by small regional breweries throughout the country.

Regional Differences

Tōkyō people are known for their candor and vigor, as compared with the refined restraint of people in the older, more provincial Kyōto. This applies as much to food as it does to language, art, and fashion. Foods in the Kansai district (including Kyōto, Nara, Ōsaka, and Kōbe) tend to be lighter, the sauces less spicy, the soups not as hardy as those of the Kantō district, of which Tōkyō is the center. How many Tōkyōites have been heard to grumble about the "weak" soba broth on their visits to Kyōto? You go to Kyōto for the delicate and formal kaiseki, to Tōkyō for sushi.

Nigiri zushi (note that the pronunciation of "sushi" changes to "zushi" when combined with certain words), with pieces of raw fish on bite-size balls of rice (the form with which most Westerners are familiar), originated in the Kantō district, where there is a bounty of fresh fish. *Saba zushi* is the specialty of landlocked Kyōto. Actually the forerunner of nigiri zushi, it is made by pressing salt-preserved mackerel onto a bed of rice in a mold.

Every island in the Japanese archipelago has its specialty, and within each island every province has its own *meibutsu ryōri,* or specialty dish. In Kyūshū try *shippoku-ryōri,* a banquet-style feast of different dishes in which you eat your way up to a large fish mousse topped with shrimp. This dish is the local specialty in Nagasaki, for centuries the only port through which Japan had contact with the West.

On the island of Shikoku, try *sawachi-ryōri,* an extravaganza of elaborately prepared platters of fresh fish dishes, which is the specialty of Kōchi, the main city on the Pacific Ocean side of the island. In Hokkaidō, where salmon dishes are the local specialty, try *ishikari-nabe,* a hearty salmon-and-vegetable stew.

The Bottom Line

A couple of things take some getting used to. Things will be easier for you in Japan if you've had some experience with chopsticks. Some of the tourist-oriented restaurants (and, of course, all those serving Western food) provide silverware, but most traditional restaurants in Japan offer only chopsticks. It's a good idea to practice. The secret is to learn to move only the chopstick on top rather than trying to move both at once.

Sitting on the floor is another obstacle for many, including the younger generation of Japanese, to whom the prospect of sitting on a cushion on tatami mats for an hour or so means nothing but stiff knees and numb feet. Because of this, many restaurants now have rooms with tables and chairs. The most traditional restaurants, however, have kept to the customary style of dining in tatami rooms. Give it a try. Nothing can compare with a full-course kaiseki meal brought to your room at a traditional inn. Fresh from the bath, robed in a cotton kimono, you are free to relax and enjoy it all, including the view. After all, the carefully landscaped garden outside your door was designed specifically to be seen from this position.

The service in Japan is usually superb, particularly at a *ryōri-ryokan,* as restaurant-inns are called. A maid is assigned to anticipate your every need (even a few you didn't know you had). "*O-kyakusama wa kamisama desu*" (the customer is god), as the old Japanese proverb goes. People who prefer to dine in privacy have been known to say the service is too much.

Other problems? "The portions are too small" is a common complaint. The solution is an adjustment in perspective. In the world of Japanese cuisine, there are colors to delight in, and shapes, textures, and flavors are balanced for your pleasure. Naturally, the aroma, flavor, and freshness of the foods have importance, but so do the dishware, the design of the room, the sound of water in a stone basin outside. You are meant to leave the table delighted—not stuffed. An appeal is made to all the senses through the food itself, the atmosphere, and appreciation for a carefully orchestrated feast in every sense of the word—these, and the luxury of time spent in the company of friends.

This is not to say that every Japanese restaurant offers aesthetic perfection. Your basic train-platform, stand-up, gulp-it-down noodle stall ("eat-and-out" in under six minutes) should leave no doubts as to the truth of the old saying that "all feet tread not in one shoe."

In the end you'll discover that the joy of eating in Japan lies in the adventure of exploring the possibilities. Along every city street you'll find countless little eateries specializing in anything you can name—and some you can't. In the major cities, you'll find French restaurants, British pubs, and little places serving Italian, Chinese, Indian, and American food. In country towns you can explore a world of regional delicacies found nowhere else. Each meal can be paired with a suitable drink, too, usually sake or beer. (For more on what to drink in Japan drinks, see the CloseUp "Japanese Beer, Wine, Spirits & Sake" in Chapter 2, Where to Eat.)

There's something for everyone and every budget—from the most exquisitely prepared and presented formal kaiseki meal to a delicately sculpted salmon mousse à la nouvelle cuisine, from skewers of grilled chicken in barbecue sauce to a steaming bowl of noodle soup at an outdoor stall. And much to the chagrin of culinary purists, Japan has no dearth of international fast-food chains—from burgers to spareribs to fried chicken to doughnuts to 31 flavors of American ice cream.

Sometimes the contradictions of this intriguing culture—as seen in the startling contrast between ancient traditions and modern industrial life—seem almost overwhelming. Who would ever have thought you could face eating a salad that included seaweed along with lettuce and tomatoes, or that you could happily dig into green-tea ice cream? As the famous potter Kanjirō Kawai once said, "Sometimes it's better if you don't understand everything . . . It makes life so much more exciting."

Tips on Dining in Japan

- Don't point or gesture with chopsticks. Licking the ends of your chopsticks is rude, as is taking food from a common serving plate with the end of the chopstick you've had in your mouth. Don't stick your chopsticks upright into your food when you're done using them; instead, allow them to rest on the side of your dish or bowl.

- There's no taboo against slurping your noodle soup, though women are generally less boisterous about it than men.

- Pick up the soup bowl and drink directly from it, rather than leaning over the table to sip it. Take the fish or vegetables from it with your chopsticks. Return the lid to the soup bowl when you are finished. The rice bowl, too, is to be picked up and held in one hand while you eat from it.

- When drinking with a friend, don't pour your own. Take the bottle and pour for the other person. She will in turn reach for the bottle and pour for you. The Japanese will attempt to top your drink off after every few sips.

- The Japanese don't pour sauces on their rice in a traditional meal. Sauces are intended for dipping foods lightly, not for dunking or soaking.

- Among faux pas that are considered nearly unpardonable, the worst perhaps is blowing your nose. Excuse yourself and leave the room if this becomes necessary.

- Although McDonald's and Häagen-Dazs have made great inroads on the custom of never eating in public, it's still considered gauche to munch on a hamburger (or an ice-cream cone) as you walk along a public street.

— by Diane Durston

ARTS & CULTURE

PAPERMAKING & CALLIGRAPHY

Papermaking

Handmade paper and shōji (paper screens) are unique and beautiful Japanese creations that are surprisingly affordable, unlike other traditional crafts. *Washi*, Japanese paper, can have a translucent quality that seems to argue against its amazing durability.

The use of paper as a decorative symbol in Shintō shrines—probably due to its purity when new—gives an added importance to the already high esteem the Japanese hold for paper and the written word. Paper is a symbol of *kami* (god), and the process to make it is almost ritualistic. Usually, the inner bark of the paper mulberry is used, but leaves, ropelike fibers, even gold flake can be added in the later steps of the process for a dramatic effect. The raw branches are steamed and bleached by exposure to cold or snow. The fibers are boiled with ash lye and subsequently rinsed. After chopping and beating the pulp, it's soaked in a starchy taro solution, and the textures or leaves are added for decoration. A screen is dipped in the floating fibers, and when the screen is pulled up evenly, a sheet of paper is formed. Amazingly, wet sheets when stacked do not stick together.

The best places to view the papermaking process are Kurodani, near Kyōto; Mino, in central Japan; and Yame, near Kurume. Different parts of Japan specialize in different products. Gifu is known for its umbrellas and lanterns, Nagasaki for its distinctive kites, and Nara for its calligraphy paper and utensils. A light, inexpensive, and excellent gift, Japanese paper is a handicraft you can easily carry home as a souvenir.

Calligraphy

Calligraphy in Japan arrived around AD 500 with Chinese characters. By 800 the *kana* of Japanese language—the two alphabets—began to be artistically written as well. The art of calligraphy lies not only in the creative execution of the characters, as in Western calligraphy, but also in the direct expression of the artist's personality and message. Thick, heavy splotches or delicate, watery lines should be viewed first without respect to their meaning, as creative forms displaying emotion. Then the meaning can come to the fore, adding substance to the art.

As with all traditional arts in Japan, there are various schools and styles of calligraphy—five in this case—each with more or less emphasis on structure and expression. The Chinese exported the *tensho* (a primitive style called "seal") and *reisho* (scribe's style, an advanced primitive form) to Japan with written Buddhist scripture. The Japanese developed three other styles: *sōsho* (cursive writing), the looser *gyōsho* (semicursive, or "running" style), and *kaisho* (block, or standard style). The first two demonstrate the Japanese emphasis on expression to convey an impromptu, flowing image unique to the moment—retouching and erasing is impossible. Kaisho has since developed into carved calligraphy on wood—either engraved or in relief—and the traditional stamp art seen at temples and in print. Avant-garde styles now popular, which are difficult even for Japanese to read, can seem the most interesting to foreigners as an art form. You'll see this style in many traditional restaurants.

Go to visitor centers if you would like to try out a brush. Reading: *The Art of Japanese Calligraphy,* by Yūjiro Nakata.

— David Miles & Barbara Blechman

CERAMICS & LACQUERWARE

Ceramics

With wares that range from clean, flawlessly decorated porcelain to rustic pieces so spirited that they almost breathe, Japanese pottery attracts its share of enthusiasts and ardent collectors for good reason. During the past several decades, it has significantly influenced North American ceramic artists. The popularity of Raku firing techniques, adapted from those of the famous Japanese pottery clan of the same name, is one example.

Japanese ceramic styles are defined regionally. Arita *yaki* (ceramic ware from Arita on Kyūshū), Tobe yaki, Kutani yaki, and Kyōto's Kyō yaki and Kiyomizu yaki are all porcelain ware. True to the nature of porcelain—a delicate fine-particled clay body—these styles are either elaborately decorated or covered with images. Stoneware decoration tends to have an earthier but no less refined appeal, befitting the rougher texture of the clay body. Mashiko yaki's brown, black, and white glazes are often applied in splatters. Celebrated potter Shōji Hamada (1894–1978) worked in Mashiko.

Other regional potters use glazes on stoneware for texture and coloristic effects—mottled, crusty Tokoname yaki; speckled, earth-tone Shigaraki yaki made near Kyōto; and the pasty white or blue-white Hagi yaki come to life with the surface and depth of their rustic glazes. Bizen yaki, another stoneware, has no liquid glaze applied to its surfaces. Pots are buried in ash, wrapped in straw, or colored in the firing process by the potters' manipulations of kiln conditions.

Unless your mind is set on the idea of kiln hopping in pottery towns like Hagi, Bizen, and Arita, you can find these wares in department stores. If you do go on a pilgrimage, call local kilns and tourist organizations to verify that what you want to see will be open and to ask about yearly pottery sales, during which local wares are discounted. Reading: *Inside Japanese Ceramics* (Weatherhill, 1999) by Richard L. Wilson.

Lacquerware

Japanese lacquerware has its origins in the Jōmon period (8,000–300 BC), when basic utensils were coated with lacquer resin made from tree sap. By the Nara period (AD 710–AD 784) most of the techniques we recognize today were being used. For example, *maki-e* (literally, "sprinkled picture") refers to several different techniques that use gold or silver powder in areas coated with liquid lacquer. In the Azuchi-Momoyama period (1568–1600), lacquerware exports made their way to Europe. The following period, the Edo (1603–1868), saw the broadening of the uses of lacquer for the newly prosperous merchant class.

The production of lacquerware starts with the draining, evaporation, and filtration of sap from lacquer trees. Successive layers of lacquer are carefully painted on basketry, wood, bamboo, woven textiles, metal, and even paper. The lacquer strengthens the object, making it durable for eating, carrying, or protecting fragile objects, such as fans. Lacquerware can be mirrorlike if polished; often the many layers contain inlays of mother-of-pearl or precious metals inserted between coats, creating a complicated design of exquisite beauty and delicacy. The best places to see lacquerware are Hōryū-ji in Nara—the temple has a beautiful display—and Wajima in Ishikawa. Expensive yet precious lacquerware remains one of the most distinctive and highest-quality crafts of Japan.

— David Miles & Barbara Blechman

JAPANESE GARDENS

WHAT MIGHT STRIKE US only second to the sense of beauty and calm that pervades Japanese gardens is how different they are from our own Western gardens. One key to understanding—and more fully enjoying—them is knowing that garden design, like all traditional Japanese arts, emerged out of the country's unique mixture of religious, philosophical, and artistic ideas.

Shintoism, Taoism, and Buddhism all stress the contemplation and re-creation of nature as part of the process of achieving understanding and enlightenment, and from these come many of the principles that most influence Japanese garden design.

From Shintoism, Japan's ancient religion, comes *genus loci* (the spirit of place) and the search for the divine presence in remarkable natural features: special mountains, trees, rocks, and so forth. Prevalent features of Tao influence are islands that act as a symbolic heaven for souls who achieve perfect harmony. Here sea turtles and cranes—creatures commonly represented in gardens—serve these enlightened souls.

Buddhist gardens function as settings for meditation, the goal of which is enlightenment. Shōgun and samurai were strongly drawn to Zen Buddhism and the achievement of enlightenment, and Zen gardens evolved as spaces for individuals to use almost exclusively for meditation and growth. The classic example from this time is the *karesansui*—dry landscape—consisting of meticulously placed rocks and raked gravel. It's a highly challenging style that reflects the skill of the designer.

Historically, the first garden designers in Japan were temple priests. Later, tea masters created gardens in order to refine the tea ceremony experience. A major contribution of the tea masters was the *roji*,

the path or dewy ground that emotionally and mentally prepares participants for the ceremony as it leads them through the garden to the teahouse.

Gradually gardens moved out of the exclusive realm to which only nobles, *daimyō*, (feudal lords) wealthy merchants, and poets had access, and the increasingly affluent middle class began to demand professional designers. In the process, aesthetic concerns came to override those of religion.

In addition to genus loci, karesansui style, and the roji mentioned above, here are a few terms that will help you more fully experience Japanese gardens.

Change and movement. Change is highlighted in Japanese gardens with careful attention to the seasonal variations that plants undergo: from cherry blossoms in spring to summer greenery to autumn leaf coloring to winter snow clinging to the garden's bare bones. A water element, either real or abstract, often represents movement, as with the use of raked gravel or a stone "stream."

Mie gakure. The "reveal-and-hide" principle dictates that from no point should all of a garden be visible, that there is always mystery and incompleteness, and that viewers move through a garden to contemplate its changing perspectives.

Miniaturized landscapes. Depicting celebrated natural and literary sites, these references have been one of the most frequently utilized design techniques in Japanese gardens. They hark back to their original inspiration—Fuji-san represented by a truncated cone of stones; Ama-no-Hashidate, the famous spit of land, by a stone bridge; or a mighty forest by a lone tree.

Shakkei. "Borrowed landscape" extends the boundaries of a garden by integrating a nearby attractive mountain, grove of trees, or a sweeping temple roofline, for example, and framing and capturing the view by echoing it with elements of similar shape or color inside the garden itself.

Symbolism. Abstract concepts and mythological legends, readily understood by Japan's homogeneous population, are part of the garden vocabulary. The use of boulders in a streambed can represent life's surmountable difficulties, a pine tree can stand for stability, or islands in a pond for a faraway paradise.

— David Miles & Barbara Blechman

JAPANESE TEXTILES

THE TOPIC OF TEXTILES is invariably linked to the history and nature of kimonos and costumes, which offered the best opportunity for weavers, dyers, and designers to exhibit their skills. Both Buddhism and Confucianism helped to create the four castes in Japan: samurai, Buddhist clerics, farmers, and townspeople (merchants and artisans) in descending order of importance. Courtesans and actors often slipped through the cracks and thus were exempt from the targets of the laws that reinforced these strata by making certain types of dress illegal for lower castes. Outer appearance helped to identify social rank and maintained order. Styles of embroidery and decoration and sumptuous clothing changed legal status in reaction to social upheavals and the eventual rise of the merchant class.

The types of the kimono—Japanese traditional dress attire is unisex in cut—are made from flat woven panels that provide the most surface for decoration. Although Western clothing follows the body line in a sculptural way, the Japanese use of fabric is more painterly and has little concern for body size and shape. No matter the wearer's height or weight, a kimono is made from one bolt of cloth cut and stitched into four panels and fitted with a collar. When creating a kimono, or the Buddhist clerics' *kesa* (a body wrap), no fabric is wasted. Shintō's emphasis is evident in the importance of natural fabrics, as the way of the gods was always concerned with purity and defilement.

Regional designs are the rule in textiles. Kyōto's heavily decorated Nishijin Ori is as sumptuous as Japanese fabric comes. Okinawa produces a variety of stunning fabrics, and both Kyōto's and Tōkyō's stencil dyeing techniques yield intricate, elegant patterns. The most affordable kimonos are used kimonos—which can be nearly flawless or in need of minor stitching. Kyōto's flea markets are a good venue for this. Also look for lighter weight *yukata* (robes), *obi* (sashes), or handkerchiefs from Arimatsu, near Nagoya, for example. Good places to see fabrics are Kyōto's Fūzoku Hakubutsukan (Costume Museum), Nishijin Orimono (Textile Center), and the Tōkyō National Museum, which displays garments of the Edo period.

BATHING:
AN IMMERSION COURSE

MANY JAPANESE CULTURAL PHE-NOMENA confound first-time visitors to the country, but few rituals are as opaque to foreigners as those surrounding bathing. Partly because of the importance of purification rites in Shintō, Japan's ancient indigenous religion, the art of bathing has been a crucial element of Japanese culture for centuries. Baths in Japan are as much about pleasure and relaxation as they are about washing and cleansing. Traditionally, communal bathhouses served as centers for social gatherings, and even though most modern houses and apartments have bathtubs, many Japanese still prefer the pleasures of communal bathing—either at *onsen* (hot springs) while on vacation or in public bathhouses closer to home.

Japanese bathtubs themselves are different from those in the West—they're deep enough to sit in upright with (very hot) water up to the neck—and the procedures for using them are quite different as well. You wash yourself in a special area outside the tub first. The tubs are for soaking, not washing; soap must not get into the bathwater.

Many hotels in major cities offer only Western-style reclining bathtubs, so to indulge in the pleasure of a Japanese bath you'll need to stay in a Japanese-style inn or find an *o-furo-ya* or *sentō* (public bathhouse). The latter are clean, hygienic, and easy to find. Japanese bath towels, which are typically called (*ta*-o-ru), are available for a fee at onsen and bathhouses. They are no larger than a hand towel, and they have three functions: covering your privates (and breasts in mixed bathing), washing before you bathe and scrubbing while you bathe (if desired), and drying off (wring them out hard and they will dry you quite well). If you want a larger towel to dry yourself off, you will have to bring one along.

You may at first feel justifiably apprehensive about bathing (and bathing *properly*) in an o-furo, but if you're well versed in bathing etiquette, you should soon feel at ease. And once you've experienced a variety of public baths—from the standard bathhouses found in every neighborhood to idyllic outdoor hot springs—you may find yourself an unlikely advocate of this ancient custom.

The first challenge in bathing is acknowledging that your Japanese bath mates will stare at your body. Take solace, however, in the fact that their apparent voyeurism most likely stems from curiosity.

When you enter the bathing room, help yourself to two towels, soap, and shampoo (often included in the entry fee), and grab a bucket and a stool. At one of the shower stations around the edge of the room, crouch on your bucket (or stand if you prefer) and use the handheld showers, your soap, and one of your towels to wash yourself thoroughly. A head-to-toe twice-over will impress onlookers. Rinse off, and then you may enter the public bath. When you do, you'll still have one dry towel. You can use it to cover yourself, or you can place it on your head (as you'll see many of your bath mates doing) while soaking. The water in the bath is as hot as the body can endure, and the reward for making it past the initial shock of the heat is the pleasure of a lengthy soak in water that does not become tepid. All you need to do then is lean back, relax, and experience the pleasures of Shintō-style purification—cleanse your body and enlighten your spirit. It seems, in Japan, cleanliness is next to godliness.

— David Miles

RITUAL & RELIGION

Buddhism

Buddhism in Japan grew out of a Korean king's symbolic gift of a statue of Shaka—the first Buddha, Prince Gautama—to the Yamato court in AD 538. The Soga clan adopted the foreign faith and used it as a vehicle for changing the political order of the day. After battling for control of the country, the Soga clan established itself as political rulers, and Buddhism took permanent hold of Japan. Shōtoku Taishi, the crown prince and regent during this period, sent the first Japanese ambassadors to China, which inaugurated the importation of Chinese culture, writing, and religion in Japan. Since that time several eras in Japanese history have seen the equation of consolidating state power with promulgating Buddhist influence and building temples. By the 8th century AD Japanese Buddhism's six schools of thought were well established, and priests from India and Persia came for the ceremonial opening of Tōdai-ji in Nara. Scholars argue that the importation of architectural styles and things Buddhist in this period may have had more to do with the political rather than religious needs of Japanese society. Likewise, the intertwining of religion and state and the importation of foreign ideas had undeniably political motivations during the Meiji Restoration and Japanese colonial expansion early in the 20th century. And the use of foreign ideas continues to be an essential component of understanding the social climate in Japan today.

Three waves in the development of Japanese Buddhism followed the religion's Nara-period (710–84) florescence. In the Heian period (794–894), two priests who studied in China—Saichō and Kūkai—introduced esoteric Buddhism. Near Kyōto, Saichō established a temple on Mt. Hiei—making it the most revered mountain in Japan after Mt. Fuji. Kūkai established the Shingon sect of Esoteric Buddhism on Mt. Kōya, south of Nara. It's said he is still in a state of meditation and will remain so until the arrival of the last bodhisattva (Buddhist messianic saint, *bosatsu* in Japanese). In Japanese temple architecture, Esoteric Buddhism introduced the separation of the temple into an interior for the initiated and an outer laypersons' area. This springs from Esoteric Buddhism's emphasis on *mikkyō* (secret rites) for the initiated.

Amidism was the second wave, and it flourished until the introduction of Zen in 1185. Its adherents saw the world emerging from a period of darkness, during which Buddhism had been in decline, and asserted that salvation was offered only to the believers in Amida, a Nyorai (Buddha), an enlightened being. Amidism's promise of salvation and its subsequent versions of heaven and hell earned it the appellation "Devil's Christianity" from visiting Christian missionaries in the 16th century.

The influences of Nichiren and Zen Buddhist philosophies pushed Japanese Buddhism in the unique direction it heads today. Nichiren (1222–82) was a monk who insisted that repetition of the phrase "Hail the miraculous law of the Lotus Sutra" would bring salvation, the Lotus Sutra being the supposed last and greatest sutra of Shaka. Zen Buddhism was attractive to the samurai class's ideals of discipline and worldly detachment and thus spread throughout Japan in the 12th century.

Japanese Buddhism today, like most religions in Japan, plays a minimal role in the daily life of the average Japanese. Important milestones in life provide the primary occasions for religious observance. Most Japanese have Buddhist burials. Weddings are usually in the Shintō style; recently, ceremonial references to Christian weddings have crept in, added mainly for romantic effect. (This mixing of religions may seem strange in the West, but it is wholly acceptable in Japan.) Outsiders have criticized the Japanese for lacking spirituality, and it is true that many Japanese don't make some kind of religious observance part of their daily or weekly lives. That said, there is a spiritual element in the people's unflinching belief in the group, and Japanese circles around very spiritual issues.

For more information on religious and political history, statuary manifestations of bosatsu and the Buddha, and architectural styles, consult *Buddhism, A History,* by Noble Ross Reat, and *Sources of Japanese Tradition,* by Tsunoda, De Bary, and Keene.

Shintō

Shintō—literally, "the way of the *kami* (god)"—does not preach a moral doctrine or code of ethics to follow. It's a form of animism, nature worship, based on myth and rooted to the geography and holy places of the land. Fog-enshrouded mountains, pairs of rocks, primeval forests, and geothermal activity are all manifestations of the *kami-sama* (honorable gods). For many Japanese the Shintō aspect of their lives is simply the realm of the kami-sama, not attached to a religious framework as it would be in the West. In that sense, the name describes more a philosophy than a religion.

Shintō rites that affect the daily lives of Japanese today are the wedding ceremony, the *matsuri* (festivals), and New Year's Day. The wedding ceremony uses an elaborate, colorful kimono for the bride and a simple, masculine *montsuki* (crested) kimono and *haori* overcoat with *hakama* pants for the groom. The number three is significant, and sake, of the fruits of the earth from the gods, is the ritual libation.

The neighborhood shrine's annual matsuri is a time of giving thanks for prosperity and of the blessing of homes and local businesses. *O-mikoshi,* portable shrines for the gods, are enthusiastically carried around the district by young local men. Shouting and much sake drinking are part of the celebration.

New Year's Day entails visiting an important local shrine and praying for health, happiness, success in school or business, or the safe birth of a child in the coming year. A traditional meal of rice cakes and sweet beans is served in stacked boxes at home, as part of a family time not unlike those of traditional Western winter holidays.

Like Buddhism, Shintō was used throughout Japanese history as a tool for affirming the might of a given ruling power. The Meiji Restoration in 1868 used Shintoism to reclaim the emperor's sacred right to rule and to wrest control from the last Tokugawa shōgun. Today shrines are more often visited for their beauty than for their spiritual importance, though there is no denying the ancient spiritual pull of shrines like the Ise Jingū, south of Nagoya.

— David Miles

THE TEA CEREMONY

T HE TEA CEREMONY was formalized by the 16th century under the patronage of the Ashikaga shōguns, but it was the Zen monks of the 12th century who started the practice of drinking tea for a refresher between meditation sessions. The samurai and tea master Sen-no-Rikyū elucidated "the Way," the meditative and spiritual aspect of the ceremony, and is the most revered figure in the history of tea. For samurai, the ceremony appealed to their ideals and their sense of discipline, and diversions in time of peace were necessary. In essence, tea ceremony is a spiritual and philosophical ritual whose prescribed steps and movements serve as an aid in sharpening the aesthetic sense.

Tea ceremony has a precisely choreographed program. Participants enter the teahouse or room and comment on the specially chosen art in the entryway. The ritual begins as the server prepares a cup of tea for the first patron. This process involves a strictly determined series of movements and actions, common to every ceremony, which include cleansing each of the utensils to be used. One by one the participants slurp up their bowl of tea, then eat the sweet cracker served with it. Finally, comments about the beauty of the bowls used are exchanged. The entire ritual involves contemplating the beauty in the smallest actions, focusing their meaning in the midst of the impermanence of life.

The architecture of a traditional teahouse is also consistent. There are two entrances: a service entrance for the host and server and a low door that requires that guests enter on their knees, in order to be humbled. Tearooms often have a flower arrangement or piece of artwork in the alcove, for contemplation and comment, and tatami (grass mat) flooring. Though much of the process may seem the same wherever you experience the ceremony, there are different schools of thought on the subject. The three best-known schools of tea are the Ura Senke, the Omote Senke, and the Musha Kōji, each with its own styles, emphases, and masters.

Most of your tea experiences will be geared toward the uninitiated: the tea ceremony is a rite that requires methodical initiation by education. If you don't go for instruction before your trip, keep two things in mind if you attend or are invited to a tea ceremony: first, be in the right frame of mind when you enter the room. Though the tea ceremony is a pleasant event, some people take it quite seriously, and boisterous behavior beforehand is frowned upon. Instead, make conversation that enhances a mood of serenity and invites a feeling of meditative quietude. Second, be sure to sit quietly through the serving and drinking—controlled slurping is expected—and openly appreciate the tools and cups afterward, commenting on their elegance and simplicity. This appreciation is an important final step of the ritual. Above all, pay close attention to the practiced movements of the ceremony, from the art at the entryway and the kimono of the server to the quality of the utensils. Reading: *The Book of Tea,* by Kakuzo Okakura; *Cha-no-Yu: The Japanese Tea Ceremony,* by A. L. Sadler.

— David Miles

GEISHA

BECAUSE THE CHARACTER FOR the *gei* in *geisha* stands for arts and accomplishments (*sha* in this case means person), the public image of geisha in Japan is one of high status. Although it's a common misconception in the West, geisha are not prostitutes. To become a geisha, a woman must perfect many talents. She must have grace and a thorough mastery of etiquette. She should have an accomplished singing voice and dance beautifully. She needs to have a finely tuned aesthetic sense—with flower arranging and tea ceremony—and should excel at the art of conversation. In short, she should be the ultimate companion.

These days geisha are a rare breed. They numbered a mere 10,000 in the late 1980s, as opposed to 80,000 in the 1920s. This is partly due to the increase of bar hostesses—who perform a similar function in nightclubs with virtually none of a geisha's training—not to mention the refinement and expense it takes to hire a geisha. Because she is essentially the most personal form of entertainer, the emphasis is on artistic and conversational skills, not solely on youth or beauty. Thus the typical geisha can work to an advanced age.

Geisha will establish a variety of relations with men. Besides maintaining a dependable amount of favorite customers, one might choose a *danna,* one man for emotional, sexual, and financial gratification. The geisha's exercise of choice in this matter is due partly to the fact that wages and tips alone must provide enough for her to survive. Some geisha marry, most often to an intimate client. When they do, they leave the profession.

A geisha typically starts her career as a servant at a house until 13. She continues as a *maiko* (dancing child) until she masters the requisite accomplishments at about 18. Before World War II full geisha status was achieved after a geisha experienced a *mizuage* (deflowering), with an important client of the house. Maiko must master the shamisen and learn the proper hairstyles and kimono fittings. They are a sight to see on the banks of the Kamogawa in the Gion district of Kyōto, or in Shimbashi, Akasaka, and Ginza in Tōkyō. Today geisha unions, restaurant unions, and registry offices regulate the times and fees of geisha. Fees are measured in "sticks"—generally, one hour—which is the time it would take a stick of *senkō* (incense) to burn.

Arthur Golden's minutely researched novel, *Memoirs of a Geisha,* offers a balanced and intelligent view of this society seldom to be found in English-language books.

— David Miles

JAPANESE SOCIETY: A FACTORY OF FADS

IT IS IMPOSSIBLE TO SUMMARIZE the life of a people in brief. Still, there are a few fascinating points about the Japanese that are nonetheless important to mention, even if only in passing.

The Japanese communicate among themselves in what Dr. Chie Nakane, in her *Japanese Society* (1972), calls a "vertical society." In other words, the Japanese constantly vary the way they speak with each other according to the gender, family and educational background, occupation and position, and age of the speakers. Japanese grammar reflects this by requiring different verbs for different levels of interaction. Since it is necessary for individuals to vary the way they speak according to the person, they are always considering the levels of the people around them. In a crowded country, this means the Japanese are often wondering what other people are thinking—often in an effort to gauge where they belong themselves. This constant consideration toward other members of their group makes the Japanese keen readers of other people's emotions and reactions.

Where much of the West—the United States in particular—has shed nearly everything but wealth as an indicator of position in society, the Japanese maintain concepts of social order that have feudal echoes, as in the ideas of *uchi* and *soto*. Uchi refers to the home, the inside group, and, ultimately, Japan and Japaneseness. Soto is everything outside. Imagine uchi being a set of concentric rings, where the most central group is the family; the next is the neighborhood or extended family; then the school, company, or association; then the prefecture, the family of companies, or the region in which they live; and, finally, Japan itself. Japanese verb forms are more casual within the various uchi, as opposed to the more polite forms for those "outside." Interestingly enough, the *gai* in the Japanese word for foreigner, *gaijin*, is the same character as *soto*. Soto—not belonging—is an undeniable barrier for non-Japanese. Translated into feelings, being the "other" can be frustrating and alienating. At the same time, it makes instances of crossing the boundary into some level of uchi that much more precious.

Despite the belief that the American presence after World War II was what built Japan, it is more correctly the sense of tribe or group the Japanese have utilized to their advantage since the Meiji Restoration that really created modern Japan. In the West we might have trouble understanding what we perceive as a lack of individuality in Japanese society, but we tend to ignore the sense of togetherness and joy that comes from a feeling of homogeneity. We might also miss any number of subtleties in interpersonal communication because we are wholly unaccustomed to them. It can take a lifetime to master the finer points of Japanese ambiguities, but even a basic appreciation of shades of meaning and the Japanese vigilance in maintaining the tightness of the group helps to see the beauty of this different way of life.

This beauty might be that much more precious in the face of change. With more of the younger generation traveling and living abroad, women especially, the group mentality and its role in supporting the Japanese socioeconomic structure are eroding rapidly.

You're bound to notice that the Japanese are extremely fond of animation, and they use it in communicating ideas and in advertising far more than we do in the West. So you'll see the anthropomorphizing of garbage cans, signage, and even huge, cute squid telephone booths. The Japanese also seem to lead the world in the production of purposeless gadgets that astound and delight, if only for a minute or two. If this is your thing, don't miss the shops in downtown Ōsaka, or Harajuku and Shibuya in Tōkyō, because you'll never find these items anywhere else. Some of them are expensive—the mooing cow clock that wakes you up with "Don't-o suleepu yo-ah lie-foo eh-way" looks hardly worth more than $10 but is nearly four times that, if you can even find one available; and the "waterfall sounds" player for shy women using the toilet can run up to $300.

There are reams of books and articles on Japanese English—and how they use and abuse it—but the topic might not come to mind until you set foot in Japan. Throughout the country, on billboards and in stores, on clothes, bags, hats, and even on cars, baffling, cryptic, often side-splitting English phrases leap out at you in the midst of your deepest cultural encounters. For example: "Woody goods: We have a woody heart, now listen to my story." What could this possibly mean? Did it make sense in the original Japanese?

Alas, friends and family might not understand why you find funny English so hilarious, without a firsthand encounter with something like CREAM SODA earnestly printed on a bodybuilder's T-shirt—or a fashion catalog that cryptically asserts "optimistic sunbeam shines beautifully for you." These tortured meanings are no doubt a compliment to the ascendancy of the English language, which on the world popular-culture stage is, in whatever form, chic and cool. You might find that on a heavy day of temple viewing, funny English might be the straightest path toward *satori* (enlightenment).

The latest obsessions in Japan can take a long time to get rolling, but when they do, they can take over the country. And Japanese homogeneity makes for a certain lemming quality that is utterly intriguing when it comes to observing fads. Take the wild popularity of Tamagotchi and Pokèmon. The international success of these techno-obsessions just goes to show how adept the Japanese are at catering to the world's unrecognized needs.

Whatever the fad is, when you're in Japan, make a note of it and try to remember the Japanese name or words associated with it. When you try to pronounce them, Japanese friends and colleagues will be immensely humored and impressed. Such is the intensity of fads that they act as barometers of the atmosphere of Japan at any given time.

— David Miles

BOOKS & MOVIES

Books

The incredible refinement of Japanese culture has produced a wealth of literature. Yet in the face of thousands of such books, where should you begin? If you are a newcomer to the subject of Japan, start with Pico Iyer's *The Lady and the Monk*, which will charm you through the first five phases of stereotypical infatuation with Japan and leave you with five times as many insights. Then read Seichō Matsumoto's *Inspector Imanishi Investigates*, a superb detective novel that says volumes about Japanese life (make a list of characters' names as you read to keep them straight). For those wanting to know more about the atomic bombing, John Hersey's *Hiroshima*, in which he records the stories of survivors, is essential reading. For a fictional retelling of this terrible period in Japan's history read Ibuse Masuji's classic novel *Black Rain*.

Art & Architecture. A wealth of literature exists on Japanese art. Much of the early writing has not withstood the test of time, but R. Paine and Alexander Soper's *Art and Architecture of Japan* remains a good place to start. A more recent survey, though narrower in scope, is Joan Stanley-Smith's *Japanese Art*.

The multivolume *Japan Arts Library* covers most of the styles and personalities of the Japanese arts. The series has volumes on castles, teahouses, screen painting, and wood-block prints. A more detailed look at the architecture of Tōkyō is Edward Seidensticker's *Low City, High City*. Kazuo Nishi and Kazuo Hozumi's *What Is Japanese Architecture?* treats the history of Japanese architecture and uses examples of buildings you will actually see on your travels.

Fiction & Poetry. The great classic of Japanese fiction is the *Tale of Genji*, written by Murasaki Shikibu, a woman of the imperial court around 1000 AD. Genji, or the Shining Prince, has long been taken as the archetype of ideal male behavior. From the same period, Japanese literature's golden age, *The Pillow Book of Sei Shōnagon* is the stylish and stylized diary of a woman's courtly life. *The Tale of Heike* is the poetic and highly moving story of the battles and eventual defeat of the ancient Taira clan by the Minamotos.

The Edo period is well covered by literary translations. Howard Hibbett's *Floating World in Japanese Fiction* gives an excellent selection with commentaries. For a selection of Edo ghost stories try Akinari Ueda's *Ugetsu Monogatari: Tales of Moonlight and Rain*, translated by Leon Zolbrod. The racy prose of late-17th-century Saikaku Ihara is translated in various books, including *Some Final Words of Advice* and *Five Women Who Loved Love*.

Modern Japanese fiction is more widely available in translation. One of the best-known writers among Westerners is Yukio Mishima, author of *The Sea of Fertility* trilogy and *The Temple of The Golden Pavilion*, among many other works. His books often deal with the effects of postwar Westernization on Japanese culture. Two superb prose stylists are Junichirō Tanizaki, author of *The Makioka Sisters, Some Prefer Nettles*, and the racy 1920s *Quicksand*; and Nobel Prize winner Yasunari Kawabata, whose superbly written novels include *Snow Country* and *The Sound of the Mountain*. Kawabata's *Thousand Cranes*, which uses the tea ceremony as a vehicle, is an elegant page-turner. Jirō Osaragi's *The Journey* is a lucid, entertaining rendering of the clash of tradition and modernity in postwar Japan. Also look for Sōseki Natsume's charming *Botchan* and delightful *I Am a Cat*.

Other novelists and works of note are Kōbō Abe, whose *Woman in the Dunes* is a 1960s landmark, and Shūsaku Endō, who brutally and breathlessly treated the early clash of Japan with Christianity in *The Samurai.*

Novelists at work in Japan today are no less interesting. Fumiko Enchi's *Masks* poignantly explores the fascinating public-private dichotomy. Haruki Murakami's *Wild Sheep Chase* is a wild ride indeed; his short stories are often bizarre and humorous, with a touch of the science fiction thrown in for good measure. Murakami's more recent *The Wind-up Bird Chronicle,* a dense and daring novel, fantastically juxtaposes the banality of modern Japanese suburbia with the harsh realities of 20th-century Japanese history. Along with Murakami's books, Banana Yoshimoto's *Kitchen* and other novels are probably the most fun you'll have with any Japanese fiction. Taeko Kōno's *Toddler-Hunting* and Yūko Tsushima's *The Shooting Gallery* are as engrossing and well crafted as they are frank about the burdens of tradition on Japanese women today. Nobel Prize winner Kenzaburō Ōe's writing similarly explores deeply personal issues, among them his compelling relationship with his disabled son. His two most important works are *A Personal Matter* and *Silent Scream.*

Haiku, the 5-7-5 syllable form that the monk Matsuo Bashō honed in the 17th century, is the flagship of Japanese poetry. His *Narrow Road to the Deep North* is a wistful prose-and-poem travelogue that is available in a few translations. But there are many more forms and authors worth exploring. Three volumes of translations by Kenneth Rexroth include numerous authors' work from the last 1,000 years: *One Hundred Poems from the Japanese, 100 More Poems from the Japanese,* and *Women Poets of Japan* (translated with Akiko Atsumi). Each has notes and brief author biographies. *Ink Dark Moon,* translated by Jane Hirshfield with Mariko Aratani, presents the remarkable poems of Ono no Komachi and Izumi Shikibu, two of Japan's earliest women poets. The Zen poems of Ryōkan represent the sacred current in Japanese poetry; look for *Dew Drops on a Lotus Leaf.* Other poets to look for are Issa, Buson, and Bonchō. Two fine small volumes that link their haiku with those of other poets, including Bashō, are *The Monkey's Raincoat* and the beautifully illustrated *A Net of Fireflies.*

Another way into Japanese culture is riding on the heels of Westerners who live or have lived in Japan. The emotional realities of such experience are engagingly rendered in *The Broken Bridge: Fiction from Expatriates in Literary Japan,* edited by Suzanne Kamata. The enormously popular tale *Memoirs of a Geisha,* by Arthur Golden, recounts the dramatic life of a geisha in the decades surrounding World War II.

History & Society. Fourteen hundred years of history are rather a lot to take in when going on a vacation, but two good surveys make the task much easier: Richard Storry's *A History of Modern Japan* (by modern, he means everything post-prehistoric) and George Sansom's *Japan: A Short Cultural History.* Sansom's three-volume *History of Japan* is a more exhaustive treatment.

If you're interested in earlier times, Tsunetomo Yamamoto's *Hagakure (The Book of the Samurai)* is an 18th-century guide of sorts to the principles and ethics of the "Way of the Samurai," written by a Kyūshū samurai. Dr. Junichi Saga's *Memories of Silk and Straw: A Self-Portrait of Small-Town Japan* is his 1970s collection of interviews with local old-timers in his hometown outside Tōkyō. Saga's father illustrated the accounts. Few books get so close to the realities of everyday life in early modern rural Japan. Elizabeth Bumiller's 1995 *The Secrets of Mariko* intimately recounts a very poignant year in the life of a Japanese woman and her family.

The Japanese have a genre they refer to as *nihon-jin-ron,* or studies of Japaneseness. A fine study of the Japanese mind is found in Takeo Doi's *The Anatomy of Dependence* and Chie Nakane's *Japanese Society.*

Karel van Wolferen's *The Enigma of Japanese Power* is an enlightening book on the Japanese sociopolitical system, especially for diplomats and businesspeople intending to work with the Japanese. And as a sounding of the experience of his years in the country, Alex Kerr's *Lost Japan* examines the directions of Japanese society past and present. This book was the first by a foreigner ever to win Japan's Shinchō Gakugei literature prize.

Language. There's an overwhelming number of books and courses available for studying Japanese. *Japanese for Busy People* uses conversational situations (rather than grammatical principles) as a means of introducing the Japanese language. With it you will also learn the two syllabaries, *hiragana* and *katakana*, and rudimentary *kanji* characters.

Religion. Anyone wanting to read a Zen Buddhist text should try *The Platform Sutra of the Sixth Patriarch,* one of the Zen classics, written by an ancient Chinese head of the sect and translated by Philip B. Yampolsky. Another Buddhist text of high importance is the *Lotus Sutra*; it has been translated by Leon Hurvitz as *The Scripture of the Lotus Blossom of the Fine Dharma: The Lotus Sutra.* Stuart D. Picken has written books on both major Japanese religions: *Shintō: Japan's Spiritual Roots* and *Buddhism: Japan's Cultural Identity.* William R. LaFleur's *Karma of Words: Buddhism and the Literary Arts in Medieval Japan* traces how Buddhism affected medieval Japanese mentality and behavior.

Travel Narratives. Two travel narratives stand out as superb introductions to Japanese history, culture, and people. Donald Richie's classic *The Inland Sea* recalls his journey and encounters on the fabled Seto Nai-kai. Leila Philip's year working in a Kyūshū pottery village became the eloquent *Road Through Miyama.*

Movies

The Japanese film industry has been active since the early days of the medium's invention. A limited number of Japanese films, however, have been transferred to video for Western audiences, and even these may be hard to locate at your local video store. Many Japanese movies fall into two genres: the *jidai-geki* period-costume films and the *gendai-geki* films about contemporary life. Period films often deal with romantic entanglements, ghosts, and samurai warriors, as in *chambara* (sword-fight) films. Movies set in more recent times often focus on lower- or middle-class family life and the world of gangsters.

Western viewers have typically encountered Japanese cinema in the works of Japan's most prolific movie directors, Kenji Mizoguchi, Yasujirō Ozu, and Akira Kurosawa. Mizoguchi's career spanned a 34-year period beginning in 1922, and three of his finest films investigate the social role of a female protagonist in feudal Japan: *The Life of Oharu* (1952), *Ugetsu* (1953), and *Sanchō the Bailiff* (1954). Ozu directed 54 films from 1927 to 1962; most of his movies explore traditional Japanese values and concentrate on the everyday life and relationships of middle-class families. Among his best works are *Late Spring* (1949), *Early Summer* (1951), *Tōkyō Story* (1953), and *An Autumn Afternoon* (1962).

Kurosawa, who began directing movies in 1943, is the best-known Japanese filmmaker among Western audiences. His film *Rashōmon* (1950), a 12th-century murder story told by four different narrators, brought him international acclaim and sparked world interest in Japanese cinema. Among his other classic period films are *Seven Samurai* (1954), *The Hidden Fortress* (1958), *Yōjimbō* (1961), *Red Beard* (1965), *Dersu Uzala* (1975), and *Kagemusha* (1980). The life-affirming

Ikiru (1952) deals with an office worker dying of cancer. *High and Low* (1963), about a kidnapping, was based on a detective novel by Ed McBain. Two of Kurosawa's most honored films were adapted from Shakespeare plays: *Throne of Blood* (1957), based on *Macbeth,* and *Ran* (1985), based on *King Lear.*

Another director in the same generation as Mizoguchi and Ozu was Teinosuke Kinugasa, whose *Gate of Hell* (1953) vividly re-creates medieval Japan. *The Samurai Trilogy* (1954), directed by Hiroshi Inagaki, follows the adventures of a legendary 16th-century samurai hero, Musashi Miyamoto. A whole new group of filmmakers came to the forefront in postwar Japan, including Kon Ichikawa, who directed two powerful antiwar movies, *The Burmese Harp* (1956) and *Fires on the Plain* (1959); and Masaki Kobayashi, whose samurai period film *Harakiri* (1962) is considered his best work. In the late '60s and '70s several new directors gained prominence, including Hiroshi Teshigahara, Shōhei Imamura, and Nagisa Ōshima. Teshigahara is renowned for the allegorical *Woman in the Dunes* (1964), based on a novel by Kōbō Abe. Among Imamura's honored works are *The Ballad of Narayama* (1983), about the death of the elderly, and *Black Rain* (1989), which deals with the atomic bombing of Hiroshima. Ōshima directed *Merry Christmas, Mr. Lawrence* (1983), about a British officer in a Japanese prisoner-of-war camp in Java during World War II.

Other Japanese filmmakers worth checking out are Yoshimitsu Morita, Jūzō Itami, Masayuki Suō, Takeshi Kitano and Shunji Iwai. Morita's *The Family Game* (1983) satirizes Japanese domestic life and the educational system. Itami won international recognition for *Tampopo* (1986), a highly original comedy about food. His other films include *A Taxing Woman* (1987), which pokes fun at the Japanese tax system, and *Mimbō* (1992), which dissects the world of Japanese gangsters. Suō's *Shall We Dance?* (1997) is a bittersweet comedy about a married businessman who escapes his daily routine by taking ballroom dance lessons. *Fireworks* (1997), by Takeshi Kitano, depicts a cop's struggle with loss in modern, frenetic Japan. Shunji Iwai's *Love Letter* (1995) is a touching story about a girl who receives a lost letter from her boyfriend after he has died.

The Japanese film industry also produces some of the best animated or anime movies in the world. The Academy Award-winning picture, *Spirited Away* (2002), available in English, is a good place to start for those interested in these kind of movies. *Kiki's Delivery Service* (1989), starring Kirsten Dunst as the voice of Kiki, is another very good choice.

FACTS & FIGURES

JAPAN AT A GLANCE

Fast Facts

Capital: Tōkyō
National anthem: *Kimigayo (The Emperor's Reign)*
Type of government: Constitutional monarchy with a parliamentary government
Administrative divisions: 47 prefectures
Independence: 660 BC (traditional founding)
Constitution: May 3, 1947
Legal system: Modeled after European civil law system with English-American influence; judicial review of legislative acts in the Supreme Court
Suffrage: 20 years of age; universal
Legislature: Bicameral Diet or Kokkai with House of Councillors (247 seats, members elected for six-year terms, half reelected every three years, 149 members in multiseat constituencies and 98 by proportional representation); House of Representatives (480 seats, members elected for four-year terms, 300 in single-seat constituencies, 180 members by proportional representation in 11 regional blocs)

Population: 127.3 million
Population density: 340 people per square km (880 people per square mi)
Median age: Female: 44.1, male: 40.5
Life expectancy: Female: 84.5; male: 77.7
Infant mortality rate: 3.3 deaths per 1,000 live births
Literacy: 99%
Language: Japanese
Ethnic groups: Japanese 99%; other (Korean, Chinese, Brazilian, Filipino) 1%
Religion: Shintō and Buddhist 84%; other 16%

In fact, the whole of Japan is a pure invention. There is no such country, there are no such people . . . The Japanese people are . . . simply a mode of style, an exquisite fancy of art.

—Oscar Wilde

Geography & Environment

Land area: 374,744 square km (144,689 square mi), slightly smaller than California
Coastline: 29,751 km (11,487 mi)
Terrain: Mostly rugged and mountainous
Islands: Bonin Islands (Ogasawara-guntō), Daito-shotō, Minami-jima, Okino-tori-shima, Ryūkyū Islands (Nansei-shotō), and Volcano Islands (Kazan-rettō)
Natural resources: Fish, mineral resources

Natural hazards: Japan has about 1,500 seismic occurrences (mostly tremors) every year; tsunamis; typhoons, volcanoes
Environmental issues: Air pollution from power plant emissions results in acid rain; acidification of lakes and reservoirs degrading water quality and threatening aquatic life; Japan is one of the largest consumers of fish and tropical timber, contributing to the depletion of these resources in Asia and elsewhere

Economy

Currency: Yen
Exchange rate: 110 yen
GDP: $3.6 trillion

Per capita income: 4 million yen ($35,610)
Inflation: -0.4%

Unemployment: 5.3%
Work force: 66.7 million; services 70%; industry 25%; agriculture 5%
Major industries: Chemicals, electronic equipment, machine tools, motor vehicles, processed foods, ships, steel and nonferrous metals, textiles
Agricultural products: Dairy products, eggs, fish, fruit, pork, poultry, rice, sugar beets, vegetables
Exports: $447.1 billion
Major export products: Chemicals, motor vehicles, office machinery, semiconductors
Export partners: U.S. 28.8%; China 9.6%; South Korea 6.9%; Taiwan 6.3%; Hong Kong 6.1%

Imports: $346.6 billion
Major import products: Chemicals, foodstuffs, fuels, machinery and equipment, raw materials, textiles
Import partners: China 18.3%; U.S. 17.4%; South Korea 4.6%; Indonesia 4.2%; Australia 4.1%

Japan has distorted its economy and depressed its living standard in order to keep its job structure and social values as steady as possible. At the government's direction, the entire economy has tried to flex almost as one, in response to the ever-changing world.

–James Fallows

Political Climate

Japan has more than 10,000 political parties and most are small, regional bodies without mass appeal. The Liberal Democratic party (LDP) held the majority of seats in the legislature since 1955, when the party was formed, with a brief ouster in the 1990s. The LDP is considered a conservative party and has supported close ties with the U.S., especially concerning security. The Democratic Party of Japan and New Kōmeitō form the largest opposition groups. Economically, deregulation and growth in the free market are important policy issues. Japan's aging population is also becoming a crucible for politicians, as the balance between the structure of the labor force and pensions and benefits for the elderly makes the government's budget a tough one to balance.

Did You Know?

• Japanese engineers have built a car that can go 11,193 miles on one gallon of fuel, a world record. The car performs best at 15 mi per hour and engineers are adapting the technology for commercial production. Japan is also home to the world's first environmentally friendly rental car company. Kōbe-Eco-Car in Kōbe has rented electric vehicles, compressed natural gas vehicles, and hybrid cars since it was founded in 1998.

• With an average life expectancy of 77.7 years for men and 84.5 years for women, the Japanese live longer than anyone else on the planet.

• To take any of the 2,200 daily trips on the East Japan Railway is to ride the world's busiest train system. It carries 16 million passengers over 4,684 mi of track, stopping at a dizzying 1,707 stations.

• The world's worst single-aircraft accident occurred in 1985 over Japan when a JAL Boeing 747 lost control over the rear of the aircraft. Fifteen crew members and 520 passengers were killed.

• The largest sumō wrestling champion in the history of the sport isn't Japanese, but American. Chad Rowan, whose sumō name is Akebono, was born in Hawaii, and reached the top ranking of *yokozuna* in 1983. He was 6 feet 8 inches and 501 pounds.

• The Japanese prime minister earns an annual salary of 69.3 million yen ($676,000), the highest of any prime minister in the world.

• Japan's Yomiuri Shimbun has more readers than any other newspaper on earth. Its combined morning and evening circulation is 14.3 million, more than 10 times larger than the New York Times.

• Japan is the third-largest consumer of cigarettes. The Japanese smoke about 325 billion cigarettes each year, about 100 billion less than Americans and more than a trillion less than the Chinese.

TŌKYŌ AT A GLANCE

Fast Facts

Type of government: Metropolitan prefecture with democratically elected governor and assembly. Wards and other subsidiary units have local assemblies.
Population: 12.4 million (city), 28 million (metro)
Population density: 5,656 people per square km (14,655 people per square mi)
Crime rate: Roughly 225 criminal cases per 10,000 residents per year

Median age: Female 41.2, male 38.2
Language: Japanese (official)
Ethnic groups: Japanese: 99.4%; other 0.6%

The Metropolis should have been aborted long before it became New York, London or Tōkyō.
— John Kenneth Galbraith

Geography & Environment

Latitude: 35°N (same as Albuquerque, New Mexico; Kabul, Afghanistan; Memphis, Tennessee)
Longitude: 139° E (same as Adelaide, Australia)
Elevation: 17 meters (59 feet)
Land area: 2,187 square km (844 square mi)
Terrain: Tōkyō sits on the Kantō plain, at the head of Tōkyō Bay, near the center of the Japanese archipelago. Edogawa River is to the east, mountains are to the west, and Tamagawa River is to the south. Mount Fuji, Japan's highest mountain, rises up 12,388 feet

about 60 mi (100 km) west of Tōkyō.
Natural hazards: Earthquakes, typhoons
Environmental issues: Tōkyō has banned trucks that don't meet strict emissions standards and ordered filters placed on many other diesel vehicles. As a result, the air quality has improved. Studies are being conducted on the so-called heat island effect, which is the raising of temperatures by air-conditioners and other exhausts emitted by buildings in the dense downtown area. Also, finding landfills for the city's garbage is a growing problem.

Economy

Per capita income: ¥4.1 million ($37,661)
Unemployment: 4.6%
Work force: 6.5 million; clerical, technical and management 46.3%; sales and services 29.2%; manufacturing and transportation 24%; agriculture,

forestry and fisheries 0.5%
Major industries: Automobiles, banking, cameras and optical goods, consumer items, electronic apparatus, equipment, financial services, furniture, publishing and printing, textiles, transport

Did You Know?

• The average Tōkyō residence is only slightly larger than a two-car garage in the U.S.

• Tōkyō has the lowest population of children aged 0 to 14 of any area of Japan.

• Japanese inventors have created a material that absorbs nitrogen and sulphur oxide gases, reducing smog. The product is now in use on bridges, buildings, and highways across Tōkyō.

• Tōkyō has the second largest homeless population in Japan. In 2003, the city counted 5,927 people. About half are estimated to be sleeping in parks and on the streets, the rest are in government shelters.

• There are eight U.S. military bases within Tōkyō, covering more than 6 square mi.

• Tōkyō's daytime population is 2.7 million people higher than its nighttime population. The change is most dramatic in the city's downtown wards—Chiyoda, Chūō, and Minato—which have only 268,000 persons by night and 2.3 million by day.

• The ginkgo biloba is the most common tree in Tōkyō and has even been adopted as the city's symbol. It's fan-shaped green leaves turn yellow every fall.

CHRONOLOGY

10,000 BC– AD 300	Neolithic Jōmon hunting and fishing culture leaves richly decorated pottery.
AD 300	Yayoi culture displays knowledge of farming and metallurgy imported from Korea.
after 300	The Yamato tribe consolidates power in the rich Kansai plain and expands westward, forming the kind of military aristocratic society that will dominate Japan's history.
ca. 500	Yamato leaders, claiming to be descended from the sun goddess, Amaterasu, take the title of emperor.
538–552	Buddhism, introduced to the Yamato court from China by way of Korea, complements rather than replaces the indigenous Shintō religion.
593–622	Prince Shōtoku encourages the Japanese to embrace Chinese culture and has Buddhist temple Hōryū-ji built at Nara in 607 (its existing buildings are among the oldest surviving wooden structures in the world).

Nara Period

710–784	Japan has first permanent capital at Nara; great age of Buddhist sculpture, piety, and poetry.

Fujiwara or Heian (Peace) Period

794–1160	The capital is moved from Nara to Heian-kyō (now Kyōto), where the Fujiwara family dominates the imperial court. Lady Murasaki's novel *The Tale of Genji*, written circa 1020, describes the elegance and political maneuvering of court life.

Kamakura Period

1185–1335	Feudalism enters, with military and economic power in the provinces and the emperor a powerless, ceremonial figurehead in Kyōto. Samurai warriors welcome Zen, a new sect of Buddhism from China.
1192	After a war with the Taira family, Yoritomo of the Minamoto family becomes the first shōgun; he places his capital in Kamakura.
1274 and 1281	The fleets sent by Chinese emperor Kublai Khan to invade Japan are destroyed by typhoons, praised in Japanese history as kamikaze, or divine wind.

Ashikaga Period

1336–1568	The Ashikaga family assumes the title of shōgun and settles in Kyōto. The Zen aesthetic flourishes in painting, landscape gardening, and tea ceremony. Nō theater emerges. The Silver Pavilion, or Ginkaku-ji, in Kyōto, built in 1483, is the quintessential example of Zen-inspired architecture. The period is marked by constant warfare but also by

increased trade with the mainland. Ōsaka develops into an important commercial city, and trade guilds appear.

1467–77 The Ōnin Wars that wrack Kyōto initiate a 100-year period of civil war.

1543 Portuguese sailors, the first Europeans to reach Japan, initiate trade relations with the lords of western Japan and introduce the musket, which changes Japanese warfare.

1549–51 St. Francis Xavier, the first Jesuit missionary, introduces Christianity.

Momoyama Period of National Unification

1568–1600 Two generals, Nobunaga Oda and Hideyoshi Toyotomi, are the central figures of this period. Nobunaga builds a military base from which Hideyoshi unifies Japan.

1592, 1597 Hideyoshi invades Korea. He brings back Korean potters, who rapidly develop a Japanese ceramics industry.

Tokugawa Period

1600–1868 Ieyasu Tokugawa becomes shōgun after the battle of Sekigahara. The military capital is established at Edo (now Tōkyō), which shows phenomenal economic and cultural growth. A hierarchical order of four social classes—warriors, farmers, artisans, then merchants—is rigorously enforced. The merchant class, however, is increasingly prosperous and effects a transition from a rice to a money economy. Merchants patronize new, popular forms of art: Kabuki, haiku, and the ukiyo-e school of painting. The life of the latter part of this era is beautifully illustrated in the wood-block prints of the artist Hokusai (1760–1849).

1618 Japanese Christians who refuse to renounce their foreign religion are persecuted.

1637–38 Japanese Christians are massacred in the Shimabara uprising. Japan is closed to the outside world except for a Dutch trading post in Nagasaki harbor.

1853 U.S. commodore Matthew Perry reopens Japan to foreign trade.

Meiji Restoration

1868–1912 Opponents of the weakened Tokugawa Shogunate support Emperor Meiji and overthrow the last shōgun. The emperor is restored (with little actual power), and the imperial capital is moved to Edo, which is renamed Tōkyō (Eastern Capital). Japan is modernized along Western lines, with a constitution proclaimed in 1889; a system of compulsory education and a surge of industrialization follow.

1902–05 Japan defeats Russia in the Russo-Japanese War and achieves world-power status.

1910 Japan annexes Korea.

1914–18 Japan joins the Allies in World War I.

1923 The Great Kantō Earthquake devastates much of Tōkyō and Yokohama.

1931 As a sign of growing militarism in the country, Japan seizes the Chinese province of Manchuria.

1937 Following years of increasing military and diplomatic activity in northern China, open warfare breaks out (and lasts until 1945); Chinese Nationalists and Communists both fight Japan.

1939–45 Japan, having signed anti-Communist treaties with Nazi Germany and Italy (1936 and 1937), invades and occupies French Indochina.

1941 The Japanese attack on Pearl Harbor on December 7 brings the United States into war against Japan in the Pacific.

1942 Japan's empire extends to Indochina, Burma, Malaya, the Philippines, and Indonesia. Japan bombs Darwin, Australia. U.S. defeat of Japanese forces at Midway turns the tide of the Pacific war.

1945 Tōkyō and 50 other Japanese cities are devastated by U.S. bombing raids. The United States drops atomic bombs on Hiroshima and Nagasaki in August, precipitating Japanese surrender.

1945–52 The American occupation under General Douglas MacArthur disarms Japan and encourages the establishment of a democratic government. Emperor Hirohito retains his position.

1953 After the Korean War, Japan begins a period of great economic growth.

1964 Tōkyō hosts the Summer Olympic games.

late 1960s Japan develops into one of the major industrial nations in the world.

mid-1970s Production of electronics, cars, cameras, and computers places Japan at the heart of the emerging Pacific Rim economic sphere and threatens to spark a trade war with the industrial nations of Europe and the United States.

1989 Emperor Hirohito dies.

1990 Coronation of Emperor Akihito. Prince Fumihito marries Kiko Kawashima.

1992 The Diet approves use of Japanese military forces under United Nations auspices.

1993 Crown Prince Naruhito marries Masako Owada.

1995 A massive earthquake strikes Kōbe and environs. Approximately 5,500 people are killed and 35,000 injured; more than 100,000 buildings are destroyed.

Members of a fringe religious organization, the Aum Shinri Kyō, carry out a series of poison-gas attacks on the transportation networks of Tōkyō and Yokohama, undermining, in a society that is a model of decorum and mutual respect, confidence in personal safety.

1997 The deregulation of rice prices and the appearance of discount gasoline stations mark a turn in the Japanese economy toward genuine privatization. These small indications constitute a break from traditional price control policies that support small merchants and producers.

1998 The Japanese economy is crippled from slumps throughout Asia. Banks merge or go bankrupt, and Japanese consumers spend less and less.

1999 In the international arena Japanese toys, films, and other accoutrements of pop culture find themselves in the spotlight like never before. The economy, however, continues to suffer as politicians debate economic measures that foreign economists have been recommending for years. Small businesses are most affected, and the attitude of the average Japanese is grim.

A nuclear accident 112 km (70 mi) northeast of Tōkyō injures few but raises many questions about Japan's vast nuclear-power industry.

2001 In support of the U.S. war against terrorism in Afghanistan, the Japanese government extends noncombat military activities abroad for the first time since World War II by sending support ships to the Indian Ocean under a reinterpretation of the existing post-1945, pacifist constitution. Asian leaders express some concern for a first step for Japanese military presence abroad since 1945.

2002 North Korea admits to the kidnapping of 11 Japanese civilians in the 1970s and '80s for use as language teachers. Japan negotiates the return of several of its citizens.

2003 Prime Minister Koizumi sends Japanese combat troops to Iraq in the first deployment of Japanese troops since WWII.

VOCABULARY & MENU GUIDE

ABOUT JAPANESE

Japanese sounds and spellings differ in principle from those of the West. We build words letter by letter, and one letter can sound different depending where it appears in a word. For example, we see *ta* as two letters, and *ta* could be pronounced three ways, as in *tat, tall,* and *tale.* For the Japanese, *ta* is one character, and it is pronounced one way: *tah.*

The *hiragana* and *katakana* (tables of sounds) are the rough equivalents of our alphabet. There are four types of syllables within these tables: the single vowels *a, i, u, e,* and *o,* in that order; vowel-consonant pairs like *ka, ni, hu,* or *ro;* the single consonant *n,* which punctuates the upbeats of the word for bullet train, *Shinkansen* (shee-n-ka-n-se-n); and compounds like *kya, chu,* and *ryo.* Remember that these compounds are one syllable. Thus Tōkyō, the capital city, has only two syllables—*tō* and *kyō*—not three. Likewise pronounce Kyōtō *kyō-tō,* not *kee-oh-to.*

Japanese vowels are pronounced as follows: *a*–ah, *i*–ee, *u*–oo, *e*–eh, *o*–oh. The Japanese *r* is rolled so that it sounds like a bounced *d.*

No diphthongs. Paired vowels in Japanese words are not slurred together, as in our words *coin, brain,* or *stein.* The Japanese separate them, as in *mae* (*ma*-eh), whch means in front of; *kōen* (*ko*-en), which means park; *byōin* (*byo*-een), which means hospital; and *tokei* (to-*keh*-ee), which means clock or watch.

Macrons. Many Japanese words, when rendered in *romaji* (roman letters), require macrons over vowels to indicate correct pronunciation, as in Tōkyō. When you see these macrons, double the length of the vowel, as if you're saying it twice: *to*-o-*kyo*-o. Likewise, when you see double consonants, as in the city name Nikkō, linger on the Ks—as in "bookkeeper"—and on the O.

Emphasis. Some books state that the Japanese emphasize all syllables in their words equally. This is not true. Take the words *sayōnara* and *Hiroshima.* Americans are likely to stress the downbeats: *sa*-yo-*na*-ra and *hi*-ro-*shi*-ma. The Japanese actually emphasize the second beat in each case: sa-*yō*-na-ra (note the macron) and hi-*ro*-shi-ma. Metaphorically speaking, the Japanese don't so much stress syllables as pause over them or race past them: Emphasis is more a question of speed than weight. In the vocabulary below, we indicate emphasis by italicizing the syllable that you should stress.

Three interesting pronunciations are in the vocabulary below. The word *desu* roughly means "is." It looks like it has two syllables, but the Japanese race past the final *u* and just say "dess." Likewise, some verbs end in *-masu,* which is pronounced "mahss." Similarly, the character *shi* is often quickly pronounced "sh," as in the phrase meaning "pleased to meet you:" *ha*-ji-me-*mash(i)*-te. Just like *desu* and *-masu,* what look like two syllables, in this case *ma* and *shi,* are pronounced *mahsh.*

Hyphens. Throughout *Fodor's Tōkyō,* we have hyphenated certain words to help you recognize meaningful patterns. This isn't conventional; it is practical. For example, *Eki-mae-dōri,* which literally means "Station Front Avenue," turns into a blur when rendered Ekimaedōri. And you'll run across a number of sight names that end in *-jingū* or *-jinja* or *-taisha.* You'll soon catch on to their meaning: Shintō shrine.

ESSENTIAL PHRASES

Basics 基本的表現

Yes/No	*ha*-i/*ii*-e	はい／いいえ
Please	o-ne-*gai* shi-masu	お願いします
Thank you (very much)	(*dō*-mo) a-*ri*-ga-to go-*zai*-ma su	(どうも)ありがとうございます
You're welcome	*dō* i-ta-shi-ma-shi-te	どういたしまして
Excuse me	su-mi-ma-*sen*	すみません
Sorry	*go*-men na-*sai*	ごめんなさい
Good morning	o-*ha*-yō *go*-zai-ma-su	お早うございます
Good day/afternoon	kon-*ni*-chi-wa	こんにちは
Good evening	kom-*ban*-wa	こんばんは
Good night	o-*ya*-su-mi na-*sai*	おやすみなさい
Goodbye	sa-*yō*-na-ra	さようなら
Mr./Mrs./Miss	-san	―さん
Pleased to meet you	*ha*-ji-me-*mashi*-te	はじめまして
How do you do?	*dō*-zo yo-*ro*-shi-ku	どうぞよろしく

Numbers 数

The first reading is used for reading numbers, as in telephone numbers, and the second is often used for counting things.

1	*i*-chi / hi-*to*-tsu	一／一つ	17	*jū*-shi-chi	十七
2	ni / fu-*ta*-tsu	二／二つ	18	*jū*-ha-chi	十八
3	san / *mit*-tsu	三／三つ	19	*jū*-kyū	十九
4	shi / *yot*-tsu	四／四つ	20	*ni*-jū	二十
5	go / i-*tsu*-tsu	五／五つ	21	*ni*-jū-i-chi	二十一
6	*ro*-ku / *mut*-tsu	六／六つ	30	*san*-jū	三十
7	*shi*-chi / *na*-na-tsu	七／七つ	40	yon-jū	四十
8	*ha*-chi / *yat*-tsu	八／八つ	50	go-jū	五十
9	kyū / *ko*-ko-no-*tsu*	九／九つ	60	*ro*-ku-jū	六十
10	jū / tō	十／十	70	na-na-jū	七十
11	*jū*-i-chi	十一	80	*ha*-chi-jū	八十
12	*jū*-ni	十二	90	kyū-jū	九十
13	*jū*-san	十三	100	*hya*-ku	百
14	*jū*-yon	十四	1000	sen	千
15	*jū*-go	十五	10,000	*i*-chi-man	一万
16	*jū*-ro-ku	十六	100,000	*jū*-man	十万

Days of the Week   曜日

Sunday	*ni*-chi yō-bi	日曜日
Monday	*ge*-tsu yō-bi	月曜日
Tuesday	*ka* yō-bi	火曜日
Wednesday	*su*-i yō-bi	水曜日
Thursday	*mo*-ku yō-bi	木曜日
Friday	*kin* yō-bi	金曜日
Saturday	*do* yō-bi	土曜日
Weekday	hei-ji-tsu	平日
Weekend	shū-ma-tsu	週末

Months   月

January	*i*-chi *ga*-tsu	一月
February	*ni* ga-tsu	二月
March	*san* ga-tsu	三月
April	*shi* ga-tsu	四月
May	*go* ga-tsu	五月
June	*ro*-ku *ga*-tsu	六月
July	*shi*-chi *ga*-tsu	七月
August	*ha*-chi *ga*-tsu	八月
September	*ku* ga-tsu	九月
October	*jū* ga-tsu	十月
November	*jū*-i-chi *ga*-tsu	十一月
December	*jū*-ni *ga*-tsu	十二月

Useful Expressions, Questions, and Answers   よく使われる表現

Do you speak English?	*ei*-go ga wa-*ka*-ri-ma-su ka	英語が わかりますか。
I don't speak Japanese.	*ni*-hon-go ga wa-*ka*-ri-ma-*sen*	日本語が わかりません。
I don't understand.	wa-*ka*-ri-ma-*sen*	わかりません。
I understand.	wa-*ka*-ri-ma-shi-*ta*	わかりました。
I don't know.	*shi*-ri-ma-*sen*	知りません。
I'm American (British).	wa-*ta*-shi wa a-*me*-ri-ka (i-*gi*-ri-su) jin *desu*	私はアメリカ (イギリス) 人 です。
What's your name?	o-*na*-ma-e wa *nan* desu ka	お名前は何ですか。
My name is . . .	. . . to *mo*-shi-*ma*-su	…..と申します。
What time is it?	*i*-ma *nan*-ji desu ka	今何時ですか。

How?	*dō* yat-te	どうやって
When?	*i*-tsu	いつ
Yesterday/today/ tomorrow	ki-*nō*/kyō/*ashi*-ta	きのう／きょう／ あした
This morning	*ke*-sa	けさ
This afternoon	*kyō* no *go*-go	きょうの午後
Tonight	*kom*-ban	こんばん
Excuse me, what?	su-*mi*-ma-*sen, nan* desu *ka*	すみません、 何ですか。
What is this/that?	*ko*-re/*so*-re wa *nan* desu *ka*	これ／ それは何ですか。
Why?	*na*-ze desu *ka*	なぜですか。
Who?	*da*-re desu *ka*	だれですか。
I am lost.	*mi*-chi ni ma-yo-i-*mash*-ta	道に迷いました。
Where is [place]	[place] wa *do*-ko desu *ka*	.....はどこですか。
Train station?	e-ki	駅
Subway station?	chi-*ka*-te-tsu-no eki	地下鉄の駅
Bus stop?	*ba*-su *no*-ri-*ba*	バス乗り場
Taxi stand?	*ta*-ku-shi-i *no*-ri-*ba*	タクシー乗り場
Airport?	kū-kō	空港
Post office?	*yū*-bin-*kyo*-ku	郵便局
Bank?	*gin*-kō	銀行
the [name] hotel?	[name] ho-*te*-ru	ホテル
Elevator?	e-re-bē-tā	エレベーター
Where are the restrooms?	*to*-i-re wa *do*-ko desu *ka*	トイレは どこですか。
Here/there/over there	*ko*-ko/*so*-ko/*a*-so-ko	ここ／そこ／あそこ
Left/right	hi-*da*-ri/*mi*-gi	左／右
Straight ahead	mas-*su*-gu	まっすぐ
Is it near (far)?	chi-*ka*-i (*tō*-i) desu *ka*	近い (遠い) ですか。
Are there any rooms?	*he*-ya *ga* a-ri-masu *ka*	部屋がありますか。
I'd like [item]	[item] ga ho-*shi*-i no desu ga	.....がほしいの ですが。
Newspaper	*shim*-bun	新聞
Stamp	*kit*-te	切手
Key	*ka*-gi	鍵
I'd like to buy [item]	[item] o kai-*ta*-i no desu ke do	.....を買いたいの ですけど。

a ticket to [event]	[event] *ma*-de no *kip*-pu	.....までの切符
Map	*chi*-zu	地図
How much is it?	i-*ku*-ra desu *ka*	いくらですか。
It's expensive (cheap).	ta-*ka*-i (ya-*su*-i) de su *ne*	高い (安い) ですね。
A little (a lot)	su-*ko*-shi (*ta*-ku-san)	少し (たくさん)
More/less	*mot*-to o-ku/ su-ku-*na*-ku	もっと多く／少なく
Enough/too much	*jū*-bun/o-su-*gi*-ru	十分／多すぎる
I'd like to exchange . . .	. . . *ryō*-ga e shi-*te* i-*ta*-da-ke-masu *ka*	.....両替して 頂けますか。
dollars to yen	*do*-ru o *en* ni	ドルを円に
pounds to yen	*pon*-do o *en* ni	ポンドを円に
How do you say . . . in Japanese?	ni-*hon*-go de . . . wa *dō* i-i-masu *ka*	日本語で.....は どう言いますか。
I am ill/sick.	wa-*ta*-shi wa *byō*-ki desu	私は病気です。
Please call a doctor.	*i*-sha o *yon*-de ku-da-*sa*-i	医者を呼んで 下さい。
Please call the police.	*ke*-i-sa-tsu o *yon*-de ku-da-*sa*-i	警察を 呼んで下さい。
Help!	*ta*-su-*ke*-te	助けて！

More Useful Phrases   よく使われる表現

Temple	tera/-dera/-ji/-in/-dō	堂／寺／院
Shrine	jinja/jingū/-gū/-dō/taisha	神社／神宮／宮／堂／大社
Castle	-jō	城
Park	kōen	公園
River	kawa/-gawa	川
Bridge	hashi/-bashi	橋
Museum	hakubutsukan	博物館
Zoo	dōbutsu-en	動物園
Botanical gardens	shokubutsu-en	植物園
Island	shima/-jima/-tō	島
Slope	saka/-zaka	坂
Hill	oka	丘
Lake	-ko	湖
Marsh	shitsugen	湿原
Pond	ike	池
Bay	wan	湾

Plain	-hara/-bara/-taira/-daira	原／平
Peninsula	hantō	半島
Mountain	yama/-san/-take	山
Cape	misaki/-sakı/-zaki	岬／崎
Sea	-kai/-nada	海／灘
Gorge	kyōkoku	峡谷
Plateau	kōgen	高原
Train line	sen	線
Prefecture	-ken/-fu	県／府
Ward	-ku	区
Exit	deguchi/-guchi	出口
Street, avenue	-dōri/-dō/michi	道
main road	kaidō/kōdō	街道／公道
In front of	mae	前
North	kita	北
South	minami	南
East	higashi	東
West	nishi	西
Shop, store	mise/-ten/-ya	店／屋
Hot-spring spa	onsen	温泉

MENU GUIDE

Restaurants　レストラン

Basics and Useful Expressions　よく使われる表現

A bottle of . . .	. . . *ip*-pon	.....一本
A glass/cup of . . .	. . . *ip*-pai	.....一杯
Ashtray	*ha*-i-*za*-ra	灰皿
Plate	*sa*-ra	皿
Bill/check	kan-*jō*	かんじょう
Bread	pan	パン
Breakfast	*chō*-sho-ku	朝食
Butter	ba-*tā*	バター
Cheers!	kam-*pai*	乾杯！
Chopsticks	*ha*-shi	箸
Cocktail	*ka*-ku-*te*-ru	カクテル
Does that include dinner?...	*yū*-sho-ku *ga tsu-ki-ma-su-ka*	夕食が付きますか。
Excuse me!	su-mi-ma-*sen*	すみません。
Fork	*fō*-ku	フォーク
I am diabetic.	wa-*ta*-shi wa tō-*nyō*-byō de su	私は糖尿病です。
I am dieting.	*da*-i-et-to *chū* desu	ダイエット中です。
I am a vegetarian.	sa-i-*sho*-ku *shū*-gi-sha de-su	菜食主義者です。
I cannot eat [item]	[item] wa *ta*-be-ra-re-ma-*sen*	.....は食べられません。
I'd like to order.	*chū*-mon o shi-*tai* desu	注文をしたいです。
I'd like [item]	[item] o o-ne-*gai*-shi-ma su	.....をお願いします。
I'm hungry.	*o*-na-ka ga *su*-i-te i-*ma su*	お腹が空いています。
I'm thirsty.	*no*-do ga ka-*wa*-i-te i-*ma su*	喉が渇いています。
It's tasty (not good)	o-i-shi-i (ma-*zu*-i) desu	おいしい (まずい) です。
Knife	*na*-i-fu	ナイフ
Lunch	*chū*-sho-ku	昼食
Menu	me-nyū	メニュー
Napkin	*na*-pu-*kin*	ナプキン
Pepper	ko-*shō*	こしょう
Please give me [item]	[item] o ku-da-*sa*-i	.....を下さい。

Salt	*shi*-o	塩
Set menu	*te*-i-sho-ku	定食
Spoon	su-*pūn*	スプーン
Sugar	sa-to	砂糖
Wine list	*wa*-i-n *ri*-su-*to*	ワインリスト
What do you recommend?	o-su-su-me *ryō*-ri wa *nan* desu *ka*	お勧め料理は 何ですか。

Meat Dishes   肉料理

焼き肉	yaki-niku	Thinly sliced meat is marinated then barbecued over an open fire at the table.
すき焼き	sukiyaki	Thinly sliced beef, green onions, mushrooms, thin noodles, and cubes of tōfu are simmered in a large iron pan in front of you. These ingredients are cooked in a mixture of soy sauce, mirin (cooking wine), and a little sugar. You are given a saucer of raw egg to cool the suki-yaki morsels before eating. Using chopsticks, you help yourself to anything on your side of the pan and dip it into the egg and then eat. Best enjoyed in a group.
しゃぶしゃぶ	shabu-shabu	Extremely thin slices of beef are plunged for an instant into boiling water flavored with soup stock and then dipped into a thin sauce and eaten.
肉じゃが	niku-jaga	Beef and potatoes stewed together with soy sauce.
ステーキ	sutēki	steak
ハンバーグ	hambāgu	Hamburger pattie served with sauce.
トンカツ	tonkatsu	Breaded deep-fried pork cutlets.
しょうが焼	shōga-yaki	Pork cooked with ginger.
酢豚	subuta	Sweet and sour pork, originally a Chinese dish.
からあげ	kara-age	deep-fried without batter
焼き鳥	yaki-tori	Pieces of chicken, white meat, liver, skin, etc., threaded on skewers with green onions and marinated in sweet soy sauce and grilled.
親子どんぶり	oyako-domburi	Literally, "mother and child bowl"—chicken and egg in broth over rice.

他人どんぶり	tanin-domburi	Literally, "strangers in a bowl"— similar to oyako domburi, but with beef instead of chicken.
ロールキャベツ	rōru kyabetsu	Rolled cabbage; beef or pork rolled in cabbage and cooked.
はやしライス	hayashi raisu	Beef flavored with tomato and soy sauce with onions and peas over rice.
カレーライス	karē-raisu	Curried rice. A thick curry gravy typically containing beef is poured over white rice.
カツカレー	katsu-karē	Curried rice with tonkatsu.
お好み焼き	okonomi-yaki	Sometimes called a Japanese pancake, this is made from a batter of flour, egg, cabbage, and meat or seafood, griddle-cooked then covered with green onions and a special sauce.
シュウマイ	shūmai	Shrimp or pork wrapped in a light dough and steamed.
ギョウザ	gyōza	Pork spiced with ginger and garlic in a Chinese wrapper and fried or steamed.

Seafood Dishes   魚貝類料理

焼き魚	yaki-zakana	broiled fish
塩焼	shio-yaki	Fish sprinkled with salt and broiled until crisp.
さんま	samma	saury pike
いわし	iwashi	sardines
しゃけ	shake	salmon
照り焼き	teri-yaki	Fish basted in soy sauce and broiled.
ぶり	buri	yellowtail
煮魚	nizakana	soy-simmered fish
さばのみそ煮	saba no miso ni	Mackerel stewed with soy-bean paste.
揚げ魚	age-zakana	deep-fried fish
かれいフライ	karei furai	deep-fried breaded flounder
刺身	sashimi	Very fresh raw fish. Served sliced thin on a bed of white radish with a saucer of soy sauce and horseradish. Eaten by dipping fish into soy sauce mixed with horseradish.
まぐろ	maguro	tuna

あまえび	ama-ebi	sweet shrimp
いか	ika	squid
たこ	tako	octopus
あじ	aji	horse mackerel
さわら	sawara	Spanish mackerel
しめさば	shimesaba	Mackerel marinated in vinegar.
かつおのたたき	katsuo no tataki	Bonito cooked just slightly on the surface. Eaten with cut green onions and thin soy sauce.
どじょうの柳川なべ	dojo no yanagawa nabe	Loach cooked with burdock root and egg in an earthen dish. Considered a delicacy.
うな重	una-jū	Eel marinated in a slightly sweet soy sauce is charcoal-broiled and served over rice. Considered a delicacy.
天重	ten-jū	Deep-fried prawns served over rice with sauce.
海老フライ	ebi furai	Deep-fried breaded prawns.
あさりの酒蒸し	asari no sakamushi	Clams steamed with rice wine.

Sushi 寿司

寿司	sushi	Basically, sushi is rice, fish, and vegetables. The rice is delicately seasoned with vinegar, salt, and sugar. There are basically three types of sushi: nigiri, chirashi, and maki.
にぎり寿司	nigiri zushi	The rice is formed into a bite-sized cake and topped with various raw or cooked fish. The various types are usually named after the fish, but not all are fish. Nigiri zushi is eaten by picking up the cakes with chopsticks or the fingers, dipping the fish side in soy sauce, and eating.
ちらし寿司	chirashi zushi	In chirashi zushi, a variety of seafood is arranged on the top of the rice and served in a bowl.
巻き寿司	maki zushi	Raw fish and vegetables or other morsels are rolled in sushi rice and wrapped in dried seaweed. Some popular varieties are listed here.
まぐろ	maguro	tuna
とろ	toro	fatty tuna

たい	tai	red snapper
さば	saba	mackerel
こはだ	kohada	gizzard shad
しゃけ	shake	salmon
はまち	hamachi	yellowtail
ひらめ	hirame	flounder
あじ	aji	horse mackerel
たこ	tako	octopus
あなご	anago	conger eel
えび	ebi	shrimp
甘えび	ama-ebi	sweet shrimp
いか	ika	squid
みる貝	miru-gai	giant clam
あおやぎ	aoyagi	round clam
卵	tamago	egg
かずのこ	kazunoko	herring roe
かに	kani	crab
ほたて貝	hotate-gai	scallop
うに	uni	sea urchin
いくら	ikura	salmon roe
鉄火巻	tekka-maki	tuna roll
かっぱ巻	kappa-maki	cucumber roll
新香巻	shinko-maki	shinko roll (shinko is a type of pickle)
カリフォルニア巻	kariforunia-maki	California roll, containing crabmeat and avocado. This was invented in the U.S. but was re-exported to Japan and is gaining popularity there.
うに	uni	Sea urchin on rice wrapped with seaweed.
いくら	ikura	Salmon roe on rice wrapped with seaweed.
太巻	futo-maki	Big roll with egg and pickled vegetables.

Vegetable Dishes   野菜料理

おでん	oden	Often sold by street vendors at festivals and in parks, etc., this is vegetables, octopus, or egg simmered in a soy fish stock.

天ぷら	tempura	Vegetables, shrimp, or fish deep-fried in a light batter. Eaten by dipping into a thin sauce containing grated white radish.
野菜サラダ	yasai sarada	vegetable salad
大学いも	daigaku imo	fried yams in a sweet syrup
野菜いため	yasai itame	stir-fried vegetables
きんぴらごぼう	kimpira gobō	Carrots and burdock root, fried with soy sauce.
煮もの	nimono	vegetables simmered in a soy- and sake-based sauce
かぼちゃ	kabocha	pumpkin
さといも	satoimo	taro root
たけのこ	takenoko	bamboo shoots
ごぼう	gobō	burdock root
れんこん	renkon	lotus root
酢のもの	sunomono	Vegetables seasoned with ginger.
きゅうり	kyūri	cucumber
和えもの	aemono	Vegetables dressed with sauces.
ねぎ	tamanegi	onions
おひたし	o-hitashi	Boiled vegetables with soy sauce and dried shaved bonito or sesame seeds.
ほうれん草	hōrenso	spinach
漬物	tsukemono	Japanese pickles. Made from white radish, eggplant or other vegetables. Considered essential to the Japanese meal.

Egg Dishes　卵料理

ベーコン・エッグ	bēkon-eggu	bacon and eggs
ハム・エッグ	hamu-eggu	ham and eggs
スクランブル・エッグ	sukuramburu eggu	scrambled eggs
ゆで卵	yude tamago	boiled eggs
目玉焼	medama-yaki	fried eggs, sunny-side up
オムレツ	omuretsu	omelet
オムライス	omuraisu	Omelet with rice inside, often eaten with ketchup.
茶わんむし	chawan mushi	Vegetables, shrimp, etc., steamed in egg custard.

Tōfu Dishes　豆腐料理

Tōfu, also called bean curd, is a white, high-protein food with the consistency of soft gelatin.

冷やっこ	hiya-yakko	Cold tōfu with soy sauce and grated ginger.
湯どうふ	yu-dōfu	boiled tōfu
あげだしどうふ	agedashi dōfu	Lightly fried plain tōfu dipped in soy sauce and grated ginger.
マーボーどうふ	mābō dōfu	Tōfu and ground pork in a spicy red sauce. Originally a Chinese dish.
とうふの田楽	tōfu no dengaku	Tōfu broiled on skewers and flavored with miso.

Rice Dishes　ごはん料理

ごはん	gohan	steamed white rice
おにぎり	onigiri	Triangular balls of rice with fish or vegetables inside and wrapped in a type of seaweed.
おかゆ	okayu	rice porridge
チャーハン	chāhan	Fried rice; includes vegetables and pork.
ちまき	chimaki	A type of onigiri made with sticky rice.
パン	pan	Bread, but usually rolls with a meal.

Soups　汁もの

みそ汁	miso shiru	Miso soup. A thin broth containing tōfu, mushrooms, or other morsels in a soup flavored with miso or soy-bean paste. The morsels are taken out of the bowl and the soup is drunk straight from the bowl without a spoon.
すいもの	suimono	Soy sauce flavored soup, often including fish and tofu.
とん汁	tonjiru	Pork soup with vegetables.

Noodles　麺類

うどん	udon	Wide flour noodles in broth. Can be lunch in a light broth or a full dinner called *nabe-yaki udon* when meat, chicken, egg, and vegetables are added.

そば	soba	Buckwheat noodles. Served in a broth like udon or, during the summer, cold on a bamboo mesh and called *zaru soba*.
ラーメン	rāmen	Chinese noodles in broth, often with *chashu* or roast pork. Broth is soy sauce, miso or salt flavored.
そう麺	sōmen	Very thin wheat noodles, usually served cold with a tsuyu or thin sauce. Eaten in summer.
ひやむぎ	hiyamugi	Similar to somen, but thicker.
やきそば	yaki-soba	Noodles fried with beef and cabbage, garnished with pickled ginger and vegetables.
スパゲッティ	supagetti	Spaghetti. There are many interesting variations on this dish, notably spaghetti in soup, often with seafood.

Fruit 果実

アーモンド	āmondo	almonds
あんず	anzu	apricot
バナナ	banana	banana
ぶどう	budō	grapes
グレープフルーツ	gurēpufurūtsu	grapefruit
干しぶどう	hoshi-budō	raisins
いちご	ichigo	strawberries
いちじく	ichijiku	figs
かき	kaki	persimmons
キーウィ	kiiui	kiwi
ココナツツ	kokonattsu	coconut
くり	kuri	chestnuts
くるみ	kurumi	walnuts
マンゴ	mango	mango
メロン	meron	melon
みかん	mikan	tangerine (mandarin orange)
桃	momo	peach
梨	nashi	pear
オレンジ	orenji	orange
パイナップル	painappuru	pineapple
パパイヤ	papaiya	papaya

ピーナッツ	piinattsu	peanuts
プルーン	purūn	prunes
レモン	remon	lemon
りんご	ringo	apple
さくらんぼ	sakurambo	cherry
西瓜	suika	watermelon

Dessert　デザート類

アイスクリーム	aisukuriimu	ice cream
プリン	purin	caramel pudding
グレープ	kurēpu	crepes
ケーキ	kēki	cake
シャーベット	shābetto	sherbet
アップルパイ	appuru pai	apple pie
ようかん	yōkan	sweet bean paste jelly
コーヒーゼリー	kōhii zerī	coffee-flavored gelatin
和菓子	wagashi	Japanese sweets

Drinks　飲物

Alcoholic　酒類

ビール	biiru	beer
生ビール	nama biiru	draft beer
カクテル	kakuteru	cocktail
ウィスキー	uisukii	whisky
スコッチ	sukocchi	scotch
バーボン	bābon	bourbon
日本酒（酒） あつかん ひや	nihonshu (sake) atsukan hiya	Sake, a wine brewed from rice. warmed sake cold sake
焼酎	shōchū	Spirit distilled from potatoes.
チューハイ	chūhai	Shōchū mixed with soda water and flavored with lemon juice or other flavors.
ワイン 赤 白 ロゼ	wain aka shiro roze	wine red white rose
シャンペン	shampen	champagne
ブランデー	burandē	brandy

Non-alcoholic　その他の飲物

コーヒー	kōhii	coffee
アイスコーヒー	aisu kōhii	iced coffee
日本茶	nihon cha	Japanese green tea
紅茶	kō-cha	black tea
レモンティー	remon tii	tea with lemon
ミルクティー	miruku tii	tea with milk
アイスティー	aisu tii	iced tea
ウーロン茶	ūron cha	oolong tea
ジャスミン茶	jasumin cha	jasmine tea
牛乳／ミルク	gyū-nyū/miruku	milk
ココア	kokoa	hot chocolate
レモンスカッシュ	remon sukasshu	carbonated lemon soft drink
ミルクセーキ	miruku sēki	milk shake
ジュース	jūsu	juice, but can also mean any soft drink
レモネード	remonēdo	lemonade

GLOSSARY OF KEY JAPANESE WORDS AND SUFFIXES

asa-ichi	朝市	morning market
banchi	番地	street number
bashi	橋	bridge
bijutsukan	美術館	art museum
-chō	町	street or block
-chōme	丁目	street
chūō	中央	central
-dake (dah-keh)	岳	peak
daimyō	大名	feudal lord
deguchi	出口	exit
-den	殿	hall
depāto (deh-pah-to)	デパート	department store
-dera	寺	Buddhist temple
-dō	堂	temple or shrine
-dōri	通（り）	avenue
tenshukaku	天守閣	castle stronghold
eki	駅	train station
-en	園／苑	garden
gaijin	外人	foreigner
gaikokujin	外国人	foreigner
-gama	窯	kiln
gawa	川、河	river
-gū	宮	Shintō shrine
-gun	郡	county or district
hakubutsukan	博物館	museum
-hama	浜	beach
-hantō	半島	peninsula
higashi	東	east
hōmotsu-kan	宝物館	treasure house
ike (ee-key)	池	pond
ijinkan	異人館	Western-style house
-in	院	Buddhist temple

izakaya	居酒屋	pub
-ji	寺	Buddhist temple
-jima	島	island
jingū	神宮	Shintō shrine
jinja	神社	Shintō shrine
-jō	城	castle
kado	角	street corner
kama	窯	kiln
-kan	館	museum hall
kawa	川、河	river
-ken	県	prefecture
kita	北	north
-ko	湖	lake
kōen	公園	park
kōgen	高原	plateau
ku	区	section or ward
kūkō	空港	airport
kyō	峡	gorge
machi	町	town
matsuri	祭り	festival
michi	道	street
minami	南	south
misaki	岬	cape
-mon	門	gate
Nihon-kai	日本海	Sea of Japan
nishi	西	west
ōhashi	大橋	large bridge
Ohōtsuku-kai	オホーツク海	Sea of Okhotsk
onsen	温泉	hot spring
-rettō	列島	island chain
rōmaji	ローマ字	Japanese words rendered in roman letters
rotemburo	露天風呂	open-air thermal bath
ryokan	旅館	traditional inn
ryūhyō	流氷	ice floes
sake	酒	rice wine
-saki	崎	cape or point

sakura	桜	cherry blossoms
-san	山	mountain, as in Kōya-san, Mt. Kōya
Seto Nai-kai	瀬戸内海	Seto Inland Sea
-shi	市	city or municipality
shima	島	island
-shotō	諸島	island chain
Shinkansen	新幹線	bullet train, literally "new trunk line",
shita	下	lower, downward
taisha	大社	big or main Shintō shrine
-take (tah-keh)	岳	peak
taki	滝	falls
-tō	島	island
tōge	峠	pass
torii (to-ree-ee)	鳥居	gate
wan	湾	bay
-ya	屋	shop, as in hon-ya, bookshop
-yaki	焼 (き)	pottery
yama	山	mountain
yamanote	山の手	the hilly part of town
-zaki	崎	cape or point
-zan	山	mountain

INDEX

NOTES

NOTES